The
Random House

Collection

# The Unfinished Nation

A CONCISE HISTORY
OF THE AMERICAN PEOPLE

# The
# Unfinished
# Nation

A CONCISE HISTORY
OF THE AMERICAN PEOPLE

**Second Edition**

# Alan Brinkley

ALFRED A. KNOPF    NEW YORK    1997

THIS IS A BORZOI BOOK
PUBLISHED BY ALFRED A. KNOPF, INC.

Copyright © 1993, 1997 by The McGraw-Hill Companies, Inc.

http://www.randomhouse.com/

Library of Congress Cataloging-in-Publication Data
Brinkley, Alan.
The unfinished nation : a concise history of the American people /
Alan Brinkley. — 2nd ed.
p.  cm.
Includes bibliographical references and index.
ISBN 0-679-45459-4
1. United States — History.  I. Title.
E178.1.B827    1997
973 — dc20                  96-1210 CIP

Manufactured in the United States of America
First edition published May 15, 1993
Second edition published October 1997

# Contents

# AMERICAN VOICES

# DEBATING THE PAST

# APPENDICES

# List of Illustrations

# List of Maps

# Preface

T he story of the American past, which is the subject of this book, has undergone a remarkable transformation in recent decades. The past itself has not changed, of course; but the way Americans understand it has changed dramatically. And in the wake of those changes have come both new forms of presentation and bitter controversies.

On the one hand, history is becoming more visible to more people than ever before as a part of American popular culture. Historical museums and exhibitions have multiplied; popular writing on history—both in novels and in nonfiction—has grown in popularity; history is a constant presence on television, in films, and, increasingly, on the Internet; it is a major element in theme parks and even shopping malls. At the same time, historical scholarship has become the source of increasing debate—both among historians themselves and among national politicians, some of whom have attacked the historical profession for what they claim is an excessively critical view of the American past.

The growing prominence of American history in popular culture and the increasing controversy over its meaning are to a large degree a result of the same things. In turbulent and confusing times, people have naturally looked to their past for guidance and reassurance—and for a reminder of what they believe was a better era. But those same times have encouraged historians to look to the past to understand the tensions and contests that preoccupy us today. In the process, they have reinterpreted much of it. As the population of the United States has become ever more diverse and as groups that once stood outside the view of scholarship thrust themselves into its center, historians have set out to reveal the immense and, until relatively recently, inadequately understood complexity of their country's past. The result has been the slow emergence of a richer and fuller history of the United States, but also a more fragmented, contentious, and controversial one. That history offers a picture of a highly diverse people. It also provides a picture of a great nation.

Threading one's way through the many, conflicting demands of contemporary scholars and contemporary readers is no easy task. But I have tried in this book to find an acceptable middle ground between the claims of diversity and the claims of unity. The United States is, indeed, a nation of many cultures. We cannot understand its history without understanding the experiences of all the different groups that have shaped American society, without understanding the particular worlds that have developed within it based on region, religion, class, ideology, race, gender, and ethnicity.

But the United States is more than just a collection of different cultures. It is also a nation. And as important as understanding its diversity is understanding the forces that have drawn it together and allowed it to survive and flourish despite division. The United States has constructed a remarkably stable and enduring political system that touches the lives of all Americans. It has developed an immense, highly productive national economy that affects the working and consuming lives of virtually everyone. It has created a mass popular culture that colors the experiences and assumptions of almost all the American people, and the people of much of the rest of the world as well. One can admire these unifying forces for their contributions to America's considerable success as a nation, or condemn them for the ways they have contributed to inequality, injustice, and failure. But no one proposing to understand the history of the United States can afford to ignore them.

In the great historical narratives of the nineteenth and early twentieth centuries, the story of America moved smoothly and triumphantly from one clearly defined era to another, focusing on great events and great men and tracing the rise of national institutions. The late twentieth century has produced a different narrative, with frequent, sometimes jarring, changes of focus and direction. It devotes attention to private as well as public events, to failure as well as success, to difference as well as to unity. And yet it remains, in the end, a narrative, a story—newly complicated, perhaps, by our understanding of the many worlds of historical experience that once eluded us—but even more remarkable and compelling for those complications.

This second edition of *The Unfinished Nation* continues the effort to tell this newer story of America for students of history and for general readers in a single, reasonably concise volume. Those familiar with the first edition will notice a number of important changes: Chapters 7 through 11 have been thoroughly reorganized to allow for a more extended and coherent discussion of antebellum American society and culture and to permit a considerable expansion of the treatment of the Old South and slavery. Chapter 15 has been restructured to link an extended description of the New South to the account of the Reconstruction process, which did much to shape it. Chapter 16 is now devoted entirely to the history of the trans-Mississippi West in the late nineteenth century and offers a considerably expanded treatment of the history of that region. And there is a new final chapter (34) which contains an account of events since the publication of the first edition and a major reorganization and expansion of the discussion of contemporary society and culture.

There are other important changes as well. Throughout the book, I have given considerably expanded attention to the American West (beginning with an extended discussion of early Spanish settlement in what is now the American Southwest and continuing to the rise of the modern "Sunbelt"). I have substantially increased the coverage of Hispanic Americans and Asian Americans. There is much new material from recent scholarship in women's history. There is a greatly expanded discussion of the complicated social and cultural history of the 1950s, a new section on the origins of the Vietnam War and a much-expanded discussion of the conflict itself, and a new section on the rise of the right in the 1960s and 1970s. There are also new illustrations and maps, two new essays on "Debating the Past," and illustrated time lines covering significant events in each chapter.

The result, I hope, is a book that will serve to introduce readers to enough different approaches to and areas of American history to make them aware of its extraordinary richness and diversity. I hope it will also give readers some sense of the shared experiences of Americans.

The title of this book, *The Unfinished Nation*, is meant to suggest several things. It is a reminder of America's exceptional diversity: of the degree to which, despite all the many efforts to build a single, uniform definition of the meaning of American nationhood, that meaning remains contested and diverse. It is a reference to the centrality of change in American history: to the way in which the nation has continually transformed itself and to how it continues to do so in our own time. And it is a description of the writing of American history itself, of the way historians are engaged in a continuing, ever unfinished, process of asking new questions of the past.

Many people contributed to this book: Lyn Uhl, Larry Goldberg, Elizabeth Strange, Kathy Bendo, Elyse Rieder, Irving Tullar, Wanda Kossak, and Wanda Lubelska at McGraw-Hill; my research assistants Thad Russell, Charlie Forcey, and Dave Ekbladh; Yanek Mieczkowski, who prepared the time lines; and several anonymous scholars who commented on the first edition and alerted me to various errors and omissions. The reviewers of the second edition made helpful suggestions and comments: Stacy Cole, Ohlone College; Randy Kelly, Community College of Allegheny; Chana Lee, Indiana University; and Ronald Petrin, Oklahoma State University. The reviewers of the text's supplements also made useful contributions: Gisela Ables, Houston Community College; Carla Joy, Red Rocks Community College; Susan Hult, Houston Community College; and Joseph Stout,

Oklahoma State University. I am grateful to them all. I will also be grateful to any readers who wish to offer comments, criticisms, and corrections as I prepare future editions. Suggestions can be sent to me in care of the Department of History, Columbia University, New York, NY 10027; I will respond to them as fully and constructively as I can.

ALAN BRINKLEY

# The
# Unfinished
# Nation

A CONCISE HISTORY
OF THE AMERICAN PEOPLE

# CHAPTER ONE

# The Meeting of Cultures

*America Before Columbus* ∼ *Europe Looks Westward*
*The Arrival of the English*

T HE DISCOVERY OF America did not begin with Christopher Columbus. It started many thousands of years earlier when human beings first crossed an ancient land bridge over the Bering Strait into what is now Alaska and—almost certainly without realizing it—began to people a new continent.

## AMERICA BEFORE COLUMBUS

No one is certain when these migrations began; recent estimates suggest that they started between 14,000 and 16,000 years ago. They were probably a result of the development of new stone-tipped spears and other hunting implements that made it possible for humans to pursue the large animals that regularly crossed between Asia and North America. Year after year, a few at a time, these nomadic peoples—apparently drawn from a Mongolian stock similar to that of modern-day eastern Siberia—entered the new continent and moved deeper into its heart. Perhaps as early as 8000 B.C., the migrations reached the southern tip of South America. By the end of the fifteenth century A.D., when the first important contact with Europeans occurred, America was the home of many millions of men and women. Scholars estimate that well over 10 million people lived in South America by 1500 and that perhaps 4 million lived in the territory that now constitutes the United States.

| TIME LINE | | | |
|---|---|---|---|
| **14,000–12,000 B.C.** | **1492** | **1497** | **1502** |
| Asians migrate to North America | Columbus discovers America | Cabot explores North America | African slaves arrive in Spanish America |
| **1518–1530** | **1519–1522** | **1558** | **1565** | **1587** |
| Smallpox ravages Indians | Magellan circumnavigates globe | Elizabeth I becomes English queen | St. Augustine, Florida founded | "Lost Colony" established on Roanoke Island |
| **1603** | **1606** | **1608** | **1609** | |
| James I becomes English king | Virginia Company established | French establish Quebec | Spanish found Sante Fe | |

## The Civilizations of the South

The most elaborate of these societies emerged in South and Central America and in Mexico. In Peru, the Incas created a powerful empire of perhaps 6 million people. They developed a complex political system and a large network of paved roads that welded together the populations of many tribes under a single government. In Central America and on the Yucatán peninsula of Mexico, the Mayas built a sophisticated culture with a written language, a numerical system similar to the Arabic, an accurate calendar, and an advanced agricultural system. They were succeeded by the Aztecs, a once-nomadic warrior tribe from the north. In the late thirteenth century, the Aztecs established a precarious rule over much of central and southern Mexico and built elaborate administrative, educational, and medical systems comparable to the most advanced in Europe at the time. The Aztecs also developed a harsh religion that required human sacrifice. Their Spanish conquerors discovered the skulls of 100,000 victims in one location when they arrived in 1519.

The economies of these societies were based primarily on agriculture, but there were also substantial cities. Tenochtitlán, the Aztec capital built on the site of present-day Mexico City, had a population of over 100,000 in 1500, which was comparable to some of the largest European cities of the time. The Mayas (at Mayapán and elsewhere) and the Incas (in such cities as Cuzco and Machu Picchu) produced elaborate settlements with striking religious and ceremonial structures. These civilizations accomplished all this without some of the important technologies that Asian and European civilizations possessed. As late as the sixteenth century, no American society had yet developed wheeled vehicles.

### The Civilizations of the North

The peoples north of Mexico—in the lands that became the United States and Canada—developed less elaborate but still substantial civilizations and political systems. Inhabitants of the northern regions of the continent subsisted on hunting, gathering, fishing, or some combination of the three. They included the Eskimos of the Arctic Circle, who fished and hunted seals and whose civilization spanned thousands of miles of largely frozen land; the big-game hunters of the northern forests, who led nomadic lives based on pursuit of moose and caribou; the tribes of the Pacific Northwest, whose principal occupation was salmon fishing and who created substantial permanent settlements along the coast; and a group of tribes spread through relatively arid regions of the Far West, who developed successful communities, many of them quite wealthy and densely populated, based on fishing, hunting small game, and gathering edible seeds, roots, and other plant materials.

Other societies in North America were primarily agricultural. Among the most developed were those in the Southwest. The people of that arid region built large irrigation systems, and they constructed substantial towns of stone and adobe structures. In the Great Plains region, too, most tribes were engaged in sedentary farming (corn and other grains) and lived in large permanent settlements, although there were some small nomadic tribes that subsisted by hunting buffalo.

The eastern third of what is now the United States—much of it covered with forests and inhabited by the Woodland Indians—had the greatest food resources of any area of the continent. The many tribes of the region engaged in farming, hunting, gathering, and fishing simultaneously. In the South there were substantial permanent settlements and large trading networks based on the corn and other grains grown in the rich lands of the Mississippi River valley. The city of Cahokia (near present-day St. Louis) was a large trading center. At its peak in A.D. 1200 it had a population of 40,000.

The agricultural societies of the Northeast were less stationary. Farming techniques there were designed to exploit the land quickly rather than to develop permanent settlements. Many of the tribes living east of the Mississippi River were linked together loosely by common linguistic roots. The largest of these language groups consisted of the Algonquin tribes, which

INDIANS FISHING The English explorer John White visited areas of the Atlantic coast in the 1580s and created a series of watercolors of native life there—among them this scene of Woodland Indians fishing from a canoe.

lived along the Atlantic seaboard from Canada to Virginia; the Iroquois Confederacy, which was centered in what is now upstate New York; and the Muskogean, which consisted of the tribes in the southernmost region of the eastern seaboard. Alliances among the various Indian societies (even among those with common languages) were fragile, since the peoples of the Americas did not think of themselves as members of a single civilization. When Europeans arrived and began to threaten their way of life, tribes only rarely were able to unite in opposition to white encroachments.

In the last centuries before the arrival of Europeans, Native Americans—like peoples in other parts of the world—were experiencing an agricultural revolution. In all areas of what is now the United States (if in varying degrees from place to place), tribes were becoming more sedentary and were developing new sources of food, clothing, and shelter. Most regions were experiencing significant population growth. And virtually all were developing the sorts of elaborate social customs and rituals that only relatively stationary societies can produce. Religion was as important to Indian society as it was to most other cultures, and it was usually closely bound up with

**Principal Subsistence Patterns of Early Native Peoples of North America**

PRINCIPAL BASIS OF SUBSISTENCE

Fish, shellfish, and sea mammals

Agricultural products

Seeds, nuts, roots, and small game

Large game

the natural world on which the tribes depended. Native Americans worshiped many gods, whom they associated variously with crops, game, forests,
rivers, and other elements of nature.

All tribes assigned women the jobs of caring for children, preparing
meals, and gathering certain foods. But the allocation of other tasks varied
from one society to another. Some tribal groups (notably the Pueblos of the
Southwest) reserved farming tasks almost entirely for men. Among others
(including the Algonquins, the Iroquois, and the Muskogean), women tended
the fields, while men engaged in hunting, warfare, or clearing land. Iroquois
women and children were often left alone for extended periods while men
were away hunting or fighting battles. As a result, women tended to control
the social and economic organization of the settlements and played powerful roles within families.

## EUROPE LOOKS WESTWARD

Europeans were almost entirely unaware of the existence of the Americas
before the fifteenth century. A few early wanderers—Leif Eriksson, an
eleventh-century Norse seaman, and perhaps others—had glimpsed parts of
the New World on their voyages. But even if their discoveries had become
common knowledge (and they did not), there would have been little incentive for others to follow, for Europe in the Middle Ages (roughly A.D.
500–1500) was so divided and decentralized, so limited in its commerce, and
so lacking in powerful political leaders that interest in great ventures remained limited. By the end of the fifteenth century, however, conditions in
Europe had changed, and the incentive for overseas exploration had grown.

### Commerce and Nationalism

Two changes in particular helped produce incentives for Europeans to look
toward new lands. One was a result of the significant growth in Europe's population in the fifteenth century. The Black Death, a catastrophic epidemic
of the bubonic plague that began in Constantinople in 1347, had killed (according to some estimates) as many as half the people of the Continent. But
a century and a half later, the population had rebounded. With that growth
came a reawakening of commerce and a general increase in prosperity. A new
merchant class was emerging to meet the rising demand for goods from
abroad. As trade increased, and as advances in navigation and shipbuilding

made long-distance sea travel more feasible, interest in expanding trade even further grew quickly.

At the same time, new governments were emerging that were more united and powerful than the feeble political entities of the feudal past. In the western areas of Europe in particular, strong new monarchs were emerging, creating centralized nation-states and growing eager to enhance the commercial development of their nations.

Ever since the early fourteenth century, when Marco Polo and other adventurers had returned from the Orient bearing exotic goods (spices, cloths, dyes) and even more exotic tales, Europeans who craved commercial glory had dreamed above all of trade with the East. For two centuries, that trade had been limited by the difficulties of the long overland journey to the Asian courts. But in the fourteenth century, as the maritime talents of several western European societies increased, there began to be talk of finding a faster, safer route to the Orient by sea. In the late fifteenth century, some of the new monarchs were ready to finance daring voyages of exploration.

The first to do so were the Portuguese. Their maritime preeminence in the fifteenth century was in large part the work of Prince Henry the Navigator, who devoted much of his life to the promotion of exploration. Some of Henry's mariners went as far south as Cape Verde, on Africa's west coast. After his death in 1460, Portuguese explorers advanced farther still. In 1486, Bartholomeu Dias rounded the southern tip of Africa (the Cape of Good Hope); and in 1497–1498, Vasco da Gama proceeded all the way around the cape to India. In 1500, the next Portuguese fleet bound for India, under the command of Pedro Cabral, was blown off course and happened upon the coast of Brazil. But by then, another man, in the service of another country, had already encountered the "New World."

### Christopher Columbus

Christopher Columbus was born and reared in Genoa, Italy, and spent his early seafaring years in the service of the Portuguese. By the time he was a young man, he had developed great ambitions. He believed he could reach the Orient by sailing west, across the Atlantic, rather than east, around Africa. Columbus's optimism rested on several basic misconceptions. He thought the world was far smaller than it actually is. He also believed that the Asian continent extended farther eastward than it actually does. Most important, he did not realize that anything lay to the west between Europe and the lands of Asia.

FROBISHER 1576–1578

HUDSON 1610

GILBERT 1583

CABOT 1497

*Hudson Bay*

HUDSON 1610

LABRADOR

CARTIER
1534, 1535

*James Bay*

CARTIER
1535

45°

CARTIER 1534

41°

CARTIER 1536

VERRAZANO 1524

*Gulf of
St. Lawrence*

*Drake's Bay*

St. Lawrence R.

Sagadoahoc

38°

*Missouri R.*

34°

*Ohio R.*

ATLANTIC OCEAN

CORONADO 1540–1542

*Arkansas R.*

VERRAZANO 1524

3

*Rio Grande*

*Pecos R.*

*Red R.*

DE SOTO

*Mississippi R.*

DE SOTO 1539–1542

St. Augustine

HAWKINS 1580

PONCE DE LEON 1513

COLUMBUS, 1492

*Gulf of Mexico*

PONCE
DE LEON

Havana

Tenochtitlan
(Mexico City)

CORTÉS 1518–1521

Mayapan

Chichen
Itza

Santiago
de Cuba

AZTEC
EMPIRE

San Juan

DRAKE 1577–1580

MAYAN
EMPIRE

YUCATAN
PENINSULA

1493

COLUMBUS 1493

PACIFIC OCEAN

HAWKINS 1580

*Caribbean
Sea*

COLUMBUS 1502

COLUMBUS 1498

BALBOA 1513

1502

*Orinoco River*

**European Journeys of
Exploration and Conquest**

SPANISH VOYAGES

ISTHMUS OF
PANAMA

●●●●●●●●● Columbus, 1492
◆ ─ ─ ─ ─ Columbus, 1493
◄ - - - - - Columbus, 1498
◄ ─ · ─ · ─ Columbus, 1502
◄──── Other Spanish routes

OTHER EUROPEAN VOYAGES

◆──── French

◄──── English

PIZARRO 1531–1533

INCA
EMPIRE

Native American empires

0          500 Miles
0          500 Kilometers

Columbus failed to convince the leaders of Portugal of the value of his plan, so he turned instead to Spain. Although the Spaniards were not yet as advanced a maritime people as the Portuguese, they were just as energetic and ambitious. And in the fifteenth century they were establishing a strong nation-state. The marriage of Spain's two most powerful regional rulers, Ferdinand of Aragon and Isabella of Castile, had produced the strongest monarchy in Europe, one that was eager to demonstrate its strength by sponsoring new commercial ventures.

Columbus appealed to Queen Isabella for support for his proposed westward voyage, and in 1492, after consolidating her position at home, she agreed. Commanding ninety men and three ships—the *Niña*, the *Pinta*, and the *Santa Maria*—Columbus left Spain in August 1492 and sailed west into the Atlantic. Ten weeks later, he sighted land and assumed he had reached an island off Asia. In fact, he had landed in the Bahamas. When he pushed on and encountered Cuba, he assumed he had reached China. He returned to Spain, bringing with him several captured natives as evidence of his achievement. (He called the natives "Indians" because he believed they were from the East Indies in the Pacific.)

But Columbus could not, of course, bring back news of the great khan's court in China or any samples of the fabled wealth of the Indies. And so a year later, he tried again, this time with a much larger expedition. As before, he headed into the Caribbean, discovering several other islands and leaving a small and short-lived colony on Hispaniola. On a third voyage, in 1498, he finally reached the mainland and cruised along the northern coast of South America. He then realized, for the first time, that he had encountered not a part of Asia but a separate continent. Still, he remained convinced that Asia was only a short distance away.

Columbus's celebrated accomplishments made him a popular hero for a time, but he ended his life in obscurity. Ultimately, he was even unable to give his name to the land he had revealed to the Europeans. That distinction went instead to a Florentine merchant, Amerigo Vespucci, a passenger on a later Portuguese expedition to the New World, who wrote a series of vivid descriptions of the lands he visited and helped popularize the idea that the Americas were new continents.

Partly as a result of Columbus's initiative, Spain began to devote greater resources and energy to maritime exploration and gradually replaced Portugal as the foremost seafaring nation. In 1513 the Spaniard Vasco de Balboa fought his way across the Isthmus of Panama and became the first European to gaze westward upon the great ocean that separated America from China. Seeking access to that ocean, Ferdinand Magellan, a Portuguese in

San Francisco (1776)
Monterey (1770)
San Luis Obispo (1772)
Los Angeles (1781)
San Juan Capistrano (1776)
San Diego de Alcala (1769)
Tucson (1709)
Taos (1609)
Santa Fe (1607)

LOUISIANA
(Spanish 1763-1800)

UNITED STATES
(from 1783)

Red R.

Rio Grande

Mississippi R.

Culiacán (1531)

Tampico

Mexico City (Tenochtitlán) (1325)

Veracruz (1519)

VICEROYALTY OF

Yucatan Peninsula

Guatemala (1519)

NEW SPAIN

Gulf of Mexico

SPANISH FLORIDA (to 1819)

St. Augustine (1565)

La Habana (1515)

Cuba (1492)
Santiago (1514)

Jamaica (to Britain 1655)

Bahamas (to Britain 1646)

Española (1492)

HAITI (French after 1697)

Puerto Rico (1502)

Santo Domingo (1496)

ATLANTIC OCEAN

World divided into Spanish and Portugue hemispheres Treaty of Tordesillas (1494)

Caribbean Sea

Panama (1519)

Caracas (1567)

Orinoco R.

Trinidad (1498)

FRENCH GUIANA (1626)

PACIFIC OCEAN

VICEROYALTY OF

Santa Fe de Bogotá (1538)

SURINAM (Dutch) (1625)

NEW GRANADA

Quito (1534)

Guayaquil (1535)

Amazon River

Ciudad de los Reyes (Lima) (1535)

Cuzco (1535)

La Paz (1548)

VICEROYALTY OF

NEW CASTILIA (Peru)

VICEROYALTY OF LA PLATA

PORTUGUESE BRAZIL

Rio c Janei (156

São P (1554

Valparaiso (1544)

Santiago (1541)

Parana R.

Montevideo (1724)

Buenos Aires (1580)

Rio de la Plata

**Spanish America**

Colonial boundaries and provincial names
are for the late 18th century

Aztec Empire at the time of Spanish conquest

Inca Empire at the time of Spanish conquest

OUTPOSTS ON THE NORTHERN FRONTIER OF NEW SPAIN
(Not simultaneous; through the 18th century)

- Missions
○ Forts (sometimes with missions)
- Settlements

Straits of Magellan
Tierra del Fuego

0   1,000 Miles
0   1,000 Kilometers

Spanish employ, found the strait that now bears his name at the southern end of South America, struggled through the stormy narrows and into the ocean (so calm by contrast that he christened it the Pacific), and then proceeded to the Philippines. There Magellan died in a conflict with the natives, but his expedition went on to complete the first known circumnavigation of the globe (1519–1522). By 1550, Spaniards had explored the coasts of North America as far north as Oregon in the west and Labrador in the east.

### The Spanish Empire

In time, Spanish explorers in the New World stopped thinking of America simply as an obstacle to their search for a route to the East and began instead to consider it a possible source of wealth in itself. The Spanish claimed for themselves the whole of the New World, except for a piece of it (today's Brazil) that was reserved by a papal decree for the Portuguese; and by the mid-sixteenth century, they were establishing a substantial American empire.

The early Spanish colonists, beginning with those Columbus brought on his second voyage, settled on the islands of the Caribbean. But then, in 1518, Hernando Cortés, who had been an unsuccessful Spanish government official in Cuba for fourteen years, decided to lead a small military expedition (about 600 men) against the Aztecs in Mexico and their powerful emperor, Montezuma, after hearing stories of great treasures there. His first assault on Tenochtitlán, the Aztec capital, failed. But Cortés and his army had, unknowingly, unleashed an assault on the Aztecs far more devastating than military attack: they had exposed the natives to smallpox. An epidemic of that deadly disease decimated the Aztec population and made it possible for the Spanish to triumph in their second attempt at conquest. Through his ruthless suppression of the surviving natives, Cortés established himself as one of the most brutal of the Spanish "conquistadores" (conquerors). Twenty years later, Francisco Pizarro conquered Peru, revealed to the European world the wealth of the Incas, and opened the way for other advances into South America.

The story of the Spanish warriors is one of great military daring and achievement. It is also a story of remarkable brutality and greed. The conquistadores subjugated and, in some areas, virtually exterminated the native populations. In this horrible way, they made possible the creation of a vast Spanish Empire in the New World.

Although the conquistadores had cleared the way for Spanish colonization of America, the task of creating settlements remained difficult. Spaniards who wished to launch expeditions to the New World had to get licenses from the crown and pay the monarch a fifth of any wealth gathered in the new

CORTÉS IN THE NEW WORLD An Aztec artist created this image of Hernando Cortés in Mexico. Cortés is visible at upper left, on horseback, wielding a sword. Other images suggest the destruction his arrival produced among the Aztecs. One of the most brutal and successful of the Spanish conquistadores, Cortés burned his ships in 1519 upon landing at Vera Cruz (where he founded a city) to prevent his men from turning back. In 1521, he captured the Aztec capital, Tenochtitlán, after a long siege.

colonies. Colonizers then had to equip and finance their expeditions without help from the government and assume the full risk of loss or ruin. They might succeed and make a fortune; they might fail and lose everything, including their lives.

The first Spanish settlers in America were interested only in exploiting the American stores of gold and silver, and they were fabulously successful. For 300 years, beginning in the sixteenth century, the mines of Spanish America yielded more than ten times as much gold and silver as the rest of the world's mines together. These riches made Spain for a time the wealthiest and most powerful nation on earth.

After the first wave of conquest, however, most Spanish settlers in America traveled to the New World for other reasons. Many went in hopes of creating a profitable agricultural economy, and they helped establish elements of European civilization permanently in America. Other Spaniards went to

America to spread the Christian religion; after the 1540s priests or friars accompanied all colonizing ventures. Through the work of zealous missionaries, the influence of the Catholic Church ultimately extended throughout South and Central America and Mexico.

### Northern Outposts

The Spanish fort of St. Augustine, established in Florida in 1565, became the first permanent European settlement in the present-day United States. But it was little more than a military outpost and a headquarters for unsuccessful missionary campaigns among North American natives that were ultimately abandoned.

A more substantial colonizing venture began in the Southwest in 1598, when Don Juan de Oñate traveled north from Mexico with a party of 500, claimed for Spain some of the lands of the Pueblo Indians in what is now New Mexico, and began to establish a colony. Oñate created *encomiendas* (large land grants to favored Spaniards, who could then exact tribute and labor from the natives). Spanish colonists founded Santa Fe in 1609.

There were tensions between the Spanish and the Pueblo Indians, whose lands they were attempting to control; but the Spanish and the Pueblos learned to cooperate in many ways and even profited at times from each other's presence. The greatest danger to the colony came from Apache and Navajo raiders, who threatened the Spanish and Pueblos alike. But the New Mexico settlement continued to grow. By 1680, there were over 2,000 Spanish colonists living among about 30,000 Pueblos. The economic heart of the colony was cattle and sheep, raised on the *ranchos* that stretched out around the small towns Spanish settlers established.

In 1680, the colony was nearly destroyed when the Pueblos rose in revolt. Despite widespread conversions to Catholicism, most natives (including the converts) continued also to practice their own religious rituals. In 1680, Spanish priests and the colonial government were engaged in one of their periodic efforts to suppress these rituals. In response, Pope, an Indian religious leader, led an uprising that killed hundreds of European settlers (including twenty-one priests), captured Santa Fe, and drove the Spanish temporarily from the region. But twelve years later the Spanish returned, resumed seizing Pueblo lands, and crushed a last revolt in 1696.

After the revolts, many Spanish colonists seemed to understand that they could not hope to prosper in New Mexico in constant conflict with a native population that greatly outnumbered them. On the one hand, the Spanish intensified their efforts to assimilate the Indians—baptizing Indian children at birth and enforcing observance of Catholic rituals. On the other hand, they now permitted the Pueblos to own land; they stopped commandeering Indian labor; they replaced the *encomienda* system with a less demanding and oppressive one; and they tacitly tolerated the survival of tribal religious rituals. There was significant intermarriage between Europeans and Indians. And increasingly, the Pueblos came to consider the Spanish their allies in the continuing battles with the Apaches and Navajos. By 1750, the Spanish population had grown modestly to about 4,000. The Pueblo population had declined (through disease, war, and migration) to about 13,000, less than half what it had been in 1680. New Mexico had by then become a reasonably stable but still weak and isolated outpost of the Spanish Empire.

### The Spanish Empire at High Tide

By the end of the sixteenth century, the Spanish Empire had become one of the largest in the history of the world. It included the Caribbean islands, Mexico, and southern North America. The Spanish Empire also spread into South America and included what is now Chile, Argentina, and Peru. In 1580, when the Spanish and Portuguese monarchies temporarily united, Brazil came under Spanish jurisdiction as well.

It was, however, a colonial empire very different from the one the English would later establish in North America. The earliest Spanish ventures in the New World had operated largely independently of the throne, but by the end of the sixteenth century the monarchy had extended its authority directly into the governance of local communities, leaving colonists few opportunities to establish political institutions independent of the crown. The Spanish were far more successful than the British would be in extracting great surface wealth—gold and silver—from their American colonies. But they concentrated relatively less energy on agriculture and commerce. The strict and inflexible commercial policies of the Spanish government made the problem worse.

But the biggest difference between the Spanish Empire and the later European colonization of North America was in the characters of the populations. The societies of English, French, and Dutch America were centered on farming and permanent settlement and emphasized family life. Hence, the Europeans in North America reproduced themselves rapidly after their first difficult years and in time came to outnumber the natives. The Spanish, by contrast, ruled their empire but did not people it. The number of European settlers in Spanish America always remained relatively small, and despite disease and war, the vast majority of the population continued to consist of natives.

## Cultural Exchanges

European and native cultures never entirely merged in the Spanish Empire. Indeed, significant differences remain today between European and Indian cultures throughout South and Central America. Nevertheless, the arrival of whites launched a process of interaction between different peoples that left no one unchanged.

That Europeans were exploring the Americas at all was a result of their early contacts with the natives, from whom they had learned of the rich deposits of gold and silver. From then on, the history of the Americas became one of increasing levels of exchanges—some beneficial, some catastrophic—among different peoples and cultures. The first and perhaps most profound result of this exchange was the importation of European diseases to the New World. It would be difficult to exaggerate the consequences of the exposure of Native Americans to such illnesses as influenza, measles, typhus, and above all smallpox—diseases to which Europeans had, over time, developed at least a partial immunity but to which Americans were tragically vulnerable. Millions died. In some areas, native populations were virtually wiped out within a few decades of their first contact with whites. On Hispaniola—where the Dominican Republic and Haiti are today and where Columbus landed and established a small, short-lived colony in the 1490s—the native population quickly declined from approximately 1 million to about 500. In the Mayan areas of Mexico, as much as 95 percent of the population perished within a few years of the natives' first contact with the Spanish. Some groups fared better than others; many (although not all) of the tribes north of Mexico, whose contact with European settlers came later and was often less intimate, were spared the worst of the epidemics. But for other areas of the New World, this was a catastrophe at least as grave as, and in some places far worse than, the Black Death that had killed as much as half the population of Europe two centuries before.

The decimation of native populations in the southern regions of the Americas was not, however, purely a result of exposure to infection. It was also a result of the conquistadores' quite deliberate policy of subjugation and extermination. Their brutality was in part a reflection of the ruthlessness with which Europeans waged war in all parts of the world. It was also a result of their conviction that the natives were "savages"—uncivilized peoples who could be treated as somehow not fully human. Ironically, it was also a consequence of the high level of development of some native societies. Organized into substantial empires, they posed a serious threat to the conquistadores' ambitions. As a result, the Spanish razed cities and dismantled temples and monuments. They destroyed records and documents. They systematically killed Indian warriors, leaders, priests, and organized elites. By the 1540s, the combined effects of European diseases and European military brutality had all but destroyed the empires of Mexico and South America and allowed the Spanish to exert their authority with few organized challenges from the natives.

Not all aspects of the exchange were so disastrous to the Indians. The Europeans introduced to America important new crops (among them sugar and bananas), domestic livestock (cattle, pigs, and sheep), and perhaps most significant the horse. Indians soon learned to cultivate the new crops, and European livestock spread widely among tribes that in the past had possessed virtually no domesticated animals other than dogs. The horse, in particular, became central to the lives of many natives and transformed their societies.

The exchange was at least as important (and more beneficial) to the Europeans. In both North and South America, the arriving white peoples learned from the natives new agricultural techniques appropriate to the demands of the new land. They discovered new crops, above all maize (corn), which Columbus took back to Europe from his first trip to America. Such foods as squash, pumpkins, beans, sweet potatoes, tomatoes, peppers, and potatoes all found their way into European diets by way of Native Americans.

In South America, Central America, and Mexico, a society emerged in which Europeans and natives lived in intimate, if unequal, contact with one another. As a result, Indians adopted many features of European civilization, although seldom did those features survive the transfer to America unchanged. Many natives gradually came to speak Spanish or Portuguese, but they created a range of dialects fusing the European languages with elements of their own. Gradually, European missionaries—through a combination of persuasion and coercion—spread Catholicism through most areas of the Spanish Empire. But native Christians combined the new religion with features of their old ones.

Colonial officials were expected to take their wives with them to America, but among the ordinary settlers—the majority—European men outnumbered European women by at least ten to one. As a result, male Spanish immigrants had substantial sexual contact with native women. Intermarriage—sometimes forcible, sometimes with the agreement of native women responding to the shortage of native men—became frequent. Before long, the population of the colonies came to be dominated (numerically, at least) by people of mixed race, or "mestizos."

Virtually all the enterprises of the Spanish and Portuguese colonists depended on an Indian work force. In some places, Indians were sold into slavery. More often, colonists used a coercive wage system by which Indians worked in the mines and on the plantations under duress for fixed periods. These indentured work forces survived in some areas of the South American mainland for many centuries. Yet even that was not, in the end, enough to meet the labor needs of the colonists—particularly since the native population had declined (and in some places virtually vanished) because of disease and war. As early as 1502, therefore, European settlers began importing slaves from Africa.

### Africa and America

Over half of all the immigrants to the New World between 1500 and 1800 were Africans, virtually all of them sent to America against their will. Most came from a large region in west Africa below the Sahara Desert, known as Guinea.

Europeans and white Americans came to portray African society as primitive and uncivilized (in part to justify the enslavement of Africa's people). But most Africans were, in fact, civilized peoples with well-developed economies and political systems. The residents of upper Guinea had substantial commercial contact with the Mediterranean world—trading ivory, gold, and slaves for finished goods—and, largely as a result, became early converts to Islam. After the collapse of the ancient kingdom of Ghana around A.D. 1100, they created the even larger empire of Mali, which survived into the fifteenth century and whose trading center at Timbuktu became fabled as a center of education and a meeting place of the peoples of many lands.

Farther south, Africans were more isolated from Europe and the Mediterranean and were more politically fragmented. The central social unit was the village, which usually consisted of members of an extended family group. Some groups of villages united in small kingdoms. But no large empires emerged in the south. Nevertheless, these southern societies developed extensive trade—in woven fabrics, ceramics, wooden and iron goods, as well as crops and livestock—both among themselves and, to a lesser degree, with the outside world.

African civilizations naturally developed economies that reflected the climates and resources of their lands. In upper Guinea, fishing and rice cultivation, supplemented by the extensive trade with Mediterranean lands, were the foundation of the economy. Farther south, Africans grew wheat and other food crops, raised livestock, and fished. There were some more nomadic tribes in the interior, who subsisted largely on hunting and gathering and had less elaborate social systems. But most Africans were sedentary, farming people.

As in many Indian societies in America, but in contrast to the European tradition, African families tended to be matrilineal. This means that people traced their heredity through and inherited property from their mothers. Women played a major role, often the dominant role, in trade; in many areas, they were the principal farmers (while the men hunted, fished, and raised livestock); and everywhere, they managed child care and food preparation. Most tribes also divided political power by gender, with men choosing leaders and systems for managing male affairs and women choosing parallel leaders to handle female matters.

In those areas of west Africa where indigenous religions had survived the spread of Islam (which included most of the lands south of the empire of Mali), people worshiped many gods, whom they associated with various aspects of the natural world and whose spirits they believed lived in trees, rocks, forests, and streams. Most Africans also developed forms of ancestor worship and took great care in tracing family lineage; the most revered priests were generally the oldest people.

Small elites of priests and nobles stood at the top of many African societies. Most people belonged to a large middle group of farmers, traders, crafts workers, and others. At the bottom of society were slaves—men and women who were put into bondage after being captured in wars, because of criminal behavior, or as a result of unpaid debts. Slavery was not usually permanent; people were generally in bondage for a fixed term, and in the meantime retained certain legal protections (including the right to marry). Children did not inherit their parents' condition of bondage. The slavery that Africans would experience at the hands of the Europeans was to be very different.

The African slave trade long preceded European settlement in the New World. As early as the eighth century, west Africans began selling slaves to traders from the Mediterranean. When Portuguese sailors began exploring the coast of Africa in the fifteenth century, they too bought slaves and took them back to Portugal, where there was a small but steady demand. In the sixteenth century, however, the market for slaves increased dramatically as a result of the growing European demand for sugar cane. The small areas of sugar cultivation in the Mediterranean were proving inadequate, and production soon moved to new areas: to the island of Madeira off the African coast, which became a Portuguese colony, and not long thereafter (still in the sixteenth century) to the Caribbean islands and Brazil. Sugar was a labor-intensive crop, and the demand for African workers in these new areas of cultivation was high. At first the slave traders were overwhelmingly Portuguese and, to a lesser extent, Spanish. By the seventeenth century, the Dutch had won control of most of the market. In the eighteenth century, the English dominated it; by then, slavery had spread well beyond its original locations in the Caribbean and South America and into the English colonies to the north.

## THE ARRIVAL OF THE ENGLISH

England's first documented contact with the New World came only five years after Spain's. In 1497, John Cabot (like Columbus, a native of Genoa) sailed to the northeastern coast of North America on an expedition sponsored by King Henry VII. Other English navigators, continuing Cabot's unsuccessful search for a northwest passage through the New World to the Orient, explored other areas of North America during the sixteenth century. But nearly a century passed before the English made any serious efforts to establish colonies there. Like other European nations, England had to experience an internal transformation before it could begin settling new lands.

### Incentives for Colonization

Interest in colonization grew in part as a response to social and economic problems of sixteenth-century England. The English people suffered from frequent and costly European wars, and they suffered from almost constant religious strife within their own land. Many suffered too from a harsh economic transformation of the countryside. Because the worldwide demand for wool was growing rapidly, landowners were converting their land from fields for crops to pastures for sheep. The result was a significant growth in the wool trade—and a reduction in the amount of land available for growing food. Many of the displaced farmers became beggars or criminals. England's food supply declined at the same time that the English population was growing—from 3 million in 1485 to 4 million in 1603. To some of the English, the New World began to seem attractive because it offered something that was growing scarce in England: land.

At the same time, new merchant capitalists were prospering by selling the products of England's growing wool-cloth industry abroad. At first, most exporters did business almost entirely as individuals. In time, however, merchants formed companies that operated on the basis of charters from the monarch giving the companies monopolies for trading in particular regions. Investors in these companies often made fantastic profits, and they were eager to expand their profitable trade.

Central to this drive was the emergence of a new concept of economic life known as mercantilism. Mercantilism rested on the belief that the world's wealth was finite, that one person or nation could grow rich only at the expense of another, and that a nation's economic health depended, therefore, on extracting as much wealth as possible from foreign lands and exporting as little wealth as possible from home. The principles of mercantilism spread throughout Europe in the sixteenth and seventeenth centuries and increased the competition among nations. Every European state was trying to find markets for its exports while trying to limit its imports. One result was the increased attractiveness of acquiring colonies, which could become the source of raw materials and a market for the colonizing power's goods.

In England, the mercantilistic program thrived at first on the basis of the flourishing wool trade with the European continent, and particularly with the great cloth market in Antwerp. In the 1550s, however, that glutted market began to collapse, and English merchants had to look elsewhere for overseas trade. The establishment of colonies seemed to be an answer to their problems. Some English also believed colonies would help alleviate poverty and unemployment by siphoning off the surplus population. Perhaps most important, colonial commerce would allow England to acquire products for which the nation had previously been dependent on foreigners—products such as lumber, naval stores, and silver and gold.

There were also religious motives for colonization. The Protestant Reformation began in Germany in 1517, when Martin Luther challenged some of the basic practices and beliefs of the Roman Catholic Church—until then, the supreme religious authority. Luther quickly won a wide following among ordinary men and women in northern Europe. When the pope excommunicated him in 1520, Luther began leading his followers out of the Catholic Church entirely.

As the spirit of the Reformation spread rapidly throughout Europe, other dissidents began offering other alternatives to Catholicism. The Swiss theologian John Calvin went even further than Luther had in rejecting the Catholic belief that human behavior could affect an individual's prospects for salvation. Calvin introduced the doctrine of predestination. God "elected" some people to be saved and condemned others to damnation; each person's destiny was determined before birth, and no one could change that predetermined fate. But those who accepted Calvin's teachings came to believe that the way they led their lives might reveal to them their chances of salvation. A wicked or useless existence would be a sign of damnation; saintliness, diligence, and success could be signs of grace. Calvinism created anxieties among its followers, but it also produced a strong incentive to lead virtuous, productive lives. The new creed spread rapidly throughout northern Europe and produced (among other groups) the Huguenots in France and the Puritans in England.

The English Reformation was less a result of these doctrinal revolts than of a political dispute between the king and the pope. In 1529 King Henry VIII, angered by the refusal of the pope to grant him a divorce from his Spanish wife, broke England's ties with the Catholic Church and established himself as the head of the Christian faith in his country. After Henry's death, his Catholic daughter, Queen Mary, restored England's allegiance to Rome and persecuted those who resisted. But when Mary died in 1558, her half-sister, Elizabeth I, became England's sovereign and once again severed the nation's connection with the Catholic Church, this time for good.

To many English people, however, the new Church of England—which differed little at first from the Catholic Church—was not reformed enough. Some had been affected by the teachings of the European Reformation, and they complained that theirs was a church that had abandoned Rome without abandoning Rome's offensive beliefs and practices. They clamored for reforms that would "purify" the church, and thus they became known as Puritans.

The most radical Puritans, known as Separatists, were determined to worship as they pleased in their own independent congregations, despite English laws that required all subjects to attend regular Anglican services. But most Puritans did not wish to leave the Church of England. They wanted, rather, to simplify Anglican forms of worship and reform the leadership of the church. Like the Separatists, they grew increasingly frustrated by the refusal of political and ecclesiastical authorities to respond to their demands.

Puritan discontent grew rapidly after the death of Elizabeth, the last of the Tudors, and the accession of James I, the first of the Stuarts, in 1603. Convinced that kings ruled by divine right, James quickly antagonized the Puritans, a group that included most of the rising businessmen, by resorting to illegal and arbitrary taxation, by favoring English Catholics in the granting of charters and other favors, and by supporting "high-church" forms of ceremony. By the early seventeenth century, some religious nonconformists were beginning to look for places of refuge outside the kingdom.

Many factors, therefore, combined to increase the interest of the English in peopling distant lands—social and economic instability, religious discontent, personal ambition, commercial greed. England's first experience with colonization, however, came not in the New World but in neighboring Ireland. The English had long laid claim to the island, but only in the late sixteenth century did serious efforts at colonization begin. The long, brutal process by which the English attempted (never entirely successfully) to subdue the Irish led to an important assumption about colonization that the English would take with them to America: the belief that settlements in foreign lands must retain a rigid separation from the native populations. Unlike the Spanish in America, the English in Ireland tried to build a separate society of their own, peopled with emigrants from England itself. They would take that concept with them to the New World.

### The French and the Dutch in America

English settlers in North America were to encounter not only natives but also other Europeans who were, like them, driven by mercantilist ideas. There were scattered North American outposts of the Spanish Empire, whose residents looked on the English as intruders. More important, there were French and Dutch settlers.

France founded its first permanent settlement in America at Quebec in 1608, less than a year after the English started their first at Jamestown. The colony's population grew very slowly, but the French exercised an influence in the New World disproportionate to their numbers, because of their relationships with Native Americans. Unlike the early English settlers, who hugged the coastline and traded with the Indians of the interior through intermediaries, the French forged close ties with natives deep inside the continent. French Jesuit missionaries established some of the first contacts between the two peoples. More important were the *coureurs de bois*— adventurous fur traders and trappers—who also penetrated far into the wilderness and developed an extensive trade that became one of the underpinnings of the French colonial economy. The French traders formed partnerships with the Indians and often became virtually a part of native society, living among the natives and at times marrying Indian women. The fur trade helped open the way for French agricultural estates (or *seigneuries*) along the St. Lawrence River and for the development of trade and military centers at Quebec and Montreal.

The English also faced competition from the Dutch in North America. Holland in the early seventeenth century was one of the leading trading nations of the world. In 1609 an English explorer in the employ of the Dutch, Henry Hudson, sailed up the river that was to be named for him in what is now New York State; and his explorations led to a Dutch claim on that territory. In 1624, not long after the first two permanent English colonies took root in Jamestown and Plymouth, the Dutch created a wedge between them when the Dutch West India Company established a series of permanent trading posts on the Hudson, Delaware, and Connecticut Rivers. The company actively encouraged settlement of the region, and the result was the colony of New Netherland and its principal town, New Amsterdam, on Manhattan Island. But the Dutch population remained relatively small.

## The First English Settlements

The first permanent English settlement in the New World was established at Jamestown, in Virginia, in 1607. But for nearly thirty years before that, English merchants and adventurers had been engaged in a series of failed efforts to create colonies in America.

Through much of the sixteenth century, the English had harbored mixed feelings about the New World. They were intrigued by its possibilities, but they were also leery of Spain, which remained the dominant force in America and the dominant naval power in Europe. In 1588, however, King Philip II of Spain sent one of the largest military fleets in the history of warfare—the Spanish Armada—across the English Channel to attack England itself. The smaller English fleet, taking advantage of its greater maneuverability, dispersed the armada and, in a single stroke, ended Spain's domination of the Atlantic and its threat to English colonization of the New World.

The pioneers of English colonization were Sir Humphrey Gilbert and his half-brother Sir Walter Raleigh—both friends of Queen Elizabeth, and both veterans of earlier colonial efforts in Ireland. In 1578 Gilbert obtained from Elizabeth a six-year patent granting him the exclusive right "to inhabit and possess any remote and heathen lands not already in the possession of any Christian prince." Five years later, after several setbacks, he led an expedition to Newfoundland and proceeded south looking for a good place to build a profitable colony. But a storm sank his ship, and he was lost at sea.

Sir Walter Raleigh was undeterred. The next year, he secured his own six-year grant from the queen and sent a small group of men on an expedition to explore the North American coast. When they returned, Raleigh named the region they had explored Virginia, in honor of Elizabeth, who was unmarried and was known as the "Virgin Queen."

In 1585 Raleigh recruited his cousin, Sir Richard Grenville, to lead a group of men to the island of Roanoke, off the coast of what is now North Carolina, to establish a colony. Grenville deposited the settlers on the island, antagonized the natives by destroying an Indian village as retaliation for a minor theft, and returned to England. The following spring, with expected supplies and reinforcements from England long overdue, Sir Francis Drake unexpectedly arrived in Roanoke. The dispirited colonists boarded his ships and left.

Raleigh tried again in 1587, sending an expedition to Roanoke carrying ninety-one men, seventeen women (two of them pregnant), and nine children. The settlers attempted to take up where the first group of colonists had left off. (Shortly after arriving, one of the women—the daughter of the commander of the expedition, John White—gave birth to a daughter, Virginia Dare, the first American-born child of English parents.) White returned to England after several weeks, in search of supplies and additional

ROANOKE A drawing by one of the English colonists in the ill-fated Roanoke expedition of 1585 became the basis for this engraving by Theodore DeBry, published in England in 1590. A small European ship carrying settlers approaches the island of Roanoke, at left. The wreckage of several larger vessels farther out to sea and the presence of Indian settlements on the mainland and on Roanoke itself suggest some of the perils the settlers encountered.

settlers, leaving his daughter and granddaughter behind. Because of a war with Spain, he was unable to return to Roanoke for three years. When he did, in 1590, he found the island utterly deserted, with no clue to the fate of the settlers other than the cryptic inscription "Croatoan" carved on a post. No solution to the mystery of the "Lost Colony" has ever been found.

The Roanoke disaster marked the end of Sir Walter Raleigh's involvement in English colonization of the New World, and no later colonizer would receive grants of land in America as vast or undefined as those Raleigh and Gilbert had acquired. But despite the discouraging example of these first experiences, the colonizing impulse remained very much alive. In the early years of the seventeenth century, a group of London merchants to whom Raleigh had assigned his charter rights decided to renew the attempt at colonization in Virginia. A rival group of merchants, from the area around Plymouth, was also interested in American ventures and was sponsoring voyages of exploration farther north. In 1606 James I issued a new charter, which divided America between the two groups. The London group got the exclusive right to colonize in the south, and the Plymouth merchants received the same right in the north. Through the efforts of these and other companies, the first enduring English colonies would be established in America.

# CHAPTER TWO

# The English "Transplantations"

*The Early Chesapeake* ⌒ *The Caribbean Colonies*
*The Growth of New England* ⌒ *The Restoration Colonies*
*The Development of Empire*

HE ROANOKE FIASCO dampened colonization enthusiasm in England for a time. But the lures of the New World—the presumably vast riches, the abundant land, the promise of religious freedom, the chance to begin anew—were too strong to be suppressed for very long. By the early seventeenth century, the effort to establish permanent English colonies in the New World resumed.

The new efforts were much like the earlier, failed ones: private ventures, with little planning or direction from the English government; small, fragile enterprises led by people unprepared for the hardships they were to face. Unlike the Roanoke experiment, they survived, but not before experiencing a series of disastrous setbacks.

Four things in particular shaped the character of these English settlements. First, the colonies were business enterprises, and one of their principal concerns was to produce a profit for their corporate sponsors. Second, because the colonies were tied only indirectly to the crown, they began from the start to develop their own political and social institutions. Third, as in Ireland, there were few efforts to blend English society with the society of the natives. The Europeans tried to isolate themselves from the Indians and created communities that would be entirely their own: "transplantations" of societies from the Old World to the New. And fourth, almost nothing worked out as they had planned.

## THE EARLY CHESAPEAKE

Once James I had issued his 1606 charters to the London and Plymouth Companies, the Plymouth group floundered and largely abandoned its ef-

## TIME LINE

| 1607 | 1619 | 1620 | 1622 | 1624 | 1630 |
|------|------|------|------|------|------|
| Jamestown founded | First African workers in Virginia | Pilgrims found Plymouth Colony | Powhatan Indians attack Virginia | Dutch settle Manhattan | Puritans establish Massachusetts Bay Colony |
| | Virginia House of Burgesses meets | | | | |

| 1634 | 1635 | 1637 | | 1663 | 1664 |
|------|------|------|--|------|------|
| Maryland founded | Roger Williams founds Rhode Island | Anne Hutchinson expelled from Massachusetts Bay Colony | | Carolina chartered | English capture New Netherlands |
| | | Pequot War | | | |

| 1675 | 1676 | 1681 | 1686 | 1689 | 1732 |
|------|------|------|------|------|------|
| King Philip's War | Bacon's Rebellion | Pennsylvania chartered | Dominion of New England | Glorious Revolution in America | Georgia chartered |

forts at settling the northern regions of British America. But the London Company moved quickly and decisively to launch a colonizing expedition headed for Virginia—a party of 144 men aboard three ships, the *Godspeed*, the *Discovery*, and the *Susan Constant*, which set sail for America early in 1607.

### The Founding of Jamestown

Only 104 men survived the journey. They reached the American coast in the spring of 1607, sailed into Chesapeake Bay and up a river they named the James, and established their colony on a peninsula. They called it Jamestown.

They chose an inland setting that they believed would offer them security from the natives. But they chose poorly. The site was low and swampy and subject to outbreaks of malaria. It was surrounded by thick woods, which were difficult to clear for cultivation. And it bordered the territories of powerful local Indians. The result could hardly have been more disastrous. For seventeen years, one wave of settlers after another attempted to make Jamestown a habitable and profitable colony. Every effort failed. The town became instead a place of misery and death, and the London Company found itself saddled with endless losses. All that could be said of Jamestown at the end of this first period of its existence was that it had survived.

The initial colonists ran into serious difficulties from the moment they landed. They had no prior exposure to the infections of the new land and were highly vulnerable to local diseases, particularly malaria. The promoters in London demanded a quick return on their investment and diverted the colonists' energies into futile searches for gold and only slightly more successful efforts to pile up lumber, tar, pitch, and iron for export. These energies would have been better spent on growing food. The promoters also had little interest in creating a family-centered community, and they sent

RECRUITING FOR THE COLONIES, 1609 This is the title page for a pamphlet that describes the attractions of settlement in the New World. Most accounts of the "excellent fruites" of life in Virginia were, like this one, written by people who had never seen America but who shared the excitement that the colonies inspired among the early-seventeenth-century English.

Growth of the Chesapeake, 1607–1750

Virginia Colony

Fairfax Proprietary

To Lord Baltimore, 1632

Granville Proprietary

(1649) Date settlement founded

virtually no women to Jamestown. Hence, settlers could not establish real households and had difficulty feeling any sense of a permanent stake in the community.

By January 1608, when ships appeared with additional men and supplies, all but 38 of the first 104 colonists were dead. Jamestown, now facing extinction, survived largely as a result of the efforts of Captain John Smith, who at age twenty-seven was already a famous world traveler. Leadership in the colony had been bitterly divided until the fall of 1608, when Smith took control. He imposed work and order on the community. He also organized raids on neighboring Indian villages to steal food and kidnap natives. During the colony's second winter, fewer than a dozen (in a population of about 200) died. By the summer of 1609, when Smith returned to England, the colony was showing promise of survival. But Jamestown's ordeal was not over yet.

## Reorganization and Expansion

As Jamestown struggled to survive, the London Company (now renamed the Virginia Company) was already dreaming of bigger things. In 1609, it obtained a new charter from the king, which increased its power and enlarged its territory; and it sent Lord De La Warr to be the colony's first governor. The company raised money by selling additional stock. It offered stock in the company to planters who were willing to migrate at their own expense. And it provided free passage to Virginia for poorer people who would agree to serve the company for seven years. In the spring of 1609, confident that it was now poised to transform Jamestown into a vibrant, successful venture, the company dispatched a fleet of nine vessels with about 600 people (including some women and children) aboard to Virginia.

Disaster followed. One of the Virginia-bound ships was lost at sea in a hurricane. Another ran aground on one of the Bermuda islands and was unable to free itself for months. Many of those who reached Jamestown, still weak from their long and stormy voyage, succumbed to fevers before winter came. The winter of 1609–1610 became known as the "starving time," a period worse than anything before. The local Indians, antagonized by hostile actions by the early English settlers, killed off the livestock in the woods and kept the colonists barricaded within their palisade. The Europeans lived on what they could find: "dogs, cats, rats, snakes, toadstools, horsehides," and even the "corpses of dead men," as one survivor recalled. When the migrants who had run aground in Bermuda finally arrived in Jamestown the following May, they found only about 60 emaciated people (out of 500 residents the previous summer) still alive. The new arrivals took the survivors onto their ship, abandoned the settlement, and sailed for home. But as the refugees proceeded down the James, they met an English ship coming up the river—part of a fleet bringing supplies and the colony's first governor, Lord De La Warr. The departing settlers agreed to return to Jamestown. New relief expeditions with hundreds of colonists soon began to arrive, and the effort to turn a profit in Jamestown resumed.

Under the leadership of its first governors, Virginia survived and even expanded. New settlements began lining the river above and below Jamestown. That was partly because of the order and discipline the governors at times managed to impose and because of increased military assaults on the local Indian tribes to protect the new settlements. But it was also because the colonists had at last discovered a marketable crop: tobacco.

Europeans had become aware of tobacco soon after Columbus's first return from the West Indies, where he had seen the Cuban natives smoking small cigars *(tabacos)*, which they inserted in the nostril. By the early seventeenth century, tobacco from the Spanish colonies was already in wide use in Europe. Then in 1612, the Jamestown planter John Rolfe, noting that local Indians were growing a strain of tobacco, began trying to cultivate the crop in Virginia. Tobacco planting soon spread up and down the James.

Almost immediately, tobacco cultivation created great pressure for territorial expansion. Tobacco growers needed large areas of farmland to grow their profitable crops; and because tobacco exhausted the soil very quickly, the demand for land increased rapidly. As a result, English farmers began establishing plantations deeper and deeper in the interior, isolating themselves from the center of European settlement, Jamestown, and penetrating farther into the territory of the native tribes.

The tobacco economy also created a heavy demand for labor. To entice new workers to the colony, the Virginia Company established what it called the "headright" system. Headrights were fifty-acre grants of land. Those who already lived in the colony received two headrights (100 acres) apiece. Each new settler received a single headright for himself or herself. This system encouraged family groups to migrate together, since the more family members traveled to America, the more land the family would receive. In addition, anyone who paid for the passage of immigrants to Virginia would receive an extra headright for each arrival, an encouragement to the prosperous to import new laborers. As a result, some colonists were able to assemble large plantations.

The company also transported ironworkers and other skilled craftsmen to Virginia to diversify the economy. In 1619, it sent 100 Englishwomen to the colony (which was still overwhelmingly male) to become the wives of male colonists. It promised the male colonists the full rights of Englishmen (as provided in the original charter of 1606), an end to strict and arbitrary rule, and even a share in self-government. On July 30, 1619, delegates from the various communities met as the House of Burgesses. It was the first meeting of an elected legislature within what was to become the United States.

A month later, Virginia established another important precedent. As John Rolfe recorded, "about the latter end of August" a Dutch ship brought in "20 and odd Negroes." There is some reason to believe that the colonists did not consider these first Africans in Virginia slaves, that they thought of them rather as servants to be held for a term of years and then freed, like the white servants with whom the planters were already familiar. For a time, moreover, the use of black labor remained limited. Although Africans trickled steadily into the colony, planters continued to prefer European indentured servants until at least the 1670s, when white servants began to become scarce and expensive. But the small group of blacks who arrived in 1619 marked the first step toward the enslavement of Africans within what was to be the American republic.

The European settlers in Virginia built their society not only on the co-erced labor of imported Africans but also on the effective suppression of the local Indians. For two years, Sir Thomas Dale, De La Warr's successor as governor, led unrelenting assaults against the Powhatan Indians, led by (and named for) their formidable chief, Powhatan. In the process, Dale kidnapped Powhatan's young daughter Pocahontas. Several years earlier, Pocahontas had played a role in mediating differences between her people and the Europeans and, according to legend, once intervened with her father to spare John Smith from execution. But now, Powhatan refused to ransom her. Living among the English, Pocahontas gradually adapted to many of their ways. She converted to Christianity and in 1614 married John Rolfe and visited England with him. As a Christian convert and a gracious woman, she stirred interest among many English in projects to "civilize" the Indians. She died shortly before her planned return to Virginia.

By the time of Pocahontas's marriage, Powhatan had ceased his attacks on the English in the face of overwhelming odds. But after his death several years later, his brother, Opechancanough, revived the effort to defend tribal lands and began secretly to plan the elimination of the English intruders. On a March morning in 1622, tribesmen called on the white settlements as if to offer goods for sale; then they suddenly attacked. Not until 347 whites of both sexes and all ages (including John Rolfe) lay dead were the Indian warriors finally forced to retreat. And not until over twenty years later were the Powhatans finally defeated.

By then, however, the Virginia Company in London was defunct. The company had poured virtually all its funds into its profitless Jamestown venture and in the aftermath of the 1622 Indian uprising faced imminent bankruptcy. In 1624, James I revoked the company's charter, and the colony at last came under the control of the crown. So it would remain until 1776.

With the stabilization of Virginia's English sponsorship, the suppression of the Indian threat, and the development of a profitable cash crop, the colony finally seemed secure. But this success had come at a terrible cost. In Virginia's first seventeen years, more than 8,500 white settlers had arrived in the colony. In 1624, the white population stood at 1,300.

### Maryland and the Calverts

The Maryland colony ultimately came to look much like Virginia, but its origins were very different from those of its southern neighbor. George

Calvert, the first Lord Baltimore, was a recent convert to Catholicism and a shrewd businessman, and he envisioned establishing a colony in America both as a great speculative venture in real estate and as a retreat for English Catholics oppressed by the Anglican establishment at home. Calvert died while still negotiating with the king for a charter to establish a colony in the Chesapeake region. But in 1632 his son Cecilius, the second Lord Baltimore, finally received the charter.

The Maryland charter was remarkable not only for the extent of the territory it granted to Calvert—an area that encompassed parts of what is now Pennsylvania, Delaware, and Virginia, in addition to present-day Maryland—but also for the powers it bestowed on him. He and his heirs were to hold their province as "true and absolute lords and proprietaries." Their only obligation to the king was paying an annual fee to the crown.

Lord Baltimore named his brother, Leonard Calvert, as governor of the colony. In March 1634, two ships—the *Ark* and the *Dove*—bearing Calvert along with 200 or 300 other colonists, entered the Potomac River, turned into one of its eastern tributaries, and established the village of St. Mary's on a high, dry bluff. Neighboring Indians befriended the settlers and provided them with temporary shelter and with stocks of corn. The early Marylanders experienced no Indian assaults, no plagues, no starving time.

The Calverts needed to attract thousands of settlers to Maryland if their expensive colonial venture was to pay. As a result, they had to encourage the immigration of Protestants as well as their fellow English Catholics. The Calverts soon realized that Catholics would always be a minority in the colony, and so they adopted a policy of religious toleration, embodied in the 1649 "Act Concerning Religion," which ensured freedom of worship for all Christians. Nevertheless, politics in Maryland remained plagued for years by tensions, and at times violence, between the Catholic minority and the Protestant majority.

The government in Maryland gradually came to resemble that of other English colonies in America in many ways. At the insistence of the first settlers, the Calverts agreed in 1635 to the calling of a representative assembly—the House of Delegates—whose proceedings were based on the rules of Parliament. But the proprietor retained absolute authority to distribute land as he wished; and since Lord Baltimore granted large estates to his relatives and to other English aristocrats, a distinct upper class soon established itself. By 1640, a severe labor shortage forced a modification of the land-grant procedure; and Maryland, like Virginia, adopted a headright system—a grant of 100 acres to each male settler, another 100 for his wife and each servant, and 50 for each of his children. But the great landlords of the colony's earliest years remained powerful even as the population grew larger and more diverse. Like Virginia, Maryland became a center of tobacco cultivation; and as in Virginia, planters worked their land with the aid, first, of indentured servants imported from England and then, beginning late in the seventeenth century, of slaves imported from Africa.

## Turbulent Virginia

By the mid-seventeenth century, the Virginia colony had survived its early disasters. Its population was growing, and its economy was becoming more complex and profitable. Soon, factions began to emerge within the colony to compete for influence within the government, and particularly for influence over policies toward the natives.

For more than thirty years, one man—Sir William Berkeley, the royal governor of Virginia—dominated the politics of the colony. He took office in 1642 at the age of thirty-six and with but one brief interruption remained in control of the government until the 1670s. In his first years as governor, he helped open up the interior of Virginia by sending explorers across the Blue Ridge Mountains and crushing a 1644 Indian uprising. The defeated Indians agreed to a treaty ceding to England most of the territory east of the mountains and establishing a boundary west of which white settlement would be prohibited. But the rapid growth of the Virginia population made this agreement difficult to sustain. By 1650, Virginia's population of 16,000 was twice what it had been ten years before; by 1660, it had more than doubled again, to 40,000. By 1652, English settlers had established three counties in the territory set aside by the treaty for the Indians. Unsurprisingly, there were frequent clashes between natives and whites.

In the meantime, Berkeley was expanding his own powers. By 1670, the vote for delegates to the House of Burgesses, once open to all white men, was restricted to landowners. Elections were rare, and the same burgesses, representing the established planters of the eastern (or tidewater) region of the colony and subservient to the governor, remained in office year after year. The more recent settlers on the frontier were underrepresented in the assembly or not represented at all.

Resentment of the power of the governor and the tidewater aristocrats grew steadily in the newly settled lands of the west (often known as the "backcountry"). In 1676, this resentment helped create a major conflict, led by Nathaniel Bacon, a young, handsome aristocrat who had arrived in Virginia in 1673. Bacon had a good farm in the west and a seat on the governor's council. But like other members of the new backcountry gentry, he was at odds in crucial ways with the governor and his tidewater allies, particularly over

Indian policy. The frontier elites were in constant danger of attack from the tribes on whose lands they were encroaching, and they chafed at the governor's attempts to hold the line of settlement steady so as to avoid antagonizing the Indians. Bacon's rift with Berkeley was also a result of resentment that he was not part of the inner circle of the governor's council and that Berkeley refused to allow him a piece of the Indian fur trade, which the governor himself controlled.

Bloody events thrust Bacon into the role of leader of an anti-Berkeley faction. In 1675, a major conflict erupted in the west between whites and natives. As the fighting escalated, Bacon and other concerned landholders demanded that the governor send the militia. Berkeley, however, simply ordered the construction of several new forts along the western border. Bacon responded by offering to organize a volunteer army of backcountry men who would do their own fighting. Berkeley, who saw Bacon as a potential rival and feared a needless slaughter of the natives, rejected the offer. Bacon ignored him and launched a series of vicious but unsuccessful pursuits of the Indian challengers. When Berkeley heard of the unauthorized military effort, he dismissed Bacon from the governor's council and proclaimed him and his men to be rebels. Bacon now turned his army against the governor and, in what became known as Bacon's Rebellion, twice led his troops east to Jamestown. The first time he won a temporary pardon from the governor; the second time, after the governor reneged on the agreement, Bacon burned the city and drove the governor into exile. But then Bacon died suddenly of dysentery; and Berkeley, his position bolstered by the arrival of British troops, soon regained control. In 1677, the Indians (aware of their inability to defeat the white forces militarily) reluctantly signed a new treaty that opened new lands to white settlement.

Bacon's Rebellion was significant for several reasons. It was evidence of the continuing struggle to define the Indian and white spheres of influence in Virginia. It revealed the bitterness of the competition among rival elites and between easterners and westerners in particular. But it also demonstrated the potential for instability in the colony's large population of free, landless men. These men—most of them former indentured servants without property or prospects—had formed the bulk of Bacon's constituency during the rebellion. Their hatred of Indians drew them to Bacon, but they also harbored a deep animosity toward the landed gentry (of which Bacon himself, ironically, was a part). One result was that landed elites in both eastern and western Virginia began to recognize a common interest in quelling social unrest from below. That was one of the reasons that they turned increasingly to the African slave trade to fulfill their need for labor. African slaves, unlike white indentured servants, did not need to be released after a fixed term and hence did not threaten to become an unstable, landless class.

## THE CARIBBEAN COLONIES

The Chesapeake was the site of the first permanent English settlements in the New World. But throughout the first half of the seventeenth century, the most important destinations for English immigrants were the islands of the Caribbean and the northern way station of Bermuda. These Caribbean societies had close ties to English North America and influenced the development of the mainland colonies in many ways.

### The West Indies

Before the arrival of the Europeans, most of the Caribbean islands had substantial native populations. But beginning with Christopher Columbus's first visit in 1492, and accelerating after 1496, when the Spanish established their first colony on Hispaniola, the native population was all but wiped out by European epidemics.

The Spanish created substantial settlements only on the largest of the islands: Cuba, Hispaniola, and Puerto Rico. English, French, and Dutch traders began settling on some of the smaller islands early in the sixteenth century, despite the Spanish claim to them. These fledgling colonies were always vulnerable to Spanish attack. But after Spain and the Netherlands went to war in 1621 (distracting the Spanish navy and leaving the English in the Caribbean relatively unmolested), the pace of English colonization increased. By midcentury, there were several important English settlements on the islands, the most important of them on Antigua, St. Kitts, Jamaica, and Barbados.

In their first years in the Caribbean, English settlers experimented unsuccessfully with tobacco and cotton. But they soon discovered that the most lucrative export crop was sugar, for which there was a substantial and growing market in Europe. Because raising sugar required a great deal of labor, and because the native population (ravaged by epidemics) was too small to provide a work force, English planters quickly found it necessary to import laborers. As in the Chesapeake, they began by bringing indentured servants from England. But the arduous work and the enervating tropical climate discouraged white laborers. By midcentury, therefore, the English

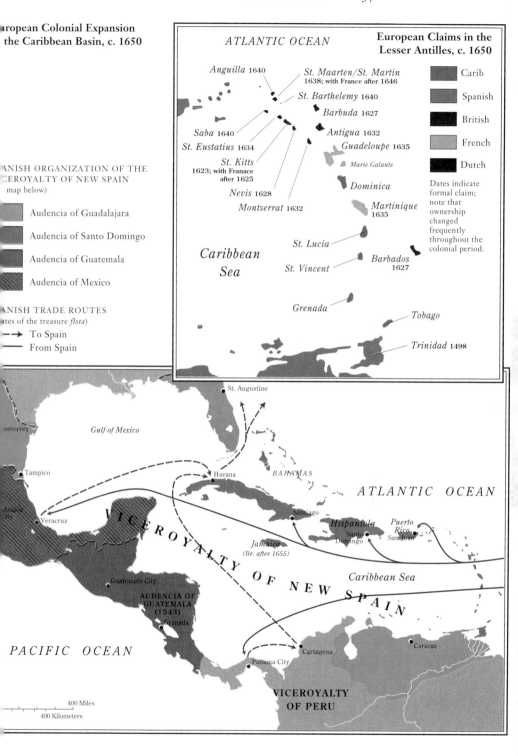

uropean Colonial Expansion
the Caribbean Basin, c. 1650

**European Claims in the Lesser Antilles, c. 1650**

ATLANTIC OCEAN

Anguilla 1640

St. Maarten/St. Martin
1638; with France after 1646

St. Barthelemy 1640

Barbuda 1627

Saba 1640

Antigua 1632

St. Eustatius 1634

Guadeloupe 1635

St. Kitts
1623; with Franace
after 1625

Marie Galante

Nevis 1628

Dominica

Montserrat 1632

Martinique
1635

St. Lucia

Caribbean
Sea

Barbados
1627

St. Vincent

Grenada

Tobago

Trinidad 1498

Carib

Spanish

British

French

Dutch

Dates indicate
formal claim;
note that
ownership
changed
frequently
throughout the
colonial period.

ANISH ORGANIZATION OF THE
CEROYALTY OF NEW SPAIN
map below)

Audencia of Guadalajara

Audencia of Santo Domingo

Audencia of Guatemala

Audencia of Mexico

ANISH TRADE ROUTES
tes of the treasure *flota*)

—→ To Spain

—— From Spain

St. Augustine

onterrey

Gulf of Mexico

Tampico

Havana

BAHAMAS

ATLANTIC OCEAN

exico
ity

Veracruz

Santiago

Hispaniola

Puerto
Rico

Santo
Domingo

San Juan

Jamaica
(Br. after 1655)

Caribbean Sea

Guatemala City

AUDENCIA OF
GUATEMALA
(1543)

Granada

PACIFIC OCEAN

Cartagena

Caracas

Panama City

VICEROYALTY
OF PERU

400 Miles

400 Kilometers

planters in the Caribbean (like the Spanish colonists) were relying more and more heavily on an enslaved African work force, which soon substantially outnumbered them.

On Barbados and other islands where a flourishing sugar economy developed, the English planters were a tough, aggressive, and ambitious breed. Some of them grew enormously wealthy; and since their livelihoods depended on their work forces, they created a rigid slave system remarkably quickly. By the late seventeenth century, African slaves outnumbered white settlers by better than four to one.

## Masters and Slaves

A small white population, much of it enjoying great economic success, and a large African population, all of it in bondage, were a potentially explosive combination. Whites in the Caribbean—fearful of slave revolts—monitored their labor forces closely and often harshly, and the English West Indians devised a rigid set of laws and practices to ensure control over their black laborers. There was little in either the law or the character of the economy to compel planters to pay much attention to the welfare of their workers. Many concluded it was cheaper to buy new slaves periodically than to protect the well-being of those they already owned, and it was not uncommon for masters literally to work their slaves to death. Few African workers survived more than a decade in the brutal Caribbean working environment. Even whites, who worked far less strenuously, often succumbed to the harsh climate; most died before the age of forty—often from tropical diseases to which they had no immunity.

Establishing a stable society and culture was extremely difficult for people living in such harsh and even deadly conditions. Many of the whites were principally interested in getting rich and had no long-term commitment to the islands. Those who could returned to England with their fortunes and left their estates in the hands of overseers. A large proportion of the European settlers either died or left at a young age, and the white population remained a distinct minority on the islands. The society of Europeans in the Caribbean lacked many of the institutions that gave stability to the North American settlements: church, family, community. The Caribbean colonies of England were governed by a small white elite ruling over a much larger population of Africans and natives.

Africans in the Caribbean faced much greater difficulties than the white settlers, but they managed to create a world of their own despite the hardships. They started families (although many of them were broken up by death or the slave trade); they sustained African religious and social traditions (and resisted Christianity); and within the rigidly controlled world of the sugar plantations, they established patterns of resistance.

The Caribbean settlements were important to the North American colonies in many ways. They were an important part of the Atlantic trading nexus in which many Americans became involved. They were the principal source of African slaves for the mainland colonies. And because Caribbean planters established an elaborate plantation system earlier than planters in North America, they provided models that many mainland people emulated.

## THE GROWTH OF NEW ENGLAND

The northern regions of British North America were slow to attract settlers, in part because the Plymouth Company was never able to mount a success-ful colonizing expedition after receiving its charter in 1606. It did, however, sponsor exploration of the region. Captain John Smith, after his departure from Jamestown, made an exploratory journey for the Plymouth merchants,

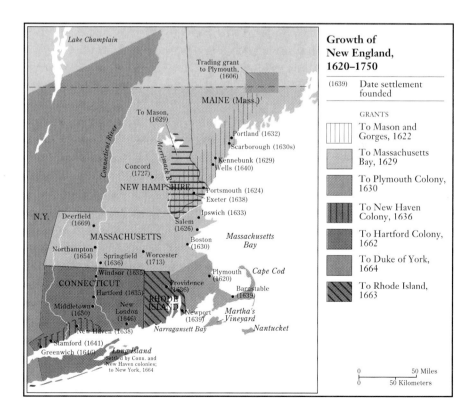

wrote an enthusiastic pamphlet about the lands he had seen, and called them New England.

### Plymouth Plantation

A discontented congregation of Puritan Separatists in England, not the Plymouth Company, established the first enduring European settlement in New England. In 1608, after years of persecution for attempting to practice their own religion, a congregation of Separatists from the hamlet of Scrooby began emigrating quietly (and illegally), a few at a time, to Leyden, Holland, where they could enjoy freedom of worship. But as foreigners in Holland, they could not join the Dutch guilds of craftsmen, and so they had to work at unskilled and poorly paid jobs. They also watched with alarm as their children began to speak Dutch, marry into Dutch families, and drift away from their church. Finally, some of the Separatists decided to move again, across the Atlantic, where they hoped to create a stable, protected community and where they could spread "the gospel of the Kingdom of Christ in those remote parts of the world."

In 1620, leaders of the Scrooby group obtained permission from the Virginia Company to settle in Virginia and received informal assurances from the king that he would "not molest them, provided they carried themselves peaceably." Several English merchants advanced the necessary funds for the venture. The "Pilgrims," as they saw themselves, sailed from Plymouth, England, in September 1620 on the *Mayflower*; thirty-five "saints" (Puritan Separatists) and sixty-seven "strangers" (people who were not part of the congregation) were aboard. In November, after a long and difficult voyage, they sighted land—the shore of what is now known as Cape Cod. That had not been their destination, but it was too late in the year to sail farther. So the Pilgrims chose a site for their settlement in the area just north of the cape, a place John Smith had labeled "Plymouth" on a map he had drawn during an earlier exploration of New England. Because Plymouth lay outside the London Company's territory, the settlers were not bound by the company's rules. So while still aboard ship, the "saints" in the group drew up an agreement, the Mayflower Compact, to establish a government for themselves. Then, on December 21, 1620, they stepped ashore at Plymouth Rock.

The Pilgrims' first winter was a difficult one. Half the colonists perished from malnutrition, disease, and exposure. But the colony survived, in large part because of crucial assistance from local Indians, who showed them how to gather seafood and cultivate corn. After the first autumn harvest, the settlers invited the natives to join them in a festival, the original Thanksgiving.

The Pilgrims could not create rich farms on the sandy and marshy soil around Plymouth, but they developed a profitable trade in fish and furs. New colonists arrived from England, and in a decade the population reached 300. The people of Plymouth Plantation chose as their governor the remarkable William Bradford, who governed successfully for many years without any serious interference from London.

The Pilgrims were always poor. As late as the 1640s, they had only one plow among them. But they were, on the whole, content to be left alone to live their lives in what they considered godly ways.

### The Massachusetts Bay Experiment

Turbulent events in England in the 1620s generated a strong interest in colonization among other groups of Puritans. James I had been creating tensions for years by his effort to assert the divine right of kings and by his harsh, repressive policies toward Puritans. In 1635, he was succeeded by his son, Charles I, who was even more autocratic than his father. The new king tried to restore Roman Catholicism to England and to destroy religious nonconformity. The Puritans were particular targets of Charles's policies; many of them were imprisoned for their beliefs. The king dissolved Parliament in 1629 (it was not to be recalled until 1640), ensuring that there would be no one in a position to oppose him.

In the midst of this turmoil, a group of Puritan merchants began organizing a new colonial venture in America. They obtained a grant of land in New England for most of the area now comprising Massachusetts and New Hampshire, and they acquired a charter from the king (who was evidently unaware of their religious inclinations) allowing them to create the Massachusetts Bay Company and to establish a colony in the New World. In 1629, they were ready to dispatch a substantial group of settlers to New England.

Some members of the Massachusetts Bay Company, however, saw the enterprise as more than a business venture. They wanted to create a refuge in New England for Puritans. After buying out the interests of company members who preferred to stay in England, the new owners elected a governor, John Winthrop, and sailed for New England in 1630. With 17 ships and 1,000 people, mostly family groups, it was the largest single migration of its kind in the seventeenth century. Winthrop carried with him the charter of the Massachusetts Bay Company, which meant that the colonists would be responsible to no company officials in England.

The Massachusetts migration quickly produced several settlements. The port of Boston, at the mouth of the Charles River, became the capital, but

A M E R I C A N V O I C E S

WILLIAM BRADFORD

## Safe Arrival of the Pilgrims at Cape Cod

BEING THUS ARRIVED in a good harbor, and brought safe to land, they fell upon their knees and blessed the God of Heaven who had brought them over the vast and furious ocean, and delivered them from all the perils and miseries thereof, again to set their feet on the firm and stable earth, their proper element. . . .

But here I cannot but stay and make a pause, and stand half amazed at this poor people's present condition; . . .they had now no friends to welcome them nor inns to entertain or refresh their weatherbeaten bodies; no houses or much less towns to repair to, to seek for succour. It is recorded in Scripture as a mercy to the Apostle and his shipwrecked company, that the barbarians showed them no small kindness in refreshing them, but these savage barbarians, when they met with them . . . were readier to fill their sides full of arrows than otherwise. . . . Besides, what could they see but a hideous and desolate wilderness, full of wild beasts and wild men—and what multitudes there might be of them they knew not. . . . Which way soever they turned their eyes (save upward to the heavens) they could have little solace or content in respect of any outward objects. For summer being done, all things stand upon them with a weatherbeaten face, and the whole country, full of woods and thickets, represented a wild and savage hue.

SOURCE: William Bradford, *Of Plymouth Plantation: 1620–1647*, ed. Samuel Eliot Morison, pp. 61–62. Copyright 1952 Samuel Eliot Morison. Reprinted by permission of Alfred A. Knopf, Inc.

in the course of the next decade colonists established several other towns in eastern Massachusetts: Charlestown, Newtown (later renamed Cambridge), Roxbury, Dorchester, Watertown, Ipswich, Concord, Sudbury, and others. John Winthrop continued to dominate the politics of Massachusetts Bay, but after 1634 he and most other officers of the colony had to face election each year.

Unlike the Separatist founders of Plymouth, the Puritan founders of Massachusetts had come to America with no intention of breaking away from the Church of England. But in every town, the community church had (in the words of the prominent minister John Cotton) "complete liberty to stand alone," without connection to Anglican hierarchy or ritual. Each congregation chose its own minister and regulated its own affairs. The result was what became the Congregational Church, a church controlled by its own congregation.

The Massachusetts Puritans were not grim or joyless, as many critics would later come to believe, but they were serious and pious. They strove to lead useful, conscientious lives of thrift and hard work, and they honored material success as evidence of God's favor. Winthrop and the other founders of Massachusetts believed they were founding a holy commonwealth, a model—a "city upon a hill"—for the corrupt world to see and emulate. But if Massachusetts was to become a beacon to others, it had first to maintain its own purity and "holiness." And to that end, the ministers and the officers of the government worked closely together. Colonial Massachusetts was a "theocracy," a society in which the church was almost indistinguishable from the state. Residents had no more freedom of worship than the Puritans themselves had had in England.

Like other new settlements, the Massachusetts Bay colony had early difficulties. During the first winter (1629–1630), nearly 200 people died and many others decided to leave. But more rapidly than Jamestown, the colony grew and prospered. The nearby Pilgrims and neighboring Indians helped with food and advice. Incoming settlers, many of them affluent, brought needed tools and other goods. The dominance of families in the colony (a sharp contrast to the early years at Jamestown) helped ensure a feeling of commitment to the community and a sense of order among the settlers, and it also ensured that the population would reproduce itself.

*Spreading Settlement*

It did not take long for English settlement to begin moving outward from Massachusetts Bay to other parts of New England and beyond. Some people migrated in search of soil more productive than the stony land around Boston provided. Others left because of the oppressiveness of the church-dominated government of Massachusetts.

The Connecticut River valley, about 100 miles west of Boston, began attracting English families as early as the 1630s—despite the presence of powerful native tribes and despite claims to those lands by the Dutch—because of the valley's fertile lands and its isolation from Massachusetts Bay. In 1635, Thomas Hooker, a minister of Newtown (Cambridge), defied the Massachusetts government, led his congregation west, and established the town of Hartford. Four years later, the people of Hartford and of two other newly founded towns nearby established a colonial government of their own and adopted a constitution known as the Fundamental Orders of Connecticut. This created a government similar to that of Massachusetts Bay but gave a larger proportion of the men the right to vote and hold office. (Women were barred from voting virtually everywhere.)

Another Connecticut colony grew up around New Haven on the Connecticut coast. Unlike Hartford, it reflected unhappiness with what its founders considered the increasing religious laxity in Boston. The Fundamental Articles of New Haven (1639) established a Bible-based government even stricter than that of Massachusetts Bay. New Haven remained independent until 1662, when a royal charter officially gave the Hartford colony jurisdiction over the New Haven settlements.

European settlement in what is now Rhode Island was a result of the religious and political dissent of Roger Williams, an engaging but controversial young minister who lived for a time in Salem, Massachusetts. Williams was a confirmed Separatist who argued that the Massachusetts church should abandon even its nominal allegiance to the Church of England. He was also friendly with the neighboring Indians and proclaimed that the land the colonists were occupying belonged to the natives and not to the king or to the Massachusetts Bay Company. The colonial government voted to deport him, but he escaped before they could do so. During the bitter winter of 1635–1636, he took refuge with Narragansett tribesmen; the following spring he bought a tract of land from them, and with a few followers, created the town of Providence on it. In 1644, after obtaining a charter from Parliament, he established a government for Providence and the surrounding settlements—a government similar to that of Massachusetts but without any ties to the church. For a time, Rhode Island was the only colony in which all faiths (including Judaism) could worship without interference.

Another challenge to the established religious order in Massachusetts Bay came from Anne Hutchinson, an intelligent and charismatic woman from a substantial Boston family. Hutchinson argued that the faithful could communicate directly with God (as she claimed she herself had done) and gain from Him assurance of grace and salvation. Such teachings (known as the Antinomian heresy) were a serious threat to the spiritual authority of the established clergy. Hutchinson also challenged prevailing assumptions about the proper role of women in Puritan society. She was not a retiring, deferential wife and mother but a powerful religious figure in her own right.

As Hutchinson's influence grew, and as she began to deliver open attacks on members of the clergy, the Massachusetts hierarchy mobilized to stop her. In 1638, she was convicted of heresy and sedition and banished.

ANNE HUTCHINSON PREACHING IN HER HOUSE IN BOSTON
Anne Hutchinson was alarming to many of Boston's religious leaders not only because she openly challenged the authority of the clergy, but also because she implicitly challenged norms of female behavior in Puritan society.

With her family and some of her followers, she moved to a point on Narragansett Bay not far from Providence. Later she moved south into New York, where in 1643 she and her family died during an Indian uprising.

The Hutchinson affair had an important impact on the settlement of the areas north of Massachusetts Bay. New Hampshire and Maine were established in 1629 by two English proprietors. But few settlers moved into these northern regions until the religious disruptions in Massachusetts Bay. In 1639, John Wheelwright, a disciple of Anne Hutchinson, led some of his fellow dissenters to Exeter, New Hampshire. Other groups—of both dissenting and orthodox Puritans—soon followed. The Massachusetts Bay Company tried to extend its authority over this entire northern territory, with partial success. New Hampshire became a separate colony in 1679, but Maine remained a part of Massachusetts until 1820.

### Settlers and Natives

The first white settlers in New England had generally amicable relations with the natives and learned much from them. Indians taught whites how to grow vital food crops such as corn, beans, pumpkins, and potatoes; they also taught them crucial agricultural techniques, such as annual burning for fertilization and planting beans to replenish exhausted soil. European farmers also benefited from the extensive lands Indians had already cleared (and either abandoned or sold). White traders used Indians as partners in some of their most important trading activities (and particularly in the creation of the thriving North American fur trade). Indeed, commerce with the Indians was responsible for the creation of some of the first great fortunes in British North America. Other white settlers attempted to educate the Indians in European religion and culture. Protestant missionaries converted some natives to Christianity, and a few Indians became at least partially assimilated into white society.

But as in other areas of white settlement, tensions soon developed—primarily as a result of the white colonists' insatiable appetite for land. The particular character of those conflicts—and the brutality with which whites assaulted their Indian foes—emerged as well out of Puritan attitudes toward the natives. The religious leaders of New England came to consider the tribes a threat to their hopes of creating a godly community in the New World, particularly once dissenters such as Roger Williams began forming close relationships with the tribes. Gradually, the image of Indians as helpful neighbors came to be replaced by the image of Indians as "heathens" and barbarians.

In 1637, hostilities broke out between English settlers in the Connecticut Valley and the Pequot Indians of the region, a conflict (known as the Pequot War) that ended disastrously for the natives. The Pequot tribe was almost wiped out. But the bloodiest and most prolonged encounter between whites and Indians in the seventeenth century began in 1675, a conflict that whites called King Philip's War. As in the Pequot War, an Indian tribe—the Wampanoags, under the leadership of a chieftain known to the white settlers as King Philip and among his own people as Metacomet—rose up to resist English encroachment on its lands and the efforts of the colonial government to impose English law on the natives. (A court in Plymouth had recently tried and hanged several Wampanoags for murdering a member of their own tribe.)

For three years, the natives inflicted terror on a string of Massachusetts towns, killing over a thousand people. But beginning in 1676, the white settlers gradually prevailed. Massachusetts leaders recruited guides and spies from rival tribes, including a group of Mohawks who ambushed Metacomet, shot and killed him, and then bore his severed head to Boston to present to the colonial leaders. Without Metacomet, the fragile alliance among the tribes collapsed, and the white settlers were soon able to crush the uprising.

Yet these victories by the white colonists did not end the danger to their settlements. This was in part because other Indians in other tribes were still capable of launching wars. It was also because the New England settlers faced competition not only from the natives but also from the Dutch and the French, who claimed the territory on which some of the outlying settlements were established.

## THE RESTORATION COLONIES

For nearly thirty years after Lord Baltimore received the charter for Maryland in 1632, no new English colonies were established in America. England was preoccupied with troubles of its own at home.

### The English Civil War

After Charles I dissolved Parliament in 1629 and began ruling as an absolute monarch, he steadily alienated a growing number of his subjects—and the members of the powerful Puritan community, above all. Finally, desperately in need of money, Charles called Parliament back into session in 1640 and asked it to levy new taxes. But he antagonized the members by dismissing them twice in two years; and in 1642, they organized a military force, thus beginning the English Civil War.

The conflict between the Cavaliers (the supporters of the king) and the Roundheads (the forces of Parliament, who were largely Puritans) lasted seven years. In 1649, the Roundheads defeated the king's forces, captured Charles himself, and beheaded the monarch. The stern Roundhead leader Oliver Cromwell replaced the king and assumed the position of "protector." But when Cromwell died in 1658, his son and heir proved unable to maintain his authority. Two years later, King Charles II, son of the beheaded monarch, returned from exile and seized the throne, in what became known as the Restoration.

Among the results of the Restoration was the resumption of colonization in America. Charles II rewarded faithful courtiers with grants of land in the New World, and in the twenty-five years of his reign he issued charters for four additional colonies: Carolina, New York, New Jersey, and Pennsylvania. The new colonies were all proprietary ventures (modeled on Maryland rather than on Virginia and Massachusetts). Unlike the private companies that had launched the first colonies in search of quick profits, the new colonial ventures sought permanent settlements that would provide proprietors with land and power.

### The Carolinas

Carolina (a name derived from the Latin word for "Charles") was, like Maryland, carved in part from the original Virginia grant. In successive charters issued in 1663 and 1665, Charles II awarded eight proprietors joint title to a vast territory stretching south to the Florida peninsula and west to the Pacific Ocean. Like Lord Baltimore, they received almost kingly powers over their grant. They reserved tremendous estates for themselves and distributed the rest through a headright system similar to those in Virginia and Maryland, after which they collected annual payments from the settlers. Although committed Anglicans themselves, they guaranteed religious freedom to all Christian faiths. They also created a representative assembly to make laws. They hoped to attract settlers from the existing American colonies and to avoid the expense of financing expeditions from England.

But their initial efforts to profit from settlement in Carolina failed dismally. A few early attempts at colonization were quickly abandoned, and most of the original proprietors soon gave up on Carolina. One man, however, persisted. Anthony Ashley Cooper convinced the other proprietors to give up on attracting settlers from other colonies and to finance expeditions to Carolina from England, the first of which set sail with 300 people in the spring of 1670. Only 100 people survived the difficult voyage; those who did established a settlement at Port Royal on the Carolina coast. Ten years later they founded a city at the junction of the Ashley and Cooper Rivers, which in 1690 became the colonial capital. They called it Charles Town (it was later renamed Charleston).

With the aid of the English philosopher John Locke, Cooper (now the earl of Shaftesbury) drew up the Fundamental Constitution for Carolina in 1669 in an attempt to create a highly ordered society. It divided the colony into counties of equal size and divided each county into equal parcels. The largest number of parcels would be distributed among the proprietors themselves (who were to be known as "seigneurs"); a local aristocracy (consisting of lesser nobles known as "landgraves" or "caciques") would receive fewer parcels; and ordinary settlers ("leet-men") would receive still less land. At the bottom of this stratified society would be poor whites, who would have few political rights, and African slaves, whose subjection would be complete. Proprietors, nobles, and other landholders would have a voice in the colonial parliament in proportion to the size of their landholdings.

In fact, however, Carolina developed along lines quite different from the carefully ordered vision of Shaftesbury and Locke. For one thing, the colony was never really united in anything more than name. The northern and southern regions of settlement were widely separated and socially and economically distinct from one another. The northern settlers were mainly backwoods farmers, scratching out a meager existence at subsistence agriculture. They developed no important aristocracy and for many years imported virtually no black slaves. In the south, fertile lands and the good harbor at Charles Town promoted a more prosperous economy and a more stratified, aristocratic society. Settlements grew up rapidly along the Ashley and Cooper Rivers, and colonists established a flourishing trade, particularly (beginning in the 1660s) in rice—which was to become the colony's principal commercial crop.

Southern Carolina very early developed close commercial ties to the large (and overpopulated) European colony on the Caribbean island of Barbados (see pp. 36–39). During the first ten years of settlement, most of the new residents in Carolina were Barbadians, some of whom arrived with large groups of black workers and established themselves as substantial landlords. African slavery had taken root on Barbados earlier than in any of the mainland colonies; and the white Caribbean migrants—tough, uncompromising profit seekers—established a similar slave-based plantation society in Carolina.

For several decades, Carolina remained one of the most divided English colonies in America. There were tensions between the small farmers of the Albemarle region in the north and the wealthy planters in the south. And there were conflicts between the rich Barbadians in southern Carolina and the smaller landowners around them. After Lord Shaftesbury's death, the proprietors proved unable to establish order. In 1719, the colonists seized control of the colony from them. Ten years later, the king divided the region into two royal colonies, North Carolina and South Carolina.

### New Netherland and New York

In 1664, Charles II granted his brother James, the duke of York, all the territory lying between the Connecticut and Delaware Rivers. But the grant faced a major challenge from the Dutch, who claimed the entire area and controlled settlements at New Amsterdam and other strategic points.

England and the Netherlands were already commercial rivals in Europe, and that rivalry now extended to America, where the Dutch served as a wedge between the northern and southern English colonies. In 1664, vessels of the English navy, under the command of Richard Nicolls, put in at New Amsterdam and extracted a surrender from the arbitrary and unpopular Dutch governor, Peter Stuyvesant. Several years later, in 1673, the Dutch reconquered and briefly held their old provincial capital. But they lost it again, this time for good, in 1674.

The duke of York, now firmly in possession of his territory, renamed it New York and set out to govern the diverse region. New York contained not only Dutch and English but Scandinavians, Germans, French, and a large number of Africans (imported as slaves by the Dutch West India Company), as well as members of several different Indian tribes. James wisely made no effort to impose his own Roman Catholicism on the colony. He delegated powers to a governor and a council but made no provision for representative assemblies.

Property holding and political power remained highly divided and highly unequal in New York. In addition to confirming the great Dutch "patroonships" already in existence, James granted large estates to some of his own political supporters. Power in the colony thus remained widely dispersed among wealthy English landlords, Dutch patroons, fur traders, and the duke's political appointees. By 1685, when the duke of York ascended the

English throne as James II, New York contained about four times as many people (around 30,000) as it had twenty years before, and it was one of the most contentious colonies in America.

Shortly after James received his charter, he gave a large part of the land south of New York to a pair of political allies, both Carolina proprietors, Sir John Berkeley and Sir George Carteret. Carteret named the territory New Jersey, after the island in the English Channel on which he had been born. But the venture in New Jersey generated few profits, and in 1674, Berkeley sold his half interest. The colony was divided into two jurisdictions, East Jersey and West Jersey, which squabbled with one another until 1702, when the two halves of the colony were again joined and became a single royal colony.

New Jersey, like New York (from which much of its population came), was a colony of enormous ethnic and religious diversity, and the weak colonial government made few efforts to impose strict control over the fragmented society. But unlike New York, New Jersey developed no important class of large landowners; most of its residents remained small farmers. Nor did New Jersey produce any single important city.

### The Quaker Colonies

Pennsylvania was born out of the efforts of a dissenting English Protestant sect, the Society of Friends, to find a home for their own distinctive social order. The society began in the mid-seventeenth century under the leadership of George Fox, a Nottingham shoemaker, and Margaret Fell. Their followers came to be known as Quakers (from Fox's instruction to them to "tremble at the name of the Lord"). Unlike the Puritans, Quakers rejected the concept of predestination and original sin. All people, they believed, had divinity within themselves and need only learn to cultivate it; all could attain salvation. Also unlike the Puritans, Quakers granted women a position within the church generally equal to that of men.

The Quakers had no formal church government and no traditional church buildings, only meetinghouses. They had no paid clergy, and in their worship they spoke up one by one as the spirit moved them. Disregarding distinctions of gender and class, they addressed one another with the terms "thee" and "thou," words commonly used in other parts of English society only in speaking to servants and social inferiors. As confirmed pacifists, they would not take part in wars. Unpopular in England both with the government and with members of other religious orders (whose services Quakers occasionally disrupted), the Quakers began looking to America for asylum. A few migrated to New

England or Carolina, but most Quakers wanted a colony of their own. As members of a despised sect, however, they could not get the necessary royal grant without the aid of someone influential at the court.

Fortunately for the Quaker cause, a number of wealthy and prominent men had converted to the faith. One of them was William Penn, whose father, Sir William Penn, was an admiral in the Royal Navy and a landlord of valuable Irish estates. Over his father's objections, the younger Penn converted to Quakerism, took up evangelism, and was sent repeatedly to prison. He soon began working with George Fox to create a Quaker colony in America. In 1681, after the death of his father, he received from the king a valuable grant of lands. Penn had inherited his father's claim to a large debt from the king. Charles II paid the debt with an enormous grant of territory between New York and Maryland, which Penn was to control as both landlord and ruler. At the king's insistence, the territory was to be named Pennsylvania, after Penn's late father.

Through his informative and honest advertising, Penn soon made Pennsylvania the best-known and most cosmopolitan of all the English colonies in America, a place to which settlers flocked from England and the Continent. More than any other English colony, Pennsylvania prospered from the outset, because of Penn's successful recruiting, his careful planning, and the region's mild climate and fertile soil. But the colony never became a great source of profit for Penn or his descendants. (Indeed, Penn himself, near the end of his life, was imprisoned in England for debt and died in poverty in 1718.)

Penn sailed to Pennsylvania in 1682 to oversee the laying out, between the Delaware and Schuylkill Rivers, of the city he named Philadelphia ("Brotherly Love"), which, with its rectangular streets, helped set the pattern for most later cities in America. Penn recognized Indians' claims to the land in the province, and he was scrupulous about reimbursing them for it. The Indians respected Penn, and during his lifetime the colony had no major battles with the natives.

But the colony was not without conflict. By the late 1690s, some residents of Pennsylvania were beginning to chafe at the nearly absolute power of the proprietor. Residents of the southern areas of the colony, in particular, complained that the government in Philadelphia was unresponsive to their needs. Pressure from these groups grew to the point that in 1701, shortly before he departed for England for the last time, Penn agreed to a Charter of Liberties for the colony. The charter established a representative assembly (consisting, alone among the English colonies, of only one house), which greatly limited the authority of the proprietor. The charter also permitted "the lower counties" of the colony to establish their own representative assembly. The three counties did so in 1703 and as a result became, in effect, a separate colony—Delaware—although until the American Revolution it continued to have the same governor as Pennsylvania.

## The Founding of Georgia

Not until 1733, decades after the founding of the Restoration colonies, did another new English settlement emerge in America: Georgia, the last English colony to be established in what would become the United States. Georgia was unlike any other colony. It was founded neither by a corporation nor by a wealthy proprietor. Its guiding purpose was neither the pursuit of profit nor the desire for a religious refuge. The founders of Georgia, led by General James Oglethorpe, were driven primarily by military and philanthropic motives. They wanted to erect a military barrier between the Spanish lands to the south and the established English colonies to the north, and they wanted to provide a refuge for the impoverished, a place where English men and women without prospects at home could begin a new life.

The need for a military buffer between South Carolina and the Spanish settlements in Florida was growing urgent in the first years of the eighteenth century. There had been tensions between the Spanish and the English in North America ever since the founding of Jamestown. And when hostilities broke out in Europe between Spain and England in 1701 (known in England as Queen Anne's War and on the Continent as the War of the Spanish Succession), fighting renewed in America as well. That war ended in 1713, but another European conflict with repercussions for the New World was continually expected.

Oglethorpe, a hero of Queen Anne's War, was aware of the military advantages of the new colony. But his own interests were primarily philanthropic. As head of a parliamentary committee investigating English prisons, he was moved by the plight of honest debtors rotting in confinement. Such prisoners, and other poor people in danger of succumbing to a similar fate, could, he believed, become the farmer-soldiers of the new colony in America.

A 1732 charter from King George II transferred the land between the Savannah and Altamaha Rivers to Oglethorpe and his fellow trustees. Oglethorpe himself led the first colonial expedition to Georgia, which built a fortified town at the mouth of the Savannah River in 1733 and later constructed additional forts south of the Altamaha. The trustees organized the colony in part to make it militarily defensible. They limited the size of landholdings to make the settlement compact and easily defended against Spanish and Indian attacks. Blacks—free or slave—were excluded; Roman Catholics were excluded; rum was prohibited; and trade with the Indians was strictly regulated—all to limit the possibility of wartime insurrection or collusion with future enemies. Only a few debtors were released from jail and sent to Georgia, but the trustees brought hundreds of needy tradesmen and artisans from England and Scotland and many religious refugees from Switzerland and Germany.

The strict rules governing life in the new colony stifled its development and created dissent in its early years. Settlers in Georgia needed a work force and almost from the start demanded the right to buy slaves. Some opposed the restrictions on the size of individual property holdings. Many resented the nearly absolute political power of Oglethorpe and the trustees. As a result, newcomers to the region generally preferred to settle in South Carolina, where there were fewer restrictive laws. Eventually, the trustees removed the limitation on individual landholdings and later the ban on slavery and the prohibition of rum. In 1751, they returned control of the colony to the king, who immediately permitted the election of a representative assembly. Georgia continued to grow more slowly than the other southern colonies, but it now developed along lines roughly similar to those of South Carolina.

## THE DEVELOPMENT OF EMPIRE

The English colonies in America had originated as separate projects, and for the most part they grew up independent of one another and subject to little more than nominal control from London. Yet by the mid-seventeenth century, the growing commercial success of the colonial ventures was producing pressure in England for a more rational, uniform structure to the empire.

### The Drive for Reorganization

Reorganization, its advocates claimed, was necessary to ensure the success of the mercantile system, the foundation of the English economy. For the new possessions truly to promote mercantilist goals, England decided it would have to exclude foreigners (as Spain had done) from its colonial trade. But in that decision were the seeds of conflict, because many American colonists had developed profitable trade with the Spanish, Dutch, and French and were likely to resist interference with it.

The English government began trying to regulate colonial trade in the

1650s, when Parliament passed laws to keep Dutch ships out of the English colonies. Later, Parliament passed three important Navigation Acts. The first of them, in 1660, closed the colonies to all trade except that carried by English ships, and it required that tobacco and other items be exported from the colonies only to England or to an English possession. The second act, in 1663, required that all goods sent from Europe to the colonies pass through England on the way, where they would be subject to English taxation. The third act, in 1673, imposed duties on the coastal trade among the English colonies, and it provided for the appointment of customs officials to enforce the Navigation Acts. These acts, with later amendments and additions, formed the legal basis of England's mercantile system in America for a century.

## The Dominion of New England

Before the Navigation Acts, all the colonial governments (except that of Virginia, a "royal colony" with a governor appointed by the king) had operated largely independently of the crown, with governors chosen by the proprietors or by the colonists themselves and with powerful representative assemblies. Officials in London recognized that to increase their control over their colonies they would have to create an instrument separate from the independent-minded colonial governments, which were unlikely to enforce the new laws.

In 1675, the king created a new body, the Lords of Trade, to make recommendations for imperial reform. Following their advice, he moved in 1679 to increase his control over Massachusetts, the most defiant of the colonies. He stripped it of its authority over New Hampshire and chartered a separate, royal colony there whose governor he would himself appoint. He also began seeking legal grounds for revoking the colony's corporate charter and making Massachusetts itself a royal colony. He soon became convinced that he had found such grounds in the defiance of the Navigation Acts by the Massachusetts General Court, which insisted that Parliament had no power to legislate for the colony. In 1684, the king finally succeeded in revoking the Massachusetts charter.

Charles II's brother James II, who succeeded him to the throne in 1685, went further. He created a single Dominion of New England, which combined the government of Massachusetts with the governments of the rest of the New England colonies and later with those of New York and New Jersey as well. He eliminated the existing assemblies within the new Dominion and appointed a single governor, Sir Edmund Andros, to supervise the entire region from Boston. Andros's rigid enforcement of the Navigation Acts and his brusque dismissal of the colonists' claims to the "rights of Englishmen" made him quickly and thoroughly unpopular.

### The "Glorious Revolution"

James II was not only losing friends in America; he was making powerful enemies in England by attempting to control Parliament and the courts and by appointing his fellow Catholics to high office. By 1688, his popular support had all but vanished, and Parliament invited his Protestant daughter Mary and her husband, William of Orange, ruler of the Netherlands, to assume the throne. James II (perhaps remembering what had happened to his father, Charles I) offered no resistance and fled to France. As a result of this bloodless coup, which the English called the "Glorious Revolution," William and Mary became joint sovereigns.

When Bostonians heard of the overthrow of James II, they moved quickly to unseat his unpopular viceroy in New England. Andros was arrested and imprisoned. The new sovereigns in England accepted the toppling of Andros, quickly abolished the Dominion of New England, and restored separate colonial governments. They did not, however, re-create them as they had been. In 1691, they combined Massachusetts with Plymouth and made it a single, royal colony. The new charter restored the General Court, but it gave the crown the right to appoint the governor. It also replaced church membership with property ownership as the basis for voting and officeholding.

Andros had been governing New York through a lieutenant governor, Captain Francis Nicholson, who enjoyed the support of the wealthy merchants and fur traders of the province. Other, less favored colonists—farmers, mechanics, small traders, and shopkeepers—had a long accumulation of grievances against Nicholson and his allies. The leadership of the New York dissidents fell to Jacob Leisler, a German immigrant and a prosperous merchant. He had married into a prominent Dutch family but had never won acceptance as one of the colony's ruling class. In May 1689, when news of the Glorious Revolution in England and the fall of Andros in Boston reached New York, Leisler raised a militia, captured the city fort, drove Nicholson into exile, and proclaimed himself the new head of government in New York. For two years, he tried in vain to stabilize his power in the colony amid fierce factional rivalry. In 1691, when William and Mary appointed a new governor, Leisler briefly resisted. Although he soon yielded, his hesitation allowed his many political enemies to charge him with treason. He was convicted and executed. Fierce rivalry between what became known as the "Leislerians" and the "anti-Leislerians" dominated the politics of the colony for many years thereafter.

In Maryland, many people erroneously assumed when they heard news of the Glorious Revolution that their proprietor, the Catholic Lord Baltimore, who was living in England, had sided with the Catholic James II and opposed William and Mary. So in 1689, an old opponent of the proprietor's government, the Protestant John Coode, led a revolt that drove out Lord Baltimore's officials and petitioned the crown for a charter as a royal colony. In 1691, William and Mary complied, stripping the proprietor of his authority. The colonial assembly established the Church of England as the colony's official religion and excluded Catholics from public office. Maryland became a proprietary colony again in 1715, but only after the fifth Lord Baltimore joined the Anglican Church.

Thus the Glorious Revolution of 1688 in England touched off revolutions, mostly bloodless ones, in several colonies. Under the new king and queen, the representative assemblies that had been abolished were revived, and the scheme for colonial unification from above was abandoned. But the Glorious Revolution in America was not, as many Americans later came to believe, a clear demonstration of American resolve to govern itself or a clear victory for colonial self-rule. In New York and Maryland, in particular, the uprisings had more to do with local factional and religious divisions than with any larger vision of the nature of the empire. And while the insurgencies did succeed in eliminating the short-lived Dominion of New England, their ultimate results were governments that actually increased the crown's potential authority. As the first century of English settlement in America came to its end, the colonists were becoming more a part of the imperial system than ever before.

CHAPTER THREE

# Life in Provincial America

*The Colonial Population* ∼ *The Colonial Economy*
*Patterns of Society* ∼ *The Colonial Mind*

A S THE EXTENT of settlement in North America grew, and as the economies of the colonies began to flourish, several distinctive ways of life emerged. The new American societies differed considerably from the society that most had attempted to re-create in the New World—the society of England. They differed as well from one another. Indeed, the pattern of society in some areas of North America seemed to resemble that of others scarcely at all. Americans would eventually decide that they had enough in common to enable them to join together and form a single nation. But regional differences would continue to shape their society throughout their history.

## THE COLONIAL POPULATION

After uncertain beginnings at Jamestown and Plymouth, the non-Indian population of English North America grew rapidly and substantially, through continued immigration and through natural increase, until by the late seventeenth century European and African immigrants outnumbered the natives along the Atlantic coast.

A few of the early settlers were members of the English upper classes, but for the most part the early colonial population was decidedly unaristocratic. It included some members of the emerging English middle class, businessmen who immigrated to America for religious or commercial reasons or both. But the dominant element was English laborers. Some came independently, such as the religious dissenters in early New England, who came as families, paid their own way, and settled on their own land. But in the

| TIME LINE | | | | |
|---|---|---|---|---|
| **1636** | **1662** | **1685** | **1692** | **1697** |
| Harvard founded | Halfway Covenant | Huguenots migrate to America | Salem witchcraft trials | Slave importations increase |

| **1720** | **1734** | **1739** | **1740s** | |
|---|---|---|---|---|
| Cotton Mather starts smallpox inoculations | Great Awakening begins <br> Zenger trial | George Whitefield arrives in America <br> Great Awakening intensifies <br> Stono slave rebellion | Indigo production begins | |

Chesapeake, at least three-fourths of the immigrants in the seventeenth century arrived as indentured servants.

### *Indentured Servitude*

The system of temporary servitude developed out of practices in England. Young men and women bound themselves to masters for fixed terms of servitude (usually four to five years) in exchange for passage to America, food, and shelter. Upon completion of their service, male indentures were supposed to receive clothing, tools, and occasionally land; in reality, however, many left service with nothing. Roughly one-fourth of the indentures in the Chesapeake were women, most of whom worked as domestic servants and could expect to marry when their terms of servitude expired, since men greatly outnumbered women in the region.

Most indentured servants came to the colonies voluntarily, but some did not. Beginning as early as 1617, the English government occasionally dumped shiploads of convicts in America to be sold into servitude. The government also transported prisoners taken in battles with the Scots and the Irish in the 1650s, as well as orphans, vagrants, and paupers. Other involuntary immigrants were victims of kidnapping, or "impressment," by unscrupulous investors and promoters.

By the late seventeenth century, the indentured servant population had become one of the largest elements of the total population and was creating serious social problems. Some former indentures managed to establish themselves successfully as farmers, tradespeople, or artisans, and some of the

A  M  E  R  I  C  A  N     V  O  I  C  E  S

GOTTLIEB MITTLEBERGER

## An Indentured Servant's Voyage from Germany to America

BOTH IN ROTTERDAM and in Amsterdam the people are packed densely, like herrings so to say, in the large sea-vessels. . . . During the voyage there is on board these ships terrible misery, stench, fumes, horror, vomiting, many kinds of sea-sickness, fever, dysentery, headache, heat, constipation, boils, scurvy, cancer, mouthrot, and the like, all of which come from old and sharply salted food and meat, also from very bad and foul water, so that many die miserably. . . . Many sigh and cry, "Oh, that I were at home again, and if I had to lie in my pigsty!" . . . Many hundred people necessarily die and perish in such misery, and must be cast into the sea, which drives their relatives . . . to such despair that it is almost impossible to pacify and console them. . . .

When the ships have landed at Philadelphia after their long voyage, no one is permitted to leave them except those who pay for their passage or can give good security; the others, who cannot pay, must remain on board the ships till they are purchased, and are released from the ships by their purchasers. The sick always fare the worst, for the healthy are naturally preferred and purchased first; and so the sick and wretched must often remain on board in front of the city for 2 or 3 weeks, and frequently die. . . . Many parents must sell and trade away their children like so many head of cattle. . . . It often happens that such parents and children, after leaving the ship, do not see each other again for many years, perhaps no more in their lives.

women married propertied men. Others (mostly males) found themselves without land, without employment, without families, and without prospects; and there grew up in some areas, particularly the Chesapeake, a large floating population of young single men—such as those who supported Bacon's Rebellion—who served as a potential (and at times actual) source of social unrest. Even those free laborers who did find employment or land for themselves and settled down with families often did not stay put for very long. Many families pulled up stakes and moved to other, more promising locations every few years.

Beginning in the 1670s, a decrease in the birth rate in England and an improvement in economic conditions there reduced the pressures on laboring men and women to emigrate, and the flow of indentured servants declined. Those who did travel to America as indentures now generally avoided the southern colonies, where working conditions were arduous and prospects for advancement were slim. In the Chesapeake, therefore, landowners were beginning to rely much more heavily on African slavery as their principal source of labor.

### Birth and Death

Although immigration remained for a time the greatest source of population growth, the most important long-range factor in the increase of the colonial population was its ability to reproduce itself. Marked improvement in the reproduction rate began in New England and the mid-Atlantic colonies in the second half of the seventeenth century, and after the 1650s natural increase became the most important source of population growth in those areas. The New England population more than quadrupled through reproduction alone in the second half of the seventeenth century. That was not just because families were having large numbers of children. It was also because life expectancy in New England was unusually high, both in comparison to that of other colonies and in comparison to that of England.

Conditions improved much more slowly in the South. The high death rates in the Chesapeake region did not begin to decline to the levels of those elsewhere until the mid-eighteenth century. Throughout the seventeenth century, the average life expectancy for men in the region was just over forty years, and for women slightly less. (In New England, life expectancy was up to thirty years longer.) One in four children died in infancy, and half died before the age of twenty. Children who survived infancy often lost one or both of their parents before reaching maturity. Widows, widowers, and orphans thus formed a substantial proportion of the Chesapeake population.

Only after settlers developed immunity to local diseases (particularly malaria) did life expectancy increase significantly. Population growth was substantial in the region, but it was largely a result of immigration.

The natural increases in the population in the seventeenth century were in large part a result of steady improvement in the balance between men and women in the colonies. In the early years of settlement, more than three-quarters of the white population of the Chesapeake consisted of men. And even in New England, which from the beginning had attracted more families (and thus more women) than the southern colonies, 60 percent of the inhabitants were male in 1650. Gradually, however, more women began to arrive in the colonies; and increasing birth rates, which of course produced roughly equal numbers of males and females, contributed to shifting the sex ratio (the balance between men and women) as well. By the late seventeenth century, the proportion of males to females in all the colonies was becoming more balanced.

### Women and Families in the Colonies

The importance of reproduction in the labor-scarce society of seventeenth-century America had significant effects on both the status and the life cycles of women. Because there were many more men than women, few women remained unmarried for long. The average European woman in America married for the first time at twenty or twenty-one years of age, considerably earlier than in England.

Because of the large numbers of indentured servants who were forbidden to marry until their terms of service expired, premarital sexual relationships were frequent. Over a third of Chesapeake marriages occurred with the bride already pregnant. Children born out of wedlock were usually taken from their mothers at a young age and bound out as indentured servants.

Women in the Chesapeake could anticipate a life consumed with childbearing. The average wife experienced pregnancies every two years. Those who lived long enough bore an average of eight children apiece (up to five of whom typically died in infancy or early childhood). Since childbirth was one of the most frequent causes of female death, many women did not survive to see their children grow to maturity.

But southern white women did enjoy certain advantages. Because men were plentiful and women scarce, females had considerable latitude in choosing husbands. And because of the high mortality rate, the traditional male-dominated (or "patriarchal") family structure of England—in which husbands and fathers exercised firm, even dictatorial control over the lives of their wives and children—was difficult to maintain. Women generally married at a much younger age than men, so they also tended to outlive their husbands. Many widows were left with several children and with responsibility for managing a farm or plantation, a circumstance of enormous hardship but one that also gave them significant economic power. Widows seldom remained unmarried for long, however. And since many widows married men who were themselves widowers, complex combinations of households were frequent.

By the early eighteenth century, the demographic character of the Chesapeake was beginning to change, and with it the nature and structure of the typical family. Life expectancy was increasing, and indentured servitude was in decline. Natural reproduction was becoming the principal source of white population growth. The sex ratio was becoming more equal. One result of these changes was that life for white people in the region became less perilous and less difficult. Another result was that women lost some of the power that their small numbers had once given them. As families grew more stable, traditional patterns of male authority revived. By the mid-eighteenth century, southern families were becoming highly patriarchal.

In New England, where many more immigrants arrived with family members and where death rates declined far more quickly, family structure was much more stable than in the Chesapeake and hence more traditional. The sex ratio was less unbalanced than in the Chesapeake, so most men could expect to marry. But there were still fewer women than men. As in the Chesapeake, women married young, began producing children early, and continued to do so well into their thirties. In contrast to the situation in the South, however, northern children were more likely to survive (the average family raised six to eight children to maturity), and their families were more likely to remain intact. Fewer New England women became widows, and those who did generally lost their husbands later in life. Hence women were less often cast in roles independent of their husbands. Young women, moreover, had less control over the conditions of marriage, both because there were fewer unmarried men vying for them and because their fathers were more likely to be alive and able to exercise control over their choices.

The longer lives in New England meant that parents continued to control their children longer than did parents in the South. They did not often actually "arrange" marriages for their children, but few sons and daughters could choose a spouse entirely independently of their parents' wishes. Men tended to rely on their fathers for land to cultivate—generally a prerequisite for beginning families of their own. Women needed dowries from their parents if they were to attract desirable husbands. Stricter parental supervision of children meant, too, that fewer women became pregnant before marriage than was the case in the South (although even in Puritan New England, the premarital pregnancy rate was as high as 20 percent in some communities).

Puritanism placed a high value on the family, which was not only the principal economic unit but the principal religious unit within every community. In one sense, then, women played important roles within the family because the position of wife and mother was highly valued in Puritan culture. At the same time, however, Puritanism served to reinforce the idea of nearly absolute male authority and the assumption of female weakness and inferiority. Women were expected to be modest and submissive. A wife was expected to devote herself almost entirely to serving the needs of her husband. Even so, women were vital to the family economy, and they continuously engaged in tasks crucial to the functioning of the farm—gardening, raising poultry, tending cattle, spinning, and weaving, as well as cooking, cleaning, and washing.

Family life in the Chesapeake colonies grew more patriarchal in the late seventeenth and early eighteenth centuries. But New England families grew somewhat less so. As settlement spread beyond the early Puritan centers, as the authority of the church began gradually to decline, and as sons began increasingly to chafe under the control of their fathers, family life became somewhat more fluid, and the rigid division of authority between generations and between the sexes that had characterized seventeenth-century communities became less universal.

### *The Beginnings of Slavery in English North America*

The demand for African servants to supplement the scarce southern labor supply existed almost from the first moments of settlement. For a time, however, the supply of black workers was limited. Not until the mid-seventeenth century, when a substantial commerce in slaves grew up between the Caribbean islands and the southern colonies, did black workers become generally available in North America.

The demand for slaves in North America helped expand the transatlantic slave trade. And as slave trading grew more extensive and more sophisticated, it also grew more horrible. Before it ended in the nineteenth century, it was responsible for the forced immigration of as many as 11 million Africans to North and South America and the Caribbean. Indeed, until the late eighteenth century, the number of African immigrants to the Americas was higher than that of Europeans. In the flourishing slave marts on the African coast, native chieftains made large numbers of blacks available by capturing

AFRICANS BOUND FOR AMERICA Shown here are the below-deck slave quarters of a Spanish vessel en route to the West Indies. A British warship captured the slaver, and a young English naval officer (Lt. Francis Meynell) made this watercolor sketch on the spot. The Africans seen in this picture appear somewhat more comfortable than prisoners on other slave ships, some of whom were chained and packed together so tightly that they had no room to stand or even sit.

members of enemy tribes in battle and bringing them out of the forests and to the ports. The terrified victims were then packed into the dark, filthy holds of ships for the horrors of the "middle passage"—the long journey to the Americas, during which the black prisoners were usually kept chained in the bowels of the slave ships and supplied with only minimal food and water. Women were often victims of rape and other sexual abuse. Those who died en route, and many did, were simply thrown overboard. Many slave traders tried to cram as many Africans as possible into their ships to ensure that enough would survive to yield a profit at journey's end. Upon arrival in the New World, slaves were auctioned off to white landowners and transported, frightened and bewildered, to their new homes.

North America was a less important direct destination for African slaves than were such other parts of the New World as the Caribbean islands and Brazil; fewer than 5 percent of the Africans imported to the Americas arrived first in the English colonies. Through most of the seventeenth century, those blacks who were transported to what became the United States came not directly from Africa but from the West Indies. Not until the 1670s did traders start importing blacks directly from Africa to North America. Even then the flow remained small for a time, mainly because a single group, the Royal African Company of England, monopolized the trade and kept prices high and supplies low.

A turning point in the history of the black population in North America was 1697, the year the Royal African Company's monopoly was broken. With the trade now open to competition, prices fell and the number of Africans greatly increased. By 1700, about 25,000 black slaves lived in English North America. That was only 10 percent of the total non-Indian population, but because blacks were so heavily concentrated in a few southern colonies, they were already beginning to outnumber whites in some areas. There were perhaps twice as many black men as black women in most areas, but in some places the African-American population grew by natural increase nevertheless. In the Chesapeake more new slaves were being born than were being imported from Africa. In South Carolina, by contrast, the arduous conditions of rice cultivation ensured that the black population would barely be able to sustain itself through natural increase until much later.

By 1760, the number of Africans in the colonies had increased to approximately a quarter of a million. A few (16,000 in 1763) lived in New England; slightly more (29,000) lived in the middle colonies. The vast majority, however, lived in the South. By then blacks had almost wholly replaced white indentured servants as the basis of the southern work force.

For a time, the legal and social status of the African laborers remained somewhat fluid. In some areas—South Carolina, for example, where the number of black arrivals swelled more quickly than anywhere else—white and black laborers worked together at first on terms of relative equality. Some blacks were treated much like white hired servants, and some were freed after a fixed term of servitude. A few blacks themselves became landowners, and some apparently owned slaves of their own. By the late seventeenth century, however, a rigid distinction was emerging between blacks and whites. White workers could not be bound to a master indefinitely, but there was no legal requirement that masters free black workers after a term of service. Gradually, the assumption spread that blacks would remain in service permanently and that black children would inherit their parents' bondage. White beliefs about the inferiority of the black race reinforced the growing rigidity of the system. That slavery was developing in a society that was already multiracial also had an impact on its evolution. Whites had long ago defined themselves as a superior race in their relations with the native Indian population; the idea of subordinating an "inferior" race was, therefore, already part of European thinking by the time substantial numbers of Africans appeared in their midst.

The system of permanent servitude—American slavery—became legal in the early eighteenth century when colonial assemblies began to pass "slave codes" granting almost absolute authority to white masters over their slaves. Only one factor determined whether a person was subject to the slave codes: color. In the colonial societies of Spanish America, people of mixed race were granted a different (and higher) status than pure Africans. English America recognized no such distinctions. Any African ancestry was enough to classify a person as black.

### Changing Sources of European Immigration

The most distinctive and enduring feature of the American population was that it brought together peoples of many different races, ethnic groups, and nationalities. North America was home to a substantial population of natives, to a growing number of English immigrants, to forcibly imported Africans, and to substantial non-English groups from Europe.

The earliest of these non-English European immigrants were the French Calvinists, or Huguenots, escaping religious persecution in Roman Catholic France. A total of about 300,000 left France, some of them for the English colonies of North America, after the Edict of Nantes, which had guaranteed them substantial liberties, was revoked in 1685. Many German Protestants suffered similarly from the arbitrary religious policies of their rulers, and all Germans suffered from the frequent wars between their principalities and France. Because of its proximity to France, the Rhineland of southwestern Germany, known as the Palatinate, was exposed to frequent invasion, which sent more than 12,000 Germans fleeing to England early in the eighteenth century; approximately 3,000 of them found their way to America. Most settled in Pennsylvania, where they ultimately became known to English settlers as the "Pennsylvania Dutch" (a corruption of the German term for their nationality, *Deutsch*). Other, later German immigrants headed to Pennsylvania as well, among them the Moravians and Mennonites, whose religious views were similar to those of the Quakers.

The most numerous of the newcomers were the so-called Scotch-Irish— Scotch Presbyterians who had settled in northern Ireland (in the province of Ulster) in the early seventeenth century. Most of the Scotch-Irish in America pushed out to the edges of European settlement and occupied land

Dominant Immigrant Groups
in Colonial America, c. 1760

English

Scotch-Irish

German

Dutch

African

without much regard for who actually claimed to own it. They were as ruthless in their displacement and suppression of the Indians as they had been with the native Irish Catholics in Ireland.

There were also immigrants from Scotland itself and from southern Ireland. Scottish Highlanders, some of them Roman Catholics, mainly immigrated into North Carolina. Scottish Presbyterian Lowlanders, fleeing high rents and unemployment, left for America in large numbers shortly before the American Revolution. The Irish migrated steadily over a long period and by the time of the Revolution were almost as numerous as the Scots. Many of them had abandoned their Roman Catholic religion and much of their ethnic identity after they arrived in America.

By 1775, the non-Indian population of the colonies was over 2 million— a nearly tenfold increase since the beginning of the century. Throughout the colonial period, the population almost doubled every twenty-five years. Its continuing and increasing ethnic diversity became one of many factors dividing colonial society from the society of England.

## THE COLONIAL ECONOMY

Farming dominated almost all areas of European and African settlement in North America throughout the seventeenth and eighteenth centuries. Even so, the economies of the different regions varied markedly from one another.

### The Southern Economy

A strong European demand for tobacco enabled some planters in the Chesapeake (Maryland and Virginia) to become enormously wealthy and at times allowed the region as a whole to prosper. But throughout the seventeenth and eighteenth centuries, production of tobacco frequently exceeded demand, and as a result the price of the crop sometimes suffered severe declines. The result was a boom-and-bust cycle in the Chesapeake economy, with the first major bust occurring in 1640.

Most of the Chesapeake planters believed that the way to protect themselves from the instability of the market was to grow more tobacco. That only made the overproduction problem worse. It also encouraged those planters who could afford to do so to expand their landholdings, enlarge their fields, and acquire additional laborers. After 1700, tobacco plantations employing several dozen slaves or more were common.

South Carolina and Georgia relied on rice production, since the low-

lying coastline with its many tidal rivers made it possible to create rice pad-
dies that could be flooded and drained. Rice cultivation was arduous work—
performed standing knee-deep in malarial swamps—a task so difficult and
unhealthy that white laborers generally refused to perform it. Hence planters
in South Carolina and Georgia were far more dependent on slaves than were
their northern counterparts. African workers were adept at rice cultivation,
in part because some of them had come from rice-producing regions of west
Africa and in part because they were generally more accustomed to the hot,
humid climate than were the Europeans.

Because of their dependence on large-scale cash crops, the southern
colonies developed less of a commercial or industrial economy than the
colonies of the North. The trading in tobacco and rice was handled largely
by merchants based in London and, later, in the northern colonies. Few cities

SELLING TOBACCO This late-seventeenth-century label was
used in the sale of American tobacco in England. The drawing
depicts Virginia as a land of bright sunshine, energetic slaves,
and prosperous, pipe-smoking planters.

of more than modest size developed in the South. A pattern was emerging that would characterize the southern economy, and differentiate it from that of other regions, for more than two centuries.

### The Northern Economy

In the North, as in the South, agriculture continued to dominate, but it was agriculture of a more diverse kind. In addition to farming, there gradually emerged an important commercial sector of the economy.

One reason that agriculture did not remain the only major economic activity in the North was that conditions for farming were less favorable than in the South. In northern New England, in particular, colder weather and hard, rocky soil made it difficult for colonists to develop the kind of large-scale commercial farming system that southerners were creating. Most New Englanders did not produce a staple crop that could become a major export item; they planted largely to meet the needs of their own families. Conditions for agriculture were better in southern New England and the middle colonies, where the soil was fertile and the weather more temperate. New York, Pennsylvania, and the Connecticut River valley were the chief suppliers of wheat to much of New England and to parts of the South.

Beginning with a failed effort to establish an ironworks in Saugus, Massachusetts, in the mid-seventeenth century, colonists in New England and the middle colonies embarked on industrial ventures as well. Almost every colonist engaged in a certain amount of industry at home. Occasionally these home industries provided families with surplus goods they could trade or sell. Beyond these domestic efforts, craftsmen and artisans established themselves in colonial towns as cobblers, blacksmiths, riflemakers, cabinetmakers, silversmiths, and printers. In some areas, entrepreneurs harnessed water power to run small mills for grinding grain, processing cloth, or milling lumber. And in several places, large-scale shipbuilding operations began to flourish.

The largest industrial enterprise anywhere in English North America was the ironworks of the German ironmaster Peter Hasenclever in northern New Jersey. Founded in 1764 with British capital, it employed several hundred laborers, many of them imported from ironworks in Germany. There were other, smaller ironmaking enterprises in every northern colony (with particular concentrations in Massachusetts, New Jersey, and Pennsylvania), and there were ironworks as well in several of the southern colonies. But these and other growing industries did not become the basis for the kind of explosive industrial growth that Great Britain experienced in the late eighteenth century—in part because English parliamentary regulations such as the Iron Act of 1750 restricted metal processing in the colonies. Similar prohibitions limited the manufacture of woolens, hats, and other goods. But the most important obstacles to industrialization in America were an inadequate labor supply, a small domestic market, and inadequate transportation facilities and energy supplies.

More important than manufacturing to the economy of the northern colonies were industries that exploited the natural resources of the continent. By the mid-seventeenth century, the flourishing fur trade of earlier years was in decline; the supply of fur-bearing animals along the Atlantic seaboard had been nearly exhausted, and the interior fur trade was largely in the hands of the Algonquins and their French allies. More important now were lumbering, mining, and fishing, particularly in the waters off the New England coast. These industries provided commodities that could be exported to England in exchange for manufactured goods. And they helped produce the most distinctive feature of the northern economy—a thriving commercial class.

### The Rise of Commerce

Perhaps the most remarkable feature of colonial commerce in the seventeenth century was that it was able to survive at all. American merchants faced such bewildering and intimidating obstacles, and lacked so many of the basic institutions of trade, that they managed to stay afloat only with great difficulty. The colonies had almost no gold or silver, and their paper currency was not acceptable as payment for goods from abroad. For many years, colonial merchants had to rely on barter or on money substitutes such as beaver skins.

A second obstacle was lack of information about supply and demand. Traders had no way of knowing what they would find in foreign ports; vessels sometimes stayed at sea for years, journeying from one port to another, trading one commodity for another, attempting to find some way to turn a profit. There was also an enormous number of small, fiercely competitive companies, which made the problem of rationalizing the system even more acute.

Nevertheless, commerce in the colonies survived and grew. There was elaborate trade among the colonies themselves and with the West Indies. The mainland colonies offered their Caribbean trading partners rum, agricultural products, meat, and fish. The islands offered sugar, molasses, and at times slaves in return. There was also trade with England, continental Europe, and the west coast of Africa. This commerce has often been described, somewhat inaccurately, as the "triangular trade," suggesting a neat process

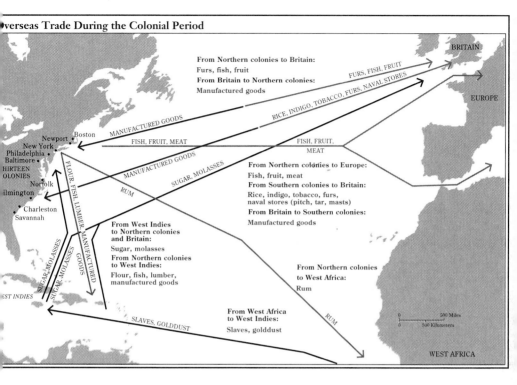

Overseas Trade During the Colonial Period

From Northern colonies to Britain:
Furs, fish, fruit
From Britain to Northern colonies:
Manufactured goods

FURS, FISH, FRUIT

RICE, INDIGO, TOBACCO, FURS, NAVAL STORES

BRITAIN

EUROPE

MANUFACTURED GOODS

FISH, FRUIT, MEAT

FISH, FRUIT, MEAT

Newport • Boston
New York
Philadelphia •
Baltimore •
THIRTEEN
COLONIES
Norfolk
Wilmington

FLOUR, FISH, LUMBER, MANUFACTURED

MANUFACTURED GOODS

RUM

SUGAR, MOLASSES

From Northern colonies to Europe:
Fish, fruit, meat
From Southern colonies to Britain:
Rice, indigo, tobacco, furs,
naval stores (pitch, tar, masts)
From Britain to Southern colonies:
Manufactured goods

• Charleston
Savannah

SUGAR, MOLASSES

SUGAR, MOLASSES

MANUFACTURED GOODS

WEST INDIES

From West Indies
to Northern colonies
and Britain:

Sugar, molasses
From Northern colonies
to West Indies:

Flour, fish, lumber,
manufactured goods

From Northern colonies
to West Africa:

Rum

SLAVES, GOLDDUST

From West Africa
to West Indies:

Slaves, golddust

RUM

0    500 Miles
0    500 Kilometers

WEST AFRICA

by which merchants carried rum and other goods from New England to Africa, exchanged their merchandise for slaves, whom they then transported to the West Indies (hence the term "middle passage" for the dread journey— it was the second of the three legs of the voyage), and then exchanged the slaves for sugar and molasses, which they shipped back to New England to be distilled into rum. In fact, the so-called triangular trade in rum, slaves, and sugar was in reality a complicated maze of highly diverse trade routes.

Out of this risky trade emerged a group of adventurous entrepreneurs who by the mid-eighteenth century were beginning to constitute a distinct merchant class concentrated in the port cities of the North. The British Navigation Acts protected them from foreign competition in the colonies. They had ready access to the market in England for such colonial products as furs, timber, and American-built ships. But they also developed markets illegally outside the British Empire—in the French, Spanish, and Dutch West Indies, where prices were often higher than in the British colonies.

During the eighteenth century, the colonial commercial system began to stabilize. But the trading sector of the American economy remained fluid, and open to newcomers, largely because it—and the society on which it was based—were expanding so rapidly.

## PATTERNS OF SOCIETY

Although there were sharp social distinctions in the colonies, the well-defined and deeply entrenched class system of England failed to reproduce itself in America. In England, land was scarce and the population large, and the relatively few landowners had enormous power over the landless. In colonial America, in contrast, land was abundant and people were scarce. Aristocracies emerged there, to be sure; but they tended to rely less on landownership than on control of a substantial work force, and they were generally less secure and less powerful than their English counterparts. More than in England, there were opportunities in America for social mobility—both up and down. There were also new forms of community in America, and they varied greatly from one region to another.

### The Plantation

The plantation system of the American South illustrated clearly the way in which colonial communities evolved in response to local conditions. The first plantations emerged in the tobacco-growing areas of Virginia and Maryland. Some of the early planters hoped to re-create in America the entrenched, landholding aristocracy of England, and in a few cases—notably in the great Maryland estates granted by Lord Baltimore to his relatives and friends—a semblance of such an aristocracy did emerge. On the whole, however, seventeenth-century colonial plantations were rough and relatively small estates. In the early days in Virginia, they were little more than crude clearings where landowners and indentured servants worked side by side in conditions so harsh that death was an everyday occurrence. Even in later years, when the death rate declined and the landholdings became more established, plantation work forces seldom exceeded thirty people. Most landowners lived in rough cabins or houses, with their servants or slaves nearby.

The economy of the plantation was a precarious one. Planters could not control their markets, so even the largest of them were constantly at risk. When prices fell—as tobacco prices did, for example, in the 1660s—planters faced the prospect of ruin. The plantation economy created many new wealthy landowners, but it also destroyed many.

Because plantations were often far from cities and towns, they tended to become self-contained communities. Some wealthier planters created something approaching a full town on their plantations. Smaller planters lived more modestly, but still in a relatively self-sufficient world. On the larger estates, plantation mistresses, unlike the wives of small farmers, had servants to perform ordinary household chores, thus freeing up time they could devote to their husbands and children. But many also had to tolerate sexual liaisons between their husbands or sons and black women of the slave community.

Even though the fortunes of planters could rise and fall quickly, there were always particularly wealthy landowners who exercised great social and economic influence. A great landowner controlled not only the lives of those who worked his own plantation but the livelihood of poorer neighbors who could not compete with him and thus depended on him to market their crops and supply them with credit. Some whites were unable to own their land and rented their farms from wealthy planters. Such independent farmers, working with few or no slaves to help them, formed the majority of the southern agrarian population, but the planters dominated the southern agrarian economy.

The enslaved African Americans, of course, lived very differently. On the smaller farms with only a handful of slaves, it was not always possible for a rigid separation to develop between whites and blacks. But over three-fourths of all blacks lived on plantations of at least ten slaves; nearly half lived in communities of fifty slaves or more. And in these places they began to develop a society and culture of their own. Although whites seldom encouraged formal marriages among slaves, blacks themselves developed a strong and elaborate family structure. Slaves attempted to construct nuclear families, and they managed at times to build stable households. But families were always precarious, because any member could be sold at any time to another planter, even to one in another colony. As a result, blacks placed special emphasis on extended kinship networks and often created surrogate "relatives" to replace missing members of their own families. There was also a distinctive slave religion, which blended Christianity with African folklore and which became a central element in the emergence of an independent black culture.

Nevertheless, black society was subject to constant intrusions from and interaction with white society. Black house servants, for example, were isolated from their own community and were under constant surveillance from whites. Black women were subject to usually unwanted sexual advances from owners and overseers and hence to bearing mulatto children, who were rarely recognized by their white fathers but were generally accepted as members of the slave community. On some plantations, black workers were treated with kindness and sometimes responded to their owners with genuine devotion. On others, they encountered physical brutality and occasionally even sadism, against which they were virtually powerless.

Slaves often resisted their masters, in large ways and small. The most serious example in the colonial period was the Stono Rebellion in South Carolina in 1739, during which about 100 blacks rose up, seized weapons, killed several whites, and attempted to escape south to Florida. The uprising was quickly crushed, and most participants were executed. A more frequent form of resistance was simply running away, but that provided no real solution either. There was nowhere to go. So for most slaves, resistance took the form of subtle, and often undetected, defiance or evasion of their masters' wishes.

Most slaves, male and female, worked as field hands (with the women shouldering the additional burdens of cooking and child rearing). But on the larger plantations that aspired to genuine self-sufficiency, some slaves learned trades and crafts: blacksmithing, carpentry, shoemaking, spinning, weaving, sewing, midwifery, and others. These skilled crafts workers were at times hired out to other planters. Some set up their own establishments in towns or cities and shared their profits with their owners. A few were able to buy their freedom. There was a small free black population living in southern cities by the time of the Revolution.

### The Puritan Community

The characteristic social unit in New England was not the isolated farm but the town. In the early years of colonization, each new settlement drew up a "covenant" binding all residents together in a religious and social unit. The structure of the towns reflected the spirit of the covenant. Colonists laid out a village, with houses and a meetinghouse arranged around a central pasture, or "common." Thus families generally lived with their neighbors close by, reinforcing the strong sense of community. They divided up the outlying fields and woodlands among the residents; the size and location of a family's field depended on the family's numbers, wealth, and social station.

Once a town was established, residents held a yearly "town meeting" to decide important questions and to choose a group of "selectmen," who ran the town's affairs. Participation in the meeting was generally restricted to adult males who were members of the church. Only those who could give evidence of grace, of being among the elect (the "visible saints") assured of salvation, were admitted to full membership, although other residents of the town were required to attend church services.

New Englanders did not adopt the English system of primogeniture— the passing of all property to the firstborn son. Instead, a father divided up his land among all his sons. His control of this inheritance gave him great power over the family. Often a son would reach his late twenties before his father would allow him to move into his own household and work his own land. Even then, sons would usually continue to live in close proximity to their fathers. Young women were generally more mobile than their brothers, since they did not stand to inherit land.

The early Puritan community was, in short, a tightly knit organism. The town as a whole was bound together by the initial covenant, by the centralized layout of the village, by the power of the church, and by the town meeting. The family was held together by the rigid patriarchal structure that limited opportunities for younger members (males in particular) to strike out on their own. Yet as the years passed and the communities grew, this communal structure experienced strains. This was partly because of the increasing commercialization of New England society, which introduced new forces and new tensions into the communities of the region. It was also partly because of population growth. As towns grew larger, residents tended to cultivate lands farther and farther from the community center and, by necessity, to live at increasing distances from the church. Often, groups of outlying residents would apply for permission to build a church of their own, usually the first step toward creation of a wholly new town. Such applications could cause bitter quarrels between the original townspeople and those who proposed to break away.

The control of land by fathers also created strains. In the first generations, fathers generally controlled enough land to satisfy the needs of all their sons. After several generations, however, when such lands were being subdivided for the third or fourth time, there was often too little to go around, particularly in communities surrounded by other towns, with no room to expand outward. The result was that in many communities, groups of younger residents broke off and moved elsewhere—at times far away—to form towns of their own.

The tensions building in Puritan communities could produce bizarre and disastrous events. One example was the widespread hysteria in the 1680s and 1690s over accusations of witchcraft (the human exercise of satanic powers) in New England. The most famous outbreak (although by no means the only one) was in Salem, Massachusetts, where adolescent girls began to exhibit strange behavior and leveled charges of witchcraft against several West Indian servants steeped in voodoo lore. Hysteria spread throughout the town, and hundreds of people (most of them women) were accused of witchcraft. Nineteen residents of Salem were put to death before the trials finally ended in 1692; the girls who had been the original accusers later recanted and admitted that their story had been fabricated.

The Salem experience was not unique. Accusations of witchcraft spread through many New England towns in the early 1690s (and indeed had emerged regularly in Puritan society for many years before). Research into

A Modeſt Enquiry
Into the Nature of

# Witchcraft,

AND

How Perſons Guilty of that Crime
may be *Convicted* : And the means
uſed for their Diſcovery Diſcuſſed,
both *Negatively* and *Affirmatively*,
according to *SCRIPTURE* and
*EXPERIENCE.*

## By John Hale,

Paſtor of the Church of Chriſt in *Beverley,*
*Anno Domini* 1697.

*When they ſay unto you, ſeek unto them that have*
*Familiar Spirits and unto Wizzards that peep,&c.*
*To the Law and to the Teſtimony ; if they ſpeak*
*not according to this word, it is becauſe there is no*
*light in them,* Iſaiah VIII. 19, 20.
*That which I ſee not teach thou me,* Job 34. 32.

*BOSTON in N. E.*
Printed by *B. Green,* and *J. Allen,* for
*Benjamin Eliot* under the Town Houſe. 1702

A STUDY OF WITCHCRAFT  This pamphlet, originally
written in 1697 near the height of the witchcraft
phenomenon in New England, was one of many
contemporary studies to take the idea of witchcraft
seriously. Belief in witches was widespread in early New
England society, and many of the charges that seem
preposterous to twentieth-century eyes appeared entirely
plausible even to educated people of the time.

the background of accused witches reveals that most were middle-aged
women, often widowed, with few or no children. Many accused witches
were of low social position, were often involved in domestic conflicts, had
frequently been accused of other crimes, and were considered abrasive by
their neighbors. Others were women who, through inheritance or hard
work, had come into possession of substantial property of their own and thus
challenged the gender norms of the community.

The witchcraft controversies were also a reflection of the highly religious
character of New England societies. New Englanders believed in the power
of Satan and his ability to assert his power in the world. Belief in witchcraft

was not a marginal superstition, rejected by the mainstream. It was a common feature of Puritan religious conviction.

## Cities

Even the largest colonial community was scarcely bigger than a modern small town. Yet by the standards of the eighteenth century, cities did exist in America. In the 1770s the two largest ports—Philadelphia and New York—had populations of 28,000 and 25,000, respectively, which made them larger than most English urban centers. Boston (16,000), Charles Town (later Charleston), South Carolina (12,000), and Newport, Rhode Island (11,000), were also substantial communities by the standards of the day.

Colonial cities served as trading centers for the farmers of their regions and as marts for international commerce. Their leaders were generally merchants who had acquired substantial estates. Class divisions in American cities were not as sharp as those in Europe. But more than in any other area of colonial life (except, of course, in the relationship between masters and slaves), social distinctions were real and visible in urban areas.

Cities were the centers of much of what industry there was in the colonies, such as distilleries for turning imported molasses into exportable rum. They were the locations of the most advanced schools and sophisticated cultural activities and of shops where imported goods could be bought. In addition, they were communities with urban social problems: crime, vice, pollution, traffic. Unlike smaller towns, cities needed to set up constables' offices and fire departments and develop systems for supporting the urban poor, whose numbers became especially large in times of economic crisis—to which cities were particularly vulnerable.

Finally, cities became places where new ideas could circulate and be discussed. There were newspapers, books, and other publications from abroad, and hence new intellectual influences. The taverns and coffeehouses of cities provided forums in which people could gather and debate the issues of the day. That is one reason why the Revolutionary crisis, when it began to build in the 1760s and 1770s, began first in the cities.

## THE COLONIAL MIND

Intellectual life in colonial America revolved around the conflict between the traditional outlook of the sixteenth and seventeenth centuries, with its emphasis on a personal God deeply involved in individual lives, and the new spirit of the Enlightenment, which was sweeping both Europe and America and which stressed the importance of science and human reason. The old views placed a high value on a stern moral code in which intellect was less important than faith. The Enlightenment suggested that people had substantial control over their own lives and societies.

## The Pattern of Religions

Religious toleration flourished in America to a degree unmatched in any European nation, not because Americans deliberately sought to produce it but because conditions virtually required it. Settlers in America brought with them so many different religious practices that it proved impossible to impose a single religious code on any large area.

The experience of the Church of England illustrated how difficult the establishment of a common religion would be in the colonies. By law, Anglicanism was established as the official faith in Virginia, Maryland, New York, the Carolinas, and Georgia. In these colonies everyone, regardless of belief or affiliation, was supposed to be taxed for the support of the church. Except in Virginia and Maryland, however, the laws establishing the Church of England as the official colonial religion were largely ignored. Missionaries of the Society for the Propagation of the Gospel, founded in 1701 to spread the Anglican faith, had some success in Massachusetts and Connecticut. But Anglicanism never succeeded in becoming a dominant religious force in America.

Even in New England, where the Puritans had originally believed that they were all part of a single faith, there was a growing tendency in the eighteenth century for different congregations to affiliate with different denominations, especially Congregationalism and Presbyterianism. In parts of New York and New Jersey, Dutch settlers had established their own Calvinist denomination, Dutch Reformed, which survived after the colonies became part of the British Empire. The American Baptists (of whom Roger Williams is considered the first) were also originally Calvinistic in their theology, but a great variety of Baptist sects emerged. They shared the belief that rebaptism, usually by total immersion, was necessary when believers reached maturity. But while some Baptists remained Calvinists, believers in predestination, others came to believe in salvation by free will.

Protestants extended toleration to one another more readily than they did to Roman Catholics. Many Protestants feared and hated the pope. New Englanders, in particular, viewed their Catholic neighbors in New France (Canada) not only as commercial and military rivals but as agents of Rome bent on frustrating their own divine mission. In most of the English colonies, however, Roman Catholics were too few to cause serious conflict. They were most numerous in Maryland, and even there they numbered no more than 3,000. Perhaps for that reason they suffered their worst persecution in that colony. After the overthrow of the original proprietors in 1691, Catholics in Maryland not only lost their political rights but were forbidden to hold religious services except in private houses.

Jews in provincial America totaled no more than about 2,000 at any time. The largest community lived in New York City. Smaller groups settled in Newport and Charleston, and there were scattered Jewish families in all the colonies. Nowhere could they vote or hold office. Only in Rhode Island could they practice their religion openly.

By the beginning of the eighteenth century, some Americans were growing troubled by the apparent decline in religious piety in their society. With so many diverse sects existing side by side, some people were tempted to doubt whether any particular denomination, even their own, possessed a monopoly of truth. The movement of the population westward and the wide scattering of settlements had caused many communities to lose touch with organized religion. The rise of commercial prosperity created a more secular outlook in urban areas. The progress of science and free thought in Europe—and the importation of Enlightenment ideas to America—caused at least some colonists to doubt traditional religious belief.

Concerns about declining piety surfaced as early as the 1660s in New England, where the Puritan oligarchy warned of a deterioration in the power of the church. Sabbath after Sabbath, ministers preached sermons of despair (known as "jeremiads"), deploring the signs of waning piety. By the standards of other societies or other eras, the Puritan faith remained remarkably strong. But New Englanders measured their faith by their own standards, and to them the "declension" of religious piety seemed a serious problem.

## The Great Awakening

By the early eighteenth century, similar concerns were emerging in other regions and among members of other faiths. Everywhere, colonists were coming to believe, religious piety was in decline and opportunities for spiritual regeneration were dwindling. The result was the first great American revival: the Great Awakening.

The Great Awakening began in earnest in the 1730s, reached its climax in the 1740s, and brought a new spirit of religious fervor that many believed was reversing the trend away from piety. The revival had particular appeal to women (who constituted the majority of converts) and to younger sons of the third or fourth generation of settlers—those who stood to inherit the least land and who faced the most uncertain futures. The rhetoric of the revival emphasized the potential for every person to break away from the constraints of the past and start anew in his or her relationship with God. Such beliefs may have reflected the desires of many people to break away from their families or communities and start a new life on earth.

Powerful evangelists from England helped spread the revival. John and Charles Wesley, the founders of Methodism, visited Georgia and other colonies in the 1730s. George Whitefield, a powerful open-air preacher and for a time an associate of the Wesleys, made several evangelizing tours through the colonies and drew tremendous crowds. But the evangelizers from abroad were less important to American revivalism in the long run than the colonial ministers attempting to restore religious fervor in America. The outstanding preacher of the Great Awakening was the New England Congregationalist Jonathan Edwards—a deeply orthodox Puritan but a highly original theologian. From his pulpit in Northampton, Massachusetts, Edwards attacked the new doctrines of easy salvation for all. He preached anew the traditional Puritan ideas of the absolute sovereignty of God, predestination, and salvation by God's grace alone. His vivid descriptions of hell could terrify his listeners.

The Great Awakening led to the division of existing congregations (between "New Light" revivalists and traditionalists) and to the founding of new ones. It also affected areas of society outside the churches. Some of the revivalists denounced book learning as a hindrance to salvation, and some communities repudiated secular education altogether. But other evangelists saw education as a means of furthering religion, and they founded or led schools for the training of New Light ministers.

*Education*

Many colonists placed a high value on education, despite the difficulties they confronted in gaining access to it. Some families tried to teach their children to read and write at home, although the heavy burden of work in most agricultural households limited the time available for schooling. In Massachusetts, a 1647 law required that every town support a public school; and even though many communities failed to comply, a modest network of public schools emerged as a result. The Quakers and other sects operated church schools, and in some communities widows or unmarried women conducted "dame schools" by holding private classes in their homes. In cities, master craftsmen set up evening schools for their apprentices.

A "DAME SCHOOL" PRIMER More than the residents of any other region of North America (and far more than those of most of Europe), the New England colonists strove to educate their children and achieved perhaps the highest level of literacy in the world. Throughout the region, young children attended institutions known as "dame schools" (because the teachers were almost always women) and learned from primers such as this one.

White male Americans, at least, achieved a high degree of literacy in the eighteenth century. By the time of the Revolution, well over half of all white men could read and write, a rate substantially higher than that in most European countries. The literacy rate for women lagged behind the rate for men until the nineteenth century; and while opportunities for education beyond the primary level were scarce for men, they were almost nonexistent for women. Nevertheless, the literacy rate for females was also substantially higher than that of their European counterparts.

African Americans, most of whom were enslaved, had virtually no access to education. Occasionally a master or mistress would teach slave children to read and write; but as the slave system became more firmly entrenched, strong social (and ultimately legal) sanctions developed to discourage such efforts, lest literacy encourage slaves to question their stations. Indians, too, remained largely outside the white educational system—to a large degree by choice: most tribes preferred to educate their children in their own way. But some white missionaries and philanthropists established schools for Native Americans and helped create a small but significant population of Indians literate in spoken and written English.

Nowhere was the intermingling of traditional religiosity and the new spirit of the Enlightenment clearer than in the colleges and universities of colonial America. Of the six colleges in operation by 1763, all but two were founded by religious groups primarily for the training of preachers. Yet in almost all, the influences of the new scientific, rational approach to knowledge could be felt.

Harvard, the first American college, was established in 1636 by Puritan theologians who wanted to create a training center for ministers. (The college was named for a Charlestown minister, John Harvard, who had left it his library and half his estate). Decades later, in 1693, William and Mary College (named for the English king and queen) was established in Williamsburg, Virginia, by Anglicans; like Harvard, it was conceived as an academy to train clergymen. And in 1701, conservative Congregationalists, dissatisfied with the growing religious liberalism of Harvard, founded Yale (named for one of its first benefactors, Elihu Yale) in New Haven, Connecticut. Out of the Great Awakening emerged the College of New Jersey, founded in 1746 and known later as Princeton (after the town in which it was located); one of its first presidents was Jonathan Edwards. Despite the religious basis of these colleges, most of them offered curricula that included not only theology but logic, ethics, physics, geometry, astronomy, rhetoric, Latin, Hebrew, and Greek. King's College, founded in New York in 1754 and later renamed Columbia, was specifically devoted to the spread of secular knowledge; it had no theological faculty and was interdenominational from the start. The Academy and College of Philadelphia, founded in 1755 and later renamed the University of Pennsylvania, was also a completely secular institution, established by a group of laymen under the inspiration of Benjamin Franklin.

After 1700, most colonial leaders received their entire education in America (rather than attending university in England, as had once been the case). But the advantages of higher education were not widely shared. Women, blacks, and Indians were excluded from all colleges and universities. And among white men, only those from relatively affluent families could afford to attend.

*Concepts of Law and Politics*

In law and politics, as in other parts of their lives, Americans in the seventeenth and eighteenth centuries believed that they were re-creating in the New World the practices and institutions of the Old. But as in other areas, they in fact created something very different.

Changes in the law in America resulted in part from the scarcity of English-trained lawyers, who were almost unknown in the colonies until after 1700. Although the American legal system adopted most of the essential elements of the English system, including such ancient rights as trial by jury, significant differences developed in court procedures, punishments, and the definition of crimes. In England, for example, a printed attack on a public official, whether true or false, was considered libelous. At the 1734 trial of the New York publisher John Peter Zenger, who was powerfully defended by the Philadelphia lawyer Andrew Hamilton, the courts ruled that criticisms of the government were not libelous if factually true—a verdict that removed some colonial restrictions on the freedom of the press.

More significant for the future of the relationship between the colonies and England were differences emerging between the American and British political systems. Because the royal government—in theory the ultimate authority over the colonies—was so far away, Americans created a group of institutions of their own that gave them a large measure of self-government. In most colonies, local communities grew accustomed to running their own affairs with minimal interference from higher authorities. The colonial assemblies came to exercise many of the powers that Parliament exercised in England. Provincial governors (appointed by the king after the 1690s) had broad powers on paper, but in fact their influence was sharply limited. Control over appointments and contracts resided largely in England or with local colonial leaders. A governor could be removed any time his patron in England lost favor. And in some cases, governors were not even familiar with the colonies they were meant to govern; most governors were Englishmen who came to the colonies for the first time to assume their offices.

The result of all this was that the focus of politics in the colonies became a local one. The provincial governments became accustomed to acting more or less independently of Parliament, and a set of assumptions and expectations about the rights of the colonists took hold in America that was not shared by policymakers in England. These differences caused few problems before the 1760s, because the British did little to exert the authority they believed they possessed. But when, beginning in 1763, the English government began attempting to tighten its control over the American colonies, a historic crisis resulted.

D E B A T I N G     T H E     P A S T

## The Origins of Slavery

THE DEBATE AMONG historians over how and why white Americans created a system of slave labor in the seventeenth century—and how and why they determined that African-Americans and no others should populate that system—has been an unusually lively one. At its center is a debate over whether slavery was a result of white racism, or whether racism was a result of slavery.

In 1950, Oscar and Mary Handlin published an influential article comparing slavery to other systems of "unfreedom" in the colonies. What separated slavery from other conditions of servitude, they argued, was that it was restricted to people of African descent, that it was permanent, and that it passed from one generation to the next. The unique characteristics of slavery, the Handlins argued, were part of an effort by colonial legislatures to increase the available labor force. White laborers needed an incentive to come to America; black laborers, forcibly imported from Africa, did not. The distinction between the conditions of white workers and the conditions of black workers was, therefore, based on legal and economic motives, not on racism.

Winthrop Jordan was one of a number of historians who later challenged the Handlins' thesis and argued that white racism, more than economic interests, produced African slavery. In *White Over Black* (1968) and other works, Jordan argued that Europeans had long viewed people of color—and black Africans in particular—as inferior beings appropriate for serving whites. Those attitudes migrated with white Europeans to the New World, and white racism shaped the treatment of Africans in America—and the nature of the slave labor system—from the beginning. Even without the economic incentives the Handlins described, in other words, whites would have been likely to oppress blacks in the New World.

Peter Wood's *Black Majority* (1974), a study of seventeenth-century South Carolina, was one of a number of works that moved the debate back towards social and economic conditions. Wood demonstrated that blacks and whites often worked together on relatively equal terms in the early years of settlement; that racism, in other words, did not inevitably shape the relationships between blacks and whites. But as rice cultivation expanded, it became more difficult to find white laborers willing to do the arduous work. The increase in the forcible importation of African workers, and the creation of a system of permanent bondage, was a response to this growing demand for labor. It was also a response to fears among whites that without slavery it would be difficult to control a labor force brought to America against its will. Edmund Morgan's *American Slavery, American Freedom* (1975) argued similarly that the southern labor system was at first relatively flexible and later grew more rigid. In colonial Virginia, he claimed, white settlers did not at first intend to create a system of permanent bondage for blacks or whites. But as the tobacco economy grew and created a high demand for cheap labor, white landowners began to feel uneasy about their dependence on a large group of dependent white workers. Such workers were difficult to recruit and control. Slavery, therefore, was less a result of racism than of the desire for whites to find a reliable and stable labor force.

In recent years, the debate over the origins of slavery has become part of a larger debate over the nature of racism in American (and world) history. Some scholars continue to argue, as Winthrop Jordan did in the 1960s, that racism is a powerful, autonomous part of white culture, which exists independent of other factors. Others argue that race as a category of distinction among human beings is itself meaningless; since there are no significant biological or genetic distinctions separating the races, the belief that there are important differences is always an invention, or "construction," designed to serve other needs. Just as historians have argued that eighteenth-century racism was a product and not a cause of slavery, so other scholars argue that racism in other times is an ideology created to justify systems of oppression that serve economic, political, or other needs.

CHAPTER FOUR

# The Empire Under Strain

*Origins of Resistance* ∼ *The Struggle for the Continent*
*The New Imperialism* ∼ *Stirrings of Revolt*
*Cooperation and War*

A S LATE AS the 1750s, few Americans objected to their membership
in the British Empire. The imperial system had commercial and
political benefits for the Americans. And it had few costs, because for the
most part the English government left the colonies alone. By the mid-1770s,
however, the relationship between the American colonies and their British
rulers had become so strained, so poisoned, so characterized by suspicion
and resentment that the empire was on the verge of unraveling. And in the
spring of 1775, the first shots were fired in a war that would ultimately win
America its independence. How had it happened? And why so quickly?

## ORIGINS OF RESISTANCE

In one sense, it had not happened quickly at all. Ever since the first days of
English settlement in North America, the ideas and institutions of the
colonies had been diverging from those in Britain in countless ways. In another sense, however, the Revolutionary crisis emerged in response to important and relatively sudden changes in the administration of the empire.
In 1763 the English government began to enforce a series of policies toward
its colonies that brought the differences between the two societies into sharp
focus.

### A Loosening of Ties

In the fifty years after the Glorious Revolution, the English Parliament
(which became the British Parliament after the union of England and Scot-

| TIME LINE | | | |
|---|---|---|---|
| **1756** | **1760** | **1763** | **1764** |
| Seven Years' War begins | George III becomes king | Peace of Paris  Proclamation of 1763 | Sugar Act |
| **1765** | **1766** | **1767** | **1770** |
| Stamp Act | Stamp Act repealed  Declaratory Act | Townshend duties | Boston Massacre  Most Townshend duties repealed |
| **1771** | **1772** | **1773** | **1774** | **1775** |
| Regulator movement in North Carolina | Committees of correspondence in Boston  Gaspée incident | Tea Act, Boston Tea Party | Intolerable Acts  First Continental Congress in Philadelphia | Battles of Lexington and Concord  American Revolution begins |

land in 1707) established a growing supremacy over the king. During the reigns of George I (1714–1727) and George II (1727–1760), both of whom were German-born and unaccustomed to English ways, the prime minister and his cabinet became the nation's real executives. They held their positions less by the king's favor than by their ability to control majorities in Parliament.

These parliamentary leaders were less inclined than the seventeenth-century monarchs had been to try to tighten control over the empire. They depended politically on the great merchants and landholders of England, most of whom feared that any such efforts would reduce the profitability of the colonial trade. As a result, administration of the colonies remained decentralized and inefficient, with no single office or agency responsible for colonial affairs.

The character of the royal officials in America—the governors and other officers of the royal colonies and (in all the colonies) the naval officers and collectors of customs—contributed further to the looseness of the imperial system. Some of these officeholders were able and intelligent; most were not. Many, perhaps most, colonial officials had used bribery to obtain their offices; many, perhaps most, accepted bribes once they assumed their offices. Some appointees remained in England and hired substitutes to take their places in America.

Resistance to imperial authority centered in the colonial legislatures. By the 1750s the assemblies had become accustomed to levying taxes, making appropriations, approving appointments, and passing laws for their respective colonies. The assemblies came to look upon themselves as little parliaments, each practically as sovereign within its colony as Parliament itself was in England.

### Intercolonial Disunity

Even so, the colonists continued to think of themselves as loyal English subjects. Many felt stronger ties to England than they did to the other American colonies, so great were the differences among the colonial societies. Yet for all their differences, the colonies could not avoid forging connections with one another. As settlement became almost continuous along the seacoast, people of the different colonies came into closer contact. The gradual construction of roads, the rise of trade, and the creation of a colonial postal service also forged intercolonial ties.

But the colonists were reluctant to cooperate in larger ways even when, in 1754, they faced a common threat from their old rivals, the French, and France's Indian allies. A conference of colonial leaders—with delegates from Pennsylvania, Maryland, New York, and New England—was meeting in Albany in that year to negotiate a treaty with the Iroquois. The delegates tentatively approved a plan offered by Benjamin Franklin to set up a "general government" in America to manage relations with the Indians on behalf of all the colonies. War with the French and Indians was already beginning when this Albany Plan was presented to the colonial assemblies. None approved it.

## THE STRUGGLE FOR THE CONTINENT

The war that raged in North America through the late 1750s and early 1760s was part of a larger struggle between England and France for dominance in world trade and naval power. The British victory in that struggle, known in Europe as the Seven Years' War, confirmed England's commercial supremacy and cemented its control of the settled regions of North America.

In America, however, the conflict was also the final stage in a long struggle among the three principal powers in northeastern North America: the English, the French, and the Iroquois. For more than a century prior to the conflict—known in America as the French and Indian War—these three groups had maintained a precarious balance of power. The events of the 1750s upset that balance, produced a prolonged and open conflict, and established a precarious dominance for the English societies throughout the region. The war also brought English America into closer contact with British authority than ever before and raised to the surface some of the underlying tensions in the colonial relationship.

### New France and the Iroquois Nation

The French and the English had coexisted relatively peacefully in North America for nearly a century. But by the 1750s, as both English and French settlements expanded, religious and commercial tensions began to produce new frictions and new conflicts. By the end of the seventeenth century, the French Empire in America comprised a vast territory. In the 1680s, French explorers journeyed as far south as the delta of the Mississippi, claimed the surrounding country for France, and named it Louisiana in honor of King Louis XIV. Subsequent traders and missionaries wandered southwest as far as the Rio Grande and west to the Rocky Mountains. The French had by then revealed the outlines of, and laid claim to, the whole continental interior.

To secure their hold on these enormous claims, they founded a string of widely separated communities, strategically located fortresses, and far-flung missions and trading posts. Would-be feudal lords established large estates (seigneuries) along the banks of the St. Lawrence River. And on a high bluff above the river stood the fortified city of Quebec, the center of the French Empire in America. Montreal to the south and Sault Sainte Marie and Detroit to the west marked the northern boundaries of French settlement. On the lower Mississippi emerged plantations much like those in the southern colonies of English America, worked by black slaves and owned by "Creoles" (white immigrants of French descent). New Orleans, founded in 1718 to service the French plantation economy, was soon as big as some of the larger cities of the Atlantic seaboard; Biloxi and Mobile to the east completed the string of French settlement.

But the French, of course, shared the continental interior with a large and powerful Indian population. Both the French and the English were aware that the battle for control of North America would be determined in part by which group could best win the allegiance of native tribes—as trading partners and, at times, as military allies. The English—with their more advanced commercial economy—could usually offer the Indians better and more plentiful goods. But the French offered something that was often more important: tolerance. Unlike the English settlers, who strove constantly to impose their own social norms on the Indians they encountered, the French settlers in the interior generally adjusted their own behavior to Indian patterns. French fur traders frequently married Indian women and adopted tribal ways; Jesuit missionaries interacted comfortably with the natives and converted them to Catholicism by the thousands without challenging most of their social customs. By the mid-eighteenth century, therefore, the French had better and closer relations with most of the Indians of the interior than did the English.

The most powerful native group, however, had a different relationship with the French. The Iroquois Confederacy—five Indian nations (Mohawk, Seneca, Cayuga, Onondaga, and Oneida) that had formed a defensive alliance in the fifteenth century—had been the most powerful native presence in the Ohio Valley and a large surrounding region since the 1640s. For nearly a century, neither the French nor the English raised any serious challenge to Iroquois control of the region, and the Iroquois maintained their autonomy by avoiding too close a relationship with either group. They traded successfully with both the English and the French and astutely played the two groups off against each other. As a result, they maintained an uneasy balance of power in the Great Lakes region.

### Anglo-French Conflicts

As long as England and France remained at peace and as long as the precarious balance in the North American interior survived, English and French colonists coexisted without serious difficulty. But after the Glorious Revolution in England, a series of Anglo-French wars erupted and continued intermittently in Europe for nearly eighty years.

The wars had important repercussions in America. King William's War (1689–1697) produced only a few, indecisive clashes between the English and the French in northern New England. Queen Anne's War, which began in 1701 and continued for nearly twelve years, generated more substantial conflicts: border fighting with the Spaniards in the South as well as with the French and their Indian allies in the North. The Treaty of Utrecht, which brought the conflict to a close in 1713, transferred substantial territory from the French to the English in North America, including Acadia (Nova Scotia) and Newfoundland.

Two decades later, disputes over British trading rights in the Spanish colonies produced a war between England and Spain that soon merged with a much larger European war, in which England and France lined up on opposite sides. The English colonists in America were soon drawn into the struggle, which they called King George's War; and between 1744 and 1748 they engaged in a series of conflicts with the French. New Englanders captured the French bastion at Louisbourg on Cape Breton Island, but the peace treaty that finally ended the conflict forced them to abandon it.

In the aftermath of King George's War, relations among the English, French, and Iroquois in North America quickly deteriorated. The Iroquois (in what appears to have been a major blunder) granted trading concessions in the interior to English merchants for the first time. The French, fearful (probably correctly) that the English were using the concessions as a first step toward expansion into French lands, began in 1749 to construct new fortresses in the Ohio Valley. The English interpreted the French activity as a threat to their western settlements, protested, and began making military preparations and building fortresses of their own. The balance of power that the Iroquois had carefully and successfully maintained for so long rapidly disintegrated.

For the next five years, tensions between the English and the French increased. In the summer of 1754 the governor of Virginia sent a militia force (under the command of an inexperienced young colonel, George Washington) into the Ohio Valley to challenge French expansion. Washington built a crude stockade (Fort Necessity) not far from Fort Duquesne, the larger outpost the French were building on the site of what is now Pittsburgh. After the Virginians staged an unsuccessful attack on a French detachment, the French countered with an assault on Fort Necessity, trapping Washington and his soldiers inside. After a third of them died in the fighting, Washington surrendered. The clash marked the beginning of the French and Indian War.

### The Great War for the Empire

The French and Indian War lasted nearly nine years, and it moved through three distinct phases. During the first of these phases, from the Fort Necessity debacle in 1754 until the expansion of the war to Europe in 1756, it was primarily a local, North American conflict. The English colonists managed the war mainly on their own, and they focused largely on defending themselves against raids on their western settlements by the Indians of the Ohio Valley. Virtually all the tribes except the Iroquois were now allied with the French; they had interpreted the defeat of the Virginians at Fort Duquesne as evidence of British weakness. Even the Iroquois, who were nominally allied with the British, feared antagonizing the French. They remained largely passive in the conflict. By late 1755, many English settlers along the frontier had withdrawn to the east of the Allegheny Mountains to escape the hostilities.

The second phase of the struggle began in 1756, when the governments of France and England formally opened hostilities and a truly international conflict (the Seven Years' War) began. The fighting now spread to the West Indies, India, and Europe itself. But the principal struggle remained the one in North America, where so far England had suffered nothing but frustration and defeat. Beginning in 1757, William Pitt, the English secretary of state (and future prime minister), began to transform the war effort in America by bringing it for the first time fully under British control. Pitt himself planned military strategy, appointed commanders, and issued orders to the colonists. Military recruitment had slowed dramatically in America, and to replenish the army British commanders began forcibly enlisting colonists (a practice known as "impressment"). Officers also seized supplies from local farmers and tradesmen and compelled colonists to offer shelter to British troops—all generally without compensation. The Americans resented these new impositions and firmly resisted them—at times, as in a 1757 riot in New York City, violently. By early 1758, the friction between the British authorities and the colonists was threatening to bring the war effort to a halt.

Beginning in 1758, therefore, Pitt initiated the third and final phase of the war by relaxing many of the policies that Americans had found obnoxious. He agreed to reimburse the colonists for all supplies requisitioned by the army. He returned control over recruitment to the colonial assemblies (which resulted in an immediate and dramatic increase in enlistments). And he dispatched large numbers of additional British troops to America. Finally, the tide of battle began to turn in England's favor. The French, who had always been outnumbered by the British colonists and who, after 1756, suffered from a series of poor harvests, were unable to sustain their early military successes. By mid-1758, the British regulars in America (who did the bulk of the actual fighting) and the colonial militias were seizing one French stronghold after another. Two brilliant English generals, Jeffrey Amherst and James Wolfe, captured the fortress at Louisbourg in July 1758; a few months later Fort Duquesne fell without a fight. The next year, at the end of a siege of Quebec, supposedly impregnable atop its towering cliff, the army of General Wolfe struggled up a hidden ravine under cover of darkness, surprised the larger forces of the Marquis de Montcalm, and defeated them in a battle in which both commanders were killed. The dramatic fall of Quebec on September 13, 1759, marked the beginning of the end of the Amer-

A LL thofe who prefer the Glory of bearing Arms to any fervile mean Employ, and have Spirit to ftand forth in **D**efence of their **K**ing and **C**ountry, againft the treacherous Defigns of *France* and *Spain*, in the

# Suffex Light Dragoons,

Commanded by

## Lt. Col. John Baker Holroyd,

Let them repair to

Where they fhall be handfomely Cloathed, moft compleatly Accoutred, mounted on noble Hunters. and treated with Kindnefs and Generofity.

RECRUITING FOR THE FRENCH AND INDIAN WAR The extravagant promises in this recruiting poster, distributed to colonists during the French and Indian War, suggest how difficult it sometimes was to persuade Americans to fight in the British army.

ican phase of the war. A year later, in September 1760, the French army formally surrendered to Amherst in Montreal.

Peace finally came in 1763, with the Peace of Paris. Under its terms, the French ceded to Great Britain some of their West Indian islands, most of their colonies in India and Canada, and all other French territory in North America east of the Mississippi. They ceded New Orleans and their claims west of the Mississippi to Spain, thus surrendering all title to the mainland of North America.

The French and Indian War had profound effects on the British Empire and the American colonies. It greatly expanded England's territorial claims in the New World. At the same time, the cost of the war greatly enlarged Britain's debt and substantially increased British resentment of the Americans. English leaders were contemptuous of the colonists for what they considered American military ineptitude during the war; they were angry that the colonists had made so few financial contributions to a struggle waged, they believed, largely for American benefit; they were particularly bitter that some colonial merchants had been selling food and other goods to the French in the West Indies throughout the conflict. All these factors combined to persuade many English leaders that a major reorganization of the empire, giving London increased authority over the colonies, would be necessary in the aftermath of the war.

The war had an equally profound but very different effect on the American colonists. It was an experience that forced them, for the first time, to act in concert against a common foe. And it seemed to establish certain precedents. The friction of 1756–1757 over British requisition and impressment policies and the 1758 return of authority to the colonial assemblies seemed to many Americans to confirm the illegitimacy of English interference in local affairs.

For the Indians of the Ohio Valley, the third major party in the French and Indian War, the British victory was disastrous. Those tribes that had allied themselves with the French had earned the enmity of the victorious English. The Iroquois Confederacy, which had allied itself with Britain, fared only slightly better. English officials saw the passivity of the Iroquois during the war (a result of their effort to hedge their bets and avoid antagonizing the French) as evidence of duplicity. In the aftermath of the peace settlement, the Iroquois alliance with the British quickly unraveled, and the Iroquois Confederacy itself began to crumble from within. The tribes would continue to contest the English for control of the Ohio Valley for another fifty years; but increasingly divided and increasingly outnumbered, they would seldom again be in a position to deal with their European rivals on terms of military or political equality.

## THE NEW IMPERIALISM

With the treaty of 1763, England found itself truly at peace for the first time in more than fifty years. Undistracted by war, the British government could now turn its attention to the organization of its empire. And after the difficult experiences of the previous decade, many English leaders were convinced that the question of imperial organization could no longer be ignored. Saddled with enormous debts from the many years of fighting, England was desperately in need of new revenues from its empire. And responsible for vast new lands in the New World, the imperial government felt compelled to expand its involvement in its colonies.

## Burdens of Empire

The experience of the French and Indian War, however, suggested that such increased involvement would not be easy to establish. Not only had the colonists proved so resistant to British control that Pitt had been forced to relax his policies in 1758, but the colonial assemblies had continued after that to respond to British needs slowly and grudgingly. Unwilling to be taxed by Parliament to support the war effort, the colonists were generally reluctant to tax themselves as well. Defiance of imperial trade regulations and other British demands continued.

With the territorial annexations of 1763, the area of the British Empire was suddenly twice as great as it had been, and the problems of governing it thus became many times more complex. Some English officials argued that the empire should restrain rapid settlement and development of the western territories to avoid costly conflicts with the Indians and the possibility of renewed battles with the many French people remaining in North America. Restricting settlement would also keep the land available for hunting and trapping. Others wanted to see the new territories opened for immediate development, but they disagreed among themselves about who should control the western lands. The existing colonial governments made fervent, and often conflicting, claims of jurisdiction. Some officials in London wanted control to remain in England and wanted the territories to be considered entirely new colonies, unlinked to the existing settlements.

At the same time, the government in London was running out of options in its effort to deal with its staggering war debt. Landlords and merchants in England itself were objecting strenuously to tax increases. And the reluctance of the colonial assemblies to pay for the war effort had suggested that England could not rely on any cooperation from them in its search for revenues. Only a system of taxation administered by London, the leaders of the empire believed, could effectively meet England's needs.

At this crucial moment in Anglo-American relations, with the imperial system in need of redefinition, the government of England was thrown into turmoil by the accession to the throne of a new king, George III, who assumed power in 1760. He brought two particularly unfortunate qualities to the office. First, he was determined, unlike his two predecessors, to reassert the authority of the monarchy. Pushed by his ambitious mother, he removed from power the relatively stable coalition of Whigs that had governed the empire for much of the century and replaced it with a new coalition of his own, assembled through patronage and bribes. The new ministries that emerged as a result of this change were very unstable, each lasting in office an average of only about two years.

HUDSON'S BAY COMPANY

QUÉBEC

Lake Superior

MAIN
(Mass

Québec

Fort Michilimackinac

Montreal

Fort
Frontenac

Palmo

La Baye

Lake Huron

Lake Michigan

Fort
Stanwix

Lake Ontario

N.H.

Portsmo

Glouce

Fort Niagara

Mohawk R.

Bennington

Boston

MASS.

Plymo

Albany

CONN

Provider

Fort Detroit

NEW YORK

Kingston

Hartford

R.I.

Newpor

Lake Erie

Poughkeepsie

New Haven

St. Joseph

Allegheny R.

PENNSYLVANIA

New York

Southampton

Maumee R.

Mountains

Perth Amboy

Reading

Trenton

NEW JERSEY

Illinois R.

Ohio R.

Fort
Duquesne

Susquehanna R.

Delaware R.

Philadelphia

Burlington

New Castle

Baltimore

Dover

St. Louis

Vincennes

Ohio R.

Shenandoah R.

Potomac R.

Annapolis

DELAWARE

MARYLAND

Wabash R.

VIRGINIA

Richmond

James R.

Williamsburg

Petersburg

Norfolk

SPANISH
LOUISIANA

Roanoke R.

ATLANTIC OCEA

Cumberland R.

Appalachian

Edenton

NORTH CAROLINA

Greensville

Mississippi R.

Tennessee R.

Fayetteville

Cape Fear R.

New Bern

Portsmouth

Wilmington

Camden

Santee R.

DISPUTED TERRITORY
(Claimed by Spain and Britain)

Columbia

Kingston

Augusta

Ashley R.

SOUTH
CAROLINA

Savannah R.

Cooper R.

Charleston

WEST FLORIDA

GEORGIA

Altamaha R.

Savannah

Mobile

Pensacola

EAST FLORIDA

St. Augustine

New Orleans

Gulf of Mexico

**The Thirteen Colon
in 1763**

NON-INDIAN SETTLEM

Before 1700

1700–1763

Frontier line
in 1763

Proclamation Li
of 1763

★ Provincial capita

0                    150 Miles

0                    200 Kilometers

The king also had serious intellectual and psychological limitations. He suffered, apparently, from a rare mental disease that produced intermittent bouts of insanity. (Indeed, in the last years of his long reign he was, according to most accounts, a virtual lunatic, confined to the palace and unable to perform any official functions.) Yet even when George III was lucid and rational, which was most of the time in the 1760s and 1770s, he was painfully immature (he had been only twenty-two when he ascended the throne) and insecure. The king's personality, therefore, contributed both to the instability and to the intransigence of the British government during these critical years.

More directly responsible for the problems that soon emerged with the colonies, however, was George Grenville, whom the king made prime minister in 1763. Grenville, though a brother-in-law of William Pitt, did not share Pitt's sympathy with the American point of view. He agreed instead with the prevailing opinion within Britain that the colonists had been too long indulged and that they should be compelled to obey the laws and to pay a part of the cost of defending and administering the empire.

### The British and the Tribes

With the defeat of the French, frontiersmen from the English colonies had begun immediately to move over the mountains and into tribal lands in the upper Ohio Valley. An alliance of Indian tribes, under the Ottawa chieftain Pontiac, struck back. To prevent an escalation of the fighting that might threaten western trade, the British government issued a ruling—the Proclamation of 1763—forbidding settlers to advance beyond the mountains that divided the Atlantic coast from the interior.

The Proclamation of 1763 gave London, rather than the provincial governments and their land-hungry constituents, power to control (and slow) the westward movement of the white population. Slower western settlement would limit costly wars with the Indians. It would also slow the population exodus from the coastal colonies, where England's most important markets and investments were. And it would reserve opportunities for land speculation and fur trading for English rather than colonial entrepreneurs.

Although Native Americans had few illusions about the Proclamation, which required them to cede land east of the mountains to the white settlers, many Indian groups supported the agreement as the best bargain available to them. The Cherokee, in particular, worked actively to hasten the drawing of the boundary, hoping finally to put an end to white encroachments. Relations between the western tribes and the British improved in at least some areas after the Proclamation, partly as a result of the work of the Indian superintendents the British appointed, who were sympathetic to tribal needs.

In the end, however, the Proclamation of 1763 failed to meet even the modest expectations of the Indians, because on the crucial point of the line of settlement it was almost completely ineffective. White settlers continued to swarm across the boundary and continued to claim lands farther and farther into the Ohio Valley. The British authorities tried repeatedly to establish limits to the expansion. In 1768, new agreements with the western tribes created a supposedly permanent boundary (which, as always, increased the area of white settlement at the expense of the Indians). But these treaties (signed respectively at Hard Labor Creek, South Carolina, and Fort Stanwix, New York) also failed to stop the white advance. Within a few years, the 1768 agreements were replaced with new ones, which pushed the line of settlement still farther west.

## The Colonial Response

The Grenville ministry soon increased its authority in the colonies more directly. Regular British troops were stationed permanently in America, and under the Mutiny Act of 1765 the colonists were required to help provision and maintain the army. Ships of the British navy patrolled American waters to search for smugglers. The customs service was reorganized and enlarged. Royal officials were required to take up their colonial posts in person instead of sending substitutes. Colonial manufacturing was restricted, so that it would not compete with rapidly expanding industries in Great Britain.

The Sugar Act of 1764, designed in part to eliminate the illegal sugar trade between the continental colonies and the French and Spanish West Indies, established new vice-admiralty courts in America to try accused smugglers—thus cutting them off from sympathetic local juries. The Currency Act of 1764 required that the colonial assemblies stop issuing paper money. Most momentously, the Stamp Act of 1765 imposed a tax on every printed document in the colonies: newspapers, almanacs, pamphlets, deeds, wills, licenses. British officials were soon collecting more than ten times as much annual revenue in America as they had been before 1763. But the new policies created many more problems than they solved.

It was difficult for the colonists to resist these unpopular new laws. For one thing, Americans continued to harbor as many grievances against one another as they did against the authorities in London. In 1763, for example, a band of Pennsylvania frontiersmen known as the Paxton Boys descended on Philadelphia to demand tax relief and financial support for their defense against Indians; bloodshed was averted only by concessions from the colonial assembly. In 1771, a small-scale civil war broke out in North Carolina when the Regulators, farmers of the Carolina upcountry, organized and armed themselves to resist the high taxes that local sheriffs (appointed by the colonial governor) collected. An army of militiamen, most of them from the eastern counties, crushed the revolt in the Battle of Alamance. Nine on each side were killed and many others wounded. Afterward, six Regulators were hanged for treason.

Despite the conflicts, however, the new policies of the British government began after 1763 to create common grievances among virtually all colonists. For under the Grenville program, as Americans saw it, all people in all colonies would suffer. Northern merchants would suffer from restraints on their commerce, from the closing of the West to land speculation and fur trading, from the restriction of opportunities for manufacturing, and from the increased burden of taxation. Southern planters, in debt to English merchants, would now have to pay additional taxes and would be unable to ease their debts by speculating in western land. Small farmers, the largest group in the colonies, would suffer from increased taxes and from the abolition of paper money, which had been the source of most of their loans. Workers in towns faced the prospect of narrowing opportunities, particularly because of the restraints on manufacturing and currency. The new restrictions came, moreover, at the beginning of a postwar economic depression in America. The British government had poured money into the colonies to finance the war, but that flow stopped after 1763. Now the authorities in London proposed to aggravate the problem by taking money out of the colonies.

In reality, most Americans soon found ways to live with (or circumvent) the new British laws. The American economy was not being destroyed. But there was still a deep sense of unease, particularly in the cities—the places most directly affected by British policies. Periodic and increasingly frequent economic slumps, the frightening depression of the early 1760s, the growth of a large group of unemployed or semiemployed—all combined to produce great distress in some colonial cities, and particularly in Boston, the city suffering the worst economic problems.

Whatever the economic burdens of the imperial program, colonists considered the political burdens worse. Americans were accustomed (and deeply attached) to wide latitude in self-government. Most important, they believed, was the right of the colonial assemblies to control appropriations for the costs of government within the colonies. By attempting to circumvent the colonial assemblies and raise extensive revenues directly from the public, the British government was challenging the basis of colonial political power.

## STIRRINGS OF REVOLT

By the mid-1760s, therefore, a hardening of positions had begun in both England and America that would bring the colonies into increasing conflict with the mother country. The result was a progression of events that, more rapidly than anyone could have imagined, destroyed the English empire in America.

### The Stamp Act Crisis

Grenville could not have devised a better method for antagonizing and unifying the colonies than the Stamp Act of 1765 if he had tried. Unlike the Sugar Act of a year earlier, which affected only a few New England merchants, the tax on printed documents fell on all Americans. The actual economic burdens of the Stamp Act were relatively light, but the precedent it seemed to set was ominous. In the past, taxes and duties on colonial trade had always been presented as measures to regulate commerce, not raise money. The Stamp Act, however, was a direct attempt by England to raise revenue in the colonies without the consent of the colonial assemblies. If Americans accepted this new tax without resistance, the door would be open for more burdensome taxation in the future.

Few colonists believed that they could do anything more than grumble until the Virginia House of Burgesses sounded a "trumpet of sedition" that aroused Americans to action almost everywhere. Foremost among the Virginia malcontents was Patrick Henry, who made a dramatic speech to the House in May 1765, concluding with a vague prediction that if present policies were not revised, George III, like earlier tyrants, might lose his head. There were shocked cries of "Treason!" and, according to one witness, an immediate apology from Henry (although many years later he was quoted as having made the defiant reply: "If this be treason, make the most of it"). Henry introduced a set of resolutions declaring that Americans possessed the same rights as the English, especially the right to be taxed only by their own representatives; that Virginians should pay no taxes except those voted by the Virginia assembly; and that anyone advocating the right of Parliament to tax Virginians should be deemed an enemy of the colony. The House of

Burgesses defeated some of Henry's resolutions, but all of them were printed and circulated as the "Virginia Resolves."

In Massachusetts at about the same time, James Otis persuaded his fellow members of the colonial assembly to call an intercolonial congress to take action against the new tax. And in October 1765, the Stamp Act Congress, as it was called, met in New York with delegates from nine colonies and petitioned the king and Parliament. The petition denied that the colonies could rightfully be taxed except through their own provincial assemblies.

Meanwhile, in several colonial cities mobs began taking the law into their own hands. During the summer of 1765 serious riots broke out up and down the coast, the largest of them in Boston. Men belonging to the newly organized Sons of Liberty terrorized stamp agents and burned stamps. The agents, themselves Americans, hastily resigned. In Boston, the mob also attacked such pro-British "aristocrats" as the lieutenant governor, Thomas Hutchinson (who had privately opposed passage of the Stamp Act but who felt obliged to support it once it became law). Hutchinson's elegant house was pillaged and virtually destroyed.

At last the crisis subsided, largely because England backed down. The authorities in London were less affected by the political protests than by economic pressure. Many New Englanders had stopped buying English goods to protest the Sugar Act of 1764. The Stamp Act caused the colonial boycott to spread, and the Sons of Liberty intimidated reluctant colonists into participating in it. The merchants of England, feeling the loss of much of their colonial market, begged Parliament to repeal the unpopular law. On March 18, 1766, the Stamp Act was repealed at the urging of the new prime minister, the marquis of Rockingham. To satisfy his strong and vociferous opponents, Rockingham also pushed through the Declaratory Act, which confirmed parliamentary authority over the colonies "in all cases whatsoever." In their rejoicing over the repeal, most Americans paid little attention to this sweeping declaration of Parliament's power, but the Declaratory Act was clear evidence of how large a gulf had emerged between the English and American views of the imperial relationship.

### The Townshend Program

The Rockingham government's policy of appeasement met substantial opposition in England. English landlords, a powerful political force, feared that they would be taxed to make up for the money lost from abandoning the colonial revenues. The king finally bowed to their pressure, dismissed the Rockingham ministry, and replaced it with a new government led by the aging but still powerful William Pitt, who was now Lord Chatham. Chatham had been a critic of the Stamp Act and had a reputation in America as a friend of the colonists. Once in office, however, he was so hobbled by gout and at times so incapacitated by mental illness that the actual leadership of his administration fell to the chancellor of the exchequer, Charles Townshend (pronounced "Townsend").

Townshend had to deal with imperial problems and colonial grievances left over from the Grenville ministry. With the Stamp Act repealed, the greatest American grievance involved the Mutiny (or Quartering) Act of 1765, which required the colonists to provide quarters and supplies for the British troops in America. The colonists did not object to quartering or supplying the troops; but they resented that these contributions were now mandatory, and they considered them another form of taxation without their consent. The Massachusetts and New York assemblies refused to vote the mandated supplies to the troops.

To enforce the law and to try again to raise revenues in the colonies, Townshend steered two measures through Parliament in 1767. First, the New York Assembly was disbanded until the colonists agreed to obey the Mutiny Act. (By singling out New York, Townshend thought he would avoid Grenville's mistake of arousing all the colonies at once.) Second, new taxes (known as the Townshend Duties) were levied on various goods imported to the colonies from England—lead, paint, paper, and tea. Townshend reasoned that since these were taxes purely on "external" transactions (imports from overseas), as opposed to the internal transactions the Stamp Act had taxed, the colonists could not object.

But the distinction between external and internal taxation meant little to the colonists. The purpose of the new duties, they claimed, was the same as that of the Stamp Act: to raise revenue from the colonists without their consent. And the suspension of the New York Assembly aroused the resentment of all the colonies. They considered this assault on the rights of one provincial government a threat to all of them.

The Massachusetts Assembly took the lead in opposing the new measures by circulating a letter to all the colonial governments urging them to stand up against every tax imposed by Parliament. At first, the document evoked little response outside Massachusetts. Then Lord Hillsborough, secretary of state for the colonies in London, warned that assemblies endorsing the Massachusetts letter would be dissolved. Massachusetts defiantly reaffirmed its support for the circular, and the other colonies supported Massachusetts.

Besides persuading Parliament to levy import duties and suspend the

New York Assembly, Townshend took steps to enforce commercial regulations in the colonies more effectively. The most important of these steps was the establishment of a board of customs commissioners in America to stop the rampant corruption in the colonial customs houses. To some extent the plan worked. The new commissioners virtually ended smuggling in Boston, where they established their headquarters, although smugglers continued to carry on a busy trade in other colonial seaports.

The Boston merchants—accustomed to loose enforcement of the Navigation Acts and aggrieved now that the new commission was diverting the lucrative smuggling trade elsewhere—took the lead in organizing another boycott. Merchants in Philadelphia and New York joined them in a nonimportation agreement in 1768, and later some southern merchants and planters also agreed to cooperate. The colonists boycotted British goods that were subject to the Townshend Duties; and throughout the colonies, American homespun and other domestic products became suddenly fashionable, while English luxuries fell from favor.

Late in 1767, Charles Townshend died—before the consequences of his ill-conceived program had become fully apparent. In March 1770, the new prime minister, Lord North, hoping to break the nonimportation agreement and divide the colonists, repealed all the Townshend Duties except the tea tax.

### The Boston Massacre

Before news of the repeal reached America, an event in Massachusetts electrified colonial opinion. The harassment of the new customs commissioners in Boston had grown so intense that the British government had placed four regiments of regular troops in the city—a constant affront to the colonists' sense of independence. Everywhere they went, Bostonians encountered British "redcoats," some of whom were arrogant, coarse, or provocative. Many poorly paid British soldiers wanted jobs in their off-duty hours, and they thus competed with local workers in an already tight labor market. Clashes between the two groups were frequent.

On the night of March 5, 1770, a few days after a particularly intense skirmish between workers at a ship-rigging factory and British soldiers who were trying to find jobs there, a mob of dockworkers, "liberty boys," and others began pelting the sentries at the customs house with rocks and snowballs. Hastily, Captain Thomas Preston of the British regiment lined up several of his men in front of the building to protect it. There was some scuffling; one of the soldiers was knocked down; and in the midst of it all, apparently,

*THE BOSTON MASSACRE* (1770), BY PAUL REVERE  This is one of many engravings, by Revere and others, of the conflict between British troops and Boston laborers that became important as propaganda for the Patriot cause in the 1770s. Among the victims of the massacre listed by Revere was Crispus Attucks, probably the first black man to die in the struggle for American independence.

several British soldiers fired into the crowd, killing five people (among them a mulatto sailor, Crispus Attucks).

This murky incident, almost certainly the result of panic and confusion, was quickly transformed by local resistance leaders into the "Boston Massacre"—a graphic symbol of British oppression and brutality. The victims became popular martyrs; the event became the subject of such lurid (and inaccurate) accounts as the widely circulated pamphlet *Innocent Blood Crying to God from the Streets of Boston*. A famous engraving by Paul Revere portrayed the massacre as a carefully organized, calculated assault on a peaceful crowd. The British soldiers, tried before a jury of Bostonians, were found guilty only of manslaughter and given token punishment. But colonial pamphlets and newspapers convinced many Americans that the soldiers were guilty of official murder. Year after year, resistance leaders marked the anniversary of the massacre with demonstrations and speeches.

The leading figure in fomenting public outrage over the Boston Massacre was Samuel Adams, the most effective radical in the colonies. He spoke frequently at Boston town meetings; and as one unpopular English policy followed another, his message attracted increasing support. England, he argued, had become a morass of sin and corruption; only in America did public virtue survive. In 1772, he proposed the creation of a "committee of correspondence" in Boston to publicize the grievances against England throughout the colony, and he became its first head. Other colonies followed Massachusetts's lead, and a loose intercolonial network of political organizations was soon established that kept the spirit of dissent alive through the 1770s.

### The Philosophy of Revolt

Although a superficial calm settled on the colonies for approximately three years after the Boston Massacre, the crises of the 1760s had helped arouse enduring ideological excitement and had produced instruments for publicizing colonial grievances. Gradually a political outlook took hold in America that would ultimately serve to justify revolt.

The ideas that would support the Revolution emerged from many sources. Some were indigenous to America, drawn from religious (particularly Puritan) sources or from the political experiences of the colonies. But these native ideas were enriched and enlarged by the importation of powerful arguments from abroad. Of most importance, perhaps, were the "radical" ideas of those in Great Britain who stood in opposition to their government. Some were Scots, who viewed the English state as tyrannical. Others were embittered "country Whigs," who felt excluded from power and considered the existing system corrupt and oppressive. Drawing from some of the great philosophical minds of earlier generations—most notably John Locke—these English dissidents framed a powerful argument against their government.

Central to this emerging ideology was a new concept of what government should be. Because humans were inherently corrupt and selfish, government was necessary to protect individuals from the evil in one another. But because any government was run by corruptible people, it needed safeguards against abuses of power. In the eyes of most English and American people, the English constitution was the best system ever devised to meet these necessities. By distributing power among the three elements of society—the monarchy, the aristocracy, and the common people—the English political system ensured that no individual or group could exercise authority unchecked by another. Yet by the mid-seventeenth century, dissidents in both England and America had become convinced that the constitution was in danger. A single center of power—the king and his ministers—was emerging, and the system was becoming a corrupt and dangerous tyranny.

Such arguments found little sympathy in most of England. The English constitution was not a written document, nor was it a fixed set of unchangeable rules. It was a general sense of the "way things are done," and most people in England were willing to accept evolutionary changes in it. Americans, by contrast, drew from their experience with colonial charters, in which the shape and powers of government were permanently inscribed on paper. They resisted the idea of a flexible, changing set of basic principles. Many colonists argued that the English constitution should itself be written down, to prevent fallible politicians from tampering with its essence.

Part of that essence, Americans believed, was their right to be taxed only with their own consent. When Townshend levied his external duties, the Philadelphia lawyer John Dickinson published a widely circulated pamphlet, *Letters of a Pennsylvania Farmer*, which argued that even external taxation was legal only when designed to regulate trade, not to raise a revenue. Gradually, most Americans ceased to accept even that distinction, and they finally took an unqualified stand: "No taxation without representation." Whatever the nature of a tax—whether internal or external, whether designed to raise revenue or to control trade—it could not be levied without the consent of the colonists themselves.

This clamor about "representation" made little sense to the English. According to the prevailing English theory, members of Parliament did not represent individuals or particular geographical areas. Instead, each member represented the interests of the whole nation and indeed the whole empire, no matter where the member happened to come from. The many unenfranchised boroughs of England, the whole of Ireland, and the colonies thousands of miles away—all were thus represented in the Parliament at London, even though they elected no representatives of their own. This was the theory of "virtual" representation. But Americans, drawing from their experiences with their town meetings and their colonial assemblies, believed in "actual" representation. Every community was entitled to its own representative, elected by the people of that community and directly responsible to them. Since they had none of their own representatives in Parliament, it followed that they were not represented there. According to the emerging American view of the empire, the colonial assemblies played the same role within the colonies—had the same powers, enjoyed the same rights—that Parliament did within England. The empire, the Americans argued, was a sort of federation of commonwealths, each with its own legislative body, all tied together by common loyalty to the king. What may have made the conflict between England and America ultimately insoluble was a fundamental difference of opinion over the nature of sovereignty. By arguing that Parliament had the right to legislate for England and for the empire as a whole, but that only the provincial assemblies could legislate for the individual colonies, Americans were in effect arguing for a division of sovereignty. Parliament would be sovereign in some matters; the assemblies would be sovereign in others. To the British, such an argument was absurd. In any system of government there must be a single, ultimate authority. And since the empire was, in their view, a single, undivided unit, there could be only one authority within it: the English government of king and Parliament. Ultimately, that presented the colonists with a stark choice: between complete subordination to England and complete independence from it. Slowly, cautiously, they began moving toward independence.

### The Tea Excitement

The apparent calm in America in the first years of the 1770s masked a growing sense of frustration and resentment about the continued and increasingly heavy-handed enforcement of the Navigation Acts. Popular anger was visible in occasional acts of rebellion. At one point, colonists seized a British revenue ship on the lower Delaware River. And in 1772, angry residents of Rhode Island boarded the British schooner *Gaspie*, set it afire, and sank it in Narragansett Bay.

What finally revived the Revolutionary fervor of the 1760s, however, was a new act of Parliament—one that the English government had expected to be relatively uncontroversial. It involved the business of selling tea. In 1773, Britain's East India Company (which possessed an official monopoly on trade with the Far East) was sitting on large stocks of tea that it could not sell in England. It was on the verge of bankruptcy. In an effort to save it, the government passed the Tea Act of 1773, which gave the company the right to export its merchandise directly to the colonies without paying any of the regular taxes that were imposed on the colonial merchants, who had traditionally served as the middlemen in such transactions. With these privileges, the company could undersell American merchants and monopolize the colonial tea trade.

The act proved inflammatory for several reasons. First, it angered influential colonial merchants, who feared being replaced and bankrupted by a powerful monopoly. More important, however, the Tea Act revived American passions about the issue of taxation without representation. The law provided no new tax on tea. But the original Townshend duty on the commodity—the only one of the original duties that had not been repealed—survived. It was the East India Company's exemption from that duty that put the colonial merchants at such a grave disadvantage in competition with the company. Lord North assumed that most colonists would welcome the new law because it would reduce the price of tea to consumers by removing the middlemen. But resistance leaders in America resented the monopolistic privileges of the company and, more important, argued that the law, in effect, represented an unconstitutional tax. The colonists responded by boycotting tea.

Unlike earlier protests, most of which had involved relatively small numbers of people, the tea boycott mobilized large segments of the population. It also helped link the colonies together in a common experience of mass popular protest. Particularly important to the movement were the activities of colonial women, who were among the principal consumers of tea and now became the leaders of the effort to boycott it. The Daughters of Liberty—a women's patriotic organization which, like the Sons of Liberty, was committed to agitating against British policies, proclaimed "that rather than Freedom, we'll part with our Tea."

In the last weeks of 1773, with strong popular support, leaders in various colonies made plans to prevent the East India Company from landing its cargoes in colonial ports. In Philadelphia and New York, determined colonists kept the tea from leaving the company's ships, and in Charleston, they stored it away in a public warehouse. In Boston, after failing to turn three ships away from the harbor, local patriots staged a spectacular drama. On the evening of December 16, 1773, three companies of fifty men each, masquerading as Mohawks, passed through a crowd of spectators, went aboard the three ships, broke open the tea chests, and heaved them into the harbor. As the electrifying news of the Boston "tea party" spread, colonists in other seaports staged similar acts of resistance.

Parliament retaliated in four acts of 1774: closing the port of Boston, drastically reducing the powers of self-government in Massachusetts, permitting royal officers to be tried in other colonies or in England when accused of crimes, and providing for the quartering of troops by the colonists. These Coercive Acts—or, as they were more widely known in America, "Intolerable Acts"—were followed by the Quebec Act, which was unrelated to them but also provocative to English Americans. The law extended the boundaries of Quebec to include the French communities between the Ohio and Mississippi Rivers. It also granted political rights to Roman Catholics and recognized the legality of the Roman Catholic Church within the enlarged province. Many colonists feared that a plot was afoot in London to subject Americans to the authority of the pope. Those interested in western lands, moreover, believed that the act would hinder westward expansion.

The Coercive Acts, far from isolating Massachusetts, made it a martyr in the eyes of residents of other colonies and sparked new resistance up and down the coast. Colonial legislatures passed a series of resolves supporting Massachusetts. Women's groups throughout the colonies mobilized to extend the boycotts of British goods and to create substitutes for the tea, textiles, and other commodities they were shunning. In Edenton, North Carolina, fifty-one women signed an agreement in October 1774 declaring their "sincere adherence" to the anti-British resolutions of their provincial assembly and proclaiming their duty to do "every thing as far as lies in our power" to support the "publick good."

## COOPERATION AND WAR

Beginning in 1765, colonial leaders developed a variety of organizations for converting popular discontent into action—organizations that in time formed the basis for an independent government.

### New Sources of Authority

The passage of authority from the royal government to the colonists themselves began on the local level. In colony after colony, local institutions responded to the resistance movement by simply seizing authority on their own. At times, entirely new institutions emerged and began to perform some of the functions of government.

The most effective of these new groups were the committees of correspondence that Samuel Adams had inaugurated in Massachusetts in 1772. Virginia later established the first intercolonial committees of correspondence, which helped make possible continuous cooperation among the colonies, and later took the greatest step of all toward united action. After the royal governor dissolved the assembly in 1774, a rump session met in the Raleigh Tavern at Williamsburg, declared that the Intolerable Acts menaced the liberties of every colony, and issued a call for a Continental Congress.

Delegates from all thirteen colonies except Georgia were present when,

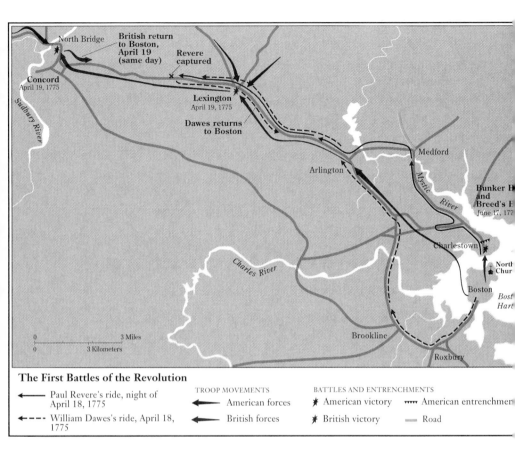

**The First Battles of the Revolution**

← Paul Revere's ride, night of
April 18, 1775

←--- William Dawes's ride, April 18,
1775

TROOP MOVEMENTS

← American forces

← British forces

BATTLES AND ENTRENCHMENTS

✱ American victory      ⌇⌇⌇ American entrenchmen

✱ British victory       ⌇⌇ Road

in September 1774, the First Continental Congress convened in Philadelphia. They made five major decisions. First, in a close vote, they rejected a plan for a colonial union under British authority. Second, they endorsed a statement of grievances that reflected the influence of moderates by seeming to concede Parliament's right to regulate colonial trade and by addressing the king as "Most Gracious Sovereign," but it also included a more extreme demand for the repeal of all oppressive legislation passed since 1763. Third, they approved a series of resolutions from a Massachusetts convention recommending that military preparations be made for defense against possible attack by the British troops in Boston. Fourth, they agreed to a series of boycotts that they hoped would stop all trade with Great Britain, and they formed a "Continental Association" to see that these agreements were enforced. And fifth, the delegates agreed to meet again the following spring, indicating that they saw the Continental Congress as a continuing organization.

During the winter, the Parliament in London debated proposals for conciliating the colonists. Lord North finally won approval early in 1775 for a series of measures known as the Conciliatory Propositions. Parliament proposed that the colonies, instead of being taxed directly by Parliament, would tax themselves at Parliament's demand. With this offer, Lord North hoped to separate the American moderates, whom he believed represented the views of the majority, from the extremist minority. But his offer was too little and too late. It did not reach America until after the first shots of war had been fired.

### Lexington and Concord

For months, the farmers and townspeople of Massachusetts had been gathering arms and ammunition and training as "minutemen," preparing to fight on a minute's notice. The Continental Congress had approved preparations for a defensive war, and the citizen-soldiers waited only for an aggressive move by the British regulars in Boston.

In Boston, General Thomas Gage, commanding the British garrison, considered his army too small to do anything without reinforcements. He resisted the advice of less cautious officers, who assured him that the Amer-

THE BRITISH RETREAT FROM CONCORD, 1775 This American cartoon satirizes the retreat of British forces from Concord after the battle there on April 19, 1775. Patriot forces are lined up on the left, and the retreating British forces (portrayed with dog heads, perhaps because many of the soldiers were "wild" Irish) straggle off at right—some fleeing in panic, others gloating over the booty they have plundered from the burning homes above.

icans would never dare actually to fight, that they would back down quickly before any show of British force. When General Gage received orders to arrest the rebel leaders Sam Adams and John Hancock, known to be in the vicinity of Lexington, he still hesitated. But when he heard that the minutemen had stored a large supply of gunpowder in Concord (eighteen miles from Boston), he decided to act. On the night of April 18, 1775, he sent a detachment of about 1,000 men out from Boston on the road to Lexington and Concord. He hoped to surprise the colonials and seize the illegal supplies without bloodshed.

But patriots in Boston were watching the British movements closely, and during the night two horsemen, William Dawes and Paul Revere, were dispatched to warn the villages and farms. When the redcoats arrived in Lexington the next day, several dozen minutemen awaited them on the town common. Shots were fired and minutemen fell; eight of them were killed and ten more were wounded. Advancing to Concord, the British discovered that the Americans had hastily removed most of the powder supply, but the redcoats burned what was left of it. All along the road from Concord back to Boston, the British were harassed by the gunfire of farmers hiding behind trees, rocks, and stone walls. By the end of the day, the British had lost almost three times as many men as the Americans.

The first shots—the "shots heard round the world," as Americans later called them—had been fired. But who had fired them first? According to one of the minutemen at Lexington, the British commander, Major Thomas Pitcairn, had shouted to the colonists on his arrival, "Disperse, ye rebels!" When they ignored him, he ordered his troops to fire. British officers and soldiers claimed that the minutemen had fired first and that only after seeing the flash of American guns had they begun to shoot. Whatever the truth, the rebels succeeded in circulating their account well ahead of the British version, adorning it with tales of British atrocities. The effect was to rally to the rebel cause thousands of colonists, North and South, who previously had little enthusiasm for it.

It was not immediately clear to the British, and even to many Americans, that the skirmishes at Lexington and Concord were the first battles of a war. But whether they recognized it at the time or not, the War for Independence had begun.

# CHAPTER FIVE

# The American Revolution

*The States United* ～ *The War for Independence*
*War and Society* ～ *The Creation of State Governments*
*The Search for a National Government*

TWO STRUGGLES OCCURRED simultaneously during the seven years of war that began in April of 1775. One was the military conflict with Great Britain. The second was a political conflict within America.

The military conflict was, by the standards of later wars, a relatively modest one. By the standards of its own day, however, it was an unusually savage conflict, pitting not only army against army but the civilian population against a powerful external force. The shift of the war from a traditional, conventional struggle to a new kind of conflict—a revolutionary war for liberation—is what made it possible for the United States to defeat the more powerful British.

At the same time, Americans were wrestling with the great political questions that the conflict necessarily produced: first, whether to demand independence from Britain; then, how to structure the new nation they had proclaimed. Only the first of these questions had been resolved by the time of the British surrender at Yorktown in 1781.

## THE STATES UNITED

Although many Americans had been expecting a military conflict with Britain for months, even years, the actual beginning of hostilities in 1775 found the colonies generally unprepared. A still-unformed nation faced the task of mobilizing for war against the world's greatest armed power. Americans faced that task deeply divided about what they were fighting for.

| TIME LINE | | | | |
|---|---|---|---|---|
| **1775** | **1776** | **1777** | **1778** | **1781** |
| Second Continental Congress | Paine's *Common Sense* | Articles of Confederation adopted | French-American alliance | Articles of Confederation ratified |
| Washington commands American forces | Declaration of Independence<br>Battle of Trenton | British defeat at Saratoga | | Cornwallis surrenders at Yorktown |

| **1783** | **1784** | | **1786** | **1787** |
|---|---|---|---|---|
| Treaty of Paris | Postwar depression begins | | Shays's Rebellion | Northwest Ordinance |

### Defining American War Aims

Three weeks after the battles of Lexington and Concord, when the Second Continental Congress met in Philadelphia, delegates from every colony except Georgia (which sent no representative until the following autumn) agreed to support the war. But they disagreed about its purpose. At one extreme was a group led by the Adams cousins (John and Samuel), Richard Henry Lee of Virginia, and others, who already favored independence; at the other extreme was a group led by such moderates as John Dickinson of Pennsylvania, who hoped for a quick reconciliation with Great Britain. Most of the delegates tried to find some middle ground between these positions. They voted for one last appeal to the king: the so-called Olive Branch Petition. Then, on July 6, 1775, they adopted the Declaration of the Causes and Necessity of Taking Up Arms. It proclaimed that the British government had left the American people with only two alternatives: "unconditional submission to the tyranny of irritated ministers or resistance by force."

Most Americans still believed they were fighting not for independence but for a redress of grievances within the British Empire. During the first year of fighting, however, many of them began to change their minds. The costs of the war—human and financial—were so high that the original war aims began to seem too modest to justify them. What lingering affection Americans retained for the mother country greatly diminished when the British began trying to recruit Indians, black slaves, and German mercenaries (the hated "Hessians") against them. When the British government rejected the Olive Branch Petition and instead enacted the Prohibitory Act, which closed the colonial ports (through a naval blockade) to all overseas trade and made no concessions to American demands except an offer to pardon repentant rebels, many colonists concluded that independence was the only remaining option.

An impassioned pamphlet crystallized these feelings in January 1776: Thomas Paine's *Common Sense*. Paine, who had emigrated from England to America less than two years before, wanted to turn the anger of Americans away from particular parliamentary measures and toward what he considered the root of the problem—the English constitution itself. It was simple common sense for Americans to break completely with a political system that could produce so corrupt a monarch as George III and could inflict such brutality on its own people. *Common Sense* sold more than 100,000 copies (an astonishing number given the size of the colonial population) in only a few months. To many of its readers it was a revelation. Although sentiment for independence was still far from unanimous, the first months of 1776 saw a rapid growth of support for the idea.

## The Decision for Independence

In the meantime, the Continental Congress in Philadelphia was moving toward a complete break with England. It opened American ports to the ships of all nations except Great Britain, began negotiating with other nations, and recommended to the colonies that they establish governments independent of the empire, as in fact most were already doing.

At the beginning of the summer, finally, Congress appointed a committee to draft a formal declaration of independence. And on July 2, 1776, it adopted a resolution: "That these United Colonies are, and, of right, ought to be, free and independent states; that they are absolved from all allegiance to the British crown, and that all political connexion between them and the state of Great Britain is, and ought to be, totally dissolved." Two days later, on July 4, Congress approved the Declaration of Independence itself, which provided formal justifications for the actions the delegates had taken two days earlier.

The Declaration was largely the work of Thomas Jefferson, a thirty-three-year-old Virginian, although it was substantially revised by other delegates. (Among other changes, Congress struck out a passage condemning the slave trade, to placate southern slaveowners.) The final document was in two parts. In the first, Jefferson restated the familiar contract theory of John Locke: the theory that governments were formed to protect what Jefferson called "life, liberty and the pursuit of happiness." In the second part, he listed the alleged crimes of the king, who, with the backing of Parliament, had violated his contract with the colonists and thus had forfeited all claim to their loyalty. Little of what Jefferson wrote was new to the document's readers; the power of the Declaration lay in the eloquence with which it expressed beliefs already widespread in America.

Having asserted their independence, the individual colonies now began to call themselves states—a reflection of their belief that each province was now a sovereign entity. By 1781, most states had produced written constitutions for themselves that established republican governments. At the national level, however, the process was more uncertain and less immediately successful. For a time, Americans were not sure whether they even wanted a real national government; virtually everyone considered the individual colonies (now states) the real centers of authority. Yet fighting a war required a certain amount of central direction. In November 1777, finally, Congress adopted a plan for union. The document was known as the Articles of Confederation. It confirmed the weak, decentralized system already in operation. (See pp. 139–140.)

### Mobilizing for War

Organizing the war effort was a formidable task for the frail Congress and the new state governments. They had to find the money to pay for the war, and they had to raise and equip an army to fight it.

Financing the war was particularly difficult, because Congress lacked the authority and the states generally lacked the inclination to impose taxes on the public. Hard currency (gold and silver) had always been scarce in America. And when Congress requisitioned money from the state governments, none contributed more than a small part of its expected share. Congress had little success borrowing from the public, since few Americans could afford to buy bonds and those who could preferred to invest in more profitable ventures, such as privateering. So there was no alternative in the end but to issue paper money. Printing presses turned out enormous amounts of "Continental currency," and the states printed currencies of their own. The result, predictably, was soaring inflation. Many American farmers and merchants began to prefer doing business with the British, who could pay for goods in gold or silver coin. (That was one reason why George Washington's troops suffered from food shortages at Valley Forge in the winter of 1777–1778; many Philadelphia merchants would not accept the paper money the army offered them.) Congress was unable to stop the inflation, and ultimately it was able to finance the war only by borrowing from other nations.

Raising and equipping the army was little easier. After the first surge of patriotism in 1775, only a small proportion of eligible men were willing to volunteer. States had to pay bounties or use a draft to recruit the needed men.

At first, militiamen remained under the control of their respective states. But Congress recognized the need for a centralized military command, and it created a Continental army with a single commander in chief: George Washington. A forty-three-year-old Virginia planter-aristocrat who had commanded colonial forces during the French and Indian War, Washington had considerable military experience and was an early advocate of independence; he was admired, respected, and trusted by nearly all Patriots. He took command of the new army in June 1775.

Washington was not without shortcomings as a military commander. Indeed, he lost more battles than he won. But whatever his faults and failures, he was indisputably a great war leader. With the aid of foreign military experts such as the Marquis de Lafayette from France and the Baron von Steuben from Prussia, he built a force that prevailed against the mightiest power in the world. Even more important, perhaps, Washington's steadiness, courage, and dedication to his cause provided the army—and the people— with a symbol of stability around which they could rally.

## THE WAR FOR INDEPENDENCE

On the surface, all the advantages in the military struggle between America and Great Britain appeared to lie with the British. They had the greatest navy and the best-equipped army in the world. They had the resources of an empire. They had a coherent structure of command. The Americans, by contrast, were struggling to create an army and a government at the same time that they were trying to fight a war. Yet the United States had advantages too. Americans were fighting on their own ground. They were more committed to the conflict than the British. And beginning in 1777, they received substantial aid from abroad.

But the American victory was not simply the result of these advantages, or even of the spirit and resourcefulness of the American people and army. It was a result, too, of a series of blunders and miscalculations by the British in the early stages of the fighting, when England could (and probably should) have won. And it was, finally, a result of the transformation of the war— through three distinct phases—into a new kind of conflict that the British military, for all its strength, was unable to win.

### The First Phase: New England

For the first year of the conflict—from the spring of 1775 to the spring of 1776—the British were not entirely sure that they were fighting a war. Many

REVOLUTIONARY SOLDIERS Jean Baptist de Verger, a French officer serving in America during the Revolution, kept a journal of his experiences illustrated with watercolors. Here he portrays four American soldiers carrying different kinds of arms: a black infantryman with a light rifle, a musketman, a rifleman, and an artilleryman.

English authorities thought that British forces were simply quelling pockets of rebellion in the contentious area around Boston.

American forces besieged the British army in Boston (under the command of General Thomas Gage) after the redcoats withdrew from Lexington and Concord. In the Battle of Bunker Hill (actually fought on Breed's Hill) on June 17, 1775, the Patriots suffered severe casualties and withdrew. But they inflicted even greater losses on the enemy (indeed, the heaviest casualties the British were to suffer in the entire war) and continued the siege. Early in 1776, the British decided that Boston was a poor place from which to fight. It was in the center of the most anti-British part of America. It was also tactically indefensible, easily isolated and besieged. And so, on March 17, 1776, the redcoats evacuated Boston for Halifax with hundreds of Loyalist refugees.

In the meantime, a band of Patriots to the south, at Moore's Creek Bridge in North Carolina, crushed an uprising of Loyalists (Americans still loyal to England and its king) on February 27, 1776, and discouraged a British plan to invade the southern states. And to the north, the Americans began an invasion of Canada—hoping to remove the British threat and to

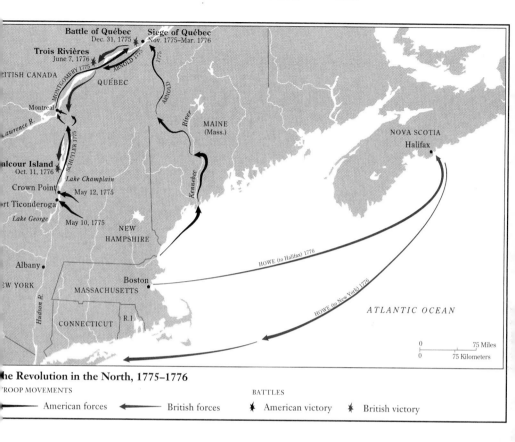

**The Revolution in the North, 1775–1776**

TROOP MOVEMENTS — American forces   ← British forces   BATTLES   ✳ American victory   ✳ British victory

win the Canadians to their cause. Generals Benedict Arnold and Richard Montgomery threatened Quebec in late 1775 and early 1776. Montgomery was killed in the assault on the city; and although a wounded Arnold kept up the siege for a time, the Quebec campaign ended in failure. Canada did not join the American Revolution.

By the spring of 1776, it had become clear to the British that the conflict was not just a local phenomenon in the area around Boston. The American campaigns in Canada, agitation in the South, and the growing evidence of colonial unity all suggested that England must prepare to fight a much larger conflict.

### The Second Phase: The Mid-Atlantic Region

During the next phase of the war, which lasted from 1776 until early 1778, the British were in a good position to win. Indeed, had it not been for a series of blunders and misfortunes, they probably would have crushed the rebellion then.

The British regrouped quickly after their retreat from Boston. During the summer of 1776, in the weeks immediately following the Declaration of Independence, hundreds of British ships and 32,000 British soldiers arrived in New York, under the command of General William Howe. Howe wanted to avoid an armed conflict with the Americans and hoped simply to awe them into submission. He offered Congress a choice between surrender with royal pardon and a battle against overwhelming odds.

To oppose Howe's great force, Washington could muster only about 19,000 inadequately armed and poorly trained soldiers; he had no navy at all. Even so, the Americans rejected Howe's offer and continued to fight. Perhaps inevitably, they suffered a succession of major defeats. The British pushed the Patriot forces off Long Island, forced them to abandon Manhattan, and then drove them in slow retreat over the plains of New Jersey, across the Delaware River, and into Pennsylvania.

**The Revolution in the Middle Colonies, 1776–1778**

A M E R I C A N    V O I C E S

JOSEPH P. MARTIN

*A Soldier's View*
*of the Battle of Long Island*

[T]HE REGIMENT was ordered to Long Island, the British having landed in force there . . . I went to the top of the house where I had a full view of that part of the island. . . . The horrors of battle there presented themselves to my mind in all their hideousness. . . . We were soon ordered to our regimental parade, from which, as soon as the regiment was formed, we were marched off for the ferry. At the lower end of the street were placed several casks of sea-bread . . . nearly hard enough for musket flints. As my good luck would have it, there was a momentary halt made; I improved the opportunity thus offered me, as every good soldier should upon all important occasions, to get as many of the biscuit as I possibly could. . . .

Our officers . . . pressed forward to the creek, where a large party of Americans and British were engaged. By the time we arrived, the enemy had driven our men into the creek . . . where such as could swim got across. Those that could not swim, and could not procure anything to buoy them up, sunk. . . . There was in this action a regiment of Maryland troops (volunteers), all young gentlemen. When they came out of the water and mud, looking like water rats, it was a truly pitiful sight. Many of them were killed in the pond, and more were drowned. Some of us went into the water . . . and took out a number of corpses and a great many arms that were sunk in the pond and creek.

The British settled down for the winter in northern and central New Jersey, with an outpost of Hessians at Trenton, on the Delaware River. But Washington did not sit still. On Christmas night 1776, he daringly recrossed the icy Delaware River, surprised and scattered the Hessians, and occupied Trenton. Then he advanced to Princeton and drove a force of redcoats from their base in the college there. But Washington was unable to hold either Princeton or Trenton and finally took refuge for the rest of the winter in the hills around Morristown. As the campaign of 1776 came to an end, the Americans could console themselves with the thought that they had won two minor victories, that their main army was still intact, and that the invaders were no nearer than before to the decisive triumph Howe had so confidently anticipated.

For the campaigns of 1777 the British devised a strategy that might have cut the United States in two and prepared the way for final victory by Great Britain—if only Howe had followed it. Howe would move from New York up the Hudson to Albany, while another force would come down from Canada to meet him. John Burgoyne secured command of this northern force and prepared a two-pronged attack to the south along both the Mohawk and the upper Hudson approaches to Albany.

But after setting the plan in motion, Howe abandoned his part of it. Instead of moving north to meet Burgoyne, he went south and attacked Philadelphia. He hoped that capturing the rebel capital would discourage the Patriots, rally the Loyalists, and bring the war to a speedy conclusion. He moved most of his forces by sea from New York to the head of Chesapeake Bay, brushed Washington aside at the Battle of Brandywine Creek on September 11, and proceeded north to Philadelphia, which he took with little resistance—sending the Continental Congress into exile in York, Pennsylvania. Washington launched an unsuccessful Patriot attack against the British on October 4 at Germantown (just outside Philadelphia); then he went into winter quarters at Valley Forge.

Howe's move to Philadelphia left Burgoyne to carry out the campaign in the north alone. He sent Colonel Barry St. Leger up the St. Lawrence River toward Lake Ontario. Burgoyne himself advanced directly down the upper Hudson Valley and easily seized Fort Ticonderoga, with its large store of powder and supplies; Congress was so dismayed by the loss that it removed General Philip Schuyler from command of American forces in the north and replaced him with Horatio Gates.

By the time Gates took over, Burgoyne had already experienced two staggering defeats. In one of them—at Oriskany, New York, on August 6—Patriots held off a force of Indians and Tories commanded by St. Leger. That allowed Benedict Arnold to close off the Mohawk Valley to St. Leger's advance. In the other battle—at Bennington, Vermont, on August 16—New England militiamen mauled a detachment that Burgoyne had sent to seek supplies. Short of materials, with all help cut off, Burgoyne fought several costly engagements and then withdrew to Saratoga, where Gates surrounded him. On October 17, 1777, Burgoyne surrendered—an event that became a major turning point in the war.

The campaign in upstate New York was not just a British defeat. It was a setback for the ambitious efforts of several Iroquois leaders. Although the Iroquois Confederacy had declared its neutrality in the Revolutionary War in 1776, not all of its members were content to remain passive. Among those who worked to expand the Indian role in the war were a Mohawk brother and sister, Joseph and Mary Brant. The Brants persuaded their own tribe to contribute to the British cause and attracted the support of the Seneca and Cayuga as well.

The alliance had unhappy consequences for the Iroquois. It further divided their already weakened Confederacy; only three of the Iroquois nations supported the British. Then, a year after their defeat at Oriskany, Indians joined British troops in a series of raids on outlying white settlements in upstate New York. Patriot forces under the command of General John Sullivan harshly retaliated, wreaking such destruction on Indian settlements that large groups of Iroquois fled north into Canada to seek refuge. Many never returned.

### Securing Aid from Abroad

The leaders of the American effort knew that victory would not be likely without aid from abroad. And their most promising ally, they realized, was France, still smarting from its defeat by the British in 1763. The astute French foreign minister, the Count de Vergennes, understood that France had much to gain from seeing Britain lose a crucial part of its empire.

From the beginning, therefore, there was interest in an alliance on both the American and the French sides. At first, France provided the United States with badly needed supplies but remained reluctant to grant formal diplomatic recognition to the United States. After the Declaration of Independence, Benjamin Franklin himself went to France to lobby for aid and diplomatic recognition. Franklin quickly became a hero to the French, but Vergennes wanted some evidence that the Americans had a real chance of winning before he would agree to open French intervention. Reports of the British defeat at Saratoga, he believed, offered that evidence.

The news from Saratoga arrived in London and Paris in early December 1777. In London, it persuaded Lord North to make a new peace offer: complete home rule within the empire for Americans if they would quit the war. That worried Vergennes, who feared the Americans might accept the offer and thus destroy France's opportunity to weaken Britain. Prompted by Franklin, he decided that French assistance might persuade the Americans to continue the struggle. On February 6, 1778, he reached agreement with American diplomats on formal recognition of the United States as a sovereign nation and on greatly expanded French assistance to the American war effort.

Once France entered the war, it became an international conflict, which in the next two years expanded into a general European war pitting France, Spain, and the Netherlands against Great Britain. That helped the Americans in two ways. It reduced the resources available for the English effort in America, and all three of Britain's foes gave financial and material assistance to the Patriots. But France was America's indispensable ally. It furnished the new nation with most of its money and munitions, and it provided a navy and an expeditionary force that were vital to the final, successful phase of the Revolutionary conflict.

## The Final Phase: The South

The failure of the British to crush the Continental army in the mid-Atlantic states, the stunning American victory at Saratoga, and the intervention of the French transformed the war and ushered it into its final phase. The British government now placed new limits on its commitment to the conflict. Instead of mounting a full-scale military struggle against the American army, the British tried to enlist the support of those elements of the American population—a majority, they continued to believe—who were still loyal to the crown; they worked, in other words, to undermine the Revolution from within. Since Loyalist sentiment was thought to be strongest in the South, and since the English also hoped slaves would rally to their cause, the main focus of the British effort shifted there.

The new strategy was a dismal failure. British forces spent three years (from 1778 to 1781) moving through the South, fighting small battles and large, and attempting to neutralize the territory through which they traveled. But the British had badly overestimated the extent of Loyalist sentiment. Even where Loyalists were most numerous, they were often afraid to help the British because they feared reprisals from the Patriots around them. There were also logistical problems. Patriot forces could move at will

**The Revolution in the South, 1778–1781**

TROOP MOVEMENTS

American forces ⟵ French fleet ⟵ British forces

BATTLES

✷ American victory

✷ British victory

throughout the region, living off the resources of the countryside, blending in with the civilian population, and leaving the British unable to distinguish friend from foe. The British, by contrast, suffered all the disadvantages of an army in hostile territory.

It was this phase of the conflict that made the war "revolutionary"—not only because it introduced a new kind of warfare, but because it had the effect of mobilizing and politicizing large groups of the population who had until then remained aloof from the struggle. With the war expanding into previously isolated communities, with many civilians forced to involve themselves whether they liked it or not, the political climate of the United States grew more heated than ever. And support for independence, far from being crushed as the British had hoped, greatly increased.

These political changes helped shape the important military encounters of the last years of the war. In the North, where significant numbers of British troops remained, the fighting settled into a stalemate. Sir Henry Clinton replaced the hapless William Howe in 1778 and moved what had been Howe's army from Philadelphia back to New York. There the British troops stayed for more than a year, with Washington and his army keeping watch around them. During that same winter, George Rogers Clark, on orders from the state of Virginia, led a Patriot expedition over the Green Mountains and captured settlements in the Illinois country from the British and their Indian allies.

During this period of relative calm, the American forces were shocked by the exposure of treason on the part of General Benedict Arnold. Arnold had been one of the early heroes of the war, but now, convinced that the American cause was hopeless, he conspired with British agents to betray the Patriot stronghold at West Point on the Hudson River. When the scheme was exposed and foiled, Arnold fled to the safety of the British camp, where he spent the rest of the war.

The British did have some significant military successes during this period. On December 29, 1778, they captured Savannah, on the coast of Georgia. On May 12, 1780, they took the port of Charleston, South Carolina. And they inspired some Loyalists to take up arms and advance with them into the interior. But although the British were able to win conventional battles, they were constantly harassed as they moved through the countryside by Patriot guerrillas led by such resourceful fighters as Thomas Sumter, Andrew Pickens, and Francis Marion, the "Swamp Fox." Penetrating to Camden, South Carolina, Lord Cornwallis (Clinton's choice as British commander in the South) met and crushed a Patriot force under Horatio Gates on August 16, 1780. Congress recalled Gates, and Washington replaced him with

Nathanael Greene, probably the ablest of all the American generals of the time next to Washington himself.

Even before Greene arrived in the war theater, the tide of battle had already begun to turn against Cornwallis. At King's Mountain (near the North Carolina–South Carolina border) on October 7, 1780, a band of Patriot riflemen from the backwoods killed, wounded, or captured every man in a force of 1,100 New York and South Carolina Tories, upon whom Cornwallis had depended as auxiliaries. Once Greene arrived, he confused and exasperated Cornwallis by dividing the American forces into fast-moving contingents while avoiding an open, conventional battle. One of the contingents inflicted what Cornwallis admitted was "a very unexpected and severe blow" at Cowpens on January 17, 1781. Finally, after receiving reinforcements, Greene combined all his forces and maneuvered to meet the British at Guilford Court House, North Carolina. After a hard-fought battle there on March 15, 1781, Greene was driven from the field; but Cornwallis had lost so many men that he decided to abandon the Carolina campaign.

Cornwallis withdrew to the port town of Wilmington, North Carolina, to receive supplies. Later he moved north, hoping to carry on raids in the interior of Virginia. But Clinton, fearful that the southern army might be destroyed, ordered him to take up a defensive position on the peninsula between the York and James Rivers and wait for transport to New York or Charleston. Cornwallis retreated to Yorktown and began to build fortifications there.

At that point, American and French forces descended on Yorktown in an effort to trap Cornwallis. Washington and the Count de Rochambeau marched a French-American army from New York to join the Marquis de Lafayette in Virginia, while Admiral de Grasse took a French fleet with additional troops up Chesapeake Bay to the York River. These joint operations caught Cornwallis between land and sea. After a few shows of resistance, he surrendered on October 17, 1781. Two days later, as a military band played the old tune "The World Turn'd Upside Down," he surrendered his whole army of more than 7,000.

### Winning the Peace

Cornwallis's defeat provoked outcries in England against continuing the war. Lord North resigned as prime minister; Lord Shelburne emerged from the political wreckage to succeed him; and British emissaries appeared in France to talk informally with the American diplomats there, of whom the three principals were Benjamin Franklin, John Adams, and John Jay.

The Americans were under instructions to cooperate fully with France in their negotiations with England. But Vergennes, the French foreign minister, insisted that France could not agree to any settlement of the war with England until its ally Spain had achieved its principal war aim: winning back Gibraltar from the British. There was no real prospect of that happening soon, and the Americans began to fear that the alliance with France might keep them at war indefinitely. As a result, Franklin, Jay, and Adams began proceeding on their own, without informing Vergennes, and soon drew up a preliminary treaty with Great Britain, which was signed on November 30, 1782. Franklin, in the meantime, skillfully pacified Vergennes and avoided an immediate rift in the French-American alliance.

The final treaty was signed September 3, 1783, when both Spain and France agreed to end hostilities. It was, on the whole, remarkably favorable to the United States in granting a clear-cut recognition of independence and a generous, though ambiguous, cession of territory—from the southern boundary of Canada to the northern boundary of Florida and from the Atlantic to the Mississippi. With good reason the American people celebrated as the last of the British occupation forces embarked from New York and General Washington, at the head of his troops, rode triumphantly into the city.


## WAR AND SOCIETY

Historians have long debated whether the American Revolution was a social as well as a political revolution. But whether or not those who launched and fought the war intended it, the conflict had important effects on the nature of American society.


### Loyalists and Minorities

Estimates differ as to how many Americans remained loyal to England during the Revolution, but it is clear that there were many—at least a fifth (and some estimate as much as a third) of the white population. Some were officeholders in the imperial government. Others were merchants whose trade was closely tied to the imperial system (although most merchants supported the Revolution). Still others were people who lived in relative isolation and had simply retained their traditional loyalties. There were also cultural and ethnic minorities who feared that an independent America would not offer them sufficient protection. And there were those who, expecting the British to win the war, were simply currying favor with the anticipated victors.

Hounded by Patriots in their communities, harassed by legislative and judicial actions, many of these Loyalists found themselves in an intolerable position during the war. Up to 100,000 fled the country. Those who could afford to—for example, the hated Tory governor of Massachusetts, Thomas Hutchinson—fled to England, where many lived in difficult and lonely exile. Others of more modest means moved to Canada, establishing the first English-speaking community in the province of Quebec. Some returned to America after the war and, as the early passions and resentments faded, managed to reenter the life of the nation. Others remained abroad for the rest of their lives.

The war had a significant effect on other minorities as well. No sect suffered more than the Anglicans, many of whose members were Loyalists and all of whom were widely identified with England. In Virginia and Maryland, the new Revolutionary regimes removed Anglicanism as the official religion and stopped funding it. In other states, Anglicans lost the economic aid they were accustomed to receiving from England. By the time the fighting ended, many Anglican parishes could no longer even afford clergymen. Anglicanism was permanently weakened from its losses during the Revolution. Also weakened were the Quakers in Pennsylvania and elsewhere, whose pacifism won them widespread unpopularity when they refused to support the war. The church was never to recover fully. Other Protestant denominations, however, grew stronger as a result of their enthusiastic support for the war. Presbyterian, Congregational, and Baptist Churches successfully tied themselves to the Patriot cause.

Most American Catholics also supported the Patriots during the war and won increased (although far from universal) popularity as a result. The church did not greatly increase its numbers as a result of the Revolution, but it did strengthen itself considerably as an institution. Shortly after the peace treaty was signed, the Vatican provided the United States with its own hierarchy and, in 1789, its first bishop.

For the largest of America's minorities—the black population—the war had limited, but nevertheless significant, effects. For some, the Revolution meant freedom. Because so much of the fighting occurred in the South during the last years of the war, many slaves came into contact with the British army, which—in the interests of disrupting and weakening the American cause—emancipated thousands of them and took them out of the country. For other African Americans, the Revolution meant exposure to the idea, although not the reality, of liberty. In towns and cities in particular, even blacks who could not read had exposure to the new ideas of liberty, and in some cases, they attempted to apply those ideas to themselves.

That was one reason why Revolutionary sentiment was more restrained in South Carolina and Georgia than in other colonies. Blacks constituted a majority in South Carolina and almost half the population in Georgia, and whites in both places feared that revolution would foment slave rebellions. The same fears discouraged English colonists in the Caribbean islands (who were even more greatly outnumbered by black slaves) from joining with the continental Americans in the revolt against Britain.

### Native Americans and the Revolution

Indians viewed the American Revolution with considerable uncertainty. Both the American Patriots and the British sought to maintain Indian neutrality, and most tribes ultimately chose to stay out of the war. But many Indians feared that the Revolution would replace a ruling group in which they had developed at least some measure of trust (the British) with one they considered generally hostile to them (the Patriots). The British had consistently sought to limit the expansion of white settlement into Indian land, even if unsuccessfully; the Americans had spearheaded the encroachments. Thus some Indians, among them those Iroquois who participated in the Burgoyne campaign in upper New York, chose to join the English cause. Still others took advantage of the conflict to launch attacks of their own.

In the western Carolinas and Virginia, the Cherokee, led by Chief Dragging Canoe, launched a series of attacks on outlying white settlements in the summer of 1776. Patriot militias responded in great force, ravaging Cherokee lands and forcing the chief and many of his followers to flee west across the Tennessee River. Those Cherokee who remained behind agreed to a new treaty by which they gave up still more land. Some Iroquois, despite the setbacks at Oriskany, continued to wage war against Americans in the West and caused widespread destruction in large agricultural areas of New York and Pennsylvania—areas whose crops were of crucial importance to the Patriot cause. And although the retaliating American armies inflicted heavy losses on the Indians, the attacks continued throughout the war.

In the end, however, the Revolution generally weakened the position of Native Americans in several ways. The Patriot victory increased white demand for western lands. Many whites resented the assistance such nations as the Mohawk had given the British and insisted on treating them as conquered people. Others derived from the Revolution a paternalistic view of the tribes that was only slightly less dangerous to the Native Americans than open hostility. Thomas Jefferson, for example, came to view the Indians as "noble savages," uncivilized in their present state but redeemable if they were willing to adapt to the norms of white society.

Among the Indians themselves, the Revolution increased their own deep internal divisions, which made it difficult for them to form a common front to resist the growing power of whites. In 1774, for example, the Shawnee in western Virginia could attract no support from neighboring tribes when they attempted to lead an uprising against white settlers moving into the lands that would later become Kentucky. They were defeated by the colonial militia and forced to cede still more land to white settlers. The Cherokee generated little support from surrounding tribes in their 1776 battles. The Iroquois, whose power had been eroding since the end of the French and Indian War, were unable to act in unison in the Revolution.

### Women's Rights and Women's Roles

The long Revolutionary War had a profound effect on American women. The departure of so many men to fight in the Patriot armies left wives, mothers, sisters, and daughters in charge of farms and businesses. Often, women handled these tasks with great success. But in many cases, inexperience, inflation, the unavailability of male labor, or the threat of enemy troops led to failure. Other women whose husbands or fathers were called away to war did not have even a farm or shop to fall back on. Cities and towns developed significant populations of impoverished women, who on occasion led protests against price increases or rioted and looted for food. On several other occasions (in New Jersey and Staten Island), women launched attacks on occupying British troops, whom they were required to house and feed at considerable expense.

Not all women stayed behind when the men went off to war. Sometimes by choice, more often by necessity, women flocked to the camps of the Patriot armies to join their male relatives. Despite many officers' disapproval of these female "camp followers," the women were of significant value to the new army, which had not yet developed an adequate system of supply and auxiliary services; the women increased army morale and provided a ready source of volunteers to do cooking, laundry, nursing, and other necessary tasks. In the rough environment of the camps, traditional gender distinctions proved difficult to maintain. Considerable numbers of women became involved, at least intermittently, in combat—including the legendary "Molly Pitcher" (so named because she carried pitchers of water to soldiers on the battlefield), who watched her husband fall during one encounter and immediately took his place at a gun. A few women even disguised themselves as men so as to be able to fight.

The emphasis on liberty and the "rights of man" led some women to begin to question their position in society. "By the way," Abigail Adams wrote to her husband John Adams in 1776, "in the new code of laws which I suppose it will be necessary for you to make, I desire you would remember the ladies and be more generous and favorable to them than your ancestors. Do not put such unlimited power into the hands of the Husbands." Adams was calling for a relatively modest expansion of women's rights: for new protections against abusive and tyrannical men. A few women, however, went further. Judith Sargent Murray, one of the leading essayists of the late eighteenth century, wrote in 1779 that women's minds were as good as those of men and that girls as well as boys therefore deserved access to education.

But little changed as a result. Under English common law, an unmarried woman had certain legal rights, but a married woman had virtually no rights at all. Everything she owned and everything she earned belonged to her husband. Because she had no property rights, she could not engage in any legal transactions on her own (buying or selling, suing or being sued, writing wills). She could not vote. She had no legal authority over her children. Nor could she obtain a divorce; that too was a right reserved almost exclusively to men. The Revolution did little to change any of these legal customs. In some states, it did become easier for women to obtain divorces. And in New Jersey, women obtained the right to vote (although that right was repealed in 1807). Otherwise, there were few advances and some setbacks—including the loss of the right of widows to regain their dowries from their husbands' estates. The Revolution, in other words, did not really challenge the patriarchal legal system. In many ways, it actually confirmed and strengthened it. Abigail Adams, in the same letter in which she asked her husband to "remember the ladies," also urged him to "regard us then as Beings placed by providence under your protection and in imitation of the Supreme Being make use of that power only for our happiness."

But the Revolution did encourage people of both sexes to reevaluate the contribution of women to the family and society. Part of this change was a result of the participation of women in the Revolutionary struggle itself. And part was a result of the reevaluation of American life after the war. As the new republic searched for a cultural identity for itself, it attributed a higher value to the role of women as mothers. The new nation was, many Americans liked to believe, producing a new kind of citizen, steeped in the principles of liberty. Mothers had a particularly important task, therefore, in instructing their children in the virtues that the republican citizenry was expected now to possess. Wives were still far from equal partners in marriage, but their ideas and interests were receiving some respect.

### The War Economy

The Revolution also produced important changes in the structure of the American economy. After more than a century of dependence on the British imperial system, American commerce suddenly found itself on its own. English ships no longer protected American vessels, but tried to drive them from the seas. British imperial ports—including those in England itself—were closed to American trade. But this disruption in traditional economic patterns served in the long run to strengthen the American economy. Colonial merchants had been violating British trade regulations for years, but the rules of empire had nevertheless served to inhibit American exploration of many markets. Now, enterprising merchants in New England and elsewhere began to develop new commerce in the Caribbean and South America. By the mid-1780s, American merchants were developing an important trade with the Orient. There was also a substantial increase in trade among the American states.

When English imports to America were cut off—first by the prewar boycott, then by the war itself—there were desperate efforts throughout the states to stimulate domestic manufacturing of certain necessities. No great industrial expansion resulted, but there was a modest increase in production and an even greater increase in expectations. Having broken politically with the British Empire, citizens of the new nation began to dream of breaking economically with it too—of developing a strong economy to rival that of the Old World.

## THE CREATION OF STATE GOVERNMENTS

At the same time that Americans were struggling to win their independence on the battlefield, they were also struggling to create new institutions of government to replace the British system they had repudiated. That struggle continued for more than fifteen years, but its most important phase occurred during the war itself, at the state level.

The formation of state governments began early in 1776. At first, the new state constitutions reflected primarily the fear of bloated executive power that had done so much to produce the break with England. Gradually, however, Americans became equally concerned about the instability of governments too responsive to popular will. In a second phase of state constitution writing, therefore, they gave renewed attention to the idea of balance in government.

### The Assumptions of Republicanism

If Americans agreed on nothing else when they began to build new governments for themselves, they agreed that those governments would be republican. To them, that meant a political system in which all power came from the people, rather than from some supreme authority (such as a king). The success of such a government depended on the nature of its citizenry. If the population consisted of sturdy, independent property owners imbued with civic virtue, then the republic could survive. If it consisted of a few powerful aristocrats and a great mass of dependent workers, then it would be in danger. From the beginning, therefore, the ideal of the small freeholder (the independent landowner) was basic to American political ideology.

Another crucial part of that ideology was the concept of equality. The Declaration of Independence had given voice to that idea in its most ringing phrase: "All men are created equal." It was a belief that stood in direct contrast to the old European assumption of an inherited aristocracy. The innate talents and energies of individuals, not their positions at birth, would determine their roles in society. Some people would inevitably be wealthier and more powerful than others. But all people would have to earn their success. There would be no equality of condition, but there would be equality of opportunity.

In reality, of course, the United States was never a nation in which all citizens were independent property holders. From the beginning, there was a sizable dependent labor force—the white members of which were allowed many of the privileges of citizenship, the black members of which were allowed virtually none. American women remained both politically and economically subordinate. Native Americans were systematically exploited and displaced. Nor was there ever full equality of opportunity. American society was more open and more fluid than that of most European nations, but wealth and privilege were often passed from one generation to another. The condition of a person's birth was almost always a crucial determinant of success.

Nevertheless, in embracing the assumptions of republicanism, Americans were adopting a powerful, even revolutionary, ideology, and their experiment in statecraft became a model for many other countries. It made the United States for a time the most admired and studied nation on earth.

## The First State Constitutions

Two states, Connecticut and Rhode Island, did not write new constitutions. They already had governments that were republican in all but name, and they simply deleted references to England and the king from their charters and adopted them as constitutions. The other eleven states, however, produced new documents.

The first and perhaps most basic decision was that the constitutions were to be written down. In England, the constitution was unwritten; it was simply a vague understanding about the nature of government. Americans believed that the vagueness had produced corruption, so they insisted that the structures of their own governments be clearly recorded so that no one could pervert them. The second decision was that the power of the executive, which Americans believed had grown too great in England, must be limited. Pennsylvania eliminated the executive altogether. Most other states inserted provisions limiting the power of the governor over appointments, reducing or eliminating his right to veto bills, and preventing him from dismissing the legislature. Most important, every state forbade the governor or any other executive officer from holding a seat in the legislature, thus ensuring that, unlike in England, the two branches of government would remain wholly separate.

But the new constitutions did not move all the way toward direct popular rule. In Georgia and Pennsylvania, the legislature consisted of one popularly elected house. But in every other state, there was an upper and a lower chamber, and in most cases, the upper chamber was designed to represent the "higher orders" of society. There were property requirements for voters—some modest, some substantial—in all states.

The initial phase of constitution writing proceeded rapidly. Ten states completed the process before the end of 1776. Georgia and New York finished by the end of 1777. Massachusetts did not finally adopt a constitution until 1780, by which time the construction of state governments had moved into a new phase.

## Revising State Governments

By the late 1770s, Americans were growing concerned about the apparent divisiveness and instability of their new state governments, which were having trouble accomplishing anything at all. Many believed the problem was one of too much democracy. As a result, most of the states began to revise their constitutions to limit popular power. Massachusetts was the first to act on the new concerns. By waiting until 1780 to ratify its first constitution,

Massachusetts allowed these changing ideas to shape its government, and the state produced a constitution that served as a model for others.

Two changes in particular characterized the Massachusetts and later constitutions. The first was a change in the process of constitution writing itself. Most of the first documents had been written by state legislatures and thus could easily be amended (or violated) by them. By 1780, sentiment was growing to find a way to protect the constitutions from those who had written them, to make it difficult to change the documents once they were approved. The solution was the constitutional convention: a special assembly of the people that would meet only for the purpose of writing the constitution and that would never (except under extraordinary circumstances) meet again. The constitution would be the product of the popular will, but once approved, it would be protected from the whims of public opinion and the political moods of the legislature.

The second change was a significant strengthening of the executive, a reaction to what many believed was the instability of the original state governments that had weak governors. The 1780 Massachusetts constitution made the governor one of the strongest in any state. He was to be elected directly by the people; he was to have a fixed salary (in other words, he would not be dependent on the good will of the legislature each year for his wages); he would have significant appointment powers and a veto over legislation. Other states followed. Those with weak or nonexistent upper houses strengthened or created them. Most increased the powers of the governor. Pennsylvania, which had no executive at all at first, now produced a strong one. By the late 1780s, almost every state had either revised its constitution or drawn up an entirely new one in an effort to produce stability in government.

### Toleration and Slavery

The new states moved far in the direction of complete religious freedom. Most Americans continued to believe that religion should play some role in government, but they did not wish to give special privileges to any particular denomination. The privileges that churches had once enjoyed were now largely stripped away. New York and the southern states stopped subsidizing the Church of England, and the New England states stripped the Congregational Church of many of its privileges. Boldest of all was Virginia. In 1786, it enacted the Statute of Religious Liberty, written by Thomas Jefferson, which called for the complete separation of church and state.

More difficult to resolve was the question of slavery. In areas where slavery was already weak—in New England, where there had never been many slaves, and in Pennsylvania, where the Quakers opposed slavery—it was abolished. Even in the South, there were some pressures to amend or even eliminate the institution; every state but South Carolina and Georgia prohibited further importation of slaves from abroad, and South Carolina banned the slave trade during the war. Virginia passed a law encouraging the freeing of slaves (manumission).

Nevertheless, slavery survived in all the southern and border states. There were several reasons: racist assumptions among whites about the inferiority of blacks; the enormous economic investments many white southerners had in their slaves; and the inability of even such men as Washington and Jefferson, who had deep moral misgivings about slavery, to envision any alternative to it. If slavery were abolished, what would happen to the black people in America? Few whites believed blacks could be integrated into American society as equals. In maintaining slavery, Jefferson once remarked, Americans were holding a "wolf by the ears." However unappealing it was to hold on to it, letting go would be even worse.

## THE SEARCH FOR A NATIONAL GOVERNMENT

Americans were much quicker to agree on state institutions than they were on the structure of their national government. At first, most believed that the central government should remain a relatively weak and unimportant force and that each state would be virtually a sovereign nation. Such beliefs reflected the assumption that were a republican government to attempt to administer too large and diverse a nation, it would founder. It was in response to such ideas that the Articles of Confederation emerged.

### The Confederation

The Articles of Confederation, which the Continental Congress had adopted in 1777, provided for a national government much like the one already in place. Congress would remain the central—indeed the only—institution of national authority. Its powers would expand to give it authority to conduct wars and foreign relations and to appropriate, borrow, and issue money. But it would not have power to regulate trade, draft troops, or levy taxes directly on the people. For troops and taxes it would have to make formal requests to the state legislatures, which could refuse them. There was to be no separate executive; the "president of the United States" would be merely the presiding officer at the sessions of Congress. Each state would have a single vote in Congress, and at least nine of the states would have to approve any important measure. All thirteen state legislatures would have to approve before the Articles could be ratified or amended.

The process of ratifying the Articles of Confederation revealed broad disagreements over the plan. The small states had insisted on equal state representation, but the larger states wanted representation to be based on population. The smaller states prevailed on that issue. More important, the states claiming western lands wished to keep them, but the rest of the states demanded that all such territory be turned over to the national government. New York and Virginia finally agreed to give up their western claims, and Maryland (the only state still holding out) then approved the Articles of Confederation. They went into effect in 1781.

The Confederation, which existed from 1781 until 1789, was not the complete failure that subsequent accounts often describe. But it was far from a success. Lacking adequate powers to deal with interstate issues or to enforce its will on the states, and lacking sufficient stature in the eyes of the world to be able to negotiate effectively, it suffered a series of damaging setbacks.

*Diplomatic Failures*

Evidence of the low esteem in which the rest of the world held the Confederation was its difficulty in persuading Great Britain (and to a lesser extent Spain) to live up to the terms of the peace treaty of 1783.

The British had promised to evacuate American soil, but British forces continued to occupy a string of frontier posts along the Great Lakes within the United States. Nor did the British honor their agreement to make restitution to slaveowners whose slaves the British army had confiscated. There were also disputes over the northeastern boundary of the new nation and over the border between the United States and Florida, which Britain had ceded back to Spain in the treaty. There were other diplomatic problems. American commerce, freed from imperial regulations, was expanding in new directions, but most American trade remained within the British Empire. Americans wanted full access to British markets; England, however, placed sharp postwar restrictions on that access.

In 1784, Congress sent John Adams as minister to London to resolve these differences, but Adams made no headway with the English, who could never be sure whether he represented a single nation or thirteen different

** te Claims to Western Lands and Cessions to National Government, 1782–1802**

| | | | |
|---|---|---|---|
| States with claims to Western lands | Virginia (1784) | South Carolina (1787) | Georgia (1802) |
| WESTERN CLAIMS (date of cession) | Massachusetts (1785, 1786) | North Carolina (1790) | Disputed |
| New York (1782) | Connecticut (1782, 1786, 1800) | | |

Map labels: Border disputed until 1842 · BRITISH POSSESSIONS · Border disputed until 1842 · Lake Superior · Claimed by N.Y. and N.H. Made a state 1791 · MAINE (Mass.) · Lake Huron · VT. · N.H. · Lake Michigan · Lake Ontario · NEW YORK · MASSACHUSETTS · Massachusetts claim ceded 1785 · Ceded 1786 · CONN. · R.I. · Lake Erie · Ceded 1782 · Connecticut claim ceded 1786 · Ceded 1800 · PENNSYLVANIA · N.J. · New York claim ceded 1782 · MD. · DEL. · Virginia claim ceded 1784 · VIRGINIA · Ohio River · UISIANA ded by Spain to France 1800 ld by France to United States 03 · North Carolina claim ceded 1790 · NORTH CAROLINA · South Carolina claim ceded 1787 · Mississippi · Georgia claim ceded 1802 · SOUTH CAROLINA · Savannah R. · GEORGIA · ATLANTIC OCEAN · Spanish claim ceded 1795 Georgia claim ceded 1802 · SPANISH POSSESSIONS · SPANISH FLORIDA · 0 200 Miles · 0 200 Kilometers · Gulf of Mexico

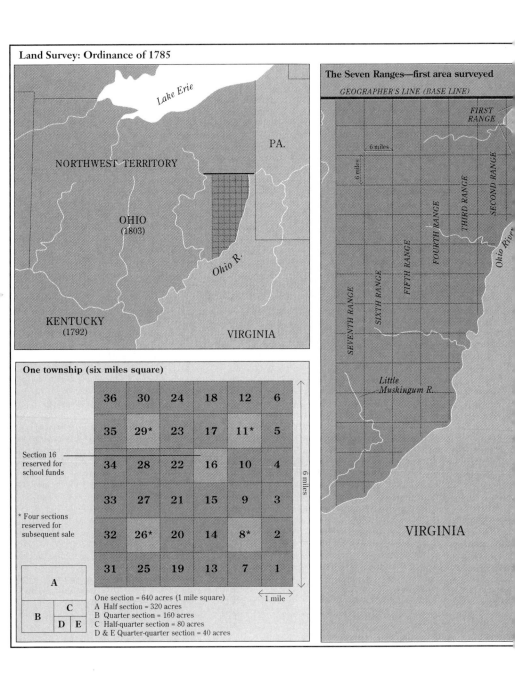

**Land Survey: Ordinance of 1785**

Lake Erie

NORTHWEST TERRITORY

PA.

OHIO
(1803)

Ohio R.

KENTUCKY
(1792)

VIRGINIA

**One township (six miles square)**

Section 16
reserved for
school funds

* Four sections
reserved for
subsequent sale

| 36 | 30 | 24 | 18 | 12 | 6 |
| 35 | 29* | 23 | 17 | 11* | 5 |
| 34 | 28 | 22 | 16 | 10 | 4 |
| 33 | 27 | 21 | 15 | 9 | 3 |
| 32 | 26* | 20 | 14 | 8* | 2 |
| 31 | 25 | 19 | 13 | 7 | 1 |

6 miles

1 mile

One section = 640 acres (1 mile square)
A  Half section = 320 acres
B  Quarter section = 160 acres
C  Half-quarter section = 80 acres
D & E Quarter-quarter section = 40 acres

A

B | C
  | D | E

**The Seven Ranges—first area surveyed**

GEOGRAPHER'S LINE (BASE LINE)

FIRST RANGE

SECOND RANGE

THIRD RANGE

FOURTH RANGE

FIFTH RANGE

SIXTH RANGE

SEVENTH RANGE

6 miles

6 miles

Ohio River

Little Muskingum R.

VIRGINIA

ones. Throughout the 1780s, the British government refused even to show the courtesy of sending a diplomatic minister to the American capital.

In dealing with the Spanish government, the Confederation demonstrated similar weakness. Its diplomats agreed to a treaty with Spain in 1786: The Spanish accepted the American interpretation of the Florida boundary. In return the Americans recognized the Spanish possessions in North America and accepted limits on the right of United States vessels to navigate the Mississippi for twenty years. But the southern states, incensed at the idea of giving up their access to the Mississippi, blocked ratification.

### The Confederation and the Northwest

The Confederation's most important accomplishment was its resolution of some of the controversies involving the western lands—although even this was a partial and ambiguous achievement.

When the Revolution began, only a few thousand whites lived west of the Appalachian divide; by 1790 their numbers had increased to 120,000. The Confederation had to find a way to include these new settlements in the political structure of the new nation. The western settlers were already often in conflict with the established centers of the East over Indian policies, trade provisions, and taxes. And Congress faced the additional difficulty of competing with state governments, some of which continued to claim jurisdiction over the regions west of the Appalachians. The landed states had begun to yield their claims to the national government in 1781, and by 1784 the Confederation controlled enough land to permit Congress to begin making policy for the national domain.

The Ordinance of 1784, based on a proposal by Thomas Jefferson, divided the western territory into ten self-governing districts, each of which could petition Congress for statehood when its population equaled the number of free inhabitants of the smallest existing state. Then, in the Ordinance of 1785, Congress created a system for surveying and selling the western lands. The territory north of the Ohio River was to be surveyed and marked off into neat rectangular townships. In every township four sections were to be set aside for the United States; the revenue from the sale of one of the others was to support creation of a public school. Sections were to be sold at auction for no less than one dollar an acre.

The original ordinances proved highly favorable to land speculators and less so to ordinary settlers, many of whom could not afford the price of the land. Congress compounded the problem by selling much of the best land to the Ohio and Scioto Companies before making it available to anyone else.

Criticism of these policies led to the passage in 1787 of another law governing western settlement—legislation that became known as the "Northwest Ordinance." The 1787 Ordinance abandoned the ten districts established in 1784 and created a single Northwest Territory out of the lands north of the Ohio; the territory might subsequently be divided into between three and five territories. It also specified a population of 60,000 as a minimum for statehood, guaranteed freedom of religion and the right to trial by jury to residents of the Northwest, and prohibited slavery throughout the territory.

The western lands south of the Ohio River received less attention from Congress, and development was more chaotic there. The region that became Kentucky and Tennessee developed rapidly in the late 1770s, and in the 1780s speculators and settlers began setting up governments and asking for recognition as states. The Confederation Congress was never able to resolve the conflicting claims in that region successfully.

*Indians and the Western Lands*

On paper at least, the western land policies of the Confederation created a system that brought order and stability to the process of white settlement in the Northwest. But in reality, order and stability came slowly and at great cost, because much of the land the Confederation was neatly subdividing and offering for sale consisted of territory claimed by the Indians of the region. Congress tried to resolve that problem in 1784, 1785, and 1786 by persuading Iroquois, Choctaw, Chickasaw, and Cherokee leaders to sign treaties ceding substantial western lands in the North and South to the United States. But those agreements proved ineffective. In 1786, the leadership of the Iroquois Confederacy repudiated the treaty it had signed two years earlier and threatened to attack white settlements in the disputed lands. Other tribes had never really accepted the treaties affecting them and continued to resist white movement into their lands.

Violence between whites and Indians on the Northwest frontier reached a crescendo in the early 1790s. In 1790 and again in 1791, the Miami, led by the famed warrior Little Turtle, defeated United States forces in two major battles near what is now the western border of Ohio; in the second of those battles, on November 4, 1791, 630 white Americans died in fighting at the Wabash River (the greatest military victory Indians had ever or would ever achieve in their battles with whites). Efforts to negotiate a settlement foundered on the Miami's insistence that no treaty was possible unless it forbade white settlement west of the Ohio River. Negotiations did not resume until after General Anthony Wayne led 4,000 soldiers into the Ohio Valley in 1794 and defeated the Indians in the Battle of Fallen Timbers.

A year later, the Miami signed the Treaty of Greenville, ceding substantial new lands to the United States (which was now operating under the Constitution of 1789) in exchange for a formal acknowledgment of their claim to the territory they had managed to retain. This was the first time the new federal government recognized the sovereignty of Indian nations; in doing so, the United States was affirming that Indian lands could be ceded only by the tribes themselves. That hard-won assurance, however, proved a frail protection against the pressure for white expansion westward in later years.

### Debts, Taxes, and Daniel Shays

The postwar depression, which lasted from 1784 to 1787, increased the perennial American problem of an inadequate money supply, a problem that bore particularly heavily on debtors. In dealing with the serious problem of debts, Congress most clearly demonstrated its weakness.

The Confederation itself had an enormous outstanding debt that it had accumulated during the Revolutionary War, and few means with which to pay it. It had sold war bonds that were now due to be repaid; it owed money to its soldiers; it had substantial debts abroad. But it had no power to tax. It could only make requisitions of the states, and it received only about one-sixth of the money it requisitioned—barely enough to meet the government's ordinary operating expenses, too little to pay the debts. The fragile new nation was faced with the grim prospect of defaulting on its obligations.

This alarming possibility brought to the fore a group of leaders who would play a crucial role in the shaping of the republic for several decades. Committed nationalists, they sought ways to increase the powers of the central government and to permit it to meet its financial obligations. Robert Morris, the head of the Confederation's treasury; Alexander Hamilton, his young protégé; James Madison of Virginia; and others called for a "continental impost"—a 5 percent duty on imported goods, to be levied by Congress and used to fund the debt.

But the scheme met with substantial opposition. Many Americans feared that the impost plan would concentrate too much financial power in the hands of Morris and his allies in Philadelphia. Congress failed to approve the impost in 1781 and again in 1783. Angry and discouraged, the nationalists largely withdrew from any active involvement in the Confederation. The states themselves generally relied on increased taxation to pay their own obligations. But poor farmers, already burdened by debt and now burdened again by new taxes on their lands, considered such policies unfair, even tyrannical. They demanded that the state governments issue paper currency to increase the money supply and make it easier for them to meet their obligations. Resentment was especially high among farmers in New England, who felt that the states were squeezing them to enrich already wealthy bondholders in Boston and other towns. Debtors who failed to pay their taxes found their mortgages foreclosed and their property seized; sometimes they found themselves in jail.

Throughout the late 1780s, therefore, mobs of distressed farmers rioted periodically in various parts of New England. They caused the most serious trouble in Massachusetts. Dissidents in the Connecticut Valley and the Berkshire Hills, many of them Revolutionary veterans, rallied behind Daniel Shays, a former captain in the Continental army. Shays issued a set of demands that included paper money, tax relief, a moratorium on debts, the re-

A SCENE FROM SHAYS'S REBELLION This woodcut depicts one of the many brawls that characterized what became known as Shays's Rebellion, which was in fact less a real insurrection than a prolonged civil disorder in a series of communities born of economic resentments.

moval of the state capital from Boston to the interior, and the abolition of imprisonment for debt. During the summer of 1786, the Shaysites concentrated on preventing the collection of debts, private or public, and used force to keep courts from sitting and sheriffs from selling confiscated property. In Boston, members of the legislature, including Samuel Adams, denounced Shays and his men as rebels and traitors.

When winter came, the rebels advanced on Springfield, hoping to seize weapons from the arsenal there. An army of state militiamen, financed by a loan from wealthy merchants who feared a new revolution, set out from Boston to confront them. In January 1787, this army met Shays's band and dispersed his ragged troops.

As a military enterprise, Shays's Rebellion was a failure. But it had important consequences for the future of the United States. In Massachusetts, it resulted in a few immediate gains for the discontented groups. Shays and his lieutenants, at first sentenced to death, were later pardoned; and Massachusetts offered the protesters some tax relief and a postponement of debt payments. More significantly, however, the rebellion added urgency to a movement already gathering support throughout the new nation—the movement to produce a new, national constitution.

D E B A T I N G    T H E    P A S T

*The American Revolution*

HE LONGSTANDING DEBATE over the origins of the American Revolution has tended to reflect two broad schools of interpretation. One sees the Revolution largely as a political and intellectual event and argues that the revolt against Britain was part of a defense of ideals and principles. The other views the Revolution as a social and economic phenomenon and contends that material interests were at the heart of the rebellion.

The Revolutionary generation itself portrayed the conflict as a struggle over ideals, and this interpretation prevailed through most of the nineteenth century. But in the early twentieth century, historians influenced by the reform currents of the progressive era began to identify social and economic forces that they believed had contributed to the rebellion. Carl Becker, for example, wrote in a 1909 study of New York that two questions had shaped the Revolution: "The first was the question of home rule; the second was the question . . . of who should rule at home." The colonists were not only fighting the British; they were also engaged in a kind of civil war, a contest for power between radicals and conservatives that led to the "democratization of American politics and society."

Other "progressive" historians elaborated on Becker's thesis. J. Franklin Jameson, writing in 1926, argued, "Many economic desires, many social aspirations, were set free by the political struggle, many aspects of society profoundly altered by the forces thus let loose." Arthur M. Schlesinger maintained in a 1917 book that colonial merchants, motivated by their own interest in escaping the restrictive policies of British mercantilism, aroused American resistance in the 1760s and 1770s.

Beginning in the 1950s, a new generation of scholars began to reemphasize the role of ideology and de-emphasize the role of economic interests. Robert E. Brown (in 1955) and Edmund S. Morgan (in 1956) both argued that most eighteenth-century Americans shared common political principles and that the social and economic conflicts the progressives had identified were not severe. The rhetoric of the Revolution, they suggested, was not propaganda but a real reflection of the ideas of the colonists. Bernard Bailyn, in *The Ideological Origins of the American Revolution* (1967), demonstrated the complex roots of the ideas behind the Revolution and argued that this carefully constructed political stance was not a disguise for economic interests but a genuine ideology, rooted in deeply held convictions about rights and power, that itself motivated the colonists to act. The Revolution, he claimed, "was above all else an ideological, constitutional, political struggle and not primarily a controversy between social groups undertaken to force changes in the organization of the society or the economy."

By the late 1960s, however, a group of younger historians—many of them influenced by the New Left—were challenging the ideological interpretation again by illuminating social and economic tensions within colonial society that they claimed helped shape the Revolutionary struggle. Jesse Lemisch and Dirk Hoerder pointed to the actions of mobs in colonial cities as evidence of popular resentment of both American and British elites. They noted, for example, that Revolutionary crowds were likely to attack all symbols of wealth and power, whether British or American; that they displayed a range of class-based grievances not rooted in elite ideologies. Joseph Ernst reemphasized the significance of economic pressures on colonial merchants and tradesmen. Gary Nash, in *The Urban Crucible* (1979), emphasized the role of growing economic distress in colonial cities in creating a climate in which Revolutionary sentiment could flourish. Edward Countryman and Rhys Isaac both pointed to changes in the nature of colonial society and culture, and in the relationship between classes in eighteenth-century America, as a crucial prerequisite for the growth of the Revolutionary movement. Many of these newer social interpretations of the Revolution do not argue that the rebellion was a class conflict or that economic interests inevitably *determined* a person's stance toward the struggle. They argue, rather, that the relationship between interests and ideology must be a part of any workable explanation of the conflict.

# CHAPTER SIX

# The Constitution
# and the New Republic

*Toward a New Government* ～ *Adoption and Adaptation*
*Federalists and Republicans* ～ *Asserting National Sovereignty*
*The Downfall of the Federalists*

Y THE LATE 1780s, many Americans had grown dissatisfied with the Confederation. It was ridden with factions, unable to deal effectively with economic problems, and frighteningly powerless in the face of Shays's Rebellion. A decade earlier, Americans had deliberately avoided creating a strong national government. Now they reconsidered. In 1787, in a burst of great political creativity, the nation produced a new constitution and a new, much more powerful government with three independent branches.

The American Constitution derived most of its principles from the state documents that had preceded it. But it was also a remarkable achievement in its own right. It created a system of government that has survived for more than two centuries as one of the stablest and most successful in the world. William Gladstone, a great nineteenth-century British statesman, once called the Constitution the "most wonderful work ever struck off at a given time by the brain and purpose of man." The American people generally agreed. Indeed, to many the Constitution took on some of the characteristics of a sacred document, an unassailable "fundamental law" from which all public policies and all political principles must spring.

Yet the adoption of the Constitution did not complete the creation of the republic. For while most Americans agreed that the Constitution was a nearly perfect document, they disagreed—at times fundamentally—on what that document meant.

## TIME LINE

| 1786 | 1787 | 1787–1788 | 1789 | 1791 |
|------|------|-----------|------|------|
| Annapolis Conference | Constitutional Convention; Constitution adopted | States ratify Constitution | Washington becomes first president<br><br>Bill of Rights adopted<br><br>French Revolution<br><br>Judiciary Act | First Bank of U.S. chartered |

| 1792 | 1793 | 1794 | | |
|------|------|------|--|--|
| Washington reelected | Genet Affair | Whiskey Rebellion<br><br>Jay's Treaty | | |

| 1795 | 1796 | 1798 | 1798–1799 | 1800 |
|------|------|------|-----------|------|
| Pinckney's Treaty | John Adams elected president | XYZ Affair<br><br>Alien and Sedition Acts<br><br>Virginia and Kentucky Resolutions | Quasi-war with France | Jefferson elected president |

# TOWARD A NEW GOVERNMENT

So unpopular and ineffectual had the Confederation Congress become by the mid-1780s that it began to lead an almost waiflike existence. In 1783, its members timidly withdrew from Philadelphia to escape army veterans demanding their back pay. They took refuge for a while in Princeton, New Jersey, then moved on to Annapolis, and in 1785 settled in New York. Through all of this, delegates were often scarce. Only with great difficulty could Congress produce a quorum to ratify the treaty with Great Britain ending the Revolutionary War. Only eight state delegations voted on the Confederation's most important piece of legislation, the Northwest Ordinance.

### Advocates of Centralization

Weak and unpopular though the Confederation was, a great many citizens—probably a majority—remained wary of a stronger central government. They had, they believed, fought the Revolutionary War to abolish remote and tyrannical authority; now they wanted to keep political power centered in the states, where it could be carefully and closely controlled. But some of the wealthiest and most powerful groups in the population were beginning to clamor in the 1780s for a more genuinely national government capable of dealing more effectively with the country's problems. By 1786, such demands had grown so intense that even defenders of the existing system reluctantly agreed that the government needed strengthening at its weakest point—its lack of power to tax.

The most resourceful advocate of centralization was Alexander Hamilton, the illegitimate son of a Scottish merchant in the West Indies, who had become a successful New York lawyer and had once served as an aide to George Washington. Hamilton had been unhappy from the start with the Articles of Confederation and the weak central government they had created. He now called for a national convention to overhaul the entire document. He found an important ally in James Madison of Virginia, who persuaded the Virginia legislature to convene an interstate conference on commercial questions. Only five states sent delegates to the meeting, which took place at Annapolis, Maryland, in 1786; but the conference approved a proposal drafted by Hamilton (representing New York) for a convention of special delegates from all the states to meet in Philadelphia the next year and consider ways to "render the constitution of the Federal government adequate to the exigencies of the union."

At that point, in 1786, there seemed little reason to believe the Philadelphia convention would generate much wider interest than the Annapolis meeting had attracted. Only by winning the support of George Washington, the centralizers believed, could they hope to prevail. But Washington at first showed little interest in joining the cause. Then, early in 1787, the news of Shays's Rebellion spread throughout the nation. Thomas Jefferson, then the American minister in Paris, was not alarmed. "I hold," he confided in a letter to James Madison, "that a little rebellion, now and then, is a good thing, and as necessary in the political world as storms in the physical." But Washington took the news less calmly. "There are combustibles in every State which a spark might set fire to," he exclaimed. "I feel infinitely more than I can express for the disorders which have arisen. Good God!" He promptly made plans to travel to Philadelphia for the Constitutional Convention. His support gave the meeting wide credibility.

## A Divided Convention

Fifty-five men, representing all the states except Rhode Island, attended one or more sessions of the convention that sat in the Philadelphia State House from May to September 1787. These "Founding Fathers," as they became known much later, were relatively young men; the average age was forty-four, and only one delegate (Benjamin Franklin, then eighty-one) was genuinely aged. They were well educated by the standards of their time. Most represented the great property interests of the country, and many feared what one of them called the "turbulence and follies" of democracy. Yet all were also products of the American Revolution and retained the Revolutionary suspicion of concentrated power.

The convention unanimously chose Washington to preside over its sessions and then closed its business to the public and the press. (If James Madison had not kept a private diary chronicling the proceedings, historians might know little about what happened in Philadelphia.) It then ruled that each state delegation would have a single vote and that major decisions would require not unanimity, as they did in Congress, but a simple majority. Almost all the delegates agreed that the United States needed a stronger central government. But there agreement ended.

Virginia, the largest state in population, sent a well-prepared delegation to Philadelphia. James Madison (thirty-six years old) was its intellectual leader. He had devised in some detail a plan for a new "national" government; the Virginians used it to control the agenda of the convention from the start.

Edmund Randolph of Virginia opened the debate by proposing a central element of the Virginia Plan: that "a national government ought to be established, consisting of a supreme Legislative, Executive, and Judiciary." It was a drastic proposal, calling for a government fundamentally different from the existing Confederation. But by then the delegates were so committed to fundamental reform that they approved the resolution after only brief debate. Then Randolph introduced the details of Madison's Virginia Plan. It called for a national legislature of two houses. In the lower house, states would be represented in proportion to their population; thus the largest state (Virginia) would have about ten times as many representatives as the smallest (Delaware). Members of the upper house were to be elected by the lower house under no rigid system of representation; thus some of the smaller states might at times have no members at all in the upper house.

The proposal aroused immediate opposition among delegates from Delaware, New Jersey, and other small states. Some of them responded by arguing that the convention had authority to do no more than revise the existing Articles of Confederation. William Paterson of New Jersey offered an alternative (the New Jersey Plan) that would have retained the essence of the existing system. It preserved the one-house legislature of the Confederation, in which all states had equal representation, but it gave Congress expanded powers to tax and to regulate commerce. The majority of the delegates voted to table Paterson's proposal.

Supporters of the Virginia Plan now realized they would have to make concessions to the small states if the delegations were ever to agree. They conceded an important point by agreeing that the members of the upper house would be elected by the state legislatures, thereby ensuring that every state would be represented.

But many questions remained unresolved. Among the most important was the question of slavery. Would slaves be counted as part of the population in determining representation in Congress? Or would they be considered property, not entitled to representation? Delegates from the states with large slave populations wanted to have it both ways. They argued that slaves should be considered persons in determining representation but as property whenever the new government levied taxes on the states on the basis of population. Representatives from states where slavery had disappeared or was expected soon to disappear argued that slaves should be included in calculating taxation but not representation. The convention never seriously considered liberating the slaves and giving them the right to vote or citizenship.

## Compromise

The delegates bickered for weeks. By the end of June, as both temperature and tempers rose to uncomfortable heights, the convention seemed in danger of collapsing. But the delegates refused to give up (partly because of the patient urging of Benjamin Franklin). Finally, on July 2, the convention created a "grand committee," chaired by Franklin and with one delegate from each state, to resolve the remaining disagreements. The committee produced a proposal that became the basis of the "Great Compromise." Its most important achievement was resolving the difficult problem of representation. The proposal called for a two-house legislature. In the lower house, the states would be represented on the basis of population; each slave would be counted as three-fifths of a free person in determining the basis for both representation and direct taxation. In the upper house, the states would be represented equally with two members apiece. On July 16, 1787, the convention voted to accept the compromise.

In the next few weeks, the convention agreed to another important compromise on the explosive issue of slavery. The representatives of the southern states feared that if the national government were granted power to regulate trade, it might interfere with slavery. The convention agreed to bar the new government from stopping the slave trade for twenty years. This was a large and difficult concession from the delegates who opposed slavery, but they agreed to it because they feared that without it the Constitution would fail.

Some significant issues remained unaddressed. Most important was the absence of a list of individual rights, which would restrain the powers of the national government in the way that bills of rights restrained the state governments. Madison opposed the idea, arguing that specifying rights that were reserved to the people would, in effect, limit those rights. Others, however, feared that without such protections the national government might abuse its new authority.

### The Constitution of 1787

Many people contributed to the creation of the American Constitution, but the most important person in the process was James Madison. Madison had devised the Virginia Plan, from which the final document ultimately emerged, and he did most of the drafting of the Constitution itself. Madison's most important achievement, however, was in helping resolve two important philosophical questions that had served as obstacles to the creation of an effective national government: the question of sovereignty and the question of limiting power.

The creation of the federal Constitution had required the resolution of difficult questions associated with sovereignty. How could a national government exercise sovereignty concurrently with state governments? Where did ultimate sovereignty lie? The answer, Madison and his contemporaries decided, was that all power, at all levels of government, flowed ultimately from the people. Thus neither the federal government nor the state governments were truly sovereign. All of them derived their authority from below. The opening phrase of the Constitution—"We the people of the United States of America"—is an expression of that belief. The resolution of the problem of sovereignty made possible one of the distinctive features of the Constitution—its division of powers between the national and state governments. The Constitution and the government it created were to be the "supreme law" of the land; no state would have the authority to defy it. The federal government would have the power to tax, to regulate commerce, and to control the currency. At the same time, the Constitution left certain important powers in the hands of the states.

In addition to solving the question of sovereignty, the Constitution produced a distinctive solution to the problem of concentrated authority. Nothing so frightened the leaders of the new nation as the prospect of creating a tyrannical government. Indeed, that fear had been one of the chief obstacles to the creation of a national government at all. Drawing from the ideas of the French philosopher Baron de Montesquieu, most Americans had long believed that the best way to avoid tyranny was to keep government close to the people. A republic must remain confined to a relatively small area; a large nation would breed corruption and despotism because the rulers would be so distant from most of the people that there would be no way to control them. In the new American nation, these assumptions had led to the belief that the individual states must remain sovereign and that a strong national government would be dangerous.

Madison, however, helped break the grip of these assumptions by arguing that a large republic would be less, not more, likely to produce tyranny, because it would contain so many different factions that no single group would ever be able to dominate it. This idea of many centers of power "checking each other" and preventing any single, despotic authority from emerging also helped shape the internal structure of the federal government. The Constitution's most distinctive feature was its "separation of powers" within the government, its creation of "checks and balances" among the legislative, executive, and judicial branches. The forces within the government would constantly compete with (and often frustrate) one another. Congress would have two chambers, each checking the other, since both would have to agree before any law could be passed. The president would have the power to veto acts of Congress. The federal courts would be protected from both the executive and the legislature, because judges, once appointed by the president and confirmed by the Senate, would serve for life.

The "federal" structure of the government was designed to protect the United States from the kind of despotism that Americans believed had emerged in England. But it was also designed to protect the nation from another kind of despotism: the tyranny of the people. Shays's Rebellion, most of the founders believed, had been only one example of what could happen if a nation did not defend itself against the unchecked exercise of popular will. Thus in the new government, only the members of the House of Representatives would be elected directly by the people. Senators, the president, federal judges—all would be insulated in varying degrees from the public.

On September 17, 1787, thirty-nine delegates signed the Constitution. Benjamin Franklin expressed the feelings of many of them at the end when

THE SIGNING OF THE CONSTITUTION This idealized
view of delegates signing the Constitution of 1787, with
George Washington presiding, is the work of the
twentieth-century artist Howard Chandler Christy. It
hangs in the United States Capitol. Benjamin Franklin
is portrayed seated at the front, center of the scene, with
Hamilton just to his left and Madison to his right.

he said: "Thus I consent, Sir, to this Constitution, because I expect no better, and because I am not sure that it is not the best."

## ADOPTION AND ADAPTATION

The delegates at Philadelphia had greatly exceeded their instructions from
Congress and the states. Instead of making simple revisions in the Articles
of Confederation, they had produced a plan for a completely different form
of government. They feared, therefore, that the Constitution would not be
ratified under the rules of the Articles of Confederation, which required
unanimous approval by the state legislatures. So the convention changed the

rules, proposing that the new government come into being when nine of the thirteen states ratified the Constitution and recommending that state conventions, not state legislatures, be called to ratify it.

### Federalists and Antifederalists

The Congress in New York, demoralized and overshadowed by the events in Philadelphia, passively accepted the convention's work and submitted it to the states for approval. All the state legislatures except Rhode Island elected delegates to ratifying conventions, most of which had begun meeting by early 1788. Even before the ratifying conventions adjourned, however, a great national debate on the new Constitution had begun—in the state legislatures, in public meetings, in newspapers, and in ordinary conversations.

CELEBRATING THE CONSTITUTION Perhaps because opposition to the Constitution had been so intense, its champions staged elaborate celebrations at the time of ratification in an effort to enhance its legitimacy. In 1788, supporters of the Constitution organized an elaborate parade down Wall Street, which included the ship on wheels (representing the "ship of state") pictured here. Alexander Hamilton, whose name is emblazoned on the ship's banners, was New York's leading advocate of the Constitution.

Supporters of the Constitution had a number of advantages. They were better organized. They had the support of the two most eminent men in America, Franklin and Washington. And they seized an appealing label for themselves: "Federalists"—a term that opponents of centralization had once used to describe themselves—thus implying that they were less committed to a "nationalist" government than in fact they were. The Federalists also had the support of the ablest political philosophers of their time: Alexander Hamilton, James Madison, and John Jay. Those three men, under the joint pseudonym "Publius," wrote a series of essays—widely published in newspapers throughout the nation—explaining the meaning and virtues of the Constitution. The essays were later issued as a book, and they are known today as *The Federalist Papers*. They are among the greatest American contributions to political theory.

The Federalists called their critics "Antifederalists," which suggested that their rivals had nothing to offer except opposition. But the Antifederalists had serious and intelligent arguments of their own. They saw themselves as the defenders of the true principles of the Revolution. The Constitution, they believed, would betray those principles by establishing a strong, potentially tyrannical, center of power in the new national government. The new government, they claimed, would increase taxes, obliterate the states, wield dictatorial powers, favor the "well-born" over the common people, and abolish individual liberty. But their biggest complaint was that the Constitution lacked a bill of rights, a concern that revealed one of the most important reasons for their opposition: their basic mistrust of human nature and of the capacity of human beings to wield power. The Antifederalists argued that any government that placed authority in the hands of a few powerful people would inevitably produce despotism. Their demand for a bill of rights was a product of this belief: no government could be trusted to protect the liberties of its citizens; only by enumerating the natural rights of the people could there be any certainty that those rights would be protected.

Despite the efforts of the Antifederalists, ratification proceeded quickly (although not without difficulty in several states) during the winter of 1787–1788. The Delaware convention was the first to act. It ratified the Constitution unanimously, as did New Jersey and Georgia. New Hampshire ratified the document in June 1788—the ninth state to do so. It was now theoretically possible for the Constitution to go into effect.

A new government could not hope to succeed, however, without Virginia and New York, whose conventions remained closely divided. But by the end of June, first Virginia and then New York had consented to the Constitution by narrow margins. The New York convention yielded to expediency—even some of the most staunchly Antifederalist delegates feared that the state's commercial interests would suffer if New York were to remain outside the new union. Massachusetts, Virginia, and New York all ratified on the assumption that a bill of rights would be added in the form of amendments to the Constitution. North Carolina's convention adjourned without taking action, waiting to see what happened to the amendments. Rhode Island did not even consider ratification.

### Completing the Structure

The first elections under the Constitution were held in the early months of 1789. Almost all the newly elected members of Congress had favored ratification, and many had served as delegates to the Philadelphia convention. There was never any doubt about who would be the first president. George Washington had presided at the Constitutional Convention, and many who had favored ratification did so only because they expected him to preside over the new government as well. Washington received the votes of all the presidential electors. John Adams, a leading Federalist, became vice president. After a journey from his estate at Mount Vernon, Virginia, marked by elaborate celebrations along the way, Washington was inaugurated in New York on April 30, 1789.

The first Congress served in many ways almost as a continuation of the Constitutional Convention, because its principal responsibility was filling in the various gaps in the Constitution. Its most important task was drafting a bill of rights. By early 1789, even Madison had come to agree that some sort of bill of rights would be essential to legitimize the new government in the eyes of its opponents. On September 25, 1789, Congress approved twelve amendments, ten of which were ratified by the states by the end of 1791. What we know as the Bill of Rights is these first ten amendments to the Constitution. Nine of them placed limitations on Congress by forbidding it to infringe on certain fundamental rights: freedom of religion, speech, and the press; immunity from arbitrary arrest; trial by jury; and others. The Tenth Amendment reserved to the states all powers except those specifically withheld from them or delegated to the federal government.

On the subject of federal courts, the Constitution said only: "The judicial power of the United States shall be vested in one Supreme Court, and in such inferior courts as the Congress may from time to time ordain and establish." It was left to Congress to determine the number of Supreme Court judges to be appointed and the kinds of lower courts to be organized. In the Judiciary Act of 1789, Congress provided for a Supreme Court of six members and a system of lower district courts and courts of appeal. In the same act, Congress gave the Supreme Court the power to make the final decision in cases involving the constitutionality of state laws.

The Constitution referred indirectly to executive departments but did not specify which ones or how many there should be. The first Congress created three such departments—state, treasury, and war—and also established the offices of the attorney general and postmaster general. To the office of secretary of the treasury Washington appointed Alexander Hamilton of New York, who at age thirty-two was an acknowledged expert in public finance. For secretary of war he chose a Massachusetts Federalist, General Henry Knox. As attorney general he named Edmund Randolph of Virginia, sponsor of the plan on which the Constitution had been based. As secretary of state he chose another Virginian, Thomas Jefferson.

## FEDERALISTS AND REPUBLICANS

The resolution of these initial issues, however, did not resolve the disagreements about the nature of the new government. The framers of the Constitution had dealt with many controversies not by solving them but by papering them over with a series of vague compromises; as a result, the disagreements survived to plague the new government, and the first twelve years under the Constitution produced a politics of unusual acrimony.

At the heart of the controversies of the 1790s was the same basic difference in philosophy that had been at the heart of the debate over the Constitution. On one side stood a powerful group who believed that America required a strong, national government: that the country's mission was to become a genuine nation-state, with centralized authority, a complex commercial economy, and a proud standing in world affairs. On the other side stood another group—a minority at first, but one that gained strength during the decade—whose members envisioned a more modest national government. The United States should not, this group believed, aspire to be a highly commercial or urban nation. It should remain predominantly rural and agrarian. The centralizers became known as the Federalists and gravitated to the leadership of Alexander Hamilton. Their opponents acquired the name Republicans and gathered under the leadership of Thomas Jefferson and James Madison.

### Hamilton and the Federalists

For twelve years, the Federalists retained firm control of the new government. That was in part because George Washington had always envisioned a strong national government and as president did little to stop those at-tempting to create one. But the president, Washington believed, should stand above political controversies, and so he avoided personal involvement in the deliberations of Congress. As a result, the dominant figure in his ad-ministration became Alexander Hamilton, who exerted more influence than anyone else on domestic and foreign policy. Of all the national leaders of his time, Hamilton was one of the most aristocratic in personal tastes and po-litical philosophy; he believed that a stable and effective government required an elite ruling class. Thus the new government needed the support of the wealthy and powerful; and to get that, it needed to give elites a stake in its success. Hamilton proposed, therefore, that the existing public debt be "funded": that the various certificates of indebtedness that the old Congress had issued during and after the Revolution—many of them now in the pos-session of wealthy speculators—be called in and exchanged for interest-bearing bonds. He also recommended that the Revolutionary state debts be "assumed," taken over by the federal government, to cause state bondhold-ers also to look to the central government for eventual payment. Hamilton did not envision paying off and thus eliminating the debt; he wanted to cre-ate a permanent national debt, with new bonds being issued as old ones were paid off. The result, he believed, would be that the wealthy classes, who were the most likely to lend money to the government, would always have a rea-son to want the government to survive.

Hamilton also wanted to create a national bank. It would provide loans and currency to businesses. It would give the government a safe place for the deposit of federal funds. It would facilitate the collection of taxes and the disbursement of the government's expenditures. And it would provide a stable center to the nation's small and feeble banking system. The bank would be chartered by the federal government and would have a monopoly of the government's own banking business, but much of its capital would come from private investors.

The funding and assumption of debts would require new sources of rev-enue for the national government. Hamilton recommended two kinds of taxes to complement the receipts anticipated from the sales of public land. One was an excise tax on alcoholic beverages, a tax that would be most bur-densome to the whiskey distillers of the backcountry, especially those in Pennsylvania, Virginia, and North Carolina—small farmers who converted part of their corn and rye crops into whiskey. The other was a tariff on im-ports, which Hamilton saw not only as a way to raise money but as a way to protect domestic industries from foreign competition. In his famous "Re-port on Manufactures" of 1791, he outlined a plan for stimulating the growth

ganize a vigorous op
political organizatic
(These first Republi
publican Party, whic
licans were going to
paratus of partisan i
societies, and caucus
other across state line
elections. And they v
ton and his supporter
interests of the natic
as a party, nor woulc
stitutionalized factic

From the begin
were Thomas Jeffers
magnetic of the two,
He promoted a visic
farm their own land
would, he assumed,
tional trade. Nor did
lieved, develop a cer
also believed that the
industrialization.

Although both p
among all classes, th
eralists were most nu
in such southern sea
merous in the rural a
philosophies was vis
progress of the Frenc
ical in the 1790s, with
monarchy, and event
alists expressed horre
tiaristocratic spirit th

When the time
1792, both Jefferson
term. The president
spect of both factions
alists than with the F
mained the dominan

of industry in the United States and spoke glowingly of the advantages to society of a healthy manufacturing sector.

The Federalists, in short, offered more than a vision of a stable new government. They offered a vision of the sort of nation America should become—a nation with a wealthy, enlightened ruling class, a vigorous, independent commercial economy, and a thriving industrial sector; a country able to play a prominent role in world economic affairs.

### Enacting the Federalist Program

Few members of Congress objected to Hamilton's plan for funding the national debt, but many did oppose his proposal to fund the debt at par, that is, to exchange new bonds for old certificates of indebtedness on a dollar-for-dollar basis. The old certificates had been issued to merchants and farmers in payment for war supplies during the Revolution and to officers and soldiers of the Revolutionary army in payment for their services. Many of these holders had been forced to sell their bonds during the hard times of the 1780s to speculators, who had bought them at a fraction of their face value. James Madison, now a representative from Virginia, argued for a plan by which the new bonds would be divided between the original purchasers and the speculators. But Hamilton's allies insisted that such a plan was both impractical and dangerous, that the honor of the government required a literal fulfillment of its earlier promises to pay whoever held the bonds. Congress finally passed the funding bill Hamilton wanted.

Hamilton's proposal that the federal government assume the state debts encountered greater difficulty. Its opponents argued that if the federal government took over the state debts, the states with few debts would have to pay taxes to service the states with large ones. Massachusetts, for example, owed much more money than did Virginia. Only by striking a bargain with the Virginians were Hamilton and his supporters able to win passage of the assumption bill.

The deal involved the location of the national capital. The Virginians wanted to create a new capital near them in the South. Hamilton and Jefferson met and agreed to exchange northern support for placing the capital in the South for Virginia's votes for the assumption bill. The bargain called for the construction of a new capital city on the banks of the Potomac River, which divided Maryland and Virginia, on land to be selected by George Washington. The government would move its operations by the beginning of the new century.

Hamilton's bank bill produced the most heated debates. Madison, Jef-

# ASSERTING NATIONAL SOVEREIGNTY

The Federalists consolidated their position—and attracted wide public support for the new national government—by acting effectively in two areas in which the old Confederation had been largely unsuccessful: the western territories and diplomacy.

### Securing the West

Despite the Northwest Ordinance, the old Congress had largely failed to tie the outlying western areas of the country firmly to the national government. Farmers in western Massachusetts had rebelled; settlers in Vermont, Kentucky, and Tennessee had flirted with seceding from the Union. At first, the new government under the Constitution faced similar problems.

In 1794, farmers in western Pennsylvania raised a major challenge to fed-

ferson, Randolph
provision for a na
poration), Congr
Hamilton's bill d
some apparent re
operations in 179

Hamilton als
farmers later forc
He failed to win |
but the tariff law

Once enacted
creditors, and oth
But others found
formed the majo
taxed excessively.
gram served the i
of this feeling an

The Constitutio
was not an oversi
ticular—believed
Disagreement wa
believed that sucl
mation of perma
Yet not many
before Madison :
lowers had becor
Federalists enact
ominously, Ham
tional network of
The Federalists |
porters and win a
associations—lar
local communitie
nents believed, th
century had done
Because the F
acing and tyranni

WASHINGTON IN COMMAND, 1794 When Pennsylvania farmers rose up in the Whiskey Rebellion in 1794, President Washington decided at once on a strong military response. This painting, credited to Frederick Kemmelmeyer, shows Washington reviewing troops in Cumberland, Maryland, as they prepare to march against the insurgents.

eral authority when they refused to pay the new whiskey excise tax and began terrorizing tax collectors in the region. But the federal government did not leave settlement of the so-called Whiskey Rebellion to the authorities of Pennsylvania as Congress had left Shays's Rebellion to the authorities of Massachusetts. At Hamilton's urging, Washington called out the militias of three states and assembled an army of nearly 15,000, a larger force than he had commanded against the British during most of the Revolution, and he personally accompanied the troops into Pennsylvania. At the approach of the militiamen, the rebellion quickly collapsed.

The federal government won the allegiance of the whiskey rebels through intimidation. It won the loyalties of other western people by accepting new states as members of the Union. The last two of the original thirteen colonies joined the Union once the Bill of Rights had been appended to the Constitution—North Carolina in 1789 and Rhode Island in 1790. Vermont became the fourteenth state in 1791 after New York and New Hampshire agreed to give up their claims to it. Next came Kentucky, in 1792, when Virginia gave up its claim to that region. After North Carolina ceded its western lands to the Union, Tennessee became a state in 1796.

The new government faced a greater challenge in more distant areas of the Northwest and the Southwest. The ordinances of 1784–1787, establishing the terms of white settlement in the West, had produced a series of border conflicts with Indian tribes that were resisting white settlement in their lands. The new government inherited these clashes, which continued with few interruptions for nearly a decade.

These clashes revealed another issue the Constitution had done little to resolve: the place of the Indian nations within the new federal structure. The Constitution made almost no mention of Native Americans. It gave Congress power to "regulate Commerce . . . with the Indian tribes." And it bound the new government to respect treaties negotiated by the Confederation, most of which had been with the tribes. But none of this did very much to clarify the precise legal standing of Indians or Indian nations within the United States. The tribes received no direct representation in the new government. Above all, the Constitution did not address the major issue that would govern relations between whites and Indians: land. Indian nations lived within the boundaries of the United States, yet they claimed (and the white government at times agreed) that they had some measure of sovereignty over their own land. But neither the Constitution nor common law offered any clear guide to the rights of a "nation within a nation" or to the precise nature of tribal sovereignty, which ultimately depended on control of land. Thus, the relationship between the tribes and the United States remained to be determined by a series of treaties, agreements, and judicial decisions in a process that has continued for more than two centuries.

### Maintaining Neutrality

Not until 1791 did Great Britain send a minister to the United States, and then only because Madison and the Republicans were threatening to place special trade restrictions on British ships. A new crisis in Anglo-American relations emerged in 1793 when the new French government established after the revolution of 1789 went to war with Great Britain. Both the president and Congress took steps to establish American neutrality in the conflict, but that neutrality was severely tested.

Early in 1794, the Royal Navy began seizing hundreds of American ships engaged in trade in the French West Indies, outraging public opinion in the United States. Anti-British sentiment rose still higher at the report that the governor general of Canada had delivered a warlike speech to the Indians on the northwestern frontier. Hamilton was deeply concerned. War would mean an end to imports from England, and most of the revenue for maintaining his financial system came from duties on those imports.

Hamilton and the Federalists did not trust the State Department, now in the hands of the ardently pro-French Edmund Randolph, to find a solution to the crisis. So they persuaded Washington to name a special commissioner to go to England and negotiate a solution: the staunch New York Federalist and chief justice of the Supreme Court, John Jay. Jay was instructed to secure compensation for the recent British assaults on American shipping, to demand withdrawal of British forces from their posts on the frontier of the United States, and to negotiate a commercial treaty with Britain compatible with America's 1778 treaty with France.

The long and complex treaty Jay negotiated in 1794 failed to achieve these goals. But it was not without merit. It settled the conflict with Britain, avoiding a likely war. It provided for undisputed American sovereignty over the entire Northwest. It produced a reasonably satisfactory commercial relationship with a nation whose trade was important to the United States. Nevertheless, when the terms became known in America, criticism was intense and Jay was burned in effigy in some places. Opponents of the treaty—who included almost all the Republicans and even many Federalists—went to great lengths to defeat it in the Senate, cheered on by agents of France. But in the end the Senate ratified what was by then known as Jay's Treaty.

Jay's Treaty paved the way for a settlement of important American disputes with Spain. Under Pinckney's Treaty (negotiated by Thomas Pinckney and signed in 1795), Spain recognized the right of Americans to navigate the Mississippi to its mouth and to deposit goods at New Orleans for reloading on oceangoing ships; agreed to fix the northern boundary of Florida where Americans always had insisted it should be, along the 31st parallel; and commanded its authorities to prevent the Indians in Florida from launching raids north across the border.

## THE DOWNFALL OF THE FEDERALISTS

Since almost everyone in the 1790s agreed that there was no place in a stable republic for organized parties, the emergence of the Republicans as a powerful and apparently permanent opposition seemed to the Federalists a grave threat to national stability. And so when major international perils confronted the government in the 1790s, the temptation to move forcefully against this "illegitimate" opposition was strong. Facing what they believed was a stark choice between respecting individual liberties and preserving stability, the Federalists chose stability. Largely as a result of that decision, the Federalists never won another national election after 1796.

### The Election of 1796

George Washington refused to run for a third term as president in 1796, thus removing the last obstacle to open expression of the partisan rivalries that had been building over the previous eight years. Jefferson was the obvious candidate of the Republicans for president that year, but the Federalists faced a more difficult choice. Hamilton had created too many enemies to be a credible candidate. Vice President John Adams, directly associated with none of the controversial Federalist achievements, received the party's nomination for president at a caucus of the Federalists in Congress.

The Federalists were still clearly the dominant party. But without Washington to mediate, they fell victim to fierce factional rivalries that almost led to their undoing. Hamilton and many other Federalists (especially in the South) were not reconciled to Adams's candidacy and supported Thomas Pinckney. Adams defeated Jefferson by only three electoral votes and assumed the presidency as head of a divided party facing a powerful opposition. Jefferson became vice president as a result of finishing second. (Not until the adoption of the Twelfth Amendment in 1804 did electors vote separately for president and vice president.)

*The Quasi War with France*

American relations with Great Britain and Spain improved as a result of Jay's and Pinckney's Treaties. But the nation's relations with revolutionary France quickly deteriorated. French vessels captured American ships on the high seas and at times imprisoned the crews. And when the South Carolina Federalist Charles Cotesworth Pinckney, brother of Thomas Pinckney, arrived in France, the government refused to receive him as the official representative of the United States.

In an effort to stabilize relations, Adams appointed a bipartisan commission to negotiate with France. When the Americans arrived in Paris in 1797, three agents of the French foreign minister, Prince Talleyrand, demanded a loan for France and a bribe for French officials before any negotiations could begin. Pinckney, now a member of the commission, responded succinctly and angrily: "No! No! Not a sixpence!"

When Adams heard of the incident, he sent a message to Congress denouncing the French insults and urging preparations for war. Before giving the commissioners' report to Congress, he deleted the names of the three French agents and designated them only as Messrs. X, Y, and Z. When the report was published, the "XYZ Affair," as it quickly became known, provoked widespread popular outrage at France's actions and strong popular support for the Federalists' response. For nearly two years, 1798 and 1799, the United States found itself engaged in an undeclared war with France.

Adams persuaded Congress to cut off all trade with France, to abrogate the treaties of 1778, and to authorize American vessels to capture French armed ships on the high seas. In 1798, Congress created the Department of the Navy and appropriated money for the construction of new warships. The navy soon won a number of duels and captured a total of eighty-five French ships, including armed merchantmen. The United States also began cooperating so closely with the British as to be virtually a cobelligerent in England's war with France. The British provided the American navy with ammunition, furnished officers to help with the training and direction of American crews, and offered signaling information so that British and American ships could communicate readily with one another.

The French, taking note of all this, tried to conciliate the United States. Adams sent another commission to Paris in 1800, and the new French government (headed now by "First Consul" Napoleon Bonaparte) agreed to a treaty with the United States that canceled the old agreements of 1778 and established new commercial arrangements. As a result, the "quasi war" came to a reasonably peaceful end, and the United States at last freed itself from the entanglements and embarrassments of its "perpetual" alliance with France.

*Repression and Protest*

The conflict with France helped the Federalists increase their majorities in Congress in 1798. Armed with this new strength, they began to consider ways to silence the Republican opposition. The result was some of the most controversial legislation in American history: the Alien and Sedition Acts.

The Alien Act placed new obstacles in the way of foreigners who wished to become American citizens, and it strengthened the president's hand in dealing with aliens. The Sedition Act allowed the government to prosecute those who engaged in "sedition" against the government. In theory, only libelous or treasonous activities were subject to prosecution; but since such activities were defined in widely varying terms, the law, in effect, gave the government authority to stifle virtually any opposition. The Republicans interpreted the new laws as part of a Federalist campaign to destroy them and fought back.

President Adams signed the new laws but was cautious in implementing them. He did not deport any aliens, and he prevented the government from launching a broad crusade against the Republicans. But the legislation did have a significant repressive effect. The Alien Act discouraged immigration and encouraged some foreigners already in the country to leave. And the administration used the Sedition Act to arrest and convict ten men, most of them Republican newspaper editors whose only crime had been criticism of the Federalists in government.

Republican leaders began to look for ways to reverse the Alien and Sedition Acts. The Supreme Court had not yet established its right to nullify congressional legislation, so Republicans looked to the state legislatures for help. They offered a theory to justify action by the states in two sets of resolutions in 1798–1799, one written (anonymously) by Jefferson and adopted by the Kentucky legislature and the other drafted by Madison and approved by the Virginia legislature. The Virginia and Kentucky Resolutions, as they were known, used the ideas of John Locke and the Tenth Amendment to the Constitution to argue that the federal government had been formed by a "compact" or contract among the states and possessed only certain delegated powers. Whenever a party to the contract, a state, decided that the central government had exceeded those powers, it had the right to "nullify" the appropriate laws.

The Republicans did not win wide support for the nullification idea; only Virginia and Kentucky declared the congressional statutes void. They did, however, succeed in elevating their dispute with the Federalists to the level of a national crisis. By the late 1790s, the entire nation was as deeply and bitterly politicized as at any time in its history. State legislatures at times re-

CONGRESSIONAL PUGILISTS, 1798 This savage cartoon was inspired
by the celebrated fight on the floor of the House of Representatives
between Matthew Lyon, a Republican representative from Vermont,
and Roger Griswold, a Federalist from Connecticut. Griswold (at
right) attacks Lyon with his cane, and Lyon retaliates with fire tongs.
Other members of Congress are portrayed enjoying the battle.

sembled battlegrounds. Even the United States Congress was plagued with
violent disagreements. In one celebrated incident in the chamber of the
House of Representatives, Matthew Lyon, a Republican from Vermont, responded to an insult from Roger Griswold, a Federalist from Connecticut,
by spitting in Griswold's eye. Griswold attacked Lyon with his cane, Lyon
fought back with a pair of fire tongs, and soon the two men were wrestling
on the floor.

### The "Revolution" of 1800

These bitter controversies shaped the presidential election of 1800. The
presidential candidates were the same as four years earlier: Adams for the
Federalists, Jefferson for the Republicans. But the campaign of 1800 was very
different from the one preceding it. Indeed, it was probably the ugliest in
American history. Adams and Jefferson themselves displayed reasonable dignity, but their supporters showed no such restraint. The Federalists accused

Jefferson of being a dangerous radical and his followers of being wild men who, if they should come to power, would bring on a reign of terror comparable to that of the French Revolution. The Republicans portrayed Adams as a tyrant conspiring to become king, and they accused the Federalists of plotting to subvert human liberty and impose slavery on the people. There was considerable personal invective as well. (It was during this campaign that the story of Jefferson's alleged romantic involvement with Sally Hemmings, a slave woman on his plantation, was first widely aired.) The election was close, and the crucial contest was in New York. There, Aaron Burr mobilized an organization of Revolutionary War veterans, the Tammany Society, to serve as a Republican political machine. And through Tammany's efforts, the party carried the city by a large majority, and with it the state. Jefferson was, apparently, elected.

But an unexpected complication soon jeopardized the Republican victory. The Constitution called for each elector to "vote by ballot for two persons." The normal practice was that an elector would cast one vote for his party's presidential candidate and another for the vice presidential candidate. To avoid a tie, the Republicans had intended that one elector would refrain from voting for the party's vice-presidential candidate, Aaron Burr. But the plan went awry. When the votes were counted, Jefferson and Burr each had 73. No candidate had a majority, and—in accordance with the Constitution—the House of Representatives had to choose between the two top candidates, Jefferson and Burr. Each state delegation would cast a single vote.

The new Congress, elected in 1800 with a Republican majority, was not to convene until after the inauguration of the president, so it was the Federalist Congress that had to decide the question. Some Federalists hoped to use the situation to salvage the election for their party; others wanted to strike a bargain with Burr and elect him. But after a long deadlock, several leading Federalists, most prominent among them Alexander Hamilton, concluded that Burr (whom many suspected of having engineered the deadlock in the first place) was too unreliable to trust with the presidency. On the thirty-sixth ballot, Jefferson was elected.

After the election of 1800, the only branch of the federal government left in Federalist hands was the judiciary. The Adams administration spent its last months in office taking steps to make the party's hold on the courts secure. By the Judiciary Act of 1801, passed by the lame duck Congress, the Federalists reduced the number of Supreme Court justiceships by one but greatly increased the number of federal judgeships as a whole. Adams quickly appointed Federalists to the newly created positions. Indeed, there were charges that he stayed up until midnight on his last day in office to finish signing the new judges' commissions. These officeholders became known as the "midnight appointments."

Even so, the Republicans viewed their victory as almost complete. The nation had, they believed, been saved from tyranny. A new era could now begin, one in which the true principles of America would once again govern the land. The exuberance with which the victors viewed the future—and the importance they ascribed to the defeat of the Federalists—was evident in the phrase Jefferson himself later used to describe his election. He called it the "Revolution of 1800." It remained to be seen how revolutionary it would really be.

# CHAPTER SEVEN

# The Jeffersonian Era

*The Rise of Cultural Nationalism* ∼ *Stirrings of Industrialism*
*Jefferson the President* ∼ *Doubling the National Domain*
*Expansion and War* ∼ *The War of 1812*

THOMAS JEFFERSON AND his followers assumed control of the national government in 1801 as the champions of a distinctive vision of America. They favored a society of sturdy, independent farmers, happily free from the workshops, the industrial towns, and the city mobs of Europe. They celebrated localism and republican simplicity. Above all, they proposed a federal government of sharply limited power, with most public authority remaining at the level of the states.

Almost nothing worked out as they had planned, for during their years in power the young republic was developing in ways that made much of their vision obsolete. The American economy in the period of Republican ascendancy became steadily more diversified and complex, making the ideal of a simple, agrarian society impossible to maintain. American cultural life was dominated by a vigorous and ambitious nationalism reminiscent of (and often encouraged by) the Federalists.

The Republicans did manage to translate some of their political ideals into reality. Jefferson dismantled much of the bureaucracy that the Federalists had erected in the 1790s and helped keep the central government small and relatively weak. Yet at the same time, he frequently encountered situations that required him to exercise strong national authority.

The Republicans did not always like these nationalizing and modernizing trends, and on occasion they resisted them. For the most part, however, they had the sense to recognize what could not be changed. In adjusting to the new realities, they themselves began to become agents of the very transformation of American life they had once resisted.

## TIME LINE

| 1793 | 1800 | 1801 | 1803 | 1804–1806 |
|------|------|------|------|-----------|
| Eli Whitney invents cotton gin | U.S. capital moves to Washington | Second Great Awakening begins<br><br>Marshall chief justice of Supreme Court | Louisiana Purchase<br><br>*Marbury* v. *Madison* | Lewis and Clark expedition |

| 1804 | 1807 | 1808 | 1809 | 1810 |
|------|------|------|------|------|
| Jefferson reelected | Embargo Act | Madison elected president | Non-Intercourse Act<br><br>Tecumseh Confederacy formed | Macon's Bill No. 2 |

| 1811 | 1812 | 1814 | 1815 |
|------|------|------|------|
| Battle of Tippecanoe | U.S. declares war on Great Britain<br><br>Madison reelected | Hartford Convention<br><br>Treaty of Ghent | Battle of New Orleans |

# THE RISE OF CULTURAL NATIONALISM

In many respects, American cultural life in the early nineteenth century reflected the Republican vision of the nation's future. Opportunities for education increased, the nation's literary and artistic life began to free itself from European influences, and American religion began to adjust to the spread of Enlightenment rationalism. In other respects, however, the new culture was posing a serious challenge to Republican ideals.

### *Educational and Literary Nationalism*

Central to the Republican vision of America was the concept of a virtuous and enlightened citizenry. An ignorant electorate could not be trusted to preserve democracy; education was essential. Republicans believed, therefore, in the creation of a nationwide system of public schools, in which all male citizens would receive free education.

Such hopes were not fulfilled. As late as 1815, no state had actually created an effective system of free schools (although several endorsed the idea). In 1789, Massachusetts reaffirmed the colonial laws by which each town was obliged to support a school, but there was little enforcement. In Virginia, the state legislature ignored Jefferson's call for universal elementary education and for advanced education for the gifted.

Instead, schooling became primarily the responsibility of private institutions, most of which were open only to those who could afford to pay for them. In the South and in the mid-Atlantic states, most schools were run by religious groups. In New England, private academies were often more secular, many of them modeled on those founded by the Phillips family at Andover, Massachusetts, in 1778, and at Exeter, New Hampshire, three years later. By 1815, there were thirty such private secondary schools in Massachusetts, thirty-seven in New York, and several dozen more scattered throughout the country. Many were frankly aristocratic in outlook, training their students to become members of the nation's elite. There were a few educational institutions open to the poor, but not nearly enough to accommodate everyone, and the education they offered was usually clearly inferior to that provided for more prosperous students.

Private secondary schools such as those in New England generally accepted only male students; even many public schools excluded females from the classroom. Yet the late eighteenth and early nineteenth centuries did see some important advances in education for women. As Americans began to place a higher value on the importance of the "republican mother" who would help train the new generation, they had to ask how mothers could raise their children to be enlightened if the mothers themselves were uneducated. Beginning as early as the 1770s and accelerating thereafter, such concerns helped speed the creation of female academies throughout the nation (usually for the daughters of affluent families). In 1789, Massachusetts required that its public schools serve females as well as males. Other states, although not all, soon followed.

Some women aspired to more. In 1784, Judith Sargent Murray published an essay defending the right of women to education, and defending it in terms very different from those used by most men. Men and women were equal in intellect and equal in potential, Murray argued. Women, therefore, should have precisely the same educational opportunities as men. What was more, they should have opportunities to earn their own livings and to establish a role for themselves in society apart from their husbands and families. Murray's ideas attracted relatively little support at the time from men or women.

Many early-nineteenth-century reformers believed in the power of education to reform and redeem "backward" people. As a result, they generated a growing interest in Indian education. Because Jefferson and his followers liked to think of Native Americans as "noble savages" (uncivilized but, unlike blacks, not necessarily innately inferior), they hoped that schooling the Indians in white culture would "uplift" the tribes. Although state and local governments did little to promote Indian education, missionaries and mission schools proliferated among the tribes. There were no comparable efforts to educate enslaved African Americans, largely because their owners preferred that they remain ignorant and thus presumably less likely to rebel.

Higher education similarly diverged from Republican ideals. The number of colleges and universities in America grew substantially, from nine at the time of the Revolution to twenty-two in 1800, and the number increased steadily thereafter. None of the new schools, however, was truly public. Even universities established by state legislatures (in Georgia, North Carolina, Vermont, Ohio, and South Carolina, for example) relied on private contributions and tuition fees to survive. Scarcely more than one white man in a thousand (and virtually no women, blacks, or Indians) had access to any college education, and those few who did attend universities were almost without exception members of prosperous, propertied families.

Now that they had won their political independence, many Americans—Federalists and Republicans alike—aspired to a form of cultural independence. They dreamed of an American literary and artistic life that would rival the greatest achievements of Europe. The 1772 "Poem on the Rising Glory of America" predicted that America was destined to become the "seat of empire" and the "final stage" of civilization, with "glorious works of high invention and of wond'rous art." The Connecticut schoolmaster and lawyer Noah Webster (author of widely used American spellers and dictionaries) echoed such sentiments, arguing that the American schoolboy should be educated as a nationalist. "As soon as he opens his lips," Webster wrote, "he should rehearse the history of his own country; he should lisp the praise of liberty, and of those illustrious heroes and statesmen who have wrought a revolution in her favor."

American writers had great difficulty getting their work published. Even so, a growing number of native authors began working to create a strong American literature. Among the most ambitious was the Philadelphia writer Charles Brockden Brown. But his fascination with horror and deviance kept him from developing a popular audience. More successful was Washington Irving of New York, whose popular folk tales, recounting the adventures of such American rustics as Ichabod Crane and Rip Van Winkle, made him the widely acknowledged leader of American literary life in the early eighteenth century.

*Religion and Revivalism*

The American Revolution had weakened traditional forms of religious practice by detaching established churches from government and by elevating ideas of individual liberty and reason that challenged many ecclesiastical traditions. By the 1790s, only a small proportion of white Americans (perhaps as few as 10 percent) were members of formal churches, and ministers were complaining often about the "decay of vital piety."

Religious traditionalists were particularly alarmed about the emergence of new, "rational" religious doctrines—theologies that reflected modern, scientific attitudes and sharply de-emphasized the role of God in the world. "Deism," which had originated among Enlightenment philosophers in France, attracted such educated Americans as Jefferson and Franklin and by 1800 was reaching a moderately broad popular audience. Deists accepted the existence of God, but they considered Him a remote being who, after having created the universe, had withdrawn from direct involvement with the human race and its sins. Religious skepticism also produced the philosophies of "universalism" and "unitarianism," which emerged at first as dissenting views within the New England Congregational Church. Disciples of these new ideas rejected the traditional Calvinist belief in predestination, arguing that salvation was available to all. They rejected, too, the idea of the Trinity. Jesus was only a great religious teacher, they claimed, not the son of God. So wide was the gulf between these dissenters and the Congregationalist establishment that a permanent schism finally occurred. The Universalist Church was founded as a separate denomination in Gloucester, Massachusetts, in 1779, and the Unitarian Church was established in Boston three years later.

Many Americans believed that the spread of rationalism foretold the end of traditional, evangelistic religion in the new nation. In reality, quite the contrary was true. Most Americans continued to hold strong religious beliefs; what had declined was their commitment to organized churches and denominations. Deism, Universalism, and Unitarianism appeared more powerful than they actually were, in part because those who clung to more traditional faiths were for a time confused and disorganized, unable to react effectively. Beginning in 1801, however, traditional religion staged a dramatic comeback in the form of a wave of revivalism known as the Second Great Awakening.

The origins of the Awakening lay in the efforts of conservative theologians of the 1790s to fight the spread of religious rationalism and in the efforts of church establishments to revitalize their organizations. Presbyterians expanded their efforts on the western fringes of white settlement, and conservatives became increasingly militant in response to dissenters. Methodism, founded in England by John Wesley, spread to America in the 1770s; authoritarian and hierarchical in structure, the Methodists sent itinerant preachers throughout the nation to win recruits for the new church, which soon became the fastest-growing denomination in America. Almost as successful were the Baptists, who were themselves relatively new to America; they found an especially fervent following in the South.

By 1800, the revivalist energies of all these denominations were combining to create the greatest surge of evangelical fervor since the first Great Awakening sixty years before. In only a few years, the revivalists mobilized a large proportion of the American people, and membership in those churches embracing revivalism—most prominently the Methodist, Baptist, and Presbyterian—was mushrooming. At Cane Ridge, Kentucky, in the summer of 1801, a group of evangelical ministers presided over the nation's first "camp meeting"—an extraordinary revival that lasted several days and impressed all who saw it with its size (some estimated that 25,000 people attended) and its fervor. Such events became common in subsequent years, as the Methodists in particular came to rely on them as a way to "harvest" new members.

The message of the Second Great Awakening was not entirely uniform, but its basic thrust was clear. Individuals must readmit God and Christ into their daily lives, must embrace a fervent, active piety, and must reject the skeptical rationalism that threatened traditional beliefs. Yet the wave of revivalism did not restore the religion of the past. Few denominations any longer accepted the idea of predestination, and the belief that a person could affect his or her own chances for salvation, rather than encouraging irreligion as many had feared, added intensity to the individual's search for salvation. The Awakening, in short, combined a more active piety with a belief in a God whose grace could be attained through faith and good works.

One of the striking features of the Awakening was the preponderance of women, particularly young women, within it. Female converts far outnumbered males. One reason for this was that women were more numerous in certain regions than men, who were more likely than women to strike out on their own and move west. Their marriage prospects thus diminished and their futures plagued with uncertainty, some women discovered in religion a foundation on which to build their lives. But even in areas where there was no shortage of men, women flocked to the revivals in enormous numbers, which suggests that they may have been responding in part to changing economic circumstances as well. The movement of industrial work out of the

THE CAMP MEETING Camp meetings became a popular feature of evangelical religion in America beginning around 1800. By the 1820s, there were about 1,000 such meetings a year, most of them in the South and the West. This lithograph, which dates from the 1830s, illustrates the central role of women in the religious revivals of the time.

home (where women had often contributed to the family economy through spinning and weaving) and into the factory—a process making rapid strides in the early nineteenth century—robbed women of one of their most important social roles. Religious enthusiasm may have compensated for the losses and adjustments these transitions produced; it also provided access to a new range of activities associated with the churches—charitable societies ministering to orphans and the poor, missionary organizations, and others—in which women came to play important roles.

Revivalism was not restricted to white society. In some areas of the country, revival meetings were open to people of all races. Many African Americans not only attended the events but embraced the new religious fervor. Out of these revivals emerged a group of black preachers who became important figures within the slave community. Some of them translated the apparently egalitarian religious message of the Awakening—that salvation was available to all—into a similarly egalitarian message for blacks in the present world. Out of black revival meetings in Virginia, for example, arose an elaborate plan in 1800 (devised by Gabriel Prosser, the brother of a black preacher) for a slave rebellion and attack on Richmond. The plan was discovered and foiled in advance by whites, but revivalism continued in subsequent years to create occasional racial unrest in the South.

The spirit of revivalism was particularly strong in these years among Native Americans, although its origins and the forms it took were very different from those in white or black society. The dislocations and military defeats Indians suffered in the aftermath of the American Revolution created a sense of crisis among many of the eastern tribes in particular; as a result, the 1790s and early 1800s became an era of Indian religious fervor and prophecy. Presbyterian and Baptist missionaries were active among the southern tribes and sparked a wave of conversions. But the most important revivalism came from the efforts of a great Indian prophet: Handsome Lake, a Seneca whose seemingly miraculous "rebirth" after years of alcoholism helped give him a special stature within his tribe. Handsome Lake, like the earlier Indian prophet Neolin, who had been active in the 1760s, called for a revival of traditional Indian ways. That meant repudiating the individualism of white society and restoring the communal quality of the Indian world. Handsome Lake's message spread through the scattered Iroquois communities that had survived the military and political setbacks of previous decades and inspired many Indians to give up whiskey, gambling, and other destructive customs derived from white society. But revivalism did not produce a restoration of traditional Iroquois culture. Handsome Lake encouraged Christian missionaries to become active within the tribes, and he urged Iroquois men to abandon their roles as hunters (partly because so much of their hunting land had been seized by whites) and become sedentary farmers instead. Iroquois women, who had traditionally done the farming, were to move into more domestic roles.

## STIRRINGS OF INDUSTRIALISM

It was not only culturally and religiously that the nation was developing in ways unforeseen by Jefferson and his followers. Economically, the United States was taking the first, tentative steps toward a transformation that would ultimately shatter forever the vision of a simple, agrarian republic.

### Technology and Transportation in America

While Americans were engaged in a revolution to win their independence, an even more important revolution was in progress in England: the emergence of modern industrialism. Power-driven machines were taking the place of hand-operated tools and were permitting manufacturing to become more rapid and extensive—with profound social and economic consequences. Not since the agrarian revolution thousands of years earlier, when humans had turned from hunting to farming for sustenance, had there been an economic change of a magnitude comparable to the industrial revolution. Centuries of traditions, of social patterns, of cultural and religious assumptions were challenged and often shattered.

Nothing even remotely comparable to the English industrial revolution occurred in America in the first two decades of the nineteenth century. Indeed, it was opposition to the kind of economic growth occurring in England that had helped the Republicans defeat the Federalists in 1800. Yet even while Jeffersonians warned of the dangers of rapid economic change, they were witnessing a series of technological advances that would ultimately help ensure that the United States too would be transformed.

Some of these technological advances were imported from England. Despite efforts by the British government to prevent the export of textile machinery or the emigration of skilled mechanics, a number of immigrants with advanced knowledge of English technology arrived in the United States eager to introduce the new machines to America. Samuel Slater, for example, used the knowledge he had acquired before leaving England to build a spinning mill in Pawtucket, Rhode Island, for the Quaker merchant Moses Brown in 1790. It was generally recognized as the first modern factory in America.

More important than imported technology was that of purely domestic origin. America in the early nineteenth century produced several notable inventors of its own. Among the most important was the Massachusetts born, Yale-educated Eli Whitney. In 1793, Whitney, who was working as a tutor on a Georgia plantation, invented a machine that performed the arduous task of removing the seeds from short-staple cotton quickly and efficiently. It was dubbed the cotton gin ("gin" being a derivative of "engine"). With the device a single operator could clean as much cotton in a few hours as a group of workers had once needed a whole day to do. The results were profound. Soon cotton growing spread throughout the South. (Previously it had been restricted largely to the coast and the Sea Islands, the only places where long-staple cotton—easily cleaned without the cotton gin—could be grown.) Within a decade, the total cotton crop increased eightfold. African-American slavery, which with the decline of tobacco production had seemed for a time to be a dwindling institution, expanded and firmly fixed itself upon the

SLATER'S MILL Samuel Slater served as an apprentice in England in the 1780s to Richard Arkwright, an inventor of machinery for the new cotton mills that were driving the English industrial revolution. In 1790 Slater, having immigrated to America, designed the first successful cotton-spinning mill in the United States at Pawtucket, Rhode Island. This drawing shows the Pawtucket bridge, falls, and mill as they appeared sometime between 1810 and 1819.

South. The large supply of domestically produced fiber also served as a strong incentive to entrepreneurs in New England and elsewhere to develop a native textile industry.

One of the prerequisites for industrialization is a transportation system that allows the efficient movement of raw materials to factories and of finished goods to markets. The United States had no such system in the early years of the republic, and thus it had no domestic market extensive enough to justify large-scale production. But projects were under way that would ultimately remove the transportation obstacle.

One such project was the development of the steamboat. Oliver Evans's high-pressure engine, lighter and more efficient than the earlier steam engine created by James Watt in England in the 1760s, made steam more feasible for powering river boats and, eventually, locomotives and mill machinery. The inventor Robert Fulton and the promoter Robert R. Livingston made further advances in steam-powered navigation. Their *Clermont*, equipped with paddle wheels and an English-built engine, sailed up the Hudson in the summer of 1807. In 1811, a partner of Livingston, Nicholas

J. Roosevelt (a remote ancestor of Theodore Roosevelt), introduced the steamboat to the West by sending the *New Orleans* from Pittsburgh down the Ohio and Mississippi. The next year, the vessel began a profitable career of service between New Orleans and Natchez.

Meanwhile, what was to become known as the "turnpike era" had begun. In 1792, a corporation constructed a toll road running the sixty miles from Philadelphia to Lancaster, with a hard-packed surface of crushed rock. This venture proved so successful that similar turnpikes (so named from the kind of tollgate frequently used) were laid out from other cities to neighboring towns. But similar highways would not be extended over the mountains until governments began to participate in the financing of the projects.

Despite all the changes and all the advances, America remained in the early nineteenth century an overwhelmingly rural and agrarian nation. Only 3 percent of the population lived in towns of more than 8,000 in 1800. Ten percent of the non-Indian population lived west of the Appalachian Mountains, far from what urban centers there were. Even the nation's largest cities could not begin to compare, either in size or in cultural sophistication, with such European capitals as London and Paris (although Philadelphia, with 70,000 residents, New York, with 60,000, and others were becoming centers of commerce, learning, and urban culture comparable to many of the secondary cities of Europe).

It was still possible in the early nineteenth century to believe that this small, half-formed nation might not become a complex modern society. But the forces already at work would, in time, lastingly transform the United States. And Thomas Jefferson, for all his commitment to the agrarian ideal, found himself, as president, obliged to confront and accommodate them.

## JEFFERSON THE PRESIDENT

Privately, Thomas Jefferson may well have considered his victory over John Adams in 1800 to be what he later termed it: a revolution "as real . . . as that of 1776." Publicly, however, he was restrained and conciliatory, attempting to minimize the differences between the two parties and calm the passions that the bitter campaign had aroused. There was no complete repudiation of Federalist policies, no true "revolution." Indeed, at times Jefferson seemed to outdo the Federalists at their own work—most notably in overseeing a remarkable expansion of the territory of the United States.

In some respects, however, the Jefferson presidency did indeed represent a fundamental change in the direction of the federal government. The new administration oversaw a drastic reduction in the powers of some national institutions, and it forestalled the development of new powers in areas where the Federalists would certainly have attempted to expand them.

## *The Federal City and the "People's President"*

The relative unimportance of the federal government during the era of Jefferson was symbolized by the character of the newly founded national capital, the city of Washington. John Adams had moved to the new seat of government during the last year of his administration. And there were many at that time who envisioned that the raw, uncompleted town would soon emerge as a great and majestic city, a focus for the growing nationalism that the Federalists were promoting. The French architect Pierre L'Enfant had designed the capital on a grand scale, with broad avenues radiating from the uncompleted Capitol building. Many Americans believed Washington would become the Paris of the United States.

In reality, throughout Jefferson's presidency—indeed, throughout most of the nineteenth century—Washington remained little more than a straggling, provincial village. Although the population increased steadily from the 3,200 counted in the 1800 census, it never rivaled that of New York, Philadelphia, or the other major cities of the nation. The city remained a raw, inhospitable community, with few public buildings of any consequence. Members of Congress viewed Washington not as a home but as a place to visit briefly during sessions of the legislature and leave as quickly as possible. Few owned houses there. Most lived in a cluster of simple boardinghouses in the vicinity of the Capitol. It was not unusual for a member of Congress to resign his seat in the midst of a session to return home if he had an opportunity to accept the more prestigious post of member of his state legislature.

As president, Jefferson acted in a spirit of democratic simplicity appropriate to the frontierlike character of the unfinished federal city. He was a wealthy and aristocratic planter by background, but he conveyed to the public an image of plain, almost crude disdain for pretension. He walked like an ordinary citizen to and from his inauguration at the Capitol, instead of riding in a coach at the head of a procession. In the presidential mansion, which had not yet acquired the name White House, he disregarded the courtly etiquette of his predecessors. He did not always bother to dress up, prompting the British ambassador to complain on one occasion of being received by the president in clothes that were "indicative of utter slovenliness and indifference to appearances."

Yet Jefferson managed nevertheless to impress most of those who knew

THOMAS JEFFERSON This 1805 portrait by the noted
American painter Rembrandt Peale shows Jefferson at
the beginning of his second term as president. It also
conveys (through the simplicity of dress and the
slightly unkempt hair) the image of democratic
simplicity that Jefferson liked to project as the
champion of the "common man."

him. He was a brilliant conversationalist, a gifted writer, and one of the nation's most intelligent and creative men, with a wider range of interests and
accomplishments than any major public figure in American history with the
possible exception of Benjamin Franklin. In addition to politics and diplomacy, he was an active architect, educator, inventor, scientific farmer, and
philosopher-scientist.

Jefferson was, above all, a shrewd and practical politician. He went to
great lengths to eliminate the aura of majesty surrounding the presidency
that he believed his predecessors had created. But he also worked hard to
exert influence as the leader of his party, giving direction to Republicans in
Congress by quiet and sometimes even devious means. Although the Republicans had objected strenuously to the efforts of their Federalist prede-

cessors to build a network of influence through patronage, Jefferson used his powers of appointment as an effective political weapon. Like Washington before him, he believed that federal offices should be filled with men loyal to the principles and policies of the administration. By the end of his second term practically all federal jobs were held by loyal Republicans. Jefferson was a popular president during his first term and had little difficulty winning reelection against the Federalist Charles C. Pinckney. The Republican ticket carried even the New England states (except Connecticut), and Jefferson won by the overwhelming electoral majority of 162 to 14. Republican membership of both houses of Congress increased.

## Dollars and Ships

Under Washington and Adams, the Republicans believed, the government had been needlessly extravagant. Yearly federal expenditures had nearly tripled between 1793 and 1800. The public debt had also risen, as Hamilton had intended. And an extensive system of internal taxation, including the hated whiskey excise tax, had been erected.

The Jefferson administration moved deliberately to reverse these trends. In 1802, the president persuaded Congress to abolish all internal taxes, leaving customs duties and the sale of western lands as the only sources of revenue for the government. Meanwhile, Secretary of the Treasury Albert Gallatin drastically reduced government spending, cutting the already small staffs of the executive departments to minuscule levels. Although Jefferson was unable entirely to retire the national debt as he had hoped, he did cut it almost in half (from $83 million to $45 million).

Jefferson also scaled down the armed forces. He reduced the already tiny army of 4,000 men to 2,500. He pared down the navy from twenty-five ships in commission to seven, cutting the number of officers and sailors accordingly. Anything but the smallest of standing armies, he argued, might menace civil liberties and civilian control of government. And a large navy, he feared, might be misused to promote overseas commerce, which Jefferson believed should remain secondary to agriculture. Yet Jefferson was not a pacifist. At the same time that he was reducing the size of the army and navy, he helped establish the United States Military Academy at West Point, founded in 1802. And when trouble started brewing overseas, he began again to build up the fleet. Such trouble appeared first in the Mediterranean, off the coast of northern Africa. For years the Barbary states of North Africa—Morocco, Algiers, Tunis, and Tripoli—had been demanding protection money, paid to avoid piracy, from all nations whose ships sailed the Mediterranean. Even Great Britain gave regular contributions to the pirates. During the 1780s and

1790s the United States too had agreed to treaties providing for annual tribute to the Barbary states, but Jefferson showed reluctance to continue this policy of appeasement.

In 1801, the pasha of Tripoli forced Jefferson's hand. Unhappy with American responses to his demands, he ordered the flagpole of the American consulate chopped down—a symbolic declaration of war. Jefferson responded cautiously and built up American naval forces in the area over the next several years. Finally, in 1805, he agreed to terms by which the United States ended the payment of tribute to Tripoli but paid a substantial (and humiliating) ransom for the release of American prisoners.

### Conflict with the Courts

Having won control of the executive and legislative branches of government, the Republicans looked with suspicion on the judiciary, which remained largely in the hands of Federalist judges. Soon after Jefferson's first inauguration, his followers in Congress launched an attack on this last preserve of the opposition. Their first step was the repeal of the Judiciary Act of 1801, thus eliminating the judgeships to which Adams had made his "midnight appointments."

The debate over the courts led to one of the most important judicial decisions in the history of the nation. Federalists had long maintained that the Supreme Court had the authority to nullify acts of Congress (although the Constitution said nothing specifically to support the claim), and the Court itself had actually exercised the power of judicial review in 1796 when it upheld the validity of a law passed by Congress. But the Court's authority in this area would not be secure, it was clear, until it actually declared a congressional act unconstitutional. In 1803, in the case of *Marbury* v. *Madison*, it did so. William Marbury, one of Adams's "midnight appointments," had been named a justice of the peace in the District of Columbia. But his commission, although signed and sealed, had not been delivered to him before Adams left office. When Jefferson took office, his secretary of state, James Madison, refused to hand over the commission. Marbury asked the Supreme Court to direct Madison to perform his official duty. But the Court ruled that while Marbury had a right to his commission, the Court had no authority to order Madison to deliver it. On the surface, therefore, the decision was a victory for the administration. But of much greater importance than the relatively insignificant matter of Marbury's commission was the Court's reasoning in the decision.

The original Judiciary Act of 1789 had given the Court the power to compel executive officials to act in such matters as the delivery of commissions, and it was on that basis that Marbury had filed his suit. But the Court ruled that Congress had exceeded its authority, that the Constitution defined the powers of the judiciary, and that the legislature had no right to expand them. The relevant section of the 1789 act was, therefore, void. In seeming to deny its own authority, the Court was in fact radically enlarging it. The justices had repudiated a relatively minor power (the power to force the delivery of a commission) by asserting a vastly greater one (the power to nullify an act of Congress).

The chief justice of the United States at the time of the ruling (and until 1835) was John Marshall, one of the towering figures in the history of American law. A leading Federalist and prominent Virginia lawyer, he had served John Adams as secretary of state. (It was Marshall, ironically, who had neglected to deliver Marbury's commission in the closing hours of the administration.) In 1801, just before leaving office, Adams had appointed him chief justice, and almost immediately Marshall established himself as the dominant figure on the Court, shaping virtually all its most important rulings—including, of course, *Marbury* v. *Madison*. Through a succession of Republican presidents, he battled to give the federal government unity and strength. And in so doing, he established the judiciary as a coequal branch of government with the executive and the legislature—a position that the founders of the republic had never clearly indicated it should occupy.

## DOUBLING THE NATIONAL DOMAIN

In the same year Jefferson was elected president of the United States, Napoleon Bonaparte made himself ruler of France with the title of first consul. In the year Jefferson was reelected, Napoleon named himself emperor. The two men had little in common. Yet for a time they were of great assistance to each other in international politics—until Napoleon's ambitions moved from Europe to America and created conflict and estrangement.

### *Jefferson and Napoleon*

Having failed in a grandiose plan to seize India from the British Empire, Napoleon began to dream of restoring French power in the New World. The territory east of the Mississippi, which France had ceded to Great Britain in 1763, was now part of the United States and lost forever. But Napoleon hoped to regain the lands west of the Mississippi, which belonged to Spain. In 1800, under the secret Treaty of San Ildefonso, France regained title to Louisiana, which included almost the whole of the Mississippi Valley to the west of the river, plus New Orleans near the river's mouth. The Louisiana Territory would, Napoleon hoped, become the heart of a great French Empire in America.

Jefferson was unaware at first of Napoleon's imperial ambitions in America, and for a time he pursued a foreign policy that reflected his well-known admiration for France. But he began to reassess American relations with the French when he heard rumors of the secret transfer of Louisiana. Particularly troubling to Jefferson was French control of New Orleans, the outlet through which the produce of the fast-growing western regions of the United States was shipped to the markets of the world. If France should actually take and hold New Orleans, Jefferson said, then "we must marry ourselves to the British fleet and nation."

Jefferson was even more alarmed when, in the fall of 1802, he learned that the Spanish intendant at New Orleans (who still governed the city, since the French had not yet taken formal possession of the region) had announced a disturbing new regulation. American ships sailing the Mississippi River had for many years been accustomed to depositing their cargoes in New Orleans for transfer to oceangoing vessels. The intendant now forbade the practice, even though Spain had guaranteed Americans that right in the Pinckney Treaty of 1795; the prohibition effectively closed the lower Mississippi to American shippers.

Westerners demanded that the federal government do something to reopen the river, and the president faced a dilemma. If he yielded to the frontier clamor and tried to change the policy by force, he would run the risk of a major war with France. If he ignored the westerners' demands, he might lose political support. But Jefferson saw another solution. He instructed Robert Livingston, the American ambassador in Paris, to negotiate for the purchase of New Orleans. Livingston on his own authority proposed that the French sell the United States the rest of Louisiana as well.

In the meantime, Jefferson persuaded Congress to appropriate funds for an expansion of the army and the construction of a river fleet, and he hinted that American forces might soon descend on New Orleans and that the United States might form an alliance with Great Britain if the problems with France were not resolved. Perhaps in response, Napoleon suddenly decided to offer the United States the entire Louisiana Territory.

Napoleon had good reasons for the decision. His plans for an empire in America had already gone seriously awry, partly because a yellow fever epidemic had wiped out much of the French army in the New World and partly because the expeditionary force he wished to send to reinforce the troops and take possession of Louisiana had been icebound in a Dutch harbor through the winter of 1802–1803. By the time the harbor thawed in the spring of 1803, Napoleon was preparing for a renewed war in Europe. He would not, he realized, have the resources to secure an empire in America.

### The Louisiana Purchase

Faced with Napoleon's sudden proposal, Livingston and James Monroe, whom Jefferson had sent to Paris to assist in the negotiations, had to decide whether they should accept it even if they had no authorization from their government to do so. But fearful that Napoleon might withdraw the offer, they decided to proceed without further instructions from home. After some haggling over the price, Livingston and Monroe signed an agreement with Napoleon on April 30, 1803.

By the terms of the treaty, the United States was to pay a total of 80 million francs ($15 million) to the French government. The United States was also to grant certain exclusive commercial privileges to France in the port of New Orleans and was to incorporate the residents of Louisiana into the Union with the same rights and privileges as other citizens. The boundaries of the purchase were not clearly defined; the treaty simply specified that Louisiana would consist of the same territory France and Spain had claimed.

In Washington, the president was both pleased and embarrassed when he received the treaty. He was pleased with the terms of the bargain; but because he believed the Constitution should be strictly observed, he was uncertain about his authority to accept it, since the Constitution said nothing about the acquisition of new territory. But Jefferson's advisers persuaded him that his treaty-making power under the Constitution would justify the purchase of Louisiana, and Congress promptly approved the treaty and appropriated money to implement it. Finally, late in 1803, General James Wilkinson, commissioner of the United States and the commander of a small occupation force, took formal control of the territory on behalf of the United States. In New Orleans, beneath a bright December sun, the French tricolor was lowered and the American flag raised.

Before long, the Louisiana Territory was organized on the general pattern of the Northwest Territory, with the assumption that it would be divided eventually into states. The first of these was admitted to the Union as the state of Louisiana in 1812.

### Exploring the West

Meanwhile, a series of explorations was revealing the geography of the far-flung new territory to white Americans. In 1803, even before Napoleon's

## A M E R I C A N   V O I C E S

LEWIS AND CLARK

# Exploring the Louisiana Territory, 1804–1806

NOV. 7, 1805. A cloudy foggey morning. Some rain. We set out early, proceeded under the stard. [starboard] side under high ruged hills with steep assent, the shore boalt and rockey, the fog so thick we could not see across the river. Two canos of Indians met and returned with us to their village which is situated on the stard. side behind a cluster of marshey islands, on a narrow chanl. of the river through which we passed to the village of 4 houses. They gave us to eat some fish, and sold us fish, *wap pa to* roots, three dogs and 2 otters skins for which we gave fish hooks principally, of which they were verry fond. . . .

After delaying at this village one hour and a half we set out piloted by an Indian dressed in a salors dress, to the main chanel of the river. . . . A large marshey island near the middle of the river near which several canoes came allong side with skins, roots, fish &c. to sell, and had a temporey residence on this island. . . .

Great joy in camp. We are in view of the ocian (in the morning when the fog cleared off just below the last village, first on leaving this village, of Warkiacum) this great Pacific Ocean which we been so long anxious to see, and the roreing or noise made by the waves brakeing on the rockey shores (as I suppose) may be heard distinctly.

SOURCE: From *Original Journals of the Lewis and Clark Expedition.*

offer to sell Louisiana, Jefferson helped plan an expedition that was to cross the continent to the Pacific Ocean, gather geographical facts, and investigate prospects for trade with the Indians. He named as its leader his private secretary and Virginia neighbor, the thirty-two-year-old Meriwether Lewis, a veteran of Indian wars who was skilled in the ways of the wilderness. Lewis chose as a colleague the twenty-eight-year-old William Clark, who—like George Rogers Clark, his older brother—was an experienced frontiersman and Indian fighter. In the spring of 1804, Lewis and Clark, with a company of four dozen men, started up the Missouri River from St. Louis. With the Shoshone woman Sacajawea as their interpreter, they eventually crossed the Rocky Mountains, descended along the Snake and Columbia Rivers, and in

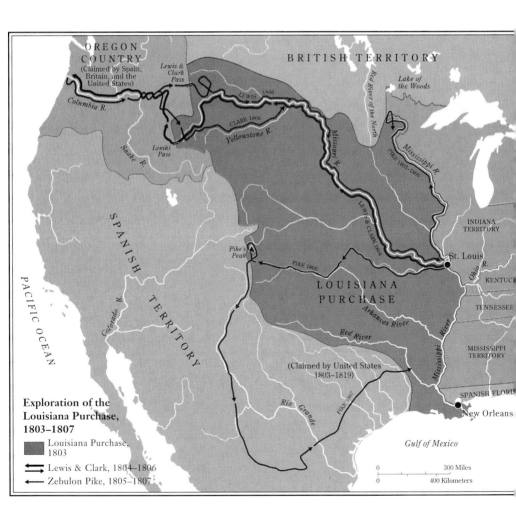

the late autumn of 1805 camped on the Pacific coast. In September 1806, they were back in St. Louis with elaborate records of the geography and the Indian civilizations they had observed along the way.

While Lewis and Clark were on their journey, Jefferson dispatched other explorers to other parts of the Louisiana Territory. Lieutenant Zebulon Montgomery Pike, twenty-six years old, led an expedition in the fall of 1805 from St. Louis into the upper Mississippi Valley. In the summer of 1806, he set out again, proceeding up the valley of the Arkansas River and into what later became Colorado, where he encountered, but failed in his attempt to climb, the peak that now bears his name. His account of his western travels helped create an enduring (and inaccurate) impression among most Americans that the land between the Missouri and the Rockies was a desert that farmers could never cultivate and that would be left forever to the nomadic Indian tribes.

### The Burr Conspiracy

Jefferson's triumphant reelection in 1804 suggested that most of the nation approved the new acquisition. But some New England Federalists raged against it. They realized that the more the West grew and the more new states joined the Union, the less power the Federalists and their region would retain. In Massachusetts, a group of the most extreme Federalists, known as the Essex Junto, concluded that the only recourse for New England was to secede from the Union and form a separate "northern confederacy." If a northern confederacy was to have any hope for lasting success as a separate nation, the Federalists believed, it would have to include New York and New Jersey as well as New England. But the leading Federalist in New York, Alexander Hamilton, refused to support the secessionist scheme.

Federalists in New York then turned to Hamilton's greatest political rival: Vice President Aaron Burr, a politician without prospects in his own party, because Jefferson had never forgiven him for the 1800 election deadlock. Burr accepted a Federalist proposal that he become their candidate for governor of New York in 1804, and there were rumors (unsupported by any evidence) that he had also agreed to support the Federalist plans for secession. Hamilton accused Burr of plotting treason and made numerous private remarks, widely reported in the press, about Burr's "despicable" character. When Burr lost the election, he blamed his defeat on Hamilton's malevolence and challenged him to a duel. Hamilton feared that refusing Burr's challenge would brand him a coward. And so, on a July morning in

1804, the two men met at Weehawken, New Jersey. Hamilton was mortally wounded; he died the next day.

The resourceful and charismatic Burr was now a political outcast, who had to flee New York to avoid an indictment for murder. He found new outlets for his ambitions in the West. Even before the duel, he had begun corresponding with prominent white settlers in the Southwest, especially with General James Wilkinson, now governor of the Louisiana Territory. Burr and Wilkinson, it seems clear, hoped to lead an expedition that would capture Mexico from the Spanish. But there were also rumors that they wanted to separate the Southwest from the Union and create a western empire that Burr would rule. There is little evidence that these rumors were true.

Whether true or not, many of Burr's opponents chose to believe the rumors—including, ultimately, Jefferson himself. When Burr led a group of armed followers down the Ohio River by boat in 1806, disturbing reports flowed into Washington (the most alarming from Wilkinson, who had suddenly turned against Burr and who now informed the president that treason was afoot) that an attack on New Orleans was imminent. Jefferson ordered the arrest of Burr and his men as traitors. Burr was brought to Richmond for trial. Jefferson carefully managed the government's case from Washington. But Chief Justice Marshall, presiding over the case on circuit duty, limited the evidence the government could present and defined the charge in such a way that the jury had little choice but to acquit Burr.

The Burr conspiracy was in part the story of a single man's soaring ambitions and flamboyant personality. But it was also a symbol of the larger perils still facing the new nation. With a central government that remained deliberately weak, with vast tracts of land only nominally controlled by the United States, with ambitious political leaders willing, if necessary, to circumvent normal channels in their search for power, the legitimacy of the federal government—and indeed the existence of the United States as a stable and united nation—remained to be fully established.

## EXPANSION AND WAR

Two very different conflicts were taking shape in the last years of Jefferson's presidency that would, together, draw the United States into a difficult and frustrating war. One was the continuing tension in Europe, which in 1803 escalated once again into a full-scale conflict (the Napoleonic Wars). As fighting between the British and the French increased, each side took steps to prevent the United States from trading with (and thus assisting) the other.

The other conflict occurred in North America itself, a result of the cease-less westward expansion of white settlement, which was now stretching to the Mississippi River and beyond, colliding again with a native population committed to protecting its lands from intruders. In both the North and the South, the threatened tribes mobilized to resist white encroachments. They began as well to forge connections with British forces in Canada and Span-ish forces in Florida. The Indian conflict on land, therefore, became inter-twined with the European conflict on the seas, and ultimately helped cause the War of 1812, an unpopular conflict with ambiguous results.

### Conflict on the Seas

Politicians at the time and historians since have argued over whether the con-flict in the West or the conflict on the seas was the real cause of the War of 1812. In fact, the war was a result of both.

In 1805, at the Battle of Trafalgar, a British fleet virtually destroyed what was left of the French navy. Because France could no longer challenge the British at sea, Napoleon now chose to pressure England in other ways. The result was what he called the Continental System, designed to close the Eu-ropean continent to British trade. Napoleon issued a series of decrees (one in Berlin in 1806 and another in Milan in 1807) barring British ships and neutral ships touching at British ports from landing their cargoes at any Eu-ropean port controlled by France or its allies. The British government replied to Napoleon's decrees by establishing—through a series of "orders in council"—a blockade of the European coast. The blockade required that any goods being shipped to Napoleon's Europe be carried either in British vessels or in neutral vessels stopping at British ports—precisely what Napoleon's policies forbade.

In the early nineteenth century, the United States had developed one of the most important merchant marines in the world, one that soon controlled a large proportion of the trade between Europe and the West Indies. But the events in Europe now challenged that control, because American ships were caught between Napoleon's Berlin and Milan decrees and Britain's orders in council. If they sailed directly for the European continent, they risked being captured by the British navy. If they sailed by way of a British port, they ran the risk of seizure by the French. Both of the warring powers were violating America's rights as a neutral nation. But most Americans considered the British, with their greater sea power, the worse offender—especially since British vessels frequently stopped American ships on the high seas and seized sailors off the decks, making them victims of "impressment."

*Impressment*

British sailors called their navy—with its floggings, its low pay, and its terrible shipboard conditions—a "floating hell." Few volunteered. Most had had to be "impressed" (forced) into the service. At every opportunity they deserted. By 1807, many of these deserters had emigrated to the United States and joined the American merchant marine or the American navy. To check this loss of manpower, the British claimed the right to stop and search American merchantmen (although not naval vessels) and reimpress deserters. They did not claim the right to take native-born Americans, but they did insist on the right to seize naturalized Americans born on British soil. In practice, the British navy often made no careful distinctions, impressing British deserters and native-born Americans alike into their service.

In the summer of 1807, the British went to more provocative extremes in an incident involving a vessel of the American navy. Sailing from Norfolk, with several alleged deserters from the British navy among the crew, the American naval frigate *Chesapeake* was hailed by the British ship *Leopard*. When the American commander, James Barron, refused to allow the British to search the *Chesapeake*, the *Leopard* opened fire. Barron had no choice but to surrender, and a boarding party from the *Leopard* dragged four men off the American frigate.

When news of the *Chesapeake-Leopard* incident reached the United States, there was a great popular clamor for revenge. But Jefferson and Madison tried to maintain the peace. Jefferson expelled all British warships from American waters to lessen the likelihood of future incidents. Then he sent instructions to his minister in England, James Monroe, to demand from the British government an end to impressment. The British government disavowed the actions of the *Leopard*'s commanding officer and recalled him; it offered compensation for those killed and wounded in the incident; and it promised to return three of the captured sailors (one of the original four had been hanged). But the British cabinet refused to renounce impressment and instead reasserted its right to recover deserting seamen.

*"Peaceable Coercion"*

In an effort to prevent future incidents that might bring the nation again to the brink of war, Jefferson persuaded Congress to pass a drastic measure late in 1807. It was known as the Embargo, and it prohibited American ships from leaving the United States for any foreign port anywhere in the world. (If it had specified only British and French ports, Jefferson reasoned, it could have been evaded with false clearance papers.)

The law was widely evaded, but it was effective enough to create a serious depression throughout most of the nation. Hardest hit were the merchants and shipowners of the Northeast, most of them Federalists. Their once-lucrative shipping business came to a virtual standstill. They became convinced that Jefferson had acted unconstitutionally.

The presidential election of 1808 came in the midst of this Embargo-induced depression. James Madison, Jefferson's secretary of state and political ally, was elected president, but the Federalist candidate, Charles Pinckney again, ran much more strongly than he had in 1804. The Federalists gained seats in Congress, although the Republicans still controlled both houses. The Embargo was clearly a growing political liability, and Jefferson decided to back down. A few days before leaving office, he approved a bill ending his experiment with what he called "peaceable coercion."

To replace the Embargo, Congress passed the Non-Intercourse Act just before Madison took office. It reopened trade with all nations but Great Britain and France. A year later, in 1810, the Non-Intercourse Act expired and was replaced by Macon's Bill No. 2, which reopened free commercial relations with Britain and France but authorized the president to prohibit commerce with either belligerent if it should continue violating neutral shipping after the other had stopped. Napoleon, in an effort to induce the United States to reimpose the Embargo against Britain, announced that France would no longer interfere with American shipping. Madison announced that an embargo against Great Britain alone would automatically go into effect early in 1811 unless Britain renounced its restrictions on American shipping.

In time, this new, limited embargo persuaded England to repeal its blockade of Europe. But the repeal came too late to prevent war. In any case, naval policies were only part of the reason for tensions between Britain and the United States.

### The "Indian Problem" and the British

Given the ruthlessness with which white settlers in North America had dislodged Indian tribes to make room for expanding settlement, it was hardly surprising that ever since the Revolution most Indians had continued to look to England—which had historically attempted to limit western expansion—for protection. The British in Canada, for their part, had relied on the Indians as partners in the lucrative fur trade and as potential military allies. There had been relative peace in the Northwest for over a decade after Jay's Treaty and Anthony Wayne's victory over the tribes at Fallen Timbers in 1794. But the 1807 war crisis following the *Chesapeake-Leopard* incident revived the conflict between Indians and white settlers. Two important (and very different) men emerged to lead it: William Henry Harrison and Tecumseh.

The Virginia-born Harrison, already a veteran Indian fighter at age twenty-six, went to Washington as the congressional delegate from the Northwest Territory in 1799. He was a committed advocate of growth and development in the western lands, and he was largely responsible for the passage in 1800 of the so-called Harrison Land Law, which enabled white settlers to acquire farms from the public domain on much easier terms than before.

In 1801, Jefferson appointed Harrison governor of Indiana Territory to administer the president's proposed solution to the "Indian problem." Jefferson offered the Indians a choice: they could convert themselves into settled farmers and become a part of white society, or they could migrate west of the Mississippi. In either case, they would have to give up their claims to their tribal lands in the Northwest.

Jefferson considered the assimilation policy a benign alternative to the continuing conflict between Indians and white settlers, a conflict he assumed the tribes were destined to lose. But to the tribes, the new policy seemed far from benign, especially given the bludgeonlike efficiency with which Harrison set out to implement it. He played off one tribe against another and used threats, bribes, trickery, and whatever other tactics he felt would help him. By 1807, the United States had extracted from reluctant tribal leaders treaty rights to eastern Michigan, southern Indiana, and most of Illinois.

Meanwhile, in the Southwest, white Americans were taking millions of acres from other tribes in Georgia, Tennessee, and Mississippi. The Indians wanted desperately to resist, but the separate tribes were helpless by themselves against the power of the United States. They might have accepted their fate passively but for the emergence of two new factors.

One factor was the policy of British authorities in Canada. After the *Chesapeake* incident and the surge of anti-British feeling throughout the United States, the British colonial authorities began to expect an American invasion of Canada and took desperate measures for their own defense. Among those measures were efforts to renew friendship with the Indians and provide them with increased supplies.

*Tecumseh and the Prophet*

The second, and more important, factor intensifying the border conflict was the rise of two remarkable native leaders. One was Tenskwatawa, a charismatic religious leader and orator known as "the Prophet." He had experienced a mystical awakening in the process of recovering from alcoholism. Having freed himself from what he considered the evil effects of white culture, he began to speak to his people of the superior virtues of Indian civilization and the sinfulness and corruption of the white world. In the process, he inspired a religious revival that spread through numerous tribes and helped unite them. The Prophet's headquarters at the meeting of Tippecanoe Creek and the Wabash River (known as Prophetstown) became a sacred place for people of many tribes and attracted thousands of Indians from throughout the Midwest. Out of their common religious experiences, they began to consider joint political and military efforts as well.

The Prophet's brother Tecumseh—"the Shooting Star," chief of the Shawnees—emerged as the leader of these more secular efforts. Tecumseh understood, as few other Indian leaders had, that only through united action could the tribes hope to resist the steady advance of white civilization. Beginning in 1809, he set out to unite all the tribes of the Mississippi Valley, north and south. Together, he promised, they would halt white expansion, recover the whole Northwest, and make the Ohio River the boundary between the United States and Indian country. He maintained that Harrison and others, by negotiating treaties with individual tribes, had obtained no real title to land. The land belonged to all the tribes; none of them could rightfully cede any of it without the consent of the others. In 1811, Tecumseh left Prophetstown and traveled down the Mississippi to visit the tribes of the South and persuade them to join the alliance.

During Tecumseh's absence, Governor Harrison saw a chance to destroy the growing influence of the two Indian leaders. With 1,000 soldiers he camped near Prophetstown, and on November 7, 1811, he provoked an armed conflict. Although the white forces suffered losses as heavy as those of the natives, Harrison drove off the Indians and burned the town. The Battle of Tippecanoe (named for the creek near which it was fought) disillusioned many of the Prophet's followers, who had believed that his magic would protect them; and Tecumseh returned to find the confederacy in disarray. But there were still warriors eager for combat, and by spring of 1812 they were active along the frontier, from Michigan to Mississippi, raiding white settlements and terrifying settlers.

The bloodshed along the western borders was largely a result of the Indians' own initiative, but Britain's agents in Canada had encouraged and helped to supply the uprising. To Harrison and most white residents of the regions, there seemed only one way to make the West safe for Americans. That was to drive the British out of Canada and annex that province to the United States—a goal that many westerners had long cherished for other reasons as well.

### The Lure of Florida

While white "frontiersmen" in the North demanded the conquest of Canada, those in the South looked to the acquisition of Spanish Florida (a territory that included the present state of Florida and the southern areas of what are now Alabama, Mississippi, and Louisiana). The territory was a continuing threat to whites in the southern United States. Slaves escaped across the Florida border; Indians in Florida launched frequent raids north into white settlements along the border. But white southerners also coveted Florida because through it ran rivers that could provide residents of the Southwest with access to valuable ports on the Gulf of Mexico.

In 1810, American settlers in West Florida (the area presently part of Mississippi and Louisiana) seized the Spanish fort at Baton Rouge and asked the federal government to annex the territory to the United States. President Madison happily agreed and then began maneuvering to get the rest of Florida too. The desire for Florida became yet another motivation for war with Britain. Spain was Britain's ally, and a war with England might provide an excuse for taking Spanish as well as British territory.

By 1812, therefore, war fever was raging on both the northern and southern borders of the United States. The demands of the residents of these areas found substantial support in Washington among a group of determined young congressmen who soon earned the name "War Hawks."

In the congressional elections of 1810, voters elected a large number of representatives of both parties eager for war with Britain. These congressmen represented a new generation, aggressive and impatient. The most influential of them came from the new states in the West or from the backcountry of the old states in the South. Two of their leaders, both recently elected to the House of Representatives, were Henry Clay of Kentucky and John C. Calhoun of South Carolina, men of great intellect, magnetism, and ambition who would play a large role in national politics for nearly forty years. Both were supporters of war with Great Britain.

Clay was elected Speaker of the House in 1811, and he appointed Calhoun to the crucial Committee on Foreign Affairs. Both men began agitating for the conquest of Canada. Madison still preferred peace but was losing control of Congress. On June 18, 1812, he approved a declaration of war against Britain.

# THE WAR OF 1812

Preoccupied with their struggle against Napoleon in Europe, the British were not eager for an open conflict with the United States. Even after the Americans declared war, Britain largely ignored them for a time. But in the fall of 1812, Napoleon launched a catastrophic campaign against Russia that left his army in disarray and his power in Europe diminished. By late 1813, with the French empire on its way to final defeat, Britain was able to turn its military attention to America.

## Battles with the Tribes

Americans entered the War of 1812 with great enthusiasm, but events on the battlefield soon cooled their ardor. In the summer of 1812, American forces invaded Canada through Detroit. They soon had to retreat back to Detroit and in August surrendered the fort there. Other invasion efforts also failed. In the meantime, Fort Dearborn (later Chicago) fell before an Indian attack.

Things went only slightly better for the United States on the seas. At first, American frigates won some spectacular victories over British warships. But by 1813, the British navy was counterattacking effectively, driving the American frigates to cover and imposing a blockade on the United States.

The United States did, however, achieve significant early military successes on the Great Lakes. First, the Americans took command of Lake Ontario; this permitted them to raid and burn York (now Toronto), the capital of Canada. American forces then seized control of Lake Erie, mainly through the work of the young Oliver Hazard Perry, who engaged and dispersed a British fleet at Put-in Bay on September 10, 1813. This made possible, at last, an invasion of Canada by way of Detroit, which Americans could now reach easily by water. William Henry Harrison, the American commander in the West, pushed up the river Thames into upper Canada and on October 5, 1813, won a victory notable for the death of Tecumseh, who was serving as a brigadier general in the British army. The Battle of the Thames

The War of 181

NAVAL AND
TROOP MOVEMENT

American force
British forces
British blockad

BATTLES
American victo
British victory
Indian battles

resulted in no lasting occupation of Canada, but it weakened and disheartened the Indians of the Northwest and greatly diminished their ability to defend their claims to the region.

In the meantime, another white military leader was striking an even harder blow at the Indians of the Southwest. The Creeks, aroused by Tecumseh on a southern visit and supplied by the Spaniards in Florida, had been attacking white settlers near the Florida border. Andrew Jackson, a wealthy Tennessee planter and a general in the state militia, temporarily abandoned plans for an invasion of Florida and set off in pursuit of the Creeks. On March 27, 1814, in the Battle of Horseshoe Bend, Jackson's men took terrible revenge on the Indians—slaughtering women and children along with warriors—and broke the resistance of the Creeks. The tribe agreed to cede most of its lands to the United States and retreated westward, farther into the interior. The battle also won Jackson a commission as major general in the United States Army, and in that capacity he led his men farther south into Florida. On November 7, 1814, he seized the Spanish fort at Pensacola.

### Battles with the British

But the victories over the tribes were not enough to win the war. After the surrender of Napoleon in 1814, England prepared to invade the United States. A British armada sailed up the Patuxent River from Chesapeake Bay and landed an army that marched to nearby Bladensburg, on the outskirts of Washington, where it dispersed a poorly trained force of American militiamen. On August 24, 1814, the British troops entered Washington and put the government to flight. Then they set fire to several public buildings, including the White House, in retaliation for the earlier American burning of the Canadian capital at York. This was the low point of American fortunes in the war.

Leaving Washington in partial ruins, the invading army proceeded up the bay toward Baltimore. But Baltimore, guarded by Fort McHenry, was prepared. To block the approaching fleet, the American garrison had sunk several ships in the Patapsco River (the entry to Baltimore's harbor), thus forcing the British to bombard the fort from a distance. Through the night of September 13, Francis Scott Key (a Washington lawyer on board one of the British ships, where he was trying to secure the release of an American prisoner) watched the bombardment. The next morning, "by the dawn's early light," he could see the flag on the fort still flying; he recorded his pride in the moment by writing a poem—"The Star-Spangled Banner." The British withdrew from Baltimore, and Key's words were soon set to the tune

THE BURNING OF WASHINGTON This dramatic engraving somewhat exaggerates the extent of the blazes in Washington when the British occupied the city in August 1814. But the invaders did set fire to the Capitol, the White House, and other public buildings in retaliation for the American burning of the Canadian capital at York.

of an old English drinking song. (In 1931, "The Star-Spangled Banner" became the official national anthem.)

Meanwhile, American forces repelled another British invasion in northern New York; at the Battle of Plattsburgh, on September 11, 1814, they turned back a much more numerous British naval and land force and secured the northern border of the United States. In the South, a formidable array of battle-hardened British veterans, fresh from the campaign against the French in Spain, landed below New Orleans and prepared to advance north up the Mississippi. Awaiting the British was Andrew Jackson with a motley collection of Tennesseans, Kentuckians, Creoles, blacks, pirates, and regular army troops drawn up behind earthen breastworks. On January 8, 1815, the redcoats advanced on the American fortifications, but the exposed British forces were no match for Jackson's well-protected men. After the Americans had repulsed several waves of attackers, the British finally retreated, leaving behind 700 dead (including their commander, Sir Edward Pakenham), 1,400 wounded, and 500 prisoners. Jackson's losses: 8 killed, 13 wounded. Only later did news reach North America that the United States and Britain had signed a peace treaty several weeks before the Battle of New Orleans.

### The Revolt of New England

With a few notable exceptions, such as the Battles of Put-in Bay and New Orleans, the military efforts of the United States between 1812 and 1815 consisted of a series of humiliating failures. As a result, the American government faced increasing popular opposition as the contest dragged on. In New England, opposition both to the war and to the Republican government that was waging it was so extreme that some Federalists celebrated British victories. In Congress, in the meantime, the Republicans had continual trouble with the Federalist opposition, led by a young congressman from New Hampshire, Daniel Webster, who missed no opportunity to embarrass the administration.

By now the Federalists were very much in the minority in the country as a whole, but they were still the majority party in New England. Some of them began to dream of creating a separate nation in that region, which they could dominate and in which they could escape what they saw as the tyranny of slaveholders and backwoodsmen. Talk of secession reached a climax in the winter of 1814–1815.

On December 15, 1814, delegates from the New England states met in Hartford, Connecticut, to discuss their grievances against the Madison administration. The would-be seceders at the Hartford Convention were outnumbered by a comparatively moderate majority. But while the convention's report only hinted at secession, it reasserted the right of nullification and proposed seven amendments to the Constitution (presumably as the condition of New England's remaining in the Union)—amendments designed to protect New England from the growing influence of the South and the West.

Because the war was going so badly, the New Englanders assumed that the Republicans would have to agree to their demands. Soon after the convention adjourned, however, the news of Jackson's victory at New Orleans reached the cities of the Northeast. A day or two later, reports arrived from abroad of a treaty of peace. In the changed atmosphere these apparent triumphs produced, the Hartford Convention and the Federalist party came to seem futile, irrelevant, even treasonable.

## The Peace Settlement

Serious negotiations between the United States and Britain began in August 1814, when American and British diplomats met in Ghent, Belgium. John Quincy Adams, Henry Clay, and Albert Gallatin led the American delegation. Although both sides began with extravagant demands, the final treaty did very little except end the fighting itself. The Americans gave up their demand for a British renunciation of impressment and for the cession of Canada to the United States. The British abandoned their call for creation of an Indian buffer state in the Northwest and made other, minor territorial concessions. The negotiators referred other disputes to arbitration. Hastily drawn up, the treaty was signed on Christmas Eve 1814.

Both sides had reason to accept this skimpy agreement. The British, exhausted and in debt from their prolonged conflict with Napoleon, were eager to settle the lesser dispute in North America. The Americans realized that with the defeat of Napoleon in Europe, the British would no longer have much incentive to interfere with American commerce. Indeed, by the end of 1815, impressment had all but ceased.

Other settlements followed the Treaty of Ghent and contributed to a long-term improvement in Anglo-American relations. A commercial treaty in 1815 gave Americans the right to trade freely with England and much of the British Empire. The Rush-Bagot agreement of 1817 provided for mutual disarmament on the Great Lakes; eventually (although not until 1872) the Canadian-American boundary became the longest "unguarded frontier" in the world.

For the other parties to the War of 1812, the Indian tribes east of the Mississippi, the conflict proved another disastrous blow to the capacity of Indians to resist white expansion. Tecumseh, their most important leader, was dead. The British, their most important allies, were gone from the Northwest. The intertribal alliance that Tecumseh and the Prophet had forged was in disarray. The end of the war served as a spur to white movement westward, into land the Indians were less than ever able to defend.

CHAPTER EIGHT

# Varieties of American Nationalism

*Stabilizing Economic Growth* ～ *Expanding Westward*
*The "Era of Good Feelings"* ～ *Sectionalism and Nationalism*
*The Revival of Opposition*

L IKE A "FIRE BELL in the night," as Thomas Jefferson put it, the issue of slavery arose after the War of 1812 to threaten the unity of the nation. The debate began when the territory of Missouri applied for admission to the Union, raising the question of whether it would be a free or a slaveholding state. But the larger issue, one that would arise again and again to plague the republic, was whether the vast new western regions of the United States would ultimately move into the orbit of the North or the South.

Yet the Missouri crisis, which Congress settled by compromise in 1820, was significant at the time not only because it was a sign of the sectional crises to come but because it stood in such sharp contrast to the rising American nationalism of the years following the war. Whatever forces might be working to pull the nation apart, stronger ones were acting for the moment to draw it together. The American economy was experiencing remarkable growth. The federal government was acting in both domestic and foreign policy to assert a vigorous nationalism. Above all, perhaps, a set of widely (although never universally) shared sentiments and ideals worked to bind the nation together: the memory of the Revolution, the veneration of the Constitution and its framers, the belief that America had a special destiny in the world. For a time, it was possible for many Americans to overlook the very different forms their nationalism took—and to ignore the large elements of their population who were excluded from the national self-definition altogether. But the vigorous economic and territorial expansion this exuberant nationalism produced ultimately brought those differences to the fore.

## TIME LINE

| 1815 | 1816 | 1818 | 1819 |
|------|------|------|------|
| U.S. takes western lands from Indians | Second Bank of U.S<br><br>Monroe elected president | Seminole War ends<br><br>Rush-Bagot agreement | Panic and depression<br><br>Dartmouth College v. Woodward; McCulloch v. Maryland |

| 1820 | 1823 | 1824 | 1828 |
|------|------|------|------|
| Missouri Compromise<br><br>Monroe reelected | Monroe Doctrine | John Quincy Adams elected | Tariff of abominations<br><br>Jackson elected president |

# STABILIZING ECONOMIC GROWTH

The end of the War of 1812 allowed the United States to resume the economic growth and territorial expansion that, despite the Republicans' aspirations, had characterized the first decade of the nineteenth century. A vigorous postwar boom led to a disastrous bust in 1819. Brief though it was, the collapse was evidence that the United States continued to lack some of the basic institutions necessary to sustain long-term growth.

### The Government and Economic Growth

The War of 1812 may have stimulated the growth of manufactures. But it also produced chaos in shipping and banking, and it exposed dramatically the inadequacy of the existing transportation and financial systems. The aftermath of the war, therefore, saw the emergence of a series of political issues connected with national economic development: reestablishing the Bank of the United States (the first Bank's charter had expired in 1811, and Congress had refused to renew it), protecting new industries, and providing a nationwide network of roads and waterways.

The wartime experience underlined the need for another national bank. After the expiration of the first Bank's charter, a large number of state banks had begun operations. They issued vast quantities of bank notes but did not always retain a large enough reserve of gold or silver to redeem the notes on demand. The notes circulated more or less as money, but their value depended on the reputation of the bank that issued them. Thus there was a

THE UNITED STATES CAPITOL IN 1824 This slightly idealized view by the American artist Charles Burton shows the approach to the west front of the United States Capitol along Pennsylvania Avenue. The large, columned dome that today rises above the building was built in the 1860s to replace the simpler dome shown in this painting.

confusing variety of notes of widely differing value in circulation at the same time. Honest business was difficult, and counterfeiting easy.

In response to these problems, Congress chartered a second Bank of the United States in 1816. It was essentially the same institution Hamilton had founded in 1791 except that it had more capital than its predecessor. The national bank could not forbid state banks from issuing notes, but its size and power enabled it to dominate the state banks. It could compel them to issue only sound notes or risk being forced out of business.

Congress also acted to promote manufacturing, which the war (by cutting off imports) had already greatly stimulated. The American textile industry had experienced a particularly dramatic growth. Between 1807 and 1815, the total number of cotton spindles in the country increased more than fifteenfold, from 8,000 to 130,000. Until 1814, the textile factories—most of them in New England—produced only yarn and thread; families operating handlooms at home did the actual weaving of cloth. Then the Boston merchant Francis Cabot Lowell, after examining textile machinery in England, developed a power loom better than its English counterpart. In 1813, in Waltham, Massachusetts, Lowell founded the first mill in America to carry on the processes of spinning and weaving under a single roof. His company was an important step in revolutionizing American manufacturing.

But the end of the war suddenly dimmed the prospects for American industry. British ships—determined to recapture their lost markets—swarmed into American ports and unloaded cargoes of manufactured goods, many priced below cost. Threatened American industries cried out for protection, arguing that they needed time to grow strong enough to withstand the foreign competition. In 1816, protectionists in Congress passed a tariff law that effectively limited competition from abroad on a wide range of items, including cotton cloth, despite objections from agricultural interests, who stood to pay higher prices for manufactured goods.

## Transportation

The nation's most pressing economic need in the aftermath of the war, however, was for improvements in its transportation system that would give manufacturers access to raw materials and markets. So an old debate resumed: Should the federal government help to finance roads and other "internal improvements"? The idea of using government funds to finance road building was not a new one. When Ohio entered the Union in 1803, the federal government agreed that part of the proceeds from the sale of public lands there should finance road construction. And in 1807, Congress enacted a law proposed by the Jefferson administration that permitted using revenues from the Ohio land sales to finance a National Road from the Potomac River to the Ohio. By 1818, the highway ran as far as Wheeling, Virginia, on the Ohio River; and the Lancaster Pike, financed in part by the state of Pennsylvania, extended westward to Pittsburgh. The roads were heavily traveled and helped lower shipping costs across the mountains.

At the same time, on the rivers and the Great Lakes, steam-powered shipping was expanding rapidly. By 1816, river steamers were beginning to journey up and down the Mississippi to the Ohio River, and up the Ohio as far as Pittsburgh. Steamboats were soon carrying more cargo on the Mississippi than all the earlier forms of river transport—flatboats, barges, and others—combined. They stimulated the agricultural economy of the West and the South by providing readier access to markets at greatly reduced cost. And they enabled eastern manufacturers to send their finished goods west much more readily.

But despite the progress with steamboats and turnpikes, there remained serious gaps in the nation's transportation network, as experience during the War of 1812 had shown. Once the British blockade cut off Atlantic shipping,

THE STEAMBOAT "WALK-IN-THE-WATER," 1818 The
inventor Robert Fulton launched the *Clermont*, the first
American steam-powered boat large enough to be
commercially useful, in 1806. By 1818, when the vessel
shown here was making regular trips on Lake Erie,
steamboat travel had become common on major rivers
and lakes throughout the eastern United States.

the coastal roads became choked by the unaccustomed volume of north-
south traffic. Merchants and consumers experienced long delays and serious shortages. In 1815, with this wartime experience in mind, President
Madison noted the "great importance of establishing throughout our country the roads and canals which can be best executed under the national authority." But when Congress passed a bill introduced by Representative
John C. Calhoun that allowed the use of government funds to finance internal improvements, Madison, on his last day in office, vetoed it. He supported the purpose of the bill, he explained, but he believed that Congress
lacked authority to fund the improvements without a constitutional amendment. And so on the issue of internal improvements, the nationalists fell short
of their goals. For a time, state governments and private enterprise were left
on their own to build the transportation network necessary for the growing
American economy.

# EXPANDING WESTWARD

One reason for the growing interest in internal improvements was the sudden and dramatic surge in westward expansion in the years following the War of 1812. "Old America seems to be breaking up and moving westward," wrote an English observer at the time. By the time of the census of 1820, white settlers had pushed well beyond the Mississippi River, and the population of the western regions was increasing more rapidly than that of the nation as a whole. Almost one of every four white Americans lived west of the Appalachians in 1820; ten years before, only one in seven had resided there.

## *The Great Migration*

The westward movement of the white American population was one of the most important developments of the century. And like earlier movements west, it thrust peoples of different cultures and traditions into intimate association with one another—with effects that were ultimately disastrous for some, but important for everyone. There were several major reasons for this expansion. Population pressures and economic pressures pushed many Americans from the East; the availability of new lands and the weakening of Indian resistance drew them to the West.

The pressures driving white Americans out of the East came in part from the continued growth of the nation's population. Between 1800 and 1820, the population nearly doubled—from 5.3 million to 9.6 million. Most Americans were still farmers, and the agricultural lands of the East were by now largely occupied or exhausted. In the South, the spread of the plantation system and its slave labor force limited opportunities for new settlers. Meanwhile, the West itself was becoming increasingly attractive to white settlers. In the aftermath of the War of 1812, the federal government continued its policy of pushing the Indian tribes farther and farther west. It also created a "factor" system, by which government factors (or agents) supplied the Indians with goods at cost. This not only worked to drive Canadian traders out of the region; it also helped create a situation of dependency that made the Indians themselves easier to control.

As fertile lands became more secure for white settlement, migrants from throughout the East flocked to what was then known as the Old Northwest (now part of the Midwest), most of them via the Ohio and Monongahela Rivers. Once on the Ohio, they floated downstream on flatboats bearing all their possessions, then left the river (often at Cincinnati, which was becoming one of the region's—and the nation's—principal cities), and pressed on overland with wagons, handcarts, packhorses, cattle, and hogs.

### White Settlers in the Old Northwest

Having arrived at their destination, preferably in the spring or early summer, most settlers built lean-tos or cabins and then hewed clearings out of the forest and planted crops of corn to supplement the wild game they caught and the domestic animals they had brought with them. It was a rough and lonely existence. Men, women, and children worked side by side in the fields—and at times had virtually no contact for weeks or months with anyone outside their own families.

Life in the western territories was not, however, entirely solitary or individualistic. Migrants often journeyed westward in groups, stayed together, and built new communities with schools, churches, stores, and other institutions. The labor shortage in the interior led neighbors to develop systems of mutual aid. They gathered periodically to raise a barn, clear land, harvest crops, or make quilts.

Another common feature of life in the Northwest (and indeed in much of early-nineteenth-century America) was mobility. Individuals and families were constantly on the move, settling for a few years in one place and then selling their land (often at a significant profit, given the rapidly rising prices in the region) and resettling somewhere else. When new areas for settlement opened farther to the west, it was often the people already on the western edges of white settlement—rather than those who remained in the East—who flocked to them first.

### The Plantation System in the Old Southwest

In the Old Southwest (now generally known as the Deep South), the new agricultural economy emerged along different lines. The market for cotton continued to grow, and in the Southwest stretched a broad zone where cotton could thrive. That zone included what was to become known as the Black Belt of central Alabama and Mississippi, a vast prairie with a dark, productive soil.

The first arrivals in the uncultivated regions of the Old Southwest were usually ordinary people like the settlers farther north, small farmers who made rough clearings in the forest. But wealthier planters soon followed. They bought up the cleared or partially cleared land, and the original settlers moved farther west and started over again. The large planters made the westward journey in a style quite different from that of the first pioneers. Over the alternately dusty and muddy roads came great caravans consisting of herds of livestock, wagonloads of household goods, long lines of slaves, and—bringing up the rear—the planter's family riding in carriages. Success in the wilderness was by no means assured, even for the wealthiest settlers. But many planters soon expanded small clearings into vast cotton fields. They replaced the cabins of the early pioneers with more sumptuous log dwellings and ultimately with imposing mansions that demonstrated the rise of a newly wealthy class.

The rapid growth of the Old Northwest and Southwest resulted in the admission of four new states to the Union in the immediate aftermath of the War of 1812: Indiana in 1816, Mississippi in 1817, Illinois in 1818, and Alabama in 1819.

### Trade and Trapping in the Far West

Not many Anglo-Americans yet knew much about or were much interested in the far western areas of the continent. But a significant trade nevertheless began to develop between these western regions and the United States early in the nineteenth century, and it grew steadily for decades.

Mexico, which continued to control Texas, California, and much of the rest of the far Southwest, won its independence from Spain in 1821. Almost immediately, it opened its northern territories to trade with the United States, hoping to revive their stagnant economy. American traders poured into the region—overland into Texas and New Mexico, by sea into California. Merchants from the United States quickly displaced Indian and Mexican traders. In New Mexico, for example, the Missouri trader William Becknell began in 1821 to offer American manufactured goods for sale, priced considerably below the inferior Mexican goods that had dominated the market in the past. Mexico effectively lost its markets in its own colony, and a steady traffic of commercial wagon trains was moving back and forth along the Santa Fe Trail between Missouri and New Mexico.

Becknell and those who followed him diverted an established trade from Mexico to the United States. But fur traders created a wholly new kind of commerce. After the War of 1812, John Jacob Astor's American Fur Company and others extended their operations from the Great Lakes area westward to the Rockies. At first, fur traders did most of their business by purchasing pelts from the Indians. But increasingly, white trappers entered the region and joined the Iroquois and other Indians in pursuit of beaver and other furs.

The trappers, or "mountain men," who began trading in and exploring the Far West were small in number. But they were developing important

THE RENDEZVOUS  The annual rendezvous of fur trappers and traders was a major event in the lives of the lonely men who made their livelihoods gathering furs. It was also a gathering of representatives of the many cultures that mingled in the Far West, among them Anglo-Americans, French Canadians, Indians, and Hispanics.

relationships with the existing residents of the West—Indian and Mexican—and altering the character of society there. White trappers were almost without exception relatively young single men. Perhaps unsurprisingly, many of them entered into sexual relationships with Indian and Mexican women. They also recruited the women as helpers in the difficult work of preparing furs and skins for trading. Perhaps two-thirds of the white trappers married Indian or Hispanic women.

In 1822, Andrew and William Ashley founded the Rocky Mountain Fur Company and recruited white trappers to move permanently into the Rockies in search of furs, which were becoming scarce farther east. The Ashleys dispatched supplies annually to their trappers in exchange for furs and skins. The arrival of the supply train became the occasion for a gathering of scores of mountain men, some of whom lived much of the year in considerable isolation.

But however isolated their daily lives, these mountain men were closely bound up with the expanding market economy of the United States. Some were employees of the Rocky Mountain Company (or some other, similar business enterprise), earning a salary in return for providing a steady supply of furs. Others were nominally independent but relied on the companies for credit; they were almost always in debt and hence economically bound to the companies. Some trapped entirely on their own and simply sold their furs for cash, but they too depended on merchants from the East for their livelihoods. Whatever the character of the transactions, the bulk of the profits from the trade flowed to the merchants.

Many trappers and mountain men lived peacefully and successfully with the Indians and Mexicans whose lands they came to share. But some did not. Jedediah S. Smith, a former Ashley partner, founded his own fur company in the northern Rockies in 1826. He also led a series of forays deep into Mexican territory that ended in disastrous battles with the Mojaves and other tribes. He escaped from an 1827 expedition to Oregon, in which sixteen members of his party of twenty died. But four years later, he was killed by Comanches while en route to the Rockies. The Indians took the weapons he was carrying and sold them to Mexican settlers.

### Eastern Images of the West

Americans in the East were only dimly aware of the world the trappers were entering and helping to reshape, and the trappers themselves, who did not often write of their lives or draw maps of the lands they explored, did little to enlighten others. More important in increasing eastern awareness of the West were explorers, many of them dispatched by the United States government with instructions to chart the territories they visited. In 1819 and 1820, with instructions from the War Department to find the source of the Red River, Stephen H. Long led nineteen soldiers on a journey up the Platte and South Platte Rivers through what is now Nebraska and eastern Colorado (where he discovered the peak that would be named for him), and then returned eastward along the Arkansas River through what is now Kansas. He failed to find the headwaters of the Red River. But he wrote an influential report on his trip, which echoed the dismissive conclusions of Zebulon Pike fifteen years before. The region "between the Missouri River and the Rocky Mountains," Long wrote, "is almost wholly unfit for cultivation, and of course uninhabitable by a people depending upon agriculture for their subsistence." On the published map of his expedition, he labeled the Great Plains the "Great American Desert."

## THE "ERA OF GOOD FEELINGS"

The expansion of the economy, the growth of white settlement and trade in the West, the creation of new states—all reflected the rising spirit of nationalism that was permeating the United States in the years following the

War of 1812. That spirit found reflection for a time in the character of national politics.

## The End of the First Party System

Ever since 1800, the presidency seemed to have been the special possession of Virginians, passing from one to another in unvarying sequence. After two terms in office Jefferson chose his secretary of state, James Madison of Virginia, to succeed him, and after two more terms, Madison secured the presidential nomination for his secretary of state, James Monroe, also of Virginia. Many in the North already were expressing impatience with the so-called Virginia Dynasty, but the Republicans had no difficulty electing their candidate in the listless campaign of 1816. Monroe received 183 ballots in the electoral college; his Federalist opponent, Rufus King of New York, only 34—from Massachusetts, Connecticut, and Delaware.

Monroe was sixty-one years old when he became president. In the course of his long career, he had served as a soldier in the Revolution, as a diplomat, and most recently as a cabinet officer. He entered office under what seemed to be remarkably favorable circumstances. With the decline of the Federalists, his party faced no serious opposition. With the conclusion of the War of 1812, the nation faced no important international threats. American politicians had dreamed since the first days of the republic of a time in which partisan divisions and factional disputes might come to an end, a time in

THE INAUGURATION OF JAMES MONROE, 1816 The ruins of part of the United States Capitol, burned by the British two years earlier late in the War of 1812, provided a bleak backdrop for James Monroe's first inauguration in 1816.

which the nation might learn to exhibit the harmony and virtue that the founders had envisioned. In the prosperous postwar years, Monroe attempted to use his office to realize that dream.

He made that clear, above all, in the selection of his cabinet. For secretary of state, he chose the New Englander and former Federalist John Quincy Adams. Jefferson, Madison, and Monroe had all served as secretary of state before becoming president; Adams, therefore, immediately became the heir apparent, suggesting that the "Virginia Dynasty" would soon come to an end. Speaker of the House Henry Clay declined an offer to be secretary of war, so Monroe named John C. Calhoun instead. In his other appointments, too, Monroe took pains to include both northerners and southerners, easterners and westerners, Federalists and Republicans—to harmonize the various interests and sections of the country in a government of national unity.

Soon after his inauguration, Monroe did what no president since Washington had done: he made a good-will tour through the country. In New England, so recently the scene of rabid Federalist discontent, he was greeted everywhere with enthusiastic demonstrations. The *Columbian Centinel*, a Federalist newspaper in Boston, commenting on the "Presidential Jubilee" in that city, observed that an "era of good feelings" had arrived. This phrase became a popular label for the presidency of Monroe. On the surface, at least, the years of Monroe's presidency did appear to be an "era of good feelings." In 1820, Monroe was reelected without opposition. For all practical purposes, the Federalist Party had now ceased to exist.

### John Quincy Adams and Florida

Like his father, the second president of the United States, John Quincy Adams had spent much of his life in diplomatic service. And he had demonstrated in all his assignments a calmness and firmness that made him one of the great diplomats in American history. He was also a committed nationalist; and when he assumed the office of secretary of state, he considered his most important task to be the promotion of American expansion.

His first challenge was Florida. The United States had already annexed West Florida, but that claim was in dispute. Most Americans, moreover, still believed the nation should gain possession of the entire peninsula. In 1817, Adams began negotiations with the Spanish minister, Luis de Onís, in hopes of resolving the dispute and gaining the entire territory for the United States.

In the meantime, however, events were taking their own course in Florida itself. Andrew Jackson, now in command of American troops along

CAPTURING THE SEMINOLES  A nineteenth-century woodcut illustrates American troops under the command of Andrew Jackson taking two Seminole chiefs into captivity in Florida in 1816.

the Florida frontier, had orders from Secretary of War Calhoun to "adopt the necessary measures" to stop the continuing raids on American territory by Seminole Indians south of the border between Georgia and Florida. Jackson used those orders as an excuse to invade Florida, seize the Spanish forts at St. Marks and Pensacola, and order the hanging of two British subjects on the charge of supplying and inciting the Indians.

Instead of condemning Jackson's raid, Adams urged the government to assume responsibility for it, because he saw a chance to win an important advantage in his negotiations with Spain. The United States, he told the Spanish, had the right under international law to defend itself against threats from across its borders. Since Spain was unwilling or unable to curb those threats, America had simply done what was necessary. Jackson's raid had demonstrated to the Spanish that the United States could easily take Florida by force. Adams implied that the nation might consider doing so.

Onís realized, therefore, that he had little choice but to come to terms with the Americans. Under the provisions of the Adams-Onís Treaty of 1819, Spain ceded all of Florida to the United States and gave up its claim to territory north of the 42nd parallel in the Pacific Northwest. In return, the American government gave up its claims to Texas.

## The Panic of 1819

But the Monroe administration had little time to revel in its diplomatic successes. At the same time that Adams was completing his negotiations with Onís, the nation was falling victim to a serious economic crisis that helped revive many of the political disputes that the "era of good feelings" had presumably settled.

The Panic of 1819 followed a period of high foreign demand for American farm goods and thus of exceptionally high prices for American farmers (all as a result of the disruption of European agriculture by the Napoleonic Wars). The rising prices for farm goods had stimulated a land boom in the western United States. Fueled by speculative investments, land prices soared well above the government-established minimum of $2 an acre; some land in the Black Belt of Alabama and Mississippi went for $100 an acre and more.

The availability of easy credit to settlers and speculators—from the government (under the land acts of 1800 and 1804), from state banks and wildcat banks, even for a time from the rechartered Bank of the United States—fueled the land boom. Beginning in 1819, however, new management at the national bank began tightening credit, calling in loans, and foreclosing mortgages. This precipitated a series of failures by state banks, which had taken out loans from the Bank of the United States. The result was a financial panic, which many Americans, particularly those in the West, blamed on the national bank. Thus began a process that would eventually make the Bank's existence one of the nation's most burning political issues.

Six years of depression followed. Prices for both manufactured goods and agricultural produce fell rapidly. Manufacturers secured passage of a new tariff in 1824 to protect them from foreign competition. Indebted farmers won some relief through the land law of 1820 and the relief act of 1821, which lowered the price of land and reduced existing debts while extending their payment schedules.

Some Americans saw the Panic of 1819 and the widespread distress that followed as a warning that rapid economic growth and territorial expansion would destabilize the nation and threaten its survival. But by 1820 most Americans were irrevocably committed to such growth and expansion. And public debate in the future would revolve less around whether such growth was good or bad than around how to encourage and control it. That debate, which the Panic of 1819 did much to encourage, created new factional divisions within the Republican Party and ultimately brought the era of nonpartisanship—the "era of good feelings"—to an acrimonious end.

# SECTIONALISM AND NATIONALISM

For a brief but alarming moment in 1819–1820, the increasing differences between the nation's two leading sections threatened the unity of the United States—until the Missouri Compromise averted a sectional crisis for a time. The forces of nationalism continued to assert themselves, and the federal government began to assume the role of promoter of economic growth.

## *The Missouri Compromise*

When Missouri applied for admission to the Union as a state in 1819, slavery was already well established there. Even so, Representative James Tallmadge, Jr., of New York, proposed an amendment to the Missouri statehood bill that would prohibit the further introduction of slaves into Missouri and

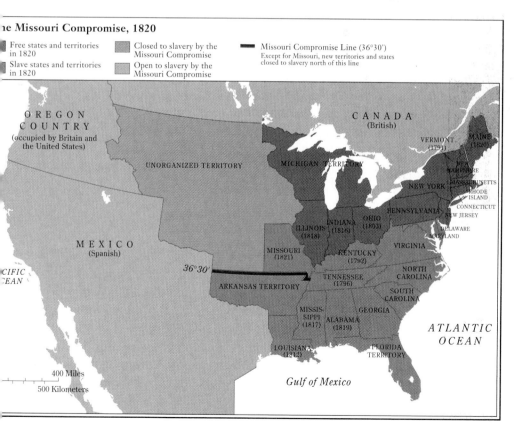

**ie Missouri Compromise, 1820**

Free states and territories in 1820
Slave states and territories in 1820
Closed to slavery by the Missouri Compromise
Open to slavery by the Missouri Compromise
Missouri Compromise Line (36°30')
Except for Missouri, new territories and states closed to slavery north of this line

provide for the gradual emancipation of those already there. The Tallmadge Amendment provoked a controversy that was to rage for the next two years.

Since the beginning of the republic, partly by chance and partly by design, new states had come into the Union more or less in pairs, one from the North, another from the South. In 1819, there were eleven free states and eleven slave states; the admission of Missouri would upset that balance and establish a precedent that in the future might increase the political power of the North over the South. Hence the controversy over slavery and freedom in Missouri.

Complicating the Missouri question was the application of Maine (previously the northern part of Massachusetts) for admission as a new (and free) state. Speaker of the House Henry Clay informed northern members that if they blocked Missouri from entering the Union as a slave state, southerners would block the admission of Maine. But Maine ultimately offered a way out of the impasse, as the Senate agreed to combine the Maine and Missouri proposals into a single bill. Maine would be admitted as a free state, Missouri as a slave state. Then Senator Jesse B. Thomas of Illinois proposed an amendment prohibiting slavery in the rest of the Louisiana Purchase territory north of the southern boundary of Missouri (the 36° 30′ parallel). The Senate adopted the Thomas Amendment, and Speaker Clay, although with great difficulty, guided the amended Maine-Missouri bill through the House.

Nationalists in both North and South hailed this settlement—which became known as the Missouri Compromise—as a happy resolution of a danger to the Union. But the debate over it had revealed a strong undercurrent of sectionalism that was competing with—although at the moment failing to derail—the powerful tides of nationalism.

### Marshall and the Court

John Marshall served as chief justice of the United States for almost thirty-five years, from 1801 to 1835, and he dominated the Court more fully than anyone else before or since. Republican presidents filled vacancies with one after another Republican justice. But Marshall continued to carry a majority with him in most of the Court's decisions. More than anyone but the framers themselves, he molded the development of the Constitution: strengthening the judicial branch at the expense of the executive and legislative branches; increasing the power of the federal government at the expense of the states; and advancing the interests of the propertied and commercial classes.

Committed to promoting commerce, the Marshall Court firmly strength-

JOHN MARSHALL Marshall became Chief Justice of the
United States Supreme Court in 1801 after establishing
himself as one of the leaders of the Federalist Party. He
served as Chief Justice for thirty-five years, longer than
anyone else in American history. And despite the frequent
opposition of a series of Republican presidents, he used his
position to make the judiciary a vigorous instrument for
asserting and strengthening American nationalism.

ened the inviolability of contracts as a cornerstone of American law. In *Fletcher*
v. *Peck* (1810), which arose out of a series of notorious land frauds in Georgia, the Court had to decide whether the Georgia legislature of 1796 could
repeal the act of the previous legislature granting lands under shady circumstances to the Yazoo Land Companies. In a unanimous decision, Marshall
held that a land grant was a valid contract and could not be repealed even if
corruption was involved.

   *Dartmouth College* v. *Woodward* (1819) further expanded the meaning of
the contract clause of the Constitution. Having gained control of the New
Hampshire state government, Republicans tried to revise Dartmouth's charter (granted by King George III in 1769) to convert the private college into
a state university. Daniel Webster, a Dartmouth graduate and brilliant orator, argued the college's case. The Dartmouth charter, he insisted, was a
contract, protected by the same doctrine that the Court had already upheld
in *Fletcher* v. *Peck*. Then, according to legend, he brought some of the jus-

tices to tears with an irrelevant passage that concluded: "It is, sir, . . . a small college. And yet there are those who love it." The Court ruled for Dartmouth, proclaiming that corporation charters such as the one the legislature had granted the college were contracts and thus inviolable. The decision placed important restrictions on the ability of state governments to control corporations.

In overturning the act of the legislature and the decisions of the New Hampshire courts, the justices also implicitly claimed for themselves the right to override the decisions of state courts. But advocates of states' rights, especially in the South, continued to challenge its right to do so. In *Cohens* v. *Virginia* (1821), Marshall explicitly affirmed the constitutionality of federal review of state court decisions. The states had given up part of their sovereignty in ratifying the Constitution, he explained, and their courts must submit to federal jurisdiction; otherwise, the federal government would be prostrated "at the feet of every state in the Union."

Meanwhile, in *McCullogh* v. *Maryland* (1819), Marshall confirmed the "implied powers" of Congress by upholding the constitutionality of the Bank of the United States. The Bank had become so unpopular in the South and the West that several of the states tried to drive branches out of business by outright prohibition or by confiscatory taxes. This case presented two constitutional questions to the Supreme Court: Could Congress charter a bank? And if so, could individual states ban it or tax it? Daniel Webster, one of the Bank's attorneys, argued that establishing such an institution came within the "necessary and proper" clause of the Constitution and that the power to tax involved a "power to destroy." If the states could tax the Bank at all, they could tax it to death. Marshall adopted Webster's words in deciding for the Bank.

In the case of *Gibbons* v. *Ogden* (1824), the Court strengthened Congress's power to regulate interstate commerce. The state of New York had granted Robert Fulton and Robert Livingston's steamboat company the exclusive right to carry passengers on the Hudson River to New York City. Fulton and Livingston then gave Aaron Ogden the business of carrying passengers across the river between New York and New Jersey. But Thomas Gibbons, with a license granted under an act of Congress, began competing with Ogden for the ferry traffic. Ogden brought suit against him and won in the New York courts. Gibbons appealed to the Supreme Court. The most important question facing the justice was whether Congress's power to give Gibbons a license to operate his ferry superseded the state of New York's power to grant Ogden a monopoly. Marshall claimed that the power of Congress to regulate interstate commerce (which, he said, included navigation) was "complete in itself" and might be "exercised to its utmost extent." Ogden's state-granted monopoly, therefore, was void.

The lasting significance of *Gibbons* v. *Ogden* was that it freed transportation systems from restraints by the states and helped pave the way for unfettered capitalist growth. But it also helped quell several political efforts by Republicans from the South and West—angry at Marshall's assertions of federal authority—to weaken the Supreme Court. The *Gibbons* decision, with its popular stand against state-granted monopolies, quieted much of the opposition.

The decisions of the Marshall Court established the primacy of the federal government over the states in regulating the economy and opened the way for an increased federal role in promoting economic growth. They protected corporations and other private economic institutions from local government interference. They were, in short, highly nationalistic decisions, designed to promote the growth of a strong, unified, and economically developed United States.

### The Court and the Tribes

The nationalist inclinations of the Marshall Court were visible as well in a series of decisions concerning the legal status of Indian tribes within the United States. But these decisions did not simply affirm the supremacy of the United States; they also carved out a distinctive position for Native Americans within the constitutional structure.

The first of the crucial Indian decisions was in the case of *Johnson* v. *McIntosh* (1823). Leaders of the Illinois and Pinakeshaw tribes had sold parcels of their land to a group of white settlers (including Johnson) but had later signed a treaty with the federal government ceding to the United States territory that included those same parcels. The government proceeded to grant homestead rights to new white settlers (among them McIntosh) on the land claimed by Johnson. The Court was asked to decide which claim had precedence. Marshall's ruling, not surprisingly, favored the United States. But in explaining it, he offered a preliminary definition of the place of Indians within the nation. The tribes had a basic right to their tribal lands, he said, that preceded all other American law. Individual American citizens could not buy or take land from the tribes; only the federal government could do that.

Eight years later, in *Cherokee Nation* v. *Georgia*, the Marshall Court refused to hear a case filed by the Cherokees against a Georgia law abolishing their tribal legislature and courts. The Cherokees argued that because the tribe was a "foreign nation," the Supreme Court (which had constitutional responsibility for mediating disputes between the states and foreign nations) had jurisdiction. Marshall's earlier and later rulings suggested considerable sympathy for tribal claims that states could not regulate them, but he could not accept the Cherokee argument in this case. The tribes were not foreign nations, he said. Rather, they had a special status within the nation. The relationship of the Indians to the United States, he wrote, "resembles that of a ward to his guardian." This was the origin of what became known as the "trust relationship," by which the United States claimed broad powers over the tribes but accepted substantial responsibility for protecting their welfare.

Most important was the Court's 1832 decision in *Worcester* v. *Georgia*, in which the Court invalidated a Georgia law that attempted to regulate access by U.S. citizens to Cherokee country. Only the federal government could do that, Marshall claimed, thus taking another important step in consolidating federal authority over the states (and over the tribes). In doing so, he further defined the nature of the Indian nations. The tribes, he explained, were sovereign entities in much the same way Georgia was a sovereign entity, "distinct political communities, having territorial boundaries within which their authority is exclusive." In defending the power of the federal government, he was also affirming, indeed expanding, the rights of the tribes to remain free from the authority of state governments.

The Marshall decisions, therefore, did what the Constitution itself had not done: they defined a place for Indian tribes within the American political system. The tribes had basic property rights. They were sovereign entities not subject to the authority of state governments. But the federal government, like a "guardian" governing its "ward," had ultimate authority over tribal affairs—even if that authority was, according to the Court, limited by the government's obligation to protect Indian welfare. These provisions were seldom enough to defend Indians from the steady westward march of white civilization. But they formed the basis of what legal protections they had.

### The Latin American Revolution and the Monroe Doctrine

Just as the Supreme Court was asserting American nationalism in the shaping of the country's economic life, so the Monroe administration was asserting nationalism in foreign policy. As always, American diplomacy was principally concerned with Europe. But in the 1820s, dealing with Europe forced the United States to develop a policy toward Latin America.

Americans looking southward in the years following the War of 1812 beheld a gigantic spectacle: the Spanish Empire in its death throes, a whole continent in revolt, new nations in the making. Already the United States had developed a profitable trade with Latin America and was rivaling Great Britain as the principal trading nation there. Many believed the success of the anti-Spanish revolutions would further strengthen America's position in the region.

In 1815, the United States proclaimed neutrality in the wars between Spain and its rebellious colonies, implying a partial recognition of the rebels' status as nations. Moreover, the United States sold ships and supplies to the revolutionaries, a clear indication that it was not genuinely neutral but was trying to help the insurgents. Finally, in 1822, President Monroe established diplomatic relations with five new nations—La Plata (later Argentina), Chile, Peru, Colombia, and Mexico—making the United States the first country to recognize them.

In 1823, Monroe went further and announced a policy that would ultimately be known (beginning some thirty years later) as the "Monroe Doctrine," even though it was primarily the work of John Quincy Adams. "The American continents," Monroe declared, ". . . are henceforth not to be considered as subjects for future colonization by any European powers." The United States would consider any foreign challenge to the sovereignty of existing American nations an unfriendly act. At the same time, he proclaimed, "Our policy in regard to Europe . . . is not to interfere in the internal concerns of any of its powers."

The Monroe Doctrine emerged directly out of America's relations with Europe in the 1820s. Many Americans feared that Spain's European allies (notably France) would assist Spain in an effort to retake its lost empire. Even more troubling to Adams (and many other Americans) was the fear that Great Britain had designs on Cuba. Adams wanted to keep Cuba in Spanish hands until it fell (as he believed it ultimately would) to the Americans.

Monroe and Adams hoped their message would rally the people of Latin America to resist foreign intervention. They also hoped it would help arouse the United States from a business depression, divert the nation from sectional politics, and increase popular interest in the otherwise lackluster administration of Monroe. It did none of those things. But the Monroe Doctrine was important nevertheless for several reasons. It was an expression of the growing spirit of nationalism in the United States in the 1820s. It was an expression of concern about the forces that were already gathering to threaten that spirit. And it established the idea of American hegemony in the Western Hemisphere that later United States governments would invoke at will to justify policies in Latin America.

# THE REVIVAL OF OPPOSITION

After 1816, the Federalist Party offered no presidential candidate and soon ceased to exist as a national political force. The Republican Party (which considered itself not a party at all but an organization representing the whole of the population) was the only organized force in national politics.

Yet the policies of the federal government continued to spark opposition, and by the late 1820s partisan divisions were emerging once again. In some respects, the division mirrored the schism that had produced the first party system in the 1790s. The Republicans had in many ways come to resemble the early Federalist regimes in their promotion of economic growth and centralization. And the opposition, like the opposition in the 1790s, objected to the federal government's expanding role in the economy. There was, however, a crucial difference. At the beginning of the century, the opponents of centralization had also often been opponents of economic growth. Now, in the 1820s, the controversy involved not whether but how the nation should continue to expand.

## The "Corrupt Bargain"

Until 1820, when the Federalist Party effectively ceased operations and James Monroe ran for reelection unopposed, presidential candidates were nominated by caucuses of the two parties in Congress. But in 1824, "King Caucus" was overthrown. The Republican caucus nominated William H. Crawford of Georgia, the secretary of the treasury and the favorite of the extreme states' rights faction of the party. But other candidates received nominations from state legislatures and won endorsements from irregular mass meetings throughout the country.

One of them was Secretary of State John Quincy Adams, who held the office that was the traditional stepping-stone to the presidency. But as he himself ruefully understood, he was a man of cold and forbidding manners, with little popular appeal. Another contender was Henry Clay, the Speaker of the House. He had a devoted personal following and a definite and coherent program: the "American System," which proposed creating a great home market for factory and farm producers by raising the protective tariff, strengthening the national bank, and financing internal improvements. Andrew Jackson, the fourth major candidate, had no significant political record—even though he had served briefly as a representative in Congress and was now a new member of the United States Senate. But he was a military hero and had the help of shrewd political allies from his home state of Tennessee.

Jackson received more popular and electoral votes than any other candidate, but not a majority. He had 99 electoral votes to Adams's 84, Crawford's 41, and Clay's 37. The Twelfth Amendment to the Constitution (passed in the aftermath of the contested 1800 election) required the House of Representatives to choose among the three candidates with the largest numbers of electoral votes. Clay was thus out of the running, but he was in a strong position to influence the result. Crawford was seriously ill and not a plausible candidate, and Jackson was Clay's most dangerous political rival in the West. Clay had no love for Adams either; but he supported him because, alone among the candidates, he was an ardent nationalist and a likely supporter of the American System. With Clay's endorsement, Adams won election in the House.

The Jacksonians believed large popular and electoral pluralities entitled their candidate to the presidency, and they were enraged when he lost. But they grew angrier still when Adams named Clay his secretary of state. The State Department was the well-established route to the presidency, and Adams thus appeared to be naming Clay as his own successor. The outrage the Jacksonians expressed at what they called a "corrupt bargain" haunted Adams throughout his presidency.

### The Second President Adams

Throughout Adams's term in the White House, the political bitterness arising from the "corrupt bargain" charges thoroughly frustrated his policies. Adams proposed an ambitiously nationalist program reminiscent of Clay's American System. But Jacksonians in Congress blocked most of it.

Adams also experienced diplomatic frustrations. He appointed delegates to an international conference that the Venezuelan liberator, Simón Bolívar, had called in Panama in 1826. But Haiti was one of the participating nations, and southerners in Congress opposed the idea of white Americans mingling with the black delegates. Supporters of Jackson charged that Adams intended to sacrifice American interests and involve the nation in an entangling alliance. Congress delayed approving the Panama mission so long that the American delegation did not arrive until after the conference was over.

Adams also lost a contest with the state of Georgia, which wished to remove the remaining Creek and Cherokee Indians from the state to gain additional soil for cotton planters. The United States government, in a 1791 treaty, had guaranteed that land to the Creeks; but in 1825, white Georgians had extracted a new treaty from William McIntosh, the leader of one faction in the tribe and a longtime advocate of Indian cooperation with the United States. Adams believed the new treaty had no legal force, since McIntosh clearly did not represent the wishes of the tribe; and he refused to enforce the treaty, setting up a direct conflict between the president and the state. The governor of Georgia defied the president and proceeded with plans for Indian removal.

Even more damaging to the administration was its support for a new tariff on imported goods in 1828. This measure originated in the demands of Massachusetts and Rhode Island woolen manufacturers, who complained that the British were dumping textiles on the American market at artificially low prices. But to win support from middle and western states, the administration had to accept duties on other items. In the process, it antagonized the original New England supporters of the bill; the benefits of protecting their manufactured goods from foreign competition now had to be weighed against the prospects of having to pay more for raw materials. Adams signed the bill, earning the animosity of southerners, who cursed it as the "tariff of abominations."

### Jackson Triumphant

By the time of the 1828 presidential election, a new two-party system had begun to emerge out of the divisions among the Republicans. On one side stood the supporters of John Quincy Adams, who called themselves the National Republicans and who supported the economic nationalism of the preceding years. Opposing them were the followers of Andrew Jackson, who took the name Democratic Republicans and who called for an assault on privilege and a widening of opportunity. Adams attracted the support of most of the remaining Federalists; Jackson appealed to a broad coalition that opposed the "economic aristocracy." But issues seemed to count for little in the end, as the campaign degenerated into a war of personal invective. The Jacksonians charged that Adams as president had been guilty of gross waste and extravagance and had used public funds to buy gambling devices (a chess set and a billiard table) for the White House.

Adams's supporters hurled even worse accusations at Jackson. They called him a murderer and distributed a "coffin handbill," which listed, within coffin-shaped outlines, the names of militiamen whom Jackson was said to have shot in cold blood during the War of 1812. (The men had been deserters who were legally executed after sentence by a court-martial.) And they called his wife a bigamist. In fact, Jackson had married his beloved Rachel at a time when the pair incorrectly believed her first husband had divorced her. (When Jackson's wife first read of the accusations against her shortly after the election, she collapsed, and a few weeks later, died; not without reason, Jackson blamed his opponents for her death.)

Jackson's victory was decisive, but sectional. He won 56 percent of the popular vote and an electoral majority of 178 votes to 83. Adams swept virtually all of New England, and he showed significant strength in the mid-Atlantic region. Nevertheless, the Jacksonians considered their victory as complete and as important as Jefferson's in 1800. Once again, the forces of privilege had been driven from Washington. Once again, a champion of democracy would occupy the White House and restore liberty to the people and to the economy. America had entered, some Jacksonians claimed, a new era of democracy, the "era of the common man."

# Jacksonian America

MANY AMERICANS WERE growing apprehensive about the future of their republic in the 1820s and 1830s, as the nation expanded both economically and territorially. Some feared that the rapid growth of the United States would produce social chaos; they insisted that the country's first priority must be to establish order and a clear system of authority. Others argued that the greatest danger facing the nation was the growth of inequality and privilege; they believed that society's goal should be to eliminate the favored status of powerful elites and make opportunity more widely available. Advocates of this latter vision seized control of the federal government in 1829 with the inauguration of Andrew Jackson.

Despite their enthusiasm for the idea of democracy, Jackson and his followers were imperfect democrats. They did nothing to challenge (and indeed much to support) the existence of slavery; they supervised one of the harshest assaults on American Indians in the nation's history; and they accepted economic, social, and gender inequality. Jackson himself was a frontier aristocrat, and most of those who served him were people of wealth and standing. But the Jacksonians were not usually aristocrats by birth. Convinced that they had risen to prominence on the basis of their own talents and energies, their goal in public life was to ensure that others like themselves would have the opportunity to do the same.

## THE RISE OF MASS POLITICS

On March 4, 1829, thousands of Americans from all regions of the country—including many farmers, laborers, and others of humble rank—crowded

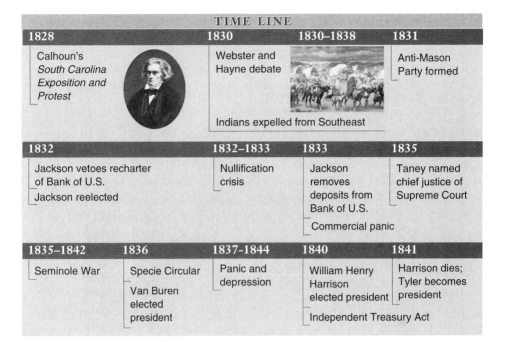

TIME LINE

| 1828 | 1830 | 1830–1838 | 1831 |
|---|---|---|---|
| Calhoun's *South Carolina Exposition and Protest* | Webster and Hayne debate | Indians expelled from Southeast | Anti-Mason Party formed |

| 1832 | 1832–1833 | 1833 | 1835 |
|---|---|---|---|
| Jackson vetoes recharter of Bank of U.S. Jackson reelected | Nullification crisis | Jackson removes deposits from Bank of U.S. Commercial panic | Taney named chief justice of Supreme Court |

| 1835–1842 | 1836 | 1837–1844 | 1840 | 1841 |
|---|---|---|---|---|
| Seminole War | Specie Circular Van Buren elected president | Panic and depression | William Henry Harrison elected president Independent Treasury Act | Harrison dies; Tyler becomes president |

before the United States Capitol to watch the inauguration of Andrew Jackson. After the ceremonies, the crowd poured into a public reception at the White House, where, in their eagerness to shake the new president's hand, they filled the state rooms to overflowing, trampled one another, soiled the carpets, and ruined the upholstery. "It was a proud day for the people," wrote Amos Kendall, one of Jackson's closest political associates. But Supreme Court justice Joseph Story, a friend and colleague of John Marshall, looked on the inaugural levee, as it was called, and remarked with disgust: "The reign of King 'Mob' seems triumphant."

In fact, the "age of Jackson" was much less a triumph of the common people than Kendall hoped and Story feared. But it did mark a transformation of American politics that extended power widely to new groups. Once restricted to a relatively small elite of property owners, politics now became open to virtually all the nation's white male citizens. In a political sense at least, the era had some claim to the title the Jacksonians gave it: the "era of the common man."

ANDREW JACKSON EN ROUTE TO WASHINGTON, 1829 Only a few weeks after Andrew Jackson's wife died (a result, he believed, of vicious attacks on her by his political enemies), the president-elect began a slow, triumphal procession from Tennessee to Washington, greeted by throngs of admirers in every town through which he passed.

## The Expanding Electorate

Until the 1820s, relatively few Americans had been permitted to vote; most states restricted the franchise to white male property owners or taxpayers or both, effectively removing a great mass of the less affluent from the voting roles. But even before Jackson's election, the franchise began to expand. Change came first in Ohio and other new states of the West, which, on joining the Union, adopted constitutions that guaranteed all adult white males the right to vote and permitted all voters the right to hold public office. Older states, concerned about the loss of their population to the West, began to grant similar political rights to their citizens, dropping or reducing their property ownership or taxpaying requirements. Eventually, every state democratized its electorate to at least some degree.

The wave of state reforms was generally peaceful, but in Rhode Island democratization efforts created considerable instability. The Rhode Island constitution (which was still basically the old colonial charter) barred more than half the adult males in the state from voting in the 1830s. The conservative legislature, chosen by this restricted electorate, consistently blocked all efforts at reform. In 1840, the lawyer and activist Thomas L. Dorr and a group of his followers formed a "People's party," held a convention, drafted a new constitution, and submitted it to a popular vote. It was overwhelmingly approved. The existing legislature rejected the Dorr document and submitted a new constitution of its own to the voters. It was narrowly defeated. The Dorrites, in the meantime, had begun to set up a new government, under their own constitution, with Dorr as governor; and so, in 1842, two governments were laying claims to legitimacy in Rhode Island. The old state government proclaimed that Dorr and his followers were rebels and began to imprison them. The Dorrites, meanwhile, made a brief and ineffectual effort to capture the state arsenal. The Dorr Rebellion, as it was known, quickly failed; Dorr himself surrendered and was briefly imprisoned. But the episode helped spur the old guard to draft a new constitution, which greatly expanded the suffrage.

The democratization process was far from complete. In much of the South, election laws continued to favor the planters and politicians of the older counties and to limit the influence of more newly settled western areas. Free blacks could not vote anywhere in the South and hardly anywhere in the North. Pennsylvania, in fact, amended its state constitution in 1838 to strip blacks of the right to vote, which they had previously held. In no state could women vote. Nowhere was the ballot secret, and often it was cast as a spoken vote rather than a written one, which meant that voters could be, and often were, bribed or intimidated.

Despite the persisting limitations, however, the number of voters increased at a much more rapid rate than did the population as a whole. Indeed, one of the most striking political trends of the early nineteenth century was the change in the method of choosing presidential electors and the dramatic increase in popular participation in the process. In 1800, the legislature had chosen the presidential electors in ten states, and the people in only six. By 1828, electors were chosen by popular vote in every state but South Carolina. In the presidential election of 1824, fewer than 27 percent of adult white males had voted. In the election of 1828, the figure was 58 percent; and in 1840, 80 percent.

The high level of voter participation was only in part the result of an expanded electorate. It was also the result of a growing popular interest in politics and a strengthening of party organization.

*The Legitimization of Party*

Although factional competition was part of American politics almost from the beginning of the republic, acceptance of the idea of party was not. For more than thirty years, most Americans who had opinions about the nature of government considered parties evils to be avoided and thought the nation should seek a broad consensus in which permanent factional lines would not exist. But in the 1820s and 1830s, those assumptions gave way to a new view: that permanent, institutionalized parties were a desirable part of the political process, that indeed they were essential to democracy.

The elevation of the idea of party occurred first at the state level, most prominently in New York. There, Martin Van Buren led a dissident political faction (known as the "Bucktails" or the "Albany Regency"). In the years after the War of 1812 this group began to challenge the established political elite—led by the aristocratic governor, De Witt Clinton—that had dominated the state for years. Factional rivalries were not new in New York, of course; what was new about this one was the way in which Van Buren and his followers posed their challenge. Refuting the traditional view of a political party as undemocratic, they argued that only an institutionalized party, based in the populace, could ensure genuine democracy. The alternative was the sort of closed elite that Clinton had created. In this new kind of party, ideological commitments would be less important than loyalty to the party itself. Above all, for a party to survive, it must have a permanent opposition. Competing parties would give each political faction a sense of purpose; they would force politicians to remain continually sensitive to the will of the people; and they would check and balance each other in much the same way that the different branches of government checked and balanced one another.

By the late 1820s, this new idea of party was spreading beyond New York. The election of Jackson in 1828, the result of a popular movement that stood apart from the usual political elites, seemed further to legitimize it. In the 1830s, finally, a fully formed two-party system began to operate at the national level, with each party committed to its own existence as an institution and willing to accept the legitimacy of its opposition. The anti-Jackson forces began to call themselves the Whigs. Jackson's followers called themselves Democrats, thus giving a permanent name to what is now the nation's oldest political party.

### President of the Common Man

The Democratic Party may have had no single ideological position, but Andrew Jackson himself did embrace a distinct, if simple, theory of democracy. Government, he said, should offer "equal protection and equal benefits" to all its white male citizens and favor no one region or class over another. In practice, that meant an assault on what Jackson and his associates considered the citadels of the eastern aristocracy and an effort to extend opportunities to the rising classes of the West and the South.

Jackson's first target was the entrenched officeholders in the federal government, many of whom had been in place for a generation or more. Jackson bitterly denounced what he considered a "class" of permanent officeholders. Offices, he said, belonged to the people, not to a self-serving bureaucracy. Equally important, a large turnover in the bureaucracy would allow him to reward his own supporters with offices.

One of Jackson's allies, William L. Marcy of New York, once explained, "To the victors belong the spoils"; and patronage, the process of giving out jobs as political rewards, became known as the "spoils system." In the end, during the eight years of his presidency Jackson removed no more than one-fifth of the federal officeholders. But by embracing the philosophy of the spoils system, a system already well entrenched in a number of state governments, the Jackson administration helped fix it firmly upon American politics.

Jackson's supporters also worked to transform the process by which presidential candidates were selected. In 1832, the president's followers staged a national convention to renominate him. In later generations, some would come to see the party convention as the source of corruption and political exclusivity, but those who created it in the 1830s considered it a great triumph for democracy. Through the convention, they believed, power in the party would arise directly from the people rather than from such elite political institutions as the congressional caucus.

The spoils system and the political convention did limit the power of two entrenched elites—permanent officeholders and the exclusive party caucus. Yet neither really transferred power to the common people. Appointments to office almost always went to prominent political allies of the president and his associates. Delegates to national conventions were less often common people than members of local party elites. Political opportunity within the party was expanding, but much less so than Jacksonian rhetoric suggested.

## "OUR FEDERAL UNION"

Jackson's commitment to extending power beyond entrenched elites led him to want to reduce the functions of the federal government. A concentration of power in Washington would, he believed, restrict opportunity to those favored few with political connections. But Jackson also believed in forceful presidential leadership and was strongly committed to the preservation of the Union. Thus at the same time that Jackson was promoting an economic program to reduce the power of the national government, he was asserting the supremacy of the Union in the face of a potent challenge. For no sooner had he entered office than his own vice president—John C. Calhoun—began to champion a controversial (and, in Jackson's view, dangerous) constitutional theory: nullification.

### Calhoun and Nullification

Calhoun was forty-six years old in 1828, with a distinguished past and an apparently promising future. But the smoldering issue of the tariff created a dilemma for him. Once he had been an outspoken protectionist and had strongly supported the tariff of 1816. But by the late 1820s, many South Car-

JOHN C. CALHOUN  This photograph, by Mathew Brady,
captured Calhoun toward the end of his life, when he was
torn between his real commitment to the ideals of the
Union and his equally fervent commitment to the interests
of the South. The younger generation of southern leaders,
who would dominate the politics of the region in the 1850s,
were less idealistic and more purely sectional in their views.

olinians had come to believe that the "tariff of abominations" was responsible for the stagnation of their state's economy—even though the stagnation was largely a result of the exhaustion of South Carolina's farmland, which could no longer compete effectively with the newly opened and fertile lands of the Southwest. Some exasperated Carolinians were ready to consider a drastic remedy—secession.

Calhoun's future political hopes rested on how he met this challenge in his home state. He did so by developing a theory that he believed offered a more moderate alternative to secession: the theory of nullification. Drawing from the ideas of Madison and Jefferson and their Virginia and Kentucky Resolutions of 1798–1799 and citing the Tenth Amendment to the Constitution, Calhoun argued that since the federal government was a creation of the states, the states—not the courts or Congress—were the final arbiters of the constitutionality of federal laws. If a state concluded that Congress had passed an unconstitutional law, then it could hold a special convention and declare the federal law null and void within the state. The nullification doctrine—and the idea of using it to nullify the 1828 tariff—quickly attracted broad support in South Carolina. But it did nothing to help Calhoun's standing within the new administration, in part because he had a powerful rival in Martin Van Buren.

### The Rise of Van Buren

Van Buren was about the same age as Calhoun and equally ambitious. He had won election to the governorship of New York in 1828 while helping Jackson win the state, and he resigned his new office in 1829 when Jackson appointed him secretary of state. Alone among the figures in the Jackson administration, Van Buren soon established himself as a member both of the official cabinet and of the president's unofficial circle of political allies, known as the "Kitchen Cabinet" (which included such Democratic newspaper editors as Isaac Hill of New Hampshire and Amos Kendall and Francis P. Blair of Kentucky). Van Buren's influence with the president was unmatched and grew stronger still as a result of a quarrel over etiquette that drove a wedge between the president and Calhoun.

Peggy O'Neale was the attractive daughter of a Washington tavern keeper with whom both Andrew Jackson and his friend John H. Eaton had taken lodgings while serving as senators from Tennessee. O'Neale was married, but rumors circulated in Washington in the mid-1820s that she and Senator Eaton were having an affair. O'Neale's husband died in 1828, and she and Eaton were soon married. A few weeks later, Jackson named Eaton secretary of war and thus made the new Mrs. Eaton a cabinet wife. The rest of the administration wives, led by Mrs. Calhoun, refused to receive her. Jackson (remembering the effects of public slander directed against his own late wife) was furious and demanded that the members of the cabinet accept her into their social world. Calhoun, under pressure from his wife, refused. Van Buren, a widower, befriended the Eatons and thus ingratiated himself with Jackson.

By 1831, partly as a result of the Peggy Eaton affair, Jackson had chosen Van Buren to succeed him in the White House. Calhoun's dreams of the presidency had all but vanished.

### The Webster-Hayne Debate

In January 1830, a great debate in the United States Senate dramatically revealed the degree to which sectional issues were intruding into national politics. The controversy grew out of a seemingly routine Senate discussion of federal policy toward the public lands in the West. In the midst of the debate, a senator from Connecticut suggested that all land sales and surveys be temporarily discontinued. Senator Thomas Hart Benton of Missouri, the Jacksonian leader in the Senate, attacked the proposal, charging that it would serve the economic needs of the Northeast at the expense of the West.

Robert Y. Hayne, a young senator from South Carolina, took up Benton's argument. He had no direct interest in the western lands, but he and other southerners saw the issue as a way to win western support for their drive to lower the tariff. Hayne argued that the South and the West were both victims of the tyranny of the Northeast and hinted that the two regions might combine to defend themselves against that tyranny.

Daniel Webster, now a senator from Massachusetts, took the floor the day after Hayne's speech. Although once an advocate of states' rights and an opponent of the tariff, he had changed his position as the sectional passions of his own region had ebbed. Now he attacked Hayne, and through him Calhoun, for what he considered their challenge to the integrity of the Union. He was, in effect, challenging Hayne to a debate not on public lands and the tariff but on the issue of states' rights versus national power. Hayne, coached by Calhoun, responded with a defense of the theory of nullification. Webster then spent two full afternoons delivering what became known as his "Second Reply to Hayne," a speech that northerners quoted and revered for years to come. He concluded with the ringing appeal: "Liberty and Union, now and for ever, one and inseparable!"

Calhoun's followers believed Hayne had the better of the argument, but their main concern was what President Jackson thought. The answer became clear at the annual Democratic Party banquet in honor of Thomas Jefferson. After dinner, guests delivered a series of toasts. The president arrived with a written text in which he had underscored certain words: "Our *Federal* Union—*It must be preserved.*" While he spoke, he looked directly at Calhoun. The diminutive Van Buren, who stood on his chair to see better, thought he saw Calhoun's hand shake and a trickle of wine run down his glass as he responded to the president's toast with his own: "The Union, next to our liberty most dear." Sharp lines had been drawn.

## The Nullification Crisis

In 1832, finally, the controversy over nullification produced a crisis when South Carolinians responded angrily to a congressional tariff bill that offered them no relief from the 1828 "tariff of abominations." Some militant South Carolinians were ready to secede from the Union, but Calhoun persuaded them to turn to nullification instead. The supporters of nullification won a substantial victory in the state elections of 1832. Almost immediately, the newly elected legislature summoned a state convention, which voted to nullify the tariffs of 1828 and 1832 and to forbid the collection of duties within the state. At the same time, South Carolina elected Hayne to serve as governor and Calhoun (who resigned as vice president) to replace Hayne as senator.

Jackson insisted that nullification was treason and that its adherents were traitors. He strengthened the federal forts in South Carolina and ordered a warship and several revenue ships to Charleston. When Congress convened early in 1833, Jackson's followers won approval of a force bill authorizing the president to use the military to see that acts of Congress were obeyed. Violence seemed a real possibility early in 1833.

Calhoun faced a predicament as he took his place in the Senate. Not a single state had come to South Carolina's support. Even South Carolina itself was divided and could not hope to prevail in a showdown with the federal government. Calhoun was saved by the timely intervention of Henry Clay, newly elected to the Senate, who devised a compromise by which the tariff would be lowered gradually until in 1842 it would reach approximately the same level as in 1816. The compromise and the force bill were passed on the same day, March 1, 1833. Jackson signed them both.

In South Carolina, the convention reassembled and repealed its nullification of the tariffs. But unwilling to allow Congress to have the last word, the convention nullified the force act—a purely symbolic act, since the tariff toward which the force act was directed had already been repealed. Calhoun and his followers claimed a victory for nullification, which had, they insisted, forced the revision of the tariff. They had some justification for doing so. But the episode taught Calhoun and his allies an important lesson: No state could defy the federal government alone.

## THE REMOVAL OF THE INDIANS

Andrew Jackson's attitude toward the Indian tribes that remained in the eastern United States was clear. He wanted them to move west, out of the way of expanding white settlement. Jackson's hostility toward the Indians was particularly intense because of his own earlier experiences leading military campaigns against the tribes. But in most respects, his views were not much different from those of most other white Americans.

### White Attitudes Toward the Tribes

In the eighteenth century, many whites had shared Thomas Jefferson's view of the Indians as "noble savages," peoples without real civilization but with an inherent dignity that made civilization possible among them. By the first decades of the nineteenth century, however, this vaguely philanthropic attitude was fading, particularly among the whites in the West. They were coming to view Native Americans simply as "savages," not only uncivilized but uncivilizable. That was one reason for the growing white commitment to removing the Indians from all the lands east of the Mississippi: the belief that whites should not be expected to live in close proximity to "savages." But white westerners also favored removal to put an end to violence and conflict in the western areas of white settlement. Most of all, however, they wanted valuable land that the tribes still possessed.

The federal government had already removed many Indians from the East before Jackson became president, but substantial tribal enclaves remained. In the Old Northwest, the long process of expelling the woodland Indians culminated in a last battle in 1831–1832. An alliance of Sauk (or Sac) and Fox Indians under the fabled and now aged warrior Black Hawk fought white settlers in Illinois in an effort to overturn a treaty ceding tribal lands in that state to the United States; Black Hawk and his followers considered the agreement, signed by a rival tribal faction, illegal. The Black Hawk War was a major defeat for the Indians, and was notable for the viciousness of the white military efforts. White forces attacked the Indians even when they attempted to surrender, pursued them as they retreated, and slaughtered many of them.

## The "Five Civilized Tribes"

More troubling to the government in the 1830s were the remaining Indian tribes of the South. In western Georgia, Alabama, Mississippi, and Florida lived what were known as the "Five Civilized Tribes"—the Cherokee, Creek, Seminole, Chickasaw, and Choctaw—most of whom lived in settled agricultural societies. They were, therefore, more closely tied to their lands than many of the more nomadic tribes to the north.

The federal government had worked steadily through the first decades of the nineteenth century to negotiate treaties with the southern Indians that would remove them to the West and open their lands for white settlement. But the negotiating process did not proceed fast enough to satisfy the region's whites. In 1830, finally, Congress passed the Removal Act, which appropriated new funds for negotiating treaties with the southern tribes and relocating them in the West. By then, several southern state governments were taking measures of their own to speed the removal. Most tribes were too weak to resist white pressures and ceded their lands in return for only token payments. Some, however, resisted.

The Cherokees tried to stop the encroachments by the state of Georgia through an appeal in the Supreme Court, and the Court's rulings in *Cherokee Nation* v. *Georgia* and *Worcester* v. *Georgia* (see pp. 227–228) supported the tribe's contention that the state had no authority to negotiate with tribal representatives. But Jackson repudiated the decisions, reportedly responding to news of the rulings with the contemptuous statement: "John Marshall has made his decision. Now let him enforce it."

In 1835, the United States government extracted a treaty from a minority faction of the Cherokees that ceded to Georgia the tribe's land in that state in return for $5 million and a reservation west of the Mississippi. The great majority of the 17,000 Cherokees did not recognize the treaty as legitimate and refused to leave their homes. But Jackson sent an army of 7,000 under General Winfield Scott to round them up and drive them westward.

## Trails of Tears

About 1,000 fled to North Carolina, where eventually the federal government provided them with a small reservation in the Smoky Mountains that survives today. But most of the rest made a long, forced trek to what is now

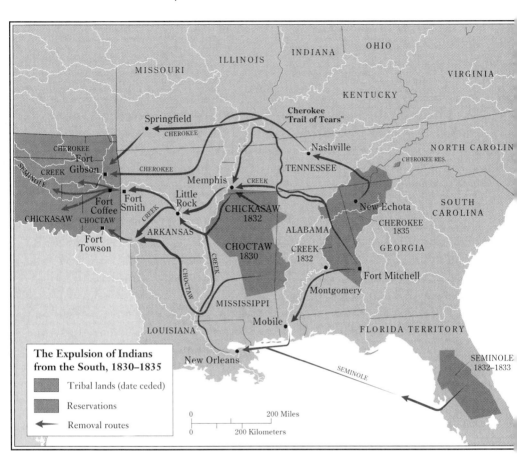

The Expulsion of Indians
from the South, 1830–1835

Tribal lands (date ceded)

Reservations

Removal routes

0    200 Miles

0    200 Kilometers

Oklahoma beginning in the winter of 1838. Thousands, perhaps a quarter or more of the émigrés, perished before reaching their unwanted destination. In the harsh new reservations in which they were now forced to live, the survivors remembered the terrible journey as "The Trail Where They Cried," the Trail of Tears.

Between 1830 and 1838, virtually all the Five Civilized Tribes were expelled from the southern states and forced to travel along their own Trails of Tears to "Indian Territory" (formally created by the Indian Intercourse Act of 1834), in what later became Oklahoma. The new territory seemed safely removed from existing white settlements and embraced land that most whites considered undesirable. It had the additional advantage, the government believed, of being bordered on the west by what explorers such as Edwin James and Stephen H. Long had christened the "Great American

Desert," land deemed unfit for habitation. Whites seemed unlikely ever to settle along the western borders of the Indian Territory, which meant that further conflict might be avoided. The Choctaws of Mississippi and western Alabama were the first to make the trek, beginning in 1830. The army moved out the Creeks of eastern Alabama and western Georgia in 1836. The Chickasaws in northern Mississippi began the long march westward a year later, and the Cherokees, finally, a year after that.

Only the Seminoles in Florida managed to resist the pressures, and even their success was limited. Like other tribes, the Seminoles had agreed under pressure to a settlement (the 1832–1833 treaties of Payne's Landing) by which they ceded their lands and agreed to move to Indian Territory within three years. Most did move west, but a substantial minority, under the leadership of the chieftain Osceola, balked and staged an uprising beginning in 1835 to defend their lands. (Joining the Indians in their struggle was a group of runaway black slaves, who had been living with the tribe.) The Seminole

*THE TRAIL OF TEARS* This twentieth-century painting by Robert Lindneux shows the forced evacuation of 18,000 Cherokee Indians from their ancestral lands in Georgia beginning in 1838. An epidemic of smallpox, along with starvation and exposure, cost thousands of Indians their lives. Here the Cherokees, guarded by soldiers carrying guns and bayonets, cross the Missouri River on their way to their new and unfamiliar homes in what is now Oklahoma.

War dragged on for years. Jackson sent troops to Florida, but the Seminoles with their black associates were masters of guerrilla warfare in the jungle-like Everglades. Finally, in 1842, the government abandoned the war. By then, many of the Seminoles had been either killed or forced westward. But the relocation of the Seminoles, unlike the relocation of most of the other tribes, was never complete.

### The Meaning of Removal

By the end of the 1830s, virtually all the important Indian societies east of the Mississippi (with a few exceptions such as remnants of the Seminoles and Cherokees) had been removed to the West. The tribes had ceded over 100 million acres of eastern land to the federal government; they had received in return about $68 million and 32 million acres in the far less hospitable lands west of the Mississippi. There they lived, divided by tribe into a series of separate reservations, in a territory surrounded by a string of United States forts to keep them in (and to keep most whites out), in a region whose climate and topography bore little relation to anything they had known before. Eventually, even this forlorn enclave would face encroachments from white civilization.

What were the alternatives to the removal of the eastern Indians? There was probably never any realistic possibility that the government could stop white expansion westward. White people had already been penetrating the West for nearly two centuries, and such penetrations were certain to continue.

But there were, in theory at least, alternatives to the brutal removal policy. The West was filled with examples of white settlers and native tribes living side by side and creating a shared (if not necessarily equal) world. In the pueblos of New Mexico, in the fur trading posts of the Pacific Northwest, in parts of Texas and California, settlers from Mexico, Canada, and the United States had created societies in which Indians and whites were in intimate contact with each other. Even the Lewis and Clark expedition, during its famous explorations, had lived with western Indians on terms of such intimacy that many of its members contracted venereal disease from Indian sexual partners. Sometimes these close contacts between whites and Indians were beneficial to both sides, even reasonably equal. Often they were cruel and exploitive. But the early multiracial societies of the West did not separate whites and Indians. They demonstrated ways in which the two cultures could interact, each shaping the other.

By the mid-nineteenth century, however, white Americans had adopted a different model as they contemplated westward expansion. Much as the early British settlers along the Atlantic coast had established "plantations," from which natives were, in theory, to be excluded, so the westering whites of later years came to view the territories they were entering as virgin land, with no preexisting civilization. Indians, they believed, could not be part-ners—either equal or subordinate—in the creation of new societies in the West. They were obstacles, to be removed and, as far as possible, isolated. Indians, Andrew Jackson once said, had "neither the intelligence, the in-dustry, the moral habits, nor the desire of improvement" to be fit partners in the project of extending white civilization westward. By dismissing Indian cultures in that way, white Americans justified to themselves a series of harsh policies that they believed (incorrectly) would make the West theirs alone.

## JACKSON AND THE BANK WAR

Jackson was quite willing to use federal power against the Indian tribes. Where white Americans were concerned, however, he was usually opposed to concentrating power either in the federal government or in elite institu-tions associated with it. An early example of that was his 1830 veto of a con-gressional measure providing a subsidy to the proposed Maysville Road in Kentucky. The bill was unconstitutional, Jackson argued, because the road in question lay entirely within Kentucky and was not, therefore, a part of "interstate commerce." But the bill was also unwise, because it committed the government to what Jackson considered extravagant expenditures. A similar resistance to federal power lay behind the most celebrated episode of Jackson's presidency: the war against the Bank of the United States.

### Biddle's Institution

The Bank of the United States had a monopoly on the deposits of the fed-eral government, which owned one-fifth of the Bank's stock; it also did a tremendous business in general banking. It provided credit to growing en-terprises; it issued bank notes which served as a dependable medium of ex-change throughout the country; and it exercised a restraining effect on the less well managed state banks. Nicholas Biddle, who ran the Bank from 1823 on from its imposing headquarters in Philadelphia, had done much to put the institution on a sound and prosperous basis. Nevertheless, Andrew Jackson was determined to destroy it.

Opposition to the Bank came from two very different groups: the "soft-money" faction and the "hard-money" faction. Advocates of soft money consisted largely of state bankers and their allies. They objected to the Bank of the United States because it restrained the state banks from issuing notes freely. The hard-money people believed that coin was the only safe currency, and they condemned all banks that issued bank notes, including the Bank of the United States. The soft-money advocates were believers in rapid economic growth and speculation; the hard-money forces embraced older ideas of "public virtue" and looked with suspicion on expansion and speculation. Jackson himself supported the hard-money position, but he was also sensitive to the complaints of his many soft-money supporters in the West and the South. He made it clear that he would not favor renewing the charter of the Bank of the United States, which was due to expire in 1836.

Biddle was a Philadelphia aristocrat, unaccustomed to politics. But in his efforts to save the Bank, he began granting banking favors to influential men. In particular, he relied on Daniel Webster, whom he named the Bank's legal counsel and director of the Boston branch. Webster was also a frequent, heavy borrower. He helped Biddle enlist the support of Henry Clay as well.

Clay, Webster, and other advisers persuaded Biddle to apply to Congress for a recharter bill in 1832, four years ahead of the expiration date. Congress passed the recharter bill; Jackson vetoed it; and the Bank's supporters in Congress failed to override the veto. The Bank question then emerged as the paramount issue of the 1832 election, just as Clay had hoped.

In 1832, Clay ran for president as the unanimous choice of the National Republicans, who held a nominating convention in Baltimore late in 1831. But the "Bank War" failed to provide Clay with the winning issue for which he had hoped. Jackson, with Van Buren as his running mate, overwhelmingly defeated Clay (and several minor-party candidates) with 55 percent of the popular vote and 219 electoral votes (more than four times as many as Clay received). The results were a defeat not only for Clay but for Biddle.

### The "Monster" Destroyed

Jackson was now more determined than ever to destroy the "monster." He could not legally abolish the institution before the expiration of its charter. But he weakened it by removing the government's deposits from the Bank. His secretary of the treasury believed that such an action would destabilize the financial system and refused to give the order. Jackson removed him and appointed a replacement. When the new secretary similarly procrastinated, Jackson named a third: Roger B. Taney, the attorney general, a close friend and loyal ally of the president.

Taney soon began taking the government's deposits out of the Bank of the United States and putting them in a number of state banks (which Jackson's enemies called "pet banks"). In response, Biddle called in loans and raised interest rates, explaining that without the government deposits the Bank's resources were stretched too thin. His actions precipitated a short recession, which Biddle thought would pressure Congress to recharter the Bank.

As financial conditions worsened in the winter of 1833–1834, supporters of the Bank organized meetings around the country and sent petitions to Washington urging a rechartering of the Bank. But the Jacksonians blamed the recession on Biddle and refused. The banker finally carried his contraction of credit too far and had to reverse himself to appease the business community. His hopes of winning a recharter of the Bank died in the process. Jackson had won a considerable political victory. But when the Bank of the United States died in 1836, the country lost an important financial institution and was left with a fragmented and chronically unstable banking system that would plague the economy for many years.

## The Taney Court

In the aftermath of the Bank War, Jackson moved against the most powerful institution of economic nationalism: the Supreme Court. In 1835, when John Marshall died, the president appointed as the new chief justice his trusted ally Roger B. Taney. Taney did not bring a sharp break in constitutional interpretation, but he did help modify Marshall's vigorous nationalism.

Perhaps the clearest indication of the new judicial mood was the celebrated case of *Charles River Bridge* v. *Warren Bridge* of 1837. The case involved a dispute between two Massachusetts companies over the right to build a bridge across the Charles River between Boston and Cambridge. One company had a longstanding charter from the state to operate a toll bridge, a charter that the firm claimed guaranteed it a monopoly of the bridge traffic. Another company had applied to the legislature for authorization to construct a second, competing bridge that would—since it would be toll-free—greatly reduce the value of the first company's charter. The first company contended that in granting the second charter, the legislature was engaging in a breach of contract; and it noted that the Marshall Court, in the *Dartmouth College* case and other decisions, had ruled that states had no right to abrogate contracts. But now Taney, speaking for the Democratic majority on the Court, supported the right of Massachusetts to award the second charter. The object of government, Taney maintained, was to promote the general happiness, an object that took precedence over the rights of property. A state, therefore, had the right to amend or abrogate a contract if such action was necessary to advance the well-being of the community. The decision reflected one of the cornerstones of the Jacksonian idea: that the key to democracy was an expansion of economic opportunity, which would not occur if older corporations could maintain monopolies and choke off competition from newer companies.

## THE EMERGENCE
## OF THE SECOND PARTY SYSTEM

Jackson's forceful—some claimed tyrannical—tactics in crushing first the nullification movement and then the Bank of the United States helped galvanize a growing opposition coalition that by the mid-1830s was ready to assert itself in national politics. It began as a gathering of national political leaders opposed to Jackson's use of power. Denouncing the president as "King Andrew I," they began to refer to themselves as Whigs, after the party in England that traditionally worked to limit the power of the king. As the new party began to develop as a national organization with constituencies in every state, its appeal became more diffuse. Nevertheless, both in its philosophy and in the nature of its membership, the Whig Party was different from the party of Jackson.

With the emergence of the Whigs, the nation once again had two competing political parties. What scholars now call the "second party system" had begun what would turn out to be its relatively brief life.

### The Two Parties

The philosophy of the Democratic Party in the 1830s bore the stamp of Andrew Jackson, but it drew from many older traditions as well. Democrats envisioned a future of steadily expanding opportunities. The function of government, therefore, was to remove artificial obstacles to that expansion and to avoid creating new obstacles of its own. The federal government should be limited in power, except to the degree that it worked to eliminate social and economic arrangements that entrenched privilege and stifled opportunity. The rights of states should be protected except to the extent that state governments interfered with social and economic mobility. Jacksonian Democrats celebrated "honest workers," "simple farmers," and "forthright businessmen" and contrasted them to the corrupt, monopolistic, aristocratic forces of established wealth.

The Jacksonians were not hostile to wealth. Most Democrats believed in material progress, and many party leaders—including Jackson himself—were wealthy men. Yet Democrats tended to look with suspicion on government efforts to stimulate commercial and industrial growth. These efforts, they believed, generally produced such menacing institutions of power as the Bank of the United States. Democrats were less likely than Whigs to support chartered banks and corporations, state-supported internal improvements, even public schools. They were more likely than Whigs to support territorial expansion, which would, they believed, widen opportunities for aspiring Americans. Among the most radical members of the party—the so-called Locofocos, mainly workingmen and small businessmen and professionals in the Northeast—sentiment was strong for a vigorous, perhaps even violent, assault on monopoly and privilege far in advance of anything Jackson himself ever contemplated.

The political philosophy that became known as Whiggery favored expanding the power of the federal government, encouraging industrial and commercial development, and knitting the country together into a consolidated economic system. Whigs embraced material progress enthusiastically, but they were cautious about westward expansion, fearful that rapid territorial growth would produce instability. Their vision of America was of a nation embracing the industrial future and rising to greatness as a commercial and manufacturing power. And although Whigs insisted that their vision would result in increasing opportunities for all Americans, they tended to attribute particular value to the elites they considered the productive, modernizing forces in society—the entrepreneurs and institutions that most effectively promoted economic growth. Thus while Democrats were inclined to oppose legislation establishing banks, corporations, and other modernizing institutions, Whigs generally favored such measures.

### Party Constituencies

To some extent, the constituencies of the two major parties were reflections of these diffuse philosophies. The Whigs were strongest among the more substantial merchants and manufacturers of the Northeast; the wealthier planters of the South (those who favored commercial development and the strengthening of ties with the North); and the ambitious farmers and rising commercial class of the West—usually migrants from the Northeast—who advocated internal improvements, expanding trade, and rapid economic progress. The Democrats drew more support from smaller merchants and the workingmen of the Northeast; from Southern planters suspicious of industrial growth; and from westerners—usually with Southern roots—who favored a predominantly agrarian economy and opposed the development of powerful economic institutions in their region. Whigs tended to be wealthier than Democrats, tended to have more aristocratic backgrounds, and tended to be more commercially ambitious.

But Whigs and Democrats alike were more interested in winning elections than in maintaining philosophical purity. And both parties made adjustments from region to region in order to attract the largest possible number of voters, often at the sacrifice of party philosophy. In New York, for example, the Whigs developed a popular following through a movement known as Anti-Masonry. The Anti-Mason Party had emerged in the 1820s in response to widespread resentment against the secret and exclusive, hence supposedly undemocratic, Society of Freemasons. Such resentment increased in 1826 when a former Mason, William Morgan, mysteriously disappeared from his home in Batavia, New York, shortly before he was scheduled to publish a book that would allegedly expose the secrets of Freemasonry. The assumption was widespread that Morgan had been abducted and murdered by the vengeful Masons. Whigs seized on the Anti-Mason frenzy to launch spirited attacks on Jackson and Van Buren (both Freemasons), implying that the Democrats were connected with the anti-democratic conspiracy. By embracing Anti-Masonry, Whigs were attacking the Democrats with the Democrats' own issues.

Religious and ethnic divisions also played an important role in determining the constituencies of the two parties. Irish and German Catholics, among the largest of the recent immigrant groups, tended to support the Democrats, who appeared to share their own vague aversion to commercial development and entrepreneurial progress and who seemed to respect and protect their cultural values and habits. Evangelical Protestants gravitated toward the Whigs because they associated the party with constant development and improvement, goals their own religion embraced. They envisioned a society progressing steadily toward unity and order, and they looked on the new immigrant communities as a threat to that progress—as groups that needed to be disciplined and taught "American" ways. In many communities, these and other local ethnic, religious, and cultural tensions were much more influential in determining party alignments than any concrete political or economic proposals.

*Party Leadership*

The Whig Party was more successful at defining its positions and attracting a constituency than it was in uniting behind a national leader. No one person was ever able to command the loyalties of the party in the way Jackson commanded the loyalties of the Democrats. Instead, Whigs tended to divide their allegiance among three major figures: Henry Clay, Daniel Webster, and John C. Calhoun.

Clay won support from many of those who favored internal improvements and economic development, what he called the American System; such improvements were especially important to people living in the western states, where the absence of good transportation routes to the markets of the east often proved crippling to commerce. But Clay's image as a devious political operator and his identification with the West proved an insuperable liability. He ran for president three times and never won. Daniel Webster, the greatest orator of his era, won broad support with his passionate speeches in defense of the Constitution and the Union; but his close connection with the Bank of the United States and the protective tariff, his reliance on rich men for financial support, and his excessive fondness for brandy prevented him from developing enough of a national constituency to win him the office he so desperately wanted. John C. Calhoun, the third member of what became known as the Great Triumvirate, never considered himself a true Whig, and his identification with the nullification controversy in effect disqualified him from national leadership in any case. Yet he sided with Clay and Webster on the issue of the national bank. And he shared with them a strong animosity toward Andrew Jackson.

The Whigs, in other words, were able to marshal an imposing array of national leaders, each with his own powerful constituency. Yet for many years they were unable to find a way to merge those constituencies into a single winning combination. The result was that while the Whigs competed relatively evenly with the Democrats in congressional, state, and local races, they managed to win only two presidential elections in the more than twenty years of their history.

Their problems became particularly clear in 1836. The Democrats were united behind Andrew Jackson's personal choice for president, Martin Van Buren. The Whigs could not even agree on a single candidate. Instead, they ran several candidates, hoping to profit from the regional strength of each. Webster represented the party in New England; Hugh Lawson White of Tennessee ran in the South; and the former Indian fighter and hero of the War of 1812, William Henry Harrison of Ohio, was the candidate in the middle states and the West. None of the three candidates could expect to get a majority in the electoral college, but party leaders hoped they might separately draw enough votes from Van Buren to prevent his getting a majority and throw the election to the House of Representatives, where the Whigs might be better able to elect one of their candidates. In the end, however, the three Whigs were no match for the one Democrat. Van Buren won easily, with 170 electoral votes to 124 for all his opponents.

## POLITICS AFTER JACKSON

Andrew Jackson retired from public life in 1837, the most beloved political figure of his age. Martin Van Buren was less fortunate. He could not match Jackson's personal magnetism, and his administration suffered from economic difficulties that hurt both him and his party.

### The Panic of 1837

Van Buren's success in the 1836 election was a result in part of a nationwide economic boom that was then reaching its height. Canal and railroad builders were at a peak of activity. Prices were rising, and credit was easy. The land business, in particular, was booming. Between 1835 and 1837, the government sold nearly 40 million acres of public land, nearly three-fourths of it to speculators who purchased large tracts in hopes of reselling them at a profit. These land sales, along with revenues the government received from the tariff of 1833, created a series of substantial federal budget surpluses and made possible a steady reduction of the national debt (something Jackson had always advocated). From 1835 to 1837, the government for the first and only time in its history was out of debt, with a substantial surplus in the Treasury.

Congress and the administration now faced the question of what to do with the Treasury surplus. Support soon grew for returning the federal surplus to the states. An 1836 "distribution" act required that the federal government pay its surplus funds to the states each year in four quarterly installments as interest-free, unsecured loans. No one expected the "loans" to be repaid. The states spent the money quickly, mainly to promote the construction of highways, railroads, and canals. The distribution of the surplus thus gave further stimulus to the economic boom. At the same time, the withdrawal of federal funds strained the state (or "pet") banks in which they had been deposited by the government; the banks had to call in their own loans to make the transfer of funds to the state governments.

Congress did nothing to check the speculative fever, with which many congressmen themselves were badly infected. But Jackson, always suspicious of paper currency, feared that the government was selling land for state bank notes of questionable value. In 1836, not long before leaving office, he issued an executive order, the "specie circular." It provided that in payment for public lands, the government would accept only gold or silver coins or currency backed by gold or silver. Jackson was right to fear the speculative fever but wrong in thinking the specie circular would cure it. On the contrary, it produced a financial panic that began in the first months of Van Buren's presidency. Hundreds of banks and hundreds of businesses failed. Unemployment grew. There were bread riots in some of the larger cities. Prices fell, especially the price of land. Many railroad and canal projects failed; several of the debt-burdened state governments ceased to pay interest on their bonds, and a few repudiated their debts, at least temporarily. It was the worst depression in American history to that point, and it lasted for five years. It was a political catastrophe for Van Buren and the Democrats.

### The Van Buren Program

The Van Buren administration, which strongly opposed government intervention in the economy, did little to fight the depression. Some of the steps it took—borrowing money to pay government debts and accepting only specie for payment of taxes—may have made things worse. Other efforts failed in Congress: a "preemption" bill that would have given settlers the right to buy government land near them before it was opened for public sale, and another bill that would have lowered the price of land. Van Buren did succeed in establishing a ten-hour workday on all federal projects by issuing a presidential order, but he had few legislative achievements.

The most important and controversial measure in the president's program was a proposal for a new financial system to replace the Bank of the United States. Under Van Buren's plan, known as the "independent treasury" or "subtreasury" system, government funds would be placed in an independent treasury in Washington and in subtreasuries in other cities. No private banks would have the government's money or name to use as a basis for speculation; the government and the banks would be "divorced." Van Buren called a special session of Congress in 1837 to consider the proposal, which failed in the House. In 1840, the administration finally succeeded in driving the measure through both houses of Congress.

### The Log Cabin Campaign

As the campaign of 1840 approached, the Whigs realized that they would have to settle on one candidate for president. Accordingly, they held their first national nominating convention in Harrisburg, Pennsylvania, in December 1839. Passing over Henry Clay, who expected the nomination, the convention chose William Henry Harrison—a descendant of the Virginia aristocracy who had spent his adult life in the Northwest. He was a renowned soldier and a popular national figure. The Democrats nominated Van Buren.

WHIG HEADQUARTERS The Whig Party managed in 1840 to disguise its relatively elitist roots by portraying its presidential candidate, the patrician General William Henry Harrison, as a product of a log cabin who enjoyed drinking hard cider from a jug. Pictures of log cabins abounded in Whig campaign posters, as seen in this drawing of a Harrison rally in Philadelphia.

The 1840 campaign illustrated how fully the ethos of party competition (the subordination of ideology to immediate political needs) had established itself in America. The Whigs—who had emerged as a party largely because of their opposition to Andrew Jackson's common-man democracy, who in most regions represented the more affluent elements of the population, who favored government policies that would aid business—presented themselves in 1840 as the party of the common people. So, of course, did the Democrats. Both parties used the same techniques of mass voter appeal, the same evocation of simple, rustic values. What mattered was not the philosophical purity of the party but its ability to win votes. The Whig campaign was particularly effective in portraying William Henry Harrison, a wealthy member of the frontier elite with a considerable estate, as a simple man of the people who loved log cabins and hard cider. The Democrats, already weakened by the depression, had no effective defense against such tactics. Harrison won the election with 234 electoral votes to 60 for Van Buren and with a popular majority of 53 percent.

## The Frustration of the Whigs

But the Whigs found the four years after their resounding victory frustrating and divisive. In large part, that was because their appealing new president died of pneumonia one month after taking office. Vice President John Tyler of Virginia succeeded him. Control of the administration thus fell to a man with whom the Whig Party leadership had relatively weak ties. Harrison had generally deferred to Henry Clay and to Daniel Webster, whom he named secretary of state. Under Tyler, things changed quickly.

Tyler was a former Democrat who had left the party in reaction to what he considered Jackson's excessively egalitarian program and his imperious methods. But there were still signs of his Democratic past in his approach to public policy. The president did agree to bills abolishing the independent-treasury system and raising tariff rates. But he refused to support Clay's attempt to recharter the Bank of the United States. And he vetoed several internal improvement bills sponsored by Clay and other congressional Whigs. Finally, a conference of congressional Whigs (many of whom referred scornfully to the new president as "His Accidency") read Tyler out of the party. Every cabinet member but Webster resigned; five former Democrats took their places. When Webster, too, left the cabinet, Tyler appointed Calhoun, who had rejoined the Democratic Party, to replace him.

A new political alignment was taking shape. Tyler and a small band of conservative southern Whigs were preparing to rejoin the Democrats. Into the common man's party of Jackson and Van Buren was arriving a faction with decidedly aristocratic political ideas, men who thought that government had an obligation to protect and even expand the institution of slavery and who believed in states' rights with almost fanatical devotion.

## Whig Diplomacy

In the midst of these domestic controversies, a series of incidents brought Great Britain and the United States to the brink of war in the late 1830s.

Anti-British factions in Canada launched an unsuccessful rebellion against the colonial government there in 1837. When the insurrection failed, some of the rebels took refuge near the United States border and chartered an American steamship, the *Caroline*, to ship them supplies across the Niagara River from New York. British authorities in Canada seized the *Caroline* and burned it, killing one American in the process. The British government refused either to disavow the attack or to provide compensation for it, and resentment in the United States grew rapidly.

At the same time, tensions flared over the boundary between Canada and Maine, which had been in dispute since the treaty of 1783. In 1838, groups of Americans and Canadians, mostly lumberjacks, began moving into the Aroostook River region in the disputed area, precipitating a violent brawl between the two groups that became known as the "Aroostook War."

Several years later, there were yet more Anglo-American problems. In 1841, an American ship, the *Creole*, sailed from Virginia for New Orleans with more than 100 slaves aboard. En route the slaves mutinied, seized possession of the ship, and took it to the Bahamas. British officials there declared the slaves free, and the English government refused to overrule them. Many Americans, especially southerners, were furious.

At this critical juncture a new government eager to reduce tensions with the United States came to power in Great Britain. It sent Lord Ashburton, an admirer of America, to negotiate an agreement on the Maine boundary and other matters. The result was the Webster-Ashburton Treaty of 1842, under which the United States received slightly more than half the disputed area and agreed to a revised northern boundary as far west as the Rocky Mountains. Ashburton also eased the memory of the *Caroline* and *Creole* affairs by expressing regret and promising no future "officious interference" with American ships. The Webster-Ashburton Treaty was popular in America, and Anglo-American relations were suddenly better than they had been for many years.

During the Tyler administration, the United States established its first diplomatic relations with China as part of an effort to win a share in the newly emerging China trade. In the Treaty of Wang Hya, concluded in 1844, American diplomats secured the same trading privileges as the English. In the next ten years, American trade with China steadily increased.

In their diplomatic efforts, at least, the Whigs were able to secure some important successes. But by the end of the Tyler administration, the party could look back on few other victories. In the election of 1844, the Whigs lost the White House. They were to win only one more national election in their history before a great sectional crisis would arise that would shatter their party and, for a time, the Union.

# D E B A T I N G    T H E    P A S T

## *Jacksonian Democracy*

O MANY AMERICANS in the 1820s and 1830s, Andrew Jackson was a champion of democracy, a symbol of the spirit of antielitism and egalitarianism that was sweeping American life. Historians, however, have disagreed sharply not only in their assessments of Jackson himself but in their portrayal of American society in his era.

The "progressive" historians of the early twentieth century tended to see Jacksonian politics as a forebear of their own battles against economic privilege and political corruption. Frederick Jackson Turner encouraged scholars to see Jacksonianism as the product of the democratic West: a protest by the people of the frontier against the conservative aristocracy of the East, which they believed restricted their own freedom and opportunity. Jackson represented those who wanted to make government responsive to the will of the people rather than to the power of special interests. The culmination of this progressive interpretation of Jacksonianism was the publication in 1945 of Arthur M. Schlesinger, Jr.'s *The Age of Jackson*. Schlesinger was less interested in the regional basis of Jacksonianism than the disciples of Turner had been. Jacksonian Democracy, he argued, was the effort "to control the power of the capitalist groups, mainly Eastern, for the benefit of non-capitalist groups, farmers and laboring men, East, West, and South." He portrayed Jacksonianism as an early version of modern reform efforts (in the progressive era and the New Deal) to "restrain the power of the business community."

Richard Hofstadter, in an influential 1948 essay, sharply disagreed. Jackson, he argued, was the spokesman of rising entrepreneurs—aspiring businessmen who saw the road to opportunity blocked by the monopolistic power of Eastern aristocrats. The Jacksonians opposed special privileges only to the extent that those privileges blocked their own road to success. They were less sympathetic to the aspirations of those below them. Bray Hammond, writing in 1957, argued similarly that the Jacksonian cause was "one of campaign against capitalist," of rising elites against entrenched ones. Other historians, exploring the ideological origins of the movement, saw Jacksonianism less as a democratic reform movement than as a nostalgic effort to restore a lost (and largely imagined) past. Marvin Meyers's *The Jacksonian Persuasion* (1957) argued that Jackson and his followers looked with misgivings on the new industrial society emerging around them and yearned instead for a restoration of the agrarian, republican virtues of an earlier time.

Historians of the 1960s began examining Jacksonianism in entirely new ways: looking less at Jackson and his supporters and more at the nature of American society in the early nineteenth century. Lee Benson's *The Concept of Jacksonian Democracy* (1961) used new quantitative techniques to demonstrate the role of religion and ethnicity in determining party divisions. If there was an egalitarian spirit alive in America in those years, he claimed, it extended well beyond the Democratic party and the followers of Jackson. Edward Pessen's *Jacksonian America* (1969) revealed that the democratic rhetoric of the age disguised the reality of an increasingly stratified society, in which inequality was growing more, not less, severe. Alan Dawley went further in 1977, arguing that the extension of political rights in the 1820s and 1830s not only failed to advance economic democracy, but undermined the ability of workers and other exploited groups to articulate and act upon their grievances.

Scholars in more recent years have continued to pay less attention to Jackson and the Democratic party than to the origins and character of democratic ideas generally. In *Chants Democratic* (1984), Sean Wilentz identified the rise in the 1820s of a powerful working-class identity, expressed through a set of ideas known as "republicanism" and stimulated (although not fundamentally shaped) by the democratic rhetoric of party politics at the time. Workers in New York, he showed, were attracted less to Jackson himself than to the idea that power in a republic should be widely dispersed. They were raising a genuinely radical challenge to the rise of laissez-faire capitalism and to an emerging wage-labor system that threatened to reduce once-independent artisans into factory laborers unable to control their own livelihoods.

CHAPTER TEN

# America's Economic Revolution

*Foundations of Economic Development*

*Transportation and Communications Revolutions* ∼ *Commerce and Industry*

*Men and Women at Work* ∼ *Patterns of Society*

*The Agricultural North*

W HEN THE UNITED STATES entered the War of 1812, it was still an essentially agrarian nation. There were, to be sure, some substantial cities in America. There was also modest but growing manufacturing, mainly in the Northeast. But the overwhelming majority of Americans were farmers and tradespeople, working within an economy that was still mainly local.

By the time the Civil War began in 1861, the United States had transformed itself. Most Americans were still rural people. But even American farmers were, with few exceptions, now part of a national, and even international, market economy. Above all, perhaps, the United States had developed a major manufacturing sector and was beginning to challenge the industrial nations of Europe for supremacy. The nation had experienced the beginning of its industrial revolution.

These dramatic changes did not have the same impact everywhere. The Northeast and its new economic ally the Northwest were rapidly developing a complex, modern economy and society, dominated by large cities, important manufacturing, and profitable commercial farming. It was in many ways an unequal society, but it was also a fluid one, firmly committed to the ideal of free labor. Relatively few white Americans yet lived west of the Mississippi River, but parts of those western lands, too, were becoming part of large-scale commercial agriculture and were creating links to the capitalist economy of the Northeast.

In the South and Southwest, there were changes too. Southern agriculture, particularly cotton farming, flourished in response to the growing de-

| TIME LINE | | | | |
|---|---|---|---|---|
| **1817–1825** | **1830** | **1830s** | **1834** | **1837** |
| Erie Canal constructed | Baltimore and Ohio Railroad begins operation | Immigration from southern Ireland begins | Lowell mills women strike<br><br>McCormick patents mechanical reaper | Native American Association fights immigration |
| **1844** | **1845** | **1846** | **1847** | **1852** |
| Morse sends first telegraph message | Irish potato famine begins<br><br>Native American Party formed | Rotary press invented | John Deere manufactures steel plows | American Party (Know Nothings) formed |

mand from textile mills in New England and elsewhere and became increasingly tied to the national and international economy. But the southern states also remained much less developed than their northern counterparts. And as the North became ever more committed to the fluidity and mobility of its free-labor system, the South was becoming more and more resolute in its defense of slavery.

The industrial revolution, which was doing so much to draw the nation into a single, integrated economy, was also working to isolate—and, increasingly, to alarm—the residents of one of its regions. It was transforming the nation. It was also dividing it.

# FOUNDATIONS OF ECONOMIC DEVELOPMENT

The American industrial revolution was a result of many factors: population growth, advances in transportation and communications, the growth of manufacturing technology, and the development of new systems of business organization. By 1860, the northern regions of the nation had acquired at least the beginnings of all those things.

## *The American Population, 1820–1840*

Three trends characterized the American population between 1820 and 1840, all of them contributing in various ways to economic growth. The population was increasing rapidly. Much of it was moving westward. And much of it was moving to towns and cities, where it provided a work force for industry.

The American population had stood at only 4 million in 1790. By 1820, it had reached 10 million; and by 1840, 17 million. The United States was growing much more rapidly in population than Britain or Europe. By 1860 it had more people than the United Kingdom and almost as many as Germany and France. One reason for the growth was improvements in public health; the number and ferocity of epidemics (such as the great cholera plague of 1832) slowly declined, as did the mortality rate as a whole. But the population increase was also a result of a high birth rate. In 1840, the birth rate for white women stood at 6.14.

The African-American population increased more slowly than the white. After 1808, when the importation of slaves became illegal, the proportion of blacks to whites in the nation as a whole steadily declined. In 1820, there was one African American to every four whites; in 1840, one to every five. The slower increase of the black population was a result of its comparatively high death rate. Slave mothers had large families, but life was shorter for both

THE PORT OF NEW YORK, 1828 This view of South Street in Manhattan shows the East River lined with docks. Other docks, similarly busy, lined the Hudson River on the opposite side of the island. The population of New York City was approaching 150,000 by 1828.

slaves and free blacks than for whites—a result of the enforced poverty in which virtually all African Americans lived.

Immigration, choked off by wars in Europe and economic crises in America, contributed little to the American population in the first three decades of the nineteenth century. Of the total 1830 population of nearly 13 million, the foreign-born numbered fewer than 500,000. Soon, however, immigration began to grow once again. Reduced transportation costs and increasing economic opportunities in America helped stimulate the immigration boom, as did deteriorating economic conditions in some areas of Europe. The migrations introduced new groups to the United States. In particular, the number of immigrants arriving from the southern (Catholic) counties of Ireland began to grow.

Much of this new European immigration flowed into the rapidly growing cities of the Northeast. But urban growth was a result of substantial internal migration as well. As the agricultural regions of New England and other areas grew less profitable, more and more people picked up stakes and moved—some to more promising agricultural regions in the West, but many to eastern cities. In 1790, one person in thirty had lived in a city (defined as a community of 8,000 or more); in 1820, one in twenty; and in 1840, one in twelve. The largest such cities were in the Northeast.

The rise of New York City was particularly dramatic. By 1810 it was the largest city in the United States. That was partly a result of its excellent natural harbor. It was also a result of the Erie Canal (completed in 1825), which gave the city unrivaled access to the interior. And it was a result, too, of liberal state laws that made the city attractive for both foreign and domestic commerce.

*Immigration and Urban Growth, 1840–1860*

The growth of cities accelerated dramatically between 1840 and 1860. The population of New York, for example, rose from 312,000 to 805,000. Philadelphia's population grew over the same twenty-year period from 220,000 to 565,000; Boston's, from 93,000 to 177,000. By 1860, 26 percent of the population of the free states was living in towns (places of 2,500 people or more) or cities, up from 14 percent in 1840. In the South, by contrast, the increase of urban residents was only from 6 percent in 1840 to 10 percent in 1860.

The booming agricultural economy of the western regions of the nation produced significant urban growth as well. Between 1820 and 1840, communities that had once been small villages or trading posts became major cities: St. Louis, Pittsburgh, Cincinnati, Louisville. Each of them benefited from a strategic position on the Mississippi River or one of its major tributaries. All of them became centers of the growing carrying trade that connected the farmers of the Midwest with New Orleans and, through it, the cities of the Northeast. After 1830, however, an increasing proportion of this shipping moved from the river to the Great Lakes and created major new urban centers that gradually superseded the river ports. Among them were Buffalo, Detroit, Milwaukee, Cleveland, and—most important in the end—Chicago.

The enlarged urban population was in part simply a reflection of the growth of the national population as a whole, which rose by more than a third—from 23 million to over 31 million—in the 1850s alone. But it was more directly a result of the flow of people into cities from two sources: the native farmers of the Northeast, who were being forced off the land by competition from the West; and, even more significantly by the 1850s, immigrants from Europe. Only 500,000 foreigners had arrived in the United States in the 1830s, in part because of the serious American depression of those years. But between 1840 and 1850, more than 1.5 million Europeans moved to America. In the 1850s, the number rose to 2.5 million. Almost half the residents of New York City in the 1850s were recent immigrants. In St. Louis, Chicago, and Milwaukee, the foreign-born outnumbered those of native birth. Few immigrants settled in the South. Only 500,000 lived in the slave states in 1860, a third of them in Missouri.

The newcomers came from many different countries, but the overwhelming majority came from Ireland and Germany, where widespread poverty and political upheavals were driving many people out. By 1860, there were more than 1.5 million Irish-born and approximately 1 million German-born people in the United States. Most of the Irish stayed in the eastern cities where they landed and swelled the ranks of unskilled labor. Germans generally moved on to the Northwest, where they became farmers or went into business in the western towns. One reason for the difference was wealth: German immigrants generally arrived with at least some money; the Irish had practically none. Another important reason was gender. Most German immigrants were members of family groups or were single men, for whom movement to the agricultural frontier was both possible and attractive. Most Irish immigrants were young, single women, for whom movement west was less plausible. They were more likely to stay in the eastern cities, where factory and domestic work was available.

## The Rise of Nativism

The new foreign-born population almost immediately became a major factor in American political life. Many politicians saw in the immigrant population a source of important potential support, and they eagerly courted the support of the new arrivals. Others, however, viewed the growing foreign population with alarm. Some argued that the immigrants were mentally and physically defective, that they bred urban slums, that they corrupted politics by selling their votes. Others complained that because the foreign-born were willing to work for low wages, they were stealing jobs from the native work force. Protestants warned that the growing Irish population was increasing the power of the Catholic Church in America. Older-stock Americans feared that immigrants would become a radical force in politics. Out of these fears and prejudices emerged a number of secret societies to combat the "alien menace."

The first was the Native American Association, founded in 1837, which in 1845 was transformed into the Native American Party. In 1850, nativist groups combined to form the Supreme Order of the Star-Spangled Banner, whose demands included banning Catholics or aliens from holding public office, enacting more restrictive naturalization laws, and establishing literacy tests for voting. The order adopted a strict code of secrecy, which included a secret password, used in lodges across the country: "I know nothing." Ultimately, members of the movement were labeled "Know-Nothings."

After the 1852 elections, the Know-Nothings created a new political organization that they called the American Party. It scored an immediate and astonishing success in the elections of 1854. The Know-Nothings did well in Pennsylvania and New York and actually won control of the state government in Massachusetts. Outside the Northeast, however, their progress was more modest. And after 1854, the strength of the Know-Nothings declined. The party's most lasting impact was its contribution to the collapse of the second party system and the creation of new national political alignments.

# TRANSPORTATION AND COMMUNICATIONS REVOLUTIONS

Just as the industrial revolution required an expanding population, it also required an efficient and effective system of transportation and communications. The first half of the nineteenth century saw dramatic changes in both.

## The Canal Age

From 1790 until the 1820s, the so-called turnpike era, the United States had relied largely on roads for internal transportation. But roads alone were not adequate for the nation's expanding needs. And so, in the 1820s and 1830s, Americans began to turn to other means of transportation as well.

The larger rivers, especially the Mississippi and the Ohio, became increasingly important as steamboats replaced the slow barges that had previously dominated water traffic. The new riverboats carried the corn and wheat of northwestern farmers and the cotton and tobacco of southwestern planters to New Orleans. From New Orleans, oceangoing ships took the cargoes on to eastern ports.

But neither the farmers of the West nor the merchants of the East were satisfied with this pattern of trade. Farmers would pay less to transport their goods (and eastern consumers would pay less for them) if they could ship them directly eastward to market, rather than by the roundabout river-sea route; and northeastern merchants, too, could sell larger quantities of their manufactured goods if they could transport their merchandise more directly

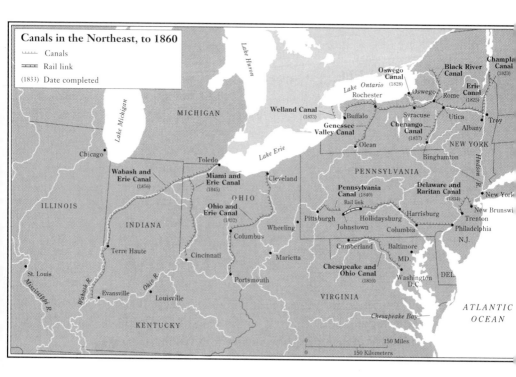

Canals in the Northeast, to 1860

and economically to the West. New highways across the mountains provided a partial solution to the problem. But the costs of hauling goods overland, although lower than before, were still too high for anything except the most compact and valuable merchandise. On a turnpike, four horses could haul one and a half tons eighteen miles in a day. But the same four horses could draw a boatload of a hundred tons twenty-four miles a day on a canal. And so interest grew rapidly in building new inland waterways.

Canal building was too expensive for private enterprise, and the job of digging canals fell largely to the states. New York was the first to act. It had the natural advantage of a good land route between the Hudson River and Lake Erie through the only break in the Appalachian chain. But the engineering tasks were still imposing. The distance was more than 350 miles, several times as long as any of the existing canals in America. The route was interrupted by high ridges and thick woods. After a long public debate over whether the scheme was practical, canal advocates prevailed when De Witt Clinton, a late but ardent convert to the cause, became governor in 1817. Digging began on July 4, 1817.

The building of the Erie Canal was the greatest construction project Americans had ever undertaken. The canal itself was simple: basically a ditch forty feet wide and four feet deep, with towpaths along the banks for the horses or mules that were to draw the canal boats. But its construction involved hundreds of difficult cuts and fills to enable the canal to pass through hills and over valleys, stone aqueducts to carry it across streams, and eighty-eight locks, of heavy masonry with great wooden gates, to permit ascents and descents. The Erie Canal was not just an engineering triumph but an immediate financial success. It opened in October 1825, amid elaborate ceremonies and celebrations, and traffic was soon so heavy that within about seven years tolls had repaid the entire cost of construction. By providing a route to the Great Lakes, the canal gave New York access to Chicago and the growing markets of the West.

The system of water transportation extended farther when the states of Ohio and Indiana, inspired by the success of the Erie Canal, provided water connections between Lake Erie and the Ohio River. These canals made it possible to ship goods by inland waterways all the way from New York to New Orleans, although it was still necessary to transfer cargoes several times between canal, lake, and river craft.

One of the immediate results of these new transportation routes was increased white settlement in the Northwest, because it was now easier for migrants to make the westward journey and to ship their goods back to eastern markets. Much of the western produce continued to go downriver to

New Orleans, but an increasing proportion (including most of the wheat of the Northwest) went east to New York. And manufactured goods from throughout the East now moved in growing volume through New York and then by the new water routes to the West.

Rival cities along the Atlantic seaboard took alarm at the prospect of New York's acquiring so vast a hinterland, largely at their expense. But they had limited success in catching up. Boston, its way to the Hudson River blocked by the Berkshire Mountains, did not even try to connect itself to the West by canal; its hinterland would remain confined largely to New England. Philadelphia and Baltimore had the still more formidable Allegheny Mountains to contend with. They made a serious effort at canal building nevertheless, but with discouraging results. Pennsylvania's effort ended in an expensive failure. Maryland began the Chesapeake and Ohio Canal in 1828, but the waterway never crossed the mountains. In the South, Richmond and Charleston also aspired to build water routes to the Ohio Valley, but also never completed them.

Canals did not provide a satisfactory way to the West for any of New York's rivals. Some cities, however, saw opportunities in a different and newer means of transportation. Even before the canal age had reached its height, the era of the railroad was already beginning.

### The Early Railroads

Railroads played a relatively small role in the nation's transportation system in the 1820s and 1830s, but railroad pioneers laid the groundwork in those years for the great surge of railroad building in midcentury that would link the nation together as never before. Eventually, railroads became the primary transportation system for the United States, and they remained so until the construction of the interstate highway system in the mid-twentieth century.

Railroads emerged from a combination of technological and entrepreneurial innovations: the invention of tracks, the creation of steam-powered locomotives, and the development of trains as public carriers of passengers and freight. By 1804, both English and American inventors had experimented with steam engines for propelling land vehicles. In 1820, John Stevens ran a locomotive and cars around a circular track on his New Jersey estate. And in 1825, the Stockton and Darlington Railroad in England opened a short length of track and became the first line to carry general traffic.

American entrepreneurs, especially in those northeastern cities that sought better communication with the West, quickly grew interested in the English experiment. The first company to begin actual operations was the

The Growth of the Railroads, 1850–1860

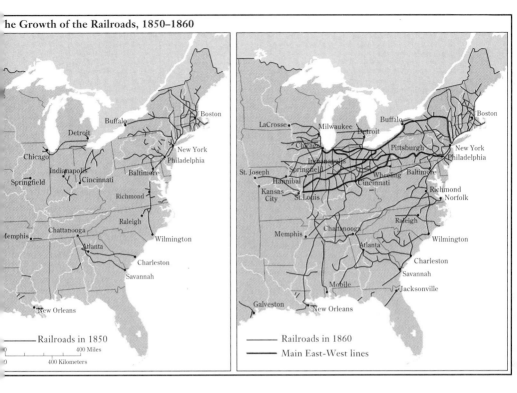

Railroads in 1850
400 Miles
400 Kilometers

Railroads in 1860
Main East-West lines

Baltimore and Ohio, which opened a thirteen-mile stretch of track in 1830. In New York, the Mohawk and Hudson began running trains along the sixteen miles between Schenectady and Albany in 1831. By 1836, more than a thousand miles of track had been laid in eleven states.

But there was not yet a true railroad system. Even the longest of the lines was comparatively short in the 1830s, and most of them served simply to connect water routes, not to link one railroad to another. Even when two lines did connect, the tracks often differed in gauge (width), so cars from one line often could not fit onto the tracks of another. Schedules were erratic, and wrecks were frequent. But railroads made some important advances in the 1830s and 1840s. The introduction of heavier iron rails improved the roadbeds. Steam locomotives became more flexible and powerful. Redesigned passenger cars became stabler, more comfortable, and larger.

Railroads and canals were soon competing bitterly. For a time, the Chesapeake and Ohio Canal Company blocked the advance of the Baltimore and Ohio Railroad through the narrow gorge of the upper Potomac, which it controlled; and the state of New York prohibited railroads from hauling

RACING ON THE RAILROAD  Peter Cooper designed and built the first steam-powered locomotives in America in 1830 for the Baltimore and Ohio railroad. On August 28 of that year, he raced his locomotive (the "Tom Thumb") against a horse-drawn railroad car. This sketch depicts the moment when Cooper's engine overtook the horse-car.

freight in competition with the Erie Canal and its branches. But railroads had so many advantages that when free competition existed they almost always prevailed.

### The Triumph of the Rails

After 1840, railroads gradually supplanted canals and all other forms of transport. In 1840, the total railroad trackage of the country was 2,818 miles; by the end of the decade, the trackage figure had risen to 9,021 miles. And an unparalleled burst of railroad construction followed in the 1850s. The amount of trackage tripled between 1850 and 1860. The Northeast developed the most comprehensive and efficient system, with twice as much trackage per square mile as the Northwest and four times as much as the South. Railroads were even crossing the Mississippi at several points by great iron bridges. Chicago became the rail center of the West, served by fifteen lines and more than a hundred daily trains.

The appearance of the great train lines diverted traffic from the main water routes—the Erie Canal and the Mississippi River. By lessening the dependence of the West on the Mississippi, the railroads also helped weaken further the connection between the Northwest and the South.

Railroad construction required massive amounts of capital. Some of it came from private sources, but much of it came from government. State and local governments invested in railroads because they were eager to have lines to serve them. Even greater assistance came from the federal government in the form of public land grants. In 1850, Senator Stephen A. Douglas of Illinois and other railroad-minded politicians persuaded Congress to grant federal lands to aid the Illinois Central, which was being extended toward the Gulf of Mexico. Other states and their railroad promoters demanded the same privileges, and by 1860, Congress had allotted over 30 million acres to eleven states to assist railroad construction.

*Innovations in Communications and Journalism*

Facilitating the operation of the railroads was an important innovation in communications: the telegraph, which burst into American life in 1844, when Samuel F. B. Morse, after several years of experimentation, succeeded in transmitting from Baltimore to Washington the news of James K. Polk's nomination for the presidency. The relatively low cost of constructing wire systems made the Morse telegraph system seem the ideal answer to the problems of train scheduling and other forms of long-distance communication. By 1860, more than 50,000 miles of wire connected most parts of the country; and a year later, the Pacific Telegraph, with 3,595 miles of wire, opened between New York and San Francisco. By then, nearly all the independent lines had joined in one organization, the Western Union Telegraph Company.

New forms of journalism also drew communities together into a common communications system. In 1846, Richard Hoe invented the steam cylinder rotary press, making it possible to print newspapers rapidly and cheaply. The development of the telegraph, together with the introduction of the rotary press, made possible much speedier collection and distribution of news than ever before. In 1846, newspaper publishers from around the nation formed the Associated Press to promote cooperative news gathering by wire; no longer did they have to depend on the cumbersome exchange of newspapers for out-of-town reports.

## COMMERCE AND INDUSTRY

By the middle years of the nineteenth century, the United States had developed the beginnings of a modern capitalist economy and an advanced industrial capacity. But this economic development had occurred along highly unequal lines—benefiting certain classes and certain regions far more than others.

## The Expansion of Business, 1820–1840

American business grew rapidly in the 1820s and 1830s, partly because of population growth and the transportation revolution, but also because of the daring, imagination, and ruthlessness of a new generation of entrepreneurs.

One important change came in the retail distribution of goods, which was becoming increasingly systematic and efficient. In the larger cities, stores specializing in groceries, dry goods, hardware, and other lines appeared, although residents of smaller towns and villages still depended on the general store and did much of their business by barter.

The organization of business was also changing. Individuals or limited partnerships continued to operate most businesses, and the dominating figures were still the great merchant capitalists, who generally had sole ownership of their enterprises. In some larger businesses, however, the individual merchant capitalist was giving way to the corporation. Corporations had the advantage of combining the resources of a large number of shareholders, and they began to develop particularly rapidly in the 1830s, when some legal obstacles to their formation were removed. Previously, a corporation could obtain a charter only by a special act of a state legislature—a cumbersome process that stifled corporate growth. By the 1830s, however, states were beginning to pass general incorporation laws, under which a group could secure a charter merely by paying a fee. The laws also permitted a system of limited liability, in which individual stockholders risked losing only the value of their own investment if a corporation should fail; they were not liable (as they had been in the past) for the corporation's larger losses. The rise of these new corporations made possible the accumulation of much greater amounts of capital and hence made possible much larger manufacturing and business enterprises.

But investment alone still provided too little capital. The most ambitious businesses relied on credit, even though credit mechanisms remained very crude. The government alone could issue currency, but there was too little official currency to support the growing demand for loans. Under pressure from corporate promoters, many banks issued large quantities of bank notes to provide capital for expanding business ventures—some doing so far in excess of their own reserves. As a result, bank failures were frequent and bank deposits often insecure.

## The Emergence of the Factory

All of these changes—increasing population, improved transportation and communications, and the expansion of business activity—contributed to perhaps the most profound economic development in mid-nineteenth-century America: the rise of the factory. Before the War of 1812, most of what manufacturing there was in the United States took place within households or in small, individually operated workshops. Early in the nineteenth century, however, New England textile manufacturers began using new machines driven by water power that allowed them to bring their operations together under a single roof. This factory system, as it came to be known, spread rapidly in the 1820s and soon penetrated the shoe industry and other industries as well.

Machine technology advanced more rapidly in the United States in the mid-nineteenth century than in any other country in the world. By the end of the 1830s, American technology had become so advanced—particularly in textile manufacturing—that industrialists in Britain and Europe were beginning to travel to the United States to learn new techniques, instead of the other way around.

## The Expansion of Industry, 1840–1860

Between 1840 and 1860, American industry experienced even more dramatic growth. In 1840, the total value of manufactured goods produced in the United States stood at $483 million; by 1860 it had climbed to nearly $2 billion. For the first time, the value of manufactured goods was roughly equal to that of agricultural products.

More than half of the approximately 140,000 manufacturing establishments in the country in 1860 were located in the Northeast, and they included most of the larger enterprises. The Northeast thus produced more than two-thirds of the manufactured goods and employed nearly three-quarters of the men and women working in manufacturing.

Even the most highly developed industries were still relatively immature. Cotton manufacturers, for example, produced goods of coarse grade; fine items continued to come from England. But technology and industrial ingenuity were preparing the way for future growth. By the 1840s, the machine tools used in the factories of the Northeast were already better than those in European factories. At the same time, the principle of interchangeable parts, first applied decades earlier in gun factories designed by

Eli Whitney and Simeon North, was being introduced into many other industries. Coal was replacing wood as an industrial fuel and was replacing water power as a fuel for the steam engines that drove most of the factory machinery in the Northeast. The production of coal, most of it mined around Pittsburgh in western Pennsylvania, leaped from 50,000 tons in 1820 to 14 million tons in 1860. The new power source made it possible to locate mills away from running streams and thus permitted industry to expand still more widely.

The great technical advances in American industry owed much to American inventors. In 1830, the number of inventions patented was 544; by 1860, it had risen to 4,778. Several industries provide particularly vivid examples of how a technological innovation could produce a major economic change. In 1839, Charles Goodyear, a New England hardware merchant, discovered a method of vulcanizing rubber; by 1860, his process had found over 500 uses and had helped create a major American rubber industry. In 1846, Elias Howe of Massachusetts constructed a sewing machine; Isaac Singer made improvements on it, and the Howe-Singer machine was soon being used in the manufacture of ready-to-wear clothing. A few years later, during the Civil War, it would supply the Northern troops with uniforms.

The merchant capitalists—entrepreneurs who were engaged primarily in foreign and domestic trade and who at times invested some of their profits in small-scale manufacturing ventures—remained figures of importance in the 1840s. In such cities as New York, Philadelphia, and Boston, influential mercantile groups operated shipping lines to southern ports—carrying off cotton, rice, and sugar—or dispatched fleets of trading vessels to the ports of Europe and the Orient. Among their vessels were the famous clippers, the fastest (and most beautiful) sailing ships afloat. In their heyday in the late 1840s and early 1850s, the clippers could average 300 miles a day, which compared favorably with the best time of contemporary steamships.

But merchant capitalism was declining by the middle of the century. This was partly because British competitors were stealing much of America's export trade. But the more important reason for the decline was the discovery by the merchants themselves that there were greater opportunities for profit in manufacturing than in trade. They reduced their mercantile investments and invested instead in factories. That was one reason why industries developed first in the Northeast: an affluent merchant class already existed there and had the money and the will to finance them. By the 1840s, particularly in the textile industry, the corporate form of organization was spreading rapidly. Ownership of American enterprise, in other words, was moving away from individuals and families and toward its highly dispersed modern form: many stockholders, each owning a relatively small proportion of the total. Whatever the form of business organization—and there continued to be many different forms—industrial capitalists soon became the new ruling class, the aristocrats of the Northeast, with far-reaching economic and political influence.

## MEN AND WOMEN AT WORK

However advanced industrial firms became technologically and administratively, manufacturers still relied above all on a supply of labor. In the 1820s and 1830s, factory labor came primarily from the native-born population. After 1840, the growing immigrant population became the most important new source of workers.

### *Recruiting a Native Work Force*

Recruiting a labor force was not an easy task in the early years of the factory system. Ninety percent of the American people in the 1820s still lived and worked on farms. Many of the relatively small number of urban residents were skilled artisans who owned and managed their own shops; they were not likely to flock to factory jobs. The available unskilled workers were not numerous enough to form a reservoir from which the new industries could draw.

But the transformation of American agriculture in the nineteenth century gradually created a supply of industrial workers. Dramatic improvements in agricultural production, particularly in the Midwest, meant that each region no longer had to feed itself; it could import the food it needed. As a result, some of the relatively unprofitable farming areas of the East began to decline, especially those in New England, and rural people began leaving the land to work in the factories.

Two systems of recruitment emerged to bring this new labor supply to the expanding textile mills. One, common in the mid-Atlantic states (especially in New York and Philadelphia), brought whole families from the farm to work together in the mill: parents alongside children, some of whom were no more than four or five years old. The second system, common in Massachusetts, enlisted young women, mostly farmers' daughters in their late teens and early twenties. It was known as the Lowell or Waltham system, after the towns in which it first emerged. Many of these women worked for several years in the factories, saved their wages, and then returned home to

NEW ENGLAND TEXTILE WORKERS Women continued to constitute the majority of the work force in the cotton mills of New England even after the carefully monitored life of the "Lowell girls" became a thing of the past—as this 1868 engraving by Winslow Homer suggests.

marry and raise children. Others married men they met in the factories or in town and remained part of the industrial world, but most eventually stopped working in the mills and took up domestic roles instead.

Labor conditions in these early years of the factory system, hard as they often were, remained significantly better than they would later become. The Lowell workers, for example, lived in clean boardinghouses and dormitories, which the factory owners maintained for them. They were well fed and carefully supervised. Employers quickly dismissed women suspected of immoral conduct. Wages for the Lowell workers were relatively generous by the standards of the time. The women even published a monthly magazine, the *Lowell Offering.*

Yet even these relatively well treated workers found the transition from farm life to factory work difficult, even traumatic. Uprooted from everything familiar, forced to live among strangers in a regimented environment, many women had difficulty adjusting to the nature of factory work—the repetition of fixed tasks hour after hour, day after day. But however uncomfortable women may have found factory work, they had few other options. Most of society considered it unthinkable for women to travel the country alone,

A  M  E  R  I  C  A  N      V  O  I  C  E  S

MARY PAUL

## Letter from the Lowell Mills, 1845

DEAR FATHER,

I received your letter on Thursday the 14th with much pleasure. I am well which is one comfort. My life and health are spared while others are cut off. Last Thursday one girl fell down and broke her neck, which caused instant death. She was going in or coming out of the mill and slipped down it being very icy. The same day a man was killed by the cars. Another had nearly all his ribs broken. Another was nearly killed by . . . having a bale of cotton fall on him. Last Tuesday we were paid. In all I had six dollars and sixty cents paid $4.68 for board. With the rest I got me a pair of rubbers and a pair of 50.cts shoes. Next payment I am to have a dollar a week beside my board. . . . Perhaps you would like something about our regulations about going in and coming out of the mill. At 5 o'clock in the morning the bell rings for the folks to get up and get breakfast. At half past six it rings for the girls to get up and at seven they are called into the mill. At half past 12 we have dinner are called back again at one and stay till half past seven. I get along very well with my work. I can doff as fast as any girl in our room. . . . I think that the factory is the best place for me and if any girl wants employment I advise them to come to Lowell.

SOURCE: Thomas Dublin, ed., *Farm to Factory: Women's Letters, 1830–1860* (New York: Columbia University Press, 1981), pp. 103–104.

as many men did, in search of opportunities. Work in the mills was in many cases virtually the only alternative to returning to farms that could no longer support them.

The paternalistic factory system of Lowell did not, in any case, survive for long. In the competitive textile market as it developed in the 1830s and 1840s—a market prey to the booms and busts that afflicted the American economy as a whole—manufacturers found it difficult to maintain the high living standards and reasonably attractive working conditions with which they had begun. Wages declined; the hours of work lengthened; the conditions of the boardinghouses deteriorated as buildings decayed and overcrowding increased. In 1834, mill workers in Lowell organized a union— the Factory Girls Association—which staged a strike to protest a 25 percent wage cut. Two years later, the association struck again—against a rent increase in the boardinghouses. Both strikes failed, and a recession in 1837 virtually destroyed the organization. Eight years later the Lowell women, led by the militant Sarah Bagley, created the Female Labor Reform Association and began agitating for a ten-hour day and for improvements in conditions in the mills. The new association not only made demands of management; it turned to state government and asked for legislative investigation of conditions in the mills. By then, however, the character of the factory work force was changing again. Many mill girls were gradually moving into other occupations: teaching, domestic service, or marriage. And textile manufacturers were turning to a less contentious labor supply: immigrants.

### The Immigrant Work Force

The increasing supply of immigrant workers after 1840 was a boon to manufacturers and other entrepreneurs. At last they had access to a cheap and plentiful source of labor. These new workers, because of their growing numbers and their unfamiliarity with their new country, had even less leverage than the women they at times displaced, and thus they often encountered far worse working conditions. Poorly paid construction gangs, made up increasingly of Irish immigrants, performed the heavy, unskilled work on turnpikes, canals, and railroads under often intolerable conditions. Many of them lived in flimsy shanties, in grim conditions that endangered the health of their families (and reinforced native prejudices toward the "shanty Irish"). Irish workers began to predominate in the New England textile mills as well in the 1840s, and their arrival accelerated the deterioration of working conditions there. Employers began paying piece rates rather than a daily wage and used other devices to speed up production and exploit the labor force more efficiently. The factories themselves were becoming large, noisy, unsanitary, and often dangerous places to work; the average workday was extending to twelve, often fourteen hours; and wages were declining. Women and children, whatever their skills, earned less than most men.

### The Factory System and the Artisan Tradition

It was not only mill workers who suffered from the transition to the modern factory system. It was also the skilled artisans whose trades the factories were displacing. The artisan tradition was as much a part of the older, republican vision of America as the tradition of sturdy yeoman farmers. Independent craftsmen considered themselves embodiments of the American ideal. They clung to a vision of economic life that was in some ways very different from the one the new capitalist class was promoting. It was a vision based not just on the idea of individual, acquisitive success (although they were not, of course, averse to profits) but also on a sense of a "moral community." Skilled artisans valued their independence; they also valued the stability and relative equality within their economic world.

The factory system threatened that world with obsolescence. Some artisans made successful transitions into small-scale industry. But others found themselves unable to compete with the new factory-made goods that sold for a fraction of the artisans' prices. In the face of this competition from industrial capitalists, craftsmen began early in the nineteenth century to form organizations—workingmen's political parties and the first American labor unions—to protect their endangered positions and to resist the new economic order in which they sensed they would have no role.

In cities such as Philadelphia, Baltimore, Boston, and New York, skilled workers of each craft formed societies for mutual aid. During the 1820s and 1830s, the craft societies began to combine on a citywide basis and set up central organizations known as trade unions. In 1834, delegates from six cities founded the National Trades' Union, and in 1836, printers and cordwainers (makers of high-quality shoes and boots) set up their own national craft unions.

This early craft union movement fared poorly. Hostile laws and hostile courts handicapped the unions. The Panic of 1837 and the depression that followed weakened the movement further. But the failure of these first organizations did not end the efforts by workers—artisans and factory operatives alike—to gain some control over their productive lives.

A TOLEWARE MAKER, C. 1850 By the middle of the nineteenth century, skilled artisans—such as this maker of handcrafted kitchenware—were rapidly being replaced by semiskilled workers producing similar goods in factories. The craftsman pictured here conveys some of the important elements of the vanishing artisanal world: formal dress in the workplace, to suggest his status as a highly skilled craftsman; pride in his workmanship; and a middle-class sensibility that, in the end, made it difficult for artisans to fight the forces driving them toward obsolescence.

## Fighting for Control

Workers at all levels of the emerging industrial economy made continuous efforts to improve their lots. They tried, with little success, to persuade state legislatures to pass laws setting a maximum workday and regulating child labor. The greatest legal victory of industrial workers came in Massachusetts in 1842, when the state supreme court, in *Commonwealth* v. *Hunt*, declared that unions were lawful organizations and that the strike was a lawful weapon. Other state courts gradually accepted the principles of the Massachusetts decision. But on the whole, the union movement of the 1830s and 1840s remained generally ineffective.

Artisans and skilled workers, despite their early setbacks, had somewhat greater success in the 1850s, when a number of new organizations took shape. But their unions often had more in common with preindustrial guilds than with modern labor organizations. In most cases, the primary purpose of these unions was to protect the favored position of their members in the labor force by restricting admission to the skilled trades.

Virtually all the early craft unions excluded women, even though female workers were numerous in almost every industry. As a result, women began establishing their own protective unions by the 1850s, often with the support of middle-class female reformers. Like the male craft unions, the female protective unions had little power in dealing with employers. They did, however, serve an important role as mutual aid societies for women workers.

Many factors combined to inhibit the growth of effective labor resistance. Among the most important was the flood of immigrant laborers into the country. The newcomers were usually willing to work for lower wages than native workers; and because they were so numerous, manufacturers had little difficulty replacing disgruntled or striking workers with eager immigrants. Ethnic divisions and tensions—both between natives and immigrants and among the various immigrant groups themselves—often led workers to channel their resentments into internal bickering rather than into their shared grievances against employers. There was, too, the sheer strength of the industrial capitalists, who had not only economic but political and social power and could usually triumph over even the most militant challenges.

## PATTERNS OF SOCIETY

The industrial revolution was making the United States—and particularly its more economically developed regions—dramatically wealthier by the year. It was also making society more unequal, and it was transforming social relationships at almost every level—from the workplace to the family.

### The Rich and the Poor

The commercial and industrial growth of the United States greatly elevated the average income of the American people. But this increasing wealth was being distributed highly unequally. Substantial groups of the population, of course, shared hardly at all in the economic growth: slaves, Indians, landless farmers, and many of the unskilled workers on the fringes of the manufacturing system. But even among the rest of the population, disparities of income were increasingly marked. Among the American people overall in 1860, according to scholarly estimates, 5 percent of the families possessed more than 50 percent of the wealth. Merchants and industrialists were accumulating enormous fortunes; and because there was now a significant number of rich people living in cities, a distinctive culture of wealth began to emerge.

In large cities, people of great wealth gathered together in neighborhoods of astonishing opulence. They founded clubs and developed elaborate social rituals. They looked increasingly for ways to display their wealth—in the great mansions they built, the showy carriages in which they rode, the lavish household goods they accumulated, the clothes they wore, the elegant social establishments they patronized. New York, which had more wealthy families than anywhere else, developed a particularly elaborate high society. The construction of the city's great Central Park, which began in the 1850s, was in part a result of pressure from the members of high society, who wanted an elegant setting for their daily carriage rides.

There was also a significant population of genuinely destitute people emerging in the growing urban centers of the nation. These were people who were not merely poor, in the sense of having to struggle to sustain themselves; most Americans were poor in that sense. They were almost entirely without resources, often homeless, dependent on charity or crime or both for survival. Substantial numbers of people actually starved to death or died of exposure.

Some of these "paupers," as contemporaries called them, were recent immigrants who had failed to find work or to adjust to life in the New World. Some were widows and orphans, stripped of the family structures that allowed most working-class Americans to survive. Some were people suffering from alcoholism or mental illness, unable to work. Others were victims of native prejudice—barred from all but the most menial employment because of race or ethnicity. The Irish were particular victims of such prejudice.

Among the worst victims were free blacks. African-American communities in antebellum northern cities were small by later standards, but most major urban areas had significant black populations. Some of these African Americans were descendants of families that had lived in the North for generations. Others were former slaves who had escaped or been released by their masters. In material terms, at least, life was not always much better for them in the North than it had been in slavery. Most had access to very menial jobs at best. In most parts of the North, blacks could not vote, could not attend public schools, indeed could not use any of the public services available to white residents. Even so, most blacks preferred life in the North, however arduous, to life in the South, because it permitted them at least some level of freedom.

### Social Mobility

Despite the contrasts between conspicuous wealth and conspicuous poverty in antebellum America, there was relatively little overt class conflict. For one thing, life, in material terms at least, was usually better for factory workers than it had been on the farms or in the European societies from which they had migrated. They ate better, they were often better clothed and housed, and they had greater access to consumer goods.

There was also a significant amount of mobility within the working class, which helped limit discontent. A few workers managed to move from poverty to riches by dint of work, ingenuity, and luck—a very small number, but enough to support the dreams of those who watched them. And a much larger number of workers managed to move at least one notch up the ladder—for example, becoming in the course of a lifetime a skilled, rather than an unskilled, laborer. Such people could envision their children and grandchildren moving up even further.

More important than social mobility was geographical mobility. America had a huge expanse of uncultivated land in the West, much of it open for settlement for the first time in the 1840s and 1850s. Some workers saved money, bought land, and moved west to farm it. But few urban workers, and even fewer poor ones, could afford to make such a move. Much more common was the movement of laborers from one industrial town to another. These migratory workers were often the victims of layoffs, looking for better opportunities elsewhere. Their search may seldom have led to a marked improvement in their circumstances, but the rootlessness of this large segment of the work force—one of the most distressed segments—made effective organization and protest more difficult.

### The Changing Family

The new industrializing society of the northern regions of the United States produced profound changes in the nature and function of the family. At the heart of the transformation was the movement of families from farms to urban areas, where jobs, not land, were the most valued commodities. The family patterns of the countryside, where powerful fathers controlled their children's futures by controlling the distribution of land to them, could not survive the move to a city or town. Sons and daughters were much more likely to leave the family in search of work than they had been in the rural world.

Another important change was the shift of income-earning work out of the home and into the shop, mill, or factory. In the early decades of the nineteenth century (and for many years before that), the family itself had been the principal unit of economic activity. Now most income earners left home each day to work elsewhere. A sharp distinction began to emerge between the public world of the workplace—the world of commerce and industry—and the private world of the family. The world of the family was now dominated not by production but by housekeeping, child rearing, and other primarily domestic concerns.

Accompanying (and perhaps in part caused by) the changing economic function of the family was a decline in the birth rate. In 1800, the average American woman could be expected to give birth to approximately seven children during her childbearing years. By 1860, the average woman bore five children. The birth rate fell most quickly in urban areas and among middle-class women.

### The "Cult of Domesticity"

The growing separation between the public and private worlds, between the workplace and the home, helped cause increasingly sharp distinctions between the social roles of men and women. Those distinctions affected not only factory workers and farmers but members of the growing middle class as well.

Traditional inequalities remained. Women had many fewer legal and political rights than did men, and within the family they remained under the virtually absolute authority of their husbands. Women were seldom encouraged—and in most cases were effectively barred—from pursuing education above the primary level. Not until 1837 did any college or university accept women students: Oberlin in Ohio, which educated both women and men; and Mt. Holyoke in Massachusetts, founded by Mary Lyon as an academy for women. Not until much later in the century were there more than a handful of others.

But however unequal the positions of men and women in the preindustrial era, those positions had generally been defined within the context of a household in which all members played important economic roles. In the middle-class family of the new industrial society, by contrast, the husband was assumed to be the principal, usually the only, income producer. The wife was now expected to remain in the home and to engage in largely domestic activities. The image of women changed from one of contributors to the family economy to one of guardians of the "domestic virtues." Middle-class women, no longer producers, now became more important as consumers. They learned to place a higher value on keeping a clean, comfortable, and well-appointed home; on entertaining; on dressing elegantly and stylishly.

Within their own separate sphere, middle-class women began to develop a distinctive female culture. A "lady's" literature began to emerge to meet the demands of middle-class women. There were romantic novels (many of them by female writers), which focused on the private sphere that middle-class women now inhabited. There were women's magazines, which focused on fashions, shopping, homemaking, and other purely domestic concerns.

Most middle-class men—and many middle-class women—considered the new female sphere a vehicle for expressing special qualities that made women in some ways superior to men. Women were to be the custodians of morality and benevolence; they were to provide religious and moral instruction to their children and to counterbalance the acquisitive, secular impulses of their husbands. This "cult of domesticity," as some scholars have called it, gave many women greater material comfort than they had in the past and placed a higher value on their "female virtues" and on their roles as wives and mothers. At the same time, it left women increasingly detached from the public world, with few outlets for their interests and energies. Except for teaching and nursing—the favored occupations of unmarried middle-class women—work by women outside the household gradually came to be seen as a lower-class preserve.

Working-class women continued to work in factories and mills, but under conditions far worse than those that the original, more "respectable" women workers of Lowell and Waltham had experienced. Domestic service became another frequent source of female employment. Now that production had moved outside the household, women who needed to earn money had to move outside their own homes to do so.

## THE AGRICULTURAL NORTH

Even in the rapidly urbanizing and industrializing Northeast, and more so in what nineteenth-century Americans called the Northwest (and what Americans today call the Midwest), most people remained tied to the agricultural world. But agriculture, like industry and commerce, was becoming increasingly a part of the new capitalist economy, linked to the national and international market.

## Northeastern Agriculture

The story of agriculture in the Northeast after 1840 is one of decline and transformation. The reason for the decline was simple: the farmers of the section could no longer compete with the new and richer soil of the Northwest. In 1840, the leading wheat-growing states were New York, Pennsylvania, Ohio, and Virginia; in 1860 they were Illinois, Indiana, Wisconsin, Ohio, and Michigan. In raising corn, Illinois, Ohio, and Missouri supplanted New York, Pennsylvania, and Virginia. In 1840 the most important cattle-raising areas in the country were New York, Pennsylvania, and New England; but by the 1850s the leading cattle states were Illinois, Indiana, Ohio, and Iowa in the West and Texas in the South.

Some eastern farmers responded to these changes by moving west themselves and establishing new farms. Still others moved to mill towns and became laborers. Some farmers, however, remained on the land and turned to the task of supplying food to the growing cities of the East; they raised vegetables (truck farming) or fruit and sold their produce in nearby towns. New York, for example, led all other states in apple production. Supplying milk, butter, and cheese to local urban markets also attracted many farmers in central New York, southeastern Pennsylvania, and various parts of New England.

But while agriculture in the region remained an important part of the economy, it was steadily becoming less important relative both to the agriculture of the Northwest and to the industrial growth of the Northeast itself. As a result, the rural population in many parts of the Northeast continued to decline.

## The Old Northwest

Life was different in the states of the Northwest in the mid-nineteenth century. There was some industry in this region, more than in the South, and in the two decades before the Civil War, the section experienced steady industrial growth. There were flourishing industrial and commercial areas in and around Cleveland, on Lake Erie, and Cincinnati, the center of meatpacking in the Ohio Valley. Farther west, the rising city of Chicago, destined to become the great metropolis of the section, was emerging as the national center of the agricultural machinery and meatpacking industries. Most of the major industrial activities of the West either served agriculture (as in the case of farm machinery) or relied on agricultural products (as in flour milling, meatpacking, whiskey distilling, and the making of leather goods). Some areas of the Northwest were not yet dominated by whites. Indians remained the most numerous inhabitants of large portions of the upper third of the Great Lakes states until after the Civil War. In those areas, hunting and fishing, along with some sedentary agriculture, remained the principal economic activities. But the tribes did not become integrated into the new commercialized economy that was emerging elsewhere in the Northwest.

For the white (and occasionally black) settlers who populated the lands farther south that they had by now largely wrested from the natives, the Northwest was primarily an agricultural region. Its rich and plentiful lands made farming a lucrative and expanding activity there, in contrast to the declining agrarian Northeast. Thus the typical citizen of the Northwest was not the industrial worker or poor, marginal farmer but the owner of a reasonably prosperous family farm. The average size of western farms was 200 acres, the great majority of them owned by the people who worked them.

Rising farm prices around the world provided a strong incentive for these western farmers to engage in commercial agriculture: to concentrate on growing a single crop for market (corn, wheat, cattle, sheep, hogs, and others). In the early years of white settlement in the Northwest, farm prices rose because Europe found it necessary to import American products to feed its people. The Northwest, with good water routes on the Mississippi for getting its crops to oceangoing vessels, profited from this international trade.

Industrialization, in both the United States and Europe, provided the greatest boost to agriculture. With the growth of factories and cities in the Northeast, the domestic market for farm goods increased dramatically. The growing national and worldwide demand for farm products resulted in steadily rising farm prices. For most farmers, the 1840s and early 1850s were years of increasing prosperity.

The expansion of agricultural markets had profound effects on sectional alignments in the United States. The Northwest sold most of its products to the Northeast and became an important market for the products of eastern industry. A strong economic relationship was emerging between the two sections that was profitable to both—and that was increasing the isolation of the South within the Union.

To meet the growing demand for the region's farm products, residents of the Northwest worked strenuously, and often frantically, to increase their productive capacities. Many tried to take advantage of the large areas of still-uncultivated land and to enlarge the area of white settlement during the 1840s. By 1850, the growing western population was moving into the prairie regions on both sides of the Mississippi: areas of Indiana, Michigan, Illinois, Missouri, Iowa, and Minnesota. These farmers cleared forest lands or made use of fields the Indians had cleared many years earlier. And they began to develop a timber industry to make use of the forests that remained. Wheat was the staple crop of the region, but other crops—corn, potatoes, and oats—and livestock were also important.

The Northwest also increased production by adopting new agricultural techniques that greatly reduced the labor necessary for producing a crop. Farmers began to cultivate new varieties of seed, notably Mediterranean wheat, which was hardier than the native type; and they imported better breeds of animals, such as hogs and sheep from England and Spain, to take the place of native stock. Most important were improved tools and farm machines. The cast-iron plow, an earlier innovation, remained popular because its parts could be replaced when broken. An even better tool appeared in 1847, when John Deere established at Moline, Illinois, a factory to manufacture plows with steel moldboards, which were more durable than those made of iron.

McCORMICK'S REAPER This 1850 advertisement for the automatic reaper created by Cyrus McCormick was aimed at farmers in Ohio and Illinois. But the reaper's greatest impact was to be in the vast grain-growing regions farther west, which were already attracting large numbers of white settlers and would attract many more in the decades to come.

Two new machines heralded a coming revolution in grain production. The most important was the automatic reaper, the invention of Cyrus H. McCormick of Virginia. The reaper took the place of sickle, cradle, and hand labor and enabled a crew of six or seven men to harvest in a day as much wheat (or any other small grain) as fifteen men could harvest using the older methods. McCormick, who had patented his device in 1834, established a factory at Chicago, in the heart of the grain belt, in 1847. By 1860, more than 100,000 reapers were in use on western farms. Almost as important to the grain grower was the thresher—a machine that separated the grain from the wheat stalks. Threshers appeared in large numbers after 1840. Before that, farmers generally flailed grain by hand (seven bushels a day was a good average for a farm) or used farm animals to tread it (twenty bushels a day on the average). A threshing machine could thresh twenty-five bushels or more in an hour. The Jerome I. Case factory in Racine, Wisconsin, manufactured most of the threshers.

The Northwest was the most self-consciously democratic section of the country. But its democracy was of a relatively conservative type—capitalistic, property-conscious, middle-class. Abraham Lincoln, an Illinois Whig, voiced the economic opinions of many of the people of his section. "I take it that it is best for all to leave each man free to acquire property as fast as he can," said Lincoln. "Some will get wealthy. I don't believe in a law to prevent a man from getting rich; it would do more harm than good. . . . When one starts poor, as most do in the race of life, free society is such that he knows he can better his condition; he knows that there is no fixed condition of labor for his whole life."

# CHAPTER ELEVEN

# Cotton, Slavery, and the Old South

*The Cotton Economy* ～ *Southern White Society*
*The "Peculiar Institution"* ～ *The Culture of Slavery*

T HE SOUTH, LIKE the North, experienced dramatic growth in the middle years of the nineteenth century. Southerners fanned out into the Southwest and established new communities, new states, and new markets. The southern agricultural economy grew increasingly productive and increasingly prosperous. Trade in such staples as sugar, rice, tobacco, and above all cotton made the South a major force in international commerce and created substantial wealth within the region. It also tied the South securely to the emerging capitalist world of the United States and its European trading partners.

Yet for all the changes, the South experienced a much less fundamental transformation in these years than did the North. It had begun the nineteenth century a primarily agricultural region; it remained overwhelmingly agrarian in 1860. It had begun the century with few important cities and little industry; and so it remained sixty years later. In 1800, a plantation system dependent on slave labor had dominated the southern economy; by 1860, that system had only strengthened its grip on the region. As one historian has written, "The South grew, but it did not develop." And as a result, it became increasingly unlike the North and increasingly sensitive to what it considered to be threats to its distinctive way of life.

## THE COTTON ECONOMY

The most important economic development in the mid-nineteenth-century South was the shift of economic power from the "upper South," the original southern states along the Atlantic coast, to the "lower South," the expanding

| TIME LINE | | | | |
|---|---|---|---|---|
| **1800** | **1808** | **1820s** | **1822** | **1831** |
| Gabriel Prosser's unsuccessful slave revolt | Slave importation banned | Depression in tobacco prices begins<br><br>High cotton production in Southwest | Denmark Vesey's conspiracy | Nat Turner slave rebellion |

| **1833** | **1837** | **1846** | **1849** | |
|---|---|---|---|---|
| John Randolph frees 400 slaves | Cotton prices plummet | *De Bow's Review* founded | Cotton production boom | |

agricultural regions in the new states of the Southwest. That shift reflected above all the growing dominance of cotton in the southern economy.

## The Rise of King Cotton

Much of the upper South continued in the nineteenth century to rely, as it always had, on the cultivation of tobacco. But the market for that crop was notoriously unstable, and tobacco rapidly exhausted the land on which it grew. By the 1830s, therefore, many farmers in the old tobacco-growing regions of Virginia, Maryland, and North Carolina were shifting to other crops—notably wheat—while the center of tobacco cultivation was moving westward, into the Piedmont area.

The southern regions of the coastal South—South Carolina, Georgia, and parts of Florida—continued to rely on the cultivation of rice, a more stable and lucrative crop. But rice demanded substantial irrigation and needed an exceptionally long growing season (nine months), so cultivation of that staple remained restricted to a relatively small area. Sugar growers along the Gulf Coast, similarly, enjoyed a reasonably profitable market for their crop. Sugar cultivation required intensive (and debilitating) labor and a long growing time; only relatively wealthy planters could afford to engage in it. And producers faced major competition from the great sugar plantations of the Caribbean. Sugar cultivation, therefore, did not spread much beyond a small area in southern Louisiana and eastern Texas. Long-staple (Sea Island) cotton was another lucrative crop, but like rice and sugar, it could grow only in a limited area—the coastal regions of the Southeast.

## Slavery and Cotton: The South in 1820 and 1860

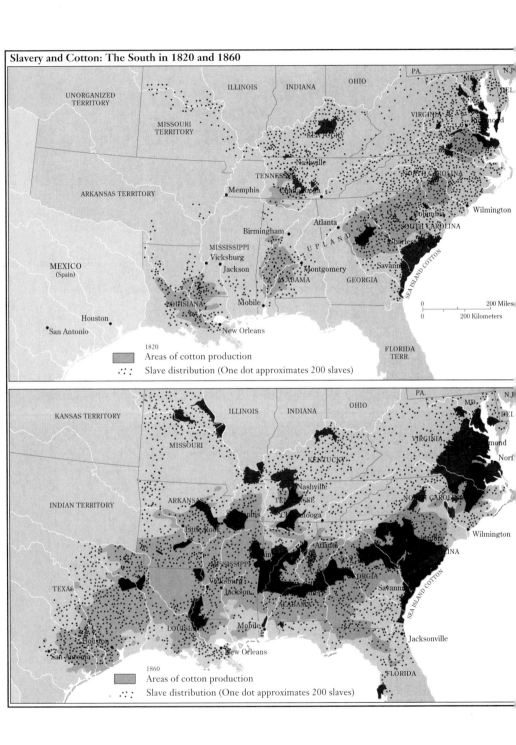

1820

▨ Areas of cotton production

⋰⋱ Slave distribution (One dot approximates 200 slaves)

1860

▨ Areas of cotton production

⋰⋱ Slave distribution (One dot approximates 200 slaves)

The decline of the tobacco economy in the upper South, and the inherent limits of the sugar, rice, and long-staple cotton economies farther south, might have forced the region to shift its attention in the nineteenth century to other, nonagricultural pursuits, had it not been for the growing importance of a new product which soon overshadowed all else: short-staple cotton. This was a hardier and coarser strain of cotton which could grow successfully in a variety of climates and in a variety of soils. It was harder to process than the long-staple variety; its seeds were more difficult to remove from the fiber. But the invention of the cotton gin (see p. 183) had largely solved that problem.

Demand for cotton increased rapidly with the growth of the textile industry in Britain in the 1820s and 1830s and in New England in the 1840s and 1850s. Beginning in the 1820s, therefore, cotton production spread rapidly. From the western areas of South Carolina and Georgia, production moved into Alabama and Mississippi and then into northern Louisiana, Texas, and Arkansas. By the 1850s, cotton had become the linchpin of the southern economy. In 1820, the South had produced only about 500,000

THE PORT OF CHARLESTON  Bales of cotton accumulate on the docks of Charleston, South Carolina, waiting to be loaded onto the ships that would take them to the textile mills in New England, Britain, and other destinations around the world.

bales of cotton. By 1860 it was producing nearly 5 million bales a year. There were periodic fluctuations in cotton prices, resulting generally from overproduction; periods of boom frequently gave way to abrupt busts. But the cotton economy continued to grow, even if in fits and starts. By the time of the Civil War, cotton constituted nearly two-thirds of the total export trade of the United States. It was little wonder that southern politicians now proclaimed: "Cotton is king!"

Cotton production dominated the relatively recently settled areas of what came to be known as the "lower South" (or, in a later era, the "Deep South"). Some began to call it the "Cotton Kingdom." The prospect of tremendous profits drew settlers to the lower South by the thousands. Some were wealthy planters from the older states who transferred their assets and slaves to new and larger plantations. Most were small slaveholders or slaveless farmers who hoped to move into the planter class.

A similar shift, if an involuntary one, occurred in the slave population. In the period 1820–1860, the number of slaves in Alabama leaped from 41,000 to 435,000, and in Mississippi from 32,000 to 436,000. Between 1840 and 1860, according to some estimates, 410,000 slaves moved from the upper South to the cotton states—either accompanying masters who were themselves migrating to the Southwest or (more often) sold to planters already there. The sale of slaves to the Southwest became an important economic activity in the upper South and helped the troubled planters of that region compensate for the declining value of their crops.

### Southern Trade and Industry

In the face of this booming agricultural expansion, other forms of economic activity developed slowly in the South. There was growing activity in flour milling and in textile and iron manufacturing, particularly in the upper South. The Tredegar Iron Works in Richmond, for example, compared favorably with the best iron mills in the Northeast. But industry remained an insignificant force in comparison with the agricultural economy. The total value of southern textile manufactures in 1860 was $4.5 million—a threefold increase over the value of those goods twenty years before, but only about 2 percent of the value of the cotton exported that year.

To the degree that the South developed a nonfarm commercial sector, it was largely to serve the needs of the plantation economy. Particularly important were the brokers, or "factors," who marketed the planters' crops. These merchants tended to live in such towns as New Orleans, Charleston, Mobile, and Savannah, where they worked to find buyers for cotton and other crops and where they purchased goods for the planters they served. The South had only a very rudimentary financial system, and the factors often also served the planters as bankers, providing them with credit. Planters frequently accumulated substantial debts, particularly during periods when cotton prices were in decline; and the southern merchant-bankers thus became figures of considerable influence and importance in the region.

The rudimentary character of the region's financial system matched a lack of development in other basic services and structures that would have been necessary for extensive industrial development. Perhaps most notable was the South's inadequate transportation system. In the North in the antebellum period, governments and entrepreneurs were investing enormous sums in roads, canals, and above all railroads to knit the region together into an integrated market. In the South there were few such investments. Canals were almost nonexistent; most roads were crude and unsuitable for heavy

*DE BOW'S COMMERCIAL REVIEW* J. D. B. De Bow, owner and editor of the South's leading magazine, presented his *Review* as a commercial publication, designed for those committed to commerce. But it also contained essays and articles promoting the South's way of life and what many white Southerners considered the region's distinctive (and superior) culture.

transport; and railroads, although they expanded substantially in the 1840s and 1850s, failed to tie the region together effectively. A few towns (Charleston, Atlanta, Savannah, Richmond, and Norfolk) had connections with Memphis, and thus with the Northwest. Most of the South, however, remained unconnected to the national railroad system. The principal means of transportation was water. Planters generally shipped their crops to market along rivers or by sea; most manufacturing was in or near port towns.

The South was, therefore, becoming more and more (and increasingly unhappily) dependent on the manufacturers, merchants, and professionals of the North. Some southerners began to champion their region's economic independence. Among the most prominent was James B. D. De Bow, a resident of New Orleans. From 1846 to 1880, he published *De Bow's Review*, a magazine advocating southern commercial and agricultural expansion and economic independence from the North. He warned constantly of the dangers of the "colonial" relationship between the sections. Yet *De Bow's Review* was itself evidence of the dependency of the South on the North. It was filled with advertisements from northern manufacturing firms; and its circulation was always modest in comparison with those of northern publications. In Charleston, for example, it sold an average of 173 copies per issue; *Harper's Magazine* of New York regularly sold 1,500 copies to South Carolinians.

### Sources of Southern Difference

Despite this growing concern about what De Bow called the region's "colonial dependency," the South made few serious efforts to build an economy that might challenge that dependency. An important question about antebellum southern history, therefore, is why the region did so little to develop a larger industrial and commercial economy of its own. Why did it remain so different from the North?

Part of the reason was the great profitability of the region's agricultural system, and particularly of cotton production. In the Northeast, many people had turned to manufacturing as the agricultural economy of the region declined. In the South, the agricultural economy was booming, and ambitious people eager to profit from the emerging capitalist economy had little incentive to look elsewhere. Another reason was that wealthy southerners had so much capital invested in their land and their slaves that they had little left for other investments. Some historians have suggested that the southern climate—with its long, hot, steamy summers—was less suitable for industrial development than the climate of the North.

But the southern failure to create a flourishing commercial or industrial economy was also in part the result of a set of values distinctive to the South that discouraged the growth of cities and industry. Many white southerners liked to think of themselves as representatives of a special way of life: one based on traditional values of chivalry, leisure, and elegance. Southerners were, they argued, "cavaliers"—people happily free from the base, acquisitive instincts of northerners, people more concerned with a refined and gracious way of life than with rapid growth and development. But appealing as the "cavalier" image was to southern whites, it conformed to the reality of southern society in very limited ways.

## SOUTHERN WHITE SOCIETY

Only a small minority of southern whites owned slaves. In 1860, when the white population was just above 8 million, the number of slaveholders was only 383,637. These figures are somewhat misleading, since each slaveholder was normally the head of a family averaging five members. But even with all members of slaveowning families included in the figures, those owning slaves still amounted to perhaps no more than one-quarter of the white population. And of this minority of whites holding slaves, only a small proportion owned them in substantial numbers.

### The Planter Class

How, then, did the South come to be seen—both by the outside world and by many southerners themselves—as a society dominated by great plantations and wealthy landowning planters? In large part, it was because the planter aristocracy—the cotton magnates, the sugar, rice, and tobacco nabobs, the whites who owned at least forty or fifty slaves and 800 or more acres—exercised power and influence far in excess of their numbers. They became a class to which all others deferred.

White southerners liked to compare their planter class to the old upper classes of England and Europe: true aristocracies, long entrenched. In fact, the southern upper class was in most cases not at all similar to the landed aristocracies of the Old World. In some areas of the upper South—the tidewater region of Virginia, for example—many of the great aristocrats were indeed people whose families had occupied positions of wealth and power for generations. In most of the South, however, there was no longstanding landed aristocracy; the "cavalier" image was largely a myth. As late as the 1850s, many of the great landowners in the lower South were still first-generation settlers, who had arrived with only modest resources, struggled for many years, and only relatively recently started to live in the comfort and luxury for which they became famous. Large areas of the "Old South" (as Americans later called the South of the pre–Civil War era) had been settled and cultivated for less than two decades at the time of the Civil War.

Nor was the world of the planter nearly as leisured and genteel as the "cavalier" myth would suggest. Growing staple crops was a business—often a big and highly profitable business. Planters were, in many respects, just as much competitive capitalists as the industrialists of the North whose lifestyles they claimed to hold in contempt. Even many affluent planters lived rather modestly, their wealth so heavily invested in land and slaves that there was little left for personal comfort. And white planters, even some substantial ones, tended to move frequently as new and presumably more productive areas opened up to cultivation.

Perhaps it was the very newness and precariousness of the plantation way of life that made many southern planters determined to portray themselves as genteel aristocrats. Having struggled so hard to reach and maintain their position, they were all the more determined to defend it. Perhaps that was why the defense of slavery and of the South's "rights" was stronger in the new, booming regions of the lower South and weaker in the more established and less flourishing areas of the tidewater.

Wealthy southern whites sustained their image of themselves as aristo-crats in many ways. They adopted an elaborate code of "chivalry," which ob-ligated white men to defend their "honor," often through dueling—which survived in the South long after it had largely vanished in the North. They avoided such "coarse" occupations as trade and commerce; those who did not become planters often gravitated toward the military, a "suitable" career for men raised in a culture in which medieval knights (as portrayed in the novels of Walter Scott) were a powerful and popular image. The aristocratic ideal also found reflection in the definition of a special role for southern white women.

### The "Southern Lady"

In some respects, affluent white women in the South occupied roles very sim-ilar to those of middle-class white women in the North. Their lives gener-ally centered in the home, where (according to the South's social ideal) they served as companions to and hostesses for their husbands and as nurturing mothers for their children. Even less frequently than in the North did "gen-teel" southern white women engage in public activities or find income-pro-ducing employment.

But the life of the "southern lady" was also in many ways very different from that of her northern counterpart. For one thing, the cult of honor in the region meant that southern white men gave particular importance to the "defense" of women. In practice, this generally meant that white men were even more dominant and white women even more subordinate in southern culture than they were in the North. George Fitzhugh, one of the South's most important social theorists, wrote in the 1850s: "Women, like children, have but one right, and that is the right to protection. The right to protection involves the obligation to obey."

More important in determining the role of southern white women, however, was that the vast majority of them lived on farms, relatively isolated from people outside their own families, with little access to the "public world" and thus few opportunities to look beyond their roles as wives and mothers. For many white women, living on farms of modest size meant a fuller engagement in the economic life of the family than was becoming typical for middle-class women in the North. These women engaged in spinning, weaving, and other production; they participated in agricultural tasks; they helped supervise the slave work force. On the larger plantations, however, even these limited roles were often considered unsuitable for white women, and the "plantation mistress" became, in some cases, more an ornament for her husband than an active part of the economy or the society. Southern white women also had less access to education than their northern counterparts. Nearly a quarter of all white women over twenty were completely illiterate; relatively few women had more than a rudimentary education. The few female "academies" in the South trained women primarily to be suitable wives.

Southern white women had other special burdens as well. The southern white birth rate remained nearly 20 percent higher than that of the nation as a whole, and infant mortality in the region remained higher than elsewhere; nearly half the children born in the South in 1860 died before they reached five years of age. The slave labor system also had a mixed impact on white women. It helped spare many of them from certain kinds of arduous labor, but it also damaged their relationships with their husbands. Male slaveowners had frequent sexual relationships with the female slaves on their plantations; the children of those unions became part of the plantation labor force and served as a constant reminder to white women of their husbands' infidelity. Black women (and men) were obviously the most important victims of such practices. But white women suffered too.

A few southern white women rebelled against their roles and against the prevailing assumptions of their region. Some became outspoken abolitionists and joined northerners in the crusade to abolish slavery. Some agitated for other reforms within the South itself. Most white women, however, expressed no open discontent with their lives or their society. Instead, they came to believe strongly in the benefits of their position and—often even more fervently than southern white men—defended the special virtues of the southern way of life.

### The Plain Folk

The typical white southerner was not a great planter and slaveholder but a modest yeoman farmer. Some of these "plain folk," as they have become known, owned a few slaves, with whom they worked and lived more closely than did the larger planters. Most (in fact, three-quarters of all white families) owned no slaves at all. Some plain folk, most of whom owned their own land, devoted themselves largely to subsistence farming; others grew cotton or other crops for the market, but usually could not produce enough to allow them to expand their operations or even get out of debt. Most yeomen knew that they had little prospect of substantially bettering their lot.

One reason was the southern educational system, which provided poor whites with few opportunities to learn and thus limited their chances of advancement. For the sons of wealthy planters, the region provided ample opportunities to gain an education. In 1860 there were 260 southern colleges and universities, public and private, with 25,000 students enrolled in them, or more than half the total number of students in the United States. But as in the rest of the United States, universities were only within the reach of the upper class. The elementary and secondary schools of the South were not only fewer than but also inferior to those of the Northeast (although not much worse than the crude schools of the Northwest). The South had more than 500,000 illiterate whites, or over half the country's total.

The subordination of the plain folk to the planter class raises an important question: Why did the plain folk not oppose the aristocratic social system in which they shared so little? Why did they not resent the system of slavery, from which they generally did not benefit?

Some nonslaveowning whites did oppose the planter elite, but for the most part in limited ways and in relatively few, isolated areas. These were the southern highlanders, the "hill people," who lived in the Appalachian ranges east of the Mississippi, in the Ozarks to the west of the river, and in other "hill country" or "backcountry" areas cut off from the more commercial world of the plantation system. Of all southern whites, they were the most isolated from the mainstream of the region's life. They practiced a simple form of subsistence agriculture, owned practically no slaves, and had a proud sense of seclusion. They were, in most respects, unconnected to the new commercial economy that dominated the great cotton-planting region of the South.

Such whites frequently expressed animosity toward the planter aristocracy of the other regions of the South. The mountain region was the only part of the South to defy the trend toward sectional conformity, and it was the only part to resist the movement toward secession when it finally developed. Even during the Civil War itself, many refused to support the Confederacy; some went so far as to fight for the Union.

Far greater in number, however, were the nonslaveowning whites who lived in the midst of the plantation system. Many, perhaps most of them, accepted that system because they were tied to it in important ways. Small farmers depended on the local plantation aristocracy for many things: access to cotton gins, markets for their modest crops and their livestock, credit or other financial assistance in time of need. In many areas, there were also extensive kinship networks linking lower- and upper-class whites. The poorest resident of a county might easily be a cousin of the richest aristocrat. Taken together, these mutual ties—a system of vaguely paternal relationships—helped mute what might otherwise have been pronounced class tensions.

Small farmers felt tied to the plantation society in other ways as well. For white men, at least, the South was an unusually democratic society, in the sense that participation in politics—both through voting and through attending campaign meetings and barbecues—was even more widespread than in the North, where participation was also high. Officeholders in the South, even more than in the North, were almost always members of the region's elites, but poorer white men felt they had participated in choosing them nevertheless. In the 1850s, moreover, the boom in the cotton economy allowed many small farmers to improve their economic fortunes. Some bought more land, became slaveowners, and moved into at least the fringes of plantation society. Others simply felt more secure in their positions as independent yeomen and hence more likely to embrace the fierce regional loyalty that was spreading throughout the white South in these years.

Small farmers, even more than great planters, were also committed to a traditional patriarchal family structure. Their household-centered economies required the participation of all family members and, they believed, a stable system of gender relations to ensure order and stability. Men were the unquestioned masters of their homes; women and children, who were both family and work force, were firmly under the master's control. As the northern attack on slavery increased in the 1840s and 1850s, it was easy for such farmers to believe—and easy for ministers, politicians, and other propagandists for slavery to persuade them—that an assault on one hierarchical system (slavery) would open the way to an assault on another such system (the family).

There were other white southerners, however, who shared almost not at all in the plantation economy and yet continued to accept its premises. These were the members of that degraded class—numbering perhaps a half-million in 1850—known variously as "crackers," "sand hillers," or "poor white trash." Occupying the infertile lands of the pine barrens, the red hills, and the swamps, they lived in genuine squalor. Many owned no land (or owned land on which virtually nothing could be grown) and supported themselves by foraging or hunting. Others worked at times as common laborers for their neighbors, although the slave system limited their opportunities to do that. Their degradation resulted partly from dietary deficiencies and disease. They resorted at times to eating clay (hence the tendency of more affluent whites to refer to them disparagingly as "clay eaters"), and they suffered from pellagra, hookworm, and malaria. Planters and small farmers alike held them in contempt. In some material respects, their plight was worse than that of the black slaves (who themselves often looked down on the poor whites).

Even among these southerners—the true outcasts of white society in the region—there was no real opposition to the plantation system or slavery. In part, undoubtedly, this was because these men and women were so benumbed by poverty that they had little strength to protest. But it resulted also from perhaps the single greatest unifying factor among the southern white population: their perception of race. However poor and miserable white southerners might be, they could still consider themselves members of a ruling race; they could still look down on the black population of the region and feel a bond with their fellow whites born of a determination to maintain their racial supremacy.

## THE "PECULIAR INSTITUTION"

White southerners often referred to slavery as the "peculiar institution." By that they meant not that the institution was odd but that it was distinctive, special. American slavery was indeed distinctive. The South in the mid-nineteenth century was the only area in the Western world—except for Brazil and Cuba—where slavery still existed. Slavery, more than any other single factor, isolated the South from the rest of American society. And as that isolation increased, so did the commitment of southerners to defend the institution.

Within the South itself, the institution of slavery had paradoxical results. On the one hand, it isolated blacks from whites, drawing a sharp and inviolable racial line dividing one group of southerners from another. As a result, African Americans under slavery began to develop a society and culture of their own. On the other hand, slavery created a unique bond between blacks and whites—masters and slaves—in the South. The two groups may have maintained separate spheres, but each sphere was deeply influenced by, indeed dependent on, the other.

### Varieties of Slavery

Slavery was an institution established and regulated in detail by law. The slave codes of the southern states forbade slaves to hold property, to leave their masters' premises without permission, to be out after dark, to congregate with other slaves except at church, to carry firearms, or to strike a white person even in self-defense. The codes prohibited whites from teaching slaves to read or write and denied slaves the right to testify in court against white people. The laws contained no provisions to legalize slave marriages or divorces. If an owner killed a slave while punishing him, the act was generally not considered a crime. Slaves, however, faced the death penalty for killing or even resisting a white person and for inciting to revolt. The codes also contained extraordinarily rigid provisions for defining a person's race. Anyone with a trace (or often even a rumor) of African ancestry was defined as black.

These and dozens of other restrictions might seem to suggest that slaves lived under a uniformly harsh and dismal regime. Had the laws been rigidly and universally enforced, that might have been the case. In fact, however, enforcement was spotty and uneven. Some slaves did acquire property, did learn to read and write, and did assemble with other slaves, in spite of laws to the contrary. Although some major slave offenses generally fell under the jurisdiction of the courts (and thus of the slave codes), white owners handled most transgressions and inflicted widely varying punishments. In other words, despite the rigid provisions of law, there was in reality considerable variety within the slave system. Some blacks lived in almost prisonlike conditions, rigidly and harshly controlled by their masters. Many (probably most) others enjoyed considerable flexibility and autonomy.

The nature of the relationship between masters and slaves depended in part on the size of the plantation. The typical master had a different image

RETURNING FROM THE COTTON FIELD In this photograph, South Carolina field workers return after a day of picking cotton, some of their harvest carried in bundles on their heads. A black slave driver leads the way.

of slavery from that of the typical slave. Most masters possessed very few slaves, and their experience with (and image of) slavery was a reflection of the special nature of slavery on the small farm. White farmers with few slaves generally supervised their workers directly and often worked closely alongside them. On such farms, blacks and whites developed a form of intimacy unknown on larger plantations. The paternal relationship between such masters and their slaves could, like relationships between fathers and children, be warm and in many ways benevolent. It could also be tyrannical and cruel. In general, the evidence suggests, African Americans themselves preferred to live on larger plantations, where they had more privacy and a chance for a social world of their own.

Although the majority of slaveowners were small farmers, the majority of slaves lived on plantations of medium or large size, with substantial slave work forces. Thus the relationship between master and slave was much less intimate for the typical slave than for the typical slaveowner. Substantial planters often hired overseers and even assistant overseers to represent them. "Head drivers," trusted and responsible slaves often assisted by several sub-drivers, acted under the overseer as foremen.

Larger planters generally used one of two methods of assigning slave labor. One was the task system, most common in rice culture, under which slaves were assigned a particular task in the morning, for example, hoeing one acre; after completing the job, they were free for the rest of the day. The other, far more common, was the gang system, employed on the cotton, sugar, and tobacco plantations, under which slaves were simply divided into groups, each of them directed by a driver, and compelled to work for as many hours as the overseer considered a reasonable workday.

### Life Under Slavery

Slaves generally received an adequate if rough diet, consisting mainly of cornmeal, salt pork, molasses, and on special occasions fresh meat or poultry. Many slaves cultivated gardens for their own use. Their masters provided them with cheap clothing and shoes. They lived in rude cabins, called slave quarters, usually clustered together in a complex near the master's house. The plantation mistress or a doctor retained by the owner provided some medical care, but slave women themselves—as "healers" and midwives, or simply as mothers—were the more important source.

Slaves worked hard, beginning with light tasks as children; and their workdays were longest at harvest time. Slave women worked particularly hard. They generally labored in the fields with the men, and they also handled cooking, cleaning, and child rearing. Many slave families were divided. Husbands and fathers often lived on neighboring plantations; at times, one spouse (usually the male) would be sold to a plantation owner far away. As a result, black women often found themselves acting in effect as single parents. Within the slave family, therefore, women had special burdens but also a special authority.

Slaves were, as a group, much less healthy than southern whites. After 1808, when the importation of slaves became illegal, the proportion of blacks to whites in the nation as a whole steadily declined. In 1820, there was one African American to every four whites; in 1840, one to every five. The slower increase of the black population was a result of its comparatively high death rate. Slave mothers had large families, but the enforced poverty in which vir-

# A M E R I C A N    V O I C E S

### JAMES L. BRADLEY

## *An African American Describes His Bondage, 1835*

 I THINK I was between two and three years old when the soul-destroyers tore me from my mother's arms, somewhere in Africa, far back from the sea. They carried me a long distance to a ship; all the way I looked back, and cried. The ship was full of men and women loaded with chains; but I was so small they let me run about on deck.

After many long days, they brought us into Charleston, South Carolina. A slaveholder bought me, and took me up into Pendleton County. I suppose that I staid with him about six months. He sold me to a Mr. Bradley, by whose name I have ever since been called. This man was considered a wonderfully kind master; and it is true that I was treated better than most of the slaves I knew. I never suffered for food, and never was flogged with the whip; but oh, my soul! I was tormented with kicks and knocks more than I can tell. . . .

I used to work very hard. I was always obliged to be in the field by sunrise, and I labored till dark stopping only at noon long enough to eat dinner. . . . My master had kept me ignorant of everything he could. . . . Yet from the time I was fourteen years old, I used to think a great deal about freedom. It was my heart's desire; I could not keep it out of my mind. Many a sleepless night I have spent in tears, because I was a slave. I looked back on all I had suffered—and when I looked ahead, all was dark and hopeless bondage.

SOURCE: John W. Blassingame, ed., *Slave Testimony* (Baton Rouge: Louisiana State University Press, 1977), pp. 687–688.

tually all African Americans lived ensured that fewer of their children would survive to adulthood than the children of white parents. Even those who did survive typically died at a younger age than the average white person.

Even so, according to some historians, the material conditions of slavery may, in fact, have been better than those of some northern factory workers and considerably better than those of both peasants and industrial workers in nineteenth-century Europe. The conditions of American slaves were certainly less severe than those of slaves in the Caribbean and much of South America. That was in part because plantations in other regions of the Americas tended to grow crops that required more arduous labor; sugar production in the Caribbean islands, in particular, involved extraordinarily back-breaking work. In addition, Caribbean and South American planters continued to use the African slave trade well into the nineteenth century to replenish their labor supply, so they had less incentive than American planters (who no longer had much access to that trade) to protect their existing laborers. Growing cotton, the activity for most slaves in the United States, was much less debilitating than growing sugar; and planters had strong economic incentives to maintain a healthy slave population. One result of this was that America became the only country where a slave population actually increased through natural reproduction (although it grew much more slowly than the white population).

Household servants had a somewhat easier life—physically at least—than did field hands. On a small plantation, the same slaves might do both field work and housework. But on a large estate, there would generally be a separate domestic staff: nursemaids, housemaids, cooks, butlers, coachmen. These people lived close to the master and his family, eating the leftovers from the family table and in some cases even sleeping in the "big house." Between the blacks and whites of such households affectionate, almost familial relationships might develop. More often, however, house servants resented their isolation from their fellow slaves and the lack of privacy that came with living in such close proximity to the master's family. Among other things, that proximity meant that their transgressions were more visible than those of field hands, and so they received punishments more often than did other slaves. When emancipation came after the Civil War, it was often the house servants who were the first to leave the plantations of their former owners.

Female household servants were especially vulnerable to sexual abuse by their masters and white overseers, who often pressured them into sexual relationships and sometimes literally raped them. In addition to being subjected to unwanted sexual attention from white men, female slaves often received vindictive treatment from white women. Plantation mistresses naturally resented the sexual liaisons between their husbands and female slaves. Punishing their husbands was not usually possible, so they often punished the slaves instead—with arbitrary beatings, increased workloads, and various forms of psychological torment.

## Slavery in the Cities

The conditions of slavery in the cities differed significantly from those in the countryside. On the relatively isolated plantations, slaves had little contact with free blacks and lower-class whites, and masters maintained a fairly direct and effective control; a deep and seemingly unbridgeable chasm yawned between slavery and freedom. In the city, however, a master often could not supervise his slaves closely and at the same time use them profitably. Even if they slept at night in carefully watched backyard barracks, they moved about during the day alone, performing errands of various kinds.

There was a considerable market in the South for common laborers, particularly since, unlike in the North, there were few European immigrants to perform menial chores. As a result, masters often hired out slaves for such tasks. Slaves on contract worked in mining and lumbering (often far from cities), but others worked on the docks and on construction sites, drove wagons, and performed other unskilled jobs in cities and towns. Slave women and children worked in the region's few textile mills. Particularly skilled workers such as blacksmiths or carpenters were also often hired out. After regular working hours, many of them fended for themselves; neither their owners nor their employers bothered to supervise them. Thus urban slaves gained numerous opportunities to mingle with free blacks and with whites. In the cities, the line between slavery and freedom became increasingly indistinct.

Indeed, white southerners generally considered slavery to be incompatible with city life; and as southern cities grew, the number of slaves in them declined, relatively if not absolutely. The reasons were social rather than economic. Fearing conspiracies and insurrections, urban slaveowners sold off much of their male property to the countryside. Remaining behind in the cities was a slave population in which black women outnumbered black men. Even while slavery in the cities was declining, forced segregation of urban blacks, both free and slave, from white society increased. Segregation was a means of social control intended to make up for the loosening of the discipline of plantation slavery itself in urban areas.

### Free Blacks

There were about 250,000 free blacks in the slaveholding states by the start of the Civil War, more than half of them in Virginia and Maryland. In some cases, they were slaves who had somehow earned money with which they managed to buy their own and their families' freedom, most often by developing a skill they could market independently of their masters. It was usually urban blacks, with their greater freedom of movement and activity, who could take that route. One example was Elizabeth Keckley, a slave woman who bought freedom for herself and her son with proceeds from sewing. She later became a seamstress, personal servant, and companion to Mary Todd Lincoln in the White House. But few masters had any incentive, or inclination, to give up their slaves, so this route was open to relatively few people.

Some slaves were set free by a master who had moral qualms about slavery, or by a master's will after his death—for example, the more than 400 slaves belonging to John Randolph of Roanoke, freed in 1833. From the 1830s on, however, state laws governing slavery became more rigid. That was in part a response to the fears Nat Turner's revolt (see p. 314) created among white southerners: free blacks, removed from close supervision by whites, might generate more violence and rebellion than would slaves. The new laws made it more and more difficult, and in some cases practically impossible, for owners to set free (or "manumit") their slaves.

A few free blacks (generally those on the northern fringes of the slaveholding regions) attained wealth and prominence. Some owned slaves themselves, usually relatives whom they had bought in order to ensure their ultimate emancipation. In a few cities—New Orleans, Natchez, and Charleston—free black communities managed to flourish relatively unmolested by whites and with some economic stability. Most free blacks, however, lived in abject poverty, under conditions worse than those of blacks in the North. Yet great as were the hardships of freedom, blacks usually preferred them to slavery.

### Slave Resistance

Few issues have sparked as much debate among historians as the effects of slavery on African Americans themselves. (See "Debating the Past," pp. 319–320.) Slaveowners, and many white Americans after emancipation, liked to argue that the slaves were generally content, "happy with their lot." That may have been true in some cases. But it is clear that the vast majority of southern blacks were not content with being slaves, that they yearned for freedom even though most realized there was little they could do to secure it. Evidence for that conclusion can be found, if nowhere else, in the reaction of slaves when emancipation finally came. Virtually all reacted to freedom with joy and celebration; relatively few chose to remain in the service of the whites who had owned them before the Civil War (although most blacks, of course, remained for many years subservient to whites in one way or another).

Rather than contented acceptance, the dominant response of blacks to slavery was a complex one: a combination of adaptation and resistance. At the extremes, slavery could produce two very different reactions, each of which served as the basis for a powerful stereotype in white society. One extreme was what became known as the "Sambo"—the shuffling, grinning, head-scratching, deferential slave who acted out the role that he recognized the white world expected of him. More often than not, the "Sambo" pattern of behavior was a charade, a façade assumed in the presence of whites. The other extreme was the slave rebel—the African American who could not bring himself or herself to either acceptance or accommodation but remained forever rebellious.

Actual slave revolts were extremely rare, but the knowledge that they were possible struck terror into the hearts of white southerners everywhere. In 1800, Gabriel Prosser gathered 1,000 rebellious slaves outside Richmond; but two Africans gave the plot away, and the Virginia militia stymied the uprising before it could begin. Prosser and thirty-five others were executed. In 1822, the Charleston free black Denmark Vesey and his followers—rumored to total 9,000—made preparations for revolt; but again word leaked out, and suppression and retribution followed. On a summer night in 1831, Nat Turner, a slave preacher, led a band of African Americans armed with guns and axes from house to house in Southampton County, Virginia. They killed sixty white men, women, and children before being overpowered by state and federal troops. More than a hundred blacks were executed in the aftermath. Nat Turner's was the only actual slave insurrection in the nineteenth-century South, but fear of slave conspiracies and renewed violence pervaded the section as long as slavery lasted.

For the most part, however, resistance to slavery took other, less drastic forms. Some blacks attempted to resist by running away. A small number managed to escape to the North or to Canada, especially after sympathetic whites began organizing the so-called underground railroad to assist them in flight. But the odds against a successful escape, particularly from the

HARRIET TUBMAN WITH ESCAPED SLAVES Harriet Tubman (c. 1820–1913) was born into slavery in Maryland. In 1849, when her master died, she escaped to Philadelphia to avoid being sold out of state. Over the next ten years, she assisted first members of her own family and then up to 300 other slaves to escape from Maryland to freedom. During the Civil War, she served alternately as a nurse and as a spy for Union forces in South Carolina. She is shown here, on the left, with some of the slaves she had helped to free.

Deep South, were almost impossibly high. The hazards of distance and the slaves' ignorance of geography were serious obstacles. So were the white "slave patrols," which stopped wandering blacks on sight throughout the South demanding to see travel permits. Without such a permit, slaves were presumed to be runaways and were taken captive. Despite all the obstacles to success, however, blacks continued to run away from their masters in large numbers. Some did so repeatedly, undeterred by the whippings and other penalties inflicted on them when captured.

But perhaps the most important method of resistance was simply a pattern of everyday behavior by which blacks defied their masters. That whites so often considered blacks to be lazy and shiftless suggests one means of resistance: refusal to work hard. Some slaves stole from their masters or from neighboring whites. Some performed isolated acts of sabotage: losing or breaking tools (southern planters gradually began to buy unusually heavy hoes because so many of the lighter ones got broken) or performing tasks improperly. In extreme cases, blacks might make themselves useless by cutting off their fingers or even committing suicide. Or, despite the terrible consequences, a few turned on their masters and killed them. The extremes, however, were very rare. For the most part, blacks resisted by building into their normal patterns of behavior subtle methods of rebellion.

## THE CULTURE OF SLAVERY

Resistance was only part of the slave response to slavery. Another was an elaborate process of adaptation—a process that did not imply contentment with bondage but a recognition that there was no realistic alternative. One of the ways blacks adapted was by developing their own, separate culture, one that enabled them to sustain a sense of racial pride and unity.

### Slave Religion

A separate slave religion was not supposed to exist. Almost all African Americans were Christians by the early nineteenth century. Some had converted voluntarily and some after coercion from their masters and Protestant missionaries who evangelized among them. Masters expected their slaves to worship under the supervision of white ministers. Indeed, autonomous black churches were banned by law, and many slaves became members of the same denominations as their owners—usually Baptist or Methodist. In the 1840s and 1850s, as slavery expanded in the South, missionary efforts increased. Vast numbers of blacks became members of Protestant churches in those years.

Nevertheless, blacks throughout the South developed their own version of Christianity, at times incorporating into it such practices as voodoo or other polytheistic religious traditions of Africa. Or they simply bent religion to the special circumstances of bondage. Natural leaders emerging within the slave community rose to the rank of preacher.

African-American religion was more emotional than its white counterparts and reflected the influence of African customs and practices. Slave prayer meetings routinely involved fervent chanting, spontaneous exclamations from the congregation, and ecstatic conversion experiences. Black religion was also more joyful and affirming than that of many white denominations. And above all, black religion emphasized the dream of freedom and deliverance. In their prayers and songs and sermons, black Christians talked and sang of the day when the Lord would "call us home," "deliver us to freedom," "take us to the Promised Land." And while their white masters generally chose to interpret such language merely as the expression of hopes for life after death, many blacks themselves used the images of Christian salvation to express their own dream of freedom in the present world. Christian images, and biblical injunctions, were central to Gabriel Prosser, Denmark Vesey, Nat Turner, and others who planned or engaged in open resistance to slavery.

In cities and towns in the South, some African Americans had their own churches, where free blacks occasionally worshiped alongside slaves. In the countryside, however, slaves usually attended the same churches as their masters. Seating in such churches was usually segregated. Blacks sat in the rear or in balconies. They held their own services later, often in secret, usually at night.

### The Slave Family

The slave family was the other crucial institution of black culture in the South. Like religion, it suffered from legal restrictions—most notably the lack of legal marriage. Nevertheless, what we now call the "nuclear family" consistently emerged as the dominant kinship model among African Americans.

Such families did not always operate according to white customs. Black women generally began bearing children at younger ages than most whites, often as early as age fourteen or fifteen. Slave communities did not condemn premarital pregnancy in the way white society did, and black couples would often begin living together before marrying. It was customary, however, for couples to marry—in a ceremony involving formal vows—soon after conceiving a child. Many marriages occurred between slaves living on neighboring plantations. Husbands and wives sometimes visited each other with the permission of their masters, but often such visits had to be in secret, at night. Family ties were generally no less strong than those of whites, and many slave marriages lasted through long lifetimes.

When marriages did not survive, it was often because of circumstances over which blacks had no control. Up to a third of all black families were broken apart by the slave trade; an average slave might expect during a lifetime to see ten or more relatives sold. That accounted for some of the other distinctive characteristics of the black family, which adapted itself to the cruel realities of its own uncertain future. Extended kinship networks—which grew to include not only spouses and their children but aunts, uncles, grandparents, even distant cousins—were strong and important and often helped compensate for the breakup of nuclear families. A slave forced suddenly to move to a new area, far from his or her family, might create fictional kinship ties and become "adopted" by a family in the new community. Even so, the impulse to maintain contact with a spouse and children remained strong long after the breakup of a family. One of the most frequent causes of flight from the plantation was a slave's desire to find a husband, wife, or child who had been sent elsewhere.

However much blacks resented their lack of freedom, they often found it difficult to maintain an entirely hostile attitude toward their owners. Not only were they dependent on whites for the material means of existence—food, clothing, and shelter; they also often derived from their masters a sense of security and protection. There was, in short, a paternal relationship between slave and master—sometimes harsh, sometimes kindly, but always important. That paternalism, in fact, became (even if not always consciously) a vital instrument of white control. By creating a sense of mutual dependence, whites helped reduce resistance to an institution that, in essence, served only the interests of the ruling race.

D  E  B  A  T  I  N  G        T  H  E        P  A  S  T

## *The Nature of Plantation Slavery*

O ISSUE IN American history has produced a richer literature or a more spirited debate than the nature of plantation slavery. The debate began even before the Civil War, when abolitionists strove to expose slavery to the world as a brutal, dehumanizing institution, while Southern defenders of slavery tried to depict it as a benevolent, paternalistic system. That same debate continued for a time after the Civil War; but by the late nineteenth century, with white Americans eager for sectional conciliation, most Northern and Southern chroniclers of slavery began to accept a romanticized and unthreatening picture of the Old South and its peculiar institution.

The first major scholarly examination of slavery was fully within this romantic tradition. Ulrich B. Phillips's *American Negro Slavery* (1918) portrayed slavery as an essentially benign institution in which kindly masters looked after submissive, childlike, and generally contented African Americans. Phillips's apologia for slavery remained the authoritative work on the subject for nearly thirty years.

In the 1940s, as concern about racial injustice increasingly engaged the attention of white Americans, challenges to Phillips began to emerge. In 1941, for example, Melville J. Herskovits challenged Phillips's contention that black Americans retained little of their African cultural inheritance. In 1943, Herbert Aptheker published a chronicle of slave revolts as a way of challenging Phillips's claim that blacks were submissive and content.

A somewhat different challenge to Phillips emerged in the 1950s from historians who emphasized the brutality of the institution. Kenneth Stampp's *The Peculiar Institution* (1956) and, even more powerfully, Stanley Elkins's *Slavery* (1959) described a labor system that did serious physical and psychological damage to its victims. Stampp and Elkins portrayed slavery as something like a prison, in which men and women had virtually no space to

*(continued on next page)*

develop their own social and cultural lives. Elkins compared the system to Nazi concentration camps during World War II and likened the childlike "Sambo" personality of slavery to the tragic distortions of character produced by the Holocaust.

In the early 1970s, an explosion of new scholarship on slavery shifted the emphasis away from the damage the system inflicted on African Americans and toward the striking success of the slaves themselves in building a culture of their own despite their enslavement. John Blassingame in 1973, echoing Herskovits's claims of thirty years earlier, argued that "the most remarkable aspect of the whole process of enslavement is the extent to which the American-born slaves were able to retain their ancestors' culture." Herbert Gutman, in *The Black Family in Slavery and Freedom* (1976), challenged the prevailing belief that slavery had weakened and even destroyed the African-American family. On the contrary, he argued, the black family survived slavery with impressive strength, although with some significant differences from the prevailing form of the white family. Eugene Genovese's *Roll, Jordan, Roll* (1974) revealed how African Americans manipulated the paternalist assumptions that lay at the heart of slavery to build a large cultural space of their own, within the system, where they could develop their own family life, social traditions, and religious patterns. That same year, Robert Fogel and Stanley Engerman published their controversial *Time on the Cross,* a highly quantitative study that supported some of the claims of Gutman and Genovese about black achievement but that went much further in portraying slavery as a successful and reasonably humane (if ultimately immoral) system. Slave workers, they argued, were better treated and lived in greater comfort than most Northern industrial workers of the same era. Their conclusions produced a storm of criticism.

Some of the most important recent scholarship on slavery extends the notion of slave autonomy to discussions of African-American women. Elizabeth Fox-Genovese's *Within the Plantation Household* (1988) examined the lives of both white and black women on the plantation. Rejecting the claims of some feminist historians that black and white women shared a common female identity born of their shared subordination to men, she portrayed slave women as defined by their dual roles as members of the plantation work force and anchors of the black family. Slave women, she argued, professed loyalty to their mistresses when forced to serve them as domestics; but their real loyalty remained to their own communities and families.

# CHAPTER TWELVE

# An Age of Reforms

*The Romantic Impulse* ∼ *Remaking Society*
*The Crusade Against Slavery*

T HE UNITED STATES in the mid-nineteenth century was growing rapidly in geographical extent, in the size and diversity of its population, and in the dimensions and complexity of its economy. And like any people faced with such rapid and fundamental change, Americans reacted with ambiguity. On the one hand, they were excited by the new possibilities that economic growth was providing. On the other hand, they were painfully aware of the dislocations that it was creating: the challenges to traditional values and institutions, the social injustice and instability, the uncertainty about the future.

One result of these conflicting attitudes was the emergence of movements to "reform" the nation. Such movements were highly diverse, but most reflected one of two basic impulses, and at times elements of both. Some rested on an optimistic faith in human nature, a belief that within every individual resided a spirit that was basically good and that society should attempt to unleash. This assumption—which produced in both Europe and America a movement known as romanticism—stood in marked contrast to the traditional Calvinist assumption that human desires and instincts were sinful and needed to be repressed.

A second impulse was a desire for order and control. With their society changing so rapidly, with their traditional values and institutions being challenged and eroded, many Americans yearned above all for a restoration of stability and discipline to their nation. Often, this impulse embodied a conservative nostalgia for better, simpler times. But it also inspired efforts to create new institutions of social control, suited to the realities of the new age.

Reform efforts took many forms and could be found in every part of the nation. By the end of the 1840s, however, one issue—slavery—had come to overshadow all others. And one group of reformers—the abolitionists—had

## TIME LINE

| 1821 | 1823 | 1826 | 1830 | 1831 |
|------|------|------|------|------|
| New York constructs first penitentiary | Hartford Female Seminary founded | American Society for the Promotion of Temperance founded | Joseph Smith publishes the *Book of Mormon* | *The Liberator* begins publication |
| | | Cooper's *The Last of the Mohicans* | | |

| 1833 | 1837 | 1840 | 1841 | 1845 |
|------|------|------|------|------|
| American Antislavery Society founded | Horace Mann secretary of Massachusetts Board of Education | Liberty Party | Brook Farm founded | Frederick Douglass's autobiography |

| 1848 | 1850 | 1851 | 1852 | 1854 | 1855 |
|------|------|------|------|------|------|
| Women's rights convention at Seneca Falls, N.Y. | Hawthorne's *The Scarlet Letter* | Melville's *Moby Dick* | Beecher Stowe's *Uncle Tom's Cabin* | Thoreau's *Walden* | Whitman's *Leaves of Grass* |
| Oneida community founded | | | | | |

become the most influential of all. At that point, the reform impulse became another wedge between the North and the South.

## THE ROMANTIC IMPULSE

"In the four quarters of the globe," wrote the English wit Sydney Smith in 1820, "who reads an American book? or goes to an American play? or looks at an American picture or statue?" The answer, he assumed, was obvious—no one.

American intellectuals were painfully aware of the low regard in which Europeans held their culture, and they tried in the middle decades of the century to create an American artistic life that would express their own nation's special virtues. At the same time, many of the nation's cultural leaders were striving for another kind of liberation, which was—ironically—largely an import from Europe: the spirit of romanticism. In literature, in philosophy, in art, even in politics and economics, American intellectuals were committing themselves to the liberation of the human spirit.

## An American Literature

The effort to create a distinctively American literature, which Washington Irving and others had begun in the first decades of the century, made considerable progress in the 1820s through the work of the first great American novelist: James Fenimore Cooper. What most distinguished his work was its evocation of the American West. Cooper had a lifelong fascination with the human relationship to nature and with the challenges (and dangers) of America's expansion westward. His most important novels—among them *The Last of the Mohicans* (1826) and *The Deerslayer* (1841)—explored the experience of rugged white frontiersmen with Indians, pioneers, violence, and the law. Cooper not only celebrated the American spirit and landscape; he also evoked the ideal of the independent individual with a natural inner goodness—an ideal that many Americans feared was in jeopardy in the expanding, industrializing world of the East.

Another later group of American writers displayed more clearly the appeal of romanticism to the nation's artists and intellectuals. In 1855, Walt Whitman published his first book of poems, *Leaves of Grass*, and established himself as one of the nation's most important writers. His poems celebrated democracy, the liberation of the individual spirit, and the pleasures of the flesh. Whitman helped liberate verse from traditional, restrictive conventions; he also expressed a yearning for emotional and physical release and personal fulfillment—a yearning perhaps rooted in part in his own experience as a homosexual living in a society profoundly intolerant of unconventional sexuality.

Less exuberant was Herman Melville, probably the greatest American writer of his era. The most important of his novels was *Moby Dick*, published in 1851—the story of Ahab, the powerful, driven captain of a whaling vessel, who was obsessed with his search for Moby Dick, the great white whale that had once maimed him. It was a story of courage and of the strength of human will. But it was also a tragedy of pride and revenge, and a metaphor for the harsh, individualistic, achievement-driven culture of nineteenth-century America.

## The Transcendentalists

One of the outstanding expressions of the romantic impulse in America came from a group of New England writers and philosophers known as the transcendentalists. Borrowing heavily from German and English writers and philosophers, the transcendentalists embraced a theory of the individual that rested on a distinction between what they called "reason" and "understanding." Reason, as they defined it, was the highest human faculty; it was the individual's innate capacity to grasp beauty and truth by giving full expression to the instincts and emotions. Understanding, by contrast, was the use of intellect in the narrow, artificial ways imposed by society; it involved the repression of instinct and the victory of externally imposed learning. Every person's goal, therefore, should be liberation from the confines of "understanding" and, instead, the cultivation of "reason." Each individual should strive to "transcend" the limits of the intellect and allow the emotions, the "soul," to create an "original relation to the Universe."

Transcendentalist philosophy emerged first in America among a small group of intellectuals centered in Concord, Massachusetts, and led by Ralph Waldo Emerson. A Unitarian minister in his youth, Emerson left the clergy in 1832 to devote himself to writing, teaching, and lecturing. In "Nature" (1836), Emerson wrote that in the quest for self-fulfillment, individuals should work for a communion with the natural world: "in the woods, we return to reason and faith. . . . Standing on the bare ground,—my head bathed by the blithe air, and uplifted into infinite space,—all mean egotism vanishes. . . . I am part and particle of God." In other essays, he was even more explicit in advocating a commitment of the individual to the full exploration of inner capacities. "Nothing is at last sacred," he wrote in "Self-Reliance" (1841), perhaps his most famous essay, "but the integrity of your own mind."

Almost as influential as Emerson was another Concord transcendentalist, Henry David Thoreau. Thoreau went even further than his friend Emerson in repudiating the repressive forces of society, which produced, he said, "lives of quiet desperation." Each individual should work for self-realization by resisting pressures to conform to society's expectations and responding instead to his or her own instincts. Thoreau's own effort to free himself—immortalized in *Walden* (1854)—led him to build a small cabin in the Concord woods on the edge of Walden Pond, where he lived alone for two years as simply as he could, attempting to liberate himself from repressive convention and from what he considered society's excessive interest in material comforts. "I went to the woods," he explained, "because I wished to live deliberately, to front only the essential facts of life, and see if I could not learn what it had to teach, and not, when I came to die, discover that I had not lived." Thoreau's rejection of what he considered the artificial constraints of society extended to his relationship with government. In 1846, he went to jail (briefly) rather than agree to pay a poll tax. He would not, he insisted, give financial support to a government that permitted the existence of slavery. In his 1849 essay "Resistance to Civil Government," he explained his refusal by arguing that a government which required an individual to violate his or her own morality had no legitimate authority. The proper response was "civil disobedience," or "passive resistance"—a public refusal to obey unjust laws.

### Visions of Utopia

Although transcendentalism was at its heart an individualistic philosophy, it helped spawn one of the most famous of all nineteenth-century experiments in communal living: Brook Farm. The dream of the Boston transcendentalist George Ripley, Brook Farm was established in 1841 as an experimental community in West Roxbury, Massachusetts. There, according to Ripley, individuals would gather to create a new society that would permit every member to have full opportunity for self-realization. All residents would share equally in the labor of the community so that all could share too in the leisure, which was essential for cultivation of the self. (Ripley was one of the first Americans to attribute positive connotations to the idea of leisure; most of his contemporaries equated it with laziness and sloth.) The tension between the ideal of individual freedom and the demands of a communal society took their toll on Brook Farm. Many residents became disenchanted and left. When a fire destroyed the central building of the community in 1847, the experiment dissolved.

Among the original residents of Brook Farm was the writer Nathaniel Hawthorne, who expressed his disillusionment with the experiment and, to some extent, with transcendentalism in a series of novels voicing some of the same concerns that his contemporary Herman Melville was articulating. In *The Blithedale Romance* (1852), he wrote scathingly of Brook Farm itself. In other novels—most notably *The Scarlet Letter* (1850) and *The House of the Seven Gables* (1851)—he wrote equally passionately about the price individuals pay for cutting themselves off from society. Egotism, he claimed (in an indirect challenge to the transcendentalist faith in the self), was the "serpent" that lay at the heart of human misery.

The failure of Brook Farm did not, however, prevent the formation of other experimental communities. The Scottish industrialist and philanthropist Robert Owen founded an experimental community in Indiana in 1825, which he named New Harmony. It was to be a "Village of Cooperation," in which every resident worked and lived in total equality. The community was an economic failure, but the vision that had inspired it continued to enchant some Americans. Dozens of other "Owenite" experiments began in other locations in the ensuing years.

*Redefining Gender Roles*

Many of the new utopian communities (and many of the new social philoso-phies on which they rested) were centrally concerned with the relationship between men and women. Some experimented with a radical redefinition of gender roles.

Such a redefinition was central to one of the most enduring of the utopian colonies of the nineteenth century: the Oneida Community, estab-lished in 1848 in upstate New York by John Humphrey Noyes. The Oneida "Perfectionists," as residents of the community called themselves, rejected traditional notions of family and marriage. All residents, Noyes declared, were "married" to all other residents; there were to be no permanent con-jugal ties. But Oneida was not, as horrified critics often claimed, an experi-ment in unrestrained "free love." It was a place where the community care-fully monitored sexual behavior; where women were protected from unwanted childbearing; and where children were raised communally, often seeing little of their own parents. The Oneidans took pride in what they con-sidered their liberation of women from the demands of male "lust" and from the traditional bonds of family.

The Shakers, too, made a redefinition of traditional gender roles cen-tral to their society. Founded by "Mother" Ann Lee in the 1770s, the soci-ety of the Shakers survived into the twentieth century. (A tiny remnant is left today.) But the Shakers attracted a particularly large following in the mid-nineteenth century and established more than twenty communities through-out the Northeast and Northwest in the 1840s. They derived their name from a unique religious ritual—a sort of dance, in which members of a con-gregation would "shake" themselves free of sin while performing a loud chant and an ecstatic dance.

The most distinctive feature of Shakerism, however, was its commitment to complete celibacy—which meant, of course, that no one could be born to Shakerism; all Shakers had to choose the faith voluntarily. Shaker com-munities attracted about 6,000 members in the 1840s, more women than men. They lived in communities where contacts between men and women were strictly limited, and they endorsed the idea of sexual equality. Within Shaker society, women exercised the most power. Shakerism, one observer wrote in the 1840s, was a refuge from the "perversions of marriage" and "the gross abuses which drag it down."

The Shakers were not, however, motivated only by a desire to escape the burdens of traditional gender roles. They were trying as well to create a society separated and protected from the chaos and disorder that they believed had come to characterize American life as a whole. In that, they were much like other dissenting religious sects and other utopian communities of their time.

## The Mormons

Perhaps the most important effort to create a new and more ordered society in America was that of the Church of Jesus Christ of Latter Day Saints, whose members are known as Mormons. Mormonism began in upstate New York as a result of the efforts of Joseph Smith, an energetic but economically unsuccessful man, who had spent most of his twenty-four years moving restlessly through New England and the Northeast. Then, in 1830, he published a remarkable document—the Book of Mormon—which he claimed was a translation of a set of golden tablets he had found in the hills of New York after a revelation by an angel of God. The Book of Mormon told the story of an ancient civilization in America, whose now vanished kingdom could become a model for a new holy community in the United States.

Gathering a small group of believers around him, Smith began in 1831 to seek a sanctuary for his new community of "saints," an effort that would continue, unhappily, for more than twenty years. Time and again, the Mormons attempted to establish their "New Jerusalem." Time and again, they met with persecution from surrounding communities suspicious of their radical religious doctrines—which included polygamy (the right of men to take several wives), a rigid form of social organization, and an intense secrecy that gave rise to wild rumors among their critics of conspiracy and depravity.

Driven from their original settlements in Independence, Missouri, and Kirtland, Ohio, the Mormons founded Nauvoo, Illinois, which in the early 1840s became an imposing and economically successful community. In 1844, however, Joseph Smith was arrested, charged with treason (for conspiring against the government to win foreign support for a new Mormon colony in the Southwest), and imprisoned in nearby Carthage, Illinois. There an angry mob attacked the jail, forced Smith from his cell, and shot and killed him. The Mormons then abandoned Nauvoo and, under the leadership of Smith's successor, Brigham Young, traveled across the desert—a society of 12,000 people, one of the largest group migrations in American history—and established a new settlement in Utah, the present Salt Lake City. There, at last, the Mormons were able to create a permanent settlement.

Like other experiments in social organization of the era, Mormonism reflected a belief in human perfectibility. God had once been a man, the church taught; and thus every man or woman could aspire to become, in ef-

THE MORMONS' TREK WESTWARD  The great Mormon migration to Utah was, like the Mormon Church itself, a family undertaking. This image, painted at the time by one of the settlers, shows women and children gathering buffalo chips (dried buffalo manure) for lighting fires as other families cross a stream on their way into camp.

fect, a god—as Joseph Smith had done. But the Mormons did not celebrate individual liberty. Instead, they created a highly organized, centrally directed, almost militarized social structure as a refuge against the disorder and uncertainty of the secular world. They placed particular emphasis on the structure of the family. The original Mormons were, for the most part, men and women who felt displaced in their rapidly changing society—economically marginal people left behind by the material growth and social progress of their era. In the new religion, they found security and order.

## REMAKING SOCIETY

The reform impulse also helped create new movements to remake mainstream society—movements in which, to a striking degree, women formed both the rank and file and the leadership. By the 1830s, such movements had taken the form of organized reform societies. The new organizations worked on behalf of a wide range of goals: temperance; education; peace; the care of the poor, the handicapped, and the mentally ill; the treatment of criminals; the rights of women; and many more. Few eras in American history have witnessed as wide a range of reform efforts. And few eras have exposed more clearly the simultaneous (and at times competing) attraction of Americans to the ideas of personal liberty and social order.

### Revivalism, Morality, and Order

The philosophy of reform arose in part from the optimistic vision of those such as the transcendentalists who preached the divinity of the individual. But another, and in many respects more important, source was Protestant revivalism—the movement that had begun with the Second Great Awakening early in the century and had, by the 1820s, evolved into a powerful force for social reform.

The New Light evangelicals embraced the optimistic belief that every individual was capable of salvation through his or her own efforts (hence the term "Free Will Baptists," by which one group described themselves). Partly as a result, revivalism soon became not only a means of personal salvation but a mandate for the reform of the larger society. In particular, revivalism produced a crusade against personal immorality. "The church," said Charles Grandison Finney, the leading revivalist of his time, "must take right ground on the subject of Temperance, the Moral Reform, and all the subjects of practical morality which come up for decision from time to time."

Evangelical Protestantism added major strength to one of the most influential reform movements of the era: the crusade against drunkenness. No social vice, temperance advocates argued, was more responsible for crime, disorder, and poverty than the excessive use of alcohol. Women, who were particularly active in the temperance movement, complained that men spent money their families needed on alcohol and that drunken husbands often beat and abused their wives. Temperance also appealed to those who were alarmed by immigration; drunkenness, many nativists believed, was responsible for violence and disorder in immigrant communities and temperance was a way to discipline them. By 1840, temperance had become a major national movement, with powerful organizations and more than a million followers who had signed a formal pledge to forgo hard liquor.

As the movement gained in strength, it became divided in purpose. Some demanded legislation to restrict the sale and consumption of alcohol (Maine passed such a law in 1851). Others insisted that temperance must rely on the conscience of the individual. Whatever their disagreements, however, most

*THE DRUNKARD'S PROGRESS* This 1846 lithograph by Nathaniel Currier shows what temperance advocates argued was the inevitable consequence of alcohol consumption. Beginning with an apparently innocent "glass with a friend," the young man rises step by step to the summit of drunken revelry, then declines to desperation and suicide while his abandoned wife and child grieve.

temperance advocates shared similar motives. By promoting abstinence, reformers were attempting to promote individual moral self-improvement. They were also trying to impose discipline on a disordered society.

### Education and Rehabilitation

One of the most important reform movements of the mid-nineteenth century was the effort to produce a system of universal public education. As of 1830, no state had such a system, although some—such as Massachusetts—were supporting limited versions. Soon after that, however, interest in public education began growing rapidly.

The greatest of the educational reformers was Horace Mann, the first secretary of the Massachusetts Board of Education, which was established in 1837. To Mann and his followers, education was the only way to "counterwork this tendency to the domination of capital and the servility of labor." It was also the only way to protect democracy, for an educated electorate was essential to the workings of a free political system. Mann reorganized the Massachusetts school system, lengthened the academic year (to six months), doubled teachers' salaries (although he did not eliminate the large disparities between the salaries of male and female teachers), broadened the curriculum, and introduced new methods of professional training for teachers. Other states followed similar courses: building new schools, creating teachers' colleges, and offering many children access to education for the first time. By the 1850s, the principle (although not yet the reality) of tax-supported elementary schools was established in every state.

Yet the quality of public education continued to vary widely. In some places—Massachusetts, for example—educators were generally capable men and women, often highly trained, who had an emerging sense of themselves as career professionals. In other areas, however, teachers were often barely literate, and funding for education was severely limited. In much of the West, where the population was highly dispersed, many children had no access to schools at all. In the South, all African Americans were barred from education (although approximately 10 percent of them managed to achieve literacy anyway), and only about a third of all white children of school age were actually enrolled in schools in 1860. In the North, 72 percent were enrolled, but even there, many students attended classes only briefly and casually.

The interest in education (and, implicitly, in the unleashing of individual talents that could result from it) was visible too in the growing movement to educate American Indians in the antebellum period. Some reformers, even many who considered black people inferior and unredeemable, believed that Indians could be "civilized" if only they could be taught the ways of the white world. Efforts by missionaries and others to educate Indians and encourage them to assimilate were particularly prominent in such areas of the Far West as Oregon, where substantial numbers of whites were beginning to settle in the 1840s and where conflicts with the natives had not yet become acute. Nevertheless, the great majority of Native Americans remained outside the reach of educational reform, either by choice or by circumstance or both.

Despite limitations and inequities, the achievements of the school reformers were impressive. By the beginning of the Civil War, the United States had one of the highest literacy rates of any nation of the world: 94 percent of the population of the North, 83 percent of the white population (and 58 percent of the total population) of the South.

The conflicting impulses that underlay the movement for school reform were visible in some of the different educational institutions that emerged. The belief in the potential of the individual sparked the creation of new institutions to help the disabled: institutions that formed part of a great network of charitable activities known as the Benevolent Empire. Among them was the Perkins School for the Blind in Boston, the first such school in America. Nothing better exemplified the romantic spirit of the era than the belief of those who founded Perkins that even society's supposedly most disadvantaged members—unsighted and otherwise handicapped—could be helped to discover their own inner strength and wisdom.

More typical of educational reform, however, were efforts to use schools to impose a set of social values on children—values that reformers and others believed were appropriate for their new, industrializing society. These values included thrift, order, discipline, punctuality, and respect for authority. Horace Mann, for example, spoke of the role of public schools in extending democracy and expanding individual opportunity. But he spoke, too, of their role in creating social order: "The unrestrained passions of men are not only homicidal, but suicidal. . . . Train up a child in the way he should go, and when he is old he will not depart from it."

Similar impulses produced another powerful movement of reform: the creation of "asylums" for criminals and the mentally ill. In advocating prison and hospital reform, Americans were reacting against one of society's most glaring ills: antiquated jails and mental institutions whose inmates lived in almost inhuman conditions. Beginning in the 1820s, many states built new penitentiaries and mental asylums. New York built the first penitentiary at Auburn in 1821. In Massachusetts, the reformer Dorothea Dix began a national movement for new methods of treating the mentally ill.

But the creation of asylums for social deviants was not simply an effort to curb the abuses of the old system. It was also an attempt to reform and rehabilitate the inmates. New forms of prison discipline were designed to rid criminals of the "laxness" that had presumably led them astray. Solitary confinement and the imposition of silence on work crews (both instituted in Pennsylvania and New York in the 1820s) were meant to give prisoners opportunities to meditate on their wrongdoings and develop "penitence" (hence the name "penitentiary"). Some reformers argued that the discipline of the asylum could serve as a model for other potentially disordered environments—for example, factories and schools.

Some of the same impulses that produced asylums underlay the emergence in the 1840s and 1850s of a new "reform" approach to the problems of Native Americans: the idea of the reservation. For several decades, the dominant thrust of the United States' policy toward the Indians in areas of white settlement had been relocation. The principal motive behind relocation was simple: getting the tribes out of the way of white civilization. But among some whites there had also been another, if secondary, intent: to move the Indians to a place where they would be protected from whites and allowed to develop to a point at which assimilation might be possible. Even Andrew Jackson, whose animus toward Indians was legendary, once described the removals as part of the nation's "moral duty . . . to protect and if possible to preserve and perpetuate the scattered remnants of the Indian race."

It was a small step from the idea of relocation to the idea of the reservation, the notion of creating an enclosed region in which Indians would live in isolation from white society. Again, the reservations served white economic purposes above all, as they involved moving Native Americans out of good lands that white settlers wanted. But they also had a reform purpose. Just as prisons, asylums, and orphanages would provide society with an opportunity to train and uplift misfits and unfortunates within white society, so the reservations might provide a way to undertake what one official called "the great work of regenerating the Indian race."

### The Rise of Feminism

Many of the women who became involved in reform movements in the 1820s and 1830s came to resent the social and legal restrictions that limited their participation. Out of their concerns emerged the first American feminist movement. Sarah and Angelina Grimké, sisters born in South Carolina who had become active and outspoken abolitionists, ignored attacks by men who claimed that their activism was inappropriate to their gender. "Men and women were *created equal*," they argued. "They are both moral and accountable beings, and whatever is right for man to do, is right for women to do." Other reformers—Catharine Beecher, Harriet Beecher Stowe (her sister), Lucretia Mott, Elizabeth Cady Stanton, and Dorothea Dix—similarly pressed at the boundaries of "acceptable" female behavior, chafing at the restrictions placed on women by men.

In 1840, American female delegates arrived at a world antislavery convention in London, only to be turned away by the men who controlled the proceedings. Angered at the rejection, several of the delegates—notably Lucretia Mott and Elizabeth Cady Stanton—became convinced that their first duty as reformers should now be to elevate the status of women. Over the next several years, Mott, Stanton, and others began drawing pointed parallels between the plight of women and the plight of slaves; and in 1848, in Seneca Falls, New York, they organized a convention to discuss the question of women's rights. Out of the meeting came the "Declaration of Sentiments and Resolutions" (patterned on the Declaration of Independence), which stated that "all men and women are created equal," that women no less than men are endowed with certain inalienable rights. In demanding the right to vote, they launched a movement for woman suffrage that would survive until the battle was finally won in 1920. The Seneca Falls document was at least equally important for its rejection of the whole notion that men and women should be assigned separate "spheres" in society.

Many of the women involved in these feminist efforts were Quakers. Quakerism had long embraced the ideal of sexual equality and had tolerated, indeed encouraged, the emergence of women as preachers and community leaders. Quakers had also been among the leaders of the antislavery movement, and Quaker women had played a leading role within those efforts. Not all Quakers went so far as to advocate full sexual equality in American society, but enough Quaker women coalesced around such demands to cause a schism in the yearly meeting of Friends in Genesee, New York, in 1848. That dissident faction formed the core of the group that organized the Seneca Falls convention. Of the women who drafted the Declaration of Sentiments there, all but Elizabeth Cady Stanton were Quakers. Stanton, joined two years later by Susan B. Anthony, led the movement to implement the Seneca Falls resolutions in the 1850s and beyond. Together, they ultimately transformed it into a powerful force for change.

Progress toward feminist goals was limited in the antebellum years, but some women did manage to break the social barriers to advancement. Elizabeth Blackwell, born in England, gained acceptance and fame as a physician. Her sister-in-law Antoinette Brown Blackwell became the first ordained woman minister in the United States, and another sister-in-law, Lucy Stone, took the revolutionary step of retaining her maiden name after marriage. Stone became a successful and influential lecturer on women's rights. Emma Willard, founder of the Troy Female Seminary in 1821, and Catharine Beecher, who founded the Hartford Female Seminary in 1823, worked on behalf of women's education.

Feminists benefited greatly from their association with other reform movements, most notably abolitionism; but they also suffered as a result. The demands of women were usually assigned—even by some women themselves—a secondary position to what many considered the far greater issue of the rights of slaves.

# THE CRUSADE AGAINST SLAVERY

The antislavery movement was not new to the mid-nineteenth century. But only in 1830 did it begin to gather the force that would ultimately enable it to overshadow virtually all other efforts at social reform.

## Early Opposition to Slavery

In the early years of the nineteenth century, those who opposed slavery were, for the most part, a calm and genteel lot, expressing moral disapproval but doing little else. To the extent that there was an organized antislavery movement, it centered on the concept of colonization—the effort to resettle American blacks in Africa or the Caribbean. In 1817, a group of prominent white Virginians organized the American Colonization Society (ACS), which tried to challenge slavery without challenging property rights or southern sensibilities. The ACS proposed a gradual freeing of slaves, with masters receiving compensation. The liberated blacks would then be transported out of the country and helped to establish a new society of their own. The ACS was not without impact. It received some funding from private donors, some from Congress, some from the legislatures of Virginia and Maryland. And it arranged to have several groups of blacks transported out of the United States, some of them to the west coast of Africa, where in 1830 they established the nation of Liberia. (In 1846, Liberia became an independent black republic, with its capital, Monrovia, named for the American president who had presided over the initial settlement.)

But the ACS was in the end a negligible force. Neither private nor public funding was nearly enough to carry out the vast projects its supporters envisioned. In the space of a decade, they managed to "colonize" fewer slaves than were born in the United States in a month. Nothing, in fact, would have been enough; there were far too many blacks in America in the nineteenth century to be transported to Africa by any conceivable program. And the ACS met resistance, in any case, from blacks themselves, many of whom were now three or more generations removed from Africa and, despite their loathing of slavery, had no wish to emigrate.

By 1830, colonization was failing rapidly, particularly since the cotton boom in the Deep South was increasing the commitment of planters to their labor system. Those opposed to slavery had reached what appeared to be a dead end.

## Garrison and Abolitionism

At this crucial juncture, with the antislavery movement seemingly on the verge of collapse, a new figure emerged to transform it: William Lloyd Garrison. Born in Massachusetts in 1805, Garrison was in the 1820s an assistant to the New Jersey Quaker Benjamin Lundy, who published the leading antislavery newspaper of the time. Garrison grew impatient with his employer's moderate tone and mild proposals for reform. In 1831, therefore, he returned to Boston to found his own weekly newspaper, the *Liberator*.

Garrison's philosophy was so simple as to be genuinely revolutionary. Opponents of slavery, he said, should not talk, as earlier reformers had done, about the evil influence of slavery on white society; they should talk about the damage the system did to blacks. And they should, therefore, reject "gradualism" and demand the immediate, unconditional, universal abolition of slavery and the extension to blacks of all the rights of American citizenship. Garrison wrote in a relentless, uncompromising tone. "I am aware," he wrote in the very first issue of the *Liberator*, "that many object to the severity of my language; but is there not cause for severity? I will be as harsh as truth, and as uncompromising as justice. . . . I am in earnest—I will not equivocate—I will not excuse—I will not retreat a single inch—and I will be heard."

Garrison soon attracted a large group of followers throughout the North, enough to enable him to found the New England Antislavery Society in 1832 and a year later, after a convention in Philadelphia, the American Antislavery Society. By 1835, there were more than 400 local societies; by 1838, there were 1,350, with more than 250,000 members.

Abolitionists were very much a part of the larger spirit of reform of their era. Like other reformers, they were calling for an unleashing of the individual human spirit, the elimination of artificial social barriers to fulfillment. Who, after all, most needed help in realizing individual potential than enslaved men and women?

## Black Abolitionists

Abolitionism had a particular appeal to the free black population of the North, which in 1850 numbered about 250,000, mostly concentrated in cities. These free blacks lived in conditions of poverty and oppression at times worse than those of their slave counterparts in the South. They were often the victims of mob violence; they had virtually no access to education; they could vote in only a few states; and they were barred from all but the most menial of occupations. Most worked either as domestic servants or as sailors

FREDERICK DOUGLASS  Frederick Douglass was the most prominent African American of the nineteenth century. Born in Maryland to an unknown white father and a slave mother, he escaped from slavery into the North in 1838. He quickly became a leader in the abolitionist movement.

in the American merchant marine, and their wages were so low that most lived in squalor. Some were kidnapped by whites and forced back into slavery.

For all their problems, however, northern blacks were fiercely proud of their freedom and sensitive to the plight of those members of their race who remained in bondage; they were aware that their own position in society would remain precarious as long as slavery existed. Many in the 1830s came to support Garrison. But they also rallied to leaders of their own.

The greatest of the black abolitionists was Frederick Douglass, one of the most electrifying orators of his time. Born a slave in Maryland, Douglass escaped to Massachusetts in 1838, became an outspoken leader of antislavery sentiment, and spent two years lecturing in England, where members of that country's vigorous antislavery movement lionized him. On his return to the United States in 1847, Douglass purchased his freedom from his Maryland owner and founded an antislavery newspaper, the *North Star*, in

Rochester, New York. He achieved wide renown as well for his autobiography, *Narrative of the Life of Frederick Douglass* (1845), in which he presented a damning picture of slavery. Douglass demanded not only freedom but full social and economic equality.

### Antiabolitionism

The rise of abolitionism was a powerful force, but it provoked a powerful opposition as well. Almost all white southerners, of course, were bitterly hostile to the movement. But even in the North, abolitionists were a small, dissenting minority whom most whites viewed as dangerous radicals. Some feared that abolitionism would produce a destructive war between the sections. Others feared that it would lead to a great influx of free blacks into the North.

The result of such fears was an escalating wave of violence directed against abolitionists in the 1830s. A mob in Philadelphia attacked the abolitionist headquarters there in 1834, burned it to the ground, and began a bloody race riot. Another mob seized Garrison on the streets of Boston in 1835 and threatened to hang him. He was saved from death only by being locked in jail. Elijah Lovejoy, the editor of an abolitionist newspaper in Alton, Illinois, was victimized repeatedly by mob violence and finally killed when he tried to defend his press from attack.

That so many men and women continued to embrace abolitionism in the face of such vicious opposition from within their own communities suggests that abolitionists were not people who made their political commitments lightly or casually. They were strong-willed, passionate crusaders who displayed not only enormous courage and moral strength but at times a fervency that many of their contemporaries (even some who shared their dislike of slavery) found deeply disturbing. The mobs were only the most violent expression of a hostility to abolitionism that many, perhaps most, other white Americans shared.

### Abolitionism Divided

By the mid-1830s, the abolitionist crusade had begun to experience serious internal strains and divisions. One reason was the violence of the antiabolitionists, which persuaded some members of the movement that a more moderate approach was necessary. Another reason was the growing radicalism of William Lloyd Garrison, who shocked even many of his own allies (including Frederick Douglass) by attacking not only slavery but the government itself. The Constitution, he said, was "a covenant with death and an agreement with hell." The nation's churches, he claimed, were bulwarks of slavery. In 1840, Garrison precipitated a formal division within the American Antislavery Society by insisting that women, who had always been central to the organization's work, be permitted to participate in the movement on terms of full equality. He continued after 1840 to arouse controversy with new and even more radical stands: an extreme pacifism that rejected even defensive wars; opposition to all forms of coercion—not just slavery but prisons and asylums; and finally, in 1843, a call for northern disunion from the South. The nation could, he suggested, purge itself of the sin of slavery by expelling the slave states from the Union.

From 1840 on, therefore, abolitionism moved in many channels and spoke with many different voices. The Garrisonians, with their radical and uncompromising moral stance, remained influential. But others operated in more moderate ways, arguing that abolition could be accomplished only as the result of a long, patient, peaceful struggle—"immediate abolition gradually accomplished," as they called it. At first, they depended on "moral suasion." They appealed to the conscience of the slaveholders, attempting to convince them that their institution was sinful. When that produced no results, they turned to political action, seeking to induce the northern states and the federal government to aid the cause. They joined the Garrisonians in helping runaway slaves find refuge in the North or in Canada through what became known as the underground railroad (although their efforts were never as highly organized as the name suggests). After the Supreme Court (in *Prigg* v. *Pennsylvania*, 1842) ruled that states need not aid in enforcing the 1793 law requiring the return of fugitive slaves to their owners, abolitionists won passage in several northern states of "personal liberty laws," which forbade state officials to assist in the capture and return of runaways. The antislavery societies also petitioned Congress to abolish slavery in places where the federal government had jurisdiction—in the territories and in the District of Columbia—and to prohibit the interstate slave trade.

Antislavery sentiment underlay the formation in 1840 of the Liberty Party, which ran Kentucky antislavery leader James G. Birney for president. But this party and its successors never campaigned for outright abolition (an illustration of the important fact that "antislavery" and "abolitionism" were not always the same thing). They stood instead for "free soil," for keeping slavery out of the territories. Some free-soilers were concerned about the welfare of blacks; others were people who cared nothing about slavery but simply wanted to keep the West a country for whites. Garrison dismissed free-soilism as "white-manism." But the free-soil position would ultimately

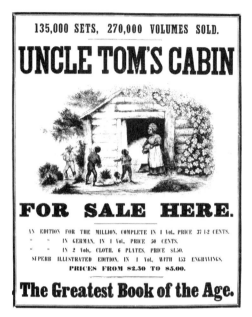

*UNCLE TOM'S CABIN* This poster (advertising, among other things, a German edition of Harriet Beecher Stowe's novel) did not exaggerate when it described *Uncle Tom's Cabin* as "The Greatest Book of the Age." There were, to be sure, greater literary accomplishments; but no American book of the nineteenth century had so profound a political impact.

do what abolitionism never could: attract the support of large numbers, even a majority, of the white population of the North.

The frustrations of political abolitionism drove some critics of slavery to embrace more drastic measures. A few began to advocate violence; it was a group of prominent abolitionists in New England, for example, who funneled money and arms to John Brown for his bloody uprisings in Kansas and Virginia. Others attempted to arouse public anger through propaganda. The most powerful of all abolitionist propaganda was Harriet Beecher Stowe's novel *Uncle Tom's Cabin*, published as a book in 1852. It rocked the nation. It sold more than 300,000 copies within a year of publication and was later issued again and again, becoming one of the most remarkable bestsellers in American history. And it succeeded in bringing the message of abolitionism to an enormous new audience—not only those who read the book but those who watched dramatizations of its story by countless theater companies across the nation. Reviled throughout the South, Stowe became a hero to many in the North. And in both regions, her novel helped inflame sectional tensions to a new level of passion. Few books in American history have had so great an impact on the course of public events.

Even divided, therefore, abolitionism remained a powerful influence on the life of the nation. Only a relatively small number of people before the Civil War ever accepted the abolitionist position that slavery must be entirely eliminated in a single stroke. But the crusade that Garrison had launched, and that thousands of committed men and women kept alive for three decades, was a constant, visible reminder of how deeply the institution of slavery was dividing America.

# CHAPTER THIRTEEN

# The Impending Crisis

*Looking Westward* ～ *Expansion and War*
*The Sectional Debate* ～ *The Crises of the 1850s*

NTIL THE 1840s, the tensions between North and South remained relatively contained. Had no new sectional issues arisen, it is possible that the two sections might have resolved their differences peaceably over time. But new issues did arise, centered around the expansion of slavery. From the North came the strident and increasingly powerful abolitionist movement. And from the West, more significantly, came a series of controversies that would ultimately tear the fragile Union apart.

## LOOKING WESTWARD

More than a million square miles of new territory came under the control of the United States during the 1840s—the greatest wave of expansion since the Louisiana Purchase nearly forty years before. By the end of the decade, the nation possessed all the territory of the present-day United States except Alaska, Hawaii, and a few relatively small areas acquired later through border adjustments. Many factors accounted for this great new wave of expansion, but one of the most important was a set of ideas—an ideology known as "Manifest Destiny."

### Manifest Destiny

Manifest Destiny reflected both the burgeoning pride that characterized American nationalism in the mid-nineteenth century and the idealistic vision of social perfection that fueled so much of the reform energy of the time. It rested on the idea that America was destined—by God and by history—to expand its boundaries over a vast area.

| TIME LINE | | | | |
|---|---|---|---|---|
| **1836** | **1844** | **1846** | **1848** | **1850** |
| Texas declares independence from Mexico | Polk elected president | Oregon boundary dispute settled

U.S. declares war on Mexico

Wilmot Proviso | Treaty of Guadalupe Hidalgo

Taylor elected president

California gold rush begins | Compromise of 1850

Taylor dies; Fillmore becomes president |
| **1852** | **1853** | **1854** | **1855–1856** | **1856** |
| Pierce elected president | Gadsden Purchase | Kansas-Nebraska Act

Republican Party formed | "Bleeding Kansas" | Buchanan elected president |
| **1857** | **1858** | **1859** | | **1860** |
| *Dred Scott* decision | Lecompton constitution defeated | John Brown raids Harper's Ferry | | Lincoln elected president |

By the 1840s, the idea of Manifest Destiny had spread throughout the nation, publicized by the new "penny press," which made newspapers available to a far greater proportion of the population than ever before, and fanned by the rhetoric of nationalist politicians. Some advocates of Manifest Destiny had relatively limited territorial goals; others envisioned a vast new "empire of liberty" that would include Canada, Mexico, Caribbean and Pacific islands, and ultimately, a few dreamed, much of the rest of the world.

Henry Clay and some other prominent politicians warned that territorial expansion would reopen the painful controversy over slavery and threaten the stability of the Union. Their voices, however, were all but drowned out in the enthusiasm over expansion in the 1840s, which began with the issues of Texas and Oregon.

### Texas

The United States had once claimed Texas—which, as the 1830s began, was part of the Republic of Mexico—as a part of the Louisiana Purchase, but it had renounced the claim in 1819. Twice thereafter, the United States had offered to buy Texas, only to meet with indignant Mexican refusals. But in the early 1820s, the Mexican government launched an ill-advised experiment.

It encouraged American immigration into Texas. The Mexicans hoped to strengthen the economy of the territory and increase their own tax revenues. An 1824 colonization law designed to attract American settlers promised the newcomers cheap land and a four-year exemption from taxes.

Thousands of Americans flocked to the rich soil in Texas. The great majority were white southerners and their slaves, intent on establishing cotton plantations. By 1830, there were about 7,000 Americans living in Texas, more than twice the number of Mexicans there.

The Mexican government offered land directly to immigrants, but most of the settlers came to Texas through the efforts of American intermediaries (known to the Mexicans as *empresarios*), who received sizable land grants from Mexico in return for promising to bring settlers into the region. The most successful of them was Stephen F. Austin, a young immigrant from Missouri who had established the first legal American settlement in Texas in 1822. Austin and others recruited many American immigrants to Texas; in the process, they created centers of power in the region that competed with the Mexican government. In 1826, one *empresario* led a revolt to establish Texas as an independent nation (which he proposed calling Fredonia.) The Mexican government quickly crushed it and, four years later, passed new laws barring any further American immigration into the region. But Americans kept flowing into the territory anyway. By 1835 over 30,000 Americans, white and black, had settled in Texas.

Friction between the American settlers and the Mexican government continued to grow. It arose, in part, from the efforts of the immigrants to create stronger bonds with the United States and also from their desire to legalize slavery, which the Mexican government banned in Texas (as it had in Mexico) in 1830. Austin and his followers continued trying to reach a peaceful settlement with Mexico that would give Texas more autonomy within the Mexican republic. Others wanted to fight for independence.

In the mid-1830s, instability in Mexico itself drove General Antonio Lopez de Santa Ana to seize power as a dictator and create a new, more autocratic regime. He increased the powers of the national government at the expense of the state governments, a measure that Texans from the United States assumed Santa Ana was aiming specifically at them. Sporadic fighting between Americans and Mexicans in Texas began in 1835 and escalated as the Mexican government sent more troops into the territory. In 1836, the American settlers defiantly proclaimed their independence from Mexico.

Santa Ana led a large army into Texas, where the American settlers were divided into several squabbling factions, unable even to agree on who their military commanders were. Mexican forces annihilated an American garrison at the Alamo mission in San Antonio after a famous, if futile, defense by a group of Texas "patriots," a group that included, among others, the renowned frontiersman and former Tennessee congressman Davy Crockett. Another garrison at Goliad suffered substantially the same fate when the Mexicans executed most of the force after it had surrendered. By the end of 1836, the rebellion appeared to have collapsed.

But General Sam Houston managed to keep a small force together. And on April 23, 1836, at the Battle of San Jacinto (near the present-day city of Houston), he defeated the Mexican army and took Santa Ana prisoner. American troops then killed many of the Mexican soldiers in retribution for the executions at Goliad. Santa Ana, under pressure from his captors, signed a treaty giving Texas independence. And while the Mexican government later repudiated the treaty, there were no further military efforts to win Texas back.

A number of Mexican residents of Texas *(Tejanos)* had fought with the Americans in the revolution. But soon after Texas won its independence, their positions grew difficult. The Americans did not trust them, feared that they were agents of the Mexican government, and in effect drove many of them out of the new republic. Most of those who stayed had to settle for a politically and economically subordinate status within the fledgling nation.

One of the first acts of the new president of Texas, Sam Houston, was to send a delegation to Washington with an offer to join the Union. There were supporters of annexation in the United States, some of whom had been encouraging the revolt against Mexico for years. But there was also opposition. Many American northerners opposed acquiring large new slave territory and increasing southern political power. One of the opponents was President Jackson, who blocked annexation and even delayed recognizing the new republic until 1837. Presidents Martin Van Buren and William Henry Harrison also avoided the issue during their terms of office.

Spurned by the United States, Texas cast out on its own. Some of its leaders dreamed of creating a vast southwestern nation that would rival the United States. When England and France, concerned about the growing power of America and seeing Texas as a possible check on its growth, began forging ties with the new republic, President Tyler persuaded Texas to apply for statehood again in 1844. But Secretary of State Calhoun presented an annexation treaty to Congress as if its only purpose were to extend slavery, and northern senators defeated it. The Texas question quickly became the central issue in the election of 1844.

## Oregon

Control of what was known as Oregon country, in the Pacific Northwest, was another major political issue in the 1840s. Its half-million square miles included the present states of Oregon, Washington, and Idaho, parts of Montana and Wyoming, and half of British Columbia. Both Britain and the United States claimed sovereignty in the region. Unable to resolve their con-

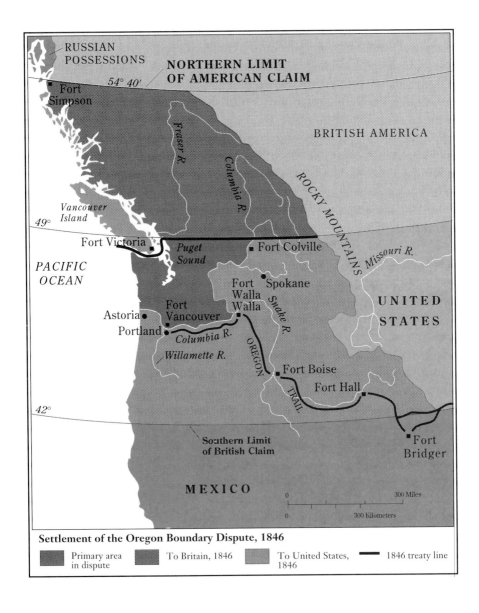

**Settlement of the Oregon Boundary Dispute, 1846**

flicting claims diplomatically, they agreed in an 1818 treaty to allow citizens of each country equal access to the territory. This arrangement, known as "joint occupation," continued for twenty years.

In fact, by the time of the treaty neither Britain nor the United States had established much of a presence in Oregon country. White settlement in the region consisted largely of American and Canadian fur traders, and the most significant white settlements were scattered fur trading posts, the largest of which was John Jacob Astor's Astoria. But American interest in Oregon grew substantially in the 1820s and 1830s. Protestant missionaries made it a target for evangelical efforts, especially after the strange appearance of four Nez Percé and Flathead Indians in St. Louis in 1831. The Indians (who spoke no English) died before whites could determine why they had come from Oregon to Missouri. But some missionaries considered the visit a divinely inspired invitation to extend their efforts westward. They had little success with the tribes they attempted to convert, and some missionaries—embittered by Indian resistance to their efforts—began encouraging white immigration into the region, arguing that by repudiating Christianity the Indians had abdicated their right to the land.

By the 1840s, white Americans substantially outnumbered the British in Oregon. They had also devastated much of the Indian population, in part through a measles epidemic that spread through the Cayuse. The tribe blamed a Protestant mission for the plague, and in 1847 the Cayuse attacked it and killed thirteen whites. But such resistance did little to stem the white immigration. By the mid-1840s, American settlements had spread up and down the Pacific Coast, and the new settlers (along with advocates of Manifest Destiny in the East) were urging the United States government to take possession of the disputed Oregon territory.

### The Westward Migration

The migrations into Texas and Oregon were part of a larger movement that took hundreds of thousands of white and black Americans into the far western regions of the continent between 1840 and 1860. Southerners flocked mainly to Texas. But the largest number of migrants came from the Old Northwest (today's Midwest)—white men and women, and a few blacks, who undertook arduous journeys in search of new opportunities. Most traveled in family groups, until the early 1850s, when the great gold rush attracted many single men. (See pp. 359–360.) Most were relatively young people. Most had undertaken earlier, if usually shorter, migrations in the past. Few were wealthy, but many were relatively prosperous. Poor people could not afford the expensive trip and the cost of settling on new land. Those without money who wished to migrate usually had to do so by joining more established families or groups as laborers—men as farm or ranch hands, women as domestic servants, teachers, or, in some cases, prostitutes. The character of the migrations varied according to the destination of the migrants. Groups headed for areas where mining or lumbering was the principal economic ac-

Western Trails, to 1860

THE OREGON TRAIL Trappers and merchants had used the Oregon Trail to reach the Far West since early in the nineteenth century, but settlers traveling by wagon train dominated traffic along the trail beginning in the 1840s. This drawing by William Henry Jackson suggests both the ruggedness of the journey and the large dimensions of the migration.

tivity consisted mostly of men. Those heading for farming regions traveled mainly as families.

All the migrants were in search of a new life, but they harbored many different visions of what the new life would bring. Some—particularly after the discovery of gold in California in 1849—hoped for quick riches. Others planned to take advantage of the vast public lands the federal government was selling at modest prices to acquire property for farming or speculation. Still others hoped to establish themselves as merchants and serve the new white communities developing in the West. Some (among them the Mormons) were on religious missions. Others were attempting to escape the epidemic diseases that were plaguing many cities in the East. But the vast majority of migrants were simply looking for economic opportunities.

Most migrants—about 300,000 between 1840 and 1860—traveled west along the great overland trails. They generally gathered in one of several major depots in Iowa and Missouri (Independence, St. Joseph, or Council Bluffs), joined a wagon train led by hired guides, and set off with their belongings piled in covered wagons, livestock trailing behind. The major route west was the 2,000-mile Oregon Trail, which stretched from Independence across the Great Plains and through the South Pass of the Rocky Mountains.

From there, migrants moved north into Oregon or south (along the California trail) to the northern California coast. Other migrations moved along the Santa Fe Trail, southwest from Independence into New Mexico.

However they traveled, overland migrants faced an arduous journey—although the death rate for travelers was only slightly higher than the rate for the American population as a whole. Most journeys lasted five or six months (from May to November), and there was always pressure to get through the Rockies before the snows began, often not an easy task given the very slow pace of most wagon trains (about fifteen miles a day). There was also the danger of disease; many groups were decimated by cholera.

Only a few expeditions experienced Indian attacks. In the twenty years before the Civil War, fewer than 400 migrants (slightly more than one-tenth of 1 percent) died in conflicts with the tribes. In fact, Indians were usually more helpful than dangerous to the white migrants. They often served as guides, and they traded horses, clothing, and fresh food with the travelers.

Life on the trail was obviously very different from life on a farm or in a town. But the society of the trail re-created some of the patterns of conventional American society. Families divided tasks along gender lines: the men driving and, when necessary, repairing the wagons or hunting game; the women cooking, washing clothes, and caring for children. Almost everyone, male or female, walked the great majority of the time, to lighten the load for the horses drawing the wagons; and so the women, many of whose chores came at the end of the day, generally worked harder than the men, who usually rested when the caravan halted.

Despite the traditional image of westward migrants as rugged individualists, most travelers found the journey a highly collective experience. That was partly because many expeditions consisted of groups of friends, neighbors, or relatives who had decided to pull up stakes and move west together. And it was partly because of the intensity of the experience: many weeks of difficult travel with no other human contacts except, occasionally, with Indians. It was a rare expedition in which there were not some internal conflicts before the trip was over; but those who made the journey successfully generally learned the value of cooperation.


## EXPANSION AND WAR

The growing number of white Americans in the lands west of the Mississippi put great pressure on the government in Washington to annex Texas, Oregon, and other territory. And in the 1840s, these expansionist pressures helped push the United States into a war that—however dubious its origins—became a triumph for the advocates of Manifest Destiny.

### The Democrats and Expansion

Most Americans had expected the election of 1844 to be a contest between two old foes: the Whig Henry Clay and the Democrat and former president Martin Van Buren. In preparing for the race, both men tried to avoid taking a stand on the controversial issue of the annexation of Texas. Their separate statements on the question were so similar that many suspected they had collaborated in preparing them. Both favored annexation, but only with the consent of Mexico. Since such consent was unlikely, the statements meant virtually nothing.

Because sentiment for expansion was mild within the Whig Party, Clay had no difficulty securing the nomination despite his noncommittal position. Among the Democrats, however, there were many supporters of annexation, particularly in the South; and they resented Van Buren's equivocal stand. The expansionists took control of the Democratic convention, passed over Van Buren, and nominated a strong supporter of annexation, James K. Polk—the first "dark horse" to win the presidential nomination of his party.

Polk was not as obscure as his Whig critics claimed. Beginning in 1825, he had represented Tennessee in the House of Representatives for fourteen years, four of them as Speaker. Subsequently, he had been governor of Tennessee. But by 1844, he had been out of public office—and for the most part out of the public mind—for three years. What made his victory possible was the belief, expressed in the Democratic platform, "that the re-occupation of Oregon and the re-annexation of Texas at the earliest practicable period are great American measures." By combining the Oregon and Texas questions, the Democrats hoped to appeal to both northern and southern expansionists.

In a belated effort to catch up with public sentiment, Clay announced in midcampaign, too late, his qualified support for annexing Texas. Polk carried the election by 170 electoral votes to 105, although his popular majority was less than 40,000. The Liberty Party, running James G. Birney a second time, polled 62,000 votes (as compared with 7,000 in 1840), mainly from antislavery Whigs who had turned against Clay.

Polk may have been obscure, but he was intelligent and energetic; and he entered office with a clear set of goals and with plans for attaining them. John Tyler accomplished the first of Polk's goals for him in the last days of his own presidency. Interpreting the election returns as a mandate for the annexation of Texas, the outgoing president won congressional approval for it in February 1845. That December, Texas became a state.

Polk himself resolved the Oregon question. The British minister in Washington brusquely rejected a compromise Polk offered that would establish the United States–Canadian border at the 49th parallel; he did not even refer the proposal to London. Incensed, Polk again asserted the American claim to all of Oregon. There was loose talk of war on both sides of the Atlantic—talk that in the United States often took the form of the bellicose slogan "Fifty-four forty or fight!" (a reference to where the Americans hoped to draw the northern boundary of their part of Oregon). But neither country really wanted war. Finally, the British government offered to accept Polk's original proposal and divide the territory at the 49th parallel. On June 15, 1846, the Senate approved a treaty that fixed the boundary at the 49th parallel, where it remains today.

### The Southwest and California

One of the reasons the Senate and the president had agreed so readily to the British offer to settle the Oregon question was that new tensions were emerging in the Southwest—tensions that ultimately led to a war with Mexico. As soon as the United States admitted Texas to statehood in 1845, the Mexican government broke diplomatic relations with Washington. To make matters worse, a dispute then developed over the boundary between Texas and Mexico. Texans claimed the Rio Grande as their western and southern border, a claim that would have added much of what is now New Mexico to Texas. Mexico still refused formally to concede the loss of Texas but argued nevertheless that the border had always been the Nueces River, to the north of the Rio Grande. Polk accepted the Texas claim, and in the summer of 1845 he sent a small army under General Zachary Taylor to the Nueces line—to protect Texas, he claimed, against a possible Mexican invasion.

Part of the area in dispute was New Mexico, one of the northernmost outposts of Mexican civilization, with its center at Santa Fe. Its Spanish and Indian residents lived in a multiracial society that had by the 1840s endured for nearly a century and a half. In the 1820s, the Mexican government had invited American traders into the region (just as it was inviting American settlers into Texas), hoping to speed development of the province. And New Mexico, like Texas, soon began to become more American than Mexican. A flourishing commerce soon developed between Santa Fe and Independence, Missouri, with long caravans moving back and forth along the Santa Fe Trail, carrying manufactured goods west and bringing gold, silver, furs, and mules east in return. The Santa Fe trade, as it was called, further increased the American presence in New Mexico and signaled to advocates of expansion another direction for their efforts.

Americans were also increasing their interest in an even more distant province of Mexico: California. In this vast region lived members of several western Indian tribes and perhaps 7,000 Mexicans, mostly descendants of Spanish colonists. Gradually, however, white Americans began to arrive: first maritime traders and captains of Pacific whaling ships, who stopped to barter goods or buy supplies; then merchants, who established stores, imported merchandise, and developed a profitable trade with the Mexicans and Indians; and finally pioneering farmers, who entered California from the east, by land, and settled in the Sacramento Valley. Some of these new settlers began to dream of bringing California into the United States.

President Polk soon came to share their dream and committed himself to acquiring both New Mexico and California for the United States. At the same time that he dispatched the troops under Taylor to the Nueces in Texas, he sent secret instructions to the commander of the Pacific naval squadron to seize the California ports if Mexico declared war. Representatives of the president quietly informed Americans in California that the United States would respond sympathetically to a revolt against Mexican authority there.

### The Mexican War

Having appeared to prepare for war, Polk turned once more to diplomacy and dispatched a special minister, John Slidell, to try to buy off the Mexicans. But Mexican leaders rejected Slidell's offer to purchase the disputed territories. And on January 13, 1846, as soon as he heard the news, Polk ordered Taylor's army in Texas to move across the Nueces to the Rio Grande. For months, the Mexicans refused to fight. But finally, according to accounts of American commanders (later disputed), some Mexican troops crossed the Rio Grande and attacked a unit of American soldiers. Polk, who had been planning to request a declaration of war even without a military provocation, now told Congress: "War exists by the act of Mexico herself." On May 13, 1846, Congress declared war by votes of 40 to 2 in the Senate and 174 to 14 in the House.

The war had many opponents in the United States. Whig critics charged from the beginning that Polk had deliberately maneuvered the country into the conflict and had staged the border incident that had precipitated the declaration. Many argued that the hostilities with Mexico were draining re-

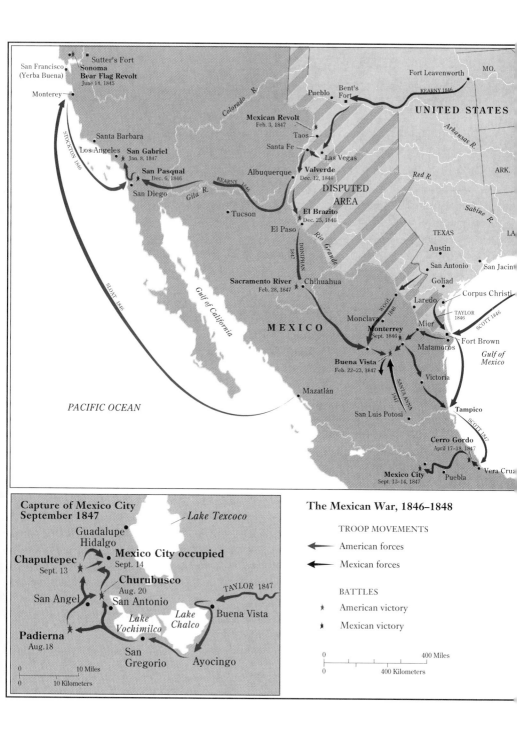

The Mexican War, 1846–1848

**Capture of Mexico City September 1847**

TROOP MOVEMENTS
← American forces
← Mexican forces

BATTLES
★ American victory
★ Mexican victory

sources and attention away from the more important issue of the Pacific Northwest; and when the United States finally reached its agreement with Britain on the Oregon question, opponents claimed that Polk had settled for less than he should have because he was preoccupied with Mexico. Opposition intensified as the war continued and as the public became aware of the casualties and expense.

American forces were generally successful in their campaigns against the Mexicans, but final victory did not come nearly as quickly as Polk had hoped. Through most of the war, the president himself planned the military strategy. He ordered Taylor to cross the Rio Grande and seize parts of northeastern Mexico, beginning with the city of Monterrey, before marching on to Mexico City itself. Taylor attacked Monterrey in September 1846 and, after a hard fight, captured it. But he let the Mexican garrison evacuate without pursuit. Polk now began to doubt the feasibility of his plan to move toward Mexico City. He feared that Taylor lacked the tactical skill for the campaign, and he became convinced that an advance south through the mountains would involve impossible supply problems. He also feared that, if successful, Taylor would become a powerful political rival (as, in fact, he did).

In the meantime, Polk ordered other offensives against New Mexico and California. In the summer of 1846, a small army under Colonel Stephen W. Kearny made the long march to Santa Fe and occupied the town with no opposition. Then Kearny proceeded to California, where he joined a conflict already in progress that was being staged jointly by American settlers, a well-armed exploring party led by John C. Frémont, and the American navy: the so-called Bear Flag Revolution. Kearny brought the disparate American forces together under his command, and by the autumn of 1846 he had completed the conquest of California.

The United States now controlled the two territories for which it had gone to war. But Mexico still refused to end the hostilities or cede the conquered territories. At this point, Polk and General Winfield Scott, the commanding general of the army and its finest soldier, launched a bold new campaign. Scott assembled an army at Tampico, which the navy transported down the Mexican coast to Veracruz. From Veracruz, Scott moved west along the National Highway to Mexico City. With an army that never numbered more than 14,000, Scott advanced 260 miles into enemy territory, kept casualties low, and finally achieved his objective without losing a battle. He inflicted a crushing defeat on the Mexican army at Cerro Gordo in the mountains and met no further resistance until he was within a few miles of Mexico City. After a hard fight on the outskirts of the capital, Americans oc-

STEPHEN KEARNY IN SANTA FE  Colonel Stephen Kearny led a small U.S. military party to Santa Fe in 1846 and seized the town without opposition. In this 1909 drawing (which the artist Kenneth Chapman acknowledged was not entirely accurate), Kearny raises the American flag over the "old palace" in Santa Fe. The image appeared on a U.S. postage stamp in 1946.

cupied the city. A new Mexican government took power and announced its willingness to negotiate a peace treaty.

President Polk was now growing thoroughly unclear about his objectives. He continued to encourage those who demanded that the United States annex much of Mexico itself. At the same time, concerned about the approaching presidential election, he was growing anxious to get the war finished quickly. Polk had sent a special presidential envoy to Mexico with the army, who was authorized to negotiate a settlement. The agent, Nicholas Trist, concluded an agreement with the new Mexican government on February 2, 1848: the Treaty of Guadalupe Hidalgo. Mexico agreed to cede California and New Mexico to the United States and acknowledge the Rio Grande as the boundary of Texas. In return, the United States promised to assume the claims of its new citizens against Mexico and pay the Mexicans $15 million. When the treaty reached Washington, Polk faced a dilemma. Trist had obtained most of Polk's original demands, but he had not satisfied the new, more expansive dreams of acquiring additional territory in Mexico itself. Polk angrily claimed that Trist had violated his instructions, but he soon realized that he had no choice but to accept the treaty. Some ardent expansionists were demanding that he hold out for annexation of—in a phrase widely bandied about at the time—"All Mexico!" Antislavery leaders, in the meantime, were charging that the demands for acquisition of Mexico were part of a southern scheme to extend slavery to new realms. To silence this bitter and potentially destructive debate, Polk submitted the Trist treaty to the Senate, which approved it by a vote of 38 to 14. The war was over, and America had gained a vast new territory. But it had also acquired a new set of troubling and divisive issues.

## THE SECTIONAL DEBATE

James Polk tried to be a president whose policies transcended sectional divisions. But conciliating the sections was becoming an ever more difficult task, and Polk gradually earned the enmity of northerners and westerners alike, who believed his policies (and particularly his enthusiasm for territorial expansion in the Southwest) favored the South at their expense.

### Slavery and the Territories

In August 1846, while the Mexican War was still in progress, Polk asked Congress to appropriate $2 million for purchasing peace with Mexico. Representative David Wilmot of Pennsylvania, an antislavery Democrat, introduced an amendment to the appropriation bill prohibiting slavery in any territory acquired from Mexico. The so-called Wilmot Proviso passed the House but failed in the Senate. It would be called up, debated, and voted on repeatedly for years. Southern militants, in the meantime, had a plan of their own. They contended that since the territories belonged to the entire nation, all Americans had equal rights in them, including the right to move their slaves (which they considered property) into them.

As the sectional debate intensified, President Polk supported a proposal to extend the Missouri Compromise line through the new territories to the Pacific coast, banning slavery north of the line and permitting it south of the line. Others supported a plan, originally known as "squatter sovereignty" and later by the more dignified phrase "popular sovereignty," which would allow the people of each territory (acting through their legislature) to decide the status of slavery there. The debate over these various proposals dragged on for many months, and the issue remained unresolved when Polk left office in 1849.

The presidential campaign of 1848 dampened the controversy for a time as both Democrats and Whigs tried to avoid the slavery question. When Polk declined to run again, the Democrats nominated Lewis Cass of Michigan, a dull, aging party regular. The Whigs nominated General Zachary Taylor of Louisiana, a hero of the Mexican War but a man with no political experience whatever. Opponents of slavery found the choice of candidates unsatisfying, and out of their discontent emerged the new Free-Soil Party, which drew from the existing Liberty Party and the antislavery wings of the Whig and Democratic Parties and which endorsed the Wilmot Proviso. Its candidate was former president Martin Van Buren.

Taylor won a narrow victory. But while Van Buren failed to carry a sin-

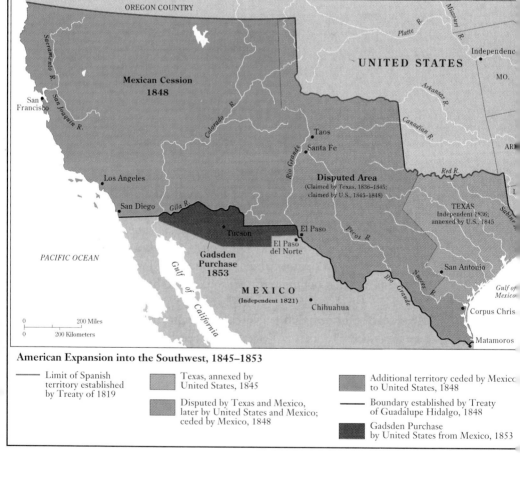

**American Expansion into the Southwest, 1845–1853**

——— Limit of Spanish territory established by Treaty of 1819

Texas, annexed by United States, 1845

Disputed by Texas and Mexico, later by United States and Mexico; ceded by Mexico, 1848

Additional territory ceded by Mexico to United States, 1848

——— Boundary established by Treaty of Guadalupe Hidalgo, 1848

Gadsden Purchase by United States from Mexico, 1853

gle state, he polled an impressive 291,000 votes (10 percent of the total), and the Free-Soilers elected ten members to Congress. Van Buren probably drew enough Democratic votes away from Cass, particularly in New York, to throw the election to Taylor. The emergence of the Free-Soil Party as an important political force, like the emergence of the Know-Nothing and Liberty Parties before it, signaled the inability of the existing parties to contain the political passions slavery was creating and was an important part of a process that would lead to the collapse of the second party system in the 1850s.

### The California Gold Rush

By the time Taylor took office, the pressure to resolve the question of slavery in the far western territories had become more urgent as a result of dramatic events in California. In January 1848, a carpenter working in a sawmill on the ranch of James Sutter (one of California's leading ranchers) found traces of gold in the foothills of the Sierra Nevada mountains. Within months, news of the discovery had spread throughout the nation and much of the world. Almost immediately, hundreds of thousands of people began flocking to California in a frantic search for gold. The non-Indian population of the territory increased nearly twentyfold in only four years.

The atmosphere in California at the peak of the gold rush was one of almost crazed excitement and greed. Most migrants to the Far West prepared carefully before making the journey. But the California migrants (known as "Forty-niners") threw caution to the winds. They abandoned farms, jobs, homes, families; they piled onto ships and flooded the overland trails—many carrying only what they could pack on their backs. The overwhelming majority of the Forty-niners (perhaps 95 percent) were men, and the society they created on their arrival in California was unusually fluid and volatile because of the almost total absence of women, children, or families.

The gold rush also attracted some of the first Chinese migrants to the western United States. News of the discoveries created great excitement in China, particularly in impoverished areas, where letters from Chinese already in California and reports from American visitors spread the word. It was, of course, extremely difficult for a poor Chinese peasant to get to America; but many young, adventurous people (mostly men) decided to go anyway—in the belief that they could quickly become rich and then return to China. Emigration brokers loaned many migrants money for passage to California, which the migrants were to pay off out of their earnings there. The migration was almost entirely voluntary (unlike the forced movement of kidnapped "coolies" to such places as Peru and Cuba at about the same time). The Chinese in California were, therefore, free laborers and merchants, looking for gold or, more often, hoping to profit from other economic opportunities the gold boom was creating.

The gold rush was producing a serious labor shortage in California, as many male workers left their jobs and flocked to the gold fields. That created opportunities for many people who needed work (including Chinese immigrants). It also led to a frenzied exploitation of Indians that resembled slavery in all but name. A new state law permitted the arrest of "loitering" or orphaned Indians and their assignment to a term of "indentured" labor.

The gold rush was of critical importance to the growth of California, but not for the reasons most of the migrants hoped. There was substantial gold in the hills of the Sierra Nevada, and many people got rich from it. But only a tiny fraction of the Forty-niners ever found gold, or even managed to stake a claim to land on which they could look for gold. Some disappointed migrants returned home after a while. But many stayed in California and swelled both the agricultural and urban populations of the territory. By 1856, for example, San Francisco—whose population had been 1,000 before the gold rush (and at one point declined to about 100 as people left for the mines)—was the home of over 50,000 people. By the early 1850s, California, which had always had a diverse population, had become even more heterogeneous. The gold rush had attracted not just white Americans but Europeans, Chinese, South Americans, Mexicans, free blacks, and slaves who accompanied southern migrants. Conflicts over gold intersected with racial and ethnic tensions to make the territory an unusually turbulent place. The gold rush, therefore, became another factor putting pressure on the United States to resolve the status of the territories—and of slavery within them.

### Rising Sectional Tensions

Zachary Taylor was a southerner and a slaveholder, but from his long years in the army he had acquired a national outlook. He recognized the importance of dealing with the problems of the newly acquired territories, which—in the absence of territorial governments—were still under the control of the military. There was particular pressure to establish a new government in California, after the enormous boom following the gold rush that began in 1848.

Taylor believed statehood could become the solution to the issue of slavery in the territories. As long as the new lands remained territories, the federal government was responsible for deciding the fate of slavery within them.

But once they became states, their own governments would be able to settle the slavery question. At Taylor's urging, California quickly adopted a constitution that prohibited slavery, and in December 1849 Taylor asked Congress to admit California as a free state. New Mexico, he added, should also be granted statehood as soon as it was ready and should, like California, be permitted to decide for itself what it wanted to do about slavery.

Congress balked, in part because of several other controversies concerning slavery that were complicating the debate. One was the effort of antislavery forces to abolish slavery in the District of Columbia, a movement bitterly resisted by southerners. Another was the emergence of personal liberty laws in northern states, which barred courts and police officers from helping to return runaway slaves to their owners. In response, southerners demanded a stringent law that would require northern states to return fugitive slaves to their owners. But the biggest obstacle to the president's pro-

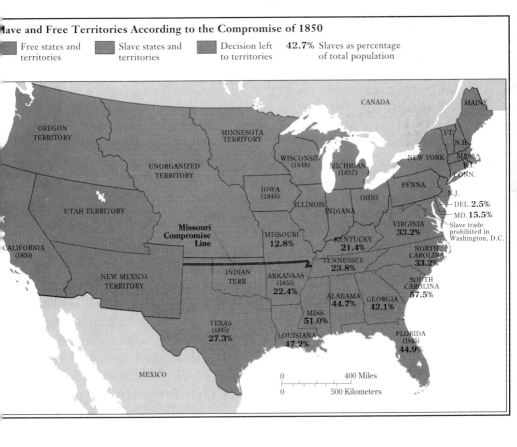

Slave and Free Territories According to the Compromise of 1850

Free states and territories

Slave states and territories

Decision left to territories

42.7% Slaves as percentage of total population

gram was the white South's fear that two new free states would be added to the northern majority. The number of free and slave states was equal in 1849—fifteen each. But the admission of California would upset the balance; and New Mexico, Oregon, and Utah might upset it further, leaving the South in a minority in the Senate, as it already was in the House.

Tempers were now rising to dangerous levels. Even many otherwise moderate southern leaders were beginning to talk about secession from the Union. In the North, every state legislature but one adopted a resolution demanding the prohibition of slavery in the territories.

### The Compromise of 1850

Faced with this mounting crisis, moderates and unionists spent the winter of 1849–1850 trying to frame a great compromise. The aging Henry Clay, who was spearheading the effort, believed that no compromise could last unless it settled all the issues in dispute between the sections. As a result, he took several measures which had been proposed separately, combined them into a single piece of legislation, and presented it to the Senate on January 29, 1850. Among the bill's provisions were the admission of California as a free state; the formation of territorial governments in the rest of the lands acquired from Mexico, without restrictions on slavery; the abolition of the slave trade, but not slavery itself, in the District of Columbia; and a new and more effective fugitive slave law. These resolutions launched a debate that raged for seven months—both in Congress and throughout the nation. The debate occurred in two phases, the differences between which revealed much about how American politics was changing in the 1850s.

In the first phase of the debate, the dominant voices in Congress were those of old men—national leaders who still remembered Jefferson, Adams, and other founders—who argued for or against the compromise on the basis of broad ideals. Clay himself, seventy-three years old in 1850, made a broad plea for sectional conciliation and appealed to shared sentiments of nationalism. Early in March, another of the older leaders—John C. Calhoun, sixty-eight years old and so ill that he had to sit grimly in his seat while a colleague read his speech for him—joined the debate. Calhoun insisted that the North grant the South equal rights in the territories, that it agree to observe the laws concerning fugitive slaves, that it cease attacking slavery, and that it amend the Constitution to create dual presidents, one from the North and one from the South, each with a veto. Calhoun was making radical demands that had no chance of passage. But like Clay, he was offering what he considered a comprehensive, permanent solution to the sectional problem that would, he believed, save the Union. After Calhoun came the third of the elder statesmen, sixty-eight-year-old Daniel Webster, one of the great orators of his time. Still nourishing presidential ambitions, he delivered an eloquent address in the Senate, trying to calm angry passions and to rally northern moderates to support Clay's compromise.

But in July, after six months of this impassioned, nationalistic debate, Congress defeated the Clay proposal. And with that, the controversy moved into its second phase, in which a very different cast of characters predominated. Clay, ill and tired, left Washington to spend the summer resting in the mountains. Calhoun had died even before the vote in July. And Webster accepted a new appointment as secretary of state, thus removing himself from the Senate and from the debate.

In place of these leaders, a new, younger group now emerged. One spokesman was William H. Seward, forty-nine years old, of New York, a wily political operator who staunchly opposed the proposed compromise. The ideals of Union were to him less important than the issue of eliminating slavery. Another was Jefferson Davis of Mississippi, forty-two years old, a representative of the new, cotton South. To him, the slavery issue was less one of principles and ideals than one of economic self-interest.

Most important of all, there was Stephen A. Douglas, a thirty-seven-year-old Democratic senator from Illinois. A westerner from a rapidly growing state, he was an open spokesman for the economic needs of his section—and especially for the construction of railroads. His was a career devoted not to any broad national goals but frankly to sectional gain and personal self-promotion.

The new leaders of the Senate were able, as the old leaders had not been, to produce a compromise. In part, they were assisted by the great prosperity of the early 1850s. Conservative economic interests everywhere wanted to end the sectional dispute and concentrate on economic growth. Another spur to the compromise was the disappearance of the most powerful obstacle to it: the president. Zachary Taylor had been adamant that only after California and possibly New Mexico were admitted as states could other measures be discussed. He had threatened not only to veto any measure that diverged from this proposal but to use force against the southern states if they attempted to secede. But on July 9, 1850, Taylor suddenly died—the victim of a violent stomach disorder. He was succeeded by Millard Fillmore of New York—a dull, handsome, dignified man who understood the political importance of flexibility. He supported the compromise and used his powers of persuasion to swing northern Whigs into line.

The new leaders also benefited, however, from their own pragmatic tactics. Douglas's first step, after the departure of Clay, was to break up the "omnibus bill" that Clay had envisioned as a great, comprehensive solution to the sectional crisis and to introduce instead a series of separate measures to be voted on one by one. Thus representatives of different sections could support those elements of the compromise they liked and oppose those they did not. Douglas also gained support with complicated backroom deals linking the compromise to such nonideological matters as the sale of government bonds and the construction of railroads. As a result of his efforts, by mid-September Congress had enacted and the president had signed all the components of the compromise.

The Compromise of 1850, unlike the Missouri Compromise thirty years before, was not a product of widespread agreement on common national ideals. It was, rather, a victory of self-interest. Still, members of Congress hailed the measure as a triumph of statesmanship; and Millard Fillmore, signing it, called it a just settlement of the sectional problem, "in its character final and irrevocable."

## THE CRISES OF THE 1850S

For a few years after the Compromise of 1850, the sectional conflict seemed briefly to be forgotten amid booming prosperity and growth. But the tensions between North and South remained, and the crisis continued to smolder until—in 1854—it once more burst into the open.

### The Uneasy Truce

Both major parties endorsed the Compromise of 1850 in their platforms in 1852, and both parties nominated presidential candidates unlikely to arouse passionate opposition in either North or South. The Democrats chose the obscure New Hampshire politician Franklin Pierce and the Whigs the military hero General Winfield Scott, a man whose political views were so undefined that no one knew what he thought about the Compromise.

But the gingerly way in which party leaders dealt with the sectional question could not prevent its divisive influence from intruding on the election. The Whigs were the principal victims. Already plagued by the defections of those antislavery northerners who had formed the Free-Soil Party in 1848, they alienated still more party members—the "Conscience" Whigs—by straddling the issue of slavery and refusing openly to condemn it. In the meantime, the Free-Soil Party was gaining in numbers and influence in the North; its presidential candidate, John P. Hale, repudiated the Compromise of 1850. The divisions among the Whigs helped produce a victory for the Democrats in 1852.

Franklin Pierce, a charming, amiable man of no particular distinction, attempted to maintain party—and national—harmony by avoiding divisive issues, and particularly by avoiding the issue of slavery. But those issues arose despite him. They arose, in particular, because of northern opposition to the Fugitive Slave Act, opposition which intensified after 1850 when southerners began appearing occasionally in northern states to pursue people they claimed were fugitives. So fervently did many opponents of slavery resent such efforts that mobs formed in many cities to prevent enforcement of the law. Several northern states also passed laws to prevent the deportation of fugitive slaves. White southerners watched with growing anger and alarm as the one element of the Compromise of 1850 that they had considered a victory seemed to become meaningless as a result of northern defiance.

### *"Young America"*

One of the ways Franklin Pierce hoped to dampen sectional controversy was through his support of a movement in the Democratic Party known as "Young America." Its adherents saw the expansion of American democracy throughout the world as a way to divert attention from the controversies over slavery. The great liberal and nationalist revolutions of 1848 in Europe stirred them to dream of a republican Europe with governments based on the model of the United States. They dreamed as well of expanding American commerce in the Pacific and acquiring new territories in the Western Hemisphere.

But efforts to extend the nation's domain could not avoid becoming entangled with the sectional crisis. Pierce had been pursuing unsuccessful diplomatic attempts to buy Cuba from Spain (efforts begun in 1848 by Polk). In 1854, however, a group of his envoys sent him a private document from Ostend, Belgium, making the case for seizing Cuba by force. When the Ostend Manifesto, as it became known, was leaked to the public, it enraged many antislavery northerners, who charged the administration with conspiring to bring a new slave state into the Union.

The South, for its part, opposed all efforts to acquire new territory that would not support a slave system. The kingdom of Hawaii agreed to join the United States in 1854, but the treaty died in the Senate because it contained a clause prohibiting slavery in the islands. A powerful movement to annex Canada to the United States—a movement that had the support of many Canadians eager for access to American markets—similarly foundered, at least in part because of slavery.

*Slavery, Railroads, and the West*

What fully revived the sectional crisis, however, was the same issue that had produced it in the first place: slavery in the territories. By the 1850s, the line of white settlement had moved beyond the boundaries of Missouri, Iowa, and what is now Minnesota into a great expanse of plains, which many white Americans had once believed was unfit for cultivation. Now it was becoming apparent that large sections of this region were, in fact, suitable for farming. In the states of the Old Northwest, therefore, prospective settlers urged the government to open the area to them, provide territorial governments, and—despite the solemn assurance the United States had earlier given the Indians of the sanctity of their reservations—dislodge the tribes located there so as to make room for white settlers. There was relatively little opposition from any segment of white society to this proposed violation of Indian rights. But the interest in further settlement raised two issues that did prove highly divisive and that gradually became entwined with each other: railroads and slavery.

As the nation expanded westward and as the problem of communication between the older states and the areas west of the Mississippi River became more and more critical, broad support began to emerge for building a transcontinental railroad. The problem was where to place it—and in particular, where to locate the railroad's eastern terminus. Northerners favored Chicago, the rapidly growing capital of the free states of the Northwest. Southerners supported St. Louis, Memphis, or New Orleans—all located in slave states. The transcontinental railroad, in other words, had become part of the struggle between the North and the South.

Pierce's secretary of war, Jefferson Davis of Mississippi, removed one obstacle to a southern route. Surveys indicated that a road with a southern terminus would have to pass through an area in Mexican territory. But in 1853 Davis sent James Gadsden, a southern railroad builder, to Mexico, where he persuaded the Mexican government to accept $10 million in exchange for a strip of land that today comprises part of Arizona and New Mexico. But the so-called Gadsden Purchase only accentuated the sectional rivalry.

*The Kansas-Nebraska Controversy*

As a senator from Illinois, a resident of Chicago, and the acknowledged leader of northwestern Democrats, Stephen A. Douglas naturally wanted the transcontinental railroad for his own city and section. He also realized the strength of the principal argument against the northern route: that west of the Mississippi it would run mostly through country with a substantial Indian population. As a result, he introduced a bill in January 1854 to organize (and thus open to white settlement) a huge new territory, known as Nebraska, west of Iowa and Missouri.

Douglas knew the South would oppose his bill because it would prepare the way for a new free state; the proposed territory was in the area of the Louisiana Purchase north of the Missouri Compromise line (36°30′) and hence closed to slavery. In an effort to make the measure acceptable to southerners, Douglas inserted a provision that the status of slavery in the territory would be determined by the territorial legislature—that is, according to "popular sovereignty." In theory, the region could choose to open itself to slavery (although few believed it actually would). When southern Democrats demanded more, Douglas agreed to two changes in the bill: an additional clause explicitly repealing the antislavery provision of the Missouri Compromise (which the popular-sovereignty provision of his original bill had done implicitly), and the division of the area into two territories, Nebraska and Kansas, instead of one. The new, second territory (Kansas) was more likely to become a slave state. In its final form the measure was known as the Kansas-Nebraska Act. President Pierce supported the bill, and after a strenuous debate, it became law in May 1854 with the unanimous support of the South and the partial support of northern Democrats.

No piece of legislation in American history produced so many immediate, sweeping, and ominous consequences. It divided and destroyed the Whig Party, which disappeared almost entirely by 1856, and along with it a conservative, nationalistic influence in American politics. It divided the northern Democrats (many of whom were appalled at the repeal of the Missouri Compromise, which they considered an almost sacred part of the fabric of the Union) and drove many of them from the party.

Most important of all, it spurred the creation of a new party that was frankly sectional in composition and creed. People in both major parties who opposed Douglas's bill began to call themselves Anti-Nebraska Democrats and Anti-Nebraska Whigs. In 1854, they formed a new organization and named it the Republican Party. It instantly became a major force in American politics. In the elections of that year, the Republicans won enough seats in Congress to permit them, in combination with allies among the Know-Nothings, to organize the House of Representatives.

### "Bleeding Kansas"

Events in Kansas itself in the next two years increased the popular excitement in the North. White settlers from both the North and the South began moving into the territory almost immediately after the passage of the Kansas-Nebraska Act. In the spring of 1855, elections were held for a territorial legislature. There were only about 1,500 legal voters in Kansas by then, but more than 6,000 people voted. That was because thousands of Missourians, some traveling in armed bands, had crossed into Kansas to vote. The result was that the pro-slavery forces elected a majority to the legislature, which proceeded immediately to enact a series of laws legalizing slavery. Outraged free-staters defied the legislature and elected delegates to a constitutional convention, which met at Topeka and adopted a constitution excluding slavery. They then chose their own governor and legislature and petitioned Congress for statehood. President Pierce denounced them as traitors and threw the full support of the federal government behind the pro-slavery territorial legislature.

A few months later a pro-slavery federal marshal assembled a large posse, consisting mostly of Missourians, to arrest the free-state leaders, who had set up their headquarters in Lawrence. The posse sacked the town, burned the "governor's" house, and destroyed several printing presses. Retribution came quickly.

Among the most fervent abolitionists in Kansas was John Brown, a grim, fiercely committed zealot who considered himself an instrument of God's will to destroy slavery. He had moved to Kansas with his sons so that they could fight to make it a free state. After the events in Lawrence, he gathered six followers (including four of his sons) and in one night murdered five pro-slavery settlers, leaving their mutilated bodies to discourage other supporters of slavery from entering Kansas. This terrible episode, known as the Pottawatomie Massacre, led to more civil strife in Kansas—irregular, guerrilla warfare conducted by armed bands, some of them more interested in land claims or loot than in ideologies. Northerners and southerners alike came to believe that the events in Kansas illustrated (and were caused by) the aggressive designs of the other section. "Bleeding Kansas" became a symbol of the sectional controversy.

Another symbol soon appeared, in the United States Senate. In May 1856, Charles Sumner of Massachusetts—a militant and passionately doctrinaire opponent of slavery—rose to give a speech entitled "The Crime Against Kansas." In it, he gave particular attention to Senator Andrew P. Butler of South Carolina, an outspoken defender of slavery. The South Carolinian was, Sumner claimed, the "Don Quixote" of slavery, having "chosen a mistress . . . who, though ugly to others, is always lovely to him, though polluted in the sight of the world, is chaste in his sight . . . the harlot slavery."

The pointedly sexual references and the general viciousness of the speech enraged Butler's nephew, Preston Brooks, a member of the House of Representatives from South Carolina. Several days after the speech, Brooks approached Sumner at his desk in the Senate chamber during a recess, raised a heavy cane, and began beating him repeatedly on the head and shoulders. Sumner, trapped in his chair, rose in agony with such strength that he tore the desk from the bolts holding it to the floor; then he collapsed, bleeding and unconscious. So severe were his injuries that he was unable to return to the Senate for four years. Throughout the North, he became a hero—a martyr to the barbarism of the South. In the South, Preston Brooks became a hero too. Censured by the House, he resigned his seat, returned to South Carolina, and stood successfully for reelection.

### The Free-Soil Ideology

What had happened to produce such deep hostility between the two sections? In part, the tensions were a reflection of the two sections' differing economic and territorial interests. But they were also a reflection of a hardening of ideas in both North and South. As the nation expanded and political power grew more dispersed, each section became concerned with ensuring that its vision of America's future would be the dominant one. And those visions were becoming—partly as a result of internal developments within the sections themselves, partly because of each region's conceptions (and misconceptions) of what was happening outside it—increasingly distinct and increasingly rigid.

In the North, assumptions about the proper structure of society came to center on the belief in "free soil" and "free labor." Although abolitionists generated some support for their argument that slavery was a moral evil and must be eliminated, theirs was never the dominant voice. Instead, an increasing number of white northerners, gradually becoming a majority, came to believe that the existence of slavery was dangerous not because of what it did to blacks but because of what it threatened to do to whites. At the heart of American democracy, they argued, was the right of all citizens to own property, to control their own labor, and to have access to opportunities for advancement. The ideal society, in other words, was one of small-scale capitalism, in which everyone could aspire to a stake and to upward mobility.

According to this vision, the South was the antithesis of democracy. It was a closed, static society, in which the slave system preserved an entrenched aristocracy, and in which common whites had no opportunity to improve themselves. While the North was growing and prospering, displaying thrift, industry, and a commitment to progress, the South—decadent, lazy, dilapidated—was stagnating, rejecting the northern values of individualism and progress. The South was, northern free-laborites further maintained, engaged in a conspiracy to extend slavery throughout the nation and thus to destroy the openness of northern capitalism and replace it with the closed, aristocratic system of the South. This "slave power conspiracy," as it came to be known, threatened the future of every white laborer and property owner in the North. The only solution was to fight the spread of slavery and work for the day when the nation's democratic (i.e., free-labor) ideals would extend to all sections of the country.

This ideology, which lay at the heart of the new Republican Party, also strengthened the commitment of Republicans to the Union. Since the idea of continued growth and progress was central to the free-labor vision, the prospect of dismemberment of the nation—a diminution of America's size and economic power—was unthinkable.

### The Pro-Slavery Argument

In the South, in the meantime, a very different ideology—entirely incompatible with the free-labor ideology—was emerging out of a rapid hardening of position among southern whites on the issue of slavery.

As late as the early 1830s, a substantial number of southern whites had harbored reservations about slavery. But by the mid-1830s, a militant defense of the system was beginning to replace this ambivalence. In part, the change was a result of events in the South. The Nat Turner uprising in 1831 terrified whites throughout the region, and they grew more determined than ever to make slavery secure. And with the expansion of the cotton economy into the Deep South, slavery—which had begun to seem unprofitable in many areas of the upper South—now became lucrative once again.

But the change was also a result of events in the North, and particularly of the growth of the Garrisonian abolitionist movement, with its strident attacks on southern society. The popularity of Harriet Beecher Stowe's *Uncle Tom's Cabin* (see pp. 340–341) was perhaps the most glaring evidence of the success of those attacks, but other abolitionist writings had been antagonizing white southerners for years.

In response to these pressures, a number of white southerners produced an intellectual defense of slavery. In 1832, Professor Thomas R. Dew of the College of William and Mary became one of the first to outline the case for slavery. Twenty years later, apologists for slavery summarized their views in an anthology that gave their ideology its name: *The Pro-Slavery Argument.* John C. Calhoun stated the essence of the case in 1837: Southerners should stop apologizing for slavery as a necessary evil and defend it as "a good—a positive good." It was good for the slaves, the southern apologists argued, because blacks, as inferior people, needed the guidance of white masters; the slaves were, moreover, better off—better fed, clothed, and housed, and more secure—than northern factory workers. Slavery was good for southern society as a whole because it was the only way the two races could live together in peace. It was good for the entire country because the southern economy, based on slavery, was the key to the prosperity of the nation.

Above all, southern apologists argued, slavery was good because it served as the basis for the southern way of life—a way of life superior to any other in the United States, perhaps in the world. White southerners looking at the North saw a society that they believed was abandoning traditional American values and replacing them with a spirit of greed, debauchery, and destructiveness. "The masses of the North are venal, corrupt, covetous, mean and selfish," wrote one southerner. Others wrote with horror of the factory system and the crowded, pestilential cities filled with unruly immigrants. The South, in contrast, was a stable, orderly society, operating at a slow and human pace. It had a labor system that avoided the feuds between capital and labor plaguing the North, a system that protected the welfare of its workers, a system that allowed the aristocracy to enjoy a refined and accomplished cultural life. It was, in short, as nearly perfect as any human civilization could become, an ideal social order in which all elements of the population were secure and content.

The defense of slavery rested, too, on increasingly elaborate arguments about the biological inferiority of African Americans, who were, white Southerners argued, inherently unfit to take care of themselves, let alone exercise the rights of citizenship. And just as abolitionist arguments drew strength from Protestant theology in the North, the pro-slavery defense mobilized the Protestant clergy in the South to give the institution a religious and biblical justification. By the 1850s, southern leaders had not only committed themselves to a militant pro-slavery ideology. Their growing intolerance of criticism of slavery further encouraged those northerners who warned of the "slave power conspiracy" against their liberties.

### Buchanan and Depression

In this unpromising climate—with the nation aroused by the Brooks assault and the continuing violence in Kansas, with each section becoming increasingly militant in support of its own ideology—the presidential campaign of 1856 began. Democratic Party leaders wanted a candidate who had not made many enemies and who was not closely associated with the explosive question of "Bleeding Kansas." They chose James Buchanan of Pennsylvania, a reliable party stalwart who as minister to England had been safely out of the country during the recent controversies. The Republicans, participating in their first presidential contest, denounced the Kansas-Nebraska Act and the expansion of slavery but also endorsed a program of internal improvements, thus combining the idealism of antislavery with the economic aspirations of the North. As eager as the Democrats to present a safe candidate, the Republicans nominated John C. Frémont, who had made a national reputation as an explorer of the Far West and who had no political record. In the meantime, the Native American, or Know-Nothing, Party was beginning to break apart. Nevertheless, it nominated former president Millard Fillmore, who also received the endorsement of a sad remnant of the Whig Party.

After a heated, even frenzied campaign, Buchanan won a narrow victory. He polled a plurality but not a majority of the popular votes: 1,833,000 to 1,340,000 for Frémont and 872,000 for Fillmore. A slight shift of votes in Pennsylvania and Illinois would have thrown those states into the Republican column and elected Frémont. More significant, perhaps, was that Frémont, who attracted virtually no votes at all in the South, outpolled all other candidates in the North.

At the time of his inauguration, Buchanan had been in public life for more than forty years. He was, at age sixty-five, the oldest president, except for William Henry Harrison, ever to have taken office. Whether because of age and physical infirmities or because of a more fundamental weakness of character, he became a painfully timid and indecisive president at a time when the nation cried out for strong, effective leadership.

In the year Buchanan took office, a financial panic struck the country, followed by a depression that lasted several years. European demand for American food had risen during the Crimean War of 1854–1856. When that demand fell off, agricultural prices declined. In the North, the depression strengthened the Republican Party. Distressed manufacturers and farmers came to believe that the hard times were the result of the unsound policies of southern-controlled Democratic administrations. They expressed their frustrations by moving into an alliance with antislavery elements and thus into the Republican Party.

### *The* Dred Scott *Decision*

The Supreme Court of the United States now projected itself into the sectional controversy with one of the most controversial decisions in its history—its ruling in the case of *Dred Scott* v. *Sanford*, handed down two days after Buchanan was inaugurated. Dred Scott was a Missouri slave, once owned by an army surgeon who had taken Scott with him to the North. Some abolitionists persuaded Scott to sue for his freedom in the Missouri courts on the ground that residence in a free territory had made him a free man. The state supreme court decided against him. By then, the surgeon had died and ownership of Scott had been transferred to his widow's brother, J. F. A. Sanford, an abolitionist who lived in New York. Now Scott's lawyers could get the case into the federal courts on the ground that the suit lay between citizens of different states. The case was no longer to determine Scott's fate; his abolitionist owners were determined to free him. It was now a case to force a federal decision on the status of slavery in the territories.

The Supreme Court was so divided that it was unable to issue a single ruling on the case. The thrust of the various rulings, however, was a stunning defeat for the antislavery movement. Chief Justice Roger Taney, who wrote one of the majority opinions, declared that Scott could not bring a suit in the federal courts because he was not a citizen. Blacks had no claim to citizenship, Taney argued, and in fact virtually no rights at all under the Constitution. Slaves were property, and the Fifth Amendment prohibited Congress from taking property without "due process of law." Consequently, Taney concluded, Congress possessed no authority to pass a law depriving persons of their slave property in the territories. The Missouri Compromise, therefore, had always been unconstitutional.

The ruling did nothing to challenge the right of an individual state to prohibit slavery within its borders, but the statement that the federal government was powerless to act on the issue was a drastic and startling one. Few judicial opinions have ever created as much controversy. Southern whites were elated: the highest tribunal in the land had sanctioned parts of the most extreme southern argument. In the North, the decision produced widespread dismay. Republicans threatened that when they won control of the national government, they would reverse the decision—by "packing" the Court with new members.

### Deadlock over Kansas

President Buchanan timidly endorsed the *Dred Scott* decision. At the same time, he tried to resolve the controversy over Kansas by supporting its admission to the Union as a slave state. In response, the pro-slavery territorial legislature called an election for delegates to a constitutional convention. The free-state residents refused to participate, claiming that the legislature had discriminated against them in drawing district lines. As a result, the pro-slavery forces won control of the convention, which met in 1857 at Lecompton, framed a constitution legalizing slavery, and refused to give voters a chance to reject it. When an election for a new territorial legislature was called, the antislavery groups turned out to vote and won a majority. The new legislature promptly submitted the Lecompton constitution to the voters, who rejected it by more than 10,000 votes.

Both sides had resorted to fraud and violence, but it was clear nevertheless that a majority of the people of Kansas opposed slavery. Buchanan, however, ignored the evidence and pressured Congress to admit Kansas under the Lecompton constitution. Stephen A. Douglas and other western Democrats refused to support the president; and while Buchanan's proposal passed the Senate, western Democrats helped block it in the House. Finally, in April 1858, Congress approved a compromise: The Lecompton constitution would be submitted to the voters of Kansas again. If the document won approval, Kansas would be admitted to the Union; if it was rejected, statehood would be postponed until the population of the territory reached the level required for a representative in Congress. Again, Kansas voters decisively rejected the Lecompton constitution. Not until the closing months of Buchanan's administration in 1861, when a number of southern states had withdrawn from the Union, did Kansas enter the Union—as a free state.

### The Emergence of Lincoln

Given the gravity of the sectional crisis, the congressional elections of 1858 took on a special importance. Of particular note was the United States Senate election in Illinois, which pitted Stephen A. Douglas, the most prominent northern Democrat, against Abraham Lincoln, who was largely unknown outside Illinois but who quickly emerged as one of the most skillful politicians in the Republican Party.

Lincoln was a successful lawyer who had long been involved in state politics. He had served several terms in the Illinois legislature and one undistinguished term in Congress. But he was not a national figure like Douglas, and so he tried to increase his visibility by engaging Douglas in a series of debates. The Lincoln-Douglas debates attracted enormous crowds and received wide attention. By the time they ended, Lincoln's increasingly eloquent and passionate attacks on slavery had made him nationally prominent.

The content of the debates revealed the deep disagreements between the two parties in the North. Douglas, defending popular sovereignty, accused the Republicans of promoting a war of sections, of wishing to interfere with

THE LINCOLN-DOUGLAS DEBATES, ILLINOIS, 1858  The still clean-shaven Abraham Lincoln lost in his 1858 bid to replace Stephen Douglas as United States senator from Illinois, but he gained wide national recognition for his performance in the debates between the two candidates during the campaign.

slavery in the South, and of advocating social equality of the races. Lincoln denied these charges (properly, since neither he nor his party had ever advocated any of these things). He, in turn, accused the Democrats of conspiring to extend slavery into the territories and possibly into the free states as well (a charge that was equally unfounded).

At the heart of the debates, however, was a basic difference on the issue of slavery. Douglas appeared to have no moral position on the issue and, Lincoln claimed, did not care whether slavery was "voted up, or voted down." Lincoln's opposition to slavery was more fundamental. If the nation could accept that blacks were not entitled to basic human rights, he argued, then it could accept that other groups—immigrant laborers, for example—could be deprived of rights too. And if slavery were to extend into the western territories, he argued, opportunities for poor white laborers to better their lots there might be lost. The nation's future, he argued (reflecting the central idea of the Republican Party), rested on the spread of free labor.

Lincoln believed slavery was morally wrong, but he was not an abolitionist. That was in part because he could not envision an easy alternative to it in the areas where it already existed. He shared the prevailing view among northern whites that the black race was not prepared (and perhaps never would be) to live on equal terms with whites. He and his party would "arrest the further spread" of slavery, that is, prevent its expansion into the territories; they would not directly challenge it where it already existed, but would trust that the institution would gradually die out there of its own accord. Yet the implications of Lincoln's argument were more sweeping than this relatively moderate formula suggests, for both he and other Republicans believed that by restricting slavery to the South, they would be consigning slavery to its "ultimate extinction."

Douglas's position satisfied his followers sufficiently to win him reelection to the Senate, but it aroused little enthusiasm and did nothing to enhance his national political ambitions. Lincoln, by contrast, lost the election but emerged with a growing following both in and beyond the state. And outside Illinois, the elections went heavily against the Democrats, who lost ground in almost every northern state. The party retained control of the Senate but lost its majority in the House, with the result that the congressional sessions of 1858 and 1859 were bitterly deadlocked.

### John Brown's Raid

The battles in Congress, however, were almost entirely overshadowed by a spectacular event that enraged and horrified the entire South and greatly hastened the rush toward disunion. In the fall of 1859, John Brown, the antislavery zealot whose bloody actions in Kansas had inflamed the crisis there, staged an even more dramatic episode, this time in the South itself. With private encouragement and financial aid from some prominent eastern abolitionists (a group sometimes known as the "Secret Six"), he made elaborate plans to seize a mountain fortress in Virginia from which, he believed, he could foment a slave insurrection in the South. On October 16, he and a group of eighteen followers attacked and seized control of a United States arsenal in Harpers Ferry, Virginia. But the slave uprising Brown hoped to inspire did not occur, and he quickly found himself besieged in the arsenal

JOHN BROWN Even in this formal photographic portrait
(taken in 1859, the last year of his life), John Brown
conveys the fierce sense of righteousness that fueled his
extraordinary activities in the fight against slavery.

by citizens, local militia companies, and before long United States troops
under the command of Robert E. Lee. After ten of his men were killed,
Brown surrendered. He was promptly tried in a Virginia court for treason
against the state, found guilty, and sentenced to death. He and six of his followers were hanged.

No other single event did more than the Harpers Ferry raid to convince
white southerners that they could not live safely in the Union. Despite their
passionate defense of slavery, many were consumed with one great, if often
secret, fear: the possibility of a general slave insurrection. And John Brown's
raid, which many southerners believed (incorrectly) had the support of the
Republican Party, suggested that the North was now committed to producing just such an insurrection.

### The Election of Lincoln

The presidential election of 1860 had the most momentous consequences
of any in American history. It was also among the most complex.

The Democratic Party was torn apart by a battle between southerners, who demanded a strong endorsement of slavery, and westerners, who supported the idea of popular sovereignty. The party convention met in April in Charleston, South Carolina—an inopportune location since South Carolina was the center of pro-slavery extremism. When the convention endorsed popular sovereignty, delegates from eight states in the lower South walked out. The remaining delegates could not agree on a presidential candidate and finally adjourned the convention to meet again in Baltimore in June. The decimated convention at Baltimore nominated Stephen Douglas for president. In the meantime, disenchanted southern Democrats met in Richmond and nominated John C. Breckinridge of Kentucky. Later, a group of conservative ex-Whigs met in Baltimore to form the Constitutional Union Party, with John Bell of Tennessee as their presidential candidate. They endorsed the Union and remained silent on slavery.

The Republican leaders, in the meantime, were working to broaden the base of their party. No longer content to present themselves simply as opponents of slavery, they tried now to appeal to every major interest group in the North that feared the South was blocking its economic aspirations. The platform endorsed such traditional Whig measures as a high tariff, internal improvements, a homestead bill, and a Pacific railroad to be built with federal financial assistance. It supported the right of each state to decide the status of slavery within its borders. But it also insisted that neither Congress nor territorial legislatures could legalize slavery in the territories. The Republican convention chose Abraham Lincoln as the party's presidential nom-

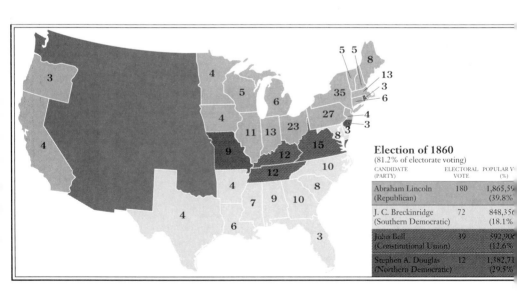

**Election of 1860**
(81.2% of electorate voting)

| CANDIDATE (PARTY) | ELECTORAL VOTE | POPULAR V. (%) |
|---|---|---|
| Abraham Lincoln (Republican) | 180 | 1,865,5% (39.8%) |
| J. C. Breckinridge (Southern Democratic) | 72 | 848,35( (18.1% |
| John Bell (Constitutional Union) | 39 | 592,90( (12.6%) |
| Stephen A. Douglas (Northern Democratic) | 12 | 1,382,71 (29.5% |

inee. Lincoln was appealing because of his growing reputation for eloquence, because of his firm but moderate position on slavery, and because his relative obscurity ensured that he would have none of the drawbacks of other, more prominent (and therefore more controversial) Republicans. He was a representative of the West, a considerable asset in a race against Douglas.

In the November election, Lincoln won the presidency with a majority of the electoral votes but only about two-fifths of the fragmented popular vote. The Republicans, moreover, failed to win a majority in Congress, and, of course, they did not control the Supreme Court. Even so, the election of Lincoln became the final signal to many white southerners that their position in the Union was hopeless. And within a few weeks of Lincoln's victory, the process of disunion began—a process that would quickly lead to a prolonged and bloody war between two groups of Americans, each heir to more than a century of struggling toward nationhood, each now convinced that it shared no common ground with the other.

# CHAPTER FOURTEEN

# The Civil War

*The Secession Crisis* ∼ *The Mobilization of the North*
*The Mobilization of the South* ∼ *Strategy and Diplomacy*
*Campaigns and Battles*

Y THE END OF 1860, the cords that had once bound the Union together seemed to have snapped. The almost mystical veneration
of the Constitution and the romantic vision of America's great national destiny had now taken very different forms in the North and the South. The
relatively stable second party system had collapsed, replaced by a new one
that accentuated rather than muted regional controversy. The federal government was no longer the remote, unthreatening presence it once had
been; the need to resolve the status of the territories had made it necessary
for Washington to deal directly with sectional issues. The election of 1860
brought these tensions to a head.

## THE SECESSION CRISIS

Almost as soon as the news of Abraham Lincoln's election reached the
South, the militant leaders of the region began to demand an end to the
Union. Within weeks, the process of secession had begun.

### The Withdrawal of the South

South Carolina, long the hotbed of southern separatism, seceded first, on
December 20, 1860. By the time Lincoln took office, six other southern
states—Mississippi (January 9, 1861), Florida (January 10), Alabama (January 11), Georgia (January 19), Louisiana (January 26), and Texas (February 1)—had withdrawn from the Union. In February 1861, representatives
of the seven seceded states met at Montgomery, Alabama, and formed a new

nation—the Confederate States of America. President James Buchanan told Congress in December 1860 that no state had the right to secede from the Union but that the federal government had no authority to stop a state if it did.

The seceding states immediately seized the federal property—forts, arsenals, government offices—within their boundaries. But they did not at first have sufficient military power to seize two fortified offshore military installations: Fort Sumter, on an island in the harbor of Charleston, South Carolina, garrisoned by a small force under Major Robert Anderson; and Fort Pickens, in the harbor of Pensacola, Florida. Buchanan, timid though he was, refused to yield Fort Sumter when South Carolina demanded it. Instead, in January 1861, he ordered an unarmed merchant ship to proceed to Fort Sumter with additional troops and supplies. Confederate guns turned it back. Still, neither section was yet ready to concede that war had begun. And in Washington, efforts began once more to forge a compromise.

### The Failure of Compromise

Gradually, the compromise efforts came together around a proposal first submitted by Senator John J. Crittenden of Kentucky and known as the Crittenden Compromise. It called for constitutional amendments to guarantee the permanent existence of slavery in the slave states and satisfy other southern demands. But the heart of Crittenden's plan was a proposal to reestablish the Missouri Compromise line and extend it westward, so that it would

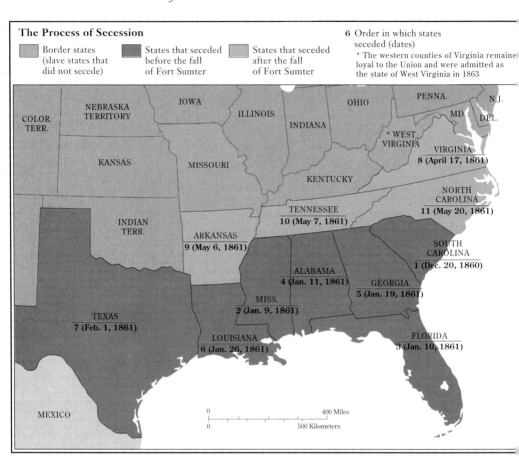

**The Process of Secession**

Border states (slave states that did not secede)

States that seceded before the fall of Fort Sumter

States that seceded after the fall of Fort Sumter

6 Order in which states seceded (dates)
* The western counties of Virginia remaine loyal to the Union and were admitted as the state of West Virginia in 1863

COLOR. TERR.

NEBRASKA TERRITORY

IOWA

ILLINOIS

INDIANA

OHIO

PENNA.

N.J.

MD.

DEL.

* WEST VIRGINIA

VIRGINIA
8 (April 17, 1861)

KANSAS

MISSOURI

KENTUCKY

NORTH CAROLINA
11 (May 20, 1861)

INDIAN TERR.

ARKANSAS
9 (May 6, 1861)

TENNESSEE
10 (May 7, 1861)

SOUTH CAROLINA
1 (Dec. 20, 1860)

ALABAMA
4 (Jan. 11, 1861)

GEORGIA
5 (Jan. 19, 1861)

MISS.
2 (Jan. 9, 1861)

TEXAS
7 (Feb. 1, 1861)

LOUISIANA
6 (Jan. 26, 1861)

FLORIDA
3 (Jan. 10, 1861)

MEXICO

0    400 Miles
0    500 Kilometers

divide all the present and future territory of the United States: slavery would be prohibited north of the line and permitted south of it. Southerners in the Senate seemed willing to accept the plan. But the compromise would have required the Republicans to abandon their most fundamental position—that slavery not be allowed to expand—and they rejected it.

And so nothing had been resolved when Abraham Lincoln arrived in Washington for his inauguration—arriving in the city in disguise on a night train to avoid assassination as he passed through the slave state of Maryland. In his inaugural address, Lincoln insisted that since the Union was older than the Constitution, no state could leave it. Acts of force or violence to support secession were insurrectionary, he said, and the government would "hold, occupy, and possess" federal property in the seceded states—a clear reference to Fort Sumter.

But Union forces at Fort Sumter were running short of supplies; unless they received fresh provisions, they would have to evacuate the fort. Lincoln knew that if he surrendered Sumter, his commitment to maintaining the Union would no longer be credible. So he sent a relief expedition to the fort and informed the South Carolina authorities that there would be no attempt to send troops or munitions unless the supply ships met with resistance. The new Confederate government now faced a dilemma. Permitting the expedition to land would seem to be a tame submission to federal authority. Firing on the ships or the fort would seem (to the North at least) to be aggression. Confederate leaders finally decided that to appear cowardly would be worse than to appear belligerent; they ordered General P. G. T. Beauregard, commander of Confederate forces at Charleston, to take the fort, by force if necessary. When Anderson refused to give up, the Confederates bombarded it for two days, April 12–13, 1861. On April 14, Anderson surrendered. The Civil War had begun.

Almost immediately, Lincoln began mobilizing the North for war. Equally promptly, four more slave states seceded from the Union and joined the Confederacy: Virginia (April 17, 1861), Arkansas (May 6), Tennessee (May 7), and North Carolina (May 20). The four remaining slave states, Maryland, Delaware, Kentucky, and Missouri—under heavy political and even military pressure from Washington—remained in the Union.

## The Opposing Sides

All the important material advantages for waging war lay with the North. Its population was more than twice as large as that of the South (and more than four times as large as the nonslave population of the South). The North had an advanced industrial system and was able by 1862 to manufacture almost all its own war materials. The South had almost no industry at all.

In addition, the North had a much better transportation system than did the South, and in particular more and better railroads: twice as much trackage and a much better integrated system of lines. During the war, the already inferior Confederate railroad system steadily deteriorated and by the beginning of 1864 had almost collapsed.

At the start of the war, however, the material advantages of the North were not as decisive as they eventually became. The Southern armies were, for the most part, fighting a defensive war on familiar land and had the advantage of local support. The Northern armies, on the other hand, were fighting mostly within the South amid hostile local populations; they had to maintain long lines of communications and had access only to the South's own inadequate transportation system. The commitment of the white population of the South to the war was, with limited exceptions, clear and firm. In the North, opinion about the war was more divided, and support for it remained shaky until very near the end. A major Southern victory at any one of several crucial moments might have proved decisive by breaking the North's will to continue the struggle. Finally, the dependence of the English and French textile industries on American cotton inclined many leaders in those countries to favor the Confederacy; and Southerners hoped, with some reason, that one or both might intervene on their behalf.

## THE MOBILIZATION OF THE NORTH

In the North, the war produced considerable discord, frustration, and suffering. But it also produced prosperity and economic growth by giving a major stimulus to both industry and agriculture. With Southern forces now gone from Congress, the Republican Party had almost unchallenged supremacy. During the war, it enacted an aggressively nationalistic program to promote economic development.

### Economic Measures

Two acts of 1862 assisted the rapid development of the West. The Homestead Act permitted any citizen or prospective citizen to purchase 160 acres of public land for a small fee after living on it for five years. The Morrill Act transferred substantial public acreage to the state governments; they were to sell the land and use the proceeds to finance public education. This act led to the creation of many new state colleges and universities, the so-called land-grant institutions. Congress also passed a series of tariff bills that by the end of the war had raised duties to the highest level in the nation's history—a great boon to domestic industries eager for protection from foreign competition, but a hardship for many farmers and other consumers.

Congress also moved to spur completion of a transcontinental railroad. It created two new federally chartered corporations: the Union Pacific Railroad Company, which was to build westward from Omaha, and the Central Pacific, which was to build eastward from California. The two projects were to meet in the middle and complete the link. The government provided free public lands and generous loans to the companies.

The National Bank Acts of 1863–1864 created a new national banking system. Existing or newly formed banks could join the system if they had enough capital and were willing to invest one-third of it in government securities. In return, they could issue United States Treasury notes as currency. The new system eliminated much of the chaos and uncertainty in the nation's currency and created a uniform system of national bank notes.

More difficult than promoting economic growth was financing the war itself. The government tried to do so in three ways: levying taxes, issuing paper currency, and borrowing. Congress levied new taxes on almost all goods and services; and in 1861 the government levied an income tax for the first time, with rates that eventually rose to 10 percent on incomes above $5,000. But taxation raised only a small proportion of the funds necessary for financing the war, and strong popular resistance prevented the government from raising the rates.

At least equally controversial was the printing of paper currency, or "greenbacks." The new currency was backed not by gold or silver but simply by the good faith and credit of the government (much like today's currency). The value of the greenbacks fluctuated according to the fortunes of the Northern armies. Early in 1864, with the war effort bogged down, a greenback dollar was worth only 39 percent of a gold dollar. Even at the close of the war, it was worth only 67 percent of a gold dollar. Because of the difficulty of making purchases with this uncertain currency, the government used greenbacks sparingly. The Treasury issued only $450 million worth of paper currency—a small proportion of the cost of the war but enough to inflate prices by over 80 percent in the course of the war.

By far the largest source of financing for the war was loans. The Treasury persuaded ordinary citizens to buy over $400 million worth of bonds—the first example of mass financing of a war in American history. But public bond purchases constituted only a small part of the government's borrowing, which in the end totaled $2.6 billion, most of it from banks and large financial interests.

### Raising the Union Armies

Over 2 million men served in the Union military forces during the Civil War. But at the beginning of 1861, the regular army of the United States consisted of only 16,000 troops, many of them stationed in the West to protect white settlers from Indians. So the Union, like the Confederacy, had to raise its army mostly from scratch. Lincoln called for an increase of 23,000 in the regular army, but the bulk of the fighting, he knew, would have to be done by the volunteers in state militias. When Congress convened in July

1861, it authorized enlisting 500,000 volunteers for three-year (as opposed to the customary three-month) terms.

This voluntary system of recruitment produced adequate forces only briefly, during the first flush of enthusiasm for the war. By March 1863, Congress was forced to pass a national draft law. Virtually all young adult males were eligible to be drafted, but a man could escape service by hiring someone to go in his place or by paying the government a fee of $300. Only about 46,000 men were ever actually conscripted, but the draft greatly increased voluntary enlistments.

To a people accustomed to a remote and inactive national government, conscription was strange and threatening. Opposition to the law was widespread, particularly among laborers, immigrants, and Democrats opposed to the war. Occasionally it erupted into violence. Demonstrators against the draft rioted in New York City for four days in July 1863, killed over 100 people, mostly blacks (whom many opponents of the war blamed for the conflict), and burned down African-American homes, businesses, and even an orphanage. It was the bloodiest riot in American history. Only the arrival of federal troops halted the violence.

### Wartime Politics

When Abraham Lincoln arrived in Washington early in 1861, many Republicans—noting his lack of national experience and his folksy, unpretentious manner—considered him a minor politician from the prairies, a man who would be easily controlled by the real leaders of his party. The new president understood his (and his party's) weaknesses, and he assembled a cabinet representing every faction of the Republican Party and every segment of Northern opinion—men of exceptional prestige, influence, and in some cases arrogance, several of whom believed that they, not Lincoln, should be president. But Lincoln was a man of great self-confidence, and he was not cowed by the distinguished figures around him. He moved boldly as well to use the war powers of the presidency, blithely ignoring inconvenient parts of the Constitution because, he said, it would be foolish to lose the whole by being afraid to disregard a part.

He sent troops into battle without asking Congress for a declaration of war, arguing that the conflict was a domestic insurrection and that no congressional authorization was necessary. He increased the size of the regular army without receiving legislative authority to do so. He unilaterally proclaimed a naval blockade of the South.

Lincoln's greatest political problem was the widespread popular opposition to the war, mobilized by those in the Democratic Party who were known as Peace Democrats (or, by their enemies, "Copperheads"). Lincoln used extraordinary methods to suppress them. He ordered military arrests of civilian dissenters and suspended the right of habeas corpus (the right of an arrested person to receive a speedy trial). At first, Lincoln used these methods only in sensitive areas such as the border states; but in 1862, he proclaimed that all persons who discouraged enlistments or engaged in disloyal practices were subject to martial law. In all, more than 13,000 persons were arrested and imprisoned for varying periods.

By the time of the presidential election of 1864, the North was in political turmoil. The Republicans had suffered heavy losses in 1862, and in response leaders of the party tried to create a broad coalition of all the groups that supported the war. They called the new organization the Union Party, but it was, in reality, little more than the Republican Party and a small faction of War Democrats. The Union Party nominated Lincoln for another term as president and Andrew Johnson of Tennessee, a War Democrat who had opposed his state's decision to secede, for the vice presidency.

The Democrats nominated George B. McClellan, a celebrated former Union general who had been relieved of his command by Lincoln, and adopted a platform denouncing the war and calling for a truce. McClellan repudiated that demand, but the Democrats were clearly the peace party in the campaign, trying to profit from growing war weariness and from the Union's discouraging military position in the summer of 1864. For a time, Lincoln's prospects for reelection seemed doubtful.

At this crucial moment, however, several Northern military victories, particularly the capture of Atlanta, Georgia, early in September, rejuvenated Northern morale and boosted Republican prospects. Lincoln won reelection comfortably, with 212 electoral votes to McClellan's 21; the president carried every state except Kentucky, New Jersey, and Delaware. But Lincoln's lead in the popular vote was a more modest 10 percent. Had Union victories not occurred when they did, and had Lincoln not made special arrangements to allow Union troops to vote, the Democrats might have won.

## The Politics of Emancipation

Despite their surface unity in supporting the war and their general agreement on most economic matters, the Republicans disagreed sharply with one another on the issue of slavery. Radicals—led in Congress by such men as Representative Thaddeus Stevens of Pennsylvania and Senators Charles

Sumner of Massachusetts and Benjamin Wade of Ohio—wanted to use the war to abolish slavery immediately and completely. Conservatives either opposed abolition altogether or, more often, favored a slower, more gradual, and, they believed, less disruptive process for ending slavery—in part so as to placate the border slave states that remained, precariously, within the Union. In the beginning, at least, the president seemed to side with the conservative gradualists.

Despite the president's cautious view of emancipation, momentum began to gather behind it early in the war. In 1861, Congress passed the Confiscation Act, which declared that all slaves used for "insurrectionary" purposes (that is, in support of the Confederate military effort) would be considered freed. Subsequent laws in the spring of 1862 abolished slavery in the District of Columbia and in the western territories and provided for the compensation of owners. In July 1862, the Radicals pushed through Congress the second Confiscation Act, which declared free the slaves of persons supporting the insurrection (whether or not the slaves themselves were doing so) and authorized the president to employ blacks, including freed slaves, as soldiers.

As the war progressed, many in the North seemed slowly to accept emancipation as a central war aim; nothing less, they believed, would justify the enormous sacrifices of the struggle. As a result, the Radicals gained increasing influence within the Republican Party—a development that did not go unnoticed by the president, who decided to seize the leadership of the rising antislavery sentiment himself.

On September 22, 1862, after the Union victory at the Battle of Antietam, the president announced his intention to use his war powers to issue an executive order freeing all slaves in the Confederacy. And on January 11, 1863, he formally signed the Emancipation Proclamation, which declared forever free the slaves inside the Confederacy. The proclamation did not apply to the border slave states, which had never seceded from the Union; nor did it affect those parts of the Confederacy already under Union control (Tennessee, western Virginia, and southern Louisiana).

The immediate effect of the proclamation was thus limited. It applied only to slaves over which the Union had no control. But the document was of great importance because it clearly and irrevocably established that the war was being fought not only to preserve the Union but also to eliminate slavery. Eventually, as federal armies occupied much of the South, the proclamation became a practical reality and led directly to the freeing of thousands of slaves. About 186,000 of these emancipated blacks served as soldiers, sailors, and laborers for the Union forces.

Even in areas not directly affected by the proclamation, the antislavery impulse gained strength. By the end of the war, two Union slave states (Maryland and Missouri) and three Confederate states occupied by Union forces (Tennessee, Arkansas, and Louisiana) had abolished slavery. The final step came in 1865, when Congress approved and the states ratified the Thirteenth Amendment, which abolished slavery as an institution in all parts of the United States, not just the areas covered by the Emancipation Proclamation. After more than two centuries, legalized slavery finally ceased to exist in the United States.

### The War and Economic Development

The Civil War did not, as some historians used to claim, transform the North from an agrarian to an industrial society. Industrialization was already far advanced when the war began, and in some areas, the war actually retarded growth by diverting labor and resources to military purposes.

On the whole, however, the war sped the economic development of the North. That was in part a result of the political dominance of the Republican Party and its promotion of nationalistic economic legislation. But it was also because the war itself required the expansion of certain sectors of the economy. Coal production increased by nearly 20 percent during the war. Railroad facilities improved—mainly through the adoption of a standard gauge (track width) on new lines. The loss of farm labor to the military forced many farmers to increase the mechanization of agriculture.

The war was a difficult experience for many American workers. Industrial laborers suffered a substantial loss of purchasing power, as prices in the North rose by more than 80 percent during the war while wages rose only about 40 percent. Wages remained low because liberalized immigration laws permitted a flood of new workers to enter the labor market and because the increasing mechanization of production eliminated the jobs of many skilled workers. One result was a substantial increase in union membership in some industries and the creation of several national unions, for coal miners, railroad engineers, and others—organizations bitterly opposed and rigorously suppressed by employers.

### Women, Nursing, and the War

The war thrust women into new and often unfamiliar roles, by choice and by necessity. They took over positions vacated by men as teachers, salesclerks, office workers, and mill and factory hands. They did so not only to

THE U.S. SANITARY COMMISSION  Mathew Brady took this photograph of female nurses and Union soldiers standing before an infirmary at Brandy Station, Virginia, near Petersburg, in 1864. The infirmary was run by the U.S. Sanitary Commission, the government-supported nursing corps that became indispensable to the medical care of wounded soldiers during the Civil War.

meet the needs of employers for additional labor but to meet their own, often desperate, need for money. With husbands and fathers away in the army, many women were left destitute—particularly since military pay was small and erratic.

Above all, women entered nursing, a field previously dominated by men. The United States Sanitary Commission, an organization of civilian volunteers led by Dorothea Dix, mobilized large numbers of female nurses to serve in field hospitals. By the end of the war, women were the dominant force in nursing; by the end of the century, nursing had become an almost entirely female profession.

Female nurses encountered considerable resistance from male doctors, many of whom considered women too weak for medical work and many of whom thought it inappropriate for women to be taking care of male strangers. The Sanitary Commission countered such arguments by presenting nursing in domestic terms: as a profession that made use of the same maternal, nurturing roles women played as wives and mothers.

Some women, especially those who had been committed to feminist causes earlier, came to see the war as an opportunity to win support for their own goals. Elizabeth Cady Stanton and Susan B. Anthony, who together founded the National Woman's Loyal League in 1863, worked simultaneously for the abolition of slavery and the awarding of suffrage to women.

## THE MOBILIZATION OF THE SOUTH

Early in February 1861, representatives of the seven states that had seceded from the Union met at Montgomery, Alabama, to create a new Southern nation. When Virginia seceded several months later, the government of the Confederacy moved to Richmond—one of the few Southern cities large enough to house a government.

White Southerners boasted loudly of the differences between their new nation and the nation they had left. Those differences were real. But there were also important similarities between the Union and the Confederacy, which became particularly clear as the two sides mobilized for war: similarities in their political systems, in the methods they used for financing the war and conscripting troops, and in the way they fought.

### Confederate Government

The Confederate constitution was almost identical to the Constitution of the United States, with several significant exceptions. It explicitly acknowledged the sovereignty of the individual states (although not the right of secession). And it specifically sanctioned slavery and made its abolition (even by one of the states) practically impossible.

The constitutional convention at Montgomery named a provisional president and vice president: Jefferson Davis of Mississippi and Alexander H. Stephens of Georgia, who were later chosen by the general electorate, without opposition, for six-year terms. Davis had been a moderate secessionist before the war. Stephens had argued against secession. The Confederate government, like the Union government, was dominated throughout the war by men of the center. It was also, like the Union government, dominated less by the old aristocracy of the East than by the newer aristocrats of the West, of whom Davis was the most prominent example.

Davis was, in the end, an unsuccessful president. He was a reasonably able administrator and the dominating figure in his government, encountering little interference from the generally tame members of his unstable cabinet and serving, in effect, as his own secretary of war. But he rarely provided genuinely national leadership. He spent too much time on routine items, and unlike Lincoln, he displayed a punctiliousness about legal and constitutional niceties inappropriate to the needs of a new nation at war. One shrewd Confederate official wrote: "All the revolutionary vigor is with the enemy. . . . With us timidity—hair splitting."

There were no formal political parties in the Confederacy, but its congressional and popular politics were badly divided nevertheless. Some white Southerners (and most blacks who were aware of the course of events) opposed secession and war altogether. Many white people in poorer "backcountry" and "upcountry" regions, where slavery was limited, refused to recognize the new Confederate government or to serve in the Southern army; some worked or even fought for the Union. Most white Southerners supported the war, but as in the North many were openly critical of the government and the military, particularly as the tide of battle turned against the South and the Confederate economy decayed.

### Money and Manpower

Financing the Confederate war effort was a monumental and ultimately impossible task. The Confederate Congress tried at first not to tax the people directly but to requisition funds from the individual states; but most of them were also unwilling to tax their citizens and paid their shares, when they paid them at all, with bonds or notes of dubious worth. In 1863, therefore, the congress enacted an income tax. But taxation produced only about 1 percent of the government's total income. Borrowing was not much more successful. The Confederate government issued bonds in such vast amounts that the public lost faith in them and stopped buying them, and efforts to borrow money in Europe using cotton as collateral fared no better.

As a result, the Confederacy had to pay for the war through the least stable, most destructive form of financing: paper currency, which it began issuing in 1861. By 1864, the Confederacy had issued the staggering total of $1.5 billion in paper money, more than three times what the Union had produced. And unlike the Union, the Confederacy had no uniform currency system; the national government, states, cities, and private banks all issued their own notes, producing widespread chaos and confusion. The result was a disastrous inflation—a 9,000 percent increase in prices in the course of the war (in contrast to 80 percent in the North)—with devastating effects on Confederate morale.

Like the United States, the Confederacy first raised armies by calling for volunteers. And as in the North, by the end of 1861 voluntary enlistments were declining. In April 1862, therefore, the congress enacted the Con-

CONFEDERATE VOLUNTEERS Smiling and apparently confident, young Southern soldiers pose for a photograph in 1861, shortly before the first Battle of Bull Run. The Civil War was one of the first military conflicts extensively chronicled by photographers.

scription Act, which subjected all white males between the ages of eighteen and thirty-five to military service for three years. As in the North, a draftee could avoid service if he furnished a substitute. But since the price of substitutes was high, the provision aroused such opposition from poorer whites that it was repealed in 1863. Even more controversial were other provisions of the draft, especially the exemption of one white man on each plantation with twenty or more slaves, a provision that caused some smaller farmers to complain: "It's a rich man's war but a poor man's fight."

Even so, conscription worked for a time, in part because enthusiasm for the war was intense and widespread among white men in most of the South. At the end of 1862, about 500,000 soldiers were in the Confederate army. That number did not include the many slave men and women recruited by the military to perform such services as cooking, laundry, and manual labor, hence freeing additional white manpower for fighting. After 1862, however, conscription began producing fewer men, and the armed forces steadily decreased in size.

As 1864 opened, the Confederate government faced a critical manpower shortage. The congress began trying to draft men as young as seventeen and as old as fifty. But in a nation suffering from intense war weariness, where many had concluded that defeat was inevitable, nothing could attract or retain an adequate army any longer. In 1864–1865, there were 100,000 desertions. In a frantic final attempt to raise men, the congress authorized the conscription of 300,000 slaves, but the war ended before the government could attempt this incongruous experiment.

### States' Rights Versus Centralization

The greatest sources of division in the South were not differences of opinion over the war, which most white Southerners generally supported, but the products of the doctrine of states' rights. States' rights had become such a cult among many white Southerners that they resisted virtually all efforts to exert national authority, even those necessary to win the war. States' rights enthusiasts restricted Davis's ability to impose martial law and suspend habeas corpus. They obstructed conscription. Recalcitrant governors such as Joseph Brown of Georgia and Zebulon M. Vance of North Carolina tried at times to keep their own troops apart from the Confederate forces and insisted on hoarding surplus supplies for their own states' militias.

Even so, by the end of the war, the Confederate bureaucracy was larger than its counterpart in Washington. The national government experimented, successfully for a time, with a "food draft" which permitted soldiers to feed themselves by seizing crops from farms in their path. The government impressed slaves, often over the objections of their owners, to work as laborers on military projects. The Confederacy seized control of the railroads and shipping; it imposed regulations on industry; it limited corporate profits. States' rights sentiment was a significant handicap, but the South nevertheless took dramatic steps in the direction of centralization—becoming in the process increasingly like the region whose institutions it was fighting to escape.

### Economic and Social Effects of the War

The war had a devastating effect on the South's economy. It cut off Southern planters and producers from markets in the North and made the sale of cotton overseas much more difficult (because of the Northern blockade); it robbed farms and industries without large slave populations of a male work force. In the North, production of all goods increased during the war; in the

South, it declined by more than a third. Above all, the fighting itself—almost all of which occurred inside the Confederacy—wreaked havoc on the Southern landscape, destroying farmland, towns, cities, and railroads.

As the war continued, the shortages, the inflation, and the suffering created increasing instability in Southern society. There were major food riots (some led by women) in cities in Georgia, North Carolina, and Alabama in 1863, as well as a large and violent demonstration in Richmond. Resistance to conscription, food impressment, and taxation increased throughout the Confederacy, as did hoarding and black-market commerce.

The long-range results of the war for Southern women are difficult to measure but certainly profound. The war forced many women (and some men) to question the prevailing assumption of their society that females were not suited for the public sphere, since so many women had to perform untraditional, nondomestic tasks during the conflict. A more concrete legacy was the decimation of the male population and the creation of a major gender imbalance in the region. After the war, women outnumbered men in most Southern states by significant margins. The result, of course, was a large number of unmarried or widowed women who, both during and after the war, had no choice but to find employment.

Even before emancipation, the war had far-reaching effects on the lives of slaves. Confederate leaders were more terrified of slave revolts during the war than they had been in peacetime, and they enforced slave codes with particular severity. Even so, many slaves—especially those near the front—escaped their masters and crossed Union lines.

## STRATEGY AND DIPLOMACY

Militarily, the initiative in the Civil War lay mainly with the North, since it needed to defeat the Confederacy while the South needed only to avoid defeat. Diplomatically, however, the initiative lay with the South. It needed to enlist the recognition and support of foreign governments; the Union wanted only to preserve the status quo.

### The Commanders

The most important Union military commander was Abraham Lincoln, whose previous military experience consisted only of brief service in his state militia. Lincoln made many mistakes, to be sure, but he was on the whole a successful commander in chief because he realized that numbers and resources were on his side and because he knew how to exploit the North's material advantages. He realized, too, that the proper objective of his armies was the destruction of the Confederate armies and not the occupation of Southern territory. It was fortunate for the North that Lincoln had a good grasp of strategy, because many of his generals did not. The problem of finding adequate commanders for the troops in the field plagued him throughout the first three years of the war.

From 1861 to 1864, Lincoln tried time and again to find a chief of staff capable of orchestrating the Union war effort. He turned first to General Winfield Scott, the aging hero of the Mexican War. But Scott was unprepared for the magnitude of the new conflict and retired on November 1, 1861. Lincoln then appointed the young George B. McClellan, who was the commander of the Union forces in the East, the Army of the Potomac; but the proud, arrogant McClellan had a wholly inadequate grasp of strategy and in any case returned to the field in March 1862. For most of the rest of the year, Lincoln had no chief of staff at all. And when he eventually appointed General Henry W. Halleck to the post, he found him an ineffectual strategist who left all substantive decision making to the president or the generals in the field. Not until March 1864 did Lincoln finally find a general he trusted to command the war effort: Ulysses S. Grant, who shared Lincoln's belief in making enemy armies and resources, not enemy territory, the target of military efforts. Lincoln gave Grant a relatively free hand, but the general always submitted at least the broad outlines of his plans to the president for advance approval.

Lincoln's handling of the war effort faced constant scrutiny from the Committee on the Conduct of the War, a joint investigative committee of the two houses of Congress and the most powerful voice the legislative branch has ever had in formulating war policies. Established in December 1861 and chaired by Senator Benjamin E. Wade of Ohio, it complained constantly of the inadequate ruthlessness of Northern generals, which Radicals on the committee attributed (largely inaccurately) to a secret sympathy among the officers for slavery. The committee's efforts often seriously interfered with the conduct of the war.

Southern military leadership centered on President Davis, who unlike Lincoln was a trained professional soldier but who, also unlike Lincoln, failed ever to create an effective central command system. Early in 1862, Davis named General Robert E. Lee as his principal military adviser. But in fact, Davis had no intention of sharing control of strategy with anyone. After a few months, Lee left Richmond to command forces in the field, and for the next two years Davis planned strategy alone. In February 1864, he named General Braxton Bragg as a military adviser, but Bragg never provided much more than technical advice. Not until February 1865 did the Confederate Congress create the formal position of general in chief. Davis named Lee to the post, but the war ended before the new command structure had time to take shape.

At lower levels of command, men of markedly similar backgrounds controlled the war in both the North and the South. Many of the professional officers on both sides were graduates of the United States Military Academy at West Point and the United States Naval Academy at Annapolis and thus had been trained in similar ways. Many were closely acquainted, even friendly, with their counterparts on the other side. Amateur officers played an important role in both armies as commanders of volunteer regiments. In both North and South, such men were usually economic or social leaders in their communities who appointed themselves officers and rounded up troops to lead. Although occasionally this system produced officers of real ability, more often it did not.

*The Role of Sea Power*

The Union had an overwhelming advantage in naval power, and it gave its navy two important roles in the war. One was enforcing a blockade of the Southern coast, which the president ordered on April 19, 1861. The other was assisting the Union armies in field operations.

The blockade of the South was never fully effective. The United States Navy could generally keep oceangoing ships out of Confederate ports, but for a time small blockade runners continued to slip through. Gradually, however, federal forces tightened the blockade by seizing the ports themselves. The last important port in Confederate hands—Wilmington, North Carolina—fell to the Union early in 1865.

The Confederates made bold attempts to break the blockade with new weapons. Foremost among them was an ironclad warship, constructed by plating with iron a former United States frigate, the *Merrimac*, which the Union navy had scuttled in Norfolk harbor when Virginia seceded. On March 8, 1862, the refitted *Merrimac*, renamed the *Virginia*, left Norfolk to attack a blockading squadron of wooden ships at nearby Hampton Roads. It destroyed two of the ships and scattered the rest. But the Union government had already built ironclads of its own. And one of them, the *Monitor*, arrived off the coast of Virginia only a few hours after the *Virginia*'s dramatic foray.

The next day, it met the *Virginia* in the first battle ever between ironclad ships. Neither vessel was able to sink the other, but the *Monitor* put an end to the *Virginia*'s raids and preserved the blockade.

The Union navy was particularly important in the western theater of the war—the vast region between the Appalachian Mountains and the Mississippi River—where the larger rivers were navigable by large vessels. The navy transported supplies and troops and joined in attacking Confederate strong points. The South had no significant navy of its own and could defend against the Union gunboats only with ineffective fixed land fortifications.

### Europe and the Disunited States

Judah P. Benjamin, the Confederate secretary of state for most of the war, was an intelligent but undynamic man who attended mostly to routine administrative tasks. William Seward, his counterpart in Washington, gradually became one of the outstanding American secretaries of state. He had invaluable assistance from Charles Francis Adams, the American minister to London, who had inherited the considerable diplomatic talents of his father, John Quincy Adams, and his grandfather, John Adams.

At the beginning of the war, the sympathies of the ruling classes of England and France, the two nations whose support was most crucial to both sides, lay largely with the Confederacy. That was partly because the two nations imported much Southern cotton; but it was also because they were eager to weaken the United States, an increasingly powerful rival to them in world commerce, and because many leaders of the two monarchies admired the South's defense of aristocracy. But France was unwilling to take sides in the conflict unless England did so first. And in England, the government was reluctant to act because there was powerful popular support for the Union—particularly from the large and influential English antislavery movement. After Lincoln issued the Emancipation Proclamation, antislavery groups worked particularly avidly for the Union.

Southern leaders hoped to counter the strength of the British antislavery forces by arguing that access to Southern cotton was vital to the English and French textile industries, an approach known as "King Cotton diplomacy." But English manufacturers had a surplus of both raw cotton and finished goods on hand in 1861 and could withstand a temporary loss of access to American cotton. Later, as the supply of cotton began to diminish, both England and France managed to keep at least some of their mills open by importing cotton from Egypt, India, and other sources. Equally important, even the 500,000 English textile workers thrown out of jobs as a result of mill closings continued to support the North. In the end, therefore, no European nation offered diplomatic recognition to the Confederacy or intervened in the war. No nation wanted to antagonize the United States unless the Confederacy seemed likely to win, and the South never came close enough to victory to convince its potential allies to support it.

Even so, there was considerable tension, and on occasion near hostilities, between the United States and Britain, beginning in the first days of the war. Great Britain, France, and other nations declared themselves neutral early in the war. The Union government was furious. Neutrality implied that the two sides to the conflict had equal stature, but Washington was insisting that the conflict was simply a domestic insurrection, not a war between two legitimate governments.

A more serious crisis, the so-called *Trent* affair, began in late 1861. Two Confederate diplomats, James M. Mason and John Slidell, had slipped through the then-ineffective Union blockade to Havana, Cuba, where they boarded an English steamer, the *Trent*, for England. Waiting in Cuban waters was the American frigate *San Jacinto*, commanded by the impetuous Charles Wilkes. Acting without authorization, Wilkes stopped the British vessel, arrested the diplomats, and carried them in triumph to Boston. The British government demanded the release of the prisoners, reparations, and an apology. Lincoln and Seward, aware that Wilkes had violated maritime law and unwilling to risk war with England, spun out the negotiations until American public opinion had cooled off; then they released the diplomats with an indirect apology.

A second diplomatic crisis produced problems that lasted for years. Unable to construct large ships itself, the Confederacy bought six ships, known as commerce destroyers, from British shipyards. The best known of them were the *Alabama*, the *Florida*, and the *Shenandoah*. The United States protested that this sale of military equipment to a belligerent violated the laws of neutrality, and the protests became the basis, after the war, of a prolonged battle over damage claims by the United States against Great Britain.

## CAMPAIGNS AND BATTLES

In the absence of direct intervention by the European powers, the two contestants in North America were left to resolve the conflict between themselves. They did so in four long years of bloody combat that produced more carnage than any other war in American history, before or since. More than 618,000 Americans died in the course of the Civil War, far more than the

115,000 who perished in World War I or the 318,000 who died in World War II—more, indeed, than died in all other American wars prior to Vietnam combined. There were nearly 2,000 deaths for every 100,000 of population during the Civil War. In World War I, the comparable figure was only 109; in World War II, 241.

Despite the gruesome cost, the Civil War has become the most romanticized and the most intently studied of all American wars. In part, that is because the conflict produced—in addition to hideous fatalities—a series of military campaigns of classic strategic interest and a series of military leaders who displayed unusual brilliance and daring.

## *The Opening Clashes, 1861*

The Union and the Confederacy fought their first major battle of the war in northern Virginia. A Union army of over 30,000 men under the command of General Irvin McDowell was stationed just outside Washington. About thirty miles away, at Manassas, was a slightly smaller Confederate army under P. G. T. Beauregard. If the Northern army could destroy the Southern one, Union leaders believed, the war might end at once. In mid-July, McDowell marched his inexperienced troops toward Manassas. Beauregard moved his troops behind Bull Run, a small stream north of Manassas, and called for reinforcements, which reached him the day before the battle. The two armies were now approximately the same size.

On July 21, in the First Battle of Bull Run, or First Battle of Manassas, McDowell almost succeeded in dispersing the Confederate forces. But the Southerners managed to stop a last strong Union assault and then began a savage counterattack. The Union troops, exhausted after hours of hot, hard fighting, suddenly panicked. They broke ranks and retreated chaotically. McDowell was unable to reorganize them, and he had to order a retreat to Washington—a disorderly withdrawal complicated by the presence along the route of many civilians, who had ridden down from the capital, picnic baskets in hand, to watch the battle from nearby hills. The Confederates, as disorganized by victory as the Union forces were by defeat, and short of supplies and transportation, did not pursue. The battle was a severe blow to Union morale and to the president's confidence in his officers. It also dispelled the illusion that the war would be a quick one.

Elsewhere, Union forces achieved some small but significant victories in 1861. In Missouri, rebel forces gathered behind Governor Claiborne Jackson and other state officials who wanted to take the state out of the Union. Nathaniel Lyon, who commanded a small regular army force in St.

**The Virginia Theater, 1861–1863**

TROOP MOVEMENTS

Union forces

Confederate forces

BATTLES

⭑ Union victories

⭑ Confederate victories

⭑ Inconclusive

Louis, moved his troops into southern Missouri to face the secessionists. On August 10, at the Battle of Wilson's Creek, he was defeated and killed—but not before he had seriously weakened the striking power of the Confederates. Union forces were subsequently able to hold most of the state.

Meanwhile, a Union force under George B. McClellan moved east from Ohio into western Virginia. By the end of 1861, it had "liberated" the antisecession mountain people of the region, who created their own state government loyal to the Union; the state was admitted to the Union as West Virginia in 1863. The occupation of western Virginia was of limited military value, since the mountains cut the area off from the rest of Virginia. It was, however, an important propaganda victory for the North.

## The Western Theater, 1862

After the battle at Bull Run, military operations in the East settled into a long and frustrating stalemate. The first decisive operations in 1862 occurred, therefore, in the western theater. Here the Union forces were trying to seize control of the southern part of the Mississippi River; this would divide the Confederacy and give the North easy transportation into the heart of the South. Northern soldiers advanced on the southern Mississippi from both the north and south, moving down the river from Kentucky and up from the Gulf of Mexico toward New Orleans.

In April, a Union squadron of ironclads and wooden vessels commanded by David G. Farragut gathered in the Gulf of Mexico, then smashed past weak Confederate forts near the mouth of the Mississippi, and from there sailed up to New Orleans. The city was virtually defenseless because the Confederate high command had expected the attack to come from the north. The surrender of New Orleans on April 25, 1862, was the first major Union victory and an important turning point in the war. From then on, the mouth of the Mississippi was closed to Confederate trade, and the South's largest city and most important banking center was in Union hands.

Farther north in the western theater, Confederate troops under the command of Albert Sidney Johnston were stretched out in a long defensive line, whose center was at two forts in Tennessee, Fort Henry and Fort Donelson, on the Tennessee and Cumberland Rivers respectively. But the forts were located well behind the main Southern flanks, a fatal weakness that Union commanders recognized and exploited. Early in 1862, Ulysses S. Grant attacked Fort Henry, whose defenders, awed by the ironclad riverboats accompanying the Union army, surrendered with almost no resistance on February 6. Grant then moved both his naval and ground forces to Fort Donelson, where the Confederates put up a stronger fight but finally, on February 16, had to surrender. By cracking the Confederate center, Grant had gained control of river communications and forced Confederate forces out of Kentucky and half of Tennessee.

With about 40,000 men, Grant now advanced south along the Tennessee River to seize control of railroad lines vital to the Confederacy. From Pittsburg Landing, he marched to nearby Shiloh, Tennessee, where a force

**The War in the West, 1861–1863**

Under Union control, January 1, 1862

Union gains

TROOP MOVEMENTS
Union forces
Confederate forces

BATTLES
Union victories
Confederate victories
Siege line

almost equal to his own and commanded by Albert Sidney Johnston and P. G. T. Beauregard caught him by surprise. The result was the Battle of Shiloh, April 6–7. In the first day's fighting (during which Johnston was killed), the Southerners drove Grant back to the river. But the next day, reinforced by 25,000 fresh troops, Grant recovered the lost ground and forced Beauregard to withdraw. After the narrow Union victory at Shiloh, Northern forces occupied Corinth, Mississippi, the hub of several important railroads, and took control of the Mississippi River as far south as Memphis.

Braxton Bragg, now in command of the Confederate army in the West, gathered his forces at Chattanooga, in eastern Tennessee, which the Confederacy still controlled. He hoped to win back the rest of the state and then move north into Kentucky. But first he had to face a Union army (commanded first by Don Carlos Buell and then by William S. Rosecrans), whose assignment was to capture Chattanooga. The two armies maneuvered for advantage inconclusively in northern Tennessee and southern Kentucky for several months until they finally met, on December 31–January 2, in the Battle of Murfreesboro, or Stone's River. Bragg was forced to withdraw to the south, his campaign a failure.

By the end of 1862, therefore, Union forces had made considerable progress in the West. But the major conflict remained in the East, and the North was having much less success there.

### The Virginia Front, 1862

George B. McClellan, commander of the Army of the Potomac and the most controversial general of the war, was in command of Union operations as 1862 began. McClellan was a superb trainer of men, but he often seemed reluctant to commit his troops to battle. Opportunities for important engagements came and went, and McClellan seemed never to take advantage of them—claiming always that he was not ready or that his troops were outnumbered.

During the winter of 1861–1862, McClellan concentrated on training his army of 150,000 men near Washington. Finally, he designed a spring campaign whose purpose was to capture the Confederate capital at Richmond. But instead of heading overland directly toward Richmond, McClellan chose a complicated, roundabout route that he thought would circumvent the Confederate defenses. The navy would carry his troops down the Potomac to a peninsula east of Richmond, between the York and James Rivers; the army would approach the city from there. The combined operations became known as the Peninsular campaign.

McClellan began the campaign with only part of his army. Approximately 100,000 men accompanied him down the Potomac. Another 30,000, under General Irvin McDowell, remained behind to protect Washington. McClellan insisted that Washington was safe as long as he was threatening

Richmond, and he finally persuaded Lincoln to send him the additional men. But before the president could do so, a Confederate army under Thomas J. ("Stonewall") Jackson changed his plans. Jackson staged a rapid march north through the Shenandoah Valley, as if he were planning to cross the Potomac and attack Washington. Alarmed, Lincoln dispatched Mc-Dowell's corps to head off Jackson. In the brilliant Valley campaign of May 4–June 9, 1862, Jackson defeated two separate Union forces and slipped away before McDowell could catch him.

Meanwhile, Confederate troops under Joseph E. Johnston were attacking McClellan's advancing army outside Richmond. But in the two-day Battle of Fair Oaks, or Seven Pines (May 31–June 1), they could not repel the Union forces. Johnston, badly wounded, was replaced by Robert E. Lee, who then recalled Stonewall Jackson from the Shenandoah Valley. With a combined force of 85,000 to face McClellan's 100,000, Lee launched a new offensive, known as the Battle of the Seven Days (June 25–July 1). Lee wanted to cut McClellan off from his base on the York River and then destroy the isolated Union army. But McClellan fought his way across the peninsula and set up a new base on the James. There, with naval support, the Army of the Potomac was safe.

McClellan was now only twenty-five miles from Richmond, with a secure line of water communications, and thus in a good position to renew the campaign. But despite continuing pressure from Lincoln, he did not advance. Instead of replacing McClellan with a more aggressive commander, as many were urging him to do, the president finally ordered the army to move back to northern Virginia and join a smaller force under John Pope. The president hoped to begin a new offensive against Richmond on the direct overland route that he himself had always preferred. As the Army of the Potomac left the peninsula by water, Lee moved north with the Army of Northern Virginia to strike Pope before McClellan could join him. Pope was as rash as McClellan was cautious, and he attacked the approaching Confederates without waiting for the arrival of all of McClellan's troops. In the ensuing Second Battle of Bull Run, or Second Battle of Manassas (August 29–30), Lee threw back the assault and routed Pope's army, which fled to Washington. With hopes for an overland campaign against Richmond now in disarray, Lincoln removed Pope from command and put McClellan back in charge of all the federal forces in the region.

Lee soon went on the offensive again, heading north through western Maryland, and McClellan moved out to meet him. McClellan had the good luck to get a copy of Lee's orders, which revealed that a part of the Confederate army, under Stonewall Jackson, had separated from the rest to at-

SKIRMISH AT ANTIETAM The American public followed the course of the Civil War through newspaper reports and, at times, through published drawings of the battlefields by traveling artists who sketched important events for publication. Photographers chronicled the war as well. But cameras in the 1860s could not easily capture action scenes, and very few newspapers or magazines were technologically equipped to publish photographs. So drawings such as this one by A. R. Waud—of a Brooklyn, N.Y., regiment fighting Southern cavalry at the battle at Antietam—were much in demand.

tack Harpers Ferry. But instead of attacking quickly before the Confederates could recombine, McClellan stalled and gave Lee time to pull most of his forces together behind Antietam Creek, near the town of Sharpsburg. There, on September 17, in the bloodiest engagement of the war, McClellan's 87,000-man army repeatedly attacked Lee's force of 50,000, with staggering casualties on both sides. In all, 6,000 men were killed, 17,000 wounded. Late in the day, just as the Confederate line seemed ready to break, the last of Jackson's troops arrived from Harpers Ferry to reinforce it. McClellan might have broken through with one more assault. Instead, he allowed Lee to retreat into Virginia. Technically, Antietam was a Union victory; but in reality, McClellan had squandered an opportunity to destroy much of the Confederate army. In November, Lincoln finally removed McClellan from command for good.

McClellan's replacement, Ambrose E. Burnside, was a short-lived mediocrity. He tried to move toward Richmond by crossing the Rappahannock River at Fredericksburg, the strongest defensive point on the river. There, on December 13, he launched a series of attacks against Lee, all of them bloody, all of them hopeless. After losing a large part of his army, he withdrew to the north bank of the Rappahannock. He was relieved at his own request. The year 1862 ended, therefore, with a series of frustrations for the Union.

## *1863: Year of Decision*

At the beginning of 1863, General Joseph Hooker was commanding the still-formidable Army of the Potomac, whose 120,000 troops remained north of the Rappahannock, opposite Fredericksburg. But despite his formidable reputation (his popular nickname was "Fighting Joe"), Hooker showed little resolve as he launched his own campaign in the spring. Taking part of his army, Hooker crossed the river above Fredericksburg and moved toward the town and Lee's army. But at the last minute, he apparently lost his nerve and drew back to a defensive position in a desolate area of brush and scrub trees known as the Wilderness. Lee had only half as many men as Hooker had, but he boldly divided his forces for a dual assault on the Union army. In the Battle of Chancellorsville, May 1–5, Stonewall Jackson attacked the Union right and Lee himself charged the front. Hooker barely managed to escape with his army. Lee had frustrated Union objectives, but it was not an entirely happy victory. He had not destroyed the Union army. And his ablest officer, Jackson, was fatally wounded in the course of the battle.

While the Union forces were suffering repeated frustrations in the East, they were winning some important victories in the West. In the spring of 1863, Ulysses S. Grant was driving at Vicksburg, Mississippi, one of the Confederacy's two remaining strongholds on the southern Mississippi River. Vicksburg was well protected, surrounded by rough country on the north and low, marshy ground on the west, and had good artillery coverage of the river itself. But in May, Grant boldly moved men and supplies—over land and by water—to an area south of the city, where the terrain was better. He then attacked Vicksburg from the rear. Six weeks later, on July 4, Vicksburg—whose residents were by then literally starving as a result of a prolonged siege—surrendered. At almost the same time, the other Confederate strong point on the river, Port Hudson, Louisiana, also surrendered to a Union force that had moved north from New Orleans. The Union had achieved one of its basic military aims: control of the whole length of the Mississippi. The Confederacy was split in two, with Louisiana, Arkansas, and

Texas cut off from the other seceded states. The victories on the Mississippi were one of the great turning points of the war.

During an early stage of the siege of Vicksburg, Lee proposed an invasion of Pennsylvania, which would, he argued, divert Union troops north and remove the pressure on the lower Mississippi. Further, he argued, if he could win a major victory on Northern soil, England and France might come to the Confederacy's aid. The war-weary North might even quit the war before Vicksburg fell.

In June 1863, Lee moved up the Shenandoah Valley into Maryland and then entered Pennsylvania. The Union Army of the Potomac, commanded first by Hooker and then (after June 28) by George C. Meade, moved north too, paralleling the Confederates' movement and staying between Lee and Washington. The two armies finally encountered one another at the small town of Gettysburg, Pennsylvania. There, on July 1–3, 1863, they fought the most celebrated battle of the war.

Meade's army established a strong, well-protected position on the hills south of the town. The confident and combative Lee attacked, even though his army of 75,000 was outnumbered by Meade's 90,000. His first assault on the Union forces on Cemetery Ridge failed. A day later, he ordered a second, larger effort. In what is remembered as Pickett's Charge, a force of 15,000 Confederate soldiers advanced for almost a mile across open country while being swept by Union fire. Only about 5,000 made it up the ridge, and this remnant finally had to surrender or retreat. By now, Lee had lost nearly a third of his army. On July 4, the same day as the surrender of Vicksburg, he withdrew from Gettysburg. The retreat was another major turning point in the war. Never again were the weakened Confederate forces able seriously to threaten Northern territory.

Before the end of the year, there was another important turning point, this one in Tennessee. After occupying Chattanooga on September 9, Union forces under William Rosecrans began an unwise pursuit of Bragg's retreating Confederate forces. Bragg was waiting for them just across the Georgia line, with reinforcements from Lee's army. The two armies engaged in the Battle of Chickamauga (September 19–20), one of the few battles in which the Confederates enjoyed a numerical superiority (70,000 to 56,000). Union forces could not break the Confederate lines and retreated back to Chattanooga.

Bragg now began a siege of Chattanooga itself, seizing the heights nearby and cutting off fresh supplies to the Union forces. Grant came to the rescue. In the Battle of Chattanooga (November 23–25), the reinforced Union army drove the Confederates back into Georgia. Northern troops

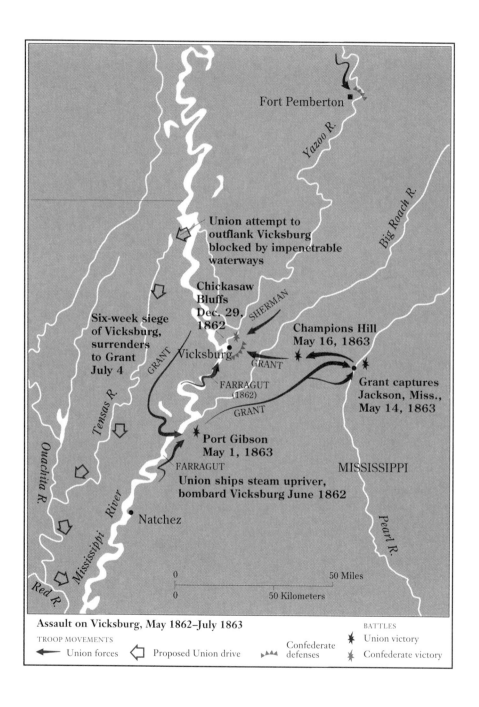

Fort Pemberton

*Yazoo R.*

*Big Roach R.*

Union attempt to outflank Vicksburg blocked by impenetrable waterways

Chickasaw Bluffs Dec. 29, 1862

SHERMAN

Six-week siege of Vicksburg, surrenders to Grant July 4

GRANT

Vicksburg

Champions Hill May 16, 1863

GRANT

FARRAGUT (1862)

GRANT

Grant captures Jackson, Miss., May 14, 1863

*Tensas R.*

*Ouachita R.*

Port Gibson May 1, 1863

FARRAGUT

Union ships steam upriver, bombard Vicksburg June 1862

MISSISSIPPI

*Mississippi River*

Natchez

*Pearl R.*

*Red R.*

| 0 | | 50 Miles |

| 0 | | 50 Kilometers |

**Assault on Vicksburg, May 1862–July 1863**

TROOP MOVEMENTS

◄— Union forces ◁ Proposed Union drive ►▲▲▲ Confederate defenses

BATTLES

✸ Union victory

✹ Confederate victory

The Battle of Gettysburg, July 1–3, 1863

TROOP MOVEMENTS
← Union (Federal) forces
← Confederate forces

TROOP POSITIONS
■ Union forces
■ Confederate forces
— Roads

then occupied most of eastern Tennessee. Union forces had now achieved a second important objective: control of the Tennessee River. Four of the eleven Confederate states were now effectively cut off from the Southern nation. No longer could the Confederacy hope to win independence through a decisive military victory. It could hope to win only by holding on and exhausting the Northern will to fight.

## The Last Stage, 1864–1865

By the beginning of 1864, Ulysses S. Grant had become general in chief of all the Union armies. At long last, the president had found a general whom he could rely on to pursue the war doggedly and tenaciously. Grant was not a subtle strategic or tactical general; he simply believed in using the North's great advantage in troops and material resources to overwhelm the South. He was not afraid to absorb massive casualties as long as he was inflicting similar or greater casualties on his opponents.

Grant planned two great offensives for 1864. In Virginia, the Army of the Potomac would advance toward Richmond and force Lee into a decisive battle. In Georgia, the western army, under William T. Sherman, would advance east toward Atlanta and destroy the remaining Confederate force, which was now under the command of Joseph E. Johnston.

The northern campaign began when the Army of the Potomac, 115,000 strong, plunged into the rough, wooded Wilderness area of northwestern Virginia in pursuit of Lee's 75,000-man army. After avoiding an engagement for several weeks, Lee turned Grant back in the Battle of the Wilderness (May 5–7). But Grant was undeterred. Without stopping to rest or reorganize, he resumed his march toward Richmond. He met Lee again in the bloody, five-day Battle of Spotsylvania Court House, in which 12,000 Union

ULYSSES S. GRANT  One observer said of Grant (photographed here during the Wilderness campaign of 1864): "He habitually wears an expression as if he had determined to drive his head through a brick wall, and was about to do it." It was an apt metaphor for Grant's military philosophy, which relied on constant, unrelenting assault.

troops and a large, but unknown, number of Confederates fell. Despite the enormous losses, Grant kept moving. But victory continued to elude him. Lee kept his army between Grant and the Confederate capital and on June 1–3 repulsed the Union forces again, just northeast of Richmond, at Cold Harbor. The month-long Wilderness campaign had cost Grant 55,000 men (killed, wounded, or captured) compared with Lee's 31,000. And Richmond still had not fallen.

Grant now changed his strategy. He moved his army east of Richmond, bypassing the capital altogether, and headed south toward the railroad center at Petersburg. If he could seize Petersburg, he could cut off the capital's communications with the rest of the Confederacy. But Petersburg had strong defenses; and once Lee came to the city's relief, the assault became a prolonged siege, which lasted nine months.

In Georgia, meanwhile, Sherman was facing a less ferocious resistance. With 90,000 men, he confronted Confederate forces of 60,000 under Johnston, who was unwilling to risk a direct engagement. As Sherman advanced, Johnston tried to delay him by maneuvering. The two armies fought only one real battle—Kennesaw Mountain, northwest of Atlanta, on June 27—where Johnston scored an impressive victory. Even so, he was unable to stop the Union advance toward Atlanta. Davis replaced Johnston with the combative John B. Hood, who twice daringly attacked Sherman's army but accomplished little except seriously weakening his own forces. Sherman took Atlanta on September 2. News of the victory electrified the North and helped unite the previously divided Republican Party behind President Lincoln.

Hood now tried unsuccessfully to draw Sherman out of Atlanta by moving back up through Tennessee and threatening an invasion of the North. Sherman did not take the bait. But he did send Union troops to reinforce Nashville. In the Battle of Nashville on December 15–16, 1864, Northern forces practically destroyed what was left of Hood's army.

Meanwhile, Sherman had left Atlanta to begin his soon-to-be-famous "March to the Sea." Living off the land, destroying supplies it could not use, his army cut a sixty-mile-wide swath of desolation across Georgia. "War is all hell," Sherman had once said. By that he meant not that war is terrible, and to be avoided, but that it should be made as horrible and costly as possible for the opponent. He sought not only to deprive the Confederate army of war materials and railroad communications but also to break the will of the Southern people by burning towns and plantations along his route. By December 20, he had reached Savannah, which surrendered two days later. Sherman offered it to President Lincoln as a Christmas gift. Early in 1865, Sherman continued his destructive march, moving northward through South

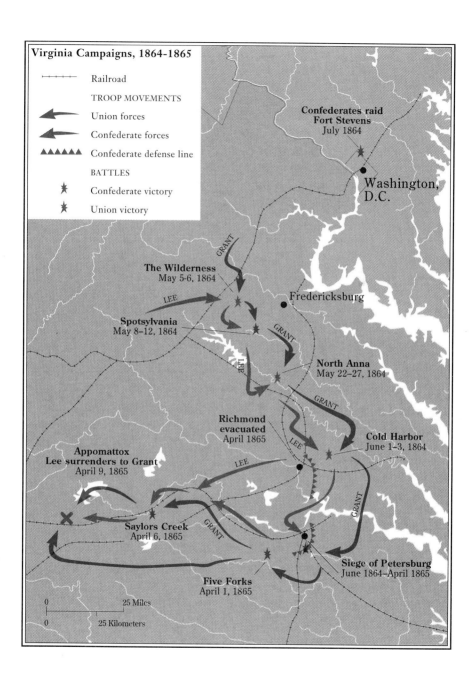

**Virginia Campaigns, 1864-1865**

Railroad

TROOP MOVEMENTS

Union forces

Confederate forces

Confederate defense line

BATTLES

Confederate victory

Union victory

Confederates raid
Fort Stevens
July 1864

Washington,
D.C.

GRANT

The Wilderness
May 5-6, 1864

Fredericksburg

LEE

Spotsylvania
May 8–12, 1864

GRANT

North Anna
May 22–27, 1864

LEE

GRANT

Richmond
evacuated
April 1865

LEE

Cold Harbor
June 1-3, 1864

Appomattox
Lee surrenders to Grant
April 9, 1865

LEE

Saylors Creek
April 6, 1865

GRANT

GRANT

Siege of Petersburg
June 1864–April 1865

Five Forks
April 1, 1865

0          25 Miles

0          25 Kilometers

Carolina. He was virtually unopposed until he was well inside North Carolina, where a small force under Johnston could do no more than cause a brief delay.

In April 1865, Grant's Army of the Potomac—still engaged in the prolonged siege at Petersburg—finally captured a vital railroad junction southwest of the town. Without rail access to the South, cut off from other Confederate forces, plagued by heavy casualties and massive desertions, Lee informed the Confederate government that he could no longer defend Richmond. Within hours, Jefferson Davis, his cabinet, and as much of the white population as could find transportation fled along with Lee's soldiers. That night, mobs roamed the city, setting devastating fires. And the next morning, Northern forces (led by an African-American infantry brigade) entered the Confederate capital. With them was Abraham Lincoln, who walked through the streets of the burned-out city surrounded by black men and women cheering him as the "Messiah" and "Father Abraham." In one particularly stirring moment, the president turned to a former slave kneeling on the street before him and said: "Don't kneel to me. . . . You must kneel to God only, and thank Him for the liberty you will enjoy hereafter."

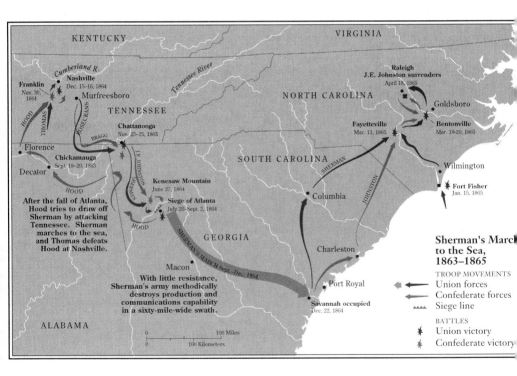

# A M E R I C A N   V O I C E S

### J. J. HILL

## *The 29th Connecticut Colored Infantry Enters Richmond, April 1865*

ALL WAS QUIET here until the 1st of April, when all was in readiness, and the order was given to strike tents and move on to Richmond. . . . On our march to Richmond, we captured 500 pieces of artillery, some of the largest kind, 6,000 stand of small arms, and the prisoners I was not able to number. The road was strewed with all kinds of obstacles, and men were lying all along the distance of seven miles. The main body of the army went up the New Market road. The 29th skirmished all the way, and arrived in the city at 7 A.M., and were the first infantry that entered the city. . . .

The 3rd [of April] President Lincoln visited the city. No triumphal march of a conqueror could have equalled in moral sublimity the humble manner in which he entered Richmond. I was standing on the bank of the James River viewing the scene of desolation when a boat, pulled by twelve sailors, came up the stream. It contained President Lincoln and his son. In some way the colored people on the bank of the river ascertained that the tall man wearing the black hat was President Lincoln. . . . As he approached, I said to a woman, "Madam, that is the man that made you free." . . . She gazed at him with clasped hands and said, "Glory to God, Give him the praise for his goodness," and she shouted till her voice failed her. . . . It was a man of the people among the people. It was a great deliverer among the delivered. No wonder tears came to his eyes. . . . After visiting Jeff Davis's Mansion, he proceeded to the rebel capital and from the steps delivered a short speech to the colored people as follows: ". . . God has made you free. Although you have been deprived of your God-given rights by your so-called masters, you are now as free as I am, and if those that claim to be your superiors do not know that you are free, take the sword and bayonet and teach them that you are—for God created all men free, giving to each the same rights of life, liberty, and the pursuit of happiness."

With the remnant of his army, now about 25,000 men, Lee began moving west in the forlorn hope of finding a way around the Union forces so that he could move south and link up with Johnston in North Carolina. But the Union army pursued him and blocked his escape route. Lee finally recognized that further bloodshed was futile. He arranged to meet Grant at a private home in the small town of Appomattox Courthouse, Virginia, where on April 9 he surrendered what was left of his forces. Nine days later, near Durham, North Carolina, Johnston surrendered to Sherman.

In military terms, at least, the long war was now effectively over, even though Jefferson Davis refused to accept defeat. He moved south after leaving Richmond, hoping to reach Texas and continue the struggle from there. He was finally captured in Georgia. A few Southern diehards continued to fight, but even their resistance collapsed before long. And well before the last shot was fired, the difficult process of reuniting the shattered nation had begun.

D E B A T I N G    T H E    P A S T

## The Causes of the Civil War

HE OUTLINES OF the scholarly debate over the causes of the Civil War became visible even before the war itself began. In 1858, Senator William H. Seward of New York took note of the two competing explanations of the sectional tensions that were then inflaming the nation. On one side, he said, stood those who believed the conflicts to be "accidental, unnecessary, the work of interested or fanatical agitators." Opposing them stood those (among them Seward himself) who believed there to be "an irrepressible conflict between opposing and enduring forces." Without realizing it, Seward had identified a division of opinion that would survive among historians for more than a century.

The irrepressible-conflict argument dominated historical discussion of the war from the 1860s to the 1920s. War was inevitable, some historians claimed, because there was no room for compromise on the central issue of slavery. Others de-emphasized slavery and pointed to the economic differences between the agrarian South and the industrializing North. Charles and Mary Beard, for example, wrote in 1927 of the "inherent antagonisms" between the interests of planters and those of industrialists. Each group was seeking to control the federal government to promote its own economic interests. Still others cited social and cultural differences between the two sections as the source of an irrepressible conflict. Slavery, the historian Allan Nevins argued, was only one factor in the cultural divergence that was making residents of the North and South "separate peoples." There were fundamental differences in "assumptions, tastes, and cultural aims" that made it virtually impossible for the two societies to live together in peace.

*(continued on next page)*

More recent proponents of "irrepressible-conflict" arguments similarly emphasize culture and ideology but define the concerns of the North and the South in different terms. Eric Foner, writing in 1970, argued that the moral concerns of abolitionists and the economic concerns of industrialists were less important in explaining Northern hostility to the South than was the broad-based "free-labor" ideology of the region. Northerners opposed slavery because they feared it might spread into their own region and threaten the position of free white laborers. Hence their insistence that it not be allowed to expand into the West.

Other historians have taken a very different view of the Civil War. Rather than arguing over what factors made the war inevitable, they have suggested that the differences between North and South were not so great as to require a conflict. The modern version of this position began to emerge in the 1920s, among a group known as the "revisionists." James G. Randall, for example, saw in the social and economic systems of the North and the South no differences so fundamental as to require a war. By the time the war began, he argued, slavery was already "crumbling in the presence of nineteenth century tendencies." The failures of a "blundering generation" of political leaders, not irrepressible differences, caused the Civil War. Avery Craven, writing in 1942, argued similarly that slavery was on the road to "ultimate extinction" and that skillful and responsible leaders could have produced a compromise solution that would have avoided war. David Donald, writing in 1960, agreed with Randall and Craven that compromise should have been possible. He was less critical than they of the political leaders of the 1850s; he argued, rather, that the rapid extension of democracy in both North and South had made it more difficult for "statesmen" to guard against popular passions. Michael Holt revived the "revisionist" argument in a 1978 book, in which he too emphasized the partisan ambitions of politicians who used sectional rivalries to advance their own aims. "Much of the story of the coming of the Civil War," he argued, "is the story of the successful efforts of Democratic politicians in the South and Republican politicians in the North to keep the sectional conflict at the center of the political debate."

Like the proponents of the "irrepressible conflict" interpretation, the "revisionists" have differed among themselves in important ways. But the explanation of the coming of the Civil War continues, more than a century later, to reflect the two schools of thought William Seward identified in 1858.

# CHAPTER FIFTEEN

# Reconstruction and the New South

EW PERIODS IN the history of the United States have produced as much bitterness or created such enduring controversy as the era of Reconstruction—the years following the Civil War during which Americans attempted to reunite their shattered nation. Those who lived through Reconstruction viewed it in sharply different ways. To many white Southerners, it was a vicious and destructive experience—a period when vindictive Northerners inflicted humiliation and revenge on the prostrate South and unnecessarily delayed a genuine reunion of the sections. Northern defenders of Reconstruction, in contrast, argued that their policies were the only way to prevent unrepentant Confederates from restoring Southern society as it had been before the war; without forceful federal intervention, there would be no way to forestall the reemergence of a backward aristocracy and the continued subjugation of former slaves—no way, in other words, to prevent the same sectional problems that had produced the Civil War in the first place.

To most African Americans at the time, and to many people of all races since, Reconstruction was notable for other reasons. Neither a vicious tyranny, as white Southerners charged, nor a thoroughgoing reform, as many Northerners claimed, it was, rather, a small but important first step in the effort to secure civil rights and economic power for the former slaves. Reconstruction did not provide African Americans with either the legal protections or the material resources to assure them anything like real equality. And when it came to an end in the late 1870s—as a result of an economic crisis, a lack of political will in the North, and organized, at times violent, resistance by white Southerners—the freed slaves found themselves abandoned by the federal government to face a system of economic peonage and

## TIME LINE

| 1863 | 1864 | 1865 | 1866 | 1867 |
|---|---|---|---|---|
| Lincoln announces Reconstruction plan | Lincoln vetoes Wade-Davis bill | Lincoln assassinated; Johnson becomes president | Republicans gain in congressional elections | Congressional Reconstruction begins |
|  |  | Freedmen's Bureau established |  |  |
|  |  | Joint Committee on Reconstruction established |  |  |

| 1868 | 1869 | 1872 | 1873 | 1875 |
|---|---|---|---|---|
| Grant elected president | Congress passes 15th Amendment | Grant reelected | Panic and depression | "Whiskey ring" scandal |

| 1877 | 1883 | 1890s | 1895 | 1896 |
|---|---|---|---|---|
| Hayes wins disputed election | Supreme Court upholds segregation | Jim Crow laws in South | Atlanta Compromise | *Plessy* v. *Ferguson* |
| Compromise of 1877 ends Reconstruction |  |  |  |  |

legal subordination. For the remainder of the nineteenth century, those black men and women who continued to live in what came to be known as the New South had little power to resist their oppression.

And yet for all its shortcomings, Reconstruction did help African Americans create institutions and legal precedents that helped them survive and that ultimately, well into the twentieth century, became the basis of later efforts to win freedom and equality.

## THE PROBLEMS OF PEACEMAKING

In 1865, when it became clear that the war was almost over, no one in Washington knew quite what to do. Abraham Lincoln could not negotiate a treaty with the defeated government; he continued to insist that the Confederate government had no legal right to exist. Yet neither could he simply readmit the Southern states into the Union as if nothing had happened.

### *The Aftermath of War and Emancipation*

The South after the Civil War was a desolate place. Towns had been gutted, plantations burned, fields neglected, bridges and railroads destroyed. Many white Southerners—stripped of their slaves through emancipation and stripped of the capital they had invested in now worthless Confederate bonds and currency—had almost no personal property. More than 258,000 Confederate soldiers had died in the war, and thousands more returned home wounded or sick. Many families had to rebuild their fortunes without the help of adult males. Some white Southerners faced starvation and homelessness.

If conditions were bad for Southern whites, they were far worse for Southern blacks—the 4 million men and women now emerging from

CHARLESTON, 1865  Not until 1864 did substantial fighting and destruction begin to take place in the urban South. But in the last year of the war, several major cities (and many towns and smaller communities) experienced devastation at the hands of the Northern armies—among them Richmond, Atlanta, and (as seen here) Charleston.

bondage. As soon as the war ended, hundreds of thousands of them—young and old, many of them ill and feeble—left the plantations in search of a new life in freedom. But most had nowhere to go, and few had any possessions except the clothes they wore.

Despite the disarray of Southern society, almost everyone faced the future with some very clear aspirations. For blacks and whites alike, Reconstruction became a struggle to define the meaning of freedom. But the former slaves and the defeated whites had very different conceptions of what freedom meant.

For African Americans, freedom meant above all an end to slavery. But it also meant acquiring rights and protections that would enable them to live as free people, just as whites did. Some blacks believed the only way to secure freedom was to have the government take land away from white people, who owned virtually all of it, and give it to black people, who owned virtually none. Others asked only for legal equality, confident that they could advance successfully in American society once the formal obstacles to their advancement disappeared. But whatever their particular demands, virtually all former slaves were united in their desire for independence from white control. Throughout the post–Civil War South, African Americans separated themselves from white institutions—pulling out of white-controlled churches and establishing their own, creating clubs and societies for their own people, in some cases starting their own schools.

For most white Southerners, freedom meant something very different. It meant the ability to control their own destinies without interference from the North or the federal government. And in the immediate aftermath of the war, they attempted to exercise this version of freedom by trying to restore their society to its antebellum form. When these white Southerners fought for what they considered freedom, they were fighting above all to preserve local and regional autonomy and white supremacy.

The federal government kept troops in the South to preserve order and protect the freedmen. And in March 1865, Congress established the Freedmen's Bureau, an agency of the army directed by General Oliver O. Howard. The Freedmen's Bureau distributed food to millions of former slaves. It established schools, staffed by missionaries and teachers who had been sent to the South by Freedmen's Aid Societies and other private and church groups in the North. It made a modest effort to settle blacks on lands of their own. (The bureau also offered considerable assistance to poor whites, many of whom were similarly destitute and homeless after the war.) But the Freedmen's Bureau was not a permanent solution. It had authority to operate for only one year, and it was, in any case, far too small to deal effectively with the enormous problems facing Southern society. By the time the war ended, other proposals for reconstructing the defeated South were emerging.

### Plans for Reconstruction

Most Democrats favored a Reconstruction process that would readmit the former Confederate states to the Union quickly and painlessly. (That was in part because the Democratic Party had the most to gain from the readmission of the South, most of whose voters were likely to be Democrats.) But control of Reconstruction remained largely in the hands of the Republicans, who had substantial majorities in both houses of Congress. And the Republicans were divided in their approach to the issue. Conservatives within the party insisted that the South accept the abolition of slavery, but they proposed few other conditions for the readmission of the seceded states. The Radicals, led by Representative Thaddeus Stevens of Pennsylvania and Senator Charles Sumner of Massachusetts, urged a much harsher course, including disenfranchising large numbers of Southern whites, protecting black civil rights, and confiscating the property of wealthy white Southerners who had aided the Confederacy and distributing the land among the freedmen. There was also a group of Republican Moderates, who rejected the most stringent demands of the Radicals but supported extracting at least some concessions from the South on black rights.

President Lincoln's sympathies lay with the Moderates and Conservatives of his party. He favored a lenient Reconstruction policy, and he believed that Southern Unionists (mostly former Whigs) could become the nucleus of new, loyal state governments in the South. Lincoln announced his Reconstruction plan in December 1863, more than a year before the war ended. It offered a general amnesty to white Southerners—other than high officials of the Confederacy—who would pledge an oath of loyalty to the government and accept the elimination of slavery. When 10 percent of a state's total number of voters in 1860 took the oath, those loyal voters could set up a state government. Lincoln also proposed extending suffrage to those blacks who were educated, owned property, and had served in the Union army. Three Southern states—Louisiana, Arkansas, and Tennessee, all under Union occupation—reestablished loyal governments under the Lincoln formula in 1864.

The Radical Republicans were outraged at the mildness of Lincoln's program and refused to admit representatives from the three "reconstructed"

ABRAHAM LINCOLN  Lincoln was the subject of many
photographic portraits, of which this one, by
Mathew Brady, is one of the most famous.

states to Congress. In July 1864, they pushed their own plan through Congress in the form of the Wade-Davis Bill. It called for the president to appoint a provisional governor for each conquered state. When a majority (not Lincoln's 10 percent) of the white males of a state pledged their allegiance to the Union, the governor could summon a state constitutional convention, whose delegates were to be elected by voters who had never borne arms against the United States (again, a major departure from Lincoln's plan). The new state constitutions would be required to abolish slavery, disenfranchise Confederate civil and military leaders, and repudiate debts accumulated by the state governments during the war. Only then would Congress readmit the states to the Union. Like the president's proposal, the Wade-Davis Bill left up to the states the question of political rights for blacks.

Congress passed the bill a few days before it adjourned in 1864, and Lincoln disposed of it with a pocket veto. His action enraged the Radical leaders, and the pragmatic Lincoln realized he would have to accept at least some of the Radical demands. In the first weeks of 1865, he began to move toward a new approach to Reconstruction.

## The Death of Lincoln

What plan he might have produced no one can say. On the night of April 14, 1865, Lincoln and his wife attended a play at Ford's Theater in Washington. As they sat in the presidential box, John Wilkes Booth, an actor obsessed with aiding the Southern cause, entered the box from the rear and shot Lincoln in the head. Early the next morning, the president died.

The circumstances of Lincoln's death earned him immediate martyrdom. They also produced something close to hysteria throughout the North, especially because it quickly became clear that Booth had been the leader of a conspiracy. One of his associates shot and wounded Secretary of State William Seward on the night of the assassination, and another abandoned at the last moment a scheme to murder Vice President Andrew Johnson. Booth himself escaped on horseback into the Maryland countryside, where, on April 26, he was cornered by Union troops and shot to death in a blazing barn. Eight other people were convicted by a military tribunal of participating in the conspiracy (at least two of them on the basis of virtually no evidence). Four were hanged.

To many Northerners, however, the murder of the president seemed evidence of an even greater conspiracy—one masterminded and directed by the unrepentant leaders of the defeated South. Militant Republicans exploited such suspicions relentlessly in the ensuing months, ensuring that Lincoln's death would help doom his plans for a relatively easy peace.

## Johnson and "Restoration"

Leadership of the Moderates and Conservatives fell to Lincoln's successor, Andrew Johnson of Tennessee, who was not well suited, either by circumstance or personality, for the task. A Democrat until he had joined the Union ticket with Lincoln in 1864, he became president at a time of growing partisan passions. And Johnson himself was an intemperate and tactless man, filled with resentments and insecurities.

Johnson revealed his plan for Reconstruction—or "Restoration," as he preferred to call it—soon after he took office, and he implemented it during the summer of 1865 when Congress was in recess. Like Lincoln, he offered some form of amnesty to Southerners who would take an oath of allegiance. In most other respects, however, his plan resembled that of the Wade-Davis Bill. The president appointed a provisional governor in each state and charged him with inviting qualified voters to elect delegates to a constitutional convention. In order to win readmission to Congress, a state had to revoke its ordinance of secession, abolish slavery and ratify the Thirteenth Amendment, and repudiate Confederate and state war debts—essentially the same terms as in Wade-Davis.

By the end of 1865, all the seceded states had formed new governments—some under Lincoln's plan, some under Johnson's—and awaited congressional approval of them. But Radicals in Congress vowed not to recognize the Johnson governments, just as they had previously refused to recognize the Lincoln regimes, for by now, Northern opinion had become more hostile toward the South than it had been a year earlier when Congress passed the Wade-Davis Bill. Delegates to the Southern conventions had angered much of the North by their apparent reluctance to abolish slavery and by their refusal to grant suffrage to any blacks. Southern states had elected prominent Confederate leaders to represent them in Congress, among them Alexander H. Stephens, former vice president of the Confederacy, who was selected as a United States senator from Georgia.

## RADICAL RECONSTRUCTION

Reconstruction under Johnson's plan—often known as "presidential Reconstruction"—continued only until Congress reconvened in December 1865. At that point, Congress refused to seat the representatives of the "restored" states and created a new Joint Committee on Reconstruction to frame a Reconstruction policy of its own. The period of "congressional" or "Radical" Reconstruction had begun.

### The Black Codes

Meanwhile, events in the South were driving Northern opinion in even more radical directions. Throughout the South in 1865 and early 1866, state legislatures were enacting sets of laws known as the Black Codes, designed to give whites substantial control over former slaves. The codes authorized local officials to apprehend unemployed blacks, fine them for vagrancy, and hire them out to private employers to satisfy the fine. Some of the codes forbade blacks to own or lease farms or to take any jobs other than as plantation workers or domestic servants. To many Northerners, and to most African Americans, the Black Codes represented a return to slavery in all but name.

Congress first responded to the Black Codes by passing an act extending the life of the Freedmen's Bureau and widening its powers. The bureau could now establish special courts, which could nullify work agreements forced on freedmen under the Black Codes. Then, in April, Congress passed the first Civil Rights Act, which declared blacks to be citizens of the United States and gave the federal government power to intervene in state affairs to protect the rights of citizens. Johnson vetoed both the Freedmen's Bureau and Civil Rights Acts, but Congress overrode him.

### The Fourteenth Amendment

In April 1866, the Joint Committee on Reconstruction proposed a new amendment to the Constitution, which Congress approved in early summer and sent to the states for ratification. Eventually, it became one of the most important of all the provisions in the Constitution.

The Fourteenth Amendment offered the first constitutional definition of American citizenship. Everyone born in the United States, and everyone naturalized, was automatically a citizen and entitled to all the "privileges and immunities" guaranteed by the Constitution, including equal protection of the laws by both the state and national governments. There could be no other requirements for citizenship. The amendment also imposed penalties—reduction of representation in Congress and in the electoral college—on states that denied suffrage to any adult male inhabitants. (The wording reflected the prevailing view in Congress and elsewhere that the franchise was properly restricted to men.) Finally, it prohibited former members of Congress or other former federal officials who had aided the Confederacy from holding any state or federal office unless two-thirds of Congress voted to pardon them.

Congressional Radicals offered to readmit to the Union any state whose legislature ratified the Fourteenth Amendment. Only Tennessee did so. All the other former Confederate states, along with Delaware and Kentucky, refused to do so. That denied the amendment the necessary approval of three-fourths of the states and temporarily derailed it.

But in the meantime, the Radicals were growing more confident and determined. Bloody race riots in New Orleans and other Southern cities—riots in which blacks were the principal victims—were among the events that strengthened their hand. In the 1866 congressional elections, Johnson actively campaigned for Conservative candidates, but he did his own cause more harm than good with his intemperate speeches. The voters returned an overwhelming majority of Republicans, most of them Radicals, to Congress. In the Senate, there were now 42 Republicans to 11 Democrats; in the House, 143 Republicans to 49 Democrats. (The South remained largely unrepresented in both chambers.) Congressional Republicans, who until this point had served mainly as an obstacle to the president's plans for Reconstruction, were now strong enough to produce a plan of their own.

## The Congressional Plan

The Radicals passed three Reconstruction bills early in 1867 and overrode Johnson's vetoes of all of them. These bills established finally, nearly two years after the end of the war, a coherent plan for Reconstruction.

Under the congressional plan, Tennessee, which had ratified the Fourteenth Amendment, was promptly readmitted. But Congress rejected the Lincoln-Johnson governments of the other ten Confederate states and, instead, combined those states into five military districts. A military commander governed each district and had orders to register qualified voters (defined as all adult black males and those white males who had not participated in the rebellion). Once registered, voters would elect conventions to prepare new state constitutions, which had to include provisions for black suffrage. Once voters ratified the new constitutions, they could elect state governments. Congress had to approve a state's constitution, and the state legislature had to ratify the Fourteenth Amendment. Once that happened, and once enough states ratified the amendment to make it part of the Constitution, then the former Confederate states could be restored to the Union.

By 1868, seven of the ten former Confederate states (Arkansas, North Carolina, South Carolina, Louisiana, Alabama, Georgia, and Florida) had fulfilled these conditions (including ratification of the Fourteenth Amendment, which now became part of the Constitution) and were readmitted to the Union. Conservative whites held up the return of Virginia and Texas until 1869 and Mississippi until 1870. By then, Congress had added an additional requirement for readmission—ratification of another constitutional amendment, the Fifteenth, which forbade the states and the federal government to deny suffrage to any citizen on account of "race, color, or previous condition of servitude." Several Northern and border states refused to approve the Fifteenth Amendment, and it was adopted only with the support of the three Southern states that had to ratify it in order to be readmitted to the Union.

To stop the president from interfering with their plans, the congressional Radicals passed two remarkable laws of dubious constitutionality in 1867. One, the Tenure of Office Act, forbade the president to remove civil officials, including members of his own cabinet, without the consent of the Senate. The principal purpose of the law was to protect the job of Secretary of

A CELEBRATION OF RECONSTRUCTION  The celebrated
cartoonist Thomas Nast—best known for his savage
caricatures of machine politicians in New York's Tammany
Hall—drew this celebratory, and optimistic, image of
Reconstruction not long after the end of the
Civil War: a classical goddess restoring the former
Confederate states to their rightful place within symbolic
fasces that represented union. In fact, the Reconstruction
process proved much more difficult than this hopeful
image suggested.

War Edwin M. Stanton, who was the only Lincoln appointee still in Johnson's cabinet and who was cooperating with the Radicals. The other law, the
Command of the Army Act, prohibited the president from issuing military
orders except through the commanding general of the army (General Grant),
whose headquarters were to be in Washington and who could not be relieved
or assigned elsewhere without the consent of the Senate.

The congressional Radicals also took action to stop the Supreme Court from interfering with their plans. In 1866, the Court had declared in the case of *Ex parte Milligan* that military tribunals were unconstitutional in places where civil courts were functioning, a decision that seemed to threaten the system of military government the Radicals were planning for the South. Radicals in Congress immediately proposed several bills that would require two-thirds of the justices to support any decision overruling a law of Congress, would deny the Court jurisdiction in Reconstruction cases, would reduce its membership to three, and would even abolish it. The justices apparently took notice. Over the next two years, the Court refused to accept jurisdiction in any cases involving Reconstruction (and the congressional bills concerning the Court never passed).

## The Impeachment of the President

President Johnson had long since ceased to be a serious obstacle to the passage of Radical legislation, but he was still the official charged with administering the Reconstruction programs. As such, the Radicals believed, he remained a serious impediment to their plans. Early in 1867, they began looking for a way to get rid of him. Under the Constitution, Congress could impeach a President and remove him from office only for "high crimes or misdemeanors," so Republicans were seeking a basis for such charges. Johnson finally gave them what they considered a plausible reason for impeachment when he dismissed Secretary of War Stanton despite Congress's refusal to agree, thus deliberately violating the Tenure of Office Act in hopes of testing the law before the courts. Elated Radicals in the House quickly impeached the president on eleven charges and sent the case to the Senate for trial. Nine counts dealt with the violation of the Tenure of Office Act. The others charged Johnson with slandering Congress and not enforcing the Reconstruction Acts.

The trial before the Senate lasted throughout April and May 1868. The Radicals put heavy pressure on all the Republican senators, but the Moderates (who were losing faith in the Radical program) vacillated. On the first three charges to come to a vote, seven Republicans joined the twelve Democrats to support acquittal. The vote was 35 to 19, one short of the constitutionally required two-thirds majority. After that, the Radicals dropped the impeachment campaign.

# THE SOUTH IN RECONSTRUCTION

When white Southerners spoke bitterly in later years of the effects of Reconstruction, they referred most frequently to the governments Congress imposed on them—governments that were, they claimed, both incompetent and corrupt, that saddled the region with enormous debts, and that trampled on the rights of citizens. When black Southerners and their defenders condemned Reconstruction, in contrast, they spoke of its failure to guarantee to freedmen even the most elemental rights of citizenship—a failure that resulted in a new and cruel system of economic subordination.

## *The Reconstruction Governments*

In the ten states of the South that were reorganized under the congressional plan, approximately one-fourth of the white males were at first excluded from voting or holding office, which produced black majorities among voters in South Carolina, Mississippi, and Louisiana (where blacks were also a majority of the population) and in Alabama and Florida (where they were not). But federal officials soon lifted most suffrage restrictions so that nearly all white males could vote. After that, Republicans could maintain control only with a combination of black and white support.

Critics labeled Southern white Republicans with the derogatory terms "scalawags" and "carpetbaggers." Many of the "scalawags" were former Whigs who had never felt comfortable in the Democratic Party or farmers who lived in remote areas where there had been little or no slavery; most of these Republicans hoped the party's program of internal improvements would help end their economic isolation. The "carpetbaggers" were white men from the North, most of them veterans of the Union army who looked on the South as a new frontier, more promising than the West. They had settled there at war's end as hopeful planters, businessmen, or professionals.

The most numerous Republicans in the South were the black freedmen, most of whom had no previous experience in politics and tried, therefore, to build institutions through which they could learn to exercise their power. In several states, African-American voters held their own conventions to chart their future course. One such "colored convention," as Southern whites called it, assembled in Alabama in 1867 and announced: "We claim exactly the same rights, privileges and immunities as are enjoyed by white men—we ask nothing more and will be content with nothing less." The black churches freedmen created after emancipation, when they withdrew from the white-dominated churches they had been compelled to attend under slavery, also helped give them unity and political self-confidence.

African Americans played a significant role in the politics of the Reconstruction South. They served as delegates to the constitutional conventions. They held public offices of practically every kind. Between 1869 and 1901, twenty blacks served in the United States House of Representatives, two in the Senate. They served, too, in state legislatures and in various other state offices. Southern whites complained loudly (both at the time and for generations to come) about "Negro rule" during Reconstruction, but no such thing ever actually existed in any of the states. No black man was ever elected governor of a Southern state (although P. B. S. Pinchback, the African-American lieutenant governor of Louisiana, was acting governor briefly). Blacks never controlled any of the state legislatures (although African Americans did once win a majority of seats in South Carolina's lower house). In the South as a whole, the percentage of black officeholders was always far lower than the percentage of blacks in the population.

The record of the Reconstruction governments is mixed. Critics at the time and later denounced them for corruption and financial extravagance, and there is some truth to both charges. Officeholders in many states enriched themselves through graft and other illicit activities. State budgets expanded to hitherto unknown totals, and state debts soared to previously undreamed-of heights. But the corruption in the South, real as it was, was hardly unique to the Reconstruction governments. Corruption had been rife in some antebellum and Confederate governments, and it was at least as rampant in the Northern states. In some of the Southern state governments, moreover, corruption continued and even grew worse after the end of Reconstruction.

The large state expenditures of the Reconstruction years were huge only in comparison with the meager budgets of the antebellum era. They represented an effort to provide the South with desperately needed services that antebellum governments had never offered: public education, public works programs, poor relief, and other costly new commitments. There were, to be sure, graft and extravagance in Reconstruction governments; there were also positive and permanent accomplishments.

Perhaps the most important of those accomplishments was a dramatic improvement in Southern education—an improvement that benefited both whites and blacks. In the first years of Reconstruction, much of the impetus for educational reform in the South came from outside groups—from the Freedmen's Bureau, from Northern private philanthropic organizations, from the many Northern white women who traveled to the South to teach in freedmen's schools—and from African Americans themselves. Over the opposition of many Southern whites, who feared that education would give blacks "false notions of equality," these reformers established a large network of schools for former slaves—4,000 schools by 1870, staffed by 9,000 teachers (half of them black), teaching 200,000 students (about 12 percent of the total school-age population of the freedmen). In the 1870s, Reconstruction governments began to build a comprehensive public school system in the South. By 1876, more than half of all white children and about 40 percent of all black children were attending schools in the South (although almost all such schools were racially segregated). Several black "academies," offering more advanced education, also began operating. Gradually, these academies grew into an important network of black colleges and universities.

### Landownership

The most ambitious goal of the Freedmen's Bureau, and of some Republican Radicals in Congress, was to reform landownership in the South. The effort failed. By June 1865, the bureau had settled nearly 10,000 black families on their own land—most of it drawn from abandoned plantations in areas occupied by the Union armies. By the end of that year, however, Southern plantation owners were returning and demanding the restoration of their property. President Johnson supported their demands, and the government eventually returned most of the confiscated lands to their original white owners. Congress never had much stomach for the idea of land redistribution, and the experiment quickly died.

Even so, the distribution of landownership in the South changed considerably in the postwar years. Among whites, there was a striking decline in landownership, from 80 percent before the war to 67 percent by the end of Reconstruction. Some whites lost their land because of unpaid debt or increased taxes; some left the marginal lands they had owned to move to more fertile areas, where they rented. Among blacks, during the same period, the proportion who owned land rose from virtually none to more than 20 percent.

Still, most blacks, and a growing minority of whites, did not own their own land during Reconstruction, and some who acquired land in the 1860s had lost it by the 1890s. Instead, they worked for others in one form or another. Many black agricultural laborers—perhaps 25 percent of the total—simply worked for wages. Most, however, became tenants of white landowners—that is, they worked their own plots of land and paid their landlords either a fixed rent or a share of their crop (hence the term "sharecropping").

AFTER SLAVERY Although most freed slaves remained agricultural laborers after Emancipation, a considerable number moved off the land in search of new occupations and new homes. For many, that meant living for some time without stable employment or a permanent home. This photograph from the late 1860s shows a group of former slaves at a county almshouse in the South.

The new system represented a repudiation by blacks of the gang-labor system of the antebellum plantation, in which slaves had lived and worked together under the direction of a master. As tenants and sharecroppers, blacks enjoyed at least a physical independence from their landlords and had the sense of working their own land, even if in most cases they could never hope to buy it. But tenantry also benefited landlords in some ways, relieving them of the cost of purchasing slaves and of any responsibility for the physical well-being of their workers.

### Incomes and Credit

In some respects, the postwar years were a period of remarkable economic progress for African Americans in the South. When the material benefits they had received under slavery are calculated as income, prewar blacks had earned about a 22 percent share of the profits of the plantation system. By the end of Reconstruction, they were earning 56 percent. Measured another way, the per capita income of blacks rose 46 percent between 1857 and

1879, while the per capita income of whites declined 35 percent. This represented one of the most significant redistributions of income in American history.

But those figures tell only part of the story. The black share of profits was increasing, but the total profits of Southern agriculture were declining—a result of the dislocations of the war and a reduction in the world market for cotton. And while African Americans were earning a greater return on their labor than they had under slavery, they were also working less. Women and children were less likely to labor in the fields than they had been in the past. Adult men tended to work shorter days. In all, the black labor force worked about one-third fewer hours during Reconstruction than it had been compelled to do under slavery—a reduction that brought the working schedule of blacks roughly into accord with that of white farm laborers. Nor did the income redistribution of the postwar years lift many blacks out of poverty. Black per capita income rose from about one-quarter of white per capita income to about one-half in the first few years after the war. After this initial increase, it rose hardly at all.

For blacks and poor whites alike, whatever gains there might have been as a result of land and income redistribution were often overshadowed by the ravages of the crop-lien system. Few of the traditional institutions of credit in the South—the "factors" and banks—returned after the war. In their stead emerged a new system of credit, centered in large part on local country stores—some of them owned by planters, others owned by independent merchants. Blacks and whites, landowners and tenants—all depended on these stores for such necessities as food, clothing, seed, and farm implements. And since farmers do not have the same steady cash flow as other workers, customers usually had to rely on credit from these merchants in order to purchase what they needed. Most local stores had no competition (and went to great lengths to ensure that things stayed that way). As a result, they were able to set interest rates as high as 50 or 60 percent. Farmers had to give the merchants a lien (or claim) on their crops as collateral for the loans (thus the term "crop-lien system," generally used to describe Southern farming in this period). Farmers who suffered a few bad years in a row, as many did, could become trapped in a cycle of debt from which they could never escape.

One effect of this burdensome credit system was that some blacks who had acquired land during the early years of Reconstruction gradually lost it as they fell into debt. So, to a lesser extent, did white small landowners. Another was that Southern farmers became almost wholly dependent on cash crops—and most of all on cotton—because only such marketable commodities seemed to offer any possibility of escape from debt. The relentless planting of cotton contributed to an exhaustion of the soil. The crop-lien system, in other words, was not only helping to impoverish small farmers; it was also contributing to a general decline in the Southern agricultural economy.

## The African-American Family in Freedom

One of the most striking features of the black response to Reconstruction was the effort to build or rebuild family structures and to protect them from the interference they had experienced under slavery. A major reason for the rapid departure of so many blacks from plantations was the desire to find lost relatives and reunite families. Thousands of African Americans wandered through the South looking for husbands, wives, children, or other relatives from whom they had been separated. Former slaves rushed to have their marriages, previously without legal standing, sanctified by church and law. Black families resisted living in the former slave quarters and moved instead to small cabins scattered widely across the countryside, where they could enjoy at least some privacy.

Within the black family, the definition of male and female roles quickly came to resemble that within white families. Many women and children ceased working in the fields. Such work, they believed, was a badge of slavery. Instead, many women restricted themselves largely to domestic tasks—cooking, cleaning, gardening, raising children, attending to the needs of their husbands. Still, economic necessity often compelled black women to engage in income-producing activities: working as domestic servants, taking in laundry, or helping their husbands in the fields. By the end of Reconstruction, half of all black women over the age of sixteen were working for wages. And unlike white working women, most black female income earners were married.

## THE GRANT ADMINISTRATION

Exhausted by the political turmoil of the Johnson administration, American voters in 1868 yearned for a strong, stable figure to guide them through the troubled years of Reconstruction. They did not find one. Instead, they turned trustingly to General Ulysses S. Grant, the hero of the war and, by 1868, a revered national idol. Grant was a disastrous president. During his two terms in office, he faced problems that would have taxed the abilities of a master of statecraft. Grant, however, had few political skills and little vision.

## The Soldier President

Grant could have had the nomination of either party in 1868. But believing that Republican Reconstruction policies were more attuned to public opinion than the Democratic alternatives, he accepted the Republican nomination. The Democrats nominated former governor Horatio Seymour of New York. The campaign was a bitter one, and Grant's triumph was surprisingly narrow. He carried twenty-six states to Seymour's eight, but his popular majority was a scant 310,000 votes. Without the 500,000 black Republican voters in the South, he would have had a minority of the popular vote.

Grant entered the White House with no political experience, and his performance was clumsy and ineffectual from the start. Except for Hamilton Fish, whom Grant appointed secretary of state and who served for eight years with great distinction, most members of the cabinet were as inept as the president. Grant relied chiefly, and increasingly, on the machine leaders in the party—the group most ardently devoted to the spoils system; consequently, his administration used the spoils system even more blatantly than most of his predecessors. The result was the emergence of a growing sentiment among reformers and others for a civil service system, which would fill many government positions on "merit" and not through patronage. Grant also attracted the hostility of many of his fellow Republicans, particularly as Northerners grew disillusioned with the Radical Reconstruction policies Grant continued to support. Some Republicans suspected, correctly, that there was also corruption in the Grant administration itself.

By the end of Grant's first term, therefore, members of a substantial faction of the party—who referred to themselves as Liberal Republicans—had come to oppose what they called "Grantism." In 1872, hoping to prevent Grant's reelection, they bolted the party and nominated their own presidential candidate: Horace Greeley, veteran editor and publisher of the New York *Tribune*. The Democrats, somewhat reluctantly, named Greeley their candidate as well, hoping that the alliance with the Liberals would enable them to defeat Grant. But the effort was in vain. Grant won a substantial victory, polling 286 electoral votes and 3,597,000 popular votes to Greeley's 66 and 2,834,000. Three weeks later, apparently crushed by his defeat, Greeley died.

## The Grant Scandals

During the 1872 campaign, the first of a series of political scandals came to light that would plague Grant and the Republicans for the next eight years.

It involved the French-owned Crédit Mobilier construction company, which had helped build the Union Pacific Railroad. The heads of Crédit Mobilier had used their positions as Union Pacific stockholders to steer large fraudulent contracts to their construction company, thus bilking the Union Pacific (and the federal government, which provided large subsidies to the railroad) of millions. To prevent investigations, the directors had given Crédit Mobilier stock to key members of Congress. But in 1872, Congress did conduct an investigation, which revealed that some highly placed Republicans—including Schuyler Colfax, now Grant's vice president—had accepted stock.

One dreary episode followed another in Grant's second term. Benjamin H. Bristow, Grant's third Treasury secretary, discovered that some of his officials and a group of distillers operating as a "whiskey ring" were cheating the government out of taxes by filing false reports. Then a House investigation revealed that William W. Belknap, secretary of war, had accepted bribes to retain an Indian-post trader in office (the so-called Indian ring). Other, lesser scandals added to the growing impression that "Grantism" had brought rampant corruption to government.

### The Greenback Question

Compounding Grant's, and the nation's, problems was the financial crisis known as the Panic of 1873. It began with the failure of a leading investment banking firm, Jay Cooke and Company, which had invested too heavily in postwar railroad building. There had been panics before—in 1819, 1837, and 1857—but this was the worst one yet. The depression it produced lasted four years.

Debtors now pressured the government to inflate the value of their currency, which would have made it easier for them to pay their debts. More specifically, they urged the government to redeem federal war bonds with greenbacks, paper currency of the sort printed during the Civil War, which would increase the amount of money in circulation. But Grant and most Republicans wanted a "sound" currency—based solidly on gold reserves—which would favor the interests of banks and other creditors.

The greenback question would not go away. There was approximately $356 million in paper currency issued during the Civil War that was still in circulation. And in 1873, when the Supreme Court ruled in *Knox* v. *Lee* that greenbacks were legal, the Treasury issued more in response to the panic. The following year, Congress voted to raise the total further. But Grant, under pressure from eastern financial interests, vetoed the measure.

In 1875, Republican leaders in Congress, in an effort to crush the greenback movement for good, passed the Specie Resumption Act. This law provided that after January 1, 1879, the greenback dollars, whose value constantly fluctuated, would be redeemed by the government and replaced with new certificates, firmly pegged to the price of gold. The law satisfied creditors, who had worried that debts would be repaid in paper currency of uncertain value. But "resumption" made things more difficult for debtors, because the gold-based money supply could not easily expand. As a result, money became scarcer.

In 1875, the "greenbackers," as the inflationists were called, formed their own political organization: the National Greenback Party. It was active in the next three presidential elections, but it failed to gain widespread support. It did, however, keep the money issue alive. The question of the proper composition of the currency was to remain one of the most controversial and enduring issues in late-nineteenth-century American politics.

## Republican Diplomacy

The Johnson and Grant administrations achieved their greatest successes in foreign affairs. The accomplishments were the work not of the presidents themselves, who displayed little aptitude for diplomacy, but of two outstanding secretaries of state: William H. Seward, who had served Lincoln and who remained in office until 1869; and Hamilton Fish, who served throughout the two terms of the Grant administration.

An ardent expansionist, Seward acted with as much daring as the demands of Reconstruction politics and the Republican hatred of President Johnson would permit. Seward accepted a Russian offer to sell Alaska to the United States for $7.2 million, despite criticism from many who considered Alaska a useless frozen wasteland and derided it as "Seward's Folly." In 1867, Seward also engineered the American annexation of the tiny Midway Islands, west of Hawaii.

Hamilton Fish was also a firm and decisive diplomat. His first major challenge was resolving a longstanding controversy with England. Many Americans believed that the British government had violated the neutrality laws during the Civil War by permitting English shipyards to build ships (among them the *Alabama*) for the Confederacy. American demands that England pay for the damage these vessels had caused became known as the "Alabama claims." In 1871, after a number of failed efforts, Fish forged an agreement, the Treaty of Washington, which provided for international arbitration and in which Britain expressed regret for the escape of the *Alabama* from England.

# THE ABANDONMENT OF RECONSTRUCTION

As the North grew increasingly preoccupied with its own political and economic problems, interest in Reconstruction began to wane. The Grant administration continued to protect Republican governments in the South, although less because of any interest in helping the freedmen than because of
a desire to prevent the reemergence of a strong Democratic Party in the region. But even the presence of federal troops was not enough to prevent
white Southerners from overturning the Reconstruction regimes. By the
time Grant left office, Democrats had taken back (or, as white Southerners
liked to put it, "redeemed") seven of the governments of the former Confederate states.

For three other states—South Carolina, Louisiana, and Florida—the end
of Reconstruction had to wait for the withdrawal of the last federal troops
in 1877, a withdrawal that was the result of a long process of political bargaining and compromise at the national level.

## The Southern States "Redeemed"

In the states where whites constituted a majority—the states of the upper
South—overthrowing Republican control was relatively simple. By 1872, all
but a handful of Southern whites had regained suffrage. Now a clear majority, they needed only to organize and elect their candidates.

In other states, where blacks were a majority or the populations of the
two races were almost equal, whites used intimidation and violence to undermine the Reconstruction regimes. Secret societies—the Ku Klux Klan,
the Knights of the White Camellia, and others—used terrorism to frighten
or physically bar blacks from voting or otherwise exercising citizenship.
Paramilitary organizations—the Red Shirts and White Leagues—armed
themselves to "police" elections and worked to force all white males to join
the Democratic Party and to exclude all blacks from meaningful political activity. Strongest of all, however, was the simple weapon of economic pressure. Some planters refused to rent land to Republican blacks; storekeepers
refused to extend them credit; employers refused to give them work.

In the meantime, Southern blacks were losing the support of many of
their former advocates in the North. After the adoption of the Fifteenth
Amendment in 1870, some reformers convinced themselves that their long
campaign in behalf of black people was now over, that with the vote blacks
ought to be able to take care of themselves. Former Radical leaders such as
Charles Sumner and Horace Greeley now began calling themselves Liber-

als, cooperating with the Democrats, and at times outdoing even the Democrats in denouncing what they viewed as black-and-carpetbag misgovernment. Within the South itself, many white Republicans joined the Liberals and moved into the Democratic Party.

The Panic of 1873 further undermined support for Reconstruction. In the congressional elections of 1874, the Democrats won control of the House of Representatives for the first time since 1861. Grant took note of the changing temper of the North and reduced the use of military force to prop up the Republican regimes that were still standing in the South.

By the end of 1876, only three states were left in the hands of the Republicans—South Carolina, Louisiana, and Florida. In the state elections that year, Democrats (after using terrorist tactics) claimed victory in all three. But the Republicans claimed victory as well and were able to remain in office because of the presence of federal troops. If the troops were to be withdrawn, the last of the Republican regimes would fall.

## The Compromise of 1877

Grant had hoped to run for another term in 1876, but most Republican leaders—shaken by recent Democratic successes, afraid of the scandals with which Grant was associated, and worried about the president's failing health—resisted. Instead, they sought a candidate not associated with the problems of the Grant years, one who might entice Liberals back and unite the party again. They settled on Rutherford B. Hayes, a former Union army officer and congressman, three times governor of Ohio, and a champion of civil service reform. The Democrats united behind Samuel J. Tilden, the reform governor of New York, who had been instrumental in overthrowing the corrupt Tweed Ring of New York City's Tammany Hall.

Although the campaign was a bitter one, there were few differences of principle between the candidates, both of whom were conservatives committed to moderate reform. The November election produced an apparent Democratic victory. Tilden carried the South and several large Northern states, and his popular margin over Hayes was nearly 300,000 votes. But disputed returns from Louisiana, South Carolina, Florida, and Oregon, whose electoral votes totaled 20, threw the election in doubt. Tilden had undisputed claim to 184 electoral votes, only one short of the majority. But Hayes could still win if he managed to receive all 20 disputed votes.

The Constitution had established no method to determine the validity of disputed returns. It was clear that the decision lay with Congress, but it was not clear with which house or through what method. (The Senate was

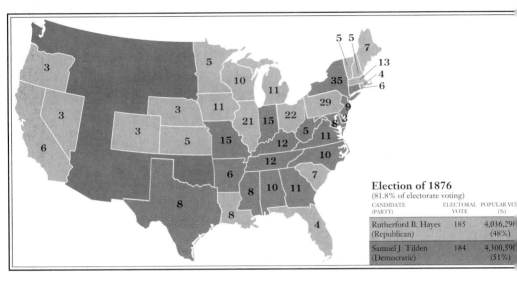

**Election of 1876**
(81.8% of electorate voting)

| CANDIDATE (PARTY) | ELECTORAL VOTE | POPULAR VOTE (%) |
|---|---|---|
| Rutherford B. Hayes (Republican) | 185 | 4,036,298 (48%) |
| Samuel J. Tilden (Democratic) | 184 | 4,300,590 (51%) |

Republican, and the House was Democratic.) Members of each party naturally supported a solution that would yield them the victory.

Finally, late in January 1877, Congress tried to break the deadlock by creating a special electoral commission to judge the disputed votes. The commission was to be composed of five senators, five representatives, and five justices of the Supreme Court. The congressional delegation would consist of five Republicans and five Democrats. The Court delegation would include two Republicans, two Democrats, and the only independent, Justice David Davis. But when the Illinois legislature elected Davis to the United States Senate, the justice resigned from the commission. His seat went instead to a Republican justice. The commission voted along straight party lines, 8 to 7, awarding every disputed vote to Hayes. Congress accepted the verdict on March 2. Two days later, Hayes was inaugurated.

Behind the resolution of the deadlock, however, lay a series of elaborate compromises among leaders of both parties. When a Democratic filibuster threatened to derail the commission's report, Republican Senate leaders met secretly with Southern Democratic leaders to work out terms by which the Democrats would support Hayes. As the price of their cooperation, the Southern Democrats (among them some former Whigs) exacted several pledges from the Republicans: the appointment of at least one Southerner to the Hayes cabinet, control of federal patronage in their areas, generous internal improvements, federal aid for the Texas and Pacific Railroad, and withdrawal of the troops. Many powerful Southern Democrats supported industrializing the region. They believed that Republican programs of federal support for business would aid their region more than the states' rights policies of the Democrats.

In his inaugural address, Hayes announced that the South's most pressing need was the restoration of "wise, honest, and peaceful local self-government"—a signal that he planned to withdraw the troops and let white Democrats take over the state governments. The statement, and Hayes's subsequent actions, supported the widespread charges that he was paying off the South for acquiescing in his election and strengthened those who referred to him as "His Fraudulency." But the election had already created such bitterness that there was probably nothing Hayes could have done to mollify his critics, not even his promise to serve only one term.

The president and his party hoped to build up a "new Republican" organization in the South drawn from Whiggish conservative white groups and committed to modest support for black rights. But all such efforts failed. Although many white Southern leaders sympathized with Republican economic policies, resentment of Reconstruction was so deep that supporting the party was politically impossible. The "solid" Democratic South, which would survive until the mid-twentieth century, was taking shape. And the withdrawal of federal troops was a signal that the national government was giving up its attempt to control Southern politics and to improve the lot of blacks in Southern society.

## The Legacy of Reconstruction

Reconstruction made important contributions to the efforts of former slaves to achieve dignity and equality in American life. There was a significant redistribution of income, from which blacks benefited. There was a more limited but not unimportant redistribution of landownership, which enabled some former slaves to acquire property. There was both a relative and an absolute improvement in the economic circumstances of most blacks. Perhaps most of all, there was a large, and largely successful, effort by blacks themselves to carve out a society and culture of their own within the American South, to create or strengthen their own institutions, and to convince themselves that they were, indeed, no longer slaves.

Nor was Reconstruction as disastrous an experience for Southern white elites as most believed at the time. Within little more than a decade after the end of a devastating war, the white South had regained control of its own institutions and, to a great extent, restored its traditional ruling class to power. Former Confederate leaders received no severe punishments. The federal government imposed no drastic economic reforms on the region, and indeed few lasting political changes of any kind other than the abolition of slavery. Not many conquered peoples have fared as well.

But Reconstruction was also notable for its limitations. For in those years the United States failed in its first serious effort to resolve its oldest and deepest social problem—the problem of race. What was more, the experience so disappointed, disillusioned, and embittered white Americans that it would be nearly a century before they would try again in any serious way. Why did this great assault on racial injustice not achieve more? In part, it was because of the weaknesses and errors of the people who directed it. But in greater part, it was because attempts to produce solutions ran up against conservative obstacles so deeply embedded in the nation's life that they could not be dislodged: among them, a profound respect for private property and free enterprise and a pervasive belief among many of even the most liberal whites that African Americans were inherently inferior. Given the odds confronting them, therefore, African Americans had reason for considerable pride in the gains they were able to make during Reconstruction. And future generations could be grateful for two great charters of freedom—the Fourteenth and Fifteenth Amendments to the Constitution—which, although widely ignored at the time, would one day serve as the basis for a "Second Reconstruction" that would renew the drive to bring freedom to all Americans.

## THE NEW SOUTH

The agreement between southern Democrats and northern Republicans that helped settle the disputed election of 1876 was supposed to be the first step toward developing a stable, permanent Republican Party in the South. In that respect, at least, it failed. In the years following the end of Reconstruction, white southerners established the Democratic Party as the only viable political organization for the region's whites. Even so, the South did change in the years after Reconstruction in some of the ways the framers of the Compromise of 1877 had hoped.

### The "Redeemers"

By the end of 1877—after the last withdrawal of federal troops—every southern state government had been "redeemed." That is, political power had been restored to white Democrats. Many white southerners rejoiced at the restoration of what they liked to call "home rule." But in reality, political power in the region was soon more restricted than at any time since the Civil War. Once again, the South fell under the control of a powerful, conservative oligarchy, whose members were known variously as the "Redeemers" or the "Bourbons."

In some places, this post-Reconstruction ruling class was much the same as the ruling class of the antebellum period. In Alabama, for example, the old planter elite—despite challenges from new merchant and industrial forces—retained much of its former power and continued largely to dominate the state for decades. In other areas, however, the Redeemers constituted a genuinely new ruling class. They were merchants, industrialists, railroad developers, and financiers. Some of them were former planters, some of them northern immigrants who had been absorbed into the region's life, some of them ambitious, upwardly mobile white southerners from the region's lower social tiers. They combined a commitment to "home rule" and social conservatism with a commitment to economic development.

The various Bourbon governments of the New South behaved in many respects quite similarly. Conservatives had complained that the Reconstruction governments fostered widespread corruption, but the Redeemer regimes were, if anything, even more awash in waste and fraud. (In this, they were little different from governments in every region of the country.) At the same time, virtually all the new Democratic regimes lowered taxes, reduced spending, and drastically diminished state services. One state after another eliminated or reduced its support for public school systems.

## Industrialization and the "New South"

Many white southern leaders in the post-Reconstruction era hoped to see their region become the home of a vigorous industrial economy, a "New South." Henry Grady, editor of the *Atlanta Constitution*, and other prominent spokesmen for a New South seldom challenged white supremacy, but they did advocate other important changes in southern values. Above all, they promoted the virtues of thrift, industry, and progress—qualities that prewar southerners had often denounced in northern society.

New South enthusiasts helped southern industry expand dramatically in the years after Reconstruction and become a more important part of the region's economy than ever before. Most visible was the growth in textile manufacturing, which increased ninefold in the last twenty years of the century. In the past, southern planters had usually shipped their cotton out of the region to manufacturers in the North or in Europe. Now textile factories appeared in the South itself—many of them drawn to the region from New

England by the abundance of water power, the ready supply of cheap labor, the low taxes, and the accommodating conservative governments. The tobacco-processing industry, similarly, established an important foothold in the region. In the lower South, and particularly in Birmingham, Alabama, the iron (and, later, steel) industry grew rapidly. By 1890, the southern iron and steel industry represented nearly a fifth of the nation's total capacity.

Railroad development also increased substantially in the post-Reconstruction years—at a rate far greater than that of the nation at large. Between 1880 and 1890, trackage in the South more than doubled. And the South took a major step toward integrating its transportation system with that of the rest of the country when, in 1886, it changed the gauge (width) of its trackage to correspond with the standards of the North. No longer would it be necessary for cargoes heading into the South to be transferred from one train to another at the borders of the region.

Yet southern industry developed within strict limits, and its effects on the region were never even remotely comparable to the effects of industrialization on the North. The southern share of national manufacturing doubled in the last twenty years of the century, but it was still only 10 percent of the total. The region's per capita income increased 21 percent in the same period, but average income in the South was still only 40 percent of that in the North; in 1860 it had been more than 60 percent. And even in those industries where development had been most rapid—textiles, iron, railroads—much of the capital had come from, and many of the profits thus flowed to, the North.

The growth of industry in the South required the region to recruit a substantial industrial work force for the first time. From the beginning, a high percentage of the factory workers (and an especially high percentage of textile workers) were women. Heavy male casualties in the Civil War had helped create a large population of unmarried women who desperately needed employment. Factories also hired entire families, many of whom moved into towns from failed farms. Hours were long (often as much as twelve hours a day), and wages were far below the northern equivalent; indeed, one of the greatest attractions of the South to industrialists was that employers were able to pay workers there as little as one-half what northern workers received. Life in most mill towns was rigidly controlled by the owners and managers of the factories. They rigorously suppressed attempts at protest or union organization. Company stores sold goods to workers at inflated prices and issued credit at exorbitant rates (much like country stores in agrarian areas), and mill owners ensured that no competitors were able to establish themselves in the community.

Some industries, such as textiles, offered virtually no opportunities to

African-American workers. Others—tobacco, iron, and lumber, for example—did provide some employment for blacks, usually the most menial and lowest-paid positions. Some mill towns, therefore, were places where the black and white cultures came into close contact. That contributed less to the growth of racial harmony than to the determination of white leaders to take additional measures to protect white supremacy.

### Tenants and Sharecroppers

Despite significant growth in southern industry, the region remained primarily agrarian. The most important economic reality in the post-Reconstruction South, therefore, was the impoverished state of agriculture. The 1870s and 1880s saw an acceleration of the process that had begun in the immediate postwar years: the imposition of systems of tenantry and debt peonage on much of the region; the reliance on a few cash crops rather than on a diversified agricultural system; and increasing absentee ownership of valuable farmlands. During Reconstruction, perhaps a third or more of the farmers in the South were tenants; by 1900 the figure had increased to 70 percent. That was in large part the result of the crop-lien system that had emerged in the aftermath of the Civil War. Farmers who owned their own land often lost it as merchants seized it for payment of debts. Farmers who rented could never accumulate enough capital to buy land.

Tenantry, which now dominated Southern agriculture, took several forms. Farmers who owned tools, equipment, and farm animals—or who had the money to buy them—usually paid an annual cash rent for their land. But many farmers (including most black ones) had no money or equipment at all. Landlords would supply them with land, a crude house, a few tools, seed, and sometimes a mule. In return, the farmers would promise the landlord a large share of the annual crop. After paying their landlords and their local furnishing merchants (who were often the same people), these "sharecroppers" seldom had anything left to sell on their own.

The crop-lien system was particularly devastating to southern blacks, few of whom owned their own land to begin with. These economic difficulties were compounded by social and legal discrimination, which in the post-Reconstruction era began to take new forms and to inspire new responses.

### African Americans and the New South

The "New South creed" was not the property of whites alone. Many African Americans were attracted to the vision of progress and self-improvement as well. Some blacks succeeded in elevating themselves into a distinct middle class—even if one far less prosperous than the white middle class. These were former slaves (and, as the decades passed, their offspring) who managed to acquire property, establish small businesses, or enter professions.

This rising group of African Americans believed strongly that education was vital to the future of their people. With the support of northern missionary societies and, to a far lesser extent, a few southern state governments, they expanded the network of black colleges and institutes that had taken root during Reconstruction into an important educational system.

The chief spokesman for this commitment to education, and for a time the most prominent spokesman for black people as a whole, was Booker T. Washington, founder and president of the Tuskegee Institute in Alabama. Born into slavery, Washington had worked his way out of poverty after acquiring an education (at Virginia's Hampton Institute). He urged other blacks to follow the same road to self-improvement.

Washington's message was both cautious and hopeful. African Americans should attend school, learn skills, and establish a solid footing in agriculture and the trades. Industrial, not classical, education should be their goal. Blacks should, moreover, refine their speech, improve their dress, and adopt habits of thrift and personal cleanliness; they should, in short, adopt the standards of the white middle class. Only thus, he claimed, could they win the respect of the white population, the prerequisite for any larger social gains.

In a famous speech in Georgia in 1895, Washington outlined a controversial philosophy of race relations that became widely known as the Atlanta Compromise. Blacks, he said, should forgo agitating for political rights and concentrate on self-improvement and preparation for equality. If blacks were ever to win the rights and privileges of citizenship, they must first show that they were "prepared for the exercise of these privileges." Washington offered a powerful challenge to those whites who wanted to discourage African Americans from acquiring an education or winning any economic gains. But his message was also intended to assure whites that blacks would not challenge the system of segregation, which southern governments were in the process of creating.

### The Birth of Jim Crow

Few white southerners had ever accepted the idea of racial equality. That the former slaves acquired any legal and political rights at all after emancipation was in large part the result of their own efforts and critical federal support. That outside support all but vanished after 1877. Federal troops withdrew. Congress lost interest. And the Supreme Court effectively stripped the Fourteenth and Fifteenth Amendments of much of their significance. In the so-called civil rights cases of 1883, the Court ruled that the Fourteenth Amendment prohibited state governments from discriminating against people because of race but did not restrict private organizations or individuals from doing so. Thus railroads, hotels, theaters, and the like could legally practice segregation.

Eventually, the Court also validated state legislation that institutionalized the separation of the races. In *Plessy* v. *Ferguson* (1896), a case involving a Louisiana law that required separate seating arrangements for the races on railroads, the Court held that separate accommodations did not deprive blacks of equal rights if the accommodations were equal, a decision that survived for years as part of the legal basis of segregated schools. In *Cumming* v. *County Board of Education* (1899), the Court ruled that communities could establish schools for whites only even if there were no comparable schools for blacks.

Even before these decisions, white southerners were working to separate the races to the greatest extent possible. One illustration of this movement from subordination to segregation was black voting rights. In some states, disfranchisement had begun almost as soon as Reconstruction ended. But in other areas, black voting continued for some time after Reconstruction—largely because conservative whites believed they could control the black electorate and use it to beat back the attempts of poor white farmers to take control of the Democratic Party.

In the 1890s, however, franchise restrictions became much more rigid. During those years, some small white farmers began to demand complete black disfranchisement—both because of racial prejudice and because they objected to the black vote being used against them by the Bourbons. At the same time, many members of the conservative elite began to fear that poor whites might unite politically with poor blacks to challenge them. They too began to support further franchise restrictions.

In devising laws to disfranchise black males (black females, like white women, had never voted), the southern states had to find ways to evade the Fifteenth Amendment, which prohibited states from denying anyone the right to vote because of race. Two devices emerged before 1900 to accomplish this goal. One was the poll tax or some form of property qualification; few blacks were prosperous enough to meet such requirements. Another was the "literacy" or "understanding" test, which required voters to demonstrate an ability to read and to interpret the Constitution. Even those African

Americans who could read had a hard time passing the difficult test white officials gave them. The laws affected poor white voters as well as blacks. By the late 1890s, the black vote had decreased by 62 percent, the white vote by 26 percent. The Supreme Court proved as compliant in upholding the disfranchising laws as it was in dealing with the civil rights cases.

Laws restricting the franchise and segregating schools were only part of a network of state and local statutes—known as the Jim Crow laws—that by the first years of the twentieth century had institutionalized an elaborate system of segregation reaching into almost every area of southern life. Blacks and whites could not ride together in the same railroad cars, sit in the same waiting rooms, use the same washrooms, eat in the same restaurants, or sit in the same theaters. Blacks had no access to many public parks, beaches, picnic areas; they could not be patients in many hospitals. Much of the new legal structure did no more than confirm what had already been widespread social practice in the South since well before the end of Reconstruction. But the Jim Crow laws also stripped blacks of many of the modest social, economic, and political gains they had made in the more fluid atmosphere of the late nineteenth century. They served, too, as a means for whites to retain control of social relations between the races in the rapidly growing cities and towns of the South, where traditional patterns of subjugation were more difficult to preserve than in the countryside.

More than legal efforts were involved in this process. The 1890s witnessed a dramatic increase in white violence against blacks, which, along with the Jim Crow laws, served to inhibit black agitation for equal rights. The worst such violence—lynching of blacks by white mobs, either because the victims were accused of crimes or because they had seemed somehow to violate their proper station—reached appalling levels. In the nation as a whole in the 1890s, there was an average of 187 lynchings each year, more than 80 percent of them in the South. The vast majority of victims were black. Those involved in lynchings often saw their actions as a legitimate form of law enforcement, and some victims of lynchings had in fact committed crimes. But lynchings were also a means by which whites controlled the black population through terror and intimidation.

The rise of lynchings shocked the conscience of many white Americans in a way that other forms of racial injustice did not. In 1892 Ida B. Wells, a committed black journalist, launched what became an international anti-lynching movement with a series of impassioned articles after the lynching of three of her friends in Memphis, Tennessee, her home. The movement gradually gathered strength in the first years of the twentieth century, attracting substantial support from whites in both the North and South (par-

LYNCH MOB, 1893 White Southerners sometimes traveled many miles to watch a lynching, such as this one of a black man accused of killing a three-year-old white girl. More common than these large public lynchings, however, were less conspicuous vigilante murders by small groups of whites.

ticularly from white women). Its goal was a federal antilynching law, which would allow the national government to do what state and local governments in the South were generally unwilling to do: punish those responsible for lynchings.

But the substantial southern white opposition to lynchings stood as an exception to the general white support for suppression of African Americans. Indeed, just as in the antebellum period, the shared commitment to white supremacy helped dilute class animosities between poorer whites and the Bourbon oligarchies. Economic issues tended to play a secondary role to race in southern politics, distracting people from the glaring social inequalities that afflicted blacks and whites alike. The commitment to white supremacy, in short, was a burden for poor whites as well as for blacks.

D E B A T I N G    T H E    P A S T

## *Reconstruction*

D EBATE OVER THE nature of Reconstruction has been unusually intense, not only among historians but among much of the larger
public as well. Indeed, few issues in American history have raised such deep
and enduring passions.

Beginning in the late nineteenth century and continuing well into the
twentieth, a relatively uniform and highly critical view of Reconstruction prevailed among historians—a reflection of a broad consensus among white
Americans about the inferiority of blacks and of a yearning in both the
North and the South for sectional reconciliation. William A. Dunning's *Reconstruction, Political and Economic* (1907) was the principal scholarly expression of this prevailing view. Dunning portrayed Reconstruction as a corrupt
and oppressive outrage imposed on a prostrate South by a vindictive group
of Northern Republican radicals. Unscrupulous carpetbaggers flooded the
South and plundered the region. Ignorant African Americans were thrust
into political offices for which they were unfit. Reconstruction governments
were awash in corruption and compiled enormous levels of debt. The Dunning interpretation dominated several generations of historical scholarship.
It also helped shape such popular images of Reconstruction as those in the
novel and film *Gone with the Wind*.

Among historians, at least, the Dunning interpretation gradually lost
credibility in the face of a series of challenges. W. E. B. Du Bois, the great
African-American scholar, offered one of the first alternative views in *Black
Reconstruction* (1935). To Du Bois, Reconstruction was an effort by freed
blacks (and their white allies) to create a more democratic society in the

South, and it was responsible for many valuable social innovations. In the early 1960s, John Hope Franklin and Kenneth Stampp, building on a generation of work by other scholars, published new histories of Reconstruction that also radically revised the Dunning interpretation. Reconstruction, they argued, was a genuine, if flawed, effort to solve the problem of race in the South. The Reconstruction governments were not perfect, but they were bold experiments in interracial politics. Congressional radicals were not saints, but they were genuinely concerned with protecting the rights of former slaves. Reconstruction had brought important, if temporary, progress to the South and had created no more corruption there than governments were creating in the North at the same time. What was tragic about Reconstruction, the revisionists claimed, was not what it did to Southern whites but what it failed to do for Southern blacks. It was, in the end, too weak and too short-lived to guarantee African Americans genuine equality.

In more recent years, some historians have begun to question the assessment of the first revisionists that, in the end, Reconstruction accomplished relatively little. Leon Litwack argued in *Been in the Storm So Long* (1979) that former slaves used the protections Reconstruction offered them to carve out a certain level of independence for themselves within southern society: strengthening churches, reuniting families, and resisting the efforts of white planters to revive the gang labor system.

Eric Foner's *Reconstruction: America's Unfinished Revolution* (1988) also emphasized how far African Americans moved toward freedom and independence in a short time, how much of lasting value they were able to accomplish despite imposing obstacles, and how important they were in shaping the execution of Reconstruction policies. Reconstruction, he argues, "can only be judged a failure" as an effort to secure "blacks' rights as citizens and free laborers." But it "closed off even more oppressive alternatives. . . . The post-Reconstruction labor system embodied neither a return to the closely supervised gang labor of antebellum days, nor the complete dispossession and immobilization of the black labor force and coercive apprenticeship systems envisioned by white Southerners in 1865 and 1866. Nor were blacks, as in twentieth-century South Africa, barred from citizenship, herded into labor reserves, or prohibited by law from moving from one part of the country to another. . . . The doors of economic opportunity that had opened could never be completely closed."

# CHAPTER SIXTEEN

# The Conquest of the Far West

*The Societies of the Far West* ∼ *The Changing Western Economy*
*The Dispersal of the Tribes* ∼ *The Rise and Decline of the Western Farmer*

T hrough much of the first half of the nineteenth century, relatively few English-speaking Americans considered moving into the vast and presumably arid lands west of the Mississippi River. By the mid-1840s, however, migrants from the eastern regions of the nation had settled in the West in substantial numbers. Farmers, ranchers, and miners all found opportunity in the western lands. By the end of the Civil War, the West had become legendary in the eastern states. No longer the Great American Desert, it was now the "frontier": an empty land awaiting settlement and civilization; a place of wealth, adventure, opportunity, and untrammeled individualism.

In fact, the real West of the mid-nineteenth century bore little resemblance to its popular image. It was a diverse land, with many different regions, many different climates, many different stores of natural resources. And it was extensively populated, with a number of well-developed societies and cultures. The English-speaking migrants of the late nineteenth century did not find an empty, desolate land. They found Indians, Mexicans, French and British Canadians, Asians, and others, some of whose families had been living in the West for generations.

The Anglo-American settlers tried, with considerable success, to conquer and disperse many of the peoples already living in the region, but they were never able to make the West theirs alone. Almost everything the Anglo-Americans did and built reflected the influence of the other cultures of the region. Nevertheless, English-speaking Americans transformed the West by connecting it with, and making it part of, the growing capitalist economy of the East. And despite their self-image as rugged individualists, they relied heavily on assistance from the federal government—land grants, subsidies, and military protection—as they developed the region.

| TIME LINE | | | |
|---|---|---|---|
| 1862 | 1865-1867 | 1866 | 1869 |
| Homestead Act | Sioux War | Western cattle bonanza | Transcontinental railroad completed |

| 1873 | 1874 | 1876 | 1877 | 1882 |
|---|---|---|---|---|
| Barbed wire invented | Black Hills gold rush | Battle of Little Bighorn | Desert Land Act | Chinese Exclusion Act |

| 1885 | 1887 | 1889 | 1890 | 1893 |
|---|---|---|---|---|
| Twain's *Huckleberry Finn* | Dawes Act | Oklahoma opened to white settlement | Battle of Wounded Knee | Turner's "Frontier Thesis" |

# THE SOCIETIES OF THE FAR WEST

The Far West—the region beyond the Mississippi River into which millions of Anglo-Americans moved in the years after the Civil War—was in fact many lands. It contained some of the most arid territory in the United States, and some of the wettest and lushest. It contained the flattest plains and the highest mountains. And it contained many peoples.

## The Western Tribes

The largest and most important western population group before the great American migration was the Indian tribes. Some were members of eastern tribes—Cherokee, Creek, and others—who had been forcibly resettled west of the Mississippi to "Indian Territory" (later Oklahoma) and elsewhere before the Civil War. But most were members of tribes indigenous to the West.

The western tribes had developed a number of patterns of civilization. More than 300,000 Indians (among them the Serrano, Chumash, Pomo, Maidu, Yurok, and Chinook) had lived on the Pacific Coast before the arrival of Spanish settlers, supporting themselves through a combination of fishing, foraging, and simple agriculture. Disease and dislocation decimated the tribes, but in the mid-nineteenth century 150,000 Indians remained—some living within the Hispanic society the Spanish and Mexican settlers had created, many still living within their own tribal communities.

The Pueblos of the Southwest had long lived largely as farmers and had established permanent settlements there even before the Spanish arrived in the seventeenth century. The Pueblos grew corn; they built towns and cities of adobe houses; they practiced elaborate forms of irrigation; and they participated in trade and commerce. In the eighteenth and nineteenth centuries, their intimate relationship with the Spanish (later Mexicans) produced, in effect, an alliance against the Apaches, Navajos, and Commanches of the region.

The most widespread Indian groups in the West were the Plains Indians. They were, in fact, many different tribal and language groups. Some lived more or less sedentary lives as farmers; others were highly nomadic hunters. Despite their differences, however, the tribes shared some traits. Their cultures were based on close, extended family networks and on an intimate relationship with nature. Women's roles were largely domestic and artistic: raising children, cooking, gathering roots and berries, preparing hides, and tending fields and gardens in those places where bands remained settled long enough to raise crops. Men worked as hunters and traders and supervised religious and military life. Most of the Plains Indians practiced a religion centered on a belief in the spiritual power of the natural world—of plants and animals and the rhythms of the days and the seasons.

Many of the Plains tribes—including some of the most powerful tribes in the Sioux nation—subsisted largely through hunting buffalo. Riding small but powerful horses, the tribes moved through the grasslands following the herds. Permanent settlements were rare. When a band halted, it constructed tepees as temporary dwellings; when it departed, it left the landscape almost completely undisturbed.

The buffalo, or bison, which the Indians so relentlessly pursued, provided the economic basis for the Plains Indians' way of life. The flesh of the large animal was their principal source of food, and its skin supplied materials for clothing, shoes, tepees, blankets, robes, and utensils. "Buffalo chips"—dried manure—provided fuel; buffalo bones became knives and arrow tips; buffalo tendons formed the strings of bows.

The Plains Indians were proud and aggressive warriors, schooled in warfare from their frequent (and usually brief) skirmishes with rival tribes. By the early nineteenth century, the Sioux had become the most powerful tribe in the Missouri River valley and had begun expanding west and south until they dominated much of the plains and were the most important military force in the region.

The Plains warriors proved to be the most formidable foes white settlers encountered. But they also suffered from several serious weaknesses. One was the inability of the various tribes (and often even of the bands within tribes) to unite against white aggression. Not only were they seldom able to draw together a coalition large enough to counter white power; they were also frequently distracted from their battles with whites by conflicts among the tribes themselves. And at times, tribal warriors faced white forces who were being assisted by guides and even fighters from other, usually rival, tribes.

Even so, some tribes were at times able to overcome their divisions and unite effectively. By the mid-nineteenth century, for example, the Sioux, Arapaho, and Cheyenne had forged a powerful alliance that dominated the northern plains. The more important weaknesses of the western tribes in their contest with white society were, in fact, ecological and economic. Indians were tragically vulnerable to eastern infectious diseases. Smallpox epidemics, for example, decimated the Pawnees in Nebraska in the 1840s and many of the California tribes in the early 1850s. And the tribes were, of course, at a considerable disadvantage in any long-term battle with an economically and industrially advanced people. They were, in the end, outmanned and outgunned.

### Hispanic New Mexico

For centuries, much of the Far West had been part of, first, the Spanish Empire and, later, the Mexican Republic. When the United States acquired its new lands there in the 1840s, it acquired many Mexican residents at the same time.

In New Mexico, the centers of Spanish-speaking society were the farming and trading communities the Spanish had established in the seventeenth century. Descendants of the original Spanish settlers (and more recent migrants from Mexico) lived alongside the Pueblo Indians and some American traders and engaged primarily in cattle and sheep ranching. When the United States acquired title to New Mexico in the aftermath of the Mexican War, General Stephen Kearny—who had commanded the American troops in the region during the conflict—tried to establish a territorial government there. He drew most of the officials from among the approximately 1,000 Anglo-Americans in the region, ignoring the over 50,000 Hispanics. There were widespread fears among Hispanics and Indians alike that the new American rulers of the region would confiscate their lands and otherwise threaten their societies. In 1847, Taos Indians rebelled; they killed the new governor and other Anglo-American officials before being subdued by United States Army forces. New Mexico remained under military rule for three years, until the United States finally organized a territorial government there in 1850.

Even without its former political power, Hispanic society in New Mexico survived and even grew in the face of the expansion of Anglo-American settlement in the Southwest. The United States Army finally did what the Hispanic residents had been unable to accomplish for 200 years: it broke the power of the Navajo, Apache, and other tribes that had long prevented the residents of New Mexico from expanding their society and commerce. The defeat of the tribes led to substantial Hispanic migration into other areas of the Southwest and as far north as Colorado. Most of the expansion involved peasants and small tradespeople who were looking for land or new opportunities for commerce.

The Anglo-American presence in the Southwest grew rapidly once the railroads established lines into the region in the 1880s and early 1890s. With the railroads came extensive new ranching, farming, and mining. The expansion of economic activity in the region attracted a new wave of Mexican immigrants—perhaps as many as 100,000 by 1900—who moved across the border (which was unregulated until World War I) in search of work. But unlike the earlier Hispanic residents of the Southwest, the new immigrants entered a society in which the best opportunities were now reserved for Anglo-Americans. The English-speaking proprietors of the new enterprises restricted most Mexicans to the lowest-paying and least stable jobs.

### Hispanic California and Texas

In California, Spanish settlement began in the eighteenth century with a string of Christian missions along the Pacific coast. The missionaries and the soldiers who accompanied them gathered most of the coastal Indians into their communities, some forcibly and some by persuasion. The Indians were targets of the evangelizing efforts of the missionaries, who baptized over 50,000 of them. They were also a labor force for the flourishing and largely self-sufficient economies the missionaries created; the Spanish forced most of these laborers into a state of servitude little different from slavery.

In the 1830s, after the new Mexican government began reducing the power of the church, the mission society largely collapsed. In its place emerged a secular Mexican aristocracy, which controlled a chain of large estates (some of them former missions) in the fertile lands west of the Sierra mountains. For them, the arrival of Anglo-Americans before and after the Civil War was disastrous. So vast were the numbers of English-speaking immigrants that the *californios* (as the Hispanic residents of the region were known) had little power to resist the onslaught. English-speaking prospectors organized to exclude them, sometimes violently, from the mines during the gold rush. Many *californios* also lost their lands—either through corrupt business deals or through outright seizure (sometimes with the help of the courts and often through simple occupation by squatters).

In the southern areas of California, where there were at first fewer English-speaking migrants, some Mexican landowners managed to hang on for a time. The booming Anglo communities in the north of the state created a large market for the cattle that southern *rancheros* were raising. But a combination of reckless expansion, growing indebtedness, and a severe drought in the 1860s devastated the Mexican ranching culture. By the 1880s, the Hispanic aristocracy in California had largely ceased to exist.

Increasingly, Mexicans and Mexican Americans became part of the lower end of the state's working class, clustered in barrios in Los Angeles or elsewhere or laboring as migrant farmworkers. Even small Hispanic landowners who managed to hang on to their farms found themselves unable to raise livestock, as the once-communal grazing lands fell under the control of powerful Anglo ranchers.

A similar pattern occurred in Texas. After the territory joined the United States, many Mexican landowners lost their land—some as a result of fraud and coercion, some because even the most substantial Mexican ranchers could not compete with the enormous Anglo-American ranching kingdoms that were emerging. In 1859, angry Mexicans, led by the rancher Juan Cortina, raided the jail in Brownsville and freed all the Mexican prisoners inside. But such resistance had little long-term effect. As in California, Mexicans in southern Texas (who constituted nearly three-quarters of the population there) became an increasingly impoverished working class relegated largely to unskilled farm or industrial labor.

### The Chinese Migration

At the same time that ambitious or impoverished Europeans were crossing the Atlantic in search of opportunities in the New World, many Chinese were crossing the Pacific in hopes of better lives than they could expect in their own poverty-stricken land. Not all came to the United States. Many Chinese moved to Hawaii, Australia, Latin America, South Africa, and even the Caribbean—some as "coolies" (indentured servants whose condition was close to slavery).

A few Chinese traveled to the American West even before the gold rush, but after 1848 the flow increased dramatically. By 1880, more than 200,000 Chinese had settled in the United States, mostly in California, where they constituted nearly a tenth of the population. Almost all came as free laborers. For a time, white Americans welcomed the Chinese as a conscientious, hardworking people. Very quickly, however, white opinion turned hostile—in part because the Chinese were so industrious and successful that some white Americans began considering them rivals, even threats.

In the early 1850s, large numbers of Chinese immigrants worked in the gold mines. Many of them were well-organized, hardworking prospectors, and for a time some of them enjoyed considerable success. But opportunities for Chinese to prosper in the mines were fleeting. In 1852, the California legislature began trying to exclude the Chinese from gold mining by enacting a "foreign miners" tax (which also helped exclude Mexicans). Gradually, the effect of the discriminatory laws, the hostility of white miners, and the declining profitability of the surface mines drove most Chinese out of prospecting.

As mining declined as a source of wealth and jobs for the Chinese, railroad employment grew. Beginning in 1865, over 12,000 Chinese found work building the transcontinental railroad. In fact, Chinese workers formed 90 percent of the labor force of the Central Pacific and were mainly responsible for construction of the western part of the new road. The company preferred them to white workers because they worked hard, made few demands, and accepted relatively low wages.

Work on the Central Pacific was arduous and often dangerous, and the company made few concessions to the difficult conditions. In the winter, many Chinese tunneled into snow banks at night to create warm sleeping areas for themselves, even though such tunnels frequently collapsed, suffocating those inside. In the spring of 1866, 5,000 Chinese railroad workers rebelled against the terrible conditions of their work and went on strike demanding higher wages and a shorter workday. The company isolated them, surrounded them with strikebreakers, and starved them into submission. The strike failed, and most of the workers returned to their jobs.

In 1869 the transcontinental railroad was completed. Thousands of Chinese were now out of work. Some moved into agricultural work, usually in menial positions. Increasingly, however, the Chinese flocked to cities. By 1900, nearly half the Chinese population of California lived in urban areas. By far the largest single Chinese community was in San Francisco. Much of community life there, and in other "Chinatowns" throughout the West, revolved around organizations—usually formed by people from the same clan or community in China—that functioned as something like benevolent societies and filled many of the roles that political machines often served in immigrant communities in eastern cities. They were often led by prominent

CHINESE WORKERS ON THE UNION PACIFIC RAILROAD  The Union Pacific Railroad, which moved east from California en route to its meeting with the Central Pacific in Utah, was one of the great engineering feats of the nineteenth century. It was also one of the largest employers of its day, and the captains of the project made heavy use of Chinese laborers—because they accepted low wages, because they worked reliably and hard, and because they seldom complained about the arduous conditions under which they were often forced to live.

merchants. (In San Francisco, the leading merchants—known as the "Six Companies"—often worked together to advance their interests in the larger community of the city and state.) These organizations became, in effect, employment brokers, unions, arbitrators of disputes, defenders of the community against outside persecution, and dispensers of social services. They also organized the elaborate festivals and celebrations that were such a conspicuous and important part of life in Chinatowns.

Other Chinese organizations were secret societies, known as "tongs." And some of the tongs were violent criminal organizations, involved in the opium trade and prostitution. Few people outside the Chinese communities were aware of their existence, except when rival tongs engaged in violent conflict (or "tong wars"), as occurred frequently in San Francisco in the 1880s.

In San Francisco and other western cities, the Chinese usually occupied the lower rungs of the employment ladder. Many worked as common laborers, servants, and unskilled factory hands. Some established their own small businesses, especially laundries. They moved into this business not because of experience—there were few commercial laundries in China—but because laundries could be started with very little capital and required only limited command of English. By the 1890s, Chinese constituted over two-thirds of all the laundry workers in California, many of them in shops they themselves owned and ran.

During the earliest Chinese migrations to California, virtually all the relatively small number of women who made the journey did so because they had been sold into prostitution in China. As late as 1880, nearly half the Chinese women in California were prostitutes. Gradually, however, the number of Chinese women increased (both through immigration and birth), and Chinese men in America became more likely to seek companionship in families.

### Anti-Chinese Sentiments

As Chinese communities grew larger and more conspicuous in western cities, anti-Chinese sentiment among white residents became increasingly virulent. In fact, next to the Indians, the Chinese probably suffered the most intense persecution from white Americans in the West. Anti-Chinese activities, some of them violent, reflected the resentment of many white workers toward Chinese laborers for accepting low wages and thus undercutting union members. As the political value of attacking the Chinese grew in California, the Democratic Party took up the call. So did the Workingmen's Party of California—created in 1878 by Denis Kearney, an Irish immigrant—which gained significant political power in the state in large part on the basis of its hostility to the Chinese. By the mid-1880s, anti-Chinese agitation and violence had spread up and down the Pacific Coast and into other areas of the West—combining economic and racist resentments.

In 1882, Congress responded to the political pressure and the growing violence by passing the Chinese Exclusion Act, which banned Chinese immigration into the United States for ten years and barred Chinese already in the country from becoming naturalized citizens. Congress renewed the law for another ten years in 1892 and made it permanent in 1902. It had a dramatic effect on the Chinese population, which declined by more than 40 percent in the forty years after the act's passage.

### Migration from the East

The great wave of new settlers in the West from the eastern United States after the Civil War followed important earlier migrations. But the scale of the postwar migration dwarfed everything that had preceded it. In previous decades, the settlers had come in thousands. Now they came in millions, spreading throughout the vast western territories—into empty and inhabited lands alike. Most of the new settlers were from the established Anglo-American societies of the eastern United States, but substantial numbers— over 2 million between 1870 and 1900—were foreign-born immigrants from Europe: Scandinavians, Germans, Irish, Russians, Czechs, and others.

They came to the West for many reasons. Settlers were attracted by gold and silver deposits, by the shortgrass pasture for cattle and sheep, and ultimately by the sod of the plains and the meadowlands of the mountains, which they discovered were suitable for farming or ranching. The completion of the great transcontinental railroad line in 1869, and the construction of the many subsidiary lines that spread out from it, encouraged settlement. So did the land policies of the federal government. The Homestead Act of 1862 permitted settlers to buy plots of 160 acres for a small fee if they occupied the land they purchased for five years and improved it.

Supporters of the Homestead Act believed it would create new markets and new outposts of commercial agriculture for the nation's growing economy. But a unit of 160 acres, while ample in much of the East, was too small for the grazing and grain farming of the Great Plains. Although over 400,000 homesteaders stayed on Homestead Act claims long enough to gain title to their land, a much larger number abandoned the region before the end of the necessary five years, unable to cope with the bleak life and the economic hardships on the windswept plains.

Not for the last time, beleaguered westerners looked to the federal government for solutions to their problems. In response to their demands, Congress increased the homestead allotments. The Timber Culture Act (1873) permitted homesteaders to receive grants of 160 additional acres if they planted 40 acres of trees on them. The Desert Land Act (1877) provided that claimants could buy 640 acres at $1.25 an acre provided they irrigated part of their holdings within three years. These and other laws ultimately made it possible for individuals to acquire as much as 1,280 acres of land at little cost. Some enterprising settlers got much more. Fraud ran rampant in the administration of the acts. Lumber, mining, and cattle companies, by employing "dummy" registrants and using other illegal devices, seized millions of acres of the public domain.

Political organization followed on the heels of settlement. By the close of the 1860s, territorial governments were in operation in the new provinces of Nevada, Colorado, Dakota, Arizona, Idaho, Montana, and Wyoming. Statehood rapidly followed. Nevada became a state in 1864, Nebraska in

1867, and Colorado in 1876. In 1889, North and South Dakota, Montana, and Washington won admission; Wyoming and Idaho entered the next year. Congress denied Utah statehood until its Mormon leaders convinced the government in 1896 that polygamy (the practice of men taking several wives) had been abandoned. At the turn of the century, only Arizona, New Mexico, and Oklahoma—all with small white populations—remained outside the Union.

## THE CHANGING WESTERN ECONOMY

Among many other things, the new wave of Anglo-American settlement transformed the economy of the Far West. The new American settlers tied the West firmly to the growing industrial economy of the East (and of much of the rest of the world).

### Labor in the West

As commercial activity increased, many farmers, ranchers, and miners found it necessary to recruit a paid labor force—not an easy task for those far away from major population centers and unable or unwilling to hire Indian workers. The labor shortage of the region led to higher wages for some workers than were typical in most areas of the East. But working conditions were often arduous, and job security was almost nonexistent. Once a railroad was built, a crop harvested, a herd sent to market, a mine played out, hundreds and even thousands of workers could find themselves suddenly unemployed. Competition from Chinese immigrants, whom employers could usually hire for considerably lower wages than they had to pay whites, also forced some Anglo-Americans out of work.

Even more than in many parts of the East, the western working class was highly multiracial. English-speaking whites worked alongside African Americans and immigrants from southern and eastern Europe, as they did in the East. Even more, they worked with Chinese, Filipinos, Mexicans, and Indians. But the work force was highly stratified along racial lines. In almost every area of the western economy, white workers (whatever their ethnicity) occupied the upper tiers of employment: management and skilled labor. The lower tiers—unskilled and often arduous work in the mines, on the railroads, or in agriculture—consisted overwhelmingly of nonwhites.

This dual labor system rested in part on a set of racial myths—arguments for the inherent inferiority of nonwhite workers. Such myths served the interests of employers, because it helped keep the work force divided. But many white workers embraced them too. That was in part because the myths supported a system that reserved whatever mobility there was largely for whites. Poor whites in the American South often believed they had more in common with wealthy planters than they did with black workers. Similarly in the West, white laborers—when forced to choose sides—often supported white bosses over nonwhite fellow workers.

The western economy was, however, no more a single entity than the economy of the East. In the late nineteenth century, the region produced three major industries, each with a distinctive history and distinctive characteristics: mining, ranching, and commercial farming.

### The Arrival of the Miners

The first economic boom in the Far West came in mining. The life span of the mining boom was relatively brief. It began in earnest around 1860 (although there had, of course, been some earlier booms, most notably in California), and it flourished until the 1890s. And then it abruptly declined.

News of a gold or silver strike in an area would start a stampede reminiscent of the California gold rush of 1849, followed by several stages of settlement. Individual prospectors would exploit the first shallow deposits of ore largely by hand, with pan and placer mining. After these surface deposits dwindled, corporations moved in to engage in lode or quartz mining, which dug deeper beneath the surface. Then, as those deposits dwindled, commercial mining either disappeared or continued on a restricted basis, and ranchers and farmers moved in and established a more permanent economy.

The first great mineral strikes (other than the California gold rush) occurred just before the Civil War. In 1858, gold was discovered in the Pike's Peak district of what would soon be the territory of Colorado; the following year, 50,000 prospectors stormed in from California, the Mississippi Valley, and the East. Denver and other mining camps blossomed into "cities" overnight. Almost as rapidly as it had developed, the boom ended. Later, the discovery of silver near Leadville supplied a new source of mineral wealth.

While the Colorado rush of 1859 was still in progress, news of another strike drew miners to Nevada. Gold had been found in the Washoe district, but the most valuable ore in the great Comstock Lode (first discovered in 1858 by Henry Comstock) and other veins was silver. The first prospectors to reach the Washoe fields came from California, and from the beginning, Californians dominated the settlement and development of Nevada. In a remote desert without railroad transportation, the territory produced no supplies of its

COLORADO BOOM TOWN  After a prospector discovered silver nearby in 1890, miners flocked to the town of Creede, Colorado. For a time in the early 1890s, 150 to 300 people arrived there daily. Although the town was located in a canyon so narrow that there was room for only one street, buildings sprouted rapidly to serve the growing community. Like other such boom towns, however, Creede's prosperity was short-lived. In 1893 the price of silver collapsed, and by the end of the century, Creede was almost deserted.

own, and everything—from food and machinery to whiskey and prostitutes— had to be shipped from California to Virginia City, Carson City, and other roaring camp towns. When the first placer (or surface) deposits ran out, Californian and eastern capitalists bought the claims of the pioneer prospectors and began to use the more difficult process of quartz mining, which enabled them to retrieve silver from deeper veins. For a few years these outside owners reaped tremendous profits; from 1860 to 1880 the Nevada lodes yielded bullion worth $306 million. After that, the mines quickly played out.

The next important mineral discoveries came in 1874, when gold was found in the Black Hills of southwestern Dakota Territory. Prospectors swarmed into the area, then (and for years to come) accessible only by stagecoach. Like the others, the boom flared for a time, until surface resources faded and corporations took over from the miners. One enormous company, the Homestake, came to dominate the fields. The Dakotas, like other boom areas of the mineral empire, ultimately developed a largely agricultural economy.

Although the gold and silver discoveries generated the most popular excitement, in the long run other, less glamorous natural resources proved more important to the development of the West. The great Anaconda copper mine launched by William Clark in 1881 marked the beginning of an industry that would remain important to Montana for many decades. In other areas, mining operations had significant success with lead, tin, quartz, and zinc.

Life in the mining boomtowns had a hectic tempo and a gaudy flavor unknown in any other part of the Far West. A speculative spirit, a mood of heady optimism, gripped almost everyone and dominated every phase of community activity. And while very few of the prospectors and miners ever "struck it rich," there was at least some truth to the popular belief that mining provided opportunities for sudden wealth. The "bonanza kings"—the miners who did become enormously wealthy off a strike—were much more likely to have come from modest or impoverished backgrounds than the industrial tycoons of the East.

The conditions of mine life in the boom period—the presence of precious minerals, the vagueness of claim boundaries, the cargoes of gold being shipped out—attracted to the camps outlaws and "bad men," operating as individuals or gangs. When the situation became intolerable in a community, those members interested in order began enforcing their own laws through vigilance committees, an unofficial system of social control used earlier in California. Vigilantes were unconstrained by the legal system, and they often imposed their notion of justice arbitrarily and without regard for any form of due process. Some vigilantes continued to operate as private "law" enforcers even after the creation of regular governments.

Men greatly outnumbered women in the mining towns, and younger men in particular had difficulty finding female companions of comparable age. Those women who did gravitate to the new communities often came with their husbands, and their activities were generally (although not always) confined to the same kinds of domestic tasks that eastern women performed. Single women, or women whose husbands were earning no money, did work for wages at times, as cooks, laundresses, and tavern keepers. And in the sexually imbalanced mining communities, there was always a ready market for prostitutes.

The thousands of people who flocked to the mining towns in search of quick wealth and failed to find it often remained as wage laborers in corporate mines after the boom period, working in almost uniformly terrible conditions. In the 1870s, before technological advances eliminated some of the dangers, one worker in every thirty was disabled in the mines, and one in every eighty was killed. That rate fell later in the nineteenth century, but mining remained one of the most dangerous and arduous working environments in the United States.

### The Cattle Kingdom

A second important element of the changing economy of the Far West was cattle ranching. The open range—the vast grasslands of the public domain—provided a huge area on the Great Plains where cattle raisers could graze their herds free of charge and unrestricted by the boundaries of private farms. The railroads gave birth to the range-cattle industry by giving it access to markets. Eventually, the same railroads ended it by bringing farmers to the plains and thus destroying the open range.

The western cattle industry was Mexican and Texan by ancestry. Long before citizens of the United States entered the Southwest, Mexican ranchers had developed the techniques and equipment that the cattlemen and cowboys of the Great Plains later employed: branding (a device known in all frontier areas where stock was grazing in common areas), roundups, roping, and the gear of the herders—their lariats, saddles, leather chaps, and spurs. Americans in Texas adopted these methods and carried them to the northernmost ranges of the cattle kingdom. Texas also had the largest herds of cattle in the country. From Texas, too, came the small, muscular horses (broncos and mustangs) that enabled cowboys to control the herds.

At the end of the Civil War, an estimated 5 million cattle roamed the Texas ranges. Eastern markets were offering fat prices for steers in any condition, and the challenge facing the cattle industry was getting the animals from the range to the railroad centers. Early in 1866, some Texas cattle ranchers began driving their combined herds, some 260,000 head, north to Sedalia, Missouri, on the Missouri Pacific Railroad. The caravan suffered heavy losses. But the drive proved that cattle could be driven to distant markets and pastured along the trail, and that they would even gain weight during the journey. This earliest of the "long drives," in other words, established the first, tentative link between the isolated cattle breeders of west Texas and the booming urban markets of the East. It laid the groundwork for the explosion of the industry—for the creation of the "cattle kingdom."

With the precedent of the long drive established, the next step was to find an easier route through more accessible country. Market facilities grew up at Abilene, Kansas, on the Kansas Pacific Railroad, and for years the town reigned as the railhead of the cattle kingdom. But by the mid-1870s, agricultural development in western Kansas was eating away at the open-range

The Cattle Kingdom, c. 1866–1887

Open range

—— Railroads

CATTLE TRAILS

Sedalia and Baxter Springs Trail

Chisholm Trail

Western Trail

Goodnight-Loving Trail

land. Cattlemen had to develop other trails and other market outlets. As the railroads began to reach farther west, Dodge City and Wichita in Kansas, Ogallala and Sidney in Nebraska, Cheyenne and Laramie in Wyoming, and Miles City and Glendive in Montana all began to rival Abilene as major centers of stock herding.

There had always been an element of risk and speculation in the open-range cattle business. At any time, "Texas fever"—a disease transmitted to cattle by parasite-carrying ticks—might decimate a herd. Rustlers and Indians frequently seized large numbers of animals. But as settlement of the plains increased, new forms of competition joined these traditional risks. Sheep breeders from California and Oregon brought their flocks onto the range to compete for grass. Farmers ("nesters") from the East threw fences around their claims, blocking trails and breaking up the open range. A series of "range wars"—between sheepmen and cattlemen, between ranchers and farmers—erupted out of the tensions between these competing groups. Some of the wars resulted in significant loss of life and extensive property damage.

Accounts of the lofty profits to be made in the cattle business—it was said that an investment of $5,000 would return $45,000 in four years—tempted eastern, English, and Scottish capital to the plains. Increasingly, the structure of the cattle economy became corporate; in one year, twenty corporations with a combined capital of $12 million were chartered in Wyoming. The result of this frenzied, speculative expansion was that the ranges, already severed and shrunk by the railroads and the farmers, became overstocked. There was not enough grass to support the crowding herds or sustain the long drives. Two severe winters, in 1885–1886 and 1886–1887, with a searing summer between them, stung and scorched the plains. Hundreds of thousands of cattle died; streams and grass dried up; princely ranches and costly investments disappeared in a season.

The open-range industry never recovered; the long drive disappeared for good. Railroads displaced the trail as the route to market for livestock. But established cattle ranches—with fenced-in grazing land and stocks of hay for winter feed—survived, grew, and prospered, eventually producing more beef than ever.

Although the cattle industry was overwhelmingly male in its early years, there were always a few women involved in ranching and driving. And as ranching became more sedentary, the presence of women greatly increased. By 1890, more than 250,000 women owned ranches or farms in the western states (many of them as proxies for their husbands or fathers, but some in their own right). Indeed, the region provided women with many opportunities that were closed to them in the East—including the opportunity to participate in politics. Wyoming was the first state in the Union to guarantee woman suffrage.

## THE DISPERSAL OF THE TRIBES

Having imagined the West as a "virgin land" awaiting civilization by white people, many Americans tried to force the region to match their image of it. That meant, above all, ensuring that the Indian tribes would not remain obstacles to the spread of white society.

## White Tribal Policies

The traditional policy of the federal government was to regard the tribes simultaneously as independent nations (with which the United States could negotiate treaties) and as wards of the president (who would exercise paternalistic authority over the Indians). The concept of Indian sovereignty had supported the government's attempt before 1860 to erect a permanent frontier between whites and Indians and to reserve the region west of the bend of the Missouri River as a permanent Indian country separated from the rest of the United States. But the belief in tribal sovereignty, and the treaties or agreements with the Indians, were not strong enough to withstand the pressure of white settlers eager for access to Indian lands. The history of relations between the United States and the Native Americans was, therefore, one of nearly endless broken promises—as the national government used its allegedly paternalistic responsibilities to abrogate treaties and seize Indian lands.

By the early 1850s, the idea of establishing one great enclave in which many tribes could live gave way, in the face of white demands for access to lands in Indian Territory, to a new reservations policy, known as "concentration." In 1851, the government assigned each tribe its own defined reservation, confirmed by separate treaties—treaties often illegitimately negotiated with unauthorized "representatives" chosen by whites, people known sarcastically as "treaty chiefs." The new arrangement had many benefits for whites and few for the Indians. It divided the tribes from one another and made them easier to control. It allowed the government to force tribes into scattered locations and to take over the most desirable lands for white settlement. But it did not survive as the basis of Indian policy for long.

In 1867, in the aftermath of a series of bloody conflicts, Congress established the Indian Peace Commission, composed of both soldiers and civilians, to recommend a new and presumably permanent Indian policy. The commission recommended replacing the "concentration" policy with a new one. The government would move all the Plains tribes into two large reservations—one in Indian Territory (Oklahoma), the other in the Dakotas. At a series of meetings with the tribes, government agents cajoled, bribed, and tricked representatives of the Arapaho, Cheyenne, Sioux, and other tribes into agreeing to treaties establishing the new reservations.

But this "solution" worked little better than previous ones. Part of the problem was the way in which the government administered the reservations it had established. White management of Indian matters was entrusted to the Bureau of Indian Affairs, located in the Department of the Interior. The

BUFFALO HIDES The appetite for buffalo hides in the urban East grew rapidly in the late nineteenth century, creating an incentive for hunters to decimate the massive herds. This photograph shows 40,000 buffalo hides pile up in a yard in Dodge City, Kansas, in 1878. Within a few years after that, the buffalo herds were almost extinct.

bureau was responsible for distributing land, making payments, and supervising the shipment of supplies. Its record was abysmal. The bureau's agents in the West, products of political patronage, were often men of extraordinary incompetence and dishonesty. But even the most honest and diligent agents were generally ill-prepared for their jobs. The poor and usually corrupt administration of the reservations was one reason for the constant conflicts between the tribes and the whites who were surrounding them.

But the problem was also a result of the relentless slaughtering by whites of the buffalo herds that supported the tribes' way of life. Even in the 1850s, whites had been killing buffalo at a rapid rate to provide food and supplies for the large bands of migrants traveling to the gold rush in California. After the Civil War, white demand for buffalo hides (especially in the East) became a national phenomenon. Professional and amateur hunters, even casual visitors shooting from passing trains, swarmed over the plains killing the huge animals. Some Indian tribes (notably the Blackfeet) also began killing large numbers of buffalo to sell in the booming new market. The buffalo suffered too from the ecological changes white settlement brought to the region—the reduction and in some areas virtual disappearance of the open plains on which the buffalo depended. The southern herd was virtually exterminated by 1875, and within a few years the smaller northern herd had met the same fate. In 1865, there had been at least 15 million buffalo; a decade later, fewer than a thousand of the great beasts survived. By destroying the buffalo herds, whites were destroying the Indians' source of food and supplies and their ability to resist the white advance. They were also inadvertently contributing to a climate in which Indian warriors felt the need to fight to preserve their way of life.

## The Indian Wars

There was almost incessant fighting between whites and Indians from the 1850s to the 1880s, as Indians struggled against the growing threats to their civilizations. Indian warriors, usually traveling in raiding parties of thirty to forty men, attacked wagon trains, stagecoaches, and isolated ranches, often in retaliation for earlier attacks on them by whites. As the United States Army became more deeply involved in the fighting, the tribes began to focus more of their attacks on white soldiers.

At times, this small-scale fighting escalated into something close to a war. During the Civil War, the eastern Sioux in Minnesota, cramped on a small reservation and exploited by corrupt white agents, suddenly rebelled. Led by Little Crow, they killed more than 700 whites before being subdued by a force of regulars and militiamen. Thirty-eight of the Indians were hanged, and the tribe was exiled to the Dakotas.

At the same time, fighting flared up in eastern Colorado, where the Arapaho and Cheyenne were coming into conflict with white miners settling in the region. Bands of Indians attacked stagecoach lines and settlements in an effort to regain territory they had lost. In response to these incidents, whites called up a large territorial militia, and the army issued dire threats of retribution. The governor urged all friendly Indians to congregate at army posts for protection before the army began its campaign. One Arapaho and Cheyenne band under Black Kettle, apparently in response to the invitation, camped near Fort Lyon on Sand Creek in November 1864. Some members of the party were warriors, but Black Kettle believed he was under official protection and exhibited no hostile intention. Nevertheless, Colonel J. M. Chivington, apparently encouraged by the army commander of the district, led a volunteer militia force—largely consisting of unemployed miners, many of whom were apparently drunk—to the unsuspecting camp and massacred 133 people, 105 of them women and children. Black Kettle himself escaped the Sand Creek massacre. But four years later, in 1868, he and his Cheyennes, some of whom were now at war with the whites, were caught on the Washita River, near the Texas border, by Colonel George A. Custer. White troops killed the chief and his people.

At the end of the Civil War, white troops stepped up their wars against the western Indians on several fronts. The most serious and sustained conflict was in Montana, where the army was attempting to build a road, the Bozeman Trail, to connect Fort Laramie, Wyoming, to the new mining centers. The western Sioux resented this intrusion into the heart of their buffalo range. Led by one of their great chiefs, Red Cloud, they so harried the soldiers and the construction party—among other things, burning the forts that were supposed to guard the route—that the road could not be used.

But it was not only the United States military that harried the tribes. It was also unofficial violence by white vigilantes who engaged in what became known as "Indian hunting." In California, in particular, tracking down and killing Indians became for some whites a kind of sport. Sometimes the killing was in response to Indian raids on white communities. But considerable numbers of whites were committed to the goal of literal "elimination" of the tribes whatever their behavior, a goal that rested on the belief in the essential inhumanity of Indians and the impossibility of white society's coexisting with them. In California, civilians killed close to 5,000 Indians between 1850 and 1880—one of many factors (disease and poverty being the more important) that reduced the Indian population of the state from 150,000 before the Civil War to 30,000 in 1870.

The treaties negotiated in 1867 brought a temporary lull to many of the conflicts. But new forces soon shattered the peace again. In the early 1870s, more waves of white settlers, mostly miners, began to penetrate some of the lands in Dakota Territory supposedly guaranteed to the tribes in 1867. At the same time, the federal government, responding to the recommendations of a commission, decided that it would no longer recognize the tribes as independent entities and would no longer negotiate with tribal chiefs. This step was intended to undermine the collective nature of Indian life and to force the Indians to assimilate into white culture—a goal cherished by many white reformers, who believed that only through assimilation could the Indians achieve genuine "civilization."

Indian resistance flared anew, this time with even greater strength. In the northern plains, the Sioux rose up in 1875 and left their reservation. When white officials ordered them to return, bands of warriors gathered in Montana and united under two great leaders: Crazy Horse and Sitting Bull. Three army columns set out to round them up and force them back onto the reservation. With the expedition, as colonel of the famous Seventh Cavalry, was the colorful and controversial George A. Custer. At the Battle of the Little Bighorn in southern Montana in 1876—perhaps the most famous of all conflicts between whites and Indians—an unprecedentedly large army of up to 4,000 tribal warriors surprised Custer and part of his regiment, surrounded them, and killed every man.

But the Indians did not have the political organization or the supplies to keep their troops united. Soon the warriors drifted off in bands to elude pursuit or search for food, and the army ran them down singly and returned them to Dakota. The power of the Sioux—and of their proud leaders, Crazy Horse and Sitting Bull—soon collapsed. They accepted defeat and life on reservations.

One of the most dramatic episodes in Indian history occurred in Idaho in 1877. The Nez Percé were a small and relatively peaceful tribe, some of whose members had managed to live unmolested in Oregon into the 1870s without ever signing a treaty with the United States. But under pressure from white settlers, the government forced them to move into a reservation that another branch of the tribe had accepted by treaty in the 1850s. With no realistic prospect of resisting, the Indians began the journey to the reservation; but on the way, several younger Indians, drunk and angry, killed four white settlers.

The leader of the band, Chief Joseph, persuaded his followers to flee from the expected retribution. American troops pursued and attacked them, only to be driven off in a battle at White Bird Canyon. After that, the Nez Percé scattered in several directions and became part of a remarkable chase. Joseph moved with 200 men and 350 women, children, and old people in an effort to reach Canada and take refuge with the Sioux there. Pursued by four columns of American soldiers smarting from their defeat at White Bird Canyon, the Indians covered 1,321 miles in seventy-five days, repelling or evading the army time and again. They were finally caught just short of the Canadian boundary. Some escaped and slipped across the border; but Joseph and most of his followers, weary and discouraged, finally gave up. "Hear me, my chiefs," Joseph said after meeting with the American general Nelson Miles. "I am tired. My heart is sick and sad. From where the sun now stands, I will fight no more forever." He surrendered, and the Nez Percé were shipped from one place to another for several years; in the process, many of them died of disease and malnutrition (although Joseph himself lived until 1908).

The last Indians to maintain organized resistance against the whites were the Chiricahua Apaches, who fought intermittently from the 1860s to the late 1880s. The two ablest chiefs of this fierce tribe were Mangas Colorados and Cochise. Mangas was murdered during the Civil War by white

# A M E R I C A N  V O I C E S

## *Two Indian Leaders Face Conquest*

CHIEF JOSEPH SURRENDERS, 1877
I am tired of fighting. The old men are all dead. [My brother] who led the young men is dead. It is cold, and we have no blankets. The little children are freezing to death. My people, some of them, have run away to the hills. No one knows where they are. I want to have some time to look for my children. Maybe I shall find them among the dead.

Hear me, my chiefs. From where the sun now stands, I will fight no more forever.

SITTING BULL SPEAKS OF LIFE ON THE SIOUX RESERVATION, 1883
Whatever you wanted of me I have obeyed. The Great Father sent me word that whatever he had against me in the past had been forgiven and thrown aside, and I accepted his promises and came in [the reservation]. And he told me not to step aside from the white man's path, and I am doing my best to travel in that path. I sit here and look around me now, and I see my people starving. We want cattle to butcher. That is the way you live, and we want to live the same way. When the Great Father told me to live like his people, I told him to send me six teams of mules, because that is the way the white people make a living. I asked for a horse and buggy for my children; I was advised to follow the ways of the white man, and that is why I asked for those things.

THE SURRENDER OF GERONIMO  The great Apache warrior Geronimo
(front row, third from right) sits with members of his diminished band
after surrendering to United States troops in 1886. The two men at
front row, left, are Geronimo's half brothers. The young boy at front
row, right, is his son.

soldiers who tricked him into surrendering, and in 1872 Cochise agreed to
peace in exchange for a reservation that included some of the tribe's traditional land. But Cochise died in 1874, and his successor, Geronimo—unwilling to bow to white pressures to assimilate—fought on for more than a
decade longer, establishing bases in the mountains of Arizona and Mexico
and leading warriors in intermittent raids against white outposts. With each
raid, however, the number of warring Apaches dwindled, as some warriors
died and others drifted away to the reservation. By 1886, Geronimo's plight
was hopeless. His band consisted of only about 30 people, including women
and children, while his white pursuers numbered perhaps 10,000. Geronimo recognized the odds and surrendered, an event that marked the end of
formal warfare between Indians and whites.

The Apache wars were the most violent of all the Indian conflicts, perhaps because the tribes were now the most desperate. But it was the whites

who committed the most flagrant and vicious atrocities. In 1871, for example, a mob of white miners invaded an Apache camp, slaughtered over a hundred Indians, and captured children, whom they sold as slaves to rival tribes. On other occasions, white troops murdered Indians who responded to invitations to peace conferences, once killing them with poisoned food.

Nor did the brutality end with the conclusion of the Apache wars. Another tragic encounter occurred in 1890 as a result of a religious revival among the Sioux—a revival that itself symbolized the catastrophic effects of the white assaults on Indian civilization. The Sioux were by now aware that their culture and their glories were irrevocably fading; some were also near starvation because corrupt government agents had reduced their food rations. As other tribes had done in trying times in the past, many of these Indians turned to a prophet who led them in a religious revival.

This time the prophet was Wovoka, a Paiute who inspired a fervent spiritual awakening that began in Nevada and spread quickly to the plains. The new revival emphasized the coming of a messiah, but its most conspicuous feature was a mass, emotional "Ghost Dance," which inspired ecstatic visions that many participants believed were genuinely mystical. Among these visions were images of a retreat of white people from the plains and a restoration of the great buffalo herds. White agents on the Sioux reservation watched the dances in bewilderment and fear; some believed they might be the preliminary to hostilities.

On December 29, 1890, the Seventh Cavalry (which had once been Custer's regiment) tried to round up a group of about 350 cold and starving Sioux at Wounded Knee, South Dakota. Fighting broke out in which about 40 white soldiers and more than 300 of the Indians, including women and children, died. An Indian may well have fired the first shot, but the battle soon turned into a one-sided massacre, as the white soldiers turned their new machine guns on the Indians and mowed them down in the snow.

*The Dawes Act*

Even before the Ghost Dance and the Wounded Knee tragedy, the federal government had moved to destroy forever the tribal structure that had always been the cornerstone of Indian culture. Reversing its policy of nearly fifty years of creating reservations in which the tribes would be isolated from white society, Congress abolished the practice by which tribes owned reservation lands communally. Some supporters of the new policy believed they were acting for the good of the Indians, whom they considered a "vanishing race" in need of rescue by white society. But the action was frankly designed to force Indians to become landowners and farmers, to abandon their collective society and culture and become part of white civilization.

The Dawes Severalty Act of 1887 (usually known simply as the Dawes Act) provided for the gradual elimination of most tribal ownership of land and the allotment of tracts to individual owners: 160 acres to the head of a family, 80 acres to a single adult or orphan, 40 acres to each dependent child. Adult owners were given United States citizenship, but unlike other citizens, they could not gain full title to their property for twenty-five years (supposedly to prevent them from selling the land to speculators). The act applied to most of the western tribes.

In applying the Dawes Act, the Bureau of Indian Affairs relentlessly promoted the idea of assimilation that lay behind it. Not only did agents of the bureau try to move Indian families onto their own plots of land; they also took Indian children away from their families and sent them to boarding schools run by whites, where they believed the young people could be educated to abandon tribal ways. They also moved to stop Indian religious rituals and encouraged the spread of Christianity and the creation of Christian churches on the reservations.

Few Indians were prepared for this wrenching change. In any case, white administration of the Dawes Act was so corrupt and inept that ultimately the government simply abandoned most efforts to enforce it. Much of the reservation land, therefore, was never distributed to individual owners. Congress attempted to speed assimilation with the Burke Act of 1906, but Indians continued to resist.

## THE RISE AND DECLINE
## OF THE WESTERN FARMER

The arrival of the miners, the empire building of the cattle ranchers, the dispersal of the Indian tribes—all served as a prelude to the decisive phase of white settlement of the Far West. Even before the Civil War, farmers had begun moving into the plains region, challenging the dominance of the ranchers and the Indians and occasionally coming into conflict with both. By the 1870s, what was once a trickle had become a deluge. Farmers poured into the plains and beyond, enclosed land that had once been hunting territory for Indians and grazing territory for cattle, and established a new agricultural region.

For a time in the late 1870s and early 1880s, the new western farmers flourished, enjoying the fruits of an agricultural economic boom comparable in many ways to the booms that eastern industry periodically enjoyed. Beginning in the mid-1880s, however, the boom turned to bust, and the western agricultural economy began a long, steady decline.

### Farming on the Plains

Many factors combined to produce the surge of western agricultural settlement, but the most important was the railroads. Before the Civil War, the Great Plains had been accessible only through a difficult journey by wagon. But beginning in the 1860s, a great new network of railroad lines developed, spearheaded by the transcontinental route Congress had authorized and subsidized in 1862. They made huge new areas of settlement accessible.

The building of the transcontinental line—completed in 1869 when the two lines met at Promontory Point, Utah—was a dramatic and monumental achievement. But while this first transcontinental line captured the public imagination, the construction of subsidiary lines in the following years proved of greater importance to the West. State governments, imitating Washington, subsidized railroad development by offering direct financial aid, favorable loans, and more than 50 million acres of land (on top of the 130 million acres the federal government had already provided). Although built and operated by private corporations, the railroads were in many respects public projects.

The railroads spurred agricultural settlement by making access to the Great Plains easier. But the railroad companies also actively promoted settlement, both to provide themselves with customers for their services and to increase the value of their vast landholdings. The companies set rates so low for settlers that almost anyone could afford the trip west. And they sold much of their land at very low prices and with liberal credit to prospective settlers.

Contributing further to the great surge of white agricultural expansion was a pronounced but temporary change in the climate of the Great Plains. For several years in succession, beginning in the 1870s, rainfall in the plains states was well above average. White Americans now rejected the old idea that the region was the Great American Desert. Some even claimed that cultivation of the plains actually encouraged rainfall.

Even under the most favorable conditions, farming on the plains presented special problems. First was the problem of fencing. Farmers had to enclose their land, if for no other reason than to protect it from the herds of the open-range cattlemen. But materials for traditional wood or stone fences were unavailable, and in any case, such fences would be ineffective as barriers to cattle. In the mid-1870s, however, two Illinois farmers, Joseph H. Glidden and I. L. Ellwood, solved this problem by developing and marketing barbed wire, which became standard equipment on the plains and revolutionized fencing practices all over the country and the world.

The second problem was water. Water was scarce even when rainfall was above average. After 1887, a series of dry seasons began, and lands that had been fertile now returned to semidesert. Some farmers dealt with the problem by using deep wells pumped by steel windmills, or by turning to what was called dryland farming (a system of tillage designed to conserve moisture in the soil by covering it with a dust blanket), or by planting drought-resistant crops. In many areas of the plains, however, only large-scale irrigation could save the endangered farms. But irrigation projects of the necessary magnitude required government assistance, and neither the federal nor the state governments were prepared to fund the projects.

Most of the people who moved into the region had previously been farmers in the Middle West, the East, or Europe. In the booming years of the early 1880s, with land values rising, the new farmers had no problem obtaining extensive and easy credit and had every reason to believe they would soon be able to retire their debts. But the arid years of the late 1880s—during which crop prices were falling while production was becoming more expensive—changed that prospect. Tens of thousands of farmers could not pay their debts and were forced to abandon their farms. There was, in effect, a reverse migration: white settlers moving back east, sometimes turning once-flourishing communities into desolate ghost towns. Those who remained continued to suffer from falling prices (for example, wheat, which had sold for $1.60 a bushel at the end of the Civil War, dropped to 49 cents in the 1890s) and persistent indebtedness.

### Commercial Agriculture

American farming by the late nineteenth century no longer bore very much relation to the comforting image many Americans continued to cherish. The sturdy, independent farmer of popular myth was being replaced by the commercial farmer—attempting to do in the agricultural economy what industrialists were doing in the manufacturing economy.

Commercial farmers were not self-sufficient and made no effort to become so. They specialized in cash crops which they sold in national or world markets. They did not often make their own household supplies or grow their own food but bought them from merchants. This kind of farming, when it was successful, raised farmers' living standards. But it also made them dependent on bankers and interest rates, railroads and freight rates, national and European markets, world supply and demand. And unlike the capitalists of the industrial order, they could not regulate their production or influence the prices of what they sold.

Between 1865 and 1900, agriculture became an international business. Farm output increased dramatically, not only in the United States but in Brazil, Argentina, Canada, Australia, New Zealand, Russia, and elsewhere. At the same time, modern forms of communication and transportation—the telephone, the telegraph, steam navigation, railroads—were creating new markets around the world for agricultural goods. American commercial farmers, constantly opening new lands, produced much more than the domestic market could consume; they relied on the world market to absorb their surplus, but in that market they faced major competition. Cotton farmers depended on export sales for 70 percent of their annual income, wheat farmers for 30 to 40 percent; but the volatility of the international market put them at great risk. Beginning in the 1880s, worldwide overproduction led to a drop in prices for most agricultural goods and hence to great economic distress for many of the more than 6 million American farm families. By the 1890s, 27 percent of the farms in the country were mortgaged; by 1910, 33 percent. In 1880, 25 percent of all farms had been operated by tenants; by 1910, the proportion had grown to 37 percent. Commercial farming made some people fabulously wealthy. But the farm economy as a whole was suffering a significant decline relative to the rest of the nation.

### The Farmers' Grievances

American farmers were painfully aware that something was wrong. But few yet understood the implications of national and world overproduction. Instead, they concentrated their attention and anger on more immediate, more comprehensible—and no less real—problems: inequitable freight rates, high interest charges, and an inadequate currency.

The farmers' first and most burning grievance was against the railroads. In many cases, the railroads charged higher rates for farm goods than for other goods, and higher rates in the South and West than in the Northeast. Railroads also controlled elevator and warehouse facilities in buying centers and charged arbitrary storage rates.

Farmers also resented the institutions controlling credit—banks, loan companies, insurance corporations. Since sources of credit in the West and South were few, farmers had to take loans on whatever terms they could get, often at interest rates of from 10 to 25 percent. Many farmers had to pay these loans back in years when prices were dropping and currency was becoming scarce. As a result, expansion of the currency became an increasingly important issue to farmers.

A third grievance concerned prices—both the prices farmers received for their products and the prices they paid for goods they bought. Farmers sold their products in a competitive world market over which they had no control and of which they had no advance knowledge. A farmer could plant a large crop at a moment when its price was high and find that by the time of the harvest the price had declined. Farmers' fortunes rose and fell in response to unpredictable forces. But many farmers became convinced (often with some reason) that "middlemen"—speculators, bankers, regional and local agents—were conspiring with one another to fix prices so as to benefit themselves at the growers' expense. Many farmers also came to believe (again, not entirely without reason) that manufacturers in the East were colluding to keep the prices of farm goods low and the prices of industrial goods high. Although farmers sold their crops in a competitive world market, they bought manufactured goods in a domestic market protected by tariffs and dominated by trusts and corporations.

### The Agrarian Malaise

These economic difficulties produced a series of social and cultural resentments. In part, this was a result of the isolation of farm life. Farm families in some parts of the country—particularly in the prairie and plains regions, where large farms were scattered over vast areas—were virtually cut off from the outside world. During the winter months and spells of bad weather, the loneliness and boredom could become nearly unbearable. Many farmers lacked access to adequate education for their children, to proper medical facilities, to recreational or cultural activities, to virtually anything that might give them a sense of being members of a community. Older farmers felt the sting of watching their children leave the farm for the city. They felt the humiliation of being ridiculed as "hayseeds" by the new urban culture that was coming to dominate American life.

The result of this sense of isolation and obsolescence was a growing malaise among many farmers, a discontent that would help create a great national political movement in the 1890s. It found reflection, too, in the literature that emerged from rural America. Writers in the late nineteenth century might romanticize the rugged life of the cowboy and the western miner. For the farmer, however, the image was usually different. Hamlin Garland, for example, reflected the growing disillusionment in a series of novels and short stories. In the past, Garland wrote in the introduction to his novel *Jason Edwards* (1891), the agrarian frontier had seemed to be "the Golden West, the land of wealth and freedom and happiness. All of the associations called up by the spoken word, the West, were fabulous, mythic, hopeful." Now, however, the bright promise had faded. The trials of rural life were crushing the human spirit. "So this is the reality of the dream!" a character in Jason Edwards exclaims. "A shanty on a barren plain, hot and lone as a desert. My God!" Once, sturdy yeoman farmers had viewed themselves as the backbone of American life. Now they were becoming painfully aware that their position was declining in relation to the rising urban-industrial society to the east.

D E B A T I N G    T H E    P A S T

## The Frontier and the West

HE EMERGENCE OF the history of the American West as an important field of scholarship can be traced to the paper Frederick Jackson Turner delivered at a meeting of the American Historical Association in 1893: "The Significance of the Frontier in American History." The "Turner thesis," or "frontier thesis," as his argument became known, shaped both popular and scholarly views of the West for two generations.

Turner stated his thesis simply. The settlement of the West by white Americans—"the existence of an area of free land, its continuous recession, and the advance of American settlement westward"—was the central story of the nation's history. The process of westward expansion had transformed a desolate and savage land into modern civilization. It had also continually renewed American ideas of democracy and individualism.

In the first half of the twentieth century, virtually everyone who wrote about the West echoed at least part of Turner's argument. Ray Allen Billington's *Westward Expansion* (1949), the standard textbook in the field for decades, was almost wholly consistent with the Turnerian model. In *The Great Plains* (1931) and *The Great Frontier* (1952), Walter Prescott Webb similarly emphasized the bravery and ingenuity of white settlers in the Southwest.

Serious efforts to displace the Turner thesis as the explanation of western American history began after World War II. In *Virgin Land* (1950), Henry Nash Smith examined many of the same heroic images of the West that Turner and his disciples had presented; but he treated those images less as descriptions of reality than as myths. Earl Pomeroy challenged Turner's notion of the West as a place of individualism, innovation, and democratic renewal. "Conservatism, inheritance, and continuity bulked at least as large," he claimed. Howard Lamar, in *Dakota Territory, 1861–1889* (1956) and *The Far Southwest* (1966), emphasized the highly diverse characters of different areas of the West and thus challenged the Turnerian idea that a distinctive western environment shaped the western experience.

(continued on next page)

The western historians who began to emerge in the late 1970s launched an even more emphatic attack on the Turner thesis and the idea of the "frontier." Echoing the interest of other historians in issues of race, gender, ethnicity, and culture, "new" western historians such as Richard White, Patricia Nelson Limerick, William Cronon, Donald Worster, Peggy Pascoe, and many others challenged the Turnerians on a number of points.

Turner saw the nineteenth-century West as "free land" awaiting the expansion of Anglo-American settlement and American democracy. The "new western historians" have rejected the concept of an empty "frontier" and emphasize, instead, the elaborate and highly developed civilizations (Native American, Hispanic, mixed-blood, and others) that already existed in the region. White, English-speaking Americans, they have argued, did not so much settle the West as conquer it. And Anglo-Americans in the West continue to share the region not only with the Indians and Hispanics who preceded them there, but also with African Americans, Asians, Latin Americans, and others who flowed into the West at the same time they did.

The Turnerian West was a place of heroism, triumph, and above all progress, dominated by the feats of brave white men. The West the new historians describe is a less triumphant (and less masculine) place in which bravery and success coexist with oppression, greed, and failure; in which decaying ghost towns, bleak Indian reservations, impoverished barrios, and ecologically devastated landscapes are as characteristic of western development as great ranches, rich farms, and prosperous cities; and in which women are as important as men in shaping the societies that emerged.

To Turner and his disciples, the nineteenth-century West was a place where rugged individualism flourished and replenished American democracy. The new scholars consider that belief a self-serving myth. Western "pioneers" were never self-sufficient. The region was inextricably tied to a national and international capitalist economy. Westerners depended on government-subsidized railroads for access to markets, federal troops for protection from Indians, and (later) government-funded dams and canals for irrigating their fields and sustaining their towns.

And while Turner defined the West as a process—a process of settlement that came to an end with the "closing of the frontier" in the late nineteenth century—the new historians see the West as a region. Its history does not end in 1890. It continues into our own time.

# CHAPTER SEVENTEEN

# Industrial Supremacy

*Sources of Industrial Growth* ∼ *Capitalism and Its Critics*
*The Ordeal of the Worker*

ITH A STRIDE that astonished statisticians, the conquering hosts of business enterprise swept over the continent; twenty-five years after the death of Lincoln, America had become, in the quantity and value of her products, the first manufacturing nation of the world. What England had accomplished in a hundred years, the United States had achieved in half the time." So wrote the historians Charles and Mary Beard in the 1920s, expressing the amazement many Americans felt when they considered the remarkable expansion of their industrial economy in the late nineteenth century.

In fact, America's rise to industrial supremacy was not as sudden as such observers suggested. The nation had been building a manufacturing economy since early in the nineteenth century; industry was well established before the Civil War. But Americans were clearly correct in observing that the accomplishments of the last three decades of the nineteenth century overshadowed all the earlier progress. Those years witnessed nothing less than the transformation of the nation.

The remarkable growth did much to increase the wealth and improve the lives of many Americans. But such benefits were far from equally shared. While industrial titans and a growing middle class were enjoying a prosperity without precedent in the nation's history, workers, farmers, and others were experiencing an often painful ordeal that slowly edged the United States toward a great economic and political crisis.

## SOURCES OF INDUSTRIAL GROWTH

Many factors contributed to the growth of American industry: abundant raw materials; a large and growing labor supply; a surge in technological innovation; the emergence of a talented, ambitious, and often ruthless group of

| TIME LINE | | | | |
|---|---|---|---|---|
| **1859** | **1866** | **1870** | **1873** | **·1876** |
| First oil well drilled | National Labor Union founded<br><br>First transatlantic cable | Rockefeller founds Standard Oil | Carnegie Steel founded<br><br>Economic panic | Bell invents telephone |
| **1877** | **1879** | **1881** | **1886** | **1887** | **1892** |
| Nationwide railroad strike | Edison invents electric light bulb | American Federation of Labor founded | Haymarket bombing | Bellamy's *Looking Backward* | Homestead Steel strike |
| **1893** | **1899** | **1901** | **1903** | **1914** | |
| Depression begins | Pullman strike | Morgan creates U.S. Steel | Wright brothers' airplane flight | Ford introduces factory assembly lines | |

entrepreneurs; a federal government eager to assist the growth of business; and a great and expanding domestic market for the products of manufacturing.

### Industrial Technology

The rapid emergence of new technologies, together with the discovery of new materials and productive processes, was one of the principal sources of late-nineteenth-century industrial growth.

Some of the most important innovations were in communications. In 1866, Cyrus W. Field laid a transatlantic telegraph cable to Europe. During the next decade, Alexander Graham Bell developed the first commercially useful telephone; and by the 1890s, the American Telephone and Telegraph Company, which handled his interests, had installed nearly half a million telephones in American cities. Other inventions that speeded the pace of business organization were the typewriter (by Christopher L. Sholes in 1868), the cash register (by James Ritty in 1879), and the calculating or adding machine (by William S. Burroughs in 1891).

Among the most revolutionary innovations was the introduction in the 1870s of electricity as a source of light and power. Among the pioneers of electric lighting were Charles F. Brush, who devised the arc lamp for street illumination, and Thomas A. Edison, who invented the incandescent lamp (or light bulb), which could be used for both street and home lighting. Edison and others designed improved generators and built large power plants to furnish electricity to whole cities. By the turn of the century, electric power was becoming commonplace in street railway systems, in the elevators of urban skyscrapers, in factories, and increasingly in offices and homes.

A process by which iron could be transformed into steel—a much more durable and versatile material—had been discovered simultaneously in the 1850s by an Englishman, Henry Bessemer, and an American, William Kelly. (The process consisted of blowing air through molten iron to burn out the impurities.) After the Civil War, the new process transformed the metal industry. In 1868, the New Jersey ironmaster Abram S. Hewitt introduced from Europe another method of making steel—the open-hearth process. These techniques made possible the production of steel in great quantities and large dimensions, for use in the manufacture of locomotives, steel rails, and girders for the construction of tall buildings.

The steel industry emerged first in western Pennsylvania and eastern Ohio, a region where iron ore and coal were abundant and where there was already a flourishing iron industry. Pittsburgh quickly became the center of the steel world. But the industry was growing so fast that new sources of ore were soon necessary. The upper peninsula of Michigan, the Mesabi range in Minnesota, and the area around Birmingham, Alabama, became important ore-producing centers by the end of the century, and new centers of steel production grew up near them: Cleveland, Detroit, Chicago, and Birmingham, among others.

The oil industry emerged in the late nineteenth century largely in response to the steel industry's need for lubrication for its machines. (Not until later did oil become important primarily for its potential as a fuel.) The existence of petroleum reserves in western Pennsylvania had been common knowledge for some time. Not until the 1850s, however, after Pennsylvania businessman George Bissell showed that the substance could be burned in lamps and that it could also yield such products as paraffin, naphtha, and lubricating oil, was there any sense of its commercial value. Bissell raised money to begin drilling; and in 1859, Edwin L. Drake, one of Bissell's employees, established the first oil well near Titusville, Pennsylvania, which was soon producing 500 barrels of oil a month. Demand for petroleum grew quickly, and promoters soon developed other fields in Pennsylvania, Ohio, and West Virginia. By the 1870s, oil had advanced to fourth place among the nation's exports.

Other great innovations were emerging by the beginning of the twentieth century. The Italian inventor Guglielmo Marconi was taking the first steps toward the development of radio in the 1890s. The Wright brothers launched the first airplane flight at Kitty Hawk, North Carolina, in 1903. Other inventors were developing the automobile. As early as the 1870s, designers in France, Germany, and Austria—inspired by the success of railroad engines—had begun to develop an "internal combustion engine," which used the expanding power of burning gas to drive pistons; and with this new engine, they created the first automobiles.

The American automobile industry developed rapidly soon thereafter. Charles and Frank Duryea built the first gasoline-driven motor vehicle in America in 1903. Three years later, Henry Ford produced the first of the famous cars that would bear his name. By 1910, the industry had become a major force in the economy, and the automobile was beginning to reshape

THE ASSEMBLY LINE AT FORD  Henry Ford helped revolutionize automobile manufacturing when he introduced the moving assembly line, pictured here, to his plants in Dearborn, Michigan. Manufacturers all over the world followed his example, and in many places—among them the Soviet Union—the modern science of mass production came to be known as "Fordism."

American social and cultural life. In 1895, there were only four automobiles on the American highways. By 1917, there were nearly 5 million.

## The Science of Production

Central to the growth of the automobile and other industries were changes in the techniques of production. By the turn of the century, many industrialists were embracing the new principles of "scientific management," often known as "Taylorism" after its leading theoretician, Frederick Winslow Taylor. Taylor himself, and his many admirers, argued that scientific management was a way to manage human labor to make it compatible with the demands of the machine age. But scientific management was also a way to increase the employer's control of the workplace, to make working people less independent. Taylor urged employers to reorganize the production process by subdividing tasks. This would speed up production; it would also make workers more interchangeable (less skilled, less in need of training) and thus diminish a manager's dependence on any particular employee. If properly managed by trained experts, he claimed, workers using modern machines could perform simple tasks at much greater speed, greatly increasing productive efficiency.

The most important change in production technology in the industrial era was the emergence of mass production and, along with it, the moving assembly line, which Henry Ford introduced in his automobile plants in 1914. This revolutionary technique cut the time for assembling a chassis from twelve and a half hours to one and a half hours. It enabled Ford to raise the wages and reduce the hours of his workers while cutting the base price of his Model T from $950 in 1914 to $290 in 1929. It became a standard for many other industries.

## Railroad Expansion and the Corporation

But the principal agent of industrial development in the late nineteenth century was the expansion of the railroads. Railroads were the nation's primary method of transportation and gave industrialists access to distant markets and distant sources of raw materials. They were the nation's largest businesses and created new forms of corporate organization that served as models for other industries. And they were America's biggest investors, stimulating economic growth through their own enormous expenditures on construction and equipment.

Total railroad trackage increased dramatically in the last forty years of the nineteenth century: from 30,000 miles in 1860 to 193,000 in 1900. Subsidies from federal, state, and local governments (along with foreign loans and investments) were vital to this expansion, which required far more capital than private entrepreneurs could raise by themselves. Equally important was the emergence of great railroad combinations, many of them dominated by one or two individuals. The achievements (and excesses) of these tycoons—Cornelius Vanderbilt, James J. Hill, Collis R. Huntington, and others—became symbols to much of the nation of concentrated economic power. But railroad development was less significant for the individual barons it created than for its contribution to the growth of a new institution: the modern corporation.

There had been various forms of corporations in America since colonial times, but the modern corporation emerged as a major force only after the Civil War. By then, railroad magnates and other industrialists realized that their great ventures could not be financed by any single person, no matter how wealthy, or even by any single group of partners.

Under the laws of incorporation passed in many states in the 1830s and 1840s, business organizations could raise money by selling stock to members of the public; after the Civil War, one industry after another began doing so. What made the stocks more appealing than they had been in the past was that investors now had only "limited liability"—that is, they risked only the amount of their investments; they were not liable for any debts the corporation might accumulate beyond that point. The ability to sell stock to a broad public made it possible for entrepreneurs to gather vast sums of capital and undertake great projects.

The Pennsylvania and other railroads were among the first to adopt the new corporate form of organization. But incorporation quickly spread beyond the railroad industry. In steel, the central figure was Andrew Carnegie, a Scottish immigrant who had worked his way up from modest beginnings and in 1873 opened his own steelworks in Pittsburgh. Soon he dominated the industry. With his associate Henry Clay Frick, he bought up coal mines and leased part of the Mesabi iron range in Minnesota, operated a fleet of ore ships on the Great Lakes, and acquired railroads. Ultimately, he controlled the processing of his steel from mine to market. He financed his vast undertakings not only out of his own profits but out of the sale of stock. Then, in 1901, he sold out for $450 million to the banker J. Pierpont Morgan, who merged the Carnegie interests with others to create the giant United States Steel Corporation—a $14 billion enterprise that controlled almost two-thirds of the nation's steel production.

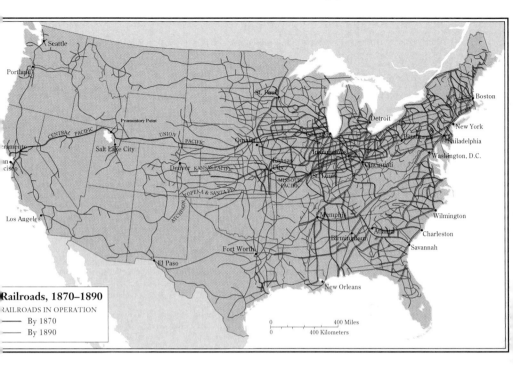

**Railroads, 1870–1890**
RAILROADS IN OPERATION
—— By 1870
—— By 1890

0          400 Miles
0      400 Kilometers

There were similar developments in other industries. Gustavus Swift developed a relatively small meatpacking company into a great national corporation. Isaac Singer patented a sewing machine in 1851 and created I. M. Singer and Company—one of the first modern manufacturing corporations.

Large, national business enterprises needed more systematic administrative structures than the limited, local ventures of the past. As a result, corporate leaders introduced a set of managerial techniques—the genesis of modern business administration—that relied on systematic division of responsibilities, a carefully designed hierarchy of control, careful cost-accounting procedures, and perhaps above all a new breed of business executive: the "middle manager," who formed a layer of command between workers and owners. Efficient administrative capabilities helped make possible another major feature of the modern corporation: consolidation.

Businessmen created large, consolidated organizations primarily through two methods. One was "horizontal integration"—the combining of a number of firms engaged in the same enterprise into a single corporation. The consolidation of many different railroad lines into one company was an example. Another method, which became popular in the 1890s, was "vertical integration"—the taking over of all the different businesses on which a company relied for its primary function. Carnegie Steel, which came to control not only steel mills but mines, railroads, and other enterprises, was an example of vertical integration.

The most celebrated corporate empire of the late nineteenth century was John D. Rockefeller's Standard Oil, a great combination created through both horizontal and vertical integration. Shortly after the Civil War, Rockefeller launched a refining company in Cleveland and immediately began trying to eliminate his competition. Allying himself with other wealthy capitalists, he proceeded methodically to buy out competing refineries. In 1870, he formed the Standard Oil Company of Ohio, which in a few years had acquired twenty of the twenty-five refineries in Cleveland, as well as plants in Pittsburgh, Philadelphia, New York, and Baltimore.

So far, Rockefeller had expanded only horizontally. But soon he began expanding vertically as well. He built his own barrel factories, terminal warehouses, and pipelines. Standard Oil owned its own freight cars and developed its own marketing organization. By the 1880s, Rockefeller had established such dominance within the petroleum industry that to much of the nation he served as the leading symbol of monopoly. He controlled access to 90 percent of the nation's refined oil.

Rockefeller and other industrialists saw consolidation as a way to cope with what they believed was the greatest curse of the modern economy: "cutthroat competition." Most businessmen claimed to believe in free enterprise and a competitive marketplace, but in fact they feared that substantial competition could spell instability and ruin for all. A successful enterprise, many capitalists believed (but did not say), was one that could eliminate or absorb its competitors.

As the movement toward combination accelerated, new vehicles emerged to facilitate it. The railroads began with so-called pool arrangements—informal agreements among various companies to stabilize rates and divide markets (arrangements that would, in later years, be known as cartels). But if even a few firms in an industry were unwilling to cooperate (as was almost always the case), the pool arrangements collapsed.

The failure of the pools led to new techniques of consolidation. At first, the most successful such technique was the creation of the "trust"—pioneered by Standard Oil in the early 1880s and perfected by the banker J. P. Morgan. Over time, the word "trust" became a popular term for describing any great economic combination, but the trust was in fact a particular kind of organization. Under a trust agreement, stockholders in individual corporations transferred their stocks to a small group of trustees in exchange for shares in the trust itself. Owners of trust certificates often had no direct control over the decisions of the trustees; they simply received a share of the profits of the combination. The trustees themselves, on the other hand, might literally own only a few companies but could exercise effective control over many.

In 1889, the state of New Jersey helped produce a third form of consolidation by changing its laws of incorporation to permit companies to buy up other companies. Other states soon followed. That made the trust unnecessary and permitted actual corporate mergers. Rockefeller, for example, quickly relocated Standard Oil in New Jersey and created there what became known as a "holding company"—a central corporate body that would buy up the stock of various members of the Standard Oil trust and establish direct, formal ownership of the corporations in the trust.

By the end of the nineteenth century, as a result of corporate consolidation, 1 percent of the corporations in America were able to control more than 33 percent of the manufacturing. A system of economic organization was emerging that lodged enormous power in the hands of very few men— the great bankers of New York such as J. P. Morgan, industrial titans such as Rockefeller (who himself gained control of a major bank), and others.

The industrial giants of the era were clearly responsible for substantial economic growth. They were also creating the basis for one of the greatest public controversies of their era: a raging debate over concentrated economic and political power that continued well into the twentieth century.

## CAPITALISM AND ITS CRITICS

The rise of big business was not without its critics. Farmers and workers saw in the growth of the new corporate power centers a threat to notions of a republican society in which wealth and authority were widely distributed. Middle-class critics pointed to the corruption that the new industrial titans seemed to produce in their own enterprises and in local, state, and national politics. The growing criticisms challenged the captains of industry to create a defense of the new corporate economy.

### Survival of the Fittest

The new rationale for capitalism rested squarely on an older ideology of individualism. The new industrial economy, its defenders argued, was not shrinking opportunities for individual advancement. It was expanding those opportunities. It was providing every individual with a chance to succeed and attain great wealth.

There was an element of truth in such claims, but only a small element. Before the Civil War there had been few millionaires in America; by 1892 there were more than 4,000. Some of them—Carnegie, Rockefeller, and a few others—were in fact what almost all millionaires claimed to be: "self-made men." But most of the new business tycoons had begun their careers from positions of comfort, privilege, and wealth. Nor was their rise to power and prominence always a result simply of hard work and ingenuity, as they liked to claim. It was also a result of ruthlessness and, at times, rampant corruption.

Nevertheless, most tycoons continued to claim that they had attained their wealth and power through hard work, acquisitiveness, and thrift—the traditional virtues of Protestant America. Those who succeeded, they argued, deserved their success, and those who failed had earned their failure through their own laziness, stupidity, or carelessness. Such assumptions became the basis of a popular social theory of the late nineteenth century: Social Darwinism, the application to human society of Charles Darwin's laws of evolution and natural selection among species. Just as only the fittest survived in the process of evolution, the Social Darwinists argued, so in human society only the fittest individuals survived and flourished in the marketplace.

The English philosopher Herbert Spencer was the first and most important proponent of this theory. Society, he argued, benefited from the elimination of the unfit and the survival of the strong and talented. Spencer's teachings found prominent supporters among American intellectuals, most notably William Graham Sumner of Yale, who promoted similar ideas in lectures, articles, and a famous 1906 book, *Folkways*. Sumner did not agree with everything Spencer wrote, but he did share Spencer's belief that individuals must have absolute freedom to struggle, to compete, to succeed, or to fail.

Social Darwinism appealed to corporate leaders because it seemed to legitimize their success and confirm their virtues. It was not, however, an ideology that had very much to do with the realities of the corporate economy. At the same time that businessmen were celebrating the virtues of competition and the free market, they were making active efforts to protect themselves from competition and to replace the natural workings of the marketplace with control by great combinations. Vicious competitive battle—which Spencer and Sumner celebrated and called a source of healthy progress—was in fact the very thing that American businessmen most feared and tried to eliminate.

## The Gospel of Wealth

Some businessmen attempted to temper the harsh philosophy of Social Darwinism with a gentler, if in some ways equally self-serving, idea: the "gospel of wealth." People of great wealth, advocates of this idea argued, had not only great power but great responsibilities. It was their duty to use their riches to advance social progress. Andrew Carnegie elaborated on the creed in his 1901 book, *The Gospel of Wealth*, in which he wrote that people of wealth should consider all revenues in excess of their own needs as "trust funds" to be used for the good of the community. Carnegie was only one of many great industrialists who devoted large parts of their fortunes to philanthropic works.

The notion of private wealth as a public blessing existed alongside another popular concept: the notion of great wealth as something available to all. Russell H. Conwell, a Baptist minister, became the most prominent spokesman for the idea by delivering one lecture, "Acres of Diamonds," more than 6,000 times between 1880 and 1900. Conwell told a series of stories, which he claimed were true, of individuals who had found opportunities for extraordinary wealth in their own backyards. (One such story involved a modest farmer who discovered a vast diamond mine in his own fields in the course of working his land.) Most of the millionaires in the country, Conwell claimed (inaccurately), had begun on the lowest rung of the economic ladder and had worked their way to success. Every industrious individual had the chance to do likewise.

Horatio Alger was the most famous promoter of the success story. Alger was originally a minister in a small town in Massachusetts but was driven from his pulpit as a result of a scandal connected to his active, but hidden, homosexuality. He moved to New York, where he wrote his celebrated novels: *Ragged Dick, Tom the Bootblack, Sink or Swim*, and many others, more than 100 in all, which together sold more than 20 million copies. The titles and characters varied, but the story and message were invariably the same: a poor boy from a small town went to the big city to seek his fortune. By work, perseverance, and luck, he became rich.

## Alternative Visions

Alongside the celebrations of competition, the justifications for great wealth, and the legitimization of the existing order stood a group of alternative philosophies, challenging the corporate ethos and at times capitalism itself.

One such philosophy emerged in the work of the sociologist Lester Frank Ward. Ward was a Darwinist, but he rejected the application of Darwinian laws to human society. In *Dynamic Sociology* (1883) and other books, he argued that civilization was not governed by natural selection but by human intelligence, which was capable of shaping society as it wished. In contrast to Sumner, who believed that state intervention to remodel the environment was futile, Ward thought that an active government engaged in positive planning was society's best hope.

Other Americans skeptical of the laissez-faire ideas of the Social Darwinists adopted more radical approaches to reform. Some dissenters found a home in the Socialist Labor Party, founded in the 1870s and led for many years by Daniel De Leon, an immigrant from the West Indies. Although De Leon attracted a modest following in the industrial cities, the party never became a major political force and never polled more than 82,000 votes. A dissident faction of De Leon's party, eager to forge stronger ties with organized labor, broke away and in 1901 formed the more enduring American Socialist Party.

Other radicals gained a wider following. One of the most influential was the California writer and activist Henry George. His angrily eloquent *Progress and Poverty*, published in 1879, became one of the best-selling nonfiction works in American publishing history. George blamed social problems on the ability of a few monopolists to grow wealthy as a result of rising land values. An increase in the value of land, he claimed, was not a result of any effort by the owner. It was an "unearned increment," produced by the growth of society around the land. Such profits were rightfully the property of the community. And so George proposed a "single tax" on land, to replace all other taxes, which would return the increment to the people. The tax, he argued, would destroy monopolies, distribute wealth more equally, and eliminate poverty. Single-tax societies sprang up in many cities, and in 1886, George, with the support of labor and the socialists, narrowly missed being elected mayor of New York.

Rivaling George in popularity was Edward Bellamy, whose utopian novel *Looking Backward*, published in 1888, sold more than 1 million copies. It described the experiences of a young Bostonian who went into a hypnotic sleep in 1887 and awoke in the year 2000 to find a new social order in which want, politics, and vice were unknown. The new society had emerged through a peaceful, evolutionary process: the large trusts of the late nineteenth century had continued to grow in size and to combine with one another until ultimately they formed a single, great trust, controlled by the government, which distributed the abundance of the industrial economy equally among all the people. "Fraternal cooperation" had replaced competition. Class divisions had disappeared. Bellamy labeled the philosophy behind this vision "nationalism," and his work inspired the formation of more than 160 Nationalist Clubs to propagate his ideas.

### The Problems of Monopoly

Relatively few Americans shared the views of those who questioned capitalism itself. But as time went on, a growing number of people were becoming deeply concerned about a particular, glaring aspect of capitalism: the growth of monopoly.

By the end of the century, a wide range of groups had begun to assail monopoly and economic concentration. Workers, farmers, consumers, small manufacturers, conservative bankers and financiers, advocates of radical change—all joined the attack. They blamed monopoly for creating artificially

THE FEAR OF MONOPOLY As corporate organizations grew ever larger in the late nineteenth century, the fear of "monopoly power" became a potent force in American life. This cartoon from the political magazine *Puck* suggests something of the horror with which many Americans viewed the rise of monopoly and the tyranny they believed monopoly power exercised over the nation.

high prices. And they blamed it for America's highly unstable economy, which, beginning in 1873, fluctuated erratically, producing severe recessions every five or six years.

Adding to the resentment of monopoly was the emergence of a new class of enormously and conspicuously wealthy people, whose lifestyles became an affront to those struggling to stay afloat in the erratic economy. According to one estimate early in the century, 1 percent of the families in the United States controlled nearly 88 percent of the nation's assets. Some of the wealthy—Andrew Carnegie, for example—lived relatively modestly and donated large sums to philanthropic causes. Others, however, lived in almost grotesque luxury. Observing them were the four-fifths of the American people who lived modestly, and at least 10 million people who lived below the commonly accepted poverty line.


## THE ORDEAL OF THE WORKER

The American working class was both a beneficiary and a victim of the growth of industrial capitalism. Most workers in the late nineteenth century experienced a real rise in their standard of living. But they did so at the cost of arduous and often dangerous working conditions, diminishing control over their own work, and a growing sense of powerlessness.


### The Immigrant Work Force

The industrial work force expanded dramatically in the late nineteenth century as demand for factory labor grew. The source of that expansion was a massive migration into industrial cities—immigration of two sorts. The first was the continuing flow of rural Americans into factory towns and cities—people disillusioned with or bankrupted by life on the farm and eager for new economic and social opportunities. The second was the great wave of immigration from abroad (primarily from Europe, but also from Asia, Canada, and other areas) in the decades following the Civil War—an influx greater than that of any previous era. The 25 million immigrants who arrived in the United States between 1865 and 1915 were more than four times the number who had arrived in the fifty years before.

In the 1870s and 1880s, most of the immigrants came from the nation's traditional sources: England, Ireland, and northern Europe. By the end of the century, however, the major sources of immigrants had shifted, with large numbers of southern and eastern Europeans (Italians, Poles, Russians,

Greeks, Slavs, and others) moving into the country and into the industrial work force.

The new immigrants were coming to America in part to escape poverty and oppression in their homelands. But they were also lured to the United States by expectations of new opportunities. Some such expectations were unrealistic, the result of false promises. Railroads tried to lure immigrants into their western landholdings by distributing misleading advertisements overseas. Industrial employers actively recruited immigrant workers under the Labor Contract Law, which—until its repeal in 1885—permitted them to pay for the passage of workers in advance and deduct the amount later from their wages. Even after the repeal of the law, employers continued to encourage the immigration of unskilled laborers, often with the assistance of foreign-born labor brokers, such as the Greek and Italian *padrones*, who recruited work gangs of their fellow nationals.

The arrival of these new groups introduced heightened ethnic tensions into the dynamics of the working class. Low-paid Poles, Greeks, and French Canadians began to displace higher-paid British and Irish workers in the textile factories of New England. Italians, Slavs, and Poles emerged as a major source of labor for the mining industry, traditionally dominated by native workers or northern European immigrants. Chinese and Mexicans competed with Anglo-Americans and African Americans in mining, farmwork, and factory labor in California, Colorado, and Texas.

*Wages and Working Conditions*

At the turn of the century, the average income of the American worker was $400 to $500 a year—below the $600 figure that many believed was the minimum required to maintain a reasonable level of comfort. Nor did workers have much job security. All were vulnerable to the boom-and-bust cycle of the industrial economy, and some lost their jobs because of technological advances or because of the cyclical or seasonal nature of their work. Even those who kept their jobs could find their wages suddenly and substantially cut in hard times. Few workers, in other words, were ever very far from poverty.

American laborers faced a wide array of other hardships as well. For first-generation workers accustomed to the patterns of agrarian life, there was a difficult adjustment to the nature of modern industrial labor: the performance of routine, repetitive tasks, often requiring little skill, on a strict and monotonous schedule. To skilled artisans whose once-valued tasks were now performed by machines, the new system was impersonal and demeaning. Factory laborers worked ten-hour days, six days a week; in the steel industry they worked twelve hours a day. Industrial accidents were frequent and severe.

### Women and Children at Work

The decreasing need for skilled work in factories induced many employers to increase the use of women and children, whom they could hire for lower wages than adult males. By 1900, 20 percent of all manufacturing workers were women, and 20 percent of all women (well over 5 million) were wage earners. Women worked in all areas of industry, even in some of the most arduous jobs. Most women, however, worked in a few industries where unskilled and semiskilled machine labor (as opposed to heavy manual labor) prevailed. The textile industry remained the largest single industrial employer of women. (Domestic service remained the most common female occupa-

CHILD LABOR Many working-class children of the early twentieth century found employment as "breaker boys," picking pieces of slate out of piles of coal. The coal dust was often so thick that they could hardly see one another, as this Lewis Hine photograph suggests.

tion overall.) Women worked for wages well below the minimum necessary for survival (and well below the wages paid to men working the same jobs).

At least 1.7 million children under sixteen years of age were employed in factories and fields, more than twice the number of thirty years before; 10 percent of all girls aged ten to fifteen, and 20 percent of all boys, held jobs. Under public pressure, thirty-eight states passed child labor laws in the late nineteenth century. But 60 percent of child workers were employed in agriculture, which was typically exempt from the laws. And even for children employed in factories, the laws merely set a minimum age of twelve years and a maximum workday of ten hours, standards that employers often ignored in any case.

### Emerging Unionization

Laborers attempted to fight back against such conditions by adopting one of the same tactics their employers had used so effectively: creating large combinations—national unions. By the end of the century, however, their efforts had met with little success.

There had been craft unions in America, representing small groups of skilled workers, since well before the Civil War. Alone, however, individual unions could not hope to exert significant power in the economy. And during the recession years of the 1870s, unions faced the additional problem of widespread public hostility. When labor disputes with employers turned bitter and violent, as they occasionally did, much of the public instinctively blamed the workers (or the "radicals" and "anarchists" they believed were influencing the workers) for the trouble, rarely the employers. Particularly alarming to middle-class Americans was the emergence of the "Molly Maguires," in the anthracite coal region of western Pennsylvania. This militant labor organization occasionally used violence and even murder in its battle with coal operators. Much of the violence attributed to the Molly Maguires, however, was deliberately instigated by informers and agents employed by the mine owners, who wanted a pretext for ruthless measures suppressing unionization.

Excitement over the Molly Maguires paled beside the near hysteria that gripped the country during the railroad strike of 1877, which began when the eastern railroads announced a 10 percent wage cut and which soon expanded into something approaching a class war. Strikers disrupted rail service from Baltimore to St. Louis, destroyed equipment, and rioted in the streets of Pittsburgh and other cities. State militias were called out, and in July President Hayes ordered federal troops to suppress the disorders in West Virginia. In

Baltimore, eleven demonstrators died and forty were wounded in a conflict between workers and militiamen. In Philadelphia, the state militia killed twenty people when the troops opened fire on thousands of workers and their families who were attempting to block the railroad crossings. In all, over 100 people died before the strike finally collapsed several weeks after it had begun. The great railroad strike was America's first major, national labor conflict, and it illustrated that disputes between labor and capital could no longer be localized in the increasingly national economy.

### The Knights of Labor

The first major effort to create a genuinely national labor organization was the founding in 1869 of the Noble Order of the Knights of Labor, under the leadership of Uriah S. Stephens. Membership was open to all who "toiled," a definition that included all workers, most business and professional people, and virtually all women—whether they worked in factories, as domestic servants, or in their own homes. The only excluded groups were lawyers, bankers, liquor dealers, and professional gamblers. The Knights of Labor was loosely organized, without much central direction. Its program was similarly vague. Although its leaders championed an eight-hour workday and the abolition of child labor, they were more interested in long-range reform of the economy. The Knights hoped to replace the "wage system" with a new "cooperative system," in which workers would themselves control a large part of the economy.

For several years, the Knights remained a secret fraternal organization. But in the late 1870s, under the leadership of Terence V. Powderly, the order moved into the open and entered a period of spectacular expansion. By 1886, it claimed a total membership of over 700,000, including some militant elements that the moderate leadership could not always control. Local unions or assemblies associated with the Knights launched a series of railroad and other strikes in the 1880s in defiance of Powderly's wishes. Their failure helped discredit the organization. By 1890, the membership of the Knights had shrunk to 100,000. A few years later, the organization disappeared altogether.

### The AFL

Even before the Knights began to decline, a rival association based on a very different organizational concept appeared. In 1881, representatives of a number of craft unions formed the Federation of Organized Trade and

Labor Unions of the United States and Canada. Five years later, this body took the name it has borne ever since, the American Federation of Labor (AFL), and it soon became the most important labor group in the country.

Rejecting the Knights' idea of one big union for everybody, the Federation was an association of essentially autonomous craft unions and represented mainly skilled workers. Samuel Gompers, the powerful leader of the AFL, accepted the basic premises of capitalism; his goal was simply to secure for the workers he represented a greater share of capitalism's material rewards. The AFL concentrated on labor's immediate objectives: wages, hours, and working conditions. While it hoped to attain its ends by collective bargaining, it was ready to use strikes if necessary.

As one of its first objectives, the AFL demanded a national eight-hour workday and called for a general strike if the goal was not achieved by May 1, 1886. On that day, strikes and demonstrations for a shorter workday took place all over the country, most of them staged by AFL unions but a few by more radical groups.

In Chicago, a center of labor and radical strength, a strike was already in progress at the McCormick Harvester Company. City police had been harassing the strikers, and labor and radical leaders called a protest meeting at Haymarket Square. When the police ordered the crowd to disperse, someone threw a bomb that killed seven policemen and injured sixty-seven others. The police, who had killed four strikers the day before, fired into the crowd and killed four more people. Conservative, property-conscious Americans—frightened and outraged—demanded retribution, even though no one knew who had thrown the bomb. Chicago officials finally rounded up eight anarchists and charged them with murder, on the grounds that their statements had incited whoever had hurled the bomb. All eight scapegoats were found guilty after a remarkably injudicious trial. Seven were sentenced to death. One of them committed suicide, four were executed, and two had their sentences commuted to life imprisonment.

To most middle-class Americans, the Haymarket bombing was an alarming symbol of social chaos and radicalism. "Anarchism" now became in the public mind a code word for terrorism and violence, even though most anarchists were relatively peaceful visionaries dreaming of a new social order. For the next thirty years, the specter of anarchism remained one of the most frightening concepts in the American imagination. It was a constant obstacle to the goals of the AFL and other labor organizations, and it did particular damage to the Knights of Labor. However much they tried to distance themselves from radicals, labor leaders were always vulnerable to accusations of anarchism, as the violent strikes of the 1890s occasionally illustrated.

## The Homestead Strike

The Amalgamated Association of Iron and Steel Workers, which was affiliated with the American Federation of Labor, was the most powerful trade union in the country. Its members were skilled workers, in great demand by employers, and thus had long been able to exercise significant power in the workplace. In the mid-1880s, however, demand for skilled workers was in decline as new production methods changed the steelmaking process. In the Carnegie system, which was coming to dominate the steel industry, the union was able to maintain a foothold in only one of the corporation's three major factories—the Homestead plant near Pittsburgh.

By 1890, Carnegie and his chief lieutenant, Henry Clay Frick, had decided that the Amalgamated "had to go" even at Homestead. Over the next two years, they repeatedly cut wages at Homestead. At first, the union acquiesced, aware that it was not strong enough to wage a successful strike.

BREAKING THE HOMESTEAD STRIKE, 1892 State militiamen enter Homestead, Pennsylvania, to put an end to the Amalgamated union's violent strike by opening the Carnegie-owned steel plant to strikebreaking workers. This double photograph forms a "stereograph," which, when viewed through a special lens (a "stereoscope"), gave the impression of a three-dimensional scene.

But in 1892, when the company stopped even discussing its decisions with the union and gave it two days to accept another wage cut, the Amalgamated called for a strike.

Frick abruptly shut down the plant and called in 300 guards from the Pinkerton Detective Agency to enable the company to hire nonunion workers. The hated Pinkertons were well-known strikebreakers, and their presence alone was often enough to incite workers to violence. They approached the plant by river, on barges, on July 6, 1892. The strikers poured gasoline on the water, set it on fire, and then met the Pinkertons at the docks with guns and dynamite. A pitched battle broke out. After several hours of fighting, which brought death to three guards and ten strikers and injuries to many others, the Pinkertons surrendered and were escorted roughly out of town.

But the workers' victory was temporary. The governor of Pennsylvania, at the company's request, sent the state's entire National Guard contingent, some 8,000 men, to Homestead. Production resumed, with strikebreakers now protected by troops. And public opinion turned against the strikers when a radical made an attempt to assassinate Frick. Slowly, workers drifted back to their jobs, and finally—four months after the strike began—the Amalgamated surrendered. By 1900, every major steel plant in the Northeast had broken with the Amalgamated, which now had virtually no power to resist. Its membership shrank from a high of 24,000 in 1891 (two-thirds of all eligible steelworkers) to fewer than 7,000 a decade later.

### The Pullman Strike

A dispute of greater magnitude and equal bitterness, if less violence, was the Pullman strike in 1894. The Pullman Palace Car Company manufactured sleeping and parlor cars for railroads, which it built and repaired at a plant near Chicago. There the company constructed a 600-acre town, Pullman, and rented its trim, orderly houses to the employees. George M. Pullman, owner of the company, saw the town as a model—a solution to the problems of industrial workers; he referred to the workers as his "children." But many residents chafed at the regimentation (and the high rents). In the winter of 1893–1894, the Pullman Company slashed wages by about 25 percent, citing its own declining revenues in the depression. At the same time, Pullman refused to reduce rents in its model town, which were 20 to 25 percent higher than those for comparable accommodations in surrounding areas. Workers went on strike and persuaded the militant American Railway Union, led by Eugene V. Debs, to support them by refusing to handle Pullman cars and equipment. Within a few days thousands of railroad workers in twenty-seven states and territories were on strike, and transportation from Chicago to the Pacific Coast was paralyzed.

Most state governors responded readily to appeals from strike-threatened businesses; but the governor of Illinois, John Peter Altgeld, was a man with demonstrated sympathies for workers and their grievances. He refused to call out the militia to protect employers now. Bypassing Altgeld, railroad operators asked the federal government to send regular army troops to Illinois, using the pretext that the strike was preventing the movement of mail on the trains. In July 1894, President Grover Cleveland, over Altgeld's objections, ordered 2,000 troops to the Chicago area. A federal court issued an injunction forbidding the union to continue the strike. When Debs and his associates defied it, they were arrested and imprisoned. With federal troops protecting the hiring of new workers and with the union leaders in a federal jail, the strike quickly collapsed.

### Sources of Labor Weakness

The last decades of the nineteenth century were years in which labor, despite its occasionally militant organizing efforts, made few real gains. Industrial wages rose hardly at all. Labor leaders won a few legislative victories—the abolition by Congress in 1885 of the Contract Labor Law; the establishment by Congress in 1868 of an eight-hour day on public works projects and in 1892 of the same workday for government employees; and state laws governing hours of labor and safety standards and establishing systems for compensating workers injured on the job. But many such laws were not enforced. There were widespread strikes and protests, and many other working-class forms of resistance, large and small, but few real gains. The end of the century found most workers with less political power and less control of the workplace than they had had forty years before.

Workers failed to make greater gains for many reasons. The principal labor organizations represented only a small percentage of the industrial work force; the AFL, the most important, excluded unskilled workers, who were emerging as the core of the industrial work force, and along with them most women, blacks, and recent immigrants. Divisions within the work force contributed further to union weakness. Tensions among different ethnic and racial groups kept laborers divided.

Another source of labor weakness was the shifting nature of the work force. Many immigrant workers came to America intending to remain only briefly, to earn some money and then return home. The assumption that they had no long-range future in the country, even if that assumption was often inaccurate, eroded their willingness to organize. Other workers—natives and immigrants alike—were in constant motion, moving from one job to another, one town to another, seldom in a single place long enough to establish any institutional ties or exert any real power.

Above all, perhaps, workers made few gains in the late nineteenth century because of the strength of the forces arrayed against them. They faced corporate organizations of vast wealth and power, which were generally determined to crush any efforts by workers to challenge their prerogatives. And as the Homestead and Pullman strikes suggest, the corporations usually had the support of local, state, and federal authorities, who were willing to send in troops to "preserve order" and crush labor uprisings on demand.

Despite the creation of new labor unions, despite a wave of strikes and protests that in the 1880s and 1890s reached startling proportions, workers in the late nineteenth century failed on the whole to create successful organizations or to protect their interests in the way the large corporations managed to do. In the battle for power within the emerging industrial economy, almost all the advantages seemed to lie with capital.

# CHAPTER EIGHTEEN

# The Age of the City

*The New Urban Growth* ～ *Society and Culture in Urbanizing America*
*High Culture in the Urban Age*

T HE INDUSTRIALIZATION AND commercialization of America changed the face of society in countless ways. No change was more profound, however, than the growing size and influence of cities. Having begun its life as a primarily agrarian republic, the United States in the late nineteenth century was becoming an urban nation—with a culture increasingly shaped and dominated by its cities.

## THE NEW URBAN GROWTH

The great movement of people from the countryside to the city was not unique to the United States. It was occurring simultaneously throughout much of the Western world in response to industrialization and the factory system. But America, a society with little experience of great cities, found urbanization particularly jarring. The city attracted people because it offered conveniences, entertainments, and cultural experiences unavailable in rural communities. But it attracted people most of all because it offered more and better-paying jobs than were available in the countryside. Whatever the reasons, the urban population of America increased sevenfold in the half-century after the Civil War. And in 1920, the census revealed that for the first time, a majority of the American people lived in "urban" areas—defined as communities of 2,500 people or more.

Natural increase accounted for only a small part of the urban growth. Urban families experienced a high rate of infant mortality, a declining fertility rate, and a high death rate from disease. Without immigration, cities would have grown relatively slowly.

| TIME LINE | | | | |
|---|---|---|---|---|
| **1869** | **1870** | **1871** | **1872** | **1876** |
| First intercollegiate football game | NYC opens first elevated railroads | Boston and Chicago fires | Boss Tweed convicted | Baseball's National League founded |

| **1882** | **1884** | **1890** | **1891** | **1894** | **1895** |
|---|---|---|---|---|---|
| Congress restricts Chinese immigration | First "skyscraper" in Chicago | Riis's *How the Other Half Lives* | Basketball invented | Immigration Restriction League | Crane's *The Red Badge of Courage* |

| **1897** | **1901** | **1903** | **1906** | **1910** |
|---|---|---|---|---|
| Boston opens first subway in America | Baseball's American League founded | First World Series | San Francisco earthquake and fire Sinclair's *The Jungle* | NCAA founded |

*The Migrations*

The late nineteenth century was an age of unprecedented geographical mobility, as Americans left the declining agricultural regions of the East at a dramatic rate. Some of those who left were moving to the newly developing farmlands of the West. But almost as many were moving to the cities of the East and the Midwest.

Among those leaving rural America for industrial cities in the 1880s were southern blacks. They were escaping the poverty, debt, violence, and oppression they faced in the South. They were also seeking new opportunities in cities—opportunities that were limited but usually an improvement over what they left behind. Factory jobs for blacks were rare and professional opportunities almost nonexistent. Urban blacks tended to work as cooks, janitors, and domestic servants, as well as in other service occupations. Since many such jobs were considered women's work, black women often outnumbered black men in the cities. By the end of the nineteenth century, there were substantial black communities (10,000 people or more) in over thirty cities.

The most important source of urban population growth in the late nineteenth century, however, was the arrival of great numbers of new immigrants from abroad. Some came from Canada, Latin America, and—particularly on the West Coast—China and Japan. But the greatest number came from Europe. After 1880, the flow of new arrivals began to include large numbers of people from southern and eastern Europe. By the 1890s, more than half of all immigrants came from these new regions, as opposed to fewer than 2 percent in the 1860s.

In earlier years, most new immigrants from Europe (particularly Germans and Scandinavians) had arrived with at least some money and education. Most of them had headed west—either to be farmers or to work as businessmen, professionals, or skilled laborers in midwestern cities such as St. Louis, Cincinnati, and Milwaukee. But the new immigrants of the late nineteenth century generally lacked the capital to buy farmland and lacked the education to establish themselves in professions. So, like similarly poor Irish immigrants before the Civil War, they settled overwhelmingly in industrial cities, where they occupied largely unskilled jobs.

### The Ethnic City

By 1890, most of the population of the major urban areas consisted of immigrants: 87 percent of the population in Chicago, 80 percent in New York, 84 percent in Milwaukee and Detroit. (London, the largest industrial city in Europe, had by contrast a population that was 94 percent native.)

Equally striking was the diversity of the new immigrant populations. In other countries experiencing heavy immigration in this period, most of the new arrivals were coming from one or two sources. But in the United States, no single national group dominated. In the last four decades of the nineteenth century, substantial groups arrived from Italy, Germany, Scandinavia, Austria, Hungary, Russia, Great Britain, Ireland, Poland, Greece, Canada, Japan, China, Holland, Mexico, and other nations. In some towns, a dozen different ethnic groups might find themselves living in close proximity to one another.

Most of the new immigrants were rural people, and their adjustment to city life was often a painful one. To help ease the transition, many national groups formed close-knit ethnic communities within the cities: neighborhoods (often called "immigrant ghettoes") that attempted to re-create in the New World many of the features of the Old. Some ethnic neighborhoods consisted of people who had migrated to America together from the same province, town, or village. Even when the population was more diverse, however, the community offered newcomers much that was familiar. They could find newspapers and theaters in their native languages, stores selling their native foods, and church and fraternal organizations that provided links with their national pasts. Many immigrants also maintained close ties with their native countries. They stayed in touch with relatives who had remained be-

A  M  E  R  I  C  A  N     V  O  I  C  E  S

ANZIA YEZIERSKA

*A Jewish Immigrant Strains*
*Against the Past*

FOR SEVENTEEN YEARS I had stood [my father's] preaching and his bullying. But now all the hammering hell that I had to listen to since I was born cracked my brain. His heartlessness to Mother, his pitiless driving away Bessie's only chance to love, bargaining away Fania to a gambler and Mashah to a diamond-faker—when they each had the luck to win lovers of their own—all these tyrannies crashed over me. Should I let him crush me as he crushed them? No. This is America, where children are people. . . .

Blindly, I grabbed my things together into a bundle. I didn't care where I was going or what was to become of me. Only to break away from my black life. Only not to hear Father's preaching voice again. . . .

As I came through the door with my bundle, Father caught sight of me. "What's this?" he asked. "Where are you going?"

"I'm going back to work, in New York. . . . I've got to live my own life. It's enough that Mother and the others lived for you. . . . Thank God, I'm not living in olden times. Thank God I'm living in America! You made the lives of the other children. I'm going to make my own life!"

"You blasphemer!" His hand flung out and struck my cheek. "Denier of God! I'll teach you respect for the law!"

I leaped back and dashed for the door. The Old World had struck its last on me.

SOURCE: Selections from *Bread Givers* by Anzia Yezierska, copyright © 1925 by Doubleday, copyright renewed 1952 by Anzia Yezierska, transferred to Louise Levitas Henriksen in 1970. Reprinted by permission of Persea Books, Inc.

hind. Some (perhaps as many as a third in the early years) returned to their homelands after a relatively short time; others helped bring the rest of their families to America.

The cultural cohesiveness of the ethnic communities clearly eased the pain of separation from the immigrants' native lands. What role it played in helping immigrants become absorbed into the economic life of America is a more difficult question to answer. It is clear that some ethnic groups (Jews and Germans in particular) advanced economically more rapidly than others (for example, the Irish). One explanation is that, by huddling together in ethnic neighborhoods, immigrant groups tended to reinforce the cultural values of their previous societies. When those values were particularly well suited to economic advancement—as was, for example, the high value Jews placed on education—ethnic identification may have helped members of a group to improve their lots. When other values predominated—maintaining community solidarity, strengthening family ties, preserving order—progress could be less rapid.

But other factors were at least as important in determining how well immigrants fared. Immigrants who aroused strong racial prejudice among native-born whites—most notably African Americans, Asians, and Mexicans—found it very difficult to advance whatever their talents. Those who arrived with a valuable skill or with some capital did better than those who did not. And over time, those who lived in cities where people of their own nationality came to predominate—for example, the Irish in New York and Boston, or the Germans in Milwaukee—gained an advantage as they learned to exert their political power.

### Assimilation and Exclusion

Despite the many differences among the various immigrant communities, virtually all groups had certain things in common. Most immigrants shared the experience of living in cities (and of adapting from a rural past to an urban present). Most were young; the majority of newcomers were between fifteen and forty-five years old. And in most foreign-born immigrant communities, the strength of ethnic ties had to compete against another powerful force: the desire for assimilation.

Many of the new arrivals had come to America with romantic visions of the New World. And however disillusioning they might find their first contact with the United States, they usually retained the dream of becoming true "Americans." Second-generation immigrants were particularly likely to attempt to break with the old ways, to assimilate themselves completely into what they considered the real American culture. Some even looked with contempt on parents and grandparents who continued to defend traditional ethnic habits and values. Young women, in particular, sometimes rebelled against parents who tried to arrange (or prevent) marriages or who opposed women entering the workplace.

Assimilation was not, of course, entirely a matter of choice. Native-born Americans encouraged it, both deliberately and inadvertently, in countless ways. Public schools taught children in English, and employers often insisted that workers speak English on the job. Most stores sold mainly American products, forcing immigrants to adapt their diets, clothing, and lifestyles to American norms. Church leaders were often native-born Americans or more assimilated immigrants who encouraged their parishioners to adopt American ways. Some even reformed their religion to make it more compatible with the norms of the new country. Reform Judaism, imported from Germany in the late nineteenth century, was an effort by American Jewish leaders (as it had been by German ones) to make their faith less "foreign" to the dominant culture of a largely Christian nation.

The arrival of these vast numbers of new immigrants, and the way many of them clung to old ways and created distinctive communities, provoked fear and resentment among some native-born Americans in much the same way earlier arrivals had done. Some people reacted against the immigrants out of generalized fears and prejudices, seeing in their "foreignness" the source of all the disorder and corruption of the urban world. Native laborers were also often incensed by the willingness of the immigrants to accept lower wages and to take over the jobs of strikers.

The rising nativism provoked political responses. In 1887, Henry Bowers, a self-educated lawyer obsessed with a hatred of Catholics and foreigners, founded the American Protective Association, a group committed to stopping immigration. By 1894, membership in the organization reportedly reached 500,000, with chapters throughout the Northeast and Midwest. That same year, five Harvard alumni founded a more genteel organization—the Immigration Restriction League—in Boston. They proposed screening immigrants through literacy tests and other standards, to separate the "desirable" from the "undesirable."

Even before the rise of these new organizations, politicians were struggling with the "immigration question." In 1882 Congress had responded to strong anti-Asian sentiment in California and elsewhere and excluded the Chinese. In the same year, Congress denied entry to "undesirables"—

convicts, paupers, the mentally incompetent—and placed a tax of 50 cents on each person admitted. Later legislation of the 1890s enlarged the list of those barred from immigrating and increased the tax.

But these laws kept out only a small number of aliens, and more ambitious restriction proposals made little progress in Congress. That was because immigration was providing a cheap and plentiful labor supply to the rapidly growing economy, and many argued that America's industrial (and indeed agricultural) development would be impossible without it.

## The Urban Landscape

The city was a place of remarkable contrasts. It had homes of almost unimaginable size and grandeur and hovels of indescribable squalor. It had conveniences unknown to earlier generations and problems that seemed beyond the capacity of society to solve. Both the attractions and the problems were a result of the stunning pace at which cities were growing. The expansion of the urban population helped spur important new technological and industrial developments. But the rapid growth also produced misgovernment, poverty, congestion, filth, epidemics, and great fires. The rate of growth was simply too fast for planning and building to keep pace.

One of the greatest problems was providing housing for the thousands of new residents who were pouring into the cities every day. For the prosperous, housing was seldom a worry. The availability of cheap labor and the increasing accessibility of tools and materials reduced the cost of building in the late nineteenth century and permitted anyone with even a moderate income to afford a house. Some of the richest urban residents lived in palatial mansions in the heart of the city. Many of the moderately well-to-do took advantage of less expensive land on the edges of the city and settled in new suburbs, linked to the downtowns by trains or streetcars.

Most urban residents, however, could not afford either to own a house in the city or to move to the suburbs. Instead, they stayed in the city centers and rented. Landlords tried to squeeze as many rent-paying residents as possible into the smallest available space. In Manhattan, for example, the average population density in 1894 was 143 people per acre—a rate higher than that of the most crowded cities of Europe (Paris had 127 per acre, Berlin 101) and far higher than that of any other American city then or since. In the cities of the South—Charleston, New Orleans, Richmond—poor blacks lived in crumbling former slave quarters. In Boston, immigrants moved into cheap three-story wooden houses ("triple deckers"), many of them decaying fire hazards. In Baltimore and Philadelphia, the new arrivals crowded into narrow brick row houses. And in New York and many other cities, they lived in tenements.

The word "tenement" had originally referred simply to a multiple-family rental building, but by the late nineteenth century it had become a term for slum dwellings only. The first tenements, built in 1850, had been hailed as a great improvement in housing for the poor. But most were, in fact, miserable places, with many windowless rooms, little or no plumbing or heating, and often a row of privies in the basement. Jacob Riis, a Danish immigrant and New York newspaper reporter and photographer, shocked many middle-class Americans with his sensational (and some claimed sensationalized) descriptions and pictures of tenement life in his 1890 book, *How*

A NEW YORK TENEMENT, 1910 This photograph of a woman and her children in a rear tenement bedroom was meant to illustrate the crowding and squalor of urban immigrant life. The photographer was Lewis Hine, who from 1907 to 1914 worked for a government committee investigating child labor and whose efforts to expose social conditions helped spur legislative action.

*the Other Half Lives.* But the solution reformers often adopted was simply to raze slum dwellings without building any new housing to replace them.

Urban growth posed monumental transportation challenges. Old downtown streets were often too narrow for the heavy traffic that was beginning to move over them. Most were without a hard, paved surface and resembled either a sea of mud or a cloud of dust, depending on the weather. But it was not simply the conditions of the streets that impeded urban transportation. It was the numbers of people who needed to move every day from one part of the city to another, numbers that mandated the development of mass transportation. Streetcars drawn on tracks by horses had been introduced into some cities even before the Civil War. But the horsecars were not fast enough, so many communities developed new forms of mass transit. In 1870, New York opened its first elevated railway, whose noisy, filthy steam-powered trains moved rapidly above the city streets on massive iron structures. New York, Chicago, San Francisco, and other cities also experimented with cable cars, towed by continuously moving underground cables. Richmond, Virginia, introduced the first electric trolley line in 1888, and in 1897 Boston opened the first American subway. At the same time, cities were developing new techniques of road and bridge building. One of the great technological marvels of the 1880s was the completion of the Brooklyn Bridge in New York—a dramatic steel-cable suspension span designed by John A. Roebling.

Cities were growing upward as well as outward. In Chicago, the construction of the first modern "skyscraper"—by later standards a relatively modest building, ten stories high—launched a new era in urban architecture. Once builders perfected the technique of constructing tall buildings with cast iron and then steel beams, and once other inventors produced the electric elevator, no obstacle remained to even higher buildings.

### Strains of Urban Life

The increasing congestion of the city and the absence of adequate public services produced serious hazards. One was fire. In one major city after another, fires destroyed large downtown areas. Chicago and Boston suffered "great fires" in 1871. Other cities—among them Baltimore and San Francisco, where a tremendous earthquake produced a catastrophic fire in 1906—experienced similar disasters. The great fires were terrible experiences, but they were also important events in the development of the cities involved. They encouraged the construction of fireproof buildings and the development of professional fire departments. They also forced cities to rebuild at a time when new technological and architectural innovations were available. Some of the modern, high-rise downtowns of American cities arose out of the rubble of great fires.

An even greater hazard than fire was disease, especially in poor neighborhoods with inadequate sanitation facilities. But an epidemic that began in a poor neighborhood could (and often did) spread easily into other neighborhoods as well. Few municipal officials recognized the relationship of improper sewage disposal and water contamination to such epidemic diseases as typhoid fever and cholera; many cities lacked adequate systems for disposing of human waste until well into the twentieth century.

Above all, perhaps, the expansion of the city spawned widespread and often desperate poverty. Despite the rapid growth of urban economies, the sheer number of new residents ensured that many people would be unable to earn enough for a decent subsistence. Public agencies and private philanthropic organizations offered some relief. But they were generally dominated by middle-class people who believed that too much assistance would breed dependency and that poverty was the fault of the poor themselves.

Poverty and crowding naturally bred crime and violence. The American murder rate rose rapidly in the late nineteenth century (even as such rates were declining in Europe), from 25 murders for every million people in 1880 to over 100 by the end of the century. The rising crime rates encouraged many cities to develop larger and more professional police forces. But police forces themselves could spawn corruption and brutality, particularly since jobs on them were often filled through political patronage.

Americans and Europeans alike reacted to the city with marked ambivalence. It was a place of strong allure and great excitement. Yet it was also a place of alienating impersonality, a new feeling of anonymity, a different kind of work with which the individual could feel only limited identification. To some, it was also a place of degradation and exploitation. Theodore Dreiser's novel *Sister Carrie* (1900) exposed one troubling aspect of urban life: the plight of single women (like Dreiser's heroine, Carrie) who moved from the countryside into the city and found themselves without any means of support. Carrie first took an exhausting and ill-paying job in a Chicago shoe factory; then she drifted into a life of "sin," exploited by predatory men. Many women were experiencing in reality the dilemmas Carrie experienced in fiction. Living in conditions of extreme poverty and hardship, some moved into prostitution—which, degrading and dangerous as it was, produced a livelihood and some sense of community for desperate people.

## The Machine and the Boss

Newly arrived immigrants, many of whom could not speak English, were much in need of institutions to help them adjust to American urban life. For many residents of the inner cities, the principal source of assistance was the political "machine."

The urban machine was one of America's most distinctive political institutions. It owed its existence to the power vacuum that the chaotic growth of cities (and the very limited growth of governments) had created. It was also a product of the potential voting power of large immigrant communities. Any politician who could mobilize that power stood to gain enormous influence or public office. And so there emerged a group of "urban" bosses, themselves often of foreign birth or parentage. Many were Irish, because they spoke English and because some had previous political experience from the long Irish struggle against the English at home.

The principal function of the political boss was simple: to win votes for his organization. That meant winning the loyalty of his constituents. To do so, a boss might provide them with occasional relief—a basket of groceries or a bag of coal. He might step in to save those arrested for petty crimes from jail. When he could, he found work for the unemployed. Above all, he rewarded many of his followers with patronage: with jobs in city government or in such city agencies as the police (which the machine's elected officials often controlled); with jobs building or operating the new transit systems; and with opportunities to rise in the political organization itself.

Machines were also vehicles for making money. Politicians enriched themselves and their allies through various forms of graft and corruption. Some of it might be fairly open—what George Washington Plunkitt of New York's Tammany Hall called "honest graft." For example, a politician might discover in advance where a new road or streetcar line was to be built, buy land near it, and sell it at a profit to the city or to developers when property values rose as a result of the construction. There was also covert graft. Officials received kickbacks from contractors in exchange for contracts to build streets, sewers, public buildings, and other projects, and they sold franchises for the operation of such public utilities as street railways, waterworks, and electric light and power systems. The most famously corrupt city boss was William M. Tweed, boss of New York City's Tammany Hall in the 1860s and 1870s, whose extravagant use of public funds on projects that paid kickbacks to the organization finally landed him in jail in 1872.

Middle-class critics cited corruption as the principal characteristic of the machine, but it was also notable for other things. Political organizations contributed to modernizing city infrastructures, to expanding the role of government, and to creating stability in a political and social climate that otherwise would have lacked a center.

Several factors made boss rule possible. One was the power of immigrant voters, who were less concerned with middle-class ideas of political morality than with obtaining the services that machines provided and reformers did not. Another was the link between the political organizations and many wealthy, prominent citizens who profited from their dealings with bosses and resisted efforts to overthrow them.

The urban machine was not without competition. Reform groups frequently mobilized public outrage at the corruption of the bosses and often succeeded in driving machine politicians from office. Tammany, for example, saw its candidates for mayor and other high city offices lose almost as often as they won in the last decades of the nineteenth century. But the reform organizations typically lacked the permanence of the machine, and more often than not, their power faded after a few years.

## SOCIETY AND CULTURE IN URBANIZING AMERICA

For urban middle-class Americans, the last decades of the nineteenth century were a time of dramatic advances. Indeed, it was in those years that a distinctive middle-class culture began to exert a powerful influence over the whole of American life. Other groups in society advanced less rapidly, or not at all, but almost no one was unaffected by the rise of the new urban, consumer culture.

### The Rise of Mass Consumption

The growth of American industry could not have occurred without the expansion of markets for the goods being produced. Much of the emerging mass market for industrial goods consisted of the increasingly wealthy middle class. But much of it also consisted of less affluent people who consumed more because mass production and mass distribution were making consumer goods less expensive.

Incomes were rising for almost everyone in the industrial era, although at highly uneven rates. The most conspicuous result of the new economy was the creation of vast fortunes, but perhaps the most important result for society as a whole was the growth and increasing prosperity of the middle class. The salaries of clerks, accountants, middle managers, and other "white-collar" workers rose by an average of a third between 1890 and 1910—and in some parts of the middle class, much higher. Doctors, lawyers, and other professionals, for example, experienced a particularly dramatic increase in both the prestige and the profitability of their professions. Working-class incomes rose too in those years, although from a much lower base and often more slowly. The iron and steel industries saw workers' hourly wages increase by a third between 1890 and 1910; but industries with large female work forces—shoes, textiles, and paper—saw more modest increases, as did almost all industries in the South. Wages for African Americans, Mexicans, and Asians also tended to rise more slowly than those for other workers.

The new mass market was also a result of the development of affordable products and the creation of new merchandising techniques, which made many consumer goods available to a mass market for the first time. A good example of such changes was the emergence of ready-made clothing. In the early nineteenth century, most Americans had made their own clothing—usually from cloth they bought from merchants, at times from fabrics they spun and wove themselves. The invention of the sewing machine and the spur that the Civil War (and its demand for uniforms) gave to the manufacture of clothing helped create an enormous industry devoted to producing ready-made garments. By the end of the century, virtually all Americans bought their clothing from stores. Partly as a result, much larger numbers of people became concerned with personal style. Interest in women's fashion, for example, had once been a luxury reserved for the relatively affluent. Now middle-class and even working-class women could strive to develop a distinctive style of dress.

Buying and preparing food also became a critical part of the new consumerism. The development and mass production of tin cans in the 1880s created a large new industry devoted to packaging and selling canned food and condensed milk. Refrigerated railroad cars made it possible for perishables—meats, vegetables, dairy products, and other foodstuffs—to be transported over long distances without spoiling. Artificially frozen ice enabled many households to afford iceboxes. Among other things, the changes meant improved diets and better health. Life expectancy rose six years in the first two decades of the twentieth century.

Changes in marketing also altered the way Americans bought goods. New "chain stores" could usually offer a wider array of goods at lower prices than the small local stores with which they competed. The Atlantic and Pacific Tea Company (the A & P) began a national network of grocery stores

THE DEPARTMENT STORE, C. 1892 This detail from an advertisement shows an interior cross section of the Abraham and Straus department store in Brooklyn, New York. Early department stores boasted not just of the variety of their merchandise but also of the almost magical consumer world they created.

in the 1870s. F. W. Woolworth built a chain of dry goods stores. Sears and Roebuck established a large market for its mail-order merchandise by distributing an enormous catalog each year. Even people in remote rural areas could order its products.

In larger cities, the emergence of great department stores helped transform buying habits and turn shopping into a more alluring and glamorous activity. Marshall Field in Chicago created one of the first American department stores—a place deliberately designed to produce a sense of wonder and excitement. Similar stores emerged in New York, Brooklyn, Boston, Philadelphia, and other cities.

The rise of mass consumption had particularly dramatic effects on American women, who were generally the primary consumers within families. Women's clothing styles changed much more rapidly and dramatically than those of men. Women generally bought and prepared food for their families, so the availability of new food products changed not only the way everyone ate but the way women shopped and cooked. Canning and refrigeration meant greater variety in the diet. It also meant that food did not always have to be purchased on the day it was eaten. The consumer economy also produced new employment opportunities for women as salesclerks in department stores and as waitresses in rapidly proliferating restaurants. And it spawned the creation of a new movement in which women were to play a vital role: the consumer protection movement. The National Consumers

League, formed in the 1890s under the leadership of Florence Kelley, attempted to mobilize the power of women as consumers to force retailers and manufacturers to improve wages and working conditions.

### Leisure and Sport

Closely related to the growth of consumption was a growing interest in leisure time, which for many people was increasing rapidly. Members of the urban middle and professional classes had large blocks of time during which they were not at work—evenings, weekends, even paid vacations. Working hours in many factories declined, from an average of nearly seventy hours a week in 1860 to under sixty in 1900. Even farmers found that the mechanization of agriculture gave them more free time. The lives of many Americans were becoming more compartmentalized, with clear distinctions between work and leisure that had not existed in the past. The change produced a search for new forms of recreation and entertainment.

Among the most important responses to this search was the rise of organized spectator sports, and especially baseball, which by the end of the century was well on its way to becoming the "national pastime." A game much like baseball—known as "rounders" and derived from cricket—had enjoyed limited popularity in Great Britain in the early nineteenth century. Versions of the game began to appear in America in the early 1830s, well before Abner Doubleday supposedly "invented" baseball. (Doubleday, in fact, had almost nothing to do with the creation of baseball and actually cared little for sports. Alexander Cartwright, a member of a New York City baseball club, defined many of the rules and features of the game as we know it today in the 1840s.)

By the end of the Civil War, interest in the game had grown rapidly. More than 200 amateur or semiprofessional teams and clubs existed, many of which joined a national association and proclaimed a set of standard rules. As the game grew in popularity, it offered opportunities for profit. The first salaried team, the Cincinnati Red Stockings, was formed in 1869. Other cities soon fielded professional teams, and in 1876 the teams banded together in the National League. A rival league, the American Association, soon appeared. It eventually collapsed, but in 1901 the American League emerged to replace it. And in 1903, the first modern World Series was played, in which the American League Boston Red Sox beat the National League Pittsburgh Pirates. By then, baseball had become an important business and a great national preoccupation (at least among men), attracting paying crowds at times as large as 50,000.

Baseball had great appeal to working-class males. The second most popular game, football, appealed at first to a more elite segment of the male population, in part because it originated in colleges and universities. The first intercollegiate football game in America occurred between Princeton and Rutgers in 1869, and soon the game began to become entrenched as part of collegiate life. Early intercollegiate football bore only an indirect relation to the modern game; it was more similar to what is now known as rugby. By the late 1870s, however, the game was becoming standardized and was taking on the outlines of its modern form.

Basketball was invented in 1891 at Springfield, Massachusetts, by Dr. James A. Naismith, a Canadian working as athletic director for a local college. Boxing, which had long been a disreputable activity concentrated primarily among the urban lower classes, became by the 1880s a more popular and in some places more reputable sport.

The major spectator sports of the era were activities open almost exclusively to men. But a number of other sports were emerging in which women became important participants. Golf and tennis seldom attracted crowds in the late nineteenth century, but both experienced a rapid increase in participation among relatively wealthy men and women. Bicycling and croquet also enjoyed widespread popularity in the 1890s among women as well as men. Women's colleges introduced their students to more strenuous sports as well—track, crew, swimming, and (beginning in the late 1890s) basketball—challenging the once-prevalent notion that vigorous exercise was dangerous to women.

### Leisure and Popular Culture

Other forms of popular entertainment developed in the cities in response to the large potential markets there. Many ethnic communities maintained their own theaters, in which immigrants heard the music of their homelands and listened to comedians making light of their experiences in the New World. Urban theaters also introduced some of the most distinctively American entertainment forms: the musical comedy, which evolved gradually from the comic operettas of European theater; and vaudeville, a form of theater adapted from French models, which remained the most popular urban entertainment in the first decades of the twentieth century. Even saloons and small community theaters could afford to offer their customers vaudeville, which consisted of a variety of acts (musicians, comedians, magicians, jugglers, and others) and was, at least in the beginning, inexpensive to produce. As the economic potential of vaudeville grew, some promoters—most prominently Florenz Ziegfeld of New York—staged much more elaborate spectacles.

Vaudeville was also one of the few entertainment media open to black performers. They brought to it elements of the minstrel shows they had earlier developed for black audiences in the late nineteenth century. Some minstrel singers (including the most famous, Al Jolson) were whites wearing heavy makeup (or "blackface"), but most were black. Entertainers of both races performed music based on the gospel and folk tunes of the plantation and on the jazz and ragtime of black urban communities. Performers of both races also tailored their acts to prevailing white prejudices, ridiculing blacks by acting out demeaning stereotypes.

The most important form of mass entertainment (until the invention of radio and television), and the one that reached most widely across the nation, was the movies. Thomas Edison and others had created the technology of the motion picture in the 1880s. Soon after that, short films became available to individual viewers watching peepshows in pool halls, penny ar-

A NICKELODEON  An early movie theater, with musicians providing a live accompaniment to a silent film. The first feature-length sound picture (or "talkie"), *The Jazz Singer*, appeared in 1927.

cades, and amusement parks. Soon, larger projectors made it possible to project the images onto big screens, which permitted substantial audiences to see films in theaters. By 1900, Americans were becoming attracted in large numbers to these early movies—usually plotless films of trains or waterfalls or other spectacles designed mainly to show off the technology. The great D. W. Griffith carried the motion picture into a new era with his silent epics—*The Birth of a Nation* (1915), *Intolerance* (1916), and others—which introduced serious (if notoriously racist) plots and elaborate productions to filmmaking. Motion pictures were the first truly mass entertainment medium—one that reached all areas of the country and most groups in the population.

Particularly striking about popular entertainment in the late nineteenth and early twentieth centuries was its public quality. Many Americans spent their leisure time in places where they would find not only entertainment but also other people. Thousands of working-class New Yorkers flocked to the amusement park at Coney Island, for example, not just for the rides and shows but for the excitement of the crowds, as did the thousands who spent evenings in dance halls, vaudeville houses, and concert halls. More affluent New Yorkers enjoyed afternoons in Central Park, where a principal attraction was seeing other people (and being seen by them). Moviegoers were attracted not just by the movies themselves but by the energy of the audiences at the lavish "movie palaces" that began to appear in cities in the early twentieth century, just as sports fans were drawn by the crowds as well as by the games.

Mass entertainment did not usually bridge differences of class or race; there were relatively few places where people of widely diverse backgrounds gathered together. When members of different classes or races did meet in public spaces—as they did, for example, in city parks—there was often considerable conflict over what constituted appropriate public behavior. Elites in New York City, for example, tried to prohibit anything but quiet, "genteel" activities in Central Park, while working-class people wanted to use the public spaces for sports and entertainments. But even divided by class, new forms of popular entertainment helped sustain a vigorous public culture.

Not all popular entertainment, however, involved public events. Many Americans amused themselves privately by reading novels and poetry. The so-called dime novels, cheaply bound and widely circulated, became popular after the Civil War, with detective stories, tales of the "Wild West," sagas of scientific adventure (such as the Tom Swift stories), and novels of "moral uplift" (among them those of Horatio Alger). Publishers also distributed sentimental novels of romance, which developed a large audience among women, as did books about animals and about young children growing up. Louisa May Alcott's *Little Women*, most of whose readers were women, sold more than 2 million copies.

### Mass Communications

Urban-industrial society created a vast market for news and information. And so American publishing and journalism experienced an important change in the decades following the Civil War. Between 1870 and 1910, the circulation of daily newspapers increased nearly ninefold (from under 3 million to more than 24 million), a rate three times as great as the rate of population increase. And while standards varied widely from one paper to another, American journalism was developing the beginnings of a professional identity. Salaries of reporters increased; many newspapers began separating the reporting of news from the expression of opinion; and newspapers themselves became important businesses.

One striking change was the emergence of national press services, which made use of the telegraph to supply papers throughout the country with news and features and which contributed, as a result, to a standardization of the product. By the turn of the century important newspaper chains had emerged as well. The most powerful was owned by William Randolph Hearst, who by 1914 controlled nine newspapers and two magazines. Hearst and rival publisher Joseph Pulitzer helped popularize what became known as "yellow journalism"—a deliberately sensational, even lurid, style of reporting presented in bold graphics, designed to reach a mass audience uninterested in the sober, detailed reporting of more traditional newspapers.

Another major change occurred in the nature of American magazines. Beginning in the 1880s, a new kind of magazine appeared, designed to achieve a mass circulation. One of the pioneers in this field was Edward W. Bok, who took over the *Ladies' Home Journal* in 1899 and, by targeting a mass female audience, built the circulation of the journal to over 700,000.

## HIGH CULTURE IN THE URBAN AGE

In addition to the important changes in popular culture that accompanied the rise of cities and industry, there were profound changes in the realm of "high culture"—in the ideas and activities of intellectuals and elites. Even the idea of a distinction between "highbrow" and "lowbrow" culture was largely new to the industrial era. In the early nineteenth century, most cultural activities had attracted people of widely varying backgrounds and targeted people of all classes. By the late nineteenth century, however, elites were developing a cultural and intellectual life quite separate from the popular amusements of the urban masses.

### The Literature of Urban America

The high culture of late-nineteenth-century America was shaped profoundly by the growth of industry and the rise of the city. Some writers and artists—the local-color writers of the South, for example, and Mark Twain, in such novels as *Huckleberry Finn* and *Tom Sawyer*—responded to the new civilization by evoking an older, more natural world. But others grappled directly with the modern, urban order.

One of the strongest impulses in late-nineteenth- and early-twentieth-century American literature was the effort to re-create urban social reality. This trend toward realism found an early voice in Stephen Crane, who—although best known for his novel of the Civil War, *The Red Badge of Courage* (1895)—created a sensation in 1893 when he published *Maggie: A Girl of the Streets*, a grim picture of urban poverty and slum life. Theodore Dreiser, Frank Norris, and Upton Sinclair—whose 1906 novel, *The Jungle*, inspired federal legislation with its exposure of abuses in the meatpacking industry—were similarly drawn to social issues as themes. Kate Chopin, a southern writer who explored the oppressive features of traditional marriage, encountered widespread public abuse (and in some places formal bans) after publication of her shocking novel, *The Awakening*, in 1899. It described a young wife and mother who abandoned her family in search of personal fulfillment. William Dean Howells, in *The Rise of Silas Lapham* and other works, described what he considered the shallowness and corruption in ordinary American lifestyles.

Other critics of American society responded to the new civilization not by attacking it but by withdrawing from it. The historian Henry Adams published an autobiography in 1906, *The Education of Henry Adams*, which portrayed a man disillusioned with and unable to relate to his society, even though he continued to live in it. The novelist Henry James lived the major part of his adult life in England and Europe and produced a series of coldly realistic novels—*The American* (1877), *Portrait of a Lady* (1881), *The Ambassadors* (1903), and others—that showed his ambivalence about the merits of both American and European civilization.

*Art in the Age of the City*

American art through most of the nineteenth century had been overshadowed by the art of Europe. By 1900, however, a number of American artists,
although some continued to study and even live in Europe, broke from the
Old World traditions and experimented with new styles. Winslow Homer
was vigorously American in his paintings of New England maritime life and
other native subjects. James McNeil Whistler was one of the first western
artists to appreciate the beauty of Japanese color prints and to introduce Oriental themes into American and European art.

By the first years of the new century, some American artists were turning decisively away from the traditional academic style (a style perhaps best

EDWARD HOPPER, *AUTOMAT*  Edward Hopper was one of a growing group of
American painters in the early twentieth century who chose to chronicle not the
world of wealth and power, the characteristic subject of earlier artists, but the
harsh, gritty world of the modern city. Hopper's work was distinctive for its
evocation of the loneliness of urban life. This 1927 painting of a scene in an
"automat" in New York City is characteristic of his work.

exemplified in America by the brilliant portraitist John Singer Sargent). Instead, many younger painters were exploring the same grim aspects of modern life that were becoming the subject of American literature. Members of the so-called Ashcan School produced work startling in its naturalism and stark in its portrayal of the social realities of the era. John Sloan portrayed the dreariness of American urban slums; George Bellows caught the vigor and violence of his time in paintings and drawings of prizefights; Edward Hopper explored the starkness and loneliness of the modern city. The Ashcan artists were also among the first Americans to appreciate expressionism and abstraction; and they showed their interest in new forms in 1913 when they helped stage the famous "Armory Show" in New York City, which displayed works of the French postimpressionists and of some American moderns.

The work of these and other artists marked the beginning in America of an artistic movement known as modernism, a movement that had counterparts in many other areas of cultural and intellectual life as well. Rejecting the heavy reliance on established forms that characterized the "genteel tradition" of the nineteenth-century art world, modernists embraced new subjects and new forms. The genteel tradition emphasized the "dignified" and "elevated" aspects of civilization (and glorified the achievements of gifted elites); modernism gloried in the ordinary, even the coarse. The genteel tradition placed great importance on respect for the past and maintenance of "standards"; modernism looked to the future and gloried in the new. Eventually, modernism developed strict orthodoxies of its own. But in its early stages, it seemed to promise an escape from rigid, formal traditions and an unleashing of individual creativity.

### The Impact of Darwinism

The single most profound intellectual development in the late nineteenth century was the widespread acceptance of the theory of evolution, associated most prominently with the English naturalist Charles Darwin. Darwinism argued that the human species had evolved from earlier forms of life (and most immediately from simian creatures similar to apes) through a process of "natural selection." History, Darwinism suggested, was not the working out of a divine plan, as most Americans had always believed. It was a random process dominated by the fiercest or luckiest competitors.

The theory of evolution met widespread resistance at first from educators, theologians, and even many scientists. By the end of the century, however, the evolutionists had converted most members of the urban professional and educated classes. Even many middle-class Protestant religious leaders had accepted the doctrine, making significant alterations in theology to accommodate it. Evolution had become enshrined in schools and universities; virtually no serious scientist any longer questioned its basic validity. Unseen by most urban Americans at the time, however, the rise of Darwinism was contributing to a deep schism between the new, cosmopolitan culture of the city—which was receptive to new ideas such as evolution—and the more traditional, provincial culture of some rural areas—which remained wedded to fundamentalist religious beliefs and older values. Thus the late nineteenth century saw not only the rise of a liberal Protestantism in tune with new scientific discoveries but also the beginning of an organized Protestant fundamentalism, which would make its presence felt politically in the 1920s and beyond.

Darwinism helped spawn other new intellectual currents. There was the Social Darwinism of William Graham Sumner and others, which industrialists used so enthusiastically to justify their favored position in American life. But there were also more sophisticated philosophies, among them a doctrine that became known as "pragmatism," which reflected Darwinism's rejection of inherited ideas and its emphasis on scientific research. William James, a Harvard psychologist (and brother of the novelist Henry James), was the most prominent publicist of the new theory, although earlier intellectuals such as Charles S. Peirce and later ones such as John Dewey were also important to its development and dissemination. According to the pragmatists, modern society should rely for guidance not on inherited ideals and moral principles but on the test of scientific inquiry. No idea or institution (not even religious faith) was valid, they claimed, unless it worked, unless it stood the test of experience.

A similar concern for scientific inquiry was intruding into the social sciences and challenging traditional orthodoxies. Sociologists such as Edward A. Ross and Lester Frank Ward urged applying the scientific method to the solution of social and political problems. Historians such as Frederick Jackson Turner and Charles Beard argued that economic factors more than spiritual ideals had been the governing force in historical development. John Dewey proposed a new approach to education that placed less emphasis on the rote learning of traditional knowledge and more on a flexible, democratic approach to schooling, one that enabled students to acquire knowledge that would help them deal with the realities of their society.

The implications of Darwinism also promoted the growth of anthropology and encouraged some scholars to begin examining other cultures—

most significantly, perhaps, the culture of American Indians—in new ways. Some white Americans began to look at Indian society as a coherent culture with its own norms and values that were worthy of respect and preservation, even though they were different from those of white society.

### Toward Universal Schooling

A society increasingly dependent on specialized skills and scientific knowledge was, of course, a society with a high demand for education. The late nineteenth century, therefore, was a time of rapid expansion and reform of American schools and universities.

One example was the spread of free public primary and secondary education. In 1860, there were only 100 public high schools in the entire United States. By 1900, the number had reached 6,000 and by 1914 over 12,000. By 1900, compulsory school attendance laws were in effect in thirty-one states and territories. But education was still far from universal. Rural areas lagged far behind urban-industrial ones in funding public education. And in the South, many blacks had access to no schools at all.

Educational reformers sought to provide educational opportunities to the Indian tribes as well, in an effort to "civilize" them and help them adapt to white society. In the 1870s, reformers recruited small groups of Indians to attend Hampton Institute (a primarily black college). In 1879 they organized the Carlisle Indian Industrial School in Pennsylvania. Like many black colleges, Carlisle emphasized the kind of practical "industrial" education that Booker T. Washington had urged on blacks. Ultimately, however, these reform efforts failed, partly because of inadequate funding and commitment and partly because the venture itself—the effort to remove Indians from their traditional surroundings and transform them into members of white society—was unpopular with its intended beneficiaries.

Colleges and universities were also proliferating rapidly in the late nineteenth century. They benefited particularly from the Morrill Land Grant Act of the Civil War era, by which the federal government had donated land to states for the establishment of colleges. After 1865, states in the South and West took particular advantage of the law. In all, sixty-nine "land-grant" institutions were established in the last decades of the century—among them the state university systems of California, Illinois, Minnesota, and Wisconsin. Other universities benefited from millions of dollars contributed by business and financial tycoons. Rockefeller, Carnegie, and others gave generously to such schools as Columbia, Chicago, Harvard, Northwestern,

Princeton, Syracuse, and Yale. Other philanthropists founded new universities or reorganized older ones and perpetuated their family names—Vanderbilt, Johns Hopkins, Cornell, Duke, Tulane, and Stanford.

## Education for Women

The post–Civil War era saw, too, an important expansion of educational opportunities for women, although such opportunities continued to lag far behind those available to men and were almost without exception denied to black women.

Most public high schools accepted women readily, but opportunities for higher education were fewer. At the end of the Civil War, only three American colleges were coeducational. In the years after the war, many of the land-grant colleges and universities in the Midwest and such private universities as Cornell and Wesleyan began to admit women along with men. But co-education was less crucial to women's education in this period than was the creation of a network of women's colleges. Mount Holyoke in central Massachusetts had begun its life in 1836 as a "seminary" for women; it became a full-fledged college in the 1880s, at about the same time that entirely new female institutions were emerging: Vassar, Wellesley, Smith, Bryn Mawr, Wells, and Goucher. A few of the larger private universities created separate colleges for women on their campuses (Barnard at Columbia and Radcliffe at Harvard, for example). Proponents of women's colleges saw the institutions as places where female students would not be treated as "second-class citizens" by predominantly male student bodies and faculties.

The female college was part of an important phenomenon in the history of modern American women: the emergence of distinctive women's communities. Most faculty members and many administrators were women (usually unmarried). And the life of the college produced a spirit of sorority and commitment among educated women that had important effects in later years, as women became the leaders of many reform activities. Most female college graduates ultimately married, but they married at a more advanced age than their noncollege counterparts. A significant minority, perhaps over 25 percent, did not marry at all, but devoted themselves to careers. The growth of female higher education clearly became for some women a liberating experience, persuading them that they had roles to perform in their rapidly changing urban-industrial society other than as wives and mothers.

# CHAPTER NINETEEN

# From Stalemate to Crisis

*The Politics of Equilibrium* ~ *The Agrarian Revolt*
*The Crisis of the 1890s*

T HE ENORMOUS CHANGES America was experiencing in the late nineteenth century strained not only the nation's traditional social arrangements but its political institutions as well. Industrialization and urbanization were responsible for considerable progress and substantial achievements. They also produced disorder and despair. Gradually, Americans began to look to government for leadership in their search for stability and social justice.

Yet American government during much of this period was ill equipped to deal with the new challenges confronting it. In the face of unprecedented dilemmas, it responded with apparent passivity and confusion. Its leaders, for the most part, seemed political mediocrities. The issues with which it was concerned generally had little to do with the nation's most important problems. Rather than taking active leadership of America's dramatic transformation, the American political system for nearly two decades after the end of Reconstruction (a period sometimes described by a phrase Mark Twain coined for it, "the Gilded Age") was locked in a rigid stalemate—watching the remarkable changes that were occurring in the nation and doing relatively little to affect them. The result was a set of problems and grievances that festered and grew without any natural outlet. It was not surprising, under the circumstances, that in the 1890s the United States entered a period of national crisis.

## THE POLITICS OF EQUILIBRIUM

To modern eyes, the nature of the American political system in the late nineteenth century appears in many ways paradoxical. The two political parties enjoyed a strength and stability during those years that neither was ever to

535

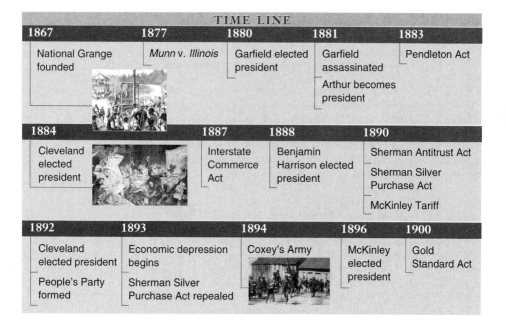

| TIME LINE | | | | |
|---|---|---|---|---|
| **1867** | **1877** | **1880** | **1881** | **1883** |
| National Grange founded | *Munn* v. *Illinois* | Garfield elected president | Garfield assassinated | Pendleton Act |
| | | | Arthur becomes president | |
| **1884** | | **1887** | **1888** | **1890** |
| Cleveland elected president | | Interstate Commerce Act | Benjamin Harrison elected president | Sherman Antitrust Act |
| | | | | Sherman Silver Purchase Act |
| | | | | McKinley Tariff |
| **1892** | **1893** | **1894** | **1896** | **1900** |
| Cleveland elected president | Economic depression begins | Coxey's Army | McKinley elected president | Gold Standard Act |
| People's Party formed | Sherman Silver Purchase Act repealed | | | |

know again. And yet the federal government, which the two parties were struggling to control, was doing relatively little of importance. In fact, most Americans in those years engaged in political activity not because of an interest in particular issues but because of broad regional, ethnic, or religious sentiments. Party loyalty had less to do with positions on public policy than with the way Americans defined themselves socially and culturally.

### The Party System

The most striking feature of the late-nineteenth-century party system was its remarkable stability. From the end of Reconstruction until the late 1890s, the electorate was divided almost precisely evenly between the Republicans and the Democrats. Loyalties fluctuated almost not at all. Sixteen states were solidly and consistently Republican, and fourteen states (most of them in the South) were solidly and consistently Democratic. Only five states (the most important of them New York and Ohio) were usually in doubt, and their voters generally decided the results of national elections, often on the basis of voter turnout. The Republican Party captured the presidency in all but two of the elections of the era, but the party was not really as dominant as those victories suggest. In the five presidential elections beginning in

1876, the average popular-vote margin separating the Democratic and Republican candidates was 1.5 percent. The congressional balance was similarly stable, with the Republicans generally controlling the Senate and the Democrats generally controlling the House.

As striking as the balance between the parties was the intensity of public loyalty to them. In most of the country, Americans viewed their party affiliations with a passion and enthusiasm that is difficult for later generations to understand. Voter turnout in presidential elections between 1860 and 1900 averaged over 78 percent of all eligible voters (as compared with only slightly over 50 percent in the 1980s and 1990s). Even in nonpresidential years, from 60 to 80 percent of the voters turned out to cast ballots for congressional candidates. Large groups of potential voters were disfranchised in these years: women in most states; almost all blacks and many poor whites in the South. But for adult white males outside the South, there were few franchise restrictions. The remarkable turnout represented a genuinely mass-based politics.

What explains this extraordinary loyalty to the two political parties? It was not, certainly, because the parties took distinct positions on important public issues. They did so rarely. Party loyalties reflected other factors. Region was perhaps the most important. To white southerners, loyalty to the Democratic Party was a matter of unquestioned faith. It was the vehicle by which they had triumphed over Reconstruction, the vehicle by which they preserved white supremacy. To many northerners, white and black, Republican loyalties were equally intense for the opposite reason. The party of Lincoln remained what it had been during the Civil War: a bulwark against slavery and treason.

Religious and ethnic differences also shaped party loyalties. The Democratic Party attracted most of the Catholic voters, most of the recent immigrants, and most of the poorer workers; those three groups, of course, often overlapped. The Republican Party appealed to northern Protestants, citizens of old stock, and much of the middle class; those groups, too, had considerable overlap. Among the few substantive issues on which the parties took clearly different stands were matters connected with immigrants. Republicans tended to support measures restricting immigration and to favor temperance legislation, which many believed would help discipline immigrant communities. Catholics and immigrants viewed such proposals as assaults on them and their cultures and opposed them; the Democratic Party followed their lead.

Party identification, then, was usually more a reflection of cultural inclinations than a calculation of economic interest. Individuals might affiliate with a party because their parents had done so, or because it was the party of their region, their church, or their ethnic group. Most clung to their party loyalties with great persistence and passion.

### The National Government

One reason the two parties managed to avoid substantive issues was that the federal government (and for the most part state and local governments as well) did relatively little. The government in Washington was responsible for delivering the mails, for maintaining a national military, for conducting foreign policy, and for collecting tariffs and taxes. It had few other responsibilities and few institutions with which it could have undertaken additional responsibilities even if it had chosen to do so.

There was one significant exception. From the end of the Civil War to the early twentieth century, the federal government administered a system of annual pensions for Union Civil War veterans who had retired from work and for their widows. At its peak, this pension system was making payments to a majority of the male citizens (black and white) of the North and to many women as well. Some reformers hoped to make the system permanent and universal; they pressured the government to create a system of old-age pensions for all Americans. But their efforts failed. That was in part because the Civil War pension system was awash in party patronage and corruption. Other reformers—believers in "good government"—saw elimination of the pension system as a way to fight graft, corruption, and party rule. When the Civil War generation died out, the pension system died with it.

In most other respects, the United States in the late nineteenth century was a society without a modern, national government. The most powerful national political institutions were the two political parties (and the bosses and machines that dominated them) and the federal courts. The national leaders of both parties were primarily concerned not with policy but with office—with winning elections and controlling patronage.

### Presidents and Patronage

The power of party bosses had an important effect on the power of the presidency. The office had great symbolic importance, but its occupants were unable to do very much except distribute government appointments. A new president and his tiny staff had to make almost 100,000 appointments (most of them in the post office, the only really large government agency); and even in that function, presidents had limited latitude, since they had to avoid offending the various factions within their own parties.

Sometimes that proved impossible, as the presidency of Rutherford B. Hayes (1877–1881) demonstrated. By the end of his term, two groups—the Stalwarts, led by Roscoe Conkling of New York, and the Half-Breeds, captained by James G. Blaine of Maine—were competing for control of the Republican Party and threatening to split it. The dispute between the Stalwarts and the Half-Breeds was characteristic of the political battles of the era. It had little basis in substance. Rhetorically, the Stalwarts favored traditional, professional machine politics, while the Half-Breeds favored reform. In fact,

REVOLT AMONG REPUBLICANS Many Republican reformers, believers in "good government," were aghast when their party nominated James G. Blaine for president in 1884. Blaine, a former Speaker of the House, U.S. senator, and secretary of state, was the leader of the "Half-Breed" faction of the party, the faction that claimed to support cautious reform. But he was controversial even among reformers after a long career of wily political maneuvering and because of the scandals that continually attached themselves to his name. This cartoon by Joseph Keppler in the political magazine *Puck* shows Republican leaders responding with horror to "the writing on the wall," and to the dire consequences they believed would follow the nomination of Blaine. Blaine himself, at left, hides behind the *New York Herald-Tribune*, the principal organ of the reformers and a critic of Blaine.

both groups were mainly interested in a larger share of the patronage pie. Hayes tried to satisfy both and ended up satisfying neither.

The battle over patronage overshadowed all else during Hayes's unhappy presidency. His one important substantive initiative—an effort to create a civil service system—attracted no support from either party. And his early announcement that he would not seek reelection only weakened him further. He had virtually no power in Congress. The Democrats controlled the House throughout his presidency and the Senate during the last two years of his term. And Senate Republicans, led by Roscoe Conkling, opposed his efforts to defy the machines in making appointments. (His popularity with politicians in Washington was not enhanced by the unwillingness of his wife, a temperance advocate widely known as "Lemonade Lucy," to permit alcoholic beverages to be served in the White House.) Hayes's presidency was a study in frustration.

The Republicans managed to retain the presidency in 1880 in part because they managed to agree on a ticket that included a Stalwart and a Half-Breed. After a long convention deadlock, they nominated James A. Garfield, a veteran congressman from Ohio and a Half-Breed, for president and Chester A. Arthur of New York, a Stalwart and Conkling henchman, for vice president. The Democrats nominated General Winfield Scott Hancock, a minor Civil War commander with no national following. Benefiting from the end of the recession of 1879, Garfield won a decisive electoral victory, although his popular-vote margin was very thin. The Republicans also captured both houses of Congress.

Garfield began his presidency by trying to defy the Stalwarts in his appointments and by showing support for civil service reform. He soon found himself embroiled in an ugly public quarrel with both Conkling and other Stalwarts. It was never resolved. On July 2, 1881, only four months after his inauguration, Garfield was shot twice while standing in the Washington railroad station by an apparently deranged gunman (and unsuccessful office seeker) who shouted, "I am a Stalwart and Arthur is president now!" Garfield lingered for nearly three months but finally died, a victim as much of inept medical treatment as of the wounds themselves.

Chester A. Arthur, who succeeded Garfield, had spent a political lifetime as a devoted, skilled, and open spoilsman and a close ally of Roscoe Conkling. But on becoming president, he tried—like Hayes and Garfield before him—to follow an independent course and even to promote reform, aware no doubt that the Garfield assassination had to some degree discredited the traditional spoils system. To the dismay of the Stalwarts, Arthur kept most of Garfield's appointees in office and supported civil service reform, aware that the legislation was likely to pass whether he supported it or not. In 1883, Congress passed the first national civil service measure, the Pendleton Act, which required that some federal jobs be filled by competitive written examinations rather than by patronage. Relatively few offices fell under civil service at first, but its reach extended steadily so that by the mid-twentieth century most federal employees were civil servants.

## Cleveland, Harrison, and the Tariff

In the unsavory election of 1884, the Republican candidate for president was Senator James G. Blaine of Maine—known to his adoring admirers as "the Plumed Knight" but to thousands of other Americans as a symbol of seamy party politics. A group of disgruntled "liberal Republicans," known derisively by their critics as the "mugwumps," announced they would bolt the party and support an honest Democrat. Rising to the bait, the Democrats nominated Grover Cleveland, the "reform" governor of New York. He differed from Blaine on no substantive issues but had acquired a reputation as an enemy of corruption.

In a campaign filled with personal invective, what may have decided the election was the last-minute introduction of a religious controversy. Shortly before the election, a delegation of Protestant ministers called on Blaine in New York City; their spokesman, Dr. Samuel Burchard, referred to the Democrats as the party of "rum, Romanism, and rebellion." Blaine was slow to repudiate Burchard's indiscretion, and Democrats quickly spread the news that Blaine had tolerated a slander on the Catholic Church. Cleveland's narrow victory was probably a result of an unusually heavy Catholic vote for the Democrats in New York. Cleveland won 219 electoral votes to Blaine's 182; his popular margin was only 23,000.

Grover Cleveland was respected, if not often liked, for his stern and righteous opposition to politicians, grafters, pressure groups, and Tammany Hall. He had become famous as the "veto governor," as an official who was not afraid to say no. He was the embodiment of an era in which few Americans believed the federal government could, or should, do very much. Cleveland had always doubted the wisdom of protective tariffs (taxes on imported goods designed to protect domestic producers). The existing high rates, he believed, were responsible for the annual surplus in federal revenues, which was tempting Congress to pass "reckless" and "extravagant" legislation, which he frequently vetoed. In December 1887, therefore, he asked Congress to reduce the tariff rates. Democrats in the House approved a tariff reduction, but Senate Republicans defiantly passed a bill of their own actually raising the rates. The resulting deadlock made the tariff an issue in the election of 1888.

The Democrats renominated Cleveland and supported tariff reductions. The Republicans settled on former senator Benjamin Harrison of Indiana, who was obscure but respectable (and the grandson of President William Henry Harrison); and they endorsed protection. The campaign was the first since the Civil War to involve a clear question of economic difference between the parties. It was also one of the most corrupt (and one of the closest) elections in American history. Harrison won an electoral majority of 233 to 168, but Cleveland's popular vote exceeded Harrison's by 100,000.

## Changing Issues

Benjamin Harrison's record as president was little more substantial than that of his grandfather, who had died a month after taking office. Harrison had few visible convictions, and he made no effort to influence Congress. And yet during Harrison's passive administration, public opinion was beginning to force the government to confront some of the pressing social and economic issues of the day. Most notably, perhaps, sentiment was rising in favor of legislation to curb the power of trusts.

By the mid-1880s, fifteen western and southern states had adopted laws prohibiting combinations that restrained competition. But corporations found it easy to escape limitations by incorporating in states such as New Jersey and Delaware that offered them special privileges. If antitrust legislation was to be effective, its supporters believed, it would have to come from the national government. Responding to growing popular demands, both houses of Congress passed the Sherman Antitrust Act in July 1890, almost without dissent. Most members of Congress saw the act as a largely symbolic measure, one that would help deflect public criticism but was not likely to have any real effect on corporate power. And for over a decade after its passage, the Sherman Act—indifferently enforced and steadily weakened by the courts—had virtually no impact. As of 1901, the Justice Department had instituted many antitrust suits against unions, but only fourteen against business combinations; there had been few convictions.

The Republicans were more interested, however, in the issue they believed had won them the 1888 election: the tariff. Representative William McKinley of Ohio and Senator Nelson W. Aldrich of Rhode Island drafted the highest protective measure ever proposed to Congress. Known as the McKinley Act, it became law in October 1890. But Republican leaders apparently misinterpreted public sentiment, for the party suffered a stunning reversal in the 1890 congressional election. The Republicans' substantial Senate majority was slashed to 8; in the House, the party retained only 88 of the 323 seats. McKinley himself was among those who went down to defeat. Nor were the Republicans able to recover in the course of the next two years. In the presidential election of 1892, Benjamin Harrison once again supported protection; Grover Cleveland, renominated by the Democrats, once again opposed it. A new third party, the People's Party, with James B. Weaver as its candidate, advocated more substantial economic reform. Cleveland won 277 electoral votes to Harrison's 145 and had a popular margin of 380,000. Weaver showed some significant strength, but still ran far behind. For the first time since 1878, the Democrats won a majority of both houses of Congress.

The policies of Cleveland's second term were much like those of his first—devoted to minimal government and hostile to active efforts to deal with social or economic problems. Again, he supported a tariff reduction, which the House approved but the Senate weakened. Cleveland denounced the result but allowed it to become law as the Wilson-Gorman Tariff. It included only a few, very modest reductions.

But public pressure was growing in the 1880s for other reforms, among them regulation of the railroads. Farm organizations in the Midwest (most notably the Grangers) had persuaded several state legislatures to pass regulatory legislation in the early 1870s. But in 1886, the Supreme Court—in *Wabash, St. Louis, and Pacific Railway Co.* v. *Illinois*, known as the *Wabash* case—ruled one of the Granger Laws in Illinois unconstitutional. According to the Court, the law was an attempt to control interstate commerce and thus infringed on the exclusive power of Congress. Later, the courts limited the powers of the states to regulate commerce even within their own boundaries.

Effective railroad regulation, it was now clear, could come only from the federal government. Congress grudgingly responded to public pressure in 1887 with the Interstate Commerce Act, which banned discrimination in rates between long and short hauls, required that railroads publish their rate schedules and file them with the government, and declared that all interstate rail rates must be "reasonable and just"—although the act did not define what that meant. A five-person agency, the Interstate Commerce Commission (ICC), was to administer the act. But it had to rely on the courts to enforce its rulings. For almost twenty years after its passage, the Interstate Commerce Act—which was, like the Sherman Act, haphazardly enforced and narrowly interpreted by the courts—was without much practical effect.

The agitation over the tariff, the trusts, and the railroads was a sign that the dramatic changes in the American economy were creating problems that much of the public considered too important and dangerous to ignore. But the federal government lacked both the will and the institutional capacity to respond effectively to those problems. The effort to create a government capable of doing more would dominate much of American public life in the coming decades. That effort first became visible in a dramatic dissident movement that helped shatter the political equilibrium the nation had experienced for the previous twenty years.

## THE AGRARIAN REVOLT

No group watched the performance of the federal government in the 1880s with more dismay than American farmers. Isolated from the urban-industrial society that was beginning to dominate national life, suffering from a long, painful economic decline, afflicted with a sense of obsolescence, rural Americans were keenly aware of the problems of the modern economy and particularly eager for government assistance in dealing with them. The result was the emergence of one of the most powerful movements of political protest in American history: what became known as Populism.

### The Grangers

Farmers had been making efforts to organize politically for several decades before the 1880s. The first major farm organization had its origins shortly after the Civil War in a tour through the South by a minor Agriculture Department official, Oliver H. Kelley, who became appalled by what he considered the isolation and drabness of rural life. In 1867 he left the government and helped found the National Grange of the Patrons of Husbandry, from which emerged a network of local organizations. At first, the Granges simply tried to teach new scientific agricultural techniques and attempted to create a feeling of community, to relieve the loneliness of rural life. But when the depression of 1873 caused a sharp decline in farm prices, membership rapidly increased and the direction of the organization changed. Granges in the Midwest began to organize marketing cooperatives, which would allow farmers to circumvent the hated middlemen. And they promoted political action to curb the monopolistic practices of the railroads and warehouses. The Granges succeeded for a time both in creating an impressive network of farm cooperatives and in putting effective pressure on state legislatures. At their peak, their supporters controlled the legislatures in

A MEETING OF THE GRANGE, 1873 The Grange attracted broad and enthusiastic support from midwestern farmers in the 1870s. They were attracted by the political message of its leaders, who championed the cause of farmers against railroads, food processors, and others whom they charged with exploiting agricultural producers. But farmers liked the Grange, too, as a social organization—as a vehicle through which men and women who lived much of their lives in relative isolation could gather together. This sketch depicts a great Grange meeting in Edwardsville, Illinois.

most of the midwestern states. The result was the Granger Laws of the early 1870s, by which many states imposed strict regulations on railroad rates and practices. But the destruction of the new regulations by the courts, combined with the political inexperience of many Grange leaders and the return of prosperity in the late 1870s, produced a dramatic decline in the power of the association by the end of the decade.

### The Alliances

The successor to the Granges as the leading vehicle of agrarian protest began to emerge even before the Granger movement had faded. As early as 1875, farmers in parts of the South (most notably in Texas) were banding together in so-called Farmers' Alliances. By 1880, the Southern Alliance had more than 4 million members; and a comparable Northwestern Alliance was taking root in the plains states and the Midwest and developing ties with its southern counterpart.

Like the Granges, the Alliances formed cooperatives and other marketing mechanisms. They established stores, banks, processing plants, and other facilities for their members—to free them from dependence on the hated "furnishing merchants" who kept so many farmers in debt. Some Alliance leaders, however, saw the movement in larger terms: as an effort to build a new society in which economic competition might give way to cooperation. Alliance lecturers traveled throughout rural areas lambasting the concentrated power of the great corporations and financial institutions.

Although the Alliances quickly became far more widespread than the Granges had ever been, they suffered from similar problems. Their cooperatives did not always work well, partly because the market forces operating against them were sometimes too strong to be overcome and partly because the cooperatives themselves were often mismanaged. These economic frustrations helped push the movement into a new phase at the end of the 1880s: the creation of a national political organization.

In 1889, the Southern and Northwestern Alliances, despite continuing differences between them, agreed to a loose merger. The next year the Alliances held a national convention at Ocala, Florida, and issued the so-called Ocala Demands, which were, in effect, a party platform. In the 1890 off-year elections, candidates supported by the Alliances won partial or complete control of the legislatures in twelve states. They also won six governorships, three seats in the Senate, and approximately fifty in the House of Representatives. Many of the successful Alliance candidates were simply Democrats who had benefited—often passively—from Alliance endorsements. But dissident farmers drew enough encouragement from the results to contemplate further political action, including forming a party of their own.

Alliance leaders discussed plans for a third party at meetings in Cincinnati in May 1891 and St. Louis in February 1892—meetings attended by many northern Alliance members, a smaller but still significant number of Southern Alliance leaders, and representatives of the fading Knights of Labor, whom some farm leaders hoped to bring into the coalition. Then, in July 1892, 1,300 exultant delegates poured into Omaha, Nebraska, to proclaim the creation of the new party, approve an official set of principles, and nominate candidates for the presidency and vice presidency. The new organization's official name was the People's Party, but the movement was more commonly referred to as Populism.

The election of 1892 demonstrated the potential power of the new movement. The Populist presidential candidate—James B. Weaver of Iowa, a former Greenbacker—polled more than 1 million votes, 8.5 percent of the total, and carried six mountain and plains states for 22 electoral votes. Nearly 1,500 Populist candidates won election to state legislatures and local offices. The party elected three governors, five senators, and ten congressmen. It could also claim the support of many Republicans and Democrats in Congress who had been elected by appealing to Populist sentiment.

### The Populist Constituency

Already, however, there were signs of the limits of Populist strength. Populism had great appeal to farmers, and particularly to small farmers with little long-range economic security—people whose operations were only minimally mechanized, if at all, who relied on one crop, and who had little access to credit. But Populism failed to move much beyond that group. Its leaders made energetic efforts to include labor within the coalition. In addition to courting the Knights of Labor, the new party added a labor plank to its platform—calling for shorter hours for workers and restrictions on immigration, and denouncing the use of private detective agencies as strikebreakers in labor disputes. But Populism never attracted any substantial labor support, in part because the economic interests of labor and the interests of farmers were often at odds.

In the South in particular, white Populists struggled with the question of accepting African Americans in the party, since their numbers and their poverty made them potentially valuable allies. And indeed there was an important black component to the movement—a network of "Colored Alliances" that by 1890 numbered over 1.25 million members. But most white Populists were willing to accept the assistance of blacks only as long as it was clear that whites would remain indisputably in control. When southern conservatives began to attack the Populists for undermining white supremacy, the interracial character of the movement quickly faded.

### Populist Ideas

The reform program of the Populists was spelled out first in the Ocala Demands of 1890 and then, even more clearly, in the Omaha platform of 1892. It proposed a system of "subtreasuries," which would replace and strengthen the cooperatives with which the Granges and Alliances had been experimenting for years. The national government would establish a network of warehouses, where farmers could deposit their crops. Using those crops as collateral, growers could then borrow money from the government at low rates of interest and wait for the price of their goods to go up before selling them. In addition, the Populists called for the abolition of national banks, which they believed were dangerous institutions of concentrated power; the end of absentee ownership of land; the direct election of United States senators (which would weaken the power of conservative state legislatures); and other devices to improve the ability of the people to influence the political process. They called as well for regulation and (after 1892) government ownership of railroads, telephones, and telegraphs. And they demanded a system of government-operated postal savings banks, a graduated income tax, the inflation of the currency, and, later, the remonetization of silver.

Some Populists were openly anti-Semitic. Others were anti-intellectual, antieastern, and antiurban. But bigotry was not the dominant force behind Populism. The movement was a serious and often intelligent effort to find solutions to real problems. Populists emphatically rejected the laissez-faire orthodoxies of their time, the idea that the rights of ownership are absolute. Populism was less a critique of industrialization or capitalism than a challenge, one of the most powerful such challenges of the era, to what the Populists considered the brutal and chaotic way in which the economy was developing. Progress and growth should continue, they urged, but it should be strictly defined by the needs of individuals and communities.

## THE CRISIS OF THE 1890S

The rising agrarian protest was only one of many indications of the national political crisis emerging in the 1890s. There was a severe depression, which began in 1893. There was widespread labor unrest and violence, culminating in the tumultuous strikes of 1894. There was the continuing failure of either major party to respond to the growing distress. And there was the rigid conservatism of Grover Cleveland, who took office for the second time just at the moment that the economy collapsed. Out of this growing sense of crisis came some of the most heated political battles in American history, culminating in the dramatic campaign of 1896, which many Americans came to believe would determine the future of the nation.

### The Panic of 1893

The Panic of 1893 precipitated the most severe depression the nation had ever experienced. It began in March 1893, when the Philadelphia and Reading Railroads declared bankruptcy, unable to meet demands for payment by British banks from which they had borrowed large sums. Two months later, the National Cordage Company failed as well. Together, the two corporate failures triggered a collapse of the stock market. And since many of the major New York banks were heavy investors in the market, a wave of bank failures soon began. That caused a contraction of credit, which meant that many of the new, aggressive businesses that had recently begun operations soon went bankrupt because they were unable to secure the loans they needed.

There were other, longer-range causes of the financial collapse. Depressed prices in agriculture since 1887 had weakened the purchasing power of farmers, the largest group in the population. Depression conditions that had begun earlier in Europe were resulting in a loss of American markets abroad and a withdrawal by foreign investors of gold invested in the United States. Railroads and other major industries had expanded too rapidly, well beyond market demand. The depression reflected, too, the degree to which all parts of the American economy were now interconnected, the degree to which failures in one area affected all other areas. And the depression showed how dependent the economy was on the health of the railroads, which remained the nation's most powerful corporate and financial institutions. When the railroads suffered, as they did beginning in 1893, everything suffered.

Once the panic began, its effects spread with startling speed. Within six months, more than 8,000 businesses, 156 railroads, and 400 banks failed. Already low agricultural prices tumbled further. Up to 1 million workers, 20 percent of the labor force, lost their jobs—the highest level of unemployment in American history to that point, a level comparable to that of the Great Depression of the 1930s. The depression was unprecedented not only in its severity but also in its persistence. Although there was slight improvement beginning in 1895, prosperity did not fully return until after 1898.

The depression produced widespread social unrest, not least among the enormous numbers of unemployed workers. In 1894, Jacob S. Coxey, an Ohio businessman and Populist, began advocating an inflation of the currency and a massive public works program to create jobs for the unemployed. When it became clear that his proposals were making no progress in Congress, Coxey organized a march of the unemployed (known as "Coxey's Army") to Washington to present his demands to the government. Congress took no action on the demands.

There were major labor upheavals as well during the decade—of which the Homestead and Pullman strikes were only the most prominent exam-

COXEY'S ARMY Jacob S. Coxey's "army" of the unemployed marches toward Washington in 1894 to demand relief from the federal government. Although several thousand people started out from various parts of the country to join the army, only about 400 actually reached the Capitol. The protest disbanded after Coxey and several others were arrested for "trespassing" on the grounds of the United States Capitol.

ples. (See pp. 506–508.) To many middle-class Americans, the worker unrest was a sign of dangerous social instability, even perhaps a revolution. Labor radicalism—some of it real, much of it imagined by the frightened middle class—was seldom far from the public mind, heightening the general sense of crisis.

### The Silver Question

Debate over the causes of the depression centered increasingly on the currency. Populists, and many others, blamed the crisis on an inadequate supply of money. Conservatives blamed it on a lack of commitment to a "sound currency." The "money question," therefore, became one of the burning issues of the era.

The currency issue is a complicated and confusing one, and it has often been difficult for later generations to understand the enormous passions the controversy aroused. The heart of the debate was over what would form the basis of the dollar, what would lie behind it and give it value. Today, the value of the dollar rests on little more than public confidence in the government. But in the nineteenth century, most people assumed that currency was worthless if there was not something concrete behind it—precious metal (specie), which holders of paper money could collect if they presented their currency to a bank or to the Treasury.

During most of its existence as a nation, the United States had recognized two metals—gold and silver—as a basis for the dollar, a formula known as "bimetallism." In the 1870s, however, that had changed. The official ratio of the value of silver to the value of gold for purposes of creating currency (the "mint ratio") was 16 to 1: sixteen ounces of silver equaled one ounce of gold. But the actual commercial value of silver (the "market ratio") was much higher than that. Owners of silver could get more by selling it for manufacture into jewelry and other objects than they could by taking it to the mint for conversion to coins. So they stopped taking it to the mint, and the mint stopped coining silver.

In 1873, Congress passed a law that seemed simply to recognize the existing situation by officially discontinuing silver coinage. Few objected at the time. But later in the 1870s, the market value of silver fell well below the official mint ratio of 16 to 1. (Sixteen ounces of silver, in other words, were now worth less, not more, than one ounce of gold.) Silver was suddenly available for coinage again, and it soon became clear that Congress had foreclosed a potential method of expanding the currency. Before long, many Americans concluded that a conspiracy of big bankers had been responsible for the "demonetization" of silver, and they referred to the law as the "Crime of '73."

Two groups of Americans were especially determined to undo the "Crime of '73." One consisted of silver-mine owners and their allies, now understandably eager to have the government take their surplus silver and pay them much more than the market price. The other group consisted of discontented farmers, who wanted an increase in the quantity of money—an inflation of the currency—as a means of raising the prices of farm products and easing payment of the farmers' debts. The inflationists demanded that the government return at once to "free silver"—that is, to the "free and unlimited coinage of silver" at the old ratio of 16 to 1. In 1893, Congress responded weakly to these demands with the Sherman Silver Purchase Act of 1893, which required the government to purchase (but not coin) silver and pay for it in gold. That provided some relief to silver miners, but it did nothing to expand the currency.

At the same time, the nation's gold reserves were steadily dropping. And the Panic of 1893 intensified the demands on those reserves. President Cleveland believed that the chief cause of the weakening gold reserves was the Sherman Silver Purchase Act. Early in his second administration, therefore, Congress responded to his request and repealed the act—although only after a bitter and divisive battle that helped create a permanent split in the Democratic Party. The president's gold policy had aligned the southern and western Democrats in a solid phalanx against him and his eastern followers. Only substantial Republican support had allowed the bill to pass.

By now, both sides had invested the currency question with great symbolic and emotional importance. Supporters of the gold standard considered its survival essential to the honor and stability of the nation. Because the supply of gold was limited, a gold-based currency would be assured of stable, long-term value. Supporters of free silver were equally passionate. They considered the gold standard an instrument of tyranny and silver an instrument of liberation. The issue achieved an intensity rarely seen in the politics of the era, culminating in the tumultuous presidential election of 1896.

### "A Cross of Gold"

Republicans, watching the failure of Cleveland and the Democrats to deal effectively with the depression, were confident of success in 1896. Party leaders, led by the Ohio boss Marcus A. Hanna, settled on former congressman William McKinley, author of the 1890 tariff act and now governor of Ohio, as the party's presidential candidate. The tariff, they believed, should be the principal issue in the campaign. But their platform also opposed the free coinage of silver except by agreement with the leading commercial nations (which everyone realized was unlikely). Thirty-four delegates from the mountain and plains states walked out in protest and joined the Democratic Party.

The Democratic convention of 1896 was unusually tumultuous. Southern and western delegates, eager for a way to compete with the populists, were determined to seize control of the party from conservative easterners and incorporate some Populist demands—among them free silver—into the Democratic platform. They wanted as well to nominate a pro-silver candidate. The divided platform committee presented two reports to the convention. The majority report, the work of westerners and southerners, called for tariff reduction, an income tax, "stricter control" of trusts and railroads, and—most prominently—free silver. The minority report, the product of the party's eastern wing, echoed the Republican platform by opposing the free coinage of silver except by international agreement. The debate over the two competing platforms dominated the convention.

Defenders of the gold standard seemed to prevail in the debate, until the final speech. Then William Jennings Bryan, a handsome, thirty-six-year-old congressman from Nebraska, already well known as an effective orator, mounted the podium to address the convention. His great voice echoed through the hall as he delivered a defense of free silver that became one of the most famous political speeches in American history. The closing passage sent his audience into something close to a frenzy: "If they dare to come out in the open and defend the gold standard as a good thing, we will fight them to the uttermost. Having behind us the producing masses of this nation and the world, supported by the commercial interests, the laboring interests and the toilers everywhere, we will answer their demand for a gold standard by saying to them: 'You shall not press down upon the brow of labor this crown of thorns; you shall not crucify mankind upon a cross of gold.'" It became known as the "Cross of Gold" speech.

In the glow of Bryan's speech, the convention voted to adopt the pro-silver platform. Perhaps more important, the agrarians embraced Bryan as their leader. The following day, Bryan (as he had eagerly, and not entirely

WILLIAM JENNINGS BRYAN Bryan addresses a crowd late in his career, displaying the flamboyant oratorical style that characterized his public life from the beginning. The poster at the lower left of the platform shows him as he appeared in the 1890s, when, as a young congressman from Nebraska, he became known as the "Boy Orator of the Platte" and the leader of the national free-silver movement.

secretly, hoped) was nominated for president on the fifth ballot. He remains the youngest man ever nominated for president by a major party.

The choice of Bryan and the nature of the Democratic platform created a quandary for the Populists. They had expected both major parties to adopt conservative programs and nominate conservative candidates, leaving the Populists to represent the growing forces of protest. But now the Democrats had stolen much of their thunder. The Populists faced the choice of naming their own candidate and splitting the protest vote or endorsing Bryan and losing their identity as a party. The Populists supported the free-silver cause, but without Bryan's passion; they considered other issues more important. Many Populists argued that "fusion" with the Democrats—who had endorsed free silver but ignored the other, more important Populist demands—would destroy their party. But the majority concluded that there was no viable alternative. Amid considerable acrimony, the convention voted to support Bryan. In a feeble effort to maintain their independence, the Populists repudiated the Democratic nominee for vice president and chose their own, Tom Watson of Georgia.

## The Conservative Victory

The campaign of 1896 produced desperation among conservatives. The business and financial community, frightened beyond reason at the prospect of a Bryan victory, contributed lavishly to the Republican campaign, which may have spent as much as $7 million, as compared with the Democrats' $300,000. From his home at Canton, Ohio, McKinley conducted a dignified "front-porch" campaign before pilgrimages of the Republican faithful, customary behavior in an age when many Americans considered it undignified to campaign too openly for the presidency.

Bryan showed no such restraint. He became the first presidential candidate in American history to stump the country systematically, to appear in villages and hamlets—indeed, the first to say frankly to the voters that he wanted to be president. He traveled 18,000 miles (mostly in the West and South) and addressed an estimated 5 million people. But Bryan may have done himself more harm than good. His revivalistic, camp-meeting style pleased old-stock Protestants, but it alienated many of the immigrant Catholics and other ethnics who normally voted Democratic. Employers, meanwhile, warned workers that a Bryan victory would cost them their jobs, thus intimidating many traditional Democrats into supporting McKinley or not voting at all.

On election day, McKinley polled 271 electoral votes to Bryan's 176 and

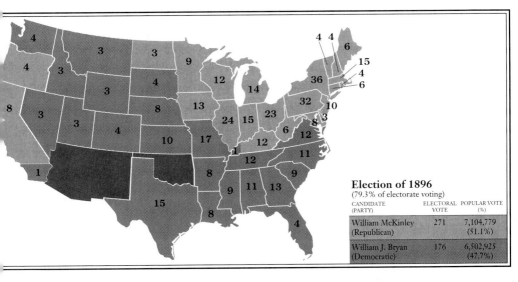

**Election of 1896**
(79.3% of electorate voting)

| CANDIDATE (PARTY) | ELECTORAL VOTE | POPULAR VOTE (%) |
|---|---|---|
| William McKinley (Republican) | 271 | 7,104,779 (51.1%) |
| William J. Bryan (Democratic) | 176 | 6,502,925 (47.7%) |

received 51.1 percent of the popular vote to Bryan's 47.7. Bryan carried only those areas of the South and West where miners or struggling staple farmers predominated. The Democratic program, like that of the Populists, had been too narrow to win a national election.

For the Populists and their allies, the election results were a disaster. They had gambled everything on their "fusion" with the Democratic Party and lost. Within months of the election, the People's Party began to dissolve. Never again would American farmers unite so militantly to demand economic reform. And never again would so large a group of Americans raise so forceful a protest against the nature of the industrial economy.

### McKinley and Prosperity

The administration of William McKinley, which began in the aftermath of turmoil, saw a return to relative calm. The labor and agrarian protests that had dominated the early 1890s subsided; the depression began to ease; and the McKinley administration shrewdly committed itself to a reassuring stability.

McKinley and his allies worked actively and energetically on only one issue, one on which they knew virtually all Republicans were agreed: the need for higher tariff rates. Within weeks of McKinley's inauguration, the administration won approval of the Dingley Tariff, raising duties to the highest point in American history. The administration dealt more gingerly with the explosive silver question (an issue McKinley himself had never considered very important in any case). McKinley sent a commission to Europe to explore the possibility of a silver agreement with Great Britain and France. As he and everyone else anticipated, the effort produced no agreement. The Republicans then enacted the Currency, or Gold Standard, Act of 1900, which confirmed the nation's commitment to the gold standard.

And so the "battle of the standards" ended in victory for the forces of conservatism. Economic developments at the time seemed to vindicate them. Prosperity returned beginning in 1898. Foreign crop failures sent United States farm prices surging upward, and American business entered another cycle of booming expansion. Prosperity and the gold standard, it seemed, were closely allied.

But while the free-silver movement had failed, it had raised an important question for the American economy. In the quarter-century before 1900, the countries of the Western world had experienced a spectacular growth in productive facilities and population. Yet the supply of money had not kept pace with economic progress, because the supply was tied to gold and the amount of gold had remained practically constant. Had it not been for a dramatic increase in the gold supply in the late 1890s (a result of new techniques for extracting gold from low-content ores and the discovery of huge new gold deposits in Alaska, South Africa, and Australia), Populist predictions of financial disaster might in fact have proved correct. In 1898, two and a half times as much gold was produced as in 1890, and the currency supply was soon inflated far beyond anything Bryan and the free-silver forces had proposed.

By then, however, Bryan—like many other Americans—was becoming engaged with another major issue: the nation's growing involvement in world affairs and its increasing flirtation with imperialism.

# D E B A T I N G    T H E    P A S T

## *Populism*

HE SCHOLARLY DEBATES over the nature of Populism have tended to reflect a larger debate over the nature of popular mass movements. To some historians, mass uprisings seem dangerous and potentially antidemocratic; and to them, the Populist movement has usually appeared ominous. To others, such insurgency is evidence of a healthy democratic resistance to oppression; and to them, Populism has generally seemed more appealing.

The latter view shaped the first, and for many years the only, general history of Populism: John D. Hicks's *The Populist Revolt* (1931). Reflecting the influence of Frederick Jackson Turner, Hicks portrayed Populism as an expression of the healthy, democratic sentiments of the West. (He paid relatively little attention to the South.) Populists were reacting rationally and constructively to the harsh impact of eastern industrial growth on agrarian society, and they were proposing potentially valuable reforms to restrict the power of the new financial titans. Populism was, he wrote, "the last phase of a long and perhaps a losing struggle—the struggle to save agricultural America from the devouring jaws of industrial America."

In the early 1950s, scholars sensitive to the nature of European fascism and contemporary communism took a more suspicious view of mass popular politics and a more hostile view of Populism. The leading figure in this reinterpretation was Richard Hofstadter. In *The Age of Reform* (1955), he conceded that the Populists had genuine grievances and advanced some sensible reforms. But he concentrated on revealing what he called the "soft" and "dark" sides of the movement. Populism, Hofstadter claimed, rested on a romanticized and obsolete vision of the role of farmers in American society. And it was permeated with bigotry and ignorance.

*(continued on next page)*

Hofstadter's harsh portrait inspired a series of spirited challenges. Norman Pollack, beginning in 1962, argued that the agrarian revolt rested not on nostalgic and romantic concepts but on a sophisticated and even radical vision of reform. A year later, Walter T. K. Nugent attempted to show that Populists were not bigoted, that they not only tolerated but welcomed Jews and other minorities into their party. And in 1976, Lawrence Goodwyn published *Democratic Promise*, the first full-scale history of the Populist movement since Hicks's study forty-five years earlier. Goodwyn described Populism as a "cooperative crusade," battling against the "coercive potential of the emerging corporate state." It was offering a genuine alternative to the inequities of modern, corporate capitalism; and it was promoting that alternative by developing an intensely democratic popular movement.

At the same time that historians were debating the meaning of Populism, they were also arguing over who the Populists were. Hicks, Hofstadter, and Goodwyn, for all their many disagreements, shared a belief that Populists were victims of economic distress—usually one-crop farmers in economically marginal regions victimized by drought and debt. Others, however, have suggested that this description is, if not wrong, at least inadequate. Sheldon Hackney maintained in 1969 that Populists in Alabama were not only economically troubled but socially rootless, "only tenuously connected to society by economic function, by personal relationships, by stable community membership, by political participation, or by psychological identification with the South's distinctive myths." Peter Argersinger, Stanley Parsons, James Turner, and others have similarly suggested that Populists tended to be people who were socially and even geographically isolated. Steven Hahn's 1983 study *The Roots of Southern Populism* described the poor farmers of "upcountry" Georgia who became Populists as people almost entirely unconnected to the modern capitalist economy. They were reacting not simply to the distress of being "left behind," but also to a real economic threat to their way of life from the intrusion into their world of a new commercial order of which they were not a part and from which they were unlikely to benefit.

There has, finally, been continuing disagreement over whether Populism has survived into the twentieth century—whether it is part of an enduring political language used by such later popular leaders as Huey Long, George Wallace, or even Ross Perot, or whether the idea of Populism has meaning only in reference to the insurgents of the 1890s.

# CHAPTER TWENTY

# The Imperial Republic

*Stirrings of Imperialism* ～ *War with Spain*
*The Republic as Empire*

T HE AMERICAN REPUBLIC had been an expansionist nation since the earliest days of its existence. Throughout the first half of the nineteenth century, as the population of the United States grew and pressed westward, the government, through purchase or conquest, had continually acquired new lands: the trans-Appalachian West, the Louisiana Territory, Florida, Texas, Oregon, California, New Mexico, Alaska. It was the nation's "Manifest Destiny," many Americans believed, to expand into new realms.

In the last years of the nineteenth century, with little room left for territorial growth on the North American continent, expansionism moved into a new phase. In the past, the nation had generally annexed land adjacent to its existing boundaries; American citizens could move there relatively easily, and the new lands could ultimately become states of the Union. But the expansionism of the 1890s, the new Manifest Destiny, involved acquiring possessions separate from the continental United States: distant island territories, many thickly populated, most of which were unlikely to attract massive settlement from America, few of which were expected to become states of the Union. The United States was joining England, France, Germany, and others in the great imperial drive that was, by the end of the century, to bring much of the nonindustrial world under the control of the industrial powers of the West.

## STIRRINGS OF IMPERIALISM

For over two decades after the Civil War, the United States expanded geographically hardly at all. By the 1890s, however, some Americans were ready—indeed, eager—to resume the course of Manifest Destiny that had

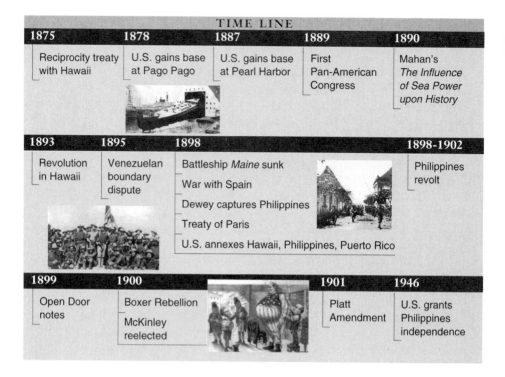

## TIME LINE

| 1875 | 1878 | 1887 | 1889 | 1890 |
|---|---|---|---|---|
| Reciprocity treaty with Hawaii | U.S. gains base at Pago Pago | U.S. gains base at Pearl Harbor | First Pan-American Congress | Mahan's *The Influence of Sea Power upon History* |

| 1893 | 1895 | 1898 | | 1898-1902 |
|---|---|---|---|---|
| Revolution in Hawaii | Venezuelan boundary dispute | Battleship *Maine* sunk<br>War with Spain<br>Dewey captures Philippines<br>Treaty of Paris<br>U.S. annexes Hawaii, Philippines, Puerto Rico | | Philippines revolt |

| 1899 | 1900 | | 1901 | 1946 |
|---|---|---|---|---|
| Open Door notes | Boxer Rebellion<br>McKinley reelected | | Platt Amendment | U.S. grants Philippines independence |

inspired their ancestors to wrest an empire from Mexico in the expansionist 1840s.

### The New Manifest Destiny

Several developments helped shift American attention to lands across the seas. The experience of subjugating the Indian tribes had established a precedent for exerting colonial control over dependent peoples. The supposed "closing of the frontier," widely heralded by Frederick Jackson Turner and others in the 1890s, produced fears that natural resources would soon dwindle and that alternative sources must be found abroad. The depression that began in 1893 encouraged some businessmen to look for new markets abroad. The bitter social protests of the time—the Populist movement, the free-silver crusade, the bloody labor disputes—led some politicians to urge a more aggressive foreign policy as an outlet for frustrations that would otherwise destabilize domestic life.

Foreign trade was becoming increasingly important to the American economy in the late nineteenth century. The nation's exports had totaled about $392 million in 1870; by 1900, the figure had reached $1.4 billion. Many Americans began to argue that colonies could expand overseas markets further. Americans were, moreover, well aware of the imperialist fever that was raging through Europe. It was leading the major powers to partition most of Africa among themselves and to turn covetous eyes on the Far East and the feeble Chinese Empire. Some Americans feared that their nation would soon be left out, that the Europeans would seize all these potential markets for themselves.

Scholars and others found a philosophic justification for expansionism in Charles Darwin's theories. They contended that nations or "races," like biological species, struggled constantly for existence and that only the fittest could survive. For strong nations to dominate weak ones was, therefore, in accordance with the laws of nature. (This was an application to world affairs of the same strained reinterpretation of Darwinism that industrialists and

LAUNCHING THE *MAINE*, 1889 The battleship *Maine* played a major role in American military history when it blew up in the harbor of Havana, Cuba, in 1898, and helped precipitate the Spanish-American War. But it was also significant as part of the growing naval strength the United States was developing in the late nineteenth century. This engraving from *Harper's Weekly* portrays the launching of the *Maine* from the New York Navy Yard in November 1889.

others had been applying to domestic economic affairs in the form of Social Darwinism.)

The ablest and most effective apostle of imperialism was Alfred Thayer Mahan, a captain and later admiral in the navy. Mahan's thesis—presented in *The Influence of Sea Power upon History* (1890) and other works—was simple: Countries with sea power were the great nations of history; the greatness of the United States, bounded by two oceans, would rest on naval power. Effective sea power required, among other things, colonies. Mahan believed America should, at the least, acquire defensive bases in the Caribbean and the Pacific and take possession of Hawaii and other Pacific islands.

Mahan feared that the United States did not have a large enough navy to play the great role he envisioned. But during the 1870s and 1880s, the government launched a shipbuilding program that by 1898 had moved the United States to fifth place among the world's naval powers, and by 1900 to third.

### Hemispheric Hegemony

James G. Blaine, who served as secretary of state in the Republican administrations of the 1880s, led the early efforts to expand American influence into Latin America, where, Blaine believed, the United States must look for markets for its surplus goods. In October 1889, he helped organize the first Pan-American Congress, which attracted delegates from nineteen nations. The delegates agreed to create the Pan-American Union, a weak international organization located in Washington that served as a clearinghouse for distributing information to the member nations. But they rejected Blaine's more substantive proposals: an inter-American customs union and arbitration procedures for hemispheric disputes.

The second Cleveland administration took a similarly lively interest in Latin America. In 1895, it supported Venezuela in a dispute with Great Britain over the boundary between Venezuela and British Guiana. When the British ignored American demands that the matter be submitted to arbitration, Secretary of State Richard Olney charged that Britain was violating the Monroe Doctrine. When Britain still did not act, Cleveland created a special commission to determine the boundary line; if Britain resisted the commission's decision, he insisted, the United States should be willing to go to war to enforce it. As war talk raged throughout the country, the British government finally realized that it had stumbled into a genuine diplomatic crisis and agreed to arbitration.

## Hawaii and Samoa

The islands of Hawaii in the mid-Pacific had been an important way station for American ships in the China trade since the early nineteenth century. By the 1880s, officers of the expanding United States Navy were looking covetously at Pearl Harbor on the island of Oahu as a possible permanent base for American ships. Pressure for an increased American presence in Hawaii was emerging from another source as well: the growing number of Americans who had settled on the islands and who had gradually come to dominate their economic and political life.

In doing so, the Americans were wresting authority away from the leaders of an ancient civilization. Settled by Polynesian people beginning in about 1500 B.C., Hawaii had developed an agricultural and fishing society in which different islands (and different communities on the same islands), each with its own chieftain, lived more or less self-sufficiently. When the first Americans arrived in Hawaii in the 1790s on merchant ships from New England, there were perhaps a half-million people living there.

Battles among rival communities were frequent, as ambitious chieftains tried to consolidate power over their neighbors. In 1810, after a series of such battles, King Kamehameha I established his dominance over the other chieftains on Hawaii. He welcomed American traders and helped them develop a thriving trade between Hawaii and China, from which the natives profited along with the merchants. But Americans soon wanted more than trade. Missionaries began settling there in the early nineteenth century, and in the 1830s, William Hooper, a Boston trader, became the first of many Americans to buy land and establish a sugar plantation on the islands.

The arrival of these merchants, missionaries, and planters was devastating to native Hawaiian society. The newcomers inadvertently brought infectious diseases to which the Hawaiians, like the American Indians before them, were tragically vulnerable. By the mid-nineteenth century, more than half the native population had died. By the turn of the century, disease had cut the population by more than half again. But the Americans brought other incursions as well. Missionaries worked to replace native religion with Christianity. Other white settlers introduced liquor, firearms, and a commercial economy, all of which eroded the traditional character of Hawaiian society. By the 1840s, American planters had spread throughout the islands; and an American settler, G. P. Judd, had become prime minister of Hawaii under King Kamehameha III, who had agreed to establish a constitutional monarchy. Judd governed Hawaii for over a decade.

In 1887, the United States negotiated a treaty with Hawaii that permitted it to open a naval base at Pearl Harbor. By then, growing sugar for export to America had become the basis of the Hawaiian economy—as a result of an 1875 agreement allowing Hawaiian sugar to enter the United States duty-free. The American-dominated sugar plantation system displaced native Hawaiians from their lands and relied heavily for workers on Asian immigrants, whom the Americans considered more reliable and more docile than the natives. Indeed, finding adequate labor, and keeping it under control, was the principal concern of many planters. Some deliberately sought to create a mixed-race work force (Chinese, Japanese, native Hawaiian, Filipinos, Portuguese, and others) as a way to keep the workers divided and unlikely to challenge them.

Native Hawaiians did not accept these changes without protest. In 1891, they elevated a powerful nationalist to the throne: Queen Liliuokalani, who set out to challenge the growing American control of the islands. But she remained in power only two years. In 1890, the United States had eliminated the 1875 exemption from tariffs for Hawaiian sugar planters. The result was devastating to the economy of the islands, and American planters concluded that the only way for them to recover was to become part of the United States (and hence exempt from its tariffs). In 1893 they staged a revolution and called on the United States for protection. After the American minister ordered marines from a warship in Honolulu harbor to go ashore to aid the rebels, the queen yielded her authority.

A provisional government, dominated by Americans (who constituted less than 5 percent of the population of the islands), immediately sent a delegation to Washington to negotiate a treaty of annexation. President Harrison signed an annexation agreement in February 1893, just before leaving office. But the Senate, controlled by Democrats after the 1892 election, refused to ratify the treaty, and Grover Cleveland, the new president, refused to support it. Debate over the annexation of Hawaii continued until 1898, when the Republicans, back in power, approved the agreement.

Three thousand miles south of Hawaii, the Samoan islands had also long served as a way station for American ships in the Pacific trade. As American commerce with Asia increased, business groups in the United States regarded Samoa with new interest, and the American navy began eyeing the Samoan harbor at Pago Pago. In 1878, the Hayes administration extracted a treaty from Samoan leaders for an American naval station at Pago Pago. It bound the United States to arbitrate any differences between Samoa and other nations. Clearly, the United States now expected to have a voice in Samoan affairs.

But Great Britain and Germany were also interested in the islands, and they too secured treaty rights from the native princes. For the next ten years the three powers jockeyed for dominance in Samoa, playing off one native ruler against another and coming dangerously close to war. Finally, the three powers agreed to create a tripartite protectorate over Samoa, with the native chiefs exercising only nominal authority. The three-way arrangement failed to halt the intrigues and rivalries of its members, and in 1899, the United States and Germany divided the islands between them, compensating Britain with territories elsewhere in the Pacific. The United States retained the harbor at Pago Pago.

## WAR WITH SPAIN

Imperial ambitions had thus begun to stir within the United States well before the late 1890s. But a war with Spain in 1898 turned those stirrings into overt expansionism. The war transformed America's relationship to the rest of the world, and it left the nation with a far-flung overseas empire.

### Controversy over Cuba

The Spanish-American War emerged out of events in Cuba, which along with Puerto Rico represented virtually all that remained of Spain's once-extensive American empire. Cubans had been resisting Spanish rule intermittently since at least 1868, when they began a long but ultimately unsuccessful fight for independence. Many Americans had sympathized with the Cubans during that ten-year struggle, but the United States did not intervene.

In 1895, the Cubans rose up again. (Although their goal was an end to Spanish misrule, the island's problems were now in part a result of the Wilson-Gorman Tariff of 1894, whose high duties on sugar had prostrated Cuba's important sugar economy by cutting off exports to the United States, the island's principal market.) This rebellion produced a ferocity on both sides that horrified Americans. The Cubans deliberately devastated the island to force the Spaniards to leave. The Spanish, commanded by General Valeriano Weyler (known in the American press as "Butcher" Weyler), confined civilians in certain areas to hastily prepared concentration camps, where they died by the thousands, victims of disease and malnutrition. The Spanish had used equally savage methods during the earlier struggle in Cuba without shocking American sensibilities. But the revolt of 1895 was reported more fully and floridly by American newspapers, and particularly by the new "yellow press" of William Randolph Hearst and Joseph Pulitzer, who were engaged in a ruthless circulation war with each other in New York City and elsewhere. In their effort to play to popular sentiment, they gave the impression that all the cruelties were being perpetrated by the Spaniards.

A growing population of Cuban émigrés in the United States—centered in Florida, New York, Philadelphia, and Trenton, New Jersey—gave extensive support to the Cuban Revolutionary Party (whose headquarters was in New York) and helped publicize its leader, José Martí, who was killed in Cuba in 1895. Later, Cuban Americans formed other clubs and associations to support the cause of *Cuba Libre* (Free Cuba). In some areas of the country, their efforts were as important as those of the yellow journalists in generating popular support for the revolution. The mounting storm of indignation against Spain did not persuade President Cleveland to intervene in the conflict. He proclaimed American neutrality and tried to stop the agitation by Cuban refugees in New York City. But when McKinley became president in 1897, he took a stronger stand. He formally protested Spain's "uncivilized and inhuman" conduct, causing the Spanish government (fearful of American intervention) to recall Weyler, modify the concentration policy, and grant the island a qualified autonomy. At the end of 1897, with the insurrection losing ground, it seemed that American involvement in the war might be averted.

But whatever chances there were for a peaceful settlement vanished as a result of two dramatic incidents in February 1898. The first occurred when a Cuban agent in Havana stole a private letter written by Dupuy de Lôme, the Spanish minister in Washington, and turned it over to the American press. It described McKinley as a weak man and "a bidder for the admiration of the crowd." This was no more than what many Americans, including some Republicans, were saying about their president (Assistant Secretary of the Navy Theodore Roosevelt once described McKinley as having "no more backbone than a chocolate eclair"). But coming from a foreigner, it created intense popular anger. Dupuy de Lôme promptly resigned.

While excitement over the de Lôme letter was still high, the American battleship *Maine* blew up in Havana harbor with a loss of more than 260 people. The ship had been ordered to Cuba in January to protect American lives and property against possible attacks by Spanish loyalists. Many Americans assumed that the Spanish had sunk the ship, particularly when a naval court of inquiry reported that an external explosion by a submarine mine had caused the disaster. (Later evidence suggested that the disaster was actually the result of an accidental explosion inside one of the engine rooms.) War hysteria swept the country, and Congress unanimously appropriated $50 million for military preparations. "Remember the *Maine!*" became a national chant for revenge.

McKinley still hoped to avoid a conflict. But others in his administration (including Theodore Roosevelt) were clamoring for war. In March 1898, the president asked Spain to agree to an armistice, negotiations for a permanent peace, and an end to the concentration camps. Spain agreed to stop the fighting and eliminate the concentration camps, but it refused to negotiate with the rebels and reserved the right to resume hostilities at its discretion. That satisfied neither public opinion nor Congress. A few days later, McKinley asked for and, on April 25, received a congressional declaration of war.

### "A Splendid Little War"

Secretary of State John Hay called the Spanish-American conflict "a splendid little war," an opinion that most Americans—with the exception of many of the enlisted men who fought in it—seemed to share. Declared in April, it was over in August. That was in part because Cuban rebels had already greatly weakened the Spanish resistance, which made the American intervention in many respects little more than a "mopping up" exercise. Only 460 Americans were killed in battle or died of wounds, although some 5,200 perished of disease: malaria, dysentery, and typhoid, among others. Casualties among Cuban insurgents, who continued to bear the brunt of the struggle, were much higher.

Yet the American war effort was not without difficulties. United States soldiers faced serious supply problems: a shortage of modern rifles and ammunition, uniforms too heavy for the warm Caribbean weather, inadequate medical services, and skimpy, almost indigestible food. The regular army numbered only 28,000 troops and officers, most of whom had experience in quelling Indian outbreaks but none in larger-scale warfare. That meant that, as in the Civil War, the United States had to rely heavily on National Guard units, organized by local communities and commanded for the most part by local leaders without military experience. The entire mobilization process was conducted with remarkable inefficiency.

There were also racial conflicts. A significant proportion of the American invasion force consisted of black soldiers. Some were volunteer troops

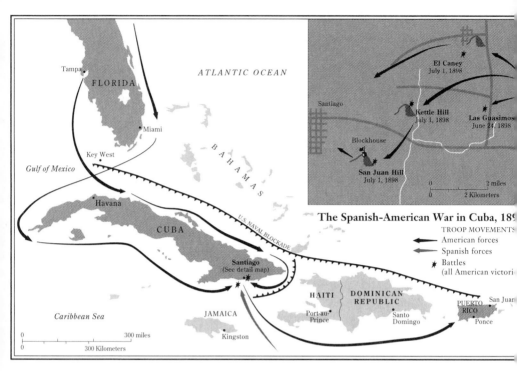

The Spanish-American War in Cuba, 189

TROOP MOVEMENTS
- ◄ — American forces
- ◄ — Spanish forces
- ✳ Battles (all American victori

put together by black communities (although some governors refused to allow the formation of such units). Others were members of the four black regiments in the regular army, who had been stationed on the frontier to defend white settlements against Indians and were now transferred east to fight in Cuba. As the black soldiers traveled through the South toward the training camps, they chafed at the rigid segregation to which they were subjected and occasionally openly resisted the restrictions. Black soldiers in Georgia deliberately made use of a "whites only" park; in Florida, they beat a soda-fountain operator for refusing to serve them; in Tampa, white provocations and black retaliation led to a night-long riot that left thirty wounded.

Racial tensions continued in Cuba itself, where African Americans played crucial roles in some of the important battles of the war (including the famous charge at San Juan Hill) and won many medals. Nearly half the Cuban insurgents fighting with the Americans were black, but unlike their American counterparts they were fully integrated into the rebel army. (Indeed, one of the leading insurgent commanders, Antonio Maceo, was a black man.) The sight of black Cuban soldiers fighting alongside whites as equals gave African Americans a stronger sense of the injustice of their own position.

## Seizing the Philippines

No agency in the American military had clear authority over strategic planning. Only the navy had worked out an objective, but its objective had little to do with freeing Cuba. Assistant Secretary of the Navy Theodore Roosevelt was an ardent imperialist, an active proponent of war, and a man uninhibited by the fact that he was a relatively lowly figure in the military chain of command. Roosevelt unilaterally strengthened the navy's Pacific squadron and instructed its commander, Commodore George Dewey, to attack Spanish naval forces in the Philippines, a colony of Spain, in the event of war.

Immediately after war was declared, Dewey sailed for the Philippines. On May 1, 1898, he steamed into Manila Bay and completely destroyed the aging Spanish fleet there. Only one American sailor died in the battle (of heatstroke), and George Dewey, immediately promoted to admiral, became the first hero of the war. Several months later, after the arrival of an American expeditionary force, the Spanish surrendered the city of Manila itself. In the rejoicing over Dewey's victory, few Americans paused to note that the character of the war was changing. What had begun as a war to free Cuba was becoming a war to seize Spain's colonies.

## The Battle for Cuba

Cuba, however, remained the principal focus of American military efforts. At first, the American commanders planned a long period of training before actually sending troops into combat. But when a Spanish fleet under Admiral Pascual Cervera slipped past the American navy into Santiago harbor, on the southern coast of Cuba, plans changed quickly. The American Atlantic fleet quickly bottled Cervera up in the harbor. And the army's commanding general, Nelson A. Miles, hastily altered his strategy and ordered a force of 17,000 to leave Tampa in June to attack Santiago. Both the departure from Florida and the landing in Cuba were scenes of fantastic incompetence. It took five days for the relatively small army to get ashore, and that was with the enemy offering no opposition.

General William R. Shafter, the American commander in Cuba, moved toward Santiago, which he planned to surround and capture. On the way he met and defeated Spanish forces at Las Guasimas and, a week later, in two simultaneous battles, El Caney and San Juan Hill. At the center of the fighting (and on the front pages of the newspapers) during all these engagements was a cavalry unit known as the Rough Riders. Nominally commanded by General Leonard Wood, its real leader was Colonel Theodore Roosevelt,

THE ROUGH RIDERS Theodore Roosevelt, center, poses with some of the Rough Riders after their famous charge in the Battle of San Juan Hill. The brigade had an unofficial anthem: "Rough, rough, we're the stuff. We want to fight, and we can't get enough."

who had resigned from the Navy Department to get into the war and who had struggled with an almost desperate fury to ensure that his regiment made it to the front before the fighting ended. Roosevelt rapidly emerged as a hero of the conflict. His fame rested in large part on his role in leading a bold, if perhaps reckless, charge up Kettle Hill (a charge that was a minor part of the larger battle for the adjacent San Juan Hill) directly into the face of Spanish guns. Roosevelt himself emerged unscathed, but nearly a hundred of his soldiers were killed or wounded. He remembered the battle as "the great day of my life."

Although Shafter was now in position to assault Santiago, his army was so weakened by sickness that he feared he might have to abandon his position, particularly as the commander of the American naval force blockading Santiago refused to enter the harbor because of mines. Disaster seemed imminent. But unknown to the Americans, the Spanish government had by now decided that Santiago was lost and had ordered Cervera to evacuate. On July 3, even though he knew the effort was hopeless, Cervera tried to escape the harbor. The waiting American squadron destroyed his entire fleet. On July

16, the commander of the Spanish ground forces in Santiago surrendered. At about the same time, an American army landed in Puerto Rico and occupied it against virtually no opposition. On August 12, the United States accepted an end to the war when Spain signed an armistice recognizing Cuban independence, ceding Puerto Rico to the United States, and accepting American occupation of Manila until the two nations reached a final agreement on the Philippines.

## Puerto Rico and the United States

The annexation of Puerto Rico produced relatively little controversy in the United States—ironically, since of all the territory America acquired as a result of the Spanish-American War, Puerto Rico would be the most important to the nation's future.

The island of Puerto Rico had been a part of the Spanish Empire since Ponce de León arrived there in 1508, and it had contained Spanish settlements since the founding of San Juan in 1521. The native people of the island, the Arawaks, disappeared almost entirely as a result of infectious diseases, Spanish brutality, and poverty. Puerto Rican society developed, therefore, with a Spanish ruling class and a large African work force for the coffee and sugar plantations that came to dominate its economy.

As Puerto Rican society became increasingly distinctive, resistance to Spanish rule began to emerge, just as it had emerged in Cuba. Uprisings occurred intermittently beginning in the 1820s; the most important of them—the so-called Lares Rebellion—was, like the others, effectively crushed by the Spanish in 1868. But the growing resistance did prompt some reforms: the abolition of slavery in 1873, representation in the Spanish parliament, and other changes. Demands for independence continued to grow, and in 1898, in response to political pressure organized by Luis Muñoz Rivera, Spain granted the island a degree of independence. But before the changes had any chance to take effect, control of Puerto Rico shifted to the United States.

American military forces occupied the island during the war. They remained in control until 1900, when the Foraker Act ended military rule and established a formal colonial government: an American governor, a two-chamber legislature (the members of the upper chamber appointed by the United States, the members of the lower elected by the Puerto Rican people). The United States could amend or veto any legislation the Puerto Ricans passed. Agitation for independence continued. And in 1917, under pressure to clarify the relationship between Puerto Rico and America, Congress passed the Jones Act, which declared Puerto Rico to be United States territory and made all Puerto Ricans American citizens.

The Puerto Rican sugar industry flourished as it took advantage of the American market that was now open to it without tariffs. As in Hawaii, Americans began establishing large sugar plantations on the island and hired natives to work them; many of the planters did not even live in Puerto Rico. The growing emphasis on sugar as a cash crop and the transformation of many Puerto Rican farmers into paid laborers led to a reduction in the growing of food for the island. Puerto Ricans became increasingly dependent on imported food and hence increasingly a part of the international commercial economy. When international sugar prices were high, Puerto Rico did well. When they dropped, the island's economy sagged, pushing the many plantation workers—already desperately poor—into destitution. Unhappy with the instability, the poverty among natives, and the American threat to Hispanic culture, many Puerto Ricans continued to agitate for independence. Others, however, began to envision closer relations with the United States, even statehood.

### The Debate over the Philippines

If the annexation of Puerto Rico produced relatively little controversy, the annexation of the Philippines occasioned a long and impassioned debate. Controlling a nearby Caribbean island fit reasonably comfortably into America's sense of itself as the dominant power in the Western Hemisphere. Controlling a large and densely populated territory thousands of miles away seemed different and, to many Americans, more ominous.

McKinley claimed to be reluctant to support annexation. But, according to his own accounts, he emerged from an "agonizing night of prayer" convinced that there were no acceptable alternatives. Returning the Philippines to Spain would be "cowardly and dishonorable," he claimed. Turning the islands over to another imperialist power (France, Germany, or Britain) would be "bad business and discreditable." Granting them independence would be irresponsible; the Filipinos were "unfit for self government." The only solution was "to take them all and to educate the Filipinos, and uplift and Christianize them, and by God's grace do the very best we could by them." Growing popular support for annexation and the pressure of the imperialist leaders of his party undoubtedly helped him reach this decision of conscience.

The Treaty of Paris, signed in December 1898, brought a formal end to the Spanish-American War. It confirmed the terms of the armistice concerning Cuba, Puerto Rico, and Guam. But American negotiators startled the Spanish by demanding that they cede the Philippines to the United States. The Spanish objected briefly, but an American offer of $20 million for the islands softened their resistance. They accepted all the American terms.

In the United States Senate, however, resistance was fierce. During debate over ratification of the treaty, a powerful anti-imperialist movement arose throughout the country to oppose acquisition of the Philippines. Among the anti-imperialists were some of the nation's wealthiest and most influential figures: Andrew Carnegie, Mark Twain, Samuel Gompers, Senator John Sherman, and others. Their motives were various. Some believed simply that imperialism was immoral, a repudiation of America's commitment to human freedom. Some feared "polluting" the American population by introducing "inferior" Asian races into it. Industrial workers feared being undercut by a flood of cheap laborers from the new colonies. Conservatives feared that the large standing army and entangling foreign alliances they thought imperialism would require would threaten American liberties. Sugar growers and others feared unwelcome competition from the new territories. The Anti-Imperialist League, established by upper-class Bostonians, New Yorkers, and others late in 1898 to fight against annexation, attracted a widespread following in the Northeast and waged a vigorous campaign against ratification of the Paris treaty.

Favoring ratification was an equally varied group. There were the exuberant imperialists such as Theodore Roosevelt, who saw the acquisition of empire as a way to reinvigorate the nation, to keep alive what they considered the healthy, restorative influence of the war. Some businessmen saw opportunities in the Philippines and believed annexation would position the United States to dominate the Oriental trade. And most Republicans saw partisan advantages in acquiring valuable new territories through a war fought and won by a Republican administration. Perhaps the strongest argument in favor of annexation, however, was the apparent ease with which it could be accomplished. The United States, after all, already possessed the islands.

When anti-imperialists warned of the danger of acquiring heavily populated territories whose people might have to become citizens, the imperialists had a ready answer: The nation's longstanding policies toward Indians—treating them as dependents rather than as citizens—had created a precedent for annexing land without absorbing people. Senator Henry Cabot

Lodge of Massachusetts, one of the leading imperialists in Congress, made the point explicitly:

> The other day . . . a great Democratic thinker announced that a Republic can have no subjects. He seems to have forgotten that this Republic not only has held subjects from the beginning, . . . but [that we have] acquired them by purchase. . . . [We] denied to the Indian tribes even the right to choose their allegiance, or to become citizens.

The fate of the treaty remained in doubt for weeks, until it received the unexpected support of William Jennings Bryan. Bryan was a fervent anti-imperialist who hoped to move the issue out of the Senate and make annexation the subject of a national referendum in 1900, when he expected to be the Democratic presidential candidate again. Bryan persuaded a number of anti-imperialist Democrats to support the treaty so as to set up the 1900 debate. The Senate ratified it finally on February 6, 1899.

But Bryan miscalculated. If the election of 1900 was in fact a referendum on the Philippines, as Bryan tried to make it, it proved beyond doubt that the nation had decided in favor of imperialism. Once again, Bryan ran against McKinley, and once again, McKinley won—even more decisively than in 1896. It was not only the issue of the colonies, however, that ensured McKinley's victory. The Republicans were the beneficiaries of growing national prosperity—and also of the colorful personality of their vice presidential candidate, Colonel Theodore Roosevelt, the hero of San Juan Hill.

## THE REPUBLIC AS EMPIRE

The new American empire was a small one by the standards of the great imperial powers of Europe. But it created large problems. It embroiled the United States in the politics of both Europe and the Far East in ways the nation had always tried to avoid in the past. It also drew Americans into a brutal war in the Philippines.

### Governing the Colonies

Three of the new American dependencies—Hawaii, Alaska, and Puerto Rico—presented relatively few problems. They received territorial status (and their residents American citizenship) relatively quickly: Hawaii in 1900, Alaska in 1912, and Puerto Rico (in stages) by 1917. The navy took control

"MEASURING UNCLE SAM FOR A NEW SUIT," BY J. S. PUGHE, IN *PUCK*
MAGAZINE, 1900 President William McKinley is approvingly depicted
here as a tailor, measuring his client for a suit large enough to
accommodate the new possessions the United States obtained in the
aftermath of the Spanish-American War. The cartoon tries to link
this expansion with earlier, less controversial ones such as the
Louisiana Purchase.

of Guam and Tutuila. The United States had also acquired some of the
smallest, least populated Pacific islands; it simply left them alone.

Cuba was a thornier problem. American military forces, commanded by
General Leonard Wood, remained there until 1902 to prepare the island for
independence. They built roads, schools, and hospitals; reorganized the
legal, financial, and administrative systems; and introduced medical and sanitation reforms. But the United States was also laying the basis for years of
American economic domination of the island. When Cuba drew up a constitution that made no reference to the United States, Congress responded
by passing the Platt Amendment in 1901 and pressuring Cuba into incorporating the amendment's terms into its constitution. The Platt Amendment
barred Cuba from making treaties with other nations (thus, in effect, giving
the United States effective control of Cuban foreign policy); it gave the
United States the right to intervene in Cuba to preserve independence, life,
and property; and it required Cuba to permit American naval stations on its
territory. The amendment left Cuba only nominally independent politically.
And American capital, which quickly took over the island's economy, made

the new nation an American economic appendage as well. American investors poured into Cuba, buying up plantations, factories, railroads, and refineries. Absentee American ownership of many of the island's most important resources was the source of resentment and agitation for decades. Resistance to "Yankee imperialism" produced intermittent revolts against the Cuban government—revolts that at times prompted United States military intervention. American troops occupied the island from 1906 to 1909 after one such rebellion; they returned again in 1912, to suppress a revolt by black plantation workers. As in Puerto Rico and Hawaii, sugar production—spurred by access to the American market—increasingly dominated the island's economy and subjected it to the same cycle of booms and busts that so plagued other sugar-producing appendages of the United States economy.

### The Philippine War

Americans did not like to think of themselves as imperial rulers in the European mold. Yet like other imperial powers, the United States soon discovered—as it had discovered at home in its relations with the Indians—that subjugating another people required more than ideals; it also required strength and at times brutality. That, at least, was the lesson of the American experience in the Philippines, where American forces soon became engaged in a long and bloody war with insurgent forces fighting for independence.

The conflict in the Philippines is the least remembered of all American wars. It was also one of the longest (it lasted from 1898 to 1902) and one of the most vicious. It involved 200,000 American troops and resulted in 4,300 American deaths, nearly ten times the number who had died in combat in the Spanish-American War. The number of Filipinos killed in the conflict is still in dispute, but it seems likely that at least 50,000 natives (and perhaps many more) died. The American occupiers faced guerrilla tactics in the Philippines very similar to those the Spanish occupiers had faced prior to 1898 in Cuba. And they soon found themselves drawn into the same pattern of brutality that had outraged so many Americans when Weyler had used them in the Caribbean.

The Filipinos had been rebelling against Spanish rule even before 1898. And as soon as they realized the Americans had come to stay, they rebelled against them as well. Ably led by Emilio Aguinaldo, who claimed to head the legitimate government of the nation, Filipinos harried the American army of occupation from island to island for more than three years. At first, American commanders believed the rebels had only a small popular following. But by early 1900, General Arthur MacArthur, an American commander in the islands (and the father of General Douglas MacArthur), was writing: "I have been reluctantly compelled to believe that the Filipino masses are loyal to Aguinaldo and the government which he heads."

To MacArthur and others, that was not a reason to moderate American tactics or conciliate the rebels. It was a reason to adopt more severe measures. Gradually, the American military effort became more systematically vicious and brutal. Captured Filipino guerrillas were treated not as prisoners of war but as murderers. Most were summarily executed. On some islands, entire communities were evacuated—the residents forced into concentration camps while American troops destroyed their villages, farms, crops, and livestock. A spirit of savagery grew among American soldiers, who came to view the Filipinos as almost subhuman and at times seemed to take pleasure in killing almost arbitrarily.

By 1902, reports of the brutality and of the American casualties had soured the American public on the war. But by then, the rebellion had largely exhausted itself and the occupiers had established control over most of the islands. The key to their victory was the March 1901 capture of Aguinaldo, who later signed a document in which he urged his followers to stop fighting and declared his own allegiance to the United States. (Aguinaldo then re-

WAR IN THE PHILIPPINES American troops take possession of a war-scarred village in the Philippines during the long, bloody conflict that followed the U.S. annexation of the islands after the Spanish-American War.

tired from public life and lived quietly until 1964.) Fighting continued in some places for another year, and the war revived intermittently until as late as 1906; but American possession of the Philippines was now secure.

In the summer of 1901, the military transferred authority over the islands to William Howard Taft, who became the first civilian governor. Taft announced that the American mission in the Philippines was to prepare the islands for independence, and he gave the Filipinos broad local autonomy. The Americans also built roads, schools, bridges, and sewers; instituted major administrative and financial reforms; and established a public health system. Filipino self-rule slowly increased. But not until July 4, 1946, did the islands finally gain their independence.

## *The Open Door*

The acquisition of the Philippines greatly increased the already strong American interest in Asia. Americans were particularly concerned about the future of China, with which the United States already had an important trading relationship and which was now so enfeebled that it provided a tempting target for exploitation by stronger countries. By 1900, England, France, Germany, Russia, and Japan were beginning to carve up China among themselves, pressuring the Chinese government for "concessions" that gave them effective economic control over various regions. In some cases, they simply seized Chinese territory and claimed it as their own "spheres of influence." Many Americans feared the process would soon cut them out of the China trade altogether.

Eager for a way to protect American interests in China without risking war, McKinley issued a statement in September 1898 saying the United States wanted access to China but no special advantages there: "Asking only the open door for ourselves, we are ready to accord the open door to others." Later, Secretary of State John Hay translated the president's words into policy when he addressed identical messages—which became known as the "Open Door notes"—to England, Germany, Russia, France, Japan, and Italy. He asked them to approve three principles: Each nation with a "sphere of influence" in China was to respect the rights and privileges of other nations in its sphere; Chinese officials were to continue to collect tariff duties in all spheres (the existing tariff favored the United States); and nations were not to discriminate against other nations in levying port dues and railroad rates within their own spheres. Together, these principles would allow the United States to trade freely with the Chinese without fear of interference and without having to become militarily involved in the region.

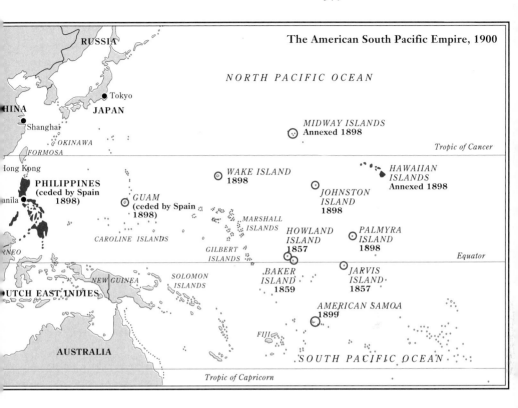

The American South Pacific Empire, 1900

RUSSIA

NORTH PACIFIC OCEAN

Tokyo

JAPAN

CHINA

Shanghai

OKINAWA

FORMOSA

Hong Kong

PHILIPPINES
(ceded by Spain
1898)

Manila

GUAM
(ceded by Spain
1898)

CAROLINE ISLANDS

BORNEO

NEW GUINEA

DUTCH EAST INDIES

AUSTRALIA

MIDWAY ISLANDS
Annexed 1898

Tropic of Cancer

WAKE ISLAND
1898

MARSHALL
ISLANDS

GILBERT
ISLANDS

SOLOMON
ISLANDS

FIJI

JOHNSTON
ISLAND
1898

HAWAIIAN
ISLANDS
Annexed 1898

HOWLAND
ISLAND
1857

PALMYRA
ISLAND
1898

BAKER
ISLAND
1859

JARVIS
ISLAND
1857

AMERICAN SAMOA
1899

Equator

SOUTH PACIFIC OCEAN

Tropic of Capricorn

But the Open Door proposals were coolly received in Europe and Japan. Russia openly rejected them; each of the other powers claimed to accept them in principle but to be unable to act unless all the other powers agreed. Hay refused to consider this a rebuff. He announced that all the powers had accepted the principles of the Open Door and that the United States expected them to observe those principles. But unless the United States was willing to resort to war, it could not prevent any nation that wanted to violate the Open Door from doing so.

No sooner had the diplomatic maneuvering over the Open Door ended than the Boxers, a secret Chinese martial-arts society, launched a revolt against foreigners in China. The climax of the Boxer Rebellion was a siege of the entire foreign diplomatic corps in the British embassy in Beijing (Peking). The imperial powers (including the United States) sent an international expeditionary force into China to rescue the diplomats. In August 1900, it fought its way into Beijing and broke the siege.

McKinley and Hay had agreed to American participation so as to secure a voice in the settlement of the uprising and to prevent the partition of China. Hay now won support for his Open Door approach from England and Germany and then induced the other participating powers to accept compensation from the Chinese for the damages the Boxer Rebellion had caused. Chinese territorial integrity survived at least in name, and the United States retained access to its lucrative trade.

### A Modern Military System

The war with Spain had revealed glaring deficiencies in the American military system. The army had exhibited the greatest weaknesses, but the entire military organization had failed to coordinate its efforts. Had the United States been fighting a more powerful nation, disaster might have resulted. After the war, McKinley appointed Elihu Root, an able New York corporate lawyer, as secretary of war to supervise a major overhaul of the armed forces. (Root was one of the first of several generations of attorney-statesmen who moved easily between public and private roles and became the core of what later came to be called the American "foreign policy establishment.") Between 1900 and 1903, Root created a new military system.

The Root reforms enlarged the regular army from 25,000 to a maximum of 100,000. They established federal command of the National Guard, ensuring that never again would the nation fight a war with volunteer regiments over which the federal government had only limited control. They sparked the creation of a system of officer training schools, including the Army Staff College (later the Command and General Staff School) at Fort Leavenworth, Kansas, and the Army War College in Washington, D.C. And in 1903, they established a general staff (now known as the Joint Chiefs of Staff) to act as military advisers to the secretary of war. As a result of the new reforms, the United States entered the twentieth century with something resembling a modern military system. The country would make substantial use of it in the turbulent century to come.

# CHAPTER TWENTY-ONE

# The Rise of Progressivism

*The Progressive Impulse* ～ *Women and Reform*
*The Assault on the Parties* ～ *Sources of Progressive Reform*
*Crusades for Order and Reform*

ELL BEFORE THE TURN of the century, many Americans had become convinced that the rapid industrialization and urbanization of their society had created intolerable problems—that the nation's most pressing need was to impose order on the growing chaos and to curb industrial society's most glaring injustices. In the early years of the new century, that outlook acquired a name: progressivism.

Not even those who called themselves progressives could always agree on what the word "progressive" really meant. Indeed, more than one historian has suggested that the word ultimately came to mean so many different things to so many different people that it ceased to mean anything at all. Yet if progressivism was a phenomenon of great scope and diversity, it was also one that rested on an identifiable set of central assumptions. It was, first, an optimistic vision. Progressives believed, as their name implies, in the idea of progress. They believed that society was capable of improvement, even of something close to perfection, and that continued growth and advancement were the nation's destiny. But progressives believed, too, that growth and progress could not continue to occur recklessly, as they had in the late nineteenth century. The "natural laws" of the marketplace, and the doctrines of laissez faire and Social Darwinism that celebrated those laws, were not sufficient to create the order and stability that the growing society required. Purposeful human intervention was necessary to solve the nation's problems. Progressives did not always agree on the form that intervention should take, but most believed that government should play an important role in the process.

## TIME LINE

| 1873 | 1889 | 1893 | 1895 | 1899 |
|------|------|------|------|------|
| Women's Christian Temperance Union founded | Jane Addams opens Hull House | Anti-Saloon League founded | National Association of Manufacturers founded | Veblen's *A Theory of the Leisure Class* |

| 1900 | 1902 | 1905 | 1909 |
|------|------|------|------|
| Galveston, Texas creates commission government — Robert La Follette elected Wisconsin governor | Ida Tarbell's exposé of Standard Oil | National Education Association founded | Croly's *The Promise of American Life* |

| 1911 | 1912 | 1919 | 1920 |
|------|------|------|------|
| Triangle Shirtwaist fire | U.S. Chamber of Commerce founded | 18th Amendment (prohibition) | 19th Amendment (women's suffrage) |

# THE PROGRESSIVE IMPULSE

Beyond these central premises, progressivism flowed outward in a number of different directions. One powerful impulse was the spirit of "antimonopoly," the fear of concentrated power and the urge to limit and disperse authority and wealth. A second progressive impulse was a belief in the importance of social cohesion: the belief that individuals are not autonomous but part of a great web of social relationships, that the welfare of any single person is dependent on the welfare of society as a whole. And a third progressive impulse was a belief in organization and efficiency: the belief that social order was a result of intelligent social organization and rational procedures for guiding social and economic life. These varied reform impulses were not entirely incompatible with one another. Many progressives made use of all these ideas at times as they tried to restore order and stability to their turbulent society.

### The Muckrakers and the Social Gospel

Among the first to articulate the new spirit of reform was a group of crusading journalists who began in the late nineteenth and early twentieth centuries to direct public attention toward social, economic, and political injustices. They became known as the "muckrakers" after Theodore Roosevelt accused one of them of raking up muck through his writings. They were committed to exposing scandal, corruption, and injustice to public view.

At first, their major targets were the trusts and particularly the railroads, which the muckrakers considered dangerously powerful and deeply corrupt. Exposés of the great corporate organizations began to appear as early as the 1860s, when Charles Francis Adams, Jr., and others uncovered corruption among the railroad barons. Decades later, Ida Tarbell produced a scorching study of the Standard Oil trust, keeping the issue of corporate power alive. By the turn of the century, however, many muckrakers were turning their attention to government and particularly to the urban political machines. The most influential, perhaps, was Lincoln Steffens, a reporter for *McClure's Magazine*. His portraits of "machine government" and "boss rule";

*MCCLURE'S MAGAZINE*, May 1903 *McClure's* was the leading outlet for a form of journalism known as "muckraking," which exposed social and economic scandals in the hope of promoting reform. This issue contains articles by two of the leading muckrakers, Lincoln Steffens and Ida Tarbell.

his exposures of "boodlers" in cities as diverse as St. Louis, Minneapolis, Cleveland, Cincinnati, Chicago, Philadelphia, and New York; his tone of studied moral outrage (as reflected in the title of his series and of the book that emerged from it, *The Shame of the Cities*)—all helped arouse sentiment for urban political reform. The muckrakers reached the peak of their influence in the first decade of the twentieth century. They investigated governments, labor unions, and corporations. They explored the problems of child labor, immigrant ghettoes, prostitution, and family disorganization. They denounced waste and destruction of natural resources, the subjugation of women, even occasionally the oppression of blacks.

The moralistic tone of the muckrakers' exposés reflected one important aspect of emerging progressive sentiment: a sense of outrage at social and economic injustice. That outrage, combined with a humanitarian sense of social responsibility, helped produce one of the central missions of many reformers: the pursuit of "social justice." A clear expression of that concern was the rise of what became known as the "Social Gospel." By the early twentieth century, it had become a powerful movement within American Protestantism (and, to a lesser extent, within American Catholicism and Judaism) to redeem the nation's cities. The Salvation Army, which began in England but soon spread to the United States, was a Christian social welfare organization with a vaguely military structure. By 1900, it had recruited 3,000 "officers" and 20,000 "privates" and was offering both material aid and spiritual service to the urban poor. In addition, many ministers, priests, and rabbis left traditional parish work to serve in the troubled cities. Charles Sheldon's *In His Steps* (1898), the story of a young minister who abandoned a comfortable post to work among the needy, sold more than 15 million copies and established itself as the most successful novel of the era. The engagement of religion with reform helped bring to progressivism a powerful moral impulse and a concern for the plight of some of society's most impoverished and degraded people.

### The Settlement House Movement

One of the strongest elements of progressive thought was the belief that the environment shaped individual development. Social Darwinists such as William Graham Sumner had argued that people's fortunes reflected their inherent "fitness" for survival. Most progressive theorists disagreed. Ignorance, poverty, even criminality, they argued, were not the result of inherent moral or genetic failings or of the workings of providence. They were, rather, the effects of an unhealthy environment. To elevate the distressed,

A M E R I C A N     V O I C E S

JANE ADDAMS

## First Days at Hull House

 FROM THE FIRST it seemed understood that we were ready to perform the humblest neighborhood services. We were asked to wash the newborn babies, and to prepare the dead for burial, to nurse the sick, and to "mind the children." Occasionally these neighborly offices unexpectedly uncovered ugly human traits. . . . a little Italian bride of fifteen sought shelter with us one November evening, to escape her husband who had beaten her every night for a week when he returned home from work, because she had lost her wedding ring; two of us officiated quite alone at the birth of an illegitimate child because the doctor was late in arriving, and none of the honest Irish matrons would "touch the likes of her." . . .

We were . . . early impressed with the curious isolation of many of the immigrants; an Italian woman once expressed her pleasure in the red roses that she saw at one of our receptions in surprise that they had been "brought so fresh all the way from Italy." She would not believe for an instant that they had been grown in America. . . . Her conception of America had been the untidy street in which she lived and had made her long struggle to adapt herself to American ways.

But in spite of some untoward experiences, we were constantly impressed with the uniform kindness and courtesy we received. Perhaps these first days laid the simple human foundations which are certainly essential for continuous living among the poor: . . . the conviction . . . that the things which make men alike are finer and better than the things that keep them apart, and that these basic likenesses, if they are properly accentuated, easily transcend the less essential differences of race, language, creed, and tradition.

SOURCE: Jane Addams, *Twenty Years at Hull House* (New York: The Macmillan Company, 1910), pp. 88–89.

therefore, required an improvement of the conditions in which the distressed lived.

Nothing produced more distress, many reformers believed, than the crowded immigrant neighborhoods of American cities. One response to the problems of such communities, borrowed from England, was the settlement house. The most famous, and one of the first, was Hull House, which opened in 1889 in Chicago as a result of the efforts of Jane Addams. It became a model for more than 400 similar institutions throughout the nation. Staffed by members of the educated middle class, settlement houses sought to help immigrant families adapt to the language and customs of their new country. Settlement houses avoided the condescension and moral disapproval of earlier philanthropic efforts. But they generally embodied a belief that middle-class Americans had a responsibility to impart their own values to immigrants. Even the word "settlement" suggested as much: middle-class people "settling" in the inner city and bringing civilization to the urban frontier.

Central to the settlement houses were the efforts of college women. Indeed, the movement became a training ground for many important female leaders of the twentieth century, among them Eleanor Roosevelt. The settlement houses also helped spawn another important institution of reform: the profession of social work—a profession in which women were to play an important role. The professional social worker combined a compassion for the poor with a commitment to the values of bureaucratic progressivism: scientific study, efficient organization, reliance on experts.

### The Allure of Expertise

As the emergence of the social work profession suggests, progressives involved in humanitarian efforts often placed high value on knowledge and expertise. Even nonscientific problems, they believed, could be analyzed and solved scientifically. Many reformers came to believe that only enlightened experts and well-designed bureaucracies could create the stability and order America needed.

This belief found expression in many ways, among them through the writings of a new group of scholars and intellectuals. Unlike the Social Darwinists of the nineteenth century, these theorists were no longer content with merely justifying the existing industrial system. They spoke instead of the creation of a new civilization, one in which the expertise of scientists and engineers could be brought to bear on the problems of the economy and society. Among the most influential was the social scientist Thorstein Veblen.

Harshly critical of the industrial tycoons of the late nineteenth century—the "leisure class," as he satirically described them in his first major work, *A Theory of the Leisure Class* (1899)—Veblen proposed instead a new economic system in which power would reside in the hands of highly trained engineers. Only they, he argued, could fully understand the "machine process" by which modern society must be governed.

In practical terms, the impulse toward expertise and organization helped produce the idea of scientific management, or "Taylorism." (See p. 491.) It encouraged the development of modern mass-production techniques and, above all, the assembly line. It inspired a revolution in American education and the creation of a new area of inquiry—social science, the use of scientific techniques in the study of society and its institutions. It produced a generation of bureaucratic reformers concerned with the structure of organizations and committed to building new political and economic institutions capable of managing a modern society. It also helped create a movement toward organization among the expanding new group of middle-class professionals.

### *The Professions*

The late nineteenth century saw a dramatic expansion in the number of Americans engaged in administrative and professional tasks. Industries needed managers, technicians, and accountants as well as workers. Cities required commercial, medical, legal, and educational services. The new technology required scientists and engineers, who, in turn, required institutions and instructors to train them. By the turn of the century, the people performing these services had come to constitute a distinct social group—what some have called a new middle class.

The new middle class placed a high value on education and individual accomplishment. By the early twentieth century, its millions of members were building organizations and establishing standards to secure their position in society. As their principal vehicle, they created the modern, organized professions. The idea of professionalism had been a frail one in America even as late as 1880. But as the demand for professional services increased, so did the pressures for reform.

Among the first to respond was the medical profession. Throughout the 1890s, doctors who considered themselves trained professionals began forming local associations and societies. In 1901, they reorganized the American Medical Association (AMA) into a national professional society. By 1920, nearly two-thirds of all American doctors were members. The AMA quickly called for strict, scientific standards for admission to the practice of medicine, with doctors themselves serving as protectors of the standards. State and local governments responded by passing new laws that required the licensing of all physicians and that restricted licenses to those practitioners approved by the profession.

There was similar movement in other professions. By 1916, lawyers in all forty-eight states had established professional bar associations, virtually all of which had succeeded in creating central examining boards, composed of lawyers, to regulate admission to the profession. Increasingly, aspiring lawyers found it necessary to enroll in graduate programs, and the nation's law schools accordingly expanded greatly, both in numbers and in the rigor of their curricula. Businessmen supported the creation of schools of business administration and created their own national organizations: the National Association of Manufacturers in 1895 and the United States Chamber of Commerce in 1912. Even farmers, long the symbol of the romantic spirit of individualism, responded to the new order by forming, through the National Farm Bureau Federation, a network of agricultural organizations designed to spread scientific farming methods, teach sound marketing techniques, and lobby for the interests of their members.

Among the chief purposes of the new professionalism was guarding entry into the professions. This was only partly an effort to defend the professions from the untrained and incompetent. The admission requirements also protected those already in the professions from excessive competition and lent prestige and status to the professional label. Some professions used their entrance requirements to exclude blacks, women, immigrants, and other "undesirables" from their ranks. Others used them simply to keep the numbers down, to ensure that demand for the services of existing members would remain high.

### Women and the Professions

American women found themselves excluded—both by custom and by active barriers of law and prejudice—from most of the emerging professions. But a substantial number of middle-class women—particularly those emerging from the new women's colleges and from the coeducational state universities—nevertheless entered professional careers.

A few women managed to establish themselves as physicians, lawyers, engineers, scientists, and corporate managers. Several leading medical schools admitted women, and about 5 percent of all American physicians were female in 1900 (a proportion that remained unchanged until the 1960s).

SETTLEMENT HOUSE WORKERS Nurses from the Henry
Street settlement in New York leave their headquarters to
begin their visits to the homes of poor immigrants in lower
Manhattan. This photograph dates from the early 1900s.

Most, however, turned by necessity to those professions that society considered suitable for women. Settlement houses and social work provided two
"appropriate" professional outlets for women. The most important, however,
was teaching. Indeed, in the late nineteenth century, more than two-thirds
of all grammar-school teachers were women, and perhaps 90 percent of all
professional women were teachers. For educated black women, in particular, teaching was often the only professional opportunity they could hope to
find. The existence of segregated black schools in the South created a substantial market for African-American teachers.

Women also dominated other professional activities. Nursing had become
primarily a women's field around the time of the Civil War, when it was still

considered a menial occupation, akin to domestic service. But by the early twentieth century, it too was adopting professional standards. Prospective nurses generally needed certification from schools of nursing and could not simply learn on the job. Women also found opportunities as librarians, another field beginning to define itself in professional terms. And many women entered academia—often studying at predominantly male institutions that permitted women to earn advanced degrees, among them the University of Chicago, MIT, and Columbia—and finding professional opportunities in the new and expanding women's colleges.

The "women's professions" had much in common with other professions: the value they placed on training and expertise, the creation of professional organizations and a professional "identity," the monitoring of admission to professional work. But they also had distinctive qualities. Careers such as teaching, nursing, and library work were "helping" professions. They involved working primarily with other women or with children. Their activities occurred in places that seemed different from the offices that dominated the predominantly male business and professional worlds; such places as schools, hospitals, and libraries had a vaguely "domestic" or "feminine" image, which enabled men (and, indeed, most women) to reconcile the idea of female professional work with prevailing ideas about the proper role of women in society.

## WOMEN AND REFORM

The prominent role of women in reform movements is one of the most striking features of progressivism. Women became important reformers even though they could not vote in most states, seldom held office, and had footholds in only a few professions. But their relative insulation from political and professional life in some ways enhanced their ability to wield influence, for it enabled them to tie their causes to the idea of a nonpartisan, nurturing culture uncontaminated by economic or political interests.

### The "New Woman"

The phenomenon of the "new woman," widely remarked upon at the time, was a product of the social and economic changes of the era. By the end of the nineteenth century, almost all income-producing activity had moved out of the home and into the factory or the office. At the same time, many women were having fewer children, and their children were beginning school at earlier ages and spending more time there. For wives and mothers who did not work for wages, home and family were less all-consuming. Hence more and more women began looking for activities outside the home.

There were also more women who lived outside traditional families altogether. Some educated women shunned marriage entirely, believing that only by remaining single could they play the roles they envisioned in the public world; approximately 10 percent of all American women in the last decades of the nineteenth century never married—a high proportion of them middle-class women. Single women were among the most prominent female reformers of the time. Some of these women lived alone. Others lived with other women, often in long-term relationships—some of them secretly romantic—that were known at the time as "Boston marriages." The divorce rate also rose rapidly in the late nineteenth century, from one divorce for every twenty-one marriages in 1880 to one in nine by 1916; women initiated the great majority of them.

Higher levels of education also contributed to the prominence of women in reform activities. The proliferation of women's colleges and of coeducational public universities in the late nineteenth century produced the first generation of women in which significant numbers had education above the high-school level. (See p. 534.) The new colleges also helped create female communities, within which women could find support for their ambitions and companionship for their activities.

There was no single profile for the "new woman." But a growing number of American women at the beginning of the twentieth century were defining their lives in ways that included a substantial amount of activity outside the home, and they were deriving from their identity as women a set of distinctive concerns that defined—and limited—their public activities.

### The Clubwomen

In the vanguard of progressive social reforms was a large network of women's clubs, which proliferated rapidly beginning in the 1880s and 1890s. The women's clubs began largely as cultural organizations to provide middle- and upper-class women with an outlet for their intellectual energies. In 1892, when women formed the General Federation of Women's Clubs to coordinate the activities of local organizations, there were more than 100,000 members in nearly 500 clubs. By 1917, there were over 1 million members.

By the early twentieth century, the clubs were becoming less concerned with cultural activities and more concerned with making a contribution to social reform. Much of what they did was uncontroversial: planting trees;

supporting schools, libraries, and settlement houses; building hospitals and parks. But clubwomen also supported such controversial measures as child labor laws, worker compensation, pure food and drug legislation, occupational safety, reforms in Indian policy, and—beginning in 1914—woman suffrage. Because many club members were from wealthy families, some organizations had substantial funds at their disposal to make their influence felt.

Black women occasionally joined clubs dominated by whites. But African Americans also formed clubs of their own, some of which affiliated with the General Federation, but more of which became part of the independent National Association of Colored Women. They modeled themselves on their white counterparts, but some black clubs took positions on issues of particular concern to blacks. Some crusaded against lynching and called for congressional legislation to make lynching a federal crime. Others protested aspects of segregation.

The women's club movement raised few overt challenges to prevailing assumptions about the proper role of women in society. But, like the limited movement of women into professions, it did represent an important effort by women to extend their influence beyond the traditional female sphere within the home and the family. Few clubwomen were willing to accept the arguments of such committed feminists as Charlotte Perkins Gilman, who in her 1898 book, *Women and Economics*, argued that the traditional definition of sexual roles was exploitive and obsolete. The club movement, rather, allowed women to define a space for themselves in the public world without openly challenging the existing, male-dominated order.

But the importance of the club movement did not lie simply in what it did for middle-class women. It lay also in what those women did for the working-class people they attempted to help. The women's club movement was an important force in winning passage of state (and ultimately federal) laws that regulated the conditions of woman and child labor, that established government inspection of workplaces, that regulated the food and drug industries, and that applied new standards to urban housing. In many of these efforts, the clubwomen formed alliances with such other women's groups as the Women's Trade Union League, founded in 1903 by female union members and upper-class reformers and committed to persuading women to join unions.

### Woman Suffrage

Perhaps the largest single reform movement of the progressive era, indeed one of the largest in American history, was the fight for woman suffrage—a movement that attracted support from both women and men. It was the culmination of many decades of struggle by women to obtain basic political rights. But it was also the product of forces peculiar to the early twentieth century.

It is sometimes difficult for today's Americans to understand why the suffrage (or right-to-vote) issue could have become the source of such enormous controversy in the early twentieth century. But at the time, suffrage seemed to many of its critics a very radical demand—in part because of the rationale some of its supporters used to advance it. Throughout the late nineteenth century, many suffrage advocates presented their views in terms of "natural rights," arguing that women deserved the same rights as men—including, first and foremost, the right to vote. Elizabeth Cady Stanton, for example, wrote in 1892 of woman as "the arbiter of her own destiny. . . . if we are to consider her as a citizen, as a member of a great nation, she must have the same rights as all other members." A woman's role as "mother, wife, sister, daughter" was "incidental" to her larger role as a part of society.

This was an argument that boldly challenged the views of many men (and even many women) who believed that society required a distinctive female "sphere" in which women would serve first and foremost as wives and mothers. And so a powerful antisuffrage movement emerged, which challenged this apparent threat to the existing social order. There were antisuffrage organizations, newspapers, and political crusades. Antisuffragists associated suffrage with divorce, promiscuity, and neglect of children. Throughout much of the late nineteenth century, they effectively stymied most efforts by women to gain the vote.

The suffrage movement began to overcome this opposition and to win some substantial victories in the first years of the twentieth century. That was in part because suffragists were becoming better organized and more politically sophisticated than their opponents. Under the leadership of Anna Howard Shaw, a Boston social worker, and Carrie Chapman Catt, a journalist from Iowa, the National American Woman Suffrage Association grew from a membership of about 13,000 in 1893 to over 2 million in 1917. The involvement of such well-known and widely admired women as Jane Addams gave added respectability to the cause.

But the movement also gained strength because many of its most prominent leaders began to justify suffrage in "safer," less threatening ways. Suffrage, some supporters began to argue, would not challenge the "separate sphere" in which women resided. It would allow women to bring their special and distinct virtues more widely to bear on society's problems. It was, they claimed, precisely because women occupied a distinct sphere—because as mothers and wives and homemakers they had special experiences and spe-

SUFFRAGISTS  Suffrage activists hang posters along
the boardwalk in the beachfront town of Long
Branch, New Jersey. Twenty-nine states had
permitted women at least some access to the ballot
before ratification of the Nineteenth Amendment in
1920. New Jersey was not one of them.

cial sensitivities to bring to public life—that woman suffrage could make such
an important contribution to politics. In particular, many suffragists argued
that enfranchising women would help the temperance movement, by giving
its largest group of supporters a political voice. Some suffrage advocates
claimed that once women had the vote, war would become a thing of the
past, since women would—through their maternal instincts and their calm-
ing, peaceful influence—help curb the natural belligerence of men. That was
one reason why World War I gave the final, decisive push to the movement
for suffrage.

Not all suffragists narrowed their arguments. Among working-class,
immigrant, and black women in particular, suffrage continued to generate
substantial support precisely because it seemed so radical, because it promised to reshape the role of women and reform the social order. But among

members of the middle class, the separation of the suffrage movement from more radical feminist goals, and its association with other reform causes of concern to many Americans, helped it gain widespread support.

The principal triumphs of the suffrage movement began in 1910. That year, Washington became the first state in fourteen years to extend suffrage to women. California joined it a year later, and in 1912 four other western states did the same. In 1913, Illinois became the first state east of the Mississippi to embrace woman suffrage. And in 1917 and 1918, New York and Michigan—two of the most populous states in the Union—gave women the vote. By 1919, thirty-nine states had granted women the right to vote in at least some elections; fifteen had allowed them full participation. In 1920, finally, suffragists won ratification of the Nineteenth Amendment, which guaranteed political rights to women throughout the nation.

To some feminists, however, the victory seemed less than complete. Alice Paul, the head of the militant National Woman's Party (founded in 1916), never accepted the relatively conservative "separate sphere" justification for suffrage. She argued that the Nineteenth Amendment alone would not be sufficient to protect women's rights. Women needed more: a constitutional amendment that would provide clear, legal protection for their rights and would prohibit all discrimination on the basis of sex. But Alice Paul's argument found limited favor even among many of the most important leaders of the recently triumphant suffrage crusade.

## THE ASSAULT ON THE PARTIES

Sooner or later, most progressive goals required the involvement of government. Only government, reformers agreed, could effectively counter the powerful private interests that threatened the nation. But American government at the dawn of the new century was, progressives believed, poorly adapted to perform their ambitious tasks. At every level, political institutions were outmoded, inefficient, and corrupt. Before society could be effectively reformed, it would be necessary to reform government itself. In the beginning, at least, many progressives believed that such reform should start with an assault on the domination of government and politics by the political parties, which they thought had become corrupt, undemocratic, and reactionary.

## Early Attacks

Attacks on party dominance had been frequent in the late nineteenth century. Greenbackism and Populism, for example, had been efforts to break the hammerlock with which the Republicans and Democrats controlled public life. The Independent Republicans (or mugwumps) had attempted to challenge the grip of partisanship, and former mugwumps became important supporters of progressive political reform activity in the 1890s and later.

The early assaults enjoyed some success. In the 1880s and 1890s, for example, most states adopted the secret ballot. Prior to that, the political parties themselves had printed ballots (or "tickets") with only the party's candidates listed, which they distributed to their supporters, who then simply went to the polls to deposit the tickets in the ballot box. The old system had made it possible for bosses to monitor the voting behavior of their constituents; it had also made it very difficult for voters to "split" their tickets—to vote for candidates of different parties for different offices. The new ballot—printed by the government and distributed at the polls, where it was filled out and deposited in secret—helped chip away at the power of the parties over the voters. (It also excluded many illiterate and non-English-speaking voters.)

By the late 1890s, critics of the parties were expanding their goals. Party rule could be broken, they believed, in one of two ways. It could be broken by increasing the power of the people, by permitting them to circumvent partisan institutions and express their will directly at the polls. Or it could be broken by placing more power in the hands of nonpartisan, nonelective officials, insulated from political life. Reformers promoted measures that moved along both those paths.

## Municipal Reform

Many progressives believed the impact of party rule was most damaging in the cities. Municipal government, therefore, became the first target of those working for political reform. Muckraking journalists such as Lincoln Steffens were especially successful in arousing public outrage at corruption and incompetence in city politics.

The muckrakers struck a responsive chord among a powerful group of urban middle-class progressives. For several decades after the Civil War, most "respectable" citizens of the nation's large cities had avoided participation in municipal government. Viewing politics as a debased and demeaning activity, they shrank from contact with the "vulgar" elements who were coming to dominate public life. By the end of the century, however, a new generation of activists—some of them members of old aristocratic families, others newly part of the middle class—were taking a revived interest in government.

They faced a formidable array of opponents. In addition to challenging the powerful city bosses and their entrenched political organizations, they were attacking a large group of special interests: saloon owners, brothel keepers, businessmen who had established lucrative relationships with the urban machines and viewed reform as a threat to their profits, and many influential newspapers, which ridiculed the reformers as naïve do-gooders. Finally, there was the great constituency of urban working people, many of them recent immigrants, for whom the machines were a source of needed jobs and services. Gradually, however, the reformers gained in political strength—in part because of their own growing numbers, in part because of the failures of the existing political leadership. And in the first years of the twentieth century, they began to score some important victories.

An early and influential success came in Galveston, Texas, where the old city government proved completely unable to deal with the effects of a destructive tidal wave in 1900. Capitalizing on public dismay, reformers (many of them local businessmen) won approval of a new city charter that replaced the mayor and council with an elected, nonpartisan commission. In 1907, Des Moines, Iowa, adopted its own version of the commission plan, and other cities soon followed.

Another approach to reform, similarly motivated by the desire to remove city government from the hands of the parties, was the city-manager plan (first adopted in Staunton, Virginia, in 1908), by which elected officials hired an outside expert—often a professionally trained business manager or engineer—to take charge of the government. The city manager would presumably remain untainted by the corrupting influence of politics. By the end of the progressive era, almost 400 cities were operating under commissions, and another 45 employed city managers.

In most urban areas, and in the larger cities in particular, the enemies of party had to settle for less absolute victories. Some cities made the election of mayors nonpartisan (so that the parties could not choose the candidates) or moved them to years when no presidential or congressional races were in progress (to reduce the influence of the large turnouts that party organizations produced on such occasions). Reformers tried to make city-council members run at large so as to limit the influence of ward leaders and district bosses. They tried to strengthen the power of the mayor at the expense of the city council, on the assumption that reformers were more likely to get a sympathetic mayor elected than to win control of the entire council.

### Statehouse Progressivism

But the assault on boss rule in the cities often did not produce results satisfying to reformers. Consequently, many progressives turned to state government as an agent for reform. These state-level progressives, like their municipal counterparts, considered existing state governments unfit to provide reform. They looked with particular scorn on state legislatures, whose ill-paid, relatively undistinguished members were, they believed, generally incompetent, often corrupt, and almost always controlled by party bosses. Many reformers began looking for ways to circumvent the legislatures (and the party bosses who controlled them) by increasing the power of the electorate.

Two of the most important changes were innovations first proposed by Populists in the 1890s: the initiative and the referendum. The initiative allowed reformers to circumvent state legislatures altogether by submitting new legislation directly to the voters in general elections. The referendum provided a method by which actions of the legislature could be returned to the electorate for approval. By 1918, more than twenty states had enacted one or both of these reforms.

The direct primary and the recall were, similarly, efforts to limit the power of parties and improve the quality of elected officials. The primary election was an attempt to take the selection of candidates away from the bosses and give it to the people. (In the South, it was also a device for excluding African Americans from voting.) The recall gave voters the right to remove a public official from office through a special election, which could be called after a sufficient number of citizens had signed a petition. By 1915 every state in the nation had instituted primary elections for at least some offices. The recall encountered more strenuous opposition, but some states adopted it as well.

Reform efforts proved most effective in states that elevated vigorous and committed politicians to positions of leadership. In New York, Governor Charles Evans Hughes exploited progressive sentiment to create a commission to regulate public utilities. In California, Governor Hiram Johnson promoted reforms to limit the political power of the Southern Pacific Railroad. In New Jersey, Woodrow Wilson, the Princeton University president who was elected governor in 1910, used executive leadership to win reforms designed to end New Jersey's widely denounced position as the "mother of trusts."

But the most celebrated state-level reformer was Robert M. La Follette of Wisconsin. Elected governor in 1900, he helped turn his state into what reformers across the nation described as a "laboratory of progressivism." The Wisconsin progressives won approval of direct primaries, initiatives, and referendums. They regulated railroads and utilities. They passed laws to regulate the workplace and provide compensation for laborers injured on the job. They instituted graduated taxes on inherited fortunes, and they nearly doubled state levies on railroads and other corporate interests. Ultimately, La Follette would find himself overshadowed by other national progressive leaders. In the early years of the century, however, few men were as effective in publicizing the message of reform. None was as successful in bending state government to that goal.

### Parties and Interest Groups

The reformers did not, of course, eliminate parties from American political life. But they did diminish the parties' centrality. Evidence of that came from, among other things, the decline in voter turnout. In the late nineteenth century, up to 81 percent of eligible voters routinely turned out for national elections. In the early twentieth century, while turnout remained very high by today's standards, the figure declined markedly. In the presidential election of 1900, 73 percent of the electorate voted. By 1912, the figure had dropped to about 59 percent. Never again did voter turnout reach as high as 70 percent.

At the same time that parties were declining, other power centers were emerging to compete with them: what have become known as "interest groups." Beginning late in the nineteenth century and accelerating rapidly in the twentieth, new organizations emerged, outside the party system, that were designed to pressure government to do the bidding of their members: professional organizations; trade associations, representing particular businesses and industries; labor organizations; farm lobbies; and many others. Social workers, the settlement house movement, women's clubs, and others learned to operate as interest groups to advance their demands. A new pattern of politics, in which many individual interests organized to influence government directly rather than operating through party structures, was emerging. It would become the characteristic form of American politics in the twentieth century.

## SOURCES OF PROGRESSIVE REFORM

Middle-class reformers, most of them from the East, dominated the public image and much of the substance of progressivism in the late nineteenth and early twentieth centuries. But they were not alone in seeking to improve social conditions. Working-class Americans, African Americans, westerners, even party bosses also played crucial roles in advancing some of the important reforms of the era.

### *Labor, the Machine, and Reform*

Although the American Federation of Labor, and its leader Samuel Gompers, remained largely aloof from many of the reform efforts of the time (reflecting Gompers's firm belief that workers should not rely on government to improve their lot), some unions nevertheless played important roles in reform battles. In San Francisco, for example, workers in the Building Trades Council spearheaded the formation of the new Union Labor Party, committed to a program of reform almost indistinguishable from that of middle-class and elite progressives in the city. Between 1911 and 1913, in significant part because of the new party's efforts, California passed a child labor law, a workmen's compensation law, and a limitation on working hours for women. Union pressures contributed to the passage of similar laws in many other states as well.

One result of the assault on the parties was a change in the party organizations themselves, which attempted to adapt to the new realities so as to preserve their influence. Some party machines emerged from the progressive era almost as powerful as they had entered it. This was largely because bosses themselves recognized that they must change in order to survive. Thus they sometimes allowed their machines to become vehicles of social reform. One example was New York's Tammany Hall, the nation's oldest and most notorious city machine. Its astute leader, Charles Francis Murphy, began in the early years of the century to fuse the techniques of boss rule with some of the concerns of social reformers. Murphy did nothing to challenge the fundamental workings of Tammany Hall. But Tammany began to take an increased interest in state and national politics, which it had traditionally scorned; and it used its political power on behalf of legislation to improve working conditions, protect child laborers, and eliminate the worst abuses of the industrial economy.

In 1911, a terrible fire swept through the factory of the Triangle Shirtwaist Company in New York; 146 workers, most of them women, died. Many of them had been trapped inside the burning building because management had locked the emergency exits to prevent malingering. For the next three years, a state commission studied not only the background of the fire but the general condition of the industrial workplace. It was responding to intense public pressure from women's groups and New York City labor unions—and to less-public pressure from Tammany Hall. By 1914, the commission had issued a series of reports calling for major reforms in the conditions of modern labor.

The report itself was a classic progressive document, based on the testimony of experts, filled with statistics and technical data. Yet when its recommendations reached the New York legislature, its most effective supporters were not middle-class progressives but two Tammany Democrats from working-class backgrounds: Senator Robert F. Wagner and Assemblyman Alfred E. Smith. With the support of Murphy and the backing of other Tammany legislators, they steered through a series of pioneering labor laws that imposed strict regulations on factory owners and established effective mechanisms for enforcement.

### Western Progressives

The American West produced some of the most notable progressive leaders of the time: Hiram Johnson of California, George Norris of Nebraska, William Borah of Idaho, and others—almost all of whom spent at least some of their political careers in the United States Senate. That was because for western states, the most important target of reform energies was not state or local governments, which had relatively little power, but the federal government, which exercised a kind of authority in the West that it had never possessed in the East.

Many of the most important issues to the future of the West required action above the state level. Disputes over water, for example, almost always involved rivers and streams that crossed state lines. More significant, perhaps, the federal government exercised enormous power over the lands and resources of the western states and provided substantial subsidies to the region in the form of land grants and support for railroad and water projects. Huge areas of the West remained (and still remain) public lands, controlled by Washington—a far greater proportion than in any states east of the Mississippi; and much of the growth of the West was (and continues to be) a result of federally funded dams and water projects.

Because so much authority in the region rested in federal bureaucracies which state and local governments could not control, political parties in most of the West were relatively weak. That was one reason why western states could move so quickly and decisively to embrace reforms that parties did not like: the initiative, the referendum, the recall, direct primaries. It is also why aspiring politicians were much quicker to look to Washington as a place from which they could influence the future of their region.

### African Americans and Reform

One social question that received relatively little attention from white progressives was race. But among African Americans themselves, the progressive era produced some significant challenges to existing racial norms.

African Americans faced greater obstacles than any other group in challenging their own oppressed status and seeking reform. That was one reason why so many embraced the message of Booker T. Washington in the late nineteenth century, to "put down your bucket where you are," to work for immediate self-improvement rather than long-range social change. Not all blacks, however, were content with this approach. And by the turn of the century a powerful challenge was emerging—to the philosophy of Washington and, more important, to the entire structure of race relations. The chief spokesman for this new approach was W. E. B. Du Bois, a Harvard-trained sociologist and historian with a more expansive view than Washington of the future of his race.

In *The Souls of Black Folk* (1903), Du Bois launched an open attack on Washington's "Atlanta Compromise," which urged blacks to postpone efforts to achieve political equality and concentrate on self-improvement. Du Bois accused Washington of encouraging white efforts to impose segregation and of unnecessarily limiting the aspirations of his race. Rather than content themselves with education at the trade and agricultural schools, Du Bois advocated, talented blacks should accept nothing less than a full university education. They should aspire to the professions. They should, above all, fight for immediate progress on civil rights, not simply wait for them to be granted as a reward for patient striving. In 1905, Du Bois and a group of his supporters met at Niagara Falls—on the Canadian side of the border because no hotel on the American side of the Falls would have them—and launched what became known as the Niagara Movement. Four years later, after a race riot in Springfield, Illinois, they joined with white progressives sympathetic to their cause to form the National Association for the Advancement of Colored People (NAACP). In the years that followed, the new organization led the drive for equal rights, using as its principal weapon lawsuits in the federal courts.

W. E. B. DU BOIS AT HIS DESK  Although W. E. B. Du Bois, unlike Booker T. Washington, never developed a large popular following, he was the acknowledged leader of the black elite in the late nineteenth and early twentieth centuries. He was the first African American to earn a doctorate at Harvard University, and he published a number of distinguished works of history and sociology during his long career. He also served as editor of *The Crisis*, the newspaper of the NAACP (which he had helped to found). He died in 1963, at the age of ninety-five.

The NAACP was not a radical, or even an egalitarian, organization. It relied, rather, on the efforts of the most intelligent and educated members of the black race, the "talented tenth" as Du Bois called them. And it stressed not so much the elevation of all blacks from poverty and oppression as the opportunity for exceptional blacks to gain positions of full equality. Ultimately, its members believed, such efforts would benefit all blacks. By creating a trained elite, blacks would in effect be creating a leadership group capable of fighting for the rights of the race as a whole.

## CRUSADES FOR ORDER AND REFORM

Reformers directed many of their energies at the political process. But they also crusaded on behalf of what they considered moral issues. There were campaigns to eliminate alcohol from national life, to curb prostitution, to regulate divorce. There were efforts to restrict immigration and to curb the power of monopoly in the industrial economy. There were crusades to resolve what many considered longstanding injustices, of which the most prominent was the campaign for woman suffrage. Proponents of each of those reforms believed that success would help regenerate society as a whole.

### The Temperance Crusade

Many progressives considered the elimination of alcohol from American life a necessary step in restoring order to society. Workers in settlement houses and social agencies abhorred the effects of drinking on working-class families: scarce wages vanished as workers spent hours in saloons; drunkenness spawned violence, and occasionally murder, within urban families. Women, in particular, saw alcohol as a source of some of the greatest problems of working-class wives and mothers, and hoped through temperance to reform abusive or irresponsible male behavior and thus improve women's lives. Employers regarded alcohol as an impediment to industrial efficiency; workers often missed time on the job because of drunkenness or, worse, came to the factory intoxicated and performed their tasks sloppily and dangerously. Critics of economic privilege denounced the liquor industry as one of the nation's most sinister trusts. And political reformers, who looked on the saloon (correctly) as one of the central institutions of the machine, saw an attack on drinking as part of an attack on the bosses. Out of such varied sentiments emerged the temperance movement.

Temperance had been a major reform movement before the Civil War, mobilizing large numbers of people (and particularly large numbers of women) in a crusade with strong religious overtones. Beginning in the 1870s, it experienced a major resurgence. As in the antebellum years, it was a movement led and supported primarily by women. In 1873, temperance advocates formed the Women's Christian Temperance Union (WCTU), led after 1879 by Frances Willard. By 1911, it had 245,000 members and had become the largest single women's organization in American history to that point. The WCTU publicized the evils of alcohol and the connection between drunkenness and family violence, unemployment, poverty, and disease. In 1893, the Anti-Saloon League joined the temperance movement and, along with the WCTU, began to press for a specific legislative solution: the legal abolition of saloons. Gradually, that demand grew to include the complete prohibition of the sale and manufacture of alcoholic beverages.

Despite substantial opposition from immigrant and working-class voters, pressure for prohibition grew steadily through the first decades of the new century. By 1916, nineteen states had passed prohibition laws. But since the consumption of alcohol was actually increasing in many unregulated areas, temperance supporters were beginning to advocate national prohibition. American entry into World War I, and the moral fervor it unleashed, provided the last push to the advocates of prohibition. In 1917, with the support of rural fundamentalists who opposed alcohol on moral and religious grounds, progressive advocates of prohibition steered through Congress a constitutional amendment embodying their demands. Two years later, after ratification by every state in the nation except Connecticut and Rhode Island (with large populations of Catholic immigrants opposed to prohibition), the Eighteenth Amendment became law, to take effect in January 1920.

## Immigration Restriction

Virtually all reformers agreed that the growing immigrant population had created social problems, but there was wide disagreement on how best to respond. Some progressives believed that helping the new residents adapt to American society was the proper approach. Others argued that efforts at assimilation had failed and that the only solution was to limit the flow of new arrivals.

In the first decades of the century, the arguments of this second, more pessimistic, group gradually gained strength; and pressure grew to close the nation's gates. New scholarly theories, appealing to the progressive respect for expertise, argued that the introduction of immigrants into American society was diluting the purity of the nation's racial stock. The spurious "science" of eugenics spread the belief that human inequalities were hereditary and that immigration was contributing to the multiplication of the unfit. A special federal commission of "experts," chaired by Senator William P. Dillingham of Vermont, issued an elaborate report filled with statistics and scholarly testimony. It argued that the newer immigrant groups—largely southern and eastern Europeans—had proved themselves less assimilable than earlier immigrants. Immigration, the report implied, should be restricted by nationality. Even many people who rejected racial arguments supported limiting immigration as a way to solve such urban problems as overcrowding, unemployment, strained social services, and social unrest.

The combination of these concerns gradually won for the nativists the support of some of the nation's leading progressives: Theodore Roosevelt, Senator Henry Cabot Lodge, and others. Powerful opponents—employers who saw immigration as a source of cheap labor, immigrants themselves, and the immigrants' political representatives—managed to block the restriction movement for a time. But by the beginning of World War I (which itself effectively blocked immigration temporarily), the nativist tide was clearly rising.

### The Dream of Socialism

At no time in the history of the United States to that point, and in few times after it, did radical critiques of the capitalist system attract more support than in the period between 1900 and 1914. Although never a force to rival, or even seriously threaten, the two major parties, the Socialist Party of America grew during the progressive era into a force of considerable strength. In the election of 1900, it had attracted the support of fewer than 100,000 voters; in 1912, its durable leader and perennial presidential candidate, Eugene V. Debs, received nearly 1 million ballots. Strongest in urban immigrant communities (particularly among Germans and Jews), it attracted the loyalties, too, of a substantial number of Protestant farmers in the South and Midwest. Socialists won election to over 1,000 state and local offices. And they had the support at times of such intellectuals as Lincoln Steffens, the crusader against municipal corruption, and Walter Lippmann, the brilliant young journalist and social critic. Florence Kelley, Frances Willard, and other women reformers were attracted to socialism because of its support for pacifism and labor militancy.

Virtually all socialists agreed on the need for basic structural changes in the economy, but they differed widely on the extent of those changes and the tactics necessary to achieve them. Some endorsed the radical goals of European Marxists (a complete end to capitalism and private property); others envisioned a more moderate reform that would allow small-scale private enterprise to survive but would nationalize major industries. Militant groups within the party favored direct, even revolutionary action. Most conspicuous was the radical labor union the Industrial Workers of the World (IWW), whose members were known to their opponents as "Wobblies." Under the leadership of William ("Big Bill") Haywood, the IWW advocated a single union for all workers, making it one of the few labor organizations of its time committed to organizing the unskilled, and abolition of the "wage slave" system; it rejected political action in favor of strikes—especially the general strike. The Wobblies were widely believed to have been responsible for the dynamiting of railroad lines and power stations and other acts of terror, although evidence of their actual participation in such activities is slim.

More moderate socialists, who advocated peaceful change through political struggle, dominated the party. They emphasized a gradual education of the public to the need for change and patient efforts within the system to achieve it. But by the end of World War I, because the party had refused to support the war effort and because of a growing wave of antiradicalism that subjected the socialists to enormous harassment and persecution, socialism was in decline as a significant political force.

## Decentralization and Regulation

Many reformers agreed with the socialists that the greatest threat to the nation's economy was excessive centralization of power and concentration of wealth, but they retained a faith in the possibilities of reform within a capitalist system. Rather than nationalize basic industries, they hoped to restore the economy to a more human scale. Few envisioned a return to a society of small, local enterprises; some consolidation, they recognized, was inevitable. They did, however, argue that the federal government should work to break up the largest combinations and enforce a balance between the need for bigness and the need for competition. This viewpoint came to be identified particularly closely with Louis D. Brandeis, a brilliant lawyer and later a justice of the Supreme Court, who spoke and wrote widely (most notably in his 1913 book, *Other People's Money*) about the "curse of bigness."

Other progressives were less enthusiastic about the virtues of competition. More important to them was efficiency, which they believed economic concentration encouraged. What government should do, they argued, was not fight "bigness" but guard against abuses of power by large institutions. It should distinguish between "good trusts" and "bad trusts," encouraging the good while disciplining the bad. Since economic consolidation was destined to remain a permanent feature of American society, continuing oversight by a strong, modernized government, led by a strong president, was essential. One of the most important spokesmen for this emerging "nationalist" position was Herbert Croly, whose 1909 book, *The Promise of American Life*, became an influential progressive document.

Opinions varied widely on how to achieve economic order. But increasingly, attention focused on some form of coordination of the industrial economy. To some, that meant businesses themselves should learn new ways of cooperation and self-regulation; some of the most energetic "progressive" reformers of the period, in fact, were businessmen searching for ways to bring order to their own troubled world. To others, the solution was for government to play a more active role in regulating and planning economic life. One of those who came to endorse that position (although not fully until after 1910) was Theodore Roosevelt, who became for a time the most powerful symbol of the reform impulse at the national level.

DEBATING THE PAST

## *Progressivism*

UNTIL THE EARLY 1950s, most historians seemed to agree on the central characteristics of early twentieth-century progressivism. It was just what many progressives themselves had said it was: a movement by the "people" to curb the power of "special interests." More specifically, it was a protest by an aroused citizenry against the excessive power of urban bosses, corporate moguls, and corrupt elected officials.

In 1951, George Mowry began the process of challenging these assumptions by examining progressives in California and describing them as a small, privileged elite of business and professional figures: people who considered themselves the natural leaders of society and who were trying to recover their fading influence from the new capitalist institutions that had displaced them. Progressivism was not, in other words, a popular, democratic movement; it was the effort of a displaced elite to restore its authority. Richard Hofstadter expanded on this idea in *The Age of Reform* (1955) by describing reformers as people afflicted by "status anxiety," fading elites suffering not from economic but from psychological discontent.

The Mowry-Hofstadter argument soon encountered a range of challenges. In 1963, Gabriel Kolko published his influential study *The Triumph of Conservatism*, in which he rejected both the older "democratic" view of progressivism and the newer "status-anxiety" view. Progressive reform, he argued, was not an effort to protect the people from the corporations; it was, rather, a vehicle through which corporate leaders used the government to protect themselves from competition. Regulation, Kolko argued, was "invariably controlled by the leaders of the regulated industry and directed towards ends they deemed acceptable or desirable."

A more moderate reinterpretation came from historians embracing what would later be called the "organizational" approach to twentieth-century

American history. First Samuel Hays, in *The Response to Industrialism* (1957), and then Robert Wiebe, in *The Search for Order* (1967), portrayed progressivism as a broad effort by businessmen, professionals, and other middle-class people to bring order and efficiency to political and economic life. In the new industrial society, economic power was increasingly concentrated in large, national organizations, while social and political life remained centered primarily in local communities. Progressivism, Wiebe argued, was the effort of a "new middle class"—a class tied to the emerging national economy—to stabilize and enhance its position in society by bringing those two worlds together.

In the 1970s and 1980s, scholarship on progressivism moved in so many different directions that some historians came to despair of finding any consistent meaning in the term. Much of the new scholarship focused on discovering new groups among whom "progressive" ideas and efforts flourished. Historians found evidence of progressivism in the rising movement by consumers to define their interests; in the growth of reform movements among African Americans; in the changing nature of urban political machines; and in the political activism of working people and labor organizations. Particularly influential was the effort to reveal the crucial role of women in promoting reform as a way of protecting their interests within a rapidly changing domestic sphere or of expanding their role in the public world.

Other scholars attempted to identify progressivism with broad changes in the structure and culture of politics. Richard McCormick, writing in 1981, argued that the crucial change in the "progressive era" was the decline of political parties and the corresponding rise of interest groups working for particular social and economic goals. Progressivism, he and others have suggested, was not so much a coherent "movement" as part of the broader process by which Americans adapted their political and social systems to the realities of the modern industrial age. At the same time, many historians were arguing that the role of women in progressive efforts helped determine the nature of early-twentieth-century reform, that women not only dominated many reform activities but shaped them to serve what they perceived to be the interests of their gender.

The search for the "essence" of progressivism will undoubtedly continue. But the scholarship of recent decades suggests that the real answer to the nature of progressive reform may be a recognition of its enormous diversity.

# CHAPTER TWENTY-TWO

# The Battle for National Reform

*Theodore Roosevelt and the Progressive Presidency*
*The Troubled Succession* ∼ *Woodrow Wilson and the New Freedom*
*The "Big Stick": America and the World, 1901–1917*

EFFORTS TO REFORM the industrial economy encountered repeated frustrations at the state and local levels. The great combinations were national in scope, and reformers gradually concluded that only national action could effectively control their power. Beginning early in the twentieth century, they began to look to the federal government.

But just as at the state and local levels, the national government—mired in partisan politics—seemed poorly suited to serve as an agent of reform. Progressives attempted to make it more responsive to their demands. Some reformers, for example, urged an end to the system by which state legislatures elected the members of the United States Senate; they proposed instead a direct popular election, which they believed would force the Senate to react more directly to public demands. The Seventeenth Amendment, passed by Congress in 1912 and ratified by the states in 1913, provided for that change.

But even a reformed Congress, progressives believed, could not be expected to provide the kind of coherent leadership their agenda required. Congress was too clumsy, too divided, too tied to local, parochial interests. If the federal government was truly to fulfill its mission, most reformers agreed, it would require leadership from the one office capable of providing "modern," "efficient" leadership: the presidency.

## THEODORE ROOSEVELT AND
## THE PROGRESSIVE PRESIDENCY

To a generation of progressive reformers, Theodore Roosevelt was more than an admired public figure; he was an idol. No president before and few after attracted such attention and devotion. Yet for all his popularity among

## TIME LINE

| 1901 | 1902 | 1903 | 1904 |
|------|------|------|------|
| McKinley assassinated<br><br>Theodore Roosevelt becomes president<br><br>Hay-Pauncefote Treaty | Northern Securities antitrust case | Department of Commerce and Labor created | Roosevelt Corollary<br><br>Panamanian independence<br><br>Roosevelt elected |

| 1906 | 1908 | 1909 | 1912 |
|------|------|------|------|
| Hepburn Railroad Regulation Act<br><br>Meat Inspection Act | Taft elected president | Payne-Aldrich Tariff<br><br>U.S. troops in Nicaragua | Wilson elected president |

| 1913 | 1914 | 1916 |
|------|------|------|
| 16th Amendment (income tax)<br><br>17th Amendment (direct election of U.S. senators)<br><br>Federal Reserve Act | Federal Trade Commission Act<br><br>Panama Canal opened<br><br>U.S. troops in Haiti | U.S. troops in Mexico |

reformers, Roosevelt was in many respects decidedly conservative. He earned his extraordinary popularity less because of the extent of his reforms than because of his ebullient public personality and because he brought to his office a broad conception of its powers and invested the presidency with something of its modern status as the center of national political life.

### The Accidental President

When President William McKinley suddenly died in September 1901, the victim of an assassination, Roosevelt (who had been elected vice president less than a year before) was only forty-two years old, the youngest man ever to assume the presidency. Already, however, he had achieved a reputation within the Republican Party as something of a wild man. Party leaders sensed his independence and despaired of controlling him. Mark Hanna, who had warned McKinley against selecting Roosevelt as his running mate, exclaimed, "Now look, that damned cowboy is president of the United States!" But Roosevelt as president never openly rebelled against the leaders of his party. He became, rather, a champion of cautious, moderate change.

Roosevelt envisioned the federal government not as the agent of any particular interest but as a mediator of the public good, with the president at its center. This attitude found expression in Roosevelt's policies toward the great industrial combinations. He was not opposed to the principle of economic concentration, but he acknowledged that consolidation produced dangerous abuses of power. He allied himself, therefore, with those progressives who urged regulation (but not destruction) of the trusts.

At the heart of Roosevelt's policy was his desire to win for government the power to investigate the activities of corporations and publicize the results. The pressure of educated public opinion, he believed, would alone eliminate most corporate abuses. Government could legislate solutions for those that remained.

Roosevelt engaged in a few highly publicized efforts to break up combinations, among them a 1902 suit against a great new railroad combination in the Northwest, the Northern Securities Company. But he was not a trust-buster at heart, and his occasional use of antitrust law did not mark any serious effort to reverse the prevailing trend toward economic concentration.

A similar commitment to establishing the government as an impartial regulatory mechanism shaped Roosevelt's policy toward labor. In the past, federal intervention in industrial disputes had almost always meant action on behalf of employers. Roosevelt was willing to consider labor's position as well. When a bitter 1902 strike by the United Mine Workers against the anthracite coal industry dragged on long enough to endanger coal supplies for the coming winter, Roosevelt asked both the operators and the miners to accept impartial federal arbitration; and he threatened to dispatch federal troops to seize the mines when the owners refused. They soon relented. Arbitrators awarded the strikers a 10 percent wage increase and a nine-hour day. Despite such episodes, Roosevelt viewed himself as no more the champion of labor than of management. On several occasions, he ordered federal troops to intervene in strikes on behalf of employers.

Reform was not Roosevelt's main priority during his first years as president. He was principally concerned with winning an election in his own right, which meant not antagonizing the conservative Republican Old Guard. By early 1904, Roosevelt had all but neutralized his opposition within the party. He won its presidential nomination with ease. And in the general election, where he faced a pallid conservative Democrat, Alton B. Parker, he captured over 57 percent of the popular vote and lost no states outside the South.

### The Square Deal

During the 1904 campaign, Roosevelt boasted that he had worked in the anthracite coal strike to provide everyone with a "square deal." In his second term, he set out to extend this square deal further, although some of his efforts were more symbolic than substantive. One of his first targets was the powerful railroad industry. The Interstate Commerce Act of 1887, establishing the Interstate Commerce Commission (ICC), had been an early effort to regulate the industry, but over the years the courts had sharply limited its influence. The Hepburn Railroad Regulation Act of 1906 sought to restore some regulatory authority to the government by giving the ICC authority to inspect the books of railroad companies, a relatively modest expansion of its power.

Roosevelt also pressured Congress to enact the Pure Food and Drug Act, which restricted the sale of dangerous or ineffective medicines but had very modest enforcement mechanisms. When Upton Sinclair's powerful novel *The Jungle* appeared in 1906, featuring appalling descriptions of conditions

MAKING SAUSAGES The shockingly unsanitary conditions by which meatpackers (such as those shown here in the Chicago stockyards) made sausages inspired Upton Sinclair's novel *The Jungle*, which in turn precipitated federal legislation, the Meat Inspection Act of 1906, establishing government inspection of meat products.

in the meatpacking industry, Roosevelt insisted on passage of the Meat Inspection Act, which ultimately helped eliminate many diseases once transmitted in impure meat. Starting in 1907, he proposed even more stringent measures: an eight-hour day for workers, broader compensation for victims of industrial accidents, inheritance and income taxes, regulation of the stock market, and others. He also started openly to criticize conservatives in Congress and the judiciary, who were obstructing these programs. The result was not only a general stalemate in Roosevelt's reform agenda but a widening gulf between the president and the conservative wing of his party.

Roosevelt's aggressive policies on behalf of conservation contributed to that gulf. A lifelong sportsman and naturalist, he had long been concerned about the unchecked exploitation of America's natural resources and its remaining wilderness. Using executive powers, he limited private development on millions of acres of undeveloped government land by adding them to the previously modest national forest system. When conservatives in Congress restricted his authority over public lands in 1907, Roosevelt and his chief forester, Gifford Pinchot, worked furiously before the bill became law to

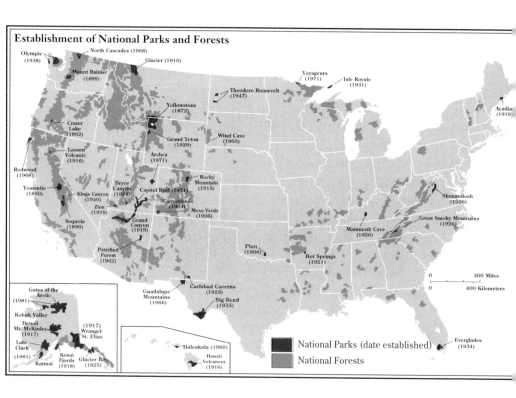

**Establishment of National Parks and Forests**

Olympic (1938)
North Cascades (1968)
Glacier (1910)
Mount Rainier (1899)
Voyageurs (1971)
Isle Royale (1931)
Theodore Roosevelt (1947)
Yellowstone (1872)
Acadia (1919)
Crater Lake (1902)
Grand Teton (1929)
Wind Cave (1903)
Lassen Volcanic (1916)
Arches (1971)
Redwood (1968)
Rocky Mountain (1915)
Yosemite (1890)
Bryce Canyon (1924)
Capitol Reef (1971)
Shenandoah (1926)
Kings Canyon (1940)
Zion (1919)
Canyonlands (1964)
Mesa Verde (1906)
Sequoia (1890)
Grand Canyon (1919)
Great Smoky Mountains (1926)
Mammoth Cave (1926)
Petrified Forest (1962)
Platt (1906)
Hot Springs (1921)
Gates of the Arctic (1981)
Guadalupe Mountains (1966)
Carlsbad Caverns (1923)
Big Bend (1935)
Kobuk Valley
Denali
Mt. McKinley (1917)
Wrangel-St. Elias (1917)
Lake Clark (1981)
Kenai Fjords (1918)
Glacier Bay (1925)
Katmai
Haleakala (1960)
Hawaii Volcanoes (1916)
Everglades (1934)

0  300 Miles
0  400 Kilometers

National Parks (date established)
National Forests

seize all the forests and many of the water power sites still in the public domain.

Roosevelt was the first president to take an active interest in the new and struggling American conservation movement, and his policies had a lasting effect on national environmental policies. More than most public figures, he was sympathetic to the concerns of the naturalists—those within the movement committed to protecting the natural beauty of the land. But Roosevelt's policies more often favored another faction within the conservation movement—those who believed in carefully managed development. That was in part a result of the influence of Pinchot, the first director of the National Forest Service, who supported rational and efficient human use of the wilderness.

The Old Guard may have opposed Roosevelt's efforts to extend government control over vast new lands. But they eagerly supported another important aspect of Roosevelt's natural resource policy: public reclamation and irrigation projects. In 1902, the president backed the Newlands Reclamation Act, which provided federal funds for the construction of dams, reservoirs, and canals in the West—projects to open new lands for cultivation and, years later, to provide cheap electric power. It was the beginning of many years of federal aid for irrigation and power development in the western states.

Despite the flurry of reforms Roosevelt was able to enact, the government still had relatively little control over the industrial economy. That became clear in 1907, when a serious recession began. Conservatives blamed Roosevelt's "mad" economic policies for the disaster. And while the president, naturally (and correctly), disagreed, he nevertheless acted quickly to reassure business leaders that he would not interfere with their private recovery efforts.

The great financier J. P. Morgan helped construct a pool of the assets of several important New York banks to prop up shaky financial institutions. The key to the arrangement, Morgan told the president, was the purchase by U.S. Steel of the shares of the Tennessee Coal and Iron Company, currently held by a threatened New York bank. He would, he insisted, need assurances that the purchase would not prompt antitrust action. Roosevelt tacitly agreed, and the Morgan plan proceeded. Whether or not as a result, the panic soon subsided.

Roosevelt loved being president, and many people assumed he would run for the office again in 1908 despite the longstanding tradition of presidents' serving no more than two terms. But the Panic of 1907, combined with Roosevelt's growing "radicalism" during his second term, so alienated conservatives in his own party that he might have had difficulty winning the Republican nomination for another term despite his great popularity. In 1904, moreover, he had made a public promise to step down four years later. And so, after nearly eight energetic years in the White House, during which he had transformed the role of the presidency in American government, Theodore Roosevelt, fifty years old, retired from public life—briefly.

## THE TROUBLED SUCCESSION

William Howard Taft, who assumed the presidency in 1909, had been Theodore Roosevelt's most trusted lieutenant and his hand-picked successor; progressive reformers believed him to be one of their own. But Taft had also been a restrained and moderate jurist, a man with a punctilious regard for legal process; conservatives expected him to abandon Roosevelt's aggressive use of presidential powers. By seeming acceptable to almost everyone, Taft won election to the White House in 1908 with almost ridiculous ease. He received his party's nomination virtually uncontested. His victory in the general election in November—over William Jennings Bryan, running forlornly for the Democrats for the third time—was a foregone conclusion. Taft entered the White House on a wave of good feeling.

Four years later, however, Taft would leave office the most decisively defeated president of the twentieth century, his party deeply divided and the government in the hands of a Democratic administration for the first time in twenty years. Taft's failure was a result in part of his own character and style: his cautious, limited use of presidential powers; his failure to match Roosevelt's personal dynamism. (Contributing to Taft's image as a less than vigorous man was his enormous weight, which at times rose to 350 pounds.) More significant, however, was that having come into office as the darling of progressives and conservatives alike, he soon found that he could not please both groups. Gradually he found himself, without really intending it, pleasing the conservatives and alienating the progressives.

### Taft and the Progressives

Taft's first problem arose in the opening months of the new administration, when he called Congress into special session to lower protective tariff rates, an old progressive demand. But the president made no effort to overcome the opposition of the congressional Old Guard, arguing that it would violate the constitutional doctrine of separation of powers if he were to intervene in legislative matters. The result was the feeble Payne-Aldrich Tariff, which reduced tariff rates scarcely at all and in some areas actually raised them. Progressives resented the president's passivity and were suspicious of his motives.

A sensational controversy broke out late in 1909 that helped destroy Taft's popularity with reformers for good. Many progressives had been unhappy when Taft replaced Roosevelt's secretary of the interior, James R. Garfield, an aggressive conservationist, with Richard A. Ballinger, a more conservative corporate lawyer. Suspicion of Ballinger grew when he attempted to invalidate Roosevelt's removal of nearly 1 million acres of forests and mineral reserves from the public lands available for private development.

In the midst of this mounting concern, Louis Glavis, an Interior Department investigator, charged the new secretary with having once connived to turn over valuable public coal lands in Alaska to a private syndicate for personal profit. Glavis took the evidence to Gifford Pinchot, still head of the Forest Service and a critic of Ballinger's policies. Pinchot took the charges to the president. Taft investigated them and decided they were groundless. But Pinchot was not satisfied, particularly after Taft fired Glavis for his part in the episode. He leaked the story to the press and asked Congress to investigate the scandal. The president discharged him for insubordination, and the congressional committee appointed to study the controversy, dominated by Old Guard Republicans, exonerated Ballinger. But progressives throughout the country supported Pinchot. The controversy aroused as much public passion as any dispute of its time; and when it was over, Taft had alienated the supporters of Roosevelt completely and, it seemed, irrevocably.

### The Return of Roosevelt

During most of these controversies, Theodore Roosevelt was far away: on a long hunting safari in Africa and an extended tour of Europe. To the American public, however, Roosevelt remained a formidable presence. His return to New York in the spring of 1910 was a major public event.

Roosevelt insisted that he had no plans to reenter politics, but his resolve lasted less than a week. Politicians began flocking immediately to his Long Island home for conferences. Roosevelt took an active role in several New York political controversies, and within a month, he announced that he would embark on a national speaking tour before the end of the summer. Furious with Taft, he was becoming convinced that he alone was capable of reuniting the Republican Party.

ROOSEVELT AT OSAWATOMIE  Roosevelt's famous speech at Osawatomie, Kansas, in 1910 was the most radical of his career and openly marked his break with the Taft administration and the Republican leadership.

The real signal of Roosevelt's decision to assume leadership of Republican reformers came in a speech he gave on September 1, 1910, in Osawatomie, Kansas. In it he outlined a set of principles, which he labeled the "New Nationalism," that made clear he had moved a considerable way from the cautious conservatism of the first years of his presidency. He argued that social justice was possible only through the vigorous efforts of a strong federal government whose executive acted as the "steward of the public welfare." Those who thought primarily of property rights and personal profit "must now give way to the advocate of human welfare." He supported graduated income and inheritance taxes, workers' compensation for industrial accidents, regulation of the labor of women and children, tariff revision, and firmer regulation of corporations.

### Spreading Insurgency

The congressional elections of 1910 provided further evidence of how far the progressive revolt had spread. In primary elections, conservative Republicans suffered defeat after defeat while almost all the progressive incumbents were reelected. In the general election, the Democrats, who were now offering progressive candidates of their own, won control of the House of Representatives for the first time in sixteen years and gained strength in the Senate. Reform sentiment seemed clearly on the rise. But Roosevelt still denied any presidential ambitions and claimed that his real purpose was to pressure Taft to return to progressive policies. Two events, however, changed his mind. The first was an antitrust decision by the Taft administration. On October 27, 1911, the administration announced a suit against U.S. Steel, charging, among other things, that the 1907 acquisition of the Tennessee Coal and Iron Company had been illegal. Roosevelt had approved that acquisition in the midst of the 1907 panic, and he was enraged by the implication that he had acted improperly.

But Roosevelt was reluctant at first to become a candidate for president, largely because Senator Robert La Follette, the great Wisconsin progressive, had been working since 1911 to secure the presidential nomination for himself. But La Follette's candidacy stumbled in February 1912. Exhausted, and distraught over the illness of a daughter, he appeared to suffer a nervous breakdown during a speech in Philadelphia. Roosevelt announced his candidacy on February 22.

### T. R. Versus Taft

La Follette retained some diehard support. But for all practical purposes, the campaign for the Republican nomination had now become a battle between Roosevelt, the champion of the progressives, and Taft, the candidate of the conservatives. Roosevelt scored overwhelming victories in all thirteen presidential primaries. Taft, however, remained the choice of most party leaders, whose preference was decisive.

The battle for the nomination at the Chicago convention revolved around an unusually large number of contested delegates: 254 in all. Roosevelt needed fewer than half the disputed seats to clinch the nomination. But the Republican National Committee, controlled by the Old Guard, awarded all but 19 of them to Taft. At a rally the night before the convention opened, Roosevelt addressed 5,000 cheering supporters and announced that if the party refused to seat his delegates, he would continue his own candidacy outside the party. "We stand at Armageddon," he told the roaring crowd, "and we battle for the Lord." The next day, he led his supporters out of the convention, and out of the party. The convention then quietly nominated Taft on the first ballot.

Roosevelt summoned his supporters back to Chicago in August for another convention, this one to launch the new Progressive Party and nominate himself as its presidential candidate. Roosevelt approached the battle feeling, as he put it, "fit as a bull moose" (thus giving his new party an enduring nickname). But by then, he was aware that his cause was virtually hopeless. That was partly because many of the insurgents who had supported him during the primaries refused to follow him out of the Republican Party. It was also because of the man the Democrats had nominated for president.

## WOODROW WILSON
## AND THE NEW FREEDOM

The 1912 presidential contest was not simply one between conservatives and reformers. It was also one between two brands of progressivism that reflected two different views of America's future. And it was one that matched the two most important national leaders of the early twentieth century in unequal contest.

### Woodrow Wilson

Reform sentiment had been gaining strength within the Democratic as well as the Republican Party in the first years of the century. At the 1912 Democratic convention in Baltimore in June, Champ Clark, the conservative Speaker of the House, was unable to assemble the necessary two-thirds majority because of progressive opposition. Finally, on the forty-sixth ballot, Woodrow Wilson, the governor of New Jersey and the only genuinely progressive candidate in the race, emerged as the party's nominee.

Wilson had risen to political prominence by an unusual path. He had been a professor of political science at Princeton until 1902, when he was named president of the university. Elected governor of New Jersey in 1910, he demonstrated a commitment to reform that he had already displayed as a university president, and during his two years in the statehouse, he earned a national reputation for winning passage of progressive legislation. As a presidential candidate in 1912, Wilson presented a progressive program that came to be called the "New Freedom." Wilson's New Freedom differed from Roosevelt's New Nationalism most clearly in its approach to economic policy and the trusts. Roosevelt believed in accepting economic concentration and using government to regulate and control it. Wilson seemed to side with those who (like Brandeis) believed that bigness was both unjust and inefficient, that the proper response to monopoly was not to regulate it but to destroy it.

The 1912 presidential campaign was something of an anticlimax. William Howard Taft, resigned to defeat, delivered a few desultory, conservative speeches and then lapsed into silence. Roosevelt campaigned energetically (until a gunshot wound from a would-be assassin forced him to the sidelines during the last weeks before the election), but he failed to draw any significant numbers of Democratic progressives away from Wilson. In November, Roosevelt and Taft split the Republicans; Wilson held onto most Democrats and won. He polled only a plurality of the popular vote: 42 percent, compared with 27 percent for Roosevelt, 23 percent for Taft, and 6 percent for the socialist Eugene Debs. But in the electoral college, Wilson won 435 of the 531 votes. Roosevelt had carried only six states, Taft two, Debs none.

### The Scholar as President

Wilson was a bold and forceful president. More than William Howard Taft, more even than Theodore Roosevelt, he concentrated the powers of the executive branch in his own hands. He exerted firm control over his cabinet, and he delegated real authority only to those whose loyalty to him was beyond question. Perhaps the clearest indication of his style of leadership was the identity of his most powerful adviser: Colonel Edward M. House, an intelligent and ambitious Texan who held no office and whose only claim to authority was his personal intimacy with the president.

In legislative matters, Wilson skillfully used his position as party leader to weld together a coalition that would support his program. Democratic majorities in both houses of Congress made his task easier. Wilson's first triumph as president was the fulfillment of an old Democratic (and progressive) goal: a substantial lowering of the protective tariff. The Underwood-Simmons Tariff, passed in a special session of Congress that Wilson summoned shortly after his inauguration, provided cuts substantial enough, progressives believed, to introduce real competition into American markets and thus to help break the power of trusts. It passed easily in the House, and despite Senate efforts to weaken its provisions, the bill survived more or less intact. To make up for the loss of revenue under the new tariff, Congress approved a graduated income tax, which the recently adopted Sixteenth Amendment to the Constitution now permitted. This first modern income tax imposed a 1 percent tax on individuals and corporations earning over $4,000, with rates ranging up to 6 percent on incomes over $500,000.

Wilson held Congress in session through the summer to work on a major reform of the American banking system: the Federal Reserve Act,

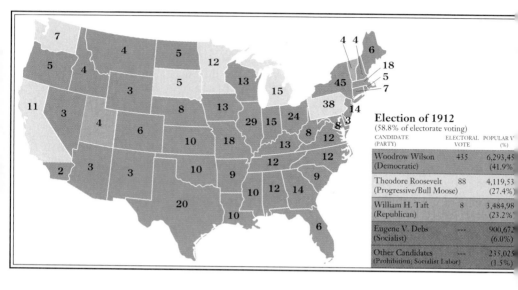

**Election of 1912**
(58.8% of electorate voting)

| CANDIDATE (PARTY) | ELECTORAL VOTE | POPULAR V (%) |
|---|---|---|
| Woodrow Wilson (Democratic) | 435 | 6,293,45 (41.9%) |
| Theodore Roosevelt (Progressive/Bull Moose) | 88 | 4,119,53 (27.4%) |
| William H. Taft (Republican) | 8 | 3,484,98 (23.2% |
| Eugene V. Debs (Socialist) | --- | 900,67. (6.0%) |
| Other Candidates (Prohibition; Socialist Labor) | --- | 235,025 (1.5%) |

which Congress passed and which the president signed on December 23, 1913. It was the most important piece of domestic legislation of Wilson's administration. The Federal Reserve Act created twelve regional banks, each to be owned and controlled by the individual banks of its district. The regional Federal Reserve banks would hold a certain percentage of the assets of their member banks in reserve; they would use those reserves to support loans to private banks at an interest (or "discount") rate that the Federal Reserve system would set; they would issue a new type of paper currency—Federal Reserve notes—which would become the nation's basic medium of trade and would be backed by the government. Most important, perhaps, they would serve as central institutions able to shift funds quickly to troubled areas—to meet increased demands for credit or to protect imperiled banks. Supervising and regulating the entire system was a national Federal Reserve Board, whose members were appointed by the president. All "national" banks were required to join the system; smaller banks were encouraged to do the same. Nearly half the nation's banking resources were represented in the system within a year, and 80 percent by the late 1920s.

In 1914, turning to the central issue of his 1912 campaign, Wilson proposed two measures to deal with the problem of monopoly. In the process, he revealed how his own approach to the issue was beginning to change. There was a proposal to create a federal agency through which the government would help business police itself—in other words, a regulatory commission of the type Roosevelt had advocated in 1912. There were, in addition, proposals to strengthen the government's power to prosecute and dismantle the trusts—a decentralizing approach more characteristic of Wilson's campaign. The two measures took shape, ultimately, as the Federal Trade Commission Act and the Clayton Antitrust Act.

The Federal Trade Commission Act created a regulatory agency that would help businesses determine in advance whether their actions would be acceptable to the government. The agency would also have authority to launch prosecutions against "unfair trade practices," which the law did not define, and it would have wide power to investigate corporate behavior. The act, in short, increased the government's regulatory authority significantly. Wilson signed it happily. But he seemed to lose interest in the Clayton Antitrust Bill and did little to protect it from conservative assaults, which greatly weakened it. The vigorous legal pursuit of monopoly that Wilson had promised in 1912 never materialized. The future, he had apparently decided, lay with government supervision.

### Retreat and Advance

By the fall of 1914, Wilson believed that the program of the New Freedom was essentially complete and that agitation for reform would now subside. He refused to support the movement for national woman suffrage. Deferring to southern Democrats, and reflecting his own southern background, he condoned the reimposition of segregation in the agencies of the federal government (in contrast to Theodore Roosevelt, who had ordered the elimination of many such barriers). When congressional progressives attempted to enlist his support for new reform legislation, he dismissed their proposals as unconstitutional or unnecessary.

The congressional elections of 1914, however, shattered the president's complacency. Democrats suffered major losses in the House of Representatives, and voters who in 1912 had supported the Progressive Party began returning to the Republicans. Wilson would not be able to rely on a divided opposition when he ran for reelection in 1916. By the end of 1915, therefore, Wilson had begun to support a second flurry of reforms. In January 1916, he appointed Louis Brandeis to the Supreme Court, making him not only the first Jew but the most advanced progressive to serve there. Later, he supported a measure to make it easier for farmers to receive credit and one creating a system of workers' compensation for federal employees.

Much of this renewed effort at reform suggested that Wilson had moved even closer to the New Nationalism. He was sponsoring measures that expanded the role of the national government in important ways, giving it new instruments by which it could regulate the economy and help shape the nation's economic and social structure. In 1916, for example, Wilson supported the Keating-Owen Act, the first federal law regulating child labor. The measure prohibited the shipment of goods produced by underage children across state lines, thus giving an expanded importance to the constitutional clause assigning Congress the task of regulating interstate commerce. (It would be some years before the Supreme Court would uphold this interpretation of the clause; the Court invalidated the Keating-Owen Act in 1918.) The president similarly supported measures that used federal taxing authority as a vehicle for legislating social change. After the Court struck down Keating-Owen, a new law attempted to achieve the same goal by imposing a heavy tax on the products of child labor. (The Court later struck it down too.) And the Smith-Lever Act of 1914 demonstrated another way in which the federal government could influence local behavior; it offered matching federal grants to states that agreed to support agricultural extension education.

## THE "BIG STICK": AMERICA AND THE WORLD, 1901–1917

American foreign policy during the progressive years reflected many of the same impulses that were motivating domestic reform. But more than that, it reflected the nation's new sense of itself as a world power with far-flung economic and political interests.

### Roosevelt and "Civilization"

Theodore Roosevelt was well suited, both by temperament and by ideology, for an activist foreign policy. He believed in the value and importance of using American power in the world (a conviction he once described by citing the proverb, "Speak softly, but carry a big stick"). But he had two different standards for using that power.

Roosevelt believed that an important distinction existed between the "civilized" and "uncivilized" nations of the world. "Civilized" nations, as he defined them, were predominantly white and Anglo-Saxon or Teutonic; "uncivilized" nations were generally nonwhite, Latin, or Slavic. But racism was only partly the basis of the distinction. At least as important was economic development. He believed, therefore, that Japan, a rapidly industrializing society, had earned admission to the ranks of the civilized.

Civilized nations were, by Roosevelt's definition, producers of industrial goods; uncivilized nations were suppliers of raw materials and markets. There was, he believed, an economic relationship between the two parts that was vital to both of them. A civilized society, therefore, had the right and duty to intervene in the affairs of a "backward" nation to preserve order and stability—for the sake of both nations. That belief was one important reason for Roosevelt's early support of the development of American sea power. By 1906, the American navy had attained a size and strength surpassed only by that of Great Britain (although Germany was fast gaining ground).

### Protecting the "Open Door" in Asia

Roosevelt considered the "Open Door" vital for maintaining American trade in the Pacific and for preventing any single nation from establishing dominance there. He looked with alarm, therefore, at the military rivalries involving Japan, Russia, Germany, and France in Asia.

In 1904 the Japanese staged a surprise attack on the Russian fleet at Port Arthur in southern Manchuria, a province of China that both Russia and Japan hoped to control. Roosevelt, hoping to prevent either nation from becoming dominant there, agreed to a Japanese request to mediate an end to the conflict. Russia, faring badly in the war, had no choice but to agree. At a peace conference in Portsmouth, New Hampshire, in 1905, Roosevelt extracted from the embattled Russians a recognition of Japan's territorial gains and from the Japanese an agreement to cease the fighting and expand no further. At the same time, he negotiated a secret agreement with the Japanese to ensure that the United States could continue to trade freely in the region. Roosevelt won the Nobel Peace Prize in 1906 for his work in ending the Russo-Japanese War. But in the years that followed, relations between the United States and Japan steadily deteriorated. Having destroyed the Russian fleet at Port Arthur, Japan now emerged as the preeminent naval power in the Pacific and soon began to exclude American trade from many of the territories it controlled.

It did not help matters that in 1906 the school board of San Francisco voted to segregate the city's Asian schoolchildren in separate schools or that, a year later, the California legislature attempted to pass a law limiting the immigration of Japanese laborers into the state. Anti-Asian riots in California and inflammatory stories in the Hearst papers about the "Yellow Peril" further fanned resentment in Japan. The president persuaded the San Francisco school board to rescind its edict in return for a Japanese agreement to stop the flow of agricultural immigrants into California. Then, lest the Japanese government construe his actions as a sign of weakness, Roosevelt sent sixteen battleships of the new American navy (known as the "Great White Fleet") on an unprecedented voyage around the world that included a call on Japan—to remind the Japanese of the potential might of the United States.

### The Iron-Fisted Neighbor

Roosevelt took a particular interest in events in what he (and most other Americans) considered the nation's special sphere of interest: Latin America. Unwilling to share trading rights, let alone military control, with any other nation, Roosevelt embarked on a series of ventures in the Caribbean and South America. He established a pattern of American intervention in the region that would long survive his presidency.

Crucial to Roosevelt's thinking was an incident early in his administration. In 1902, the financially troubled government of Venezuela began to renege on debts to European bankers. Naval forces of Britain, Italy, and Germany blockaded the Venezuelan coast in response. Then German ships began to bombard a Venezuelan port amid rumors that Germany planned to establish a permanent base in the region. Roosevelt used the threat of American naval power to pressure the German navy to withdraw.

The incident helped persuade Roosevelt that European intrusions into Latin America could result not only from aggression but from instability or irresponsibility (such as defaulting on debts) within the Latin American nations themselves. As a result, in 1904 he announced what came to be known as the "Roosevelt corollary" to the Monroe Doctrine. The United States, he claimed, had the right not only to oppose European intervention in the Western Hemisphere but to intervene itself in the domestic affairs of its neighbors if those neighbors proved unable to maintain order and national sovereignty on their own.

The immediate motivation for the Roosevelt corollary, and the first opportunity for using it, was a crisis in the Dominican Republic. A revolution had toppled its corrupt and bankrupt government in 1903, but the new regime proved no better able than the old to make good on the country's $22 million in debts to European nations. Using the rationale provided by the Roosevelt corollary, Roosevelt established, in effect, an American receivership, assuming control of Dominican customs and distributing 45 percent of the revenues to the Dominicans and the rest to foreign creditors. This arrangement lasted, in one form or another, for more than three decades.

In 1902, the United States granted political independence to Cuba, but

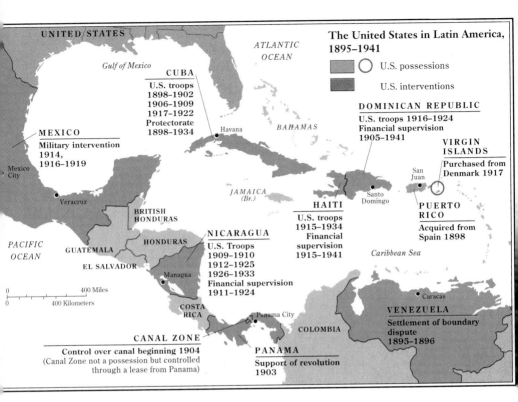

The United States in Latin America, 1895–1941

U.S. possessions

U.S. interventions

**UNITED STATES**

*Gulf of Mexico*

**CUBA**
U.S. troops
1898–1902
1906–1909
1917–1922
Protectorate
1898–1934

*ATLANTIC OCEAN*

*BAHAMAS*

*Havana*

**MEXICO**
Military intervention
1914,
1916–1919

*Mexico City*

*Veracruz*

*JAMAICA (Br.)*

**BRITISH HONDURAS**

**DOMINICAN REPUBLIC**
U.S. troops 1916–1924
Financial supervision
1905–1941

**HAITI**
U.S. troops
1915–1934
Financial
supervision
1915–1941

*Santo Domingo*

**VIRGIN ISLANDS**
Purchased from
Denmark 1917

*San Juan*

**PUERTO RICO**
Acquired from
Spain 1898

*Caribbean Sea*

**PACIFIC OCEAN**

**GUATEMALA**

**HONDURAS**

**EL SALVADOR**

*Managua*

**NICARAGUA**
U.S. Troops
1909–1910
1912–1925
1926–1933
Financial supervision
1911–1924

0    400 Miles

0    400 Kilometers

**COSTA RICA**

**CANAL ZONE**
Control over canal beginning 1904
(Canal Zone not a possession but controlled
through a lease from Panama)

*Panama City*

**COLOMBIA**

**PANAMA**
Support of revolution
1903

*Caracas*

**VENEZUELA**
Settlement of boundary
dispute
1895–1896

only after the new government had agreed to the so-called Platt Amendment (named after Senator Thomas Platt of Pennsylvania) to its constitution. The amendment gave the United States the right to prevent any foreign power from intruding into the new nation. In 1906, when domestic uprisings seemed to threaten the internal stability of the island, Roosevelt reasoned that America must intervene to "protect" Cuba from possible intervention by others. American troops landed in Cuba, quelled the fighting, and remained there for three years.

## The Panama Canal

The most celebrated accomplishment of Roosevelt's presidency was the construction of the Panama Canal. Linking the Atlantic and the Pacific by creating a channel through Central America had been an unfulfilled dream of many nations since the mid-nineteenth century. Roosevelt was determined to achieve it.

The first step was the 1901 Hay-Pauncefote Treaty between America and Britain, canceling an 1850 pact in which the two nations had agreed to construct any such canal together. The United States was now free to act alone. The next step was to choose a site for the canal. At first, Roosevelt and many others favored a route across Nicaragua, which would permit a sea-level canal requiring no locks. But they soon turned instead to the narrow Isthmus of Panama in Colombia, the site of an earlier, failed effort by a French company to construct a channel. Although the Panama route was not at sea level (and would thus require locks), it was shorter than the one in Nicaragua. And construction was already about 40 percent complete. When the French company lowered the price for its holdings from $109 million to $40 million, the United States chose Panama.

Roosevelt dispatched John Hay, his secretary of state, to negotiate an agreement with Colombian diplomats in Washington that would allow construction to begin without delay. Under heavy American pressure, the Colombian chargé d'affaires, Tomas Herrán, unwisely signed an agreement giving the United States perpetual rights to a six-mile-wide "canal zone" across Colombia; in return, the United States would pay Colombia $10 million and an annual rental of $250,000. The treaty produced outrage in the Colombian senate, which refused to ratify it. Colombia then sent a new representative to Washington with instructions to demand at least $20 million from the Americans plus a share of the payment to the French.

Roosevelt was furious and began to look for ways to circumvent the Colombian government. Philippe Bunau-Varilla, chief engineer of the French canal project, was a ready ally. In November 1903, he helped organize and finance a revolution in Panama. There had been many previous revolts, all of them failures. But this one had the support of the United States. Roosevelt landed troops from the U.S.S. *Nashville* in Panama to "maintain order." Their presence prevented Colombian forces from suppressing the rebellion, and three days later Roosevelt recognized Panama as an independent nation. The new Panamanian government quickly agreed to the terms the Colombian senate had rejected. Work on the canal proceeded rapidly, and it opened in 1914.

### Taft and "Dollar Diplomacy"

Like his predecessor, William Howard Taft worked to advance the nation's economic interests overseas. But he showed little interest in Roosevelt's larger vision of world stability. Taft's secretary of state, the corporate attorney Philander C. Knox, worked aggressively to extend American investments into less developed regions. Critics called his policies "Dollar Diplomacy."

The Taft-Knox foreign policy faced its severest test, and encountered its greatest failure, in the Far East. Ignoring Roosevelt's tacit 1905 agreement with Japan to limit American involvement in Manchuria, the new administration responded to pressure from American bankers and moved aggressively to increase America's economic influence in the region. In particular, Knox worked to include the United States in a consortium of Western powers formed to build railroads in China; and when the Europeans agreed, he went further and tried to exclude the Japanese from any role in Manchuria's railroads. When Japan responded by forming a loose alliance with Russia, the entire railroad project quickly collapsed.

In the Caribbean, the new administration continued and even expanded upon Roosevelt's policies of limiting European and expanding American influence in the region. That meant, Taft and Knox believed, not only preventing disorder but establishing a significant American economic presence there—replacing the investments of European nations with investments from the United States. But Dollar Diplomacy also had a more violent side. When a revolution broke out in Nicaragua in 1909, the administration quickly sided with the insurgents (who had been inspired to revolt by an

OPENING THE PANAMA CANAL The Panama Canal, the greatest engineering feat of the early twentieth century and one of the most notable achievements of Theodore Roosevelt's presidency, opened to shipping in 1913. This photograph shows the Tugboat *Gatun*, the first ship to travel through the canal to the Atlantic, in one of the canal's great locks.

American mining company) and sent American troops into the country to seize the customs houses. As soon as peace was restored, Knox encouraged American bankers to offer substantial loans to the new government, thus increasing Washington's financial leverage over the country. When the new pro-American government faced an insurrection less than two years later, Taft again landed American troops in Nicaragua, this time to protect the existing regime. The troops remained there for more than a decade.

### Diplomacy and Morality

Woodrow Wilson entered the presidency with relatively little interest or experience in international affairs. Yet he faced international challenges of a scope and gravity unmatched by those of any president before him. Although the greatest test of Wilsonian diplomacy did not occur until World War I, many of the qualities that he would bring to that ordeal were evident in his foreign policy from his first moments in office, and particularly in his dealings with Latin America.

Having already seized control of the finances of the Dominican Republic in 1905, the United States established a military government there in 1916 when the Dominicans refused to accept a treaty that would have made the country a virtual American protectorate. The military occupation lasted eight years. In Haiti, which shares the island of Hispaniola with the Dominican Republic, Wilson landed the marines in 1915 to quell a revolution in the course of which a mob had murdered an unpopular president. American military forces remained in the country until 1934, and American officers drafted the new Haitian constitution adopted in 1918. When Wilson began to fear that the Danish West Indies might be about to fall into the hands of Germany, he bought the colony from Denmark and renamed it the Virgin Islands. Concerned about the possibility of European influence in Nicaragua, he signed a treaty with that country's government ensuring that no other nation would build a canal there and winning for the United States the right to intervene in Nicaragua's internal affairs to protect American interests. In all of these actions, Wilson was displaying an approach to Latin America very similar to the approaches of Roosevelt and Taft.

But Wilson's view of America's role in the Western Hemisphere (and the world) was not entirely similar to the views of his predecessors. That became clear in his dealings with Mexico. For many years, under the friendly auspices of the corrupt dictator Porfirio Díaz, American businessmen had been establishing an enormous economic presence in Mexico. In 1910, however, Díaz had been overthrown by the popular leader Francisco Madero, who promised democratic reform but who also seemed hostile to American businesses in Mexico. The United States quietly encouraged a reactionary general, Victoriano Huerta, to depose Madero early in 1913, and the Taft administration, in its last weeks in office, prepared to recognize the new Huerta regime and welcome back a receptive environment for American investments in Mexico. Before it could do so, however, the new government murdered Madero, and Woodrow Wilson took office in Washington. The new president instantly announced that he would never recognize Huerta's "government of butchers."

The conflict dragged on for years. At first, Wilson hoped that simply by refusing to recognize Huerta he could help topple the regime and bring to power the opposing Constitutionalists, led by Venustiano Carranza. But when Huerta, with the support of American business interests, established a full military dictatorship in October 1913, the president became more assertive. He pressured the British to stop supporting Huerta. Then he offered to send American troops to assist Carranza. Carranza, aware that such an open alliance with the United States would undermine his popular support in Mexico, declined the offer, but he did secure the right to buy arms in the United States.

In April 1914, a minor naval incident provided the president with an excuse for more open intervention. An officer in Huerta's army briefly arrested several American sailors from the U.S.S. *Dolphin* who had gone ashore in Tampico. The men were immediately released, but the American admiral—unsatisfied with the apology he received—demanded that the Huerta forces fire a twenty-one-gun salute to the American flag as a public display of penance. The Mexicans refused. Wilson used the trivial incident as a pretext for seizing the Mexican port of Veracruz.

Wilson had envisioned a bloodless action, but in a clash with Mexican troops in Veracruz, the Americans killed 126 of the defenders and suffered 19 casualties of their own. Now at the brink of war, Wilson began to look for a way out. His show of force, however, had helped strengthen the position of the Carranza faction, which captured Mexico City in August and forced Huerta to flee the country. At last, it seemed, the crisis might be over.

But Wilson was not yet satisfied. He reacted angrily when Carranza refused to accept American guidelines for the creation of a new government, and he briefly considered throwing his support to still another aspirant to leadership: Carranza's erstwhile lieutenant Pancho Villa, who was now leading a rebel army of his own. When Villa's military position deteriorated, however, Wilson abandoned him and finally, in October 1915, granted preliminary recognition to the Carranza government. By now, however, he had

PANCHO VILLA AND HIS SOLDIERS In 1913, when this photograph was taken, Pancho Villa (second from right) was still on good terms with the government of Woodrow Wilson, which viewed him as a fighter for democracy in Mexico. Three years later, Wilson declared Villa a "bandit" and sent American troops into Mexico in a futile effort to capture him.

created yet another crisis. Villa, angry at what he considered an American betrayal, retaliated in January 1916 by taking sixteen American mining engineers from a train in northern Mexico and shooting them. Two months later, he led his soldiers (or "bandits," as the United States preferred to call them) across the border into Columbus, New Mexico, where they killed seventeen more Americans. His goal, apparently, was to destabilize relations between Wilson and Carranza and provoke a war between them, which might provide him with an opportunity to improve his own declining fortunes.

With the permission of the Carranza government, Wilson ordered General John J. Pershing to lead an American expeditionary force across the Mexican border in pursuit of Villa. The American troops never found Villa, but they did engage in two ugly skirmishes with Carranza's army, in which forty Mexicans and twelve Americans died. Again, the United States and Mexico stood at the brink of war. But at the last minute, Wilson drew back. He quietly withdrew American troops from Mexico, and in March 1917, he at last granted formal recognition to the Carranza regime. By now, however, Wilson's attention was turning elsewhere—to the far greater international crisis engulfing the European continent and ultimately much of the world.

# CHAPTER TWENTY-THREE

# America and the Great War

*The Road to War* ∼ *"War Without Stint"*
*The Search for a New World Order* ∼ *A Society in Turmoil*

T HE GREAT WAR, as it was known to a generation unaware that another, greater war would soon follow, began quietly in August 1914 when Austria-Hungary invaded the tiny Balkan nation of Serbia. Within weeks, however, it had grown into a conflagration engaging the armies of most of the major nations of Europe and shattering forever the delicate balance of power that had maintained a general peace on the Continent since the early nineteenth century. Americans looked on with horror as the war became the most savage in history and as it dragged on, murderously and inconclusively, for two and a half years. But Americans also believed at first that the conflict had little to do with them. They were wrong. After nearly three years of attempting to affect the outcome of the conflict without becoming embroiled in it, the United States formally entered the war in April 1917.

## THE ROAD TO WAR

The causes of the war in Europe have been the subject of continued debate for nearly eighty years. But it is clear that the European nations had by 1914 created an unusually precarious international system that careened into war very quickly on the basis of what most historians agree was a minor series of provocations.

### The Collapse of the European Peace

The major powers of Europe were organized by 1914 in two great, competing alliances. The "Triple Entente" linked Britain, France, and Russia. The "Triple Alliance" united Germany, the Austro-Hungarian Empire, and

## TIME LINE

| 1914 | 1915 | 1916 | 1917 |
|---|---|---|---|
| World War I begins | *Lusitania* torpedoed | Wilson reelected | German unrestricted submarine warfare |
| | Wilson supports preparedness | | U.S. enters World War I |
| | | | Selective Service Act |
| | | | War Industries Board created |

| 1918 | 1919 | 1920 | 1927 |
|---|---|---|---|
| Sedition Act | Senate rejects Treaty of Versailles | 19th Amendment ratified | Sacco and Vanzetti executed |
| Wilson's Fourteen Points | | Palmer Raids and Red Scare | |
| Armistice ends war | Race riots (in Chicago and other cities) | | |
| Paris Peace Conference | | Harding elected president | |
| | Steel strike and other labor actions | | |

Italy. The chief rivalry, however, was not between the two alliances but between the great powers that dominated them: Great Britain and Germany—the former long established as the world's most powerful colonial and commercial nation, the latter ambitious to expand its own empire and become at least Britain's equal.

The Anglo-German rivalry may have been the most important underlying source of the tensions that led to World War I, but it was not the immediate cause of its outbreak. The conflict emerged most directly out of a controversy involving nationalist movements within the Austro-Hungarian Empire. On June 28, 1914, the Archduke Franz Ferdinand, heir to the throne of the tottering empire, was assassinated while paying a state visit to Sarajevo. Sarajevo is the capital of Bosnia, then a province of Austria-Hungary, which Slavic nationalists wished to annex to neighboring Serbia; the archduke's assassin was a Serbian nationalist.

This local controversy quickly escalated through the workings of the system of alliances that the great powers had constructed. Germany supported Austria-Hungary's decision to launch a punitive assault on Serbia. The Serbians called on Russia to help with their defense. The Russians began mobilizing their army on July 30. Things quickly careened out of control. By August 3, Germany had declared war on both Russia and France and had invaded Belgium in preparation for a thrust across the French border. On

August 4, Great Britain—ostensibly to honor its alliance with France, but more importantly to blunt the advance of its principal rival—declared war on Germany. Russia and the Austro-Hungarian Empire formally began hostilities on August 6. Within months, Italy, the Ottoman Empire (Turkey), and other, smaller nations all joined the fighting. By early 1915, virtually the entire European continent (and part of Asia) was embroiled in a major war.

### Wilson's Neutrality

Wilson called on his fellow citizens in 1914 to remain "impartial in thought as well as deed." But that was impossible, for several reasons. For one thing, many Americans were not, in fact, genuinely impartial. Some sympathized with the German cause (German Americans, because of affection for Germany; Irish Americans, because of hatred of Britain). Many more (including Wilson himself) sympathized with Britain. Lurid reports of German atrocities in Belgium and France, skillfully exaggerated by British propagandists, strengthened the hostility of many Americans toward Germany.

Economic realities also made it impossible for the United States to deal with the belligerents on equal terms. The British had imposed a naval blockade on Germany to prevent munitions and supplies from reaching the enemy. As a neutral, the United States had the right, in theory, to trade with Germany. A truly neutral response to the blockade would be either to defy it or to stop trading with Britain as well. But while the United States could survive an interruption of its relatively modest trade with the Central Powers (Germany, the Austro-Hungarian Empire, and the Ottoman Empire), it could not easily weather an embargo on its much more extensive trade with the Allies (Britain, France, Italy, and Russia), particularly when war orders from Britain and France soared after 1914, helping produce one of the greatest economic booms in the nation's history. So America tacitly accepted the blockade of Germany and continued trading with Britain. By 1915, the United States had gradually transformed itself from a neutral power into the arsenal of the Allies.

The Germans, in the meantime, were resorting to a new and, in American eyes, barbaric tactic: submarine warfare. Unable to challenge British domination on the ocean's surface, Germany began early in 1915 to use the newly improved submarine to try to stem the flow of supplies to England. Enemy vessels, the Germans announced, would be sunk on sight. Months later, on May 7, 1915, a German submarine sank the British passenger liner *Lusitania* without warning, causing the deaths of 1198 people, 128 of them

Americans. The ship was, it later became clear, carrying not only passengers but munitions; but most Americans considered the attack an unprovoked act.

Wilson angrily demanded that Germany promise not to repeat such outrages and that the Central Powers affirm their commitment to neutral rights (among which, he implausibly insisted, was the right of American citizens to travel on the nonmilitary vessels of belligerents). The Germans finally agreed to Wilson's demands, but tensions between the nations continued to grow. Early in 1916, in response to an announcement that the Allies were now arming merchant ships to sink submarines, Germany proclaimed that it would fire on such vessels without warning. A few weeks later, it attacked the unarmed French steamer *Sussex*, injuring several American passengers. Again, Wilson demanded that Germany abandon its "unlawful" tactics; again, the German government relented.

### *Preparedness Versus Pacifism*

Despite the president's increasing bellicosity in 1916, he was still far from ready to commit the United States to war. One obstacle was American domestic politics. Facing a difficult battle for reelection, Wilson could not ignore the powerful factions that continued to oppose intervention.

The question of whether America should make military and economic preparations for war provided a preliminary issue over which pacifists and interventionists could debate. Wilson at first sided with the antipreparedness forces, denouncing the idea of an American military buildup as needless and provocative. As tensions between the United States and Germany grew, however, he changed his mind. In the fall of 1915, he endorsed an ambitious proposal by American military leaders for a large and rapid increase in the nation's armed forces. By midsummer 1916, armament for a possible conflict was well under way.

Still, the peace faction wielded considerable political strength, as became clear at the Democratic convention in the summer of 1916. The convention became almost hysterically enthusiastic when the keynote speaker, enumerating Wilson's accomplishments, punctuated his list of the president's diplomatic achievements with the chant, "What did we do? What did we do? . . . We didn't go to war! We didn't go to war!" That speech helped produce one of the most prominent slogans of Wilson's reelection campaign: "He kept us out of war." During the campaign, Wilson did nothing to discourage those who argued that the Republican candidate, the progressive New York governor Charles Evans Hughes, was more likely than he to lead the nation into war. Wilson ultimately won reelection by one of the smallest margins for an incumbent in American history: fewer than 600,000 popular votes and only 23 electoral votes. The Democrats retained a precarious control over Congress.

## A War for Democracy

The election was behind him. Tensions between the United States and Germany remained high. But Wilson still required a justification for American intervention that would unite public opinion and satisfy his own sense of morality. In the end, he created that rationale himself. The United States, Wilson insisted, had no material aims in the conflict. The nation was, rather, committed to using the war as a vehicle for constructing a new world order, one based on the same progressive ideals that had motivated a generation of reform efforts in America. In a speech before a joint session of Congress in January 1917, he presented a plan for a postwar order in which the United

WOODROW WILSON ASKING FOR WAR  Wilson appears before a joint session of Congress on April 2, 1917, and asks for a declaration of war against Germany and its allies in Europe. His impassioned speech did not persuade everyone. Debate over the resolution consumed nearly four days, and when it was over 56 members of Congress continued to oppose it.

States would help maintain peace through a permanent league of nations—a "peace without victory." These were, Wilson believed, goals worth fighting for if there was sufficient provocation. That provocation came quickly.

In January, after months of bloody but inconclusive warfare in the trenches of France, the military leaders of Germany decided on one last dramatic gamble to achieve victory. They would launch a series of major assaults on the enemy's lines in France. At the same time, they would begin unrestricted submarine warfare (against American as well as Allied ships) to cut Britain off from vital supplies. Then, on February 25, the British gave Wilson an intercepted telegram from the German foreign minister, Arthur Zimmermann, to the government of Mexico. It proposed that in the event of war between Germany and the United States, the Mexicans should join with Germany against the Americans. In return, they would regain their "lost provinces" in the north (Texas and much of the rest of the American Southwest) when the war was over. Widely publicized by British propagandists and in the American press, the Zimmermann telegram inflamed public opinion and helped build up popular sentiment for war.

Wilson drew additional comfort from another event, in March 1917. A revolution in Russia toppled the reactionary czarist regime and replaced it with a new, republican government. The United States would now be spared the embarrassment of allying itself with a despotic monarchy. The war for a progressive world order could proceed untainted.

On the rainy evening of April 2, two weeks after German submarines had torpedoed three American ships, Wilson appeared before a joint session of Congress and asked for a declaration of war. Even then, opposition remained. For four days, pacifists in Congress carried on their futile struggle. When the declaration of war finally passed on April 6, fifty representatives and six senators had voted against it.

## "WAR WITHOUT STINT"

Armies on both sides in Europe were decimated and exhausted by the time of Woodrow Wilson's declaration of war. The German offensives of early 1917 had failed to produce an end to the struggle, and French and British counteroffensives had accomplished little beyond adding to the appalling casualties. The Allies looked desperately to the United States for help. Wilson, who had called on the nation to wage war "without stint or limit," was eager to oblige.

## The Military Struggle

American intervention had its most immediate effect on the conflict at sea. By the spring of 1917, Great Britain was suffering such vast losses from attacks by German submarines—one of every four ships setting sail from British ports never returned—that its ability to continue receiving vital supplies from across the Atlantic was in question. Within weeks of joining the war the United States had begun to alter the balance. A fleet of American destroyers aided the British navy in its assault on the U-boats. Other American warships escorted merchant vessels across the Atlantic. Americans also helped plant antisubmarine mines in the North Sea. The results were dramatic. Sinkings of Allied ships had totaled nearly 900,000 tons in the month of April 1917; by December, the figure had dropped to 350,000; by October 1918, it had declined to 112,000.

Many Americans had hoped that providing naval assistance alone would be enough to turn the tide in the war, but it quickly became clear that a major commitment of American ground forces would be necessary as well to shore up the tottering Allies. Britain and France had few remaining reserves. By early 1918, Russia had withdrawn from the war altogether. After the Bol-

LONGPONT, FRANCE, 1918 American soldiers lead German prisoners-of-war through the streets of a French town shortly before the end of World War I. The devastation was typical of many areas of France where heavy fighting occurred.

shevik Revolution in November 1917 toppled the republican regime created the previous March, the new communist government, led by V. I. Lenin, negotiated a hasty and costly peace with the Central Powers, thus freeing German troops to fight on the western front.

But the United States did not have a large enough standing army to provide the necessary ground forces in 1917. Some (including Theodore Roosevelt, who hoped to raise and lead a regiment himself, much as he had done in the Spanish-American War) urged a voluntary recruitment process. The president, however, decided that only a national draft could provide the needed men. Despite protests, he won passage of the Selective Service Act in mid-May. The draft brought nearly 3 million men into the army; another 2 million joined various branches of the armed services voluntarily.

The engagement of these forces in combat was brief but intense. Not until the spring of 1918 were significant numbers of American troops available for battle. Eight months later, the war was over. Under the command of General John J. Pershing, the American troops joined the existing Allied forces in turning back a series of new German assaults. In early June, they assisted the French in repelling a bitter German offensive at Château-Thierry, near Paris. Six weeks later, the American Expeditionary Force (AEF) helped turn away another assault, at Rheims, farther south. By July 18, the German advance had been halted, and the Allies were beginning a successful offensive of their own. On September 26, an American fighting force of over 1 million soldiers advanced against the Germans in the Argonne Forest as part of a 200-mile attack that lasted nearly seven weeks. By the end of October, the force had helped push the Germans back toward their own border and had cut the enemy's major supply lines to the front.

Faced with an invasion of their own country, German military leaders now began to seek an armistice—an immediate cease-fire that would, they hoped, serve as a prelude to negotiations among the belligerents. Pershing wanted to drive on into Germany itself; but other Allied leaders, after first insisting on terms that made the agreement (in their eyes at least) little different from a surrender, accepted the German proposal. On November 11, 1918, more than four years after it began, the Great War shuddered to a close.

*Organizing the Economy for War*

By the time the war ended, the federal government had appropriated $32 billion for expenses directly related to the conflict. This was a staggering sum at the time. The entire federal budget had seldom exceeded $1 billion be-

America in World War I:
The Western Front, 1918

fore 1915, and the nation's entire gross national product had been only $35 billion as recently as 1910. To raise the money, the government relied on two devices. First, it launched a major drive to solicit loans from the American people by selling "Liberty Bonds" to the public. By 1920, the sale of bonds, accompanied by elaborate patriotic appeals, had produced $23 billion. At the same time, new taxes were bringing in an additional sum of nearly $10 billion—some from levies on the "excess profits" of corporations, much from new, steeply graduated income and inheritance taxes that ultimately rose as high as 70 percent in some brackets.

An even greater challenge was organizing the economy to meet war needs. The administration tried two very different approaches. In 1916, Wilson established the Council of National Defense, composed of members of his cabinet, and the Civilian Advisory Commission, which set up local defense councils in every state and locality. Economic mobilization, according to this first plan, was to rest on a large-scale dispersal of power to local communities.

But this early administrative structure soon proved completely unworkable, and members of the Council of National Defense urged a more centralized approach. Instead of dividing the economy geographically, they proposed dividing it functionally by organizing a series of planning bodies, each to supervise a specific sector of the economy. Thus one agency would control transportation, another agriculture, another manufacturing. The administrative structure that slowly emerged from such proposals was dominated by a series of "war boards," one to oversee the railroads (led by Secretary of the Treasury William McAdoo), one to supervise fuel supplies (largely coal), another to handle food (a board that helped elevate to prominence the brilliant young engineer and business executive Herbert Hoover). The boards were not without weaknesses, but they generally succeeded in meeting essential war needs without paralyzing the domestic economy.

At the center of the effort to rationalize the economy was the War Industries Board (WIB), an agency created in July 1917 to coordinate government purchases of military supplies. Casually organized at first, it stumbled badly until March 1918, when Wilson restructured it and placed it under the control of the Wall Street financier Bernard Baruch. From then on, the board wielded powers greater (in theory at least) than any government agency had ever possessed. Baruch decided which factories would convert to the production of which war materials, and he set prices for the goods they produced. When materials were scarce, Baruch decided to whom they should go. When corporations were competing for government contracts, he chose

WOMEN WORKERS DURING WORLD WAR I With much of the male work force fighting overseas, women moved into occupations that in other times would have been considered unsuitable for them. One such occupation, pictured here, was delivering huge blocks of ice daily to households to be used (in this age before electric refrigeration) in wooden iceboxes.

among them. He was, it seemed, providing the centralized regulation of the economy that some progressives had long urged.

In reality, the vaunted efficiency of the WIB was something of a myth. The agency was, in fact, plagued by mismanagement and inefficiency and was less responsible for the nation's ability to meet its war needs than the sheer extent of American resources and productive capacities. Nor was the WIB in any real sense an example of state control of the economy. Baruch viewed himself, openly and explicitly, as a partner of business; and within the WIB, businessmen themselves—the so-called dollar-a-year men, who took paid leave from their corporate jobs and worked for the government for a token salary—supervised the affairs of the private economy. Rather than working to restrict private power and limit corporate profits, as many progressives had urged, the government was working to enhance the private sector through a mutually beneficial alliance.

This link between the public and the private sectors extended, although in very different form, to labor. The National War Labor Board, established in April 1918, served as the final mediator of labor disputes. It pressured industry to grant important concessions to workers: an eight-hour day, the maintenance of minimal living standards, equal pay for women doing equal work, recognition of the right of unions to organize and bargain collectively. In return, it insisted that workers forgo strikes and that employers not engage in lockouts. Membership in labor unions increased by more than 1.5 million between 1917 and 1919.

The effort to organize the economy for war produced some spectacular accomplishments: Hoover's efficient organization of food supplies, McAdoo's success in establishing state control of the railroads, and others. In some areas, however, progress was so slow that the war was over before many of the supplies ordered for it were ready. Even so, many leaders of both government and industry emerged from the experience convinced of the advantages of a close, cooperative relationship between the public and the private sectors. Some hoped to continue and extend the wartime experiments in the peacetime world.

### The Search for Social Unity

The idea of unity—not only in the direction of the economy but in the nation's social purpose—had been the dream of many progressives for decades. To them, the war seemed to offer an unmatched opportunity for the United States to close ranks behind a great common cause. In the process, they hoped, society could achieve a lasting sense of collective purpose. In fact, however, the search for unity produced considerable repression.

Government leaders were painfully aware that public sentiment about American involvement in the war had been divided before April 1917 and remained so even after the declaration of war. Many believed that a crucial prerequisite for victory was uniting public opinion behind the war effort. The government approached that task in several ways.

The most conspicuous of its efforts was a vast propaganda campaign aimed at drumming up enthusiasm for the conflict. It was orchestrated by the Committee on Public Information (CPI), under the direction of the Denver journalist George Creel. The CPI supervised the distribution of over 75 million pieces of printed material and controlled much of the information available for newspapers and magazines. Creel encouraged journalists to exercise "self-censorship" when reporting war news, and most journalists—fearful of more coercive measures—complied by covering the war largely as the government wished. The CPI attempted at first to distribute only the "facts," believing that the truth would speak for itself. By 1918, however, government-distributed posters and films were offering lurid (and exaggerated) portrayals of the savagery of the Germans.

The government also soon began efforts to suppress dissent. CPI-financed advertisements in magazines appealed to citizens to report to the authorities any evidence among their neighbors of disloyalty, pessimism, or yearning for peace. The Espionage Act of 1917 gave the government new tools with which to combat spying, sabotage, or obstruction of the war effort (crimes that were often broadly defined). More repressive were two measures of 1918: the Sabotage Act of April 20 and the Sedition Act of May 16. These bills expanded the meaning of the Espionage Act to make illegal any public expression of opposition to the war; in practice, they allowed officials to prosecute anyone who criticized the president or the government.

The most frequent targets of the new legislation (and one of the reasons for its enactment in the first place) were such anticapitalist groups as the Socialist Party and the Industrial Workers of the World (IWW). Unlike their counterparts in Europe, American socialists had not dropped their opposition to the war after their country had decided to join it. Many Americans had favored the repression of socialists and radicals even before the war; the wartime policies now made it possible to move against them with full legal sanction. Eugene V. Debs, the humane leader of the Socialist Party and an opponent of the war, was sentenced to ten years in prison in 1918. (A pardon by President Warren G. Harding ultimately won his release in 1921.) Big Bill Haywood and members of the IWW were especially energetically prosecuted. Only by fleeing to the Soviet Union did Haywood avoid a long imprisonment. In all, more than 11,500 people were arrested in 1918 for the crime of criticizing the government.

State and local governments, corporations, universities, and private citizens contributed as well to the climate of repression. Vigilante mobs sprang up to "discipline" those who dared challenge the war. A cluster of citizens' groups emerged to mobilize "respectable" members of their communities to root out disloyalty. The most frequent victims of such activities were immigrants: Irish Americans, because of their historic animosity toward the British and because some had, before 1917, expressed hopes for a German victory; Jews, because many had expressed opposition to the anti-Semitic policies of the Russian government, until 1917 one of the Allies; and others.

The greatest target of abuse was the German-American community. Its members had unwittingly contributed to their plight. In the first years of the war in Europe, some had openly advocated American assistance to the Central Powers, and many had opposed United States intervention on behalf of the Allies. But while most German Americans supported the American war effort once it began, public opinion turned bitterly hostile. A campaign to purge society of all things German quickly gathered speed, at times assuming ludicrous forms. Performances of German music were frequently banned. German books were removed from the shelves of libraries. Courses in the German language were dropped from school curricula. Germans were routinely fired from jobs in war industries, lest they "sabotage" important tasks. Some were fired from positions entirely unrelated to the war, among them Karl Muck, the German-born conductor of the Boston Symphony Orchestra. Many Americans came to agree with the belief of the eminent psychologist G. Stanley Hall that "there is something fundamentally wrong with the Teutonic soul."

## THE SEARCH FOR A NEW WORLD ORDER

Woodrow Wilson had led the nation into war promising a just and stable peace at its conclusion. Even before the armistice, he was preparing to lead the fight for what he considered a democratic postwar settlement—for a set of war aims resting on a vision of a new world order that became known as Wilsonian internationalism.

### The Fourteen Points

On January 8, 1918, Wilson appeared before Congress to present the principles for which he claimed the nation was fighting. He grouped the war aims under fourteen headings, widely known as the Fourteen Points. They fell into three broad categories. First, Wilson's proposals contained a series of eight specific recommendations for adjusting postwar boundaries and for establishing new nations to replace the defunct Austro-Hungarian and Ottoman Empires. Those recommendations reflected his belief in the right of all peoples to self-determination. Second, there was a set of five general principles to govern international conduct in the future: freedom of the seas, open covenants instead of secret treaties, reductions in armaments, free trade, and impartial mediation of colonial claims. Finally, there was a proposal for a "League of Nations" that would help implement these new principles and territorial adjustments and resolve future controversies.

There were serious flaws in Wilson's proposals. For example, he provided no formula for deciding how to implement the "national self-determination" he promised for subjugated peoples. Nevertheless, Wilson's international vision quickly came to enchant not only much of his own generation (in both America and Europe) but members of generations to come. It reflected his belief, strongly rooted in the ideas of progressivism, that the world was as capable of just and efficient government as were individual nations—that once the international community accepted certain basic principles of conduct, and once it constructed modern institutions to implement them, the human race could live in peace.

Wilson was confident, as the war neared its end, that popular support would enable him to win Allied approval of his peace plan. There were, however, ominous signs both at home and abroad that his path might be more difficult than he expected. In Europe, leaders of the Allied powers were preparing to resist him even before the armistice was signed. Britain and France in particular, having suffered terrible losses and having developed great bitterness toward Germany as a result, were in no mood for a benign and generous peace. David Lloyd George, the British prime minister, had campaigned for reelection in 1918 by calling for the execution of Kaiser Wilhelm II.

At the same time, Wilson was encountering problems at home. In 1918, with the war almost over, Wilson unwisely appealed to the American voters to support his peace plans by electing Democrats to Congress in the November elections. Days later, the Republicans captured majorities in both houses. Domestic economic troubles, more than international issues, had been the most important factor in the voting; but because of the president's ill-timed appeal, the results damaged his ability to claim broad popular support for his peace plans.

The leaders of the Republican Party, in the meantime, were developing their own reasons for opposing Wilson. Many were angry that he had tried to make the 1918 balloting a referendum on his war aims, especially since many Republicans had been supporting the Fourteen Points. Wilson further antagonized them when he refused to appoint any important Republicans to the negotiating team that would represent the United States at the peace conference in Paris.

But the president considered such matters unimportant. There would be only one member of the American negotiating team with any real authority: Wilson himself. And once he had produced a just and moral treaty, he believed, the weight of world and American opinion would compel his enemies to support him.

### The Paris Peace Conference

Wilson arrived in Europe to a welcome such as few men in history have experienced. To the war-weary people of the Continent, he was nothing less than a savior, the man who would create a new and better world. When he entered Paris on December 13, 1918, he was greeted, some claimed, by the largest crowd in the history of France. The conference itself, however, proved less satisfying.

The principal figures in the negotiations were the leaders of the victorious Allied nations: David Lloyd George, the prime minister of Great Britain; Georges Clemenceau, the president of France; Vittorio Orlando, the prime minister of Italy; and Wilson, who hoped to dominate them all.

From the beginning, the atmosphere of idealism Wilson had sought to create competed with a spirit of national self-interest. There was also a pervasive sense of unease about the unstable situation in eastern Europe and the threat of communism. Russia, whose new Bolshevik government was still fighting "White" counterrevolutionaries, was unrepresented in Paris; but the radical threat it seemed to pose to Western governments was never far from the minds of the delegates. Wilson himself had sent American troops into Russia in 1918, allegedly to protect Czech forces trapped there, but really, many believed, to support the anti-Bolshevik forces in the civil war.

In this tense and often vindictive atmosphere, Wilson was unable to win approval of many of the broad principles he had espoused: freedom of the seas, which the British refused even to discuss; free trade; "open covenants openly arrived at" (the Paris negotiations themselves were often conducted in secret). His pledge of "national self-determination" for all peoples suffered numerous assaults. Economic and strategic demands were constantly coming into conflict with the principle of cultural nationalism.

Where the treaty departed most conspicuously from Wilson's ideals was on the question of reparations. When the conference began, the president opposed demanding reparations from the defeated Central Powers. The other Allied leaders, however, insisted on them, and slowly Wilson gave way and accepted the principle of reparations, the specific sum to be set later by a commission. The final amount, established in 1921, was less than some earlier demands but far more than the crippled German economy could absorb.

Wilson did manage to win some important victories in Paris in setting boundaries and dealing with former colonies. But his most visible triumph, and the one of most importance to him, was the creation of a permanent international organization to oversee world affairs and prevent future wars. On January 25, 1919, the Allies voted to accept the "covenant" of the League of

Nations; and with that, Wilson believed, the peace treaty was transformed from a disappointment into a success. Any mistakes and inequities that had emerged from the peace conference, he was certain, the League could correct later.

### The Ratification Battle

Wilson was well aware of the political obstacles awaiting him at home. Many Americans, accustomed to their nation's isolation from Europe, questioned the wisdom of this major new commitment to internationalism. Others had serious reservations about specific features of the treaty and the covenant. After a brief trip to Washington in February 1919, during which he listened to harsh objections to the treaty from members of the Senate and others, he returned to Europe and insisted on certain modifications in the covenant (limiting America's obligations to the League) to satisfy his critics. The changes were not enough to mollify his opponents, but Wilson refused to go further.

Wilson presented the Treaty of Versailles (which took its name from the former royal palace outside Paris where the final negotiating sessions had taken place) to the Senate on July 10, 1919. But members of the Senate had many objections to the treaty. Some—the so-called irreconcilables, many of them Western isolationists—opposed the agreement in principle. But many other opponents, with less fervent convictions, were principally concerned with constructing a winning issue for the Republicans in 1920. Most notable of these was Senator Henry Cabot Lodge of Massachusetts, the powerful chairman of the Foreign Relations Committee, who loathed the president. ("I never thought I could hate a man as I hate Wilson," Lodge once said.) He used every possible tactic to obstruct, delay, and amend the treaty.

Public sentiment clearly favored ratification, so at first Lodge could do little more than play for time. Gradually, however, Lodge's general opposition to the treaty crystallized into a series of "reservations"—amendments to the League covenant further limiting American obligations to the organization. Wilson might still have won approval at this point if he had agreed to some relatively minor changes in the language of the treaty. But the president refused to yield. The United States had a moral obligation, he claimed, to respect the terms of the agreement precisely as they stood. When he realized the Senate would not budge, he decided to appeal to the public.

He embarked on a grueling, cross-country speaking tour to arouse public support for the treaty. For more than three weeks, he traveled over 8,000 miles by train, speaking as often as four times a day, resting hardly at all. Finally, he reached the end of his strength. After speaking at Pueblo, Colorado, on September 25, 1919, he collapsed with severe headaches. Canceling the rest of his itinerary, he rushed back to Washington, where, a few days later, he suffered a major stroke. For two weeks, he was close to death; for six weeks more, he was so seriously ill that he could conduct virtually no public business. His wife and his doctor formed an almost impenetrable barrier around him, shielding the president from any official pressures that might impede his recovery and preventing the public from receiving any accurate information about the gravity of his condition.

Wilson ultimately recovered enough to resume a limited official schedule, but he was essentially an invalid for the remaining eighteen months of his presidency. His left side was partially paralyzed; more important, his mental and emotional state was unstable. His condition only intensified what had already been his strong tendency to view public issues in moral terms and to resist any attempts at compromise. When the Foreign Relations Committee finally sent the treaty to the Senate, recommending nearly fifty amendments and reservations, Wilson refused to consider any of them. When the full Senate voted in November to accept fourteen of the reservations, Wilson gave stern directions to his Democratic allies: they must vote only for a treaty with no changes whatsoever; any other version must be defeated. On November 19, 1919, forty-two Democrats, following the president's instructions, joined thirteen Republican "irreconcilables" to reject the amended treaty. When the Senate voted on the original version without any reservations, thirty-eight senators, all but one a Democrat, voted to approve it; fifty-five voted no.

There were sporadic efforts to revive the treaty over the next few months. But Wilson's opposition to anything but the precise settlement he had negotiated in Paris remained too formidable an obstacle to surmount. He was, moreover, becoming convinced that the 1920 national election would serve as a "solemn referendum" on the League. By now, however, public interest in the peace process had begun to fade—partly as a reaction against the tragic bitterness of the ratification fight, but more in response to a series of other crises.

## A SOCIETY IN TURMOIL

Even during the Paris Peace Conference, many Americans were concerned less about international matters than about turbulent events at home. Some of this unease was a legacy of the almost hysterical social atmosphere of the war years; some of it was a response to issues that surfaced after the armistice.

## The Unstable Economy

The war ended sooner than almost anyone had anticipated, and without warning, without planning, the nation lurched into the difficult task of economic reconversion. At first, the boom continued. But the postwar prosperity rested largely on the lingering effects of the war (government deficit spending continued for some months after the armistice) and on sudden, temporary demands (a booming market for scarce consumer goods at home and a strong market for American products in the war-ravaged nations of Europe). The postwar boom was accompanied, moreover, by raging inflation, a result in part of the sudden abandonment of wartime price controls. Through most of 1919 and 1920, prices rose at an average of more than 15 percent a year.

Finally, late in 1920, the economic bubble burst as many of the temporary forces that had created it disappeared and as inflation began killing the market for consumer goods. Between 1920 and 1921, the gross national product declined nearly 10 percent; 100,000 businesses went bankrupt; 453,000 farmers lost their land; and nearly 5 million Americans lost their jobs.

Well before this severe recession began, there was a dramatic increase in labor unrest. The raging inflation of 1919 wiped out the modest wage gains workers had achieved during the war; many laborers were worried about job security as hundreds of thousands of veterans returned to the work force; arduous working conditions—such as the twelve-hour day in the steel industry—continued to be a source of discontent. Employers aggravated the resentment by using the end of the war (and the end of government controls) to rescind benefits they had been forced to concede to workers in 1917 and 1918—most notably recognition of unions. The year 1919, therefore, saw an unprecedented wave of strikes—more than 3,600 in all, involving over 4 million workers. In January, a walkout by shipyard workers in Seattle, Washington, evolved into a general strike that brought the entire city to a virtual standstill. In September, there was a strike by the Boston police force, which was demanding recognition of its union in the wake of substantial layoffs and wage cuts. Seattle had remained generally calm; but with its police off the job, Boston erupted in violence and looting.

These and other strikes aroused widespread middle-class hostility to the unions, a hostility that played a part in defeating the greatest strike of 1919: a steel strike that began in September, when 350,000 steelworkers in several midwestern cities demanded an eight-hour day and recognition of their union. The steel strike was long and bitter and climaxed in a riot in Gary,

Indiana, in which eighteen strikers were killed. Steel executives managed to keep most plants running with nonunion labor, and public opinion was so hostile to the strikers that the AFL timidly repudiated them. By January, the strike had collapsed.

The wave of strikes was a reflection of the high expectations workers had in the aftermath of a war that they believed had been fought, in part, to secure their rights. It was also a reflection of the power of the forces arrayed against them. An official of the War Labor Board, observing the dismal postwar experience of unions, said in 1919: "The workers of the Allied world have been told that they were engaged in a democracy. . . . They are asking now, 'Where is that democracy for which we fought?' "

### The Demands of African Americans

The black men who had served in the armed forces during the war (367,000 of them) came home in 1919 and marched down the main streets of the industrial cities with other returning troops. And then (in New York and other cities) they marched again through the streets of black neighborhoods such as Harlem, led by jazz bands, cheered by thousands of African Americans, who believed that the glory of black heroism in the war would make it impossible for white society ever again to treat African Americans as less than equal citizens.

In truth, the fact that black soldiers had fought in the war had almost no impact at all on white attitudes. But it did have a profound effect on black attitudes: it accentuated African-American bitterness—and increased blacks' determination to fight for their rights. Veterans expected a reward for their service. But for many other American blacks, the war raised expectations in other ways. Nearly half a million migrated from the rural South to industrial cities (often enticed by northern "labor agents," who offered them free transportation) in search of the factory jobs the war was rapidly generating. This was the beginning of what became known as the "Great Migration." Within a few years, the nation's racial demographics were transformed; suddenly there were large black communities crowding into northern cities, in some of which very few African Americans had lived in the past. Just as black soldiers expected their military service to enhance their social status, so black factory workers regarded their move north as an escape from racial prejudice and an opportunity for economic gain.

By 1919, however, the racial climate had become savage and murderous. In the South, there was a sudden increase in lynchings: more than seventy blacks, some of them war veterans, died at the hands of white mobs in 1919 alone. In the North, black factory workers faced widespread layoffs as returning white veterans displaced them from their jobs. Black veterans found no significant new opportunities. And as whites became convinced that black workers with lower wage demands were hurting them economically, animosity grew rapidly.

Wartime riots in East St. Louis and elsewhere were a prelude to a summer of much worse racial violence in 1919. In Chicago, a black teenager swimming in Lake Michigan on a hot July day happened to drift toward a white beach. Whites on shore allegedly stoned him unconscious; he sank and drowned. Angry blacks gathered in crowds and marched into white neighborhoods to retaliate; whites formed even larger crowds and roamed into black neighborhoods shooting, stabbing, and beating passersby and destroying homes and properties. For more than a week, Chicago was virtually at war. In the end, 38 people died—15 whites and 23 blacks—and 537 were injured; over 1,000 people were left homeless. The Chicago riot was the worst but not the only racial violence during the so-called red summer of 1919; in all, 120 people died in such racial outbreaks in the space of little more than three months.

Racial violence, and even racially motivated urban riots, were not new. But the 1919 riots were different in one respect: they did not just involve white people attacking blacks; they also involved blacks fighting back. The NAACP signaled this change by urging blacks not just to demand government protection but also to retaliate, to defend themselves. The poet Claude McKay, one of the major figures of what would shortly be known as the Harlem Renaissance, wrote a poem after the Chicago riot called "If We Must Die": "Like men we'll face the murderous cowardly pack. Pressed to the wall, dying, but fighting back."

At the same time, a black Jamaican, Marcus Garvey, began to attract a wide following in the United States, mostly among poor urban blacks, with his ideology of black nationalism. Garvey encouraged African Americans to reject assimilation into white society and develop pride in their own race and culture (which was, he claimed, superior to that of white society). His United Negro Improvement Association (UNIA) launched a chain of black-owned grocery stores and pressed for the creation of other black businesses. Eventually, Garvey began urging his supporters to leave America and return to Africa, where they could create a new society of their own. In the 1920s, the Garvey movement experienced explosive growth for a time. It began to decline, however, after Garvey was indicted in 1923 on charges of business

MARCUS GARVEY, 1924 Garvey attracted a broad
following in the early 1920s with his message of black
nationalism and self-help. He often dressed in
semimilitary regalia and organized meetings and parades
with a vaguely martial tone. His influence declined after
he was convicted of fraud for misuse of funds he had
raised to launch an African-American steamship
company. He served a short term in jail and in 1927 was
deported to his native Jamaica, where he died in 1940 in
relative obscurity.

fraud. He was deported to Jamaica two years later. But the allure of black nationalism, which he helped make visible to millions of African Americans, survived in black culture long after Garvey himself was gone.

## The Red Scare

Much of the public considered the industrial warfare and the racial violence in 1919 a frightening omen of instability and radicalism. This was in part because other evidence emerging at the same time also seemed to suggest the existence of a radical menace. After the Russian Revolution of November 1917, communism was no longer simply a theory; it was now the basis of an important regime. Concerns about the communist threat grew in 1919 when the Soviet government announced the formation of the Communist International (or Comintern), whose purpose was to export revolution around the world.

In America, meanwhile, there were, in addition to the great number of imagined radicals, a modest number of real ones. These small groups of radicals were presumably responsible for a series of bombings in the spring of 1919 that produced great national alarm. In April, the post office intercepted several dozen parcels addressed to leading businessmen and politicians that were triggered to explode when opened. Two months later, eight bombs exploded in eight cities within minutes of one another, suggesting a nationwide conspiracy. One of them damaged the façade of United States Attorney General A. Mitchell Palmer's home in Washington.

In response to these and other provocations, what became known as the Red Scare began. Nearly thirty states enacted new peacetime sedition laws imposing harsh penalties on those who promoted revolution; some 300 people went to jail as a result. There were spontaneous acts of violence against supposed radicals in some communities, and more calculated efforts by universities and other institutions to expel radicals from their midst. But the greatest contribution to the Red Scare came from the federal government. On New Year's Day, 1920, Attorney General A. Mitchell Palmer and his ambitious young assistant, J. Edgar Hoover, orchestrated a series of raids on alleged radical centers throughout the country and arrested more than 6,000 people. The Palmer Raids had been designed to uncover huge caches of weapons and explosives; they netted a total of three pistols. Most of those arrested were ultimately released, but about 500 who were not American citizens were summarily deported.

The ferocity of the Red Scare soon abated, but its effects lingered well into the 1920s, most notably in the celebrated case of Sacco and Vanzetti.

In May of 1920, two Italian immigrants, Nicola Sacco and Bartolomeo Vanzetti, were charged with the murder of a paymaster in Braintree, Massachusetts. The case against them was questionable and suffused with nativist prejudices and fears; but because both men were confessed anarchists, they faced a widespread public presumption of guilt. They were convicted and sentenced to death. Over the next several years, public support for Sacco and Vanzetti grew to formidable proportions. But all requests for a new trial or a pardon were denied. On August 23, 1927, amid widespread protests around the world, Sacco and Vanzetti, still proclaiming their innocence, died in the electric chair.

## The Retreat from Idealism

On August 26, 1920, the Nineteenth Amendment, guaranteeing women the right to vote, became part of the Constitution. To the woman suffrage movement, this was the culmination of nearly a century of struggle. To many progressives, who had seen the inclusion of women in the electorate as a way of bolstering their political strength, it seemed to promise new support for reform. Yet the passage of the Nineteenth Amendment marked not the beginning of an era of progressive reform but the end of one.

Economic problems, labor unrest, racial tensions, and the intensity of the antiradicalism they helped create—all combined in the years immediately following the war to produce a general sense of disillusionment. That became particularly apparent in the election of 1920. Woodrow Wilson wanted the campaign to be a referendum on the League of Nations, and the Democratic candidates, Governor James M. Cox of Ohio and Assistant Secretary of the Navy Franklin D. Roosevelt, dutifully tried to keep Wilson's ideals alive. The Republican presidential nominee, however, offered a different vision. He was Warren Gamaliel Harding, an obscure Ohio senator whom party leaders had chosen as their nominee confident that he would do their bidding once in office. Harding offered no ideals, only a vague promise of a return, as he later phrased it, to "normalcy." He won in a landslide. The Republican ticket received 61 percent of the popular vote and carried every state outside the South. The party made major gains in Congress as well. To many Americans it seemed that, for better or worse, a new era had begun.

# CHAPTER TWENTY-FOUR

# The New Era

*The New Economy* ∼ *The New Culture*
*A Conflict of Cultures* ∼ *Republican Government*

T HE 1920S ARE OFTEN remembered as an era of affluence, conservatism, and cultural frivolity: the Roaring Twenties, the age of what Warren G. Harding once called "normalcy." In reality, however, the decade was a time of significant, even dramatic social, economic, and political change. It was an era in which the American economy not only enjoyed spectacular growth but developed new forms of organization. It was a time in which American popular culture reshaped itself to reflect the increasingly urban, industrial, consumer-oriented society of the United States. And it was a decade in which American government, for all its apparent conservatism, experimented with new approaches to public policy that helped pave the way for the important period of reform that was to follow. That was why contemporaries liked to refer to the 1920s as the "New Era"—an age in which America was becoming a modern nation.

At the same time, however, the decade saw the rise of a series of spirited and at times effective rebellions against the modern developments that were transforming American life. The intense cultural conflicts that characterized the 1920s were evidence of how much of American society remained unreconciled to the modernizing currents of the New Era.

## THE NEW ECONOMY

After the recession of 1921–1922, the United States began a long period of almost uninterrupted prosperity and economic expansion. Less visible at the time, but equally significant, was the survival (and even the growth) of severe inequalities and imbalances.

657

| TIME LINE | | | | |
|---|---|---|---|---|
| **1914-1920** | **1920** | **1922** | **1923** | |
| Great Migration of blacks to North | Prohibition begins<br><br>Harding elected president | Lewis's *Babbitt*<br><br>Motion Picture Association founded | Harding dies; Coolidge becomes president<br><br>Harding administration scandals revealed<br><br>Ku Klux Klan membership peaks | |

| **1924** | **1925** | **1927** | **1928** | **1929** |
|---|---|---|---|---|
| National Origins Act passed<br><br>Coolidge elected president | Fitzgerald's *The Great Gatsby*<br><br>Scopes Trial | Lindbergh's solo transatlantic flight<br><br>First sound motion picture, *The Jazz Singer* | Hoover elected president | Faulkner's *The Sound and the Fury* |

## Economic Growth and Organization

No one could deny the remarkable, some believed miraculous, feats of the American economy in the 1920s. The nation's manufacturing output rose by more than 60 percent during the decade. Per capita income grew by a third. Inflation was negligible. A mild recession in 1923 interrupted the pattern of growth; but when it subsided early in 1924, the economy expanded with even greater vigor than before.

The economic boom was a result of many things, but one of the most important causes was technology, and the great industrial expansion it made possible. The automobile industry, as a result of the development of the assembly line and other innovations, now became one of the most important industries in the nation. It stimulated growth in other, related industries as well. Auto manufacturers purchased the products of steel, rubber, glass, and tool companies. Auto owners bought gasoline from the oil corporations. Road construction in response to the proliferation of motor vehicles became an important industry. The increased mobility that the automobile made possible increased the demand for suburban housing, fueling a boom in the construction industry.

Other new industries benefiting from technological innovations contributed as well to the economic growth. Radio became a booming concern within a few years of its commercial debut in 1920. The motion picture industry expanded dramatically, especially after the introduction of sound in 1927. Aviation, electronics, home appliances, plastics, synthetic fibers, aluminum, magnesium, oil, electric power, and other industries fueled by technological advances—all grew dramatically and spurred the economic boom.

Large sectors of American business were accelerating their drive toward national organization and consolidation. Certain industries—notably those such as steel and automobiles, dependent on large-scale mass production—seemed naturally to move toward concentrating production in a few large firms. Others—industries less dependent on technology and less susceptible to great economies of scale—proved resistant to consolidation, despite the efforts of many businessmen to promote it.

Some industries less prone to domination by a few great corporations attempted to stabilize themselves not through consolidation but through cooperation. An important vehicle was the trade association—a national organization created by various members of an industry to encourage coordination in production and marketing techniques. But trade associations worked best in the mass-production industries that had already succeeded in limiting competition through consolidation. In more decentralized industries, such as cotton textiles, their effectiveness was limited.

The strenuous efforts by industrialists throughout the economy to find ways to curb competition through consolidation or cooperation reflected a strong fear of overcapacity. Even in the booming 1920s, industrialists remembered how too-rapid expansion and overproduction had helped produce recessions in 1893, 1907, and 1920. The great, unrealized dream of the New Era was to find a way to stabilize the economy so that such collapses would never occur again.

### Workers in an Age of Capital

The remarkable economic growth was accompanied by a continuing, and in some areas even increasing, maldistribution of wealth and purchasing power. More than two-thirds of the American people in 1929 lived at no better than what one major study described as the "minimum comfort level." Half of those languished at or below the level of "subsistence and poverty." Large segments of society, unable to organize, were without power to protect their economic interests.

American labor experienced both the successes and the failures of the 1920s as much as any other group. On the one hand, most workers saw their standard of living rise during the decade; many enjoyed greatly improved working conditions and other benefits. Some employers in the 1920s, eager to avoid disruptive labor unrest and forestall the growth of unions, adopted paternalistic techniques that came to be known as "welfare capitalism."

THE STEAMFITTER Lewis Hine was among the first
American photographers to recognize his craft as an art. In
this carefully posed photograph from the mid-1920s, Hine
made a point that many other artists were making in other
media: The rise of the machine could serve human beings,
but might also bend them to its own needs.

Henry Ford, for example, shortened the workweek, raised wages, and instituted paid vacations. By 1926, nearly 3 million industrial workers were eligible for at least modest pensions on retirement. When labor grievances surfaced despite these efforts, workers could voice them through the so-called
company unions that were emerging in many industries—workers' councils
and shop committees, organized by the corporations themselves. But welfare capitalism, in the end, gave workers no real control over their own
fates. Company unions were feeble vehicles. And welfare capitalism survived
only as long as industry prospered. After 1929, with the economy in crisis,
the entire system collapsed.

Welfare capitalism affected only a relatively small number of workers
in any case. Most laborers worked for employers interested primarily in

keeping their labor costs low. Workers as a whole, therefore, received wage increases that were proportionately far below the growth of the economy as a whole. Unskilled workers, in particular, saw their wages increase hardly at all—by only a little over 2 percent between 1920 and 1926. At the end of the decade, the average annual income of a worker remained below $1,500 a year when $1,800 was considered necessary to maintain a minimally decent standard of living. Only by relying on the earnings of several family members at once could many working-class families make ends meet.

The New Era was a bleak time for labor organization, in part because many unions themselves were relatively conservative and failed to adapt to the realities of the modern economy. The American Federation of Labor (led by the cautious William Green) remained wedded to the concept of the craft union, in which workers were organized on the basis of particular skills. The AFL sought peaceful cooperation with employers, without strikes. In the meantime, the number of unskilled industrial workers, many of them recent immigrants from southern or eastern Europe, was rising rapidly. They received little attention from the craft unions.

But whatever the weaknesses of the unions, the strength of the corporations was the principal reason for the absence of effective labor organization in the 1920s. After the turmoil of 1919, corporate leaders worked hard to spread the doctrine that unionism was somehow subversive, that a crucial element of democratic capitalism was the protection of the "open shop" (a shop in which no worker could be required to join a union). The crusade for the open shop, euphemistically titled the "American Plan," became a pretext for a harsh campaign of union busting across the country. As a result, union membership fell from more than 5 million in 1920 to under 3 million in 1929.

### Women and Minorities in the Work Force

A growing proportion of the work force consisted of women, who were concentrated in what have since become known as "pink-collar" jobs—low-paying service occupations with many of the same problems as manufacturing employment. Large numbers of women worked as secretaries, salesclerks, and telephone operators and in other nonmanual service capacities. Because technically such positions were not industrial jobs, the AFL and other labor organizations were uninterested in organizing these workers. Similarly, the half-million African Americans who had migrated from the rural South into the cities during the Great Migration after 1914 had few opportunities for union representation. The skilled crafts represented in the AFL often worked actively to exclude blacks from their trades and organizations. Most blacks, however, worked in jobs in which the AFL took no interest at all—as janitors, dishwashers, garbage collectors, domestics, and other service capacities. A. Philip Randolph's Brotherhood of Sleeping Car Porters was one of the few important unions dominated and led by African Americans.

In the West and the Southwest, the ranks of the unskilled included considerable numbers of Asians and Hispanics, few of them organized, most actively excluded from white-dominated unions. In the wake of the Chinese Exclusion Acts, Japanese immigrants increasingly took the place of the Chinese in menial jobs in California, despite the continuing hostility of the white population. They worked on railroads, construction sites, and farms and in many other low-paying workplaces. Some Japanese managed to escape the ranks of the unskilled by forming their own small businesses or setting themselves up as truck farmers; and many of the Issei (Japanese immigrants) and Nisei (their American-born children) enjoyed significant economic success—so much so that California passed laws in 1913 and 1920 to make it more difficult for them to buy land. Other Asians—most notably Filipinos—also swelled the unskilled work force and generated considerable hostility. Anti-Filipino riots in California beginning in 1929 helped produce legislation in 1934 virtually eliminating immigration from the Philippines.

Mexican immigrants formed a major part of the unskilled work force throughout the Southwest and California. Nearly half a million Mexicans entered the United States in the 1920s, more than any other national group, increasing the total Mexican population to over a million. Most lived in California, Texas, Arizona, and New Mexico; and by 1930, most lived in cities. Large Mexican barrios—usually raw urban communities, often without even such basic services as plumbing and sewerage—grew up in Los Angeles, El Paso, San Antonio, Denver, and many other cities and towns. Some of the residents found work locally in factories and shops; others traveled to mines or did migratory labor on farms but returned to the cities between jobs. Mexican workers, too, faced hostility and discrimination from the Anglo population of the region, but there were few efforts actually to exclude them. Employers in the relatively underpopulated West needed this ready pool of low-paid, unskilled, and unorganized workers.

### The Plight of the Farmer

Like industry, American agriculture in the 1920s was embracing new technologies for increasing production. The number of tractors on American farms, for example, quadrupled during the 1920s, helping to open 35 million new acres to cultivation. Agricultural production was increasing in other parts of the world as well. But the demand for agricultural goods was not rising as fast as production. The result was substantial surpluses, a disastrous decline in food prices, and a severe drop in farmers' income beginning early in the 1920s. More than 3 million people left agriculture altogether in the course of the decade. Of those who remained, many lost ownership of their lands and had to rent instead from banks or other landlords.

In response, some farmers began to demand relief in the form of government price supports. One price-raising scheme in particular came to dominate agrarian demands: the idea of "parity." Under parity, corn, for example, would bring a price that bore the same relation to the prices of all goods that it had in the period 1909–1913 (a good time for farmers.) Its purpose was to ensure that farmers would earn back at least their production costs no matter how the national or world agricultural market might fluctuate. Champions of parity urged high tariffs against foreign agricultural goods and a government commitment to buy surplus domestic crops at parity and sell them abroad at whatever the market would bring.

The legislative expression of the demand for parity was the McNary-Haugen Bill, named after its two principal sponsors in Congress and introduced repeatedly between 1924 and 1928. In 1926, Congress (where farm interests enjoyed disproportionate influence) approved a bill requiring parity for grain, cotton, tobacco, and rice, but President Coolidge vetoed it. In 1928, the bill won congressional approval again, only to succumb to another presidential veto.

## THE NEW CULTURE

The increasingly urban and consumer-oriented culture of the 1920s helped Americans in all regions to live their lives and perceive their world in increasingly similar ways. That same culture exposed them to a new set of values that reflected both the prosperity and complexity of the modern economy. But the new mass culture could not, of course, erase the continuing, and indeed increasing, diversity of the United States. That culture reached Americans divided by region, race, religion, gender, and class, and they responded to the cultural messages they received in very different ways.

## Consumerism and Communications

The United States of the 1920s was a consumer society—a society in which increasing numbers of men and women could afford more than simply what was necessary to survive. Many more people than ever before could buy items not just because of need but for convenience and pleasure. Middle-class families purchased electric refrigerators, washing machines, and vacuum cleaners. People wore wristwatches and smoked cigarettes. Women purchased cosmetics and mass-produced fashions. Above all, Americans bought automobiles. By the end of the decade, there were more than 30 million cars on American roads.

No group was more aware of the emergence of consumerism (or more responsible for creating it) than the advertising industry. The first advertising and public relations firms (N. W. Ayer and J. Walter Thompson) had

THE ELECTRIC REFRIGERATOR The development of new appliances for the home was an important part of the boom in the production and sale of consumer goods in the 1920s. Executives of the Delcom Light Company, a subsidiary of General Motors, pose here in front of the first Frigidaire electric refrigerator as it is readied for shipping from Dayton, Ohio, in 1921.

appeared well before World War I, but in the 1920s, partly as a result of techniques pioneered by wartime propaganda, advertising came of age. Publicists no longer simply conveyed information; they sought to identify products with a particular lifestyle. They also encouraged the public to absorb the values of promotion and salesmanship and to admire those who were effective "boosters" and publicists. One of the most successful books of the 1920s was *The Man Nobody Knows*, by advertising executive Bruce Barton. It portrayed Jesus Christ as not only a religious prophet but also a "super salesman." Barton's message, a message apparently in tune with the new spirit of the consumer culture, was that Jesus had been a man concerned with living a full and rewarding life in this world and that twentieth-century men and women should be concerned with doing the same.

The advertising industry could never have had the impact it did without the emergence of new vehicles of communication that made it possible

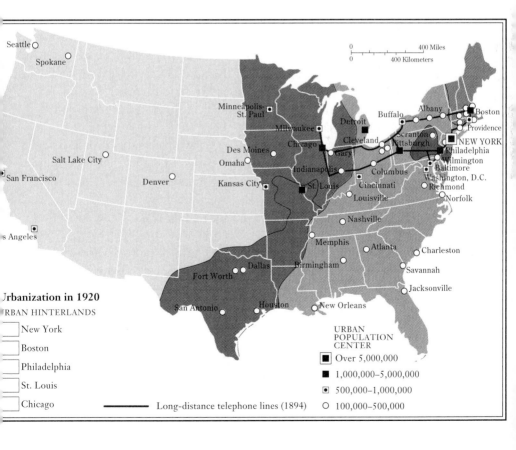

Urbanization in 1920

URBAN HINTERLANDS

- New York
- Boston
- Philadelphia
- St. Louis
- Chicago

URBAN POPULATION CENTER

- ■ Over 5,000,000
- ■ 1,000,000–5,000,000
- ◙ 500,000–1,000,000
- ○ 100,000–500,000

——— Long-distance telephone lines (1894)

to reach large audiences quickly and easily. Newspapers were being absorbed into national chains. Mass-circulation magazines—*Collier's, Ladies' Home Journal,* the *Saturday Evening Post, Time, Reader's Digest,* and others—attracted broad, national audiences. The movies were becoming an ever more popular and powerful form of mass communication; over 100 million people saw films in 1930, as compared with 40 million in 1922.

The most important communications vehicle, however, was the only one truly new to the 1920s: radio. The first commercial radio station in America, KDKA in Pittsburgh, began broadcasting in 1920, and the first national radio network, the National Broadcasting Company, was formed in 1927. By 1923, there were more than 500 radio stations, covering virtually every area of the country; by 1929, more than 12 million families owned radio sets.

## *Women in the New Era*

College-educated women were no longer pioneers in the 1920s. There were now two and even three generations of graduates of women's or coeducational colleges and universities, and some were making their presence felt in professional areas that in the past women had rarely penetrated. Still, professional opportunities for women remained limited by society's assumptions about what were suitable occupations for them. Although there were notable success stories about female business executives, journalists, doctors, and lawyers, most professional women remained confined to such traditionally "feminine" fields as fashion, education, social work, and nursing or to the lower levels of business management. The "new professional woman" was a vivid and widely publicized image in the 1920s. In reality, however, most employed women were nonprofessional, lower-class workers. Middle-class women, in the meantime, remained largely in the home.

Yet the 1920s constituted a new era for middle-class women nonetheless. In particular, the decade saw a redefinition of motherhood. Shortly after World War I, an influential group of psychologists—the "behaviorists," led by John B. Watson—began to challenge the long-held assumption that women had an instinctive capacity for motherhood. Maternal affection was not, they claimed, sufficient preparation for child rearing. Instead, mothers should rely on the advice and assistance of experts and professionals: doctors, nurses, and trained educators in nursery schools and kindergartens.

For many middle-class women, these changes devalued what had been an important and consuming activity. Many attempted to compensate by devoting new attention to their roles as wives and companions. A woman's relationship with her husband assumed a greatly enhanced importance. And many women now openly considered their sexual relationships with their husbands not simply as a means of procreation, as earlier generations had been taught to do, but an important and pleasurable experience in its own right, as the culmination of romantic love.

One result was growing interest in birth control. The pioneer of the American birth-control movement, Margaret Sanger, began her career as a promoter of the diaphragm and other birth-control devices out of a concern for working-class women; she believed that large families were among the major causes of poverty and distress in poor communities. By the 1920s (partly because she had limited success in persuading working-class women to accept her teachings), she was becoming more concerned with and more effective in persuading middle-class women to see the benefits of birth control. Nevertheless, some birth control devices remained illegal in many states (and abortion remained illegal nearly everywhere).

The new, more secular view of womanhood had effects on women beyond the middle class as well. Some women concluded that in the New Era it was no longer necessary to maintain a rigid, Victorian female "respectability." They could smoke, drink, dance, wear seductive clothes and makeup, and attend lively parties. Those assumptions became the basis of the "flapper"—the modern woman whose liberated lifestyle found expression in dress, hairstyle, speech, and behavior. The flapper lifestyle had a particular impact on lower-middle-class and working-class single women, who were flocking to new jobs in industry and the service sector. (The young, middle-class, "Bohemian" women most often associated with the flapper image were, in fact, imitating a style that emerged among this larger group.) At night, such women flocked to clubs and dance halls in search of excitement and companionship.

Despite all the changes, most women remained highly dependent on men—both in the workplace and in the home—and relatively powerless when men exploited that dependence. The realization that the "new woman" was as much myth as reality inspired some American feminists to continue their crusade for reform. The National Woman's Party, under the leadership of Alice Paul, pressed on with its campaign for the Equal Rights Amendment, although it found little support in Congress (and met continued resistance from other feminist groups). Nevertheless, women's organizations and female political activities grew in many ways in the 1920s. Responding to the suffrage victory, women organized the League of Women Voters and the women's auxiliaries of both the Democratic and Republican Parties. Female-dominated consumer groups grew rapidly and increased the range and energy of their efforts.

Women activists won an apparent triumph in 1921 when they helped secure passage of a measure in keeping with the traditional feminist goal of securing "protective" legislation for women: the Sheppard-Towner Act. It provided federal funds to states to establish prenatal and child health-care programs. From the start, however, it produced controversy. Alice Paul and her supporters opposed the measure, complaining that it classified all women as mothers. Margaret Sanger complained that the new programs would discourage birth-control efforts. More important, the American Medical Association fought Sheppard-Towner, warning that it would introduce untrained outsiders into the health-care field. In 1929, Congress terminated the program.

## The Disenchanted

Many artists and intellectuals coming of age in the 1920s were experiencing a disenchantment with modern America so fundamental that they were often able to view it only with contempt. As a result, they adopted a role different from that of most intellectuals of earlier eras. Rather than trying to influence and reform their society, they isolated themselves from it. At the heart of their disaffection was a sense of personal alienation, a belief that contemporary America no longer provided the individual with avenues by which he or she could achieve personal fulfillment.

One result of this alienation was a series of savage critiques of modern society by a wide range of writers, some of whom were known as the "debunkers." Among them was the Baltimore journalist H. L. Mencken, who delighted in ridiculing everything Americans held dear: religion, politics, the arts, even democracy itself. Sinclair Lewis, the first American to win a Nobel Prize in literature, published a series of savage novels—*Main Street* (1920), *Babbitt* (1922), *Arrowsmith* (1925), and others—in which he lashed out at one aspect of modern bourgeois society after another. Intellectuals of the 1920s claimed to reject the "success ethic" that they believed dominated American life (even though many of them hoped for—and a few achieved—commercial and critical success on their own terms). The novelist F. Scott Fitzgerald, for example, attacked the American obsession with material success in *The Great Gatsby* (1925).

Some artists and intellectuals expressed their disillusionment by leaving America to live in France, making Paris for a time a center of American artistic life. Others moved to the southwestern United States—to the art colonies at Taos and Santa Fe, New Mexico—attracted by the cultural and geographical distinctiveness of the region. Some adopted hedonistic lifestyles,

A M E R I C A N  V O I C E S

LANGSTON HUGHES

## *I, Too (1926)*

I, too, sing America.

I am the darker brother.
They send me to eat in the kitchen
When company comes,
But I laugh,
And eat well,
And grow strong.

Tomorrow,
I'll be at the table
When company comes.
Nobody'll dare
Say to me,
'Eat in the kitchen,'
Then.

Besides,
They'll see how beautiful I am
And be ashamed—

I, too, am America.

SOURCE: From *Collected Poems* by Langston Hughes. Copyright © 1994 by the Estate of Langston Hughes. Reprinted by permission of Alfred A. Knopf, Inc.

involving alcohol, drugs, casual sex, and wild parties. Most of these young men and women, however, believed the only real refuge from the travails of modern society was art. Only art, they argued, could allow them full individual expression; only the act of creation could offer them fulfillment.

Whether or not they found that fulfillment, they produced an extraordinary body of work. The roster of important American writers active in the 1920s may have no equal in any other period: Ernest Hemingway, Fitzgerald, Lewis, Thomas Wolfe, John Dos Passos, Ezra Pound, T. S. Eliot, Gertrude Stein, Edna Ferber, William Faulkner, and Eugene O'Neill.

To some intellectuals, the solution to contemporary problems lay neither in escapism nor in progressivism but in an exploration of their own cultural or regional origins. In New York City, a new generation of black intellectuals created a flourishing African-American culture widely described as the "Harlem Renaissance." The Harlem poets, novelists, and artists drew heavily from their African roots in an effort to prove the richness of their own racial heritage and to provide a basis for a cultural and political challenge to racial injustice. The poet Langston Hughes captured much of the spirit of the movement in a single sentence: "I am a Negro—and beautiful." Other black writers in Harlem and elsewhere—James Weldon Johnson, Countee Cullen, Zora Neale Hurston, Claude McKay, Alain Locke—as well as black artists and musicians helped to establish a thriving, and at times highly politicized, culture rooted in the historical legacy of their race.

## A CONFLICT OF CULTURES

The modern, secular culture of the 1920s did not go unchallenged. It grew up alongside an older, more traditional culture, with which it continually and often bitterly competed. The older culture expressed the outlook of generally less affluent, less urban, more provincial Americans—men and women who continued to revere traditional values and customs and who feared and resented modernist threats to their way of life. The result of their fears was a series of harsh cultural controversies.

### Prohibition

When the prohibition of the sale and manufacture of alcohol went into effect in January 1920, it had the support of most members of the middle class and most of those who considered themselves progressives. Within a year, however, it had become clear that the "noble experiment," as its defenders called it, was not working well. Prohibition did substantially reduce drinking in most parts of the country. But it also produced conspicuous and growing violations that made the law an almost immediate source of disillusionment and controversy.

The government hired only 1,500 agents to enforce prohibition, and in many places they received little help from local law enforcement agencies. Before long, it was almost as easy to acquire illegal alcohol in many parts of the country as it had once been to acquire legal alcohol. And since an enormous, lucrative industry was now barred to legitimate businessmen, organized-crime figures took it over.

Many middle-class progressives who had originally supported prohibition soon soured on the experiment. But an enormous constituency of provincial, largely rural, Protestant Americans continued vehemently to defend it. To them, prohibition had always meant more than stopping drinking. It represented the effort of an older America to maintain its dominance in a society in which they were becoming relatively less powerful. Drinking, which they associated with the modern city and with Catholic immigrants, became a symbol of the new culture they believed was displacing them.

As the decade proceeded, opponents of prohibition (or "wets," as they came to be known) gained steadily in influence. Not until 1933, however, when the Great Depression added weight to their appeals, were they finally able effectively to challenge the "drys" and win repeal of the Eighteenth Amendment.

### Nativism and the Klan

The fear of immigrants that many prohibitionists expressed found other expressions as well. Agitation for a curb on foreign immigration to the United States had begun in the nineteenth century, and as with prohibition, it had gathered strength in the years before the war largely because of the support of middle-class progressives. Such concerns had not been sufficient in the first years of the century to win passage of curbs on immigration; but in the years immediately following the war, when immigration began to be associated with radicalism, popular sentiment on behalf of restriction grew rapidly.

In 1921, Congress passed an emergency immigration act, establishing a quota system by which annual immigration from any country could not exceed 3 percent of the number of persons of that nationality who had been in the United States in 1910. The new law cut immigration from 800,000 to 300,000 in any single year, but the nativists remained unsatisfied. The National Origins Act of 1924 banned immigration from east Asia entirely, a measure clearly directed against Japan, since Chinese immigration was already illegal. It also reduced the quota for Europeans from 3 to 2 percent. The quota would be based, moreover, not on the 1910 census, but on the census of 1890, a year in which there had been far fewer southern and eastern Europeans in the country. What immigration there was, in other words, would heavily favor northwestern Europeans—people of "Nordic" or "Teutonic" stock. Five years later, a further restriction set a rigid limit of 150,000 immigrants a year. In the years that followed, immigration officials seldom permitted even half that number actually to enter the country.

But the nativism of the 1920s extended well beyond restricting immigration. To defenders of an older, more provincial America, the growth of large communities of foreign peoples, alien in their speech, their habits, and their values, came to seem a direct threat to their own embattled way of life. Among other things, this provincial nativism helped instigate the rebirth of the Ku Klux Klan as a major force in American society. The first Klan, founded during Reconstruction, had died in the 1870s. But in 1915, a new group of white southerners met on Stone Mountain near Atlanta and established a modern version of the society. Nativist passions had swelled in Georgia and elsewhere in response to the case of Leo Frank, a Jewish factory manager in Atlanta convicted in 1914 (on very flimsy evidence) of murdering a female employee; a mob stormed Frank's jail and lynched him. The premiere (also in Atlanta) of D. W. Griffith's film *The Birth of a Nation*, which glorified the early Klan, also helped inspire white southerners to join a new one.

At first the new Klan, like the old, was largely concerned with intimidating blacks. After World War I, however, concern about blacks gradually became secondary to concern about Catholics, Jews, and foreigners. At that point, membership in the Klan expanded rapidly and dramatically, not just in the small towns and rural areas of the South but in industrial cities in the North and Midwest. By 1924, there were reportedly 4 million members, and the largest state Klan was not in the South but in Indiana. Beginning in 1925, a series of scandals involving the organization's leaders precipitated a slow but steady decline in the Klan's influence.

Most Klan units (or "klaverns") tried to present their members as patriots and defenders of morality, and some did nothing more menacing than stage occasional parades and rallies. Often, however, the Klan also operated as a brutal, even violent, opponent of "alien" groups and as a defender of traditional, fundamentalist morality. Klansmen systematically terrorized blacks, Jews, Catholics, and foreigners. At times, they did so violently, through public whipping, tarring and feathering, arson, and lynching. What the Klan feared, however, was not simply "foreign" or "racially impure" groups; it was anyone who posed a challenge to traditional values. Klansmen persecuted not only immigrants and blacks but those white Protestants they considered guilty of irreligion, sexual promiscuity, or drunkenness. The Ku Klux Klan, in short, was fighting not just to preserve racial homogeneity but to defend its definition of traditional culture against what its members believed to be the values and morals of modernity.

### Religious Fundamentalism

Another cultural controversy of the 1920s was the result of a bitter conflict over the place of religion in contemporary society. By 1921, American Protestantism was already divided into two warring camps. On one side stood the modernists: mostly urban, middle-class people who were attempting to adapt religion to the teachings of modern science and to the realities of their modern, secular society. On the other side stood the fundamentalists: provincial, largely (although far from exclusively) rural men and women fighting to preserve traditional faith and to maintain the centrality of religion in American life. The fundamentalists insisted the Bible was to be interpreted literally. Above all, they opposed the teachings of Charles Darwin, who had openly challenged the biblical story of the Creation.

By the mid-1920s, to the great alarm of modernists, fundamentalism was gaining political strength in some states with its demands for legislation to forbid the teaching of evolution in the public schools. In Tennessee in March 1925, the legislature actually adopted a measure making it illegal for any public school teacher "to teach any theory that denies the story of the divine creation of man as taught in the Bible."

When the fledgling American Civil Liberties Union (ACLU) offered free counsel to any Tennessee educator willing to defy the law and become the defendant in a test case, a twenty-four-year-old biology teacher in the town of Dayton, John T. Scopes, agreed to have himself arrested. And when the ACLU decided to send the famous attorney Clarence Darrow to defend Scopes, the aging William Jennings Bryan (now an important fundamentalist spokesman) announced that he would travel to Dayton to assist the prosecution. Journalists from across the country flocked to Tennessee to cover

**DARROW AND BRYAN IN DAYTON** Although the Scopes trial was chiefly significant
for the issues it raised, it attracted national attention in 1925 at least as much
because of its two celebrated attorneys: Clarence Darrow, the best-known defense
attorney in America and a personification of the modern, skeptical, secular
intellect; and William Jennings Bryan, the great political leader who had become,
in the last years of his life, an ardent defender of Christian fundamentalism.

the trial, which opened in a circuslike atmosphere. Scopes had, of course,
clearly violated the law; and a verdict of guilty was a foregone conclusion,
especially when the judge refused to permit "expert" testimony by evolution
scholars. Scopes was fined $100, and the case was ultimately dismissed in a
higher court because of a technicality. Nevertheless, Darrow scored an important victory for the modernists by calling Bryan himself to the stand to
testify as an "expert on the Bible." In the course of the cross-examination,
which was broadcast by radio to much of the nation, Darrow made Bryan's
stubborn defense of biblical truths appear foolish and finally tricked Bryan
into admitting the possibility that not all religious dogma was subject to only
one interpretation.

The Scopes trial put fundamentalists on the defensive and discouraged
many of them from participating openly in politics. But it did not resolve

the conflict between fundamentalists and modernists. Four other states soon proceeded to pass antievolution laws of their own, and the issue continued to smolder for decades.

### The Democrats' Ordeal

The anguish of provincial Americans attempting to defend an embattled way of life proved particularly troubling to the Democratic Party, which was seriously debilitated during the 1920s as a result of tensions between its urban and rural factions. More than the Republicans, the Democrats consisted of a diverse coalition of interest groups, linked to the party more by local tradition than common commitment. Among those interest groups were prohibitionists, Klansmen, and fundamentalists on one side and Catholics, urban workers, and immigrants on the other.

In 1924, the tensions between them proved devastating. At the Democratic National Convention in New York that summer, a bitter conflict broke out over the platform when the party's urban wing attempted to win approval of planks calling for the repeal of prohibition and a denunciation of the Klan. Both planks narrowly failed. More serious was a deadlock in the balloting for a presidential candidate. Urban Democrats supported Alfred E. Smith, the Irish Catholic Tammanyite who had risen to become a progressive governor of New York; rural Democrats backed William McAdoo, Woodrow Wilson's Treasury secretary (and son-in-law), later to become a senator from California, who had skillfully positioned himself to win the support of southern and western delegates suspicious of Tammany Hall and modern urban life. For 103 ballots, the convention dragged on, until finally both Smith and McAdoo withdrew and the party settled on a compromise: the corporate lawyer John W. Davis.

A similar schism plagued the Democrats again in 1928, when Al Smith finally secured his party's nomination for president after another acrimonious but less prolonged battle. He was not, however, able to unite his divided party—in part because of widespread anti-Catholic sentiment, especially in the South, and in part because of Smith's own conspicuous New York provincialism. He was the first Democrat since the Civil War not to carry the entire South. Elsewhere, although he did well in large cities, he carried no states at all except Massachusetts and Rhode Island. Smith's opponent, and the victor in the presidential election, was a man who perhaps more than any other personified the modern, prosperous, middle-class society of the New Era: Herbert Hoover. The business civilization of the 1920s, with its new institutions, fashions, and values, continued to arouse the animosity of large portions of the population, but the majority of the American people appeared to have accepted and approved it.

## REPUBLICAN GOVERNMENT

For twelve years, beginning in 1921, both the presidency and the Congress rested in the hands of the Republican Party—a party in which the power of reformers had greatly dwindled. For most of those years, the federal government enjoyed a warm and supportive relationship with the American business community. Yet the government of the New Era was more than the passive, pliant instrument that critics often described. It attempted to serve in many respects as an active agent of economic change.

### Harding and Coolidge

Nothing seemed more clearly to illustrate the unadventurous character of 1920s politics than the characters of the two men who served as president during most of the decade: Warren G. Harding and Calvin Coolidge.

Harding was elected to the presidency in 1920, having spent many years in public life doing little of note. An undistinguished senator from Ohio, he had received the Republican presidential nomination as a result of an agreement among leaders of his party, who considered him, as one noted, a "good second-rater." Harding appointed capable men to the most important cabinet offices; he attempted to stabilize the nation's troubled foreign policy; and he displayed on occasion a vigorous humanity, as when he pardoned socialist Eugene V. Debs in 1921. But even as he attempted to rise to his office, he seemed baffled by his responsibilities, as if he recognized his own unfitness. "I am a man of limited talents from a small town," he reportedly told friends on one occasion. "I don't seem to grasp that I am President." Harding's intellectual limits were compounded by personal weaknesses: his penchant for gambling, illegal alcohol, and attractive women. Unsurprisingly, perhaps, Harding soon found himself delegating much of his authority to others: to members of his cabinet, to political cronies, to Congress, to party leaders.

Harding realized the importance of capable subordinates in an administration in which the president himself was reluctant to act. But he lacked the strength to abandon the party hacks who had helped create his political success. One of them, Harry Daugherty, the Ohio party boss principally responsible for his meteoric political ascent, he appointed attorney general. Another, New Mexico Senator Albert B. Fall, he made secretary of the interior. Members of the so-called Ohio Gang filled important offices throughout the administration.

Unknown to the public (and perhaps also to Harding), Daugherty, Fall, and others were engaged in fraud and corruption. The most spectacular scandal involved the rich naval oil reserves at Teapot Dome, Wyoming, and Elk Hills, California. At the urging of Fall, Harding transferred control of those reserves from the Navy Department to the Interior Department. Fall then secretly leased them to two wealthy businessmen and received in return nearly half a million dollars in "loans" to ease his private financial troubles. Fall was ultimately convicted of bribery and sentenced to a year in prison; Harry Daugherty barely avoided a similar fate for his part in another scandal.

In the summer of 1923, only months before Senate investigations and press revelations brought the scandals to light, a tired and depressed Harding left Washington for a speaking tour in the West and a visit to Alaska. In Seattle late in July, he suffered severe pain, which his doctors wrongly diagnosed as food poisoning. A few days later, in San Francisco, he died. He had suffered two major heart attacks.

In many ways, Calvin Coolidge, who succeeded Harding in the presidency, was utterly different from his predecessor. Where Harding was genial, garrulous, and debauched, Coolidge was dour, silent, even puritanical. And while Harding was, if not perhaps personally corrupt, then at least tolerant of corruption in others, Coolidge seemed honest beyond reproach. In other ways, however, Harding and Coolidge were similar figures. Both took an essentially passive approach to their office.

Like Harding, Coolidge had risen to the presidency on the basis of few substantive accomplishments. Elected governor of Massachusetts in 1919, he had won national attention with his laconic response to the Boston police strike that year: "There is no right to strike against the public safety." That was enough to make him his party's vice presidential nominee in 1920. Three years later, after Harding's death, he took the oath of office from his father, a justice of the peace, by the light of a kerosene lamp.

If anything, Coolidge was even less active as president than Harding, partly as a result of his conviction that government should interfere as little as possible in the life of the nation. He proposed no significant legislation and took little part in the running of the nation's foreign policy. In 1924, he received his party's presidential nomination virtually unopposed. Running against John W. Davis, he won a comfortable victory: 54 percent of the popular vote and 382 of the 531 electoral votes. Robert La Follette, the candidate of the reincarnated Progressive Party, received 16 percent of the popular vote but carried only his home state of Wisconsin. Coolidge probably could have won renomination and reelection in 1928. Instead, in characteristically laconic fashion, he walked into a press room one day and handed each reporter a slip of paper containing a single sentence: "I do not choose to run for president in 1928."

## Government and Business

The story of Harding and Coolidge themselves, however, is only a part—and by no means the most important part—of the story of their administrations. However passive the New Era presidents may have been, much of the federal government was working effectively and efficiently during the 1920s to adapt public policy to the widely accepted goal of the time: helping business and industry operate with maximum efficiency and productivity. The close relationship between the private sector and the federal government that had been forged during World War I continued. Secretary of the Treasury Andrew Mellon, a wealthy steel and aluminum tycoon, devoted himself to working for substantial reductions in taxes on corporate profits and personal incomes and inheritances. Largely because of his efforts, Congress cut them all by more than half. Mellon also worked closely with President Coolidge after 1924 on a series of measures to trim dramatically the already modest federal budget. The administration even managed to retire half the nation's World War I debt.

The most prominent member of the cabinet was Commerce Secretary Herbert Hoover, who considered himself, and was considered by others, a notable progressive. During his eight years in the Commerce Department, Hoover constantly encouraged voluntary cooperation in the private sector as the best avenue to stability. But the idea of voluntarism did not require that the government remain passive; on the contrary, public institutions, Hoover believed, had a duty to play an active role in creating the new, cooperative order. Above all, Hoover became the champion of the concept of business "associationalism"—a concept that envisioned the creation of national organizations of businessmen in particular industries. Through these trade associations, private entrepreneurs could, Hoover believed, stabilize their industries and promote efficiency in production and marketing.

The probusiness policies of the Republican administrations were not without their critics. In Congress, progressive reformers of the old school continued to criticize the monopolistic practices of big business, to attack

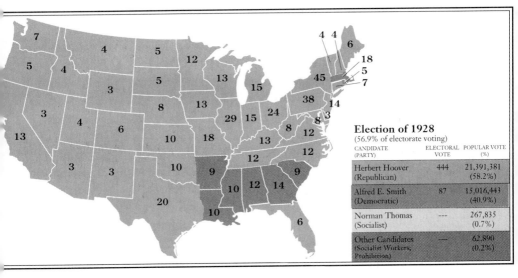

**Election of 1928**
(56.9% of electorate voting)

| CANDIDATE (PARTY) | ELECTORAL VOTE | POPULAR VOTE (%) |
|---|---|---|
| Herbert Hoover (Republican) | 444 | 21,391,381 (58.2%) |
| Alfred E. Smith (Democratic) | 87 | 15,016,443 (40.9%) |
| Norman Thomas (Socialist) | --- | 267,835 (0.7%) |
| Other Candidates (Socialist Workers, Prohibition) | --- | 62,890 (0.2%) |

government's alliance with the corporate community, and to decry social injustices. Occasionally, they were able to mobilize enough support to win congressional approval of progressive legislation, most notably the McNary-Haugen plan for farmers and an ambitious proposal to use federal funds to develop public electric power projects on the Tennessee River at Muscle Shoals. But the progressive reformers lacked the power to override the presidential vetoes that their bills almost always received.

Some progressives derived encouragement from the election of Herbert Hoover—widely regarded as the most progressive member of the Harding and Coolidge administrations—to the presidency in 1928. Hoover easily defeated Al Smith, the Democratic candidate. And he entered office promising bold new efforts to solve the nation's remaining economic problems. But Hoover had few opportunities to prove himself. Less than a year after his inauguration, the nation plunged into the severest and most prolonged economic crisis in its history—a crisis that brought many of the optimistic assumptions of the New Era crashing down and launched the nation into a period of unprecedented social innovation and reform.

# CHAPTER TWENTY-FIVE

# The Great Depression

*The Coming of the Depression*  ⁓  *The American People in Hard Times*
*The Ordeal of Herbert Hoover*

E IN AMERICA TODAY," Herbert Hoover proclaimed in August 1928, not long before his election to the presidency, "are nearer to the final triumph over poverty than ever before in the history of any land. The poorhouse is vanishing from among us." Only fifteen months later, those words would return to haunt him, as the nation plunged into the severest and most prolonged economic depression in its history—a depression that continued in one form or another for a full decade, not only in the United States but throughout much of the world. The Depression was a traumatic experience for individual Americans, who faced unemployment, the loss of land and other property, and in some cases homelessness and starvation. It also placed great strains on the political and social fabric of the nation.

## THE COMING OF THE DEPRESSION

The sudden financial collapse in 1929 came as an especially severe shock because it followed so closely a period in which the New Era seemed to be performing another series of economic miracles—miracles that seemed most clearly evident in the remarkable performance of the stock market.

In February 1928, stock prices began a steady ascent that continued, with only a few temporary lapses, for a year and a half. Between May 1928 and September 1929, the average price of stocks rose over 40 percent. The stocks of the major industrials—the stocks that were used to determine the Dow Jones Industrial Average—doubled in value in that same period. Trading mushroomed from 2 or 3 million shares a day to over 5 million, and at times to as many as 10 or 12 million. There was, in short, a widespread specula-

| TIME LINE | | | |
|---|---|---|---|
| **1929** | **1930** | **1931** | **1932** |
| Stock market crash; Great Depression begins | Hawley-Smoot Tariff | Scottsboro defendants arrested | Glass-Steagall Banking Act |
| | Drought begins in Dust Bowl | | Reconstruction Finance Corporation established |
| Agricultural Marketing Act | | | Bonus Army in Washington |
| | | | Franklin D. Roosevelt elected president |

| **1934** | **1935** | **1936** | **1939** | **1940** |
|---|---|---|---|---|
| Southern Tenant Farmers Union organized | American Communist Party proclaims Popular Front | Mitchell's *Gone with the Wind* | Steinbeck's *The Grapes of Wrath* | Wright's *Native Son* |
| | | | | Hemingway's *For Whom the Bell Tolls* |

tive fever that grew steadily more intense, particularly once brokerage firms began encouraging the mania by offering absurdly easy credit to those buying stocks.

### The Great Crash

In the autumn of 1929, the market began to fall apart. On October 21 and again on October 24, there were alarming declines in stock prices, in both cases followed by a temporary recovery. But on October 29, "Black Tuesday," all efforts to save the market failed. Sixteen million shares of stock were traded; the industrial index dropped 43 points (or nearly 10 percent), wiping out all the gains of the previous year; stocks in many companies became virtually worthless. Within a month stocks had lost half their September value, and despite occasional, short-lived rallies, they continued to decline for several years after that. In July 1932, the industrial index—which had stood at 452 in September 1929—bottomed out at 58. The market did not fully recover for over a decade.

Popular folklore has established the stock market crash as the beginning, and even the cause, of the Great Depression. But although October 1929 might have been the most visible early sign of the crisis, the Depression had earlier beginnings and more important causes.

*Causes of the Depression*

Economists, historians, and others have argued for decades about the causes of the Great Depression. But most agree on several things. They agree, first, that what is remarkable about the crisis is not that it occurred; periodic recessions are a normal feature of modern economies. What is remarkable is that it was so severe and that it lasted so long. The important question, therefore, is not so much why there was a depression but why it was such a bad one. Most observers agree, too, that a number of different factors account for the severity of the crisis, even if there is considerable disagreement about which was the most important.

One of those factors was a lack of diversification in the American economy in the 1920s. Prosperity had depended excessively on a few basic industries, notably construction and automobiles. In the late 1920s, those industries began to decline. Expenditures on construction fell from $11 billion to under $9 billion between 1926 and 1929. Automobile sales fell by more than a third in the first nine months of 1929. Newer industries were emerging to take up the slack—among them petroleum, chemicals, and plastics—but had not yet developed enough strength to compensate for the decline in other sectors.

A second important factor was the maldistribution of purchasing power and, as a result, a weakness in consumer demand. As industrial and agricultural production increased, the proportion of the profits going to farmers, workers, and other potential consumers was too small to create an adequate market for the goods the economy was producing. Even in 1929, after nearly a decade of economic growth, more than half the families in America lived on the edge of or below the minimum subsistence level—too poor to buy the goods the industrial economy was producing.

A third major problem was the credit structure of the economy. Farmers were deeply in debt—their land was mortgaged, and crop prices were too low to allow them to pay off what they owed. Small banks, especially those tied to the agricultural economy, were in constant trouble in the 1920s as their customers defaulted on loans; many of them failed. Large banks were in trouble too. Although most American bankers were very conservative, some of the nation's biggest banks were investing recklessly in the stock market or making unwise loans. When the market crashed and the loans went bad, some banks failed and others made the crisis worse by contracting the already scarce credit and calling in loans that borrowers could not pay.

A fourth factor contributing to the Depression was America's position in international trade. Late in the 1920s, European demand for American goods began to decline. That was partly because European industry and agriculture were becoming more productive and partly because some European nations were having financial difficulties of their own and could not afford to buy goods from overseas. But it was also because the European economy was being destabilized by the international debt structure that had emerged in the aftermath of World War I.

The international debt structure, therefore, was a fifth factor contributing to the Depression. When the war came to an end in 1918, all the European nations that had been allied with the United States owed large sums of money to American banks, sums much too large to be repaid out of their shattered economies. That was one reason why the Allies had insisted (over Woodrow Wilson's objections) on reparation payments from Germany and Austria. Reparations, they believed, would provide them with a way to pay off their own debts. But Germany and Austria were themselves in economic trouble after the war; they were no more able to pay the reparations than the Allies were able to pay their debts.

The American government refused to forgive or reduce the debts. Instead, American banks began making large loans to European governments, which used them to pay off their earlier loans. Thus debts (and reparations) were being paid only by piling up new and greater debts. In the late 1920s, and particularly after the American economy began to weaken in 1929, the European nations found it much more difficult to borrow money from the United States. At the same time, American protective tariffs—many raised to their highest level ever by the Hawley-Smoot Tariff of 1930—were making it difficult for them to sell their goods in American markets. Without any source of foreign exchange with which to repay their loans, they began to default. The collapse of the international credit structure was one of the reasons the Depression spread to Europe (and grew much worse in America) after 1931.

### Progress of the Depression

The stock market crash of 1929 did not so much cause the Depression, then, as help trigger a chain of events that exposed larger weaknesses in the American economy. During the next three years, the crisis grew steadily worse.

The most serious problem at first was the collapse of much of the banking system. Over 9,000 American banks either went bankrupt or closed their doors to avoid bankruptcy between 1930 and 1933. Depositors lost over $2.5 billion in deposits. Partly as a result of these banking closures, the nation's money supply fell, according to some measurements, by more than a third between 1930 and 1933. The declining money supply meant a decline in purchasing power, and thus deflation. Manufacturers and merchants began reducing prices, cutting back on production, and laying off workers. Some economists argue that a severe depression could have been avoided if the Federal Reserve system had acted responsibly. But late in 1931, in a misguided effort to build international confidence in the dollar, it raised interest rates, which contracted the money supply even further and hastened the demise of many banks and corporations.

The collapse was both rapid and devastating. The American gross national product plummeted from over $104 billion in 1929 to $76.4 billion in 1932—a 25 percent decline in three years. In 1929, Americans had spent $16.2 billion to promote capital growth; in 1933, they invested only a third of a billion. The consumer price index declined 25 percent between 1929 and 1933; the wholesale price index, 32 percent. Gross farm income dropped from $12 billion to $5 billion in four years. By 1932, according to the relatively crude estimates of the time, 25 percent of the American work force was unemployed. (Some believe the figure was even higher.) For the rest of the decade, unemployment averaged nearly 20 percent, never dropping

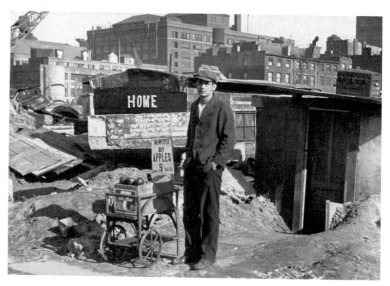

SELLING APPLES, NEW YORK CITY  In the fall of 1931 and again in the fall of 1932, large numbers of unemployed took to selling apples on the streets of major cities and became in the process a popular symbol of economic despair.

below 15 percent. Up to another one-third of the work force was "under-employed"—experiencing major reductions in wages, hours, or both.

## THE AMERICAN PEOPLE IN HARD TIMES

Someone asked the British economist John Maynard Keynes in the 1930s whether he was aware of any historical era comparable to the Great Depression. "Yes," Keynes replied. "It was called the Dark Ages, and it lasted 400 years." The Depression did not last 400 years. It did, however, bring unprecedented despair to the economies of the United States and much of the Western world. And it had far-reaching effects on American society and culture.

### Unemployment and Relief

The suffering extended into every area of society. In the industrial Northeast and Midwest, cities were becoming virtually paralyzed by unemployment. Cleveland, Ohio, for example, had an unemployment rate of 50 percent in 1932; Akron, 60 percent; Toledo, 80 percent. Unemployed workers walked through the streets day after day looking for jobs that did not exist. An increasing number of families were turning to state and local public relief systems, just to be able to eat. But those systems, which in the 1920s had served only a small number of indigents, were totally unequipped to handle the new demands being placed on them. In many cities, therefore, relief simply collapsed. Private charities attempted to supplement the public relief efforts, but the problem was far beyond their capabilities as well. State governments felt pressure to expand their own assistance to the unemployed; but tax revenues were declining along with everything else, and state leaders balked at placing additional strains on already tight budgets.

In rural areas conditions were in many ways worse. Farm income declined by 60 percent between 1929 and 1932. A third of all American farmers lost their land. In addition, a large area of agricultural settlement in the Great Plains was suffering from a catastrophic natural disaster: one of the worst droughts in the history of the nation. Beginning in 1930, the region, which came to be known as the "Dust Bowl" and which stretched north from Texas into the Dakotas, experienced a steady decline in rainfall and an accompanying increase in heat. The drought continued for a decade, turning what had once been fertile farm regions into virtual deserts. It is a measure of how productive American farmers were and how depressed the market for agricultural goods had become that even with these disastrous conditions, the farm economy continued through the 1930s to produce far more than American consumers could afford to buy.

Many farmers, like many urban unemployed, left their homes in search of work. In the South, in particular, many dispossessed farmers—black and white—simply wandered from town to town, hoping to find jobs or hand-outs. Hundreds of thousands of families from the Dust Bowl (often known as "Okies," since many came from Oklahoma) traveled to California and other states, where they found conditions little better than those they had left. Owning no land of their own, many worked as agricultural migrants, traveling from farm to farm picking fruit and other crops at starvation wages.

### African Americans and the Depression

Most African Americans had not shared very much in the prosperity of the previous decade. They now experienced more unemployment, homelessness, malnutrition, and disease than they had in the past, and more than most whites experienced.

As the Depression began, over half of all black Americans still lived in the South. Most were farmers. The collapse of prices for cotton and other staple crops left some with no income at all. Many left the land altogether—either by choice or because they had been evicted by landlords who no longer found the sharecropping system profitable. Some migrated to southern cities. But there, unemployed whites believed they had first claim to what work there was, and some now began to take positions as janitors, street cleaners, and domestic servants, displacing the blacks who formerly occupied those jobs. By 1932, over half the blacks in the South were without employment. And what limited relief there was went almost invariably to whites first.

Unsurprisingly, therefore, many black southerners—perhaps 400,000 in all—left the South in the 1930s and journeyed to the cities of the North. There they generally found less blatant discrimination. But conditions were in most respects little better than those in the South. In New York, black unemployment was nearly 50 percent. In other cities, it was higher. Two million African Americans—half the total black population of the country—were on some form of relief by 1932.

Traditional patterns of segregation and disfranchisement in the South survived the Depression largely unchallenged. But a few particularly notorious examples of racism did attract the attention of the nation. The most celebrated was the Scottsboro case. In March 1931, nine black teenagers were taken off a freight train in northern Alabama (in a small town near Scotts-boro) and arrested for vagrancy and disorder. Later, two white women who had also been riding the train accused them of rape. In fact, there was over-whelming evidence, medical and otherwise, that the women had not been raped at all; they may have made their accusations out of fear of being ar-rested themselves. Nevertheless, an all-white jury in Alabama quickly con-victed all nine of the "Scottsboro boys" (as they were known to both friends and foes) and sentenced eight of them to death.

The Supreme Court overturned the convictions in 1932, and a series of new trials began that gradually attracted national attention. The Interna-tional Labor Defense, an organization associated with the Communist Party, came to the aid of the accused youths and began to publicize the case. The trials continued throughout the 1930s. Although the white southern juries who sat on the case never acquitted any of the defendants, all of the accused eventually gained their freedom—four because the charges were dropped, four because of early paroles, and one because he escaped. The last of the Scottsboro defendants did not leave prison until 1950.

The Depression was a time of important changes in the role and behavior of leading black organizations. The NAACP, for example, began to work diligently to win a position for blacks within the emerging labor movement, supporting the formation of the Congress of Industrial Organizations and helping break down racial barriers within labor unions. Partly as a result of such efforts, more than half a million blacks were able to join labor unions. In the steelworkers union, for example, African Americans constituted about 20 percent of the membership.

### Hispanics and Asians in Depression America

Similar patterns of discrimination confronted many Mexicans and Mexican Americans. The Hispanic population of the United States had been grow-ing steadily since early in the century, largely in California and other areas of the Southwest through massive immigration from Mexico (which was specifically excluded from the immigration restriction laws of the 1920s). Chicanos (as Mexican Americans are sometimes known) filled many of the same menial jobs there that blacks had traditionally filled in other regions. Some farmed small, marginal tracts. Some became agricultural migrants, traveling from region to region harvesting fruit, lettuce, and other crops. Even during the prosperous 1920s, it had been a precarious existence. The Depression made things significantly worse. As in the South, unemployed whites in the Southwest demanded jobs held by Hispanics, jobs that whites had previously considered beneath them. Thus Mexican unemployment rose quickly to levels far higher than those for whites. Some Mexicans were, in effect, forced to leave the country by officials who arbitrarily removed them from relief rolls or simply rounded them up and transported them across the border. Perhaps half a million Chicanos left the United States for Mexico, many involuntarily, in the first years of the Depression.

Those who remained faced persistent discrimination. Most relief programs excluded Mexicans from their rolls or offered them benefits far below those available to whites. Hispanics generally had limited access to American schools. Many hospitals refused them admission. Unlike African Americans, who had established certain educational and social facilities of their own in response to discrimination, Hispanics generally had nowhere to turn. Even many who possessed American citizenship found themselves treated like foreigners.

There were, occasionally, signs of organized resistance by Mexican Americans themselves, most notably in California, where some formed a union of migrant farmworkers. But harsh repression by local growers and the public authorities allied with them prevented such organizations from having much impact. As a result, many Hispanics, like many African-American farmworkers, began to migrate to cities such as Los Angeles, where they lived in a poverty comparable to that of urban blacks in the South and Northeast.

For Asian Americans, too, the Depression reinforced longstanding patterns of discrimination and economic marginalization. In California, where the largest Japanese-American and Chinese-American populations were, even educated Asians had always found it difficult, if not impossible, to move into mainstream professions. Japanese-American college graduates often found themselves working in family fruit stands; 20 percent of all people of Japanese descent in Los Angeles worked at such stands at the end of the 1930s. For those who found jobs (usually poorly paid) in the industrial or service economy, employment was precarious; like blacks and Hispanics, they often lost jobs to white Americans desperate for work—jobs that a few years earlier the whites would not have considered. Japanese farmworkers, like Chicano farmworkers, suffered from the increasing competition for even these low-paying jobs from white migrants from the Great Plains.

In California, younger Japanese Americans tried to challenge the obstacles facing them through politics. They organized Japanese American Democratic Clubs in several cities, which worked for, among other things, laws protecting racial and ethnic minorities from discrimination. At the same time, some Japanese-American businessmen and professionals tried to overcome obstacles by encouraging members of their communities to become more assimilated, more "American." They formed the Japanese American Citizens League in 1930 to promote their goals. By 1940, it had nearly 6,000 members.

Chinese Americans fared no better. The overwhelming majority worked, as they had for many years, in Chinese-owned laundries and restaurants. Those who moved outside the Asian community could rarely find jobs above the entry level. Chinese women, for example, might find work as stock girls in department stores but almost never as salesclerks. Educated Chinese men and women could hope for virtually no professional opportunities outside the world of the Chinatowns.

### Women and Families in the Great Depression

The economic crisis served in many ways to strengthen the widespread belief that a woman's proper place was in the home. Most men and many women believed that with employment so scarce, what work there was should go to men. There was a particularly strong belief that no woman whose husband was employed should accept a job. Indeed, from 1932 until 1937, it was illegal for more than one member of a family to hold a federal civil service job.

But the widespread assumption that married women, at least, should not work outside the home did not stop them from doing so. Both single and married women worked in the 1930s, despite public condemnation of the practice, because they or their families needed the money. In fact, the largest new group of female workers consisted of precisely those people who, according to popular attitudes, were supposed to be leaving the labor market: wives and mothers. By the end of the Depression, 25 percent more women were working than had been doing so at the beginning. This occurred despite considerable obstacles. Professional opportunities for women declined because unemployed men began moving into professions such as teaching and social work that had previously been considered women's fields. Female industrial workers were more likely to be laid off or to experience wage reductions than their male counterparts. But white women also had certain advantages in the workplace. The nonprofessional jobs that women traditionally held—salesclerks, stenographers, and other service positions—were less likely to disappear than the predominantly male jobs in heavy industry.

Black women enjoyed few such advantages. In the South, in particular, they suffered massive unemployment because of a great reduction of domestic service jobs. As many as half of all black working women lost their jobs in the 1930s. Even so, at the end of the 1930s, 38 percent of black women were employed, as compared with 24 percent of white women. That was because black women—both married and unmarried—had always been more likely to work than white women, less out of preference than out of economic necessity.

For American feminists, the Depression years were, on the whole, a time of frustration. Although economic pressures pushed more women into the work force, those same pressures helped to erode the frail support feminists had won in the 1920s for the idea of women becoming economically and professionally independent. In the difficult years of the 1930s, such aspirations seemed to many to be less important than dealing with economic hardship. By the end of the 1930s, American feminism had reached its lowest ebb in nearly a century.

The economic hardships of the Depression years placed great strains on American families. Middle-class families that had become accustomed in the 1920s to a steadily increasing standard of living now found themselves plunged suddenly into uncertainty, because of unemployment or the reduction of incomes among those who remained employed. Some working-class families too had achieved a precarious prosperity in the 1920s and saw their gains disappear in the 1930s.

Such circumstances caused many families to change the way they lived. Some women returned to sewing clothes for themselves and their families and to preserving their own food. Others engaged in home businesses such as taking in laundry or boarders. Many households expanded to take in relatives (grandparents, grandchildren, and others) who needed assistance.

But the Depression also worked to erode the strength of many family units. There was a decline in the divorce rate, but largely because divorce was now too expensive for some. More common was the informal breakup of families, particularly the desertion of families by unemployed men trying to escape the humiliation of being unable to earn a living. The marriage rate and the birth rate both declined for the first time since the early nineteenth century.

### Values and Culture

Prosperity and industrial growth had done much to shape American values in the 1920s. Mainstream culture, at least, had celebrated affluence and consumerism and had stressed the importance of personal gratification through both. Many Americans assumed, therefore, that the experience of hard times would have profound effects on the nation's social values. In general, however, American social values seemed to change relatively little in response to the Depression. Rather, many people responded to hard times by redoubling their commitment to familiar ideas and goals.

No assumption would seem to have been more vulnerable to erosion during the Depression than the belief that the individual was in control of his or her own fate, that anyone displaying sufficient talent and industry could become a success. And in some respects, the economic crisis did work to undermine the traditional "success ethic" in America. Many people began to look to government for assistance; many learned to blame corporate moguls, international bankers, "economic royalists," and others for their distress. Yet the Depression did not destroy the success ethic.

The survival of the ideals of work and individual advancement was evident in many ways, not least in the reactions of those most traumatized by the Depression: conscientious working people who suddenly found themselves without employment. Some expressed anger and struck out at the economic system. Many, however, seemed to blame themselves. That was one reason why the effects of the Depression were sometimes hard to see: many of the unemployed tended to hide themselves, unwilling to display to the world what they considered their own personal failure. At the same time, millions responded eagerly to reassurances that they could, through their own efforts, restore themselves to prosperity and success. Dale Carnegie's *How to Win Friends and Influence People* (1936), a self-help manual preaching individual initiative, was one of the best-selling books of the decade.

Not all Americans, of course, responded to the crisis of the Depression so passively. Among the many people who saw the hard times as evidence of deep-rooted social injustice were many artists and intellectuals. There was, for example, a broad effort to dramatize the problem of rural poverty and to use it as an indictment of the failures of the economic system. Among those engaged in this effort were a group of documentary photographers, many of them employed by the federal Farm Security Administration in the late 1930s, who traveled through the South recording the nature of agricultural life. Men such as Roy Stryker, Walker Evans, Arthur Rothstein, and Ben Shahn and women such as Margaret Bourke-White and Dorothea Lange produced memorable studies of farm families and their surroundings, studies designed to show the savage impact of a hostile environment on its victims.

Many writers, similarly, turned away from the personal concerns of the 1920s and devoted themselves to exposés of social injustice. Erskine Caldwell's *Tobacco Road* (1932), which later became a long-running play, was an exposé of poverty in the rural South. James Agee's *Let Us Now Praise Famous*

AUCTIONING OFF A FARM  Farm auctions such as this one, photographed in 1940 near Hastings, Nebraska, by the Farm Security Administration photographer Arthur Rothstein, were common sights in rural America during the Great Depression. Even after New Deal farm programs improved the fortunes of the agricultural economy as a whole, many small farmers continued to face debts they could not pay and hence foreclosure on their lands.

*Men* (1941), with photographs by Walker Evans, was a careful, nonjudgmental description of the lives of three poor rural families in the South. Richard Wright, a major African-American novelist, exposed the plight of residents of the urban ghetto in *Native Son* (1940). John Steinbeck's *The Grapes of Wrath* (1939) portrayed the trials of a migrant family in California, concluding with an open call for collective social action against injustice.

But the cultural products of the 1930s that attracted the widest popular audiences were those that diverted attention away from the Depression. The two most powerful instruments of popular culture in the 1930s—radio and the movies—provided mostly light and diverting entertainment. Although radio stations occasionally carried socially and politically provocative programs, the staple of broadcasting was escapism: comedies such as *Amos 'n Andy*, adventures such as *Superman*, *Dick Tracy*, and *The Lone Ranger*, and other entertainment programs. Hollywood continued to exercise tight control over its products through its resilient censor Will Hays, who ensured that most movies carried only safe, conventional messages. A few films, such as the adaptation of *The Grapes of Wrath* (1940), did explore political themes. Director Frank Capra provided a muted social message in several of his comedies—*Mr. Deeds Goes to Town* (1936), *Mr. Smith Goes to Washington* (1939), and *Meet John Doe* (1941)—which celebrated the virtues of the small town and the decency of the common people in contrast to the selfish, corrupt values of the city and the urban rich. Gangster films and westerns celebrated violence and implicitly glamorized resistance to authority. More often, however, the commercial films of the 1930s were deliberately and explicitly escapist: lavish musicals and "wacky" comedies designed to divert audiences from their troubles and, very often, satisfy their fantasies about quick and easy wealth.

### The Allure of the Left

For some Americans—intellectuals, artists, workers, African Americans, and others who became disenchanted for various reasons with the prevailing values of American life—the Depression produced a commitment, for a time at least, to radical politics.

The importance of the 1936 Spanish Civil War to many American intellectuals was a good example of how the left produced a sense of commitment and purpose in individual lives. The battle against the Spanish fascists of Francisco Franco (who was receiving support from Hitler and Mussolini) attracted a substantial group of young Americans, more than 3,000 in all, who formed the "Abraham Lincoln brigade" and traveled to Spain to join in the fight. About a third of its members died in combat, but those who survived remembered the experience with pride, as one of the great moments of their lives.

Instrumental in creating the Lincoln brigade, and directing many of its activities, was the American Communist Party. Its membership reached perhaps 100,000 at its peak in the mid-1930s. One reason for its growth was the party's shift in tactics beginning in 1935, when it dropped its insistence on working completely apart from other organizations and began to advocate a democratic alliance of all antifascist groups in the United States, a "Popular Front." Communists began to praise Franklin Roosevelt and John L. Lewis, a powerful (and strongly anticommunist) labor leader. The party adopted the slogan "Communism is twentieth-century Americanism."

The American Communist Party was active in organizing the unemployed in the early 1930s and staged a hunger march in Washington, D.C., in 1931. Party members were among the most effective union organizers in some industries. And the party was one of the few political organizations to take a firm stand in favor of racial justice; its active defense of the Scottsboro defendants was but one example of its efforts to ally itself with the aspirations of African Americans. It also helped organize a union of black sharecroppers in Alabama, which resisted—in several instances violently—efforts of white landowners and authorities to displace its members from their farms.

But despite its progressive achievements and its efforts to appear a patriotic organization, the American Communist Party was always under the close and rigid supervision of the Soviet Union. Its leaders took their orders from the Comintern in Moscow. Most members obediently followed the "party line." The subordination of the party leadership to the Soviet Union was most clearly demonstrated in 1939, when Stalin signed a nonaggression pact with Nazi Germany. Moscow then sent orders to the American Communist Party to abandon the Popular Front idea and return to its old stance of harsh criticism of American liberals; and the leaders in the United States immediately obeyed—although thousands of disillusioned members left the party as a result.

The Socialist Party of America, now under the leadership of Norman Thomas, also cited the economic crisis as evidence of the failure of capitalism and sought vigorously to win public support for its own political program. Among other things, it attempted to mobilize support among the rural poor. The Southern Tenant Farmers Union (STFU), supported by the party, attempted to create a biracial coalition of sharecroppers, tenant farmers, and others to demand economic reform. Neither the STFU nor the party itself, however, made any real progress toward establishing socialism as a major force in American politics. By 1936, in fact, membership in the Socialist Party had fallen below 20,000.

## THE ORDEAL OF HERBERT HOOVER

Herbert Hoover began his presidency in March 1929 believing, like most Americans, that the nation faced a bright and prosperous future. For the first six months of his administration, he attempted to expand the policies he had advocated during his eight years as secretary of commerce, policies that would, he believed, complete a stable system of cooperative individualism and sustain a successful economy. The economic crisis that began before the year was out forced the president to deal with a new set of problems, but for most of the rest of his term, he continued to rely on the principles that had always governed his public life.

*The Hoover Program*

Hoover's first response to the Depression was to attempt to restore public confidence in the economy. "The fundamental business of this country, that is, production and distribution of commodities," he said in 1930, "is on a sound and prosperous basis." He then summoned leaders of business, labor, and agriculture to the White House and urged them to adopt a program of voluntary cooperation for recovery. He implored businessmen not to cut production or lay off workers; he talked labor leaders into forgoing demands for higher wages or better hours. But by mid-1931, economic conditions had deteriorated so much that the structure of voluntary cooperation he had erected collapsed. Frightened industrialists began cutting production, laying off workers, and slashing wages.

Hoover also attempted to use government spending as a tool for fighting the Depression. The president proposed to Congress an increase of $423 million—a significant sum by the standards of the time—in federal public works programs, and he exhorted state and local governments to fund public construction. But the spending was not nearly enough in the face of such devastating problems. And when economic conditions worsened, he became less willing to increase spending, worrying instead about keeping the budget balanced. In 1932, at the depth of the Depression, he proposed a tax increase to help the government avoid a deficit.

Even before the stock market crash, Hoover had begun to construct a program to assist the troubled agricultural economy. In April 1929, he proposed the Agricultural Marketing Act, which established the first major government program to help farmers maintain prices. A federally sponsored Farm Board would make loans to national marketing cooperatives or establish corporations to buy surpluses and thus raise prices. At the same time, Hoover attempted to protect American farmers from international competition by raising agricultural tariffs. The Hawley-Smoot Tariff of 1930 contained increased protection on seventy-five farm products.

Neither the Agricultural Marketing Act nor the Hawley-Smoot Tariff ultimately helped American farmers significantly. The Marketing Act relied on voluntary cooperation among farmers and gave the government no authority to do what the agricultural economy most badly needed: limit production. Prices continued to fall despite its efforts. The Hawley-Smoot Tariff provoked foreign governments to enact trade restrictions of their own in reprisal, further diminishing the market for American agricultural goods.

By the spring of 1931, Herbert Hoover's political position had deteriorated considerably. In the 1930 congressional elections, Democrats won control of the House and made substantial inroads in the Senate by promising increased government assistance to the economy. Many Americans held the president personally to blame for the crisis and began calling the shantytowns that unemployed people established on the outskirts of cities "Hoovervilles." Democrats urged the president to support more vigorous programs of relief and public spending. Hoover, instead, seized on a slight improvement in economic conditions early in 1931 as proof that his policies were working.

The international financial panic of the spring of 1931 destroyed the illusion that the economic crisis was coming to an end. Throughout the 1920s, European nations had depended on loans from American banks to allow them to make payments on their debts. After 1929, when they could no longer get such loans, the financial fabric of several European nations began to unravel. In May 1931, the largest bank in Austria collapsed. Over the next several months, panic gripped the financial institutions of neighboring countries. The American economy rapidly declined to new lows.

By the time Congress convened in December 1931, conditions had grown so desperate that Hoover supported a series of measures designed to keep endangered banks afloat and protect homeowners from foreclosure on their mortgages. More important was a bill passed in January 1932 establishing the Reconstruction Finance Corporation (RFC), a government agency whose purpose was to provide federal loans to troubled banks, railroads, and other businesses. It even made funds available to local governments to support public works projects and assist relief efforts. Unlike some earlier Hoover programs, it operated on a large scale. In 1932, the RFC had a budget of $1.5 billion for public works alone.

Nevertheless, the new agency failed to deal directly or forcefully enough with the real problems of the economy to produce any significant recovery. The RFC lent funds only to financial institutions with sufficient collateral, and so much of its money went to large banks and corporations. At Hoover's insistence, it helped finance only those public works projects that promised ultimately to pay for themselves (toll bridges, public housing, and others). Above all, the RFC did not have enough money to make any real impact on the Depression, and it did not even spend all the money it had. Of the $300 million available to support local relief efforts, the RFC lent out only $30 million in 1932. Of the $1.5 billion public works budget, it released only about 20 percent.

## Popular Protest

For the first several years of the Depression, most Americans were either too stunned or too confused to raise any effective protest. By the middle of 1932, however, dissident voices began to be heard.

In the summer of 1932, a group of unhappy farm owners gathered in Des Moines, Iowa, to establish a new organization: the Farmers' Holiday Association, which endorsed the withholding of farm products from the market—in effect a farmers' strike. The strike began in August in western Iowa, spread briefly to a few neighboring areas, and succeeded in blockading several markets, but in the end it dissolved in failure. The scope of the effort was too modest to affect farm prices, and many farmers in the region refused to cooperate in any case. Nevertheless, the uprising created considerable consternation in state governments in the farm belt and even more in Washington, where the president and much of Congress were facing a national election.

A more celebrated protest movement emerged from American veterans. In 1924, Congress had approved the payment of a $1,000 bonus to all those who had served in World War I, the money to be paid beginning in 1945.

THE BONUS MARCH The 1932 march on Washington by the so-called Bonus Army ended in violent disarray. But it began in high spirits and something close to military precision—as this march along Independence Avenue suggests.

By 1932, however, many veterans were demanding that the bonus be paid immediately. Hoover, concerned about balancing the budget, rejected their appeal. In June, more than 20,000 veterans, members of the self-proclaimed Bonus Expeditionary Force, or "Bonus Army," marched into Washington, built crude camps around the city, and promised to stay until Congress approved legislation to pay the bonus. Some of the veterans departed in July, after Congress had voted down their proposal. Many, however, remained where they were.

Their continued presence in Washington was an embarrassment to Herbert Hoover. Finally, in mid-July, he ordered police to clear the marchers out of several abandoned federal buildings in which they had been staying. A few marchers threw rocks at the police, and someone opened fire; two veterans fell dead. Hoover called the incident evidence of violence and radicalism. He ordered the United States Army to assist the police in clearing out the buildings.

General Douglas MacArthur, the army chief of staff, carried out the mission himself (with the assistance of his aide, Dwight D. Eisenhower) and greatly exceeded the president's orders. He led the Third Cavalry (under the command of George S. Patton), two infantry regiments, a machine-gun detachment, and six tanks down Pennsylvania Avenue in pursuit of the Bonus Army. The veterans fled in terror. MacArthur followed them across the Anacostia River, where he ordered the soldiers to burn their tent city to the ground. More than 100 marchers were injured. One baby died.

The incident served as perhaps the final blow to Hoover's already battered political standing. Hoover's own cold and gloomy personality reinforced the public image of him as aloof and unsympathetic to distressed people. The Great Engineer, the personification of the optimistic days of the 1920s, had become a symbol of the nation's failure to deal effectively with its startling reversal of fortune.

### The Election of 1932

As the 1932 presidential election approached, few people doubted the outcome. The Republican Party dutifully renominated Herbert Hoover for a second term in office, but the gloomy atmosphere of the convention made it clear that few delegates believed he could win. The Democrats, in the meantime, gathered jubilantly in Chicago to nominate the governor of New York, Franklin Delano Roosevelt.

Roosevelt had been a well-known figure in the party for many years already. A Hudson Valley aristocrat, a distant cousin of Theodore Roosevelt

ROOSEVELT AND SMITH Franklin Roosevelt, the 1932
Democratic presidential nominee, and Al Smith, the 1928
candidate, appear together at a rally for Roosevelt at the
Brooklyn Academy of Music in the fall of 1932. The two
men had once been close political allies; but by 1932, they
were already at odds. Not long after Roosevelt became
president, Smith turned against him publicly and remained
an outspoken critic.

(a connection strengthened by his marriage in 1904 to the president's niece,
Eleanor), and a handsome, charming young man, he progressed rapidly: from
a seat in the New York State legislature to a position as assistant secretary
of the navy under Woodrow Wilson during World War I to his party's vice
presidential nomination in 1920 on the ill-fated ticket with James M. Cox.
Less than a year later, he was stricken with polio. Although he never regained
use of his legs (and could walk only by using crutches and braces), he built
up sufficient physical strength to return to politics in 1928. When Al Smith
received the Democratic nomination for president that year, Roosevelt was
elected to succeed him as governor. In 1930, he easily won reelection.

Roosevelt worked no miracles in New York, but he did initiate enough

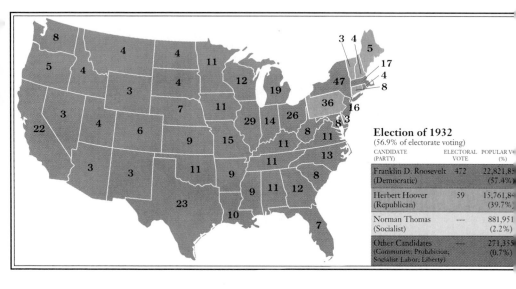

**Election of 1932**

(56.9% of electorate voting)

| CANDIDATE (PARTY) | ELECTORAL VOTE | POPULAR VOTE (%) |
|---|---|---|
| Franklin D. Roosevelt (Democratic) | 472 | 22,821,85 (57.4%) |
| Herbert Hoover (Republican) | 59 | 15,761,84 (39.7%) |
| Norman Thomas (Socialist) | --- | 881,951 (2.2%) |
| Other Candidates (Communist; Prohibition; Socialist Labor; Liberty) | --- | 271,355 (0.7%) |

positive programs of government assistance to be able to present himself as a more energetic and imaginative leader than Hoover. In national politics, he avoided such divisive cultural issues as religion and prohibition and emphasized the economic grievances that most Democrats shared. He was able as a result to assemble a broad coalition within the party and win his party's nomination. In a dramatic break with tradition, he flew to Chicago to address the convention in person and accept the nomination.

In the course of his acceptance speech, Roosevelt aroused the delegates with his ringing promise: "I pledge you, I pledge myself, to a new deal for the American people," giving his future program a name that would long endure. Neither then nor in the subsequent campaign did Roosevelt give much indication of what that program would be. But Herbert Hoover's unpopularity virtually ensured Roosevelt's election.

In November, to the surprise of no one, Roosevelt won by a landslide. He received 57.4 percent of the popular vote to Hoover's 39.7. In the electoral college, the result was even more overwhelming. Hoover carried Pennsylvania, Connecticut, Vermont, New Hampshire, and Maine. Roosevelt won everything else. Democrats won majorities in both houses of Congress. It was a broad and convincing mandate, but it was not yet clear what Roosevelt intended to do with it.

### The "Interregnum"

The period between the election and the inauguration (which in the early 1930s lasted more than four months) was a season of growing economic crisis. Presidents-elect traditionally do not involve themselves directly in government. But in a series of brittle exchanges with Roosevelt in the months following the election, Hoover tried to exact from the president-elect a pledge to maintain policies of economic orthodoxy. Roosevelt genially refused.

In February, only a month before the inauguration, a new crisis developed when the collapse of the American banking system suddenly and rapidly accelerated. Public confidence in the banks was ebbing; depositors were withdrawing their money in panic; and one bank after another was closing its doors and declaring bankruptcy. In mid-February, the governor of Michigan, one of the states hardest hit by the panic, ordered all banks temporarily closed. Other states soon followed, and by the end of the month banking activity was restricted drastically in every state but one. Hoover again asked Roosevelt to give prompt public assurances that there would be no tinkering with the currency, no heavy borrowing, no unbalancing of the budget. Roosevelt again refused.

March 4, 1933, was, therefore, a day of both economic crisis and considerable personal bitterness. On that morning, Herbert Hoover, convinced that the United States was headed for disaster, rode glumly down Pennsylvania Avenue with a beaming, buoyant Franklin Roosevelt, who would shortly be sworn in as the thirty-second president of the United States.

# CHAPTER TWENTY-SIX

# The New Deal

*Launching the New Deal* ∼ *The New Deal in Transition*
*The New Deal in Disarray* ∼ *Limits and Legacies of the New Deal*

RANKLIN ROOSEVELT SERVED longer as president than anyone else before or since, and during his twelve years in office he became more central to the life of the nation than any chief executive had ever been. Most important, his administration constructed a series of programs that permanently altered the federal government and its relationship to society.

By the end of the 1930s, the New Deal (as the Roosevelt administration was called) had created many of the broad outlines of the political world we know today. It had constructed the beginnings of a modern welfare system. It had extended federal regulation over new areas of the economy. It had presided over the birth of the modern labor movement. It had made the government a major force in the agricultural economy. It had created a powerful coalition within the Democratic Party that would dominate American politics for most of the next thirty years. And it had produced the beginnings of a new liberal ideology that would govern reform efforts for several decades after the war. One thing the New Deal had not done, however, was end the Great Depression. It helped stabilize the economy in 1933, and there was a limited, if erratic, recovery after that. But by the end of 1939, many of the basic problems of the Depression remained unsolved.

## LAUNCHING THE NEW DEAL

Roosevelt's first task upon taking office was to alleviate the panic that was threatening to create chaos in the financial system. He did so in part by force of personality and in part by constructing very rapidly an ambitious and diverse program of legislation.

## TIME LINE

| 1933 | 1934 | 1935 |
|---|---|---|
| "First New Deal" legislation | American Liberty League founded | Supreme Court invalidates NRA |
| Prohibition ends | Long's Share-Our-Wealth Society established | "Second New Deal" legislation |
| | | Lewis breaks with AFL |

| 1936 | 1937 | 1938 | 1939 |
|---|---|---|---|
| Supreme Court invalidates Agricultural Adjustment Act | Roosevelt's "court-packing" plan | Fair Labor Standards Act | Marian Anderson sings at Lincoln Memorial |
| CIO established | Supreme Court invalidates Wagner Act | | |
| Roosevelt reelected | | | |
| Sit-down strikes | Severe recession | | |

## *Restoring Confidence*

Much of Roosevelt's early success was a result of his ebullient personality. He was the first president to make regular use of the radio; and his friendly "fireside chats," during which he explained his programs and plans to the people, helped build public confidence in the administration. Roosevelt held frequent informal press conferences and won both the respect and the friendship of most reporters.

But Roosevelt could not rely on image alone. On March 6, two days after taking office, he issued a proclamation closing all American banks for four days until Congress could meet in special session to consider banking reform legislation. So great was the panic about bank failures that the "bank holiday," as the president euphemistically described it, created a general sense of relief and hope.

Three days later, Roosevelt sent to Congress the Emergency Banking Act, a generally conservative bill (much of it drafted by holdovers from the Hoover administration) designed primarily to protect the larger banks from being dragged down by the weakness of smaller ones. The bill provided for Treasury Department inspection of all banks before they would be allowed to reopen, for federal assistance to some troubled institutions, and for a thorough reorganization of those banks in the greatest difficulty. A confused and frightened Congress passed the bill within a few hours of its introduction. Whatever else the new law accomplished, it helped dispel the panic. Three-quarters of the banks in the Federal Reserve system reopened within the next

THE ROOSEVELT SMILE  The battered hat, the uptilted cigarette holder, the jaunty smile—all were hallmarks of Franklin Roosevelt's ebullient public personality. In part, at least, the president's hearty optimism was a deliberate pose, adopted to distract attention from the paralysis that had denied him the use of his legs since 1921.

three days, and $1 billion in hoarded currency and gold flowed back into them within a month. The immediate banking crisis was over.

On the morning after passage of the Emergency Banking Act, Roosevelt sent to Congress another measure—the Economy Act—designed to convince the public (and especially the business community) that the federal government was in safe, responsible hands. The act proposed to balance the federal budget by cutting the salaries of government employees and reducing pensions to veterans by as much as 15 percent. Otherwise, the president warned, the nation faced a $1 billion deficit. Like the banking bill, this one passed through Congress almost instantly—despite heated protests from some congressional progressives. Later that spring, Roosevelt signed the Glass-Steagall Act of June 1933, which gave the government authority to curb irresponsible speculation by banks. More important, perhaps, it established the Federal Deposit Insurance Corporation, which guaranteed all bank deposits up to $2,500. In other words, even if a bank should fail, small depositors would be able to recover their money. (Later, in 1935, Congress passed a major banking act that transferred much of the authority once wielded by the regional Federal Reserve banks to the Federal Reserve Board in Washington.)

To restore confidence in the stock market, Congress passed the so-called Truth in Securities Act of 1933, requiring corporations issuing new securities to provide full and accurate information about them to the public. Another act, of June 1934, established the Securities and Exchange Commission (SEC) to police the stock market.

Roosevelt also moved in his first days in office to put to rest one of the divisive issues of the 1920s. He supported and then signed a bill to legalize the manufacture and sale of beer with a 3.2 percent alcohol content—an interim measure pending the repeal of prohibition, for which a constitutional amendment (the Twenty-first) was already in process. The amendment was ratified later in 1933.

### Agricultural Adjustment

These initial actions were largely stopgaps, to buy time for more comprehensive programs. The first such program was the Agricultural Adjustment Act, which Congress passed in May 1933. Its most important feature was its provision for reducing crop production to end agricultural surpluses and halt the downward spiral of farm prices.

Under the "domestic allotment" system of the act, producers of seven basic commodities (wheat, cotton, corn, hogs, rice, tobacco, and dairy products) would decide on production limits for their crops. The government, through the Agricultural Adjustment Administration (AAA), would then tell individual farmers how much they should produce and would pay them subsidies for leaving some of their land idle. A tax on food processing (for example, the milling of wheat) would provide the funds for the new payments. Farm prices were to be subsidized up to the point of parity.

The AAA helped bring about a rise in prices for farm commodities in the years after 1933. Gross farm income increased by half in the first three years of the New Deal, and the agricultural economy as a whole emerged from the 1930s much more stable and prosperous than it had been in many years. The AAA did, however, favor larger farmers over smaller ones, particularly since local administration of its programs often fell into the hands of the most powerful producers in a community. By distributing payments to landowners, not those who worked the land, the government did little to discourage planters who were reducing their acreage from evicting tenants and sharecroppers and firing field hands.

In January 1936, the Supreme Court struck down the crucial provisions of the Agricultural Adjustment Act, arguing that the government had no constitutional authority to require farmers to limit production. But within a few weeks the administration had secured passage of new legislation (the Soil Conservation and Domestic Allotment Act), which permitted the government to pay farmers to reduce production so as to "conserve soil," prevent erosion, and accomplish other secondary goals. The Court did not interfere with the new laws.

The new legislation also attempted to correct one of the injustices of the original act: its failure to protect sharecroppers and tenant farmers. It required landlords to share the payments they received for cutting back production with those who worked their land. (The new requirements were, however, largely evaded.) The administration launched other efforts to assist poor farmers as well. The Resettlement Administration, established in 1935, and its successor, the Farm Security Administration, created in 1937, provided loans to help farmers cultivating submarginal soil to relocate on better lands. But the programs never moved more than a few thousand farmers. More effective was the Rural Electrification Administration, created in 1935, which worked to make electric power available for the first time to thousands of farmers through utility cooperatives.

*Industrial Recovery*

The Roosevelt administration considered rescuing the industrial economy from the spiraling deflation of the early 1930s at least as important as rescuing agriculture. Ever since 1931, leaders of the United States Chamber of Commerce and many others had been urging the government to adopt an antideflation scheme that would permit trade associations to cooperate in stabilizing prices within their industries. Existing antitrust laws clearly forbade such practices, and Herbert Hoover had refused to endorse suspension of the laws. The Roosevelt administration was more receptive. In exchange for relaxing antitrust provisions, however, New Dealers insisted on other provisions. Businesspeople would have to make important concessions to labor—recognize the workers' right to bargain collectively through unions—to ensure that the incomes of workers would rise along with prices. And to help create jobs and increase consumer buying power, the administration

THE BLUE EAGLE  The leaders of the National Recovery Administration, one of
the first great New Deal experiments, believed that public support for the
project was as important as the particular policies it pursued. As a result, they
encouraged even the smallest businesses to sign an NRA "code" and to display
the agency's symbol—a blue eagle above the phrase "We Do Our Part"—in
their windows. The owners of this tailor shop proudly complied.

added a major program of public works spending. The result of these and
many other impulses was the National Industrial Recovery Act, which Congress passed in June 1933.

At first, the new program appeared to work miracles. At its center was
a new federal agency, the National Recovery Administration (NRA), under
the direction of the flamboyant and energetic Hugh S. Johnson. Johnson
called on every business establishment in the nation to accept a temporary
"blanket code": a minimum wage of between 30 and 40 cents an hour, a maximum workweek of thirty-five to forty hours, and the abolition of child
labor. Adherence to the code, he claimed, would raise consumer purchasing
power and increase employment. At the same time, Johnson negotiated another, more specific set of codes with leaders of the nation's major industries. These industrial codes set floors below which no company would lower
prices or wages in its search for a competitive advantage, and they included

provisions for maintaining employment and production. He quickly won agreements from almost every major industry in the country.

From the beginning, however, the NRA encountered serious difficulties. The codes themselves were hastily and often poorly written. Administering them was beyond the capacities of federal officials with no prior experience in running so vast a program. Large producers consistently dominated the code-writing process and ensured that the new regulations would work to their advantage and to the disadvantage of smaller firms. And the codes at times did more than simply set floors under prices; they actively and artificially raised them—sometimes to levels higher than the market could sustain.

Other NRA goals did not progress as quickly as the efforts to raise prices. Section 7(a) of the National Industrial Recovery Act promised workers the right to form unions and engage in collective bargaining and encouraged many workers to join unions for the first time. But Section 7(a) contained no enforcement mechanisms. Hence recognition of unions by employers (and thus the significant wage increases the unions were committed to winning) did not follow. The Public Works Administration (PWA), established to administer the National Industrial Recovery Act's spending programs, only gradually allowed the $3.3 billion in public works funds to trickle out. Not until 1938 was the PWA budget pumping an appreciable amount of money into the economy.

Perhaps the clearest evidence of the NRA's failure was that industrial production actually declined in the months after the agency's establishment—from an index of 101 in July 1933 to 71 in November—despite the rise in prices that the codes had helped to create. By the spring of 1934, the NRA was besieged by criticism, and businessmen were flaunting many of its provisions. That fall, Roosevelt pressured Johnson to resign and established a new board of directors to oversee the NRA. Then in 1935, the Supreme Court intervened.

The constitutional basis for the NRA had been Congress's power under the Constitution to regulate interstate commerce, a power the administration had interpreted very broadly. In 1935, a case came before the Court involving alleged NRA code violations by the Schechter brothers, who operated a wholesale poultry business confined to Brooklyn, New York. The Court ruled unanimously that the Schechters were not engaged in interstate commerce and, further, that Congress had unconstitutionally delegated legislative power to the president to draft the NRA codes. The justices struck down the legislation establishing the agency. Roosevelt denounced the justices for their "horse-and-buggy" interpretation of the interstate commerce clause. He was rightly concerned, for the reasoning in the Schechter case threatened many other New Deal programs as well. But the Court's destruction of the NRA itself gave the New Deal a convenient excuse for ending a failed experiment.

## Regional Planning

The AAA and the NRA largely reflected the beliefs of New Dealers who favored economic planning but wanted private interests (farmers or business leaders) to dominate the planning process. Other reformers believed that the government itself should be the chief planning agent in the economy. Their most conspicuous success, and one of the most celebrated accomplishments of the New Deal, was an unprecedented experiment in regional planning: the Tennessee Valley Authority (TVA).

The TVA had its roots in a political controversy of the 1920s. Progressive reformers had agitated for years for public development of the nation's water resources as a source of cheap electric power. In particular, they had urged completion of a great dam at Muscle Shoals on the Tennessee River in Alabama—a dam begun during World War I but left unfinished when the war ended. But opposition from the utilities companies had been too powerful to overcome.

In 1932, however, one of the great utility empires—that of the electricity magnate Samuel Insull—collapsed spectacularly, amid widely publicized exposés of corruption. Hostility to the utilities soon grew so intense that the companies were no longer able to block the public power movement. The result was legislation supported by the president and enacted by Congress in May 1933 creating the Tennessee Valley Authority. The TVA was authorized not only to complete the dam at Muscle Shoals and build others in the region, and not only to generate and sell electricity from them to the public at reasonable rates. It was also intended to be an agent for a comprehensive redevelopment of the entire region: for stopping the disastrous flooding that had plagued the Tennessee Valley for centuries, for encouraging the development of local industries, for supervising a substantial program of reforestation, and for helping farmers improve productivity.

Opposition by conservatives within the administration ultimately blocked many of the ambitious social planning projects proposed by the more visionary TVA administrators, but the Authority revitalized the region in numerous ways. It improved water transportation. It virtually eliminated flooding in the region. It provided electricity to thousands who had never before had it. Throughout the country, largely because of the "yardstick" provided by the TVA's cheap production of electricity, private power rates declined. Still, the Authority worked no miracles. The Tennessee Valley remained a generally impoverished region despite its efforts. And like many other New Deal programs, it made no serious effort to challenge local customs and racial prejudices.

## The Growth of Federal Relief

Millions of Americans were unemployed and in desperate need of assistance in 1933, and the relief efforts of private organizations and state and local governments were unable to meet the demand. The Roosevelt administration did not consider relief its most important task, but it recognized the necessity of doing something to help impoverished Americans survive until the government could revive the economy to the point where relief might not be necessary.

Among Roosevelt's first acts as president was the establishment of the Federal Emergency Relief Administration (FERA), which provided cash grants to states to prop up bankrupt relief agencies. To administer the program, he chose the director of the New York State relief agency, Harry Hopkins, who disbursed the FERA grants widely and rapidly. But both Hopkins and Roosevelt had misgivings about establishing a government "dole."

They felt somewhat more comfortable with another form of government assistance: work relief. Thus when it became clear that the FERA grants were not enough, the administration established a second program: the Civil Works Administration (CWA). Between November 1933 and April 1934, it put more than 4 million people to work on temporary projects. Some of the projects were of lasting value, such as the construction of roads, schools, and parks; others were little more than make-work. To Hopkins, however, the important thing was pumping money into an economy badly in need of it and providing assistance to people with nowhere else to turn.

Roosevelt's favorite relief project was the Civilian Conservation Corps (CCC). Established in the first weeks of the new administration, the CCC was designed to provide employment to the millions of young men who could find no jobs in the cities and who many feared might become a source of urban crime and violence. At the same time, it was intended to advance the work of conservation and reforestation—goals Roosevelt had long cherished. The CCC created camps in national parks and forests and in other rural and wilderness settings. There young men (women were excluded from the program) worked in a semimilitary environment on such projects as planting trees, building reservoirs, developing parks, and improving agricultural irrigation. CCC camps were segregated by race. The vast majority of them were restricted to whites, but a few were reserved for blacks, Mexicans, and Indians.

Mortgage relief was a pressing need for millions of farm owners and homeowners. The Farm Credit Administration, which within two years refinanced one-fifth of all farm mortgages in the United States, was one response to that problem. The Frazier-Lemke Farm Bankruptcy Act of 1933 was another. It enabled some farmers to regain their land even after the foreclosure of their mortgages. Despite such efforts, however, 25 percent of all American farm owners had lost their land by 1934. Homeowners were similarly troubled, and in June 1933 the administration established the Home Owners' Loan Corporation, which by 1936 had refinanced the mortgages of more than 1 million householders. A year later, Congress established the Federal Housing Administration to insure mortgages for new construction and home repairs.

## THE NEW DEAL IN TRANSITION

Seldom has an American president enjoyed such remarkable popularity as Franklin Roosevelt did during his first two years in office. But by early 1935, with no end to the Depression yet in sight, the New Deal found itself the target of fierce public criticism. In the spring of 1935, partly in response to these growing attacks, Roosevelt launched an ambitious new program of legislation that has often been called the "Second New Deal."

### Critics of the New Deal

Some of the most strident attacks on the New Deal came from critics on the right. Roosevelt had tried for a time to conciliate conservatives and business leaders. By the end of 1934, however, it was clear that the American right in general, and much of the corporate world in particular, had become irreconcilably hostile to the New Deal. In August 1934, a group of the most fervent (and wealthiest) Roosevelt opponents, led by members of the Du Pont family, formed the American Liberty League, designed specifically to arouse public opposition to the New Deal's "dictatorial" policies and its supposed attacks on free enterprise. But the new organization was never able to expand its constituency much beyond the northern industrialists who had founded it.

Roosevelt's critics on the far left also managed to produce alarm among some supporters of the administration, but like the conservatives, they proved to have only limited strength. The Communist Party, the Socialist Party, and other radical and semiradical organizations were at times harshly critical of the New Deal. But they too failed ever to attract genuine mass support.

More menacing to the New Deal than either the far right or the far left was a group of dissident political movements that defied easy ideological classification. Some gained substantial public support within particular states and regions. And three men succeeded in mobilizing genuinely national followings. Dr. Francis E. Townsend, an elderly California physician, rose from obscurity to lead a movement of more than 5 million members with his plan for federal pensions for the elderly. According to the Townsend Plan, all Americans over the age of sixty would receive monthly government pensions of $200, provided they retired (thus freeing jobs for younger, unemployed Americans) and spent the money in full each month (which would pump needed funds into the economy). By 1935, the Townsend Plan had attracted the support of many older men and women. And while the plan itself made little progress in Congress, the public sentiment behind it helped build support for the Social Security system, which Congress did approve in 1935.

Father Charles E. Coughlin, a Catholic priest in the Detroit suburb of Royal Oak, Michigan, achieved even greater renown through his weekly sermons broadcast nationally over the radio. He proposed a series of monetary reforms—remonetization of silver, issuing of greenbacks, and nationalization of the banking system—that he insisted would restore prosperity and ensure economic justice. At first a warm supporter of Franklin Roosevelt, by late 1934 he had become disheartened by what he claimed was the president's failure to deal harshly enough with the "money powers." In the spring of 1935, he established his own political organization, the National Union for Social Justice. He was widely believed to have one of the largest regular radio audiences of anyone in America.

Most alarming of all to the administration was the growing national popularity of Senator Huey P. Long of Louisiana. Long had risen to power in his home state through his strident attacks on the banks, oil companies, and utilities and on the conservative political oligarchy allied with them. Elected governor in 1928, he launched an assault on his opponents so thorough and forceful that they were soon left with virtually no political power whatever. Many claimed that he had, in effect, become a dictator. But he also maintained the overwhelming support of the Louisiana electorate, in part because of his flamboyant personality and in part because of his solid record of conventional progressive accomplishment: building roads, schools, and hospitals; revising the tax codes; distributing free textbooks; lowering utility rates.

HUEY LONG  Few public speakers could arouse a crowd
more effectively than Huey Long of Louisiana, known to
many as "the Kingfish" (a nickname borrowed from the
popular radio show *Amos 'n Andy*). It was Long's effective
use of radio, however, that contributed most directly to his
spreading national popularity in the early 1930s.

Barred by law from succeeding himself as governor, he ran in 1930 for a seat
in the United States Senate and won easily.

Long, like Coughlin, supported Franklin Roosevelt for president in
1932. But within six months of Roosevelt's inauguration he had broken with
the president. As an alternative to the New Deal, he advocated a drastic program of wealth redistribution, a program he ultimately named the Share-
Our-Wealth Plan. The government, he claimed, could end the Depression
easily by using the tax system to confiscate the surplus riches of the wealthiest men and women in America and distribute these surpluses to the rest of
the population. That would, he claimed, allow the government to guaran-

tee every family a minimum "homestead" of $5,000 and an annual wage of $2,500. In 1934, Long established his own national organization: the Share-Our-Wealth Society, which soon attracted a large following through much of the nation. A poll by the Democratic National Committee in the spring of 1935 disclosed that Long might attract more than 10 percent of the vote if he ran as a third-party candidate, enough to tip a close election to the Republicans.

Members of the Roosevelt administration considered dissident movements—and the broad popular discontent they represented—a genuine threat to the president. An increasing number of advisers were warning Roosevelt that he would have to do something dramatic to counter their strength.

## The "Second New Deal"

Roosevelt launched the so-called Second New Deal in the spring of 1935 in response both to the growing political pressures and to the continuing economic crisis. The new proposals represented, if not a new direction, at least a shift in the emphasis of New Deal policy. Perhaps the most conspicuous change was in the administration's attitude toward big business. Symbolically at least, the president was now willing to attack corporate interests openly. In March, for example, he proposed to Congress an act designed to break up the great utility holding companies, and he spoke harshly of monopolistic control of their industry. The Holding Company Act of 1935 was the result, although furious lobbying by the utilities led to amendments that sharply limited its effects.

Equally alarming to affluent Americans was a series of tax reforms proposed by the president in 1935, a program conservatives quickly labeled a "soak-the-rich" scheme. Apparently designed to undercut the appeal of Huey Long's Share-Our-Wealth Plan, the Roosevelt proposals called for establishing the highest and most progressive peacetime tax rates in history—although the actual impact of these rates was limited, and many wealthy people found ways to escape them altogether.

The Supreme Court decision in 1935 to invalidate the National Industrial Recovery Act meant that Section 7(a) of the now defunct act, which had guaranteed workers the right to organize and bargain collectively, was now gone. A group of progressives in Congress led by Senator Robert E. Wagner of New York introduced what became the National Labor Relations Act of 1935. The new law, popularly known as the Wagner Act, provided workers with more federal protection than Section 7(a) of the National Industrial Recovery Act had offered. It created a crucial enforcement mechanism, the National Labor Relations Board (NLRB), which would have power to compel employers to recognize and bargain with legitimate unions. The president was not entirely happy with the bill, but he signed it anyway. That was in large part because American workers themselves had by 1935 become so important and vigorous a force that Roosevelt realized his own political future would depend in part on responding to their demands.

### Labor Militancy

The emergence of a powerful trade union movement in the 1930s was one of the most important social and political developments of the decade. It occurred partly in response to government efforts to enhance the power of unions, but it was also a result of the increased militancy of American workers and their leaders. During the 1920s, most workers had displayed relatively little militancy in challenging employers or demanding recognition of their unions. In the 1930s, however, many of the factors that had impeded militancy vanished or grew weaker. Business leaders and industrialists lost (at least temporarily) the ability to control government policies. Both Section 7(a) of the National Industrial Recovery Act of 1933 and the Wagner Act of 1935 were passed over the strong objections of most (although not all) corporate leaders. Equally important, new and more militant labor organizations emerged to challenge the established, relatively conservative unions.

The growing militancy first became obvious in 1934, when newly organized workers (many of them inspired by the collective bargaining provisions of the National Industrial Recovery Act) demonstrated an assertiveness and at times radicalism seldom seen in recent years. Some became involved in violent confrontations with employers and local authorities. Despite the new militancy, however, it was clear that without stronger legal protection, most organizing drives would end in frustration. Once the Wagner Act became law, the search for more effective forms of organization rapidly gained strength in labor ranks.

The American Federation of Labor remained committed to the idea of the craft union: organizing workers on the basis of their skills. But that concept had little to offer unskilled laborers, who now constituted the bulk of the industrial work force. During the 1930s, therefore, a newer concept of labor organization challenged the craft union ideal: industrial unionism. Advocates of this approach argued that all the workers in a particular industry should be organized in a single union, regardless of what functions the workers performed. All autoworkers should be in a single automobile union; all steelworkers should be in a single steel union. United in this way, workers would greatly increase their power.

Leaders of the AFL craft unions for the most part opposed the new concept. But industrial unionism found a number of important advocates, most prominent among them John L. Lewis, the talented, flamboyant, and eloquent leader of the United Mine Workers. At first, Lewis and his allies attempted to work within the AFL, but friction between the new industrial organizations Lewis was promoting and the older craft unions grew rapidly. At the 1935 AFL convention, Lewis became embroiled in a series of angry confrontations (and one celebrated fistfight) with craft union leaders before finally walking out. A few weeks later, he created the Committee on Industrial Organization—a body officially within the AFL but unsanctioned by its leadership. After a series of bitter jurisdictional conflicts, the AFL finally expelled the new committee from its ranks, and along with it all the industrial unions it represented. In response, Lewis renamed the committee the Congress of Industrial Organizations (CIO), established it in 1936 as an organization directly rivaling the AFL, and became its first president. The schism clearly weakened the labor movement in many ways. But by freeing the advocates of industrial unionism from the restrictive rules of the AFL, it gave impetus to the creation of powerful new organizations.

The CIO also expanded the constituency of the labor movement. It was more receptive to women and to blacks than the AFL had been, in part because women and blacks were more likely to be relegated to unskilled jobs and in part because CIO organizing drives targeted previously unorganized industries (textiles, laundries, tobacco factories, and others) where women and minorities constituted much of the work force. The CIO was also a more militant organization than the AFL. By the time of the 1936 schism, it was already engaged in major organizing battles in the automobile and steel industries.

### Organizing Battles

Out of several competing auto unions, the United Auto Workers (UAW) was gradually emerging preeminent in the early and mid-1930s. But although it was gaining recruits, it was making little progress in winning recognition from the corporations. In December 1936, however, autoworkers employed a controversial and effective new technique for challenging corporate opposition: the sit-down strike. Employees in several General Motors plants in Detroit simply sat down inside the plants, refusing either to work or to leave, thus preventing the company from using strikebreakers. The tactic spread to other locations, and by February 1937 strikers had occupied seventeen GM plants. The strikers ignored court orders and local police efforts to force them to vacate the buildings. When Michigan's governor, Frank Murphy, a liberal Democrat, refused to call up the National Guard to clear out the strikers, and when the federal government also refused to intervene on behalf of employers, General Motors relented. In February 1937, it became the first major manufacturer to recognize the UAW; other automobile companies soon did the same. The sit-down strike proved effective for rubber workers and others as well, but it survived only briefly as a labor technique. Its apparent illegality aroused so much public opposition that labor leaders soon abandoned it.

In the steel industry, the battle for unionization was less easily won. In 1936, the Steel Workers' Organizing Committee (SWOC; later the United Steelworkers of America) began a major organizing drive involving thousands of workers and frequent, at times bitter, strikes. These conflicts were notable not only for the militancy of the (predominantly male) steelworkers themselves but for the involvement of thousands of women (many of them wives or relatives of workers), who provided important logistical support for the strikers and who at times took direct action by creating a buffer between strikers and the police.

In March 1937, to the surprise of almost everyone, United States Steel, the giant of the industry, recognized the union rather than risk a costly strike at a time when it sensed itself on the verge of recovery from the Depression. But the smaller companies (known collectively as "Little Steel") were less accommodating. On Memorial Day 1937, a group of striking workers from Republic Steel gathered with their families for a picnic and demonstration in South Chicago. When they attempted to march peacefully (and legally) toward the steel plant, police opened fire on them. Ten demonstrators were killed; another ninety were wounded. Despite a public outcry against the "Memorial Day Massacre," the harsh tactics of Little Steel succeeded. The 1937 strike failed.

But the victory of Little Steel was one of the last gasps of the kind of brutal strikebreaking that had proved so effective in the past. In 1937 alone, there were 4,720 strikes—over 80 percent of them settled in favor of the unions. By the end of the year, more than 8 million workers were members of unions recognized as official bargaining units by employers (as compared with 3 million in 1932). By 1941, that number had expanded to 10 million and included the workers of Little Steel, whose employers had finally recognized the SWOC.

## Social Security

From the first moments of the New Deal, important members of the administration, most notably Secretary of Labor Frances Perkins, had been lobbying for a system of federally sponsored social insurance for the elderly and the unemployed. In 1935, Roosevelt gave public support to what became the Social Security Act, which Congress passed the same year. It established several distinct programs. For the elderly, there were two types of assistance. Those who were presently destitute could receive up to $15 a month in federal assistance. More important for the future, many Americans presently working were incorporated into a pension system, to which they and their employers would contribute by paying a payroll tax; it would provide them with an income on retirement. Pension payments would not begin until 1942 and even then would provide only $10 to $85 a month to recipients. And broad categories of workers (including domestic servants and agricultural laborers, occupations with disproportionate numbers of blacks and women) were excluded from the program. But the act was a crucial first step in building the nation's most important social program for the elderly.

In addition, the Social Security Act created a system of unemployment insurance, which employers alone would finance and which made it possible for workers laid off from their jobs to receive temporary government assistance. It also established a system of federal aid to disabled people and a program of aid to dependent children.

The framers of the Social Security Act wanted to create a system of "insurance," not "welfare." And the largest programs (old-age pensions and unemployment insurance) were in many ways similar to private insurance programs, with contributions from participants and benefits available to all. But the act also provided considerable direct assistance based on need—to the elderly poor, to the disabled, to dependent children and their mothers. These groups were widely perceived to be small and genuinely unable to support themselves. But in later generations the programs for these groups would expand until they assumed dimensions that the planners of Social Security had neither foreseen nor desired.

The distinction built into the Social Security Act between "insurance" and "public assistance" reflected a set of cultural assumptions that would continue to influence the politics of welfare for the rest of the twentieth century. New Dealers, like most other Americans, believed that some people had "earned" social protection—either because they (or their employers) had contributed to the programs from which they drew, as was the case with old-age pensions and unemployment insurance, or because they had performed some special service to the nation, as had been the case in the past for Civil War and World War I veterans. Other people (many of them women) "needed" benefits because they were incapable of supporting themselves; and while New Dealers (and progressive reformers before them) were willing to provide such benefits, they did so less generously than they did for those they believed had earned them. Whatever its limits, however, it is clear that the 1935 act was the most important single piece of social welfare legislation in American history.

### New Directions in Relief

Social Security was designed primarily to fulfill long-range goals. But millions of unemployed Americans had immediate needs. To help meet them, the administration established in 1935 the Works Progress Administration (WPA). Like the Civil Works Administration and other earlier efforts, the WPA established a system of work relief for the unemployed. But it was much bigger than the earlier agencies, both in the size of its budget ($5 billion at first) and in the energy and imagination of its operations.

Under the direction of Harry Hopkins, the WPA was responsible for building or renovating 110,000 public buildings (schools, post offices, government office buildings) and for constructing almost 600 airports, more than 500,000 miles of roads, and over 100,000 bridges. In the process, the WPA kept an average of 2.1 million workers employed and pumped needed money into the economy.

The WPA also displayed remarkable flexibility and imagination in offering assistance to those whose occupations did not fit into any traditional category of relief. The Federal Writers Project of the WPA, for example, gave unemployed writers a chance to do their work and receive a government salary. The Federal Arts Project, similarly, helped painters, sculptors, and others to continue their careers. The Federal Music Project and the Federal Theater Project oversaw the production of concerts and plays, creating work for unemployed musicians, actors, and directors. Other relief agencies emerged alongside the WPA. The National Youth Administration (NYA) provided work and scholarship assistance to high-school and college-age men and women. The Emergency Housing Division of the Public Works Administration began federal sponsorship of public housing.

WPA ART The Federal Art Project of the Works Progress Administration funded many kinds of projects, but it was probably best known for the striking murals it commissioned for post offices and other government buildings. Here, FAP artist Lucile Lloyd works on a mural portraying the history of California, which she painted for a government office building in Los Angeles.

The hiring practices of the WPA, the NYA, and other work-relief programs revealed another important, if at the time largely unrecognized, feature of the New Deal welfare system. Men and women alike were in distress in the 1930s (as in all difficult times). But the new welfare system dealt with members of the two sexes in very different ways. For men, the government concentrated mainly on work relief—on such programs as the CCC, the CWA, and the WPA, all of which were overwhelmingly male. The principal government aid to women was not work relief but cash assistance—most notably through the Aid to Dependent Children program of Social Security, which was designed largely to assist single mothers. This disparity in treatment reflected a widespread assumption that men constituted the bulk of the paid work force and that women needed to be treated within the context of the family. In fact, millions of women were already employed by the 1930s.

## The 1936 "Referendum"

The presidential election of 1936, it was clear from the start, was to be a national referendum on Franklin Roosevelt and the New Deal. And while in 1935 there had been reason to question the president's political prospects, by the middle of 1936—with the economy visibly reviving—there could be little doubt that he would win a second term. The Republican Party nominated the moderate governor of Kansas, Alf M. Landon, who waged a generally pallid campaign. Republican conservatives seemed impotent even within their own party. Roosevelt's dissident challengers now appeared similarly powerless. One reason was the violent death of their most effective leader, Huey Long, who was assassinated in Louisiana in September 1935. Another reason was the ill-fated alliance among Father Coughlin, Dr. Townsend, and Gerald L. K. Smith (an intemperate henchman of Huey Long), who joined forces that summer to establish a new political movement—the Union Party, which nominated an undistinguished North Dakota congressman, William Lemke, for president.

The result was the greatest landslide in American history to that point. Roosevelt polled just under 61 percent of the vote to Landon's 36 percent and carried every state except Maine and Vermont. The Democrats increased their already large majorities in both houses of Congress. The Union Party received fewer than 900,000 votes.

The election results demonstrated the party realignment that the New Deal had produced. The Democrats now controlled a broad coalition of western and southern farmers, the urban working classes, the poor and unemployed, and the black communities of northern cities, as well as traditional progressives and committed new liberals—a coalition that constituted a substantial majority of the electorate. It would be decades before the Republican Party could again create a lasting majority coalition of its own.

## THE NEW DEAL IN DISARRAY

Roosevelt emerged from the 1936 election at the zenith of his popularity. Within months, however, the New Deal was mired in serious new difficulties—a result of continuing opposition, the president's own political errors, and major economic setbacks.

### The Court Fight and the "Purge"

The 1936 mandate, Franklin Roosevelt believed, made it possible for him to do something about the problem of the Supreme Court. No program of reform, he had become convinced, could long survive the obstructionist justices, who had already struck down the NRA and the AAA and threatened to invalidate even more legislation.

In February 1937, Roosevelt sent a surprise message to Capitol Hill proposing a general overhaul of the federal court system; included among the many provisions was one to add up to six new justices to the Supreme Court. The courts were "overworked," he claimed, and needed additional manpower and younger blood to enable them to cope with their increasing burdens. But Roosevelt's real purpose was to give himself the opportunity to appoint new, liberal justices and change the ideological balance of the Court.

Conservatives were outraged at the "Court-packing plan," and even many Roosevelt supporters were disturbed by what they considered evidence of the president's hunger for power. Still, Roosevelt might well have persuaded Congress to approve at least a compromise measure had not the Supreme Court itself intervened. Four justices consistently opposed the New Deal, and three generally supported it. Of the remaining two, Chief Justice Charles Evans Hughes often sided with the progressives and Associate Justice Owen J. Roberts usually voted with the conservatives. On March 29, 1937, Roberts, Hughes, and the three progressive justices voted together to uphold a state minimum-wage law—in the case of *West Coast Hotel* v. *Parrish*—thus reversing a 5-to-4 decision of the previous year invalidating a similar law. Two weeks later, again by a 5-to-4 margin, the Court upheld the Wagner Act, and in May it validated the Social Security Act. The Court had prudently moderated its position to make the Court-packing bill unnecessary. Congress ultimately defeated it.

On one level, the affair was a significant victory for Franklin Roosevelt. The Court was no longer an obstacle to New Deal reforms, particularly after the older justices began to retire, to be replaced by Roosevelt appointees. But the Court-packing episode did lasting political damage to the administration. From 1937 on, southern Democrats and other conservatives voted against his measures much more often than they had in the past.

A year later, the president's political situation deteriorated further. Roosevelt was determined to regain the initiative in his legislative battles, and in several primary campaigns in spring 1938 he openly spoke against members of his own party who had opposed his programs. Not only was he un-

able to unseat any of the five Democratic senators against whom he campaigned, but his "purge" efforts drove an even deeper wedge between the
administration and its conservative opponents.

### Retrenchment and Recession

By the summer of 1937, the national income, which had dropped from $82
billion in 1929 to $40 billion in 1932, had risen to nearly $72 billion. Other
economic indices showed similar advances. Roosevelt seized on these improvements as an excuse to try to balance the federal budget, convinced by
Treasury secretary Henry Morgenthau and many economists that the real
danger now was no longer depression but inflation. Between January and August 1937, for example, he cut the WPA in half, laying off 1.5 million relief
workers. A few weeks later, the fragile boom collapsed. The index of industrial production dropped from 117 in August 1937 to 76 in May 1938. Four
million additional workers lost their jobs. Economic conditions were soon
almost as bad as they had been in the bleak days of 1932–1933.

The recession of 1937 was a result of many factors. But to many observers at the time (including, apparently, Roosevelt), it seemed to be a direct result of the administration's unwise decision to reduce spending. And
so the new crisis forced a reevaluation of policies. The advocates of government spending as an antidote to the Depression stood vindicated, it
seemed; and the notion of using government deficits to stimulate the economy established a timid foothold in American public policy. In April 1938,
the president asked Congress for an emergency appropriation of $5 billion
for public works and relief programs, and government funds soon began
pouring into the economy once again. Within a few months, another tentative recovery seemed to be under way, and the advocates of spending
pointed to it as proof of the validity of their approach.

At the same time, a group of younger liberals in the administration who
saw the recession as the result of excessively concentrated corporate power
were urging the president to launch a new assault on monopoly. In April
1938, Roosevelt sent a stinging message to Congress, vehemently denouncing what he called an "unjustifiable concentration of economic power"
and asking for the creation of a commission to examine that concentration
with an eye to major reforms in the antitrust laws. In response, Congress established the Temporary National Economic Committee (TNEC), whose
members included representatives of both houses of Congress and officials
from several executive agencies. At about the same time, Roosevelt appointed a new head of the antitrust division of the Justice Department:

Thurman Arnold, a Yale Law School professor who soon proved to be the most vigorous director ever to serve in that office.

By the end of 1938, however, it was becoming clear that these ambitious new goals faced an uncertain future. For the New Deal had by then essentially come to an end. Congressional opposition now made it difficult for the president to enact any major new programs. But more important, perhaps, the threat of world crisis hung heavy in the political atmosphere, and Roosevelt was gradually growing more concerned with persuading a reluctant nation to prepare for war than with pursuing new avenues of reform.

## LIMITS AND LEGACIES OF THE NEW DEAL

The New Deal made major changes in American government, some of them still controversial today. It also left important problems unaddressed.

### African Americans and the New Deal

One group the New Deal did relatively little to assist was African Americans. The administration was not hostile to black aspirations. On the contrary, the New Deal was probably more sympathetic to them than any previous government of the twentieth century had been. Eleanor Roosevelt spoke throughout the 1930s on behalf of racial justice and put continuing pressure on her husband and others in the federal government to ease discrimination against blacks. The president himself appointed a number of blacks to significant second-level positions in his administration, creating an informal network of officeholders that became known as the "Black Cabinet." Eleanor Roosevelt, Interior secretary Harold Ickes, and WPA director Harry Hopkins all made efforts to ensure that New Deal relief programs did not exclude blacks, and by 1935 an estimated 30 percent of all African Americans were receiving some form of government assistance. One result was a historic change in black electoral behavior. As late as 1932, most American blacks were voting Republican, as they had been doing since the Civil War. By 1936, more than 90 percent of them were voting Democratic—the beginnings of a political alliance that would endure for many decades.

Blacks supported Franklin Roosevelt because they knew he was not their enemy. But they had few illusions that the New Deal represented a millennium in American race relations. The president was, for example, never will-

ELEANOR ROOSEVELT AND MARY MCLEOD BETHUNE  Mrs. Roosevelt was a leading champion of racial equality within her husband's administration, and her commitment had an important impact on the behavior of the government even though she held no official post. She is seen here meeting in 1937 with Aubrey Williams, executive director of the National Youth Administration, and Mary McLeod Bethune, the agency's Director of Negro Affairs.

ing to risk losing the support of southern Democrats by supporting legislation to make lynching a federal crime or to ban the poll tax, one of the most potent tools by which white southerners kept blacks from voting.

New Deal relief agencies did not challenge, and indeed reinforced, existing patterns of discrimination. The Civilian Conservation Corps established separate black camps. The NRA codes tolerated paying blacks less than whites doing the same jobs. African Americans were largely excluded from employment in the TVA. The Federal Housing Administration refused to provide mortgages to blacks moving into white neighborhoods, and the first public housing projects financed by the federal government were racially segregated. The WPA routinely relegated black and Hispanic workers to the least skilled and lowest-paying jobs; when funding ebbed, African Americans, like women, were among the first to be dismissed.

The New Deal was not hostile to black Americans, and it made some contributions to their progress. But it refused to make the issue of race a significant part of its agenda.

### The New Deal and the "Indian Problem"

New Deal policy toward the Indian tribes marked a significant break from the approach in the years before Roosevelt, largely because of the efforts of the extraordinary commissioner of Indian affairs in the 1930s, John Collier. Collier was greatly influenced by the work of twentieth-century anthropologists who advanced the idea of cultural relativism—the theory that every culture should be accepted and respected on its own terms and that no culture is inherently superior to another. Cultural relativism was a challenge to the three-centuries-old assumption among white Americans that Indians were "savages" and that white society was inherently superior and more "civilized."

Collier favored legislation that would, he hoped, reverse the pressures on Native Americans to assimilate and allow them to remain Indians. Not all tribal leaders agreed with Collier. Indeed, his belief in the importance of preserving Indian culture would not find its greatest support among the tribes until the 1960s. Nevertheless, Collier effectively promoted legislation—which became the Indian Reorganization Act of 1934—to advance his goals. Among other things, it restored to the tribes the right to own land collectively (reversing the allotment policy adopted in 1887, which encouraged the breaking up of tribal lands into individually owned plots) and to elect tribal governments. In the thirteen years after passage of the 1934 bill, tribal land increased by nearly 4 million acres, and Indian agricultural income increased dramatically (from under $2 million in 1934 to over $49 million in 1947).

Even with the redistribution of lands under the 1934 act, however, Indians continued to possess, for the most part, only territory whites did not want—much of it arid, some of it desert. And as a group, they continued to constitute the poorest segment of the population. The efforts of the 1930s did not solve, or even greatly alleviate, what some called the "Indian problem." They did, however, provide Indians with some tools for rebuilding the viability of the tribes.

### Women and the New Deal

Symbolically, at least, the New Deal marked a breakthrough in the role of women in public life. Roosevelt appointed the first female member of the cabinet in the nation's history, Secretary of Labor Frances Perkins. He also named more than 100 other women to positions at lower levels of the federal bureaucracy. But New Deal support for women operated within limits.

Even many of the women in the administration were concerned not so much about achieving gender equality as about obtaining special protections for women.

The New Deal generally supported the belief (not always matched by practice) that in hard times women should withdraw from the workplace to open up more jobs for men. Frances Perkins, for example, spoke out against what she called the "pin-money worker"—the married woman working to earn extra money for the household. New Deal relief agencies offered relatively little employment for women. The NRA sanctioned sexually discriminatory wage practices. The Social Security program excluded domestic servants, waitresses, and other predominantly female occupations.

As with African Americans, so also with women: The New Deal was not actively hostile to feminist aspirations; in many ways, it was unprecedentedly supportive. It did, however, accept prevailing cultural norms. There was not yet sufficient political pressure from women themselves to persuade the administration to do otherwise. Indeed, some of the most important supporters of policies that reinforced traditional gender roles (such as Social Security) were themselves women.

### The New Deal and the West

One part of American society that did receive special attention from the New Deal was the American West, which benefited disproportionately from federal relief and public works programs. The West received more government funds per capita through New Deal relief programs than any other region.

Most westerners were eager for the assistance New Deal agencies provided, but their political leaders were not always as supportive. In Colorado, for example, the state legislature refused to provide the required matching funds for FERA relief in 1933. When, in response, Harry Hopkins cut Colorado off from the program, unemployed people rioted in Denver and looted food stores. Only then did the legislature reverse course and provide funding.

Just as in the South locally administered relief programs did not challenge prevailing racial norms, so in the West New Deal programs sustained existing racial and ethnic prejudices. In several states, relief agencies paid different groups at different rates: white Anglos received the most generous aid; blacks, Indians, and Mexican Americans received lower levels of support. In the CCC camps in New Mexico, Hispanics and Anglos sometimes worked in the same camps, but there were frequent tensions and occasional conflicts between them.

But the main reason for the New Deal's particular impact on the West was that conditions in the region made the government's programs especially important. Federal agricultural programs had an enormous impact on the West because farming remained so much more central to the economy of the region than it did in much of the East. The largest New Deal public works programs—the great dams and power stations—were mainly in the West, both because the best locations for such facilities were there and because the West had the most need for new sources of water and power. The Grand Coulee dam on the Columbia River was the largest public works project in American history to that point, and it provided cheap electric power for much of the Northwest. Its construction, and the construction of other, smaller dams and water projects, created a basis for economic development in the region.

Without this enormous public investment by the federal government, much of the economic growth that transformed the West after World War II would have been much more difficult, if not impossible, to achieve. For generations after the Great Depression, the federal government maintained a much greater and more visible bureaucratic presence in the West than in any other region.

### The New Deal and the Economy

The most frequent criticisms of the New Deal involve its failure genuinely to revive or reform the American economy. New Dealers never fully recognized the value of government spending as a vehicle for recovery, and their efforts along other lines never succeeded in ending the Depression. The economic boom sparked by World War II, not the New Deal, finally ended the crisis. Nor did the New Deal substantially alter the distribution of power within American capitalism, and it had only a small impact on the distribution of wealth among the American people.

Nevertheless, the New Deal did have a number of important and lasting effects on both the behavior and the structure of the American economy. It helped elevate new groups—workers, farmers, and others—to positions from which they could at times effectively challenge the power of the corporations. It increased the regulatory functions of the federal government in ways that helped stabilize previously troubled areas of the economy: the stock market, the banking system, and others. And the administration helped establish the basis for new forms of federal fiscal policy, which in the postwar years would give the government tools for promoting and regulating economic growth.

The New Deal also created the rudiments of the American welfare state, through its many relief programs and above all through the Social Security system. The conservative inhibitions New Dealers brought to this task ensured that the welfare system that ultimately emerged would be limited in its impact (at least in comparison with the systems of other industrial nations), would reinforce some traditional patterns of gender and racial discrimination, and would be expensive and cumbersome to administer. But for all its limits, the new system marked a historic break with the nation's traditional reluctance to offer any public assistance whatever to its neediest citizens.

### The New Deal and American Politics

Perhaps the most dramatic effect of the New Deal was its impact on the structure and behavior of American government and on the character of American politics. Franklin Roosevelt helped enhance the power of the federal government as a whole. By the end of the 1930s, state and local governments were clearly of secondary importance to the government in Washington; in the past, that had not always been clear. Roosevelt also established the presidency as the preeminent center of authority within the federal government. Not for many years would Congress wield as much independent power as it had in the years before the New Deal.

Finally, the New Deal had a profound impact on how the American people defined themselves politically. It took a weak, divided Democratic Party, which had been a minority force in American politics for many decades, and turned it into a mighty coalition that would dominate national party competition for more than thirty years. It turned the attention of many voters away from some of the cultural issues that had preoccupied them in the 1920s and awakened in them an interest in economic matters of direct importance to their lives. And it created among the American people greatly increased expectations of government—expectations that the New Deal itself did not always fulfill but that survived for generations to become the basis of new liberal crusades in the postwar era.

D  E  B  A  T  I  N  G     T  H  E     P  A  S  T

## The New Deal

ONTEMPORARIES OF FRANKLIN ROOSEVELT debated the impact of the
New Deal with ferocious intensity: conservatives complaining of a
menacing tyranny of the state, liberals celebrating the New Deal's progressive achievements, people on the left charging that the reforms of the 1930s
were largely cosmetic and ignored the nation's fundamental problems. Although the conservative critique has found relatively little scholarly expression since Roosevelt's death, the liberal and left positions continued for many
years to shape the way historians described the Roosevelt administration.

The dominant view from the beginning was an approving liberal interpretation, and its most important early voice was that of Arthur M.
Schlesinger, Jr. He argued in the three volumes of *The Age of Roosevelt*
(1957–1960) that the New Deal marked a continuation of the long struggle
between public power and private interests, a struggle Roosevelt had moved
to a new level as the unconstrained influence of business elites finally encountered an effective challenge. Workers, farmers, consumers and others
now had much more protection than they had enjoyed in the past.

At almost the same time, however, other historians were offering more
qualified assessments of the New Deal, even if ones that remained securely
within the liberal framework. Richard Hofstadter argued in 1955 that the
New Deal was a "drastic new departure . . . different from anything that had
yet happened in the United States"; that it gave American liberalism a "so-
cial-democratic tinge that had never before been present in American reform movements"; but that its highly pragmatic approach lacked a central,
guiding philosophy. James MacGregor Burns argued in 1956 that Roosevelt
failed to make full use of his potential as a leader and had accommodated
himself unnecessarily to existing patterns of power.

William Leuchtenburg's *Franklin D. Roosevelt and the New Deal* (1963)
was the first systematic "revisionist" interpretation. Leuchtenburg was a
sympathetic critic, arguing that most of the limitations of the New Deal were
the result of political and ideological constraints over which Roosevelt had

little control. But he challenged the views of earlier scholars who had proclaimed the New Deal a "revolution" in social policy. Leuchtenburg could muster only enough enthusiasm to call it a "halfway revolution," one that helped some previously disadvantaged groups (most notably farmers and workers) but that did little or nothing for many others (blacks, sharecroppers, the urban poor).

Harsher criticisms soon emerged. Barton Bernstein in a 1968 essay compiled a dreary chronicle of missed opportunities and inadequate responses to problems and concluded that the New Deal had saved capitalism, but at the expense of the least powerful. Ronald Radosh, Paul Conkin, and, more recently, Thomas Ferguson and Colin Gordon expanded on these criticisms; the New Deal, they contended, was part of the twentieth-century tradition of "corporate liberalism"—a tradition in which reform is closely wedded to the needs and interests of capitalism.

Most scholars in the 1980s and 1990s, however, seemed largely to have accepted the revised liberal view: that the New Deal was a significant (and most agree valuable) chapter in the history of reform, but one that worked within rigid, occasionally crippling limits. Much of the recent work on the New Deal, therefore, has focused on the constraints it faced. Some scholars (notably the sociologist Theda Skocpol) have emphasized the issue of "state capacity"—the absence of a government bureaucracy with sufficient strength and expertise to shape or administer many programs. James T. Patterson, Barry Karl, Mark Leff, and others have emphasized the political constraints the New Deal encountered—the conservative inhibitions about government that remained strong in Congress and among the public. Frank Freidel, Ellis Hawley, Herbert Stein, and many others point as well to the ideological constraints affecting Franklin Roosevelt and his supporters, the limits of their own understanding of their time. Alan Brinkley, in *The End of Reform* (1995), described an ideological shift within New Deal liberalism that marginalized older concerns about wealth and monopoly power.

The phrase "New Deal liberalism" has come in the postwar era to seem synonymous with modern ideas of aggressive federal management of the economy, elaborate welfare systems, a powerful bureaucracy, and large-scale government spending. But many historians of the New Deal would argue that the modern idea of New Deal liberalism bears only a limited relationship to the ideas that New Dealers themselves embraced.

# CHAPTER TWENTY-SEVEN

# The Global Crisis, 1921–1941

*The Diplomacy of the New Era* ~ *Isolationism and Internationalism*
*From Neutrality to Intervention*

ENRY CABOT LODGE of Massachusetts, chairman of the Senate Foreign Relations Committee and one of the most powerful figures in the Republican Party, led the fight against ratification of the Treaty of Versailles in 1918 and 1919. In part because of his efforts, the treaty was defeated. The United States failed to join the League of Nations; and American foreign policy embarked on an independent course that for the next two decades would attempt, but ultimately fail, to expand American influence and maintain international stability without committing the United States to any lasting relationships with other nations.

Lodge was not an isolationist. He recognized that America had emerged from World War I the most powerful nation in the world. He believed the United States should exert its influence internationally. But he believed, too, that America's expanded role in the world should reflect the nation's own interests and its own special virtues; the United States should remain unfettered with obligations to anyone else. He said in 1919:

> We are a great moral asset of Christian civilization. . . . How did we get there? By our own efforts. Nobody led us, nobody guided us, nobody controlled us. . . . I would keep America as she has been—not isolated, not prevent her from joining other nations for . . . great purposes—but I wish her to be master of her own fate.

In the end, the limited American internationalism of the interwar years proved insufficient to protect the interests of the United States, to create global stability, or to keep the nation from becoming involved in the most catastrophic war in human history.

| TIME LINE | | | | |
|---|---|---|---|---|
| **1924** | **1928** | **1931** | **1933** | **1937** |
| Dawes Plan | Kellogg-Briand Pact | Japan invades Manchuria | U.S. recognizes Soviet Union<br><br>Good Neighbor Policy | Roosevelt's "quarantine" speech |

| **1938** | **1939** | **1940** | **1941** |
|---|---|---|---|
| Munich Conference | Nazi-Soviet nonaggression pact<br><br>World War II begins | Tripartite Pact<br><br>America First Committee founded<br><br>Roosevelt reelected<br><br>Destroyers-for-bases deal | Lend-lease plan<br><br>Atlantic Charter<br><br>Japan attacks Pearl Harbor<br><br>U.S. enters World War II |

# THE DIPLOMACY OF THE NEW ERA

Critics of American foreign policy in the 1920s often described it with a single word: isolationism. But in reality, the United States played a more active role in world affairs in the 1920s than it had at almost any previous time in its history.

## Replacing the League

By the time the Harding administration took office in 1921, American membership in the League of Nations was no longer a realistic possibility. But Secretary of State Charles Evans Hughes wanted to find something with which to replace the League as a guarantor of world peace and stability. He embarked on a series of efforts to build safeguards against future wars—safeguards, however, that would not hamper American freedom of action in the world.

The most important of such efforts was the Washington Conference of 1921—an attempt to prevent a destabilizing naval armaments race among the United States, Britain, and Japan. Hughes proposed a plan for dramatic reductions in the fleets of all three nations and a ten-year moratorium on the construction of large warships. To the surprise of almost everyone, the conference ultimately agreed to accept most of Hughes's terms. The Five-Power Pact of February 1922 established limits for total naval tonnage and a ratio of armaments among the signatories. For every 5 tons of American and British warships, Japan would maintain 3 and France and Italy 1.75 each.

The Washington Conference began the New Era effort to protect world peace (and the international economic interests of the United States) without accepting international obligations. The Kellogg-Briand Pact of 1928 concluded it. When the French foreign minister, Aristide Briand, asked the United States in 1927 to join an alliance against Germany, Secretary of State Frank Kellogg (who had replaced Hughes in 1925) proposed instead a multilateral treaty outlawing war as an instrument of national policy. Fourteen nations signed the agreement in Paris on August 27, 1928, amid great solemnity and wide international acclaim. Forty-eight other nations later joined the pact. It contained no instruments of enforcement.

### Debts and Diplomacy

The first responsibility of diplomacy, Hughes, Kellogg, and others agreed, was to ensure that American overseas trade faced no obstacles. Preventing a dangerous and expensive armaments race and reducing the possibility of war were two steps to that end. So were new financial arrangements to deal with international debts. The Allied powers of Europe were struggling to repay $11 billion in loans they had contracted with the United States during and shortly after the war. At the same time, Germany was attempting to pay the reparations levied by the Allies. With the financial structure of Europe on the brink of collapse as a result, the United States stepped in with a solution.

Charles G. Dawes, an American banker, negotiated an agreement in 1924 among France, Britain, Germany, and the United States under which American banks would provide enormous loans to the Germans, enabling them to meet their reparations payments; in return, Britain and France would agree to reduce the amount of those payments. The Dawes Plan became the source of a troubling circular pattern in international finance. The United States would lend money to Germany, which would use that money to pay reparations to France and England, which would in turn use those funds (as well as large loans they themselves were receiving from American banks) to repay war debts to the United States. The flow was able to continue only by virtue of the enormous debts Germany and the other European nations were acquiring to American banks and corporations. Some in the American government warned that the reckless expansion of overseas loans and investments threatened disaster—that the United States was becoming too dependent on unstable European economies. Such warnings fell, for the most part, on deaf ears, and the American economic involvement in Europe continued to expand until the worldwide depression shattered the system in 1931.

The government felt even fewer reservations about assisting American economic expansion in Latin America. During the 1920s, American military forces maintained a presence in Nicaragua, Panama, and several other countries in the region, while United States investments in Latin America more than doubled. American banks were offering large loans to Latin American governments, just as they were in Europe; and just as in Europe, the Latin Americans were having difficulty earning the money to repay them in the face of the formidable United States tariff barrier.

### Hoover and the World Crisis

After the relatively placid international climate of the 1920s, the diplomatic challenges facing the Hoover administration must have seemed bewildering. The world financial crisis that had begun in 1929 and greatly intensified after 1931 was producing a dangerous nationalism in Europe, toppling some existing political leaders and replacing them with powerful, belligerent governments committed to expansion as a solution to their economic problems. An expansionist government in Japan was creating similar problems in Asia. Hoover was confronted with the beginning of a process that would ultimately lead to war.

In Latin America, Hoover tried to repair some of the damage earlier American policies had created. He made a ten-week good-will tour through the region before his inauguration. Once in office, he generally abstained from intervening in the internal affairs of neighboring nations and moved to withdraw American troops from Nicaragua and Haiti. When economic distress led to the collapse of several Latin American regimes, Hoover announced a new policy: America would grant diplomatic recognition to any sitting government in the region without questioning the means it had used to obtain power. He even repudiated the Roosevelt corollary to the Monroe Doctrine by refusing to permit American intervention when several Latin American countries defaulted on debt obligations to the United States in October 1931.

In Europe, the administration enjoyed few successes in its efforts to promote economic stability. When Hoover's proposed moratorium on debts failed to attract broad support or produce financial stability, he refused to cancel all war debts to the United States as many economists advised him to do. Several European nations promptly went into default. Efforts to extend the 1921 limits on naval construction fell victim to French and British fears of German and Japanese militarism. And the World Disarmament Conference in Geneva in 1932 similarly ended in frustration.

HITLER AND MUSSOLINI  The German and Italian dictators, shown here reviewing troops together in Berlin in the mid-1930s, acted publicly as if they were equals. Privately, however, Hitler viewed Mussolini with contempt, and the Italian dictator complained frequently of being treated as a junior partner by his ally.

The ineffectiveness of American diplomacy in Europe was particularly troubling in light of the new governments on the Continent. Benito Mussolini's Fascist Party had been in control of Italy since the early 1920s and had become increasingly nationalistic and militaristic. Still more ominous was the growing power of the National Socialist (or Nazi) Party in Germany. By the late 1920s, the Weimar Republic, the nation's government since the end of World War I, had been largely discredited by, among other things, a ruinous inflation. Adolf Hitler, the leader of the Nazis, was growing rapidly in popular favor and would take power in 1933. Hitler believed in the genetic superiority of the Aryan (German) people and in extending German territory to provide Lebensraum (living space) for the German "master race." He also displayed a pathological anti-Semitism and a passionate militarism.

More immediately alarming to the Hoover administration was a major crisis in Asia—another early step toward World War II. The Japanese, suffering from an economic depression of their own, were concerned about the increasing power of the Soviet Union and of Chiang Kai-shek's nationalist China. In particular, they were alarmed at Chiang's insistence on expanding his government's power in Manchuria, which remained officially a part of China but over which the Japanese had maintained informal economic control since 1905. In 1933, Japan's military leaders staged what was, in effect, a coup and took control of the government in Tokyo. Weeks later, they launched an invasion of northern Manchuria. They had conquered the region by the end of the year. Hoover permitted Secretary of State Henry Stimson to issue stern warnings to the Japanese but barred him from cooperating with the League of Nations to impose economic sanctions against them. Early in 1932, Japan expanded its aggression further into China, attacking the city of Shanghai and killing thousands of civilians.

By the time Hoover left office, early in 1933, the international system the United States had attempted to create in the 1920s—a system based on voluntary cooperation among nations and on an American refusal to commit itself to any collective obligations—had collapsed. The United States faced a choice. It could adopt a more energetic form of internationalism and enter into firmer and more meaningful associations with other nations. It could resort to nationalism and try to deal with international problems alone. Or it could ignore global problems altogether. For the next six years, it experimented with elements of all three approaches.

## ISOLATIONISM AND INTERNATIONALISM

The administration of Franklin Roosevelt faced a dual challenge as it entered office in 1933. It had to deal with the worst economic crisis in the nation's history, and it had to deal as well with the effects of a decaying international structure. The two problems were not unrelated, for it was the Depression itself that was producing much of the political chaos throughout the world.

### Depression Diplomacy

Perhaps Roosevelt's sharpest break with the policies of his predecessor was on the question of American economic relations with Europe. Hoover had argued that only by resolving the question of war debts and reinforcing the gold standard could the American economy hope to recover. He had, therefore, agreed to participate in the World Economic Conference, to be held in London in June 1933, to attempt to resolve these issues. By the time the conference assembled, however, Roosevelt had already become convinced that the gold value of the dollar had to be allowed to fall in order for American goods to be able to compete in world markets. Shortly after the conference convened, he released what became known as the "bombshell message," repudiating the orthodox views of most of the delegates and rejecting any agreement on currency stabilization. The conference quickly dissolved without reaching agreement.

At the same time, Roosevelt abandoned the commitments of the Hoover administration to settle the issue of war debts through international agreement. In April 1934 he signed a bill that prohibited American banks from making loans to any nation in default on its debts. The legislation ended the old, circular system by which debt payments continued only by virtue of increasing American loans; within months, war-debt payments from every nation except Finland stopped for good.

The United States and Russia had viewed each other with mistrust and even hostility since the Bolshevik Revolution of 1917, and the American government still had not officially recognized the Soviet regime in 1933. But a growing number of influential Americans were urging a change in policy—largely because the Soviet Union appeared to be a possible source of trade. The Russians, for their part, were hoping for American cooperation in containing Japan. In November 1933, the United States and the Soviet Union agreed to open formal diplomatic relations.

Despite this promising beginning, however, relations with the Soviet Union soon soured once again. American trade failed to establish a foothold in Russia, disappointing hopes in the United States; and the American government did little to reassure the Soviets that it was interested in stopping Japanese expansion in Asia, dousing expectations in Russia. By the end of 1934, the Soviet Union and the United States were once again viewing each other with considerable mistrust. And the Soviet leader, Josef Stalin, was beginning to consider making agreements of his own with the fascist governments of Japan and Germany.

### The Good Neighbor Policy

The United States succeeded during the 1930s in increasing both its exports to and its imports from Latin America by over 100 percent. At the same time, the Roosevelt administration was taking a new approach toward Latin America, an approach which became known as the "Good Neighbor Policy" and which expanded on the changes the Hoover administration had made. At the Inter-American Conference in Montevideo, Uruguay, in December 1933, Secretary of State Cordell Hull signed a formal convention declaring: "No state has the right to intervene in the internal or external affairs of another." By repudiating military intervention, Roosevelt, like Hoover, eased tensions between the United States and its neighbors considerably. But the Good Neighbor Policy did little to stem the growing American domination of the Latin American economy.

## The Rise of Isolationism

With the international system of the 1920s now decayed beyond repair, the United States faced a choice between more active efforts to stabilize the world and more energetic attempts to isolate itself from it. Most Americans unhesitatingly chose the latter. Support for isolationism emerged from many quarters. Some Wilsonian internationalists had grown disillusioned with the League of Nations and its inability to stop Japanese aggression in Asia. Other Americans were listening to the argument that powerful business interests—Wall Street, munitions makers, and others—had tricked the United States into participating in World War I. An investigation by a Senate committee chaired by Senator Gerald Nye of North Dakota claimed to have produced evidence of exorbitant profiteering and tax evasion by many corporations during the war, and it suggested that bankers had pressured Wilson to intervene in the war so as to protect their loans abroad. (Few historians now lend much credence to these charges.)

Roosevelt himself was sympathetic to some of the isolationist arguments. But he continued to hope for at least a modest American role in maintaining world peace. In 1935, he proposed to the Senate a treaty to make the United States a member of the World Court—a largely symbolic gesture. Nevertheless, isolationists such as Father Coughlin and William Randolph Hearst aroused popular opposition to the agreement, and the Senate voted it down. The president would not soon again attempt to challenge the isolationist tide.

In the summer of 1935, it became clear that Mussolini's Italy was preparing to invade Ethiopia. Fearing the invasion would provoke a new European war, American legislators began to design legal safeguards to prevent the United States from being dragged into the conflict. The result was the Neutrality Act of 1935, followed by additional acts in 1936 and 1937. The 1935 law established a mandatory arms embargo against both sides in any military conflict and directed the president to warn American citizens against traveling on the ships of warring nations. Thus, isolationists believed, the "protection of neutral rights" could not again become an excuse for American intervention in war. The 1936 Neutrality Act renewed these provisions, and the 1937 law added new ones, establishing the so-called cash-and-carry policy, by which belligerents could purchase only nonmilitary goods from the United States and could do so only by paying cash and shipping their purchases themselves.

Isolationist sentiment showed its strength again in 1936–1937 in response to the civil war in Spain. The Falangists of General Francisco Franco, a group much like the Italian fascists, revolted in July 1936 against the existing republican government. Hitler and Mussolini supported Franco, both vocally and with weapons and supplies. Some individual Americans traveled to Spain to assist the republican cause, but the United States government joined with Britain and France in an agreement to offer no assistance to either side.

Roosevelt, however, was slowly becoming convinced that the course of international events required some more forceful American response. Particularly disturbing was the deteriorating situation in Asia. In the summer of 1937, Japan intensified its six-year-old assault on Manchuria and attacked China's five northern provinces. Roosevelt responded in a speech in Chicago in October 1937. He warned of the dangers of the Japanese actions and argued that aggressors should be "quarantined" by the international community to prevent the contagion of war from spreading. He was deliberately vague about what such a "quarantine" would mean. Even so, public response to the speech was disturbingly hostile, and Roosevelt drew back. On December 12, 1937, Japanese aviators bombed and sank the United States gunboat *Panay*, almost certainly deliberately, as it sailed the Yangtze River in China. But so reluctant was the Roosevelt administration to antagonize the isolationists that the United States eagerly seized on Japanese claims that the bombing had been an accident, accepted Japan's apologies, and overlooked the attack.

### The Failure of Munich

In 1936, Hitler had moved the revived German army into the Rhineland, rearming an area that France had, in effect, controlled since World War I. In March 1938, German forces marched into Austria, and Hitler proclaimed a union (or *Anschluss*) between Austria, his native land, and Germany, his adopted one. Neither in America nor in most of Europe was there much more than a murmur of opposition.

The Austrian invasion, however, soon created another crisis, for Germany had by now occupied territory surrounding three sides of western Czechoslovakia, a region Hitler dreamed of annexing. In September 1938, he demanded that Czechoslovakia cede him part of that region, the Sudetenland, an area in which many ethnic Germans lived. Although Czechoslovakia was prepared to fight to stop Hitler, it needed assistance from other nations. But most Western governments, including the United States, were willing to pay almost any price to settle the crisis peacefully. On September 29, Hitler met with the leaders of France and Great Britain at Munich in an effort to resolve the crisis. The French and British agreed to accept the German demands in Czechoslovakia in return for Hitler's promise to expand no farther.

The Munich agreement, which Roosevelt applauded at the time, was the

THE BLITZ, LONDON  The German Luftwaffe terrorized London and other British cities in 1940–1941 and again late in the war by bombing civilian areas indiscriminately in an effort to break the spirit of the English people. The effort failed, and the fortitude of the British did much to arouse support for their cause in the United States.

most prominent element of a policy that came to be known as "appeasement" and that came to be identified (not altogether fairly) largely with British Prime Minister Neville Chamberlain. Whoever was to blame, the policy was a failure. In March 1939, Hitler occupied the remaining areas of Czechoslovakia, violating the Munich agreement unashamedly. And in April, he began issuing threats against Poland.

At that point, both Britain and France gave assurances to the Polish government that they would come to its assistance in case of an invasion; they even tried, too late, to draw the Soviet Union into a mutual defense agreement. But Stalin, who had not even been invited to the Munich Conference, had already decided he could expect no protection from the West. He signed a nonaggression pact with Hitler in August 1939, freeing the Germans for the moment from the danger of a two-front war. Shortly after that, Hitler staged an incident on the Polish border to allow him to claim that Germany had been attacked, and on September 1, 1939, he launched a full-scale invasion of Poland. Britain and France, true to their pledges, declared war on Germany two days later. World War II had begun.

## FROM NEUTRALITY TO INTERVENTION

"This nation will remain a neutral nation," the president declared shortly after the hostilities began in Europe, "but I cannot ask that every American remain neutral in thought as well." There was never any question that both he and the majority of the American people favored Britain, France, and the other Allied nations in the contest. The question was how much the United States was prepared to do to assist them.

### Neutrality Tested

At the very least, Roosevelt believed, the United States should make armaments available to the Allied armies to help them counter the military advantage the large German munitions industry gave Hitler. In September 1939, he asked Congress to revise the Neutrality Acts and lift the arms embargo against any nation engaged in war. Powerful isolationist opposition forced Congress to maintain the prohibition on American ships entering war zones. But the 1939 law did permit belligerents to purchase arms on the same cash-and-carry basis that the earlier Neutrality Acts had established for the sale of nonmilitary materials.

For a time, it was possible to believe that little more would be necessary. After the German armies quickly subdued Poland, the war in Europe settled into a long, quiet lull that lasted through the winter and spring—a "phony war," some called it. (In the meantime, the Soviet Union overran the small Baltic republics of Latvia, Estonia, and Lithuania and then, in late November, established effective control over Finland. The United States responded with nothing more than an ineffective "moral embargo" on the shipment of armaments to Russia.)

Whatever illusions Americans had harbored about the war in western Europe were shattered in the spring of 1940 when Germany launched a massive invasion to the west—first attacking Denmark and Norway, sweeping next across the Netherlands and Belgium, and driving finally deep into the heart of France. Allied efforts proved futile against the Nazi blitzkrieg. One western European stronghold after another fell into German hands. On June 10, Mussolini invaded France from the south as Hitler was attacking from the north. On June 22, finally, France fell, and Nazi troops marched into Paris. A new collaborationist French regime assembled in Vichy; and in all Europe, only the shattered remnants of the British and French armies, rescued from the beaches of Dunkirk, remained to oppose the Axis forces.

On May 16, in the midst of the offensive, Roosevelt asked Congress for an additional $1 billion for defense and received it quickly. That was one day after Winston Churchill, the new British prime minister, had sent Roosevelt the first of many long lists of requests for armaments, without which, he insisted, England could not long survive. Some Americans (including the United States ambassador to London, Joseph P. Kennedy) argued that the British plight was already hopeless, that any aid to the English was a wasted effort. But the president was determined to make war materials available to Britain. He even circumvented the cash-and-carry provisions of the Neutrality Acts by giving England fifty American destroyers (most of them left over from World War I) in return for the right to build American bases on British territory in the Western Hemisphere, and he returned to the factories a number of new airplanes purchased by the American government so that the British could buy them instead.

Roosevelt was able to take such steps in part because of a major shift in American public opinion. By July 1940, more than 66 percent of the public (according to opinion polls) believed that Germany posed a direct threat to the United States. Congress was, therefore, more willing to permit expanded American assistance to the Allies. Congress was also becoming more concerned about the need for internal preparations for war, and in September it approved the Burke-Wadsworth Act, inaugurating the first peacetime military draft in American history.

But the isolationists were far from finished. A powerful new isolationist lobby—the America First Committee, whose members included such prominent Americans as Charles Lindbergh and Senators Gerald Nye and Burton Wheeler—joined the debate over American policy toward the war. The lobby had at least the indirect support of a large proportion of the Republican Party. The debate was a bitter one. Through the summer and fall of 1940, moreover, it was complicated by a presidential campaign.

The biggest political question of 1940 was whether Franklin Roosevelt would break with tradition and run for an unprecedented third term. The president himself did not reveal his own wishes. But by refusing to withdraw from the contest, he made it impossible for any rival Democrat to establish a claim to the nomination. And when, just before the Democratic Convention in July, he let it be known that he would accept a "draft" from his party, the issue was virtually settled. The Democrats quickly renominated him and even reluctantly swallowed his choice for vice president: Agriculture secretary Henry A. Wallace, a man too liberal and too controversial for the taste of many party leaders.

The Republicans, again uncertain how to oppose Roosevelt effectively, nominated for president a politically inexperienced Indiana businessman, Wendell Willkie, who benefited from a powerful grassroots movement. Both the candidate and the party platform took positions little different from Roosevelt's: they would keep the country out of war but would extend generous assistance to the Allies. Willkie was an appealing figure and a vigorous campaigner, and he managed to evoke more public enthusiasm than any Republican candidate in decades. The election was closer than in either 1932 or 1936, but Roosevelt still won decisively. He received 55 percent of the popular vote to Willkie's 45 percent, and he won 449 electoral votes to Willkie's 82.

### Neutrality Abandoned

In the last months of 1940, with the election behind him and with the situation in Europe deteriorating, Roosevelt began to make subtle but profound changes in the American role in the war. Great Britain was virtually bankrupt and could no longer meet the cash-and-carry requirements imposed by the Neutrality Acts. The president, therefore, proposed a new system for supplying Britain: "lend-lease." It would allow the government not only to sell but to lend or lease armaments to any nation deemed pivotal to the defense of the United States." In other words, America could funnel weapons to England on the basis of no more than Britain's promise to return them when the war was over. Isolationists attacked the measure bitterly, but Congress enacted the bill by wide margins.

With lend-lease established, Roosevelt soon faced another serious problem. Attacks by German submarines had made shipping lanes in the Atlantic extremely dangerous. The British navy was losing ships more rapidly than it could replace them and was finding it difficult to transport materials across the Atlantic from America. Secretary of War Henry Stimson (who had been Hoover's secretary of state and who returned to the cabinet at Roosevelt's request in 1940) argued that the United States should itself convoy vessels to England; but Roosevelt took a more limited approach. He argued that the western Atlantic was a neutral zone and the responsibility of the American nations. By July 1941, therefore, American ships were patrolling the ocean as far east as Iceland.

At first, Germany did little to challenge these obviously hostile American actions. By September 1941, however, the situation had changed. Nazi forces had invaded the Soviet Union in June of that year. When the Soviets did not surrender, as many had predicted they would, Roosevelt persuaded Congress to extend lend-lease privileges to them. Now American industry was providing vital assistance to Hitler's foes on two fronts, and the American navy was protecting the flow of those goods to Europe. In September, Nazi submarines began a concerted campaign against American vessels. Roosevelt ordered American ships to fire on German submarines "on sight." In October, Nazi submarines hit two American destroyers and sank one of them, the *Reuben James*, killing many American sailors. Congress now voted to allow the United States to arm its merchant vessels and to sail all the way into belligerent ports. The United States had, in effect, launched a naval war against Germany.

In August 1941, Roosevelt met with Churchill aboard a British vessel off the coast of Newfoundland. The president made no military commitments, but he did join with the prime minister in releasing a document that became known as the Atlantic Charter, in which the two nations set out "certain common principles" on which to base "a better future for the world." It called openly for "the final destruction of the Nazi tyranny" and for a new world order in which every nation controlled its own destiny. It was, in effect, a statement of war aims.

### The Road to Pearl Harbor

Japan, in the meantime, was taking advantage of events in Europe to extend its empire in the Pacific. In September 1940, the Japanese signed the Tripartite Pact, a loose defensive alliance with Germany and Italy (although in reality, the European Axis powers never developed a very strong relationship with Japan). In July 1941, imperial troops moved into Indochina and seized the capital of Vietnam, a colony of France. The United States, having broken Japanese codes, knew their next target would be the Dutch East Indies; and when Tokyo failed to respond to Roosevelt's stern warnings, the president froze all Japanese assets in the United States, severely limiting Japan's ability to purchase needed American supplies.

Tokyo now faced a choice. Either it would have to repair relations with the United States to restore the flow of supplies or it would have to find those supplies elsewhere, most notably by seizing British and Dutch possessions

PEARL HARBOR Virtually no one in authority in Hawaii or Washington imagined that the Japanese were capable of launching an attack on a place as far from Japan as Pearl Harbor. That is one reason why intelligence experts failed to predict the attack, despite the many clues they received from deciphering secret Japanese messages. It also helps to explain why so many ships remained bunched together helplessly in the harbor, easy prey to the Japanese bombers.

in the Pacific. At first, the Tokyo government seemed willing to negotiate. But in October, militants in Tokyo forced the moderate prime minister out of office and replaced him with the leader of the war party, General Hideki Tojo. There seemed little alternative now to war.

For several weeks, the Tojo government maintained a pretense of wanting to continue negotiations. But Tokyo had already decided it would not yield on the question of China, and Washington had made clear that it would accept nothing less than a reversal of that policy. By late November, the State Department had given up on the possibility of a peaceful settlement. American intelligence, meanwhile, had decoded Japanese messages that made clear a Japanese attack was imminent. But Washington did not know where the attack would take place. Most officials continued to believe that the Japanese would move first not against American territory but against British or Dutch possessions to the south. A combination of confusion and miscalculation caused the government to overlook indications that Japan intended a direct attack on American forces.

At 7:55 A.M. on Sunday, December 7, 1941, a wave of Japanese bombers attacked the United States naval base at Pearl Harbor in Hawaii. A second wave came an hour later. Within two hours, the United States lost 8 battleships, 3 cruisers, 4 other vessels, 188 airplanes, and several vital shore installations. More than 2,400 soldiers and sailors died, and another 1,000 were injured. The Japanese suffered only light losses.

American forces were now greatly diminished in the Pacific (although by a fortunate accident, no American aircraft carriers—the heart of the Pacific fleet—had been at Pearl Harbor on December 7). Nevertheless, the raid on Hawaii unified the American people behind war. On December 8, after a stirring speech by the president, the Senate voted unanimously and the House voted 388 to 1 to approve a declaration of war against Japan. Three days later, Germany and Italy, Japan's European allies, declared war on the United States; on the same day, December 11, Congress reciprocated without a dissenting vote.

# CHAPTER TWENTY-EIGHT

# America in a World at War

*War on Two Fronts* ∼ *The American People in Wartime*
*The Defeat of the Axis*

HE ATTACK ON PEARL Harbor had thrust the United States into the greatest and most terrible war in the history of humanity. World War I had destroyed centuries-old European social and political institutions. But World War II created unprecedented carnage and horror, not only in Europe but around much of the rest of the globe. And in the end, it changed the world as profoundly as any event of the twentieth century, perhaps any century.

But World War II also transformed the United States in profound, if not always readily visible, ways. The story of American involvement in the war, therefore, is the story of the creation of a new world, both abroad and at home.

## WAR ON TWO FRONTS

Whatever political disagreements and social tensions there may have been among the American people during World War II, there was striking unity of opinion about the conflict itself. But both unity and confidence faced severe tests in the first, troubled months of 1942.

### Containing the Japanese

Ten hours after the strike at Pearl Harbor, Japanese airplanes attacked the American airfields at Manila in the Philippines, destroying much of America's remaining air power in the Pacific. Three days later Guam, an American possession, fell to Japan; Wake Island and Hong Kong followed. The

| TIME LINE | | | |
|---|---|---|---|
| **1942** | **1943** | **1944** | **1945** |
| Battle of Midway | Americans capture Guadalcanal | Allies invade Normandy | Roosevelt dies; Truman becomes president |
| Campaign in Northern Africa | | Roosevelt reelected | Germany surrenders |
| Japanese-Americans interned | Allied invasion of Italy | Americans capture Philippines | U.S. drops atomic bombs on Hiroshima, Nagasaki |
| Manhattan Project begins | | | |
| CORE founded | | | Japan surrenders |
| | Soviet victory at Stalingrad | | |

great British fortress of Singapore in Malaya surrendered in February 1942, the Dutch East Indies in March, Burma in April. In the Philippines, exhausted Filipino and American troops gave up their defense of the islands on May 6.

American strategists planned two broad offensives to turn the tide against the Japanese. One, under the command of General Douglas MacArthur, would move north from Australia, through New Guinea, and eventually to the Philippines. The other, under Admiral Chester Nimitz, would move west from Hawaii toward major Japanese island outposts in the central Pacific. Ultimately, strategists predicted, the two offensives would come together to invade Japan itself.

The Allies achieved their first important victory in the Battle of the Coral Sea, just northwest of Australia, on May 7–8, 1942, when American forces turned back the previously unstoppable Japanese. A month later, there was an even more important turning point northwest of Hawaii. An enormous battle raged for four days, June 3–6, 1942, near the small American outpost at Midway Island, at the end of which the United States, despite great losses, was clearly victorious. The American navy destroyed four Japanese aircraft carriers and lost only one of its own; the action regained control of the central Pacific for the United States.

The Americans took the offensive for the first time several months later in the southern Solomon Islands, to the east of New Guinea. In August 1942, American forces assaulted three of the islands: Gavutu, Tulagi, and Guadalcanal. A struggle of terrible ferocity developed at Guadalcanal and contin-

**World War II in the Pacific**

| | |
|---|---|
| ▨ | Farthest extent of Japanese expansion (to August 1942) |

NAVAL AND TROOP MOVEMENTS

⬅ Japanese forces

⬅ Allied forces

BATTLES

✻ Japanese victories

✻ Allied victories

▼ Atomic bombings

— Supply route

ued for six months, inflicting heavy losses on both sides. In the end, however, the Japanese were forced to abandon the island—and with it their last chance of launching an effective offensive to the south. In both the southern and the central Pacific, therefore, the initiative had shifted to the United States by mid-1943. The Japanese advance had been halted. The Americans, with aid from the Australians and the New Zealanders, now began the slow, arduous process of moving toward the Philippines and Japan itself.

GUADALCANAL  The battle of Guadalcanal, in the Solomon Islands, was the scene of some of the bloodiest and most protracted combat of the Pacific war. United States Marines are shown here charging ashore in August 1942, in the first stages of what became a six-month campaign.

## Holding Off the Germans

In the European war, the United States was fighting in cooperation with, among others, Britain and the exiled "Free French" forces in the west; and it was trying also to conciliate its new ally, the Soviet Union, which was now fighting Hitler in the east. The army chief of staff, General George C. Marshall, supported a plan for a major Allied invasion of France across the English Channel in the spring of 1943, and he placed a hitherto little-known general, Dwight D. Eisenhower, in charge of planning the operation. But the American plan faced challenges from the other Allies. The Soviet Union, which was absorbing the brunt of the German war effort (as it would through most of the conflict), wanted the Allied invasion to begin at the earliest possible moment. The British, on the other hand, wanted first to launch a series of Allied offensives around the edges of the Nazi empire—in northern Africa and southern Europe—before undertaking the major invasion of France.

Roosevelt was torn, but he ultimately decided to support the British plan—in part because he was eager to get American forces into combat quickly and feared that a cross-Channel invasion would take a long time to prepare. At the end of October 1942, the British opened a counteroffensive against Nazi forces in North Africa under General Erwin Rommel, who was threatening the Suez Canal. In a major battle at El Alamein, they forced the Germans to retreat from Egypt. On November 8, Anglo-American forces landed at Oran and Algiers in Algeria and at Casablanca in Morocco—areas under the Nazi-controlled French government at Vichy—and began moving east toward Rommel. The Germans threw the full weight of their forces in Africa against the inexperienced Americans and inflicted a serious defeat on them the Kasserine Pass in Tunisia. General George S. Patton, however, regrouped the American troops and began an effective counteroffensive. With the help of Allied air and naval power and of British forces attacking from the east under Field Marshall Bernard Montgomery (the hero of El Alamein), the American offensive finally drove the last Germans from Africa in May 1943.

The North African campaign had tied up a large proportion of the Allied resources. That was one reason why the planned May 1943 cross-Channel invasion of France had to be postponed, despite angry complaints from the Soviet Union. By now, however, the threat of a Soviet collapse seemed much diminished, for during the winter of 1942–1943, the Red Army had successfully held off a major German assault at Stalingrad in southern Russia. Hitler had committed such enormous forces to the battle, and had suffered such appalling losses, that he could not continue his eastern offensive.

The Soviet successes persuaded Roosevelt to agree, in a January 1943 meeting with Churchill in Casablanca, to a British plan for an Allied invasion of Sicily. Churchill argued that the operation in Sicily might knock Italy out of the war and tie up German divisions that might otherwise be stationed in France. On the night of July 9, 1943, American and British armies landed in southeast Sicily; thirty-eight days later, they had conquered the island and were moving onto the Italian mainland. In the face of these setbacks, Mussolini's government collapsed and the dictator himself fled north toward Germany. Although Mussolini's successor, Pietro Badoglio, quickly committed Italy to the Allies, Germany moved eight divisions into the country and established a powerful defensive line south of Rome. The Allied offensive on the Italian peninsula, which began on September 3, 1943, soon bogged down. Not until May 1944 did the Allies break through the German defenses to resume their northward advance. On June 4, 1944, they captured Rome.

The invasion of Italy contributed to the Allied war effort in several important ways. But it contributed to postponing the invasion of France by as

World War II in North Africa and Italy: The Allied Counteroffensive, 1942–1943

much as a year, deeply embittering the Soviet Union and giving the Soviets time to begin moving toward the countries of eastern Europe.

### America and the Holocaust

In the midst of this intensive fighting, the leaders of the American government found themselves confronted with one of history's great tragedies: the Nazi campaign to exterminate the Jews of Europe—the Holocaust. As early as 1942, high officials in Washington had incontrovertible evidence that Hitler's forces were rounding up Jews and others (including Poles, homosexuals, and communists) from all over Europe, transporting them to concentration camps in eastern Germany and Poland, and systematically murdering them. (The death toll would ultimately reach 6 million Jews and at least 4 million others.) News of the atrocities was reaching the public as well, and pressure began to build for an Allied effort to end the killing or at least to rescue some of the surviving Jews.

The American government consistently resisted almost all such entreaties. Although Allied bombers were flying missions within a few miles of the most notorious death camp, at Auschwitz in Poland, the War Department rejected pleas that the planes try to destroy the crematoria at the camp as militarily unfeasible. American officials also refused requests that the Allies try to destroy railroad lines leading to the camp. And the United States resisted pleas that it admit large numbers of the Jewish refugees attempting to escape Europe.

After 1941, there was probably little American leaders could have done, other than defeat Germany in the war, to save most of Hitler's victims. But more forceful action by the United States (and Britain, which was even less amenable to Jewish requests for assistance) might well have saved at least some lives. That they did not take such action, it seems clear in retrospect, constituted a considerable moral failure. But policymakers found it possible to justify ignoring pleas to help the Jews by insisting that they needed to focus exclusively on the larger goal of winning the war. Any diversion of energy and attention to other purposes, they apparently believed, would distract them from the overriding goal of victory.

## THE AMERICAN PEOPLE IN WARTIME

Not since the Civil War had the United States been involved in so prolonged and consuming a military experience as World War II. American armed forces engaged in combat around the globe for nearly four years. American society, in the meantime, experienced changes that reached into virtually every corner of the nation.

### Prosperity and the Rights of Labor

World War II had its most profound impact on American domestic life by ending the Great Depression at last. By the middle of 1941, the economic problems of the 1930s—unemployment, deflation, industrial sluggishness—had virtually vanished before the great wave of wartime industrial expansion.

The most important agent of the new prosperity was government spending, which after 1939 was pumping more money into the economy each year than all the New Deal relief agencies combined had done. In 1939, the federal budget had been $9 billion; by 1945, it had risen to $100 billion. Largely as a result, the gross national product soared: from $91 billion in 1939 to $166 billion in 1945. Personal incomes in some regions grew by as much as

100 percent or more. The demands of wartime production created a shortage of consumer goods, so many wage earners diverted much of their new affluence into savings, which would later help keep the economic boom alive in the postwar years.

The impact of government spending was perhaps most dramatic in the West. The West Coast, naturally, became the launching point for most of the naval war against Japan, and the government created large manufacturing facilities in California and elsewhere to serve the needs of its military. Altogether, the government made almost $40 billion worth of capital investments (factories, military and transportation facilities, highways, power plants) in the West during the war, more than in any other region. Ten percent of all the money the federal government spent between 1940 and 1945 went to California alone. By the end of the war, the economy of the Pacific Coast and, to a lesser extent, other areas of the West had been transformed. The Pacific Coast had become the center of the growing American aircraft industry. New yards in southern California, Washington State, and elsewhere made the West a center of the shipbuilding industry. Los Angeles, formerly a medium-sized city notable chiefly for its film industry, now became a major industrial center as well.

Instead of the prolonged and debilitating unemployment that had been the most troubling feature of the Depression economy, the war created a serious labor shortage. The armed forces took over 15 million men and women out of the civilian work force at the same time that the demand for labor was rising rapidly. Nevertheless, the civilian work force increased by almost 20 percent during the war. The 7 million who had previously been unemployed accounted for some of the increase; the employment of many people previously considered inappropriate for the work force—the very young, the elderly, minorities, and, most important, several million women—accounted for the rest of it.

The war gave an enormous boost to union membership, which rose from about 10.5 million in 1941 to over 3 million in 1945. But it also created important new restrictions on the ability of unions to fight for their members' demands. The government was principally interested in keeping production moving without disruption and preventing inflation. It managed to win two important concessions from union leaders toward those ends. One was the "no-strike" pledge, by which unions agreed not to stop production in wartime. Another was the so-called Little Steel formula, which set a 15 percent limit on wage increases. In return, the government provided labor with a "maintenance-of-membership" agreement, which ensured that the thousands of new workers pouring into unionized defense plants would be automatically enrolled in the unions. The agreement guaranteed the continued health of the union organizations, but in return workers had to give up the right to demand major gains during the war.

Despite the no-strike pledge, there were nearly 15,000 work stoppages during the war, mostly wildcat strikes (strikes unauthorized by the union leadership), many protesting harsh working conditions and high levels of stress. When the United Mine Workers defied the government by striking in May 1943, Congress reacted by passing, over Roosevelt's veto, the Smith-Connally Act (War Labor Disputes Act), which required that unions wait thirty days before striking and which empowered the president to seize a struck war plant. In the meantime, public animosity toward labor rose rapidly, and many states passed laws to limit union power.

### Stabilizing the Boom and Mobilizing Production

The fear of deflation, the central concern of the 1930s, gave way during the war to a fear of inflation, particularly after prices rose 25 percent in the two years before Pearl Harbor. In October 1942, Congress grudgingly responded to the president's request and passed the Anti-Inflation Act, which gave the administration authority to freeze agricultural prices, wages, salaries, and rents throughout the country. Enforcement of these provisions was the task of the Office of Price Administration (OPA), led first by Leon Henderson and then by Chester Bowles. In part because of its success, inflation was a much less serious problem during World War II than it had been during World War I. Even so, the OPA was never popular. There was widespread resentment of its controls over wages and prices. And there was only grudging acquiescence to its complicated system of rationing scarce consumer goods: coffee, sugar, meat, butter, canned goods, shoes, tires, gasoline, and fuel oil. Black-marketing and overcharging grew in proportions far beyond OPA policing capacity.

From 1941 to 1945, the federal government spent a total of $321 billion—twice as much as it had spent in the entire 150 years of its existence to that point, and ten times as much as the cost of World War I. The national debt rose from $49 billion in 1941 to $259 billion in 1945. The government borrowed about half the revenues it needed by selling $100 billion worth of bonds. Much of the rest it raised by radically increasing income-tax rates, through the Revenue Act of 1942. To simplify collection, Congress enacted a withholding system of payroll deductions in 1943.

The search for an effective mechanism to mobilize the economy for war began as early as 1939 and continued for nearly four years. One failed agency after another attempted to bring order to the mobilization effort. Finally, in January 1942, the president responded to widespread criticism by creating the War Production Board (WPB), under the direction of former Sears Roebuck executive Donald Nelson. In theory, the WPB was to be a "superagency," with broad powers over the economy. In fact, it never had as much authority as its World War I equivalent, the War Industries Board.

Throughout its troubled history, the WPB found itself constantly outmaneuvered and frustrated. It was never able to win complete control over military purchases; the army and navy often circumvented the board entirely in negotiating contracts with producers. It was never able to satisfy the complaints of small business, which charged (correctly) that most contracts were going to large corporations. Gradually, the president transferred much of the WPB's authority to a new office located within the White House: the Office of War Mobilization (OWM). But the OWM was only slightly more successful than the WPB.

Despite the administrative problems, however, the war economy managed to meet almost all of the nation's critical war needs. By the beginning of 1944, American factories were, in fact, producing more than the government needed. Their output was twice that of all the Axis countries combined.

### African Americans and the War

During World War I, many African Americans had eagerly seized the chance to serve in the armed forces, believing that their patriotic efforts would win them an enhanced position in postwar society. They had been cruelly disappointed. As World War II approached, blacks were again determined to use the conflict to improve the position of their race—this time, however, not by currying favor but by making demands.

In the summer of 1941, A. Philip Randolph, president of the Brotherhood of Sleeping Car Porters, an important union with a primarily black membership, began to insist that the government require companies receiving defense contracts to integrate their work forces. To mobilize support for the demand, Randolph planned a massive march on Washington. Roosevelt finally persuaded Randolph to cancel the march in return for a promise to establish what became the Fair Employment Practices Commission (FEPC) to investigate discrimination against blacks in war industries. The FEPC's enforcement powers, and thus its effectiveness, were limited, but its creation was a rare symbolic victory for African American demands of the government.

The need for labor in war plants greatly increased the migration of blacks from the rural areas of the South into industrial cities. The migration bettered the economic condition of many African Americans, but it also created urban tensions and occasionally violence. The most serious conflict occurred in Detroit in 1943, when racial friction in the city produced a major riot in which thirty-four people died, twenty-five of them blacks.

Despite such tensions, the leading black organizations redoubled their efforts during the war to challenge the system of segregation. The Congress of Racial Equality (CORE), organized in 1942, mobilized mass popular resistance to discrimination in a way that the older, more conservative organizations had never done. Randolph, Bayard Rustin, James Farmer, and other, younger black leaders helped organize sit-ins and demonstrations in segregated theaters and restaurants. Their defiant public spirit would survive into the 1950s and help produce the civil rights movement.

Pressure for change was also growing within the military. At first, the armed forces maintained their traditional practice of limiting blacks to the most menial assignments, keeping them in segregated training camps and units, and barring them entirely from the Marine Corps and the Army Air Force. Gradually, however, military leaders were forced to make adjustments—in part because of public and political pressures, but also because they recognized that these forms of segregation were wasting manpower. By the end of the war, the number of black servicemen had increased sevenfold, to 700,000; some training camps were being at least partially integrated; blacks were being allowed to serve on ships with white sailors; and more black units were being sent into combat. But tensions remained. In some of the partially integrated army bases—Fort Dix, New Jersey, for example—riots occasionally broke out when blacks protested having to serve in segregated divisions. Substantial discrimination survived in all the services until well after the war. But within the military, as within society at large, the traditional pattern of race relations was slowly eroding.

### Indians and the War

Approximately 25,000 Indians performed military service during World War II. Many Native Americans served in combat. Others (mostly Navajos) became "code-talkers," working in military communications and speaking their own language (which enemy forces would be unlikely to understand) over the radio and the telephones. The war had important effects on the Indians who served in the military. It brought them into intimate contact (often for the first time) with white society, and it awakened among some of them a taste for the material benefits of life in capitalist America that they would retain after the war. Some never returned to the reservations, but chose to remain in the non-Indian world and assimilate to its ways.

The war had important effects, too, on those Native Americans who stayed on the reservations. Little war work reached the tribes. Government subsidies dwindled. Talented young people left the reservations to serve in the military or work in war production, creating manpower shortages in some tribes. The wartime emphasis on national unity undermined support for the revitalization of tribal autonomy that the Indian Reorganization Act of 1934 had launched. New pressures emerged to eliminate the reservation system and require the tribes to assimilate into white society—pressures so severe that John Collier, the energetic director of the Bureau of Indian Affairs who had done so much to promote the reinvigoration of the reservations, resigned in 1945.

### Mexican-American War Workers

Large numbers of Mexican workers entered the United States during the war in response to labor shortages on the Pacific coast and in the Southwest. The American and Mexican governments agreed in 1942 to a program by which *braceros* (contract laborers) would be admitted to the United States for a limited time to work at specific jobs, and American employers in some parts of the Southwest began actively recruiting Hispanic workers. During the Depression, many Mexican farmworkers had been deported to make room for desperate white workers. The wartime labor shortage caused farm owners to begin hiring them again. More important, however, Mexicans were able for the first time to find significant numbers of factory jobs. They formed the second-largest group of migrants (after blacks) to American cities in the 1940s. They were concentrated mainly in the West, but there were significant Mexican communities in Chicago, Detroit, and other industrial cities in the Midwest and East.

The sudden expansion of Mexican-American neighborhoods created tensions and occasionally conflict in some American cities. White residents of Los Angeles became alarmed at the activities of Mexican-American teenagers, many of whom were joining street gangs *(pachucos)*. The youths were particularly distinctive because of their style of dress, which some whites considered outrageous. They wore long, loose jackets with padded shoulders, baggy pants tied at the ankles, long watch chains, broad-brimmed hats, and greased, ducktail hairstyles. The outfit was known as a "zoot suit."

In June 1943, animosity toward the "zoot-suiters" produced a four-day riot in Los Angeles, during which white sailors stationed at a base in Long Beach invaded Mexican-American communities and attacked zoot-suiters (in response to alleged attacks by them on servicemen). The police did little to restrain the sailors, who grabbed Hispanic teenagers, tore off and burned their clothes, cut off their ducktails, and beat them. When Mexicans tried to fight back, the police moved in and arrested them. In the aftermath of the "zoot-suit riots," Los Angeles passed a law prohibiting the wearing of zoot suits.

### Women and Children in Wartime

The war drew increasing numbers of women into roles from which they had previously been largely barred by custom or law. The number of women in the work force increased by nearly 60 percent, as many women took indus-

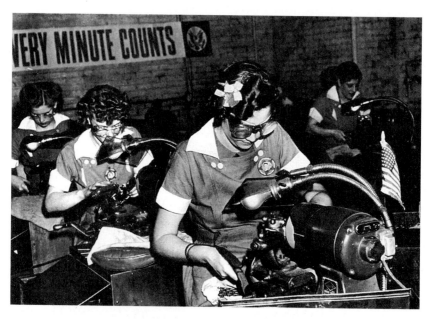

WOMEN WORKERS DURING WORLD WAR II Women—including many who had never worked for pay before—took over a broad range of traditionally male industrial jobs during World War II, replacing men serving in the armed forces. Some did so as a patriotic duty, some because they needed the money. But most also came to enjoy the independence paid employment provided, one reason why the number of women in the work force did not decline dramatically after the war.

trial jobs to replace male workers serving in the military. And these wage-earning women were more likely to be married and were on the whole older than most of those who had entered the work force in the past.

But while economic and military necessity eroded some of the popular objections to women in the workplace, obstacles remained. Many factory owners continued to categorize jobs by gender, reserving the most lucrative positions for men. (Female work, like male work, was also categorized by race: black women were usually assigned more menial tasks, and paid at a lower rate, than their white counterparts.) Still, women did make important inroads in industrial employment during the war. Women had been working in industry for over a century, but some began now to take on heavy industrial jobs that had long been considered "men's work." The famous wartime image of "Rosie the Riveter" symbolized the new importance of the female industrial worker. Women joined unions in substantial numbers, and they helped erode at least some of the prejudice, including the prejudice against mothers working, that had previously kept many of them from paid employment.

In the end, however, most women workers during the war were employed not in factories but in service-sector jobs. Above all, they worked for the government, whose bureaucratic needs expanded dramatically alongside its military and industrial needs. Even within the military, which enlisted substantial numbers of women as WAACs (army) and WAVEs (navy), most female work was clerical.

The new opportunities produced new problems. Many mothers whose husbands were in the military had to combine working with caring for their children. The scarcity of child-care facilities or other community services meant that some women had no choice but to leave young children—often known as "latchkey children" or "eight-hour orphans"—at home alone (or sometimes locked in cars in factory parking lots) while they worked.

Perhaps in part because of the family dislocations the war produced, juvenile crime rose markedly in the war years. Young boys were arrested at rapidly increasing rates for car theft and other burglary, vandalism, and vagrancy. The arrest rate for prostitutes, many of whom were teenage girls, rose too, as did the incidence of venereal disease. For many children, however, the distinctive experience of the war years was not crime but work. More than a third of all teenagers between the ages of fourteen and eighteen were employed late in the war, causing some reduction in high-school enrollments.

The return of prosperity helped increase the marriage rate and lower the age at which people married, but many marriages were unable to sur-

# A M E R I C A N    V O I C E S

SARAH KILLINGSWORTH

## *An African-American Woman Encounters the Wartime Industrial Boom*

 THE WAR STARTED and jobs kinda opened up for women that the men had. . . . They started takin' applications at Douglas, to work in a defense plant. I was hired.

I didn't want a job on the production line. I heard so many things about accidents. . . . I was frightened. All I wanted to do was get in the factory, because they were payin' more than what I'd been makin'. . . . I got the job workin' nights in the ladies' rest room, which wasn't hard. . . .

I do know one thing, this place was very segregated when I first come here. Oh, Los Angeles, you just couldn't go and sit down like you do now. You had certain places you went. You had to more or less stick to the restaurants and hotels where black people were. It wasn't until the war that it really opened up. 'Cause when I come out here it was awful, just like bein' in the South. . . .

For a person that grew up and knew nothin' but hard times to get out on my own at eighteen years old and make a decent livin' and still make a decent person outa myself, I really am proud of me. . . .

In ways it was too bad that so many lives were lost. But I think it was for a worthy cause, because it did make a way for us. And we were able to really get out.

SOURCE: Studs Terkel, *The Good War*, pp. 113–116. Copyright © 1984 by Studs Terkel. Reprinted by permission of Pantheon Books.

vive the pressures of wartime separation. The divorce rate rose rapidly. The rise in the birth rate that accompanied the increase in marriages was the first sign of what would become the great postwar "baby boom."

## The Internment of the Japanese Americans

During World War I, popular prejudice against the German people—and against German Americans—had run high. No such passions emerged against Germans, Italians, or Americans of German and Italian descent during World War II. The same could not be said, however, about the Japanese. After the attack on Pearl Harbor, government propaganda and popular culture combined to create an image of the Japanese as a devious, malign, and savage people.

Predictably, this racial animosity soon extended to Americans of Japanese descent. There were not many Japanese Americans in the United States—only about 127,000, most of them concentrated in a few areas in California. About a third of them were unnaturalized, first-generation immigrants (Issei); two-thirds were naturalized or native-born citizens of the United States (Nisei). Because they generally kept to themselves and preserved traditional Japanese cultural patterns, it was possible for others to imagine that the Japanese Americans were engaged in conspiracies on behalf of their ancestral homeland. (There is no evidence to suggest that they actually were.) Public pressure to remove the "threat" grew steadily.

Finally, in February 1942, in response to pressure from military officials and political leaders on the West Coast and recommendations from the War Department, the president authorized the army to "intern" the Japanese Americans. More than 100,000 people (Issei and Nisei alike) were rounded up, told to dispose of their property however they could (which often meant simply abandoning it), and taken to what the government euphemistically termed "relocation centers" in the "interior." In fact, they were facilities little different from prisons, many of them located in the western mountains and desert. Conditions in the internment camps were not brutal, but they were harsh and uncomfortable. More important, loyal, hardworking people (many of them citizens of the United States) were forced to spend up to three years in grim, debilitating isolation, barred from lucrative employment, provided with only minimal medical care, and deprived of decent schools for their children. (In Hawaii, by contrast, residents of Japanese descent encountered little harassment, perhaps because they were more numerous and more crucial to the economy of the islands.) The Supreme Court upheld the evacuation in a 1944 decision; and although most of the Japanese Americans were released later that year, they were largely unable to win any compensation for their losses until Congress finally acted to redress the wrongs in the late 1980s.

## The Retreat from Reform

Late in 1943, Franklin Roosevelt publicly suggested that "Dr. New Deal," as he called it, had served its purpose and should now give way to "Dr. Win-the-War." The statement reflected the president's own genuine shift in concern: victory was now more important than reform. But it reflected, too, the political reality that had emerged during the first two years of war. Liberals in government were finding themselves unable to enact new programs. They were even finding it difficult to protect existing ones from conservative assault.

The greatest assault on New Deal reforms came from conservatives in Congress, who seized on the war as an excuse to do what many had wanted to do in peacetime: dismantle many of the achievements of the New Deal. They were assisted by the end of mass unemployment, which decreased the need for such relief programs as the Civilian Conservation Corps and the Works Progress Administration (both of which Congress abolished). They were assisted, too, by their own increasing numbers. In the congressional elections of 1942, Republicans gained 47 seats in the House and 10 in the Senate.

Republicans approached the 1944 election determined to exploit what they believed was resentment of wartime regimentation and unhappiness with Democratic reform. They nominated as their candidate the young and vigorous governor of New York, Thomas E. Dewey. Roosevelt was unopposed within his party, but Democratic leaders pressured him to abandon Vice President Henry Wallace, an advanced New Dealer and hero of the CIO, and replace him with a more moderate figure. Roosevelt reluctantly acquiesced in the selection of Senator Harry S. Truman of Missouri, who had won acclaim as chairman of the Senate War Investigating Committee (known as the Truman Committee). It had compiled an impressive record uncovering waste and corruption in wartime production.

The conduct of the war was not an issue in the campaign. Instead, the election revolved around domestic economic issues and, indirectly, the president's health. The president was, in fact, gravely ill, suffering from, among other things, arteriosclerosis. It is not too much to say that he was dying. But the campaign seemed momentarily to revive him. He made several strenuous public appearances late in October, which dispelled popular doubts about his health and ensured his reelection. He captured 53.5 percent of the popular vote to Dewey's 46 percent. (It was a substantial margin of victory, but the lowest percentage of his four campaigns). He won 432 electoral votes to Dewey's 99. Democrats lost 1 seat in the Senate, gained 20 in the House, and maintained control of both.

## THE DEFEAT OF THE AXIS

By the middle of 1943, America and its allies had succeeded in stopping the Axis advance both in Europe and in the Pacific. In the next two years, the Allies themselves seized the offensive and launched a series of powerful drives that rapidly led the way to victory.

### The Liberation of France

By early 1944, American and British bombers were attacking German industrial installations and other targets almost around the clock, drastically cutting production and impeding transportation. Especially devastating was the massive bombing of such German cities as Leipzig, Dresden, and Berlin. A February 1945 incendiary raid on Dresden created a great firestorm that destroyed three-fourths of the previously undamaged city and killed approximately 135,000 people, almost all civilians. The morality of such attacks has been much debated in the years since the war; but at the time, few Americans questioned the claims of military leaders that the bombing cleared the way for the great Allied invasion of France in the late spring.

An enormous offensive force had been gathering in England for two years before the spring of 1944: almost 3 million troops, and perhaps the greatest array of naval vessels and armaments ever assembled in one place. On the morning of June 6, 1944, this vast invasion force moved into action. The landing came not at the narrowest part of the English Channel, where the Germans had expected and prepared for it, but along sixty miles of the Cotentin Peninsula on the coast of Normandy. While airplanes and battleships offshore bombarded the Nazi defenses, 4,000 vessels landed troops and supplies on the beaches. (Three divisions of paratroopers had been dropped behind the German lines the night before.) Fighting was intense along the beach, but the superior manpower and equipment of the Allied forces gradually prevailed. Within a week, the German forces had been dislodged from virtually the entire Normandy coast.

For the next month, further progress remained slow. But in late July in the Battle of Saint-Lô, General Omar Bradley's First Army smashed through the German lines. George S. Patton's Third Army, spearheaded by heavy tank attacks, then moved through the hole Bradley had created and began a drive into the heart of France. On August 25, Free French forces arrived in Paris and liberated the city from four years of German occupation. By mid-September the Allied armies had driven the Germans almost entirely out of France and Belgium.

The great Allied drive came to a halt, however, at the Rhine River against a firm line of Nazi defenses. In mid-December, German forces struck in desperation along fifty miles of front in the Ardennes Forest. In the Battle of the Bulge (named for a large bulge that appeared in the American lines as the Germans pressed forward), they drove fifty-five miles toward Antwerp before they were finally stopped at Bastogne. It was the last major battle on the western front.

While the Allies were fighting their way through France, Soviet forces were sweeping westward into central Europe and the Balkans. In late January 1945, the Russians launched a great offensive toward the Oder River, inside Germany. By early spring, they were ready to launch a final assault against Berlin. General Omar Bradley, in the meantime, was pushing toward the Rhine from the west. Early in March, his forces captured the city of Cologne, on the river's west bank. The next day, he discovered and seized an undamaged bridge over the river at Remagen; Allied troops were soon

A VICTORY CELEBRATION IN SAN FRANCISCO Soldiers and sailors in San Francisco react jubilantly to the news that the war in Europe has ended. But the news they celebrate was, in fact, one of the many false rumors of surrender circulating in the spring of 1945. The actual V-E Day occurred several weeks later.

pouring across the Rhine. In the following weeks the British commander, Montgomery, with a million troops, pushed into Germany in the north while Bradley's army, sweeping through central Germany, completed the encirclement of 300,000 German soldiers in the Ruhr.

The German resistance was now broken on both fronts. American forces were moving eastward faster than they had anticipated and could have beaten the Russians to Berlin and Prague. The American and British high commands decided, instead, to halt the advance along the Elbe River in central Germany to await the Russians. That decision enabled the Soviets to occupy eastern Germany and Czechoslovakia.

On April 30, with Soviet forces on the outskirts of Berlin, Adolf Hitler killed himself in his bunker in the capital. And on May 8, 1945, the remaining German forces surrendered unconditionally. V-E (Victory in Europe) Day prompted great celebrations in western Europe and in the United States, tempered by the knowledge of the continuing war against Japan.

## The Pacific Offensive

In February 1944, American naval forces under Admiral Chester Nimitz won a series of victories in the Marshall Islands and cracked the outer perimeter of the Japanese Empire. Within a month, the navy had destroyed other vital Japanese bastions. American submarines, in the meantime, were decimating Japanese shipping and crippling Japan's domestic economy.

A more frustrating struggle was in progress in the meantime on the Asian mainland. In 1942, the Japanese had forced General Joseph H. Stilwell of the United States out of Burma and had moved their own troops as far west as the mountains bordering on India. For a time, Stilwell supplied the isolated Chinese forces still fighting Japan with an aerial ferry over the Himalayas. In 1943, finally, he led Chinese, Indian, and a few American troops back through northern Burma, constructing a road and pipeline across the mountains into China (the Burma Road, also known as the Ledo Road or Stilwell Road); the road opened in the fall of 1944.

By then, however, the Japanese had launched a major counteroffensive and had driven so deep into the Chinese interior that they threatened the terminus of the Burma Road and the center of Chinese government at Chungking. The Japanese offensive precipitated a long-simmering feud between General Stilwell and Premier Chiang Kai-shek of China. Stilwell was indignant because Chiang was using many of his troops to maintain an armed frontier against the Chinese communists and would not deploy those troops against the Japanese.

The decisive battles of the war against Japan, however, occurred in the Pacific. In mid-June 1944, an enormous American armada struck the heavily fortified Mariana Islands and, after some of the bloodiest operations of the war, captured Tinian, Guam, and Saipan, 1,350 miles from Tokyo. In September, American forces landed on the western Carolines. And on October 20, General MacArthur's troops landed on Leyte Island in the Philippines. The Japanese now employed virtually their entire fleet against the Allied invaders in three major encounters—which together constituted the decisive Battle of Leyte Gulf, the largest naval engagement in history. American forces held off the Japanese onslaught and sank four Japanese carriers, all but destroying Japan's capacity to continue a serious naval war. Nevertheless, as American forces advanced closer to the Japanese mainland early in 1945, the imperial forces seemed only to increase their resistance. In February 1945, American marines seized the tiny volcanic island of Iwo Jima, only 750 miles from Tokyo, but only after the costliest battle in the history of the Marine Corps.

The battle for Okinawa, an island only 370 miles south of Japan, was further evidence of the strength of the Japanese resistance in these last desperate days. Week after week, the Japanese sent kamikaze (suicide) planes against American and British ships, sacrificing 3,500 of them while inflicting great damage. Japanese troops on shore launched desperate nighttime attacks on the American lines. The United States and its allies suffered nearly 50,000 casualties before finally capturing Okinawa in late June 1945. Over 100,000 Japanese died in the siege.

It seemed that the same kind of bitter fighting would await the Americans when they invaded Japan. But there were signs early in 1945 that such an invasion might not be necessary. The Japanese had almost no ships or planes left with which to fight. The firebombing of Tokyo in May, in which American bombers dropped napalm on the city and created a firestorm in which over 80,000 people died, further weakened the Japanese will to resist. Moderate Japanese leaders, who had long since concluded the war was lost, were increasing their power within the government and were looking for ways to bring the fighting to an end, although they continued to face powerful opposition from military leaders. Whether the moderates could ultimately have prevailed is a question about which historians and others continue to disagree. In any case, their efforts became superfluous in August 1945, when the United States made use of a terrible new weapon it had been developing throughout the war.

## The Manhattan Project and Atomic Warfare

Reports had reached the United States in 1939 that Nazi scientists had taken the first step toward the creation of an atomic bomb, a weapon more powerful than any ever previously devised. The United States and Britain immediately began a race to develop the weapon before the Germans did.

Over the next three years, the government secretly poured nearly $2 billion into the so-called Manhattan Project—a massive scientific effort conducted at hidden laboratories in Oak Ridge, Tennessee; Los Alamos, New Mexico; and other sites. (The name of the project had emerged earlier, when many of the atomic physicists had been working at Columbia University in New York.) The scientists pushed ahead much faster than anyone had predicted. Even so, the war in Europe ended before they were ready to test the first bomb. Just before dawn on July 16, 1945, in the desert near Alamogordo, New Mexico, the scientists gathered to witness the first atomic explosion in history: a blinding flash of light brighter than any ever seen on earth, and a huge, billowing mushroom cloud.

News of the explosion reached President Harry S. Truman (who had taken office in April on the death of Roosevelt) in Potsdam, Germany, where he was attending a conference of Allied leaders. He issued an ultimatum to the Japanese (signed jointly by the British) demanding that they surrender by August 3 or face utter devastation. When the Japanese failed to meet the deadline, Truman ordered the air force to use the new atomic weapons against Japan.

Controversy has continued for decades over whether Truman's decision to use the bomb was justified and what his motives were. Some have argued that the atomic attack was unnecessary—that had the United States agreed to the survival of the emperor (which it ultimately did agree to in any case), or had it waited only a few more weeks, the Japanese would have surrendered. Others argue that nothing less than the atomic bombs could have persuaded the Japanese to surrender without a costly American invasion. Some critics of the decision, including some of the scientists involved in the Manhattan Project, have argued that whatever the Japanese intentions, the United States, as a matter of morality, should not have used the terrible new weapon.

The nation's military and political leaders, however, showed little concern about such matters. Truman, who had not even known of the existence of the Manhattan Project until he became president, was, apparently, making what he believed to be a simple military decision. A weapon was available that would end the war quickly; he could see no reason not to use it.

On August 6, 1945, an American B-29, the *Enola Gay*, dropped an atomic

HIROSHIMA AFTER THE BOMB Where once a bustling city stood, only rubble remains. This photograph shows the center of Hiroshima shortly after it was devastated by the first of two atomic bombs the United States dropped on Japan in the last days of World War II.

weapon on the Japanese industrial center at Hiroshima. With a single bomb, the United States completely incinerated a four-square-mile area at the center of the previously undamaged city. More than 80,000 civilians died, according to later American estimates. Many more survived to suffer the crippling effects of radioactive fallout or to pass those effects on to their children in the form of birth defects.

The Japanese government, stunned by the attack, was at first unable to agree on a response. Two days later, on August 8, the Soviet Union declared war on Japan. And the following day, another American plane dropped another atomic weapon—this time on the city of Nagasaki—inflicting 100,000 deaths and horrible damage on yet another unfortunate community. Finally, the emperor intervened to break the stalemate in the cabinet, and on August 14 the government announced that it was ready to give up. On September 2, 1945, on board the American battleship *Missouri*, anchored in Tokyo Bay, Japanese officials signed the articles of surrender.

The greatest war in the history of mankind had come to an end, and the United States had emerged from it not only victorious but in a position of unprecedented power, influence, and prestige. It was a victory, however, that few could greet with unambiguous joy. Fourteen million combatants had died in the struggle. Many more civilians had perished. The United States had suffered only light casualties in comparison with some other nations, but the cost had still been high: 322,000 dead, another 800,000 injured. And despite the sacrifices, the world continued to face an uncertain future, menaced by the threat of nuclear warfare and by an emerging antagonism between the world's two strongest nations—the United States and the Soviet Union—that would darken the peace for many decades to come.

# CHAPTER TWENTY-NINE

# America and the Cold War

*Origins of the Cold War*  ∽  *The Collapse of the Peace*
*America After the War*  ∽  *The Korean War*
*The Crusade Against Subversion*

VEN BEFORE WORLD WAR II ended, there were signs of tension between the United States and the Soviet Union. Once the hostilities were over, those tensions quickly grew to create what became known as the "Cold War"—a tense and dangerous rivalry between the two former allies that would cast its shadow over international affairs for decades. The Cold War also had profound effects on American domestic life, ultimately producing the most corrosive outbreak of antiradical hysteria of the century. America in the postwar years was both powerful and prosperous, but it was also for a time troubled and uncertain about its future.

## ORIGINS OF THE COLD WAR

No issue in twentieth-century American history has aroused more debate than the question of the origins of the Cold War. (See "Debating the Past," pp. 801–802.) Some have claimed that Soviet duplicity and expansionism created the international tensions, others that American provocations and imperial ambitions were at least equally to blame. Most historians agree, however, that wherever the preponderance of blame may lie, both the United States and the Soviet Union contributed to the atmosphere of hostility and suspicion that quickly clouded the peace.

### Sources of Soviet-American Tension

At the heart of the rivalry between the United States and the Soviet Union in the 1940s was a fundamental difference in the ways the great powers envisioned the postwar world. One vision was that of many people in the

| TIME LINE | | | |
|---|---|---|---|
| **1945** | **1946** | **1947** | **1948** |
| Yalta and Potsdam Conferences | Atomic Energy Commission established | Truman Doctrine | Berlin blockade |
| | | Marshall Plan proposed | Truman elected president |
| | Iran crisis | National Security Act | |
| | | Taft-Hartley Act | Hiss case begins |
| United Nations founded | | | |
| **1949** | **1950** | **1951** | **1952** |
| NATO established | NSC-68 | Truman fires MacArthur | American occupation of Japan ends |
| Soviet Union explodes A-bomb | Korean War begins | | |
| | McCarthy's anticommunism campaign begins | | Eisenhower elected president |

United States. First openly outlined in the Atlantic Charter in 1941, it was a vision of a world in which nations abandoned their traditional belief in military alliances and spheres of influence and governed their relations with one another through democratic processes, with an international organization serving as the arbiter of disputes and the protector of every nation's right of self-determination.

The other vision was that of the Soviet Union and to some extent, it gradually became clear, of Great Britain. Both Stalin and Churchill had signed the Atlantic Charter. But Britain had always been uneasy about the implications of the self-determination ideal for its own enormous empire. And the Soviet Union was determined to create a secure sphere for itself in Central and Eastern Europe as protection against possible future aggression from the West. Both Churchill and Stalin, therefore, tended to envision a postwar structure in which the great powers would control areas of strategic interest to them, in which something vaguely similar to the traditional European balance of power would reemerge.

By the end of the war Roosevelt was able to win at least the partial consent of Winston Churchill to his principles; but although he believed at times that Stalin would similarly relent, he never managed to steer the Soviets from their determination to control Central and Eastern Europe and from their vision of a postwar order in which each of the great powers would dominate its own sphere. Gradually, the differences between these two positions would turn the peacemaking process into a form of warfare.

*Wartime Diplomacy*

Serious strains had already begun to develop in the alliance with the Soviet Union in January 1943, when Roosevelt and Churchill met in Casablanca, Morocco, to discuss Allied strategy. (Stalin had declined Roosevelt's invitation to attend.) The two leaders could not accept Stalin's most important demand—the immediate opening of a second front in western Europe. But they tried to reassure Stalin by announcing that they would accept nothing less than the unconditional surrender of the Axis powers. It was a signal that the Americans and British would not negotiate a separate peace with Hitler and leave the Soviets to fight on alone.

In November 1943, Roosevelt and Churchill traveled to Teheran, Iran, for their first meeting with Stalin. By now, however, Roosevelt's most effective bargaining tool—Stalin's need for American assistance in his struggle against Germany—had been largely removed. The German advance against Russia had been halted; Soviet forces were now launching their own westward offensive. Meanwhile, new tensions had emerged in the alliance as a result of the refusal by the British and Americans to allow any Soviet participation in the creation of a new Italian government following the fall of Mussolini.

Nevertheless, the Teheran Conference seemed in most respects a success. Roosevelt and Stalin established a cordial personal relationship. Stalin agreed to an American request that the Soviet Union enter the war in the Pacific soon after the end of hostilities in Europe. Roosevelt, in turn, promised that an Anglo-American second front would be established within six months. All three leaders agreed in principle to a postwar international organization and to efforts to prevent a resurgence of German expansionism.

On other matters, however, the origins of future disagreements were already visible. Most important was the question of the future of Poland. Roosevelt and Churchill were willing to agree to a movement of the Soviet border westward, allowing Stalin to annex some historically Polish territory. But on the nature of the postwar government in the portion of Poland that would remain independent, there were sharp differences. Roosevelt and Churchill supported the claims of the Polish government-in-exile that had been functioning in London since 1940; Stalin wished to install another, pro-communist exiled government that had spent the war in Lublin, in the Soviet Union. The three leaders avoided a bitter conclusion to the Teheran Conference only by leaving the issue unresolved.

## Yalta

For more than a year after Teheran, the Grand Alliance among the United States, Britain, and the Soviet Union alternated between high tension and warm amicability. In February 1945, Roosevelt joined Churchill and Stalin for a great peace conference in the Soviet city of Yalta. On a number of issues, the Big Three reached mutually satisfactory agreements. In return for Stalin's renewed promise to enter the Pacific war, Roosevelt agreed that the Soviet Union should receive some of the territory in the Pacific that Russia had lost in the 1904 Russo-Japanese War.

The negotiators also agreed to accept a plan for a new international organization, a plan that had been hammered out the previous summer at a conference in Washington, D.C., at the Dumbarton Oaks estate. The new United Nations would contain a General Assembly, in which every member would be represented, and a Security Council, with permanent representatives of the five major powers (the United States, Britain, France, the Soviet Union, and China), each of which would have veto power. The Security Council would also have temporary delegates from several other nations. These agreements became the basis of the United Nations charter, drafted at a conference of fifty nations beginning April 25, 1945, in San Fran-

YALTA, 1945 Churchill *(left)* and Stalin *(right)* were shocked at the physical appearance of Franklin Roosevelt *(center)* when he arrived for their critical meeting at Yalta. Roosevelt had enough energy to perform capably at the conference, but he was in fact gravely ill. Two months later, not long after he gave Congress what turned out to be an unrealistically optimistic report of the prospects for postwar peace, he died.

cisco. The United States Senate ratified the charter in July by a vote of 80 to 2 (a striking contrast to the slow and painful defeat it had administered to the charter of the League of Nations twenty-five years before).

On other issues, however, the Yalta Conference produced no real accord. Basic disagreement remained about the postwar Polish government. Stalin, whose armies now occupied Poland, had already installed a government composed of the pro-communist "Lublin" Poles. Roosevelt and Churchill insisted that the pro-Western "London" Poles must be allowed a place in the Warsaw regime. Roosevelt envisioned a government based on free, democratic elections—which both he and Stalin recognized the pro-Western forces would win. Stalin agreed only to a vague compromise by which an unspecified number of pro-Western Poles would be granted a place in the government. He reluctantly consented to hold "free and unfettered elections" in Poland, but he made no commitment to a date for them. They did not take place for more than forty years.

Nor was there agreement about the future of Germany. Roosevelt seemed to want a reconstructed and reunited Germany—one that would be permitted to develop a prosperous, modern economy while remaining under the careful supervision of the Allies. Stalin wanted to impose heavy reparations on Germany and to ensure a permanent dismemberment of the nation. The final agreement was, like the Polish accord, vague and unstable. The decision on reparations would be referred to a future commission. The United States, Great Britain, France, and the Soviet Union would each control its own "zone of occupation" in Germany—the zones to be determined by the position of troops at the end of the war. Berlin, the German capital, was already well inside the Soviet zone, but because of its symbolic importance it would itself be divided into four sectors, one for each nation to occupy. At an unspecified date, Germany would be reunited; but there was no agreement on how the reunification would occur. As for the rest of Europe, the conference produced a murky accord on the establishment of interim governments "broadly representative of all democratic elements." They would be replaced ultimately by permanent governments "responsible to the will of the people" and created through free elections. Once again, no specific provisions or timetables accompanied the agreements.

The Yalta accords, in other words, were less a settlement of postwar issues than a set of loose principles that sidestepped the most divisive questions. Roosevelt, Churchill, and Stalin returned home from the conference each apparently convinced that he had signed an important agreement. But the Soviet interpretation of the accords differed so sharply from the Anglo-American interpretation that the illusion endured only briefly. In the weeks following the Yalta Conference, Roosevelt watched with growing alarm as the Soviet Union moved systematically to establish pro-communist governments in one Central or Eastern European nation after another and as Stalin refused to make the changes in Poland that the president believed he had promised.

But Roosevelt did not abandon hope. Still believing the differences could be settled, he left Washington early in the spring for a vacation at his retreat in Warm Springs, Georgia. There, on April 12, 1945, he suffered a sudden, massive stroke and died.

## THE COLLAPSE OF THE PEACE

Harry S. Truman, who succeeded Roosevelt in the presidency, had almost no familiarity with international issues. Nor did he share Roosevelt's faith in the flexibility of the Soviet Union. Roosevelt had believed that Stalin was, essentially, a reasonable man with whom an ultimate accord could be reached. Truman, in contrast, sided with those in the government (and there were many) who considered the Soviet Union fundamentally untrustworthy and viewed Stalin himself with suspicion and even loathing.

### The Failure of Potsdam

Truman had been in office only a few days before he decided to "get tough" with the Soviet Union. Stalin had made what the new president considered solemn agreements with the United States at Yalta. The United States should insist that the Soviets honor them. Truman met on April 23 with Soviet Foreign Minister Molotov and sharply chastised him for violations of the Yalta accords.

In fact, Truman had only limited leverage by which to compel the Soviet Union to carry out its agreements. Russian forces already occupied Poland and much of the rest of Central and Eastern Europe. Germany was already divided among the conquering nations. The United States was still engaged in a war in the Pacific and was neither able nor willing to enter into a second conflict in Europe. Truman insisted that the United States should be able to get "85 percent" of what it wanted, but he was ultimately forced to settle for much less.

He conceded first on Poland. When Stalin made a few minor concessions to the pro-Western exiles, Truman recognized the Warsaw government, hoping that noncommunist forces might gradually expand their influence there. Until the 1980s, they did not. Other questions remained, above all the question of Germany. To settle them, Truman met in July at Potsdam, in Russian-occupied Germany, with Churchill (who, after elections in Britain, was replaced as prime minister by Clement Attlee in the midst of the negotiations) and Stalin. Truman reluctantly accepted adjustments of the Polish-German border that Stalin had long demanded; he refused, however, to permit the Russians to claim any reparations from the American, French, and British zones of Germany. This stance effectively confirmed that Germany would remain divided, with the western zones united into one nation, friendly to the United States, and the Russian zone surviving as another nation, with a pro-Soviet, communist government. Soon, the Soviet Union was siphoning between $1.5 and $3 billion a year out of its zone of occupation.

### The China Problem

Central to American hopes for an open, peaceful world "policed" by the great powers was a strong, independent China. But even before the war ended, the American government was aware that those hopes faced a major, perhaps insurmountable obstacle: the Chinese government of Chiang Kai-shek. Chiang was generally friendly to the United States, but he had few other virtues. His government was corrupt and incompetent. His popular legitimacy was feeble. And Chiang himself lived in a world of almost surreal isolation, unable or unwilling to face the problems that were threatening to engulf him. Ever since 1927, the nationalist government he headed had been engaged in a prolonged and bitter rivalry with the communist armies of Mao Zedong. So successful had the communist challenge grown that Mao was in control of one-fourth of the population by 1945.

At Potsdam, Truman had managed to persuade Stalin to recognize Chiang as the legitimate ruler of China; but Chiang was rapidly losing his grip on his country. Some Americans urged the government to try to find a "third force" to support as an alternative to either Chiang or Mao. A few argued that the United States should try to reach some accommodation with Mao. Truman, however, decided reluctantly that he had no choice but to continue supporting Chiang. For the next several years, as the long struggle between the nationalists and the communists erupted into a full-scale civil war, the United States continued to pump money and weapons to Chiang, even as it was becoming clear that the cause was lost. But Truman was not prepared to intervene militarily to save the nationalist regime.

Instead, the American government was beginning to consider an alternative to China as the strong, pro-Western force in Asia: a revived Japan.

Abandoning the strict occupation policies of the first years after the war (when General Douglas MacArthur had governed the nation), the United States lifted all restrictions on industrial development and encouraged rapid economic growth in Japan. The vision of an open, united world was giving way in Asia, as it was in Europe, to an acceptance of a divided world with a strong, pro-American sphere of influence.

### The Containment Doctrine

By the end of 1945, the Grand Alliance was a shambles. With its passing went any realistic hope of a postwar world constructed according to the Atlantic Charter ideals Roosevelt and others had supported. Instead, a new American policy was slowly emerging. It became known as containment. Rather than attempting to create a unified, "open" world, the West would work to "contain" the threat of further Soviet expansion. The United States would be the leading force in that effort.

The new doctrine emerged in part as a response to events in Europe in 1946. In Turkey, Stalin was trying to win some control over the vital sea lanes to the Mediterranean. In Greece, communist forces were again threatening the pro-Western government; the British had announced they could no longer provide assistance. Faced with these challenges, Truman decided to enunciate a firm new policy. In doing so, he drew from the ideas of the influential American diplomat George F. Kennan, who had warned not long after the war that in the Soviet Union the United States faced "a political force committed fanatically to the belief that with the U.S. there can be no permanent modus vivendi," and that the only answer was "a long-term, patient but firm and vigilant containment of Russian expansive tendencies." On March 12, 1947, Truman appeared before Congress and used Kennan's warnings as the basis of what became known as the Truman Doctrine. "I believe," he argued, "that it must be the policy of the United States to support free peoples who are resisting attempted subjugation by armed minorities or by outside pressures." In the same speech he requested $400 million—part of it to bolster the armed forces of Greece and Turkey, another part to provide economic assistance to Greece. Congress quickly approved the measure.

The American commitment ultimately helped ease Soviet pressure on Turkey and helped the Greek government defeat the communist insurgents. More important, it established a basis for American foreign policy that would survive for more than thirty years. On the one hand, the Truman Doctrine was a way of accommodating the status quo: it accepted that there was no immediate likelihood of overturning the communist governments Stalin had established in Eastern Europe. On the other hand, it was a strategy for the future: communism was an innately expansionist force, and it must be contained within its present boundaries.

*The Marshall Plan*

An integral part of the containment policy was a proposal to aid in the economic reconstruction of Western Europe. There were many motives: humanitarian concern for the European people; a fear that Europe would re-

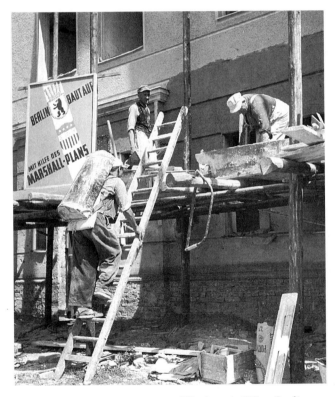

THE MARSHALL PLAN, 1950 Workers in West Berlin rebuild the war-damaged city with the aid of money funneled to them from the United States through the European Recovery Program, better known as the Marshall Plan. This photograph shows repair work in progress on Titania Palace, Berlin's biggest concert hall.

main an economic drain on the United States if it could not quickly rebuild and begin to feed itself; a desire for a strong European market for American goods. But above all, American policymakers believed that unless something could be done to strengthen the shaky pro-American governments in Western Europe, those governments might fall under the control of rapidly growing domestic communist parties.

In June 1947, therefore, Secretary of State George C. Marshall announced a plan to provide economic assistance to all European nations (including the Soviet Union) that would join in drafting a program for recovery. Although Russia and its Eastern satellites quickly and predictably rejected the plan, sixteen Western European nations eagerly participated. Whatever domestic opposition there was in the United States largely vanished after a sudden coup in Czechoslovakia in February 1948 that established a Soviet-dominated communist government there. In April, Congress approved the creation of the Economic Cooperation Administration, the agency that would administer the Marshall Plan, as it became known. And over the next three years, the Marshall Plan channeled over $12 billion of American aid into Europe, helping to spark a substantial economic revival. By the end of 1950, European industrial production had risen 64 percent, communist strength in the member nations was declining, and opportunities for American trade had revived.

*Mobilization at Home*

That the United States had fully accepted a continuing commitment to the containment policy became clear in 1947 and 1948 through a series of measures designed to maintain American military power at near wartime levels. In 1948, at the president's request, Congress approved a new military draft and revived the Selective Service System. In the meantime, the United States, having failed to reach agreement with the Soviet Union on international control of nuclear weapons, redoubled its own efforts in atomic research, elevating nuclear weaponry to a central place in its military arsenal. The Atomic Energy Commission, established in 1946, became the supervisory body charged with overseeing all nuclear research, civilian and military alike. And in 1950, the Truman administration approved the development of the new hydrogen bomb, a nuclear weapon far more powerful than the bombs the United States had used in 1945.

Particularly important was the National Security Act of 1947, which reshaped the nation's major military and diplomatic institutions. A new Department of Defense would oversee all branches of the armed services, com-

**Divided Europe After World War II**

NATO countries   Warsaw Pact countries

Berlin

Rejkjavik
ICELAND

Tegel
WEST
BERLIN
Gatow
Tempelhof
EAST
BERLIN

ATLANTIC OCEAN

EAST GERMANY

NORWAY   FINLAND

OCCUPATION ZONES
U.S.   French   Airports
British   Soviet

SWEDEN
Oslo   Helsinki
Stockholm

North
Sea   Baltic
Sea   Moscow
0   400 Miles
0   400 Kilometers

IRELAND   DENMARK
Dublin   GREAT
BRITAIN   Copenhagen

SOVIET UNION

The
Hague NETH.   Berlin POLAND
London   Bonn EAST
Brussels   GERMANY   Warsaw
BEL.   Prague
Paris   LUX.   WEST   CZECH.
GERMANY
Bern   Vienna   Budapest
FRANCE   SWITZ. AUSTRIA   HUNGARY
ROMANIA

Caspian
Sea

PORTUGAL   SPAIN   Belgrade   Bucharest   Black
Sea
Lisbon   Madrid   ITALY   YUGOSLAVIA   BULGARIA
Rome   ALB.   Sofia

TURKEY   IRAN

Mediterranean Sea   Athens

SYRIA

MOROCCO   ALGERIA   TUNISIA   IRAQ

bining functions previously performed separately by the War and Navy departments. A National Security Council (NSC), operating out of the White House, would govern foreign and military policy. A Central Intelligence Agency (CIA) would replace the wartime Office of Strategic Services and would be responsible for collecting information through both open and covert methods; as the Cold War continued, it would also engage secretly in political and military operations on behalf of American goals. The National Security Act, in other words, gave the president expanded powers with which to pursue the nation's international goals.

## The Road to NATO

At about the same time, the United States was moving to strengthen the military capabilities of Western Europe. Convinced that a reconstructed Germany was essential to the hopes of the West, Truman reached an agreement with England and France to merge the three western zones of occupation into a new West German republic (which would include the American, British, and French sectors of Berlin, even though that city lay well within the Soviet zone). Stalin responded quickly. On June 24, 1948, he imposed a tight blockade around the western sectors of Berlin. If Germany was to be officially divided, he was implying, then the country's Western government would have to abandon its outpost in the heart of the Soviet-controlled eastern zone. Truman refused to do so. Unwilling to risk war through a military response to the blockade, he ordered a massive airlift to supply the city with food, fuel, and other needed goods. The airlift continued for more than ten months, transporting nearly 2.5 million tons of material, keeping a city of 2 million people alive, and transforming West Berlin into a symbol of the West's resolve to resist communist expansion. In the spring of 1949, Stalin lifted the now ineffective blockade. And in October, the division of Germany into two nations—the Federal Republic in the west and the Democratic Republic in the East—became official.

The crisis in Berlin accelerated the consolidation of what was already in effect an alliance among the United States and the countries of Western Europe. On April 4, 1949, twelve nations signed an agreement establishing the North Atlantic Treaty Organization (NATO) and declaring that an armed attack against one member would be considered an attack against all. The NATO countries would, moreover, maintain a standing military force in Europe to defend against what many believed was the threat of a Soviet invasion. The American Senate quickly ratified the treaty, which fused European nations that had been fighting one another for centuries into a strong and enduring alliance. The formation of NATO spurred the Soviet Union to create an alliance of its own with the communist governments in Eastern Europe—an alliance formalized in 1955 by the Warsaw Pact.

## Reevaluating Cold War Policy

For a time, some American leaders believed that these initial achievements had turned the tide of the battle against communism. But a series of events in 1949 eroded that confidence and propelled the Cold War in new directions. An announcement in September that the Soviet Union had successfully exploded its first atomic weapon, years earlier than predicted, shocked and frightened many Americans. So did the collapse of Chiang Kai-shek's nationalist government in China, which occurred with startling speed in the last months of 1949. Chiang fled with his political allies and the remnants of his army to the offshore island of Formosa (Taiwan), and the entire Chinese mainland came under the control of a communist government that many Americans believed to be an extension of the Soviet Union. Few policymakers shared the belief of the so-called China lobby that the United States should now commit itself to the rearming of Chiang Kai-shek. But neither would the United States recognize the new communist regime. The Chinese mainland would remain almost entirely closed to the West for a generation. The United States, in the meantime, would devote increased attention to the revitalization of Japan as a buffer against Asian communism, ending the American occupation in 1952.

In this atmosphere of escalating crisis, Truman called for a thorough review of American foreign policy. The result was a National Security Council report, issued in 1950 and commonly known as NSC-68, which outlined a shift in the American position. The first statements of the containment doctrine—the writings of George Kennan, the Truman Doctrine speech—had made at least some distinctions between areas of vital interest to the United States and areas of less importance to the nation's foreign policy. They also had viewed containment as a commitment shared among the United States and its allies. But the April 1950 document argued that the United States could no longer rely on other nations to take the initiative in resisting communism. It must itself establish firm and active leadership of the noncommunist world. And it must move to stop communist expansion virtually anywhere it occurred, regardless of the intrinsic strategic or economic value of the lands in question. Among other things, the report called for a major expansion of American military power, with a defense budget almost four times the previously projected figure.

## AMERICA AFTER THE WAR

The crises overseas were not the only frustrations the American people encountered after the war. The nation also faced serious, if short-lived, economic difficulties in adapting to the peace. And it suffered from an exceptionally heated political climate that produced a new wave of insecurity and repression.

## The Problems of Reconversion

Despite predictions that the end of the war would return America to Depression conditions, economic growth continued after 1945. Pent-up consumer demand from workers who had accumulated substantial savings during the war helped spur the boom. So did a $6 billion tax cut. The Servicemen's Readjustment Act of 1944, better known as the GI Bill of Rights, provided housing, education, and job training subsidies to veterans and increased spending even further.

This flood of consumer demand ensured that there would be no new depression, but it contributed to more than two years of serious inflation, during which prices rose at rates of 14 to 15 percent annually. In the summer of 1946, the president vetoed an extension of the authority of the wartime Office of Price Administration, thus eliminating price controls. (He was opposed not to the controls but to congressional amendments that had weakened the OPA.) Inflation soared to 25 percent before he relented a month later and signed a bill little different from the one he had rejected.

Compounding the economic difficulties was a sharp rise in labor unrest, driven in part by the impact of inflation. By the end of 1945, there had already been major strikes in the automobile, electrical, and steel industries. In April 1946, John L. Lewis led the United Mine Workers out on strike, shutting down the coal fields for forty days. Fears grew rapidly that without vital coal supplies, the entire nation might virtually grind to a halt. Truman finally forced coal production to resume by ordering government seizure of the mines. But in the process, he pressured mine owners to grant the union most of its demands, which he had earlier denounced as inflationary. Almost simultaneously, the nation's railroads suffered a total shutdown—the first in the nation's history—as two major unions walked out on strike. By threatening to use the army to run the trains, Truman pressured the strikers back to work after only a few days.

Reconversion was particularly difficult for the millions of women and minorities who had entered the work force during the war. With veterans returning home and looking for jobs in the industrial economy, employers tended to push women, blacks, Hispanics, and others out of the plants to make room for white males. Some of the war workers, particularly women, left the work force voluntarily, out of a desire to return to their former domestic lives. But as many as 80 percent of women workers, and virtually all black and Hispanic males, wanted to continue working. The postwar inflation, the pressure to meet the growing expectations of a high-consumption society, the rising divorce rate (which left many women responsible for their own economic well-being)—all combined to create a high demand for paid employment among women. As they found themselves excluded from industrial jobs, therefore, women workers moved increasingly into other areas of the economy (above all, the service sector).

### The Fair Deal Rejected

Days after the Japanese surrender, Truman submitted to Congress a twenty-one-point domestic program outlining what he later termed the "Fair Deal." It called for expansion of Social Security benefits, the raising of the legal minimum wage from 40 to 65 cents an hour, a program to ensure full employment through aggressive use of federal spending and investment, a permanent Fair Employment Practices Act, public housing and slum clearance, long-range environmental and public works planning, and government promotion of scientific research. Weeks later he added other proposals: federal aid to education, government health insurance, prepaid medical care, funding for the St. Lawrence Seaway, and nationalization of atomic energy. The president was declaring an end to the wartime moratorium on liberal reform.

But the Fair Deal programs fell victim to the same public and congressional conservatism that had crippled the last years of the New Deal. Indeed, that conservatism seemed to be intensifying, as the November 1946 congressional elections suggested. Using the simple but devastating slogan "Had Enough?" the Republican Party won control of both houses of Congress. The new Republican Congress quickly moved to reduce government spending and chip away at New Deal reforms. Its most notable action, perhaps, was its assault on the Wagner Act of 1935. Conservatives had always resented the new powers the legislation had granted unions, and in response to the labor difficulties during and after the war, such resentments intensified sharply. The result was the Labor-Management Relations Act of 1947, better known as the Taft-Hartley Act. It made illegal the closed shop (a workplace in which no one can be hired without first being a member of a union). And although it continued to permit the creation of union shops (in which workers must join a union after being hired), it permitted states to pass "right-to-work" laws prohibiting even that. This provision, the controversial Section 14(b), remained a target of the labor movement for decades. The Taft-Hartley Act also empowered the president to call for a ten-week "cooling-off" period before a strike by issuing an injunction against any work stoppage that endangered national safety or health. Outraged workers and union leaders denounced the measure as a "slave labor bill." Truman vetoed it. But both houses easily overruled him the same day. The Taft-Hartley Act did not destroy the labor movement, as many union leaders had predicted. But it did damage weaker unions in relatively lightly organized industries such as chemicals and textiles, and it made much more difficult the organizing of workers who had never been union members at all, especially in the South and West.

## The Election of 1948

Truman and his advisers believed that the American public was not ready to abandon the achievements of the New Deal, despite the 1946 election results. As they planned strategy for the 1948 campaign, therefore, they placed their hopes in an appeal to enduring Democratic loyalties. Throughout 1948, Truman proposed one reform measure after another (including, on February 2, the first major civil rights bill of the century). To no one's surprise, Congress ignored or defeated them all. The president was building campaign issues for the fall.

There remained, however, the problem of Truman's personal unpopularity—the assumption among much of the electorate that he lacked stature and that his administration was weak and inept—and the deep divisions within the Democratic Party. At the Democratic Convention that summer, two factions abandoned the party altogether. Southern conservatives were angered by Truman's proposed civil rights bill and by the approval at the convention of a civil rights plank in the platform (engineered by Hubert Humphrey, the reform mayor of Minneapolis). They walked out and formed the States' Rights (or "Dixiecrat") Party, with Governor Strom Thurmond of South Carolina as its nominee. At the same time, some members of the party's left wing joined the new Progressive Party, whose candidate was Henry A. Wallace. Wallace supporters objected to what they considered the slow and ineffective domestic policies of the Truman administration, but they resented even more the president's confrontational stance toward the Soviet Union.

Many Democratic liberals who were unhappy with Truman were unwilling to leave the party. They attempted instead to replace the president as the party's nominee in 1948. The Americans for Democratic Action (ADA), a coalition of liberals, tried to entice Dwight D. Eisenhower, the popular war hero, to contest the nomination. Only after Eisenhower had refused did liberals bow to the inevitable and concede the nomination to Truman. The Republicans, in the meantime, had once again nominated Governor Thomas E. Dewey of New York, whose substantial reelection victory in 1946 had made him one of the nation's leading political figures. Austere, dignified, and competent, he seemed to offer an unbeatable alternative to the president.

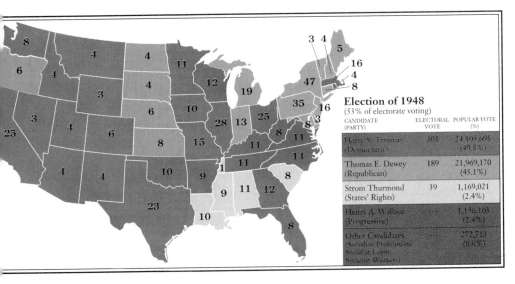

Election of 1948
(53% of electorate voting)

| CANDIDATE (PARTY) | ELECTORAL VOTE | POPULAR VOTE (%) |
| --- | --- | --- |
| Harry S. Truman (Democratic) | 303 | 24,105,695 (49.5%) |
| Thomas E. Dewey (Republican) | 189 | 21,969,170 (45.1%) |
| Strom Thurmond (States' Rights) | 39 | 1,169,021 (2.4%) |
| Henry A. Wallace (Progressive) | — | 1,156,103 (2.4%) |
| Other Candidates (Socialist, Prohibition, Socialist Labor, Socialist Workers) | | 272,713 (0.6%) |

Only Truman, it seemed, believed he could win. As the campaign gathered momentum, he became ever more aggressive, turning the fire away from himself and toward Dewey and the "do-nothing, good-for-nothing" Republican Congress, which was, he told the voters, responsible for fueling inflation and abandoning workers and common people. To dramatize his point, he called Congress into special session in July to give it a chance, he said, to enact the liberal measures the Republicans had recently written into their platform. Congress met for two weeks and, predictably, did almost nothing.

The president traveled nearly 32,000 miles and made 356 speeches, delivering blunt, extemporaneous attacks. He had told Alben Barkley, his running mate, "I'm going to fight hard. I'm going to give them hell." He called for repeal of the Taft-Hartley Act, increased price supports for farmers, and strong civil rights protection for African Americans. (He was the first president to campaign in Harlem since it had become a predominantly black community.) He sought, in short, to re-create much of Franklin Roosevelt's New Deal coalition. To the surprise of virtually everyone, he succeeded. On election night, he won a narrow but decisive victory: 49.5 percent of the popular vote to Dewey's 45.1 percent (with the two splinter parties dividing the small remainder evenly between them), and an electoral margin of 303 to 189. Democrats, in the meantime, had regained both houses of Congress by substantial margins. It was perhaps the most dramatic comeback in the history of presidential elections.

*The Fair Deal Revived*

Despite the Democratic victories, the Eighty-first Congress was no more hospitable to Truman's Fair Deal reform than its Republican predecessor had been. Truman did win some important victories, to be sure. Congress raised the legal minimum wage from 40 cents to 75 cents an hour. It approved an important expansion of the Social Security system, increasing benefits by 75 percent and extending them to 10 million additional people. And it passed the National Housing Act of 1949, which provided for the construction of 810,000 units of low-income housing accompanied by long-term rent subsidies. (Inadequate funding plagued the program for years, and the initial goal was reached only in 1972.)

But on other issues—national health insurance and aid to education among them—Truman made little progress. Nor was he able to persuade Congress to accept the civil rights legislation he proposed in 1949, legislation that would have made lynching a federal crime, provided federal protection of black voting rights, abolished the poll tax, and established a new Fair Employment Practices Commission to curb discrimination in hiring. Southern Democrats filibustered to kill the bill.

Truman did proceed on his own to battle several forms of racial discrimination. He ordered an end to discrimination in the hiring of government employees. He began to dismantle segregation within the armed forces. And he allowed the Justice Department to become actively involved in court battles against discriminatory statutes. The Supreme Court, in the meantime, signaled its own growing awareness of the issue by ruling, in *Shelley* v. *Kraemer* (1948), that the courts could not be used to enforce private "covenants" meant to bar blacks from residential neighborhoods. The achievements of the Truman years made only minor dents in the structure of segregation, but they were the tentative beginnings of a federal commitment to confront the problem of race.

## THE KOREAN WAR

On June 24, 1950, the armies of communist North Korea swept across their southern border and invaded the pro-Western half of the Korean peninsula to the south. Within days, they had occupied much of South Korea, including Seoul, its capital. Almost immediately, the United States committed itself to the conflict. It was the first American military engagement of the Cold War.

## The Divided Peninsula

The Korean conflict was the result of several years of tension within the peninsula. By the summer of 1945, both the United States and the Soviet Union had sent troops into Korea against the Japanese. When World War II ended, neither the Americans nor the Soviets were willing to leave. Instead, they divided the nation, supposedly temporarily, along the 38th par-

The Korean War, 1950–1953

North Korean attack (June 25, 1950–Sept. 10, 1950)

U.N. counterattack (Sept. 15, 1950–Nov. 24, 1950)

Chinese and North Korean counterattack (Nov. 26, 1950–Jan. 24, 1951)

Final U.N. counterattack (Jan. 25, 1951–April 21, 1951)

allel. The Russians finally departed in 1949, leaving behind a communist government in the north with a strong, Soviet-equipped army. The Americans left a few months later, handing control to the pro-Western government of Syngman Rhee, anticommunist but only nominally democratic. He had a relatively small military, which he used primarily to suppress internal opposition.

The relative weakness of the south offered a strong temptation to nationalists in the North Korean government who wanted to reunite the country. The temptation grew stronger when the American government implied that it did not consider South Korea within its own "defense perimeter." The role of the Soviet Union remains unclear; there is some reason to believe that the North Koreans acted without Stalin's approval. But the Soviets supported the offensive once it began.

MACARTHUR IN KOREA, 1950 General Douglas MacArthur visits Marines along the fighting front in Korea in September 1950. Revered by those who fought under him, MacArthur was nevertheless a persistent irritant to policymakers in Washington with his demands for widening the conflict—demands that grew more frequent and more public after the Chinese entered the war about two months after this photograph was taken.

The Truman administration responded quickly. On June 27, 1950, the president ordered limited American military assistance to South Korea, and on the same day he appealed to the United Nations to intervene. The Soviet Union was boycotting the Security Council at the time (to protest the council's refusal to recognize the new communist government of China) and was thus unable to exercise its veto power. As a result, American delegates were able to win UN agreement to a resolution calling for international assistance to the Rhee government. On June 30, the United States ordered its own ground forces into Korea, and Truman appointed General Douglas MacArthur to command the UN operations there. (Several other nations provided assistance and troops, but the "UN" armies were, in fact, overwhelmingly American.)

The intervention in Korea was the first expression of the newly expansive American foreign policy outlined in NSC-68. But the administration quickly went beyond NSC-68. It decided that the war would be an effort not simply at containment but also at "liberation." After a surprise American invasion at Inchon in September had routed the North Korean forces from the south and sent them fleeing back across the 38th parallel, Truman gave MacArthur permission to pursue the communists into their own territory. His aim, as an American-sponsored UN resolution proclaimed in October, was to create "a unified, independent and democratic Korea."

*From Invasion to Stalemate*

For several weeks, MacArthur's invasion of North Korea proceeded smoothly. On October 19, the capital, Pyongyang, fell to the UN forces. Victory seemed near—until the Chinese government, alarmed by the movement of American forces toward its border, intervened. By November 4, eight divisions of the Chinese army had entered the war. The UN offensive stalled and then collapsed. Through December 1950, outnumbered American forces fought a bitter, losing battle against the Chinese divisions, retreating at almost every juncture. Within weeks, communist forces had pushed the Americans back below the 38th parallel once again and had recaptured the South Korean capital of Seoul. By mid-January 1951 the rout had ceased; and by March the UN armies had managed to regain much of the territory they had recently lost, taking back Seoul and pushing the communists north of the 38th parallel for the second time. But with that, the war degenerated into a protracted stalemate.

From the start, Truman had been determined to avoid a direct conflict with China, which he feared might lead to a new world war. Once China entered the war, he began seeking a negotiated solution to the struggle; and for the next two years, he insisted that there be no wider war. But he faced a formidable opponent in General MacArthur, who resisted any limits on his military discretion. The United States was really fighting the Chinese, MacArthur argued. It should, therefore, attack China itself, if not through an actual invasion, then at least by bombing communist forces massing north of the Chinese border. In March 1951, he indicated his unhappiness in a public letter to House Republican leader Joseph W. Martin that concluded: "There is no substitute for victory." His position had wide popular support.

The Martin letter came after nine months during which MacArthur had resisted Truman's decisions. More than once, the president had warned the general to keep his objections to himself. The release of the Martin letter, therefore, struck the president as intolerable insubordination. On April 11, 1951, he relieved MacArthur of his command.

There was a storm of public outrage. Sixty-nine percent of the American people supported MacArthur, a Gallup poll reported. When the general returned to the United States later in 1951, he was greeted with wild enthusiasm. Public criticism of Truman finally abated somewhat when a number of prominent military figures, including General Omar Bradley, publicly supported the president's decision. But substantial hostility toward Truman remained.

In the meantime, the Korean stalemate continued. Negotiations between the opposing forces began at Panmunjom in July 1951, but the talks— and the war—dragged on until 1953.

### Limited Mobilization

Just as the war in Korea produced only a limited American military commitment abroad, so it created only a limited economic mobilization at home. Still, the government did try to control the wartime economy in several important ways.

First, Truman set up the Office of Defense Mobilization to fight inflation by holding down prices and discouraging high union wage demands. When these cautious regulatory efforts failed, the president took more drastic action. Railroad workers walked off the job in 1951, and Truman, who considered the workers' demands inflationary, ordered the government to seize control of the railroads. That helped keep the trains running, but it had no effect on union demands. Workers ultimately got most of what they had demanded. In 1952, during a nationwide steel strike, Truman seized the steel mills, citing his powers as commander in chief. But in a 6-to-3 decision, the

Supreme Court ruled that the president had exceeded his authority, and Truman was forced to relent.

The Korean War gave a significant boost to economic growth by pumping new government funds into the economy at a point when many believed it was about to decline. But the war had other, less welcome effects. It came at a time of rising insecurity about America's position in the world and intensified anxiety about communism. As the long stalemate continued, producing 140,000 American dead and wounded, frustration turned to anger. The United States, which had recently won the greatest war in history, seemed unable to conclude what many Americans considered a minor border skirmish in a small country. Many began to believe that something must be deeply wrong—not only in Korea but within the United States as well. Such fears contributed to the rise of the second major campaign of the century against domestic communism.

## THE CRUSADE AGAINST SUBVERSION

Why did the American people develop a growing fear of internal communist subversion—a fear that by the early 1950s had reached the point of near hysteria? There are many possible answers, but no single definitive explanation.

One factor was obvious. Communism was not an imagined enemy in the 1950s. It had tangible shape, in Josef Stalin and the Soviet Union. Adding to the concern were the setbacks America had encountered in its battle against communism: the Korean stalemate, the "loss" of China, the Soviet development of an atomic bomb. Searching for someone to blame, many were attracted to the idea of a communist conspiracy within American borders. But there were other factors as well, rooted in events in American domestic politics.

### HUAC and Alger Hiss

Much of the anticommunist furor emerged out of the search by the Republican Party for an issue with which to attack the Democrats, and out of the efforts of the Democrats to take that issue away from them. Beginning in 1947, the House Un-American Activities Committee (HUAC) held widely publicized investigations to prove that, under Democratic rule, the government had tolerated (if not actually encouraged) communist subversion. The committee turned first to the movie industry, arguing that communists had

A M E R I C A N V O I C E S

WHITTAKER CHAMBERS

## The Hiss Case

I BELIEVED THAT I was not meant to be spared from testifying [against Alger Hiss]. I sensed, with a force greater than any fear or revulsion, that it was for this that my whole life had been lived. For this I had been a Communist, for this I had ceased to be a Communist. . . . This challenge was the terrible meaning of my whole life, of all that I had done that was evil, of all that I had sought that was good, of my weakness and my strength. . . .

For the moment had arrived when some man must be a witness. . . . The danger to the nation from Communism had now grown acute, both within its own house and abroad. Its existence was threatened. And the nation did not know it. For the first time, the [House Unamerican Activities] Committee's subpoena gave me an opportunity to tell what I knew about that danger. . . .

I did not wish to harm, more than was unavoidable, those whom I must testify against. . . . But I must testify that they had been concealed Communists and that an underground had existed in the Government. . . . They and I must stand up in face of the nation and confess what we had been that it might take alarm, throw off its apathy and skepticism, see that the enemy really was embedded in its midst, and be given time to act and save itself. That was the least that we could do in atonement.

SOURCE: Whittaker Chambers, *Witness*, pp. 533–534. Copyright © 1952 by Whittaker Chambers. Reprinted by permission of Random House, Inc.

infiltrated Hollywood and tainted American films with propaganda. Writers and producers, some of them former communists, were called to testify; and when some of them ("the Hollywood Ten") refused to answer questions about their own political beliefs and those of their colleagues, they were sent to jail for contempt. Others were barred from employment in the industry when Hollywood, attempting to protect its public image, adopted a "blacklist" of those of "suspicious loyalty."

More alarming to the public was HUAC's investigation into charges of disloyalty leveled against a former high-ranking member of the State Department: Alger Hiss. In 1948, Whittaker Chambers, a self-avowed former communist agent, now a conservative editor at *Time* magazine, told the

ALGER HISS No single figure did more to polarize opinion about the dangers of domestic communism than Alger Hiss, the respected diplomat accused in 1948 of having been a spy in the 1930s for the Soviet Union and later convicted of perjury for testifying falsely before a congressional committee. Even half a century later, opinions remain sharply divided about Hiss's guilt.

committee that Hiss had passed classified State Department documents to him in 1937 and 1938. When Hiss sued him for slander, Chambers produced microfilms of the documents (called the "pumpkin papers," because Chambers had kept them hidden in a pumpkin in his vegetable garden). Hiss could not be tried for espionage because of the statute of limitations (a law that protects individuals from prosecution for most crimes after seven years have passed). But largely because of the relentless efforts of Richard M. Nixon, a freshman Republican congressman from California and a member of HUAC, Hiss was convicted of perjury and served several years in prison. The Hiss case not only discredited a prominent young diplomat; it cast suspicion on a generation of liberal Democrats and made it possible for the public to believe that communists had actually infiltrated the government. It also transformed Nixon into a national figure and helped him win a seat in the United States Senate in 1950.

### The Federal Loyalty Program and the Rosenberg Case

Partly to protect itself against Republican attacks, partly to encourage support for the president's foreign policy initiatives, the Truman administration in 1947 initiated a widely publicized program to review the "loyalty" of federal employees. In August 1950, the president authorized some agencies to fire people deemed no more than "bad security risks." By 1951, more than 2,000 government employees had resigned under pressure and 212 had been dismissed.

The employee loyalty program became a signal throughout the executive branch to launch a major assault on subversion. The attorney general established a widely cited list of supposedly subversive organizations. The director of the Federal Bureau of Investigation (FBI), J. Edgar Hoover, investigated and harassed alleged radicals. The anticommunist frenzy quickly grew so intense that even a Democratic Congress felt obliged to bow to it. In 1950, Congress passed the McCarran Internal Security Act, which, among other restrictions on "subversive" activity, required that all communist organizations register with the government and publish their records. Truman vetoed the bill. Congress easily overrode his veto.

The successful Soviet detonation of an atomic bomb in 1949, earlier than generally expected, suggested to some people that there had been a conspiracy to pass American atomic secrets to the Russians. In 1950, Klaus Fuchs, a young British scientist, seemed to confirm those fears when he testified that he had delivered to the Russians details of the manufacture of the bomb. The case ultimately settled on an obscure New York couple, Julius and Ethel Rosenberg, members of the Communist Party. The government claimed the Rosenbergs had received secret information from Ethel's brother, a machinist on the Manhattan Project in New Mexico, and had passed it on to the Soviet Union through other agents (including Fuchs). The Rosenbergs were convicted and, on April 5, 1951, sentenced to death. After two years of appeals and public protests, they died in the electric chair on June 19, 1953, proclaiming their innocence to the end.

All these factors—the HUAC investigations, the Hiss trial, the loyalty investigations, the McCarran Act, the Rosenberg case—combined with other concerns by the early 1950s to create a fear of communist subversion that seemed to grip the entire country. State and local governments, the judiciary, schools and universities, labor unions—all sought to purge themselves of real or imagined subversives. A pervasive fear settled on much of the country—not only the fear of communist infiltration but the fear of being suspected of communism. It was a climate that made possible the rise of an extraordinary public figure, whose behavior at any other time might have been dismissed as preposterous.

### McCarthyism

Joseph McCarthy was an undistinguished, first-term Republican senator from Wisconsin when, in February 1950, he suddenly burst into national prominence. In the midst of a speech in Wheeling, West Virginia, he lifted up a sheet of paper and claimed to "hold in my hand" a list of 205 known communists currently working in the American State Department. No person of comparable stature had ever made so bold a charge against the federal government; and in the weeks to come, as McCarthy repeated and expanded on his accusations, he emerged as the nation's most prominent leader of the crusade against domestic subversion.

Within weeks of his charges against the State Department, McCarthy was leveling accusations at other agencies. After 1952, with the Republicans in control of the Senate and McCarthy the chairman of a special subcommittee, he conducted highly publicized investigations of subversion in many areas of the government. McCarthy never produced conclusive evidence that any federal employee was a Communist. But a growing constituency adored him nevertheless for his coarse, "fearless" assaults on a government establishment that many considered arrogant, effete, even traitorous. Republicans, in particular, rallied to his claims that the Democrats had been responsible for "twenty years of treason" and that only a change of parties could rid the country of subversion. McCarthy, in short, provided his followers with an issue into which they could channel a wide range of resentments: fear of communism, animosity toward the country's "eastern establishment," and frustrated partisan ambitions. For a time, McCarthy intimidated all but a few people from opposing him. Even the highly popular Dwight D. Eisenhower, running for president in 1952, did not speak out against him, although he disliked McCarthy's tactics and was outraged at, among other things, McCarthy's attacks on General George Marshall.

### The Republican Revival

Public frustration over the stalemate in Korea and popular fears of internal subversion combined to make 1952 a bad year for the Democratic Party. Truman, whose own popularity had diminished almost to the vanishing point, wisely withdrew from the presidential contest. The party united instead behind Governor Adlai E. Stevenson of Illinois. Stevenson's dignity, wit, and eloquence made him a beloved figure to many liberals and intellectuals. But those same qualities seemed only to fuel Republican charges that Stevenson lacked the strength or the will to combat communism sufficiently.

Stevenson's greatest problem, however, was the Republican candidate opposing him. Rejecting the efforts of conservatives to nominate Robert Taft or Douglas MacArthur, the Republicans turned to a man who had no previous identification with the party: General Dwight D. Eisenhower—military hero, commander of NATO, president of Columbia University in New York—who won nomination on the first ballot. He chose as his running mate the young California senator who had gained national prominence through his crusade against Alger Hiss: Richard M. Nixon.

In the fall campaign, Eisenhower attracted support through his geniality and his statesmanlike pledges to settle the Korean conflict. Nixon (after surviving early accusations of financial improprieties, which he effectively neutralized in a famous television address, the "Checkers speech") exploited the issue of domestic anticommunism by attacking the Democrats for "cowardice" and "appeasement." The response at the polls was overwhelming. Eisenhower won both a popular and an electoral landslide: 55 percent of the popular vote to Stevenson's 44 percent, 442 electoral votes to Stevenson's 89. Republicans gained control of both houses of Congress for the first time since 1946. The election of 1952 ended twenty years of Democratic dominance. And while it might not have seemed so at the time, it also signaled the end of some of the worst turbulence of the postwar era.

D E B A T I N G    T H E    P A S T

## *The Cold War*

OR MORE than a decade after the beginning of the Cold War, few historians saw any reason to challenge the official American interpretation of its origins. The breakdown of relations between the United States and the Soviet Union was, most agreed, a direct result of Soviet expansionism and of Stalin's violation of the wartime agreements forged at Yalta and Potsdam. The Soviet imposition of communist regimes in Eastern Europe was part of a larger ideological design to spread communism throughout the world. American policy was the logical and necessary response: a firm commitment to oppose Soviet expansionism and to keep American forces in a continual state of readiness.

Disillusionment with the official justifications for the Cold War began to find expression even in the late 1950s, when anticommunist sentiment in America remained strong and pervasive. William Appleman Williams's *The Tragedy of American Diplomacy* (1959) insisted that the Cold War was simply the most recent version of a consistent American effort in the twentieth century to preserve an "open door" for American trade in world markets. The confrontation with the Soviet Union, he argued, was less a response to Soviet aggressive designs than an expression of the American belief in the necessity of capitalist expansion.

As the Vietnam War grew larger and more unpopular in the 1960s, the scholarly critique of the Cold War quickly gained intensity. Walter LaFeber's *America, Russia, and the Cold War*, first published in 1967, maintained that America's supposedly idealistic internationalism at the close of

*(continued on next page)*

the war was in reality an effort to ensure a postwar order shaped in the American image—with every nation open to American influence (and to American trade). That was why the United States was so apt to misinterpret Soviet policy, much of which reflected a perfectly reasonable commitment to ensure the security of the Soviet Union itself, as part of a larger aggressive design. Important to many revisionist arguments has been the American decision to use atomic weapons against Japan in 1945. Gar Alperovitz's *Atomic Diplomacy* (1965) and *The Decision to Use the Atomic Bomb* (1995) expanded on arguments that had begun to appear as early as 1948 and claimed that American decision makers used the bombs not to win the war (for Japan was already effectively defeated) but to impress and intimidate the Soviet Union. In fact, Alperovitz argued, this atomic diplomacy had the opposite effect: it convinced the Soviet Union of America's hostile intentions and helped speed the onset of the Cold War.

The revisionist interpretations of the Cold War ultimately produced a reaction of their own: what has come to be known as "postrevisionist" scholarship. The most important works in this school have attempted to strike a balance between orthodoxy and revisionism and to identify areas of blame and patterns of misconception on both sides of the conflict. Thomas G. Patterson, John Lewis Gaddis, Melvin Leffler, and others have presented a picture of two nations—each with a highly inadequate understanding of the other—struggling to preserve a wartime alliance that had in fact temporarily disguised a basic difference in outlook and interests. "The United States and the Soviet Union were doomed to be antagonists," Ernest May wrote in 1984. "There probably was never any real possibility that the post-1945 relationship could be anything but hostility verging on conflict."

The collapse of Soviet communism and the dissolution of the Soviet empire will undoubtedly stimulate new interpretations of the Cold War and will (by facilitating the opening of Soviet archives) cast new light on many contested issues. For the moment, however, the dominant scholarly view is one that de-emphasizes the question of who is to blame and emphasizes the ways in which both sides learned to manage a conflict that neither could easily have avoided.

# CHAPTER THIRTY

# The Affluent Society

*Abundance and Society* ∿ *The Other America*
*The Rise of the Civil Rights Movement* ∿ *Eisenhower Republicanism*
*Eisenhower, Dulles, and the Cold War*

I F AMERICA EXPERIENCED a golden age in the 1950s and early 1960s, as many Americans believed at the time and many continue to believe today, it was largely a result of two developments. One was a booming national prosperity, which profoundly altered the social, economic, and even physical landscape of the United States, as well as the way many Americans thought about their lives and their world. The other was the continuing struggle against communism, a struggle that created considerable anxiety but that also encouraged Americans to look even more approvingly at their own society.

But if these powerful forces created a widespread sense of national purpose and self-satisfaction, they also helped blind many Americans to serious problems plaguing large groups of the population. More than 30 million Americans, according to some estimates, continued to live in poverty in the 1950s. And significant minorities—most prominently the 10 percent of the American people who were black, but also Hispanics, Asians, Indians, gays and lesbians—continued to suffer social, political, and economic discrimination. Many American women, too, were chafing at obstacles to personal and professional fulfillment. The very things that made America seem so successful in the 1950s also contributed, in the end, to making the nation's social problems more difficult to avoid.

## ABUNDANCE AND SOCIETY

Perhaps the most striking feature of American society in the 1950s and early 1960s was the booming, almost miraculous economic growth that made even the heady 1920s seem pale by comparison. It was a better-balanced and

## TIME LINE

| 1947 | 1952 | 1953 | 1954 | 1955 |
|------|------|------|------|------|
| Levittown construction begins | Eisenhower elected | Korean War ends | *Brown* v. *Board of Education*<br><br>Army-McCarthy hearings | Montgomery bus boycott |

| 1956 | 1957 | 1959 | 1960 | 1961 | 1969 |
|------|------|------|------|------|------|
| Federal Highway Act<br>Eisenhower reelected<br>Suez crisis | Sputnik launched<br>Kerouac's *On the Road*<br>Little Rock desegregation crisis | Castro seizes power in Cuba | U-2 incident | First American in space | Americans land on moon |

more widely distributed prosperity than that of thirty years earlier. It was not, however, as universal as some Americans liked to believe.

### Economic Growth

By 1949, despite the continuing problems of postwar reconversion, an economic expansion had begun that would continue with only brief interruptions for almost twenty years. Between 1945 and 1960, the gross national product grew by 250 percent, from $200 billion to over $500 billion. Unemployment, which during the Depression had averaged between 15 and 25 percent, remained at about 5 percent or lower throughout the 1950s and early 1960s. Inflation, in the meantime, hovered around 3 percent a year or less.

The causes of this growth were varied. Government spending, which had ended the Depression in the 1940s, continued to stimulate growth through public funding of schools, housing, veterans' benefits, welfare, and interstate highways. Above all, there was military spending. Economic growth was at its peak during the first half of the 1950s, when military spending was highest because of the Korean War. In the late 1950s, with spending on armaments in decline, the rate of growth declined by half.

The national birth rate reversed a long pattern of decline with the so-called baby boom, which had begun during the war and peaked in 1957. The nation's population rose almost 20 percent in the decade, from 150 million in 1950 to 179 million in 1960. The baby boom meant increased consumer demand and expanding economic growth.

The rapid expansion of suburbs—whose population grew 47 percent in the 1950s—helped stimulate growth in several important sectors of the economy. The number of privately owned cars (more essential for suburban than for urban living) more than doubled in a decade, sparking a great boom in the automobile industry. Demand for new homes helped sustain a vigorous housing industry. The construction of roads, which was both a cause and a result of the growth of suburbs, stimulated the economy as well.

These forces helped the American economy to grow nearly ten times as fast as the population in the thirty years after the war. And while that growth was far from equally distributed, it affected most of society. The average American in 1960 had over 20 percent more purchasing power than in 1945, and more than twice as much as during the prosperous 1920s. The American people had achieved the highest standard of living of any society in the history of the world.

## The Rise of the Modern West

No region of the country experienced more dramatic changes as a result of the new economic growth than the American West. Its population expanded dramatically; its cities boomed; its industrial economy flourished. Before World War II, most of the West had been, economically at least, an appendage of the great industrial economy of the East—providing it with raw materials and agricultural goods. By the 1960s, some parts of the West were among the most important (and populous) industrial and cultural centers of the nation in their own right.

As during World War II, much of the growth of the West was a result of federal spending and investment—on the dams, power stations, highways, and other infrastructure projects that made economic development possible; and on the military contracts that continued to flow disproportionately to factories in California and Texas, many of them built with government funds during the war. But other factors played a role as well. The enormous increase in automobile use after World War II—a result, among other things, of suburbanization and improved highway systems—gave a large stimulus to the petroleum industry and contributed to the rapid growth of oil fields in Texas and Colorado and of the metropolitan centers serving them: Houston, Dallas, and Denver. State governments in the West invested heavily in their universities. The University of Texas and University of California systems, in particular, became among the nation's largest and best;

as centers of research, they helped attract technology-intensive industries to the region. Climate also contributed. Once they had the infrastructure (and, most important, the water supplies) to sustain large populations, southern California, Nevada, and Arizona, in particular, attracted many migrants from the East because of their warm, dry climates. The growth of Los Angeles after World War II was a remarkable phenomenon: more than 10 percent of all new businesses in the United States between 1945 and 1950 began in Los Angeles. Its population rose by over 50 percent between 1940 and 1960.

## Capital and Labor

There were more than 4,000 corporate mergers in the 1950s. To a greater extent than ever before, a relatively small number of large-scale organizations controlled an enormous proportion of the nation's economic activity. By the end of the decade, half of the net corporate income in the nation was going to only slightly more than 500 firms, or one-tenth of 1 percent of the total number of corporations.

A similar consolidation was occurring in the agricultural economy. Increasing mechanization reduced the need for farm labor, and the agricultural work force declined by more than half in the two decades after the war. Mechanization also endangered one of the most cherished American institutions: the family farm. By the 1960s, relatively few individuals could any longer afford to buy and equip a modern farm, and much of the nation's most productive land had been purchased by financial institutions and corporations.

Corporations enjoying booming growth were reluctant to allow strikes to interfere with their operations; and since the most important labor unions were now so large and entrenched that they could not easily be suppressed or intimidated, leaders of large businesses made important concessions to them. As early as 1948, Walter Reuther, president of the United Automobile Workers, obtained a contract from General Motors that included a built-in "escalator clause"—an automatic cost-of-living increase pegged to the consumer price index. In 1955, Reuther received a guarantee from Ford Motor Company that it would continue wages to autoworkers even during layoffs. A few months later, steelworkers in several corporations won a guaranteed annual salary. By the mid-1950s, factory wages in all industries had risen substantially, to an average of $80 per week.

The labor movement enjoyed significant success in winning better wages and benefits for workers already organized in strong unions. For the majority of laborers who were as yet unorganized, however, there were fewer advances. Total union membership remained relatively stable, at about 16 million, throughout the 1950s; and while this was in part a result of a shift in the work force from blue-collar to white-collar jobs, it was also a result of new obstacles to organization. The Taft-Hartley Act and the state right-to-work laws that the act spawned made it more difficult to create new unions powerful enough to demand recognition from employers.

The economic successes of the 1950s helped pave the way for a reunification of the labor movement. In December 1955, the American Federation of Labor and the Congress of Industrial Organizations ended their twenty-year rivalry and merged to create the AFL-CIO, under the leadership of George Meany.

But success also bred stagnation and corruption in some union bureaucracies. In 1957, the powerful Teamsters Union became the subject of a congressional investigation, and its president, David Beck, was charged with the misappropriation of union funds. Beck ultimately stepped down to be replaced by Jimmy Hoffa, whom government investigators pursued for nearly a decade before finally winning a conviction against him (for tax evasion) in 1967. The United Mine Workers, similarly, became tainted by violence and charges of corruption.

## Consumerism and Suburbanization

Among the most striking social developments of the immediate postwar era was the rapid extension of a middle-class lifestyle and outlook to an expanding portion of the population. The American middle class was becoming a larger, more powerful, and more self-conscious force than it had ever been before.

At the center of middle-class culture in the 1950s was a growing absorption with consumer goods. That was a result of increased prosperity, of the increasing variety and availability of products, and of the adeptness of advertisers in creating a demand for those products. It was also a result of the growth of consumer credit, which increased by 800 percent between 1945 and 1957 through the development of credit cards, revolving charge accounts, and easy-payment plans. Prosperity fueled such longtime consumer crazes as the automobile, and Detroit responded to the boom with ever-flashier styling and accessories. Consumers also responded eagerly to the development of such new products as dishwashers, garbage disposals, televisions, and high-fidelity and stereo record players.

A third of the nation's population lived in suburbs by 1960. The growth of suburbs was a result not only of increased affluence but of important innovations in home building, which made single-family houses affordable to millions of new people. The most famous of the suburban developers, William Levitt, came to symbolize the new suburban growth with his use of mass-production techniques to construct large housing developments, the first of which was on Long Island, near New York City. The houses sold for under $10,000. Young couples—often newly married war veterans eager to start a family rushed to purchase the inexpensive homes, not only in the "Levittowns" but in the many other relatively inexpensive developments that soon began appearing throughout the country.

Why did so many Americans want to move to the suburbs? One reason was the enormous importance postwar Americans placed on family life after five years of war during which families had often been separated or otherwise disrupted. Suburbs provided families with larger homes than they could find (or afford) in the cities, and thus made it easier to raise larger numbers of children. They provided privacy. They also provided a sense of security

LEVITTOWN BEFORE THE TREES A section of the Levittown on Long Island in New York, photographed in July 1948 a few months after the first families moved in. The Levitt family pioneered techniques in constructing mass-produced housing that made possible the proliferation of similar inexpensive suburbs in many areas of the country.

from the noise and dangers of urban living. They offered space for the new consumer goods—the appliances, cars, boats, outdoor furniture, and other products that middle-class Americans craved.

For many Americans, suburban life also helped provide a sense of community that was sometimes difficult to develop in large, crowded, impersonal urban areas. In later years, the suburbs would come under attack for their supposed conformity, homogeneity, and isolation. But in the 1950s, many people were attracted by the idea of living in a community populated largely by people of similar age and background, and they found it easier to form friendships and social circles there than in the city. Women in particular often valued the presence of other nonworking mothers living nearby to share the tasks of child raising.

Another factor motivating white Americans to move to the suburbs was race. Most suburbs were restricted to white inhabitants—both because relatively few blacks could afford to live in them and because formal and informal barriers kept even prosperous blacks out of all but a few. In an era when the black population of most cities was rapidly growing, many white families fled to the suburbs to escape the integration of urban neighborhoods and schools.

## The Suburban Family

For professional men (who tended to work in the city, at some distance from their homes), suburban life generally meant a rigid division between their working and personal worlds. For many middle-class women, it meant an increased isolation from the workplace. The enormous cultural emphasis on family life in the 1950s strengthened popular prejudices against women entering the professions or occupying any paid job at all. Many middle-class husbands considered it demeaning for their wives to be employed. And many women themselves shied away from the workplace when they could afford to, in part because of prevailing ideas about motherhood (popularized by such widely consulted books as Dr. Benjamin Spock's *Baby and Child Care*, first published in 1946) that instructed women to stay at home with their children.

Affluent women, then, faced heavy pressures—both externally and internally imposed—to remain in the home and concentrate on raising their children. Some women, however, had to balance these pressures against other, contradictory ones. As expectations of material comfort rose, many middle-class families needed a second income to maintain the standard of living they desired. As a result, the number of married women working out-

THE BABY BOOM IN THE SUBURBS Mothers of young children cluster outside a shopping center in Levittown, New York in the spring of 1949, during the peak of the postwar "baby boom." The rapid population growth the "baby boom" produced, and the massive movement of middle-class families into suburbs that accompanied it, were among the most important demographic trends of the postwar era.

side the home actually increased in the postwar years—even as the social pressure for them to stay out of the workplace grew. By 1960, nearly a third of all married women were part of the paid work force.

### The Birth of Television

Television, perhaps the most powerful medium of mass communication in history, was central to the culture of the postwar era. Experiments in broadcasting pictures (along with sound) had begun as early as the 1920s, but commercial television began only shortly after World War II. It experienced a phenomenally rapid growth. In 1946, there were only 17,000 television sets in the country; by 1957, there were 40 million sets in use—almost as many sets as there were families. More people had television sets, according to one report, than had refrigerators.

The impact of television on American life was rapid, pervasive, and profound. By the late 1950s, television news had replaced newspapers, magazines, and radios as the nation's most important vehicle of information. Television advertising helped create a vast market for new fashions and products. Televised athletic events gradually made professional and college sports one of the important sources of entertainment (and one of the biggest businesses) in America. Television entertainment programming, almost all of it controlled by the three national networks (and their corporate sponsors), replaced movies and radio as the principal source of diversion for American families.

Much of the programming of the 1950s and early 1960s created a relatively uniform image of American life—an image that was predominantly white, middle-class, and suburban, an image epitomized by such popular situation comedies as *Ozzie and Harriet* and *Leave It to Beaver*. But television

THE MICKEY MOUSE CLUB  In an early example of the highly integrated marketing for which it is now famous, the Walt Disney Corporation created this successful television program for children in the mid-1950s. It coincided with, and helped to promote, the opening in 1955 of Disneyland—the company's enormously profitable theme park near Los Angeles.

also conveyed other images: the gritty, urban working-class families in Jackie Gleason's *The Honeymooners*; the childless show-business family of the early *I Love Lucy*; the unmarried professional women in *Our Miss Brooks* and *My Little Margie*. Television not only sought to create an idealized image of a homogeneous suburban America. It also sought to convey experiences at odds with that image in warm, unthreatening terms—taking social diversity and cultural conflict and domesticating them, turning them into something benign and even comic.

Yet television also, inadvertently, created conditions that could accentuate social conflict. Even those unable to share in the affluence of the era could, through television, acquire a vivid picture of how the rest of their society lived. At the same time that television was reinforcing the homogeneity of the white middle class, therefore, it was also contributing to the sense of alienation and powerlessness among groups excluded from the world it portrayed. And when social conflict began to accelerate, television made that conflict seem vivid and immediate to a far-flung audience and helped it to spread.

## Science and Space

In 1961, *Time* magazine chose as its "man of the year" not a specific person but "the American Scientist." The choice was an indication of the widespread fascination with which Americans in the age of atomic weapons viewed science and technology. Major medical advances accounted for much of that fascination. Jonas Salk's vaccine to prevent polio was provided free to the public by the federal government beginning in 1955, and within a few years it (and the Sabin vaccine that soon followed) had virtually eliminated the much feared polio from American life. Other dread diseases such as diphtheria and tuberculosis also all but vanished from society as new drugs and treatments were discovered. Infant mortality and the death rate among young children both declined significantly in the first twenty-five years after the war (although less than in Western Europe). Average life expectancy in that same period rose by five years, to seventy-one.

But Americans were at least equally attracted to other scientific and technological innovations: the jet plane, the computer, synthetics, new types of commercially prepared foods. And nothing better illustrated the nation's veneration of scientific expertise than the popular enthusiasm for the American space program.

The program began in large part because of the Cold War. When the Soviet Union announced in 1957 that it had launched a satellite—*Sputnik*—

into outer space, the American government (and much of society) reacted with alarm, as if the Soviet achievement was also a massive American failure. Federal policy began encouraging (and funding) strenuous efforts to improve scientific education in the schools, to create more research laboratories, and, above all, to speed the development of America's own exploration of outer space. The centerpiece of that exploration was the manned space program, established in 1958 with the selection of the first American space pilots, or "astronauts," who quickly became the nation's most revered heroes. On May 5, 1961, Alan Shepard became the first American launched into space (several months after a Soviet "cosmonaut," Yuri Gagarin, had made a similar, if longer, flight). On February 2, 1962, John Glenn (later a United States senator) became the first American to orbit the globe (again, only after Gagarin had already done so).

Interest in the space program remained high in the summer of 1969, when Neil Armstrong and Edwin Aldrin became the first men to walk on the surface of the moon. Not long after that, however, the government began to cut the funding for future missions, and popular enthusiasm for the program began to wane.

### Organized Society and Its Detractors

Large-scale organizations and bureaucracies increased their influence over American life in the postwar era, as they had been doing for many decades before. White-collar workers came to outnumber blue-collar laborers for the first time, and an increasing proportion of them worked in corporate settings with rigid hierarchical structures. Industrial workers also confronted large bureaucracies both in the workplace and in their own unions.

As in earlier eras, Americans reacted to these developments with ambivalence, often hostility. The debilitating impact of bureaucratic life on the individual slowly became one of the central themes of popular and scholarly debate. William H. Whyte, Jr., produced one of the most widely discussed books of the decade: *The Organization Man* (1956), which attempted to describe the special mentality of the worker in a large, bureaucratic setting. Self-reliance, Whyte claimed, was losing place to the ability to "get along" and "work as a team" as the most valuable trait in the modern character. The sociologist David Riesman made similar observations in *The Lonely Crowd* (1950), in which he argued that the traditional "inner-directed man," who judged himself on the basis of his own values and the esteem of his family, was giving way to a new "other-directed man," more concerned with winning the approval of the larger organization or community.

The most derisive critics of bureaucracy, and of middle-class society generally, were a group of young poets, writers, and artists known as the "beats" (or, by derisive critics, as "beatniks"). They wrote harsh critiques of what they considered the sterility and conformity of American life, the meaninglessness of American politics, and the banality of popular culture. Allen Ginsberg's dark, bitter poem *Howl* (1955) decried the "Robot apartments! invincible suburbs! skeleton treasuries! blind capitals! demonic industries!" of modern life. Jack Kerouac produced what may have been the central document of the Beat Generation in his novel *On the Road* (1957), an account of a cross-country automobile trip that depicted the rootless, iconoclastic lifestyle of Kerouac and his friends. Other, less starkly alienated writers— among them Saul Bellow, J. D. Salinger, John Updike, and John Cheever— also used their work to express misgivings about the enormity, the impersonality, and what they considered the hollowness of modern society.

## THE OTHER AMERICA

It was relatively easy for white, middle-class Americans in the 1950s to believe that the world they knew—a world of economic growth, personal affluence, and cultural homogeneity—was the world virtually all Americans knew, that the values and assumptions they shared were ones that most other Americans shared too. But such beliefs were false. Even within the middle class, there was considerable restiveness—among women, intellectuals, young people, and others who found the middle-class consumer culture somehow unsatisfying, even stultifying. More importantly, large groups of Americans remained outside the circle of abundance and shared neither in the affluence of the middle class nor in many of its values.

### *On the Margins of the Affluent Society*

In 1962, the socialist writer Michael Harrington published a celebrated book called *The Other America*, in which he chronicled the continuing existence of poverty in the United States. The conditions he described were not new. Only the attention he was bringing to them was.

The great economic expansion of the postwar years reduced poverty dramatically but did not eliminate it. In 1960, at any given moment, more than a fifth of all American families (over 30 million people) continued to live below what the government defined as the poverty line (down from a third of all families fifteen years before). Many millions more lived just above the official poverty line, but with incomes that gave them little comfort and no security.

Most of the poor—up to 80 percent—experienced poverty intermittently and temporarily. But approximately 20 percent of the poor were people for whom poverty was a continuous, debilitating reality from which there was no easy escape. That included approximately half the nation's elderly and a significant proportion of African Americans and Hispanics. Native Americans constituted the single poorest group in the country, a result in part of government policies that had undermined the economies of the reservations and driven many Indians into cities, where—unprepared for urban life— some lived in a poverty worse than that they had left.

This "hard-core" poverty rebuked the assumptions of those who argued that economic growth would eventually lead everyone into prosperity— that, as many claimed, "a rising tide lifts all boats." It was a poverty that the growing prosperity of the postwar era seemed to affect hardly at all, a poverty, as Harrington observed, that appeared "impervious to hope."

### Rural Poverty

Among those on the margins of the affluent society were many rural Americans. In 1948, farmers had received 8.9 percent of the national income; in 1956, they received only 4.1 percent. In part, this decline reflected the steadily shrinking farm population; in 1956 alone, nearly 10 percent of the rural population moved into or was absorbed by cities. But it also reflected declining farm prices. Because of enormous surpluses in basic staples, prices fell 33 percent in those years, even though national income as a whole rose 50 percent at the same time. Even most farmers who managed to survive experienced substantial losses of income at the same time that the prices of many consumer goods rose.

Not all farmers were poor. Some were quite affluent. But the agrarian economy did produce substantial numbers of genuinely impoverished people. Black sharecroppers and tenant farmers continued to live at or below subsistence level throughout the rural South—in part because of the mechanization of cotton picking beginning in 1944, in part because of the development of synthetic fibers that reduced demand for cotton generally. (Two-thirds of the cotton acreage of the South went out of production between 1930 and 1960.) Migrant farmworkers, a group concentrated especially in the West and Southwest and containing many Mexican-American and Asian-American workers, lived in similarly dire circumstances. In rural areas without much commercial agriculture—such as the Appalachian region in the

East, where the decline of the coal economy reduced the one significant source of support for the region—whole communities lived in desperate poverty, increasingly cut off from the market economy. All these groups were vulnerable to malnutrition and even starvation.

## The Inner Cities

As prospering white families moved from cities to suburbs in vast numbers, more and more inner-city neighborhoods became repositories for the poor, "ghettoes" from which there was no easy escape. The growth of these neighborhoods owed much to a vast migration of African Americans out of the countryside (where the cotton economy was in decline) and into industrial cities. Not all these migrants were poor, and many found in the city some of the same routes to economic progress that many whites were finding. But African Americans were substantially more likely to live in poverty than most other groups, in part because of the persistence of historic patterns of discrimination that denied them any real opportunities.

More than 3 million black men and women moved from the South to northern cities between 1940 and 1960, many more than had made the same journey in the Great Migration during and after World War I. Chicago, Detroit, Cleveland, New York, and other eastern and midwestern industrial cities experienced a major expansion of their black populations—both in absolute numbers and, even more, as a percentage of the whole, since so many whites were leaving at the same time.

Similar migrations from Mexico and Puerto Rico expanded poor Hispanic neighborhoods in many American cities at the same time. Between 1940 and 1960, nearly a million Puerto Ricans moved into American cities (the largest group to New York). Mexican workers crossed the border into Texas and California and swelled the already substantial Latino communities of such cities as San Antonio, Houston, San Diego, and Los Angeles (which by 1960 had the largest Mexican-American population of any city, approximately 500,000 people).

Why these inner-city communities, populated largely by racial and ethnic minorities, remained so poor in the midst of growing affluence has been the subject of considerable, and very heated, debate. But it is indisputable that inner cities were filling up with poor minority residents at the same time that the unskilled industrial jobs they were seeking were diminishing. Employers were moving factories and mills from old industrial cities to new locations in suburbs, smaller cities, and even abroad—places where the cost of labor or other things were lower. Even in the factories that remained, automation was reducing the number of unskilled jobs. The economic opportunities that had helped earlier immigrant groups to rise up from poverty were unavailable to many of the postwar migrants. Nor can there be any doubt that historic patterns of racial discrimination in hiring, education, and housing doomed many members of these communities to continuing, and in some cases increasing, poverty.

One result of inner-city poverty was a rising rate of juvenile crime. Indeed, "juvenile delinquency" was one of the few results of poverty that middle-class Americans discussed and worried about with any consistency. A 1955 book, *One Million Delinquents*, called juvenile crime a "national epidemic" and described a troubling subculture of inner-city youth—embittered, rebellious adolescents with no hope of advancement and no sense of having a stake in the structure of their society.

## THE RISE OF THE CIVIL RIGHTS MOVEMENT

After decades of skirmishes, an open battle began in the 1950s against racial segregation and discrimination, a battle that would prove to be one of the longest and most difficult social struggles of the century. White Americans played an important role in the civil rights movement. But pressure from African Americans themselves was the crucial element in raising the issue of race to prominence.

### *The* Brown *Decision and "Massive Resistance"*

On May 17, 1954, the Supreme Court announced one of the most important decisions in its history in the case of *Brown* v. *Board of Education of Topeka*. In considering the legal segregation of a Kansas public school system, the Court rejected its own 1896 *Plessy* v. *Ferguson* decision, which had ruled that communities could provide blacks with separate facilities as long as the facilities were equal to those of whites. The *Brown* decision unequivocally declared the segregation of public schools on the basis of race unconstitutional. The justices argued that school segregation inflicted unacceptable damage on those it affected, regardless of the relative quality of the separate schools. Chief Justice Earl Warren explained the unanimous opinion of his colleagues: "We conclude that in the field of public education the doctrine of 'separate but equal' has no place. Separate educational facilities are inherently unequal." The following year, the Court issued another decision (known as *Brown II*) to provide rules for implementing the 1954 order. It ruled that communities must work to desegregate their schools "with all deliberate speed," but it set no timetable and left specific decisions up to lower courts.

In some communities, for example, Washington, D.C., compliance came relatively quickly and quietly. More often, however, strong local opposition (what came to be known in the South as "massive resistance") produced long delays and bitter conflicts. Some school districts ignored the ruling altogether. Others attempted to circumvent it with purely token efforts to integrate. More than 100 southern members of Congress signed a "manifesto" in 1956 denouncing the *Brown* decision and urging their constituents to defy it. Southern governors, mayors, local school boards, and nongovernmental pressure groups (including hundreds of White Citizens' Councils) all worked to obstruct desegregation. By the fall of 1957, only 684 of 3,000 affected

CONFRONTATION IN LITTLE ROCK, 1957 After the governor of Arkansas, Orval Faubus, refused to call the National Guard to enforce court-ordered integration of Central High School in Little Rock, President Eisenhower federalized the troops and ordered them to protect the nine black students who were attempting to begin school. Conflicts over school integration would continue into the 1970s and beyond.

school districts in the South had even begun to desegregate their schools. The *Brown* decision, far from ending segregation, had launched a prolonged battle between federal authority and state and local governments.

The Eisenhower administration was not eager to commit itself to that battle. But in September 1957, it faced a case of direct state defiance of federal authority and felt compelled to act. Federal courts had ordered the desegregation of Central High School in Little Rock, Arkansas. An angry white mob tried to block implementation of the order by blockading the entrances to the school, and Governor Orval Faubus refused to do anything to stop the obstruction. President Eisenhower finally responded by sending federal troops to Little Rock to keep the peace and ensure that the court orders would be obeyed. Only then did Central High School admit its first black students.

## The Expanding Movement

The *Brown* decision helped spark a growing number of popular challenges to segregation in the South. On December 1, 1955, Rosa Parks, an African-American woman, was arrested in Montgomery, Alabama, when she refused to give up her seat on a Montgomery bus to a white passenger (as required by the Jim Crow laws that regulated race relations in the city and throughout most of the South). Parks, an active civil rights leader in the community, had apparently decided spontaneously to resist the order to move. The arrest of this admired woman produced outrage in the city's African-American community, which organized a boycott of the bus system to demand an end to segregated seating.

Once launched, the boycott was almost completely effective. It put economic pressure not only on the bus company (a private concern) but on many Montgomery merchants, because the bus boycotters found it difficult to get to downtown stores and tended to shop instead in their own neighborhoods. Even so, the boycott might well have failed had it not been for a Supreme Court decision late in 1956, inspired in part by the protest, that declared segregation in public transportation to be illegal. The buses in Montgomery abandoned their discriminatory seating policies, and the boycott came to a close.

Perhaps the most important accomplishments of the Montgomery boycott were the legitimization of a new form of racial protest and the elevation to prominence of a new figure in the movement for civil rights. The man chosen to lead the boycott movement once it was launched was a local

Baptist pastor, Martin Luther King, Jr., the son of a prominent Atlanta minister, a powerful orator, and a gifted leader. King's approach to black protest was based on the doctrine of nonviolence—that is, of passive resistance even in the face of direct attack. And he produced an approach to racial struggle that captured the moral high ground for his supporters. For the next thirteen years—as leader of the Southern Christian Leadership Conference (SCLC), an interracial group he founded shortly after the bus boycott—he was the most influential and most widely admired black leader in the country. The popular movement he came to represent soon spread throughout the South and throughout the country.

## EISENHOWER REPUBLICANISM

Dwight D. Eisenhower was the least experienced politician to serve in the White House in the twentieth century. He was also among the most popular and politically successful presidents of the postwar era. At home, he pursued essentially moderate policies, avoiding most new initiatives but accepting the work of earlier reformers. Abroad, he continued and even intensified American commitments to oppose communism but brought to some of those commitments a measure of restraint that his successors did not always match.

### "What's Good for . . . General Motors"

The first Republican administration in twenty years staffed itself with men drawn from the same quarter as those who had staffed Republican administrations in the 1920s: the business community. But many in the American business community had acquired a very different social and political outlook by the 1950s from that of their predecessors of earlier decades. Above all, many of the nation's leading businessmen and financiers had reconciled themselves to at least the broad outlines of the Keynesian welfare state the New Deal had launched. Indeed, some corporate leaders had come to see it as something that actually benefited them—by helping maintain social order, by increasing mass purchasing power, and by stabilizing labor relations.

To his cabinet, Eisenhower appointed wealthy corporate lawyers and business executives who were not apologetic about their backgrounds. Charles Wilson, president of General Motors, assured senators considering his nomination for secretary of defense that he foresaw no conflict of interest because he was certain that "what was good for our country was good for General Motors, and vice versa." But missing from most members of this business-oriented administration was the deep hostility to "government interference" that had so dominated corporate attitudes three decades before.

Eisenhower's consistent inclination was to limit federal activities and encourage private enterprise. He supported the private rather than public development of natural resources (and once talked about selling the Tennessee Valley Authority to a private company). To the chagrin of farmers, he lowered federal support for farm prices. He also removed the last limited wage and price controls maintained by the Truman administration. He opposed the creation of new social service programs such as national health insurance. He strove constantly to reduce federal expenditures (even during the recession of 1958) and balance the budget. He ended 1960, his last full year in office, with a $1 billion budget surplus.

The president took few new initiatives in domestic policy, but he resisted pressure from the right wing of his party to dismantle those welfare policies of the New Deal that had survived the conservative assaults of the war years and after. Indeed, during his term, he agreed to extend the Social Security system to an additional 10 million people and unemployment compensation to an additional 4 million people, and he agreed to increase the minimum hourly wage from 75 cents to $1. Perhaps the most significant legislative accomplishment of the Eisenhower administration was the Federal Highway Act of 1956, which authorized $25 billion for a ten-year effort to construct over 40,000 miles of interstate highways. The program was to be funded through a highway "trust fund," whose revenues would come from new taxes on the purchase of fuel, automobiles, trucks, and tires.

In 1956, Eisenhower ran for a second term, even though he had suffered a serious heart attack the previous year. With Adlai Stevenson opposing him once again, he won by another, even greater landslide, receiving nearly 57 percent of the popular vote and 457 electoral votes to Stevenson's 73. Still, Democrats retained the control of both houses of Congress they had won back in 1954. And in 1958—during a serious recession—they increased that control by substantial margins.

### The Decline of McCarthyism

The Eisenhower administration did little in its first years in office to discourage the anticommunist furor that had gripped the nation. Indeed, in many ways it helped sustain it. The president intensified the search for sub-

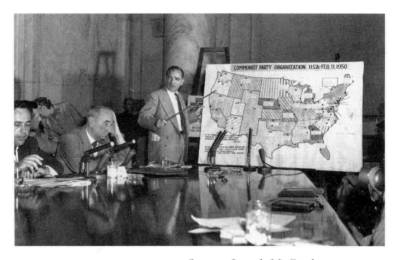

THE ARMY-MCCARTHY HEARINGS Senator Joseph McCarthy uses a map
to show the supposed distribution of communists throughout the
United States during the televised 1954 Senate hearings to mediate
the dispute between McCarthy and the U.S. Army. Joseph Welch,
chief counsel for the army, remains conspicuously unimpressed.

versives in the government, which Truman had begun several years earlier.
More than 2,220 federal employees resigned or were dismissed as a result
of security investigations.

By 1954, however, such policies were beginning to produce significant
popular opposition—an indication that the anticommunist passion of several years earlier was beginning to abate. The clearest signal of that change
was the political demise of Senator Joseph McCarthy.

During the first year of the Eisenhower administration, McCarthy continued to operate with impunity. But McCarthy finally overreached himself
in January 1954 when he attacked Secretary of the Army Robert Stevens and
the armed services in general. At that point, the administration and influential members of Congress organized a special investigation of the charges,
which became known as the Army-McCarthy hearings. They were among
the first congressional hearings to be nationally televised.

The result was devastating to McCarthy. Watching McCarthy in
action—bullying witnesses, hurling groundless (and often cruel) accusations, evading issues—much of the public began to see him as a villain, and
even a buffoon. In December 1954, the Senate voted 67 to 22 to condemn

him for "conduct unbecoming a senator." Three years later, with little public support left, he died—a victim, apparently, of complications arising from alcoholism.

## EISENHOWER, DULLES, AND THE COLD WAR

The threat of nuclear war with the Soviet Union created a sense of high anxiety in international relations in the 1950s. But the nuclear threat had another effect as well. With the potential devastation of an atomic war so enormous, both superpowers began to edge away from direct confrontations. The attention of both the United States and the Soviet Union began to turn to the rapidly escalating instability in the nations of the Third World.

### Dulles and "Massive Retaliation"

Eisenhower's secretary of state, and (except for the president himself) the dominant figure in the nation's foreign policy in the 1950s, was John Foster Dulles, an aristocratic corporate lawyer with a stern moral revulsion to communism. He entered office denouncing the containment policies of the Truman years as excessively passive, arguing that the United States should pursue an active program of "liberation," which would lead to a "rollback" of communist expansion. Once in power, however, he had to defer to the far more moderate views of the president himself, and he began to develop a new set of doctrines that reflected the impact of nuclear weapons on the world.

The most prominent of those doctrines was the policy of "massive retaliation," which Dulles announced early in 1954. The United States would, he explained, respond to communist threats to its allies not by using conventional forces in local conflicts (a policy that had led to so much frustration in Korea) but by relying on "the deterrent of massive retaliatory power" (by which he clearly meant nuclear weapons).

In part, the new doctrines reflected Dulles's inclination for tense confrontations, an approach he once defined as "brinksmanship"—pushing the Soviet Union to the brink of war in order to exact concessions. But the real force behind the massive-retaliation policy was economics. With pressure growing both in and out of government for a reduction in American military expenditures, an increasing reliance on atomic weapons seemed to promise, as some advocates put it, "more bang for the buck."

## France, America, and Vietnam

What had been the most troubling foreign policy concern of the Truman years—the war in Korea—plagued the Eisenhower administration only briefly. On July 27, 1953, negotiators at Panmunjom finally signed an agreement ending the hostilities. Each antagonist was to withdraw its troops a mile and a half from the existing battle line, which ran roughly along the 38th parallel, the prewar border between North and South Korea. A conference in Geneva was to consider means by which to reunite the nation peacefully—although in fact the 1954 meeting produced no agreement and left the cease-fire line as the apparently permanent border between the two countries.

Almost simultaneously, however, the United States was being drawn into a long, bitter struggle in Southeast Asia. Ever since 1945, France had been attempting to restore its authority over Vietnam, its one-time colony, which it had to abandon to the Japanese towards the end of World War II. Opposing the French, however, were the powerful nationalist forces of Ho Chi Minh, determined to win independence for their nation. Ho had hoped for American support in 1945, on the basis of the anticolonial rhetoric of the Atlantic Charter and Franklin Roosevelt's speeches, and also because he had received support from American intelligence forces during World War II while he was fighting the Japanese. But he was then, as he had been for many years, not only a committed nationalist but a committed communist. The Truman administration ignored him and supported the French, one of America's most important Cold War allies.

By 1954, Ho was receiving aid from communist China and the Soviet Union. America, in the meantime, had been paying most of the costs of France's ineffective military campaign in Vietnam since 1950. Early in 1954, 12,000 French troops became surrounded in a disastrous siege at the city of Dien Bien Phu. Only American intervention, it was clear, could prevent the total collapse of the French military effort. Yet despite the urgings of Secretary of State Dulles, Vice President Nixon, and others, Eisenhower refused to permit direct American military intervention in Vietnam, claiming that neither Congress nor America's other allies would support such action.

Without American aid, the French defense of Dien Bien Phu finally collapsed on May 7, 1954, and France quickly agreed to a settlement of the conflict at the same conference in Geneva that summer that was considering the Korean settlement. The Geneva accords on Vietnam of July 1954, to which the United States was not a direct party, established a supposedly temporary division of Vietnam along the 17th parallel. The north would be governed by Ho Chi Minh, the south by a pro-Western regime. Democratic elections would be the basis for uniting the nation in 1956. The agreement marked the end of the French commitment to Vietnam and the beginning of an expanded American presence there. The United States helped establish a pro-American government in the south, headed by Ngo Dinh Diem, a member of his country's Roman Catholic minority. Diem, it was clear, would not permit the 1956 elections, which he knew he would lose. He felt secure in his refusal because the United States had promised to provide him with ample military assistance against any attack from the north. (There is some evidence that the Soviet Union, eager to avoid a confrontation with the United States at this point, was at the same time pressuring Ho and his regime not to press for an election.)

### Cold War Crises

American foreign policy in the 1950s rested on a reasonably consistent foundation: the containment policy, as revised by the Eisenhower administration. But the nation's leaders spent much of their time reacting to both real and imagined crises in far-flung areas of the world. Among them were a series of crises in the Middle East, a region in which the United States had been little involved until after World War II.

On May 14, 1948, after years of Zionist efforts and a dramatic decision by the new United Nations, the nation of Israel proclaimed its independence. President Truman recognized the new Jewish homeland the next day. But the creation of Israel, while it resolved some conflicts, created others. Palestinian Arabs, unwilling to accept being displaced from what they considered their own country, fought determinedly against the new state in 1948—the first of several Arab-Israeli wars.

Committed as the American government was to Israel, it was also concerned about the stability and friendliness of the Arab regimes in the oil-rich region, in which American petroleum companies had major investments. Thus the United States reacted with alarm as it watched Mohammed Mossadegh, the nationalist prime minister of Iran, begin to resist the presence of Western corporations in his nation in the early 1950s. In 1953, the American CIA joined forces with conservative Iranian military leaders to engineer a coup that drove Mossadegh from office. To replace him, the CIA helped elevate the young Shah of Iran, Mohammed Reza Pahlevi, from his position as token constitutional monarch to that of virtually absolute ruler. The Shah remained closely tied to the United States for the next twenty-five years.

American policy was less effective in dealing with the nationalist government of Egypt, under the leadership of General Gamal Abdel Nasser, which began to develop a trade relationship with the Soviet Union in the early 1950s. In 1956, to punish Nasser for his friendliness toward the communists, Dulles withdrew American offers to assist in building the great Aswan Dam across the Nile. A week later, Nasser retaliated by seizing control of the Suez Canal from the British, saying that he would use the income from it to build the dam himself.

On October 29, 1956, Israeli forces attacked Egypt. The next day the British and French landed troops in the Suez to drive the Egyptians from the canal. Dulles and Eisenhower feared that the Suez crisis would drive the Arab states toward the Soviet Union and precipitate a new world war. By refusing to support the invasion, and by joining in a United Nations denunciation of it, the United States helped pressure the French and British to withdraw and helped persuade Israel to agree to a truce with Egypt.

Cold War concerns affected American relations in Latin America as well. In 1954, the Eisenhower administration ordered the CIA to help topple the new, leftist government of Jacobo Arbenz Guzmán in Guatemala, a regime that Dulles (responding to the entreaties of the United Fruit Company, a major investor in Guatemala fearful of Arbenz) argued was potentially communist.

No nation in the region had been more closely tied to America than Cuba. Its leader, Fulgencio Batista, had ruled as a military dictator since 1952, when with American assistance he had toppled a more moderate government. Cuba's relatively prosperous economy had become a virtual fiefdom of American corporations, which controlled almost all the island's natural resources and had cornered over half the vital sugar crop. American organized-crime syndicates controlled much of Havana's lucrative hotel and nightlife business. In 1957, a popular movement of resistance to the Batista regime began to gather strength under the leadership of Fidel Castro. On January 1, 1959, with Batista having fled to exile in Spain, Castro marched into Havana and established a new government.

Castro soon began implementing drastic policies of land reform and expropriating foreign-owned businesses and resources. Cuban-American relations deteriorated rapidly as a result. When Castro began accepting assistance from the Soviet Union in 1960, the United States cut back the "quota" by which Cuba could export sugar to America at a favored price. Early in 1961, as one of its last acts, the Eisenhower administration severed diplomatic relations with Castro. Isolated by the United States, Castro soon cemented an alliance with the Soviet Union.

## Europe and the Soviet Union

Although the problems of the Third World were moving slowly toward the center of American foreign policy, the direct relationship with the Soviet Union and the effort to resist communist expansion in Europe remained the principal concerns of the Eisenhower administration. In 1955, Eisenhower and other NATO leaders met with the Soviet premier, Nikolai Bulganin, at a cordial summit conference in Geneva. But when a subsequent conference of foreign ministers met to try to resolve specific issues, they could find no basis for agreement. Relations between the Soviet Union and the West soured further in 1956 in response to the Hungarian Revolution. Hungarian dissidents had launched a popular uprising in November to demand democratic reforms. Before the month was out, Soviet tanks and troops entered Budapest to crush the uprising and restore an orthodox, pro-Soviet regime. The Eisenhower administration refused to intervene. But the suppression of the uprising convinced many American leaders that Soviet policies had not softened.

## The U-2 Crisis

In November 1958, Nikita Khrushchev, who had succeeded Bulganin as Soviet premier and Communist Party chief earlier that year, renewed the demands of his predecessors that the NATO powers abandon West Berlin. When the United States and its allies predictably refused, Khrushchev suggested that he and Eisenhower discuss the issue personally, both in visits to each other's countries and at a summit meeting in Paris in 1960. The United States agreed. Khrushchev's 1959 visit to America produced a cool but polite public response. Plans proceeded for the summit conference and for Eisenhower's visit to Moscow shortly thereafter. Only days before the scheduled beginning of the Paris meeting, however, the Soviet Union announced that it had shot down an American U-2, a high-altitude spy plane, over Russian territory. Its pilot, Francis Gary Powers, was in captivity. Khrushchev lashed back angrily, breaking up the Paris summit almost before it could begin and withdrawing his invitation to Eisenhower to visit the Soviet Union. But the U-2 incident may have been only a pretext. By the spring of 1960, Khrushchev was under pressure from hard-liners in the Kremlin to toughen his stance toward the West; he also knew that no agreement was possible on the Berlin issue. The U-2 incident may simply have been an excuse to avoid what he believed would be fruitless negotiations.

The events of 1960 provided a somber backdrop for the end of the Eisenhower administration. After eight years in office, Eisenhower had failed to eliminate, and in some respects had actually increased, the tensions between the United States and the Soviet Union. Yet Eisenhower had brought to the Cold War his own sense of the limits of American power. He had resisted military intervention in Vietnam. And he had placed a measure of restraint on those who urged the creation of an enormous American military establishment. In his farewell address in January 1961, he warned of the "unwarranted influence" of a vast "military-industrial complex." His caution, in both domestic and international affairs, stood in marked contrast to the attitudes of his successors, who argued that the United States must act more boldly and aggressively on behalf of its goals at home and abroad.

# CHAPTER THIRTY-ONE

# The Ordeal of Liberalism

*Expanding the Liberal State* ~ *The Battle for Racial Equality*
*"Flexible Response" and the Cold War* ~ *Vietnam*
*The Traumas of 1968*

B Y THE LATE 1950s, a growing restlessness was becoming visible beneath the apparently placid surface of American society. Anxiety about America's position in the world, growing pressures from African Americans and other minorities, the increasing visibility of poverty, the rising frustrations of women, and other long-suppressed discontents were beginning to make themselves felt in the nation's public life. Ultimately, that restlessness would make the 1960s one of the most turbulent and divisive eras of the twentieth century. But at first, it contributed to a bold and confident effort by political leaders to attack social and international problems within the framework of conventional liberal politics.

## EXPANDING THE LIBERAL STATE

Those who yearned for a more active government in the late 1950s and who accused the Eisenhower administration of allowing the nation to "drift" looked above all to the presidency for leadership. The two men who served in the White House through most of the 1960s—John Kennedy and Lyndon Johnson—seemed for a time to be the embodiment of these liberal hopes.

### John Kennedy

The campaign of 1960 produced two young candidates who claimed to offer the nation active leadership. The Republican nomination went almost uncontested to Vice President Richard Nixon, who promised moderate reform. The Democrats, in the meantime, emerged from a spirited primary cam-

| TIME LINE | | | |
|---|---|---|---|
| **1960** | **1961** | **1962** | **1963** |
| Kennedy elected president | Freedom rides<br><br>Bay of Pigs<br><br>Berlin Wall erected | Cuban missile crisis | March on Washington<br><br>Kennedy assassinated; Johnson becomes president |
| **1964** | **1965** | **1967** | **1968** |
| Johnson launches war on poverty<br><br>Civil Rights Act<br><br>Gulf of Tonkin Resolution<br><br>Johnson elected president | Malcolm X assassinated<br><br>Voting Rights Act<br><br>U.S. troops in Vietnam | Antiwar movement grows | Tet offensive<br><br>Martin Luther King, Jr. assassinated<br><br>Robert Kennedy assassinated<br><br>Nixon elected president |

paign united, somewhat uneasily, behind John Fitzgerald Kennedy, an attractive and articulate senator from Massachusetts who had narrowly missed being the party's vice presidential candidate in 1956.

John Kennedy was the son of the wealthy, powerful, and highly controversial Joseph P. Kennedy, former American ambassador to Britain. But while he had grown up in a world of ease and privilege, he became a spokesman for energy and sacrifice. He premised his campaign, he said, "on the single assumption that the American people are uneasy at the present drift in our national course." But his appealing public image was at least as important as his political positions in attracting popular support. He overcame doubts about his youth (he turned forty-three in 1960) and religion (he was a Catholic) to win with a tiny plurality of the popular vote—49.9 percent to Nixon's 49.6 percent and only a slightly more comfortable electoral majority—303 to 219.

Kennedy had campaigned promising a set of domestic reforms more ambitious than any since the New Deal, a program he described as the "New Frontier." But his thin popular mandate and a Congress dominated by a coalition of Republicans and conservative Democrats frustrated many of his hopes. As a result, the president had to look elsewhere for opportunities to display positive leadership. One area where he believed he could do that was the economy. Economic growth was sluggish in 1961 when Kennedy entered the White House, with unemployment hovering at about 6 percent of the work force. Kennedy initiated a series of tariff negotiations with foreign governments—the "Kennedy Round"—in an effort to stimulate American

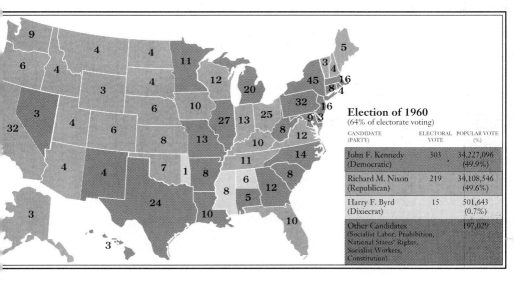

**Election of 1960**
(64% of electorate voting)

| CANDIDATE (PARTY) | ELECTORAL VOTE | POPULAR VOTE (%) |
|---|---|---|
| John F. Kennedy (Democratic) | 303 | 34,227,096 (49.9%) |
| Richard M. Nixon (Republican) | 219 | 34,108,546 (49.6%) |
| Harry F. Byrd (Dixiecrat) | 15 | 501,643 (0.7%) |
| Other Candidates (Socialist Labor, Prohibition, National States' Rights, Socialist Workers, Constitution) | | 197,029 |

exports. He began to consider an expanded use of Keynesian fiscal and monetary tools—culminating in his 1962 proposal for a substantial federal tax cut to stimulate the economy.

He also used his personal prestige to battle inflation. In 1962, several steel companies, led by U.S. Steel, announced that they were raising their prices by $6 a ton, a move certain to trigger similar action by the rest of the industry. Kennedy put heavy pressure on U.S. Steel president Roger Blough and other steel executives to rescind the increase. The companies soon relented. But it was a fleeting victory, which permanently strained Kennedy's relationship with the corporate community. A few months later the steel companies quietly raised prices again. The president did not protest.

More than any other president of the century (except perhaps the two Roosevelts and, later, Ronald Reagan), Kennedy made his own personality an integral part of his presidency and a central focus of national attention. Nothing illustrated that more clearly than the popular reaction to the tragedy of November 22, 1963. Kennedy had traveled to Texas with his wife and Vice President Lyndon Johnson for a series of political appearances. While the presidential motorcade rode slowly through the streets of Dallas, shots rang out. Two bullets struck the president—one in the throat, the other in the head. He was sped to a nearby hospital, where minutes later he was pronounced dead. Lee Harvey Oswald, who appeared to be a confused and embittered Marxist, was arrested for the crime later that day, and then mysteriously murdered by a Dallas nightclub owner, Jack Ruby, two days later as he was being moved from one jail to another. The popular assumption at

JOHN F. KENNEDY AND HIS ADVISERS Kennedy meets in the
White House with Robert McNamara and General Maxwell
Taylor, two men who would play important roles in the
process that would lead to full-scale American military
intervention in Vietnam.

the time was that both Oswald and Ruby had acted alone, assumptions endorsed by a federal commission, chaired by Chief Justice Earl Warren, that
was appointed to investigate the assassination. In later years, however, many
Americans came to believe that the Warren Commission report had ignored evidence of a wider conspiracy behind the murders.

### Lyndon Johnson

The Kennedy assassination was a national trauma—a defining event for almost everyone old enough to be aware of it. At the time, however, much of
the nation took comfort in the personality and performance of Kennedy's
successor in the White House, Lyndon Baines Johnson. Johnson was a native of the poor "hill country" of west Texas and had risen to become majority leader of the U.S. Senate by dint of extraordinary, even obsessive ef-

fort and ambition. Having failed to win the Democratic nomination for president in 1960, he surprised many who knew him by agreeing to accept the second position on the ticket with Kennedy. The events in Dallas thrust him into the White House.

Johnson's rough-edged, even crude personality could hardly have been more different from Kennedy's. But like Kennedy, Johnson was a man who believed in the active use of power. And he proved, in the end, more effective than his predecessor in translating his goals into reality. Between 1963 and 1966, he compiled the most impressive legislative record of any president since Franklin Roosevelt. He was aided by the tidal wave of emotion that followed the death of President Kennedy, which helped win support for many New Frontier proposals. But Johnson constructed a remarkable reform program of his own, one that he ultimately labeled the "Great Society." And he won approval of much of it through the same sort of skillful lobbying in Congress that had made him an effective majority leader.

Johnson envisioned himself as a great "coalition builder." He wanted the support of everyone, and for a time he very nearly got it. His first year in office was, by necessity, dominated by the campaign for reelection. There was little doubt that he would win—particularly after the Republican Party fell under the sway of its right wing and nominated the conservative Senator Barry Goldwater of Arizona. In the November election, the president received a larger plurality, over 61 percent, than any candidate before or since. Goldwater managed to carry only his home state of Arizona and five states in the Deep South. Record Democratic majorities in both houses of Congress, many of whose members had been swept into office only because of the margin of Johnson's victory, ensured that the president would be able to fulfill many of his goals.

### The Assault on Poverty

For the first time since the 1930s, the federal government took steps in the 1960s to create important new social welfare programs. The most important of these, perhaps, was Medicare: a program to provide federal aid to the elderly for medical expenses. Its enactment in 1965 came at the end of a bitter, twenty-year debate between those who believed in the concept of national health assistance and those who denounced it as "socialized medicine." But the program as it went into effect placated many critics. For one thing, it avoided the stigma of "welfare" by making Medicare benefits available to all elderly Americans, regardless of need (just as Social Security had done with pensions). That created a large middle-class constituency for the program. The program also defused the opposition of the medical community by allowing doctors serving Medicare patients to practice privately and to charge their normal fees; Medicare simply shifted responsibility for paying those fees from the patient to the government. In 1966, Johnson steered to passage the Medicaid program, which extended federal medical assistance to welfare recipients and other indigent people of all ages.

Medicare and Medicaid were the first steps in a much larger assault on poverty—one that Kennedy had been planning in the last months of his life and that Johnson launched only weeks after taking office. The centerpiece of this "war on poverty," as Johnson called it, was the Office of Economic Opportunity (OEO), which created an array of new educational, employment, housing, and health-care programs. But the OEO was controversial from the start, in part because of its commitment to the idea of "community action."

Community action was an effort to involve members of poor communities themselves in the planning and administration of the programs designed to help them. The Community Action programs provided jobs for many poor people and gave them valuable experience in administrative and political work. Many men and women who went on to significant careers in politics or community organizing, including many black and Hispanic politicians, as well as many Indians, got their start in Community Action programs.

But despite its achievements, the Community Action approach proved impossible to sustain. Many programs fell victim to mismanagement or to powerful opposition from the local governments with which they were at times competing. Some activists in Community Action agencies employed tactics that mainstream politicians considered frighteningly radical. The apparent excesses of a few agencies damaged the popular image of the Community Action programs, and indeed the war on poverty, as a whole.

The OEO spent nearly $3 billion during its first two years of existence, and it helped reduce poverty in some areas. But it fell far short of eliminating poverty altogether. That was in part because of the weaknesses of the programs themselves and in part because funding for them, inadequate from the beginning, dwindled as the years passed and a costly war in Southeast Asia became the nation's first priority.

### Cities, Schools, and Immigration

Closely tied to the antipoverty program were federal efforts to promote the revitalization of decaying cities and to strengthen the nation's schools. The Housing Act of 1961 offered $4.9 billion in federal grants to cities for the preservation of open spaces, the development of mass-transit systems, and the subsidization of middle-income housing. In 1966, Johnson established a new cabinet agency, the Department of Housing and Urban Development (whose first secretary, Robert Weaver, was the first African American ever to serve in the cabinet). Johnson also inaugurated the Model Cities program, which offered federal subsidies for urban redevelopment.

Kennedy had long fought for federal aid to public education, but he had failed to overcome two important obstacles: Many Americans feared that aid to education was the first step toward federal control of the schools, and Catholics insisted that federal assistance must extend to parochial as well as public schools. Johnson managed to circumvent both objections with the Elementary and Secondary Education Act of 1965 and a series of subsequent measures. The bills extended aid to both private and parochial schools and based the aid on the economic conditions of the students, not on the needs of the schools themselves. Total federal expenditures for education and technical training rose from $5 billion to $12 billion between 1964 and 1967.

The Johnson administration also supported the Immigration Act of 1965, one of the most important pieces of legislation of the 1960s, even if largely unnoticed at the time. The law maintained a strict limit on the number of newcomers admitted to the country each year (170,000), but it eliminated the "national origins" system established in the 1920s, which gave preference to immigrants from northern Europe over those from other parts of the world. It continued to restrict immigration from some parts of Latin America, but it allowed people from all parts of Europe, Asia, and Africa to enter the United States on an equal basis. By the early 1970s, the character of American immigration had changed, with members of new national groups—and particularly large groups of Asian—entering the United States and changing the character of the American population.

### Legacies of the Great Society

Taken together, the Great Society reforms meant a significant increase in federal spending. For a time, rising tax revenues from the growing economy nearly compensated for the new expenditures. In 1964, Johnson managed to win passage of the $11.5 billion tax cut that Kennedy had first proposed in 1962. The cut increased the federal deficit, but it helped produce substantial economic growth over the next several years that made up for much of the revenue initially lost. As Great Society programs began to multiply, however, and particularly as they began to compete with the escalating costs of America's military ventures, the federal budget rapidly outpaced increases in revenues. In 1961, the federal government had spent $94.4 billion. By 1970, that sum had risen to $196.6 billion.

The high costs of the Great Society programs and the inability of the government to find the revenues to pay for them contributed to a growing disillusionment in later years with the idea of federal efforts to solve social problems. By the 1980s, many Americans had become convinced that the Great Society efforts had not worked and that, indeed, government programs to solve social problems could not work. But the Great Society was far from a failure. It significantly reduced hunger in America. It made medical care available to millions of elderly and poor people who would otherwise have had great difficulty affording it. And it contributed to the greatest reduction in poverty in American history. In 1959, according to the most widely accepted estimates, 21 percent of the American people lived below the officially established poverty line. By 1969, only 12 percent remained below that line. The improvements affected blacks and whites in about the same proportion: 56 percent of the black population had lived in poverty in 1959, while only 32 percent did so ten years later—a 42 percent reduction; 18 percent of all whites had been poor in 1959, but only 10 percent were poor a decade later—a 44 percent reduction. Much of that progress was a result of economic growth, but some of it was a result of Great Society programs.

## THE BATTLE FOR RACIAL EQUALITY

The nation's most important domestic initiative in the 1960s was the effort to provide justice and equality to African Americans. It was the most difficult commitment, the one that produced the severest strains on American society. But it was one that could not be avoided. African Americans were themselves ensuring that the nation would have to deal with the problem of race.

### Expanding Protests

John Kennedy had long been sympathetic to the cause of racial justice, but he was hardly a committed crusader. Like presidents before him, he feared alienating southern Democratic voters and powerful southern Democrats in Congress. His administration hoped to contain the racial problem by expanding enforcement of existing laws and supporting litigation to overturn existing segregation statutes.

But the pressure for change could not long be contained. In February 1960, black college students in Greensboro, North Carolina, staged a sit-in at a segregated Woolworth's lunch counter; and in the following months, such demonstrations spread throughout the South, forcing many merchants to integrate their facilities. In the fall of 1960, some of those who had participated in the sit-ins formed the Student Nonviolent Coordinating Committee (SNCC)—a student branch of Martin Luther King, Jr.'s Southern Christian Leadership Council; SNCC worked to keep the spirit of resistance alive.

In 1961, an interracial group of students, working with the Congress of Racial Equality (CORE), began what they called "freedom rides." Traveling by bus throughout the South, they tried to force the desegregation of bus stations. They were met in some places with such savage violence on the part of whites that the president finally dispatched federal marshals to help keep the peace and ordered the integration of all bus and train stations.

Events in the Deep South in 1963 helped bring the growing movement to something of a climax. In April, Martin Luther King, Jr., helped launch a series of nonviolent demonstrations in Birmingham, Alabama, a city unsurpassed in the strength of its commitment to segregation. Police Commissioner Eugene "Bull" Connor personally supervised a brutal effort to break up the peaceful marches, arresting hundreds of demonstrators and using attack dogs, tear gas, electric cattle prods, and fire hoses—at times even against small children—as much of the nation watched televised reports in horror. Two months later, Governor George Wallace stood in the doorway of a building at the University of Alabama to prevent the court-ordered enrollment of several black students. Only after the arrival of federal marshals did he give way. The same night, NAACP official Medgar Evers was murdered in Mississippi.

### A National Commitment

The events in Alabama and Mississippi were a warning to the president that he could not any longer contain or avoid the issue of race. In an important television address the night of the University of Alabama confrontation, Kennedy spoke eloquently of the "moral issue" facing the nation. Days later, he introduced a series of new legislative proposals prohibiting segregation in "public accommodations" (stores, restaurants, theaters, hotels), barring discrimination in employment, and increasing the power of the government to file suits on behalf of school integration.

To generate support for the legislation, and to dramatize the power of

THE MARCH ON WASHINGTON, 1963 Martin Luther King, Jr. waves to the vast crowd spreading out from the Lincoln Memorial shortly after delivering his famous "I Have a Dream" speech—the centerpiece of the March on Washington. Initially envisioned as a broad and militant protest against discrimination, it became in the end a moderate, interracial demonstration of support for the civil rights bill President Kennedy had recently proposed to Congress, which passed in 1964.

the growing movement, more than 200,000 demonstrators marched down the Mall in Washington, D.C., in August 1963 and gathered before the Lincoln Memorial for the largest civil rights demonstration in the nation's history. Martin Luther King, Jr., in one of the greatest speeches of his distinguished oratorical career, aroused the crowd with a litany of images prefaced again and again by the phrase "I have a dream."

The assassination of President Kennedy three months later gave new impetus to the battle for civil rights legislation. The ambitious measure that Kennedy had proposed in June 1963 was stalled in the Senate after having passed through the House of Representatives with relative ease. Early in 1964, after Johnson had applied both public and private pressure, supporters of the measure finally mustered the two-thirds majority necessary to close debate and end a filibuster by southern senators; and the Senate passed the most comprehensive civil rights bill in the history of the nation.

## The Battle for Voting Rights

Having won a significant victory in one area, the civil rights movement shifted its focus to another: voting rights. During the summer of 1964, thousands of civil rights workers, black and white, northern and southern, spread out through the South, but primarily in Mississippi, to work on behalf of black voter registration and participation. The campaign was known as "Freedom Summer," and it produced a violent response from some southern whites. Three of the first freedom workers to arrive in the South—two whites, Andrew Goodman and Michael Schwerner, and one black, James Chaney—were murdered. Local law enforcement officials were involved in the crime.

The "Freedom Summer" also produced the Mississippi Freedom Democratic Party (MFDP), an integrated alternative to the regular state party organization. Under the leadership of Fannie Lou Hamer and others, the MFDP challenged the regular party's right to its seats at the Democratic National Convention that summer. President Johnson, with King's help, managed to broker a compromise by which members of the MFDP could be seated as observers, with promises of party reforms later on, while the regular party retained its official standing. Many MFDP members rejected the agreement and left the convention embittered.

A year later, in March 1965, King helped organize a major demonstration in Selma, Alabama, to press the demand for the right of blacks to register to vote. Selma sheriff Jim Clark led local police in a brutal attack on the demonstrators—which, as in Birmingham, was televised to a horrified nation. Two northern whites participating in the Selma march were murdered in the course of the effort there—one, a minister, beaten to death in the streets of the town; the other, a Detroit housewife, shot as she drove along a highway at night. The national outrage that followed the events in Alabama helped push Lyndon Johnson to propose and win passage of the Civil Rights Act of 1965, which provided federal protection to African Americans attempting to exercise their right to vote. But important as such gains were, they failed to satisfy the rapidly rising expectations of American blacks, as the focus of the movement began to move from political to economic issues.

## The Changing Movement

For decades, the nation's African-American population had been undergoing a major demographic shift. By 1966, 69 percent of American blacks were living in metropolitan areas and 45 percent outside the South. Although the economic condition of much of American society was improving, in many of the poor urban communities in which much of the black population was becoming concentrated, things were getting significantly worse. More than half of all American nonwhites lived in poverty at the beginning of the 1960s; black unemployment was twice that of whites.

By the mid-1960s, therefore, the issue of race was moving out of the South and into the rest of the nation. The legal battle for school integration was moving beyond the issue of formal, legal segregation to an attack on the informal practices that often sustained separation of the races. That carried the fight into northern cities, which had no Jim Crow laws but much segregation. Many African-American leaders (and their white supporters) were demanding, similarly, that the battle against job discrimination move to a new level. They argued that the only way for employers to prove that they were not discriminating against African Americans was for them to demonstrate that they were hiring minorities. If necessary, they should adopt positive measures to recruit minorities. Lyndon Johnson gave his support to the concept of "affirmative action" in 1965. Over the next decade, affirmative action guidelines gradually extended to virtually all institutions doing business with or receiving funds from the federal government (including schools and universities)—and to many others as well.

A symbol of the movement's new direction, and of the problems it would cause, was a major campaign in the summer of 1966 in Chicago, in which King played a prominent role. Organizers of the Chicago campaign hoped to direct national attention to housing and employment discrimination in northern industrial cities in much the same way that similar campaigns had exposed legal racism in the South. But the Chicago campaign not only evoked vicious and at times violent opposition from white residents of that city; it failed to attract wide attention or support in the way events in the South had done.

### Urban Violence

Well before the Chicago campaign, the problem of urban poverty had thrust itself into national prominence when riots broke out in black neighborhoods in major cities. There were a few scattered disturbances in the summer of 1964, most notably in New York City's Harlem. The first large race riot since the end of World War II occurred the following summer in the Watts section of Los Angeles. In the midst of a traffic arrest, a white police officer struck a protesting black bystander with his club. The incident triggered a storm of anger and a week of violence. Thirty-four people died during the uprising, which was eventually quelled by the National Guard. In the summer of 1966, there were forty-three additional outbreaks, the most serious of them in Chicago and Cleveland. And in the summer of 1967, there were eight major riots, including the largest of them all—a racial clash in Detroit in which forty-three people died.

Televised reports of the violence alarmed millions of Americans and created both a new sense of urgency and a growing sense of doubt among some whites who had embraced the cause of racial justice only a few years before. A special Commission on Civil Disorders, created by the president in response to the riots, issued a celebrated report in the spring of 1968 recommending massive spending to eliminate the abysmal conditions of the ghettoes. To many white Americans, however, the lesson of the riots was the need for stern measures to stop violence and lawlessness.

### Black Power

Disillusioned with the ideal of peaceful change through cooperation with whites, an increasing number of African Americans were turning to a new approach to the racial issue: the philosophy of "black power." Black power could mean many different things. But in all its forms, it suggested a shift away from the goal of assimilation and toward increased awareness of racial distinctiveness.

Perhaps the most enduring impact of the black-power ideology was a social and psychological one: instilling racial pride in African Americans who had been taught by their nation's dominant culture to think of themselves as somehow inferior to whites. But black power took political forms as well, and it created a deep schism within the civil rights movement. Traditional black organizations that emphasized cooperation with sympathetic whites—groups such as the NAACP, the Urban League, and King's Southern Christian Leadership Conference—now faced competition from more radical groups. The Student Nonviolent Coordinating Committee and the Congress of Racial Equality had both begun as relatively moderate, interracial organizations. By the mid-1960s, however, these and other groups were calling for more radical and occasionally even violent action against the racism of white society and were openly rejecting the approaches of older, more established black leaders.

The most radical expressions of the black-power idea came from such revolutionary organizations as the Black Panthers, based in Oakland, California, and the separatist group, the Nation of Islam, which denounced whites as "devils" and appealed to blacks to embrace the Islamic faith and

A M E R I C A N   V O I C E S

MALCOLM X

## The Angriest Negro in America

THEY CALLED me "the angriest Negro in America." I wouldn't deny that charge. I spoke exactly as I felt. "I *believe* in anger. The Bible says there is a *time* for anger." They called me "a teacher, a fomentor of violence." I would say point blank, "That is a lie. I'm not for wanton violence, I'm for justice. I feel that if white people were attacked by Negroes—if the forces of law prove unable, or inadequate, or reluctant to protect those whites from those Negroes—then those white people should protect and defend themselves from those Negroes, using arms if necessary. And I feel that when the law fails to protect Negroes from whites' attack, then those Negroes should use arms, if necessary, to defend themselves." . . .

What was wrong with that? I'll tell you what was wrong. I was a black man talking about physical defense against the white man. The white man can lynch and burn and bomb and beat Negroes—that's all right: "Have patience" . . . "The customs are entrenched" . . . "Things are getting better."

Well, I believe it's a crime for anyone who is being brutalized to continue to accept that brutality without doing something to defend himself. . . . I don't go for non-violence if it also means a delayed solution. To me a delayed solution is a non-solution.

SOURCE: *The Autobiography of Malcolm X*, pp. 366–367. © 1964 by Alex Haley and Malcolm X, © 1965 by Malcolm X and Betty Shabazz. Reprinted by permission of Ballantine Books.

work for complete racial separation. The most celebrated of the Black Muslims, as whites often termed them, was Malcolm Little, who had adopted the name Malcolm X ("X" to denote his lost African surname). He died in 1965 when black gunmen, presumably under orders from rivals within the Nation of Islam, assassinated him. But he remained a major figure in many black communities long after his death—as important to and revered by many African Americans as Martin Luther King, Jr.

## "FLEXIBLE RESPONSE" AND THE COLD WAR

In international affairs as much as in domestic reform, the optimistic liberalism of the Kennedy and Johnson administrations dictated a more active and aggressive approach to dealing with the nation's problems than that of the 1950s.

### Diversifying Foreign Policy

The Kennedy administration entered office convinced that the United States needed to be able to counter communist aggression in more flexible ways than the atomic weapons–oriented defense strategy of the Eisenhower years permitted. In particular, Kennedy was unsatisfied with the nation's ability to meet communist threats in "emerging areas" of the Third World—the areas in which, Kennedy believed, the real struggle against communism would be waged in the future. He gave enthusiastic support to the expansion of the Special Forces (or "Green Berets," as they were soon known)—soldiers trained specifically to fight guerrilla conflicts and other limited wars.

Kennedy also favored expanding American influence through peaceful means. To repair the badly deteriorating relationship with Latin America, he proposed an "Alliance for Progress": a series of projects for peaceful development and stabilization of the nations of that region. Kennedy also inaugurated the Agency for International Development (AID) to coordinate foreign aid. And he established what became one of his most popular innovations: the Peace Corps, which sent young American volunteers abroad to work in developing areas.

Among the first foreign policy ventures of the Kennedy administration was a disastrous assault on the Castro government in Cuba. The Eisenhower administration had launched the project; and by the time Kennedy took office, the CIA had been working for months to train a small army of anti-

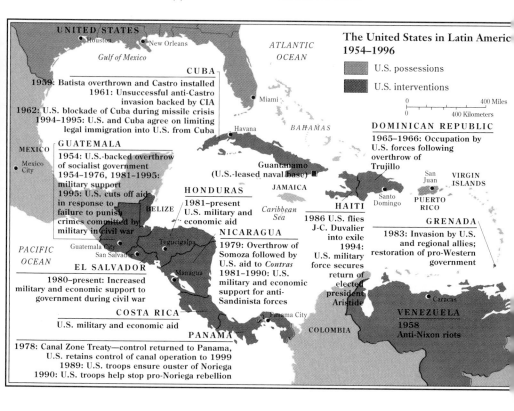

**The United States in Latin America 1954–1996**

- U.S. possessions
- U.S. interventions

0 — 400 Miles
0 — 400 Kilometers

UNITED STATES
Houston · New Orleans
Gulf of Mexico
*ATLANTIC OCEAN*

Miami

Havana · *BAHAMAS*

**CUBA**
1959: Batista overthrown and Castro installed
1961: Unsuccessful anti-Castro invasion backed by CIA
1962: U.S. blockade of Cuba during missile crisis
1994–1995: U.S. and Cuba agree on limiting legal immigration into U.S. from Cuba

MEXICO
Mexico City

**GUATEMALA**
1954: U.S.-backed overthrow of socialist government
1954–1976, 1981–1995: military support
1995: U.S. cuts off aid in response to failure to punish crimes committed by military in civil war

Guatemala City · BELIZE
San Salvador

**HONDURAS**
1981–present
U.S. military and economic aid

Tegucigalpa

*Caribbean Sea*

Guantanamo
(U.S.-leased naval base)

JAMAICA

**HAITI**
1986 U.S. flies J-C. Duvalier into exile
1994: U.S. military force secures return of elected president Aristide

Santo Domingo

**DOMINICAN REPUBLIC**
1965–1966: Occupation by U.S. forces following overthrow of Trujillo

San Juan · **VIRGIN ISLANDS**

**PUERTO RICO**

**GRENADA**
1983: Invasion by U.S. and regional allies; restoration of pro-Western government

*PACIFIC OCEAN*

**EL SALVADOR**
1980–present: Increased military and economic support to government during civil war

Managua

**NICARAGUA**
1979: Overthrow of Somoza followed by U.S. aid to *Contras*
1981–1990: U.S. military and economic support for anti-Sandinista forces

**COSTA RICA**
U.S. military and economic aid

Panama City

COLOMBIA

**VENEZUELA**
1958
Anti-Nixon riots

Caracas

**PANAMA**
1978: Canal Zone Treaty—control returned to Panama, U.S. retains control of canal operation to 1999
1989: U.S. troops ensure ouster of Noriega
1990: U.S. troops help stop pro-Noriega rebellion

Castro Cuban exiles in Central America. On April 17, 1961, with the approval of the new president, 2,000 of the armed exiles landed at the Bay of Pigs in Cuba, expecting first American air support and then a spontaneous uprising by the Cuban people on their behalf. They received neither. At the last minute, as it became clear that things were going badly, Kennedy withdrew the air support, fearful of involving the United States too directly in the invasion. The expected uprising did not occur. Instead, well-armed Castro forces easily crushed the invaders, and within two days the entire mission had collapsed.

### Confrontations with the Soviet Union

In the grim aftermath of the Bay of Pigs, Kennedy traveled to Vienna in June 1961 for his first meeting with Soviet Premier Nikita Khrushchev. Their frosty exchange of views did little to reduce tensions between the two nations. Nor did Khrushchev's veiled threat of war unless the United States ceased to support a noncommunist West Berlin in the heart of East Germany.

Khrushchev was particularly unhappy about the mass exodus of residents of East Germany to the West through the easily traversed border in the center of Berlin. But he ultimately found a method short of war to stop it. Before dawn on August 13, 1961, the East German government, complying with directives from Moscow, constructed a wall between East and West Berlin. Guards fired on those who continued to try to escape. For nearly thirty years, the Berlin Wall served as the most potent physical symbol of the conflict between the communist and noncommunist worlds.

The rising tensions culminated the following October in the most dangerous and dramatic crisis of the Cold War. During the summer of 1962, American intelligence agencies had become aware of the arrival of a new wave of Soviet technicians and equipment in Cuba and of military construction in progress. On October 14, aerial reconnaissance photos produced clear evidence that the Soviets were constructing sites on the island for offensive nuclear weapons. To the Soviets, placing missiles in Cuba probably seemed a reasonable—and relatively inexpensive—way to counter the presence of American missiles in Turkey (and a way to deter any future American invasion of Cuba). But to Kennedy and most other Americans, the missile sites represented an act of aggression by the Soviets toward the United States. Almost immediately, the president decided that the weapons could not be allowed to remain. On October 22, he ordered a naval and air blockade around Cuba, a "quarantine" against all offensive weapons. Preparations were under way for an American air attack on the missile sites when, late in the evening of October 26, Kennedy received a message from Khrushchev implying that the Soviet Union would remove the missile bases in exchange for an American pledge not to invade Cuba. Ignoring other, tougher Soviet messages, the president agreed. The crisis was over.

### Johnson and the World

Lyndon Johnson entered the presidency lacking even John Kennedy's limited prior experience with international affairs. He was eager, therefore, not only to continue the policies of his predecessor but to prove quickly that he too was a strong and forceful leader.

An internal rebellion in the Dominican Republic gave him an early opportunity to do so. A 1961 assassination had toppled the repressive dictatorship of General Rafael Trujillo, and for the next four years various factions in the country had struggled for dominance. In the spring of 1965, a conservative military regime began to collapse in the face of a revolt by a broad range of groups on behalf of the left-wing nationalist Juan Bosch. Arguing (without any evidence) that Bosch planned to establish a pro-Castro, communist regime, Johnson dispatched 30,000 American troops to quell the disorder. Only after a conservative candidate defeated Bosch in a 1966 election were the forces withdrawn.

From Johnson's first moments in office, however, his foreign policy was almost totally dominated by the bitter civil war in Vietnam and by the expanding involvement of the United States there.

## VIETNAM

George Kennan, who helped devise the containment doctrine in the name of which America went to war in Vietnam, once called the conflict "the most disastrous of all America's undertakings over the whole 200 years of its history." In retrospect, few would now wholly disagree. Yet at first, the conflict in Vietnam seemed simply one more Third World struggle on the periphery of the Cold War.

### The First Indochina War

Vietnam had been a colony of France since the mid-nineteenth century. And like other European possessions in Asia, it fell under the control of Japan during World War II. After the defeat of Japan, the question arose of what was to happen to Vietnam in the postwar world. The French wanted to reassert their control over Vietnam. Challenging them was a powerful nationalist movement within Vietnam committed to creating an independent nation. The nationalists were organized into a political party, the Vietminh, which had been created in 1941 and led ever since by Ho Chi Minh, a communist educated in Paris and Moscow, and a fervent believer in Vietnamese independence. The Vietminh had fought against Japan throughout World War II (unlike the French colonial officials who had remained in Vietnam until the last year of the war—as representatives of the Vichy regime—and had collaborated with the Japanese). In the fall of 1945, after the collapse of Japan and before the Western powers had time to return, the Vietminh declared Vietnam an independent nation and set up a government under Ho Chi Minh in Hanoi.

Ho had worked closely during the war with American intelligence forces in Indochina in fighting the Japanese; he apparently considered the United

States something like an ally. When the war ended in 1945, he began writing President Truman asking for support in his struggle against the French. He received no reply to his letters, probably because no one in the State Department had heard of him. At the same time, Truman was under heavy pressure from both the British and the French to support France in its effort to reassert its control over Vietnam. The French argued that without Vietnam, their domestic economy would collapse. And since the economic revival of Western Europe was quickly becoming one of the Truman administration's top priorities, the United States did nothing to stop (although, at first, also relatively little to encourage) the French as they moved back into Vietnam in 1946 and began a struggle with the Vietminh to regain control over the country.

At first, the French had little difficulty reestablishing control. They drove Ho Chi Minh out of Hanoi. But the Vietminh continued to challenge the French-dominated regime and slowly increased its control over large areas of the countryside. The French appealed to the United States for support, and in February 1950, the Truman administration agreed to provide them with direct military and economic aid.

For the next four years, during what has become known as the First Indochina War, Truman and then Eisenhower continued to support the French military campaign against the Vietminh; by 1954, by some calculations, the United States was paying 80 percent of France's war costs. But the war went badly for the French anyway. Finally, late in 1953, Vietminh forces surrounded the French during a major battle in the far northwest corner of the country, at Dien Bien Phu. The result was a prolonged siege, with the French position steadily deteriorating. It was at this point that the Eisenhower administration decided not to intervene to save the French (see p. 824). The defense of Dien Bien Phu soon collapsed, and the French government decided the time had come to get out. The First Indochina War had come to an end.

### Geneva and the Two Vietnams

An international conference at Geneva, planned many months before to settle the Korean dispute and other controversies, now took up the fate of Vietnam as well. The United States was only indirectly involved in the Vietnam phase of the Geneva Conference and never signed the accords. Even so, the Geneva Conference produced an agreement to end the Vietnam conflict. There would be an immediate cease-fire in the war; Vietnam would be temporarily partitioned along the 17th parallel, with the Vietminh in control of

CHINA

Lao Cai

Than Uyen

Red River

Yen Bay

NORTH VIETNAM

BURMA

Dienbienphu

Hanoi ☆

Haiphong

Red River
Delta

Pak Seng

PLAIN
OF JARS

Ban Ban

Gulf of Tonkin

Luang
Prabang

L A O S

Hainan

Vang Vieng

Vientiane ☆

Udon Thani

Vinh

Phanom

Dong Hoi

Mekong R.

Vinh Linh

DMZ (Demilitarized Zone)

Khesanh

QUANG TRI
PROVINCE

Hue

THAILAND

FRIENDSHIP HIGHWAY

Phu Bai

Da Nang

South China Sea

Takhli

Hoi An
Tamky

Don Muang

Udon Ratchathani

My Lai

Lop Buri

Ratchasima

Chulai

Quang Ngai

Dak To

Kontum

PLATEAU OF KONTUM

Ankhe

Pleiku

Quinhon

Bangkok ☆

Angkor Wat

PLATEAU
OF DARLAC

Battambang

Sattahip

Tonle Sap

CAMBODIA

Ban Me Thuot

Nhatrang

Kompong
Chom

Da Lat

Camranh Bay

Phnom
Penh ☆

Prey
Veng

Bo Duc

Phanrang

Gulf of Thailand

1970:
U.S. and South Vietnam
troops entered Viet Cong
strongholds inside Cambodia

Tay Ninh

Ben Cat

SOUTH

VIETNAM

Bienhua

Sihanoukville

Tan Son Nhut
Airbase

Saigon ☆

MEKONG DELTA

Vung Tau

Rach Gia

Cantho

The War in Vietnam and
Indochina, 1964–1975

Quan Long

0        100 Miles

0        100 Kilometers

CA MAU
PENINSULA

Con Son

□  U.S. bases

U.S. and South Vietnam
invasion of Cambodia

Ho Chi Minh Trail
(communist supply route

North Vietnam, and a pro-Western regime in control of South Vietnam. In 1956, elections would be held to reunite the country under a single government.

The partition of Vietnam was, therefore, an essentially artificial one. But there were, in fact, real and important differences between North and South Vietnam. North Vietnam, the area now to be controlled by the Vietminh, was the heart of traditional Vietnamese society, the area where French influence had been the weakest. It had remained a reasonably stable, reasonably homogeneous culture, most of whose people lived in very close-knit, traditional villages. Northern Vietnam was also the poorest and most populous region of the country.

South Vietnam, by contrast, was a much more recently settled area. Even in the 1950s, most of its people had been there only three generations or less. It was a looser, more heterogeneous, more individualistic society than that of the north. It was highly factionalized—religiously, politically, and ethnically—with powerful sects (and even a powerful mafia) all competing for dominance, which made it a very difficult region to unite and govern. It was also more prosperous and fertile than the north. South Vietnam had no legacy of strong commitment to the Vietminh and a much less fervent commitment than did the north to national unification. It was the area where the influence of the French had been strongest and where there was a substantial, westernized middle class.

### America and Diem

As soon as the Geneva accords established the partition, the French left Vietnam altogether. The United States almost immediately stepped into the vacuum and became the principal benefactor of the new government in the south, led by Ngo Dinh Diem.

Diem was an aristocratic Catholic from central Vietnam, an outsider in the south. But he was also a nationalist, uncontaminated by collaboration with the French. And he was, for a time, apparently successful. With the help of the American CIA, Diem waged an effective campaign against some of the powerful religious sects and the South Vietnamese mafia, which had challenged the authority of the central government. As a result, the United States came to regard Diem as a powerful and impressive alternative to Ho Chi Minh.

The American government supported Diem's refusal in 1956 to permit the elections called for by the Geneva accords, reasoning, almost certainly correctly, that Ho Chi Minh would easily win any such election. In the meantime, the United States poured military and economic aid into South Vietnam. By 1956, it was the second-largest recipient of American military aid in the world, after Korea.

Diem's early successes in suppressing the sects in Vietnam led him in 1959 to begin a similar campaign to eliminate the Vietminh supporters who had stayed behind in the south after the partition. That campaign persuaded Ho Chi Minh and his supporters to resume his armed struggle for national unification. In 1959, the Vietminh cadres in the south created the National Liberation Front (NLF), known to many Americans as the Viet Cong—an organization closely allied with the North Vietnamese government. It was committed to overthrowing the "puppet regime" of Diem and reuniting the nation. In 1960, under orders from Hanoi, and with both material and man-power support from North Vietnam, the NLF began military operations in the south. This marked the beginning of the Second Indochina War.

By 1961, NLF forces had established effective control over many areas of the countryside. Diem was also by now losing the support of many other groups in South Vietnam, and he was even losing support within his own military. In 1963, the Diem regime precipitated a major crisis by trying to discipline and repress the South Vietnamese Buddhists in an effort to make Catholicism the dominant religion of the country. The Buddhists began to stage enormous antigovernment demonstrations, during which several monks doused themselves with gasoline, sat cross-legged in the streets of downtown Saigon, and set themselves on fire—in view of photographers and television cameras.

American officials pressured Diem to reform his now tottering government, but the president made no significant concessions. As a result, in the fall of 1963, Kennedy gave his tacit approval to a plot by a group of South Vietnamese generals to topple Diem. In early November 1963, the generals staged the coup, assassinated Diem and his brother and principal adviser, Ngo Dinh Nhu (killings the United States had not wanted or expected), and established the first of a series of new governments, which were, for over three years, even less stable than the one they had overthrown. A few weeks after the coup, John Kennedy too was dead.

### From Aid to Intervention

Lyndon Johnson, therefore, inherited what was already a substantial American commitment to the survival of an anticommunist South Vietnam. During his first months in office, he expanded the American involvement in Vietnam only slightly, sending an additional 5,000 military advisers there and preparing to send 5,000 more. Then, early in August 1964, the president announced that American destroyers on patrol in international waters in the Gulf of Tonkin had been attacked by North Vietnamese torpedo boats. Later information raised serious doubts as to whether the administration reported the attacks accurately. At the time, however, virtually no one questioned Johnson's portrayal of the incident as a serious act of aggression or his insistence that the United States must respond. By a vote of 416 to 0 in the House and 88 to 2 in the Senate, Congress hurriedly passed the Gulf of Tonkin Resolution, which authorized the president to "take all necessary measures" to protect American forces and "prevent further aggression" in

ON PATROL IN VIETNAM, JUNE 1965  Several weeks before President Johnson announced that American ground troops would enter the Vietnam War, United States soldiers were already engaged in combat. These marines, patrolling the area around the American base at Da Nang, were ambushed by communist guerrillas moments after this photograph was taken. One marine was killed and three were wounded.

Southeast Asia. The resolution became, in Johnson's view at least, an open-ended legal authorization for escalation of the conflict.

With the South Vietnamese leadership still in disarray and the communist military pressure on the south growing stronger, more and more of the burden of opposition to the Viet Cong fell on the United States. In February 1965, after communist forces attacked an American military base at Pleiku, Johnson ordered American bombings of the north, in an attempt to destroy the depots and transportation lines responsible for the flow of North Vietnamese soldiers and supplies into South Vietnam. The bombing continued intermittently until 1972. A month later, in March 1965, two battalions of American marines landed at Da Nang in South Vietnam. There were now more than 100,000 American troops in Vietnam.

Four months later, the president finally admitted that the character of the war had changed. American soldiers would now, he announced, begin playing an active combat role in the conflict. By the end of the year, there were more than 180,000 American combat troops in Vietnam; in 1966, that number doubled; and by the end of 1967, there were over 500,000 American soldiers there. In the meantime, the air war had intensified until the tonnage of bombs dropped ultimately exceeded that in all theaters during World War II. And American casualties were mounting. By the spring of 1966, more than 4,000 Americans had been killed.

### The Quagmire

For more than seven years, American combat forces remained bogged down in a war that the United States was never able either to win or fully to understand. Combating a foe whose strength lay less in weaponry than in its infiltration of the population, the United States responded with heavy-handed technological warfare designed for conventional battles against conventional armies.

Central to the American war effort was the strategy known to the military as "attrition," one premised on the belief that the United States could inflict more damage on the enemy than the enemy could absorb. But the attrition strategy failed because the North Vietnamese were willing to commit many more soldiers and resources to the conflict than the United States had expected.

It failed, too, because the United States relied so heavily on its bombing of the north to eliminate the communists' war-making capacity. American bombers attacked almost every identifiable strategic target in North Vietnam as well as jungle areas in Cambodia and Laos thought to shelter the "Ho Chi Minh Trail," by which Hanoi sent troops and supplies into the south. But North Vietnam was not a modern industrial society, and it had relatively few of the sorts of targets against which bombing is effective. And the North Vietnamese responded to the bombing with great ingenuity: creating a network of underground tunnels, shops, and factories; securing substantial aid from the Soviet Union and China; and continually moving the Ho Chi Minh Trail to make it elusive to American bombers. Far from breaking the north's resolve, the bombing seemed actually to strengthen popular commitment to the war.

Another important part of the American strategy was the "pacification" program, whose purpose was to push the Viet Cong from particular regions and then "pacify" those regions by winning the "hearts and minds" of the people. Routing the Viet Cong was often possible, but the subsequent pacification was more difficult. American forces were not adept at establishing rapport with provincial Vietnamese, and the American military never gave that part of the program a very high priority in any case. Gradually, the pacification program gave way to the more heavy-handed relocation strategy, through which American troops uprooted villagers from their homes, sent them fleeing to refugee camps or into the cities (producing by 1967 more than 3 million refugees), and then destroyed the vacated villages and surrounding countryside.

As the war dragged on and victory remained elusive, some American officers and officials began to urge the president to expand the military efforts. But the Johnson administration resisted—in part because it was beginning to encounter obstacles and frustrations at home.

## The War at Home

Few Americans, and even fewer influential ones, had protested the American involvement in Vietnam as late as the end of 1965. But as the war dragged on and came to seem increasingly futile, political support for it began to erode.

By the end of 1967, American students opposed to the war had become a significant political force. Enormous peace marches in New York, Washington, D.C., and other cities drew broad public attention to the antiwar movement. In the meantime, a growing number of journalists, particularly reporters who had spent time in Vietnam, helped sustain the movement with their frank revelations about the brutality and apparent futility of the war.

The growing chorus of popular protest helped stimulate opposition to the war from within the government. Senator J. William Fulbright of

Arkansas, chairman of the powerful Senate Foreign Relations Committee, turned against the war and in January 1966 began to stage highly publicized and occasionally televised congressional hearings to air criticisms of it. Other members of Congress joined Fulbright in opposing Johnson's policies—including, in 1967, Robert F. Kennedy, brother of the slain president, now a senator from New York. Even within the administration, the consensus seemed to be crumbling. Robert McNamara, who had done much to help extend the American involvement in Vietnam, quietly left the government, disillusioned, in 1968. His successor as secretary of defense, Clark Clifford, became a quiet but powerful voice within the administration on behalf of a cautious scaling down of the commitment.

In the meantime, the American economy was beginning to suffer. Johnson's commitment to fighting the war while continuing his Great Society reforms helped cause a rise in the inflation rate, from the 2 percent level it had occupied through most of the early 1960s to 3 percent in 1967, 4 percent in 1968, and 6 percent in 1969. In August 1967, Johnson asked Congress for a tax increase to avoid even more ruinous inflation. In return, congressional conservatives demanded and received a $6 billion reduction in the funding for Great Society programs.

## THE TRAUMAS OF 1968

By the end of 1967, the twin crises of the war in Vietnam and the deteriorating racial situation at home had produced great social and political tensions. In the course of 1968, those tensions seemed suddenly to burst to the surface and threaten national chaos.

### The Tet Offensive

On January 31, 1968, the first day of the Vietnamese New Year (Tet), communist forces launched an enormous, concerted attack on American strongholds throughout South Vietnam. A few cities, most notably Hue, fell temporarily to the communists. Others suffered major disruptions. But what made the Tet offensive so shocking to the American people, who saw vivid reports of it on television, was the sight of communist forces in the heart of Saigon, setting off bombs, shooting down South Vietnamese officials and troops, and holding down fortified areas (including, briefly, the grounds of

JOHNSON AND HUMPHREY, MARCH 27, 1968 Four days before announcing he would not run for reelection, a grim and tired Lyndon Johnson, accompanied by Vice President Hubert Humphrey, receives a briefing on the military situation in Vietnam.

the American embassy). The Tet offensive also suggested to the American public something of the brutality of the fighting in Vietnam. In the midst of the fighting, television cameras recorded the sight of a South Vietnamese officer shooting a captured Viet Cong soldier in the head in the streets of Saigon.

American forces soon dislodged the Viet Cong from most of the positions they had seized, and the Tet offensive in the end cost the communists such appalling casualties that they were significantly weakened for months to come. Indeed, the Tet defeats permanently depleted the ranks of the NLF and forced North Vietnamese troops to take on a much larger share of the subsequent fighting. But all that had little impact on American opinion. Tet may have been a military victory for the United States, but it was a political defeat for the administration, a defeat from which it would never fully recover.

In the following weeks, opposition to the war grew substantially. Leading newspapers and magazines, television commentators, and mainstream politicians began taking public stands in favor of de-escalation of the conflict. Within weeks of the Tet offensive, public opposition to the war had almost doubled. And Johnson's personal popularity rating had slid to 35 percent, the lowest of any president since Harry Truman.

## The Political Challenge

Beginning in the summer of 1967, dissident Democrats tried to mobilize support behind an antiwar candidate who would challenge Lyndon Johnson in the 1968 primaries. When Robert Kennedy turned them down, they recruited Senator Eugene McCarthy of Minnesota. A brilliantly orchestrated campaign by young volunteers in the New Hampshire primary produced a startling showing by McCarthy in March; he nearly defeated the president.

A few days later, Robert Kennedy finally entered the campaign, embittering many McCarthy supporters but bringing his own substantial strength among blacks, poor people, and workers to the antiwar cause. Polls showed the president trailing badly in the next scheduled primary, in Wisconsin. On March 31, 1968, Johnson went on television to announce a limited halt in the bombing of North Vietnam—his first major concession to the antiwar forces—and, much more surprising, his withdrawal from the presidential contest.

Robert Kennedy quickly established himself as the champion of the Democratic primaries, winning one election after another. In the meantime, however, Vice President Hubert Humphrey, with the support of President Johnson, entered the contest and began to attract the support of party leaders and of the many delegations that were selected not by popular primaries but by state party organizations. He soon appeared to be the front-runner in the race.

## The King Assassination

On April 4, Martin Luther King, Jr., who had traveled to Memphis, Tennessee, to lend his support to striking black sanitation workers in the city, was shot and killed while standing on the balcony of his motel. The assassin, James Earl Ray, who was captured days later in London, had no apparent motive. Subsequent evidence suggested that he had been hired by others to do the killing, but he himself never revealed the identity of his employers.

King's tragic death produced a great outpouring of grief. Among American blacks, it also produced anger. In the days after the assassination, major riots broke out in more than sixty American cities. Forty-three people died; more than 3,000 suffered injuries; as many as 27,000 people were arrested.

## The Kennedy Assassination and Chicago

Late in the night of June 6, Robert Kennedy appeared in the ballroom of a Los Angeles hotel to acknowledge his victory in that day's California primary. As he left the ballroom after his victory statement, Sirhan Sirhan, a young Palestinian apparently enraged by pro-Israeli remarks Kennedy had recently made, emerged from a crowd and shot him in the head. Early the next morning, Kennedy died. The shock of this second tragedy in two months cast a deep pall over the remainder of the presidential campaign.

When the Democrats finally gathered in Chicago in August, for a convention in which Hubert Humphrey was now the only real contender, even the most optimistic observers were predicting turbulence. Inside the hall, delegates bitterly debated an antiwar plank in the party platform that both Kennedy and McCarthy supporters favored. Miles away, in a downtown park, thousands of antiwar protesters were staging demonstrations. On the third night of the convention, as the delegates were beginning their balloting on the now virtually inevitable nomination of Hubert Humphrey, demonstrators and police clashed in a bloody riot in the streets of Chicago. Hundreds of protesters were injured as police attempted to disperse them with tear gas and billy clubs. Aware that the violence was being televised to the nation, the demonstrators taunted the authorities with the chant, "The whole world is watching!" And Hubert Humphrey, who had spent years dreaming of becoming his party's candidate for president, received a nomination that night which appeared at the time to be almost worthless.

## The Conservative Response

The turbulent events of 1968 persuaded many observers that American society was in the throes of revolutionary change. In fact, however, the response of most Americans to the turmoil was a conservative one.

The most visible sign of the conservative backlash was the surprising success of the campaign of George Wallace for the presidency. Wallace had established himself in 1963 as one of the leading spokesmen for the defense of segregation when, as governor of Alabama, he had attempted to block the admission of black students to the University of Alabama. In 1968, he became a third-party candidate for president, basing his campaign on a host of conservative grievances. He denounced the forced busing of students, the proliferation of government regulations and social programs, and the permissiveness of authorities toward crime, race riots, and antiwar demonstrations. There was never any serious chance that Wallace would win the election, but his standing in the polls rose at times to over 20 percent.

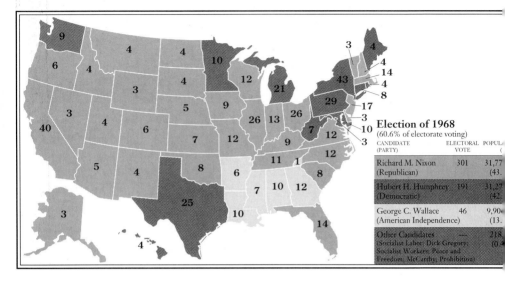

Election of 1968
(60.6% of electorate voting)

| CANDIDATE (PARTY) | ELECTORAL VOTE | POPUL. ( |
|---|---|---|
| Richard M. Nixon (Republican) | 301 | 31,77 (43. |
| Hubert H. Humphrey (Democratic) | 191 | 31,27 (42. |
| George C. Wallace (American Independence) | 46 | 9,90 (13. |
| Other Candidates (Socialist Labor: Dick Gregory; Socialist Workers; Peace and Freedom; McCarthy; Prohibition) | — | 218 (0. |

A more effective effort to mobilize the conservative middle in favor of
order and stability was under way within the Republican Party. Richard
Nixon, whose political career had seemed at an end after his losses in the
presidential race of 1960 and a California gubernatorial campaign two years
later, reemerged as the preeminent spokesman for what he sometimes called
the "silent majority." Nixon recognized that many Americans were tired of
hearing about their obligations to the poor, tired of hearing about the sacrifices necessary to achieve racial justice, tired of judicial reforms that seemed
designed to help criminals. By offering a vision of stability, law and order,
government retrenchment, and "peace with honor" in Vietnam, he easily
captured the nomination of his party for the presidency. And despite a last-
minute surge by Humphrey, he hung on to eke out a victory almost as narrow as his defeat in 1960. He received 43.4 percent of the popular vote to
Humphrey's 42.7 percent (a margin of only about 500,000 votes), and 301
electoral votes to Humphrey's 191. George Wallace, who like most third-
party candidates faded in the last weeks of the campaign, still managed to
poll 13.5 percent of the popular vote and to carry five southern states with
a total of 46 electoral ballots. Nixon had hardly won a decisive personal mandate. But the election made clear that a majority of the American electorate
was more interested in restoring stability than in promoting social change.

D E B A T I N G  T H E  P A S T

## The Vietnam Commitment

HE DEBATE over why the United States became involved in the conflict in Vietnam (which is only one of many debates about the meaning of the war) has centered on two different, if related, questions. One is an effort to assess the broad objectives Americans believed they were pursuing in Vietnam. The other is an effort to explain how and why policymakers made the specific decisions that led the United States to a military commitment in Indochina.

Scholars and writers such as Norman Podhoretz, Guenter Lewy, and R. B. Smith, echoing elements of the official government explanation of American intervention in the war, have argued that the communist aggression in Vietnam was part of a Chinese and Soviet design to spread revolution throughout Asia. America, therefore, was not only protecting Vietnam, although that was an important part of its mission; it was also defending the rest of Asia, which would soon be threatened by communism if Vietnam fell. The intervention in Vietnam was a rational and even necessary expression of America's legitimate security interests and its belief in democracy.

Most scholars, however, have been more skeptical. Historians on the left argue that America's intervention in Vietnam was a form of imperialism— part of a larger effort by the United States after World War II to impose a particular political and economic order on the world. "The Vietnam War," Gabriel Kolko wrote in 1985, "was for the United States the culmination of its frustrating postwar effort to merge its arms and politics to halt and re-

*(continued on next page)*

verse the emergence of states and social systems opposed to the international order Washington sought to establish." Others argued that the United States fought in Vietnam to serve the domestic economic interests that had a stake in the region or in the arms production the war stimulated. Other, more moderate critics blame the Vietnam intervention on the myopia of a foreign policy elite unwilling to question its own unreflective commitment to containing communism everywhere and unable to distinguish between international aggression and domestic insurgency.

Those who have looked less at the nation's broad objectives than at the workings of the policymaking process have also produced competing explanations. David Halberstam's *The Best and the Brightest* (1972) argued that policymakers deluded themselves into thinking they could achieve their goals in Vietnam by ignoring, suppressing, or dismissing information that should have suggested that they were wrong; because of arrogance or ideological rigidity, they simply refused to consider that victory was beyond their grasp.

Larry Berman, writing in 1982, offered a different view. Neither Johnson nor his advisers were unaware of the obstacles to success in Vietnam. Almost everyone suspected that victory would be difficult, even impossible, to attain. The president was not misled or misinformed. But Johnson committed troops to the war anyway, because he feared that allowing Vietnam to fall would ruin him politically and destroy his hopes for building his "Great Society" at home. Leslie Gelb and Richard Betts made a related argument in 1979. Vietnam, they claimed, was the logical, perhaps inevitable result of a political and bureaucratic order shaped by the ideology of the Cold War. However costly the intervention in Vietnam, policymakers concluded, the costs of not intervening and allowing South Vietnam to fall always seemed higher. The war escalated in the 1960s not because American aims changed but because the situation in Vietnam deteriorated to the point where nothing short of intervention would prevent defeat. Only when the national and international political situation itself shifted in the late 1960s and early 1970s—only when it became clear that the political costs of staying in Vietnam were higher than the political costs of getting out—was it possible for the United States to begin disengaging.

# CHAPTER THIRTY-TWO

# The Crisis of Authority

*The Turbulent Society* ～ *The Mobilization of Minorities* ～ *The New Feminism*
*Nixon, Kissinger, and the War* ～ *Nixon, Kissinger, and the World*
*Politics and Economics in the Nixon Years* ～ *The Watergate Crisis*

T HE ELECTION OF Richard Nixon in 1968 was the result of more than the unpopularity of Lyndon Johnson and the war. It was the result, too, of a broad popular reaction against what many Americans considered a dangerous assault on the foundations of their society and culture. In Richard Nixon they found a man who seemed perfectly to match their mood. Himself a product of a hardworking, middle-class family, he projected an image of stern dedication to traditional values. Yet the presidency of Richard Nixon, far from returning calm and stability to American politics, coincided with, and helped to produce, more years of crisis.

## THE TURBULENT SOCIETY

Perhaps most alarming to many conservatives in the 1960s and 1970s was a pattern of social and cultural protest by younger Americans, who were giving vent to two related impulses. One was the impulse, emerging from the political left, to create a great new community of "the people," which would rise up to break the power of elites and force the nation to end the war, pursue racial and economic justice, and transform its political life. The other, at least equally powerful impulse was related to, but not entirely compatible with, the first: the vision of personal "liberation." It found expression in part through the efforts of many groups—African Americans, Indians, Hispanics, women, gay people, and others—to define and assert themselves and make demands on the larger society. It also found expression through the efforts of individuals to create a new culture—one that would allow them to escape from what some considered the dehumanizing pressures of the modern "technocracy."

## TIME LINE

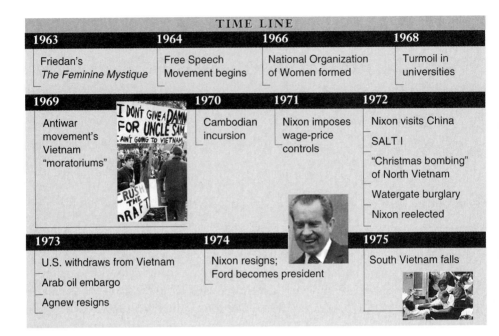

| 1963 | 1964 | 1966 | 1968 |
|---|---|---|---|
| Friedan's *The Feminine Mystique* | Free Speech Movement begins | National Organization of Women formed | Turmoil in universities |

| 1969 | 1970 | 1971 | 1972 |
|---|---|---|---|
| Antiwar movement's Vietnam "moratoriums" | Cambodian incursion | Nixon imposes wage-price controls | Nixon visits China<br>SALT I<br>"Christmas bombing" of North Vietnam<br>Watergate burglary<br>Nixon reelected |

| 1973 | 1974 | 1975 |
|---|---|---|
| U.S. withdraws from Vietnam<br>Arab oil embargo<br>Agnew resigns | Nixon resigns; Ford becomes president | South Vietnam falls |

*The New Left*

Among the products of the racial crisis and the war in Vietnam was a radicalization of many American students, who in the course of the 1960s formed what became known as the New Left. The New Left emerged from many sources, but from nothing so much as the civil rights movement, in which many idealistic young white Americans had become involved in the early 1960s. Within a few years, some white civil rights activists were beginning to consider broader political commitments. In 1962, a group of students (most of them white) gathered in Michigan to form an organization to give voice to their demands: Students for a Democratic Society (SDS). Their declaration of beliefs, the Port Huron Statement, expressed their disillusionment with the society they had inherited and their determination to build a new politics. In the following years, SDS became the leading organization of student radicalism.

Since most members of the New Left were students, much of their radicalism centered for a time on issues related to the modern university. A 1964 dispute at the University of California at Berkeley over the rights of students to engage in political activities on campus—the Free Speech Movement—was the first outburst of what was to be nearly a decade of campus turmoil.

Students at Berkeley and elsewhere protested the impersonal character of the modern university, and they denounced the role of educational institutions in sustaining what they considered corrupt or immoral public policies. The antiwar movement greatly inflamed and expanded the challenge to the universities; and beginning in 1968, campus demonstrations, riots, and building seizures became almost commonplace. At Columbia University in New York, students seized the offices of the president and other members of the administration and occupied them for several days until local police forcibly ejected them. Over the next several years, hardly any major university was immune to some level of disruption. Small groups of especially dogmatic radicals—among them the "Weathermen," an offshoot of SDS—were responsible for a few cases of arson and bombing that destroyed campus buildings and claimed several lives.

Not many people ever accepted the radical political views that lay at the heart of the New Left. But many supported the position of SDS and other groups on particular issues, and above all on the Vietnam War. Between 1967 and 1969, student activists organized some of the largest political demonstrations in American history—in Washington, D.C., and around the country—to protest the war. They helped thrust the issue of Vietnam into the center of American politics.

Closely related to opposition to the war—and another issue that helped fuel the antiwar movement—was opposition to the military draft. The gradual abolition of many traditional deferments—for graduate students, teachers, husbands, fathers, and others—swelled the ranks of those faced with conscription (and thus likely to oppose it). Draft card burnings became common features of antiwar rallies on college campuses. Many draft-age Americans simply refused induction, accepting what were occasionally long terms in jail as a result. Thousands of others fled to Canada, Sweden, and elsewhere (where they were joined by many deserters from the armed forces) to escape conscription. Not until 1977, when President Jimmy Carter issued a general pardon to draft resisters and a far more limited amnesty for deserters, did the Vietnam exiles begin to return to the country in substantial numbers.

### The Counterculture

Closely related to the New Left was a new youth culture openly scornful of the values and conventions of middle-class society. The most visible characteristic of the counterculture, as it became known, was a change in lifestyle. As if to display their contempt for conventional standards, young Americans flaunted long hair, shabby or flamboyant clothing, and a rebellious disdain

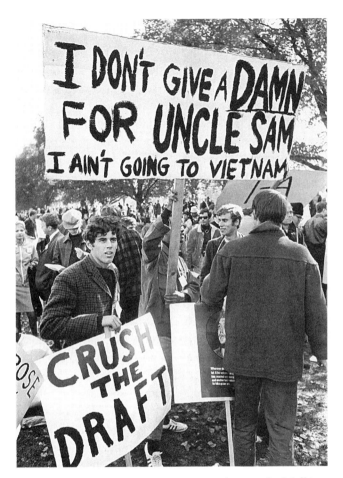

THE WAR AT HOME  Demonstrators gather on the Mall in Washington in the fall of 1967 for one of the first of the great antiwar demonstrations of the late 1960s. Over time, the antiwar movement helped erode the national consensus on the conflict in Vietnam. But the principal basis for opposing the war was never the moral or economic arguments of the left; it was simply the frustration among many Americans of seeing a war continuing too long and too inconclusively.

for traditional speech and decorum. Central to the counterculture were drugs: marijuana smoking—which after 1966 became almost as common a youthful diversion as beer drinking had once been—and the use of other, more potent hallucinogens, such as LSD. There was also a new, more permissive view of sex.

The counterculture's iconoclasm and hedonism sometimes obscured the philosophy behind it, which offered a fundamental challenge to the American middle-class mainstream. Like the New Left, with which it in many ways overlapped, the counterculture challenged the structure of modern American society, attacking its banality, its hollowness, its artificiality, its isolation from nature. The most committed adherents of the counterculture—the hippies, who came to dominate the Haight-Ashbury neighborhood of San Francisco and other places, and the social dropouts, many of whom retreated to rural communes—rejected modern society altogether and attempted to find refuge in a simpler, more "natural" existence. But even those whose commitment to the counterculture was less intense shared a commitment to the idea of personal fulfillment through rejecting the inhibitions and conventions of middle-class culture and giving fuller expression to personal instinct and desire. The first responsibility of the individual, the counterculture seemed to suggest, is cultivation of the self, the unleashing of one's own full potential for pleasure and fulfillment.

The counterculture was in many ways only an exaggerated expression of impulses that were coursing through the larger society. A new set of social norms emerged among many young people (and some adults) whose links to the counterculture were otherwise negligible. Long hair and freakish clothing became the badge not only of hippies and radicals but of an entire generation. The use of marijuana, the freer attitudes toward sex, the iconoclastic (and often obscene) language—all spread far beyond the realm of the true devotees of the counterculture. And perhaps the most pervasive element of the new youth society was one that even the least radical members of the generation embraced: rock music. Rock's driving rhythms, its undisguised sensuality, its often harsh and angry tone—all made it an appropriate vehicle for expressing the social and political restlessness of the late 1960s.

## THE MOBILIZATION OF MINORITIES

The growth of black protest, and of a significant white response to it, both preceded the political and cultural upheavals of the 1960s and helped to produce them. It also encouraged other minorities to assert themselves and demand redress of their grievances. For Indians, Hispanic Americans, gay men and lesbians, and others, the late 1960s and 1970s were a time of growing self-expression and political activism.

### Seeds of Indian Militancy

Few minorities had deeper or more justifiable grievances against the prevailing culture than American Indians—or Native Americans, as some began defiantly to call themselves in the 1960s. Indians were the least prosperous, least healthy, and least stable group in the nation. Average annual family income for Indians was $1,000 less than that for blacks. The Native American unemployment rate was ten times the national rate. Joblessness was particularly high on the reservations, where nearly half of all Indians lived. But even most Indians living in cities were victims of limited education and training and could find only menial jobs. Life expectancy among Indians was more than twenty years less than the national average. Suicides among Indian youths were a hundred times more frequent than among white youths. And while black Americans attracted the attention (for good or for ill) of many whites, Indians for many years remained largely ignored.

For much of the postwar era, and particularly after the resignation of John Collier as commissioner of Indian affairs in 1945, federal policy toward the tribes had been shaped by a determination to incorporate Indians into mainstream American society whether Indians wanted to assimilate or not. Two laws passed in 1953 established the basis of a new policy, which became known as "termination." Through termination, the federal government withdrew all official recognition of the tribes as legal entities, administratively separate from state governments, and made them subject to the same local jurisdictions as white residents. At the same time, the government encouraged Indians to assimilate into the white world and worked to funnel Native Americans into cities, where, presumably, they would adapt themselves to the larger society and lose their cultural distinctiveness.

To some degree, the termination and assimilation policies achieved their objectives. The tribes grew weaker as legal and political entities. Many Native Americans adapted to life in the cities, at least to a degree. On the whole, however, the new policies were a disastrous failure. Indians themselves fought so bitterly against them that in 1958 the Eisenhower administration barred further "terminations" without the consent of the affected tribes. In the meantime, the struggle against termination had mobilized a new generation of Indian militants and had breathed life into the principal

Native American organization, the National Congress of American Indians, which had been created in 1944.

The Democratic administrations of the 1960s did not disavow the termination policy, but neither did they make any effort to revive it. Instead, they made modest efforts to restore at least some degree of tribal autonomy. The funneling of OEO money to tribal organizations through the Community Action program was one prominent example. In the meantime, the tribes themselves were beginning to fight for self-determination—partly in response to the black civil rights movement and partly in response to other social and cultural changes (among them, the expanding mobility and rising educational levels of younger Indians, who were becoming more aware of the world around them and of their own anomalous place within it). The new militancy also benefited from the rapid increase in the Indian population, which was growing much faster than that of the rest of the nation (nearly doubling between 1950 and 1970 to a total of about 800,000).

## The Indian Civil Rights Movement

In 1961, more than 400 members of 67 tribes gathered in Chicago to discuss ways of bringing all Indians together in an effort to redress common wrongs. The manifesto they issued, the Declaration of Indian Purpose, stressed the "right to choose our own way of life" and the "responsibility of preserving our precious heritage."

The 1961 meeting was only one example of a growing Indian self-consciousness. The National Indian Youth Council, created in the aftermath of the 1961 Chicago meeting, promoted the idea of Indian nationalism and intertribal unity. In 1968, a group of young, militant Indians established the American Indian Movement (AIM), which drew its greatest support from those Indians who lived in urban areas but which soon established a significant presence on the reservations as well.

The new activism had some immediate political results. In 1968, Congress passed the Indian Civil Rights Act, which guaranteed reservation Indians many of the protections accorded other citizens by the Bill of Rights but which also recognized the legitimacy of tribal laws within the reservations. But leaders of AIM and other insurgent groups were not satisfied and turned increasingly to direct action. In 1968, Indian fishermen, citing old treaty rights, clashed with Washington State officials on the Columbia River and in Puget Sound. The following year, members of several tribes occupied the abandoned federal prison on Alcatraz Island in San Francisco Bay, claiming the site "by right of discovery."

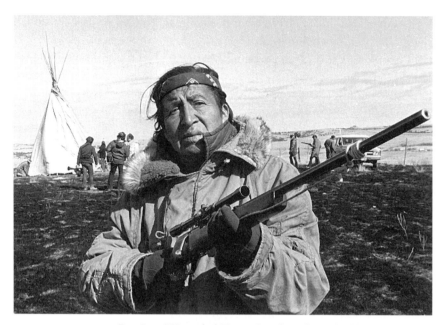

WOUNDED KNEE  In 1890, Wounded Knee, South Dakota, had been the site of a bloody conflict between white troops and Sioux Indians, a conflict that turned into a notorious massacre in which over 300 Indians died. In 1973, the American Indian Movement chose the same place as a site for a militant protest against conditions on the Pine Ridge Indian reservation.

In response to the growing pressure, the new Nixon administration appointed Louis Bruce, a Mohawk-Sioux, to the position of commissioner of Indian affairs in 1969; and in 1970 the president promised both increased tribal self-determination and an increase in federal aid. But the protests continued. In November 1972, nearly a thousand demonstrators, most of them Lakota (or Sioux) Indians, forcibly occupied the building of the Bureau of Indian Affairs in Washington for six days. A more celebrated protest occurred later that winter at Wounded Knee, South Dakota, the site of the 1890 massacre of Sioux by federal troops. In February 1973, members of AIM seized and occupied the town of Wounded Knee for two months, demanding radical changes in the administration of the reservation and insisting that the government honor its long-forgotten treaty obligations. A brief clash between the occupiers and federal forces left one Indian dead and another wounded. Shortly thereafter the siege came to an end.

The Indian civil rights movement, like other civil rights movements of the same time, fell far short of winning full justice and equality for Native

Americans. But it helped the tribes win a series of new legal rights and protections that, together, gave them a stronger position than they had enjoyed at any previous time in the twentieth century. It also helped many Indians gain a renewed awareness of and pride in their identity as Indians and as part of a distinct community within the larger United States.

### Hispanic-American Activism

More numerous and more visible than Indians were Hispanic Americans (sometimes known as Latinos), the fastest-growing minority group in the United States. Large numbers of Mexicans had entered the country during World War II in response to the wartime labor shortage, and many had remained in the cities of the Southwest and the Pacific Coast. By 1960, there were substantial Mexican-American neighborhoods (or barrios) in American cities from El Paso to Detroit. The largest (with more than 500,000 people, according to census figures) was in Los Angeles, which by then had a bigger Mexican population than anyplace except Mexico City.

But the greatest expansion in the Hispanic population of the United States was yet to come. In 1960, the census reported slightly more than 3 million Hispanics living in the United States. By 1970, that number had grown to 9 million and by 1990 to 20 million. Hispanics constituted more than a third of all legal immigrants to the United States after 1960. Since there was also an uncounted but very large number of illegal immigrants in those years (estimates ranged from 7 million to 12 million), the real percentage of Hispanic immigrants was undoubtedly much larger.

Large numbers of Puerto Ricans (who were entitled to American citizenship by birth) migrated to eastern urban areas, particularly New York, where they formed one of the poorest communities in the city. South Florida's substantial Cuban population began with a wave of middle-class refugees fleeing the Castro regime in the early 1960s. These first Cuban migrants quickly established themselves as a successful and highly assimilated part of Miami's middle class. In 1980, a second, much poorer wave of Cuban immigrants—the so-called Marielietos, named for the port from which they left Cuba—arrived in Florida when Castro temporarily relaxed exit restrictions. (This group included a large number of criminals, whom Castro had, in effect, expelled from the country.) This second wave was less welcomed by the government (and the existing Cuban community) and less easily assimilated. Later in the 1980s, large numbers of immigrants (both legal and illegal) began to arrive from Central and South America—from Guatemala, Nicaragua, El Salvador, Peru, and other countries. The most numerous

Hispanic group, however, remained the Mexican Americans, who were concentrated in the Southwest and California but who were also spreading throughout the nation's interior.

Many Hispanic Americans were affluent and successful people. But most of the newer immigrants were less well educated than either "Anglo" or black Americans and hence less well prepared for high-paying jobs. The fact that many spoke English poorly or not at all further limited their employment prospects. As a result, they found themselves concentrated in poorly paid service jobs.

Like blacks and Indians, many Hispanic Americans responded to the highly charged climate of the 1960s by strengthening their ethnic identification and by organizing for political and economic power. Affluent Hispanics in Miami filled influential positions in the professions and local government; in the Southwest, they elected Mexican Americans to seats in Congress and to governorships. A Mexican-American political organization, La Raza Unida, exercised influence in southern California and elsewhere in the Southwest in the 1970s and beyond.

One of the most visible efforts to organize Hispanics occurred in California, where an Arizona-born farmworker of Mexican descent, César Chávez, created an effective union of itinerant farmworkers: the United Farm Workers (UFW), a largely Hispanic organization. For most Hispanics, however, the path to economic and political power was more difficult. Partly because of language barriers, partly because of ineffective organization, and partly because of discrimination, Mexican Americans and others were slow to develop political influence in proportion to their numbers. In the meantime, Hispanics formed one of the poorest segments of the United States population.

### Challenging the "Melting Pot" Ideal

The efforts of blacks, Hispanics, Indians, and others to forge a clearer group identity challenged a longstanding premise of liberal political thought—the idea of the "melting pot." Older, European immigrant groups liked to believe that they had advanced in American society by adopting the values and accepting the rules of the world to which they had moved and by advancing within it on its own terms. The more militant ethnic groups of the 1960s were less willing to accept the standards of the larger society and more likely to demand recognition of their own ethnic identity. African Americans, Indians, and Hispanics all challenged the assimilationist idea and advocated instead a culturally pluralist society, in which racial and ethnic groups would preserve not only a sense of their heritage (which older, more "assimilationist" ethnic groups did as well) but also their own social and cultural norms.

To a large degree, the advocates of cultural pluralism succeeded. Recognition of the special character of particular groups was embedded in federal law through a wide range of affirmative action programs, which extended not only to blacks but to Indians, Hispanics, and others as well. Ethnic studies programs proliferated in schools and universities. Eventually, this impulse led to an even more assertive (and highly controversial) cultural movement that in the 1980s and 1990s became known as "multiculturalism," which challenged the "Eurocentric" basis of American education and culture and demanded that non-European civilizations be accorded at least equal attention.

### Gay Liberation

The last important liberation movement to emerge in the 1960s, and the most unsettling to some Americans, was the effort by gay men and lesbians to win political and economic rights and, more important, social acceptance. Homosexuality has been a generally unacknowledged reality through most of American history. Nonheterosexual men and women were forced for generations either to suppress their sexual preferences, to exercise them surreptitiously, or to live within isolated and often persecuted communities. But by the late 1960s, the liberating impulses that had affected other groups helped mobilize gay men and lesbians to fight for their own rights.

On June 27, 1969, police officers raided the Stonewall Inn, a gay nightclub in New York City's Greenwich Village, and began arresting patrons simply for frequenting the place. The raid was not unusual, but the response was. Gay onlookers taunted the police and then attacked them. Someone started a blaze in the Stonewall Inn itself, almost trapping the policemen inside. Rioting continued throughout Greenwich Village (the center of New York's gay community) through much of the night.

The "Stonewall Riot" marked the beginning of the gay liberation movement—one of the most controversial challenges to traditional values and assumptions of its time. New organizations—among them the Gay Liberation Front, founded in New York in 1969—sprang up around the country. Public discussion and media coverage of homosexuality, long subject to an unofficial taboo, quickly and dramatically increased. Gay activists were having some success in challenging the longstanding assumption that ho-

mosexuality was aberrant behavior and were arguing that no sexual preference was any more normal than another.

Most of all, however, the gay liberation movement transformed the outlook of many gay men and lesbians themselves. It helped them to "come out,"
to express their preferences openly and unapologetically, and to demand
from society a recognition that gay relationships could be as significant and
worthy of respect as heterosexual ones. Some gays advocated not only an acceptance of homosexuality as a valid and "normal" preference but a change
in the larger society as well: a redefinition of personal identity to give much
greater importance to erotic impulses. There was much resistance to such
efforts. But by the early 1980s, the gay liberation movement had made remarkable strides. Even the ravages of the AIDS epidemic, which, in the beginning at least, affected the gay community more disastrously than it affected any other group, failed to halt the growth of gay liberation. In many
ways, it strengthened it.

By the early 1990s, gay men and lesbians were achieving many of the
same milestones that other oppressed minorities had attained in earlier
decades. Openly gay politicians were winning election to public office. Universities were establishing gay and lesbian studies programs. And laws prohibiting discrimination on the basis of sexual preference were making slow,
halting progress at the state and local levels. But gay liberation produced a
powerful backlash as well, as became evident in 1993 when President Bill
Clinton's effort to end the ban on gay men and lesbians serving in the military met a storm of criticism from members of Congress and within the military itself. At the same time, voters in some cities and states were approving referendum questions on their ballots outlawing civil rights protections
for gay men and lesbians.

## THE NEW FEMINISM

American women constitute over 50 percent of the population. But during
the 1960s and 1970s, many women began to identify with minority groups
as they renewed demands for a liberation of their own. Sexual discrimination was so deeply embedded in the fabric of society that when feminists first
began to denounce it, many men (and even many women) responded with
bafflement and anger. By the mid-1970s, however, public awareness of the
issue had increased greatly, and the role of women in American life was
changing more rapidly and dramatically than that of any other group in the
nation.

## *The Rebirth*

Feminism had been a weak and often embattled force in American life for more than forty years after the adoption of the woman suffrage amendment in 1920. A few determined women kept feminist political demands alive in the National Woman's Party and other organizations. Many more women expanded the acceptable bounds of female activity by entering new areas of the workplace or engaging in political activities. Nevertheless, through the 1950s and early 1960s, active feminism was often difficult to detect.

The 1963 publication of Betty Friedan's *The Feminine Mystique* is often cited as the first event of contemporary women's liberation. Friedan, who had been a writer for women's magazines in the 1950s, traveled around the country interviewing the women who had graduated with her from Smith College in 1947. Most of these women were living out the dream that post-war American society had created for them: they were affluent wives and mothers living in comfortable suburbs. And yet many of them were deeply frustrated and unhappy, with no outlets for their intelligence, talent, and education. By chronicling their unhappiness and frustration, Friedan's book had a powerful impact. But it did not so much cause the revival of feminism as help give voice to a movement that was already stirring.

By the time *The Feminine Mystique* appeared, John Kennedy had established the President's Commission on the Status of Women, which brought national attention to sexual discrimination and helped create important networks of feminist activists who would lobby for legislative redress. Also in 1963, the Kennedy administration helped win passage of the Equal Pay Act, which barred the pervasive practice of paying women less than men for equal work. A year later, Congress incorporated into the Civil Rights Act of 1964 an amendment—Title VII—that extended to women many of the same legal protections against discrimination that were being extended to blacks.

In 1966, Friedan joined with other feminists to create the National Organization for Women (NOW), which was to become the nation's largest and most influential feminist organization. NOW reflected the varying constituencies of the emerging feminist movement. It responded to the complaints of the women Friedan's book had examined—affluent suburbanites with no outlet for their interests—by demanding greater educational opportunities for women and denouncing the domestic ideal and the traditional concept of marriage. But the heart of the movement, at least in the beginning, was directed toward the needs of women in the workplace. NOW denounced the exclusion of women from professions, from politics, and from countless other areas of American life.

## Women's Liberation

By the late 1960s, new and more radical feminist demands were also attracting a large following, especially among younger, white, educated women. Many of them drew inspiration from the New Left and the counterculture. Some were involved in the civil rights movement, others in the antiwar crusade. Many had found that even within those movements, they faced discrimination and exclusion and were subordinated to male leaders.

In its most radical form, the new feminism rejected the whole notion of marriage, family, and even heterosexual intercourse (a vehicle, some women claimed, of male domination). Not many women, not even many feminists, embraced such extremes. But by the early 1970s large numbers of women were coming to see themselves as an exploited group banding together against oppression and developing a culture of their own. The women's liberation movement inspired the creation of grassroots organizations and activities through which women not only challenged sexism and discrimination but created communities of their own. In cities and towns across the country, feminists opened women's bookstores, bars, and coffee shops. They founded feminist newspapers and magazines. They created centers to assist victims of rape and abuse, women's health clinics (and, particularly after 1973, abortion clinics), and day-care centers.

## Expanding Achievements

By the early 1970s, the public and private achievements of the women's movement were already substantial. In 1971, the government extended its affirmative action guidelines to include women—linking sexism with racism as an officially acknowledged social problem. Women were making rapid progress, in the meantime, in their efforts to move into the economic and political mainstream. The nation's major all-male educational institutions began to open their doors to women. (Princeton and Yale did so in 1969, and most others soon did the same.) Some women's colleges, in the meantime, began accepting male students.

Women were also becoming an important force in business and the professions. Nearly half of all married women held jobs by the mid-1970s, and almost 90 percent of all women with college degrees worked. The two-career family, in which both the husband and the wife maintained active professional lives, was becoming a widely accepted middle-class norm. (It had been common within the working class for decades.) Some middle-class women were postponing marriage or motherhood for the sake of their careers. There were also important symbolic changes, such as the refusal of many women to adopt their husbands' names when they married and the use of the term "Ms." in place of "Mrs." or "Miss" to denote the irrelevance of a woman's marital status in the professional world.

In politics, women began to compete effectively with men for both elected and appointive positions in the 1970s. By the mid-1980s, women were serving in both houses of Congress, on the Supreme Court, in numerous federal cabinet positions, as governors of several states, and in many other political positions. In 1981, Ronald Reagan named the first female Supreme Court justice, Sandra Day O'Connor; in 1993, Bill Clinton named the second, Ruth Bader Ginsburg. In 1984, the Democratic Party chose a woman, Representative Geraldine Ferraro of New York, as its vice presidential candidate. In academia, women were expanding their presence in traditional scholarly fields; they were also creating new fields—women's and gender studies, which in the 1980s and 1990s were among the fastest-growing areas of American scholarship.

In 1972, Congress approved the Equal Rights Amendment (ERA) to the Constitution, which some feminists had been promoting since the 1920s, and sent it to the states. For a while ratification seemed almost certain. By the late 1970s, however, the momentum behind the amendment had died. The ERA was in trouble not because of indifference but because of a rising chorus of objections to it from people (including many antifeminist women) who feared that it would disrupt traditional social patterns. In 1982, the amendment finally died when the ten years allotted for ratification expired.

### The Abortion Controversy

A major element of American feminism since the 1920s has been the effort by women to win greater control of their own sexual and reproductive lives. In its least controversial form, this impulse helped produce an increasing awareness in the 1960s and 1970s of the problems of rape, sexual abuse, and wife beating. There continued to be some controversy over the dissemination of contraceptives and birth-control information, but that issue, at least, seemed to have lost much of the explosive character it had once possessed. A related issue, however, stimulated as much popular passion as any question of its time: abortion.

Abortion had once been legal in much of the United States, but by the beginning of the twentieth century it was banned by statute in most of the country and remained so into the 1960s (although many abortions continued to be performed quietly, and often dangerously, out of sight of the law).

The women's movement created strong new pressures on behalf of the legalization of abortion. Several states had abandoned restrictions on abortion by the end of the 1960s. And in 1973, the Supreme Court's decision in *Roe v. Wade*, based on a new theory of a constitutional "right to privacy" first recognized by the Court only a few years earlier, invalidated all laws prohibiting abortion during the "first trimester"—the first three months of pregnancy. The issue, it seemed, was finally settled. But it soon became clear that it was not.

In many ways, feminism was much like other "liberation" movements of the 1960s and 1970s. But it differed from them in one fundamental respect: its success. The women's movement may not have fulfilled all its goals. But it achieved fundamental and permanent changes in the position of women in American life, and it promised to do much more.

## NIXON, KISSINGER, AND THE WAR

Richard Nixon assumed office in 1969 committed not only to restoring stability at home but to creating a new and more stable order in the world. Central to Nixon's hopes for international stability was a resolution of the stalemate in Vietnam. Yet the new president felt no freer than his predecessor to abandon the American commitment there.

### *Vietnamization*

Despite Nixon's own deep interest in international affairs, he brought with him into government a man who seemed to overshadow the president himself at times in the conduct of diplomacy: Henry Kissinger, a Harvard professor whom Nixon appointed as his special assistant for national security affairs. Kissinger quickly established dominance over the secretary of state, William Rogers, and the secretary of defense, Melvin Laird, who were both more experienced in public life. That was in part a result of Nixon's passion for concentrating decision making in the White House. But Kissinger's keen intelligence, his bureaucratic skills, his penchant for secrecy, and his success in handling the press were at least equally important. Together, Nixon and Kissinger set out to find an acceptable solution to the stalemate in Vietnam.

The new Vietnam policy moved along several fronts. One was an effort to limit domestic opposition to the war so as to give the administration more political space in which to maneuver. The administration moved, therefore, to "Vietnamize" the war—that is, to train and equip the South

Vietnamese military to assume the burden of combat in place of American forces. In the fall of 1969, Nixon announced the withdrawal of 60,000 American ground troops from Vietnam, the first reduction in United States troop strength since the beginning of the war. The withdrawals continued steadily for more than three years, so that by the fall of 1972 relatively few American soldiers remained in Indochina. From a peak of more than 540,000 in 1969, the number had dwindled to about 60,000.

Vietnamization (and the decreased draft calls it produced) did help quiet domestic opposition to the war for a time. It did nothing, however, to break the stalemate in the negotiations with the North Vietnamese in Paris. The new administration quickly decided that new military pressures would be necessary to do that.

### Escalation

By the end of their first year in office, Nixon and Kissinger had decided that the most effective way to tip the military balance in America's favor was to destroy the bases in Cambodia and Laos from which the American military believed the North Vietnamese were launching many of their attacks. Very early in his presidency, Nixon ordered the air force to begin bombing Cambodian and Laotian territory to destroy the enemy sanctuaries. He kept the raids secret from Congress and the public. In the spring of 1970, and many believed with American encouragement and support, conservative military leaders overthrew the neutral government of Cambodia and established a new, pro-American regime under General Lon Nol. Lon Nol quickly gave his approval to American incursions into his territory; and on April 30, Nixon went on television to announce that he was ordering American troops across the border into Cambodia to "clean out" the bases that the enemy had been using for its "increased military aggression."

Literally overnight, the Cambodian invasion restored the dwindling antiwar movement to vigorous life. The first days of May saw the most widespread and vocal antiwar demonstrations ever. A mood of crisis was already mounting when, on May 4, four college students were killed and nine others injured after members of the National Guard opened fire on antiwar demonstrators at Kent State University in Ohio. Ten days later, police killed two black students at Jackson State University in Mississippi during a demonstration there.

The clamor against the war spread into the government and the press. Congress angrily repealed the Gulf of Tonkin Resolution in December, stripping the president of what had long served as the legal basis for the war.

Nixon ignored the action. Then, in June 1971, first the *New York Times* and later other newspapers began publishing excerpts from a secret study of the war prepared by the Defense Department during the Johnson administration. The so-called Pentagon Papers, leaked to the press by former Defense official Daniel Ellsberg, confirmed what many had long believed: the government had been dishonest, both in reporting the military progress of the war and in explaining its own motives for American involvement. The administration went to court to suppress the documents, but the Supreme Court ruled that the press had the right to publish them.

Particularly troubling, both to the public and to the government itself, were signs of decay within the American military itself. Morale and discipline among American troops in Vietnam, who had been fighting a savage and inconclusive war for more than five years, were rapidly deteriorating. The trial and conviction in 1971 of Lieutenant William Calley, who was charged with overseeing a massacre of more than 100 unarmed South Vietnamese civilians in 1968 near the village of My Lai, attracted wide public attention to the dehumanizing impact of the war on those who fought it—and to the terrible consequences for the Vietnamese people of that dehumanization. Less publicized were other, more widespread problems among American troops in Vietnam: desertion, drug addiction, racial bias, refusal to obey orders, even the killing of unpopular officers by enlisted men.

The continuing carnage, the increasing savagery, and the social distress at home had largely destroyed public support for the war. By 1971, nearly two-thirds of those interviewed in public opinion polls were urging American withdrawal from Vietnam. President Nixon, however, was determined to resist, and if possible destroy, his critics, convinced that a defeat in Vietnam would cause unacceptable damage to the nation's (and his own) credibility. The FBI, the CIA, the White House itself, and other federal agencies increased their efforts to discredit and harass antiwar and radical groups, often through illegal means.

In Indochina, meanwhile, the fighting raged on. In February 1971, the president ordered the air force to assist the South Vietnamese army in an invasion of Laos—a test, as he saw it, of his Vietnamization program. Within weeks, the South Vietnamese scrambled back across the border in defeat. American bombing in Vietnam and Cambodia increased, despite its apparent ineffectiveness. In March 1972, the North Vietnamese mounted their biggest offensive since 1968 (the so-called Easter offensive). American and South Vietnamese forces managed to halt the communist advance, but it was clear that without American support the South Vietnamese would not have succeeded. At the same time, Nixon ordered American planes to bomb targets near Hanoi, the capital of North Vietnam, and Haiphong, its principal port, and called for the mining of seven North Vietnamese harbors (including Haiphong).

### *"Peace with Honor"*

As the 1972 presidential election approached, the administration stepped up its effort to produce a breakthrough in negotiations with the North Vietnamese. In April 1972, the president dropped his longtime insistence on a removal of North Vietnamese troops from the south before any American withdrawal. Meanwhile, Henry Kissinger was meeting privately in Paris with the North Vietnamese foreign secretary, Le Duc Tho, to work out terms for a cease-fire. On October 26, only days before the presidential election, Kissinger announced that "peace is at hand."

Several weeks later (after the election), negotiations broke down once again. Although both the American and the North Vietnamese governments were ready to accept the Kissinger-Tho plan for a cease-fire, President Nguyen Van Thieu of South Vietnam balked, still insisting on a full withdrawal of North Vietnamese forces from the south. Kissinger tried to win additional concessions from the communists to meet Thieu's objections, but on December 16 talks broke off.

The next day, December 17, American B-52s began the heaviest and most destructive air raids of the entire war on Hanoi, Haiphong, and other North Vietnamese targets. Civilian casualties were high. And fifteen American B-52s were shot down by the North Vietnamese; in the entire war to that point, the United States had lost only one of the giant bombers. On December 30, Nixon terminated the "Christmas bombing." The United States and the North Vietnamese returned to the conference table. And on January 27, 1973, they signed an "agreement on ending the war and restoring peace in Vietnam." Nixon claimed that the Christmas bombing had forced the North Vietnamese to relent. At least equally important, however, was the enormous American pressure on Thieu to accept the cease-fire.

The terms of the Paris accords were little different from those Kissinger and Tho had accepted in principle a few months before. There would be an immediate cease-fire. The North Vietnamese would release several hundred American prisoners of war, whose fate had become an emotional issue of great importance within the United States. The Thieu regime would survive for the moment, but North Vietnamese forces already in the south would remain there. An undefined committee would work out a permanent settlement.

## Defeat in Indochina

American forces were hardly out of Indochina before the Paris accords collapsed. In March 1975, finally, the North Vietnamese launched a full-scale offensive against the now greatly weakened forces of the south. Thieu appealed to Washington for assistance. The president (now Gerald Ford) appealed to Congress for additional funding; Congress refused. Late in April 1975, communist forces marched into Saigon, shortly after officials of the Thieu regime and the staff of the American embassy had fled the country in humiliating disarray. The communist forces quickly occupied the capital, renamed it Ho Chi Minh City, and began the process of reuniting Vietnam under the harsh rule of Hanoi. At about the same time, the Lon Nol regime in Cambodia fell to the murderous forces of the Khmer Rouge—whose brutal policies led to the death of more than a third of the country's people over the next several years.

Such were the dismal results of more than a decade of direct American military involvement in Vietnam. More than 1.2 million Vietnamese soldiers had died in combat, along with countless civilians throughout the region. A

THE FALL OF SAIGON The chaotic evacuation of Americans from Saigon in the spring of 1975, only hours before victorious North Vietnamese troops entered the city, was a humiliating spectacle. Desperate South Vietnamese soldiers and officials fought with American soldiers and diplomats for space on the few airplanes and helicopters available.

beautiful land had been ravaged, its agrarian economy left in ruins; until an economic revival began in the early 1990s, Vietnam remained one of the poorest and most politically oppressive nations in the world. The United States had paid a heavy price as well. The war had cost the nation almost $150 billion in direct costs and much more indirectly. It had resulted in the deaths of over 57,000 young Americans and the injury of 300,000 more. And the nation had suffered a blow to its confidence and self-esteem from which it would not soon recover.

## NIXON, KISSINGER, AND THE WORLD

The continuing war in Vietnam provided a dismal backdrop to what Nixon considered his larger mission in world affairs: the construction of a new international order. The president had become convinced that the old assumptions of a "bipolar" world—in which the United States and the Soviet Union were the only real great powers—were now obsolete. America must adapt to the new "multipolar" international structure, in which China, Japan, and Western Europe were becoming major, independent forces. Nixon and Kissinger believed it was possible to construct something like the "balance of power" that had permitted nineteenth-century Europe to enjoy nearly a century of relative stability. To do so, however, required a major change in several longstanding assumptions of American foreign policy.

### The China Initiative and Détente

For more than twenty years, ever since the fall of Chiang Kai-shek in 1949, the United States had treated China, the second-largest nation on earth, as if it did not exist. Instead, America recognized the forlorn regime-in-exile on Taiwan as the legitimate government of mainland China. Nixon and Kissinger wanted to forge a new relationship with the Chinese communists—in part to strengthen them as a counterbalance to the Soviet Union. The Chinese, for their part, were eager to forestall the possibility of a Soviet-American alliance against China and to end China's own isolation from the international arena.

On July 1971, Nixon sent Henry Kissinger on a secret mission to Beijing. When Kissinger returned, the president made the startling announcement that he would visit China himself within the next few months. That fall, with American approval, the United Nations admitted the communist government of China and expelled the representatives of the Taiwan regime. Finally, in February 1972, Nixon paid a formal visit to China and, in a single stroke, erased much of the deep American animosity toward the Chinese communists. Nixon did not yet formally recognize the communist regime, but in 1972 the United States and China began low-level diplomatic relations.

The initiatives in China coincided with (and probably assisted) an effort by the Nixon administration to improve relations with the Soviet Union. In 1969, American and Soviet diplomats met in Helsinki, Finland, to begin talks on limiting nuclear weapons. In 1972, they produced the first Strategic Arms Limitation Treaty (SALT I), which froze some nuclear missiles (ICBMs) of both sides at present levels. In May of that year, the president traveled to Moscow to sign the agreement. The next year, the Soviet premier, Leonid Brezhnev, visited Washington.

DÉTENTE AT HIGH TIDE The visit of Soviet Premier Leonid Brezhnev to Washington in 1973 was a high-water mark in the search for détente between the two nations. Here, Brezhnev and Nixon share friendly words on the White House balcony.

A M E R I C A N    V O I C E S

RICHARD NIXON

## The China Trip, 1972

ON FEBRUARY 17, 1972, at 10:35 A.M. we left Andrews Air Force Base for Peking. . . . We stopped briefly in Shanghai . . . ; an hour and a half later we prepared to land in Peking. I looked out the window. It was winter, and the countryside was drab and gray. The small towns and villages looked like pictures I had seen of towns in the Middle Ages. . . .

Chou En-lai stood at the foot of the ramp, hatless in the cold. Even a heavy overcoat did not hide the thinness of his frail body. When we were about halfway down the steps, he began to clap. I paused for a moment and then returned the gesture, according to the Chinese custom.

I knew that Chou had been deeply insulted by Foster Dulles's refusal to shake hands with him at the Geneva Conference in 1954. When I reached the bottom step, therefore, I made a point of extending my hand as I walked toward him. When our hands met, one era ended and another began. . . .

I stood on Chou's left while the band played the anthems. "The Star-Spangled Banner" had never sounded so stirring to me as on that windswept runway in the heart of Communist China. . . .

Chou and I rode into the city in a curtained car. As we left the airport, he said, "Your handshake came over the vastest ocean in the world—twenty-five years of no communication." When we came into Tienamen Square at the center of Peking . . . I noticed that the streets were empty.

SOURCE: *RN: The Memoirs of Richard Nixon*, pp. 559–560. Copyright © 1978 by Richard Nixon. Reprinted by permission of Warner Books, Inc.

*The Problems of Multipolarity*

The policies of rapprochement with communist China and détente with the Soviet Union reflected Nixon's and Kissinger's belief in the importance of stable relationships among the great powers. But great-power relationships could not alone ensure international stability, for the Third World remained the most volatile and dangerous source of international tension.

Central to the Nixon-Kissinger policy toward the Third World was the effort to maintain the status quo without involving the United States too deeply in local disputes. In 1969 and 1970, the president described what became known as the Nixon Doctrine, by which the United States would "participate in the defense and development of allies and friends" but would leave the "basic responsibility" for the future of those "friends" to the nations themselves. In practice, the Nixon Doctrine meant a declining American interest in contributing to Third World development; a growing contempt for the United Nations, where underdeveloped nations were gaining influence through their sheer numbers; and increasing support to authoritarian regimes attempting to withstand radical challenges from within.

In 1970, for example, the CIA poured substantial funds into Chile to help support the established government against a communist challenge. When the Marxist candidate for president, Salvador Allende, came to power anyway through an open election, the United States began funneling more money to opposition forces in Chile to help destabilize the new government. In 1973, a military junta seized power from Allende, who was subsequently murdered. The United States developed a friendly relationship with the new, repressive military government of General Augusto Pinochet.

In the Middle East, conditions grew more volatile in the aftermath of the 1967 war, in which Israel had occupied substantial new territories. Palestinian Arabs continued to claim the lands now controlled by Israel; many of them had been dislodged from their homes, and the refugees were a source of considerable instability in Jordan, Lebanon, and the other surrounding countries into which they moved.

In October 1973, on the Jewish high holy day of Yom Kippur, Egyptian and Syrian forces attacked Israel. For ten days, the Israelis struggled to recover from the surprise attack; finally, they launched an effective counteroffensive against Egyptian forces in the Sinai. At that point, the United States intervened, placing heavy pressure on Israel to accept a cease-fire rather than press its advantage.

The imposed settlement of the Yom Kippur War demonstrated the growing dependence of the United States and its allies on Arab oil. Permitting Israel to continue its drive into Egypt might have jeopardized the ability of the United States to purchase needed petroleum from the Arab states. A brief but painful embargo by the Arab governments on the sale of oil to America in 1973 provided an ominous warning of the costs of losing access to the region's resources. The lesson of the Yom Kippur War, therefore, was that the United States could not ignore the interests of the Arab nations in its efforts on behalf of Israel.

A larger lesson of 1973 was that the nations of the Third World could no longer be expected to act as passive, cooperative "client states." And the United States could not depend on cheap, easy access to raw materials as it had in the past.

## POLITICS AND ECONOMICS IN THE NIXON YEARS

For a time in the late 1960s, it had seemed to many Americans that forces of chaos and radicalism were taking control of the nation. The domestic policy of the Nixon administration was, the president claimed, an attempt to restore order. In the end, however, economic and political crises sharply limited the administration's ability to fulfill its domestic goals.

### Domestic Initiatives

Many of Nixon's domestic policies were a response to what he believed to be the demands of his constituency—conservative, middle-class people, the "silent majority" who he believed wanted to reduce federal "interference" in local affairs. He tried, unsuccessfully, to persuade Congress to pass legislation prohibiting school desegregation through the use of forced busing. He forbade the Department of Health, Education, and Welfare to cut off federal funds from school districts that had failed to comply with court orders to integrate. At the same time, he began to reduce or dismantle many of the social programs of the Great Society and the New Frontier. In 1973, he abolished the Office of Economic Opportunity, the centerpiece of the antipoverty program of the Johnson years.

Yet Nixon's domestic policies had progressive and creative elements as well. He signed legislation creating the Environmental Protection Agency and establishing the most stringent environmental regulations in the nation's history. He ordered the first affirmative action program for workers on federally funded projects. One of the administration's boldest efforts was an attempt to overhaul the nation's enormous welfare system. Nixon proposed replacing the existing system, which almost everyone agreed was cumbersome, expensive, and inefficient, with what he called the Family Assistance Plan (FAP). It would in effect have created a guaranteed annual income for all Americans: $1,600 in federal grants, which could be supplemented by outside earnings up to $4,000. The FAP won approval in the House in 1970, but concerted attacks by welfare recipients (who considered the benefits inadequate), members of the welfare bureaucracy (whose own influence stood to be sharply diminished by the bill), and conservatives (who opposed a guaranteed income on principle) helped kill it in the Senate.

### From the Warren Court to the Nixon Court

Of all the liberal institutions that aroused the enmity of the "silent majority" in the 1950s and 1960s, none evoked more anger and bitterness than the Supreme Court. Not only did its rulings on racial matters disrupt traditional social patterns in both the North and the South, but its staunch defense of civil liberties directly contributed, in the eyes of many Americans, to the increase in crime, disorder, and moral decay. In *Engel* v. *Fitak* (1962), the Court ruled that prayers in public schools were unconstitutional, sparking outrage among religious fundamentalists and others. In *Roth* v. *United States* (1957), the Court had sharply limited the authority of local governments to curb pornography. In a series of other decisions, the Court greatly strengthened the civil rights of criminal defendants and, many Americans believed, greatly weakened the power of law enforcement officials to do their jobs. For example, in *Gideon* v. *Wainwright* (1963), the Court ruled that every felony defendant was entitled to a lawyer regardless of his or her ability to pay. In *Escobedo* v. *Illinois* (1964), it ruled that a defendant must be allowed access to a lawyer before questioning by police. In *Miranda* v. *Arizona* (1966), the Court confirmed the obligation of authorities to inform a criminal suspect of his or her rights. By 1968, the Warren Court had become the target of Americans of all kinds who felt the balance of power in the United States had shifted too far toward the poor, the dispossessed, and the criminal at the expense of the middle class.

Nixon was determined to use his judicial appointments to give the Court a more conservative cast. When Chief Justice Earl Warren resigned early in 1969, Nixon replaced him with a federal appeals court judge of known conservative leanings, Warren Burger. A few months later, Associate Justice Abe Fortas resigned his seat after the disclosure of a series of alleged financial improprieties. To replace him, Nixon named Clement F. Haynsworth, a respected federal circuit court judge from South Carolina. But Haynsworth came under fire from Senate liberals, black organizations, and labor unions for his conservative record on civil rights and for what some claimed was a conflict of interest in several of the cases on which he had sat. The Senate rejected him. Nixon's next choice was G. Harrold Carswell, a judge of the Florida federal appeals court almost entirely lacking in distinction and widely considered unfit for the Supreme Court. The Senate rejected his nomination too.

Nixon angrily denounced the votes. But he was careful thereafter to choose men of standing within the legal community to fill vacancies on the Supreme Court: Harry Blackmun, a moderate jurist from Minnesota; Lewis E. Powell, Jr., a respected judge from Virginia; and William Rehnquist, a member of the Nixon Justice Department. In the process, he transformed the Court.

The new Court, however, fell short of what the president and many conservatives had expected. Rather than retreating from its commitment to social reform, the Court in many areas actually moved further toward it. In *Swann* v. *Charlotte-Mecklenburg Board of Education* (1971), it ruled in favor of the use of forced busing to achieve racial balance in schools. Not even the intense and occasionally violent opposition of local communities as diverse as Boston and Louisville, Kentucky, was able to weaken the judicial commitment to integration. In *Furman* v. *Georgia* (1972), the Court overturned existing capital punishment statutes and established strict new guidelines for such laws in the future. In *Roe* v. *Wade* (1973), it struck down laws forbidding abortions.

In other decisions, however, the Burger Court did demonstrate a more conservative temperament than the Warren Court had shown. Although the justices approved busing as a tool for achieving integration, they rejected, in *Milliken* v. *Bradley* (1974), a plan to transfer students across district lines (in this case, between Detroit and its suburbs) to achieve racial balance. While the Court upheld the principle of affirmative action in its celebrated 1978 decision in *Bakke* v. *Board of Regents of California*, it established restrictive new guidelines for such programs in the future. In *Stone* v. *Powell* (1976), the Court agreed to certain limits on the right of a defendant to appeal a state conviction to the federal judiciary.

## The Election of 1972

However unsuccessful the Nixon administration may have been in achieving some of its specific goals, Nixon entered the presidential race in 1972 with a substantial reserve of strength. The events of that year improved his position immeasurably. His energetic reelection committee collected enormous sums of money to support the campaign. The president himself used the powers of incumbency to strengthen his political standing in strategic areas.

Nixon was most fortunate in 1972, however, in his opposition. George Wallace, partly at Nixon's urging, entered the Democratic primaries and helped divide the party until a would-be assassin shot the Alabama governor during a rally at a Maryland shopping center in May. Paralyzed from the waist down, Wallace was unable to continue campaigning. In the meantime, the most liberal factions of the party were succeeding in establishing their candidate, Senator George S. McGovern of South Dakota, as the front-runner for the nomination. An outspoken critic of the war, a forceful advocate of advanced liberal positions on virtually every social and economic issue, McGovern profited greatly from party reforms (which he himself had helped to draft) that gave increased influence to women, blacks, and young people in the selection of the Democratic ticket. But in the process, the McGovern campaign came to be associated with aspects of the turbulent 1960s that many middle-class Americans were eager to reject.

On election day, Nixon won reelection by one of the largest margins in history: 60.7 percent of the popular vote compared with 37.5 percent for the forlorn McGovern, and an electoral margin of 520 to 17. The Democratic candidate had carried only Massachusetts and the District of Columbia. But serious problems, some beyond the president's control and some of his own making, were already lurking in the wings.

### The Troubled Economy

Although it was political scandal that would ultimately destroy the Nixon presidency, the most important national crisis of the early 1970s was the beginning of a long-term transformation of the American economy. For three decades, that economy had been the envy of the world. It had produced as much as a third of the world's industrial goods and had dominated international trade. The American dollar had been the strongest currency in the world, and the American standard of living had risen steadily and consistently from its already substantial heights, improving the lives of the vast majority of the nation's citizens. Most Americans had come to assume that this remarkable prosperity was the normal condition of their society. In fact, however, it rested in part on several artificial conditions that were by the late 1960s rapidly disappearing.

The most immediate change was the end of the nation's easy access to cheap raw materials, a change that became a major cause of the serious inflation that plagued the economy through much of the 1970s. Large increases in federal deficit spending in the 1960s were responsible for some of the inflation. But at least equally important was the rising price of energy.

More than any nation on earth, the United States based its economy on the easy availability of cheap and plentiful fuels. No society was more dependent on the automobile; none was more wasteful in its use of oil and gas in its homes, schools, and factories. Domestic petroleum reserves were no longer sufficient to meet this demand, and the nation was growing increasingly dependent on imports from the Middle East and Africa.

For many years, the Organization of Petroleum Exporting Countries (OPEC) had operated as an informal bargaining unit for the sale of oil by Third World nations but had seldom managed to exercise any real strength. But in the early 1970s, OPEC began to assert itself, to use its oil both as an economic tool and as a political weapon. In 1973, in the midst of the Yom Kippur War, Arab members of OPEC announced that they would no longer ship petroleum to nations supporting Israel—that is, to the United States and its allies in Western Europe. At about the same time, the OPEC nations agreed to raise their prices 500 percent (from $3 to $15 a barrel). These twin shocks produced momentary economic chaos in the West. The United States suffered its first fuel shortage since World War II. And although the crisis eased a few months later, the price of energy continued to skyrocket.

The energy crisis eventually subsided, but another, longer-term change in the American economy was the transformation of the nation's manufacturing sector. Ever since World War II, American industry had enjoyed relatively little competition from the rest of the world in its search for export markets and even less competition in its domination of the American domestic market. By the end of the 1960s, however, both Western Europe and Japan had recovered from the damage their manufacturing sectors had absorbed during World War II; by the early 1970s, they were providing stiff competition to American firms in the sale of automobiles, steel, and many other products both in world markets and, more importantly at first, within the United States. Many American corporations responded to these new conditions at first with confusion and bewilderment. Gradually, however, some of the nation's major industries restructured themselves to become more competitive again in world markets. In the process, they closed many older plants and eliminated hundreds of thousands of once-lucrative manufacturing jobs. The high-wage, high-employment industrial economy that had been a central fact of American life since the 1940s was gradually disappearing.

## The Nixon Response

Nixon's initial answer to these mounting economic problems was a conventional anti-inflationary one. He reduced spending and raised taxes. But those policies produced both congressional and popular protest, and Nixon turned increasingly to an economic tool more readily available to him: control of the currency. Placing conservative economists at the head of the Federal Reserve Board, he ensured sharply higher interest rates and a contraction of the money supply. But the tight money policy did little to curb inflation. The cost of living rose a cumulative 15 percent during Nixon's first two and a half years in office. Economic growth, in the meantime, declined. The United States was encountering a new and puzzling dilemma: "stagflation," a combination of rising prices and general economic stagnation.

In the summer of 1971, Nixon imposed a ninety-day freeze on all wages and prices at their existing levels. Then, in November, he launched Phase II of his economic plan: mandatory guidelines for wage and price increases, to be administered by a federal agency. Inflation subsided temporarily, but the recession continued. Fearful that the recession would be more damaging than inflation in an election year, the administration reversed itself late in 1971: interest rates were allowed to drop sharply, and government spending increased—producing the largest budget deficit since World War II. The new tactics helped revive the economy in the short term, but inflation rose substantially—particularly after the administration abandoned the strict Phase II controls and replaced them with a set of voluntary, and almost entirely ineffective, guidelines. In 1973, prices rose 9 percent; in 1974, after the Arab oil embargo and the OPEC price increases, they rose 12 percent— the highest rate since shortly after World War II. The value of the dollar continued to slide, and the nation's international trade continued to decline. The new energy crisis, in the meantime, was quickly becoming a national preoccupation. But while Nixon talked often about the need to achieve "energy independence," he offered few concrete proposals.

The erratic economic programs of the Nixon administration were a sign of a broader national confusion about the longer-term causes of American economic decline. The Nixon pattern—of lurching from a tight money policy to curb inflation at one moment to a spending policy to cure recession at the next—repeated itself during the two administrations that followed. Nowhere was there any serious attempt to address the deeper problems that lay at the heart of the erosion of the American economy.

# THE WATERGATE CRISIS

Although economic problems greatly concerned the American people in the 1970s, another stunning development almost entirely preoccupied the nation beginning early in 1973: the fall of Richard Nixon. The president's demise was a result in part of his own personality. Defensive, secretive, resentful of his critics, he brought to his office an element of mean-spiritedness that helped undermine even his most important accomplishments. But the larger explanation for the crisis lay in Nixon's view of American society and the world, and of his own role in both. The president believed the United States faced grave dangers from the radicals and dissidents who were challenging his policies. He came increasingly to consider any challenge to his policies a threat to "national security." By identifying his own political fortunes with those of the nation, Nixon was creating a climate in which he and those who served him could justify almost any tactics to stifle dissent and undermine opposition.

## The Scandals

Nixon's approach to his office was in part a culmination of long-term changes in the presidency. Public expectations of the president had increased dramatically in the years since World War II, yet the constraints on the authority of the office had grown as well. In response, a succession of presidents had sought new methods for exercising power, often stretching the law, occasionally breaking it.

Nixon not only continued but greatly accelerated these trends. Facing a Democratic Congress hostile to his goals, he attempted to find ways to circumvent the legislature whenever possible. Saddled with a federal bureaucracy unresponsive to his wishes, he constructed a hierarchy of command in which virtually all executive power became concentrated in the White House. Operating within a rigid, even autocratic staff structure, the president became a solitary, brooding figure, whose contempt for his opponents and impatience with obstacles to his policies festered and grew. Unknown to all but a few intimates, he also became mired in a pattern of illegalities and abuses of power that late in 1972 began to break through to the surface.

Early on the morning of June 17, 1972, police arrested five men who had broken into the offices of the Democratic National Committee in the Watergate office building in Washington, D.C. Two others were seized a short time later and charged with supervising the break-in. When reporters for the *Washington Post* began researching the backgrounds of the culprits,

they discovered that among those involved in the burglary were former employees of the Committee for the Re-Election of the President (CRP). One
of them had worked in the White House itself. They had, moreover, been
paid for the break-in from a secret fund of the reelection committee, a fund
controlled by, among others, members of the White House staff.

Public interest in the disclosures grew slowly in the last months of 1972.
Early in 1973, however, the Watergate burglars went on trial; and under
prodding from federal judge John J. Sirica, one of the defendants, James W.
McCord, agreed to cooperate both with the grand jury and with a special
Senate investigating committee recently established under Senator Sam J.
Ervin of North Carolina. McCord's testimony opened a floodgate of con-
fessions, and for months a parade of White House and campaign officials
exposed one illegality after another. Foremost among them was a member
of the inner circle of the White House, John Dean, counsel to the president,
who leveled allegations against Nixon himself.

Two different sets of scandals were emerging from the investigations.
One was a general pattern of abuses of power involving both the White
House and the Nixon campaign committee, which included, but was not limited to, the Watergate break-in. The other scandal, and the one that became
the major focus of public attention for nearly two years, was the way in which
the administration tried to manage the investigations of the Watergate
break-in and other abuses—a pattern of behavior that became known as the
"cover-up." There was never any conclusive evidence that the president had
planned or approved the burglary in advance. But there was mounting evidence that he had been involved in illegal efforts to obstruct investigations
of and withhold information about the episode. As interest in the case grew
to something approaching a national obsession, the investigation focused increasingly on a single question: in the words of Senator Howard Baker of
Tennessee, a member of the Ervin Committee, "What did the President
know and when did he know it?"

Nixon accepted the departure of those members of his administration
implicated in the scandals. But the president continued to insist on his own
innocence. There the matter might have rested had it not been for the disclosure during the Senate hearings of a White House taping system that had
recorded virtually every conversation in the president's office during the period in question. All those investigating the scandals sought access to the
tapes; Nixon, pleading "executive privilege," refused to release them. A special prosecutor appointed by the president to handle the Watergate cases,
Harvard law professor Archibald Cox, took Nixon to court in October 1973
in an effort to force him to relinquish the recordings. Nixon, now clearly

growing desperate, fired Cox and suffered the humiliation of watching both Attorney General Elliot Richardson and his deputy resign in protest. This "Saturday night massacre" made the president's predicament much worse. Not only did public pressure force him to appoint a new special prosecutor, Texas attorney Leon Jaworski, who proved just as determined as Cox to subpoena the tapes; but the episode precipitated an investigation by the House of Representatives into the possibility of impeachment.

## The Fall of Richard Nixon

Nixon's situation deteriorated further in the following months. Late in 1973, Vice President Spiro Agnew became embroiled in a scandal of his own when evidence surfaced that he had accepted bribes and kickbacks while serving as governor of Maryland and even as vice president. In return for a Justice Department agreement not to press the case, Agnew pleaded no contest to a lesser charge of income-tax evasion and resigned from the government. With the controversial Agnew no longer in line to succeed to the presidency, the prospect of removing Nixon from the White House became less worrisome to his opponents. The new vice president (the first appointed under the terms of the Twenty-fifth Amendment, which had been adopted in 1967) was House Minority Leader Gerald Ford, an amiable and popular Michigan congressman.

The impeachment investigation quickly gathered momentum. In April 1974, in an effort to head off further subpoenas of the tapes, the president released transcripts of a number of relevant conversations, claiming that they proved his innocence. Investigators and much of the public felt otherwise. Even these edited tapes seemed to suggest Nixon's complicity in the cover-up. In July, the crisis reached a climax. First the Supreme Court ruled unanimously, in *United States* v. *Richard M. Nixon*, that the president must relinquish the tapes to Special Prosecutor Jaworski. Days later, the House Judiciary Committee voted to recommend three articles of impeachment.

Even without additional evidence, Nixon might well have been impeached by the full House and convicted by the Senate. Early in August, however, he provided at last the "smoking gun"—the concrete proof of his guilt—that his defenders had long contended was missing from the case against him. Among the tapes that the Supreme Court compelled Nixon to relinquish were several that offered apparently incontrovertible evidence of his involvement in the Watergate cover-up. Only three days after the burglary, the recordings disclosed, the president had ordered the FBI to stop investigating the break-in. Impeachment and conviction now seemed inevitable.

For several days, Nixon brooded in the White House, on the verge, some claimed, of a breakdown. Finally, on August 8, 1974, he announced his resignation—the first president in American history ever to do so. At noon the next day, while Nixon and his family were flying west to their home in California, Gerald Ford took the oath of office as president.

Many Americans expressed relief and exhilaration that, as the new president put it, "our long national nightmare is over." They were relieved to be rid of Richard Nixon, who had lost the great popularity that had won him

---

# D E B A T I N G   T H E   P A S T

## Women's History

**T**HE REVIVAL OF feminism as a powerful social and political force in the 1960s and 1970s brought with it a dramatic rise of interest in, and a transformation of, women's history.

Both men and women have been writing histories of women for centuries, but during much of the twentieth century, women's history remained in the shadows of other fields. However, as modern feminism began to sweep across society in the 1960s and 1970s, interest in women's history revived as well. For a time, the new women's history replicated the pattern of earlier studies of women. Much of the early work was in the "contributionist" tradition, revealing ways in which women had contributed more to American history than scholars had previously recognized. Other work stressed ways in which women had been victimized by their subordination to men and by their powerlessness within the industrial economy.

Many historians developed their feminist sensibilities under the influence of the civil rights movement; and in the 1960s and 1970s they tended to emphasize the artificiality of gender distinctions, just as early civil rights activists emphasized the artificiality of racial distinctions. The difference between women and men in the public world, they argued, was "socially constructed," not inherent in the biological differences between the sexes. Much of the history of women was, therefore, the history of how men (with the his landslide reelection victory only two years before. And they were exhilarated that, as some boasted, "the system had worked." But the wave of good feeling could not obscure the deeper and more lasting damage of the Watergate crisis. In a society in which distrust of leaders and institutions of authority was already widespread, the fall of Richard Nixon confirmed for many Americans their most cynical assumptions about the character of American public life.

---

unwitting help of many women) had created and maintained a set of fictions about women's capacities that late-twentieth-century women were now attempting to shatter.

By the late 1970s, however, some feminists were beginning to argue that there were basic differences between women and men—not just biological differences, but differences in values, sensibilities, and culture. These differences were not evidence of women's incapacities. Instead, feminist historians argued, they were evidence of an alternative female culture capable of challenging (and improving) the male-dominated world. Historians of women, therefore, began exploring areas of female experience that revealed the special character of women's culture and values: family, housework, motherhood, women's clubs and organizations, female literature, the social lives of working-class women, women's sexuality, and many other subjects that suggested "difference" more than "contributions" or "victimization." Partly in response, some historians began to make the same argument about men—that understanding "masculinity" and its role in shaping men's lives is as important as understanding notions of "femininity" in explaining the history of women.

The notion of gender as a source of social and cultural difference was responsible for the most powerful challenge women's history raised to the way in which scholars viewed the past. Gender, they argued, is a critical element of the explanation for many kinds of historical experiences, not just women's experiences. Historians in all fields need to incorporate gender into their "categories of analysis" and make it stand alongside such other categories as race, class, ethnicity, religion, and region as a major element of any historical explanation.

# CHAPTER THIRTY-THREE

# The Age of Limits

*Politics and Diplomacy After Watergate*
*The Rise of the American Right* ∼ *The "Reagan Revolution"*

T HE FRUSTRATIONS OF the early 1970s—the defeat in Vietnam, the Watergate crisis, the decay of the American economy—inflicted damaging blows to the confident, optimistic nationalism that had characterized so much of the postwar era. At first some Americans responded to these problems by announcing the arrival of an "age of limits," in which America would have to learn to live with increasingly constricted expectations. By the end of the decade, however, the contours of another response to the challenges had become visible in both American culture and American politics. It was a response that combined a conservative retreat from some of the heady visions of the 1960s with a reinforced commitment to the idea of economic growth, international power, and American exceptionalism.

## POLITICS AND DIPLOMACY AFTER WATERGATE

In the aftermath of Richard Nixon's ignominious departure from office, many wondered whether faith in the presidency, and in the government as a whole, could easily be restored. The administrations of the two presidents who succeeded Nixon did little to answer those questions.

### The Ford Custodianship

Gerald Ford inherited the presidency under unenviable circumstances. He had to try to rebuild confidence in government after the Watergate scandals. And he had to try to restore prosperity in the face of unprecedented

| TIME LINE | | | | |
|---|---|---|---|---|
| **1974** | **1976** | **1977** | **1978** | |

"Stagflation"

Ford pardons Nixon

Carter elected president

Panama Canal treaties signed

Camp David accords

American hostages in Iran

Soviet Union invades Afghanistan

U.S. and China restore relations

| **1980** | **1981** | **1982** | **1983** | **1984** |
|---|---|---|---|---|

U.S. boycotts Moscow Olympics

Reagan elected president

American hostages in Iran released

Reagan wins tax and budget cuts

U.S. military buildup begins

Severe recession

U.S. invades Grenada

Reagan reelected

domestic and international challenges to the American economy. He enjoyed some success in the first of these efforts but very little in the second.

The new president's effort to establish himself as a symbol of political integrity suffered a setback only a month after he took office, when he granted Richard Nixon "a full, free, and absolute pardon" for any crimes he may have committed during his presidency. Ford explained that he was attempting to spare the nation the ordeal of years of litigation and to spare Nixon himself any further suffering. But much of the public suspected a secret deal with the former president. The pardon caused a decline in Ford's popularity from which he never fully recovered. Nevertheless, most Americans considered Ford a decent man; his honesty and amiability did much to reduce the bitterness and acrimony of the Watergate years.

The Ford administration enjoyed less success in its effort to solve the problems of the American economy. In his attempts to curb inflation, the president rejected the idea of wage and price controls and called instead for largely ineffective voluntary efforts. After supporting high interest rates, opposing increased federal spending (through liberal use of his veto power), and resisting pressures for a tax reduction, Ford had to deal with a serious recession in 1974 and 1975. Central to the economic problems was the continuing energy crisis. In the aftermath of the Arab oil embargo of 1973, the OPEC cartel began to raise the price of oil—by 400 percent in 1974 alone. Even so, American dependence on OPEC supplies continued to grow—one of the principal reasons why inflation reached 11 percent in 1976.

At first it seemed that the foreign policy of the new administration would differ little from that of its predecessor. The new president retained Henry Kissinger, whom Nixon had appointed secretary of state in 1973, and continued the general policies of the Nixon years. Late in 1974, Ford met with Leonid Brezhnev at Vladivostok in Siberia and signed an arms control accord that was to serve as the basis for SALT II, thus achieving a goal the Nixon administration had long sought. The following summer, after a European security conference in Helsinki, Finland, the Soviet Union and Western nations agreed to ratify the borders that had divided Europe since 1945; and the Soviets pledged to increase respect for human rights within their own country. In the Middle East, in the meantime, Henry Kissinger helped produce a new accord by which Israel agreed to return large portions of the occupied Sinai to Egypt; the two nations pledged not to resolve future differences by force.

Nevertheless, as the 1976 presidential election approached, Ford's policies were coming under attack from both the right and the left. In the Republican primary campaign, Ford faced a powerful challenge from former California governor Ronald Reagan, leader of the party's conservative wing, who spoke for many on the right who were unhappy with any conciliation of communists. The president only barely survived the assault to win his party's nomination. The Democrats, in the meantime, were gradually uniting behind a new and, before 1976, almost entirely unknown candidate:

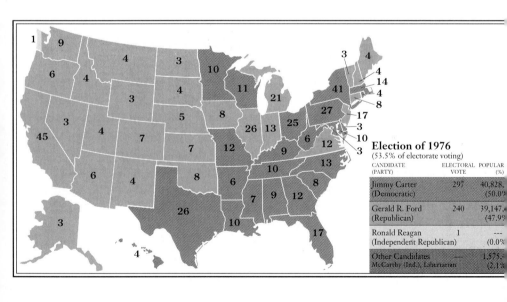

**Election of 1976**
(53.5% of electorate voting)

| CANDIDATE (PARTY) | ELECTORAL VOTE | POPULAR (%) |
| --- | --- | --- |
| Jimmy Carter (Democratic) | 297 | 40,828, (50.0% |
| Gerald R. Ford (Republican) | 240 | 39,147, (47.9% |
| Ronald Reagan (Independent Republican) | 1 | --- (0.0% |
| Other Candidates McCarthy (Ind.), Libertarian | --- | 1,575, (2.1% |

Jimmy Carter, a former governor of Georgia who organized a brilliant primary campaign and appealed to the general unhappiness with Washington by offering honesty, piety, and an outsider's skepticism of the federal government. And while Carter's mammoth lead dwindled to almost nothing by election day, unhappiness with the economy and a general disenchantment with Ford enabled the Democrat to hold on for a narrow victory. Carter emerged with 50 percent of the popular vote to Ford's 47.9 percent and 297 electoral votes to Ford's 240.

### The Trials of Jimmy Carter

Like Ford, Jimmy Carter assumed the presidency at a moment when the nation faced problems of staggering complexity and difficulty. Perhaps no leader could have thrived in such inhospitable circumstances. But Carter seemed at times to make his predicament worse by a style of leadership that many considered self-righteous and inflexible. He left office in 1981 as one of the least popular presidents of the century.

Carter had campaigned for the presidency as an "outsider," representing Americans suspicious of entrenched bureaucracies and complacent public officials. He carried much of that suspiciousness with him to Washington. He surrounded himself in the White House with a group of close-knit associates from Georgia, and in the beginning, at least, he seemed deliberately to spurn assistance from more experienced political figures.

Carter devoted much of his time to the problems of energy and the economy. Entering office in the midst of a recession, he moved first to reduce unemployment by raising public spending and cutting federal taxes. Unemployment declined, but inflation soared—less because of Carter's fiscal policies than because of the escalating cost of oil. During Carter's last two years in office, prices rose at an annual rate of well over 10 percent. Like Nixon and Ford before him, Carter responded with a combination of tight money and calls for voluntary restraint. He appointed first G. William Miller and then Paul Volcker, conservative economists, to head the Federal Reserve Board, thus ensuring a policy of high interest rates and reduced currency supplies. By 1980, interest rates had risen to the highest levels in American history; at times, they exceeded 20 percent.

The problem of energy also grew steadily more troublesome in the Carter years. In the summer of 1979, instability in the Middle East produced a second major fuel shortage in the United States. In the midst of the crisis, OPEC announced another major price increase, clouding the economic picture still further. Faced with increasing pressure to act (and with public opinion polls showing his approval rating at a dismal 26 percent), Carter withdrew to Camp David, the presidential retreat in the Maryland mountains. Ten days later, he emerged to deliver a remarkable television address. It included a series of proposals for resolving the energy crisis. But it was most notable for Carter's bleak assessment of the national condition. Speaking with unusual fervor, he complained of a "crisis of confidence" that had struck "at the very heart and soul of our national will." The address became known as the "malaise" speech (although Carter himself had never used that word), and it helped fuel attacks that the president was trying to blame his own problems on the American people. Carter's sudden firing of several members of his cabinet a few days later deepened his political problems.

### Human Rights and National Interests

Among Jimmy Carter's most frequent campaign promises was a pledge to build a new basis for American foreign policy, one in which the defense of "human rights" would replace the pursuit of "selfish interests." Carter spoke out sharply and often about violations of human rights in many countries (including, most prominently, the Soviet Union). Beyond that general commitment, the Carter administration focused on several more traditional concerns. Carter completed negotiations begun several years earlier on a pair of treaties to turn over control of the Panama Canal to the government of Panama. Domestic opposition to the treaties was intense, especially among conservatives who viewed the new arrangements as part of a general American retreat from international power. But the administration argued that relinquishing the canal was the best way to improve relations with Latin America and avoid violence in Panama. After an acrimonious debate, the Senate ratified the treaties by 68 to 32, only one vote more than the necessary two-thirds.

Far more popular, within the United States at least, was Carter's success in arranging a peace treaty between Egypt and Israel—the crowning achievement of his presidency. Middle East negotiations had seemed hopelessly stalled when a dramatic breakthrough occurred in November 1977. The Egyptian president, Anwar Sadat, accepted an invitation from Prime Minister Menachem Begin to visit Israel. In Tel Aviv, Sadat announced that Egypt was now willing to accept the state of Israel as a legitimate political entity. But translating these good feelings into an actual peace treaty proved more difficult.

When talks between Israeli and Egyptian negotiators stalled, Carter invited Sadat and Begin to a summit conference at Camp David in September

FORGING THE CAMP DAVID ACCORDS  Probably the greatest achievement of Jimmy Carter's generally frustrating presidency was his success in guiding Israel and Egypt toward a peaceful settlement of their longstanding grievances. While hosting Israeli Prime Minister Menachem Begin *(right)* and Egyptian President Anwar Sadat *(left)* at his Camp David retreat in September 1978, he helped the two leaders reach a historic agreement.

1978, holding them there for two weeks while he and others helped mediate the disputes between them. On September 17, Carter escorted the two leaders into the White House to announce agreement on a framework for an Egyptian-Israeli peace treaty. Carter intervened again several months later, when talks stalled once more, and helped produce a compromise on the most sensitive issue between the two parties: the Palestinian refugee issue. On March 26, 1979, Begin and Sadat returned together to the White House to sign a formal peace treaty between their two nations.

Carter responded eagerly to the overtures of Deng Xiaoping, the new Chinese leader who was attempting to open his nation to the outside world. On December 15, 1978, Washington and Beijing announced the resumption of formal diplomatic relations between the two nations. A few months later, Carter traveled to Vienna to meet with the aging and visibly ailing Brezhnev to finish drafting the new SALT II arms control agreement. The treaty set limits on the number of long-range missiles, bombers, and nuclear warheads on each side. Almost immediately, however, SALT II met with fierce conservative opposition in the United States. Central to the arguments against the treaty was a fundamental distrust of the Soviet Union that nearly a decade of détente had failed to destroy. By the fall of 1979, with the Senate scheduled to begin debate over the treaty shortly, ratification was already in jeopardy. Events in the following months provided a final blow, both to the treaty and to the larger framework of détente.

## The Year of the Hostages

Ever since the early 1950s, the United States had provided political support and, more recently, massive military assistance to the government of the Shah of Iran, hoping to make his nation a bulwark against Soviet expansion in the Middle East. By 1979, however, the Shah was in deep trouble with his own people. Iranians resented the repressive, authoritarian tactics through which the Shah had maintained his autocratic rule. At the same time, Islamic clergy (and much of the fiercely religious populace) opposed his efforts to modernize and westernize a fundamentalist society. The combination of resentments produced a powerful revolutionary movement. In January 1979, the Shah fled the country.

The United States made cautious efforts in the first months after the Shah's abdication to establish cordial relations with the succession of increasingly militant regimes that followed. By late 1979, however, revolutionary chaos in Iran was making any normal relationships impossible. What power there was resided with a zealous religious leader, the Ayatollah Ruhollah Khomeini, whose hatred of the West in general and the United States in particular was intense.

In late October 1979, the deposed Shah arrived in New York to be treated for cancer. Days later, on November 4, an armed mob invaded the American embassy in Teheran, seized the diplomats and military personnel inside, and demanded the return of the Shah to Iran in exchange for their freedom. Fifty-three Americans remained hostages in the embassy for over a year. Coming after years of what many Americans considered international humiliations and defeats, the hostage seizure released a deep well of anger and emotion.

Only weeks after the hostage seizure, on December 27, 1979, Soviet troops invaded Afghanistan, the mountainous nation bordering the Soviet Union and Iran. The Soviet Union had, in fact, been a power in Afghanistan for years, and the dominant force since April 1978, when a coup had estab-

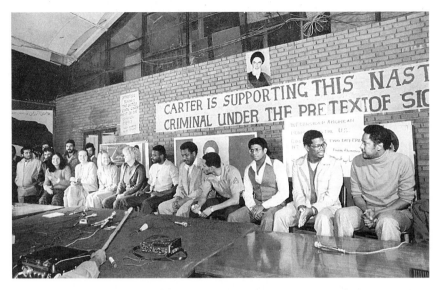

THE HOSTAGES ON DISPLAY The holding hostage of American diplomats in Iran for over a year beginning in November 1979 was always as much an effort to generate publicity as a real negotiating tactic. Anti-western Iranians wasted few opportunities to display their grievances against the United States for its long support of the Shah, and they were eager to present the hostages themselves as evidence of their ability to humble the mighty United States. Here a number of the fifty-three hostages sit on display under signs written in English for the American television audience.

lished a Marxist government there with close ties to the Kremlin. Knowledgeable observers argued that the Soviet invasion was a Russian attempt to secure the status quo against a growing rebel movement. Others—most notably the president—claimed that the invasion was a Russian "stepping stone to their possible control over much of the world's oil supplies." It was also the "gravest threat to world peace since World War II." Carter angrily imposed a series of economic sanctions on the Russians, canceled American participation in the 1980 summer Olympic Games in Moscow, and announced the withdrawal of SALT II from Senate consideration.

The combination of domestic economic troubles and international crises created widespread anxiety, frustration, and anger in the United States—damaging President Carter's already low standing with the public, and giving added strength to an alternative political force that had already made great strides.

# THE RISE OF THE AMERICAN RIGHT

The jarring public events of the 1960s and 1970s, and the broader changes in the character of America's economy, society, and culture, disillusioned many liberals, perplexed the already weakened left, and provided the right with its most important opportunity in generations to seize a position of authority in American life.

## *The Sunbelt and Its Politics*

One of the major demographic events of the 1970s was the rise of what became known as the "Sunbelt," a group of regions that included some of the most dynamically growing parts of the country. The Sunbelt included the Southeast (particularly Florida), the Southwest (particularly Texas), and above all, California, which became the nation's most populous state in 1964. By 1980, more people lived in the Sunbelt than lived in the industrial regions of the North and East.

Among other things, the rise of the Sunbelt helped produce a change in the political climate. The strong populist traditions in the South and the West—and the high emphasis on individual liberty in particular—were capable of producing progressive and even radical politics; but more often in the late twentieth century, they produced a strong opposition to the growth of government, and to government regulations in particular. Many federal regulations and restrictions—environmental laws, land-use restrictions, even the fifty-five-mile-per-hour speed limit created during the energy crisis to force motorists to conserve fuel—affected the West more than any other region.

The so-called Sagebrush Rebellion, which emerged in parts of the West in the late 1970s, mobilized conservative opposition to environmental laws and restrictions on development. It also sought to portray the West (which had probably benefited more than any other region from federal investment) as a victim of government control. Its members complained about the very large amounts of land the federal government owned in many western states and demanded that they be opened for development.

The South as a whole was considerably more conservative than other parts of the nation, and its growth served to increase the power of the right in the 1960s and 1970s. The West had not, on the whole, been more conservative than other regions historically; but in the postwar period, the West produced some of the most numerous and powerful conservative movements in the nation—particularly in southern California, where Orange

County (a large suburban area south of Los Angeles) emerged as one of the most important centers of right-wing politics in the country.

*Religious Revivalism*

The United States experienced the beginning of a major religious revival in the 1970s which continued in various forms into the 1990s. Some of the new religious enthusiasm found expression in the rise of cults and pseudo-faiths: the Church of Scientology; the Unification Church of the Reverend Sun Myung Moon; even the tragic People's Temple, whose members committed mass suicide in their jungle retreat in Guyana in 1978. But the most important impulse of the religious revival was the growth of evangelical Christianity. Evangelicism is the basis of many forms of Christian faith. But evangelicals have in common a belief in personal conversion through direct communication with God.

For many years, the evangelicals had gone largely unnoted by much of the media and the secular public, which had dismissed them as a limited, provincial phenomenon. By the late 1970s, it was no longer possible to do so. Earlier in the century, many (although never all) evangelicals had been relatively poor rural people. But the great capitalist expansion after World War II had lifted many of these people out of poverty and into the middle class, where they were more visible and more assertive. Over 70 million Americans now described themselves as "born-again" Christians—men and women who had established a "direct personal relationship with Jesus." Christian evangelicals owned their own newspapers, magazines, radio stations, and television networks. They operated their own schools and universities. One of them occupied the White House itself—Jimmy Carter, who during the 1976 campaign had talked proudly of his own "conversion experience" and who continued openly to proclaim his "born-again" Christian faith during his years in office.

For Jimmy Carter and for some others, evangelical Christianity had formed the basis for a commitment to racial justice and world peace. But many evangelicals in the 1970s became active on the political and cultural right. They were alarmed by what they considered the spread of immorality and disorder in American life; and they were concerned about the way a secular and, as they saw it, godless culture was intruding into their communities and families—through popular culture, through the schools, and through government policies. Particularly alarming to them were Supreme Court decisions eliminating prayer from schools and, later, guaranteeing women the right to an abortion.

By the late 1970s, the "Christian right" had become a visible and increasingly powerful political force. Jerry Falwell, a fundamentalist minister in Virginia with a substantial television audience, launched a movement he called the Moral Majority, which attacked the rise of "secular humanism" in American culture. The Moral Majority and other, similar organizations denounced abortion, divorce, feminism, and homosexuality, defended unrestricted free enterprise, and supported a strong American posture in the world. Some evangelicals reopened issues that had long seemed closed. For example, many fundamentalist Christians denied the scientific doctrine of evolution and instead urged the teaching in schools of the biblical story of the Creation. Others advocated various forms of censorship of books, films, plays, and other works of art whose content they considered immoral.

## The New Right

Evangelical Christians were an important part, but only a part, of what became known as the New Right—a diverse but powerful movement that enjoyed rapid growth in the 1970s and early 1980s. It had begun to take shape after the 1964 election, in which Barry Goldwater had suffered his shattering defeat. Richard Viguerie, a remarkable conservative activist and organizer, took a list of 12,000 contributors to the Goldwater campaign and used it to develop a formidable conservative communications and fund-raising organization. By the mid-1970s, he had gathered a list of 4 million contributors and 15 million supporters. Gradually these direct-mail operations helped create a much larger conservative infrastructure, designed to match and even exceed what the right saw as the powerful liberal infrastructure. By the late 1970s, there were right-wing think tanks, consulting firms, lobbyists, foundations, and scholarly centers. Another factor in the revival of the right was the emergence of credible leadership. Chief among this new generation of conservative leaders was Ronald Reagan, once a moderately successful film actor, who had become deeply involved in right-wing politics in California and, in 1966, won election as governor of the state. His engaging, self-assured demeanor and his smooth, eloquent speeches in defense of individual freedom and private enterprise won him increasing national recognition.

The presidency of Gerald Ford also played an important role in the rise of the right, by destroying the fragile equilibrium that had enabled the right wing and the moderate wing of the Republican Party to coexist. Ford appointed as vice president Nelson Rockefeller, the liberal Republican governor of New York and an heir to one of America's great fortunes; many conservatives had been demonizing Rockefeller and his family for more than twenty years. Ford proposed an amnesty program for draft resisters, embraced and even extended the hated Nixon-Kissinger policies of détente, presided over the fall of Vietnam, and agreed to cede the Panama Canal to Panama. When Reagan challenged Ford in the 1976 Republican primaries, the president survived, barely, only by dropping Nelson Rockefeller from the ticket and agreeing to a platform largely written by one of Reagan's principal allies, Senator Jesse Helms of North Carolina. Reagan hailed that platform by saying that the party "must raise a banner of no pale pastels, but bold colors which make it unmistakably clear where we stand on all the issues troubling the people."

## The Tax Revolt

At least equally important to the success of the new right was a new and potent conservative issue: the tax revolt. It had its public beginnings in 1978, when Howard Jarvis, a conservative activist, launched a successful tax revolt in California with Proposition 13, a referendum question on the state ballot rolling back property-tax rates. Similar antitax movements soon began in other states and eventually spread to national politics.

For more than thirty years after the New Deal, Republican conservatives had struggled to halt and even reverse the growth of the federal government. But during most of those years, as right-wing politicians from Robert Taft to Barry Goldwater discovered, attacking government programs did not succeed in attracting majority support. Every federal program had a political constituency, and the biggest and most expensive programs had the broadest support. Proposition 13 and similar initiatives gave members of the right a better way to undermine government than by attacking specific programs: attacking taxes. By separating the issue of taxes from the issue of what taxes supported, the right found a way to achieve the most controversial elements of its own agenda (eroding the government's ability to launch new ventures and even to sustain old ones) without openly antagonizing the millions of voters who supported specific programs. Virtually no one liked to pay taxes, and as the economy grew weaker and the relative burden of paying taxes grew heavier, that resentment naturally rose. The right exploited that resentment and, in the process, expanded its constituency far beyond anything it had known before. The 1980 presidential election propelled it to a historic victory.

## The Campaign of 1980

By the time of the crises in Iran and Afghanistan, Jimmy Carter was in desperate political trouble. His standing in popularity polls was lower than that of any president in history. Senator Edward Kennedy, younger brother of John and Robert Kennedy, was preparing to challenge him in the primaries. For a short while, the seizure of the hostages and the stern American response to the Soviet invasion revived Carter's candidacy. But as the hostage crisis dragged on, public impatience grew. Kennedy won a series of victories over the president in the later primaries. And while Carter managed in the end to stave off Kennedy's challenge and win his party's nomination, it was an unhappy convention that heard the president's listless call to arms.

The Republican Party, in the meantime, had rallied enthusiastically behind Ronald Reagan, a man whom, not many years before, many Americans had considered a frightening reactionary. But he now emerged not just as a poised and articulate campaigner but as a spokesman for the public's growing discontent with its leadership and its government.

On election day 1980, the anniversary of the seizure of the hostages in Iran, Reagan swept to victory with 51 percent of the vote to 41 percent for Jimmy Carter and 7 percent for John Anderson—a moderate Republican congressman from Illinois who had mounted an independent campaign. Carter carried only five states and the District of Columbia, for a total of 49 electoral votes to Reagan's 489. The Republican Party won control of the

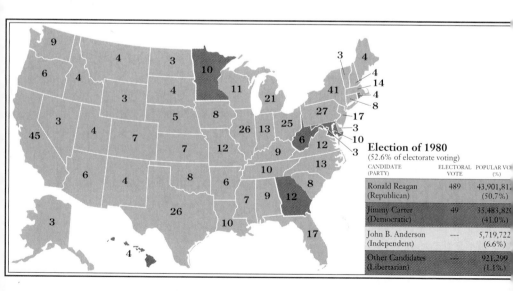

**Election of 1980**
(52.6% of electorate voting)

| CANDIDATE (PARTY) | ELECTORAL VOTE | POPULAR VOTE (%) |
|---|---|---|
| Ronald Reagan (Republican) | 489 | 43,901,812 (50.7%) |
| Jimmy Carter (Democratic) | 49 | 35,483,820 (41.0%) |
| John B. Anderson (Independent) | --- | 5,719,722 (6.6%) |
| Other Candidates (Libertarian) | --- | 921,299 (1.1%) |

Senate for the first time since 1952; and although the Democrats retained a narrow majority in the House, the lower chamber too seemed firmly in the hands of conservatives.

On the day of Reagan's inauguration, the American hostages in Iran were released after their 444-day ordeal, as a result of negotiations Jimmy Carter had concluded in the last hours of his presidency. Americans welcomed the hostages home with demonstrations of euphoria and patriotism not seen since the end of World War II. But while the celebration in 1945 had marked a great American triumph, the euphoria in 1981 marked something quite different—a troubled nation grasping for reassurance. Ronald Reagan set out to provide it.

## THE "REAGAN REVOLUTION"

Ronald Reagan assumed the presidency in January 1981 promising a change in government more profound than any since the New Deal of fifty years before. His eight years in office produced a significant shift in public policy, but they brought nothing so fundamental as many of his supporters had hoped or his opponents had feared. There was, however, no ambiguity about his administration's purely political achievements. Ronald Reagan succeeded brilliantly in making his own engaging personality the central fact of American politics in the 1980s.

### Reagan in the White House

Even many people who disagreed with the president's policies found themselves drawn to his attractive and carefully honed public image. Reagan was a master of television and a gifted public speaker. He was the oldest man ever to serve as president, but he seemed vigorous, resilient, even youthful. When he was wounded in an assassination attempt in 1981, he joked with doctors on his way into surgery and appeared to bounce back from the ordeal with remarkable speed. Four years later, he seemed to rebound from cancer surgery with similar zest. He had few visible insecurities. Even when things went wrong, as they often did, the blame seemed seldom to attach to Reagan himself (inspiring some Democrats to begin referring to him as "the Teflon president").

Reagan was not much involved in the day-to-day affairs of running the government; he surrounded himself with tough, energetic administrators who insulated him from many of the pressures of the office and apparently

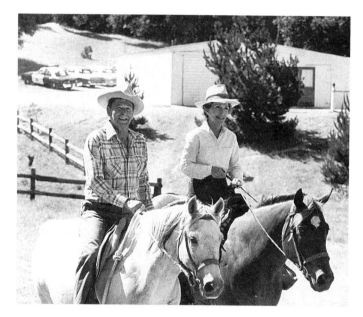

THE REAGANS IN SANTA BARBARA  In the weeks before the 1980 Republican convention, at which he was nominated for the presidency, Ronald Reagan and his wife Nancy spent time relaxing, very publicly, at their ranch near Santa Babara, California. Reagan returned often to his ranch during his presidency and, indeed, spent more days vacationing than any president in decades.

relied on him largely for general guidance, not specific decisions. But Reagan did make active use of his office to generate support for his administration's programs, by appealing repeatedly to the public over television and by fusing his proposals with a highly nationalistic rhetoric.

### "Supply-Side" Economics

Reagan's 1980 campaign for the presidency had promised, among other things, to restore the economy to health by a bold experiment that became known as "supply-side" economics or, to some, "Reaganomics." Supply-side economics operated from the assumption that the woes of the American economy were in large part a result of excessive taxation, which left inadequate capital available to investors to stimulate growth. The solution, therefore, was to reduce taxes, with particularly generous benefits to corporations and wealthy individuals, in order to encourage new investments. The result would be a general economic revival that would help everyone. Because a tax cut would reduce government revenues (at least at first), it would also be necessary to reduce government expenses. Another cornerstone of the Reagan economic program, therefore, was a dramatic cut in the federal budget, which would, the administration promised, bring it into balance within a few years.

In its first months in office, accordingly, the new administration hastily assembled a legislative program based on the supply-side idea. It proposed $40 billion in budget cuts and managed to win congressional approval of almost all of them. In addition, the president proposed a bold, three-year rate reduction on both individual and corporate taxes. In the summer of 1981, Congress passed it too. Not since Lyndon Johnson had a president compiled so impressive a legislative record in his first months in office.

By early 1982, the nation had sunk into the most severe recession since the 1930s. The Reagan economic program was not directly to blame for the problems, but critics claimed that the administration's policies were doing nothing to improve the situation. In fact, however, the economy recovered more rapidly and impressively than almost anyone had expected. By the middle of 1983, unemployment (which had reached nearly 11 percent in 1982, the highest level in over forty years) had fallen to 8.2 percent. The gross national product had grown 3.6 percent, the largest increase since the mid-1970s. Inflation had fallen below 5 percent. The economy continued to grow, and both inflation and unemployment remained low (at least by the new and more pessimistic standards the nation seemed now to have accepted) through most of the decade.

The recovery was a result of many things. Years of tight money policies by the Federal Reserve Board had helped lower inflation. A worldwide "energy glut," the virtual collapse of the OPEC cartel, and the deregulation of natural-gas production had produced at least a temporary end to the inflationary pressures of spiraling fuel costs. And staggering federal budget deficits were pumping billions of dollars into the flagging economy but also, many warned, threatening ultimately to destroy the recovery they were helping to create.

### The Fiscal Crisis

By the mid-1980s, the growing fiscal crisis had become one of the central issues in American politics. Having entered office promising a balanced budget within four years, Reagan presided over record budget deficits and accumulated more debt in his eight years in office than the American government had accumulated in its entire previous history. Before the 1980s, the highest single-year budget deficit in American history had been $66 billion (in 1976). Throughout the 1980s, the annual budget deficit consistently exceeded $100 billion (and in 1986 peaked at $221 billion). The national debt rose from $907 billion in 1980 to nearly $3 trillion by 1990.

The enormous deficits had many causes, some of them stretching back over decades of American public policy decisions. In particular, the budget suffered from enormous increases in the costs of "entitlement" programs (especially Social Security and Medicare), a result of the aging of the population and dramatic increases in the cost of health care. But some of the causes of the deficit lay in the policies of the Reagan administration. The 1981 tax cuts, the largest in American history, sharply eroded the revenue base of the federal government and accounted for a large percentage of the deficit. The massive increase in military spending (a proposed $1.6 trillion over five years) on which the Reagan administration insisted added more to the federal budget than its cuts in domestic spending removed.

In the face of these deficits, the administration refused to consider raising income taxes (although it did agree to a major increase in the Social Security tax). It would not agree to reductions in military spending. It was not willing to take the unpopular steps necessary to reduce the costs of entitlement programs, and it could do nothing to reduce interest payments on the massive (and growing) debt. Its answer to the fiscal crisis, therefore, was further cuts in "discretionary" domestic spending, which included many programs aimed at the poorest (and politically weakest) Americans. There were reductions in funding for food stamps; a major cut in federal subsidies for low-income housing; strict new limitations on Medicare and Medicaid payments; reductions in student loans, school lunches, and other educational programs; and an end to many forms of federal assistance to the states and cities—which helped precipitate years of local fiscal crises as well.

By the end of Reagan's third year in office, funding for domestic programs had been cut nearly as far as Congress (and, apparently, the public) was willing to tolerate. Congress responded with the Gramm-Rudman-Hollings Act, passed late in 1985, which mandated major deficit reductions over five years and provided for automatic budget cuts in all areas of government spending should the president and Congress fail to agree on an alternative solution. Under Gramm-Rudman-Hollings, the budget deficit did decline for several years from its 1983 high. But much of that decline was a result of a substantial surplus in the Social Security trust fund (which the sharply increased Social Security taxes had produced), not of any larger fiscal successes.

## Reagan and the World

Reagan encountered a similar combination of triumphs and difficulties in international affairs. Determined to restore American pride and prestige in the world, he argued that the United States should once again become active and assertive in opposing communism and supporting friendly governments whatever their internal policies.

Relations with the Soviet Union, which had been steadily deteriorating in the last years of the Carter administration, grew still more chilly in the first years of the Reagan presidency. The president spoke harshly of the Soviet regime (which he once called the "evil empire"), accusing it of sponsoring world terrorism and declaring that any armaments negotiations must be linked to negotiations on Soviet behavior in other areas. Relations with the Russians deteriorated further after the government of Poland (under strong pressure from Moscow) imposed martial law on the country in the winter of 1981 to crush a growing challenge from an independent labor organization, Solidarity.

Although the president had long denounced the SALT II arms control treaty as unfavorable to the United States, he continued to honor its provisions. But the Reagan administration at first made little progress toward arms control in other areas, despite the growing political power of a popular antinuclear movement in both Europe and the United States. In fact, the president proposed the most ambitious new military program in many years: the Strategic Defense Initiative (SDI), widely known as "Star Wars" (after a popular science-fiction movie). Reagan claimed that SDI, through the use of lasers and satellites, could provide an effective shield against incoming missiles and thus make nuclear war obsolete. The Soviet Union claimed that the new program would elevate the arms race to new and more dangerous levels and insisted that any arms control agreement begin with an American abandonment of SDI.

At the same time, the Reagan administration began, rhetorically at least, to support opponents of communism anywhere in the world, whether or not the regimes they were challenging were directly allied to the Soviet Union. This policy became known as the Reagan Doctrine, and it meant, above all, a new American activism in the Third World. The most conspicuous examples of the new activism came in Latin America. In October 1983, the ad-

ministration sent American soldiers and marines to the tiny Caribbean island of Grenada to oust an anti-American Marxist regime that was forging
a relationship with the Soviet Union. In El Salvador, where first a repressive military regime and later a moderate civilian one were engaged in murderous struggles with left-wing revolutionaries (who were supported, according to the Reagan administration, by Cuba and the Soviet Union), the
president provided increased military and economic assistance. In neighboring Nicaragua, a pro-American dictatorship had fallen to the revolutionary "Sandinistas" in 1979; the new government had grown increasingly
anti-American (and increasingly Marxist) throughout the early 1980s. The
administration gave both rhetorical and material support to the so-called
contras, a guerrilla movement drawn from several antigovernment groups
and fighting (without great success) to topple the Sandinista regime. Indeed,
support of the contras became a mission of special importance to the president, and later the source of some of his greatest difficulties.

In other parts of the world, the administration's bellicose rhetoric
seemed to hide an instinctive restraint. In June 1982, the Israeli army
launched an invasion of Lebanon in an effort to drive guerrillas of the Palestinian Liberation Organization from the country. The United States supported the Israelis rhetorically but also worked to permit PLO forces to leave
Lebanon peacefully. An American peacekeeping force entered Beirut to supervise the evacuation. American marines then remained in the city, apparently to protect the fragile Lebanese government, which was embroiled in
a vicious civil war. Now identified with one faction in the struggle, Americans themselves became the targets; a 1983 terrorist bombing of a United
States military barracks in Beirut left 241 marines dead. Rather than become
more deeply involved in the Lebanese struggle, Reagan withdrew the American forces.

### The Election of 1984

Reagan approached the campaign of 1984 at the head of a united Republican Party firmly committed to his candidacy. The Democrats, as had become
their custom, followed a more fractious course. In the end, however, former
vice president Walter Mondale withstood a series of vigorous challenges to
capture the nomination. He brought momentary excitement to the Democratic Convention in San Francisco that summer by selecting a woman,
Representative Geraldine Ferraro of New York, to be his running mate and
the first female candidate ever to appear on a major-party national ticket.

The Republican Party, in the meantime, rallied comfortably behind its revered leader, whose triumphant campaign that fall scarcely took note of his opponents. Reagan's victory in 1984 was decisive. He won approximately 59 percent of the vote, and he carried every state except Mondale's native Minnesota and the District of Columbia. But Reagan was stronger than his party. Democrats gained a seat in the Senate and maintained only slightly reduced control of the House of Representatives.

The triumphant reelection of Ronald Reagan was the high-water mark up to that point of conservative, and Republican, fortunes in the postwar era. It reflected satisfaction with the impressive performance of the economy under the Republican economic program, and pride in the new assertiveness the United States was showing in the world. To many Reagan supporters, the 1984 election seemed to be the dawn of a new conservative era. Few anticipated that it also coincided with the beginning of a revolutionary change in the world order, and the United States' place in it. The election of 1984 was less the first of a new era than the last of the old one. It was the final campaign of the Cold War.

CHAPTER THIRTY-FOUR

# Beyond the Cold War

*America and the Waning of the Cold War* ∼ *Modern Times*

O N NOVEMBER 8, 1989, East German soldiers stood guard at the Berlin Wall—keeping westerners out and easterners in—as they had done every day for more than twenty-eight years. The next day they were gone. Within hours, thousands of citizens of both sides of the divided city were swarming over the wall in celebration. Within weeks, bulldozers were tearing it down. Within a year, East and West Germany—divided by the Cold War for forty-five years—had reunited.

The breaching of the Berlin Wall and the reunification of Germany were among the most dramatic of a series of changes between 1986 and 1991 that radically transformed the world order. The Cold War, which as late as 1985 had seemed a permanent fact of international life, came to an end. A new world order, the outlines of which were still only dimly visible, was in the process of being born.

The Cold War had shaped the foreign policy and many aspects of the domestic life of the United States for nearly half a century. Its sudden end changed the character of national politics, economics, and culture. But America in the late 1980s and early 1990s was also encountering a series of other important social and economic changes, many of them unrelated to the Cold War. As the end of the twentieth century approached, most Americans were uncertain whether the changes would bring a better, safer world or a harsher and more dangerous one.

## AMERICA AND THE WANING OF THE COLD WAR

Many factors contributed to the collapse of the Soviet empire. The long, stalemated war in Afghanistan proved at least as disastrous to the Soviet Union as the Vietnam War had been to America. The government in Mos-

## TIME LINE

| 1979 | 1981 | 1985 | 1986 |
|---|---|---|---|
| Three Mile Island nuclear accident | AIDS first reported in U.S. | Reagan and Gorbachev meet<br><br>Crack cocaine appears in U.S. cities | U.S. bombs Libya<br><br>Iran-Contra scandal revealed |

| 1987 | 1988 | 1989 | 1990 |
|---|---|---|---|
| Gorbachev visits U.S.<br><br>Stock market falls | Bush elected president | Berlin Wall dismantled<br><br>Communist regimes collapse<br><br>American troops in Panama | Iraq invades Kuwait |

| 1991 | 1992 | | 1993 |
|---|---|---|---|
| Collapse of Soviet regime<br><br>Persian Gulf War | Los Angeles race riots<br><br>Clinton elected president | | North American Free Trade Agreement ratified<br><br>Health care reform fails |

cow had failed to address a long-term economic decline in the Soviet republics and the Eastern-bloc nations. Restiveness with the heavy-handed
policies of communist police states was growing throughout much of the Soviet empire. But the most visible factor at the time was the emergence of a
single man: Mikhail Gorbachev, who succeeded to the leadership of the Soviet Union in 1985 and, to the surprise of almost everyone (including, perhaps, himself), very quickly became the most revolutionary figure in world
politics in at least four decades.

### The Fall of the Soviet Union

Gorbachev quickly transformed Soviet politics with two dramatic new initiatives. The first he called *glasnost* (openness): the dismantling of many of
the repressive mechanisms that had been conspicuous features of Soviet life
for over half a century. The other policy Gorbachev called *perestroika* (reform): an effort to restructure the rigid and unproductive Soviet economy
by introducing, among other things, such elements of capitalism as private
ownership and the profit motive. He also began to transform Soviet foreign
policy.

The severe economic problems at home evidently convinced Gorbachev
that the Soviet Union could no longer sustain its extended commitments

SMASHING THE WALL Once it became clear in November 1989 that the East German government was no longer defending the wall that had divided Berlin for nearly thirty years, Germans on both sides of the divide swarmed over it in celebration. Here, a West German takes a sledgehammer to the already battered wall as East German border guards passively look on.

around the world. As early as 1987, he began reducing Soviet influence in Eastern Europe. And in 1989, in the space of a few months, every communist state in Europe—Poland, Hungary, Czechoslovakia, Bulgaria, Romania, East Germany, Yugoslavia, and Albania—either overthrew its government or forced it to transform itself into an essentially noncommunist (and in some cases, actively anticommunist) regime. The Communist Parties of Eastern Europe all but collapsed. Gorbachev and the Soviet Union actively encouraged the changes.

The challenges to communism were not successful everywhere. In May 1989, students in China launched a mass movement calling for greater democratization. But in June, hard-line leaders seized control of the government and sent military forces to crush the uprising. The result was a bloody massacre on June 3, 1989, in Tiananmen Square in Beijing, in which a still-unknown number of demonstrators died. The assault crushed the democracy movement and restored the hard-liners to power. It did not, however, stop China's efforts to modernize and even westernize its economy.

But China was an exception to the worldwide movement toward democratization, which even extended to parts of the world far removed from the Soviet empire. Early in 1990, the government of South Africa, long an international pariah for its rigid enforcement of "apartheid" (a system designed to protect white supremacy) began a cautious retreat from its traditional policies. Among other things, it legalized the chief black party in the nation, the African National Congress (ANC), which had been banned for decades; and on February 11, 1990, it released from prison the leader of the ANC, and a revered hero to black South Africans, Nelson Mandela, who had been in jail for twenty-seven years. Over the next several years, the South African government repealed its apartheid laws. And in 1994, there were national elections in which all South Africans could participate. As a result, Nelson Mandela became the first black president of South Africa.

In 1991, communism began to collapse at the site of its birth: the Soviet Union itself. An unsuccessful coup by hard-line Soviet leaders on August 19 precipitated a dramatic unraveling of communist power. Within days, the coup itself collapsed in the face of resistance from the public and, more important, crucial elements within the military. Mikhail Gorbachev returned to power, but it soon became evident that the legitimacy of both the Communist Party and the central Soviet government had been fatally injured. By the end of August, almost every republic in the Soviet Union had declared independence; the Soviet government was clearly powerless to stop the fragmentation. Gorbachev himself finally resigned as leader of the now virtually powerless Communist Party and Soviet government, and the Soviet Union ceased to exist.

### Reagan and Gorbachev

The last years of the Reagan administration coincided with the first years of the Gorbachev regime; and while Reagan was skeptical of Gorbachev at first, he gradually became convinced that the Soviet leader was sincere in his desire for reform. At a summit meeting with Reagan in Reykjavik, Iceland, in 1986, Gorbachev proposed reducing the nuclear arsenals of both sides by 50 percent or more, although continuing disputes over Reagan's commitment to the SDI program derailed agreements. But in 1988, after Reagan and Gorbachev exchanged cordial visits to each other's capital, the two superpowers signed a treaty eliminating American and Soviet intermediate-range nuclear forces (INF) from Europe—the most significant arms control agreement of the nuclear age. At about the same time, Gorbachev ended the Soviet Union's long and frustrating military involvement in Afghanistan, removing one of the principal irritants in the relationship between Washington and Moscow.

## The Fading of the Reagan Revolution

For a time, the dramatic changes around the world and Reagan's personal popularity deflected attention from a series of scandals that might well have destroyed another administration. There were revelations of illegality, corruption, and ethical lapses in the Environmental Protection Agency, the CIA, the Department of Defense, the Department of Labor, the Department of Justice, and the Department of Housing and Urban Development. A more serious scandal emerged within the savings and loan industry, which the Reagan administration had helped deregulate in the early 1980s. Many savings banks had responded by rapidly, often recklessly, and sometimes corruptly, expanding. By the end of the decade the industry was in chaos, and the government was forced to step in to prevent a complete collapse. Government insurance covered the assets of most savings and loan depositors; the cost of the debacle to the public eventually ran to more than half a trillion dollars.

But the most politically damaging scandal of the Reagan years came to light in November 1986, when the White House conceded that it had sold weapons to the revolutionary government of Iran as part of a largely unsuccessful effort to secure the release of several Americans being held hostage by radical Islamic groups in the Middle East. Even more damaging was the revelation that some of the money from the arms deal with Iran had been covertly and illegally funneled into a fund to aid the contras in Nicaragua.

In the months that followed, aggressive reporting and a highly publicized series of congressional hearings exposed a widespread pattern of covert activities orchestrated by the White House and dedicated to advancing the administration's foreign policy aims through secret and at times illegal means. The principal figure in this covert world appeared at first to be an obscure marine lieutenant colonel assigned to the staff of the National Security Council, Oliver North. But gradually it became clear that North was acting in concert with other, more powerful figures in the administration. The Iran-contra scandal, as it became known, did serious damage to the Reagan presidency—even though the investigations were never able decisively to tie the president himself to the most serious violations of the law.

## The Election of 1988

The fraying of the Reagan administration helped the Democrats regain control of the United States Senate in 1986 and fueled hopes in the party for a presidential victory in 1988. Even so, several of the most popular figures in the Democratic Party refused to run, and the nomination finally went to a previously little-known figure: Michael Dukakis, a three-term governor of Massachusetts. Dukakis was a dry, even dull campaigner. But Democrats were optimistic about their prospects in 1988, largely because of the identity of their opponent, Vice President George Bush, who had captured the Republican nomination without great difficulty but had failed to spark any real public enthusiasm. He entered the last months of the campaign well behind Dukakis.

Beginning at the Republican Convention, however, Bush staged a remarkable turnaround by making his campaign a long, relentless attack on Dukakis, tying him to all the unpopular social and cultural stances Americans had come to identify with "liberals." Indeed, the Bush campaign was almost certainly the most savage of the twentieth century. It was also, apparently, one of the most effective, although the listless, indecisive character of the Dukakis effort contributed to the Republican cause as well. Bush won a substantial victory in November: 54 percent of the popular vote to Dukakis's 46, and 426 electoral votes to Dukakis's 112. But Bush carried few Republicans into office with him; the Democrats retained secure majorities in both houses of Congress.

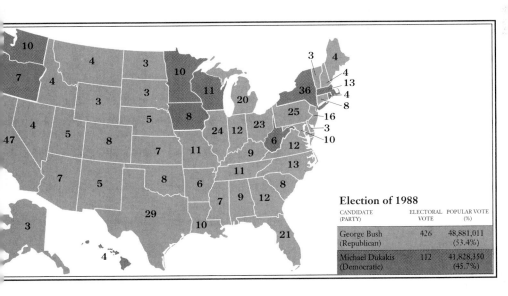

**Election of 1988**

| CANDIDATE (PARTY) | ELECTORAL VOTE | POPULAR VOTE (%) |
| --- | --- | --- |
| George Bush (Republican) | 426 | 48,881,011 (53.4%) |
| Michael Dukakis (Democratic) | 112 | 41,828,350 (45.7%) |

## The Bush Presidency

The Bush presidency was notable for a series of dramatic developments in international affairs and an almost complete absence of initiatives or ideas on domestic issues. For a time, Bush's achievements in foreign policy managed to obscure the absence of a domestic agenda. By early 1992, however, with the nation in the second year of a serious recession, the president's popularity had begun to fray.

The broad popularity Bush enjoyed during his first three years in office was partly because of his subdued, unthreatening public image. But it was primarily because of the wonder and excitement with which Americans viewed the dramatic events in the rest of the world.

Bush moved cautiously at first in dealing with the changes in the Soviet Union. But like Reagan, he eventually embraced Gorbachev and reached a series of significant agreements with the Soviet Union in its waning years. In the three years after the INF agreement in 1988, the United States and the Soviet Union moved rapidly toward even more far-reaching arms reduction agreements, including major troop reductions in Europe and the dismantling of new categories of strategic weapons.

On domestic issues, the Bush administration was less successful—partly because the president himself seemed to have little interest in promoting a domestic agenda and partly because he faced serious obstacles. His administration inherited a staggering burden of debt and a federal deficit that had been out of control for nearly a decade. Any domestic agenda that required significant federal spending was, therefore, incompatible with the president's pledge to reduce the deficit and his 1988 campaign promise of "no new taxes." Bush faced a Democratic Congress with an agenda very different from his own. And he was constantly concerned about the right wing of his own party and, in his eagerness to ingratiate himself with it, took divisive positions on such cultural issues as abortion and affirmative action that further damaged his ability to work with Congress.

Despite this political stalemate, Congress and the White House managed on occasion to agree on significant measures. They cooperated in producing a plan to salvage the floundering savings and loan industry. In 1990, the president bowed to congressional pressure and agreed to a significant tax increase as part of a multiyear "budget package" designed to reduce the deficit. In 1991, after almost two years of acrimonious debate, the president and Congress agreed on a civil rights bill to combat job discrimination.

But the most serious domestic problem facing the Bush administration was one to which neither the president nor Congress had any answer: a recession that began late in 1990 and slowly increased its grip on the national economy in 1991 and 1992. Because of the enormous level of debt that corporations (and individuals) had accumulated in the 1980s, the recession caused an unusual number of bankruptcies. It also created growing fear and frustration among middle- and working-class Americans and increasing pressure on the government to address such problems as the rising cost of health care.

### The Gulf War

The events of 1989–1991 had left the United States in the unanticipated position of being the only real superpower in the world. The Bush administration, therefore, had to consider what to do with America's formidable political and military power in a world in which the major justification for that power—the Soviet threat—was now gone.

The events of 1989–1991 suggested two possible answers, both of which had some effect on policy. One was that the United States would reduce its military strength dramatically and concentrate its energies and resources on pressing domestic problems. And, indeed, there was considerable movement in that direction both in Congress and within the administration. The other was that America would continue to use its power actively, not to fight communism but to defend its regional and economic interests. In 1989, that led the administration to order an invasion of Panama, which overthrew the unpopular military leader Manuel Noriega (under indictment in the United States for drug trafficking) and replaced him with an elected, pro-American regime. And in 1990, that same impulse drew the United States into the turbulent politics of the Middle East.

On August 2, 1990, the armed forces of Iraq invaded and quickly overwhelmed their small, oil-rich neighbor, the emirate of Kuwait. Saddam Hussein, the militaristic leader of Iraq, soon announced that he was annexing Kuwait and set out to entrench his forces there. After some initial indecision, the Bush administration agreed to join with other nations to force Iraq out of Kuwait—through the pressure of economic sanctions if possible, through military force if necessary. Within a few weeks, Bush had persuaded virtually every important government in the world, including the Soviet Union and almost all the Arab and Islamic states, to join in a United Nations–sanctioned trade embargo of Iraq.

At the same time, the United States and its allies (including the British, French, Egyptians, and Saudis) began deploying a massive military force along the border between Kuwait and Saudi Arabia, a force that ultimately reached 690,000 troops (425,000 of them American) and that assembled the largest and most sophisticated collection of military technology ever used in warfare. On November 29, the United Nations, at the request of the United States, voted to authorize military action to expel Iraq from Kuwait if Iraq did not leave by January 15, 1991. On January 12, both houses of Congress voted to authorize the use of force against Iraq, although many Democrats opposed the resolution, arguing that sanctions should be given more time to work. And on January 16, American and allied air forces began a massive bombardment of Iraqi forces in Kuwait and of military and industrial installations in Iraq itself.

The allied bombing continued for six weeks, meeting only token resistance from the small Iraqi air force and ground defenses. And on February 23, allied (primarily American) forces under the command of General Norman Schwarzkopf began a major ground offensive—not primarily against the heavily entrenched Iraqi forces along the Kuwait border, as expected, but into Iraq itself. The allied armies encountered almost no resistance and suffered only light casualties (141 fatalities). There were no reliable figures for the number of Iraqi military casualties, but some estimated the deaths (most as a result of the bombing) to be 100,000 or more. There were also a significant, if unverifiable, number of civilian casualties. On February 28, Iraq announced its acceptance of allied terms for a cease-fire, and the brief war came to an end.

The quick and (for America) relatively painless victory over Iraq was highly popular in the United States. But the longer-range results of the Gulf War were more difficult to assess. The tyrannical regime of Saddam Hussein survived, in a weakened form but showing few signs of retreat from its militaristic ambitions. And Kuwait returned to the control of its prewar government, an undemocratic monarchy increasingly unpopular with its own people.

## The Election of 1992

President Bush's popularity reached a record high in the immediate aftermath of the Gulf War. But the glow of that victory faded quickly as the recession worsened in late 1991, and as the administration declined to propose any policies for combating it. The president's popularity soon eroded.

Because the early maneuvering for the 1992 presidential election occurred when President Bush's popularity remained high, many leading Democrats declined to run. That gave Bill Clinton, the young five-term governor of Arkansas, an opportunity to emerge early as the front-runner, as a result of a skillful campaign that emphasized broad economic issues instead of the racial and cultural questions that had so divided the Democrats in the past. Clinton survived a bruising primary campaign and a series of damaging personal controversies to win his party's nomination. And George Bush withstood an embarrassing primary challenge from the conservative journalist Pat Buchanan to become the Republican nominee again.

Complicating the campaign was the emergence of Ross Perot, a blunt, forthright Texas billionaire who became an independent candidate by tapping popular resentment of the federal bureaucracy and by promising tough, uncompromising leadership to deal with the fiscal crisis and other problems of government. Particularly appealing to many voters were Perot's attacks on corruption in the political system and his insistence that his own campaign (funded by his personal fortune, not by special-interest lobbies) was a pure reflection of the will of the people. At several moments in the spring, Perot led both Bush and Clinton in public opinion polls. In July, as he began to face hostile scrutiny from the media, he abruptly withdrew from the race. But early in October, he reentered and soon regained much (although never all) of his early support.

After a campaign in which the economy and the president's unpopularity were the principal issues, Clinton won a clear, but hardly overwhelming, victory over Bush and Perot. He received 43 percent of the vote in the three-way race, to the president's 38 percent and Perot's 19 percent (the best

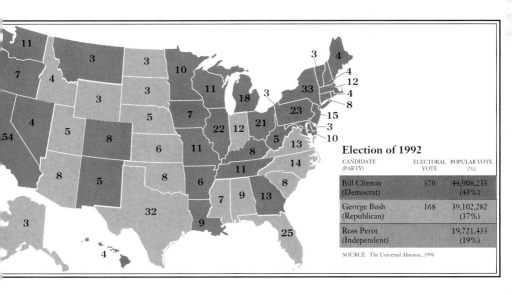

**Election of 1992**

| CANDIDATE (PARTY) | ELECTORAL VOTE | POPULAR VOTE (%) |
| --- | --- | --- |
| Bill Clinton (Democrat) | 370 | 44,908,233 (43%) |
| George Bush (Republican) | 168 | 39,102,282 (37%) |
| Ross Perot (Independent) | | 19,721,433 (19%) |

SOURCE: The Universal Almanac, 1996

showing for a third-party or independent candidate since Theodore Roosevelt in 1912). Clinton won 370 electoral votes to Bush's 168; Perot won none. Democrats retained control of both houses of Congress.

*Launching the Clinton Presidency*

Bill Clinton was the first Democratic president since Jimmy Carter and the first real activist to be president since Lyndon Johnson. He entered office carrying the extravagant expectations of liberals who had spent a generation in exile and with a domestic agenda more ambitious than that of any president since Lyndon Johnson. But Clinton also had significant political weaknesses. Having won the votes of well under half the electorate, he enjoyed no powerful mandate. Democratic majorities in Congress were frail, and Democrats in any case had grown unaccustomed to bowing to presidential leadership. The Republican leadership in Congress was highly adversarial and opposed the president with unusual unanimity on many issues.

The new administration compounded its problems with a series of missteps and misfortunes in its first months. The president's effort to end the longtime ban on gay men and lesbians serving in the military met with ferocious resistance from the armed forces themselves and from many conservatives in both parties. He was forced to settle for a pallid compromise. Several of his early appointments—to the Justice Department, in particular—became so controversial that he had to withdraw them. A longtime friend of the president from Arkansas serving in the office of the White House counsel committed suicide in the summer of 1993. His death helped spark an escalating inquiry into some banking and real estate ventures involving the President and his wife in the early 1980s; and the clumsy actions of some administration officials raised suspicions that the White House was attempting to interfere with the investigation into what became known as the Whitewater affair. A special prosecutor began examining these issues in 1993, and several congressional committees began hearings that continued into 1996.

Despite its many problems, the Clinton administration could boast of some significant achievements in its first year. The president narrowly (by a single vote in the Senate) won approval of a budget that marked a significant turn away from the policies of the Reagan-Bush years. It included a substantial tax increase on the wealthiest Americans, a significant reduction in many areas of government spending, and a major expansion of tax credits to low-income working people, designed to help lift many struggling families out of poverty. And after a long and difficult battle against, among others,

Ross Perot, the AFL-CIO, and many Democrats in Congress, he won approval of the North American Free Trade Agreement, which eliminated most trade barriers among the United States, Canada, and Mexico.

But the administration's substantial achievements were overshadowed by a large failure. The president's most important and ambitious initiative—the project that he hoped would define his presidency—was a major reform of the nation's health-care system. Early in 1993, he appointed a task force chaired by his wife, Hillary Rodham Clinton, which proposed a sweeping reform designed to guarantee coverage to every American and hold down the costs of medical care. (In the process of heading the task force, Mrs. Clinton emerged as the most powerful first lady in American history). The Clinton plan relied heavily on existing institutions, most notably private insurance companies, and some critics from the left complained that the new system would rely too heavily on an unreliable market. But the most substantial opposition came from those who believed the reform would transfer too much power to the government; and that opposition—combined with the determination of Republican leaders to deny the president any kind of victory on this potent issue—doomed the plan. There was particular opposition to the proposed tax on employers to finance the plan, a tax that small businesses claimed would be too burdensome for them. But there were complaints, too, from doctors, drug companies, insurance companies, and many people who were content with their existing insurance plans and feared the new system would treat them less favorably. In September 1994, after a series of compromises failed to attract majorities, Congress abandoned the health reform effort—a tremendous blow to the president's, and the Democratic party's, political fortunes.

The foreign policy of the Clinton administration was at first cautious and even tentative—a reflection, perhaps, of the president's relative inexperience in international affairs, but also of the rapidly changing character of the world order. Clinton presided over (although his administration had played a small role in creating) a historic agreement between Israel and the Palestinian Liberation Organization to end their long struggle over the lands Israel had occupied in 1967. His administration reached an agreement with Ukraine for an elimination of the nuclear weapons that had been positioned there when the republic had been part of the Soviet Union. And the president helped broker an agreement that led to the departure of a brutal military government from Haiti; American troops arrived to help preserve order as the elected president of Haiti returned from exile and established a new civilian regime.

The most troubling international question of the early 1990s emerged in eastern Europe. Yugoslavia, a nation created after World War I out of a group of small Balkan countries formerly part of the Austro-Hungarian Empire, dissolved into several new nations in the wake of the collapse of communism in Europe after 1989. Bosnia was among the new nations, and it quickly became embroiled in a bloody civil war between its two major ethnic groups: one Muslim, the other Serbian and Christian. All efforts by the other European nations and the United States to negotiate an end to the struggle failed until 1995, when the American negotiator Richard Holbrooke finally brought the warring parties together and crafted an agreement to partition Bosnia. The United States was among the nations to send peacekeeping troops to Bosnia to police the fragile settlement.

## The Republican Resurgence

The trials of the Clinton administration, and the failure of the health-care reform in particular, proved enormously damaging to the Democratic Party as it faced the congressional elections of 1994. Few doubted that the Republicans would make significant gains that year, but almost everyone was surprised by the dimensions of their victory. Every Republican incumbent won reelection. Democrats lost in droves. For the first time in forty years, Republicans seized control of both houses of Congress.

Several months before the election, Representative Newt Gingrich of Georgia released a set of campaign promises signed by almost all Republican candidates for the House and called it the "Contract with America." It called for dramatic changes in federal spending to produce a balanced budget, tax reductions, and a host of other measures consistent with the longtime goals of the Republican Party's conservative wing. Opinion polls suggested that few voters in 1994 were aware of the "Contract" at the time they voted. But Gingrich and the new Republican congressional leadership nevertheless interpreted the election results as a mandate for their program.

Throughout 1995, the Republican Congress worked at a sometimes feverish pace to construct one of the most ambitious and even radical legislative programs in modern times. The leaders proposed a series of measures to transfer important powers from the federal government to the states (including a proposal to abolish welfare as it had existed since the 1930s and replace it with block grants to state governments). They proposed dramatic reductions in federal spending, including a major restructuring of the once-sacrosanct Medicare program to reduce costs. They attempted to scale back a wide range of federal regulatory functions. In all these efforts, they could count on an unprecedentedly disciplined Republican majority in the House

CLINTON AND THE NEW CONGRESSIONAL LEADERSHIP In the aftermath of the dramatic Republican victories in the 1994 congressional elections, President Clinton vowed to cooperate with the new leaders of the House and Senate. He meets here, on January 5, 1995, with Speaker of the House Newt Gingrich, who spearheaded the campaign that put Congress in Republican hands for the first time in forty years, and Senate Majority Leader Robert Dole, who was already preparing to challenge President Clinton in the 1996 election.

and an only slightly less united Republican majority in the Senate. The Republican agenda, if successfully enacted, would represent the most substantial shift in the distribution of public authority in at least fifty years.

President Clinton responded to the 1994 election results by shifting his own agenda conspicuously to the center and calling for his own plan to cut taxes and balance the budget. Indeed, the gap between the Democratic White House and the Republican Congress on most major issues was relatively small. But because the legislative politics of 1995 was becoming part of the presidential politics of 1996, compromise between the president and Congress became very difficult. In November 1995 and again in January 1996, the federal government literally shut down because the president and Congress could not agree on a budget. By early 1996, public opinion seemed to be turning against much of the Republican agenda—and against the man most clearly identified with it. Gingrich was one of the most unpopular political leaders in the nation, while Clinton was slowly improving his standing in the polls. Even so, the events of 1994 and 1995 marked a re-markable change in American politics—a culmination, of sorts, of nearly thirty years of conservative efforts. Whatever the extent of the Republican legislative victories, it was clear that American politics had moved into a new era, the full outlines of which remained undefined.


## MODERN TIMES

The widespread popular suspicion of politics and government that charac-terized American life in the 1980s and 1990s was in part a result of decades of crises and scandals in public life. But it reflected, too, a series of major changes in the character and behavior of the American economy and Amer-ican society, changes more rapid—and more jarring—than those of any since at least the 1930s.


### *The Two-Tiered Economy*

Foremost among these changes was the dramatic transformation of the American economy, a transformation that had begun in earnest in the early 1970s and that continued unabated in the mid-1990s. The new economy cre-ated dazzling new miracles of technology that transformed the lives of al-most everyone. It created enormous new wealth that enriched those talented, or lucky, enough to profit from the areas of growth. And it produced enor-mous disparities in income, wealth, and opportunity that contributed to deep and increasingly corrosive divisions in American society.

The jarring changes in America's relationship to the world economy that had begun in the 1970s—the loss of cheap and easy access to raw materials, the penetration of the American market by foreign competitors, the re-structuring of American heavy industry so that it produced fewer jobs and paid lower wages—continued and in some respects accelerated through the last decades of the century. Economic growth continued, but at a slower rate than before. In the twenty years after World War II, the gross national prod-uct grew, on average, by 3.8 percent a year. In the 1970s and 1980s, the GNP grew by an average of less than 2.6 percent. Productivity grew 2.6 percent a year in the 1950s and 1960s; in the 1970s and 1980s it grew by less than 1 percent. The national savings rate—the rate at which individuals and insti-tutions saved income, which then became available for investment—peaked at around 10 percent between 1948 and 1973. The highest single-year rate in the 1980s was 3.2 percent.

For many families and individuals, the results of these contractions were jarring. In the first twenty years after World War II, it was possible for many, perhaps most, Americans to sustain themselves on a single (usually male) income. In later years, more and more families required two incomes to maintain their standards of living, and even that was often not enough. In the 1950s and 1960s, most Americans could expect to live more comfortably as adults than their parents had; in the 1980s and 1990s, increasing numbers of Americans were finding it impossible even to live as well as the generation before them. From 1973 to 1989, median family income increased less than 2 percent after inflation (from $33,656 a year to $34,213 in constant dollars), even though many families added a second income in those years.

Poverty in America had declined steadily and at times dramatically in the years after World War II, so that by the mid-1970s the percentage of people living in poverty had dropped to 12.3 percent (from 22.2 percent in 1960). By the early 1980s, the poverty rate was beginning to rise, and it reached 15 percent in 1993. As always, this increase in poverty affected women, children, and minorities far more than any other groups.

The increasingly unequal distribution of wealth and income in the United States accentuated these changes. Over 94 percent of the new wealth created by the American economy in the 1980s went to the wealthiest 20 percent of the population; over 50 percent went to the top 1 percent. In the meantime, the middle 40 percent of the population experienced an actual decline in wealth. Forty-seven percent of the total income in the United States in 1993 went to the wealthiest 20 percent of the population, and over 20 percent to the wealthiest 5 percent. Less than 30 percent of the income went to the bottom 60 percent of families, and only 4 percent to the bottom 20 percent. It was little wonder that the economic anxieties of the working and middle classes became one of the central issues in American politics in the late 1980s and early 1990s.

The new economy caused a real decline in the standard of living of most working-class Americans and even of many members of the middle class. But it created enormous rewards for others. The most dramatic area of growth in the 1980s and 1990s was technology, a field in which the United States continued to be highly competitive internationally. Biotechnology—which included pioneering new areas of medical research—was one sector of the economy that produced a bonanza. Even more important were computers, whose impact on American life exploded beginning in the 1980s and showed no signs of slowing as the century neared its close. Many of the greatest fortunes of the late twentieth century went to those men and women who capitalized on the growing market for computers and the services they provided.

The wealthiest man in America in the mid-1990s was William Gates, the founder and president of Microsoft—the software company whose operating systems served the vast majority of the world's computers. But Gates was only the most fabulously successful of large numbers of people who earned great wealth through technology and, in the process, created flourishing new areas of the national and international economies.

It became a cliché of public rhetoric that the new economy rewarded education, skills, and knowledge; but like many clichés, this one was largely true. Older sectors that relied on heavy machinery, large labor forces, and big corporate organizations did not disappear; in many cases, they restructured themselves and became more profitable—although often at the expense of their workers. But the "knowledge-based economy" was creating a disproportionate amount of the wealth and the bulk of the highly paid jobs of the 1990s.

The result was what many began to call a "two-tiered economy"—an increasingly affluent group at the top, constituting a quarter of the population or less; a struggling middle class faced with stagnating incomes and increasing insecurity; and an impoverished bottom, at times approaching a quarter of the population, with decreasing prospects for advancement in a world in which unskilled and semiskilled labor had much less value than in the past.

### "Globalization"

Perhaps the most important change, and certainly the one whose impact was the most difficult to gauge, was what became known as the "globalization" of the economy. The great prosperity of the 1950s and 1960s had rested on, among other things, the relative insulation of the United States from the pressures of international competition. As late as 1970, only 9 percent of the goods made in America were exported. More important, fewer than a third of the goods produced in America faced competition from abroad for the domestic market. The United States was an important participant in international trade. But in 1970, international trade still played a relatively small role in the American economy as a whole, which thrived on the basis of the huge domestic market in North America.

By the end of the 1970s, the world had intruded into the American economy in profound ways, and that intrusion increased unabated for the next twenty years. Exports rose, both in absolute numbers and as a percentage of goods produced: from just under $43 billion in 1970 to nearly $513 billion in 1994. More important, imports rose even more dramatically:

from just over $40 billion in 1970 to over $663 billion in 1994. As early as 1980, over 70 percent of American products faced foreign competition inside the United States, most notably some of the products whose role in creating and sustaining prosperity was especially important: steel and automobiles. America had made 76 percent of the world's automobiles in 1950 and 48 percent in 1960. By 1990, that share had dropped to 20 percent; and in 1994, even after a substantial revival of the automobile industry, the American share had risen only to 25 percent.

America was the largest exporter in the world in the 1980s and 1990s, and yet it had a huge trade imbalance (meaning it was importing much more than it was exporting). That was a reflection of how many competitors it faced and how deeply they had penetrated the United States market. The first American trade imbalance in the postwar era was in 1971; only twice since then, in 1973 and 1975, has the balance been favorable.

Globalization brought many benefits for the American consumer: new and more varied products, and lower prices for many of them. Most economists, and most national leaders, welcomed the process and worked to encourage it through lowering trade barriers. The North American Free Trade Agreement (NAFTA), ratified by the United States Senate in 1993, and the General Agreement on Tariffs and Trade (GATT), ratified a year later, were the boldest of a long series of treaties lowering trade barriers stretching back to the 1960s. But globalization was also enormously destabilizing. It was particularly hard on industrial workers, who were affected in two important ways. First, American workers lost industrial jobs as American companies lost market share. As foreign, especially Japanese, competition cut into steel, automobiles, and other heavy industries in the 1970s and beyond, the work forces in those industries declined. Second, American workers lost jobs as American companies began exporting work: building plants in Mexico, Asia, and other lower-wage countries to avoid having to pay the high wages workers had won in America. More than half of the production costs of making American cars were spent outside the United States by the 1990s. That was one reason for the rising unpopularity of free trade among many working-class people—an unpopularity effectively exploited by such self-proclaimed "populist" politicians as Ross Perot and Pat Buchanan, the conservative Republican who was running for president in 1996, and whose surprising victory in the New Hampshire primary thrust trade issues into the center of Republican Party debate for a time.

Globalization was also visible in the increasing presence of non-American investors and corporations within the American economy. Japanese and German automobile companies built new plants in the United

States. European and Asian corporations established large presences in America and sometimes bought major American companies. A group of Japanese investors bought the Columbia motion picture studio in 1989, and foreign companies purchased American corporations as large and visible as RCA, Goodyear, and Pillsbury.

### The Graying of America

After decades of steady growth, the nation's birth rate began to decline in the 1970s and remained low through the 1980s and early 1990s. In 1970, there were 18.4 births for every 1,000 people in the population. By 1975, the rate had declined to 14.6, the lowest in the twentieth century. And despite a modest increase in the 1980s, the rate remained below 16 in the mid-1990s. The declining birth rate and a significant rise in life expectancy produced a substantial increase in the proportion of elderly citizens. There were 17 million Americans over sixty-five years old in 1960 and 33 million in 1994. Over 12 percent of the population was more than sixty-five years old by 1990, as compared with 8 percent in 1970. That figure was projected to rise to over 20 percent by the end of the century as the members of the postwar baby boom began to enter old age. In 1994 the median age was thirty-four years, as compared with twenty-eight in 1970.

The aging of the population had important political and economic implications. It was a cause of the increasing costliness of Social Security pensions, and of steadily rising payroll taxes to sustain the system. It helped cause dramatic increases in health costs, both for the federal Medicare and Medicaid systems and for private hospitals and insurance companies. One of the reasons for the enormous federal deficits that came to dominate American political life in the late twentieth century was the rapidly rising cost of these pensions and medical programs for the elderly. But the changing demography also ensured that the aged, who already formed one of the most powerful interest groups in America, would remain politically formidable well into the twenty-first century.

### The Changing Profile of Immigration

Perhaps the most striking demographic change in America in the 1980s and 1990s, and one of those likely to have the farthest-reaching consequences, was the enormous change in both the extent and the character of immigration. Immigration had steadily declined for sixty years until the 1970s, when it began to increase sharply. In the 1970s, more than 4 million legal immigrants entered the United States. In the 1980s and early 1990s, the number rose to more than 6 million. (In 1994 alone, over 800,000 legal immigrants entered the United States.) When the uncounted but very large numbers of illegal immigrants in those years are included, the wave of immigration in the quarter-century after 1970 is almost certainly the largest of the twentieth century. In 1994, 8.7 percent of the American population was foreign-born—the largest percentage since 1940 and an 80 percent increase from 1970.

Equally striking was the character of the new immigration. The Immigration Reform Act of 1965 (see p. 835) had eliminated quotas based on national origin; from then on, newcomers from regions other than Latin America were generally admitted on a first-come, first-served basis. In 1965, 90 percent of the immigrants to the United States came from Europe. Twenty years later, only 10 percent of the new arrivals were Europeans. The three largest groups of foreign-born Americans in 1994 were, in order, Mexicans, Filipinos, and Cubans. The extent and character of the new immigration was causing a dramatic change in the composition of the American population. Already by the early 1990s, people of white European background constituted under 80 percent of the population (as opposed to 90 percent a half-century before). It seemed likely that by the middle of the twenty-first century, whites of European heritage would constitute less than 50 percent of the population.

Particularly important to the new immigration were two groups: Hispanics and Asians. Both had been significant segments of the American population for many decades—Hispanics since the very beginning of the nation's history, Asians since the waves of Chinese and Japanese immigration in the nineteenth century. But both groups experienced enormous, indeed unprecedented, growth after 1965.

People from Latin America—from Cuba, El Salvador, the Dominican Republic, and above all Mexico—constituted more than a third of the total number of legal immigrants to the United States in every year after 1965—and a much larger proportion of the total number of illegal immigrants. In California and the Southwest, in particular, they became an increasingly important presence. There were also substantial Hispanic populations in Illinois, New York, and Florida. High birth rates among Hispanic communities already in the United States further increased their numbers. In the 1980 census, 6 percent of the population was listed as being of Hispanic origin. The 1990 census showed an increase to 9 percent—or 20 million people. (Twenty years earlier, the number had been 7 million.) Economic problems and political repression in Mexico and other Latin American and Caribbean nations propelled the new immigrants to the United States; but in most of the areas to which they moved, opportunities were hard to find. Mexican Americans had an official poverty rate of 20 percent in 1990 (and a real poverty rate that was probably much higher, given the number of illegal immigrants who evaded official statistics). The poverty rate among Puerto Ricans was 30 percent. For illegal immigrants, conditions were particularly dire. Because they were subject to deportation if they came to the attention of the government, they had no legal recourse to being exploited by employers. Most worked for subsistence wages in menial jobs, constantly fearful of exposure.

The growing Hispanic presence became a political issue of increasing importance in the 1980s and 1990s, both to "Anglos" and, of course, to Hispanics themselves. The Immigration Reform and Control (or Simpson-Mazzoli) Act of 1987 reflected the political power of both groups. Its principal goal was to respond to the demands of whites in the Southwest and California by stemming the flow of illegal immigrants (mostly from Mexico). To that end, it placed the burden on employers for the first time to confirm the legal status of their employees. Those who failed to do so faced economic and even criminal penalties. Hispanics charged that the bill would increase discrimination in hiring, and in the first years after its passage there was considerable evidence that such charges were well founded. At the same time, the act responded to the growing political influence of Hispanics by offering amnesty to all undocumented workers who had entered the country before 1982. By the early 1990s, however, it seemed clear that the law was failing. Illegal immigration from Mexico and elsewhere was continuing at near-record levels.

White residents of areas in which the Hispanic populations were growing rapidly often reacted with alarm, fearing that they would soon become a minority in what they considered their own cities. Such fears lay behind efforts to bar the use of the Spanish language in public schools and other measures to force Hispanic immigrants to assimilate more quickly and completely.

In the 1980s and early 1990s, Asian immigrants arrived in numbers almost equal to those of Hispanics. Over 6 million of the foreign-born in America in 1994 were from Asian nations (most notably the Philippines, China, Korea, Vietnam, and India). They swelled the already substantial Chinese communities in California and elsewhere. And they created substantial new communities of immigrants from other areas of Asia. By 1990, there were more than 7 million Asian Americans in the United States, more than twice the number of ten years before. Like Hispanics, they were concentrated mainly in large cities and in the West.

A  M  E  R  I  C  A  N  V  O  I  C  E  S

# A Vietnamese Immigrant Describes Her Life in America, 1984

HERE IN AMERICA, I just remain. I don't change my traditional ways. . . . My children have adapted to American customs in hair styles and dress. . . . The older women don't change much, and most of the older men don't change either.

Over here, for older people, we receive money from the government; if not, we would die of starvation because we are older and don't know what to do. In Vietnam, we have less fear of survival, but over here, I'm afraid that when I get older I'll have to go into a nursing home to stay there, because all of my children are working. . . . Old age here is scary. . . .

The difference is that over here children do not obey their parents; in Vietnam, they obeyed us more. Over here, whenever we say something, they like to argue about it. . . . Things we consider to be right they consider wrong. Like a wife they select whom we don't like. They argue with us, against it, saying that it's right for them and that they will take the responsibility for it. They claim it's their *right* and that we don't have the right to tell them what to do. It is just like we are strangers; they won't let us interfere. . . . Our children do not keep the old traditions. They live apart from one another.

SOURCE: Reprinted from *Hearts of Sorrow: Vietnamese-American Lives*, by James M. Freeman, with the permission of the publisher, Stanford University Press. © 1989 by the Board of Trustees of the Leland Stanford Junior University.

Like most new immigrant groups, Asian Americans found adjustment to the very different culture of the United States difficult and disorienting. They also experienced resentment and discrimination. Whites feared Asian competition in economic activities that they had been accustomed to controlling. For example, there were heated disputes between white and Vietnamese shrimpers on the Gulf Coast in Texas, Mississippi, and Louisiana. Some African Americans resented the success of Asian merchants in black neighborhoods (as the black filmmaker Spike Lee noted in his 1989 film *Do the Right Thing*.) In New York, racial tensions led to a black boycott of some Korean grocery stores in African American neighborhoods in 1990.

Resentment of Asian Americans may also have been a result, in part, of their remarkable success. Indeed, some Asian groups (most notably Indians, Japanese, and Chinese) were by the 1980s earning larger average annual incomes than whites. Chinese and Japanese Americans consistently ranked at or near the top of high-school and college classes in the 1980s. That was in part because Asian-American communities contained significant numbers of people who had been involved in business and the professions before coming to America and had arrived with a high degree of expertise. They also placed an unusually high value on education.

### Black America in the Postliberal Era

The vast political and economic changes of the years after the civil rights movement had contrasting effects on African Americans. On the one hand, there were increased opportunities for advancement available to those in a position to take advantage of them. On the other hand, as industrial employment declined and government services dwindled, there was a growing sense of helplessness and despair among the large groups of nonwhites who continued to find themselves barred from upward mobility.

For the black middle class, which by the late 1970s constituted nearly a third of the entire black population of America, the progress was at times astonishing. Economic disparities between black and white professionals did not vanish, but they diminished substantially. Black families moved into more affluent urban communities and, in many cases, into suburbs—at times as neighbors of whites, more often into predominantly black communities. The number of blacks attending college rose by 350 percent in the decade following the passage of the civil rights acts (in contrast to a 150 percent increase among whites); African Americans made up 12 percent of the college population in 1990 (up from 5 percent twenty-five years earlier), although by 1994 that figure had declined to just over 10 percent. The percentage of black high-school graduates going on to college was by then virtually the same as that of white high-school graduates (although a far smaller proportion of blacks than whites managed to complete high school). And African Americans were making rapid strides in many professions from which, a generation earlier, they had been barred or within which they had been segregated. They were becoming partners in major law firms and joining the staffs of major hospitals and the faculties of major universities. Nearly half of all employed blacks in the United States had white-collar jobs. There were few areas of American life from which blacks were any longer entirely excluded. Middle-class blacks, in other words, had realized great gains from the legislation of the 1960s, from the changing national mood on race, from the creation of controversial affirmative action programs, and from their own educational and professional efforts.

But the rise of a black middle class also accentuated (and perhaps even helped cause) the increasingly desperate plight of other black Americans, whom many of the liberal programs of the 1960s had never reached. This growing "underclass" made up about a third of the nation's black population. It felt the impact of the economic troubles of the 1970s and 1980s with special force. And as more successful blacks moved out of the inner cities, the poor were left virtually alone in their decaying neighborhoods. A third of all black families lived in poverty in 1993; at the same time, just over 12 percent of white families could be officially classified as poor. Fewer than half of young inner-city blacks finished high school; more than 60 percent were unemployed.

The black family structure suffered as well from the dislocations of urban poverty. There was a radical increase in the number of single-parent, female-headed black households in the 1970s and 1980s. In the early 1990s, over 60 percent of all black children were born into single-parent families, as opposed to only 15 percent of white children (also a substantial increase over earlier eras). In 1960, only 20 percent of black children had lived in single-parent homes.

Nonwhites faced many disadvantages in the changing social and economic climate of the 1980s and 1990s. Among them was a growing impatience with affirmative action and other programs designed to advance their fortunes, as symbolized by the *Bakke* case in 1978 and by a growing reluctance among federal officials after 1980 to move aggressively to enforce affirmative action guidelines. By the mid-1990s, the white assault on affirmative action had gained so much momentum that there was real doubt as to whether very much of it would survive. Nonwhites suffered as well from a steady decline in the number of unskilled jobs in the economy. They suffered from the long, steady deterioration of urban public education and of other social services, which made it more difficult for them to find opportunities for advancement. And they suffered, in some cases, from a sense of futility and despair, born of years of entrapment in brutal urban ghettoes.

By the early 1990s, whole generations of nonwhites had grown to maturity living in destitute neighborhoods where welfare, drug dealing, and other crimes were virtually the only means of support for many people. Violence was increasingly a part of daily life. While rates of violent crime were declining nationally in the late 1980s and early 1990s, violence (much of it entirely random) was escalating in many inner-city communities—a result of the drug trade, gang wars, and the proliferation of guns.

The anger and despair such conditions were creating among inner-city residents became clear in the summer of 1992 in Los Angeles. The previ-

LOS ANGELES, APRIL 1992  An aerial view of a section of south central Los Angeles in the immediate aftermath of the great riot of 1992. The decision of an all-white jury to acquit Los Angeles police officers accused of brutalizing a black suspect (a beating recorded by a bystander on video tape) created widespread outrage and crystallized a frustration that residents of this poor, crime-plagued community had been feeling for years.

ous year, a bystander had videotaped several Los Angeles police officers beating an apparently helpless black man whom they had captured after an auto chase. Broadcast repeatedly around the country, the tape evoked outrage among whites and blacks alike. But an all-white jury in a suburban community just outside Los Angeles acquitted the officers when they were tried for assault. Black residents of South Central Los Angeles, one of the poorest communities in the city, erupted in anger—precipitating the largest racial disturbance of the twentieth century. There was widespread looting and arson. More than fifty people died. In the 1960s, urban uprisings had helped produce a major (if ultimately inadequate) government effort to deal with the problems of the inner city. But in the fiscally starved 1990s, the Los Angeles riot produced no such response.

What Americans had long called "race relations," the way in which white and black Americans viewed each other, grew increasingly sour in these difficult years. White impatience with black demands grew, as did a willingness to listen to old and long-discredited arguments about genetic differences between the races. A controversial book by two social scientists, *The Bell Curve*, published in 1994, helped reopen this bitter debate about the innate capacities of members of different races. Many African Americans, for their part, developed an intensified mistrust of the institutions of white society—of the government, the corporations, the universities, and perhaps above all the system of law enforcement.

Nowhere was this mutual suspicion more evident than in the celebrated trial of the former football star O. J. Simpson, an African American, who was accused of murdering his former wife and a young man, both of whom were white, in Los Angeles in 1994. The long and costly "O. J. trial" was an enormous media sensation for over a year, and throughout the proceedings, opinions about Simpson's guilt broke down along strikingly racial lines. A vast majority of whites believed he was guilty, and a vast majority of blacks believed he was innocent. Simpson's acquittal in the fall of 1995 caused great celebrations in many black communities and a quiet disgust among many whites.

*Modern Plagues: Drugs, AIDS, and Homelessness*

Poor African Americans, new immigrants, and many others found themselves clustered, often trapped, in cities being ravaged not just by economic decline but by two new and deadly epidemics. One was a dramatic increase in drug use, which penetrated nearly every community in the nation. The enormous demand for drugs, and particularly for "crack" cocaine, spawned what was in effect a multibillion-dollar industry, and those reaping the enormous profits of the illegal trade fought strenuously and often savagely to protect their positions.

Political figures of both parties spoke heatedly about the need for a "war on drugs," but in the absence of significant funding for such programs and clear ideas about what they should accomplish, government efforts appeared to be having little effect. Drug use declined significantly among middle-class people beginning in the late 1980s, but the epidemic showed no signs of abating in the poor urban neighborhoods where it was doing the most severe damage.

The drug epidemic was directly related to another scourge of the 1980s and 1990s: the epidemic spread of a new and lethal disease first documented in 1981 and soon named AIDS (acquired immune deficiency syndrome). AIDS is the product of the HIV virus, which is transmitted by the exchange of bodily fluids (blood or semen). The virus gradually destroys the body's immune system and makes its victims highly vulnerable to a number of diseases (particularly to various forms of cancer and pneumonia) to which they would otherwise have a natural resistance. Although many of those infected with the virus (i.e., people who are "HIV positive") live for many years without developing AIDS, once they do become ill they are virtually certain to die. The first American victims of AIDS (and in the early 1990s the group among whom cases remained the most numerous) were homosexual men. But by the late 1980s, as the gay community began to take preventive measures, the most rapid increase in the spread of the disease occurred among heterosexuals, many of them intravenous drug users, who spread the virus by sharing contaminated hypodermic needles. By the early 1990s, United States government agencies were estimating that between 1 and 1.5 million Americans were infected with the HIV virus. (Worldwide, the figure was over 10 million.) Over 400,000 Americans had actually contracted AIDS, and over 280,000 had died by the mid-1990s.

A large research effort produced a wealth of new knowledge about the virus and developed several drugs that could delay or limit the effects of AIDS. But neither a cure nor a vaccine seemed imminent. Governments and private groups, in the meantime, began promoting AIDS awareness in increasingly visible and graphic ways—urging young people, in particular, to avoid "unsafe sex" through abstinence or the use of latex condoms.

The spread of AIDS had a chilling effect on the sexual revolution that had transformed behavior beginning in the 1960s. Fear of infection caused many people to avoid casual sexual relations; but the more puritanical sexual standards against which many Americans had rebelled in the 1960s—and that some conservative Americans hoped to restore—did not return.

The increasing scarcity of housing for low-income people contributed to another urban crisis of the 1980s and 1990s: homelessness. There had always been homeless men and women in most major cities, but their numbers were clearly growing at an alarming rate in the face of rising housing costs, severe cutbacks in federal support for public housing, reduced welfare assistance, deinstitutionalization of the mentally ill, the declining availability of unskilled jobs, and the increasing weakness of family structures. The phenomenon of tens of thousands of homeless people at large in the cities put pressure on municipal governments to provide shelter and assistance for the indigent, but in an age of fiscal stringency and greatly reduced federal aid, cities found it difficult to respond adequately to the dimensions of the crisis.

## Battles Against Feminism and Abortion

Among the principal goals of the New Right as it became more powerful and assertive in the 1980s and 1990s was to challenge feminism and its achievements. Leaders of the New Right had campaigned successfully against the proposed Equal Rights Amendment to the Constitution. And they played a central role in the most divisive issue of the late 1980s and early 1990s: the controversy over abortion rights.

For those who favored allowing women to choose to terminate unwanted pregnancies, the Supreme Court's decision in *Roe* v. *Wade* (1973) had seemed to settle the question. By the 1980s, abortion was the most commonly performed surgical procedure in the country. But at the same time, opposition to abortion was creating a powerful grassroots movement. The right-to-life movement, as it called itself, found its most fervent supporters among Catholics; and indeed, the Catholic Church itself lent its institutional authority to the battle against legalized abortion. Religious doctrine also motivated the antiabortion stance of Mormons, fundamentalist Christians, and other groups. The opposition of some other antiabortion activists had less to do with religion than with their commitment to traditional notions of family and gender relations. To them, abortion was a particularly offensive part of a much larger assault by feminists on the role of women as wives and mothers. It was also, many foes contended, a form of murder. Fetuses, they claimed, were human beings who had a "right to life" from the moment of conception.

Although the right-to-life movement was persistent in its demand for a reversal of *Roe* v. *Wade* or, barring that, a constitutional amendment banning abortion, it also attacked abortion in more limited ways, at its most vulnerable points. In the 1970s, Congress and many state legislatures began barring the use of public funds to pay for abortions, thus making them almost inaccessible for many poor women. The Reagan and Bush administrations imposed further restrictions on federal funding and even on the right of doctors in federally funded clinics to give patients any information on abortion. Extremists in the right-to-life movement began picketing, occupying, and at times bombing abortion clinics. One antiabortion activist murdered a doctor in Florida who performed abortions; other physicians were subject to campaigns of terrorism and harassment—part of an effort to force them to abandon serving women who wanted abortions.

The changing composition of the Supreme Court in the 1980s to early 1990s (when five new conservative justices were named by Presidents Reagan and Bush) renewed the right-to-life movement's hopes for a reversal of *Roe* v. *Wade*. In *Webster* v. *Reproductive Health Services* (1989), the Court upheld a Missouri law that forbade any institution receiving state funds from performing abortions, whether or not those funds were used to finance the abortions. But the Court stopped short of overturning its 1973 decision.

Through much of the 1970s and 1980s, defenders of abortion had remained confident that *Roe* v. *Wade* protected their right to choose abortion and that the antiabortion movement was unlikely to prevail. But the changing judicial climate of the late 1980s and early 1990s mobilized defenders of abortion as never before. They called themselves the "pro-choice" movement, because they were defending not so much abortion itself as every woman's right to choose whether and when to bear a child. It quickly became clear that the pro-choice movement was in many parts of the country at least as strong as, and in some areas much stronger than, the right-to-life movement. With the election of President Clinton in 1992, the immediate threat to *Roe* v. *Wade* seemed to fade. In his first two years in office, Clinton named two pro-choice justices to the Court—Ruth Bader Ginsburg and Stephen Breyer. But the increasing strength of the Republican right, as demonstrated in the 1994 congressional elections, suggested that the issue was far from closed.

At times the pro-choice campaign overshadowed other efforts by feminists to protect and expand the rights of women. But such efforts continued. Women's organizations and many individual women worked strenuously in the 1980s and 1990s to improve access to child care for poor women and to win the right to caregiver leaves for parents. They also worked to raise awareness of sexual harassment in the workplace, with considerable success. Colleges, universities, government agencies, even many corporations established strict new standards of behavior for their employees in dealing with members of the opposite sex and created grievance procedures for those who believed they had been harassed. Both the achievements and the limits of their progress on this issue were evident in the sensational controversy in 1991 over Judge Clarence Thomas, President Bush's nominee for a seat on the Supreme Court. Late in the confirmation proceedings, accusations of sexual harassment from Anita Hill, a law professor and former employee of Thomas, became public. Hill's testimony before the Senate Judiciary Committee dramatically polarized both the Senate and the nation. Feminists and others tended to believe the accusations and hailed the accuser for drawing national attention to the issue of harassment; but many Americans (and most members of the virtually all-male Senate) apparently did not believe her— or at least concluded that the alleged activities should not disqualify Thomas from serving on the Court. Thomas was ultimately confirmed by a narrow margin.

### The Changing Left and the New Environmentalism

The New Left of the 1960s and early 1970s did not disappear after the end of the war in Vietnam, but it faded rapidly. Many of the students who had fought in its battles grew up, left school, and entered conventional careers. Some radical leaders, disillusioned by the unresponsiveness of American society to their demands, resignedly gave up the struggle and chose instead to work "within the system." Radical ideas continued to flourish in some academic circles, but to much of the public they came to appear dated and irrelevant—particularly as, beginning in 1989, Marxist governments collapsed in disrepute.

Yet a left of sorts did survive, giving evidence in the process of how greatly the nation's political climate had changed. Where 1960s activists had rallied to protest racism, poverty, and war, their counterparts in the 1980s and 1990s more often fought to stop the proliferation of nuclear weapons and power plants, to save the wilderness, to protect endangered species, to limit reckless economic development, and otherwise to protect the environment.

Public concerns about the environment had arisen intermittently since the beginning of the industrial era and had been growing in intensity since 1962, when the publication of Rachel Carson's *Silent Spring* aroused widespread public concern about the effect of insecticides on the natural world.

Several highly visible environmental catastrophes in the 1960s and 1970s greatly increased that concern. Among them were a major oil spill off Santa Barbara, California, in 1969; the discovery of large deposits of improperly disposed toxic wastes in a residential community in upstate New York in 1978; and a frightening accident at the nuclear power plant on Three Mile Island, Pennsylvania, in 1979. These and other revelations of the extent to which human progress threatened the natural world helped produce a major popular movement.

In the spring of 1970, a nationwide "Earth Day" signaled the beginning of the modern environmental movement. It differed markedly from the "conservation" movements of earlier years. Modern environmentalists shared the concerns of such earlier figures as John Muir and Gifford Pinchot about preserving the wilderness or carefully managing the exploitation of resources. But the new activists went much further, basing their positions on the developing field of ecology, the study of the interconnections among all components of an environment. Toxic wastes, air and water pollution, the destruction of forests, the extinction of species—these were not separate, isolated problems. All elements of the earth's environment were intimately and delicately linked, ecologists claimed. Damaging any one of those elements risked damaging all the others. Only by adopting a new social ethic, in which economic growth became less important than ecological health, or a new economics, in which environmental costs were factored into economic analyses, could the human race hope to survive in a healthy world.

In the twenty years after the first Earth Day, environmental issues gained increasing attention and support. Although the federal government often displayed limited interest in the subject, environmentalists won a series of significant battles, mostly at the local level. They blocked the construction of roads, airports, and other projects (including American development of the supersonic transport airplane, or SST) that they claimed would be ecologically dangerous. By the end of the decade, the sense of urgency had grown, as scientists began warning that the release of certain industrial pollutants (most notably chlorofluorocarbons) into the atmosphere was depleting the ozone layer of the earth's atmosphere, which protects the globe from the sun's most dangerous rays. They warned, too, of the related danger of global warming, a rise in the earth's temperature as a result of emissions from the burning of fossil fuels (coal and oil).

The concern for the environment, the opposition to nuclear power, the resistance to economic development—all were reflections of a more fundamental characteristic of the post-Vietnam left. In a sharp break from the nation's long commitment to growth and progress, many dissidents argued that only by limiting growth and curbing traditional forms of progress could society hope to survive. Some of these critics of the "idea of progress" expressed a gloomy resignation, urging a lowering of social expectations and predicting an inevitable deterioration in the quality of life. Other advocates of restraint believed that change did not require decline: human beings could live more comfortably and more happily if they learned to respect the limits imposed on them by their environment. But in either case, such arguments evoked strong opposition from conservatives and others, who ridiculed the no-growth ideology as an expression of defeatism and despair. Ronald Reagan, in particular, made an attack on the idea of "limits" central to his political success.

The rising popularity of environmental issues reflected another important shift both in the character of the American left and in the tone of American public life generally. Through much of the first half of the twentieth century, American politics had been preoccupied with debates over economic power and disparities of wealth. In the late twentieth century, with concentrations of wealth and power reaching unprecedented levels, such debates had largely ceased. There were, of course, economic implications to environmentalism and other no-growth efforts. But what drove such movements was less a concern about class than a concern about the quality of individual and community life.

### The "Culture Wars"

As class-based controversies ceased to shape American public life, cultural battles gradually took their place. Indeed, few issues attracted more attention in the 1990s than the battle over what became known as "multiculturalism." Multiculturalism meant different things to different people, but at its core was an effort to legitimize the cultural pluralism of the rapidly diversifying American population. That meant acknowledging that "American culture," which had long been defined primarily by white males of European descent, also included other traditions: female, African American, Indian, and increasingly in the late twentieth-century Hispanic and Asian. Although such demands were often controversial, especially when they became the basis of assaults on traditional academic curricula, much greater acrimony emerged out of efforts by some revisionists to portray traditional Western culture as inherently racist and imperialistic. A prolonged, if somewhat muted, dispute over how to commemorate the 500th anniversary of Columbus's first voyage to the "New World" illustrated how sharply ideas of multiculturalism had changed the way Americans discussed their past. In

1892, the Columbian anniversary had been the occasion of boisterous national celebration—and a great world's fair in Chicago. In 1992, it produced agonizing debates over the impact of the European discovery on native peoples. The only world's fairs were in Italy and Spain.

Debates over multiculturalism and related issues helped produce an increasingly strained climate in academia and in the larger American intellectual world. People on the left complained that the ascendancy of conservative politics placed new and intolerable limits on freedom of expression, as efforts to restrict National Endowment for the Arts grants to controversial artists suggested. Many on the right complained equally vigorously of a

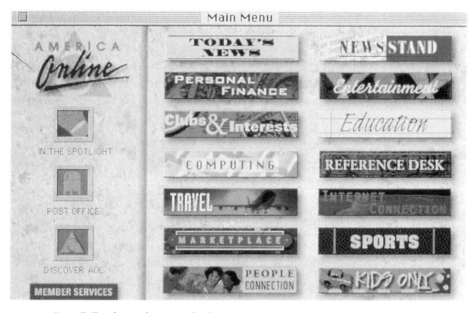

THE "NET" By the mid 1990s, the Internet—a communications system that made available vast amounts of information and entertainment through a worldwide computer network—had become something like an obsession to many Americans. Many predicted that the Internet would soon become one of the nation's primary forms of communication. Already by the mid-1990s, many people were using e-mail (electronic mail) transmitted through the Internet more often than they were using the telephone or the postal system. Access to the Internet was available at first only to employees of large institutions that had their own computer networks. But commercial services such as America Online—whose "home page" appears here—soon began to offer connections to individual consumers through their telephone lines.

tyranny of "political correctness," by which feminists, cultural radicals, and others introduced a new form of intolerance into public discourse in the name of defending the rights of women and minorities.

The controversies surrounding multiculturalism and "political correctness" were illustrations of a painful change in the character of American society. Traditional patterns of authority faced challenges from women, minorities, and others. The liberal belief in tolerance and assimilation was fraying in the face of the growing cultural separatism of members of some ethnic and racial groups. Confidence in the nation's future was declining, and with it confidence in the capacity of American society to provide justice and opportunity to all its citizens.

## The American Future

The American people approached the end of the twentieth century filled with anxieties, doubts, and resentments. Faith in the nation's institutions—most notably government—was at its lowest point in many decades. Confidence in the nation's leaders had all but vanished. Deep economic anxieties, which few Americans seemed able to translate into a coherent economic agenda, increased the nation's growing discontent.

And yet the United States in the 1990s, despite its many problems, remained a remarkably successful society—and one that had made dramatic strides in improving the lives of its citizens and dealing with many of its social problems since the end of World War II. The crisis of confidence that seemed to darken the nation's public life in the waning years of the century was not irrational, to be sure. There were many reasons for concern, even alarm, about the national condition. But crisis and division are hardly new to America's long, turbulent history. Conflict and uncertainty are, in fact, more characteristic of the national experience than the stability and consensus that many Americans believed they could restore.

The American people have seldom, if ever, been wholly content about the condition of their nation. But they have also been extraordinarily resilient—and through much of their history they have been possessed with the belief that if they tried hard enough, they could improve their world. Recovering that faith—a faith at the heart of most of the many traditions that have shaped American history—is one of the challenges of our time.

# APPENDICES

CANADA

Lake of the
Woods
onal
'alls
Duluth

*Lake Superior*

MAINE

Bangor

Sault Ste. Marie

VERMONT
Augusta

NESOTA

St. Paul
apolis

MICHIGAN

Montpelier ★ NEW Portland
HAMPSHIRE
Concord

WISCONSIN

*Lake Michigan*

*Lake Huron*

Springfield
Schenectady

Portsmouth
Boston

Green Bay

*Lake Ontario*

MASSACHUSETTS

Bay City

Rochester
Syracuse
Albany

Providence

Milwaukee

Grand
Rapids Lansing

Flint

Buffalo NEW YORK

White Plains Hartford

RHODE ISLAND
CONNECTICUT

Madison

Kalamazoo Livonia

Sterling
Heights

*Lake
Erie*

Paterson

New Haven
Stamford

y Waterloo

Rockford Chicago

Ann Arbor Detroit

Erie

Scranton

Newark

New York

IOWA
Des
ines

Cedar
Rapids
Davenport

Aurora

Gary South
Bend

Cleveland

PENNSYLVANIA

Allentown

NEW JERSEY
Trenton

Fort Wayne

Toledo Akron Youngstown

Harrisburg

Philadelphia

Peoria

Muncie

Columbus

OHIO

Pittsburgh

Dover

ILLINOIS INDIANA

Dayton

Washington, D.C.

Baltimore

DELAWARE

St. Joseph Springfield

Indianapolis

Cincinnati

WEST
VIRGINIA

Alexandria

Annapolis

MARYLAND

Kansas City
Independence

Charleston

VIRGINIA

Chesapeake Bay

Jefferson ★
City

St. Louis

Louisville

Frankfort

Lynchburg Richmond

Newport News
Hampton

Evansville

Lexington
Fayette

Roanoke

Portsmouth Norfolk
Chesapeake

ATLANTIC
OCEAN

MISSOURI

KENTUCKY

Springfield

Durham

Greensboro Raleigh

Cape Hatteras

Nashville/
Davidson

Knoxville NORTH CAROLINA

ARKANSAS

TENNESSEE

Charlotte

Chattanooga

Wilmington

Fort
Smith

Memphis

Greenville

Columbia

Cape Fear

Huntsville

Myrtle Beach

Little
Rock

Atlanta

SOUTH
CAROLINA

Texarkana

Birmingham

Augusta

Monroe

MISSISSIPPI ALABAMA

Macon

Columbus

Charleston

Shreveport

Vicksburg
Jackson

Selma

Montgomery GEORGIA

Savannah

LOUISIANA

Albany

Jacksonville

Baton Rouge

Pensacola

Tallahassee St. Augustine

ont
iston
idena
Charles
alveston

Lake Lafayette
New Orleans

FLORIDA

Daytona Beach

Orlando

Cape
Canaveral

Tampa

St. Petersburg

Sarasota

*Lake
Okeechobee*

*Gulf of Mexico*

Fort Myers

Fort Myers

Fort
Lauderdale

Hollywood
Hialeah Miami

0        300 Miles
0    400 Kilometers    Key West

## The United States in 1996

★ National Capital

★ State Capitals

URBAN POPULATION CENTERS

▪ Over 5,000,000

▪ 3,000,000–5,000,000

● 1,000,000–3,000,000

□ 500,000–1,000,000

○ 100,000–500,000

· Less than 100,000
(selected)

# United States Territorial Expansion, 1783–1898

(1859) Date of statehood

The United States in 1783

Louisiana Purchase, 1803

—— 1819 Treaty with Spain defined border of Oregon and Louisiana

West Florida annexation, 1810, 1813

Florida: East Florida cession by Spain, 1819;

Texas Annexation, 1845

- - - Texas boundary claimed by U.S., 1845–1848

Oregon Country, 1846

Mexican Cession, 1848

Gadsden Purchase 1853

Alaska Purchase 1867

Hawaii Annexation, 189

ARCTIC OCEAN

GREENLAND
(Denmark)

ALASKA
(1959)
Purchased from Russia
1867

CANADA

United States claim
ceded to Britain 1846

Ceded by Britain 1818

Disputed by United States
and Britain 1783–1842

PACIFIC OCEAN

WASH.
(1889)

British claim
ceded 1846

ORE.
(1859)

IDAHO
(1890)

MONT.
(1889)

WYO.
(1890)

N.D.
(1889)

S.D.
(1889)

NEB.
(1867)

MINN.
(1858)

IOWA
(1846)

WIS.
(1848)

ILL.
(1818)

IND.
(1816)

MICH.
(1837)

OHIO
(1803)

PA.
(1787)

N.Y.
(1788)

VT.
(1791)

ME.
(1820)

N.H. (1788)

MASS. (1788)

R.I. (1790)

CONN. (1788)

N.J. (1787)

DEL. (1787)

MD. (1788)

W.VA.
(1863)

VA.
(1788)

NEV.
(1864)

UTAH
(1896)

COLO.
(1876)

KAN.
(1861)

MO.
(1821)

KY.
(1792)

CALIF.
(1850)

ARIZ.
(1912)

N.M.
(1912)

OKLA.
(1907)

ARK.
(1836)

TENN.
(1796)

N.C.
(1789)

S.C.
(1788)

MISS.
(1817)

ALA.
(1819)

GA.
(1788)

LA.
(1812)

TEXAS
(1845)

ATLANTIC OCEA

Annexed 1813

Annexed 1810

MEXICO

Gulf of Mexico

BAHAMAS

PUERTO RIC
(1898)

CUBA

0        400 Miles
0        400 Kilometers

HAWAII
(1959)

PACIFIC
OCEAN

HAWAIIAN ISLANDS
Annexed 1898

A–4

# Documents and Tables

## THE DECLARATION OF INDEPENDENCE

*In Congress, July 4, 1776,*

THE UNANIMOUS DECLARATION OF THE THIRTEEN UNITED STATES OF AMERICA

When, in the course of human events, it becomes necessary for one people to dissolve the political bands which have connected them with another, and to assume, among the powers of the earth, the separate and equal station to which the laws of nature and of nature's God entitle them, a decent respect to the opinions of mankind requires that they should declare the causes which impel them to the separation.

We hold these truths to be self-evident, that all men are created equal; that they are endowed by their Creator with certain unalienable rights; that among these, are life, liberty, and the pursuit of happiness. That, to secure these rights, governments are instituted among men, deriving their just powers from the consent of the governed; that, whenever any form of government becomes destructive of these ends, it is the right of the people to alter or to abolish it, and to institute a new government, laying its foundation on such principles, and organizing its powers in such form, as to them shall seem most likely to effect their safety and happiness. Prudence, indeed, will dictate that governments long established, should not be changed for light and transient causes; and, accordingly, all experience hath shown, that mankind are more disposed to suffer, while evils are sufferable, than to right themselves by abolishing the forms to which they are accustomed. But, when a long train of abuses and usurpations, pursuing invariably the same object, evinces a design to reduce them under absolute despotism, it is their right, it is their duty, to throw off such government and to provide new guards for their future security. Such has been the patient sufferance of these colonies, and such is now the necessity which constrains them to alter their former systems of government. The history of the present King of Great Britain is a history of repeated injuries and usurpations, all having, in direct object, the establishment of an absolute tyranny over these States. To prove this, let facts be submitted to a candid world:

He has refused his assent to laws the most wholesome and necessary for the public good.

He has forbidden his governors to pass laws of immediate and pressing importance, unless suspended in their operation till his assent should be obtained; and, when so suspended, he has utterly neglected to attend to them.

He has refused to pass other laws for the accommodation of large districts of people, unless those people would relinquish the right of representation in the legislature; a right inestimable to them, and formidable to tyrants only.

He has called together legislative bodies at places unusual, uncomfortable, and distant from the depository of their public records, for the sole purpose of fatiguing them into compliance with his measures.

He has dissolved representative houses repeatedly for opposing, with manly firmness, his invasions on the rights of the people.

He has refused, for a long time after such dissolutions, to cause others to be elected; whereby the legislative powers, incapable of annihilation, have returned to the people at large for their exercise; the state remaining, in the meantime, exposed to all the danger of invasion from without, and convulsions within.

He has endeavored to prevent the population of these States; for that purpose, obstructing the laws for naturalization of foreigners, refusing to pass others to encourage their migration hither, and raising the conditions of new appropriations of lands.

He has obstructed the administration of justice, by refusing his assent to laws for establishing judiciary powers.

He has made judges dependent on his will alone, for the tenure of their offices, and the amount and payment of their salaries.

He has erected a multitude of new offices, and sent hither swarms of officers to harass our people, and eat out their substance.

He has kept among us, in time of peace, standing armies, without the consent of our legislatures.

He has affected to render the military independent of, and superior to, the civil power.

He has combined, with others, to subject us to a jurisdiction foreign to our Constitution, and unacknowledged by our laws; giving his assent to their acts of pretended legislation:

For quartering large bodies of armed troops among us:

For protecting them by a mock trial, from punishment, for any murders which they should commit on the inhabitants of these States:

For cutting off our trade with all parts of the world:

For imposing taxes on us without our consent:

For depriving us, in many cases, of the benefit of trial by jury:

For transporting us beyond seas to be tried for pretended offences:

For abolishing the free system of English laws in a neighboring province, establishing therein an arbitrary government, and enlarging its boundaries, so as to render it at once an example and fit instrument for introducing the same absolute rule into these colonies:

For taking away our charters, abolishing our most valuable laws, and altering, fundamentally, the powers of our governments:

For suspending our own legislatures, and declaring themselves invested with power to legislate for us in all cases whatsoever.

He has abdicated government here, by declaring us out of his protection, and waging war against us.

He has plundered our seas, ravaged our coasts, burnt our towns, and destroyed the lives of our people.

He is, at this time, transporting large armies of foreign mercenaries to complete the works of death, desolation, and tyranny, already begun, with circumstances of cruelty and perfidy scarcely paralleled in the most barbarous ages, and totally unworthy the head of a civilized nation.

He has constrained our fellow citizens, taken captive on the high seas, to bear arms against their country, to become the executioners of their friends, and brethren, or to fall themselves by their hands.

He has excited domestic insurrections amongst us, and has endeavored to bring on the inhabitants of our frontiers, the merciless Indian savages, whose known rule of warfare is an undistinguished destruction of all ages, sexes, and conditions.

In every stage of these oppressions, we have petitioned for redress, in the most humble terms; our repeated petitions have been answered only by repeated injury. A prince, whose character is thus marked by every act which may define a tyrant, is unfit to be the ruler of a free people.

Nor have we been wanting in attention to our British brethren. We have warned them, from time to time, of attempts made by their legislature to extend an unwarrantable jurisdiction over us. We have reminded them of the circumstances of our emigration and settlement here. We have appealed to their native justice and magnanimity, and we have conjured them, by the ties of our common kindred, to disavow these usurpations, which would inevitably interrupt our connections and correspondence. They, too, have been deaf to the voice of justice and consanguinity. We must, therefore, acquiesce in the necessity which denounces our separation, and hold them as we hold the rest of mankind, enemies in war, in peace, friends.

We, therefore, the representatives of the United States of America, in general Congress assembled, appealing to the Supreme Judge of the world for the rectitude of our intentions, do, in the name, and by the authority of the good people of these colonies, solemnly publish and declare, that these united colonies are, and of right ought to be, free and independent states: that they are absolved from all allegiance to the British Crown, and that all political connection between them and the state of Great Britain is, and ought to be, totally dissolved; and that, as free and independent states, they have full power to levy war, conclude peace, contract alliances, establish commerce, and to do all other acts and things which independent states may of right do. And, for the support of this declaration, with a firm reliance on the protection of Divine Providence, we mutually pledge to each other our lives, our fortunes, and our sacred honor.

The foregoing Declaration was, by order of Congress, engrossed, and signed by the following members:

John Hancock

| *New Hampshire* | *Massachusetts Bay* | *Rhode Island* |
|---|---|---|
| Josiah Bartlett | Samuel Adams | Stephen Hopkins |
| William Whipple | John Adams | William Ellery |
| Matthew Thornton | Robert Treat Paine | |
| | Elbridge Gerry | |

**Connecticut**
Roger Sherman
Samuel Huntington
William Williams
Oliver Wolcott

**New York**
William Floyd
Philip Livingston
Francis Lewis
Lewis Morris

**New Jersey**
Richard Stockton
John Witherspoon
Francis Hopkinson
John Hart
Abraham Clark

**Pennsylvania**
Robert Morris
Benjamin Rush
Benjamin Franklin
John Morton
George Clymer
James Smith
George Taylor
James Wilson
George Ross

**Delaware**
Caesar Rodney
George Read
Thomas M'Kean

**Maryland**
Samuel Chase
William Paca
Thomas Stone
Charles Carroll,
     of Carrollton

**Virginia**
George Wythe
Richard Henry Lee
Thomas Jefferson
Benjamin Harrison
Thomas Nelson, Jr.
Francis Lightfoot Lee
Carter Braxton

**North Carolina**
William Hooper
Joseph Hewes
John Penn

**South Carolina**
Edward Rutledge
Thomas Heyward, Jr.
Thomas Lynch, Jr.
Arthur Middleton

**Georgia**
Button Gwinnett
Lyman Hall
George Walton

*Resolved*, That copies of the Declaration be sent to the several assemblies, conventions, and committees, or councils of safety, and to the several commanding officers of the continental troops; that it be proclaimed in each of the United States, at the head of the army.

# THE CONSTITUTION OF THE UNITED STATES[1]

We the People of the United States, in Order to form a more perfect Union, establish Justice, insure domestic Tranquility, provide for the common defence, promote the general Welfare, and secure the Blessings of Liberty to ourselves and our Posterity, do ordain and establish this CONSTITUTION for the United States of America.

## Article I

*Section 1.*
All legislative Powers herein granted shall be vested in a Congress of the United States, which shall consist of a Senate and House of Representatives.

*Section 2.*
The House of Representatives shall be composed of Members chosen every second Year by the People of the several States, and the Electors in each State shall have the Qualifications requisite for Electors of the most numerous Branch of the State Legislature.

No Person shall be a Representative who shall not have attained to the Age of twenty-five Years, and been seven Years a Citizen of the United States, and who shall not, when elected, be an Inhabitant of that State in which he shall be chosen.

[Representatives and direct Taxes[2] shall be apportioned among the several States which may be included within this Union, according to their respective Numbers, which shall be determined by adding to the whole Number of free Persons, including those bound to Service for a Term of Years, and excluding Indians not taxed, three fifths of all other Persons.][3] The actual Enumeration shall be made within three Years after the first Meeting of the Congress of the United States, and within every subsequent Term of ten Years, in such Manner as they shall by Law direct. The Number of Representatives shall not exceed one for every thirty Thousand, but each State shall have at Least one Representative; and until such enumeration shall be made, the State of New Hampshire shall be entitled to chuse three, Massachusetts eight, Rhode-Island and Providence Plantations one, Connecticut five, New York six, New Jersey four, Pennsylvania eight, Delaware one,

---

[1] This version, which follows the original Constitution in capitalization and spelling, was published by the United States Department of the Interior, Office of Education, in 1935.
[2] Altered by the Sixteenth Amendment.
[3] Negated by the Fourteenth Amendment.

Maryland six, Virginia ten, North Carolina five, South Carolina five, and Georgia three.

When vacancies happen in the Representation from any State, the Executive Authority thereof shall issue Writs of Election to fill such Vacancies.

The House of Representatives shall chuse their Speaker and other Officers; and shall have the sole Power of Impeachment.

*Section 3.*

The Senate of the United States shall be composed of two Senators from each State, chosen by the Legislature thereof, for six Years; and each Senator shall have one Vote.

Immediately after they shall be assembled in Consequence of the first Election, they shall be divided as equally as may be into three Classes. The Seats of the Senators of the first Class shall be vacated at the Expiration of the second Year, of the second Class at the Expiration of the fourth Year, and of the third Class at the Expiration of the sixth Year, so that one-third may be chosen every second Year; and if Vacancies happen by Resignation, or otherwise, during the Recess of the Legislature of any State, the Executive thereof may make temporary Appointments until the next Meeting of the Legislature, which shall then fill such Vacancies.

No Person shall be a Senator who shall not have attained to the Age of thirty Years, and been nine Years a Citizen of the United States, and who shall not, when elected, be an Inhabitant of that State for which he shall be chosen.

The Vice President of the United States shall be President of the Senate, but shall have no vote, unless they be equally divided.

The Senate shall chuse their other Officers, and also a President pro tempore, in the absence of the Vice President, or when he shall exercise the Office of President of the United States.

The Senate shall have the sole Power to try all Impeachments. When sitting for that purpose they shall be on Oath or Affirmation. When the President of the United States is tried, the Chief Justice shall preside: And no person shall be convicted without the Concurrence of two thirds of the Members present.

Judgment in Cases of Impeachment shall not extend further than to removal from Office, and disqualification to hold and enjoy any Office of honor, Trust, or Profit under the United States: but the Party convicted shall nevertheless be liable and subject to Indictment, Trial, Judgment, and Punishment, according to Law.

*Section 4.*

The Times, Places and Manner of holding Elections for Senators and Representatives, shall be prescribed in each State by the Legislature thereof; but the Congress may at any time by Law make or alter such Regulations, except as to the Places of Chusing Senators.

The Congress shall assemble at least once in every Year, and such Meeting shall be on the first Monday in December, unless they shall by Law appoint a different Day.

*Section 5.*
Each House shall be the Judge of the Elections, Returns and Qualifications of its own Members, and a Majority of each shall constitute a Quorum to do Business; but a smaller number may adjourn from day to day, and may be authorized to compel the Attendance of absent Members, in such Manner, and under such Penalties, as each House may provide.

Each House may determine the Rules of its Proceedings, punish its Members for disorderly Behaviour, and, with the Concurrence of two thirds, expel a Member.

Each House shall keep a Journal of its Proceedings, and from time to time publish the same, excepting such Parts as may in their Judgment require Secrecy; and the Yeas and Nays of the Members of either House on any question shall, at the Desire of one fifth of those Present, be entered on the Journal.

Neither House, during the Session of Congress, shall, without the Consent of the other, adjourn for more than three days, nor to any other Place than that in which the two Houses shall be sitting.

*Section 6.*
The Senators and Representatives shall receive a Compensation for their Services, to be ascertained by Law, and paid out of the Treasury of the United States. They shall in all Cases, except Treason, Felony, and Breach of the Peace, be privileged from Arrest during their Attendance at the Session of their respective Houses, and in going to and returning from the same; and for any Speech or Debate in either House, they shall not be questioned in any other Place.

No Senator or Representative shall, during the Time for which he was elected, be appointed to any civil Office under the Authority of the United States, which shall have been created, or the Emoluments whereof shall have been increased, during such time; and no Person holding any Office under the United States shall be a Member of either House during his continuance in Office.

*Section 7.*
All Bills for raising Revenue shall originate in the House of Representatives; but the Senate may propose or concur with Amendments as on other bills.

Every Bill which shall have passed the House of Representatives and the Senate, shall, before it become a Law, be presented to the President of the United States; If he approve he shall sign it, but if not he shall return it, with his Objections, to that House in which it shall have originated, who shall enter the Objections at large on their Journal, and proceed to reconsider it. If after such Reconsideration two thirds of that House shall agree to pass the bill, it shall be sent, together with the objections, to the other House, by which it shall likewise be reconsidered, and if approved by two thirds of that House, it shall become a Law. But in all such Cases the Votes of both Houses shall be determined by Yeas and Nays, and the Names of the Persons voting for and against the Bill shall be entered on the Journal of each House respectively. If any Bill shall not be returned by the President within ten Days (Sundays excepted) after it shall have been presented to him, the Same shall be a Law, in like Manner as if he had signed it, unless the Congress by their Adjournment prevent its Return, in which Case it shall not be a Law.

Every Order, Resolution, or Vote to which the Concurrence of the Senate and House of Representatives may be necessary (except on a question of Adjournment) shall be presented to the President of the United States; and before the Same shall take Effect, shall be approved by him, or being disapproved by him, shall be repassed by two thirds of the Senate and House of Representatives, according to the Rules and Limitations prescribed in the Case of a Bill.

*Section 8.*

The Congress shall have Power To lay and collect Taxes, Duties, Imposts and Excises, to pay the Debts and provide for the common Defence and general Welfare of the United States; but all Duties, Imposts and Excises shall be uniform throughout the United States;

To borrow money on the credit of the United States;

To regulate Commerce with foreign Nations, and among the several States, and with the Indian Tribes;

To establish an uniform rule of Naturalization, and uniform Laws on the subject of Bankruptcies throughout the United States;

To coin Money, regulate the Value thereof, and of foreign Coin, and fix the Standard of Weights and Measures;

To provide for the Punishment of counterfeiting the Securities and current Coin of the United States;

To establish Post Offices and post Roads;

To promote the Progress of Science and useful Arts, by securing for limited Times to Authors and Inventors the exclusive Right to their respective Writings and Discoveries;

To constitute Tribunals inferior to the Supreme Court;

To define and punish Piracies and Felonies committed on the high Seas, and Offenses against the Law of Nations;

To declare War, grant Letters of Marque and Reprisal, and make Rules concerning Captures on Land and Water;

To raise and support Armies, but no Appropriation of Money to that Use shall be for a longer Term than two Years;

To provide and maintain a Navy;

To make Rules for the Government and Regulation of the land and naval forces;

To provide for calling forth the Militia to execute the Laws of the Union, suppress Insurrections and repel Invasions;

To provide for organizing, arming, and disciplining the Militia, and for governing such Part of them as may be employed in the Service of the United States, reserving to the States respectively, the Appointment of the Officers, and the Authority of training the Militia according to the discipline prescribed by Congress;

To exercise exclusive Legislation in all Cases whatsoever, over such District (not exceeding ten Miles square) as may, by Cession of particular States, and the acceptance of Congress, become the Seat of the Government of the United States, and to exercise like Authority over all Places purchased by the Consent of the Legislature of the State in which the Same shall be, for the Erection of Forts, Magazines, Arsenals, Dock-yards, and other needful Buildings;—And

To make all Laws which shall be necessary and proper for carrying into Execution the foregoing Powers, and all other Powers vested by this Constitution in the Government of the United States, or in any Department or Officer thereof.

*Section 9.*

The Migration or Importation of such Persons as any of the States now existing shall think proper to admit, shall not be prohibited by the Congress prior to the Year one thousand eight hundred and eight, but a tax or duty may be imposed on such Importation, not exceeding ten dollars for each Person.

The privilege of the Writ of Habeas Corpus shall not be suspended, unless when in Cases of Rebellion or Invasion the public Safety may require it.

No bill of Attainder or ex post facto Law shall be passed.

No capitation, or other direct, Tax shall be laid unless in Proportion to the Census or Enumeration herein before directed to be taken.

No Tax or Duty shall be laid on Articles exported from any State.

No Preference shall be given by any Regulation of Commerce or Revenue to the Ports of one State over those of another: nor shall Vessels bound to, or from, one State, be obliged to enter, clear, or pay Duties in another.

No Money shall be drawn from the Treasury, but in Consequence of Appropriations made by Law; and a regular Statement and Account of the Receipts and Expenditures of all public Money shall be published from time to time.

No Title of Nobility shall be granted by the United States: And no Person holding any Office of Profit or Trust under them, shall, without the Consent of the Congress, accept of any present, Emolument, Office, or Title, of any kind whatever, from any King, Prince, or foreign State.

*Section 10.*

No State shall enter into any Treaty, Alliance, or Confederation; grant Letters of Marque and Reprisal; coin Money; emit Bills of Credit; make any Thing but gold and silver Coin a Tender in Payment of Debts; pass any Bill of Attainder, ex post facto Law, or Law impairing the Obligation of Contracts, or grant any Title of Nobility.

No State shall, without the Consent of the Congress, lay any Imposts or Duties on Imports or Exports, except what may be absolutely necessary for executing its inspection Laws; and the net Produce of all Duties and Imposts, laid by any State on Imports or Exports, shall be for the use of the Treasury of the United States; and all such Laws shall be subject to the Revision and Control of the Congress.

No state shall, without the Consent of Congress, lay any duty of Tonnage, keep Troops, or Ships of War in time of Peace, enter into any Agreement or Compact with another State, or with a foreign Power, or engage in War, unless actually invaded, or in such imminent Danger as will not admit of delay.

# Article II

*Section 1.*

The executive Power shall be vested in a President of the United States of America. He shall hold his Office during the Term of four years, and, together with the Vice President, chosen for the same Term, be elected, as follows:

Each State shall appoint, in such Manner as the Legislature thereof may direct, a Number of Electors, equal to the whole Number of Senators and Representatives to which the State may be entitled in the Congress: but no Senator or Representative, or Person holding an Office of Trust or Profit under the United States, shall be appointed an Elector.

[The Electors shall meet in their respective States, and vote by Ballot for two persons, of whom one at least shall not be an Inhabitant of the same State with themselves. And they shall make a List of all the Persons voted for, and of the Number of Votes for each; which List they shall sign and certify, and transmit sealed to the Seat of the Government of the United States, directed to the President of the Senate. The President of the Senate shall, in the Presence of the Senate and House of Representatives, open all the Certificates, and the Votes shall then be counted. The Person having the greatest Number of Votes shall be the President, if such Number be a Majority of the whole Number of Electors appointed; and if there be more than one who have such Majority, and have an equal Number of Votes, then the House of Representatives shall immediately chuse by Ballot one of them for President; and if no Person have a Majority, then from the five highest on the List the said House shall in like Manner chuse the President. But in chusing the President, the Votes shall be taken by States, the Representation from each State having one Vote; a quorum for this Purpose shall consist of a Member or Members from two-thirds of the States, and a Majority of all the States shall be necessary to a Choice. In every Case, after the Choice of the President, the Person having the greatest Number of Votes of the Electors shall be the Vice President. But if there should remain two or more who have equal votes, the Senate shall chuse from them by Ballot the Vice President.]⁴

The Congress may determine the Time of chusing the Electors, and the Day on which they shall give their Votes; which Day shall be the same throughout the United States.

No person except a natural-born Citizen, or a Citizen of the United States, at the time of the Adoption of this Constitution, shall be eligible to the Office of President; neither shall any Person be eligible to that Office who shall not have attained

---

⁴ Revised by the Twelfth Amendment.

to the Age of thirty-five years, and been fourteen Years a Resident within the United States.

In Case of the Removal of the President from Office, or of his Death, Resignation, or Inability to discharge the Powers and Duties of the said Office, the same shall devolve on the Vice President, and the Congress may by Law provide for the Case of Removal, Death, Resignation, or Inability, both of the President and Vice President, declaring what Officer shall then act as President, and such Officer shall act accordingly, until the disability be removed, or a President shall be elected.

The President shall, at stated Times, receive for his Services a Compensation, which shall neither be increased nor diminished during the Period for which he shall have been elected, and he shall not receive within that Period any other Emolument from the United States, or any of them.

Before he enter on the execution of his Office, he shall take the following Oath or Affirmation:—"I do solemnly swear (or affirm) that I will faithfully execute the Office of President of the United States, and will, to the best of my Ability, preserve, protect, and defend the Constitution of the United States."

*Section 2.*
The President shall be Commander in Chief of the Army and Navy of the United States, and of the Militia of the several States, when called into the actual Service of the United States; he may require the Opinion, in writing, of the principal Officer in each of the executive Departments, upon any subject relating to the Duties of their respective Offices, and he shall have Power to Grant Reprieves and Pardons for Offenses against the United States, except in Cases of Impeachment.

He shall have Power, by and with the Advice and Consent of the Senate, to make Treaties, provided two-thirds of the Senators present concur; and he shall nominate, and by and with the Advice and Consent of the Senate, shall appoint Ambassadors, other public Ministers and Consuls, Judges of the supreme Court, and all other Officers of the United States, whose Appointments are not herein otherwise provided for, and which shall be established by Law: but the Congress may by Law vest the Appointment of such inferior Officers, as they think proper, in the President alone, in the Courts of Law, or in the Heads of Departments.

The President shall have Power to fill up all Vacancies that may happen during the Recess of the Senate, by granting Commissions which shall expire at the End of their next Session.

*Section 3.*
He shall from time to time give to the Congress Information of the State of the Union, and recommend to their Consideration such Measures as he shall judge necessary and expedient; he may, on extraordinary occasions, convene both Houses, or either of them, and in Case of Disagreement between them, with respect to the Time of Adjournment, he may adjourn them to such Time as he shall think proper; he shall receive Ambassadors and other public Ministers; he shall take care that the Laws be faithfully executed, and shall Commission all the Officers of the United States.

*Section 4.*
The President, Vice President and all civil Officers of the United States, shall be removed from Office on Impeachment for, and Conviction of, Treason, Bribery, or other high Crimes and Misdemeanors.

# Article III

*Section 1.*
The judicial Power of the United States, shall be vested in one supreme Court, and in such inferior Courts as the Congress may from time to time ordain and establish. The Judges, both of the supreme and inferior Courts, shall hold their Offices during good Behaviour, and shall, at stated Times, receive for their Services, a Compensation, which shall not be diminished during their Continuance in Office.

*Section 2.*
The judicial Power shall extend to all Cases, in Law and Equity, arising under this Constitution, the Laws of the United States, and Treaties made, or which shall be made, under their Authority;—to all Cases affecting ambassadors, other public ministers and consuls;—to all cases of admiralty and maritime Jurisdiction;—to Controversies to which the United States shall be a Party;—to Controversies between two or more States;—between a State and Citizens of another State;[5]—between Citizens of different States—between Citizens of the same State claiming Lands under Grants of different States, and between a State, or the Citizens thereof, and foreign States, Citizens, or Subjects.

In all Cases affecting Ambassadors, other public Ministers and Consuls, and those in which a State shall be Party, the supreme Court shall have original Jurisdiction. In all the other Cases before mentioned, the supreme Court shall have appellate Jurisdiction, both as to Law and Fact, with such Exceptions, and under such Regulations as the Congress shall make.

The trial of all Crimes, except in Cases of Impeachment, shall be by Jury; and such Trial shall be held in the State where the said Crimes shall have been committed; but when not committed within any State, the Trial shall be at such Place or Places as the Congress may by Law have directed.

*Section 3.*
Treason against the United States, shall consist only in levying War against them, or in adhering to their Enemies, giving them Aid and Comfort. No Person shall be convicted of Treason unless on the Testimony of two Witnesses to the same overt Act, or on Confession in open Court.

The Congress shall have power to declare the Punishment of Treason, but no Attainder of Treason shall work Corruption of Blood, or Forfeiture except during the Life of the Person attained.

---

[5] Qualified by the Eleventh Amendment.

# Article IV

*Section 1.*
Full Faith and Credit shall be given in each State to the public Acts, Records, and judicial Proceedings of every other State. And the Congress may by general Laws prescribe the Manner in which such Acts, Records and Proceedings shall be proved, and the Effect thereof.

*Section 2.*
The Citizens of each State shall be entitled to all Privileges and Immunities of Citizens in the several States.

A Person charged in any State with Treason, Felony, or other Crime, who shall flee from Justice, and be found in another State, shall on demand of the executive Authority of the State from which he fled, be delivered up, to be removed to the State having Jurisdiction of the crime.

No Person held to Service or Labour in one State, under the Laws thereof, escaping into another, shall, in Consequence of any Law or Regulation therein, be discharged from such Service or Labour, but shall be delivered up on Claim of the Party to whom such Service or Labour may be due.

*Section 3.*
New States may be admitted by the Congress into this Union; but no new State shall be formed or erected within the Jurisdiction of any other State; nor any State be formed by the Junction of two or more States, or parts of States, without the Consent of the Legislatures of the States concerned as well as of the Congress.

The Congress shall have Power to dispose of and make all needful Rules and Regulations respecting the Territory or other Property belonging to the United States; and nothing in this Constitution shall be so construed as to Prejudice any Claims of the United States, or of any particular State.

*Section 4.*
The United States shall guarantee to every State in this Union a Republican Form of Government, and shall protect each of them against Invasion; and on Application of the Legislature, or of the Executive (when the Legislature cannot be convened) against domestic Violence.

# Article V

The Congress, whenever two-thirds of both Houses shall deem it necessary, shall propose Amendments to this Constitution, or, on the Application of the Legislatures of two-thirds of the several States, shall call a Convention for proposing Amendments, which, in either Case, shall be valid to all Intents and Purposes, as part of this Constitution, when ratified by the Legislatures of three-fourths of the several States, or by Conventions in three-fourths thereof, as the one or the other Mode of Ratification may be proposed by the Congress; Provided that no Amendment which may be made prior to the Year One thousand eight hundred and eight shall in any Manner affect the first and fourth Clauses in the Ninth Section of the first Article; and that no State, without its Consent, shall be deprived of its equal Suffrage in the Senate.

## Article VI

All Debts contracted and Engagements entered into, before the Adoption of this Constitution, shall be as valid against the United States under this Constitution, as under the Confederation.

This Constitution, and the Laws of the United States which shall be made in Pursuance thereof; and all Treaties made, or which shall be made, under the Authority of the United States, shall be the supreme Law of the Land; and the Judges in every State shall be bound thereby, any Thing in the Constitution or Laws of any State to the Contrary notwithstanding.

The Senators and Representatives before mentioned, and the Members of the several State Legislatures, and all executive and judicial Officers, both of the United States and of the several States, shall be bound by Oath or Affirmation to support this Constitution; but no religious Tests shall ever be required as a qualification to any Office or public Trust under the United States.

## Article VII

The Ratification of the Conventions of nine States shall be sufficient for the Establishment of this Constitution between the States so ratifying the same.

Done in Convention by the Unanimous Consent of the States present the Seventeenth Day of September in the Year of our Lord one thousand seven hundred and Eighty seven, and of the Independence of the United States of America the Twelfth. In Witness whereof We have hereunto subscribed our Names.[6]

George Washington
*President and deputy and deputy from Virginia*

| *New Hampshire* | *Pennsylvania* | *Virginia* |
|---|---|---|
| John Langdon | Benjamin Franklin | John Blair |
| Nicholas Gilman | Thomas Mifflin | James Madison, Jr. |
| | Robert Morris | |
| *Massachusetts* | George Clymer | *North Carolina* |
| Nathaniel Gorham | Thomas FitzSimons | William Blount |
| Rufus King | Jared Ingersoll | Richard Dobbs |
| | James Wilson | Spaight |
| | Gouverneur Morris | Hugh Williamson |

[6] These are the full names of the signers, which in some cases are not the signatures on the document.

**Connecticut**
William Samuel Johnson
Roger Sherman

**New York**
Alexander Hamilton

**New Jersey**
William Livingston
David Brearley
William Paterson
Jonathan Dayton

**Delaware**
George Read
Gunning Bedford, Jr.
John Dickinson
Richard Bassett
Jacob Broom

**Maryland**
James McHenry
Daniel of
  St. Thomas Jenifer
Daniel Carroll

**South Carolina**
John Rutledge
Charles Cotesworth
  Pinckney
Charles Pinckney
Pierce Butler

**Georgia**
William Few
Abraham Baldwin

Articles in Addition to, and Amendment of, the Constitution of the United States of America, Proposed by Congress, and Ratified by the Legislatures of the Several States, Pursuant to the Fifth Article of the Original Constitution.[7]

# [Article I]

Congress shall make no law respecting an establishment of religion, or prohibiting the free exercise thereof; or abridging the freedom of speech, or of the press; or the right of the people peaceably to assemble, and to petition the Government for a redress of grievances.

# [Article II]

A well regulated Militia, being necessary to the security of a free State, the right of the people to keep and bear Arms shall not be infringed.

# [Article III]

No Soldier shall, in time of peace, be quartered in any house, without the consent of the Owner, nor in time of war, but in a manner to be prescribed by law.

# [Article IV]

The right of the people to be secure in their persons, houses, papers, and effects, against unreasonable searches and seizures, shall not be violated, and no Warrants shall issue, but upon probable cause, supported by Oath or affirmation, and

---

[7] This heading appears only in the joint resolution submitting the first ten amendments.

particularly describing the place to be searched, and the persons or things to be seized.

# [Article V]

No person shall be held to answer for a capital or otherwise infamous crime, unless on a presentment or indictment of a Grand Jury, except in cases arising in the land or naval forces, or in the Militia, when in actual service in time of War or public danger; nor shall any person be subject for the same offence to be twice put in jeopardy of life or limb; nor shall be compelled in any criminal case to be a witness against himself, nor be deprived of life, liberty, or property, without due process of law; nor shall private property be taken for public use, without just compensation.

# [Article VI]

In all criminal prosecutions, the accused shall enjoy the right to a speedy and public trial, by an impartial jury of the State and district wherein the crime shall have been committed, which district shall have been previously ascertained by law, and to be informed of the nature and cause of the accusation; to be confronted with the witnesses against him; to have compulsory process for obtaining witnesses in his favour, and to have the Assistance of Counsel for his defense.

# [Article VII]

In suits at common law, where the value in controversy shall exceed twenty dollars, the right of trial by jury shall be preserved, and no fact tried by a jury, shall be otherwise reexamined in any Court of the United States, than according to the rules of the common law.

# [Article VIII]

Excessive bail shall not be required, nor excessive fines imposed, nor cruel and unusual punishments inflicted.

# [Article IX]

The enumeration of the Constitution, of certain rights, shall not be construed to deny or disparage others retained by the people.

# [Article X]

The powers not delegated to the United States by the Constitution, nor prohibited by it to the States, are reserved to the States respectively, or to the people. [Amendments I–X, in force 1791.]

# [Article XI][8]

The Judicial power of the United States shall not be construed to extend to any suit in law or equity, commenced or prosecuted against one of the United States by Citizens of another State, or by Citizens or Subjects of any Foreign State.

# [Article XII][9]

The Electors shall meet in their respective States and vote by ballot for President and Vice-President, one of whom, at least, shall not be an inhabitant of the same State with themselves; they shall name in their ballots the person voted for as President, and in distinct ballots the person voted for as Vice-President, and they shall make distinct lists of all persons voted for as President, and of all persons voted for as Vice-President, and of the number of votes for each, which lists they shall sign and certify, and transmit sealed to the seat of the government of the United States, directed to the President of the Senate;—The President of the Senate shall, in the presence of the Senate and House of Representatives, open all the certificates and the votes shall then be counted;—The person having the greatest number of votes for President, shall be the President, if such number be a majority of the whole number of Electors appointed; and if no person have such majority, then from the persons having the highest numbers not exceeding three on the list of those voted for as President, the House of Representatives shall choose immediately, by ballot, the President. But in choosing the President, the votes shall be taken by states, the representation from each state having one vote; a quorum for this purpose shall consist of a member or members from two-thirds of the states, and a majority of all the states shall be necessary to a choice. And if the House of Representatives shall not choose a President whenever the right of choice shall devolve upon them, before the fourth day of March next following, then the Vice-President shall act as President, as in the case of the death or other constitutional disability of the President.—The person having the greatest number of votes as Vice-President, shall be the Vice-President, if such number be a majority of the whole number of Electors appointed, and if no person have a majority, then from the two highest numbers on the list, the Senate shall choose the Vice-President; a quorum for the purpose shall consist of two-thirds of the whole number of Senators, and a majority of the whole number shall be necessary to a choice. But no person constitutionally in-

---

[8] Adopted in 1798.
[9] Adopted in 1804.

eligible to the office of President shall be eligible to that of Vice-President of the United States.

# [Article XIII][10]

*Section 1.*
Neither slavery nor involuntary servitude, except as a punishment for crime whereof the party shall have been duly convicted, shall exist within the United States, or any place subject to their jurisdiction.

*Section 2.*
Congress shall have power to enforce this article by appropriate legislation.

# [Article XIV][11]

*Section 1.*
All persons born or naturalized in the United States, and subject to the jurisdiction thereof, are citizens of the United States and of the State wherein they reside. No State shall make or enforce any law which shall abridge the privileges or immunities of citizens of the United States; nor shall any State deprive any person of life, liberty, or property, without due process of law; nor deny to any person within its jurisdiction the equal protection of the laws.

*Section 2.*
Representatives shall be apportioned among the several States according to their respective numbers, counting the whole number of persons in each State, excluding Indians not taxed. But when the right to vote at any election for the choice of electors for President and Vice-President of the United States, Representatives in Congress, the Executive and Judicial officers of a State, or the members of the Legislature thereof, is denied to any of the male inhabitants of such State, being twenty-one years of age, and citizens of the United States, or in any way abridged, except for participation in rebellion, or other crime, the basis of representation therein shall be reduced in the proportion which the number of such male citizens shall bear to the whole number of male citizens twenty-one years of age in such State.

*Section 3.*
No person shall be a Senator or Representative in Congress, or elector of President and Vice-President, or hold any office, civil or military, under the United States, or under any State, who, having previously taken an oath, as a member of Congress, or as an officer of the United States, or as a member of any State legislature, or as

[10] Adopted in 1865.
[11] Adopted in 1868.

an executive or judicial officer of any State, to support the Constitution of the United States, shall have engaged in insurrection or rebellion against the same, or given aid or comfort to the enemies thereof. But Congress may by a vote of two-thirds of each House, remove such disability.

*Section 4.*
The validity of the public debt of the United States, authorized by law, including debts incurred for payment of pensions and bounties for services in suppressing insurrection or rebellion, shall not be questioned. But neither the United States nor any State shall assume or pay any debts or obligation incurred in aid of insurrection or rebellion against the United States, or any claim for the loss or emancipation of any slave; but all such debts, obligations, and claims shall be held illegal and void.

*Section 5.*
The Congress shall have the power to enforce, by appropriate legislation, the provisions of this article.

# [Article XV][12]

*Section 1.*
The right of citizens of the United States to vote shall not be denied or abridged by the United States or by any State on account of race, color, or previous condition of servitude—

*Section 2.*
The Congress shall have power to enforce this article by appropriate legislation.

# [Article XVI][13]

The Congress shall have power to lay and collect taxes on incomes, from whatever source derived, without apportionment among the several States, and without regard to any census or enumeration.

# [Article XVII][14]

The Senate of the United States shall be composed of two Senators from each State, elected by the people thereof, for six years; and each Senator shall have one vote. The electors in each State shall have the qualifications requisite for electors of the most numerous branch of the State legislatures.

[12] Adopted in 1870.
[13] Adopted in 1913.
[14] Adopted in 1913.

When vacancies happen in the representation of any State in the Senate, the executive authority of such State shall issue writs of election to fill such vacancies: *Provided,* That the legislature of any State may empower the executive thereof to make temporary appointments until the people fill the vacancies by election as the legislature may direct.

This amendment shall not be so construed as to affect the election or term of any Senator chosen before it becomes valid as part of the Constitution.

# [Article XVIII][15]

*Section 1.*
After one year from the ratification of this article the manufacture, sale, or transportation of intoxicating liquors within, the importation thereof into, or the exportation thereof from the United States and all territory subject to the jurisdiction thereof for beverage purposes is hereby prohibited.

*Section 2.*
The Congress and the several States shall have concurrent power to enforce this article by appropriate legislation.

*Section 3.*
This article shall be inoperative unless it shall have been ratified as an amendment to the Constitution by the legislatures of the several States, as provided in the Constitution, within seven years from the date of the submission hereof to the States by the Congress.

# [Article XIX][16]

The right of citizens of the United States to vote shall not be denied or abridged by the United States or by any State on account of sex.

Congress shall have power to enforce this article by appropriate legislation.

# [Article XX][17]

*Section 1.*
The terms of the President and Vice-President shall end at noon on the 20th day of January, and the terms of Senators and Representatives at noon on the 3d day of January, of the years in which such terms would have ended if this article had not been ratified; and the terms of their successors shall then begin.

[15] Adopted in 1918.
[16] Adopted in 1920.
[17] Adopted in 1933.

*Section 2.*
The Congress shall assemble at least once in every year, and such meeting shall begin at noon on the 3d day of January, unless they shall by law appoint a different day.

*Section 3.*
If, at the time fixed for the beginning of the term of the President, the President elect shall have died, the Vice-President elect shall become President. If a President shall not have been chosen before the time fixed for the beginning of his term or if the President elect shall have failed to qualify, then the Vice-President elect shall act as President until a President shall have qualified; and the Congress may by law provide for the case wherein neither a President elect nor a Vice-President elect shall have qualified, declaring who shall then act as President, or the manner in which one who is to act shall be selected, and such person shall act accordingly until a President or Vice-President shall have qualified.

*Section 4.*
The Congress may by law provide for the case of the death of any of the persons from whom the House of Representatives may choose a President whenever the right of choice shall have devolved upon them, and for the case of the death of any of the persons from whom the Senate may choose a Vice-President whenever the right of choice shall have devolved upon them.

*Section 5.*
Sections 1 and 2 shall take effect on the 15th day of October following the ratification of this article.

*Section 6.*
This article shall be inoperative unless it shall have been ratified as an amendment to the Constitution by the legislatures of three-fourths of the several States within seven years from the date of its submission.

# [Article XXI][18]

*Section 1.*
The eighteenth article of amendment to the Constitution of the United States is hereby repealed.

*Section 2.*
The transportation or importation into any State, Territory, or possession of the United States for delivery or use therein of intoxicating liquors, in violation of the laws thereof, is hereby prohibited.

[18] Adopted in 1933.

*Section 3.*
This article shall be inoperative unless it shall have been ratified as an amendment to the Constitution by conventions in the several States, as provided in the Constitution, within seven years from the date of the submission hereof to the States by the Congress.

# [Article XXII][19]

No person shall be elected to the office of the President more than twice, and no person who has held the office of President, or acted as President, for more than two years of a term to which some other person was elected President shall be elected to the office of the President more than once.

But this Article shall not apply to any person holding the office of President when this Article was proposed by the Congress, and shall not prevent any person who may be holding the office of President, or acting as President, during the term within which this Article becomes operative from holding the office of President or acting as President during the remainder of such term.

This article shall be inoperative unless it shall have been ratified as an amendment to the Constitution by the legislatures of three-fourths of the several states within seven years from the date of its submission to the states by the Congress.

# [Article XXIII][20]

*Section 1.*
The District constituting the seat of Government of the United States shall appoint in such manner as the Congress may direct:

A number of electors of President and Vice-President equal to the whole number of Senators and Representatives in Congress to which the District would be entitled if it were a State, but in no event more than the least populous State; they shall be in addition to those appointed by the States, but they shall be considered, for the purposes of the election of President and Vice-President, to be electors appointed by a State; and they shall meet in the District and perform such duties as provided by the twelfth article of amendment.

*Section 2.*
The Congress shall have power to enforce this article by appropriate legislation.

[19] Adopted in 1961.
[20] Adopted in 1961.

# [Article XXIV][21]

*Section 1.*
The right of citizens of the United States to vote in any primary or other election for President or Vice President, for electors for President or Vice President, or for Senator or Representative in Congress, shall not be denied or abridged by the United States or any state by reason of failure to pay any poll tax or other tax.

*Section 2.*
The Congress shall have the power to enforce this article by appropriate legislation.

# [Article XXV][22]

*Section 1.*
In case of the removal of the President from office or of his death or resignation, the Vice President shall become President.

*Section 2.*
Whenever there is a vacancy in the office of the Vice President, the President shall nominate a Vice President who shall take office upon confirmation by a majority vote of both Houses of Congress.

*Section 3.*
Whenever the President transmits to the President Pro Tempore of the Senate and the Speaker of the House of Representatives his written declaration that he is unable to discharge the powers and duties of his office, and until he transmits to them a written declaration to the contrary, such powers and duties shall be discharged by the Vice President as Acting President.

*Section 4.*
Whenever the Vice President and a majority of either the principal officers of the executive departments or of such other body as Congress may by law provide, transmit to the President Pro Tempore of the Senate and the Speaker of the House of Representatives their written declaration that the President is unable to discharge the powers and duties of his office, the Vice President shall immediately assume the powers and duties of the office as Acting President.

Thereafter, when the President transmits to the President Pro Tempore of the Senate and the Speaker of the House of Representatives his written declaration that no inability exists, he shall resume the powers and duties of his office unless the Vice President and a majority of either the principal officers of the executive departments or of such other body as Congress may by law provide, transmit within four days to

---

[21] Adopted in 1964.
[22] Adopted in 1967.

the President Pro Tempore of the Senate and the Speaker of the House of Representatives their written declaration that the President is unable to discharge the powers and duties of his office. Thereupon Congress shall decide the issue, assembling within forty-eight hours for that purpose if not in session. If the Congress, within twenty-one days after receipt of the latter written declaration, or, if Congress is not in session, within twenty-one days after Congress is required to assemble, determines by two-thirds vote of both Houses that the President is unable to discharge the powers and duties of his office, the Vice President shall continue to discharge the same as Acting President; otherwise, the President shall resume the powers and duties of his office.

# [Article XXVI][23]

*Section 1.*
The right of citizens of the United States, who are eighteen years of age or older, to vote shall not be denied or abridged by the United States or by any State on account of age.

*Section 2.*
The Congress shall have power to enforce this article by appropriate legislation.

# [Article XXVII][24]

No law varying the compensation for the services of the Senators and Representatives shall take effect until an election of Representatives shall have intervened.

[23] Adopted in 1971.
[24] Adopted in 1992.

# PRESIDENTIAL ELECTIONS

| Year | Candidates | Parties | Popular Vote | Percentage of Popular Vote | Electoral Vote | Percentage of Voter Participation |
|------|-----------|---------|--------------|----------------------------|----------------|-----------------------------------|
| 1789 | **GEORGE WASHINGTON (Va.)*** | | | | 69 | |
| | John Adams | | | | 34 | |
| | Others | | | | 35 | |
| 1792 | **GEORGE WASHINGTON (Va.)** | | | | 132 | |
| | John Adams | | | | 77 | |
| | George Clinton | | | | 50 | |
| | Others | | | | 5 | |
| 1796 | **JOHN ADAMS (Mass.)** | Federalist | | | 71 | |
| | Thomas Jefferson | Democratic-Republican | | | 68 | |
| | Thomas Pinckney | Federalist | | | 59 | |
| | Aaron Burr | Dem.-Rep. | | | 30 | |
| | Others | | | | 48 | |
| 1800 | **THOMAS JEFFERSON (Va.)** | Dem.-Rep. | | | 73 | |
| | Aaron Burr | Dem.-Rep. | | | 73 | |
| | John Adams | Federalist | | | 65 | |
| | C. C. Pinckney | Federalist | | | 64 | |
| | John Jay | Federalist | | | 1 | |
| 1804 | **THOMAS JEFFERSON (Va.)** | Dem.-Rep. | | | 162 | |
| | C. C. Pinckney | Federalist | | | 14 | |
| 1808 | **JAMES MADISON (Va.)** | Dem.-Rep. | | | 122 | |
| | C. C. Pinckney | Federalist | | | 47 | |
| | George Clinton | Dem.-Rep. | | | 6 | |

| Year | Candidate | Party | Popular Vote | % Popular Vote | Electoral Vote | % Voter Participation |
|---|---|---|---|---|---|---|
| 1812 | **JAMES MADISON (Va.)** | Dem.-Rep. | | | 128 | |
| | De Witt Clinton | Federalist | | | 89 | |
| 1816 | **JAMES MONROE (Va.)** | Dem.-Rep. | | | 183 | |
| | Rufus King | Federalist | | | 34 | |
| 1820 | **JAMES MONROE (Va.)** | Dem.-Rep. | | | 231 | |
| | John Quincy Adams | Dem.-Rep. | | | 1 | |
| 1824 | **JOHN Q. ADAMS (Mass.)** | Dem.-Rep. | 108,740 | 30.5 | 84 | 26.9 |
| | Andrew Jackson | Dem.-Rep. | 153,544 | 43.1 | 99 | |
| | William H. Crawford | Dem.-Rep. | 46,618 | 13.1 | 41 | |
| | Henry Clay | Dem.-Rep. | 47,136 | 13.2 | 37 | |
| 1828 | **ANDREW JACKSON (Tenn.)** | Democratic | 647,286 | 56.0 | 178 | 57.6 |
| | John Quincy Adams | National Republican | 508,064 | 44.0 | 83 | |
| 1832 | **ANDREW JACKSON (Tenn.)** | Democratic | 687,502 | 55.0 | 219 | 55.4 |
| | Henry Clay | National Republican | 530,189 | 42.4 | 49 | |
| | John Floyd | Independent | | | 11 | |
| | William Wirt | Anti-Mason | 33,108 | 2.6 | 7 | |
| 1836 | **MARTIN VAN BUREN (N.Y.)** | Democratic | 765,483 | 50.9 | 170 | 57.8 |
| | W. H. Harrison | Whig | | | 73 | |
| | Hugh L. White | Whig | | | 26 | |
| | Daniel Webster | Whig | | | 14 | |
| | W. P. Magnum | Independent | | | 11 | |

* State of residence at time of election.

# PRESIDENTIAL ELECTIONS *(cont.)*

| Year | Candidates | Parties | Popular Vote | Percentage of Popular Vote | Electoral Vote | Percentage of Voter Participation |
|---|---|---|---|---|---|---|
| 1840 | **WILLIAM H. HARRISON (Ohio)** | Whig | 1,274,624 | 53.1 | 234 | 80.2 |
| | Martin Van Buren | Democratic | 1,127,781 | 46.9 | 60 | |
| | J. G. Birney | Liberty | 7,069 | | — | |
| 1844 | **JAMES K. POLK (Tenn.)** | Democratic | 1,338,464 | 49.6 | 170 | 78.9 |
| | Henry Clay | Whig | 1,300,097 | 48.1 | 105 | |
| | J. G. Birney | Liberty | 62,300 | 2.3 | — | |
| 1848 | **ZACHARY TAYLOR (La.)** | Whig | 1,360,967 | 47.4 | 163 | 72.7 |
| | Lewis Cass | Democratic | 1,222,342 | 42.5 | 127 | |
| | Martin Van Buren | Free-Soil | 291,263 | 10.1 | — | |
| 1852 | **FRANKLIN PIERCE (N.H.)** | Democratic | 1,601,117 | 50.9 | 254 | 69.6 |
| | Winfield Scott | Whig | 1,385,453 | 44.1 | 42 | |
| | John P. Hale | Free-Soil | 155,825 | 5.0 | — | |
| 1856 | **JAMES BUCHANAN (Pa.)** | Democratic | 1,832,955 | 45.3 | 174 | 78.9 |
| | John C. Frémont | Republican | 1,339,932 | 33.1 | 114 | |
| | Millard Fillmore | American | 871,731 | 21.6 | 8 | |
| 1860 | **ABRAHAM LINCOLN (Ill.)** | Republican | 1,865,593 | 39.8 | 180 | 81.2 |
| | Stephen A. Douglas | Democratic | 1,382,713 | 29.5 | 12 | |
| | John C. Breckinridge | Democratic | 848,356 | 18.1 | 72 | |
| | John Bell | Union | 592,906 | 12.6 | 39 | |
| 1864 | **ABRAHAM LINCOLN (Ill.)** | Republican | 2,213,655 | 55.0 | 212 | 73.8 |
| | George B. McClellan | Democratic | 1,805,237 | 45.0 | 21 | |
| 1868 | **ULYSSES S. GRANT (Ill.)** | Republican | 3,012,833 | 52.7 | 214 | 78.1 |
| | Horatio Seymour | Democratic | 2,703,249 | 47.3 | 80 | |

| Year | Candidate | Party | Popular Vote | % | Electoral Vote | Turnout % |
|---|---|---|---|---|---|---|
| 1872 | **ULYSSES S. GRANT (Ill.)** | Republican | 3,597,132 | 55.6 | 286 | 71.3 |
| | Horace Greeley | Democratic; Liberal Republican | 2,834,125 | 43.9 | 66 | |
| 1876 | **RUTHERFORD B. HAYES (Ohio)** | Republican | 4,036,298 | 48.0 | 185 | 81.8 |
| | Samuel J. Tilden | Democratic | 4,300,590 | 51.0 | 184 | |
| 1880 | **JAMES A. GARFIELD (Ohio)** | Republican | 4,454,416 | 48.5 | 214 | 79.4 |
| | Winfield S. Hancock | Democratic | 4,444,952 | 48.1 | 155 | |
| 1884 | **GROVER CLEVELAND (N.Y.)** | Democratic | 4,874,986 | 48.5 | 219 | 77.5 |
| | James G. Blaine | Republican | 4,851,981 | 48.2 | 182 | |
| 1888 | **BENJAMIN HARRISON (Ind.)** | Republican | 5,439,853 | 47.9 | 233 | 79.3 |
| | Grover Cleveland | Democratic | 5,540,309 | 48.6 | 168 | |
| 1892 | **GROVER CLEVELAND (N.Y.)** | Democratic | 5,556,918 | 46.1 | 277 | 74.7 |
| | Benjamin Harrison | Republican | 5,176,108 | 43.0 | 145 | |
| | James B. Weaver | People's | 1,041,028 | 8.5 | 22 | |
| 1896 | **WILLIAM McKINLEY (Ohio)** | Republican | 7,104,779 | 51.1 | 271 | 79.3 |
| | William J. Bryan | Democratic-People's | 6,502,925 | 47.7 | 176 | |
| 1900 | **WILLIAM McKINLEY (Ohio)** | Republican | 7,207,923 | 51.7 | 292 | 73.2 |
| | William J. Bryan | Dem.-Populist | 6,358,133 | 45.5 | 155 | |
| 1904 | **THEODORE ROOSEVELT (N.Y.)** | Republican | 7,623,486 | 57.9 | 336 | 65.2 |
| | Alton B. Parker | Democratic | 5,077,911 | 37.6 | 140 | |
| | Eugene V. Debs | Socialist | 402,283 | 3.0 | — | |
| 1908 | **WILLIAM H. TAFT (Ohio)** | Republican | 7,678,908 | 51.6 | 321 | 65.4 |
| | William J. Bryan | Democratic | 6,409,104 | 43.1 | 162 | |
| | Eugene V. Debs | Socialist | 420,793 | 2.8 | — | |

# PRESIDENTIAL ELECTIONS *(cont.)*

| Year | Candidates | Parties | Popular Vote | Percentage of Popular Vote | Electoral Vote | Percentage of Voter Participation |
|------|-----------|---------|-------------|-------------|-------------|-------------|
| 1912 | **WOODROW WILSON (N.J.)** | Democratic | 6,293,454 | 41.9 | 435 | 58.8 |
| | Theodore Roosevelt | Progressive | 4,119,538 | 27.4 | 88 | |
| | William H. Taft | Republican | 3,484,980 | 23.2 | 8 | |
| | Eugene V. Debs | Socialist | 900,672 | 6.0 | — | |
| 1916 | **WOODROW WILSON (N.J.)** | Democratic | 9,129,606 | 49.4 | 277 | 61.6 |
| | Charles E. Hughes | Republican | 8,538,221 | 46.2 | 254 | |
| | A. L. Benson | Socialist | 585,113 | 3.2 | — | |
| 1920 | **WARREN G. HARDING (Ohio)** | Republican | 16,152,200 | 60.4 | 404 | 49.2 |
| | James M. Cox | Democratic | 9,147,353 | 34.2 | 127 | |
| | Eugene V. Debs | Socialist | 919,799 | 3.4 | — | |
| 1924 | **CALVIN COOLIDGE (Mass.)** | Republican | 15,725,016 | 54.0 | 382 | 48.9 |
| | John W. Davis | Democratic | 8,386,503 | 28.8 | 136 | |
| | Robert M. LaFollette | Progressive | 4,822,856 | 16.6 | 13 | |
| 1928 | **HERBERT HOOVER (Calif.)** | Republican | 21,391,381 | 58.2 | 444 | 56.9 |
| | Alfred E. Smith | Democratic | 15,016,443 | 40.9 | 87 | |
| | Norman Thomas | Socialist | 267,835 | 0.7 | — | |
| 1932 | **FRANKLIN D. ROOSEVELT (N.Y.)** | Democratic | 22,821,857 | 57.4 | 472 | 56.9 |
| | Herbert Hoover | Republican | 15,761,841 | 39.7 | 59 | |
| | Norman Thomas | Socialist | 881,951 | 2.2 | — | |
| 1936 | **FRANKLIN D. ROOSEVELT (N.Y.)** | Democratic | 27,751,597 | 60.8 | 523 | 61.0 |
| | Alfred M. Landon | Republican | 16,679,583 | 36.5 | 8 | |
| | William Lemke | Union | 882,479 | 1.9 | — | |

| Year | Candidate | Party | Popular Vote | % | Electoral | % |
|------|-----------|-------|-------------|-----|-----------|-----|
| 1940 | **FRANKLIN D. ROOSEVELT (N.Y.)** | Democratic | 27,244,160 | 54.8 | 449 | 62.5 |
| | Wendell L. Willkie | Republican | 22,305,198 | 44.8 | 82 | |
| 1944 | **FRANKLIN D. ROOSEVELT (N.Y.)** | Democratic | 25,602,504 | 53.5 | 432 | 55.9 |
| | Thomas E. Dewey | Republican | 22,006,285 | 46.0 | 99 | |
| 1948 | **HARRY S. TRUMAN (Mo.)** | Democratic | 24,105,695 | 49.5 | 304 | 53.0 |
| | Thomas E. Dewey | Republican | 21,969,170 | 45.1 | 189 | |
| | J. Strom Thurmond | State-Rights Democratic | 1,169,021 | 2.4 | 38 | |
| | Henry A. Wallace | Progressive | 1,156,103 | 2.4 | — | |
| 1952 | **DWIGHT D. EISENHOWER (N.Y.)** | Republican | 33,936,252 | 55.1 | 442 | 63.3 |
| | Adlai E. Stevenson | Democratic | 27,314,992 | 44.4 | 89 | |
| 1956 | **DWIGHT D. EISENHOWER (N.Y.)** | Republican | 35,575,420 | 57.6 | 457 | 60.6 |
| | Adlai E. Stevenson | Democratic | 26,033,066 | 42.1 | 73 | |
| | Other | — | | | 1 | |
| 1960 | **JOHN F. KENNEDY (Mass.)** | Democratic | 34,227,096 | 49.9 | 303 | 62.8 |
| | Richard M. Nixon | Republican | 34,108,546 | 49.6 | 219 | |
| | Other | — | | | 15 | |
| 1964 | **LYNDON B. JOHNSON (Tex.)** | Democratic | 43,126,506 | 61.1 | 486 | 61.7 |
| | Barry M. Goldwater | Republican | 27,176,799 | 38.5 | 52 | |
| 1968 | **RICHARD M. NIXON (N.Y.)** | Republican | 31,770,237 | 43.4 | 301 | 60.6 |
| | Hubert H. Humphrey | Democratic | 31,270,533 | 42.7 | 191 | |
| | George Wallace | American Independent | 9,906,141 | 13.5 | 46 | |

# PRESIDENTIAL ELECTIONS (cont.)

| Year | Candidates | Parties | Popular Vote | Percentage of Popular Vote | Electoral Vote | Percentage of Voter Participation |
|---|---|---|---|---|---|---|
| 1972 | **RICHARD M. NIXON (N.Y.)** | Republican | 47,169,911 | 60.7 | 520 | 55.2 |
| | George S. McGovern | Democratic | 29,170,383 | 37.5 | 17 | |
| | Other | — | — | | 1 | |
| 1976 | **JIMMY CARTER (Ga.)** | Democratic | 40,828,587 | 50.0 | 297 | 53.5 |
| | Gerald R. Ford | Republican | 39,147,613 | 47.9 | 241 | |
| | Other | — | 1,575,459 | 2.1 | — | |
| 1980 | **RONALD REAGAN (Calif.)** | Republican | 43,901,812 | 50.7 | 489 | 52.6 |
| | Jimmy Carter | Democratic | 35,483,820 | 41.0 | 49 | |
| | John B. Anderson | Independent | 5,719,722 | 6.6 | — | |
| | Ed Clark | Libertarian | 921,188 | 1.1 | — | |
| 1984 | **RONALD REAGAN (Calif.)** | Republican | 54,455,075 | 59.0 | 525 | 53.3 |
| | Walter Mondale | Democratic | 37,577,185 | 41.0 | 13 | |
| 1988 | **GEORGE BUSH (Texas)** | Republican | 47,946,422 | 54.0 | 426 | 50.2 |
| | Michael S. Dukakis | Democratic | 41,016,429 | 46.0 | 112 | |
| 1992 | **BILL CLINTON (Ark.)** | **Democratic** | 43,728,375 | 43.0 | 370 | 55.0 |
| | George Bush | Republican | 38,167,416 | 38.0 | 168 | |
| | Ross Perot | Independent | 19,237,247 | 19.0 | 0 | |

# POPULATION OF THE UNITED STATES, 1790–1994

| Year | Population | Percent Increase | Population per Square Mile | Percent Urban/ Rural | Percent White/ Nonwhite | Median Age |
|------|-----------|------------------|---------------------------|----------------------|-------------------------|------------|
| 1790 | 3,929,214 |  | 4.5 | 5.1/94.9 | 80.7/19.3 | NA |
| 1800 | 5,308,483 | 35.1 | 6.1 | 6.1/93.9 | 81.1/18.9 | NA |
| 1810 | 7,239,881 | 36.4 | 4.3 | 7.3/92.7 | 81.0/19.0 | NA |
| 1820 | 9,638,453 | 33.1 | 5.5 | 7.2/92.8 | 81.6/18.4 | 16.7 |
| 1830 | 12,866,020 | 33.5 | 7.4 | 8.8/91.2 | 81.9/18.1 | 17.2 |
| 1840 | 17,069,453 | 32.7 | 9.8 | 10.8/89.2 | 83.2/16.8 | 17.8 |
| 1850 | 23,191,876 | 35.9 | 7.9 | 15.3/84.7 | 84.3/15.7 | 18.9 |
| 1860 | 31,443,321 | 35.6 | 10.6 | 19.8/80.2 | 85.6/14.4 | 19.4 |
| 1870 | 39,818,449 | 26.6 | 13.4 | 25.7/74.3 | 86.2/13.8 | 20.2 |
| 1880 | 50,155,783 | 26.0 | 16.9 | 28.2/71.8 | 86.5/13.5 | 20.9 |
| 1890 | 62,947,714 | 25.5 | 21.2 | 35.1/64.9 | 87.5/12.5 | 22.0 |
| 1900 | 75,994,575 | 20.7 | 25.6 | 39.6/60.4 | 87.9/12.1 | 22.9 |
| 1910 | 91,972,266 | 21.0 | 31.0 | 45.6/54.4 | 88.9/11.1 | 24.1 |
| 1920 | 105,710,620 | 14.9 | 35.6 | 51.2/48.8 | 89.7/10.3 | 25.3 |
| 1930 | 122,775,046 | 16.1 | 41.2 | 56.1/43.9 | 89.8/10.2 | 26.4 |
| 1940 | 131,669,275 | 7.2 | 44.2 | 56.5/43.5 | 89.8/10.2 | 29.0 |
| 1950 | 150,697,361 | 14.5 | 50.7 | 64.0/36.0 | 89.5/10.5 | 30.2 |
| 1960 | 179,323,175 | 18.5 | 50.6 | 69.9/30.1 | 88.6/11.4 | 29.5 |
| 1970 | 203,302,031 | 13.4 | 57.4 | 73.5/26.5 | 87.6/12.4 | 28.0 |
| 1980 | 226,545,805 | 11.4 | 64.0 | 73.7/26.3 | 86.0/14.0 | 30.0 |
| 1990 | 248,709,873 | 9.9 | 70.3 | 77.5/22.5 | 80.3/19.7 | 32.9 |
| 1994 | 260,340,990 | 4.7* | NA | 79.7/20.3 | NA | 34.0† |

NA = Not available.
*Since 1990.
†Projected.

# EMPLOYMENT, 1870–1994

| Year | Number of Workers (in millions) | Male/Female Employment Ratio | Percentage of Workers in Unions |
|------|------|------|------|
| 1870 | 12.5 | 85/15 | — |
| 1880 | 17.4 | 85/15 | — |
| 1890 | 23.3 | 83/17 | — |
| 1900 | 29.1 | 82/18 | 3 |
| 1910 | 38.2 | 79/21 | 6 |
| 1920 | 41.6 | 79/21 | 12 |
| 1930 | 48.8 | 78/22 | 7 |
| 1940 | 53.0 | 76/24 | 27 |
| 1950 | 59.6 | 72/28 | 25 |
| 1960 | 69.9 | 68/32 | 26 |
| 1970 | 82.1 | 63/37 | 25 |
| 1980 | 108.5 | 58/42 | 23 |
| 1985 | 108.9 | 57/43 | 19 |
| 1988 | 114.9 | 55/45 | 17 |
| 1990 | 124.8 | 54/46 | 16 |
| 1994 | 131.1 | NA | 15.5 |

NA = Not available.

# PRODUCTION, TRADE, AND FEDERAL SPENDING/DEBT, 1790–1994

| Year | Gross National Product (GNP) (in billions $) | Balance of Trade (in millions $) | Federal Budget (in billions $) | Federal Surplus/Deficit (in billions $) | Federal Debt (in billions $) |
|---|---|---|---|---|---|
| 1790 | — | −3 | .004 | +0.00015 | .076 |
| 1800 | — | −20 | .011 | +0.0006 | .083 |
| 1810 | — | −18 | .008 | +0.0012 | .053 |
| 1820 | — | −4 | .018 | −0.0004 | .091 |
| 1830 | — | +3 | .015 | +0.100 | .049 |
| 1840 | — | +25 | .024 | −0.005 | .004 |
| 1850 | — | −26 | .040 | +0.004 | .064 |
| 1860 | — | −38 | .063 | −0.01 | .065 |
| 1870 | 7.4 | −11 | .310 | +0.10 | 2.4 |
| 1880 | 11.2 | +92 | .268 | +0.07 | 2.1 |
| 1890 | 13.1 | +87 | .318 | +0.09 | 1.2 |
| 1900 | 18.7 | +569 | .521 | +0.05 | 1.2 |
| 1910 | 35.3 | +273 | .694 | −0.02 | 1.1 |
| 1920 | 91.5 | +2,880 | 6.357 | +0.3 | 24.3 |
| 1930 | 90.7 | +513 | 3.320 | +0.7 | 16.3 |
| 1940 | 100.0 | −3,403 | 9.6 | −2.7 | 43.0 |
| 1950 | 286.5 | +1,691 | 43.1 | −2.2 | 257.4 |
| 1960 | 506.5 | +4,556 | 92.2 | +0.3 | 286.3 |
| 1970 | 992.7 | +2,511 | 196.6 | +2.8 | 371.0 |
| 1980 | 2,631.7 | +24,088 | 579.6 | −59.5 | 914.3 |
| 1990 | 5,465.1 | −100,997.1 | 1,251.8 | −220.3 | 3,223.3 |
| 1994 | 6,726.9 | −150,629.2 | 1,460.6 | −203.4 | 4,692.8 |

# Suggested Readings

CHAPTER 1 THE MEETING OF CULTURES

**Pre-Columbian America and Indian Societies.** James Axtell, *The European and the Indian: Essays in the Ethnohistory of Colonial North America* (1981), *The Invasion Within: The Contest of Cultures in Colonial North America* (1985), and *After Columbus: Essays in the Ethnohistory of Colonial North America* (1988); John Bierhorst, *The Mythology of North America* (1985); Henry Warner Bowden, *American Indians and Christian Missions* (1982). Alfred W. Crosby, Jr., *The Columbian Exchange: Biological and Cultural Consequences of 1492* (1972) and *Ecological Imperialism: The Biological Expansion of Europe, 900–1900* (1986); Carol Devens, *Countering Colonization: Native American Women and Great Lakes Missions, 1630–1900* (1992); Harold E. Driver, *Indians of North America*, 2nd ed. (1969); Stuart Fiedel, *The Prehistory of the Americas* (1987); Francisco Guerra, *The Pre-Columbian Mind* (1971); Ake Hultkrantz, *The Religions of the American Indians* (1979); Francis Jennings, *The Founders of America* (1993) and *The Invasion of America: Indians, Colonialism, and the Cant of Conquest* (1975); J. D. Jennings, ed., *Ancient North America* (1983); Alvin M. Josephy, Jr., *America in 1492* (1992) and *The Indian Heritage of America* (1968); Kenneth MacGowan and J. A. Hester, Jr., *Early Man in the New World* (1950); James H. Merrell, *The Indians' New World* (1989); Christopher L. Miller, *Prophetic Worlds: Indians and Whites on the Columbia Plateau* (1985); Gary B. Nash, *Red, White, and Black*, rev. ed. (1982); Neal Salisbury, *Manitou and Providence: Indians, Europeans, and the Making of New England* (1982); Carl Sauer, *Sixteenth-Century North America* (1985); R. F. Spencer, J. D. Jennings, et al., *The Native Americans* (1978); William C. Sturtevant et al., eds., *Handbook of North American Indians* (1986); Bruce G. Trigger, *Natives and Newcomers* (1985); Bruce G. Trigger and Wilcomb Washburn, eds., *Cambridge History of the Native Peoples of the New World*, vol. 3: *North America* (1993); Nathan Wachtel, *The Vision of the Vanquished* (1977); Wilcomb E. Washburn, *The Indian in America* (1975).

**European Explorations and Spanish America.** James Axtell, *Beyond 1492: Encounters in Colonial North America* (1992); Claudia Bushman, *America Discovers Columbus: How an Italian Explorer Became an American Hero* (1992); H. Elliott, *The Old World and the New, 1492–1650* (1970); Charles Gibson, *Spain in America* (1966); Thomas D. Hall, *Social Change in the Southwest, 1350–1880* (1989); James Lang, *Conquest and Commerce: Spain and England in the Americas* (1975); James Lockhart, *Spanish Peru, 1532–1560: A Colonial Society* (1968); Samuel Eliot Morison, *Admiral of the Ocean Sea*, 2 vols. (1942), *The European Discovery of America: The Northern Voyages* (1971), and *The European Discovery of America: The Southern Voyages* (1974); Anthony Pagden, *European Encounters with the New World: From Renaissance to Romanticism* (1993); J. H. Parry, *The Age of Reconnaissance* (1963); William H. Prescott, *History of the Conquest of Mexico*, 3 vols. (1843); David B. Quinn, *North America from Earliest Discovery to First Settlements* (1977); Kirkpatrick Sale, *The Conquest of Paradise: Christopher Columbus and the Columbian Legacy* (1990); David J. Weber, *The Spanish Frontier in North America* (1992); Donald J. Weber, *The Spanish Empire in North America* (1992); Eric Wolf, *Europe and the People Without History* (1982).

**Africa and America.** J. F. A. Ajayi and Michael Crowder, eds., *History of West Africa*, vol. 1 (1972); Philip D. Curtin, *The Atlantic Slave Trade* (1969); J. S. Fage, *A History of Africa* (1978); Patrick Manning, *Slavery and African Life: Occidental, Oriental, and African Slave Trades* (1990); Walter Rodney, *A History of the Upper Guinea Coast* (1970); Barbara L. Solow, *Slavery and the Rise of the Atlantic System* (1991); John Thornton, *Africa and Africans in the Making of the Atlantic World, 1400–1680* (1992).

**England Looks West.** Carl Bridenbaugh, *Vexed and Troubled Englishmen, 1590–1642* (1968); Nicholas Canny, *The Elizabethan Conquest of Ireland* (1976) and *Kingdom and Colony: Ireland in the Atlantic World* (1988); Patrick Collinson, *The Elizabethan Puritan Movement* (1967); C. H. George and Katherine George, *The Protestant Mind of the English Reformation* (1961); Christopher Hill, *The Century of Revolution, 1603–1714* (1961); Peter Laslett, *The World We Have Lost* (1965); W. H. McNeill, *The Rise of the West* (1963), D. W. Meinig, *The Shaping of America, vol. I: Atlantic America, 1492–1800* (1986); Wallace Notestein, *The English People on the Eve of Colonization, 1603–1630* (1954); J. H. Parry, *Europe and the New World, 1415–1715* (1949), and *The Age of Reconnaissance* (1963); David B. Quinn, *The Elizabethans and the Irish* (1966) and *North America from Earliest Discoveries to First Settlements* (1977); Margaret Spufford, *Contrasting Communities* (1974); Lawrence Stone, *The Crisis of the Aristocracy* (1965); Keith Thomas, *Religion and the Decline of Magic* (1971); David Underdown, *Pride's Purge* (1985); Michael Walzer, *The Revolution of the Saints* (1965).

**First English Colonies.** Karen Ordahl Kupperman, *Roanoke: The Abandoned Colony* (1984); David B. Quinn, *The Roanoke Voyages, 1584–1590*, 2 vols. (1955), *Raleigh and the British Empire* (1947), and *Set Fair for Roanoke* (1985); Keith Wrightson, *English Society, 1580–1680* (1982).

## CHAPTER 2 THE ENGLISH "TRANSPLANTATIONS"

**General Histories.** Charles M. Andrews, *The Colonial Period in American History*, 4 vols. (1934–1938); John E. Pomfret and F. M. Shumway, *Founding the American Colonies, 1583–1660* (1970); Clarence L. Ver Steeg, *The Formative Years, 1607–1763* (1964).

**Jamestown.** Philip L. Barbour, ed., *The Complete Works of Captain John Smith*, 3 vols. (1986), and *The Three Worlds of Captain John Smith* (1964); Bradford Smith, *Captain John Smith* (1953); Alden T. Vaughn, *American Genesis* (1975).

**The Chesapeake.** T. H. Breen, *Tobacco Culture* (1985); T. H. Breen and Stephen Innes, *"Myne Owne Ground": Race and Freedom on Virginia's Eastern Shore, 1640–1676* (1980); Lois G. Carr and David W. Jordan, *Maryland's Revolution of Government, 1689–1692* (1974); Wesley Frank Craven, *The Dissolution of the Virginia Company* (1932); *The Southern Colonies in the Seventeenth Century* (1949), and *White, Red, and Black: The Seventeenth Century Virginian* (1971); James Horn, *Adapting to a New World: English Society in the Seventeenth Century Chesapeake* (1994); David W. Jordan, *Foundations of Representative Government in Maryland, 1632–1715* (1988); Allan Kulikoff, *Tobacco and Slaves: The Development of Southern Cultures in the Chesapeake, 1680–1800* (1986); Aubrey Land et al.,

*Law, Society, and Politics in Early Maryland* (1977); Suzanne Lebsock, *A Share of Honour* (1984); Gloria L. Main, *Tobacco Colony: Life in Early Maryland, 1650–1720* (1982); Edmund S. Morgan, *American Slavery, American Freedom: The Ordeal of Colonial Virginia* (1975); Richard L. Morton, *Colonial Virginia*, 2 vols. (1960); James R. Perry, *The Formation of a Society on Virginia's Eastern Shore, 1615–1655* (1990); David B. Quinn, ed., *Early Maryland in a Wider World* (1982); Darrett B. and Anita H. Rutman, *A Place in Time: Middlesex County, Virginia, 1659–1750* (1984); Fredrick F. Siegel, *The Roots of Southern Distinctiveness: Tobacco and Society in Danville, Virginia 1780–1865* (1987); Thad Tate and David L. Ammerman, eds., *The Chesapeake in the Seventeenth Century* (1979); Wilcomb E. Washburn, *The Governor and the Rebel* (1958).

**The West Indies.**  Hilary M. Beckles, *White Servitude and Black Slavery in Barbados, 1627–1715* (1989); Richard S. Dunn, *Sugar and Slaves: The Rise of the Planter Class in the English West Indies, 1624–1713* (1972); Richard B. Sheridan, *Sugar and Slavery: An Economic History of the West Indies* (1973).

**Plymouth and Massachusetts Bay.**  Bernard Bailyn, *The New England Merchants in the Seventeenth Century* (1955); William Bradford, *Of Plymouth Plantation* (1952). David Cressy, *Coming Over: Migration and Communication Between England and New England in the Seventeenth Century* (1987); William Cronon, *Changes in the Land: Indians, Colonists, and the Ecology of New England* (1983); John Demos, *A Little Commonwealth* (1970), and *The Unredeemed Captive: A Family Story from Early America* (1994); George Langdon, *Pilgrim Colony* (1966); John Frederick Martin, *Profits in the Wilderness: Entrepreneurship and the Founding of New England Towns in the Seventeenth Century* (1991); Edmund S. Morgan, *The Puritan Dilemma: The Story of John Winthrop* (1958); Samuel Eliot Morison, *Builders of the Bay Colony* (1930); Darrett Rutman, *Winthrop's Boston* (1965); Alden T. Vaughn, *New England Frontier: Puritans and Indians* (1965); R. E. Wall, *Massachusetts Bay: The Crucial Decade, 1640–1650* (1972).

**New England Puritanism.**  Sacvan Bercovitch, *The American Jeremiad* (1978), and *The Puritan Origins of the American Self* (1975); Andrew Delbanco, *The Puritan Ordeal* (1989); Kai Erikson, *Wayward Puritans* (1966); Stephen Foster, *Their Solitary Way: The Puritan Social Ethic in the First Century of Settlement in New England* (1971), and *The Long Argument: English Puritanism and the Shaping of New England Culture, 1570–1700* (1991); Edwin S. Gaustad, *Liberty of Conscience: Roger Williams in America* (1991); Philip F. Gura, *A Glimpse of Sion's Glory* (1984); David Hall, *The Faithful Shepherd* (1972), and *Worlds of Wonder, Days of Judgement* (1989); Charles Hambrick-Stowe, *The Practice of Piety* (1982); J. V. James, *Colonial Rhode Island* (1975); M. J. A. Jones, *Congregational Commonwealth: Connecticut, 1636–1662* (1968); Janice Knight, *Orthodoxies in Massachusetts: Rereading American Puritanism* (1994); Paul R. Lucas, *Valley of Discord* (1976); Robert Middlekauff, *The Mathers* (1971); Perry Miller, *The New England Mind: The Seventeenth Century* (1939), *The New England Mind: From Colony to Province* (1953), *Orthodoxy in Massachusetts* (1933), and *Errand into the Wilderness* (1956); Edmund S. Morgan, *Visible Saints* (1963), *The Puritan Family* (1966), and *Roger Williams: The Church and the State* (1967); Norman Pettit, *The Heart Prepared: Grace and Conversion in Puritan Spiritual Life* (1989); Kenneth Silverman, *The Life and Times of Cotton Mather* (1984); W. K. B. Stoever, *A Faire and Easy Way to Heaven* (1978); Harry S. Stout, *The New England Soul* (1986); Larzer Ziff, *Puritanism in America* (1973).

**The Restoration Colonies.** Thomas J. Archdeacon, *New York City, 1664–1710* (1976); Van Cleaf Bachman, *Peltries or Plantations* (1969); Patricia Bonomi, *A Factious People* (1971); Edwin B. Bronner, *William Penn's Holy Experiment* (1962); Kenneth Coleman, *Colonial Georgia* (1976); Thomas J. Condon, *New York Beginnings* (1968); Mary Maples Dunn, *William Penn: Politics and Conscience* (1967); Roger Ekirch, *Poor Carolina* (1981); Christopher Hill, *The World Turned Upside Down* (1972); Michael Kammen, *Colonial New York* (1975); James T. Lemmon, *The Best Poor Man's Country* (1972); Barry Levy, *Quakers and the American Family* (1988); H. T. Merrens, *Colonial North Carolina* (1964); Donna Merwick, *Possessing Albany, 1630–1710: The Dutch and English Experiences* (1990); Gary B. Nash, *Quakers and Politics: Pennsylvania, 1681–1726* (1968); J. E. Pomfret, *The Province of East and West New Jersey, 1609–1702* (1956), and *The Province of East New Jersey* (1962); T. R. Reese, *Colonial Georgia: A Study in British Imperial Policy in the Eighteenth Century* (1963); Oliver A. Rink, *Holland on Hudson* (1986); Robert C. Ritchie, *The Duke's Province: A Study of New York Politics and Society, 1664–1691* (1977); M. E. Sirmans, *Colonial South Carolina* (1966); George L. Smith, *Religion and Trade in New Netherland* (1973); Alan Tully, *William Penn's Legacy* (1977); Clarence L. Ver Steeg, *Origins of a Southern Mosaic* (1975); Robert M. Weir, *Colonial South Carolina* (1983); Peter H. Wood, *Black Majority* (1974).

**The Development of Empire.** Viola Barnes, *The Dominion of New England* (1923); Thomas C. Barrow, *Trade and Empire* (1967); Lawrence Gipson, *The British Empire Before the American Revolution*, 15 vols. (1936–1970); Michael Hall, *Edward Randolph and the American Colonies* (1960); Lawrence Harper, *The English Navigation Laws* (1939); James A. Henretta, *Salutary Neglect* (1972); Richard R. Johnson, *Adjustment to Empire: The New England Colonies, 1675–1715* (1981); Michael Kammen, *Empire and Interest* (1970); Leonard Labaree, *Royal Government in America* (1964); David S. Lovejoy, *The Glorious Revolution in America* (1972); J. M. Sosin, *English America and the Revolution of 1688* (1982), and *English America and the Restoration Monarchy of Charles II* (1980); I. K. Steele, *The Politics of Colonial Policy* (1968); Stephen S. Webb, *The Governors-General* (1979); and *1676: The End of American Independence* (1984).

## CHAPTER 3 LIFE IN PROVINCIAL AMERICA

**General Social Histories.** David Hackett Fischer, *Albion's Seed* (1989); James A. Henretta and Gregory Nobles, *The Evolution of American Society, 1700–1815*, rev. ed. (1987); Richard Hofstadter, *America at 1750: A Social Portrait* (1971).

**Population and Family.** Richard Bushman, *The Refinement of America: Persons, Houses, Cities* (1992); John Putnam Demos, *Past, Present, and Personal: The Family and Life Course in American History* (1986); J. William Frost, *The Quaker Family in Colonial America* (1972); Philip Greven, *Four Generations* (1970), and *The Protestant Temperament: Patterns of Child-Rearing, Religious Experience, and the Self in Early America* (1977); Christopher Jedrey, *The World of John Cleaveland: Family and Community in Eighteenth-Century New England* (1979); Joan M. Jensen, *Loosening the Bonds: Mid-Atlantic Farm Women, 1750–1850* (1986); Lyle Koehler, *A Search for Power: "The Weaker Sex" in Seventeenth-Century New England* (1982); Judith Walzer Leavitt, *Brought to Bed: Child Bearing in America, 1750–1950* (1986); Edmund S. Morgan, *The Puritan Family* (1966); Daniel K. Richter, *The Ordeal of the Longhouse: The Peoples of the Iroquois League in the Era of Euro-*

*pean Colonization* (1992); Daniel Blake Smith, *Inside the Great House: Planter Family Life in Eighteenth Century Chesapeake Society* (1980); Roger Thompson, *Women in Stuart England and America* (1974); Laura Thatcher Ulrich, *Good Wives: Image and Reality in the Lives of Women in Northern New England, 1650–1750* (1982); Robert V. Wells, *The Population of the British Colonies in America Before 1776* (1975); Stephanie Grauman Wolf, *As Various as Their Land: The Everyday Lives of Eighteenth-Century Americans* (1993).

**Immigration.** Bernard Bailyn, *The Peopling of British North America: An Introduction* (1986), and *Voyagers to the West: A Passage in the Peopling of America on the Eve of the Revolution* (1986); R. J. Dickson, *Ulster Immigration to the United States* (1966); Albert B. Faust, *The German Element in the United States*, 2 vols. (1909); Ian C. C. Graham, *Colonists from Scotland: Emigration to North America, 1707–1783* (1956); Marcus L. Hanson, *The Atlantic Migration, 1607–1860* (1940); James Kettner, *The Development of American Citizenship* (1978); Frederic Klees, *The Pennsylvania Dutch* (1950); James G. Leyburn, *The Scotch-Irish: A Social History* (1962).

**Society and Slavery in the Colonial South.** T. H. Breen, *Tobacco Culture* (1985); T. H. Breen and Stephen Innes, *"Myne Owne Ground": Race and Freedom on Virginia's Eastern Shore* (1980); Jay Coughtry, *The Notorious Triangle: Rhode Island and the African Slave Trade, 1799–1807* (1981); Philip D. Curtin, *The Atlantic Slave Trade* (1969); David Brion Davis, *The Problem of Slavery in Western Culture* (1966); David Eltis, *Economic Growth and the Ending of the Transatlantic Slave Trade* (1987); Jean E. Friedman, *The Enclosed Garden: Women and Community in the Evangelical South* (1985); David W. Galenson, *Traders, Planters, and Slaves: Market Behavior in Early English America* (1986); Eugene Genovese, *From Rebellion to Revolution* (1979); Jack P. Greene, *Pursuits of Happiness: The Social Development of Early Modern British Colonies and the Formation of American Culture* (1988); Gwendolyn Midlo Hall, *Africans in Colonial Louisiana: The Development of Afro-Creole Culture in the Eighteenth Century* (1992); Rhys Isaac, *The Transformation of Virginia, 1740–1790* (1982); Winthrop D. Jordan, *White over Black* (1968), and *The White Man's Burden* (1974); Charles Joyner, *Down by the Riverside: A South Carolina Slave Community* (1984); Allan Kulikoff, *Tobacco and Slaves: The Development of Southern Cultures in the Chesapeake, 1680–1800* (1986); Peter Kolchin, *American Slavery, 1619–1877* (1993); Daniel Littlefield, *Rice and Slaves: Ethnicity and the Slave Trade in Colonial South Carolina* (1981); Edmund S. Morgan, *American Slavery, American Freedom: The Ordeal of Colonial Virginia* (1975); Gerald Mullin, *Flight and Rebellion* (1972); Gary B. Nash, *Red, White, and Black*, rev. ed. (1982); James R. Perry, *The Formation of a Society on Virginia's Eastern Shore, 1615–1655* (1990); Darrett B. Rutman and Anita H. Rutman, *A Place in Time: Middlesex County, Virginia, 1650–1750* (1984); Abbot E. Smith, *Colonists in Bondage* (1947); Mechal Sobel, *The World They Made Together: Black and White Values in Eighteenth-Century Virginia* (1987); Julia C. Spruill, *Women's Life and Work in the Southern Colonies* (1972); James Titus, *The Old Dominion at War: Society, Politics, and Warfare in Late Colonial Virginia* (1991); Daniel H. Usner, Jr., *Indians, Settlers, and Slaves in a Frontier Exchange Economy: The Lower Mississippi Valley Before 1783* (1992); Peter Wood, *Black Majority* (1974); J. Leitch Wright, Jr., *Anglo-Spanish Rivalry in North America* (1971), and *The Only Land They Knew: The Tragic Story of the American Indians of the Old South* (1981).

**Society and Town in Colonial New England.** Paul Boyer and Stephen Nissenbaum, *Salem Possessed* (1974); Richard Bushman, *From Puritan to Yankee* (1967); John Camp, *Out of the Wilderness: The Emergence of an American Identity in Colonial New England* (1990);

E. M. Cook, Jr., *The Fathers of Towns* (1975); John Putnam Demos, *Entertaining Satan: Witchcraft and the Culture of Early New England* (1982); Charles Grant, *Democracy in the Connecticut Frontier Town of Kent* (1961); Paul Robert Gross, *The Minutemen and Their World* (1976); David D. Hall, *Worlds of Wonder, Days of Judgment: Popular Religious Belief in Early New England* (1990); Carol Karlsen, *The Devil in the Shape of a Woman: Witchcraft in Colonial New England* (1987); Kenneth Lockridge, *A New England Town* (1970); Teresa Anne Murphy, *Ten Hours Labor: Religion, Reform, and Gender in Early New England* (1992); Carla Gardina Pestana, *Quakers and Baptists in Colonial Massachusetts* (1991); Sumner Chilton Powell, *Puritan Village* (1963); Bernard Rosenthal, *Salem Story: Reading the Witch Trials of 1692* (1993); Darrett B. Rutman, *Winthrop's Boston* (1965); Michael Zuckerman, *Peaceable Kingdoms* (1970).

**The Colonial Economy.** Carl Bridenbaugh, *Myths and Realities: Societies of the Colonial South* (1963); Stuart Bruchey, *Roots of American Economic Growth, 1607–1861* (1965); Paul G. E. Clemens, *The Atlantic Economy and Colonial Maryland's Eastern Shore: From Tobacco to Grain* (1980); David W. Galenson, *White Servitude in Colonial America: An Economic Analysis* (1982); Stephen Innes, *Labor in a New Land: Economy and Society in Seventeenth Century Springfield* (1983); Stephen Innes, ed., *Work and Labor in Early America* (1988); Alice Hanson Jones, *Wealth of a Nation to Be* (1980); Jackson Turner Main, *The Social Structure of Revolutionary America* (1965); John J. McCusker and Russell R. Menard, *The Economy of British America, 1607–1787* (1985); Harry R. Merrens, *Colonial North Carolina in the Eighteenth Century* (1964); Edmund S. Morgan, *Virginians at Home* (1952); Jacob M. Price, *France and the Chesapeake*, 2 vols. (1973), *The Tobacco Adventure to Russia* (1961), and *Capital and Credit in the British Overseas Trade: The View from the Chesapeake, 1700–1776* (1980); Sharon U. Salinger, *"To Serve Well and Faithfully": Labor and Indentured Servants in Pennsylvania, 1692–1800* (1987);

**Cities and Commerce.** Bernard Bailyn, *The New England Merchants in the Seventeenth Century* (1955); Carl Bridenbaugh, *Cities in the Wilderness* (1938), and *Cities in Revolt* (1955); Stuart Bruchey, *The Colonial Merchant* (1966); Thomas M. Doerflinger, *A Vigorous Spirit of Enterprise: Merchants and Economic Development in Revolutionary Philadelphia* (1986); Joyce D. Goodfriend, *Before the Melting Pot: Society and Culture in New York City, 1664–1730* (1992); James B. Hedges, *The Browns of Providence Plantation*, vol. 1 (1952); Arthur Jensen, *The Maritime Commerce of Colonial Philadelphia* (1963); Randolph S. Klein, *Portrait of an Early American Family* (1975); Gary B. Nash, *The Urban Crucible* (1979), and *Forging Freedom: The Formation of Philadelphia's Black Community, 1720–1840* (1988); Marcus Rediker, *Between the Devil and the Deep Sea: Merchant Seamen, Pirates, and the Anglo-American Maritime World, 1700–1750* (1987); J. F. Shepherd and G. M. Walton, *The Economic Rise of Early America* (1979); Frederick B. Tolles, *Meeting House and Counting House: The Quaker Merchants of Colonial Philadelphia, 1682–1763* (1948); G. B. Warden, *Boston, 1687–1776* (1970); Stephanie G. Wolf, *Urban Village* (1976).

**Colonial Religion.** (For studies of Puritanism, see Suggested Readings for Chapter 2.) Sidney Ahlstrom, *A Religious History of the American People* (1972); Patricia U. Bonomi, *Under the Copy of Heaven: Religion, Society, and Politics in Colonial America* (1986); Carl Bridenbaugh, *Mitre and Sceptre: Transatlantic Faiths, Ideas, Personalities, and Politics, 1689–1775* (1962); J. T. Ellis, *Catholics in America* (1965); J. R. Marcus, *Early American Jewry* (1951); William C. McLoughlin, *New England Dissent, 1630–1833*, 2 vols. (1971); Sidney Mead, *The Lively Experiment: The Shaping of Christianity in America* (1963);

W. W. Sweet, *Religion in Colonial America* (1942); Marilyn Westerkamp, *Triumph of Laity* (1988); Janet Whitman, *John Woolman, American Quaker* (1942).

**The Great Awakening.** J. M. Bumsted and John E. Van de Wetering, *What Must I Do to Be Saved? The Great Awakening in Colonial America* (1976); J. W. Davidson, *The Logic of Millennial Thought* (1977); Edwin S. Gaustad, *The Great Awakening in New England* (1957); Alan Heimert, *Religion and the American Mind* (1966). Perry Miller, *Jonathan Edwards* (1949); Patricia Tracy, *Jonathan Edwards: Pastor* (1980); Ola Winslow, *Jonathan Edwards* (1940); Conrad Wright, *The Beginnings of Unitarianism in America* (1955).

**Education.** James Axtell, *The School upon a Hill: Education and Society in Colonial New England* (1974); Bernard Bailyn, *Education in the Forming of American Society* (1960); Lawrence A. Cremin, *American Education: The Colonial Experience, 1607–1783* (1970); Jurgen Herbst, *From Crisis to Crisis* (1982); Kenneth Lockridge, *Literacy in Colonial New England* (1974); Robert Middlekauff, *Ancients and Axioms* (1963); Samuel Eliot Morison, *The Founding of Harvard College* (1935).

**Culture and the Enlightenment.** Jean-Christophe Agnew, *Worlds Apart: The Market and the Theater in Anglo-American Thought, 1550–1750* (1986); Daniel J. Boorstin, *The Americans: The Colonial Experience* (1958); Charles E. Clark, *The Public Prints: The Newspaper in Anglo-American Culture, 1665–1740* (1994); V. W. Crane, *Benjamin Franklin and a Rising People* (1954); Richard Beale Davis, *Intellectual Life in the Colonial South*, 2 vols. (1978); Brook Hindle, *The Pursuit of Science in Revolutionary America* (1956); Howard Mumford Jones, *O Strange New World* (1964); H. Leventhal, *In the Shadow of Enlightenment* (1976); Henry May, *The Enlightenment in America* (1976); Carl Van Doren, *Benjamin Franklin* (1941); Louis B. Wright, *The Cultural Life of the American Colonies* (1957).

**Law & Politics.** Bernard Bailyn, *The Origins of American Politics* (1968); J. C. D. Clark, *The Language of Liberty, 1660–1832* (1994); Thomas Curry, *The First Freedoms: Church and State in America to the Passage of the First Amendment* (1986); Robert Ferguson, *Law and Letters in American Culture* (1984); Gerald W. Gawalt, *The Promise of Power: The Emergence of the Legal Profession in Massachusetts, 1760–1840* (1979); Jack P. Greene, *The Quest for Power* (1963); Charles Hoffer, *Law and People in Colonial America* (1992); Michael Kammen, *Spheres of Liberty: Changing Perceptions of Liberty in American Culture* (1986); Leonard W. Labaree, *Royal Government in America* (1930); J. G. A. Pocock, *The Machiavellian Moment* (1975); J. R. Pole, *Political Representation in England and the Origins of the American Republic* (1966); A. G. Roeber, *Faithful Magistrates and Republican Lawyers: Creators of Virginia Legal Culture, 1680–1810* (1981); Caroline Robbins, *The Eighteenth-Century Commonwealthman* (1959); Marylynn Salmon, *Women and the Law of Property in Early America* (1986); Alan Tully, *Forming American Politics: Ideals, Interests, and Institutions in Colonial New York and Pennsylvania* (1994); Robert Zemsky, *Merchants, Farmers, and River Gods* (1971); Michael P. Zuckert, *Natural Rights and the New Republicanism* (1994).

CHAPTER 4 THE EMPIRE UNDER STRAIN

**General Histories.** J. R. Alden, *A History of the American Revolution* (1969); Charles M. Andrews, *The Colonial Background of the American Revolution* (1924, rev. 1931); Ian R. Christie, *Crisis of Empire* (1966); Ian R. Christie and Benjamin W. Labaree, *Empire or In-*

*dependence, 1760–1776* (1976); Edward Countryman, *The American Revolution* (1985); Lawrence Henry Gipson, *The Coming of the Revolution, 1763–1775* (1954); Merrill Jensen, *The Founding of a Nation* (1968); Robert Middlekauff, *The Glorious Cause: The American Revolution, 1763–1789* (1982); John C. Miller, *Origins of the American Revolution* (1957); Edmund S. Morgan, *The Birth of the Republic* (1956); Alfred E. Young, Jr., ed., *The American Revolution* (1976).

**The British Imperial System.** John Brewer, *Party Ideology and Popular Politics at the Accession of George III* (1967); John Brooke, *King George III* (1972); Richard L. Bushman, *King and People in Colonial Massachusetts* (1987); Bernard Donoughue, *British Politics and the American Revolution: The Path to War, 1773–1775* (1965); Sylvia R. Frey, *The British Soldier in America* (1981); Lawrence Henry Gipson, *The British Empire Before the American Revolution*, 15 vols. (1936–1970); Michael Kammen, *A Rope of Sand* (1968); Lewis B. Namier, *England in the Age of the American Revolution*, rev. ed. (1961); and *The Structure of Politics at the Accession of George III*, rev. ed. (1961); Robert C. Newbold, *The Albany Congress and Plan of Union of 1754* (1955); Alison Gilbert Olson, *Making the Empire Work: London and American Interest Groups, 1690–1790* (1992); Robert R. Palmer, *The Age of the Democratic Revolution:* vol. 1, *The Challenge* (1959); Richard Pares, *War and Trade in the West Indies, 1739–1763* (1936); Howard H. Peckham, *The Colonial Wars, 1689–1762* (1963); Alan Rogers, *Empire and Liberty* (1974); John Shy, *Toward Lexington: The Role of the British Army in the Coming of the American Revolution* (1965).

**The French and the Indians.** Thomas P. Abernethy, *Western Lands and the American Revolution* (1937); Fred Anderson, *A People's Army: Massachusetts Soldiers and Society in the Seven Years War* (1984); David H. Corkran, *The Cherokee Frontier* (1962), and *The Creek Frontier* (1967); R. S. Cotterill, *The Southern Indians* (1954); Gregory Evans Dowd, *A Spirited Resistance: The North American Indian Struggle for Unity, 1745–1815* (1992); Francis Jennings, *Empire of Fortune* (1988), and *The Ambiguous Iroquois Empire* (1984); Howard H. Peckham, *Pontiac and the Indian Uprising* (1947); William Pencak, *War, Politics, and Revolution in Provincial Massachusetts* (1981); Harold E. Selesky, *War and Society in Early Connecticut* (1990); J. M. Sosin, *Whitehall and the Wilderness* (1961); Richard White, *The Middle Ground: Indians, Empires, and Republics in the Great Lakes Region, 1650–1815* (1991).

**Merchants and the Empire.** Thomas C. Barrow, *Trade and Empire: The British Customs Service in Colonial America* (1967); Oliver M. Dickerson, *The Navigation Acts and the American Revolution* (1951); Thomas Doerflinger, *A Vigorous Spirit of Enterprise: Merchants and Economic Development in Revolutionary Philadelphia* (1986); Joseph Ernst, *Money and Politics in America, 1755–1775* (1973); Michael Kammen, *Empire and Interest: The American Colonies and the Politics of Mercantilism* (1970); Arthur M. Schlesinger, *The Colonial Merchants and the American Revolution* (1917); John W. Tyler, *Smugglers and Patriots: Boston Merchants and the Advent of the American Revolution* (1986).

**American Resistance.** David Ammerman, *In the Common Cause* (1974); Marc Egnal, *A Mighty Empire: The Origins of the American Revolution* (1988); Paul A. Gilje, *The Road to Mobocracy: Popular Disorder in New York City, 1763–1834* (1987); Dirk Hoerder, *Crowd Action in Revolutionary Massachusetts* (1977); Peter C. Hoffer, *Revolution and Regeneration: Life Cycle and the Historical Vision of the Generation of 1776* (1983); Benjamin W. Labaree, *The Boston Tea Party* (1964); Pauline Maier, *From Resistance to Revolution* (1972); Edmund S. Morgan and Helen M. Morgan, *The Stamp Act Crisis*, rev. ed. (1953); Peter D.

G. Thomas, *The Townshend Duties Crisis* (1987); Hiller B. Zobel, *The Boston Massacre* (1970).

**Revolutionary Ideology.** Bernard Bailyn, *The Ideological Origins of the American Revolution* (1967); Ian R. Christie, *Wilkes, Wyvil, and Reform* (1962); Nathan Hatch, *The Sacred Cause of Liberty* (1977); Rhys Isaac, *The Transformation of Virginia, 1740–1790* (1982); Isaac Kramnick, *Bolingbroke and His Circle* (1968); Richard Merritt, *Symbols of American Community, 1735–1775* (1966); Gary B. Nash, *The Urban Crucible: The Northern Seaports and the Origins of the American Revolution* (1979); Clinton Rossiter, *Seedtime of the Republic* (1953); George Rudé, *Wilkes and Liberty* (1962).

**Revolutionary Politics.** Carl Becker, *The History of Political Parties in the Province of New York* (1909); R. E. Brown and B. K. Brown, *Virginia, 1705–1786* (1964); Richard D. Brown, *Revolutionary Politics in Massachusetts* (1970); L. R. Gerlach, *Prologue to Independence* (1976); Ronald Hoffman, *A Spirit of Dissension* (1973); David Lovejoy, *Rhode Island Politics and the American Revolution* (1958); Neil R. Stout, *The Perfect Crisis: The Beginning of the Revolutionary War* (1976); Charles S. Sydnor, *Gentlemen Freeholders* (1952); Theodore Thayer, *Pennsylvania Politics and the Growth of Democracy* (1953).

## CHAPTER 5 THE AMERICAN REVOLUTION

**General Studies.** Edward Countryman, *The American Revolution* (1985); Jack P. Greene, ed., *The American Revolution: Its Character and Limits* (1987); Merrill Jensen, *The Founding of a Nation, A History of the American Revolution, 1763–1789* (1968); Michael Kammen, *A Season of Youth: The American Revolution and the Historical Imagination* (1978); Robert Middlekauff, *The Glorious Cause: The American Revolution, 1763–1789* (1982); Edmund S. Morgan, *The Birth of the Republic, 1763–1789* (1956); Gordon S. Wood, *The Radicalism of the American Revolution* (1992); Alfred E. Young, Jr., ed., *The American Revolution* (1976).

**The Road to Independence.** Carl Becker, *The Declaration of Independence* (1922); Eric Foner, *Tom Paine and Revolutionary America* (1976); David Hawke, *Paine* (1974); John R. Howe, Jr., *The Changing Political Thought of John Adams* (1966); Edmund S. Morgan, *The Meaning of Independence* (1976); Peter Shaw, *The Character of John Adams* (1976), and *American Patriots and the Rituals of Revolution* (1981); Morton White, *The Philosophy of the American Revolution* (1978); Gary Willis, *Inventing America: Jefferson's Declaration of Independence* (1978).

**The War.** John R. Alden, *The American Revolution* (1964); G. W. Allen, *Naval History of the American Revolution*, 2 vols. (1913); Richard Buel, Jr., *Dear Liberty: Connecticut's Mobilization for the Revolutionary War* (1980); E. Wayne Carp, *To Starve the Army at Pleasure: Continental Army Administration and American Political Culture, 1775–1783* (1984); Lawrence D. Cress, *Citizens in Arms: The Army and the Militia in American Society to the War of 1812* (1982); David Hackett Fischer, *Paul Revere's Ride* (1994); James T. Flexner, *George Washington in the American Revolution* (1968); Douglas Southall Freeman, *George Washington*, 7 vols. (1948–1957); T. G. Frothingham, *Washington: Commander in Chief* (1930); Ronald Hoffman and Thad W. Tate, eds., *An Uncivil War: The Southern Backcountry During the American Revolution* (1985); Don Higginbotham, *The War of Ameri-*

can Independence (1983), and George Washington and the American Military Tradition (1985); Piers Mackesy, The War for America (1964); Samuel Eliot Morison, John Paul Jones (1959); Howard H. Peckham, The War for Independence (1958); Steven Rosswurm, Arms, Country, and Class: The Philadelphia Militia and the "Lower Sort" in the Era of the American Revolution (1987); Charles Royster, A Revolutionary People at War: The Continental Army and American Character (1979), and Light-Horse Larry Lee and the Legacy of the American Revolution (1981); John Shy, A People Numerous and Armed (1976), and The American Revolution (1973); Willard Wallace, Appeal to Arms (1950); Christopher Ward, The War of the Revolution, 2 vols. (1952).

**Revolutionary Diplomacy.**  Samuel F. Bemis, The Diplomacy of the American Revolution (1935); Jonathan R. Dull, A Diplomatic History of the American Revolution (1985); E. J. Ferguson, The Power of the Purse (1961); L. S. Kaplan, Colonies into Nation: American Diplomacy, 1763–1801 (1972); Richard B. Morris, The Peacemakers (1965); Gerald Stourzh, Benjamin Franklin and American Foreign Policy, rev. ed. (1969); Clarence L. Ver Steeg, Robert Morris (1954).

**The Loyalists.**  Bernard Bailyn, The Ordeal of Thomas Hutchinson (1974); Wallace Brown, The King's Friends (1965); Robert M. Calhoon, The Loyalists in Revolutionary America (1973); Mary Beth Norton, The British Americans: The Loyalist Exiles in England 1774–1789 (1972); William H. Nelson, The American Tory (1962); Anne M. Ousterhout, A State Divided: Opposition in Pennsylvania to the American Revolution (1987); Paul H. Smith, Loyalists and Redcoats (1964); James W. St. G. Walker, The Black Loyalists (1976).

**Women, Family, and the Revolution.**  Joy Day Buel and Richard Buel, Jr., The Way of Duty: A Woman and Her Life in Revolutionary America (1984); Linda Grant DePauw, Founding Fathers (1975); Ronald Hoffman and Peter J. Albert, eds., Women in the Age of the American Revolution (1989); Joan Jensen, Loosening the Bonds: Mid-Atlantic Farm Women, 1750–1850 (1986); Linda K. Kerber, Women of the Republic: Intellect and Ideology in Revolutionary America (1980); Mary Beth Norton, Liberty's Daughters: The Revolutionary Experience of American Women, 1750–1800 (1980).

**Indians and Blacks in the Revolution.**  Ira Berlin and Ronald Hoffman, eds., Slavery in the Revolutionary Era (1982); David Brion Davis, The Problem of Slavery in the Age of Revolution (1975); Sylvia R. Frey, Water from the Rock: Black Resistance in a Revolutionary Age (1991); Barbara Graymount, The Iroquois in the American Revolution (1973); Isabel T. Kelsay, Joseph Brant, 1743–1807 (1984); Duncan McLeod, Slavery, Race and the American Revolution (1974); Edmund S. Morgan, American Slavery, American Freedom: The Ordeal of Colonial Virginia (1975); Gary B. Nash and Jean R. Soderlund, Freedom by Degrees: Emancipation in Pennsylvania and Its Aftermath (1991); Gary B. Nash, Race and Revolution (1990); James H. O'Donnell, III, Southern Indians in the American Revolution (1973); Benjamin Quarles, The Negro in the American Revolution (1961); Anthony F. C. Wallace, The Death and Rebirth of the Seneca (1969); Arthur Zilversmit, The First Emancipation (1967).

**Social and Economic Effects.**  Edward Countryman, A People in Revolution (1981); Jeffrey J. Crow and Larry E. Tise, The Southern Experience in the American Revolution (1978); Robert Gross, The Minutemen and Their World (1976); J. F. Jameson, The American Revolution Considered as a Social Movement (1962); Merrill Jensen, The American Revolution Within America (1974). Rachel N. Klein, Unification of a Slave State: The Rise of the Planter

*Class in the South Carolina Backcountry, 1760–1808* (1990); Jean B. Lee, *The Price of Nationhood: The American Revolution in Charles County* (1994); Staughton Lynd, *Class Conflict, Slavery and the United States Constitution* (1968); Jackson Turner Main, *The Social Structure of Revolutionary America* (1965); Cathy D. Matson and Peter S. Onuf, *Union of Interests: Political and Economic Thought in Revolutionary America* (1990); Richard P. McCormick, *Experiment in Independence* (1950); Jerome J. Nadlehaft, *The Disorders of War: The Revolution in South Carolina* (1981); Billy G. Smith, *"The Lower Sort": Philadelphia's Laboring People, 1750–1800* (1990); Charles G. Steffen, *The Mechanics of Baltimore: Workers and Politics in the Age of Revolution, 1763–1812* (1984); Gordon S. Wood, *The Radicalism of the American Revolution* (1992).

**State Governments.** Willi Paul Adams, *The First American Constitutions* (1980); Richard Beeman et al., eds., *Beyond Confederation: Origins of the Constitution and American National Identity* (1987); Donald S. Lutz, *Origins of American Constitutionalism* (1988); Jackson Turner Main, *Political Parties Before the Constitution* (1973), *The Sovereign States, 1775–1783* (1973), and *The Upper House in Revolutionary America, 1763–1788* (1967); Stephen E. Patterson, *Political Parties in Revolutionary Massachusetts* (1973); Irwin Polishook, *Rhode Island and the Union, 1774–1795* (1969); Gordon S. Wood, *The Creation of the American Republic* (1969).

**The Articles of Confederation.** Andrew R. L. Cayton, *The Frontier Republic: Ideology and Politics in the Ohio Country, 1780–1825* (1986); Jack Eblen, *The First and Second United States Empires* (1968); John Fiske, *The Critical Period of American History, 1783–1789* (1883); H. James Henderson, *Party Politics in the Continental Congress* (1974); Merrill Jensen, *The New Nation* (1950), and *The Articles of Confederation*, rev. ed. (1959); Jack N. Rakove, *The Beginnings of National Politics* (1979); David Szatmary, *Shays' Rebellion: The Making of an Agrarian Insurrection* (1980); Steven Watts, *The Republic Reborn: War and the Making of Liberal America, 1790–1800* (1987).

## CHAPTER 6 THE CONSTITUTION
## AND THE NEW REPUBLIC

**The Constitution.** Douglas Adair, *Fame and the Founding Fathers* (1974); Charles A. Beard, *An Economic Interpretation of the Constitution of the United States* (1913); Robert E. Brown, *Charles Beard and the Constitution* (1956); Christopher Collier and James Lincoln Collier, *Decision: Philadelphia: The Constitutional Convention of 1787* (1986); J. E. Cooke, ed., *The Federalist* (1961); Thomas Curry, *The First Freedom: Church and State in America to the Passage of the First Amendment* (1986); Linda G. DePauw, *The Eleventh Pillar: New York State and the Federal Constitution* (1966); Max Farrand, ed., *Records of the Federal Convention of 1787*, 4 vols. (1911–1937); Max Farrand, *The Framing of the Constitution of the United States* (1913); Michael Kammen, *A Machine that Would Go of Itself: The Constitution in American Culture* (1986); Leonard Levy, *Constitutional Opinions: Aspects of the Bill of Rights* (1986), and *Original Intent and the Framers' Constitution* (1988); Michael Lienesch, *New Order of the Ages: Time, the Constitution, and the Making of Modern American Political Thought* (1988); Donald S. Lutz, *Origins of American Constitutionalism* (1988); Jackson Turner Main, *The Anti-Federalists* (1961); Alpheus T. Mason, *The State Rights Debate* (1964); Forrest McDonald, *We the People: The Economic Origins of the Constitution* (1958), *E. Pluribus Unum: The Formation of the American Republic, 1776–1790* (1965), and *Novus Ordo Seclorum: The Intellectual Origins of the Constitution* (1985); William L. Miller,

*The First Liberty: Religion and the American Republic* (1986); Edmund S. Morgan, *Inventing the People: The Rise of Popular Sovereignty in England and America* (1988); Richard B. Morris, *The Forging of the Union, 1781–1789* (1987); Clinton Rossiter, *1787: The Grand Convention* (1965); Robert A. Rutland, *The Ordeal of the Constitution* (1966); Gerald Stourzh, *Alexander Hamilton and the Idea of Republican Government* (1970); Garry Wills, *Explaining America* (1981); John R. Wunder, *"Retained by the People": A History of American Indians and the Bill of Rights* (1994).

**The Federalist Era.** Leland D. Baldwin, *The Whiskey Rebels* (1939); Richard Beeman, *The Old Dominion and the New Nation, 1788–1801* (1972); Irving Brant, *The Bill of Rights* (1965); Richard Brookhiser, *Founding Father: Rediscovering George Washington* (1996); Ralph Adams Brown, *The Presidency of John Adams* (1975); Jerald A. Combs, *The Jay Treaty* (1970); Manning Dauer, *The Adams Federalists* (1953); Stanley Elkins and Eric McKitrick, *The Age of Federalism* (1993); John F. Hoadley, *Origins of American Political Parties, 1789–1803* (1986); John R. Howe, *The Changing Political Thought of John Adams* (1966); Ralph Ketcham, *Presidents Above Party: The First American Presidency, 1789–1829* (1984); Richard Kohn, *Eagle and Sword: The Federalists and the Creation of the Military Establishment in America, 1783–1802* (1975); Stephen G. Kurtz, *The Presidency of John Adams* (1957); Daniel G. Lang, *Foreign Policy in the Early Republic* (1985); Leonard Levy, *Legacy of Suppression: Freedom of Speech and Press in Early American History,* rev. ed. (1985); Forrest McDonald, *The Presidency of George Washington* (1974); John C. Miller, *Crisis in Freedom* (1951), and *The Federalist Era, 1789–1801* (1960); Carl E. Prince, *The Federalists and the Origins of the U.S. Civil Service* (1978); Thomas P. Slaughter, *The Whiskey Rebellion: Frontier Epilogue to the American Revolution* (1986); James M. Smith, *Freedom's Fetters: The Alien and Sedition Laws and American Civil Liberties* (1956); Wiley Sword, *President Washington's Indian War: The Struggle for the Old Northwest, 1790–1795* (1985); Mary K. B. Tachau, *Federal Courts in the Early Republic: Kentucky, 1789–1816* (1978); Leonard D. White, *The Federalists* (1948); Ann Fairfax Withington, *Toward A More Perfect Union: Virtue and the Formation of American Republics* (1991).

**The Jeffersonian Republicans.** Joyce Appleby, *Capitalism and a New Social Order: The Republican Vision of the 1790s* (1984); Lance Banning, *The Jeffersonian Persuasion* (1978); Charles A. Beard, *The Economic Origins of the Jeffersonian Opposition* (1915); Richard W. Buel, Jr., *Securing the Revolution: Ideology in American Politics, 1789–1815* (1972); William N. Chambers, *Political Parties in a New Nation* (1963); Joseph Charles, *The Origins of the American Party System* (1956); Noble Cunningham, *The Jeffersonian Republicans* (1957); Richard Hofstadter, *The Idea of a Party System* (1970); Drew McCoy, *The Elusive Republic: Political Economy in Jeffersonian America* (1980), and *The Last of the Fathers: James Madison and the Republican Legacy* (1989); Thomas L. Pangle, *The Spirit of Modern Republicanism: The Moral Vision of the American Founders and the Followers of Locke* (1988); Merrill D. Peterson, *Thomas Jefferson and the New Nation* (1970); Norman K. Risjord, *Chesapeake Politics, 1781–1800* (1978); Patricia Watlington, *The Partisan Spirit* (1972); Alfred F. Young, *The Democratic-Republicans of New York* (1967); John Zvesper, *Political Philosophy and Rhetoric: A Study of the Origins of American Party Politics* (1977).

**Federalist Diplomacy.** Harry Ammon, *The Genet Mission* (1973); Samuel F. Bemis, *Jay's Treaty* (1923), and *Pinckney's Treaty* (1926, rev. 1960); Alexander DeConde, *Entangling Alliance* (1958), and *The Quasi-War* (1966); Felix Gilbert, *To the Farewell Address* (1961); Lawrence S. Kaplan, *Jefferson and France* (1967); Bradford Perkins, *The Cambridge*

*History of American Foreign Relations*, vol. 1: *The Creation of a Republican Empire, 1776–1865* (1993), and *The First Rapprochment: England and the United States* (1967); Charles Ritcheson, *Aftermath of Revolution: British Policy Toward the United States, 1783–1795* (1969); Louis M. Sears, *George Washington and the French Revolution* (1960); Paul A. Varg, *Foreign Policies of the Founding Fathers* (1963).

**The Founders.** Irving Brant, *James Madison* (1950); James T. Flexner, *George Washington*, 4 vols. (1965–1972); Douglas Southall Freeman, *George Washington*, 7 vols. (1948–1957); Milton Lomask, *Aaron Burr*, 2 vols. (1979, 1982); Dumas Malone, *Jefferson and His Time*, 6 vols. (1948–1981); John C. Miller, *Alexander Hamilton* (1959); Richard B. Morris, *Witnesses at the Creation: Hamilton, Madison, Jay, and the Constitution* (1985); Merrill Peterson, *Thomas Jefferson and the New Nation* (1970); Barry Schwartz, *George Washington: The Making of a Symbol* (1987); Page Smith, *John Adams* (1962); William Stinchcombe, *The XYZ Affair* (1980); Garry Wills, *Cincinnatus: George Washington and the Enlightenment* (1984); Esmond Wright, *Franklin of Philadelphia* (1986).

CHAPTER 7 THE JEFFERSONIAN ERA

**General Histories.** Henry Adams, *History of the United States During the Administrations of Jefferson and Adams*, 9 vols. (1889–1891); Marcus Cunliffe, *The Nation Takes Shape, 1789–1832* (1959); Charles Mayfield, *The New Nation* (1981); Marshall Smelser, *The Democratic Republicans, 1801–1815* (1968).

**Society and Culture.** Sydney Ahlstrom, *A Religious History of the American People* (1972); Terry D. Bilhartz, *Urban Religion and the Second Great Awakening* (1986); John Boles, *The Great Revival in the South* (1972); Jeanne Boydston, *Home and Work: Housework, Wages, and the Ideology of Labor in the Early Republic* (1990); Priscilla F. Clement, *Welfare and the Poor in the Nineteenth-Century City* (1985); Lawrence A. Cremin, *American Education: The National Experience* (1981); Whitney R. Cross, *The Burned-Over District* (1950); Cathy Davidson, *The Revolution and the Word* (1986); Joseph J. Ellis, *After the Revolution: Profiles of Early American Culture* (1979); Carl F. Kaestle, *The Evolution of an Urban School System* (1973); Jan Lewis, *The Pursuit of Happiness: Family and Values in Jefferson's Virginia* (1983); William G. McLoughlin, *Revivals, Awakenings, and Reform* (1978); Russel B. Nye, *The Cultural Life of the New Nation* (1960); Kenneth Silverman, *A Cultural History of the American Revolution* (1976); Richard Slotkin, *Regeneration Through Violence* (1973); William W. Sweet, *Revivalism in America* (1944); Harry Warfel, *Noah Webster, Schoolmaster to America* (1936).

**Economic Growth.** W. Elliot Brownlee, *Dynamics of Ascent* (1979); Stuart Bruchey, *The Roots of American Economic Growth* (1965); Thomas C. Cochran, *Frontiers of Change: Early Industrialization in America* (1981); Arthur H. Cole, *The American Wool Manufacture*, 2 vols. (1926); C. M. Green, *Eli Whitney and the Birth of American Technology* (1956); James Henretta and Gregory Nobles, *The Evolution of American Society, 1700–1815*, rev. ed., (1987); Douglas C. North, *The Economic Growth of the United States, 1780–1860* (1961); W. J. Rorabaugh, *The Craft Apprentice: From Franklin to the Machine Age in America* (1986); Nathan Rosenberg, *Technology and American Economic Growth* (1972); Merritt Roe Smith, *Harpers Ferry Armory and the New Technology* (1977); George R. Taylor, *The Transportation Revolution* (1951); Barbara M. Tucker, *Samuel Slater and the Origins of the*

*American Textile Industry, 1790–1860* (1984); Anthony F. C. Wallace, *Rockdale* (1978); Caroline F. Ware, *Early New England Cotton Manufacture* (1931).

**Politics and Government.** Leonard Baker, *John Marshall: A Life in Law* (1974); Alexander Balinky, *Albert Gallatin: Fiscal Theories and Policy* (1958); James M. Banner, *To the Hartford Convention* (1967); Morton Borden, *Parties and Politics in the Early Republic* (1967); Noble E. Cunningham, *The Jeffersonian Republicans in Power* (1963); *The Process of Government Under Jefferson* (1978); Robert Dawidoff, *The Education of John Randolph* (1979); Richard Ellis, *The Jeffersonian Crisis: Courts and Politics in the Young Republic* (1971); David Hackett Fischer, *The Revolution of American Conservatism* (1965); Ronald P. Formisano, *The Transformation of Political Culture: Massachusetts Parties, 1790s–1840s* (1983); Robert M. Johnstone, Jr., *Jefferson and the Presidency* (1978); David P. Jordan, *Political Leadership in Jefferson's Virginia* (1983); Linda Kerber, *Federalists in Dissent* (1970); Shaw Livermore, *The Twilight of Federalism* (1962); Dumas Malone, *Jefferson the President: First Term* (1970), and *Jefferson the President: Second Term* (1974); Forrest McDonald, *The Presidency of Thomas Jefferson* (1976); Merrill Peterson, *Thomas Jefferson and the New Nation* (1970); Robert W. Tucker and David C. Hendrickson, *Empire of Liberty: The Statecraft of Thomas Jefferson* (1990); Leonard D. White, *The Jeffersonians* (1951); James S. Young, *The Washington Community* (1966).

**Jeffersonian and Madisonian Thought.** Joyce Appleby, *Capitalism and a New Social Order: The Republican Vision of the 1890s* (1984); Lance Banning, *The Jeffersonian Persuasion: Evolution of a Party Ideology* (1978); Adrienne Koch, *The Philosophy of Thomas Jefferson* (1943); Leonard W. Levy, *Jefferson and Civil Liberties: The Darker Side* (1963); Drew McCoy, *The Elusive Republic: Political Economy in Jeffersonian America* (1980), and *The Last of the Fathers: James Madison and the Republican Legacy* (1989); Merrill Peterson, *The Jeffersonian Image in the American Mind* (1960); Charles M. Wiltse, *The Jeffersonian Tradition in American Democracy* (1935).

**Foreign Policy.** Thomas P. Abernethy, *The Burr Conspiracy* (1954); Harry Ammon, *James Monroe and the Quest for National Identity* (1971); Irving Brant, *James Madison*, 6 vols. (1953–1961); George Dangerfield, *Chancellor Robert R. Livingston of New York* (1960); Alexander DeConde, *The Affair of Louisiana* (1976); Bernard De Voto, *Course of Empire* (1952); Bernard De Voto, ed., *The Journals of Lewis and Clark* (1953); Milton Lomask, *Aaron Burr*, 2 vols. (1979, 1982); Bradford Perkins, *Prologue to War: England and the United States, 1805–1812* (1961); Nathan Schachner, *Aaron Burr* (1937); Arthur P. Whitaker, *The Mississippi Question* (1934).

**Indians and the West.** Ray Allen Billington, *Westward Expansion* (1967); Gregory Evans Dowd, *A Spirited Resistance: The North American Indian Struggle for Unity, 1745–1815* (1992); R. David Edmunds, *The Shawnee Prophet* (1983), and *Tecumseh and the Quest for Indian Leadership* (1984); Reginald Horsman, *Expansion and American Indian Policy, 1783–1812* (1962), and *Matthew Elliott, British Indian Agent* (1964); Francis S. Philbrick, *The Rise of the New West* (1965); Francis P. Prucha, *American Indian Policy in the Formative Years* (1962); James P. Ronda, *Lewis and Clark Among the Indians* (1984); B. W. Sheehan, *Seeds of Extinction* (1973); Richard White, *The Roots of Dependency* (1983); Charles Wilkinson, *American Indians, Time, and the Law*, rev. ed. (1982).

**The War of 1812.** F. F. Beirne, *The War of 1812* (1949); Samuel F. Bemis, *John Quincy Adams and the Foundations of American Foreign Policy* (1949); Roger H. Brown, *The Re-*

*public in Peril: 1812* (1964); A. L. Burtt, *The United States, Great Britain, and British North America* (1940); Harry L. Coles, *The War of 1812* (1965); R. David Edmunds, *The Shawnee Prophet* (1983), and *Tecumseh and the Quest for Indian Leadership* (1984); Donald R. Hickey, *The West of 1812* (1989); Reginald Horsman, *The Causes of the War of 1812* (1962), and *The War of 1812* (1969); Alfred T. Mahan, *Sea Power in Its Relation to the War of 1812*, 2 vols. (1905); John Mahon, *The War of 1812* (1975); Bradford Perkins, *Prologue to War: England and the United States, 1805–1812* (1961), and *Castlereagh and Adams* (1964); Julius W. Pratt, *Expansionists of 1812* (1925); Robert V. Remini, *Andrew Jackson and the Course of American Empire* (1977); Robert Allen Rutland, *The Presidency of James Madison* (1990); J. C. A. Stagg, *Mr. Madison's War: Politics, Diplomacy, and Warfare in the Early American Republic, 1783–1830* (1983); Burton Spivak, *Jefferson's English Crisis: Commerce, Embargo, and the Republican Revolution* (1979); William Wood, *The War with the United States* (1915).

## CHAPTER 8 VARIETIES OF AMERICAN NATIONALISM

**Economic Growth.** George Dangerfield, *The Awakening of American Nationalism* (1965), and *The Era of Good Feelings* (1952); Bray Hammond, *Banks and Politics in America from the Revolution to the Civil War* (1957); Shaw Livermore, Jr., *The Twilight of Federalism* (1962); Murray N. Rothbard, *The Panic of 1819* (1962).

**Expanding Westward.** Thomas P. Abernethy, *The South in the New Nation* (1961); Ray Allen Billington, *The Far Western Frontier* (1965), and *Westward Expansion* (1974); Colin Calloway, *Crown and Calumet* (1987); John Mack Faragher, *Women and Men on the Overland Trail* (1979), and *Daniel Boone: The Life of and Legend of an American Pioneer* (1992); John A. Hawgood, *America's Western Frontier* (1967); Julie Roy Jeffrey, *Frontier Women: The Trans-Mississippi West* (1979); Frederick Merk, *History of the Westward Movement* (1978); Francis S. Philbrick, *The Rise of the West, 1745–1830* (1965); Glenda Riley, *The Female Frontier* (1988); Malcolm J. Rohrbough, *The Land Office Business: The Settlement and Administration of American Public Lands, 1789–1837* (1968); Frederick Jackson Turner, *The Rise of the New West* (1906), and *The Frontier in American History* (1920); Dale Van Every, *The Final Challenge* (1964).

**The "Era of Good Feelings."** Harry Ammon, *James Monroe: The Quest for National Identity* (1971); Samuel F. Bemis, *John Quincy Adams and the Union* (1956); Wesley Frank Craven, *The Legend of the Founding Fathers* (1956); George Dangerfield, *The Awakening of American Nationalism* (1965), and *The Era of Good Feelings* (1952); Don E. Fehrenbacher, *The South and Three Sectional Crises* (1980); Shaw Livermore, *The Twilight of Federalism* (1962); Glover Moore, *The Missouri Compromise* (1953); Paul C. Nagle, *One Nation Indivisible: The Union in American Thought, 1815–1828* (1965); Robert V. Remini, *The Election of Andrew Jackson* (1963); Norman K. Risjord, *The Old Republicans: Southern Conservatism in the Age of Jefferson* (1965); Glyndon Van Deusen, *The Life of Henry Clay* (1937); Charles M. Wiltse, *John C. Calhoun: American Nationalist* (1944).

**The Courts.** Leonard Baker, *John Marshall: A Life in Law* (1974); Albert J. Beveridge, *The Life of John Marshall*, 4 vols. (1916–1919); Alexander M. Bickel, *Justice Joseph Story and the Rise of the Supreme Court* (1971); D. O. Dewey, *Marshall Versus Jefferson: The Political Background of Marbury v. Madison* (1970); Richard E. Ellis, *The Jeffersonian Crisis:*

*Courts and Politics in the Young Republic* (1971); Charles G. Haines, *The Role of the Supreme Court in American Government and Politics, 1789–1835* (1970); Morton J. Horowitz, *The Transformation of American Law, 1780–1865* (1977); James McClellan, *Joseph Story and the American Constitution* (1971); R. Kent Newmyer, *The Supreme Court Under Marshall and Taney* (1968); Francis N. Stites, *John Marshall: Defender of the Constitution* (1981).

**The Monroe Doctrine.** Samuel F. Bemis, *John Quincy Adams and the Foundations of American Foreign Policy* (1940); Walter LaFeber, ed., *John Quincy Adams and the Continental Empire* (1965); Ernest R. May, *The Making of the Monroe Doctrine* (1975); Bradford Perkins, *Castlereagh and Adams: England and the United States, 1812–1823* (1964); Dexter Perkins, *The Monroe Doctrine* (1927), and *Hands Off: A History of the Monroe Doctrine* (1941); Frank Thistlethwaite, *The Anglo-American Connection in the Early Nineteenth Century* (1959); Arthur P. Whitaker, *The United States and the Independence of Latin America* (1941).

## CHAPTER 9 JACKSONIAN AMERICA

**General Histories.** James C. Curtis, *Andrew Jackson and the Search for Vindication* (1976); John Mayfield, *The New Nation, 1800–1845* (1981); Edward Pessen, *Jacksonian America*, rev. ed. (1979); Robert V. Remini, *The Jacksonian Era* (1989); Arthur M. Schlesinger, Jr., *The Age of Jackson* (1945); Charles Sellers, *The Market Revolution: Jacksonian America, 1815–1846* (1991); Glyndon Van Deusen, *The Jacksonian Era* (1959).

**Democracy.** Patrick T. Conley, *Democracy in Decline* (1977); Marvin E. Gettleman, *The Dorr Rebellion* (1973); Louis Hartz, *The Liberal Tradition in America* (1955); Michael Kammen, *Spheres of Liberty: Changing Perceptions of Liberty in American Culture* (1986); Moisie Ostrogorskii, *Democracy and the Organization of Political Parties*, 2 vols. (1902); Fred Somkin, *Unquiet Eagle: Memory and Desire in the Idea of American Freedom, 1815–1860* (1967); Alexis de Tocqueville, *Democracy in America*, 2 vols. (1835); Chilton Williamson, *American Suffrage from Property to Democracy, 1760–1860* (1960).

**Jacksonian Society.** Kenneth Cmiel, *Democratic Eloquence: The Fight over Popular Speech in Nineteenth-Century America* (1990); Nancy Hewitt, *Women's Activism and Social Change: Rochester, New York, 1822–1872* (1984); Douglas T. Miller, *Jacksonian Aristocracy* (1967); Edward Pessen, *Riches, Class, and Power Before the Civil War* (1973); Mary Ryan, *Cradle of the Middle Class: The Family in Oneida County, New York, 1790–1865* (1981); Carroll Smith-Rosenberg, *Religion and the Rise of the City* (1971); Christine Stansell, *City of Women: Sex and Class in New York, 1789–1860* (1986); Sean Wilentz, *Chants Democratic: New York City and the Rise of the American Working Class, 1788–1850* (1984).

**Jacksonian Politics.** Lee Benson, *The Concept of Jacksonian Democracy* (1961); Ronald P. Formisano, *The Birth of Mass Political Parties: Michigan, 1928–1861* (1971); Paul Goodman, *Towards a Christian Republic: Antimasonry and the Great Transition in New England, 1826–1836* (1988); Richard Hofstadter, *The American Political Tradition* (1948); Morton Horwitz, *The Transformation of American Law, 1780–1860* (1977); Richard B. Latner, *The Presidency of Andrew Jackson: White House Politics, 1829–1837* (1979); Richard B. McCormick, *The Second American Party System: Party Formation in the Jacksonian Era* (1966); Marvin Meyers, *The Jacksonian Persuasion* (1960); Robert V. Remini, *The Age of Jackson*

(1972); *Andrew Jackson and the Bank War* (1967); C. B. Swisher, *Roger B. Taney* (1936); John William Ward, *Andrew Jackson: Symbol for an Age* (1955); Harry L. Watson, *Jacksonian Politics and Community Conflict: The Emergence of the Second Party System in Cumberland County, North Carolina* (1981), and *Liberty and Power: The Politics of Jacksonian America* (1990); Leonard White, *The Jacksonians: A Study in Administrative History* (1954).

**Andrew Jackson.** Marquis James, *Andrew Jackson*, 2 vols. (1933–1937); James Parton, *Life of Andrew Jackson*, 3 vols. (1860); Robert V. Remini, *Andrew Jackson and the Course of American Empire: 1767–1821* (1977); *Andrew Jackson and the Course of American Freedom: 1822–1832* (1981); *Andrew Jackson and the Course of American Democracy* (1984), and *The Life of Andrew Jackson* (1988).

**Nullification.** Irving H. Bartlett, *John C. Calhoun: A Biography* (1993); William V. Freehling, *Prelude to Civil War: The Nullification Controversy in South Carolina* (1966); Merrill D. Peterson, *Olive Branch and Sword: The Compromise of 1833* (1983); Charles S. Sydnor, *The Development of Southern Sectionalism 1819–1848* (1948); Charles M. Wiltse, *John C. Calhoun: Nullifier* (1949).

**Indian Policies.** William Brandon, *The Last Americans* (1974); Duane Champagne, *Social Order and Political Change: Constitutional Governments Among the Cherokee, the Choctow, the Chickasaw, and the Creek* (1992); Angie Debo, *A History of the Indians of the United States* (1970); *The Road to Disappearance: A History of the Creek Indians* (1941), and *And Still the Waters Run: The Betrayal of the Five Civilized Tribes* (1973); Arthur H. DeRosier, Jr., *The Removal of the Choctaw Indians* (1970); Cecil Elby, *"That Disgraceful Affair"* (1973); Grant Foreman, *Indian Removal: The Emigration of the Five Civilized Tribes* (1932), and *Indians and Pioneers: The Story of the American Southwest Before 1830* (1936); Michael D. Green, *The Politics of Indian Removal: Cherokee Government and Society in Crisis* (1982); Daniel F. Littlefield, Jr., *Africans and Seminoles: From Removal to Emancipation* (1976); and *Africans and Creeks: From the Colonial Period to the Civil War* (1979); Theda Perdue, *Slavery and the Evolution of Cherokee Society, 1540–1866* (1979); Francis P. Prucha, *American Indian Policy in the Formative Years* (1962); Michael Rogin, *Fathers and Children: Andrew Jackson and the Destruction of American Indians* (1975); Ronald N. Satz, *American Indian Policy in the Jacksonian Era* (1975); B. W. Sheehan, *Seeds of Extinction: Jeffersonian Philanthropy and the American Indian* (1973); Anthony Wallace, *The Long Bitter Trail: Andrew Jackson and the Indians* (1993); Wilcomb E. Washburn, *The Indian in America* (1975); Richard White, *The Roots of Dependency* (1983); Thurman Wilkins, *Cherokee Tragedy* (1970).

**The Bank War.** T. P. Govan, *Nicholas Biddle, Nationalist and Public Banker* (1959); Bray Hammond, *Banks and Politics in America from the Revolution to the Civil War* (1957); John M. McFaul, *The Politics of Jacksonian Finance* (1972); Reginald C. McGrane, *The Panic of 1837* (1924); Robert V. Remini, *Andrew Jackson and the Bank War* (1967); William G. Shade, *Banks or No Banks: The Money Issue in Western Politics, 1832–1865* (1972); James R. Sharp, *The Jacksonians Versus the Banks* (1970); Peter Temin, *The Jacksonian Economy* (1969); J. A. Wilburn, *Biddle's Bank* (1967).

**Post-Jacksonian Politics.** John Ashworth, *"Agrarians" and "Aristocrats": Party Political Ideology in the United States, 1837–1846* (1983); Irving Bartlett, *Daniel Webster* (1978); Maurice C. Baxter, *One and Inseparable: Daniel Webster and the Union* (1984); John B. Brebner, *North Atlantic Triangle* (1945); Norman D. Brown, *Daniel Webster and the Politics of Availability* (1969); Thomas Brown, *Politics and Statesmanship: Essays on the American Whig Party* (1985); E. M. Carroll, *Origins of the Whig Party* (1925); Oliver P. Chitwood, *John Tyler: Champion of the Old South* (1939); Donald B. Cole, *Martin Van Buren and the American Political System* (1984); A. B. Corey, *The Crisis of 1830–1842 in Canadian-American Relations* (1941); Richard N. Current, *Daniel Webster and the Rise of National Conservatism* (1955); James C. Curtis, *The Fox at Bay: Martin Van Buren and the Presidency* (1970); Robert Dalzell, *Daniel Webster and the Trial of American Nationalism* (1973); Clement Eaton, *Henry Clay and the Art of American Politics* (1957); Claude M. Fuess, *Daniel Webster*, 2 vols. (1930). Paul Goodman, *Towards a Christian Republic: Anti-Masonry and the Great Transition in New England, 1826–1836* (1988); R. G. Gunderson, *The Log Cabin Campaign* (1957); Daniel Walker Howe, *The Political Culture of the American Whigs* (1979); Howard Jones, *To the Webster-Ashburton Treaty* (1977); Oscar D. Lambert, *Presidential Politics in the United States, 1841–1844* (1936); Sydney Nathans, *Daniel Webster and Jacksonian Democracy* (1973); John Niven, *Martin Van Buren: The Romantic Age of American Politics* (1983); Thomas H. O'Connor, *Lords of the Loom: The Cotton Whigs and the Coming of the Civil War* (1968); Merrill D. Peterson, *The Great Triumvirate: Webster, Clay, and Calhoun* (1987); George R. Poage, *Henry Clay and the Whig Party* (1936); Robert V. Remini, *Martin Van Buren and the Making of the Democratic Party* (1959), and *Henry Clay: Statesman for the Union* (1991); Alexander Saxton, *The Rise and Fall of the White Republic: Class Politics and Mass Culture in Nineteenth-Century America* (1990); William Preston Vaughn, *The Anti-Masonic Party in the United States, 1826–1843* (1983); Major L. Wilson, *The Presidency of Martin Van Buren* (1984).

## CHAPTER 10 AMERICA'S ECONOMIC REVOLUTION

**The Market Revolution.**   W. Elliot Brownlee, *Dynamics of Ascent* (1974); Stuart Bruchey, *The Growth of the Modern American Economy* (1975); Christopher Clark, *The Roots of Rural Capitalism: Western Massachusetts, 1780–1860* (1990); Thomas C. Cochran, *Frontiers of Change: Early Industrialization in America* (1981); Paul W. Gates, *The Farmer's Age* (1960); Douglass North, *The Economic Growth of the United States, 1790–1860* (1961); Charles G. Sellers, *The Market Revolution: Jacksonian America, 1815–1846* (1991); Peter Temin, *The Jacksonian Economy* (1969).

**Immigration.**   Rowland T. Berthoff, *British Immigrants in Industrial America, 1790–1950* (1953); Ray Billington, *The Protestant Crusade, 1800–1860* (1938); Theodore C. Blegen, *Norwegian Migration to America*, 2 vols. (1931–1940); John Bodnar, *The Transplanted: A History of Immigrants in America* (1985); Kathleen N. Conzen, *Immigrant Milwaukee: 1836–1860* (1976); Thomas J. Curran, *Xenophobia and Immigration, 1820–1930* (1975); Hasia Diner, *Erin's Daughters in America* (1983); Jay P. Dolan, *The Immigrant Church: New York's Irish and German Catholics* (1975); Charlotte Erickson, *Invisible Immigrants* (1972); Robert Ernst, *Immigrant Life in New York City, 1825–1863* (1949); Oscar Handlin, *The Uprooted* (1951, rev. 1973), and *Boston's Immigrants* (1941); Marcus L. Hansen, *The Immigrant in American History* (1940), and *The Atlantic Migration, 1607–1860* (1940); Maldwyn A. Jones, *American Immigration* (1960); I. M. Leonard and R. D. Parmet, *American Nativism, 1830–1860* (1971); Stuart C. Miller, *The Unwelcome Immigrant* (1969); Allan Nevins, *The Ordeal of the Union*, 2 vols. (1947); Harold Runblom and Hans Norman, *From*

*Sweden to America* (1976); Philip Taylor, *The Distant Magnet: European Emigration to the United States of America* (1971); Carl Wittke, *We Who Built America*, rev. ed. (1964); *Refugees of Revolution: The German Forty-Eighters in America* (1952), and *The Irish in America* (1956).

**Transportation and Communications.**   Collen A. Dunlavy, *Politics and Industrialization: Early Railroads in the United States and Prussia* (1994); Albert Fishlow, *American Railroads and the Transformation of the Ante-Bellum Economy* (1965); Robert W. Fogel, *Railroads and American Economic Growth* (1964); Carter Goodrich, *Government Promotion of American Canals and Railroads, 1800–1890* (1960); Eric K. Haites, James Mak, and Gary M. Walton, *Western River Transportation: The Era of Early Internal Development, 1800–1860* (1975); Nathan Miller, *The Enterprise of a Free People* (1962); Frank Luther Mott, *American Journalism* (1950); Robert J. Parks, *Democracy's Railroads: Public Enterprise in Michigan* (1972); Harry N. Scheiber, *Ohio Canal Era* (1969); Ronald E. Shaw, *Erie Water West: A History of the Erie Canal* (1966); John F. Stover, *American Railroads* (1961), *The Life and Decline of the American Railroad* (1970), and *Iron Road to the West: American Railroads in the 1850s* (1978); George R. Taylor, *The Transportation Revolution* (1951); R. L. Thompson, *Writing a Continent* (1947).

**Business and Technology.**   Menahem Blondheim, *News Over the Wires: The Telegraph and the Flow of Public Information in America, 1844–1897* (1994); Richard D. Brown, *Modernization: The Transformation of American Life, 1600–1865* (1976); Alfred D. Chandler, Jr., *The Visible Hand: The Managerial Revolution in American Business* (1977); Thomas C. Cochran, *Business in American Life* (1972); Thomas C. Cochran and William Miller, *The Age of Enterprise* (1942); E. P. Douglas, *The Coming of Age of American Business* (1971); Siegfried Giedion, *Mechanization Takes Command* (1948); H. J. Habbakuk, *American and British Technology in the Nineteenth Century* (1962); David J. Jeremy, *Transatlantic Industrial Revolution: The Diffusion of Textile Technologies Between Britain and America, 1780–1830* (1981); John F. Kasson, *Civilizing the Machine: Technology and Republican Values in America, 1776–1900* (1976); Diane Lindstrom, *Economic Development in the Philadelphia Region, 1810–1850* (1978); Otto Mayr and Robert C. Post, eds., *Yankee Enterprise: The Rise of the American System of Manufactures* (1981); Judith A. McGaw, *Most Wonderful Machine: Mechanization and Social Change in Berkshire Paper Making, 1815–1885* (1987); James Norris, *R. G. Dun & Co., 1841–1900* (1978); Nathan Rosenberg, *Technology and American Economic Growth* (1972); Merritt Roe Smith, *Harpers Ferry Armory and the New Technology* (1977); Peter Temin, *Iron and Steel in Nineteenth-Century America* (1964).

**Factories and the Working Class.**   Mary H. Blewett, *Men, Women, and Work* (1988), and *We Will Rise in Our Might: Workingwomen's Voices from Nineteenth-Century New England* (1991); Arthur H. Cole, *The American Wool Manufacture*, 2 vols. (1926); Alan Dawley, *Class and Community: The Industrial Revolution in Lynn* (1976); Thomas Dublin, *Women at Work* (1979); Susan E. Hirsch, *Roots of the American Working Class: The Industrialization of Crafts in Newark, 1800–1860* (1978); David A. Hounshell, *From the American System to Mass Production, 1800–1932: The Development of Manufacturing Technology in the United States* (1985); Alice Kessler-Harris, *Out to Work: A History of Wage-Earning Women in the United States* (1982); Bruce Laurie, *Working People of Philadelphia* (1980); Bruce Levine, *The Spirit of 1848: German Immigrants, Labor Conflict, and the Coming of the Civil War* (1992); Walter Licht, *Getting Work: Philadelphia, 1840–1950* (1992); David Montgomery, *Citizen Worker* (1993); Henry Pelling, *American Labor* (1960); David R.

Roediger, *The Wages of Whiteness: Race and the Making of the American Working Class* (1991); W. J. Rorabaugh, *The Craft Apprentice: From Franklin to the Machine Age* (1986); Steven J. Ross, *Workers on the Edge: Work, Leisure, and Politics in Industrializing Cincinnati, 1788–1890* (1985); Christine Stansell, *City of Women: Sex and Class in New York, 1789–1860* (1986); Christopher Tomlins, *Law, Labor and Ideology in the Early American Republic* (1993); Barbara M. Tucker, *Samuel Slater and the Origins of the American Textile Industry, 1790–1860* (1985); Joseph E. Walker, *Hopewell: A Social and Economic History of an Ironmaking Community* (1966); Caroline Ware, *The Early New England Cotton Manufacture* (1931); Norman Ware, *The Industrial Worker, 1840–1860* (1924); Peter Way, *Common Labor: Workers and the Digging of North American Canals, 1780–1860* (1993); Sean Wilentz, *Chants Democratic: New York City and the Rise of the American Working Class, 1788–1850* (1984); David A. Zonderman, *Aspirations and Anxieties: New England Workers and the Mechanized Factory System, 1815–1850* (1992).

**Society and Culture.** Rowland T. Berthoff, *An Unsettled People: Social Order and Disorder in American History* (1971); Stuart Blumin, *The Urban Threshold: Growth and Change in a Nineteenth-Century Community* (1976); Daniel Boorstin, *The Americans: The National Experience* (1965); John L. Brooke, *The Heart of the Commonwealth: Society and Political Culture in Worcester County, Massachusetts, 1713–1861* (1989); Leonard P. Curry, *The Free Black in Urban America, 1800–1850* (1981); Don Doyle, *The Social Order of a Frontier Community: Jacksonville, Illinois, 1825–1870* (1978); Michael Frisch, *Town into City: Springfield, Massachusetts, and the Meaning of Community, 1840–1880* (1972); Timothy J. Gilfoyle, *City of Eros: New York City, Prostitution and the Commercialization of Sex, 1790–1920* (1992); Paul A. Gilje, *The Road to Mobocracy: Popular Disorder in New York City, 1763–1834* (1987); Jonathan A. Glickstein, *Concepts of Free Labor in Antebellum America* (1991); Clyde Griffen and Sally Griffen, *Natives and Newcomers: The Ordering of Opportunity in Mid-Nineteenth-Century Poughkeepsie* (1978); Paul Johnson, *A Shopkeeper's Millennium: Society and Revivals in Rochester, New York, 1815–1837* (1978); Hannah Josephson, *The Golden Threads* (1949); Peter Knights, *The Plain People of Boston, 1830–1860* (1971); Raymond A. Mohl, *Poverty in New York, 1783–1825* (1971). Teresa Anne Murphy, *Ten Hours Labor: Religion, Reform and Gender in Early New England* (1992); Edward Pessen, *Riches, Classes, and Power Before the Civil War* (1973); David Thelen, *Paths of Resistance: Tradition and Dignity in Industrializing Missouri* (1986); Stephan Thernstrom, *Poverty and Progress* (1964); Glyndon Van Deusen, *Horace Greeley* (1953); Richard C. Wade, *The Urban Frontier, 1790–1830* (1957); Anthony F. C. Wallace, *Rockdale: The Growth of an American Village in the Early Industrial Revolution* (1977); Sam Bass Warner, Jr., *The Urban Wilderness* (1972).

**Women and Family.** Jeanne Boydston, *Home and Work* (1990); Nancy F. Cott, *The Bonds of Womanhood: "Woman's Sphere" in New England, 1780–1835* (1977); Ruth Schwartz Cowan, *More Work for Mother: The Ironies of Household Technology from the Open Hearth to the Microwave* (1983); Carl Degler, *At Odds: Women and the Family in America from the Revolution to the Present* (1980); Dolores Hayden, *The Grand Domestic Revolution: A History of Feminist Designs for American Homes, Neighborhoods, and Cities* (1981); Ellen K. Rothman, *Hands and Heart: A History of Courtship in America* (1987); Mary Ryan, *Cradle of the Middle Class: The Family in Oneida County, New York, 1790–1865* (1981); Kathryn K. Sklar, *Catherine Beecher: A Study in American Domesticity* (1973); Carroll Smith-Rosenberg, *Disorderly Conduct: Visions of Gender in Victorian America* (1985); Christine Stansell, *City of Women: Sex and Class in New York, 1789–1860* (1986); Susan Strasser, *Never Done: A His-*

*tory of American Housework* (1983); Gwendolyn Wright, *Building the Dream: A Social History of Housing in America* (1981).

## CHAPTER 11 COTTON, SLAVERY, AND THE OLD SOUTH

**Culture and Society in the White South.**  Edward L. Ayers, *Vengeance and Justice: Crime and Punishment in the Nineteenth-Century American South* (1984); David T. Bailey, *Shadow on the Church: Southwestern Evangelical Religion and the Issue of Slavery, 1783–1860* (1985); Fred Bateman, *A Deplorable Scarcity: The Failure of Industrialism in the Slave Economy* (1981); Orville Vernon Burton, *Class, Conflict, and Consensus: Antebellum Southern Community Studies* (1982), and *In My Father's House Are Many Mansions: Family and Community in Edgefield, South Carolina* (1985); Dickson D. Bruce, *Violence and Culture in the Antebellum South* (1979); W. J. Cash, *The Mind of the South* (1941); Bruce Collins, *White Society in the Antebellum South* (1985); Avery Craven, *The Growth of Southern Nationalism* (1953); Wilma A. Dunaway, *The First American Frontier: Transition to Capitalism in Southern Appalachia, 1700–1860* (1996); Clement Eaton, *Freedom of Thought in the Old South* (1940), and *The Growth of Southern Nationalism, 1848–1861* (1961); Drew Gilpin Faust, *A Sacred Circle: The Dilemma of the Intellectual in the Old South* (1977); *James Henry Hammond and the Old South: A Design for Mastery* (1982); John Hope Franklin, *The Militant South* (1956); Frank Freidel, *Francis Lieber* (1947); Steven Hahn, *The Roots of Southern Populism: Yeomen Farmers and the Transformation of the Georgia Upcountry, 1850–1890* (1983); Ann C. Loveland, *Southern Evangelicals and the Social Order, 1800–1860* (1980); Donald G. Mathews, *Religion in the Old South* (1977); John McCardell, *The Idea of a Southern Nation* (1979); Rollin G. Osterweis, *Romanticism and Nationalism in the Old South* (1949); Mitchell Snay, *Gospel of Disunion: Religion and Separation in the Antebellum South* (1993); Charles S. Sydnor, *The Development of Southern Sectionalism, 1819–1848* (1948); William R. Taylor, *Cavalier and Yankee: The Old South and American National Character* (1961); Bertram Wyatt-Brown, *Southern Honor: Ethics and Behavior in the Old South* (1982), and *Yankee Saints and Southern Sinners* (1985).

**The Plantation Economy.**  Eugene Genovese, *The Political Economy of Slavery* (1965); Lewis C. Gray, *History of Agriculture in the Southern United States to 1860*, 2 vols. (1933); J. William Harris, *Plain Folk and Gentry in a Slave Society* (1985); Peter Kolchin, *Unfree Labor: American Slavery and Russian Serfdom* (1987); Frank L. Owsley, *Plain Folk of the Old South* (1949); Ulrich B. Phillips, *Life and Labor in the Old South* (1929); Joseph P. Reidy, *From Slavery to Agrarian Capitalism in the Cotton Plantation of the South: Central Georgia, 1800–1880* (1992); R. R. Russel, *Economic Aspects of Southern Sectionalism, 1840–1861* (1924); Ralph A. Wooster, *Politicians, Planters, and Plain Folk* (1975); Gavin Wright, *The Political Economy of the Cotton South: Households, Markets, and Wealth in the Nineteenth Century* (1978).

**The Planters.**  Carol Blesser, *The Hammonds of Redcliffe* (1981); Elizabeth Fox-Genovese, *Within the Plantation Household: Black and White Women of the Old South* (1988); Eugene Genovese, *The Slaveholder's Dilemma: Freedom and Progress in Southern Conservative Thought* (1992), and *The World the Slaveholders Made* (1969); Kenneth S. Greenberg, *Masters and Statesmen: The Political Culture of American Slavery* (1985); Frances Ann Kemble, *Journal of a Residence on a Georgian Plantation in 1838–1839* (1863); Robert Manson

Myers, ed., *The Children of Pride* (1972); James Oakes, *The Ruling Race: A History of American Slaveholders* (1982), and *Slavery and Freedom: An Interpretation of the Old South* (1990); Mary D. Robertson, ed., *Lucy Breckinridge of Grove Hill* (1979).

**Southern White Women and Families.** Peter W. Bardaglio, *Reconstructing the Household: Families, Sex, and the Law in the Nineteenth-Century South* (1996); Victoria E. Bynum, *Unruly Women: The Politics of Social and Sexual Control in the Old South* (1992); Jane Turner Censer, *North Carolina Planters and Their Children, 1800–1860* (1984); Mary Boykin Chesnut, *A Diary from Dixie* (1981, C. Vann Woodward, ed.); Catherine Clinton, *The Plantation Mistress: Woman's World in the Old South* (1982); Elizabeth Fox-Genovese, *Within the Plantation Household: Black and White Women of the Old South* (1988); Suzanne Lebsock, *The Free Women of Petersburg: Status and Culture in a Southern Town* (1984); Anne Firor Scott, *The Southern Lady* (1970).

**Society, Culture, and Slavery in the Black South.** Roger D. Abrahams, *Singing the Master: The Emergence of African American Culture in the Plantation South* (1992); Herbert Aptheker, *American Negro Slave Revolts* (1943); Ira Berlin, *Slaves Without Masters* (1974); John Blassingame, *The Slave Community* (1973). John B. Boles, *Black Southerners, 1619–1869* (1983); Judith Chase, *Afro-American Art and Craft* (1971); Leonard P. Curry, *The Free Black in Urban America: The Shadow of the Dream* (1981); P. A. David et al., *Reckoning with Slavery* (1976); David Brion Davis, *Slavery and Human Progress* (1984); Carl Degler, *Neither Black nor White* (1971); Stanley Elkins, *Slavery* (1959); Dena J. Epstein, *Sinful Tunes and Spirituals: Black Folk Music to the Civil War* (1977); Barbara Jean Fields, *Slavery and Freedom on the Middle Ground* (1985); Robert Fogel, *Without Consent or Contract: The Rise and Fall of American Slavery* (1989); Robert Fogel and Stanley Engerman, *Time on the Cross*, 2 vols. (1974); Eugene Genovese, *Roll, Jordan, Roll: The World the Slaves Made* (1974); Claudia D. Goldin, *Urban Slavery in the American South, 1820–1860* (1876); Herbert Gutman, *Slavery and the Numbers Game* (1975), and *The Black Family in Slavery and Freedom* (1976); Melville J. Herskovits, *The Myth of the Negro Past* (1941); Michael P. Johnson and James L. Roark, *Black Masters* (1984); Jacqueline Jones, *Labor of Love, Labor of Sorrow: Black Women, Work, and the Family from Slavery to the Present* (1985); Lawrence W. Levine, *Black Culture and Black Consciousness: Afro-American Folk Thought from Slavery to Freedom* (1977); Leon Litwack, *North of Slavery* (1961); William S. McFeely, *Sapelo's People: A Long Walk to Freedom* (1994); Thomas D. Morris, *Southern Slavery and the Law, 1619–1860* (1996); Stephen B. Oates, *The Fires of Jubilee* (1974); Leslie Howard Owens, *This Species of Property: Slave Life and Slave Culture in the Old South* (1976); Orlando Patterson, *Slavery and Social Death: A Comparative Study* (1982); Ulrich B. Phillips, *American Negro Slavery* (1981), and *Life and Labor in the Old South* (1929); Albert J. Raboteau, *Slave Religion* (1978); George P. Rawick, *From Sundown to Sunup: The Making of the Black Community* (1973); Kenneth Stampp, *The Peculiar Institution* (1955); Robert Starobin, *Denmark Vesey* (1970), and *Industrial Slavery in the Old South* (1970); Richard C. Wade, *Slavery in the Cities* (1964); Thomas L. Weber, *Deep Like Rivers: Education in the Slave Quarters, 1831–1865* (1978); Deborah G. White, *Ar'n't I a Woman?* (1985); Joel Williamson, *New People: Miscegenation and Mulattoes in the United States* (1980).

CHAPTER 12 AN AGE OF REFORMS

**Antebellum Literature and Popular Culture.** Nina Baym, *Woman's Fiction: A Guide to Novels by and About Women in America, 1820–1870* (1978); Carl Bode, *The American*

*Lyceum: Town Meeting of the Mind* (1968); Van Wyck Brooks, *The Flowering of New England, 1815–1865* (1936); Vincent Buranelli, *Edgar Allan Poe* (1977); Ann Douglas, *The Feminization of American Culture* (1977); David Grimsted, *Melodrama Unveiled: American Theater and Culture, 1800–1850* (1968); Neil Harris, *Humbug: The Art of P. T. Barnum* (1973); Mary Kelley, *The Limits of Sisterhood* (1988); Mary Kupiec Cayton, *Emerson's Emergence: Self and Society in the Transformation of New England, 1800–1845* (1989); David Levin, *History as Romantic Art: Bancroft, Prescott, Motley, and Parkman* (1963); Kenneth S. Lynn, *Mark Twain and Southwestern Humor* (1972); Leo Marx, *The Machine and the Garden* (1964); F. O. Matthiessen, *American Renaissance* (1941); Henry F. May, *The Enlightenment in America* (1976); James Meellow, *Nathaniel Hawthorne in His Time* (1980); Vernon L. Parrington, *The Romantic Revolution in America, 1800–1860* (1927); David Reynolds, *Beneath the American Renaissance: The Subversive Imagination in the Age of Emerson and Melville* (1988), and *Walt Whitman's America: A Cultural Biography* (1995); Henry Nash Smith, *Democracy and the Novel: Popular Resistance to Classic American Writers* (1978); Robert C. Toll, *Blacking Up: The Minstrel Show in Nineteenth-Century America* (1974); Larzer Ziff, *Literary Democracy: The Declaration of Cultural Independence in America* (1981).

**Social Philosophies and Utopias.** Robert H. Abzug, *Cosmos Crumbling: American Reform and the Religious Imagination* (1994); Gay Wilson Allen, *Waldo Emerson* (1981); Arthur Bestor, *Backwoods Utopias: The Sectarian and Owenite Phases of Communitarian Socialism in America, 1663–1829* (1950); P. F. Boller, Jr., *American Transcendentalism, 1830–1860: An Intellectual Inquiry* (1974); Priscilla Brewer, *Shaker Communities and Shaker Lives* (1986); Fawn Brodie, *No Man Knows My Name: The Life of Joseph Smith* (1945); John L. Brooke, *The Refiner's Fire: The Making of Mormon Cosmology, 1644–1844* (1994); Maren L. Carden, *Oneida: Utopian Community to Modern Corporation* (1971); Henry Steele Commager, *Theodore Parker* (1936); Michael Fellman, *The Unbounded Frame: Freedom and Community in Nineteenth-Century America* (1973); Lawrence Foster, *Religion and Sexuality: The Shakers, the Mormons, and the Oneida Community* (1984), and *Women, Family, and Utopia: Communal Experiments of the Shakers, the Oneida Community, and the Mormons* (1991); Klaus J. Hansen, *Quest for Empire* (1967); J. F. C. Harrison, *Quest for the New Moral World: Robert Owen and the Owenites in Britain and America* (1969); Carol Kolmerten, *Women in Utopia* (1990); Richard Lebeaux, *Young Man Thoreau* (1977); Perry Miller, *The Transcendentalists* (1950), and *The Life of the Mind in America: From the Revolution to the Civil War* (1966); Raymond Muncy, *Sex and Marriage in Utopian Communities* (1973); Ann Rose, *Transcendentalism as a Social Movement* (1981); Arthur M. Schlesinger, Jr., *Orestes A. Brownson: A Pilgrim's Progress* (1939); Wallace Stegner, *The Gathering of Zion* (1964); R. D. Thomas, *The Man Who Would Be Perfect: John Humphrey Noyes and the Utopian Impulse* (1977).

**Antebellum Reforms.** C. C. Cole, Jr., *The Social Ideas of the Northern Evangelists, 1826–1860* (1954); Whitney R. Cross, *The Burned-Over District* (1950); James D. Davies, *Phrenology: Fad and Science* (1955); Estelle Freedman, *Their Sister's Keepers: Women's Prison Reform in America, 1830–1930* (1981); Gerald W. Grob, *Mental Institutions in America: Social Policy to 1875* (1973); Charles A. Johnson, *The Frontier Camp Meeting* (1955); Paul Johnson, *A Shopkeeper's Millennium* (1978); W. David Lewis, *From Newgate to Dannemora: The Rise of the Penitentiary* (1965); Robert Mennel, *Thorns and Thistles* (1973); William G. McLoughlin, *Revivals, Awakenings, and Reform* (1978); Stephen L. Nissenbaum, *Sex, Diet, and Debility in Jacksonian America: Sylvester Graham and Health Reform* (1980); W. J. Rorabaugh, *The Alcoholic Republic* (1979); Charles Rosenberg, *The Cholera Years: The United States in 1832, 1849, and 1866* (1962); David Rothman, *The Discovery of the Asylum* (1971); Timothy L. Smith, *Revivalism and Social Reform in Mid-*

*Nineteenth Century America* (1957); William W. Sweet, *Revivalism in America* (1949); Alice Felt Tyler, *Freedom's Ferment* (1944); Ian R. Tyrrell, *Sobering Up: From Temperance to Prohibition in Antebellum America, 1800–1860* (1979); Ronald G. Walters, *American Reformers, 1815–1860* (1978).

**Education.** Carl Bode, *The American Lyceum* (1956); Lawrence A. Cremin, *American Education: The National Experience* (1980); Michael Katz, *The Irony of Early School Reform* (1968); Jonathan Messerli, *Horace Mann* (1972); Paul Monroe, *The Founding of the American Public School System* (1949); Stanley K. Schultz, *The Culture Factory: Boston's Public Schools, 1789–1860* (1973); Robert Trennert, *Alternatives to Extinction: Federal Indian Policy and the Beginning of the Reservation System* (1975).

**Feminism.** Margaret H. Bacon, *Mothers of Feminism: The Story of Quaker Women in America* (1986); Lois Banner, *Elizabeth Cady Stanton* (1980); Kathleen Barry, *Susan B. Anthony* (1988); Barbara J. Berg, *The Remembered Gate: Origins of American Feminism: The Woman and the City* (1977); Nancy Cott, *The Bonds of Womanhood: "Woman's Sphere" in New England, 1780–1835* (1977); Carl Degler, *At Odds, Women and the Family in America from the Revolution to the Present* (1980); Ellen C. Du Bois, *Feminism and Suffrage: The Emergence of an Independent Woman's Movement in America, 1848–1860* (1978); Barbara Leslie Epstein, *The Politics of Domesticity: Women, Evangelism, and Temperance in Nineteenth-Century America* (1981); Eleanor Flexner, *Century of Struggle*, rev. ed. (1975); Lori D. Ginzberg, *Women and the Work of Benevolence: Morality, Politics, and Class in the Nineteenth-Century United States* (1990); Elisabeth Griffith, *In Her Own Right: The Life of Elizabeth Cady Stanton* (1984); Nancy A. Hewitt, *Women's Activism and Social Change: Rochester, New York, 1822–1872* (1988); William L. O'Neill, *Everyone Was Brave: The Rise and Fall of Feminism in the United States* (1970); Anne Firor Scott, *Natural Allies: Women's Associations in American History* (1991); Kathryn K. Sklar, *Catharine Beecher: A Study in American Domesticity* (1973); Jean Fagan Yellin, ed. *The Abolitionist Sisterhood: Women's Political Culture in Antebellum America* (1994).

**Antislavery and Abolitionism.** Richard H. Abbott, *Cotton and Capital: Boston Businessmen and Antislavery Reform, 1854–1868* (1991); Robert Abzug, *Theodore Dwight Weld* (1980); G. H. Barnes, *The Antislavery Impulse* (1933); Irving Bartlett, *Wendell Phillips* (1962). Arna Bontemps, *Free at Last: The Life of Frederick Douglass* (1971); David Brion Davis, *The Problem of Slavery in the Age of Revolution, 1770–1823* (1975); M. L. Dillon, *The Abolitionists* (1974); Martin Duberman, ed., *The Anti-Slavery Vanguard* (1965); Louis Filler, *The Crusade Against Slavery* (1960); Betty Fladeland, *James Gillespie Birney* (1955); George Frederickson, *The Black Image in the White Mind: The Debate on Afro-American Character and Destiny, 1817–1914* (1971); Lawrence J. Friedman, *Gregarious Saints: Self and Community in American Abolitionism* (1982); Blanche G. Hersh, *Slavery of Sex: Feminist Abolitionists in America* (1978); Nathan Huggins, *Slave and Citizen* (1980); Aileen Kraditor, *Means and Ends in American Abolitionism: Garrison and His Critics on Strategy and Tactics, 1834–1850* (1967); Alan Kraut, ed., *Crusaders and Compromisers* (1983); Gerda Lerner, *The Grimké Sisters of South Carolina: Rebels Against Slavery* (1967); William S. McFeely, *Frederick Douglass* (1991); John McKivigan, *The War Against Proslavery Religion* (1984); William H. Pease and Jane H. Pease, *They Would Be Free* (1974); Lewis Perry, *Radical Abolitionism: Anarchy and the Government of God in Antislavery Thought* (1973); Lewis Perry and Michael Fellman, eds., *Antislavery Reconsidered: New Perspectives on the Abolitionists* (1979); Benjamin Quarles, *Black Abolitionists* (1969); Leonard L. Richards,

*"Gentlemen of Property and Standing": Anti-Abolition Mobs in Jacksonian America* (1970); Gerald Sorin, *Abolitionism* (1972); James Brewer Stewart, *Holy Warriors* (1976), and *Wendell Phillips* (1987); John L. Thomas, *The Liberator* (1963); Peter F. Walker, *Moral Choices: Memory, Desire, and Imagination in Nineteenth Century Abolition* (1978); Ronald G. Walters, *The Antislavery Appeal: American Abolitionists After 1830* (1976); Bertram Wyatt-Brown, *Lewis Tappan and the Evangelical War Against Slavery* (1969); Jean Fagan Yellin, *The Antislavery Feminists in American Culture* (1989).

## CHAPTER 13 THE IMPENDING CRISIS

**Westward Expansion.**  E. C. Barker, *Mexico and Texas, 1821–1835* (1928); Ray Allen Billington, *Westward Expansion*, rev. ed. (1974), and *The Far Western Frontier, 1830–1860* (1956). William C. Brinkley, *The Texas Revolution* (1952); R. G. Cleland, *From Wilderness to Empire: A History of California, 1542–1900* (1944); R. L. Duffus, *The Santa Fe Trail* (1930); Robert R. Dystra, *Bright Radical Star: Black Freedom and White Supremacy on the Hawkeye Frontier* (1993); John M. Faragher, *Women and Men on the Overland Trail* (1979); T. R. Fehrenbach, *Lone Star: A History of Texas and the Texans* (1968); William H. Goetzmann, *Exploration and Empire* (1966); Norman A. Graebner, *Empire of the Pacific* (1955); J. S. Holiday, *The World Rushed In* (1981); David Alan Johnson, *Founding the Far West: California, Oregon, and Nevada, 1840–1890* (1992); Frederick Merk, *History of the Westward Movement* (1978), *Manifest Destiny and Mission in American History* (1963), *Fruits of Propaganda in the Tyler Administration* (1971), *Slavery and the Annexation of Texas* (1972), *The Oregon Question* (1967), and *The Monroe Doctrine and American Expansionism, 1843–1849* (1966); Francis Parkman, *The Oregon Trail* (1849); R. W. Paul, *California Gold* (1947); Henry Nash Smith, *Virgin Land* (1950); John D. Unruh, *The Plains Across: The Overland Emigrants and the Trans-Mississippi West, 1840–1860* (1979); Albert K. Weinberg, *Manifest Destiny* (1935); O. O. Winther, *The Great Northwest*, rev. ed. (1950).

**Expansion and the Mexican War.**  K. Jack Bauer, *The Mexican-American War, 1846–1848* (1974); Samuel F. Bemis, ed., *American Secretaries of State*, vols. 5 and 6 (1928); G. M. Brack, *Mexico Views Manifest Destiny, 1821–1846* (1975); S. V. Conner and O. B. Faulk, *North America Divided* (1971); C. W. Elliott, *Winfield Scott* (1937); Holman Hamilton, *Zachary Taylor, Soldier of the Republic* (1941); Robert W. Johnson, *To the Halls of Montezuma: The Mexican War in the American Imagination* (1985); Robert E. May, *The Southern Dream of a Caribbean Empire, 1854–1861* (1973); David M. Pletcher, *The Diplomacy of Annexation: Texas, Oregon, and the Mexican War* (1973); Basil Rauch, *American Interest in Cuba, 1848–1855* (1948); J. S. Reeves, *American Diplomacy Under Tyler and Polk* (1907); John H. Schroeder, *Mr. Polk's War: American Opposition and Dissent* (1973); Charles G. Sellers, *James K. Polk: Continentalist, 1843–1846* (1966); Otis A. Singletary, *The Mexican War* (1960); David J. Weber, *The Mexican Frontier, 1821–1846: The American Southwest Under Mexico* (1982).

**The Sectional Crisis: General Studies.**  William J. Cooper, *The South and the Politics of Slavery, 1828–1856* (1978), and *Liberty and Slavery* (1983); Avery Craven, *The Coming of the Civil War* (1942); William W. Freehling, *The Road to Disunion*. vol. 1: *Secessionists at Bay, 1776–1854* (1990); Michael Holt, *The Political Crisis of the 1850s* (1978); James M. McPherson, *Ordeal by Fire* (1981), and *Battle Cry of Freedom* (1988); Allan Nevins, *The Ordeal of the Union*, 2 vols. (1947), and *The Emergence of Lincoln*, 2 vols. (1950); Roy F.

Nichols, *The Disruption of American Democracy* (1948); David Potter, *The Impending Crisis, 1848–1861* (1976); James G. Randall and David Donald, *The Civil War and Reconstruction*, rev. ed. (1969); Richard H. Sewell, *A House Divided: Sectionalism and the Civil War, 1848–1865* (1988).

**The Compromise of 1850.** Kinley J. Bauer, *Cotton Versus Conscience: Massachusetts Whig Politics and Southern Expansion, 1843–1858* (1967); Richard N. Current, *Daniel Webster and the Rise of National Conservatism* (1955); Robert F. Dalzell, Jr., *Daniel Webster and the Trial of American Nationalism, 1843–1852* (1973); Holman Hamilton, *Prologue to Conflict: The Crisis and Compromise of 1850* (1964), and *Zachary Taylor: Soldier in the White House* (1951); Thelma Jennings, *The Nashville Convention* (1980); Robert W. Johannsen, *Stephen A. Douglas* (1973); Chaplain W. Morrison, *Democratic Politics and Sectionalism: The Wilmot Proviso Controversy* (1973); Robert V. Remini, *Henry Clay: Statesman for the Union* (1991); Charles M. Wiltse, *John C. Calhoun: Sectionalist, 1840–1850* (1951).

**Sectional Crises in the 1850s.** Tyler Anbinder, *Nativism and Slavery: The Northern Know Nothings and the Politics of the 1850s* (1992); Dale Baum, *The Civil War Party System: The Case of Massachusetts, 1848–1876* (1984); R. O. Boyer, *The Legend of John Brown* (1973); David Donald, *Charles Sumner and the Coming of the Civil War* (1960); Don E. Fehrenbacher, *The Dred Scott Case* (1978); Eric Foner, *Free Soil, Free Labor, Free Men* (1970), and *Politics and Ideology in the Age of the Civil War* (1980); J. C. Furnas, *The Road to Harpers Ferry* (1959); Paul W. Gates, *Fifty Million Acres: Conflict over Kansas Land Policy, 1854–1890* (1954); William E. Gienapp, *The Origins of the Republican Party, 1852–1856* (1987); William Jenkins, *Pro-Slavery Thought in the Old South* (1935); James C. Malin, *The Nebraska Question* (1953); Truman Nelson, *The Old Man: John Brown at Harpers Ferry* (1973); Stephen Oates, *To Purge This Land with Blood: A Biography of John Brown* (1970); Benjamin Quarles, *Allies for Freedom* (1974); Kenneth M. Stampp, *America in 1857: A Nation on the Brink* (1990); Harvey Wish, *George Fitzhugh: Propagandist of the Old South* (1943); Gerald Wolff, *The Kansas-Nebraska Bill* (1977).

**The Emergence of Lincoln.** Richard N. Current, *The Lincoln Nobody Knows* (1958); David Donald, *Lincoln Reconsidered* (1956); Don E. Fehrenbacher, *Prelude to Greatness: Lincoln in the 1850's* (1962); George B. Forgie, *Patricide in the House Divided* (1979); Henry V. Jaffa, *Crisis of the House Divided: An Interpretation of the Lincoln-Douglas Debates* (1959).

## CHAPTER 14 THE CIVIL WAR

**General Studies.** Bruce Catton, *This Hallowed Ground* (1956); Shelby Foote, *The Civil War: A Narrative*, 3 vols. (1958–1974); James M. McPherson, *Battle Cry of Freedom* (1988), and *Ordeal by Fire*, rev. ed. (1985); Allan Nevins, *The War for the Union*, 4 vols. (1959–1971); James G. Randall and David Donald, *The Civil War and Reconstruction*, rev. ed. (1969).

**The Secession Crisis.** William L. Barney, *The Road to Secession* (1972), and *The Secessionist Impulse: Alabama and Mississippi in 1860* (1974); Steven A. Channing, *Crisis of Fear* (1970); Daniel W. Crofts, *Reluctant Confederates: Upper South Unionists in the Secession Crisis* (1989); Richard N. Current, *Lincoln and the First Shot* (1963); Michael P. Johnson,

*Toward a Patriarchal Republic* (1977); David Potter, *Lincoln and His Party in the Secession Crisis* (1942); Kenneth M. Stampp, *And the War Came* (1950); Ralph A. Wooster, *The Secession Conventions of the South* (1962).

**Lincoln.** Robert V. Bruce, *Lincoln and the Tools of War* (1956); Harry J. Carman and Reinhard Luthin, *Lincoln and the Patronage* (1943); LaWanda Cox, *Lincoln and Black Freedom* (1981); David Donald, *Lincoln Reconsidered: Essays on the Civil War Era*, 2nd ed. (1956), and *Lincoln* (1995); William B. Hesseltine, *Lincoln and the War Governors* (1948); James M. McPherson, *Abraham Lincoln and the Second American Revolution* (1990); Mark E. Neely, *The Fate of Liberty: Abraham Lincoln and Civil Liberties* (1991), and *The Last Best Hope of Earth: Abraham Lincoln and the Promise of America* (1993); Stephen B. Oates, *With Malice Toward None: The Life of Abraham Lincoln* (1979); Phillip Shaw Pauldan, *The Presidency of Abraham Lincoln* (1994); Merrill D. Peterson, *Lincoln in American Memory* (1994); James G. Randall, *Lincoln the President*, 4 vols. (1945–1955), the final volume completed by Richard N. Current; Carl Sandburg, *Abraham Lincoln*, 6 vols. (1929–1939); Benjamin Thomas, *Abraham Lincoln* (1952); T. Harry Williams, *Lincoln and the Radicals* (1941), and *Lincoln and His Generals* (1952).

**Politics and Society in the North.** Daniel Aaron, *The Unwritten War* (1973); Iver Bernstein, *The New York City Draft Riots* (1990); John P. Bugardt, ed., *Civil War Nurse* (1980); Adrian Cook, *The Armies of the Streets: The New York City Draft Riots of 1863* (1974); David Donald, *Charles Sumner and the Rights of Man* (1970); Martin Duberman, *Charles Francis Adams* (1961); Eric Foner, *Politics and Ideology in the Age of the Civil War* (1980); George Fredrickson, *The Inner Civil War: Northern Intellectuals and the Crisis of the Union* (1965); J. Matthew Gallman, *The North Fights the Civil War: The Home Front* (1994); Paul G. Gates, *Agriculture and the Civil War* (1965); Wood Gray, *The Hidden Civil War* (1942); Alvin M. Josephy, Jr., *The Civil War in the American West* (1991); Frank L. Klement, *The Copperheads in the Middle West* (1960), and *Dark Lanterns: Secret Political Societies, Conspiracies, and Treason Trials in the Civil War* (1984); Mary E. Massey, *Bonnet Brigades: American Women and the Civil War* (1966); William Q. Maxwell, *Lincoln's Fifth Wheel: The Political History of the United States Sanitary Commission* (1956); James H. Moorhead, *American Apocalypse: Yankee Protestants and the Civil War* (1978); Grace Palladino, *Another Civil War: Labor, Capital, and the State in Anthracite Regions of Pennsylvania, 1840–1868* (1990); Philip Shaw Paludan, *"A People's Contest": The Union and the Civil War, 1861–1868* (1988); James G. Randall, *Constitutional Problems Under Lincoln* (1926); Mitchell Reid, *The Vacant Chair: The Northern Soldier Leaves Home* (1993); Susan M. Reverby, *Ordered to Care: The Dilemma of American Nursing, 1850–1945* (1987); Robert P. Sharkey, *Money, Class, and Party* (1959); Benjamin P. Thomas and Harold M. Hyman, *Stanton* (1962); Glyndon Van Deusen, *William Henry Seward* (1967); Wendy Hamand Venet, *Neither Ballots nor Bullets: Women Abolitionists and the Civil War* (1991); Edmund Wilson, *Patriotic Gore* (1962).

**African Americans and Emancipation.** Ira Berlin, Leslie Rowland, et al., eds., *Freedom: A Documentary History of Emancipation, 1861–1867, Series II: The Black Military Experience* (1982); John W. Blassingame, *Black New Orleans* (1973); Dudley T. Cornish, *The Sable Arm: Negro Troops in the Union Army* (1966); Joseph T. Glatthaar, *Forged in Battle: The Civil War Alliance of Black Soldiers and White Officers* (1990); Peter Kolchin, *First Freedom* (1972); Leon Litwack, *Been in the Storm So Long: The Aftermath of Slavery* (1979); James M. McPherson, *The Struggle for Equality* (1964), and *The Negro's Civil War* (1965);

Clarence L. Mohr, *On the Threshold of Freedom: Masters and Slaves in Civil War Georgia* (1986); Benjamin Quarles, *Lincoln and the Negro* (1962), and *The Negro in the Civil War* (1953).

**The Confederacy.** Thomas B. Alexander and Richard E. Beringer, *The Anatomy of the Confederate Congress* (1972); Stephen V. Ash, *When the Yankees Came: Conflict and Chaos in the Occupied South, 1861–1865* (1995); E. Merton Coulter, *The Confederate States of America* (1950); Clement Eaton, *A History of the Southern Confederacy* (1954), and *Jefferson Davis* (1978); Paul D. Escott, *After Secession* (1978), *Slavery Remembered* (1979), and *Many Excellent People* (1985); Drew Gilpin Faust, *The Creation of Confederate Nationalism* (1988), and *Mothers of Invention: Women of the Slaveholding South in the American Civil War* (1996); Ella Lonn, *Desertion During the Civil War* (1928); William Marvel, *Andersonville: The Last Depot* (1994); Frank L. Owsley, *State's Rights in the Confederacy* (1952); George C. Rable, *The Confederate Republic: A Revolution Against Politics* (1994); James L. Roark, *Masters Without Slaves: Southern Planters in the Civil War and Reconstruction* (1978); Charles P. Roland, *The Confederacy* (1960); Hudson Strode, *Jefferson Davis*, 3 vols. (1955–1964); Daniel E. Sutherland, *Seasons of War: The Ordeal of a Southern Community, 1861–1865* (1995); Georgia Lee Tatum, *Disloyalty in the Confederacy* (1934); Emory Thomas, *The Confederacy as a Revolutionary Experience* (1971), *The Confederate Nation* (1979), and *The Confederate State of Richmond* (1971); Bell I. Wiley, *The Life of Johnny Reb* (1943), and *The Plain People of the Confederacy* (1943); C. Vann Woodward, ed., *Mary Chesnut's Civil War* (1982); W. Buck Yearns, *The Confederate Congress* (1960).

**Diplomacy.** Stuart L. Bernath, *Squall Across the Atlantic: American Civil War Prize Cases and Diplomacy* (1970); David P. Crook, *Diplomacy During the American Civil War* (1975), and *The North, the South, and the Powers, 1861–1865* (1974); Howard Jones, *Union in Peril: The Crisis over British Intervention in the Civil War* (1992); Frank L. Owsley and Harriet Owsley, *King Cotton Diplomacy*, rev. ed. (1959); Gordon H. Warren, *Fountain of Discontent: The Trent Affair and Freedom of the Seas* (1981).

**Military Histories.** Richard E. Beringer et al., *Why the South Lost the Civil War* (1986); John Carpenter, *Ulysses S. Grant* (1976); Bruce Catton, *Mr. Lincoln's Army* (1951), *Glory Road* (1952), *A Stillness at Appomattox* (1954), *America Goes to War* (1958), *Banners at Shenandoah* (1956), and *Grant Moves South* (1960); Thomas L. Connelly, *The Marble Man* (1977); Burke Davis, *Sherman's March* (1980); David Donald, ed., *Why the North Won the Civil War* (1960); Michael Fellman, *Inside War: The Guerrilla Conflict in Missouri During the American Civil War* (1989); Shelby Foote, *The Civil War: A Narrative*, 3 vols. (1958–1974); Gary W. Gallagher, *Chancellorsville: The Battle and Its Aftermath* (1996); Douglas Southall Freeman, *Robert E. Lee*, 4 vols. (1934–1935); Herman Hattaway and Archer Jones, *How the North Won* (1983); Archer Jones et al., *Why the South Lost the Civil War* (1986); Alvin M. Josephy, *The Civil War in the American West* (1991); Gerald F. Linderman, *Embattled Courage: The Experience of Combat in the American Civil War* (1987); Thomas L. Livermore, *Numbers and Losses in the Civil War in America* (1957); C. E. MacCartney, *Mr. Lincoln's Admirals* (1956); James M. McPherson, *What They Fought For, 1861–1865* (1994); William McFeely, *Grant* (1981); John Niven, *Gideon Welles, Lincoln's Secretary of the Navy* (1973); Charles Royster, *The Destructive War: William Tecumseh Sherman, Stonewall Jackson, and the Americans* (1991); Stephen W. Sears, *George B. McClellan: The Young Napoleon* (1988), and *Landscape Turned Red: The Battle of Antietam* (1983); William N. Still, Jr., *Iron Afloat: The Story of the Confederate Armorclads* (1971), and *Con-*

*federate Shipbuilding* (1969); Richard S. West, Jr., *Mr. Lincoln's Navy* (1957); Bell Wiley, *The Life of Billy Yank* (1952); Kenneth P. Williams, *Lincoln Finds a General,* 4 vols. (1949–1952); T. Harry Williams, *McClellan, Sherman, and Grant* (1962), and *P. G. T. Beauregard, Napoleon in Gray* (1955).

## CHAPTER 15 RECONSTRUCTION AND THE NEW SOUTH

**Reconstruction: General Studies.** E. Merton Coulter, *The South During Reconstruction* (1947); W. E. B. Du Bois, *Black Reconstruction* (1935); William A. Dunning, *Reconstruction, Political and Economic, 1865–1877* (1907); Eric Foner, *Reconstruction: America's Unfinished Revolution, 1863–1877* (1988); John Hope Franklin, *Reconstruction After the Civil War* (1961); Rembert Patrick, *The Reconstruction of the Nation* (1967); Kenneth M. Stampp, *The Era of Reconstruction, 1865–1877* (1965).

**Early Reconstruction.** Richard H. Abbott, *The First Southern Strategy: The Republican Party and the South, 1855–1877* (1986); Herman Belz, *Reconstructing the Union* (1969); Louis S. Gerteis, *From Contraband to Freedman* (1973); William B. Hesseltine, *Lincoln's Plan of Reconstruction* (1960); Willie Lee Rose, *Rehearsal for Reconstruction: The Port Royal Experiment* (1964); Brooks D. Simpson, *Let Us Have Peace: Ulysses S. Grant and the Politics of War and Reconstruction, 1861–1868* (1991).

**Congressional Reconstruction.** Howard K. Beale, *The Critical Year: A Study of Andrew Johnson and Reconstruction* (1930); Herman Belz, *A New Birth of Freedom* (1976), and *Emancipation and Equal Rights* (1978); Michael Les Benedict, *A Compromise of Principle: Congressional Republicans and Reconstruction, 1863–1869* (1974), and *The Impeachment and Trial of Andrew Johnson* (1973); Richard Franklin Bensel, *Yankee Leviathan: The Origins of Central State Authority in America, 1859–1877* (1990); William R. Brock, *An American Crisis* (1963); Fawn Brodie, *Thaddeus Stevens* (1959); LaWanda Cox and John H. Cox, *Politics, Principles, and Prejudice, 1865–1867* (1963); Richard N. Current, *Old Thad Stevens* (1942); David Donald, *Charles Sumner and the Rights of Man* (1970), and *The Politics of Reconstruction* (1965); Charles Fairman, *Reconstruction and Reunion* (1971); William Gillette, *The Right to Vote* (1965); Harold Hyman, *A More Perfect Union* (1973); Stanley Kutler, *The Judicial Power and Reconstruction Politics* (1968); Eric McKitrick, *Andrew Johnson and Reconstruction* (1960); Mark W. Summers, *Railroads, Reconstruction, and the Gospel of Prosperity* (1984); Hans L. Trefousse, *The Radical Republicans* (1963), *The Impeachment of a President* (1975), and *Andrew Johnson: A Biography* (1989).

**The South in Reconstruction.** Roberta Alexander, *North Carolina Faces the Freedmen: Race Relations During Presidential Reconstruction, 1865–1867* (1985); James D. Anderson, *The Education of Blacks in the South* (1989); George Bentley, *A History of the Freedmen's Bureau* (1955); Dan Carter, *When the War Was Over: The Failure of Self-Reconstruction in the South, 1865–1867* (1985); Richard N. Current, *Those Terrible Carpetbaggers* (1988); Barbara Fields, *Slavery and Freedom on the Middle Ground* (1985); Eric Foner, *Nothing but Freedom: Emancipation and Its Legacy* (1983); William Gillette, *Retreat from Reconstruction, 1869–1879* (1980), and *The Right to Vote: Politics and Passage of the Fifteenth Amendment* (1969); William C. Harris, *The Day of the Carpetbagger: Republican Reconstruction in Mississippi, 1867–1875* (1979); Robert Higgs, *Competition and Coercion: Blacks in the American*

*Economy, 1865–1914* (1977); Thomas Holt, *Black over White: Negro Political Leadership in South Carolina During Reconstruction* (1977); Elizabeth Jacoway, *Yankee Missionaries in the South* (1979); Jacqueline Jones, *Soldiers of Light and Love: Northern Teachers and Georgia Blacks, 1865–1873* (1980), and *Labor of Love, Labor of Sorrow: Black Women, Work, and the Family from Slavery to the Present* (1985); Peter Kolchin, *First Freedom: The Responses of Alabama's Blacks to Emancipation* (1972); Leon Litwack, *Been in the Storm So Long: The Aftermath of Slavery* (1979); Richard Lowe, *Republicans and Reconstruction in Virginia, 1865–1870* (1991); Peyton McCrary, *Abraham Lincoln and Reconstruction* (1978); William S. McFeely, *Yankee Stepfather: General O. O. Howard and the Freedmen* (1968); Otto Olsen, *Carpetbagger's Crusade: Albion Winegar Tourgé* (1965); Michael Perman, *Reunion Without Compromise* (1973), and *The Road to Redemption: Southern Politics, 1869–1979* (1984); L. N. Powell, *New Masters: Northern Planters During the Civil War and Reconstruction* (1980); Roger L. Ransom and Richard Sutch, *One Kind of Freedom: The Economic Consequences of Emancipation* (1977); C. Peter Ripley, *Slaves and Freedmen in Civil War Louisiana* (1976); James Sefton, *The United States Army and Reconstruction* (1967); Crandall A. Shifflett, *Patronage and Poverty in the Tobacco South: Louisa County, Virginia, 1860–1900* (1982); Joel G. Taylor, *Louisiana Reconstructed* (1974); Allen Trelease, *White Terror: The Ku Klux Klan Conspiracy and Southern Reconstruction* (1967); Michael Wayne, *The Reshaping of Plantation Society: The Natchez District* (1983); Vernon Wharton, *The Negro in Mississippi, 1865–1890* (1965); Sarah Wiggins, *The Scalawag in Alabama Politics, 1865–1881* (1977); Joel Williamson, *After Slavery: The Negro in South Carolina During Reconstruction* (1965).

**The Grant Administration.** William B. Hesseltine, *U. S. Grant, Politician* (1935); Ari Hoogenboom, *Outlawing the Spoils* (1961); David Loth, *Public Plunder* (1938); William S. McFeely, *Grant* (1981); Allan Nevins, *Hamilton Fish* (1936); K. I. Polakoff, *The Politics of Inertia* (1973); John G. Sproat, *"The Best Men"* (1968); Margaret S. Thompson, *The "Spider Web": Congress and Lobbying in the Age of Grant* (1985); Irwin Unger, *The Greenback Era* (1964); C. Vann Woodward, *Reunion and Reaction* (1951).

**The New South.** Edward L. Ayers, *The Promise of the New South: Life After Reconstruction* (1992); Paul Buck, *The Road to Reunion* (1937); Orville Vernon Burton, *In My Father's House Are Many Mansions: Family and Community in Edgefield, South Carolina* (1985); Orville Vernon Burton and Robert C. McMath, Jr., eds., *Toward a New South? Studies in Post–Civil War Southern Communities* (1982); W. J. Cash, *The Mind of the South* (1941); Paul Gaston, *The New South Creed* (1970); J. Morgan Kousser and James M. McPherson, eds., *Region, Race, and Reconstruction* (1982); Jonathan Wiener, *Social Origins of the New South: Alabama, 1860–1885* (1978); C. Vann Woodward, *Origins of the New South* (1951), *The Burden of Southern History* (1960), *American Counterpoint* (1971), *Thinking Back* (1986), and *The Future of the Past* (1989).

**Politics in the New South.** Kenneth E. Davison, *The Presidency of Rutherford B. Hayes* (1972); Carl Degler, *The Other South: Southern Dissenters in the Nineteenth Century* (1974); Vincent P. DeSantis, *Republicans Face the Southern Question: The New Departure Years, 1877–1897* (1959); Sheldon Hackney, *Populism to Progressivism in Alabama* (1959); Stanley P. Hirshson, *Farewell to the Bloody Shirt: Northern Republicans and the Southern Negro* (1962); V. O. Key, Jr., *Southern Politics and the Nation* (1949); J. Morgan Kousser, *The Shaping of Southern Politics: Suffrage Restriction and the Establishment of the One-Party South, 1880–1910* (1974); Paul Lewinson, *Race, Class, and Party* (1932); David Potter, *The South and the Concurrent Majority* (1972); Francis B. Simkins, *Pitchfork Ben Tillman* (1944);

Joseph F. Wall, *Henry Watterson: Reconstructed Rebel* (1956); C. Vann Woodward, *Reunion and Reaction* (1951), and *Tom Watson: Agrarian Rebel* (1938).

**Race, Economics, and Social Structure.** Francis Broderick, *W. E. B. DuBois* (1959); W. Fitzhugh Brundage, *Lynching in the New South: Georgia and Virginia, 1880–1930* (1993); David Carlton, *Mill and Town in South Carolina, 1880–1920* (1982); Melvin Greenhut and W. Tate Whitman, eds., *Essays in Southern Economic Development* (1964); Steven Hahn, *The Roots of Southern Populism: Yeoman Farmers and the Transformation of the Georgia Upcountry* (1983); Steven Hahn and Jonathan Prude, eds., *The Countryside in the Age of Capitalist Transformation* (1985); Jacquelyn Dowd Hall et al., *Like a Family: The Making of a Southern Cotton Mill World* (1987); Louis R. Harlan, *Booker T. Washington: The Making of a Black Leader, 1856–1901* (1972), and *Booker T. Washington: The Wizard of Tuskegee: 1901–1915* (1983); Robert Higgs, *Competition and Coercion: Blacks in the American Economy, 1865–1914* (1977); Melton A. McLaurin, *Paternalism and Protest: Southern Cotton Mill Workers and Organized Labor* (1971); James M. McPherson, *The Abolitionist Legacy: From Reconstruction to the NAACP* (1975); August Meier, *Negro Thought in America* (1963); Cynthia Neverdon-Morton, *Afro-American Women of the South and the Advancement of the Race, 1895–1925* (1989); David Oshinsky, *Worse Than Slavery: Parchman Prison and the Ordeal of Jim Crow Justice* (1996); Howard Rabinowitz, *Race Relations in the Urban South, 1865–1890* (1978); Roger Ransom and Richard Sutch, *One Kind of Freedom* (1977); Elliott M. Rudwick, *W. E. B. DuBois: Propagandist of Negro Protest* (1968); Altina L. Waller, *Feud: Hatfields, McCoys, and Social Changes: Appalachia, 1860–1900* (1988); Joel Williamson, *After Slavery* (1965), *The Crucible of Race: Black-White Relations in the American South Since Emancipation* (1985), and *A Rage for Order* (1986), an abridgment of *The Crucible of Race*; C. Vann Woodward, *The Strange Career of Jim Crow*, rev. ed. (1974); Gavin Wright, *Old South, New South: Revolutions in the Southern Economy Since the Civil War* (1986).

## CHAPTER 16 THE CONQUEST OF THE FAR WEST

**General Works.** Ray A. Billington and Martin Ridge, *Westward Expansion*, 5th ed. (1982); Thomas D. Clark, *Frontier America* (1959); William Cronon et al., eds., *Under an Open Sky: Rethinking America's Western Past* (1992); Robert V. Hine, *The American West*, 2nd ed. (1984); Patricia Nelson Limerick, *The Legacy of Conquest: The Unbroken Past of the American West* (1987); Patricia Nelson Limerick et al., eds., *Trails: Toward a New Western History* (1992); Frederick Merk, *History of the Westward Movement* (1978); Rodman W. Paul, *The Far West and the Great Plains in Transition, 1859–1900* (1988); Rodman W. Paul and Richard W. Etulain, *The Frontier and the American West* (1977); Richard White, *"It's Your Misfortune and None of My Own": A History of the American West* (1991).

**Migrations and Communities.** Gunther Barth, *Bitter Strength: A History of the Chinese in the United States, 1850–1870* (1964); Albert Camarillo, *Chicanos in a Changing Society: From Mexican Pueblos to American Barrios in Santa Barbara and Southern California* (1979); Sucheng Chan, *This Bittersweet Soil: The Chinese in California Agriculture, 1860–1910* (1986); Richard Griswold del Castillo, *La Familia: Chicano Families in the Urban Southwest, 1848 to the Present* (1984), and *The Los Angeles Barrio, 1850–1890* (1979); Arnold De Leon, *They Called Them Greasers: Anglo Attitudes Toward Mexicans in Texas,*

*1821–1900* (1983); Sarah Deutsch, *No Separate Refuge: Culture, Class, and Gender on the Anglo-Hispanic Frontier in the Early Southwest, 1880–1940* (1987); Mario T. Garcia, *Desert Immigrants: The Mexicans of El Paso, 1880–1920* (1981); Robert V. Hine, *Community on the American Frontier* (1980); Richard Hogan, *Class and Community in Frontier Colorado* (1979); Howard R. Lamar, *Dakota Territory, 1861–1889* (1956), *The Far Southwest, 1846–1912* (1966), and *Texas Crossings: The Lone Star State and the American Far West, 1836–1986* (1991); Laurie F. Maffly-Kipp, *Religion and Society in Frontier California* (1994); Timothy R. Mahoney, *River Towns in the Great West* (1990); Dean L. May, *Three Frontiers: Family, Land, and Society in the American West, 1850–1900* (1994); Leonard Pitt, *The Decline of the Californios: A Social History of the Spanish-Speaking Californians, 1846–1890* (1960); Earl Pomeroy, *The Pacific Slope: A History of California, Oregon, Washington, Idaho, Utah, and Nevada* (1965); Andrew F. Rolle, *California: A History*, 2nd ed. (1969); Robert J. Rosenbaum, *Mexicano Resistance in the Southwest* (1981); Alexander Saxton, *The Indispensable Enemy: Labor and the Anti-Chinese Movement in California* (1971); Lillian Schlissel, *Women's Diaries of the Westward Journey* (1982); Thomas Sheridan, *Los Tucsonenses: The Mexican Community in Tucson, 1854–1941* (1986); Ronald Takaki, *Strangers from a Different Shore: A History of Asian Americans* (1989); Shih-shan Henry Tsai, *The Chinese Experience in America* (1986); Oscar O. Winther, *The Transportation Frontier: The Trans-Mississippi West, 1865–1890* (1964).

**Miners and Cattlemen.**   Andy Adams, *The Log of a Cowboy* (1927); Lewis Atherton, *The Cattle Kings* (1961); Gunther Barth, *Instant Cities* (1975); Edward E. Dale, *The Range Cattle Industry*, rev. ed. (1969); Philip Durham and Everett L. Jones, *The Negro Cowboys* (1965); Robert R. Dykstra, *The Cattle Towns* (1968); Odie B. Faulk, *Tombstone: Myth and Reality* (1972); Joe B. Frantz and Julian Choate, *The American Cowboy: The Myth and the Reality* (1955); Marion S. Goldman, *Gold Diggers & Silver Miners: Prostitution and Social Life on the Comstock* (1981); William S. Greever, *Bonanza West: Western Mining Rushes* (1963); Ralph Mann, *After the Gold Rush: Society in Grass Valley and Nevada City, California, 1849–1870* (1982); Ernest E. Osgood, *The Day of the Cattleman* (1929); Rodman W. Paul, *Mining Frontiers of the Far West, 1848–1880* (1963), and *The Far West and the Great Plains in Transition, 1859–1900* (1988); Wilson P. Rodman, *Mining Frontiers of the Far West* (1963); J. M. Skaggs, *The Cattle Trailing Industry* (1973); Richard W. Slatta, *Cowboys of the Americas* (1990); Duane A. Smith, *Rocky Mountain Mining Camps* (1967), and *Mining America: The Industry and the Environment, 1800–1980* (1987); L. Steckmesser, *The Western Hero in History and Legend* (1965); Donald E. Worcester, *The Chisholm Trail* (1980).

**Indians.**   Ralph K. Andrist, *The Long Death: The Last Days of the Plains Indians* (1964); Robert F. Berkhofer, Jr., *The White Man's Indian* (1978); Donald J. Berthrong, *The Southern Cheyennes* (1963); Dee Brown, *Bury My Heart at Wounded Knee: An Indian History of the American West* (1970); Margret Coel, *Chief Left Hand: Southern Arapaho* (1981); Angie Debo, *Geronimo* (1976); Richard Drinnon, *Facing West: The Metaphysics of Indian-Hating and Empire-Building* (1980); Thomas W. Dunlay, *Wolves for the Blue Soldiers* (1982); Loretta Fowler, *Arapahoe Politics, 1851–1978: Symbols in Crisis of Authority* (1982); William T. Hagan, *The Indian Rights Association: The Herbert Welsh Years, 1882–1904* (1985), and *American Indians* (1961); Howard L. Harrod, *Renewing the World: Plains Indians Religion and Morality* (1987); Dwight L. Hoover, *The Red and the Black* (1976); Frederick E. Hoxie, *A Final Promise: The Campaign to Assimilate the Indians, 1880–1920* (1984), and *The Crow* (1989); Peter Inverson, *The Navajos* (1990); Robert Mardock, *Reformers and the American*

*Indian* (1971); Janet A. McDonnell, *The Dispossession of the American Indian, 1887–1934* (1991); John G. Neihardt, *Black Elk Speaks* (1932); James C. Olson, *Red Cloud and the Sioux Problem* (1965); Theda Perdue, *The Cherokee* (1989); John Powell, *People of the Sacred Mountain: A History of the Northern Cheyenne Chiefs and Warrior Societies, 1830–1879*, 2 vols. (1981); Francis P. Prucha, *American Indian Policy in Crisis* (1976), and *The Great White Father: The United States Government and the American Indians* (1984); David Roberts, *Once They Moved Like the Wind: Cochise, Geronimo, and the Apache Wars* (1993); Willard H. Rollings, *The Comanche* (1989); Mari Sandoz, *Crazy Horse* (1961); Edwin R. Sweeney, *Cochise: Chiricahua Apache Chief* (1991); Robert M. Utley, *Last Days of the Sioux Nation* (1963), *Frontiersmen in Blue: The United States Army and the Indian, 1848–1865* (1967), *Frontier Regulars: The United States Army and the Indian* (1973), *The Indian Frontier of the American West, 1846–1890* (1984), and *The Lance and the Shield: The Life and Times of Sitting Bull* (1993); Wilcomb E. Washburn, *The Indian in America* (1975), and *Red Man's Land/White Man's Law* (1971); Richard White, *The Roots of Dependency: Subsistence, Environment, and Social Change Among the Choctaws, Pawnees, and Navajos* (1983); Charles F. Wilkinson, *American Indians, Time, and the Law: Native Societies in a Modern Constitutional Democracy* (1987).

**Western Women.** Susan Armitage and Elizabeth Jameson, eds., *The Women's West* (1987); John Mack Faragher, *Women and Men on the Overland Trail* (1979); Elizabeth Hampsten, *Read This Only to Yourself: The Private Writings of Midwestern Women, 1880–1910* (1982); Dolores Janiewski, *Sisterhood Denied* (1985); Julie Jeffrey, *Frontier Women: The Trans-Mississippi West, 1840–1880* (1979); Polly Welts Kaufman, *Women Teachers on the Frontier* (1984); Ruth Moynihan, *Rebel for Rights: Abigail Scott Dunaway* (1983); Sandra L. Myres, *Westering Women and the Frontier Experience, 1800–1915* (1982); Peggy Pascoe, *Relations of Rescue: The Search for Female Moral Authority in the American West, 1874–1939* (1990); Linda Peavy and Ursula Smith, *Women in Waiting in the Westward Movement: Life on the Home Frontier* (1994); Glenda Riley, *Women and Indians on the Frontier, 1825–1915* (1984), and *A Place to Grow* (1992); Joanna L. Stratton, *Pioneer Women: Voices from the Kansas Frontier* (1981).

**Western Agriculture.** Allan Bogue, *From Prairie to Corn Belt* (1963); Everett Dick, *The Sod-House Frontier* (1937); John Mack Faragher, *Sugar Creek: Life on the Illinois Prairie* (1986); Gilbert Fite, *The Farmer's Frontier, 1865–1900* (1966); Paul W. Gates, *History of Public Land Development* (1968); Norris Hundley, Jr., *The Great Thirst: Californians and Water, 1770s–1990s* (1992); D. Aidan McQuillen, *Prevailing over Time: Ethnic Adjustment on the Kansas Prairies, 1875–1925* (1990); Nell Irvin Painter, *Exodusters: Black Migration to Kansas After Reconstruction* (1976); Fred A. Shannon, *The Farmer's Last Frontier, 1860–1897* (1945); Walter Prescott Webb, *The Great Plains* (1931); Thomas A. Woods, *Knights of the Plow: Oliver H. Kelley and the Origins of the Grange in Republican Ideology* (1991). (See also Suggested Readings for Chapter 19.)

**The Idea and the Environment of the West.** Ray A. Billington, *Frederick Jackson Turner* (1973); William Cronon, *Nature's Metropolis: Chicago and the Great West* (1991); John Mack Faragher, *Daniel Boone* (1992); Richard Slotkin, *The Fatal Environment: The Myth of the Frontier in the Age of Industrialization* (1985), and *Gunfighter Nation* (1992); Henry Nash Smith, *Virgin Land* (1950); Frederick Jackson Turner, *The Frontier in American History* (1920); Donald Worster, *Under Western Skies: Nature and History in the American West* (1992), and *Rivers of Empire* (1985).

## CHAPTER 17 INDUSTRIAL SUPREMACY

**General Histories.** Daniel Boorstin, *The Americans: The Democratic Experience* (1973); Thomas C. Cochran and William Miller, *The Age of Enterprise* (1942); Carl Degler, *The Age of the Economic Revolution* (1977); John A. Garraty, *The New Commonwealth* (1968); Ray Ginger, *The Age of Excess* (1963); Samuel P. Hays, *The Response to Industrialism, 1885–1914* (1957); Robert L. Heilbroner, *The Economic Transformation of America* (1977); Robert Higgs, *The Transformation of the American Economy, 1865–1914* (1971); Edward C. Kirkland, *Industry Comes of Age: Business, Labor, and Public Policy, 1860–1897* (1961); Alan Trachtenberg, *The Incorporation of America: Culture and Society in the Gilded Age* (1982); Robert Wiebe, *The Search for Order, 1877–1920* (1968).

**Technology.** Robert W. Bruce, *Bell* (1973); Roger Burlingame, *Engines of Democracy: Inventions and Society in Mature America* (1940), and *Henry Ford* (1957); Robert Conot, *A Streak of Luck* (1979); Richard N. Current, *The Typewriter and the Men Who Made It* (1954); George Daniels, *Science and Society in America* (1971); Frank E. Hill, *Ford* (1954); Thomas P. Hughes, *Networks of Power: Electrification in Western Society, 1880–1930* (1983); Judith McGaw, *Most Wonderful Machine: Mechanization and Social Change in Berkshire Paper Making, 1801–1885* (1988); Martin V. Melosi, *Coping with Abundance: Energy and Environment in Industrial America* (1985); Elting E. Morison, *Men, Machines, and Modern Times* (1966); Lewis Mumford, *Technics and Civilization* (1934); Allan Nevins, *Ford*, 3 vols. (1954–1962); David F. Noble, *America by Design: Science, Technology, and the Rise of Corporate Capitalism* (1977); Leonard S. Reich, *The Making of American Industrial Research: Science and Business at GE and Bell, 1876–1926* (1985); Nathan Rosenberg, *Technology and American Economic Growth* (1972); Peter Temin, *Steel in Nineteenth Century America* (1964); Wyn Wachhorst, *Thomas Alva Edison: An American Myth* (1981); Frederick A. White, *American Industrial Research Laboratories* (1961).

**Railroads.** Lee Benson, *Merchants, Farmers, and Railroads* (1955); Edward G. Campbell, *The Reorganization of the American Railroad System* (1938); Thomas C. Cochran, *Railroad Leaders* (1953); Robert Fogel, *Railroads and American Economic Growth* (1964); Edward C. Kirkland, *Men, Cities, and Transportation*, 2 vols. (1948); Gabriel Kolko, *Railroads and Regulation, 1877–1916* (1965); George H. Miller, *Railroads and the Granger Laws* (1971); Richard C. Overton, *Burlington West* (1941), and *Gulf to Rockies* (1953); John F. Stover, *The Life and Decline of the American Railroad* (1970), and *The Railroads of the South, 1865–1900* (1955); George R. Taylor and I. D. Neu, *The American Railroad Network, 1861–1890* (1956); Anthony F. C. Wallace, *St. Clair: A Nineteenth-Century Coal Town's Experience with a Disaster-Prone Industry* (1987).

**The Corporation.** Alfred D. Chandler, Jr., *Strategy and Structure: Chapters in the History of the American Industrial Enterprise* (1962), *Pierre S. DuPont and the Making of the Modern Corporation* (1971), *The Visible Hand: The Managerial Revolution in American Business* (1977), and *Scale and Scope: The Dynamics of Industrial Capitalism* (1990); David F. Hawkes, *John D.: The Founding Father of the Rockefellers* (1980); Matthew Josephson, *The Robber Barons* (1934); Maury Klein, *The Life and Legend of Jay Gould* (1986); Norma R. Lamoreaux, *The Great Merger Movement in American Business, 1895–1904* (1985); Harold C. Livesay, *Andrew Carnegie and the Rise of Big Business* (1975); Allan Nevins, *Study in Power: John D. Rockefeller*, 2 vols. (1953); Glenn Porter and Harold C. Livesay, *Merchants and Manufacturers* (1971); Joseph Wall, *Andrew Carnegie* (1970); Bernard Weisberger, *The Dream Maker* (1979); Olivier Zunz, *Making America Corporate, 1870–1920* (1990).

**Ideologies.**   Charles A. Baker, *Henry George* (1955); Robert C. Bannister, *Social Darwinism: Science and Myth in Anglo-American Social Thought* (1967); Samuel Chugerman, *Lester F. Ward: The American Aristotle* (1939); Sidney Fine, *Laissez Faire and the General Welfare State: A Study of Conflict in American Thought, 1865–1901* (1956); Louis Galambos, *The Public Image of Big Business in America, 1880–1940* (1975); Richard Hofstadter, *Social Darwinism in American Thought,* rev. ed. (1955); Edward C. Kirkland, *Dream and Thought in the Business Community, 1860–1900* (1956); T. J. Jackson Lears, *No Place of Grace: Antimodernism and the Transformation of American Culture, 1880–1920* (1981); Robert G. McCloskey, *American Conservatism in the Age of Enterprise* (1951); Arthur E. Morgan, *Edward Bellamy* (1944); Daniel T. Rodgers, *The Work Ethic in Industrial America, 1850–1920* (1978); David Thelen, *Paths of Resistance: Tradition and Dignity in Industrializing Missouri* (1986); John L. Thomas, *Alternative America: Henry George, Edward Bellamy, Henry Demarest Lloyd, and the Adversary Tradition* (1983); Irvin G. Wylie, *The Self-Made Man in America* (1954).

**Labor.**   Paul Avrich, *The Haymarket Tragedy* (1984); John Bodnar, *Immigration and Industrialization: Ethnicity in an American Mill Town* (1977); Stanley Buder, *Pullman* (1967); John T. Cumbler, *Working-Class Community in Industrial America* (1979); Henry David, *The Haymarket Affair* (1936); Ileen A. DeVault, *Sons and Daughters of Labor: Class and Clerical Work in Turn-of-the-Century Pittsburgh* (1990); Melvyn Dubofsky, *Industrialism and the American Worker, 1865–1920* (1975); Melvyn Dubofsky and Warren Van Tine, eds., *Labor Leaders in America* (1987); P. K. Edwards, *Strikes in the United States, 1881–1974* (1981); Leon Fink, *Workingmen's Democracy: The Knights of Labor and American Politics* (1983); Samuel Gompers, *Seventy Years of Life and Labor,* 2 vols. (1975); David M. Gordon, Richard Edwards, and Michael Reich, *Segmented Work, Divided Workers: The Historical Transformation of Labor in the United States* (1982); Brian Greenberg, *Worker and Community: Response to Industrialization in a Nineteenth-Century American City, Albany, New York, 1850–1884* (1985); Herbert G. Gutman, *Work, Culture, and Society in Industrializing America* (1976); William F. Hartford, *Working People of Holyoke: Class and Ethnicity in a Massachusetts Mill Town, 1850–1960* (1990); Stuart Kaufman, *Samuel Gompers and the Origins of the American Federation of Labor* (1978); Alexander Keyssar, *Out of Work: The First Century of Unemployment in Massachusetts* (1986); S. J. Kleinberg, *The Shadow of the Mills: Working-Class Families in Pittsburgh, 1870–1907* (1989); David Montgomery, *Beyond Equality* (1975), *Workers' Control in America: Studies in the History of Work, Technology, and Labor Struggles* (1979), and *The Fall of the House of Labor: The Workplace, the State, and American Labor Activism, 1865–1925* (1987); Daniel Nelson, *Managers and Workers: Origins of the New Factory System in the United States, 1880–1920* (1975); Richard J. Oestreicher, *Solidarity and Fragmentation: Working People and Class Consciousness: Detroit, 1875–1900* (1986); Henry Pelling, *American Labor* (1960); Peter Rachleff, *Black Labor In Richmond, 1865–1890* (1984); Roy Rosenzweig, *"Eight Hours for What We Will": Workers and Leisure in an Industrial City, 1870–1920* (1983); Steven J. Ross, *Workers on the Edge: Work, Leisure, and Politics in Industrializing Cincinnati, 1788–1890* (1985); Peter R. Shergold, *Working Class Life* (1982); Sheldon Stromquist, *A Generation of Boomers: The Pattern of Railroad Labor Conflict in Nineteenth-Century America* (1987); Philip Taft, *The A. F. of L. in the Time of Gompers,* 2 vols. (1957–1959); Kim Voss, *The Making of American Exceptionalism: The Knights of Labor and Class Formation in the Nineteenth Century* (1993); Daniel J. Walkowitz, *Worker City, Company Town: Iron and Cotton Workers Protest in Troy and Cohoes, New York, 1855–1884* (1978); Leon Wolff, *Lockout: The Story of the Homestead Strike of 1892* (1965).

**Women.** Mary Blewett, *Men, Women, and Work Culture: Class, Gender, and Protest in the New England Shoe Industry* (1988); Patricia Cooper, *Once a Cigar Maker: Men, Women, and Work Culture in American Cigar Factories, 1900–1919* (1987); Tamara Hareven, *Family Time and Industrial Time: The Relationship Between the Family and Work in a New England Industrial Community* (1982); Paula Hyman, Charlotte Baum, and Sonya Michel, *The Jewish Woman in America* (1975); Susan E. Kennedy, *If All We Did Was to Weep at Home: A History of White Working-Class Women in America* (1979); Alice Kessler-Harris, *Out to Work: A History of Wage-Earning Women in the United States* (1982); Susan Levine, *Labor's True Women: Carpet Weavers, Industrialization, and Labor Reform in the Gilded Age* (1984); Elizabeth Anne Payne, *Reform, Labor, and Feminism* (1988); Barbara Wertheimer, *We Were There: The Story of Working Women in America* (1977).

**The Left.** Mari Jo Buhle, *Women and American Socialism, 1870–1920* (1981); Melvyn Dubofsky, *We Shall Be All: A History of the Industrial Workers of the World* (1969); Gerald N. Grob, *Workers and Utopia* (1961); J. H. M. Laslett, *Labor and the Left* (1970); Margaret M. Marsh, *Anarchist Women: 1870–1920* (1981); Nick Salvatore, *Eugene V. Debs: Citizen and Socialist* (1982).

## CHAPTER 18 THE AGE OF THE CITY

**General Histories.** Howard Chudacoff, *The Evolution of American Urban Society*, rev. ed. (1981); Charles N. Glaab and Andrew T. Brown, *A History of Urban America* (1967); Constance M. Green, *The Rise of Urban America* (1965); Blake McKelvey, *The Urbanization of America* (1963); Lewis Mumford, *The Culture of the Cities* (1938), and *The City in History* (1961); Arthur M. Schlesinger, *The Rise of the City, 1878–1898* (1933); Jon C. Teaford, *City and Suburb: The Political Fragmentation of Urban America* (1979), and *The Twentieth-Century American City: Problem, Promise, and Reality* (1986); Sam Bass Warner, Jr., *The Urban Wilderness* (1972), and *Streetcar Suburbs* (1962).

**Mobility and Race.** Howard Chudacoff, *Mobile Americans: Residential and Social Mobility in Omaha, 1880–1920* (1972); Michael Frisch, *Town into City* (1972); Clyde Griffen and Sally Griffen, *Natives and Newcomers* (1977); Gerald D. Jaynes, *Branches Without Roots: Genesis of the Black Working Class in the American South, 1862–1882* (1986); Philip Kasinitz, *Caribbean New York: Black Immigrants and the Politics of Race* (1992); David M. Katzman, *Before the Ghetto* (1966); Kenneth L. Kusmer, *A Ghetto Takes Shape* (1976); Roger Lane, *The Roots of Black Violence in Philadelphia, 1860–1900* (1986); Gilbert Osofsky, *Harlem: The Making of a Ghetto* (1966); Richard Sennett, *Families Against the City* (1970); Allan H. Spear, *Black Chicago* (1967); Stephan Thernstrom, *Poverty and Progress* (1964), and *The Other Bostonians* (1973); Stephan Thernstrom and Richard Sennett, eds., *Nineteenth Century Cities* (1969); Olivier Zunz, *The Changing Face of Inequality: Urbanization, Industrial Development, and Immigrants in Detroit, 1880–1920* (1982).

**Immigration.** Thomas J. Archdeacon, *Becoming American: An Ethnic History* (1983); Josef Barton, *Peasants and Strangers: Italians, Rumanians, and Slovaks in an American City* (1975); John Bodnar, *The Transplanted: A History of Immigrants in America* (1985), and *Immigration and Industrialization* (1977); John W. Briggs, *An Italian Passage* (1978); Jack Chen, *The Chinese of America* (1980); Robert D. Cross, *The Church and the City* (1967); Leonard Dinnerstein and David Reimers, *Ethnic Americans: A History of Immigration and*

*Assimilation* (1975); John B. Duff, *The Irish in the United States* (1971); Elizabeth Ewen, *Immigrant Women in the Land of Dollars: Life and Culture on the Lower East Side, 1890–1925* (1985); Lawrence H. Fuchs, *The American Kaleidoscope: Race, Ethnicity, and the Civic Culture* (1990); Mario T. Garcia, *Desert Immigrants: The Mexicans of El Paso, 1880–1920* (1981); Nathan Glazer and Daniel P. Moynihan, *Beyond the Melting Pot* (1963); Susan A. Glenn, *Daughters of the Shtetl: Life and Labor in the Immigrant Generation* (1990); Milton M. Gordon, *Assimilation in American Life* (1964); Victor Greene, *For God and Country: The Rise of Polish and Lithuanian Ethnic Consciousness in America* (1975); Oscar Handlin, *The Uprooted*, rev. ed. (1973); Marcus Hansen, *The Immigrant in American History* (1940); John Higham, *Strangers in the Land* (1955), and *Send These To Me: Jews and Other Immigrants in Urban America* (1975); John Higham, ed., *Ethnic Leadership in America* (1978); Bill Ong Hing, *Making and Remaking Asian America Through Immigration Policy* (1993); Francis L. K. Hsu, *The Challenge of the American Dream: The Chinese in the United States* (1971); Maldwyn A. Jones, *American Immigration* (1960); Edward R. Kantowicz, *Polish-American Politics in Chicago* (1975); Thomas Kessner, *The Golden Door: Italian and Jewish Immigrant Mobility* (1977); Harry Kitano, *Japanese-Americans: The Evolution of a Subculture* (1969); Alan M. Kraut, *The Huddled Masses: The Immigrant in American Society, 1880–1921* (1982), and *Silent Travelers: Germs, Genes, and the "Immigrant Menace"* (1994); Matt S. Maier and Feliciano Rivera, *The Chicanos: A History of Mexican-Americans* (1972); Gwendolyn Mink, *Old Labor and New Immigrants in American Political Development: Union, Party, and State, 1875–1920* (1986); Ewa Morawska, *For Bread and Butter: The Life-Worlds of East Central Europeans in Johnstown, Pennsylvania, 1890–1940* (1985); Stanley Nadel, *Ethnicity, Religion, and Class in New York City, 1845–1880* (1990); Humbert S. Nelli, *The Italians of Chicago* (1970); Moses Rischin, *The Promised City: New York's Jews* (1962); Barbara Solomon, *Ancestors and Immigrants* (1965); Thomas Sowell, *Ethnic America* (1981); Philip Taylor, *The Distant Magnet: European Emigration to the U.S.A.* (1971); David Ward, *Cities and Immigrants* (1965); Mark Wyman, *Round-Trip to America: The Immigrants Return to Europe, 1880–1900* (1993); Virginia Yans-McLaughlin, *Family and Community: Italian Immigrants in Buffalo, 1880–1930* (1977).

**Urban Poverty and Reform.**    Robert H. Bremner, *From the Depths* (1956); Stephan F. Brumberg, *Going to America, Going to School* (1986); James H. Cassedy, *Charles V. Chapin and the Public Health Movement* (1962); Allen F. Davis, *Spearheads for Reform* (1967); Barbara Gutmann Rosencrantz, *Public Health and the State* (1972); Marvin Lazerson, *Origins of the Urban School* (1971); James T. Patterson, *America's Struggle Against Poverty* (1981); Thomas L. Philpott, *The Slum and the Ghetto* (1978); James F. Richardson, *The New York Police* (1970); Jacob Riis, *How the Other Half Lives* (1890), *Children of the Poor* (1892), and *The Battle with the Slum* (1902); Selwyn K. Troen, *The Public and the Schools* (1975); David B. Tyack, *The One Best System: A History of American Urban Education* (1974).

**Urban Politics.**    John M. Allswang, *Bosses, Machines and Urban Voters* (1977); Alexander B. Callow, *The Tweed Ring* (1966); Brian J. Cudahy, *Cash, Tokens, and Transfers: A History of Urban Mass Transit in North America* (1990); Lyle Dorsett, *The Pendergast Machine* (1968); Lori Ginzberg, *Women and the Work of Benevolence: Morality, Politics, and Class in the Nineteenth-Century United States* (1990); Roger Lane, *Policing the City: Boston, 1822–1885* (1967); Seymour Mandelbaum, *Boss Tweed's New York* (1965); Christine M. Rosen, *The Limits of Power: Great Fires and the Process of City Growth in America* (1986); John Sproat, *"The Best Men": Liberal Reformers in the Gilded Age* (1968); Zane L. Miller, *Boss Cox's Cincinnati: Urban Politics in the Progressive Era* (1968).

**Social Thought and Urban Culture.** Martha Banta, *Imaging American Women: Idea and Ideals in Cultural History* (1987); Stuart Blumin, *The Emergence of the Middle Class: Social Experience in the American City, 1760–1900* (1989); Gunther Barth, *City People: The Rise of Modern City Culture in Nineteenth-Century America* (1980), and *Instant Cities: Urbanization and the Rise of San Francisco and Denver* (1975); Susan Porter Benson, *Counter Cultures: Saleswomen, Managers, and Customers in American Department Stores, 1890–1940* (1986); Henry C. Binford, *The First Suburbs: Residential Communities on the Boston Periphery, 1815–1860* (1985); Paul Boyer, *Urban Masses and Moral Order in America, 1820–1920* (1978); Marc Carnes, *Secret Ritual and Manhood in Victorian America* (1989); Clifford E. Clark, *The American Family Home, 1800–1960* (1986); Lawrence Cremin, *The Transformation of the School* (1961); Perry Duis, *The Saloon: Public Drinking in Chicago and Boston, 1880–1920* (1983); Lewis A. Erenberg, *Steppin' Out: New York Nightlife and the Transformation of American Culture, 1890–1930* (1981); Charles V. Forcey, *The Crossroads of Liberalism* (1961); Timothy J. Gilfoyle, *City of Eros: New York City, Prostitution, and the Commercialization of Sex, 1790–1920* (1992); Eliot Gorn, *The Manly Art: Bare-Knuckle Prize Fighting in America* (1986); Harvey Green, *Fit for America: Fitness, Sport, and American Society* (1986); Allen Guttmann, *A Whole New Ball Game: An Interpretation of American Sports* (1988); Karen Halttunen, *Confidence Men and Painted Women: A Study of Middle-Class Culture in America, 1830–1870* (1982); Neil Harris, *Cultural Excursions: Marketing Appetites and Cultural Tastes in Modern America* (1990); Marilyn Wood Hill, *Their Sisters' Keepers: Prostitution in New York City, 1830–1870* (1993); Daniel Horowitz, *The Morality of Spending: Attitudes Toward the Consumer Society in America, 1875–1940* (1985); Kenneth T. Jackson, *The Crabgrass Frontier: The Suburbanization of the United States* (1985); John F. Kasson, *Amusing the Million: Coney Island at the Turn of the Century* (1978), and *Rudeness and Civility: Manners in Nineteenth-Century Urban America* (1990); William Leach, *True Love and Perfect Union: The Feminist Reform of Sex and Society* (1980), and *Land of Desire: Merchants, Power, and the Rise of a New American Culture* (1993); T. J. Jackson Lears, *No Place of Grace: Antimodernism and the Transformation of American Culture, 1880–1920* (1981); T. J. Jackson Lears and Richard Wightman Fox, eds., *The Culture of Consumption* (1983); Godfrey M. Lebhar, *Chain Stores in America* (1962); Lawrence Levine, *Highbrow/Lowbrow: The Emergence of a Cultural Hierarchy in America* (1988); John A. Lucas and Ronald Smith, *Saga of American Sport* (1978); D. W. Marcell, *Progress and Pragmatism* (1974); Jay Martin, *Harvests of Change* (1967); Martin V. Melosi, ed., *Pollution and Reform in American Cities* (1980); Steven Mintz and Susan Kellogg, *Domestic Revolutions: A Social History of American Family Life* (1988); Frank Luther Mott, *American Journalism*, rev. ed. (1962); Donald R. Mrozek, *Sport and American Mentality, 1880–1910* (1983); Lewis Mumford, *The Brown Decades* (1931); David Nasaw, *Going Out: The Rise and Fall of Public Amusements* (1993), and *Schooled to Order: A Social History of Public Schooling in the United States* (1979); James D. Norris, *Advertising and the Transformation of American Society, 1865–1920* (1990); Kathy Peiss, *Cheap Amusements: Working Women and Leisure in Turn-of-the-Century New York* (1986); Roy Rosenzweig and Elizabeth Blackmar, *The Park and the People: A History of Central Park* (1992); Alexander Saxton, *The Rise and Fall of the White Republic: Class Politics and Mass Culture in Nineteenth-Century America* (1990); Robert W. Snyder, *The Voice of the City: Vaudeville and Popular Culture in New York* (1989); Dale Somers, *The Rise of Sports in New Orleans* (1972); Susan Strasser, *Satisfaction Guaranteed: The Making of the American Mass Market* (1989); William R. Taylor, *In Pursuit of Gotham: Culture and Commerce in New York* (1992); Christopher Tunnard and H. H. Reed, *American Skyline* (1955); Alexander Von Hoffman, *Local Attachments: The Making of an American Urban Neighborhood, 1850–1920* (1994); Morton White, *So-*

*cial Thought in America* (1949); Larzer Ziff, *The American 1890s: Life and Times of a Lost Generation* (1966).

## CHAPTER 19 FROM STALEMATE TO CRISIS

**General Histories.** Sean Dennis Cashman, *America and the Gilded Age* (1984); Carl N. Degler, *The Age of the Economic Revolution, 1876–1900*, 2nd ed. (1977); John H. Dobson, *Politics in the Gilded Age* (1972); Harold U. Faulkner, *Politics, Reform, and Expansion* (1959); John A. Garraty, *The New Commonwealth* (1969); Samuel P. Hays, *The Response to Industrialism, 1885–1914* (1957); Nell Irvin Painter, *Standing at Armageddon: The United States, 1877–1919* (1987); Alan Trachtenberg, *The Incorporation of America: Culture and Society in the Gilded Age* (1982); Robert Wiebe, *The Search for Order, 1877–1920* (1967); R. Hal Williams, *Years of Decision: American Politics in the 1890s* (1978).

**Politics, Reform, and the State.** Geoffrey Blodgett, *The Gentle Reformers* (1966); Ruth Bourdin, *Women and Temperance: The Quest for Power and Liberty, 1873–1900* (1980); James Bryce, *The American Commonwealth*, 2 vols. (1888); Tony Freyer, *Regulating Big Business: Antitrust in Great Britain and America, 1880–1990* (1992); Ari Hoogenboom, *Outlawing the Spoils: The Civil Service Movement* (1961); Richard Jensen, *The Winning of the Midwest: Social and Political Conflict, 1888–1896* (1971); Matthew Josephson, *The Politicos* (1963); Morton Keller, *Affairs of State* (1977); Paul Kleppner, *The Cross of Culture: A Social Analysis of Midwestern Politics, 1850–1900* (1970), and *The Third Electoral System, 1853–1892* (1979); J. Morgan Kousser, *The Shaping of Southern Politics: Suffrage Restriction and the Establishment of the One-Party South, 1880–1910* (1974); Michael P. Malone, *The Battle for Butte: Mining and Politics on the Northern Frontier, 1864–1906* (1981); Robert D. Marcus, *Grand Old Party* (1971); Gerald W. McFarland, *Mugwumps, Morals, and Politics, 1884–1920* (1975); Michael E. McGerr, *The Decline of Popular Politics* (1986); H. Wayne Morgan, *From Hayes to McKinley* (1969); Walter T. K. Nugent, *Money and American Society, 1865–1880* (1968); David J. Rothman, *Politics and Power: The United States Senate, 1869–1901* (1966); Martin J. Sklar, *The Corporate Reconstruction of American Capitalism, 1890–1916* (1988); Theda Skocpol, *Protecting Soldiers and Mothers: The Political Origins of Social Policy in the United States* (1992); Stephen Skowronek, *Building a New American State: The Expansion of National Administrative Capacities, 1877–1920* (1982); John Sproat, *"The Best Men": Liberal Reformers in the Gilded Age* (1968); Tom E. Terrill, *The Tariff, Politics, and American Foreign Policy, 1874–1901* (1973); Irwin Unger, *The Greenback Era* (1964); Leonard D. White, *The Republican Era* (1958).

**Party Leaders.** Harry Barnard, *Rutherford B. Hayes and His America* (1954); Herbert Croly, *Marcus Alonzo Hanna* (1912); Kenneth Davison, *The Presidency of Rutherford B. Hayes* (1972); Lewis L. Gould, *The Presidency of William McKinley* (1981); David Jordan, *Roscoe Conkling of New York* (1971); Margaret Leech, *In the Days of McKinley* (1959); Margaret Leech and Harry J. Brown, *The Garfield Orbit* (1978); Horace Samuel Merrill, *Bourbon Leader: Grover Cleveland and the Democratic Party* (1957); H. Wayne Morgan, *William McKinley and His America* (1963); Allan Nevins, *Grover Cleveland: A Study in Courage* (1933); Allan Peskin, *Garfield* (1978); Thomas C. Reeves, *Gentleman Boss: The Life of Chester Alan Arthur* (1975); Nick Salvatore, *Eugene V. Debs: Citizen and Socialist* (1982); Harry J. Sievers, *Benjamin Harrison*, 3 vols. (1952–1968).

**The Depression.** Ray Ginger, *Altgeld's America* (1958), and *The Bending Cross* (1949); Almot Lindsey, *The Pullman Strike* (1942); Donald McMurray, *Coxey's Army* (1929); Samuel McSeveney, *The Politics of Depression* (1972); Carlos A. Schwantes, *Coxey's Army* (1955).

**Populism.** Peter Argersinger, *Populism and Politics: William Alfred Peffer and the People's Party* (1974); O. Gene Clanton, *Populism: The Humane Preference in America, 1890–1900* (1991), and *Kansas Populism: Ideas and Men* (1969); Robert F. Durden, *The Climax of Populism: The Election of 1896* (1965); Lawrence Goodwyn, *Democratic Promise* (1976), and *The Populist Moment* (1978), an abridgment of *Democratic Promise*; Sheldon Hackney, *Populism to Progressivism in Alabama* (1969); Steven Hahn, *The Roots of Southern Populism: Yeoman Farmers and the Transformation of the Georgia Upcountry, 1850–1890* (1983); John D. Hicks, *The Populist Revolt* (1931); Richard Hofstadter, *The Age of Reform* (1954); Robert McMath, *Populist Vanguard* (1975), and *American Populism: A Social History, 1877–1898* (1993); Theodore R. Mitchell, *Political Education in the Southern Farmers Alliance, 1887–1900* (1987); Walter T. K. Nugent, *The Tolerant Populists* (1960); Bruce Palmer, *Man over Money* (1980); Stanley Parsons, *The Populist Context: Rural Versus Urban Power on a Great Plains Frontier* (1973); Norman Pollack, *The Populist Response to Industrial America* (1962), and *The Just Polity: Populism, Law, and Human Welfare* (1987); Martin Ridge, *Ignatius Donnelly: Portrait of a Politician* (1962); Theodore Saloutos, *Farmer Movements in the South, 1865–1933* (1960); Fred Shannon, *The Farmer's Last Frontier* (1945); Barton C. Shaw, *The Wool-Hat Boys: Georgia's Populist Party* (1984); Francis B. Simkins, *Pitchfork Ben Tillman* (1944); Allan Weinstein, *Prelude of Populism: Origins of the Silver Issue* (1970); C. Vann Woodward, *Origins of the New South* (1972), and *Tom Watson, Agrarian Rebel* (1938); James E. Wright, *The Politics of Populism: Dissent in Colorado* (1974).

**The "Battle of the Standards" and the Election of 1896.** Paolo Coletta, *William Jennings Bryan*, 3 vols., (1964–1969); Milton Friedman and Anna J. Schwartz, *A Monetary History of the United States* (1963); Paul Glad, *McKinley, Bryan, and the People* (1964), and *The Trumpet Soundeth* (1960); J. Rogers Hollingsworth, *The Whirligig of Politics: The Democracy of Cleveland and Bryan* (1963); Stanley Jones, *The Presidential Election of 1896* (1964).

CHAPTER 20 THE IMPERIAL REPUBLIC

**General Histories.** Robert L. Beisner, *From the Old Diplomacy to the New, 1865–1900*, 2nd ed. (1986); Charles S. Campbell, *The Transformation of American Foreign Relations, 1865–1900* (1976); John Dobson, *America's Ascent: The United States Becomes a Great Power, 1880–1914* (1978); Foster Rhea Dulles, *Prelude to World Power, 1865–1900* (1965); J. A. S. Grenville and George Berkeley Young, *Politics, Strategy and American Diplomacy: Studies in Foreign Policy, 1873–1917* (1966); David F. Healy, *U.S. Expansionism: Imperialist Urge in the 1890s* (1970); Walter LaFeber, *The Cambridge History of American Foreign Relations*, vol. 2: *The Search for Opportunity, 1865–1913* (1993), and *The New Empire* (1963); Ernest May, *Imperial Democracy* (1961), and *American Imperialism: A Speculative Essay* (1968); H. Wayne Morgan, *America's Road to Empire* (1965); Milton Plesur, *America's Outward Thrust: Approaches to Foreign Affairs, 1865–1890* (1971); David M. Pletcher, *The Awkward Years: American Foreign Relations Under Garfield and Arthur* (1962); Julius

W. Pratt, *Expansionists of 1898* (1936); Emily S. Rosenberg, *Spreading the American Dream: American Economic and Cultural Expansion, 1890–1945* (1982); Albert K. Weinberg, *Manifest Destiny: A Study in Nationalist Expansion in American History* (1935); William Appleman Williams, *The Tragedy of American Diplomacy*, rev. ed. (1972).

**The Spanish-American War.** Richard Challener, *Admirals, Generals, and American Foreign Policy, 1889–1914* (1973); Graham A. Cosmas, *An Army for Empire: The United States Army in the Spanish-American War* (1971); Philip S. Foner, *The Spanish-Cuban-American War and the Birth of American Imperialism*, 2 vols. (1972); Frank Freidel, *The Splendid Little War* (1958); Willard B. Gatewood, Jr., *Black Americans and the White Man's Burden, 1898–1903* (1975), and *"Smoked Yankees": Letters from Negro Soldiers, 1898–1902* (1971); Gerald F. Linderman, *The Mirror of War: American Society and the Spanish-American War* (1974); Walter Millis, *The Martial Spirit* (1931); Joyce Milton, *The Yellow Journalists* (1989); Edmund Morris, *The Rise of Theodore Roosevelt* (1979); John L. Offner, *An Unwanted War: The Diplomacy of the United States and Spain over Cuba, 1895–1898* (1992); Louis A. Perez, Jr., *Cuba Between Empires, 1868–1902* (1983); Hyman Rickover, *How the Battleship Maine Was Destroyed* (1976); David F. Trask, *The War with Spain in 1898* (1981); Richard S. West, Jr., *Admirals of the American Empire* (1948).

**Imperialism and Anti-Imperialism.** Robert L. Beisner, *Twelve Against Empire* (1968); Kendrick A. Clements, *William Jennings Bryan* (1983); James H. Hitchman, *Leonard Wood and Cuban Independence, 1898–1902* (1971); Frederick Merk, *Manifest Destiny and Mission in American History* (1963); Thomas J. Osborne, *"Empire Can Wait": American Opposition to Hawaiian Annexation, 1893–1898* (1891); William J. Pomeroy, *American Neo-Colonialism: Its Emergence in the Philippines and Asia* (1970); Julius W. Pratt, *America's Colonial Empire* (1950); Robert Seager II, *Alfred Thayer Mahan* (1977); E. Berkeley Tompkins, *Anti-Imperialism in the United States, 1890–1920: The Great Debate* (1970).

**The Pacific Empire.** H. W. Brands, *Bound to Empire: The United States and the Philippines* (1992); John Morgan Gates, *Schoolbooks and Krags: The United States Army in the Philippines, 1898–1902* (1971); Stanley Karnow, *In Our Image: America's Empire in the Philippines* (1989); Paul M. Kennedy, *The Samoan Tangle* (1974), Glenn A. May, *Social Engineering in the Philippines* (1980); Stuart Creighton Miller, *"Benevolent Assimilation": The American Conquest of the Philippines, 1899–1903* (1982); Daniel B. Schirmer, *Republic or Empire? American Resistance to the Philippine War* (1972); Peter Stanley, *A Nation in the Making: The Philippines and the United States* (1974); Merze Tate, *The United States and the Hawaiian Kingdom* (1965); Richard E. Welch, Jr., *Response to Imperialism: The United States and the Philippine-American War, 1899–1902* (1979); Leon Wolff, *Little Brown Brother* (1961).

**America and Asia.** Warren Cohen, *America's Response to China*, rev. ed. (1980), and *East Asian Art and American Culture: A Study in International Relations* (1992); Kenton Clymer, *John Hay: Gentleman as Diplomat* (1975); Patricia Hill, *The World Their Household: The American Women's Foreign Mission Movement and Cultural Transformation* (1985); Michael Hunt, *The Making of a Special Relationship: The United States and China to 1914* (1983); Jane Hunter, *The Gospel of Gentility: American Women Missionaries in Turn-of-the-Century China* (1984); Akira Iriye, *Across the Pacific* (1967), and *Pacific Estrangement: Japanese and American Expansion* (1972); Robert McClellan, *The Heathen Chinese: A Study of American Attitudes Toward China* (1971); Thomas J. McCormick, *China Market: America's Quest for*

*Informal Empire, 1893–1901* (1967); Charles Neu, *The Troubled Encounter* (1975); James C. Thomsen, Jr., Peter W. Stanley, and John Curtis Perry, *Sentimental Imperialists: The American Experience in East Asia* (1981); Paul Varg, *The Making of a Myth: The United States and China, 1897–1912* (1968), and *Missionaries, Chinese and Diplomats* (1958); Marilyn B. Young, *The Rhetoric of Empire: American China Policy, 1895–1901* (1968).

## CHAPTER 21 THE RISE OF PROGRESSIVISM

**Progressivism: Overviews.** John D. Buenker, John C. Burnham, and Robert M. Crunden, *Progressivism* (1977); John W. Chambers II, *The Tyranny of Change: America in the Progressive Era, 1900–1917* (1980); John Milton Cooper, *The Pivotal Decades: The United States, 1900–1920* (1990); Alan Dawley, *Struggles for Justice: Social Responsibility and the Liberal State* (1991); Richard Hofstadter, *The Age of Reform: From Bryan to FDR* (1955); Gabriel Kolko, *The Triumph of Conservatism: A Reinterpretation of American History* (1963); Arthur S. Link and Richard L. McCormick, *Progressivism* (1983); Nell Irvin Painter, *Standing at Armageddon: The United States, 1877–1919* (1987); James Weinstein, *The Corporate Ideal in the Liberal State, 1900–1918* (1969); Robert Wiebe, *The Search for Order, 1877–1920* (1967).

**The Muckrakers.** David Chalmers, *The Social and Political Ideas of the Muckrakers* (1964); Louis Filler, *The Muckrakers*, rev. ed. (1980); Leon Harris, *Upton Sinclair* (1975); Justin Kaplan, *Lincoln Steffens* (1974); C. C. Regier, *The Era of the Muckrakers* (1932); Harold S. Wilson, *McClure's Magazine and the Muckrakers* (1970).

**Progressive Thought.** Richard Abrams, *The Burdens of Progress* (1978); Carl N. Degler, *In Search of Human Nature: The Decline and Revival of Darwinism in American Social Thought* (1991); Arthur Ekirch, *Progressivism in America* (1974); Charles V. Forcey, *The Crossroads of Liberalism: Croly, Weyl, Lippmann* (1961); Sudhir Kakar, *Frederick Taylor* (1970); D. W. Marcell, *Progress and Pragmatism: James, Dewey, Beard and the American Idea of Progress* (1974); David W. Noble, ed., *The Progressive Mind*, rev. ed. (1981); Jean B. Quandt, *From the Small Town to the Great Community: The Social Thought of Progressive Intellectuals* (1970); Robert Westbrook, *John Dewey and American Democracy* (1991); Morton White, *Social Thought in America* (1949).

**Social Work and the Social Gospel.** Jane Addams, *Twenty Years at Hull House* (1910); Paul Boyer, *Urban Masses and Moral Order, 1820–1920* (1978); Mina Carson, *Settlement Folk: Social Thought and the American Settlement Movement, 1885–1930* (1990); Robert M. Crunden, *Ministers of Reform: The Progressives' Achievement in American Civilization, 1889–1920* (1982); Susan Curtis, *A Consuming Faith: The Social Gospel and Modern American Culture* (1991); Allen F. Davis, *Spearheads of Reform: The Social Settlements and the Progressive Movement, 1890–1914* (1968), and *American Heroine: The Life and Legend of Jane Addams* (1973); C. H. Hopkins, *The Rise of the Social Gospel in American Protestantism* (1940); William R. Hutchinson, *The Modernist Impulse in American Protestantism* (1982); Rivka Shpak Lissak, *Pluralism and Progressives: Hull House and the New Immigrants, 1890–1919* (1989); Roy Lubove, *The Progressives and the Slums: Tenement House Reform in New York City* (1962); Henry May, *Protestant Churches and Industrial America* (1949); Timothy Miller, *Following in His Steps: A Biography of Charles M. Sheldon* (1987).

**Education and the Professions.** Clyde W. Barrow, *Universities and the Capitalist State: Corporate Liberalism and the Reconstruction of American Higher Education, 1894–1928* (1990); Burton Bledstein, *The Culture of Professionalism* (1976); Lawrence A. Cremin, *The Transformation of the Schools: Progressivism in American Education, 1876–1957* (1971); Lynn D. Gordon, *Gender and Higher Education in the Progressive Era* (1990); Samuel Haber, *The Quest for Authority and Honor in the American Professions, 1750–1900* (1991); Barbara Harris, *Beyond Her Sphere: Women and the Professions in American History* (1978); Thomas L. Haskell, *The Emergence of Professional Social Science* (1977); Morton J. Horwitz, *The Transformation of American Law, 1870–1960: The Crisis of Legal Orthodoxy* (1992); Kenneth M. Ludmerer, *Learning to Heal: The Development of American Medical Education* (1985); Regina Markell Morantz-Sanchez, *Sympathy and Science: Women Physicians in American Medicine* (1985); Barbara Miller Solomon, *In the Company of Educated Women: A History of Women in Higher Education in America* (1985); Paul Starr, *The Social Transformation of American Medicine* (1982); David Tyack and Elizabeth Hansot, *Managers of Virtue: Public School Leadership in America, 1820–1980* (1982); Lawrence Veysey, *The Emergence of the American University* (1970).

**Municipal Reform.** John D. Buenker, *Urban Liberalism and Progressive Reform* (1973); James B. Crooks, *Politics and Progress: The Rise of Urban Progressivism in Baltimore* (1968); Oscar Handlin, *Al Smith and His America* (1958); Melvin G. Holli, *Reform in Detroit: Hazen S. Pingree and Urban Politics* (1969); J. Joseph Huthmacher, *Senator Robert F. Wagner and the Rise of Urban Liberalism* (1971); Michael Kazin, *Barons of Labor: The San Francisco Building Trades and Union Power in the Progressive Era* (1981); Zane Miller, *Boss Cox's Cincinnati* (1968); Martin J. Schiesl, *The Politics of Efficiency: Municipal Administration and Reform in America, 1880–1920* (1977).

**Women, Reform, and Suffrage.** Paula Baker, *The Moral Frameworks of Public Life: Gender, Politics, and the State in Rural New York, 1870–1930* (1991); Karen Blair, *The Clubwoman as Feminist* (1980); Mari Jo Buhle, *Women and American Socialism* (1983); Norman H. Clark, *Deliver Us from Evil: An Interpretation of American Prohibition* (1976); Mark T. Connelly, *The Response to Prohibition in the Progressive Era* (1980); Nancy Cott, *The Grounding of Modern Feminism* (1987); Ellen C. DuBois, *Feminism and Suffrage: The Emergence of an Independent Women's Movement in America, 1848–1869* (1978); Nancy Shrom Dye, *As Equal as Sisters: Feminism, The Labor Movement, and the Women's Trade Union League of New York* (1981); Eleanor Flexner, *Century of Struggle* (1959); Linda Gordon, *Woman's Body, Woman's Right: A Social History of Birth Control* (1976); Alan P. Grimes, *The Puritan Ethic and Woman Suffrage* (1967); Jacquelyn Dowd Hall, *The Revolt Against Chivalry* (1979); David M. Kennedy, *Birth Control in America: The Career of Margaret Sanger* (1970); Aileen S. Kraditor, *Ideas of the Woman Suffrage Movement* (1965); Ellen C. Lagemann, *A Generation of Women: Education in the Lives of Progressive Reformers* (1979); Elaine Tyler May, *Great Expectations: Marriage and Divorce in Post-Victorian America* (1980); David Morgan, *Suffragists and Democrats: The Politics of Woman Suffrage in America* (1972); Robyn Muncy, *Creating a Female Dominion in American Reform, 1890–1935* (1991); William O'Neill, *Divorce in the Progressive Era* (1967), and *Everyone Was Brave: The Rise and Fall of Feminism in America* (1969); Ruth Rosen, *The Lost Sisterhood: Prostitutes in America, 1900–1918* (1982); Rosalind Rosenberg, *Beyond Separate Spheres: Intellectual Roots of Modern Feminism* (1982); Elyce J. Rotella, *From Home to Office: U.S. Women and Work, 1870–1930* (1981); Sheila M. Rothman, *Woman's Proper Place* (1978); Anne F. Scott, *Making the Invisible Woman Visible* (1984).

**Racial Issues.** John Dittmer, *Black Georgia in the Progressive Era, 1900–1920* (1977); George Frederickson, *The Black Image in the White Mind* (1968); Paula Giddings, *When and Where I Enter: The Impact of Black Women on Race and Sex in America* (1984); Louis Harlan, *Booker T. Washington: The Making of a Black Leader* (1856), and *Booker T. Washington: The Wizard of Tuskegee, 1901–1915* (1983); Charles F. Kellogg, *NAACP* (1970); Jack Temple Kirby, *Darkness at Dawning: Race and Reform in the Progressive South* (1972); David L. Lewis, *W. E. B. DuBois: Biography of a Race, 1868–1919* (1993); William A. Link, *The Paradox of Southern Progressivism, 1880–1930* (1992); Ralph E. Luker, *The Social Gospel in Black and White: American Racial Reform, 1885–1912* (1991); James M. McPherson, *The Abolitionist Legacy: From Reconstruction to the NAACP* (1975); August Meier, *Negro Thought in America, 1880–1915* (1963); Cynthia Neverdon-Morton, *Afro-American Women of the South and the Advancement of the Race, 1885–1925* (1989); Elliott Rudwick, *W. E. B. Du Bois* (1969); Donald Spivey, *Schooling for the New Slavery: Black Industrial Education* (1978); Joel Williamson, *The Crucible of Race: Black-White Relations in the American South Since Emancipation* (1985).

**State-Level Reform.** Richard M. Abrams, *Conservatism in a Progressive Era: Massachusetts* (1964); Dewey Grantham, *Southern Progressivism: The Reconciliation of Progress and Tradition* (1983); Sheldon Hackney, *Populism to Progressivism in Alabama* (1969); Robert S. Maxwell, *La Follette and the Rise of Progressivism in Wisconsin* (1944); Richard L. McCormick, *From Realignment to Reform: Political Change in New York State, 1893–1910* (1981); George E. Mowry, *California Progressives* (1951); Russel B. Nye, *Midwestern Progressive Politics* (1951); David P. Thelen, *The New Citizenship: Origins of Progressivism in Wisconsin* (1972), *Robert M. La Follette and the Insurgent Spirit* (1976), and *Paths of Resistance: Tradition and Dignity in Industrializing Missouri* (1986); Robert F. Wesser, *Charles Evans Hughes: Politics and Reform in New York State, 1905–1910* (1967); C. Vann Woodward, *Origins of the New South* (1951), Irwin Yellowitz, *Labor and the Progressive Movement in New York State* (1965).

**National Issues.** Ruth Bourdin, *Women and Temperance: The Quest for Power and Liberty, 1873–1900* (1980); Melvyn Dubofsky, *We Shall Be All: A History of the Industrial Workers of the World* (1969); Sidney Fine, *Laissez Faire and the General Welfare State* (1956); Joseph Gusfield, *Symbolic Crusade: Status Politics and the Temperance Movement* (1963) John Higham, *Strangers in the Land* (1955); Michael E. McGerr, *The Decline of Popular Politics: The American North, 1865–1928* (1986); Bruno Ramirez, *When Workers Organize: The Politics of Industrial Relations in the Progressive Era, 1898–1916* (1978); James T. Timberlake, *Prohibition and the Progressive Movement* (1963); James Weinstein, *The Decline of Socialism in America* (1967); Robert Wiebe, *Businessmen and Reform: A Study of the Progressive Movement* (1962); Olivier Zunz, *Making America Corporate, 1870–1920* (1990).

## CHAPTER 22 THE BATTLE FOR NATIONAL REFORM

**General Histories.** John Milton Cooper, Jr., *The Warrior and the Priest: Woodrow Wilson and Theodore Roosevelt* (1983); Arthur Link, *Woodrow Wilson and the Progressive Era, 1910–1917* (1954); George E. Mowry, *The Era of Theodore Roosevelt* (1958). (See also Suggested Readings for Chapter 21.)

**Theodore Roosevelt.** John Morton Blum, *The Republican Roosevelt* (1954); G. Wallace Chessman, *Theodore Roosevelt and the Politics of Power* (1969); John A. Garraty, *The Life of George W. Perkins* (1960); Lewis L. Gould, *The Presidency of Theodore Roosevelt* (1991); William H. Harbaugh, *Power and Responsibility* (1961), published in paperback as *The Life and Times of Theodore Roosevelt*; Horace S. Merrill and Marion G. Merrill, *The Republican High Command* (1971); Edmund Morris, *The Rise of Theodore Roosevelt* (1979); Henry F. Pringle, *Theodore Roosevelt* (1931).

**William Howard Taft.** Donald E. Anderson, *William Howard Taft* (1973); Paolo E. Coletta, *The Presidency of William Howard Taft* (1973); George Mowry, *Theodore Roosevelt and the Progressive Movement* (1946); Henry F. Pringle, *The Life and Times of William Howard Taft*, 2 vols. (1939); Norman Wilensky, *Conservatives in the Progressive Era: The Taft Republicans of 1912* (1965).

**Woodrow Wilson.** John Morton Blum, *Joseph Tumulty and the Wilson Era* (1951), and *Woodrow Wilson and the Politics of Morality* (1956); Alexander George and Juliette George, *Woodrow Wilson and Colonel House* (1956); L. J. Holt, *Congressional Insurgents and the Party System, 1909–1916* (1967); Arthur S. Link, *Woodrow Wilson*, 5 vols. (1947–1965); Edwin A. Weinstein, *Woodrow Wilson: A Medical and Psychological Biography* (1981).

**National Issues.** O. E. Anderson, *The Health of a Nation* (1958); Stephen R. Fox, *The American Conservation Movement: John Muir and His Legacy* (1981); Samuel P. Hays, *The Gospel of Efficiency: The Progressive Conservation Movement, 1890–1920* (1962); James Holt, *Congressional Insurgents and the Party System* (1969); John M. Jordan, *Machine Age Ideology: Social Engineering and American Liberalism, 1911–1939* (1994); Susan Kleinberg, *The Shadow of the Mills: Working Class Families in Pittsburgh, 1870–1907* (1989); Naomi Lamoreaux, *The Great Merger Movement in American Business, 1895–1904* (1985); Albro Martin, *Enterprise Denied: Origins of the Decline of the American Railroads, 1897–1917* (1971); Thomas K. McCraw, ed., *Regulation in Perspective* (1981); Roderick Nash, *Wilderness and the American Mind* (1967); James Penick, Jr., *Progressive Politics and Conservation: The Ballinger-Pinchot Affair* (1968); Harold T. Pinkett, *Gifford Pinchot: Private and Public Forester* (1970); Elmo P. Richardson, *The Politics of Conservation* (1962); David Sarasohn, *The Party of Reform: The Democrats in the Progressive Era* (1989); Martin J. Sklar, *The Corporate Reconstruction of American Capitalism, 1890–1916: The Market, the Law, and Politics* (1988); Peter Temin, *Taking Your Medicine: Drug Regulation in the U.S.* (1980); Melvin I. Urofsky, *Louis D. Brandeis and the Progressive Tradition* (1981); Bernard Weisberger, *The LaFollettes of Wisconsin: Love and Politics in Progressive America* (1994); Craig West, *Banking Reform and the Federal Reserve, 1863–1923* (1977); Robert Wiebe, *Businessmen and Reform: A Study of the Progressive Movement* (1962).

**Roosevelt's Foreign Policy.** Howard K. Beale, *Theodore Roosevelt and the Rise of America to World Power* (1956); David H. Burton, *Theodore Roosevelt: Confident Imperialist* (1969); Richard Challener, *Admirals, Generals, and American Foreign Policy, 1898–1914* (1973); Raymond A. Esthus, *Theodore Roosevelt and International Rivalries* (1970); Michael H. Hunt, *The Making of a Special Relationship: The United States and China to 1914* (1983); Akira Iriye, *Pacific Estrangement: Japanese and American Expansion, 1897–1911* (1972); Richard Leopold, *Elihu Root and the Conservative Tradition* (1954); Charles E. Neu, *An Uncertain Friendship: Roosevelt and Japan, 1906–1909* (1967); Bradford Perkins, *The Great Rapprochement: England and the United States, 1895–1914* (1968); Julius W. Pratt, *Chal-*

*lenge and Rejection: The United States and World Leadership, 1900–1921* (1967); Charles Vevier, *United States and China* (1955).

**America and the Caribbean.** P. Edward Haley, *Revolution and Intervention: The Diplomacy of Taft and Wilson with Mexico, 1910–1917* (1975); David Healy, *The United States in Cuba, 1898–1902* (1963); Walter LaFeber, *The Panama Canal* (1978); Lester E. Langley, *The Banana Wars: An Inner History of American Empire, 1900–1934* (1983); David McCullough, *The Path Between the Seas* (1977); Dwight C. Miner, *Fight for the Panama Route* (1966); Dana G. Munro, *Intervention and Dollar Diplomacy in the Caribbean, 1900–1921* (1964); Louis A. Perez, Jr., *Cuba Under the Platt Amendment* (1988); Walter Scholes and Marie Scholes, *The Foreign Policies of the Taft Administration* (1970); John Womack, *Zapata and the Mexican Revolution* (1968).

**Wilson's Foreign Policy.** Kenneth Grieb, *The United States and Huerta* (1969); David Healy, *Gunboat Diplomacy in the Wilson Era: The U.S. Navy in Haiti, 1915–1916* (1976); Thomas J. Knock, *To End All Wars: Woodrow Wilson and the Quest for a New World Order* (1992); Arthur Link, *Wilson the Diplomatist* (1957), and *Woodrow Wilson: Revolution, War, and Peace* (1979); Dana Munro, *Intervention and Dollar Diplomacy in the Caribbean, 1900–1914* (1964); Robert Quirk, *An Affair of Honor: Woodrow Wilson and the Occupation of Veracruz* (1962), and *The Mexican Revolution, 1914–1915* (1960); James Reed, *The Missionary Mind and America's East Asian Policy, 1911–1915* (1983); Robert Freeman Smith, *The United States and Revolutionary Nationalism in Mexico, 1916–1932* (1972).

## CHAPTER 23 AMERICA AND THE GREAT WAR

**The Road to War.** Thomas A. Bailey and Paul B. Ryan, *The Lusitania Disaster* (1975); John Coogan, *The End to Neutrality* (1981); John Milton Cooper, Jr., *The Vanity of Power: American Isolation and the First World War* (1969); Patrick Devlin, *Too Proud to Fight: Woodrow Wilson's Neutrality* (1974); Ross Gregory, *The Origins of American Intervention in the First World War* (1971); Manfred Jonas, *The United States and Germany* (1984); C. Roland Marchand, *The American Peace Movement and Social Reform* (1973); Ernest R. May, *The World War and American Isolation* (1959); Emily Rosenberg, *Spreading the American Dream* (1982); Jeffrey J. Sanford, *Wilsonian Maritime Diplomacy* (1978); Daniel Smith, *Robert Lansing and American Neutrality* (1958), and *The Great Departure: The United States and World War I, 1914–1920,* (1965); Barbara M. Tuchman, *The Zimmermann Telegram* (1958), and *The Guns of August* (1962).

**Military Histories.** A. E. Barbeau and Florette Henri, *The Unknown Soldiers: Black American Troops in World War I* (1974); Christopher Campbell, *Aces and Aircraft of World War I* (1981); John Whiteclay Chambers, *To Raise an Army* (1987); J. Garry Clifford, *The Citizen Soldiers* (1972); Edward M. Coffman, *The War to End All Wars* (1969); Harvey A. DeWeerd, *President Wilson Fights His War* (1968); Frank Freidel, *Over There: The Story of America's First Great Overseas Crusade* (1964); Robert Jackson, *Fighter Pilots in World War I* (1977); Herbert M. Mason, Jr., *The Lafayette Escadrille* (1964); Donald Smythe, *Pershing* (1986); Lawrence Stallings, *The Doughboys: The Story of the AEF, 1917–1918* (1963); David Trask, *The United States in the Supreme War Council* (1961); Frank E. Vandiver, *Black Jack: The Life and Times of John J. Pershing* (1977); Russell Weigley, *The American Way of War* (1973).

**Wartime Diplomacy.** Kathleen Burk, *Britain, America, and the Sinews of War* (1985); W. B. Fowler, *British-American Relations, 1917–1918* (1969); John Lewis Gaddis, *Russia, the Soviet Union and the United States* (1978); George F. Kennan, *Russia Leaves the War* (1956), and *Russia and the West Under Lenin and Stalin* (1961); Carl Parrini, *Heir to Empire: United States Economic Diplomacy, 1916–1923* (1969).

**Politics and Government in Wartime.** Ray H. Abrams, *Preachers Present Arms: The Role of the American Churches and Clergy in World Wars I and II* (1969); Daniel R. Beaver, *Newton D. Baker and the American War Effort, 1917–1919* (1966); George T. Blakey, *Historians on the Homefront* (1970); William J. Breen, *Uncle Sam at Home* (1984); Zechariah Chaffee, Jr., *Free Speech in the United States* (1941); Charles Chatfield, *For Peace and Justice: Pacifism in America, 1914–1941* (1971); Edward M. Coffman, *The Hilt of the Sword: The Career of Peyton C. Marsh* (1966); Valerie Jean Conner, *The National War Labor Board* (1983); Alfred E. Conrebise, *War as Advertised: The Four Minute Men and America's Crusade, 1917–1918* (1984); Wayne Cornelius, *Building the Cactus Curtain: Mexican Migration and U.S. Responses from Wilson to Carter* (1980); Robert D. Cuff, *The War Industries Board: Business-Government Relations During World War I* (1973); Charles DeBenedettis, *Origins of the Modern Peace Movement* (1978); Harvey A. De-Weerd, *President Wilson Fights His War* (1968); Charles V. Forcey, *The Crossroads of Liberalism* (1961); Charles Gilbert, *American Financing of World War I* (1970); Otis L. Graham, Jr., *The Great Campaigns* (1971); Ellis W. Hawley, *The Great War and the Search for a Modern Order* (1979); Sondra Herman, *Eleven Against War* (1969); Donald Johnson, *The Challenge to America's Freedoms* (1963); David M. Kennedy, *Over Here* (1980); Seward Livermore, *Politics Is Adjourned* (1966); J. R. Mock and Cedric Larson, *Words That Won the War* (1939); Paul L. Murphy, *World War I and the Origins of Civil Liberties* (1984); George Nash, *The Life of Herbert Hoover: The Humanitarian, 1914–1917* (1990); Harold C. Peterson, *Propaganda for War: The Campaign Against American Neutrality, 1914–1917* (1968); Harold C. Peterson and Gilbert Fite, *Opponents of War, 1917–1918* (1957); Richard Polenberg, *Fighting Faiths: The Abrams Case, the Supreme Court, and Free Speech* (1987); William Preston, Jr., *Aliens and Dissenters: Federal Suppression of Radicals, 1903–1933* (1963); Ronald Schaffer, *America in the Great War: The Rise of the War Welfare State* (1991); Harry N. Scheiber, *The Wilson Administration and Civil Liberties, 1917–1921* (1960); Jordan Schwarz, *The Speculator: Bernard M. Baruch in Washington, 1917–1965* (1981); John A. Thomas, *Reformers and War* (1987); Stephen Vaughn, *Holding Fast the Inner Lines: Democracy, Nationalism, and the Committee on Public Information* (1979); Neil A. Wynn, *From Progressivism to Prosperity: World War I and American Society* (1986).

**Wartime Society and Culture.** Allan M. Brandt, *No Magic Bullet: A Social History of Venereal Disease in the United States* (1985); Paul Chapman, *Schools as Sorters* (1988); Stanley Cooperman, *World War I and the American Novel* (1970); Alfred W. Crosby, Jr., *Epidemic and Peace, 1918* (1976); Maurine W. Greenwald, *Women, War, and Work* (1980); Carol S. Gruber, *Mars and Minerva* (1975); John Higham, *Strangers in the Land: Patterns of American Nativism* (1955); Michael T. Isenberg, *War on Film* (1981); Frederick C. Luebke, *Bonds of Loyalty: German-Americans and World War I* (1974); Elizabeth Payne, *Reform, Labor, and Feminism: Margaret Dreier Robins and the Women's Trade Union League* (1988); Michael Pearlman, *To Make Democracy Safe for America: Patricians and Preparedness in the Progressive Era* (1984); Barbara J. Steinson, *American Women's Activism in World War I* (1982).

**Wilson and the Peace.** Lloyd Ambrosius, *Woodrow Wilson and the American Diplomatic Tradition* (1987); John Morton Blum, *Woodrow Wilson and the Politics of Morality* (1956); Robert H. Ferrell, *Woodrow Wilson and World War I* (1985); Peter Filene, *Americans and the Soviet Experiment* (1967); Denna Fleming, *The United States and the League of Nations* (1932); Inga Floto, *Colonel House at Paris* (1980); John L. Gaddis, *Russia, the Soviet Union, and the United States* (1978); Lloyd C. Gardner, *Safe for Democracy: The Anglo-American Response to Revolution, 1913–1923* (1984); John A. Garraty, *Henry Cabot Lodge* (1953); Robert Jackson, *At War with the Bolsheviks: The Allied Intervention into Russia, 1917–1920* (1972); George Kennan, *Decision to Intervene* (1958); Thomas J. Knock, *To End All Wars: Woodrow Wilson and the Quest for a New World Order* (1992); Warren F. Kuehl, *Seeking World Order* (1969); Christopher Lasch, *The American Liberals and the Russian Revolution* (1962); N. Gordon Levin, Jr., *Woodrow Wilson and World Politics* (1968); Arthur S. Link, *Woodrow Wilson*, 5 vols. (1947–1965), *Wilson the Diplomatist* (1957), and *Woodrow Wilson: War, Revolution, and Peace* (1979); Arno Mayer, *Political Origins of the New Diplomacy, 1917–1918* (1963), *Wilson vs. Lenin* (1959), and *Politics and Diplomacy of Peacemaking: Containment and Counterrevolution* (1965); David W. McFadden, *Alternative Paths: Soviets and Americans, 1917–1920* (1993); Charles L. Mee, Jr., *The End of Order: Versailles 1919* (1980); Robert E. Osgood, *Ideals and Self-Interest in American Foreign Relations* (1953); Klaus Schwabe, *Woodrow Wilson, Revolutionary Germany, and Peacemaking, 1918–1919* (1985); Gene Smith, *When the Cheering Stopped* (1964); Ronald Steel, *Walter Lippmann and the American Century* (1980); Ralph Stone, *The Irreconcilables: The Fight Against the League of Nations* (1970); Arthur Walworth, *Wilson and the Peacemakers* (1986); William C. Widenor, *Henry Cabot Lodge and the Search for an American Foreign Policy* (1980).

**Postwar America.** Wesley M. Bagby, Jr., *The Road to Normalcy* (1962); David Brody, *Steelworkers in America* (1960), and *Labor in Crisis: The Steel Strike of 1919* (1965); Stanley Coben, *A. Mitchell Palmer* (1963); David Cronon, *Black Moses* (1955); Roberta Strauss Feuerlicht, *Justice Crucified: The Story of Sacco and Vanzetti* (1977); Robert L. Friedheim, *The Seattle General Strike* (1965); Amy J. Garvey, *Garvey and Garveyism* (1963); Robert V. Haynes, *A Night of Violence: The Houston Riot of 1917* (1976); Florette Henri, *Black Migration: Movement Northward, 1900–1920* (1975); Kenneth Kusmer, *A Ghetto Takes Shape* (1976); David Montgomery, *The Fall of the House of Labor: The Workplace, the State, and American Labor Activism, 1865–1921* (1987); Robert K. Murray, *The Red Scare: A Study in National Hysteria, 1919–1920* (1955); Burl Noggle, *Into the Twenties* (1974); Stuart I. Rochester, *American Liberal Disillusionment in the Wake of World War I* (1977); Elliot Rudwick, *Race Riot at East St. Louis* (1964); Francis Russell, *A City in Terror* (1975); Alan Spear, *Black Chicago* (1967). Judith Stein, *The World of Marcus Garvey* (1986); William M. Tuttle, Jr., *Race Riot: Chicago in the Red Summer of 1919* (1970); Theodore Vincent, *Black Power and the Garvey Movement* (1971).

## CHAPTER 24 THE NEW ERA

**General Studies.** Frederick Lewis Allen, *Only Yesterday* (1931); John Braeman, Robert Bremner, and David Brody, eds., *Change and Continuity in Twentieth Century America: The 1920s* (1968); Ellis Hawley, *The Great War and the Search for a Modern Order* (1979); John D. Hicks, *Republican Ascendancy* (1960); Isabel Leighton, ed., *The Aspirin Age* (1949); William E. Leuchtenburg, *The Perils of Prosperity*, rev. ed. (1994); Donald R. McCoy, *Coming of Age* (1973); Michael Parrish, *Anxious Decades: America in Prosperity and De-*

*pression, 1920–1941* (1992); Geoffrey Perrett, *America in the Twenties* (1982); Arthur M. Schlesinger, Jr., *The Crisis of the Old Order* (1957); George Soule, *Prosperity Decade: From War to Depression* (1947).

**Labor, Agriculture, and Economic Growth.** Guy Alchon, *The Invisible Hand of Planning: Capitalism, Social Science, and the State in the 1920s* (1985); Irving Bernstein, *The Lean Years: A History of the American Worker, 1920–1933* (1960); David Brody, *Steelworkers in America* (1960), and *Workers in Industrial America* (1980); Alfred Chandler, *Strategy and Structure* (1962); Lisabeth Cohen, *Making a New Deal: Industrial Workers in Chicago, 1919–1939* (1990); Melvyn Dubofsky, *The State and Labor in Modern America* (1994); Gilbert C. Fite, *George Peek and the Fight for Farm Parity* (1954), and *American Farmers: The New Minority* (1981); Louis Galambos, *Competition and Cooperation* (1966); Louis Galambos and Joseph Pratt, *The Rise of the Corporate Commonwealth: U.S. Business and Public Policy in the Twentieth Century* (1988); Peter Gottlieb, *Making Their Own Way: Southern Blacks' Migration to Pittsburgh, 1916–1930* (1987); Jim Potter, *The American Economy Between the Wars* (1974); Theodore Saloutos and John D. Hicks, *Twentieth Century Populism* (1951); George Soule, *Prosperity Decade* (1947); Sharon Hartman Strom, *Beyond the Typewriter: Gender, Class, and the Origins of Modern American Office Work, 1900–1930* (1992); Mira Wilkins, *The Maturing of Multinational Enterprise: American Business Abroad from 1914 to 1970* (1974); Leslie Woodcock, *Wage-Earning Women* (1979); Gerald Zahavi, *Workers, Managers, and Welfare Capitalism* (1988); Robert Zieger, *Republicans and Labor* (1969).

**The New Culture.** Erik Barnouw, *A Tower in Babel: A History of American Radio to 1933* (1966); Daniel Boorstin, *The Americans: The Democratic Experience* (1973); Paul Carter, *The Twenties in America* (1968), and *Another Part of the Twenties* (1977); Stanley Coben, *Rebellion Against Victorianism: The Impetus for Cultural Change in 1920s America* (1991); Ed Cray, *Chrome Colossus* (1980); Robert Creamer, *Babe* (1974); Kenneth S. Davis, *The Hero: Charles A. Lindbergh* (1959); Ann Douglas: *Terrible Honesty: Mongrel Manhattan in the 1920s* (1995); Susan J. Douglas, *Inventing American Broadcasting* (1987); Ronald Edsforth, *Class Conflict and Cultural Consensus: The Making of a Mass Consumer Society: Flint, Michigan* (1987); Melvin Patrick Ely, *The Adventures of Amos 'n' Andy: A Social History of an American Phenomenon* (1991); Stewart Ewen, *Captains of Consciousness* (1976); James J. Flink, *The Car Culture* (1975), and *The Automobile Age* (1988); Stephen Fox, *The Mirror Makers: A History of American Advertising and Its Creators* (1984); Dana Frank, *Purchasing Power: Consumer Organizing, Gender and Seattle Labor Movement, 1919–1929* (1994); Neal Gabler, *An Empire of Their Own: How the Jews Invented Hollywood* (1988); Harvey Green, *Fit for America* (1986); Allen Guttmann, *A Whole New Ball Game* (1988); Sumiko Higashi, *Virgins, Vamps, and Flappers: The American Silent Movie Heroine* (1978); Daniel Horowitz, *The Morality of Spending: Attitudes Toward the Consumer Society in America, 1875–1940* (1985); Jackson Lears, *Fables of Abundance: A Cultural History of Advertising in America* (1994); Robert Lynd and Helen Lynd, *Middletown* (1929); Roland Marchand, *Advertising the American Dream* (1985); Lary May, *Screening Out the Past* (1980); Fred J. McDonald, *Don't Touch That Dial* (1979); Clay McShane, *Down the Asphalt Path: The Automobile and the American City* (1994); Zane Miller, *The Urbanization of America* (1973); William Leach, *Land of Desire: Merchants, Power, and the Rise of a New American Culture* (1993); Kathy H. Ogren, *The Jazz Revolution: Twenties America and the Meaning of Jazz* (1989); Michael Oriard, *Reading Football: How the Popular Press Created an American Spectacle* (1993); Kathy Peiss, *Cheap Amusements: Working Women and Leisure in Turn-of-the-*

*Century New York* (1986); Daniel Pope, *The Making of Modern Advertising* (1983); Randy Roberts, *Jack Dempsey, The Manassa Mauler* (1979); Philip T. Rosen, *The Modern Stentors: Radio Broadcasting and the Federal Government, 1920–1933* (1980); Joan Shelley Rubin, *The Making of Middlebrow Culture* (1992); Robert Sklar, *Movie-Made America* (1975); Susan Smulyan, *Selling Radio: The Commercialization of American Broadcasting*, Smithsonian Institution Press (1994); Susan Strasser, *Satisfaction Guaranteed: The Making of the American Mass Market* (1989); Bernard A. Weisberger, *The Dream Maker* (1979).

**Women, Family, and Youth.** W. Andrew Achenbaum, *Shades of Gray: Old Age, American Values, and Federal Policies Since 1920* (1983); Beth L. Bailey, *From Back Porch to Front Seat* (1988); Lois Banner, *American Beauty* (1983); Susan Porter Benson, *Counter Cultures: Saleswomen, Managers, and Customers in American Department Stores, 1890–1940* (1986); William H. Chafe, *The American Woman: Her Changing Social and Political Roles* (1972); Ellen Chesler, *Woman of Valor: Margaret Sanger and the Birth Control Movement in America* (1992); Howard P. Chudacoff, *How Old Are You? Age in American Culture* (1989); Nancy Cott, *The Grounding of American Feminism* (1987); Ruth Schwarz Cowan, *More Work for Mother* (1983); John D'Emilio and Estelle B. Friedman, *Intimate Matters: A History of Sexuality in America* (1988); Paula Fass, *The Damned and Beautiful* (1977); David H. Fischer, *Growing Old in America* (1977); Linda Gordon, *Woman's Body, Woman's Right* (1976); Helen Lefkowitz Horowitz, *Campus Life: Undergraduate Cultures from the End of the Eighteenth Century to the Present* (1987); Alice Kessler-Harris, *Out to Work: A History of Wage-Earning Women in America* (1982); J. Stanley Lemons, *The Woman Citizen: Social Feminism in the 1920s* (1973); Elizabeth Lunbeck, *The Psychiatric Persuasion: Knowledge, Gender, and Power in Modern America* (1994); Sheila Rothman, *Woman's Proper Place* (1978); Lois Scharf, *To Work and to Wed: Female Employment, Feminism, and the Great Depression* (1980); Virginia Scharff, *Taking the Wheel* (1991); Susan Strasser, *Never Done: A History of American Housework* (1982); Winifred Wandersee, *Women's Work and Family Values, 1920–1940* (1981); Renold Wilk, *Henry Ford and Grass Roots America* (1972).

**Intellectuals and the Arts.** Charles C. Alexander, *Here the Country Lies: Nationalism and the Arts in Twentieth Century America* (1980); Houston Baker, Jr., *Modernism and the Harlem Renaissance* (1987); Loren Baritz, ed., *The Culture of the Twenties* (1970); Cleanth Brooks, *William Faulkner: The Yoknapatawpha Country* (1963); Paul Conkin, *The Southern Agrarians* (1988); Malcolm Cowley, *Exiles Return* (1934); Robert Crunden, *From Self to Society: Transition in American Thought, 1919–1941* (1972); George H. Douglas, *H. L. Mencken* (1978); Frederick J. Hoffman, *The Twenties* (1949); Nathan I. Huggins, *Harlem Renaissance* (1971); Gloria T. Hull, *Color, Sex, and Poetry: Three Women Writers of the Harlem Renaissance* (1987); David L. Lewis, *When Harlem Was in Vogue* (1981); Roderick Nash, *The Nervous Generation: American Thought, 1917–1930* (1969); John Stewart, *The Burden of Time* (1965); Kenneth M. Wheeler and Virginia L. Lussier, eds., *Women, the Arts, and the 1920s in Paris and New York* (1982); Edmund Wilson, *The Twenties* (1975).

**Cultural Conflicts.** Charles C. Alexander, *The Ku Klux Klan in the Southwest* (1965); Paul Avrich, *Sacco and Vanzetti: The Anarchist Background* (1991); Herbert Asbury, *The Great Illusion* (1950); Kathleen M. Blee, *Women of the Klan: Racism and Gender in the 1920s* (1991); David Chalmers, *Hooded Americanism* (1965); Norman Clark, *Deliver Us from Evil* (1976); Elton C. Fax, *Garvey* (1972); Norman Furniss, *The Fundamentalist Controversy* (1954); Ray Ginger, *Six Days or Forever?* (1958); Joseph Gusfeld, *Symbolic Crusade* (1963);

John Higham, *Strangers in the Land* (1963); Kenneth Jackson, *The Ku Klux Klan in the City* (1965); K. Austin Kerr, *Organized for Prohibition: A New History of the Anti-Saloon League* (1985); Don Kirschner, *City and Country: Rural Responses to Urbanization in the 1920s* (1970); Lawrence Levine, *Defender of the Faith, William Jennings Bryan: The Last Decade, 1915–1925* (1965); Nancy MacLean, *Behind the Mask of Chivalry: The Making of the Second Ku Klux Klan* (1994); George M. Marsden, *Fundamentalism and American Culture* (1980); William G. McLoughlin, *Modern Revivalism* (1959); Leonard Moore, *Citizen Klansmen: The Ku Klux Klan in Indiana, 1921–1928* (1991); George J. Sanchez, *Becoming Mexican American: Ethnicity, Culture, and Identity in Chicano Los Angeles, 1900–1945* (1993); Andrew Sinclair, *The Era of Excess* (1962); Richard K. Tucker, *The Dragon and the Cross: The Rise and Fall of the Ku Klux Klan in Middle America* (1991); Theodore Vincent, *Black Power and the Garvey Movement* (1971).

**Politics and Government.** Kristi Andersen, *The Creation of a Democratic Majority, 1928–1936* (1979); LeRoy Ashby, *Spearless Leader* (1972); Christine Bolt, *American Indian Policy and American Reform* (1987); David Burner, *The Politics of Provincialism* (1967), and *Herbert Hoover* (1979); E. Paula Elder, *Governor Alfred E. Smith: The Politician as Reformer* (1983); Frank Freidel, *Franklin D. Roosevelt: The Ordeal* (1954), and *Franklin D. Roosevelt: The Triumph* (1956); James N. Giglio, *H. M. Daugherty and the Politics of Expediency* (1978); James Gilbert, *Designing the Industrial State* (1972); Oscar Handlin, *Al Smith and His America* (1958); William Harbaugh, *Lawyer's Lawyer* (1973); Ellis Hawley, *Herbert Hoover as Secretary of Commerce: Studies in New Era Thought and Practice* (1974); Robert Herzstein, *Henry R. Luce: A Political Portrait of the Man Who Created the American Century* (1994); Robert F. Himmelberg, *The Origins of the National Recovery Administration: Business, Government, and the Trade Association Issue, 1921–1933* (1976); Morton Keller, *Regulating a New Society: Public Policy and Social Change in America, 1900–1933* (1996); Alan Lichtman, *Prejudice and the Old Politics* (1979); Richard Lowitt, *George W. Norris*, vol. 2 (1971); Carol R. McCann, *Birth Control Politics in the United States, 1916–1945* (1994); Donald R. McCoy, *Calvin Coolidge* (1967); Robert K. Murray, *The Politics of Normalcy* (1973), and *The Harding Era* (1969); Burl Noggle, *Teapot Dome* (1962); Elisabeth Israels Perry, *Belle Moskowitz: Feminine Politics and the Exercise of Power in the Age of Alfred E. Smith* (1987); Francis Russell, *The Shadow of Blooming Grove* (1968); Andrew Sinclair, *The Available Man* (1965); David P. Thelen, *Robert M. La Follette and the Insurgent Spirit* (1978); George B. Tindall, *The Emergence of the New South* (1967); Eugene Trani and David Wilson, *The Presidency of Warren G. Harding* (1977); G. Edward White, *Justice Oliver Wendell Holmes: Law and the Inner Self* (1993); William Allen White, *A Puritan in Babylon* (1940); John Hoff Wilson, *Herbert Hoover: Forgotten Progressive* (1975).

## CHAPTER 25 THE GREAT DEPRESSION

**The Coming of the Depression.** Michael Bernstein, *The Great Depression: Delayed Recovery and Economic Change in America, 1929–1939* (1987); Lester V. Chandler, *America's Greatest Depression* (1970); Milton Friedman and Anna Schwartz, *The Great Contraction* (1965), or Chapter 7 of *A Monetary History of the United States* (1963); John Kenneth Galbraith, *The Great Crash* (1954); Susan E. Kennedy, *The Banking Crisis of 1933* (1973); Charles Kindelberger, *The World in Depression* (1973); Broadus Mitchell, *Depression Decade* (1947); Robert Sobel, *The Great Bull Market* (1968); Peter Temin, *Did Monetary Forces Cause the Great Depression?* (1976).

**The Impact of the Depression.** Francisco Balerman, *In Defense of La Raza: The Los Angeles Mexican Consulate and the Mexican Community, 1929–1936* (1982); Ann Banks, ed., *First-Person America* (1980); Irving Bernstein, *The Lean Years* (1960); Caroline Bird, *The Invisible Scar* (1966); Glen H. Elder, Jr., *Children of the Great Depression* (1974); Federal Writers' Project, *These Are Our Lives* (1939); James N. Gregory, *American Exodus: The Dust Bowl Migration and Okie Culture in California* (1989); Abraham Hoffman, *Unwanted Mexican-Americans in the Great Depression* (1974); Richard Lowitt and Maurine Beasley, eds., *One-Third of a Nation: Lorena Hickock Reports the Great Depression* (1981); Robert S. McElvaine, ed., *Down and Out in the Great Depression: Letters from the Forgotten Man* (1983); William Mullins, *The Depression and the Urban West Coast, 1929–1933* (1991); Janet Poppendieck, *Breadlines Knee-Deep in Wheat: Food Assistance in the Great Depression* (1986); Udo Sautter, *Three Cheers for the Unemployed: Government and Unemployment Before the New Deal* (1991); Arthur M. Schlesinger, Jr., *The Crisis of the Old Order* (1957); Walter Stein, *California and the Dust Bowl Migration* (1973); Bernard Sternsher, *Hitting Home: The Great Depression in Town and Country* (1970); Catherine McNicol Stock, *Main Street in Crisis: The Great Depression and the Old Middle Class on the Northern Plains* (1992); Studs Terkel, *Hard Times* (1970); Tom Terrill and Jerrold Hirsch, *Such as Us: Southern Voices of the Thirties* (1978); Donald Worster, *Dust Bowl: The Southern Plains in the 1930s* (1979).

**Depression-Era Culture and Society.** Charles C. Alexander, *Nationalism in American Thought, 1930–1945* (1969); Frederick Lewis Allen, *Since Yesterday* (1940); Andrew Bergman, *We're in the Money: Depression America and Its Films* (1971); Camille Guerin-Gonzales, *Mexican Workers and American Dreams: Immigration, Repatriation, and California Farm Labor, 1900–1939* (1994); Anthony Heilbut, *Exiled in Paradise: German Refugee Artists and Intellectuals in America from the 1930s to the Present* (1938); Richard Krickus, *Pursuing the American Dream* (1976); Robert Lynd and Helen Merrell Lynd, *Middletown in Transition* (1935); Alice Goldfarb Marquis, *Hopes and Ashes: The Birth of Modern Times, 1929–1939* (1986); Jeffrey Meikle, *Twentieth Century Limited: Industrial Design in America, 1925–1939* (1979); Gilbert Osofsky, *Harlem: The Making of a Ghetto* (1966); Gilman Ostrander, *American Civilization in the First Machine Age* (1970); David P. Peeler, *Hope Among Us Yet: Social Criticism and Social Thought in the Depression Years* (1987); Richard Pells, *Radical Visions and American Dreams: Culture and Social Thought in the Depression Years* (1973); Thomas Schatz, *The Genius of the System: Hollywood Film Making in the Studio Era* (1988); Ed Sikov, *Screwball: Hollywood's Madcap Romantic Comedies* (1989); Warren Susman, *Culture as History* (1984); (See Suggested Readings at the end of Chapter 26 for more literature on African Americans, Hispanic Americans, Asian Americans, Indians, and labor during the Depression.)

**Women and the Depression.** Julia K. Blackwelder, *Women of the Depression: Caste and Culture in San Antonio, 1919–1939* (1984); William Chafe, *The American Woman* (1972); Joan Jensen and Lois Scharf, eds., *Decades of Discontent: The Women's Movement, 1920–1940* (1983); Marjorie Rosen, *Popcorn Venus: Women, Movies, and the American Dream* (1971); Vicki Ruiz, *Cannery Women, Cannery Lives: Mexican Women, Unionization, and the California Food Processing Industry, 1930–1950* (1987); Lois Scharf, *To Work and to Wed: Female Employment, Feminism, and the Great Depression* (1980); Susan Ware, *Holding Their Own: American Women in the 1930s* (1982); Jeane Westin, *Making Do: How Women Survived the '30s* (1976); Patricia Zavella, *Women's Work and Chicano Families* (1987).

**The Hoover Presidency.** William J. Barber, *From New Era to New Deal: Herbert Hoover, The Economists, and American Economic Policy, 1921–1933* (1985); David Burner,

Herbert Hoover (1978); Martin Fausold, *The Presidency of Herbert C. Hoover* (1985); Martin Fausold and George Mazuzun, eds., *The Hoover Presidency* (1974), and *Herbert Hoover, The Great Depression* (1952); James S. Olsen, *Herbert Hoover and the Reconstruction Finance Corporation* (1977), and *Saving Capitalism: The Reconstruction Finance Corporation and the New Deal, 1933–1940* (1988); Albert U. Romasco, *The Poverty of Abundance* (1965); Jordan Schwarz, *The Interregnum of Despair* (1970); Harris Warren, *Herbert Hoover and the Great Depression* (1959); Joan Hoff Wilson, *Herbert Hoover: Forgotten Progressive* (1975).

**Politics and Protest.** Gary Dean Best, *FDR and the Bonus Marchers, 1933–1935* (1992); David Burner, *The Politics of Provincialism* (1967); Robert Cohen, *When the Old Left Was Young: Student Radicals and America's First Mass Student Movement, 1929–1941* (1993); Roger Daniels, *The Bonus March* (1971); Frank Freidel, *The Triumph* (1956), and *Launching the New Deal* (1973); Donald Grubbs, *Cry from the Cotton* (1971); Dorothy Healey and Maurice Isserman, *Dorothy Healey Remembers: A Life in the American Communist Party* (1990); Irving Howe and Lewis Coser, *The American Communist Party: A Critical History* (1957); Robin D. G. Kelley, *Hammer and Hoe: Alabama Communists During the Great Depression* (1990); Thomas Kessner, *Fiorello H. La Guardia and the Making of Modern New York* (1989); Harvey Klehr, *The Heyday of American Communism: The Depression Decade* (1984); Donald Lisio, *The President and Protest: Hoover, Conspiracy, and the Bonus Riot* (1974); Mark Naison, *Communists in Harlem During the Depression* (1983); Eliot Rosen, *Hoover, Roosevelt, and the Brains Trust* (1977); Arthur M. Schlesinger, Jr., *The Crisis of the Old Order* (1957); John Shover, *Cornbelt Rebellion* (1965); Rexford G. Tugwell, *The Brains Trust* (1968).

## CHAPTER 26 THE NEW DEAL

**General and Biographical Studies.** Anthony J. Badger, *The New Deal* (1989); John Braemen et al., eds., *The New Deal*, 2 vols. (1975); James MacGregor Burns, *Roosevelt: The Lion and the Fox* (1956); Blanche Wiesen Cooke, *Eleanor Roosevelt: Volume One, 1884–1933* (1992); Paul Conkin, *The New Deal*, 2nd ed. (1975); Kenneth Davis, *FDR: The New York Years: 1928–1933* (1985), and *FDR: The New Deal Years, 1933–1937* (1986); Peter Fearon, *War, Prosperity, and Depression* (1987); Steve Fraser and Gary Gerstle, eds., *The Rise and Fall of New Deal Liberalism* (1988); Frank Freidel, *Franklin D. Roosevelt*, 4 vols. (1952–1973), and *Franklin D. Roosevelt: A Rendezvous with Destiny* (1990); Joseph P. Lash, *Eleanor and Franklin* (1971); William E. Leuchtenburg, *Franklin D. Roosevelt and the New Deal* (1963), *In the Shadow of FDR* (1983), and *The FDR Years: On Roosevelt and His Legacy* (1995); Katie Louchheim, *The Making of the New Deal* (1983); Richard Lowitt, *The New Deal and the West* (1984); Robert S. McElvaine, *The Great Depression* (1984); Gerald Nash, *The Great Depression and World War II* (1979); Edgar Robinson, *The Roosevelt Leadership* (1955); Arthur M. Schlesinger, Jr., *The Age of Roosevelt*, 3 vols. (1957–1960); Harvard Sitkoff, ed., *Fifty Years Later: The New Deal Evaluated* (1985); Geoffrey Ward, *Before the Trumpet: Young Franklin Roosevelt, 1882–1905* (1985), and *A First-Class Temperament: The Emergence of Franklin Roosevelt* (1989); J. H. Wilson and Marjorie Lightman, eds., *Without Precedent: The Life and Career of Eleanor Roosevelt* (1984).

**New Deal Politics and Programs.** Mimi Abramowitz, *Regulating the Lives of Women* (1988); Bernard Bellush, *The Failure of the NRA* (1975); Donald Brand, *Corporatism and the Rule of Law* (1988); William R. Brock, *Welfare, Democracy, and the New Deal* (1987); Searle Charles, *Minister of Relief* (1963); Ralph F. De Bedts, *The New Deal's SEC* (1964);

Herbert Feis, *Characters in Crisis* (1966); Sidney Fine, *The Automobile Under the Blue Eagle* (1963); Kenneth Finegold and Theda Skocpol, *State and Party in America's New Deal* (1995); Frank Freidel, *Launching the New Deal* (1973); Gerald H. Gamm, *The Making of New Deal Democrats: Voting Behavior and Realignment in Boston, 1920–1940* (1989); Colin Gordon, *New Deals: Business, Labor, and Politics in America, 1920–1935* (1994); Otis Graham, *Encore for Reform* (1967); Nancy L. Grant, *TVA and Black Americans: Planning for the Status Quo* (1990); Ellis Hawley, *The New Deal and the Problem of Monopoly* (1966); Peter H. Irons, *The New Deal Lawyers* (1982); Mark Leff, *The Limits of Symbolic Reform: The New Deal and Taxation, 1933–1939* (1984); Thomas K. McCraw, *TVA and the Power Fight* (1970); George McJimsey, *Harry Hopkins: Ally of the Poor and Defender of Democracy* (1987); Sidney M. Milkis, *The Presidents and Their Parties: The Transformation of the American Party System Since the End of the New Deal* (1993); Raymond Moley and Eliot Rosen, *The First New Deal* (1966); Michael Parrish, *Securities Regulation and the New Deal* (1970); James T. Patterson, *America's Struggle Against Poverty, 1900–1980* (1981); Albert U. Romasco, *The Politics of Recovery: Roosevelt's New Deal* (1983); John Salmond, *The Civilian Conservation Corps* (1967); Bonnie Fox Schwartz, *The Civil Works Administration, 1933–1934* (1984); Jordan Schwarz, *The New Dealers: Power Politics in the Age of Roosevelt* (1993); Susan Ware, *Beyond Suffrage* (1981), and *Partner and I: Molly Dewson, Feminism, and New Deal Politics* (1987).

**Agriculture.**   Christina Campbell, *The Farm Bureaus* (1962); David Conrad, *The Forgotten Farmers* (1965); Lowell K. Dyson, *Red Harvest: The Communist Party and American Farmers* (1982); Gilbert Fite, *George M. Peek and the Fight for Farm Parity* (1954); David Hamilton, *From New Day to New Deal: American Farm Policy from Hoover to Roosevelt, 1928–1933* (1991); Richard S. Kirkendall, *Social Scientists and Farm Politics in the Age of Roosevelt* (1966); Paul Mertz, *The New Deal and Southern Rural Poverty* (1978); Van L. Perkins, *Crisis in Agriculture* (1969); Bruce Shulman, *From Cotton Belt to Sunbelt* (1991).

**Depression Dissidents.**   David H. Bennett, *Demagogues in the Depression* (1969); Alan Brinkley, *Voices of Protest: Huey Long, Father Coughlin, and the Great Depression* (1982); Donald Grubbs, *Cry from the Cotton* (1971); William Ivy Hair, *The Kingfish and His Realm: The Life and Times of Huey P. Long* (1991); Glen Jeansonne, *Gerald L. K. Smith: Minister of Hate* (1988); Abraham Holzman, *The Townsend Movement* (1963); R. Alan Lawson, *The Failure of Independent Liberalism* (1971); Donald McCoy, *Angry Voices* (1958); Leo Ribuffo, *The Old Christian Right: The Protestant Far Right from the Great Depression to the Cold War* (1983); Arthur M. Schlesinger, Jr., *The Politics of Upheaval* (1960); Charles J. Tull, *Father Coughlin and the New Deal* (1965); David Warren, *Radio Priest: Charles Coughlin, The Father of Hate Radio* (1996); T. Harry Williams, *Huey Long* (1969); George Wolfskill, *Revolt of the Conservatives* (1962).

**The "Second New Deal."**   Sidney Baldwin, *Poverty and Politics: The Farm Security Administration* (1968); Edward Berkowitz, *Mr. Social Security: The Life of Wilbur J. Cohen* (1995); Paul Conkin, *Tomorrow a New World* (1971); Linda Gordon, *Pitied But Not Entitled: Single Mothers and the History of Welfare* (1994); J. Joseph Huthmacher, *Senator Robert Wagner and the Rise of Urban Liberalism* (1968); Roy Lubove, *The Struggle for Social Security* (1968); William F. McDonald, *Federal Relief Administration and the Arts* (1968); Jerre Mangione, *The Dream and the Deal* (1972); Jane deHart Matthews, *The Federal Theater* (1967); W. D. Rowley, *M. L. Wilson and the Campaign for Domestic Allotment* (1970).

**The Late New Deal.** Leonard Baker, *Back to Back* (1967); Alan Brinkley, *The End of Reform: New Deal Liberalism in Recession and War* (1995); Frank Freidel, *FDR and the South* (1965); Barry Karl, *Executive Reorganization and Reform in the New Deal* (1963); William E. Leuchtenburg, *The Supreme Court Reborn: The Constitutional Revolution in the Age of Roosevelt* (1995); Dean May, *From New Deal to New Economics* (1981); James T. Patterson, *Congressional Conservatism and the New Deal* (1967), and *The New Deal and the States* (1969); Richard Polenberg, *Reorganizing Roosevelt's Government* (1966); Theodore Rosenof, *Dogma and Depression* (1972), and *Patterns of Political Economy in America* (1983); Herbert Stein, *The Fiscal Revolution in America* (1969); Charles Trout, *Boston: The Great Depression and the New Deal* (1977); George Wolfskill and John Hudson, *All But the People* (1969).

**Blacks, Hispanics, Indians.** Rodolfo Acuna, *Occupied America*, rev. ed. (1981); Francisco E. Balerman, *In Defense of La Raza* (1982); Thomas Biolsi, *Organizing the Lakota: The Political Economy of the New Deal on the Pine Ridge and Rosebud Reservations* (1992); Ralph Bunche, *The Political Status of the Negro in the Age of FDR* (1973); Dan T. Carter, *Scottsboro* (1969); Vine DeLoria, Jr., *The Nations Within* (1984); Sarah Deutsch, *No Separate Refuge: Culture, Class, and Gender on the Anglo-Hispanic Frontier in the American Southwest, 1880–1940* (1987); John Dollard, *Caste and Class in a Southern Town*, 3rd ed. (1957); Cheryl Lynn Greenberg, *"Or Does It Explode?": Black Harlem in the Great Depression* (1991); Laurence C. Kelly, *The Assault on Assimilation: John Collier and the Origins of Indian Policy Reform* (1983); John B. Kirby, *Black Americans in the Roosevelt Era* (1980); Clifford Lytle, *American Indians, American Justice* (1983); Carey McWilliams, *Factories in the Field* (1939); Donald L. Parman, *The Navajos and the New Deal* (1976); Kenneth R. Philp, *John Collier's Crusade for Indian Reform, 1920–1954* (1977); Harvard Sitkoff, *A New Deal for Blacks* (1978); Graham D. Taylor, *The New Deal and American Indian Tribalism* (1980); Nancy Weiss, *Farewell to the Party of Lincoln: Black Politics in the Age of FDR* (1983), and *The National Urban League* (1974); Raymond Wolters, *Negroes and the Great Depression* (1970); Robert L. Zangrando, *The NAACP Crusade Against Lynching* (1980).

**Labor.** Jerold Auerbach, *Labor and Liberty* (1966); John Barnard, *Walter Reuther and the Rise of the Auto Workers* (1983); Irving Bernstein, *Turbulent Years* (1970), and *A Caring Society: The New Deal, the Worker, and the Great Depression* (1985); David Brody, *Workers in Industrial America* (1980); Bert Cochran, *Labor and Communism* (1977); Lizabeth Cohen, *Making a New Deal: Industrial Workers in Chicago, 1919–1939* (1990); Melvyn Dubofsky and Warren Van Tine, *John L. Lewis* (1977); Elizabeth Faue, *Community of Suffering and Struggle: Women, Men, and the Labor Movement in Minnesota, 1915–1945* (1991); Sidney Fine, *Sit-Down* (1969); Joshua Freeman, *In Transit: The Transport Workers Union in New York City, 1933–1966* (1989); Peter Friedlander, *The Emergence of a UAW Local* (1975); Gary Gerstle, *Working-Class Americanism: The Politics of Labor in a Textile City 1914–1960* (1989); John W. Hevener, *Which Side Are You On? The Harlan County Coal Miners, 1931–1939* (1978); Nelson Lichtenstein, *The Most Dangerous Man in Detroit: Walter Reuther and the Fate of American Labor* (1995); August Meier and Elliott Rudwick, *Black Detroit and the Rise of the UAW* (1979); David Milton, *The Politics of U.S. Labor: From the Great Depression to the New Deal* (1980); Bruce Nelson, *Workers on the Waterfront: Seamen, Longshoremen, and Unionism in the 1930s* (1988); Daniel Nelson, *American Rubber Workers and Organized Labor, 1900–1941* (1988); Annelise Orleck, *Common Sense and a Little Fire: Women and Working-Class Politics in the United States, 1900–1965* (1995); Paula F. Pfeffer, *A. Philip Randolph, Pioneer of the Civil Rights Movement* (1990); Ronald W.

Schatz, *The Electrical Workers* (1983); George G. Suggs, Jr., *Union Busting in the Tristate: The Oklahoma, Kansas, and Missouri Metal Workers Strike of 1935* (1986); Christopher L. Tomlins, *The State and the Unions* (1985); Robert H. Zieger, *John L. Lewis: Labor Leader* (1988), and *American Workers, American Unions, 1920–1985* (1986).

## CHAPTER 27 THE GLOBAL CRISIS, 1921–1941

**The 1920s.** Thomas Buckley, *The United States and the Washington Conference* (1970); Warren Cohen, *America's Response to China* (1971), and *Empire Without Tears* (1987); Frank Costigliola, *Awkward Dominion: American Political, Economic, and Cultural Relations with Europe, 1919–1933* (1984); Roger Dingman, *Power in the Pacific* (1976); L. Ethan Ellis, *Republican Foreign Policy, 1921–1933* (1968); Robert H. Ferrell, *Peace in Their Time* (1952); Michael J. Hogan, *Informal Entente: The Private Structure of Cooperation in Anglo-American Economic Diplomacy, 1918–1928* (1977); Akira Iriye, *The Cambridge History of American Foreign Relations*, vol. 3: *The Globalizing of America, 1913–1945*, and *After Imperialism* (1965); William Kamman, *A Search for Stability: United States Diplomacy Toward Nicaragua, 1925–1933* (1968); Melvyn P. Leffler, *The Elusive Quest: America's Pursuit of European Stability and French Security, 1919–1933* (1979); Merlo J. Pusey, *Charles Evans Hughes*, 2 vols. (1963); Joseph Tulchin, *The Aftermath of War* (1971); William Appleman Williams, *The Tragedy of American Diplomacy* (1962); Joan Hoff Wilson, *American Business and Foreign Policy, 1920–1933* (1968), and *Ideology and Economics* (1974).

**The Hoover Years.** Alexander DeConde, *Hoover's Latin American Policy* (1951); Robert H. Ferrell, *American Diplomacy in the Great Depression* (1970); Elting Morison, *Turmoil and Tradition* (1960); Raymond O'Connor, *Perilous Equilibrium* (1962); Armin Rappaport, *Stimson and Japan* (1963).

**New Deal Diplomacy.** Edward E. Bennett, *Recognition of Russia* (1970); Dorothy Borg, *The United States and the Far Eastern Crisis of 1933–1938* (1964); Robert Browder, *The Origins of Soviet-American Diplomacy* (1953); Bruce J. Calder, *The Impact of Intervention* (1984); Robert Dallek, *Franklin D. Roosevelt and American Foreign Policy, 1932–1945* (1979); Beatrice Farnsworth, *William C. Bullitt and the Soviet Union* (1967); Peter Filene, *Americans and the Soviet Experiment, 1917–1933* (1967); Frank Freidel, *Launching the New Deal* (1973); Lloyd Gardner, *Economic Aspects of New Deal Diplomacy* (1964); Irwin F. Gellman, *Good Neighbor Diplomacy: United States Policies in Latin America, 1933–1945* (1979); David Green, *The Containment of Latin America* (1971); Warren F. Kimball, *The Juggler: Franklin Roosevelt as Wartime Statesman* (1991); Walter LaFeber, *Inevitable Revolutions* (1983); Lorenzo Meyer, *Mexico and the United States in the Oil Controversy* (1977); Bryce Wood, *The Making of the Good Neighbor Policy* (1961).

**Isolationism and Pacifism.** Selig Adler, *The Uncertain Giant* (1966), and *The Isolationist Impulse* (1957); Charles Chatfield, *For Peace and Justice: Pacifism in America, 1914–1941* (1971); Warren I. Cohen, *The American Revisionists* (1967); Wayne S. Cole, *America First* (1953); *Senator Gerald P. Nye and American Foreign Relations* (1962), *Charles A. Lindbergh and the Battle Against American Intervention in World War II* (1974), and *Roosevelt and the Isolationists, 1932–1945* (1983); Charles DeBenedetti, *Origins of the Modern American Peace Movement, 1915–1929* (1978), and *The Peace Reform in American History* (1980); Robert Divine, *The Reluctant Belligerent* (1965); Thomas N. Guinsburg, *The Pursuit of*

*Isolation in the United States Senate from Versailles to Pearl Harbor* (1982); Manfred Jonas, *Isolationism in America* (1966); Thomas C. Kennedy, *Charles A. Beard and American Foreign Policy* (1975); William Langer and S. Everett Gleason, *The Challenge to Isolation* (1952), and *The Undeclared War* (1953); Richard Lowitt, *George W. Norris*, 3 vols. (1963–1978); John K. Nelson, *The Peace Prophets* (1967); Lawrence Wittner, *Rebels Against War* (1984).

**The Coming of World War II.**   James MacGregor Burns, *Roosevelt: The Soldier of Freedom* (1970); Peter N. Carroll, *Odyssey of the Abraham Lincoln Brigade: Americans in the Spanish Civil War* (1994); Garry Clifford and Samuel R. Spencer, Jr., *The First Peacetime Draft* (1986); Roger Dingman, *Power in the Pacific* (1976); Bernard F. Donahoe, *Private Plans and Public Dangers* (1965); Herbert Feis, *The Road to Pearl Harbor* (1950); Waldo H. Heinrichs, Jr., *Threshold of War* (1988); Akira Iriye, *Across the Pacific* (1967), *After Imperialism: The Search for a New Order in the Far East, 1921–1933* (1965), and *The Origins of the Second World War in Asia and the Pacific* (1987); Manfred Jonas, *The United States and Germany* (1984); Warren Kimball, *The Most Unsordid Act: Lend-Lease, 1939–1941* (1970); Joseph Lash, *Roosevelt and Churchill* (1976); James Leutze, *Bargaining for Supremacy* (1977); Martin V. Melosi, *The Shadow of Pearl Harbor* (1977); Arnold Offner, *The Origins of the Second World War* (1975); Gordon Prange, *At Dawn We Slept* (1981), and *Pearl Harbor* (1986); Michael S. Sherry, *The Rise of American Airpower* (1987); David Reynolds, *The Creation of the Anglo-American Alliance, 1937–1941* (1982); David F. Schmitz, *The United States and Fascist Italy, 1922–1944* (1988); Jonathan Utley, *Going to War with Japan* (1985); Roberta Wohlstetter, *Pearl Harbor: Warning and Decision* (1962); David S. Wyman, *Paper Walls: America and the Refugee Crisis, 1938–1941* (1985).

## CHAPTER 28 AMERICA IN A WORLD AT WAR

**War and American Society.**   John Morton Blum, *V Was for Victory* (1976); Lewis A. Erenberg and Susan E. Hirsch, *The War in American Culture: Society and Consciousness During World War II* (1996); Mark J. Harris et al., *The Homefront* (1984); Glen Jeansonne, *Women of the Far Right: The Mothers' Movement and World War II* (1996); Richard R. Lingeman, *Don't You Know There's a War On?* (1970); Gerald D. Nash, *The American West Transformed: The Impact of the Second World War* (1985); Geoffrey Perrett, *Days of Sadness, Years of Triumph: The American People, 1939–1945* (1974); Richard Polenberg, *War and Society* (1972); Studs Terkel, *"The Good War": An Oral History of World War II* (1984).

**War Mobilization and Wartime Politics.**   Oscar E. Anderson, Jr., *The New World* (1962); Ellsworth Barnard, *Wendell Willkie* (1966); Chester Bowles, *Promises to Keep* (1971); Alan Brinkley, *The End of Reform: New Deal Liberalism in Recession and War* (1995); David Brinkley, *Washington Goes to War* (1987); James MacGregor Burns, *Roosevelt: The Soldier of Freedom* (1970); Bruce Catton, *War Lords of Washington* (1946); Lester V. Chandler, *Inflation in the United States, 1940–1948* (1951); Alan Clive, *State of War: Michigan in World War II* (1979); George Q. Flynn, *The Mess in Washington: Manpower Mobilization in World War II* (1979); Doris Kearns Goodwin, *No Ordinary Time: Franklin and Eleanor Roosevelt: The Home Front in World War II* (1994); Leslie R. Groves, *Now It Can Be Told* (1962); Howell John Harris, *The Right to Manage* (1982); Maurice Isserman, *Which Side Were You On? The American Communist Party During World War II* (1982); Eliot Janeway, *Struggle for Survival* (1951); Paul A. C. Koistinen, *The Military-Industrial Com-*

*plex: A Historical Perspective* (1980); Philip Knightley, *The First Casualty* (1975); Nelson Lichtenstein, *Labor's War at Home: The CIO in World War II* (1982); Donald Nelson, *Arsenal of Democracy* (1946); Joel Seidman, *American Labor from Defense to Reconversion* (1953); Bradley F. Smith, *The Shadow Warriors: The OSS and the Origins of the CIA* (1983); Richard Steele, *Propaganda in an Open Society* (1985); Patrick S. Washburn, *A Question of Sedition: The Federal Government's Investigation of the Black Press During World War II* (1986); Michi Weglyn, *Years of Infamy: The Untold Story of America's Concentration Camps* (1976); Alan M. Winkler, *The Politics of Propaganda; The Office of War Information, 1942–1945* (1978).

**The War and Race.** Beth Bailey and David Farber, *The First Strange Place: The Alchemy of Race and Sex in World War II Hawaii* (1993); Domenic J. Capeci, Jr., *The Harlem Riot of 1943* (1977), and *Race Relations in Wartime Detroit* (1987); Richard M. Dalfiume, *Desegregation of the U.S. Armed Forces* (1969); Roger Daniels, *The Politics of Prejudice* (1962), *Concentration Camps, USA: Japanese Americans and World War II* (1971), and *Prisoners Without Trial: Japanese Americans in World War II* (1993); John W. Dower, *War Without Mercy: Race and Power in the Pacific War* (1986); Mario T. Garcia, *Mexican-Americans: Leadership, Ideology, and Identity, 1930–1960* (1989); Herbert Garfinkel, *When Negroes March* (1959); Audrie Girdner and Anne Loftis, *The Great Betrayal* (1969); Bill Hosokawa, *Nisei* (1969); Peter Irons, *Justice at War* (1983); Thomas James, *Exiles Within: The Schooling of Japanese-Americans, 1942–1945* (1987); Valerie J. Matsumoto, *Farming the Home Place: A Japanese American Community in California, 1919–1982* (1993); Philip McGuire, ed., *Taps for a Jim Crow Army: Letters from Black Soldiers in World War II* (1982); Mauricio Mazon, *The Zoot-Suit Riots* (1984); August Meier and Elliott Rudwick, *CORE* (1973); Louis Ruchames, *Race, Jobs, and Politics* (1953); Holly Cowan Shulman, *The Voice of America* (1991); Neil Wynn, *The Afro-American and the Second World War* (1976).

**Women and the War.** Karen Anderson, *Wartime Women: Sex Roles, Family Relations, and the Status of Women During World War II* (1981); D'Ann Campbell, *Women at War with America* (1984); Sherna B. Gluck, *Rosie the Riveter Revisited* (1987); Susan Hartmann, *The Homefront and Beyond: American Women in the 1940s* (1982); Margaret R. Higgonet et al., *Behind the Lines: Gender and the Two World Wars* (1987); Maureen Honey, *Creating Rosie the Riveter: Class, Gender, and Propaganda During World War II* (1984); Ruth Milkman, *Gender at Work: The Dynamics of Job Segregation by Sex During World War II* (1987); Susan M. Reverby, *Ordered to Care: The Dilemma of American Nursing, 1850–1945* (1987); Leila Rupp, *Mobilizing Women for War* (1978).

**Wartime Military and Diplomatic Experiences.** Stephen Ambrose, *The Supreme Commander* (1970), *Eisenhower: Soldier, General of the Army, President-Elect* (1983), and *D-Day: June 6, 1944* (1994); Albert Russell Buchanan, *The United States and World War II*, 2 vols. (1962); James MacGregor Burns, *Roosevelt: The Soldier of Freedom* (1970); Winston S. Churchill, *The Second World War*, 6 vols. (1948–1953); Robert Divine, *Roosevelt and World War II* (1969), and *Second Chance* (1967); Dwight D. Eisenhower, *Crusade in Europe* (1948); John S. D. Eisenhower, *Allies: Pearl Harbor to D-Day* (1982); Kenneth Greenfield, *American Strategy in World War II* (1963); Max Hastings, *Overlord: D-Day and the Battle for Normandy* (1984); Patrick Heardon, *Roosevelt Confronts Hitler: American Entry into World War II* (1987); Godfrey Hodgson, *The Colonel: The Life and Wars of Henry Stimson, 1867–1950* (1990); Michael Howard, *The Mediterranean Strategy in World War II* (1968); Margaret Hoyle, *A World in Flames* (1970); D. Clayton James, *A Time for Gi-*

ants: *Politics of the American High Command in World War II* (1987); John Keegan, *Six Armies in Normandy: From D-Day to the Liberation of Paris, June 6–August 25, 1944* (1982); Warren Kimball, *The Juggler: Franklin Roosevelt as Wartime Statesman* (1991); E. J. Kind and W. M. Whitehill, *Fleet Admiral King* (1952); Charles B. Mcdonald, *The Mighty Endeavor* (1969); William Manchester, *American Caesar* (1979); Samuel Eliot Morison, *Strategy and Compromise* (1958), *History of United States Naval Operations in World War II*, 14 vols. (1947–1960), and *The Two Ocean War* (1963); Geoffrey Perret, *There's a War to Be Won: The United States Army in World War II* (1991); Forrest Pogue, *George C. Marshall*, 2 vols. (1963–1966); Gordon W. Prange, *At Dawn We Slept: The Untold Story of Pearl Harbor* (1981); Fletcher Pratt, *War for the World* (1951); Cornelius Ryan, *The Longest Day* (1959), and *The Last Battle* (1966); Ronald Schaffer, *Wings of Judgment: American Bombing in World War II* (1985); Michael Schaller, *The United States Crusade in China, 1938–1945* (1979); Michael Sherry, *Preparing for the Next War: American Plans for Postwar Defense, 1941–1945* (1977), and *The Rise of American Air Power* (1987); Gaddis Smith, *American Diplomacy During the Second World War* (1964); Ronald H. Spector, *Eagle Against the Sun: The American War with Japan* (1985); Mark A. Stoler, *The Politics of the Second Front: Planning and Diplomacy in Coalition Warfare, 1941–1945* (1977); Christopher Thorne, *Allies of a Kind: The United States, Britain and the War Against Japan, 1941–1945* (1978); John Toland, *The Last Hundred Days* (1966), and *The Rising Sun* (1970); Barbara M. Tuchman, *Stilwell and the American Experience in China* (1971); Russell Weigley, *The American Way of War* (1973), and *Eisenhower's Lieutenants: The Campaign of France and Germany, 1944–1945* (1981); Chester Wilmot, *The Struggle for Europe* (1952); David S. Wyman, *The Abandonment of the Jews: America and the Holocaust, 1941–1945* (1984).

**Atomic Warfare.**  Gar Alperovitz, *Atomic Diplomacy* (1965); Nuel Davis, *Lawrence and Oppenheimer* (1969); Robert Donovan, *Conflict and Crisis* (1977); Herbert Feis, *The Atomic Bomb and the End of World War II* (1966); Gregg Herken, *The Winning Weapon: The Atomic Bomb in the Cold War* (1980); John Hersey, *Hiroshima* (1946); Robert Jungk, *Brighter Than a Thousand Suns* (1958); Richard Rhodes, *The Making of the Atomic Bomb* (1987); W. S. Schoenberger, *Decision of Destiny* (1969); Martin Sherwin, *A World Destroyed* (1975); Leon V. Sigal, *Fighting to a Finish* (1988).

CHAPTER 29  AMERICA AND THE COLD WAR

**Origins of the Cold War.**  Gar Alperovitz, *Atomic Diplomacy: Hiroshima and Potsdam*, rev. ed. (1985); Stephen Ambrose, *Rise to Globalism*, 5th ed. (1988); Terry H. Anderson, *The United States, Great Britain, and the Cold War, 1944–1947* (1981); H. W. Brands, *Inside the Cold War: Loy Henderson and the Rise of the American Empire, 1918–1961* (1991); Diane Clemens, *Yalta* (1970); Warren I. Cohen, *The Cambridge History of American Foreign Relations*, vol. 4: *America in the Age of Soviet Power, 1945–1991* (1991); Herbert Feis, *Churchill, Roosevelt, and Stalin* (1957), and *Between War and Peace: The Potsdam Conference* (1960); John Lewis Gaddis, *Strategies of Containment* (1982), *The United States and the Origins of the Cold War, 1941–1947* (1972), and *The Long Peace* (1987); Lloyd C. Gardner, *Spheres of Influence: The Great Powers Partition Europe, from Munich to Yalta* (1993); Gregg Herken, *The Winning Weapon: The Atomic Bomb in the Cold War, 1945–1950* (1980); George C. Herring, Jr., *Aid to Russia* (1973); Timothy P. Ireland, *Creating the Entangling Alliance: The Origins of NATO* (1981); Bruce Kuniholm, *The Origins of the Cold War in the*

*Middle East* (1980); Walter LaFeber, *America, Russia, and the Cold War, 1945–1967*, rev. ed. (1980); Melvyn P. Leffler, *A Preponderance of Power: National Security, the Truman Administration, and the Cold War* (1992); William McNeill, *America, Britain, and Russia* (1953); Wilson D. Miscamble, *George F. Kennan and the Making of American Foreign Policy, 1947–1950* (1992); W. L. Neumann, *After Victory* (1969); Thomas G. Paterson, *Soviet-American Confrontation* (1974), *On Every Front: The Making of the Cold War* (1979), and *Meeting the Communist Threat* (1988); Robert A. Pollard, *Economic Security and the Origins of the Cold War* (1985); Martin Sherwin, *A World Destroyed* (1975); Gaddis Smith, *American Diplomacy During the Second World War* (1965), and *Dean Acheson* (1972); John L. Snell, *Illusion and Necessity* (1967); William Taubman, *Stalin's American Policy* (1982); Athan G. Theoharis, *The Yalta Myths* (1970); Adam Ulam, *The Rivals: America and Russia Since World War II* (1971); Bernard Weisberger, *Cold War, Cold Peace* (1984); Lawrence Wittner, *American Intervention in Greece, 1943–1949* (1982); Daniel Yergin, *Shattered Peace* (1977).

**Truman's Foreign Policy.**  Dean Acheson, *Present at the Creation* (1970); Hadley Arkes, *Bureaucracy, the Marshall Plan and National Interest* (1973); Richard J. Barnet, *The Alliance* (1983); Robert M. Blum, *Drawing the Line: The Origin of the American Containment Policy in East Asia* (1982); Russell D. Buhite, *Soviet-American Relations in Asia, 1945–1954* (1982); Warren I. Cohen, *America's Response to China*, rev. ed. (1980); Jeffrey Diefendorf, *American Policy and the Reconstruction of West Germany, 1945–1955* (1993); Robert Donovan, *Conflict and Crisis* (1977), and *Tumultuous Years* (1982); John King Fairbank, *The United States and China*, rev. ed. (1971); Lloyd Gardner, *Architects of Illusion* (1970); Fraser J. Harbutt, *The Iron Curtain: Churchill, America, and the Origins of the Cold War* (1986); Michael Hogan, *The Marshall Plan* (1987); Akira Iriye, *The Cold War in Asia* (1974); Laurence Kaplan, *The United States and NATO* (1984); George F. Kennan, *American Diplomacy, 1900–1950* (1952), and *Memoirs, 1925–1950* (1967); Joyce Kolko and Gabriel Kolko, *The Limits of Power* (1970); Bruce R. Koniholm, *The Origins of the Cold War in the Middle East* (1980); William R. Louis, *The British Empire in the Middle East* (1984); Gary May, *China Scapegoat* (1979); David Mayer, *George Kennan and the Dilemmas of U.S. Foreign Policy* (1988); Wilson D. Miscamble, *George F. Kennan and the Making of American Foreign Policy, 1947–1950* (1992); Brenda Gayle Plummer, *Black Americans and U.S. Foreign Affairs, 1935–1960* (1996); Edwin O. Reischauer, *The United States and Japan*, rev. ed. (1965); Lisle Rose, *Roots of Tragedy* (1976); Michael Schaller, *The U.S. Crusade in China* (1979), *Communists* (1971), and *The American Occupation of Japan: The Origins of the Cold War in Asia* (1985); Howard Schonberger, *Aftermath of War: Americans and the Remaking of Japan* (1989); Anders Stephanson, *Kennan and the Art of Foreign Policy* (1989); Michael B. Stoff, *Oil, War, and American Security* (1980); Christopher Thorne, *Allies of a Kind* (1978); Imanuel Wexler, *The Marshall Plan Revisited* (1983).

**Truman's Domestic Policies.**  Stephen K. Bailey, *Congress Makes a Law* (1950); Jack S. Ballard, *The Shock of Peace: Military and Economic Demobilization After World War II* (1983); William C. Berman, *The Politics of Civil Rights in the Truman Administration* (1970); Barton J. Bernstein, ed., *Politics and Policies of the Truman Administration* (1970); Allida M. Black, *Casting Her Own Shadow: Eleanor Roosevelt and the Shaping of Postwar Liberalism* (1996); Richard Dalfiume, *Desegregation of the U.S. Armed Forces* (1969); Richard O. Davies, *Housing Reform During the Truman Administration* (1966); John P. Diggins, *The Proud Decades, 1941–1960* (1989); Robert Donovan, *Conflict and Crisis* (1977), and

*Tumultuous Years* (1982); Andrew J. Dunar, *The Truman Scandals and the Politics of Morality* (1984); Robert H. Ferrell, *Harry S. Truman and the Modern American Presidency* (1983); Eric Goldman, *The Crucial Decade—and After: America, 1945–1960* (1961); Alonzo Hamby, *Beyond the New Deal: Harry S. Truman and American Liberalism* (1973); Susan Hartmann, *Truman and the 80th Congress* (1971); Roy Jenkins, *Truman* (1986); R. Alton Lee, *Truman and Taft-Hartley* (1967), and *Truman and the Steel Seizure Case* (1977); Arthur F. McClure, *The Truman Administration and the Problems of Postwar Labor* (1969); Donald R. McCoy, *The Presidency of Harry S. Truman* (1984); Donald R. McCoy and Richard Ruetten, *Quest and Response* (1973); David McCullough, *Truman* (1992); Maeva Marcus, *Truman and the Steel Seizure* (1977); Allen J. Matusow, *Farm Policies and Politics in the Truman Years* (1967); Merle Miller, *Plain Speaking* (1980); Richard L. Miller, *Truman: The Rise to Power* (1986); William O'Neill, *American High* (1986); William E. Pemberton, *Harry S. Truman* (1989); Monte S. Poen, *Harry S. Truman Versus the Medical Lobby* (1979); Gary Reichard, *Politics as Usual: The Age of Truman and Eisenhower* (1988); Christopher L. Tomlins, *The State and the Unions* (1985).

**Cold War Politics and Culture.** H. W. Brands, *The Devil We Knew: Americans and the Cold War* (1993); John P. Diggins, *The Proud Decades, 1941–1960* (1989); Steven M. Gillon, *Politics and Vision: The ADA and American Liberalism, 1947–1985* (1987); David Goldfield, *Black, White, and Southern: Race Relations and Southern Culture* (1990); Maurice Isserman, *If I Had a Hammer . . .: The Death of the Old Left and the Birth of the New Left* (1987); Norman Markowitz, *The Rise and Fall of the People's Century: Henry A. Wallace and American Liberalism, 1941–1948* (1973); James T. Patterson, *Mr. Republican* (1972); Richard Pells, *The Liberal Mind in a Conservative Age: American Intellectuals in the 1940s and 1950s* (1985); Irwin Ross, *The Loneliest Campaign* (1968); Richard Norton Smith, *Thomas E. Dewey and His Times* (1982); Allan M. Winkler, *Life Under a Cloud: American Anxiety About the Atom* (1993); Allen Yarnell, *Democrats and Progressives* (1974).

**The Korean War.** Carl Berger, *The Korean Knot* (1957); Ronald Caridi, *The Korean War and American Politics* (1969); Bruce Cumings, *The Origins of the Korean War* (1980), and ed., *Child of Conflict: The Korean-American Relationship, 1943–1953* (1983); Charles W. Dobbs, *The Unwanted Symbol* (1981); Joseph C. Goulden, *Korea: The Untold Story of the War* (1982); John Halliday and Bruce Cumings, *Korea: The Unknown War* (1980); Robert Leckie, *Conflict* (1962); Glenn D. Paige, *The Korean Decision* (1968); Michael Schaller, *Douglas MacArthur* (1989); Robert R. Simmons, *The Strained Alliance* (1975); John Spanier, *The Truman-MacArthur Controversy* (1959); Allen Whiting, *China Crosses the Yalu* (1960).

**Countersubversion.** Michael R. Belknap, *Cold War Political Justice: The Smith Act, the Communist Party, and American Civil Liberties* (1977); Eric Bentley, ed., *Thirty Years of Treason;* David Caute, *The Great Fear* (1978); Larry Ceplair and Steven Englund, *The Inquisition in Hollywood* (1983); Richard Freeland, *The Truman Doctrine and the Origins of McCarthyism* (1971); Richard Fried, *Men Against McCarthy* (1976), and *Nightmare in Red* (1990); Robert Griffith, *The Politics of Fear* (1970); Robert Griffith and Athan Theoharis, eds., *The Specter: Original Essays on the Cold War and the Origins of McCarthyism* (1974); Alan Harper, *The Politics of Loyalty* (1969); Stanley Kutler, *The American Inquisition* (1982); Harvey Levenstein, *Communism, Anticommunism, and the CIO* (1981); Mary Sperling McAuliffe, *Crisis on the Left* (1978); Victor Navasky, *Naming Names* (1980); William O'Neill, *A Better World* (1983); David M. Oshinsky, *A Conspiracy So Immense: The World* *of Joe McCarthy* (1983); Richard Gid Powers, *Secrecy and Power: The Life of J. Edgar Hoover* (1987); Ronald Radosh and Joyce Milton, *The Rosenberg File* (1983); Thomas C. Reeves, *The Life and Times of Joe McCarthy* (1982); Michael Paul Rogin, *The Intellectuals and McCarthy* (1967); Richard Rovere, *Senator Joe McCarthy* (1959); Walter and Miriam Schneer, *Invitation to an Inquest,* rev. ed. (1983); Ellen Schrecker, *No Ivory Tower* (1986); Edward Shils, *The Torment of Secrecy* (1956); Joseph Starobin, *American Communism in Crisis* (1972); Athan Theoharis, *Seeds of Repression* (1971), and *Spying on Americans* (1978); Athan Theoharis and John Stuart Cox, *The Boss: J. Edgar Hoover and the Great American Inquisition* (1988); Allen Weinstein, *Perjury: The Hiss-Chambers Case* (1978); Stephen J. Whitfield, *The Culture of the Cold War* (1991).

CHAPTER 30 THE AFFLUENT SOCIETY

**General Studies.** Numan V. Bartley, *The New South, 1945–1980* (1995); John Brooks, *The Great Leap* (1966); William H. Chafe, *The Unfinished Journey* (1986); Carl Degler, *Affluence and Anxiety* (1968); John P. Diggins, *The Proud Decades, 1941–1960* (1989); Eric Goldman, *The Crucial Decade and After* (1960); David Halberstam, *The Fifties* (1993); Godfrey Hodgson, *America in Our Time* (1976); William Leuchtenburg, *A Troubled Feast* (1979); Douglas T. Miller and Marion Novak, *The Fifties* (1977); William O'Neill, *American High* (1986); James T. Patterson, *Grand Expectations: Postwar America, 1945–1974* (1996).

**Economy and Labor in Postwar America.** David P. Calleo, *The Imperious Economy* (1982); Gilbert C. Fite, *American Farmers* (1981); John K. Galbraith, *The Affluent Society* (1958), and *The New Industrial State* (1967); Mark I. Gelfand, *A Nation of Cities* (1975); Robert Heilbroner, *The Limits of American Capitalism* (1965); John Hutchinson, *The Imperfect Union* (1970); C. Wright Mills, *The Power Elite* (1956); Loren J. Okroi, *Galbraith, Harrington, Heilbroner* (1986); Joel Seidman, *American Labor from Defense to Reconversion* (1953); David Stebenne, *Arthur J. Goldberg: New Deal Liberal* (1996); Harold G. Vatter, *The U.S. Economy in the 1950s* (1963).

**Culture and Ideas.** Daniel Bell, *The End of Ideology* (1960), and ed., *The Radical Right* (1963); Peter Biskind, *Seeing Is Believing: How Hollywood Taught Us to Stop Worrying and Love the Fifties* (1983); Paul Boyer, *By the Bomb's Early Light* (1986); Howard Brick, *Daniel Bell and the Decline of Intellectual Radicalism* (1986); James L. Baughman, *The Republic of Mass Culture: Journalism, Filmmaking, and Broadcasting in America Since 1941;* Paul A. Carter, *Another Part of the Fifties* (1983); Ann Charters, *Kerouac* (1973); Bruce Cook, *The Beat Generation* (1971); Thomas Cripps, *Making Movies Black: The Hollywood Message Movie from World War II to the Civil Rights Era* (1993); Tom Engelhardt, *The End of Victory Culture: Cold War America and the Disillusioning of a Generation* (1995); Edward J. Epstein, *News from Nowhere* (1973); Herbert Gans, *The Levittowners* (1967); William Graebner, *The Age of Doubt: American Thought and Culture in the 1940s* (1991); David Halberstam, *The Powers That Be* (1979); Jeffrey Hart, *When the Going Was Good: American Life in the Fifties* (1982); Dolores Hayden, *Redesigning the American Dream* (1984); Kenneth T. Jackson, *The Crabgrass Frontier: The Suburbanization of the United States* (1985); Marty Jezer, *The Dark Ages: Life in the U.S., 1945–1960* (1982); Landon Y. Jones, *Great Expectations: America and the Baby Boom Generation* (1980); Neil Jumonville, *Critical Crossings: The New York Intellectuals in Postwar America* (1991); George Lipsitz, *Class and Culture in Cold War*

*America* (1981); Roger W. Lotchin, *Fortress California, 1910–1961: From Warfare to Welfare;* Mary Sperling McAuliffe, *Crisis on the Left* (1978); Walter A. McDougall, . . . *the Heavens and the Earth: A Political History of the Space Age* (1985); Dennis McNally, *Desolate Angel* (1979); Margaret Marsh, *Suburban Lives* (1990); Douglas T. Miller and Marion Novak, *The Fifties* (1977); Zane L. Miller, *Suburb: Neighborhood and Community in Forest Park, Ohio, 1935–1976* (1981); C. Wright Mills, *White Collar* (1956); Richard H. Pells, *The Liberal Mind in a Conservative Age: American Intellectuals in the 1940s and 1950s* (1985); David Potter, *People of Plenty* (1954); David Riesman, *The Lonely Crowd* (1950); Leila Rupp and Verta Taylor, *Survival in the Doldrums* (1987); Arthur M. Schlesinger, Jr., *The Vital Center* (1949); Lynn Spigel, *Make Room for TV* (1992); Walter Sullivan, ed., *America's Race for the Moon* (1962); John Tytell, *Naked Angels* (1976); Alan M. Wald, *The New York Intellectuals* (1987); Stephen J. Whitfield, *The Culture of the Cold War* (1991); William Whyte, *The Organization Man* (1956); Tom Wolfe, *The Right Stuff* (1979); Gwendolyn Wright, *Building the American Dream: A Social History of Housing in America* (1981).

**Women and Families.** William H. Chafe, *The American Woman: Her Changing Social, Economic, and Political Roles, 1920–1970,* rev. ed. (1988); Ruth Cowan, *More Work for Mother: The Irony of Household Technology* (1983); Eugenia Kaledin, *Mothers and More: American Women in the 1950s* (1984); Susan Estabrook Kennedy, *If All We Did Was to Weep at Home: A History of White Working-Class Women in America* (1979); Alice Kessler-Harris, *Out to Work: A History of Wage-Earning Women in the United States* (1982); Elaine Tyler May, *Homeward Bound: American Families in the Cold War* (1988); Susan Strasser, *Never Done: A History of American Housework* (1982).

**Politics in the Eisenhower Years.** Sherman Adams, *Firsthand Report* (1961); Charles C. Alexander, *Holding the Line* (1975); Stephen Ambrose, *Eisenhower the President* (1984); Jean Baker, *The Stevensons: A Biography of an American Family* (1996); Brian Balogh, *Chain Reaction: Expert Debate and Public Participation in American Nuclear Commercial Power, 1945–1975* (1991); Piers Brendon, *Ike* (1986); Jeff Broadwater, *Eisenhower and the Anti-Communist Crusade* (1992); Robert F. Burk, *Dwight D. Eisenhower* (1986); Barbara B. Clowse, *Brainpower for the Cold War: The Sputnik Crisis and the National Defense Education Act of 1958* (1981); Dwight D. Eisenhower, *The White House Years,* 2 vols. (1963–1965); Fred Greenstein, *The Hidden-Hand Presidency* (1982); Emmet John Hughes, *The Ordeal of Power* (1963); Peter Lyon, *Eisenhower: Portrait of a Hero* (1974); Richard Nixon, *Six Crises* (1962); Herbert S. Parmet, *Eisenhower and the American Crusades* (1972); Nicol C. Rae, *The Decline and Fall of the Liberal Republicans* (1989); Gary Reichard, *The Reaffirmation of Republicanism* (1975), and *Politics as Usual* (1988). David W. Reinhard, *The Republican Right Since 1945* (1983); Elmo Richardson, *The Presidency of Dwight D. Eisenhower* (1979); Mark H. Rose, *Interstate: Express Highway Politics, 1941–1956* (1979); R. L. Rosholt, *An Administrative History of NASA* (1966).

**Foreign Policy.** Stephen Ambrose, *Ike's Spies* (1981); David L. Anderson, *Trapped by Success: The Eisenhower Administration and Vietnam, 1953–1961* (1991); Howard Ball, *Justice Downwind: America's Nuclear Testing Program in the 1950s* (1986); Michael Beschloss, *MAYDAY* (1986); Henry W. Brands, *Cold Warriors* (1988), and *The Specter of Neutralism: The United States and the Emergence of the Third World, 1947–1960* (1989); Blanche W. Cooke, *The Declassified Eisenhower* (1981); Chester Cooper, *Lost Crusade* (1970), and *The Lion's Last Roar* (1978); Cecil Currey, *Edward Lansdale: The Unquiet American* (1988); Robert A. Divine, *Foreign Policy and U.S. Presidential Elections,* 2 vols. (1974), and *Blow-*

*ing in the Wind: The Nuclear Test Ban Debate, 1954–1960* (1978), and *Eisenhower and the Cold War* (1981); William J. Duiker, *U.S. Containment Policy and the Conflict in Indochina* (1992); Frances Fitzgerald, *Fire in the Lake* (1972); Steven Z. Freiberger, *Dawn over Suez: The Rise of American Power in the Middle East, 1953–1957* (1992); Louis Gerson, *John Foster Dulles* (1967); Gregg Herken, *Counsels of War* (1985); George Herring, *America's Longest War* (1979); Richard G. Hewlett and Jack M. Hall, *Atoms for Peace and War, 1953–1961* (1989); Townsend Hoopes, *The Devil and John Foster Dulles* (1973); Richard Immerman, *The CIA in Guatemala* (1982); Burton Kaufman, *The Oil Cartel Case* (1978); Gabriel Kolko, *Confronting the Third World* (1988); Walter LaFeber, *Inevitable Revolutions* (1983); John T. McAlister, Jr., *Vietnam: The Origins of Revolution* (1969); Richard A. Melanson and David A. Mayers, eds., *Reevaluating Eisenhower* (1986); Stephen G. Rabe, *Eisenhower and Latin America* (1988); Kermit Roosevelt, *Counter-Coup* (1980); Andrew Rotter, *The Path to Vietnam* (1987); Richard Smoke, *National Security and the Nuclear Dilemma* (1988); Hugh Thomas, *Suez* (1967); Mira Wilkins, *The Maturing of Multinational Enterprise* (1974).

**Legal and Constitutional Issues.**  Alexander Bickel, *Politics and the Warren Court* (1965), and *The Supreme Court and the Idea of Progress* (1970); Phillip Kurland, *Politics, the Constitution, and the Warren Court* (1970); Paul Murphy, *The Constitution in Crisis Times* (1972); Bernard Schwartz, *Super Chief: Earl Warren and His Supreme Court* (1983); Philip Stern, *The Oppenheimer Case* (1969); Michael Straight, *Trial by Television* (1954); John Weaver, *Earl Warren* (1967).

**Civil Rights.**  John W. Anderson, *Eisenhower, Brownell, and the Congress* (1964); Numan V. Bartley, *The Rise of Massive Resistance* (1969); Taylor Branch, *Parting the Waters* (1988); Robert F. Burk, *The Eisenhower Administration and Black Civil Rights* (1984); William H. Chafe, *Civilities and Civil Rights: Greensboro, North Carolina, and the Black Struggle for Freedom* (1980); John Egerton, *Speak Now Against the Day: The Generation Before the Civil Rights Movement in the South* (1994); Kevin Gaines, *Uplifting the Race: Black Leadership, Politics, and Culture in the Twentieth Century* (1996); David Garrow, ed., *The Montgomery Bus Boycott and the Women Who Started It: A Memoir of Jo Ann Gibson Robinson* (1987), and *Bearing the Cross* (1986). Elizabeth Huckaby, *Crisis at Central High* (1980); Martin Luther King, Jr., *Stride Toward Freedom* (1958); Richard H. King, *Civil Rights and the Idea of Freedom* (1992); Richard Kluger, *Simple Justice* (1975); Steven Lawson, *Running for Freedom* (1991); Anthony Lewis, *Portrait of a Decade* (1964); Robert J. Norrell, *Reaping the Whirlwind: The Civil Rights Movement in Tuskegee* (1985); Howell Raines, *My Soul Is Rested* (1977); Harvard Sitkoff, *The Struggle for Black Equality, 1954–1980* (1981); Patricia Sullivan, *Days of Hope: Race and Democracy in the New Deal Era* (1996); Abigail Thernstrom, *Whose Votes Count? Affirmative Action and Minority Voting Rights* (1987); Nancy J. Weiss, *Whitney M. Young, Jr., and the Struggle for Civil Rights* (1989).

**Minorities and the Poor.**  Rodolfo Acuña, *Occupied America: A History of Chicanos* (1981); Larry W. Burt, *Tribalism in Crisis: Federal Indian Policy, 1953–1961* (1982); Donald Fixico, *Termination and Relocation: Federal Indian Policy, 1945–1970* (1986); J. Wayne Flint, *Dixie's Forgotten People: The South's Poor Whites* (1979); Michael Harrington, *The Other America* (1962); Jacqueline Jones, *The Dispossessed: America's Underclasses from the Civil War to the Present* (1992); Nicholas Lemann, *The Promised Land: The Great Black Migration and How It Changed America* (1991); Elena Padilla, *Up from Puerto Rico* (1958); Linda Reed, *Simple Decency and Common Sense* (1992).

## CHAPTER 31 THE ORDEAL OF LIBERALISM

**General Studies.** William Chafe, *The Unfinished Journey: America Since World War II*, rev. ed. (1991); Godfrey Hodgson, *America in Our Time* (1976); Allen J. Matusow, *The Unraveling of America: A History of Liberalism in the 1960s* (1984); Charles R. Morris, *A Time of Passion* (1984); Theodore H. White, *America in Search of Itself* (1982).

**Kennedy and Johnson.** Vaughn D. Bornet, *The Presidency of Lyndon B. Johnson* (1983); Thomas Brown, *JFK: The History of an Image* (1988); David Burner, *John F. Kennedy and a New Generation* (1988); Robert Caro, *The Years of Lyndon B. Johnson: The Path to Power* (1982), and *Means of Ascent* (1990); Paul K. Conkin, *Big Daddy from the Pedernales* (1986); Robert Dallek, *Lone Star Rising: Lyndon Johnson and His Times, 1908–1960* (1991); Robert A. Divine, *The Johnson Years*, vol. 3: *LBJ at Home and Abroad*; Ronnie Dugger, *The Politician* (1982); Edward J. Epstein, *Inquest* (1966), and *Legend* (1978); Henry Fairlie, *The Kennedy Promise: The Politics of Richard Reeves, President Kennedy: Profile of Power* (1993), and *Expectation* (1973); Eric Goldman, *The Tragedy of Lyndon Johnson* (1968); Richard N. Goodwin, *Remembering America* (1988); Jim Heath, *Decade of Disillusionment* (1975); Henry Hurt, *Reasonable Doubt* (1985); Lyndon B. Johnson, *Vantage Point* (1971); Doris Kearns, *Lyndon Johnson and the American Dream* (1976); Donald Lord, *John F. Kennedy: The Politics of Confrontation and Conciliation* (1977); William Manchester, *The Death of a President* (1967); Bruce Miroff, *Pragmatic Illusions: The Presidential Politics of JFK* (1976); Lewis Paper, *The Promise and the Performance* (1975); Herbert Parmet, *Jack* (1980), and *JFK* (1983); George Reedy, *The Twilight of the Presidency* (1970); Richard Reeves, *President Kennedy* (1992); Thomas Reeves, *A Question of Character: The Life of John F. Kennedy in Image and Reality* (1991); Arthur M. Schlesinger, Jr., *A Thousand Days* (1965); Theodore Sorensen, *Kennedy* (1965); Anthony Summers, *Conspiracy* (1980); Warren Commission, *The Report of the Warren Commission* (1964); Theodore H. White, *The Making of the President, 1960* (1961); Garry Wills, *The Kennedy Imprisonment* (1982).

**Domestic Policies and Politics.** Henry J. Aaron, *Politics and the Professors* (1978); William H. Chafe, *Never Stop Running: Allard Lowenstein and the Struggle to Save American Liberalism*; Greg J. Duncan, *Years of Poverty, Years of Plenty* (1984); Mark Gelfand, *A Nation of Cities* (1975); James Giglio, *The Presidency of John F. Kennedy* (1991); Hugh Davis Graham, *Uncertain Trumpet* (1984); Robert H. Haveman, ed., *A Decade of Federal Antipoverty Programs* (1977); Jim Heath, *John F. Kennedy and the Business Community* (1969); Daniel Knapp and Kenneth Polk, *Scouting the War on Poverty* (1971); Sar Levitan, *The Great Society's Poor Law* (1969); Sar Levitan and Robert Taggart, *The Promise of Greatness* (1976); Allen J. Matusow, *The Unraveling of America: A History of Liberalism in the 1960s* (1984); Charles Morris, *A Time of Passion* (1984); Charles Murray, *Losing Ground* (1984); Victor Navasky, *Kennedy Justice* (1971); James T. Patterson, *America's Struggle Against Poverty, 1900–1980* (1981); Frances Fox Piven and Richard Cloward, *Regulating the Poor* (1971); John E. Schwarz, *America's Hidden Success* (1983); James L. Sundquist, *Politics and Policy: The Eisenhower, Kennedy, and Johnson Years* (1968); Tom Wicker, *JFK and LBJ* (1968).

**Race Relations and Civil Rights.** Taylor Branch, *Parting the Waters: America in the King Years* (1988); Carl Brauer, *John F. Kennedy and the Second Reconstruction* (1977); Paul Burstein, *Discrimination, Jobs, and Politics* (1985); James Button, *Black Violence: Political Impact of the 1960s Race Riots* (1978); Stokely Carmichael and Charles Hamilton, *Black Power* (1967); Clayborne Carson, *In Struggle: SNCC and the Black Awakening of the 1960s* (1981);

William H. Chafe, *Civilities and Civil Rights: Greensboro, North Carolina, and the Black Struggle for Freedom* (1980); Joe R. Feagin and Harlan Hahn, *Ghetto Revolts* (1973); Robert Fogelson, *Violence as Protest* (1971); David Garrow, *Protest at Selma* (1978); *The FBI and Martin Luther King* (1981), and *Bearing the Cross* (1986); Hugh Davis Graham, *The Civil Rights Era* (1990); Alex Haley, *The Autobiography of Malcolm X* (1966); Martin Luther King, Jr., *Why We Can't Wait* (1964); Steven Lawson, *Black Ballots: Voting Rights in the South, 1966–1969* (1976); Nicholas Lemann, *The Promised Land: The Great Black Migration and How It Changed America* (1991); David L. Lewis, *King: A Critical Biography* (1970); Doug McAdam, *Freedom Summer* (1988); Benjamin Muse, *The American Negro Revolution* (1969); *Report of the National Advisory Commission on Civil Disorders* (1968); Stephen Oates, *Let the Trumpet Sound* (1982); Harvard Sitkoff, *The Struggle for Black Equality, 1954–1992* (1992); James R. Ralph Jr., *Northern Protest: Martin Luther King Jr., Chicago, and the Civil Rights Movement* (1993); Mark Stern, *Calculating Visions: Kennedy, Johnson and Civil Rights* (1992); Abigail Thernstrom, *Whose Votes Count? Affirmative Action and Minority Voting Rights* (1987); Robert Weisbrot, *Freedom Bound: A History of America's Civil Rights Movement* (1990); Harris Wofford, *Of Kennedy and Kings* (1980); Eugene Wolfenstein, *The Victims of Democracy: Malcolm X and the Black Revolution* (1981).

**Foreign Policy.** Elie Abel, *The Missile Crisis* (1966); Graham Allison, *Essence of Decision* (1971); Richard Barnet, *Intervention and Revolution* (1968); Michael Bechloss, *The Crisis Years* (1990); McGeorge Bundy, *Danger and Survival* (1989); Warren Cohen, *Dean Rusk* (1980); Herbert Dinerstein, *The Making of a Missile Crisis* (1976); Bernard Firestone, *The Quest for Nuclear Stability* (1982); Louise Fitzsimmons, *The Kennedy Doctrine* (1972); Philip Geyelin, *Lyndon B. Johnson and the World* (1966); John Girling, *America and the Third World* (1980); Trumbull Higgins, *The Perfect Failure: Kennedy, Eisenhower, and the CIA at the Bay of Pigs* (1987); Roger Hilsman, *To Move a Nation* (1965); Haynes Johnson, *The Bay of Pigs* (1964); Robert Kennedy, *Thirteen Days* (1969); Dan Kurzman, *Santo Domingo* (1966); Walter LaFeber, *Inevitable Revolutions: The United States in Central America* (1985); Thomas J. McCormick, *America's Half Century: United States Foreign Policy in the Cold War* (1989); Richard D. Mahoney, *JFK: Ordeal in Africa* (1983); Gerald T. Rice, *The Bold Experiment: JFK's Peace Corps* (1985); Jerome Slater, *Intervention and Negotiation* (1970); Richard Walton, *Cold War and Counterrevolution* (1972); Peter Wyden, *Bay of Pigs* (1969).

**Vietnam.** Mark Baker and Christian G. Appy, *Working-Class War: American Combat Soldiers and Vietnam* (1993), and *Nam* (1982); Lawrence Baskir and William Strauss, *Chance and Circumstance* (1978); Larry Berman, *Planning a Tragedy* (1982), and *Lyndon Johnson's War* (1989); Peter Braestrup, *Big Story* (1977; abridged ed., 1978); William Broyles, Jr., *Brothers in Arms: A Journey from War to Peace* (1986); Philip Davidson, *Vietnam at War* (1991); Gloria Emerson, *Winners and Losers* (1976); Frances Fitzgerald, *Fire in the Lake* (1972); John Galloway, *The Gulf of Tonkin Resolution* (1970); Leslie Gelb and Richard Betts, *The Irony of Vietnam: The System Worked* (1979); David Halberstam, *The Best and the Brightest* (1972); Michael Herr, *Dispatches* (1977); George C. Herring, *America's Longest War*, rev. ed. (1986); George McT. Kahin, *Intervention* (1986); Stanley Karnow, *Vietnam* (1983); Alexander Kendrick, *The Wound Within* (1974); Gabriel Kolko, *The Anatomy of a War* (1985); Robert W. Komer, *Bureaucracy at War* (1986); David Levy, *The Debate over Vietnam* (1991); Guenter Lewy, *America in Vietnam* (1978); Don Oberdorfer, *Tet* (1971); Bruce C. Palmer, Jr., *The 25-Year War* (1984); *The Pentagon Papers*, Senator Gravel edition (1975); Norman Podhoretz, *Why We Were in Vietnam* (1982); Thomas Powers, *Vietnam:*

*The War at Home* (1973); Al Santoli, *Everything We Had* (1981); Herbert Schandler, *The Unmaking of a President: Lyndon Johnson and Vietnam* (1977); Neil Sheehan, *A Bright Shining Lie* (1988); R. B. Smith, *An International History of the Vietnam War: The Kennedy Strategy* (1985); Ronald Spector, *Advice and Support* (1983); Col. Harry Summers, *On Strategy* (1981); Wallace Terry, *Bloods* (1984); Thomas C. Thayer, *War Without Fronts* (1985); Wallace J. Thies, *When Governments Collide* (1980); James Thompson, *Rolling Thunder* (1980); Kathleen J. Turner, *Lyndon Johnson's Dual War: Vietnam and the Press* (1981); Irwin Unger, *The Movement* (1974); Marilyn Young, *The Vietnam Wars* (1991).

**1968.** Dan T. Carter, *The Politics of Rage: George Wallace, The Origins of the New Conservatism, and the Transformation of American Politics* (1995); David Caute, *The Year of the Barricades* (1988); Lewis Chester, *Godfrey Hodgson, and Lewis Page, American Melodrama* (1969); David Farber, *Chicago '68* (1988); Marshall Frady, *Wallace*, rev. ed. (1976); Godfrey Hodgson, *America in Our Time* (1976); Charles Kaiser, *1968 in America* (1988); Norman Mailer, *Miami and the Siege of Chicago* (1968); Arthur M. Schlesinger, Jr., *Robert Kennedy and His Times* (1978); Ben Stavis, *We Were the Campaign* (1969); Theodore H. White, *The Making of the President, 1968* (1969).

## CHAPTER 32 THE CRISIS OF AUTHORITY

**General Studies.** John Morton Blum, *Years of Discord: American Politics and Society, 1961–1974* (1991); Peter N. Carroll, It *Seemed Like Nothing Happened* (1982); Allen J. Matusow, *The Unraveling of America: A History of Liberalism in the 1960s* (1984); Kim McQuaid, *The Anxious Years* (1989); William O'Neill, *Coming Apart* (1971).

**The New Left and the Counterculture.** Edward Bacciocco, Jr., *The New Left in America* (1974); Ronald Berman, *America in the Sixties* (1968); Wini Breines, *Community and Organization in the New Left* (1983); Peter Clecak, *Radical Paradoxes* (1973); Peter Collier and David Horowitz, *Destructive Generation: Second Thoughts About the Sixties* (1989); Margaret Cruikshank, *The Gay and Lesbian Liberation Movement in America* (1992); Morris Dickstein, *Gates of Eden* (1977); Joan Didion, *Slouching Towards Bethlehem* (1967), and *The White Album* (1979); John Diggins, *The American Left in the Twentieth Century* (1973); Sara Evans, *Personal Politics* (1979); Lewis Feuer, *The Conflict of Generations* (1969); Richard Flacks, *Youth and Social Change* (1971); Todd Gitlin, *The Whole World Is Watching* (1981), and *The Sixties: Years of Hope, Days of Rage* (1987); Paul Goodman, *Growing Up Absurd* (1960); David Harris, *Dreams Die Hard* (1983); Maurice Isserman, *"If I Had a Hammer . . .": The Death of the Old Left and the Birth of the New Left* (1987); Joseph Kelner and James Munves, *The Kent State Coverup* (1980); Kenneth Keniston, *Young Radicals* (1968), and *Youth and Dissent* (1971); Richard King, *The Party of Eros* (1972); James Kunen, *The Strawberry Statement* (1968); Lawrence Lader, *Power on the Left* (1979); Klaus Mehnert, *Twilight of the Young* (1978); James Miller, *"Democracy in the Streets": From Port Huron to the Siege of Chicago* (1987); Charles Reich, *The Greening of America* (1970); W. J. Rorabaugh, *Berkeley at War* (1989); Theodore Roszak, *The Making of a Counter Culture* (1969); Kirkpatrick Sale, *SDS* (1973); Irwin Unger, *The Movement* (1974); Milton Viorst, *Fire in the Streets* (1979); Jon Wiener, *Come Together: John Lennon in His Time* (1984).

**Indians, Hispanics, Asians.** Rodolfo Acuña, *Occupied America*, 2nd ed. (1981); Larry W. Burt, *Tribalism in Crisis: Federal Indian Policy, 1953–1961* (1982); Vine Deloria, Jr.,

*Behind the Trail of Broken Treaties* (1974), and *Custer Died for Your Sins* (1969); Ronald Dewing, *Wounded Knee: The Meaning and Significance of the Second Incident* (1985); Douglas E. Foley, *From Peones to Politicos: Class and Ethnicity in a South Texas Town, 1900–1987* (1988); Peter Iverson, *The Navajo Nation* (1981); Oscar Lewis, *La Vida* (1969); D'Arcy McNickle, *Native American Tribalism* (1973); Matt Meier and Feliciano Rivera, *The Chicanos* (1972); David M. Reimers, *Still the Golden Door: The Third World Comes to America* (1985); Julian Samora, *Los Mojados* (1971); Stan Steiner, *The New Indians* (1968); Ronald Takaki, *Strangers from a Distant Shore: A History of Asian Americans* (1989), and *A Different Mirror: A History of Multicultural America* (1993); Ronald Taylor, *Chavez and the Farm Workers* (1975); Wilcomb E. Washburn, *Red Man's Land/White Man's Law* (1971); Charles F. Wilkinson, *American Indians, Time, and the Law* (1987).

**Feminism.**   William Chafe, *The American Woman* (1972); Nancy Cott, *The Grounding of Modern Feminism* (1987); Marian Faux, *Roe v. Wade* (1988); Jo Freeman, *The Politics of Women's Liberation* (1975); Betty Friedan, *The Feminine Mystique* (1963); Carol Gilligan, *In A Different Voice* (1982); Cynthia Harrison, *On Account of Sex: The Politics of Women's Issues, 1945–1968* (1988); Susan M. Hartmann, *From Margin to Mainstream: Women and American Politics Since 1960* (1989); Alice Kessler-Harris, *Out to Work: A History of Wage-Earning Women in the United States* (1982); Ethel Klein, *Gender Politics* (1984); Kristin Luker, *Abortion and the Politics of Motherhood* (1984); Robin Morgan, ed., *Sisterhood Is Powerful* (1970); Rosalind Petchesky, *Abortion and Women's Choice* (1984); Sheila Rothman, *Woman's Proper Place* (1978); Winifred Wandersee, *On the Move: American Women in the 1970s* (1988); Gayle Yates, *What Women Want* (1975).

**Nixon and the World.**   Seyom Brown, *The Crisis of Power* (1979); Lloyd Gardner, *A Covenant with Power* (1984), and *The Great Nixon Turnaround* (1973); Seymour Hersh, *The Price of Power* (1983); Roger Hilsman, *The Crouching Future* (1975); Arnold Isaacs, *Without Honor: Defeat in Vietnam and Cambodia* (1983); Walter Isaacson, *Kissinger* (1992); Marvin Kalb and Bernard Kalb, *Kissinger* (1974); Henry A. Kissinger, *White House Years* (1979); *Years of Upheaval* (1982), and *Diplomacy* (1994); David Landau, *Kissinger: The Uses of Power* (1972); Robert S. Litwak, *Detente and the Nixon Doctrine: American Foreign Policy and the Pursuit of Stability* (1984); Timothy Lomperis, *The War Nobody Lost—and Won* (1984); Roger Morris, *Uncertain Greatness* (1977); Harland Moulton, *From Superiority to Parity* (1973); John Newhouse, *Cold Dawn* (1973); Michael Oksenberg and Robert Oxnam, eds., *Dragon and Eagle* (1978); Gareth Porter, *A Peace Denied* (1975), and *Vietnam* (1979); Thomas Powers, *The Man Who Kept the Secrets* (1979); William Quandt, *Decade of Decision* (1977); Franz Schurman, *The Foreign Policies of Richard Nixon* (1987); William Shawcross, *Sideshow: Nixon, Kissinger, and the Destruction of Cambodia* (1978); Richard Stevenson, *The Rise and Fall of Detente* (1985); John Stockwell, *In Search of Enemies* (1977); Robert Stookey, *America and the Arab States* (1975); Robert D. Schulzinger, *Henry Kissinger: Doctor of Diplomacy* (1989); Tad Szulc, *The Illusion of Peace* (1978).

**Nixon and His Presidency.**   Stephen Ambrose, *Nixon: The Triumph of a Politician, 1962–1972* (1989); Richard Barnet, *The Lean Years* (1980); Fawn Brodie, *Richard Nixon: The Shaping of His Character* (1981); Vincent Burke and Vee Burke, *Nixon's Good Deed* (1974); John Ehrlichman, *Witness to Power* (1982); John R. Greene, *The Limits of Power: The Nixon and Ford Administrations;* H. R. Haldeman, *The Haldeman Diaries: Inside the Nixon White House* (1994); Joan Hoff, *Nixon Reconsidered* (1994); J. C. Hurewitz, ed., *Oil, the Arab-Israeli Dispute, and the Industrial World* (1976); R. L. Miller, *The New Economics of Richard Nixon* (1972); Daniel P. Moynihan, *The Politics of a Guaranteed Income* (1973);

R. P. Nathan et al., *Monitoring Revenue Sharing* (1975); Richard Nixon, *RN: The Memoirs of Richard Nixon* (1978); Herbert Parmet, *Richard Nixon and His America* (1989); Raymond Price, *With Nixon* (1977); James Reichley, *Conservatives in an Age of Change: The Nixon and Ford Administrations* (1981); William Safire, *Before the Fall* (1975); Joan Edelman Spero, *The Politics of International Economic Relations* (1977); Michael Tanzer, *The Energy Crisis* (1974); Theodore H. White, *The Making of the President, 1972* (1973); Bob Woodward and Scott Armstrong, *The Brethren* (1980).

**Nixon and Watergate.** Fawn Brodie, *Richard Nixon* (1981); Richard Cohen and Jules Witcover, *A Heartbeat Away* (1974); Len Colodny and Robert Gettlin, *Silent Coup* (1991); John Dean, *Blind Ambition* (1976); James Doyle, *Not Above the Law* (1977); Fred Emery, *Watergate: The Corruption of American Politics* (1994); Stanley J. Kutler, *The Wars of Watergate* (1990); J. Anthony Lukas, *Nightmare: The Underside of the Nixon Years* (1976); Bruce Mazlish, *In Search of Nixon* (1972); Richard M. Nixon, *RN: The Memoirs of Richard Nixon* (1978); Jonathan Schell, *The Time of Illusion* (1975); Arthur M. Schlesinger, Jr., *The Imperial Presidency* (1973); Michael Schudson, *Watergate in American Memory: How We Remember, Forget, and Reconstruct the Past* (1992); William Sirica, *To Set the Record Straight* (1979); Maurice Stans, *The Terrors of Justice* (1984); Theodore H. White, *Breach of Faith* (1975); Garry Wills, *Nixon Agonistes* (1970); Bob Woodward and Carl Bernstein, *All the President's Men* (1974), and *The Final Days* (1976).

## CHAPTER 33 THE AGE OF LIMITS

**The Ford Presidency.** James M. Cannon, *Time and Chance: Gerald Ford's Appointment with History* (1994), and *Gerald Ford, A Time to Heal* (1979); John R. Greene, *The Limits of Power: The Nixon and Ford Administrations* (1992); Robert T. Hartmann, *Palace Politics* (1980); Gerald Ter Horst, *Gerald Ford* (1975); Richard Reeves, *A Ford Not a Lincoln* (1976); A. James Reichley, *Conservatives in an Age of Change: The Nixon and Ford Administrations* (1981); Edward and Frederick Schapsmeier, *Gerald R. Ford's Date with Destiny: A Political Biography* (1989); James L. Sundquist, *The Decline and Resurgence of Congress* (1981).

**The Carter Presidency.** Jack Bass and Walter Devries, *The Transformation of Southern Politics* (1976); James Bill, *The Eagle and the Lion* (1988); Zbigniew Brzezinski, *Power and Principle* (1983); Jimmy Carter, *Why Not the Best?* (1975), and *Keeping Faith* (1982); Rosalynn Carter, *First Lady from Plains* (1984); Steven Gillon, *The Democrats' Dilemma: Walter Mondale and the Liberal Legacy* (1992); Betty Glad, *Jimmy Carter* (1980); Erwin Hargrove, *Jimmy Carter as President* (1989); Steven B. Hunt, *The Energy Crisis* (1978); Haynes Johnson, *In the Absence of Power* (1980); Charles O. Jones, *The Trusteeship Presidency* (1988); Hamilton Jordan, *Crisis* (1982); Walter LaFeber, *Panama Canal* (1978); Clark Mollenhoff, *The President Who Failed* (1980); A. Glenn Mower, Jr., *Human Rights and American Foreign Policy* (1987); William B. Quandt, *Decade of Decisions* (1977), and *Camp David* (1986); Barry Rubin, *Paved with Good Intentions* (1983); Lars Schoultz, *Human Rights and U.S. Policy Toward Latin America* (1981); Gaddis Smith, *Morality, Reason, and Power* (1986); Strobe Talbott, *Endgame* (1979); Jules Witcover, *Marathon* (1977); James Wooten, *Dasher* (1978); Cyrus Vance, *Hard Choices* (1983).

**The New Right.** Sidney Blumenthal, *The Rise of the Counter-Establishment* (1986); George Nash, *The Conservative Intellectual Movement in America Since 1945* (1979); Burton Yale Pines, *Back to Basics* (1982); David W. Reinhard, *The Republican Right Since 1945*

(1983); Kirkpatrick Sale, *Power Shift: The Rise of the Southern Rim and Its Challenge to the Eastern Establishment* (1975); Peter Steinfels, *The Neo-Conservatives* (1979); John K. White, *The New Politics of Old Values* (1988); Clyde Wilcox, *God's Warriors: The Christian Right in Twentieth Century America* (1992); John Woodridge, *The Evangelicals* (1975).

**The Reagan Presidency.** Frank Ackerman, *Reaganomics* (1982); Laurence I. Barrett, *Gambling with History* (1984); Bill Boyarsky, *The Rise of Ronald Reagan* (1968); Paul Boyer, ed., *Reagan as President: Contemporary Views of the Man, His Politics, and His Policies* (1990); William J. Broad, *Teller's War: The Top-Secret Story Behind the Star Wars Deception* (1992); Lou Cannon, *Reagan* (1982), and *President Reagan: The Role of a Lifetime* (1990); Joan Claybrook, *Retreat from Safety: Reagan's Attack on American Health* (1984); Robert Dallek, *Ronald Reagan: The Politics of Symbolism* (1984); Ronnie Dugger, *On Reagan* (1983); Thomas Byrne Edsall, *The New Politics of Inequality* (1984); Anne Edwards, *Early Reagan* (1987); Rowland Evans and Robert Novak, *The Reagan Revolution* (1981); Benjamin Friedman, *Day of Reckoning: The Consequences of American Economic Policy Under Reagan and After* (1988); Jack Germond and Jules Witcover, *Blue Smoke and Mirrors: How Reagan Won and Why Carter Lost the Election of 1980* (1981), and *Wake Us When It's Over: Presidential Politics of 1984* (1985); George Gildner, *Wealth and Poverty* (1981); Fred I. Greenstein, ed., *The Reagan Presidency* (1983); William Greider, *The Education of David Stockman and Other Americans* (1982); Haynes Johnson, *Sleepwalking Through History: America in the Reagan Years* (1991); Jonathan Lash, *A Season of Spoils: The Story of the Reagan Administration's Attack on the Environment* (1984); Robert Lekachman, *Greed Is Not Enough: Reaganomics* (1982); Jane Mayer and Doyle McManus, *Landslide: The Unmaking of the President, 1984–1988* (1988); Charles Noble, *Liberalism at Work: The Rise and Fall of OSHA* (1986); Peggy Noonan, *What I Saw at the Revolution: A Political Life in the Reagan Era* (1990); John L. Palmer and Isabel V. Sawhill, eds., *The Reagan Experiment* (1982); Michael J. Piore and Charles F. Sabel, *The Second Industrial Divide* (1984); Frances Fox Piven and Richard A. Cloward, *The New Class War: Reagan's Attack on the Welfare State and Its Consequences* (1982); Nancy Reagan, *My Turn* (1989); Richard Reeves, *The Reagan Detour* (1985); Donald T. Regan, *For the Record* (1988); Michael Rogin, *Ronald Reagan: The Movie* (1987); Michael Schaller, *Reckoning with Reagan: America and Its President in the 1980s* (1992); C. Brant Short, *Ronald Reagan and the Public Lands: America's Conservation Debate, 1979–1984* (1989); Hedrick Smith, *The Power Game* (1988); Hedrick Smith et al., *Reagan: The Man, the President* (1980); David A. Stockman, *The Triumph of Politics* (1986); Sidney Weintraub and Marvin Goodstein, eds., *Reaganomics in the Stagflation Economy* (1983); F. Clifton White and William Gil, *Why Reagan Won* (1982); Theodore H. White, *America in Search of Itself* (1982); Garry Wills, *Reagan's America* (1987).

**Reagan and the World.** Seweryn Bialer and Michael Mandelbaum, eds., *Gorbachev's Russia and American Foreign Policy* (1988); Raymond Bonner, *Weakness and Deceit: U.S. Policy and El Salvador* (1984); Tom Buckley, *Violent Neighbors* (1984); Steven Emerson, *Secret Warriors: Inside the Covert Military Operations of the Reagan Era* (1988); Thomas L. Friedman, *From Beirut to Jerusalem* (1989); Alexander Haig, *Caveat: Realism, Reagan and Foreign Policy* (1984); Jane Hunter et al., *The Iran-Contra Connection* (1987); David E. Kyvig, ed., *Reagan and the World* (1990); Walter LaFeber, *Inevitable Revolutions: The United States in Central America* (1983); Richard A. Melanson, *Reconstructing Consensus: American Foreign Policy Since the Vietnam War* (1991); John Newhouse, *War and Peace in the Nuclear Age* (1989); Robert O. Pastor, *Condemned to Repetition: The United States and Nicaragua* (1987); Charles D. Smith, *Palestine and the Arab-Israeli Conflict*, 2nd ed. (1992); Strobe Talbott, *Deadly Gambits* (1984), and *The Master of the Game: Paul Nitze and the*

Nuclear Peace (1988); Daniel Wirls, Buildup: The Politics of Defense in the Reagan Era (1992); Bob Woodward, Veil: The Secret Wars of the CIA (1987).

## CHAPTER 34 BEYOND THE COLD WAR

**The Post Cold-War World.** Bernard Gwertzman and Michael T. Kaufman, eds., The Collapse of Communism (1990); Paul Kennedy, The Rise and Fall of the Great Powers (1987); Robert Kuttner, The End of Laissez Faire: National Purpose and the Global Economy After the Cold War (1991); John Mueller, Policy and Opinion in the Gulf War (1994); Henry R. Nau, The Myth of America's Decline: Leading the World Economy in the 1990s (1990); Joseph Nye, Bound to Lead: The Changing Nature of American Power (1990); H. Norman Schwarzkopf, It Doesn't Take a Hero (1992).

**Politics After Reagan.** E. J. Dionne, Why Americans Hate Politics (1991); Thomas Ferguson and Joel Rogers, Right Turn (1986); William Greider, Who Will Tell the People? (1992); Robert S. McElvaine, The End of the Conservative Era: Liberalism After Reagan (1987); Kevin Phillips, The Politics of Rich and Poor: Wealth and the American Electorate in the Reagan Aftermath (1990); Adolph L. Reed, Jr., The Jesse Jackson Phenomenon (1986); Bob Woodard, The Agenda (1994)

**Post-Liberal Culture.** Peter N. Carroll, It Seemed Like Nothing Happened (1982); Peter Clecak, America's Quest for the Ideal Self (1983); Jim Hougan, Decadence: Radical Nostalgia, Narcissism, and Decline in the Seventies (1975); Christopher Lasch, The Culture of Narcissism (1978); Edwin Schur, The Awareness Trap (1976); Daniel Yankelovich, New Rules: Search for Self-Fulfillment in a World Turned Upside Down (1981).

**Economy and Society.** Carl Abbott, The New Urban America: Growth and Politics in the Sunbelt Cities (1981); Michael A. Bernstein and David E. Adler, Understanding American Economic Decline (1994); Barry Bluestone and Bennett Harrison, The Deindustrializing of America (1982); Connie Bruck, The Predator's Ball: The Junk Bond Raiders and the Man Who Staked Them (1988); Bryan Burroughs and John Helyar, Barbarians at the Gate: The Fall of RJR Nabisco (1990); Elizabeth Fee and Daniel M. Fox, eds., AIDS: The Burdens of History (1988), and AIDS: The Making of a Chronic Disease (1992); Gerald N. Grob, From Asylum to Community: Mental Health Policy in Modern America (1991); Robert Heilbroner and Lester Thurow, Five Economic Challenges (1983); John Langone, AIDS: The Facts (1988); Frank Levy, Dollars and Dreams: The Changing American Income Distribution (1987); Michael Lewis, Liar's Poker (1989); Eric Marcus, Making History: The Struggle for Gay and Lesbian Equal Rights, 1945–1990 (1992); Robert Reich, The Work of Nations: Preparing Ourselves for Twenty-First-Century Capitalism (1991); Kirkpatrick Sale, Power Shift (1975); Jonathan Schell, The Fate of the Earth (1982); Arthur M. Schlesinger, Jr., The Disuniting of America (1992); Bruce J. Schulman, From Cotton Belt to Sunbelt: Federal Policy, Economic Development, and the Transformation of the South, 1938–1980 (1991); Randy Shilts, And the Band Played On: Politics, People, and the AIDS Epidemic (1987); James B. Stewart, Den of Thieves (1991); Studs Terkel, The Great Divide (1988); John Woodridge, The Evangelicals (1975); Daniel Yergin, The Prize (1991).

**Gender and Family.** Mary Francis Berry, Why ERA Failed (1986); Susan M. Bianchi, American Women in Transition (1987); Nancy Caraway, Segregated Sisterhood: Racism and the Politics of American Feminism (1991); Andrea Dworkin, Right-Wing Women (1983); Barbara Ehrenreich, *The Hearts of Men: American Dreams and the Flight from Commitment* (1983); Jonathan Kozol, *Rachel and Her Children: Homeless Families in America* (1988); Kristin Luker, *Abortion and the Politics of Motherhood* (1984); Jane Mansbridge, *Why We Lost the ERA* (1986); Donald G. Mathews and Jane Sherron De Hart, *Sex, Gender, and the Politics of E.R.A.: A State and the Nation* (1990); Rosalind Pechesky, *Abortion and Woman's Choice* (1984); Harrell R. Rodgers, Jr., *Poor Women, Poor Families* (1986); Hilda Scott, *Working Your Way to the Bottom: The Feminization of Poverty* (1985); Ruth Sidel, *Women and Children Last* (1986); Suzanne Staggenborg, *The Pro-Choice Movement: Organization and Activism in the Abortion Conflict* (1991); Winifred D. Wandersee, *On the Move: American Women in the 1970s* (1988).

**Nonwhites in the 1970s and 1980s.** Ken Auletta, *The Underclass* (1981); Frank D. Bean and Marta Tienda, *The Hispanic Population of the United States* (1987); Derrick Bell, *And We Are Not Saved: The Elusive Quest for Racial Justice* (1987); James D. Cockcroft, *Outlaws in the Promised Land: Mexican Immigrant Workers and America's Future* (1986); John Crewden, *The Tarnished Door: The New Immigrants and the Transformation of America* (1983); Vine Deloria, Jr., *American Indian Policy in the Twentieth Century* (1985); Leslie W. Dunbar, ed., *Minority Report* (1984); Marian Wright Edelman, *Families in Peril* (1987); Douglas Glasgow, *The Black Underclass* (1980); Andrew Hacker, *Two Nations: Black and White, Separate, Hostile, Unequal* (1992); Michael Katz, *The Undeserving Poor: From the War on Poverty to the War on Welfare* (1989); Nicholas Lemann, *The Promised Land: The Great Black Migration and How It Changed America* (1989); Carl Nightingale, *On the Edge: A History of Poor Black Children and Their American Dreams* (1993); David M. Reimers, *Still the Golden Door* (1985); Carol B. Stack, *All Our Kin: Strategies for Survival in a Black Community* (1975); William Julius Wilson, *The Truly Disadvantaged* (1987).

# Illustration Credits

# Index

NOTE: *Page numbers followed by the letter* m *refer to maps.*